www.wadsworth.com

wadsworth.com is the World Wide Web site for Wadsworth Publishing Company and is your direct source to dozens of online resources.

At *wadsworth.com* you can find out about supplements, demonstration software, and student resources. You can also send e-mail to many of our authors and preview new publications and exciting new technologies.

wadsworth.com
Changing the way the world learns®

RELATED TITLES OF INTEREST

Abnormal Child Psychology, Eric Mash and David Wolfe

Casebook in Child Behavior Disorders, Christopher Kearney

Abnormal Psychology: An Introduction, 2nd ed., V. Mark Durand and David Barlow

Abnormal Psychology: An Integrative Approach, 2nd ed., David Barlow and V. Mark Durand

Casebook in Abnormal Psychology, revised ed., Timothy Brown and David Barlow

Contemporary Behavior Therapy, 3rd ed., Michael Spiegler and David Guevremont

Culture and Mental Illness, Richard Castillo

Health Psychology, 4th ed., Linda Brannon and Jess Feist

Health Psychology, Phillip Rice

Looking into Abnormal Psychology: Contemporary Readings, Scott Lilienfeld

Meanings of Madness, Richard Castillo

Seeing Both Sides: Classic Controversies in Abnormal Psychology, Scott Lilienfeld

Stress and Health, 3rd ed., Phillip Rice

Forthcoming Titles

Community Psychology: Linking Individuals and Communities, James Dalton, Maurice Elias, and Abraham Wandersman

Forensic Psychology, Lawrence Wrightsman

Human Neuropsychology, Eric Zillmer and Mary Spiers

Clinical Psychology
Concepts, Methods, and Profession

SIXTH EDITION

Timothy J. Trull
University of Missouri–Columbia

E. Jerry Phares
Kansas State University
(Emeritus)

WADSWORTH

™

THOMSON LEARNING

Australia ■ Canada ■ Mexico ■ Singapore
Spain ■ United Kingdom ■ United States

WADSWORTH

THOMSON LEARNING ™

Psychology Editor: *Marianne Taflinger*
Assistant Editor: *Annie Berterretche*
Editorial Assistant: *Suzanne Wood*
Marketing Manager: *Marc Linsenman*
Project Editor: *Tanya Nigh*
Print Buyer: *Karen Hunt*
Permissions Editor: *Roberta Broyer*

Production Service: *Scratchgravel Publishing Services*
Text Designer: *Lisa Mirski Devenish*
Copy Editor: *Margaret C. Tropp*
Cover Designer: *Bill Stanton*
Cover Printer: *Maple-Vail*
Compositor: *Scratchgravel Publishing Services*
Printer: *Maple-Vail*

Library of Congress Cataloging-in-Publication Data
Trull, Timothy J. [date]–
    Clinical psychology : concepts, methods, and profession / Timothy J. Trull, E. Jerry Phares. — 6th ed.
        p. cm.
    Includes bibliographical references and index.
    ISBN 0-534-54856-3 (alk. paper)
    1. Clinical psychology. 2. Psychotherapy.
I. Phares, E. Jerry. II. Title.

RC467 .P48 2001
616.89—dc21   00-036663

Wadsworth/Thomson Learning
10 Davis Drive
Belmont, CA 94002-3098
USA

For more information about our products, contact us:
Thomson Learning Academic Resource Center
1-800-423-0563
http://www.wadsworth.com

International Headquarters
Thomson Learning
International Division
290 Harbor Drive, 2nd Floor
Stamford, CT 06902-7477
USA

UK/Europe/Middle East/South Africa
Thomson Learning
Berkshire House
168-173 High Holborn
London WC1V 7AA
United Kingdom

Asia
Thomson Learning
60 Albert Street, #15-01
Albert Complex
Singapore 189969

Canada
Nelson Thomson Learning
1120 Birchmount Road
Toronto, Ontario M1K 5G4
Canada

This book is printed on acid-free recycled paper.

ABOUT THE AUTHORS

Timothy J. Trull is a Professor of Psychology at the University of Missouri–Columbia. He received his B.A. from Baylor University and his M.A. and Ph.D. in clinical psychology from the University of Kentucky. Dr. Trull has published papers in the areas of psychopathology, personality assessment, personality disorders, borderline personality disorder, and substance use disorders. In addition he is co-author of a structured interview, the Structured Interview for the Five-Factor Model of Personality (SIFFM), that assesses both adaptive and maladaptive personality features. Current research projects include evaluating etiological models of borderline personality disorder, exploring the relations between personality disorders and substance use disorders, and assessing genetic and environmental influences on personality and psychopathology. His research is supported through grants from the National Institute of Health and the National Institute on Alcohol Abuse and Alcoholism, and he is a member of the scientific faculty at the Missouri Alcohol Research Center (MARC). Dr. Trull teaches a variety of courses in clinical psychology, including abnormal psychology and psychometrics, and he supervises graduate students in their research, assessment, and clinical work. In addition to his academic pursuits, Dr. Trull is a practicing clinical psychologist. Outside of work, he enjoys spending time with his family, listening to live music, playing basketball, and coaching soccer and basketball.

E. Jerry Phares received his B.A. in psychology, with honors, from the University of Cincinnati and his M.S. and then Ph.D. in clinical psychology from The Ohio State University. He is a Fellow of the American Psychological Association (Divisions 8 and 12) and is a Professor Emeritus at Kansas State University in Manhattan, Kansas. He is also the author of *Introduction to Personality*.

BRIEF CONTENTS

DETAILED CONTENTS

3 | Current Issues in Clinical Psychology   56

4 | Research Methods in Clinical Psychology   84

5 | Diagnosis and Classification of Psychological Problems 114

PART 2 CLINICAL ASSESSMENT

6 The Assessment Interview   143

7 The Assessment of Intelligence   176

8   Personality Assessment   204

9   Behavioral Assessment   240

10 Clinical Judgment 265

PART 3 CLINICAL INTERVENTIONS

11 Psychological Interventions 293

12 Psychotherapy: The Psychodynamic Perspective 326

13 Psychotherapy: Phenomenological and Humanistic-Existential Perspectives   349

14 Psychotherapy: Behavioral and Cognitive-Behavioral Perspectives   373

15 Group Therapy, Family Therapy, and Couples Therapy   405

PART 4   SPECIALTIES IN CLINICAL PSYCHOLOGY

16 Community Psychology   433

17 Health Psychology and Behavioral Medicine 458

18 Neuropsychology 485

19 Forensic Psychology 508

20 Pediatric and Clinical Child Psychology 528

PREFACE

Welcome to the sixth edition of *Clinical Psychology: Concepts, Methods, and Profession*! This new edition incorporates a number of revisions that are aimed at: (1) keeping the text at the cutting edge concerning changes and trends in the field; (2) making the book more user friendly to students and instructors; (3) incorporating more coverage of issues related to culture, gender, and diversity; (4) focusing on the impact of managed health care on the field; (5) emphasizing the importance and influence of empirically supported approaches to treatment and assessment; and (6) providing more resources to aid both students and instructors of the Clinical Psychology course. I would like to briefly highlight some of these changes.

Continuing Challenges for Clinical Psychology

In addition to general revisions related to keeping a textbook up to date, we focused more discussion on what we view as the major challenges for the field of clinical psychology. Questions that guided our revisions include the following:

- What features define clinical psychology, and what aspects of clinical psychology make it a unique specialty? These issues are discussed in Chapter 1 (Clinical Psychology: An Introduction).
- What are the current trends evident in managed health care, and how might these affect the practice of clinical psychology? We discuss these trends (e.g., rising health care costs, psychologists serving as their own

gatekeepers) and their potential impact in Chapters 3 (Current Issues in Clinical Psychology) and 11 (Psychological Interventions). These themes also surface in the chapters on various forms of psychotherapy (Chapters 12–15) and on various clinical psychology specialties (Chapters 16–20).

- What are the leading training models used to train future clinical psychologists, and which models are most likely to be successful? Chapter 3 (Current Issues in Clinical Psychology) focuses on the scientist-practitioner, clinical scientist, Psy.D., professional school, and combined professional scientific models.
- What are the leading empirically supported treatments (ESTs), and how are these implemented? Are empirically supported treatments compatible with managed health care? We discuss general issues regarding empirically supported treatments in Chapter 11 (Psychological Interventions) and then present information regarding specific empirically supported treatments in Chapters 12–15 and in some of the "specialty" chapters (Chapters 16–20).
- Which clinical assessment procedures have the most empirical support? Although this can be a complicated issue to address, we present in Chapters 6–10 the evidence (both supportive and, in some cases, not supportive) for a wide variety of assessment procedures (e.g., structured interviews, self-report measures, projective techniques, intelligence tests, behavioral assessments methods).
- How should culture, gender, and ethnicity considerations influence the practice of clini-

cal psychology? We discuss how a clinical psychologist might provide culturally sensitive mental health services throughout the book but particularly in Chapters 3 and 11.

- What specialty areas of clinical psychology are poised for growth in the future, and why? We focus on five specialty areas that fit this characterization: community psychology, health psychology and behavioral medicine, neuropsychology, forensic psychology, and pediatric and clinical child psychology (Chapters 16–20).

- How have biological and genetic viewpoints influenced the research, assessment, and treatment practices of clinical psychologists? This discussion is incorporated in chapters throughout the book, but especially in Chapters 5 (Diagnosis and Classification of Psychological Problems), 7 (The Assessment of Intelligence), 9 (Behavioral Assessment), 11 (Psychological Interventions), 17 (Health Psychology and Behavioral Medicine), 18 (Neuropsychology), and 20 (Pediatric and Clinical Child Psychology).

Culture, Gender, and Ethnicity

This edition incorporates more information concerning the important issues of culture, gender, and ethnicity. First, when available, statistics concerning these features in the context of treatment and assessment are presented (e.g., "Culturally Sensitive Mental Health Services" in Chapter 3). Second, research that examines the influence of culture, gender, and ethnicity on assessment and treatment is presented and discussed (e.g., Box 17-2, "Ethnicity and Cancer Outcomes"). Finally, there are practical suggestions regarding how clinical psychologists should incorporate these considerations into their assessment and treatment practices (e.g., Box 11-1, "Cultural Competence").

The Future of Clinical Psychology

In general, we think that the future of clinical psychology is bright. One thing that sets clinical psychologists apart from other mental health professionals is their rigorous research training as well as their training in empirically supported assessment methods and interventions. Therefore, it is likely that clinical psychologists will be asked to *plan and conduct* research on various forms of psychological problems, as well as research that evaluates assessment methods and interventions targeting these problems. We believe that in the future it is less likely that clinical psychologists will be asked to provide direct services (e.g., psychotherapy). There are many reasons for this, but the main reason is that the mental health field is becoming saturated with service providers from other disciplines. In most cases, these other mental health professionals charge less for their services. Therefore, some of the "traditional" roles played by clinical psychologists (e.g., private practice) are likely to be in less demand. Despite these trends, it is still essential that clinical psychologists obtain training in assessment and intervention. They will be asked to oversee the training of direct service providers and to evaluate the effectiveness of the interventions that are implemented.

In addition to our prognostications for the field that appear throughout the book, a feature new to this edition provides a number of very interesting viewpoints. Most of the chapters in this edition present one or two "profiles" of psychologists who are leading experts in their specialties. These profiles not only present the backgrounds of these individuals (providing, perhaps, some insight into why they became psychologists), but also their predictions for both the future of clinical psychology as well as the future of their specialties. The profiles give us a rare glimpse into the daily lives of these well-known psychologists as well as their own thoughts about clinical psychology. What they say may surprise you! Here is a list of these prominent psychologists:

Judith Beck, Ph.D., *Beck Institute of Cognitive Therapy and Research*
Yossef Ben-Porath, Ph.D., *Kent State University*
Simon Budman, Ph.D., *Innovative Training Systems*

Patrick DeLeon, Ph.D., *Staff, United States Senate*

David DuBois, Ph.D., *University of Missouri*

John Exner, Ph.D., *Rorschach Workshops*

Howard Garb, Ph.D., *Pittsburgh VA Health System*

Leslie Greenberg, Ph.D., *York University*

Stephen Haynes, Ph.D., *University of Hawaii*

Elaine Heiby, Ph.D., *University of Hawaii*

Brick Johnstone, Ph.D., *University of Missouri*

Richard McFall, Ph.D., *Indiana University*

Beth Meyerowitz, Ph.D., *University of Southern California*

Lizette Peterson, Ph.D., *University of Missouri*

Martin Seligman, Ph.D., *University of Pennsylvannia*

Kenneth Sher, Ph.D., *University of Missouri*

Hans Strupp, Ph.D., *Vanderbilt University*

Samuel Turner, Ph.D., *University of Maryland*

Thomas Widiger, Ph.D., *University of Kentucky*

Lawrence Wrightsman, Ph.D., *University of Kansas*

Resources for Student Success

We want students who use this textbook to master the material that is presented and, in addition, to be inspired to look beyond what is in this book for even more information relevant to the field of clinical psychology. This is perhaps a tall order, but toward this end we provide a number of additional resources.

- A Chapter Outline and Focus Questions are presented at the beginning of each chapter.
- Key Terms are presented and defined at the end of each chapter.
- At the end of each chapter, a Chapter Summary is presented.
- A very exciting new feature is the CD-ROM that accompanies this book. The CD-ROM presents graphic figures that are relevant to the book chapters as well as 45 video clips of patients exhibiting symptoms of a wide range of DSM-IV disorders (e.g., anxiety disorders, mood disorders, personality disorders, substance use disorders).
- At the end of each chapter, Web Sites of Interest are presented. The Internet addresses for all the web sites are listed by number in the appendix at the end of the book. These web sites can also be accessed using the CD-ROM.

- An Instructor's Manual with a Test Bank is also available. Topic summaries and suggestions to improve class presentations are included in the manual. Furthermore, the manual provides a list of film and video resources, as well as student exercises and activities relevant to the web sites that appear in the book. Directions for using the CD-ROM are also included as well as an explanation for how the CD-ROM figures and video clips correlate with the book chapters.

- Finally, InfoTrac College Edition is available (free of charge) to students who purchase this book. InfoTrac is a fully searchable online university library that contains complete articles and images from over 700 scholarly and popular publications. Such access can help students with their independent research on topics relevant to clinical psychology. Journals relevant to clinical psychology include (among others): *Behavioral Medicine, Harvard Mental Health Letter, Annual Review of Psychology, British Journal of Psychology,* and *Journal of Abnormal Child Psychology.*

So, as you can see, many changes have been incorporated into the sixth edition of *Clinical Psychology.* In the past, I have appreciated the comments and feedback from both students and instructors. I look forward to your feedback on this sixth edition as well.

Thanks and Kudos

Large projects such as this require inspiration, outside expertise, and professional guidance. This project has been inspired by so many different kinds of individuals (some of whom are even clinical psychologists). My deepest gratitude goes out to my life partner Meg, my daughters Molly and Janey, my parents, Kenny Sher, Tom Widiger, Rich Lapan, Tom DiLorenzo, Jay Farrar, and Jeff Tweedy.

I am extremely fortunate to have the benefit of the expertise of the Wadsworth staff, including: Tanya Nigh, Suzanne Wood, Stephen Rapley, Marc Linsenmann, and Annie Berterretche. I especially want to thank Marianne Taflinger and Vicki Knight whose unflagging support for this project has been a source of inspiration as well.

I also want to thank those who agreed to be "profiled" for this book (see list above). I found their comments to be both interesting and stimulating.

The feedback and comments from the reviewers of the chapters of this book were extremely helpful: Joyce Carbonnell, Florida State University; Michael Connor, CSU–Long Beach; Nancy Davis, Birmingham-Southern College; Patricia DiBartolo, Smith College; David DuBois, University of Missouri–Columbia; Jan Gillespie, SUNY–Brockport; Paul Guthrie, Midwestern State University; David Harder, Tufts University; Cooper Holmes, Emporia State University; Randolph Lee, Trinity College; Patrick Leverett, The Citadel; Raymond Lorion, University of Pennsylvania; Martin Murphy, The University of Akron; Pamela Balls Organista, University of San Francisco; Catherine Pittman, Saint Mary's College; Jeffrey Ratliff-Crain, University of Minnesota at Morris; Dennis Saccuzzo, San Diego State University Columbia; David Shapiro, John Jay College of Criminal Justice; Steven Shapiro, Auburn University Columbia; C. Rick Snyder, University of Kansas; Carol Terry, University of Oklahoma; and Peter Zachar, Auburn University at Montgomery.

In addition, I am indebted to Angie Vieth, Ph.D., for putting together the key terms and to Andy Pomerantz, Ph.D., for developing the Instructor's Manual and Test Questions.

Finally, I want to thank Janet Kelty for her help in pulling this all together. Not only did she provide clerical and editorial assistance, but her positive outlook on work and life was an inspiration as well.

Timothy J. Trull
Columbia, Missouri

Foundations of Clinical Psychology

CHAPTER ONE

Clinical Psychology: An Introduction

FOCUS QUESTIONS

1. What distinguishes a clinical psychologist from other mental health professionals?

2. How does a clinical psychologist integrate research and practice (clinical work)?

3. What current trends will likely affect the future roles of clinical psychologists?

4. What are the major components of a doctoral program in clinical psychology?

5. What are the general qualifications for graduate study in clinical psychology?

CHAPTER OUTLINE

What Is Clinical Psychology?

Closely Related Mental Health Professions
Psychiatrists
Counseling Psychologists
Other Mental Health Professionals

The Clinical Psychologist
Activities of Clinical Psychologists
Employment Sites
A Week in the Life of Dr. Karen C.
Some Demographic Notes
Research and Scientific Tradition
Art or Science?

Training: Toward a Clinical Identity
An Overview
Clinical Training Programs

Admission to Graduate Programs
Step 1: Know Your Program
Step 2: Application Materials
Essential Qualifications

A Profession in Movement
Demographics
Training Models
Clinical Practice

A Tolerance for Ambiguity and a Thirst for New Knowledge

CHAPTER SUMMARY
KEY TERMS
WEB SITES OF INTEREST

What Is Clinical Psychology?

What is a *clinical psychologist*? Although it seems as though we are inundated with real and fictional portrayals of clinical psychologists in the media, the general public remains rather confused about what psychologists do as well as their educational backgrounds (J. Peterson, 1995). Perhaps this should not be too surprising given that clinical psychologists are a heterogeneous group with respect to age, gender, theoretical allegiance, and roles (Norcross, Karg, & Prochaska, 1997a, 1997b). After all these years, people still confuse clinical psychologists with medical doctors. Some continue to believe that clinical psychology and psychoanalysis are synonymous. Others see a bit of the witch doctor in clinical psychologists, while still others view them as somewhat peculiar. Fortunately, there are many who regard them as researchers, therapists, or members of prestigious professional societies.

In a recent attempt to define and describe clinical psychology, J. H. Resnick (1991, p. 7) has proposed the following definition and description of clinical psychology:

> The field of clinical psychology involves research, teaching, and services relevant to the applications of principles, methods, and procedures for understanding, predicting, and alleviating intellectual, emotional, biological, psychological, social and behavioral maladjustment, disability and discomfort, applied to a wide range of client populations.

According to Resnick, the skill areas central to the field of clinical psychology include assessment and diagnosis, intervention or treatment, consultation, research, and application of ethical and professional principles. Clinical psychologists are distinguished by their expertise in the areas of personality and psychopathology and their integration of science, theory, and practice.

Although this definition describes what clinical psychologists do and the skills they possess, we must also take note of how others see the profession and try to correct any false images.

The main purpose of this first chapter is to clarify the nature of clinical psychology by describing what clinical psychologists do and where they do it, how they got to be clinicians, and how they differ from other professionals who also tend to people's mental health needs. In the process, we should gain a better understanding of the field of clinical psychology.

Closely Related Mental Health Professions

Before we examine the nature of clinical psychology, let us briefly review some of the other major professions in the mental health field. Because most confusion lies in contrasting clinical psychology with psychiatry and with counseling psychology, we will focus most of our discussion on these two fields. Following this review, we can better present the characteristics that give clinical psychology its unique identity.

Psychiatrists

The *psychiatrist* is a physician. Psychiatry is rooted in the medical tradition and exists within the framework of organized medicine. Thus, psychiatrists are often accorded the power and status of the medical profession, even though their intellectual heritage comes from the nonmedical contributions of Freud, Jung, Adler, and others. Although the latter were physicians, they stepped out of the medical tradition to develop a psychoanalytic system of thought that had very little to do with medicine. The psychiatric profession has vocally and effectively pushed for a superior role in the mental health professional hierarchy, and much of the profession's argument has been based on its medical background.

Because of their medical training, psychiatrists may function as physicians. They may prescribe medication, treat physical ailments, and give physical examinations. In addition to their concentration on psychotherapy and psychiatric diagnosis, psychiatrists make extensive use of a variety of medications in treating their patients' psychological difficulties. Furthermore, their medical training makes them potentially better able to recognize medical problems that may be contributing to the patient's psychological distress. However, as Box 1-1 suggests, even these traditional lines that have served to distinguish psychiatrists from clinical psychologists may become more blurred in the future.

Following completion of the medical degree and the general medical internship required of all physicians, the typical psychiatrist-to-be receives psychiatric training during a three- or four-year residency. This apprenticeship period involves supervised work with patients in an outpatient or hospital setting, sometimes accompanied by seminars, reading, discussion, and related activities. The amount of formal psychiatric coursework varies, but the core training experience is the treatment of patients under the supervision of a more experienced psychiatrist.

The following description of a psychiatrist appears on the web page of the American Psychiatric Association:

> The psychiatrist is trained to diagnose whether or not what may appear to be "psychological problems" are actually the manifestation of an underlying medical-psychiatric illness. While psychiatrists are trained in psychotherapy, psychiatrists are also trained to review medical records, examine patients, analyze laboratory reports, take detailed medical histories, and prescribe medications, and in the chemistry and biology of how medications operate and interact.

In contrast to psychiatrists, clinical psychologists typically receive little training in medicine, receive more extensive training in human behavior and formal assessment of psychological functioning, and receive extensive training in scientific research methods (Kiesler, 1977).

Psychiatry no longer enjoys the prestige and popularity it once did. The proportion of medical school graduates who choose psychiatric residencies has generally declined since 1970 (Sierles & Taylor, 1995). In 1994, only 3.4% of U.S. medical school graduates chose psychiatry, the lowest percentage since 1929 (Sierles & Taylor, 1995). Reasons offered for this decline include psychiatry's recent emphasis on biological approaches (thus making the field more conventional and similar to other medical specialties), the economic impact of managed care on psychiatric practice, and the increased competition from other mental health specialties, such as clinical psychology (Sierles & Taylor, 1995).

As for practicing psychiatrists, a recent survey highlighted several demographic trends (Zarin et al., 1998). First, a higher percentage of psychiatrists are now women (25% in 1996 versus 14.5% in 1982). In addition, recent years have seen a higher proportion of psychiatrists representing minority ethnic groups. Finally, the mean number of hours worked per week by practicing psychiatrists has been on the decrease.

Counseling Psychologists

The activities of *counseling psychologists* overlap with those of clinical psychologists. Traditionally, counseling psychologists work with normal or moderately maladjusted individuals. Their work may involve group counseling or counseling with individuals. Their principal method of assessment is usually the interview, but counseling psychologists also do testing (for example, assessment of abilities, personality, interests, and vocational aptitude). Historically, they have done a great deal of educational and occupational counseling. More recently, many counseling psychologists have begun to employ cognitive-behavioral techniques and even biofeedback.

Traditionally, the most frequent employment arenas for counseling psychologists have been educational settings, especially colleges and universities. However, counseling psychologists (like clinical psychologists) also work in hospitals, rehabilitation centers, mental health clinics, and industry. A good example of the kind of work counseling psychologists conduct within educational settings is suggested in the heading that appeared above an article in a campus newspaper several years ago: "Counseling Center Responds

BOX 1-1

But Is It the Right Prescription for Clinical Psychology?

Recently, a number of clinical psychologists have expressed the hope that they may eventually be accorded the same privilege of writing prescriptions that psychiatrists have long enjoyed. In particular, they want to prescribe psychotropic medications that affect mental activity, mood, or behavior. As Handler (1988) put it, they seem to want to "do what psychiatrists do, but do it better: a one-stop shopping approach in the best supermarket tradition . . . and thereby be more competitive in the marketplace [saving] our profession from becoming obsolete" (p. 44). Handler adds that the response of some to all this is to grumble, "If I wanted to be a psychiatrist, I would have gone to medical school." For others it is, "Do you think we really could?" Overall, the responses of many seem highly supportive.

But others would urge caution here. They suggest that the reason clinical psychology has flourished is that it is *different* from psychiatry. Clinical psychologists have developed unique skills in psychological assessment. They have built a profession on a solid scientific basis. To mimic psychiatry by an ill-advised attempt to write prescriptions would help destroy clinical psychology's very uniqueness, they say.

Clinical psychologists frequently stress to troubled clients their autonomy and the necessity that they, as clients, collaborate with the therapist in the change process. In contrast, psychiatrists often come from an authoritarian tradition. The doctor is an expert who tells patients what is wrong with them and then may prescribe medication to make things right. Traditionally, clinical psychologists have been committed to the power of words ("the talking cure") and to the process of thought and social learning. They do not subscribe to the credo of "better living through chemistry" when applied to psychological problems. Although few clinical psychologists would

argue that medication is *never* necessary, many would argue that ultimately, most clients must learn to come to grips psychologically with their problems in living. The bottom line seems to be that at present, the field has not made up its mind about the value of prescription privileges. We'll have a lot more to say about this debate in Chapter 3.

Despite the field's ambivalence, the American Psychological Association recently endorsed this pursuit (Martin, 1995). This decision has important implications for research, training, and practice. For example, major changes in graduate training would be required to prepare clinical psychologists for this new role.

What is the view of clinical training directors on this issue? Riley, Elliott, and Thomas (1992) conducted a survey of randomly selected psychology graduate and internship training directors regarding prescription privileges. To the question "Should psychology pursue prescription privileges?" the majority of training directors (66.4%) answered "definitely not," "probably not," or "unsure." Further, 66.3% of training directors indicated that their faculty would be unwilling to make changes to their respective programs if prescription privileges were granted. A majority (75%) of training directors indicated that their programs would have to be lengthened by at least one year should prescription privileges be granted to psychologists, and 21.3% reported that their programs would have to be completely revamped. As this survey indicates, there appears to be a great amount of resistance from training directors to the idea of prescription privileges for psychologists. Given this resistance, it will be interesting to see whether the APA endorsement is honored and if clinical training programs do restructure their curriculum.

to Married Students' Needs." The article went on to describe group counseling sessions designed to help students who are parents deal with the special problems that marriage and children create for them in pursuing their academic goals.

In general, counseling psychologists see themselves in the following activities: (a) preventive treatment, (b) consultation, (c) development of outreach programs, (d) vocational counseling, and (e) short-term counseling/therapy of from one to 15 sessions (Tipton, 1983). However, younger counselors seem more and more to view themselves as engaged in activities, such as psychotherapy, that are traditionally in the clinical province. Today they are frequently less interested in vocational or career counseling (Fitzgerald & Osipow, 1988) and increasingly interested in private practice (Zook & Walton, 1989).

Although there are a number of similarities between counseling and clinical psychology, there are several distinguishing features as well (Sayette, Mayne, & Norcross, 1998). The field of clinical psychology is much larger, in terms of the number of doctoral-level professionals as well as the number of accredited doctoral training programs. There are approximately three times as many accredited doctoral programs, producing four times as many graduates, in clinical psychology as in counseling psychology. In contrast to the majority of clinical psychology programs, counseling programs are less frequently housed in psychology departments. Finally, counseling psychologists are more likely to provide services for mildly disturbed or maladjusted clients, and are more likely to specialize in career or vocational assessment. Results from a recent survey (Norcross, Sayette, Mayne, Karg, & Turkson, 1998) indicate several further distinctions between doctoral programs in clinical and counseling psychology.

- About twice as many people apply to clinical programs, although acceptance rates are similar.
- Average GRE scores of accepted students are slightly higher in clinical than in counseling programs.

- Counseling programs accept a higher percentage of ethnic minority students and students with a master's degree.
- Research focusing on minority/cross-cultural issues and vocational testing is more common among counseling faculty at doctoral programs.
- Research focusing on psychological disorders and clinical health psychology is more common among clinical faculty at doctoral programs.

A total of 69 doctoral training programs in counseling psychology are accredited by the American Psychological Association (APA) (*American Psychologist*, 1998). It is estimated that more than 500 doctoral degrees in counseling psychology are granted annually (Sayette, Mayne, & Norcross, 1998).

Other Mental Health Professionals

Psychiatric Social Workers. The professional activities of *psychiatric social workers* often seem similar to those of psychiatrists and clinical psychologists. Many psychiatric social workers conduct psychotherapy on an individual or group basis and contribute to the diagnostic process as well.

In years past, social workers tended to deal with the social forces and external agents that were contributing to the patient's difficulties. The social worker would take the case history, interview employers and relatives, make arrangements for vocational placement, or counsel parents; the psychiatrist conducted psychotherapy with patients; and the clinical psychologist tested them. However, these professional roles have blurred over the years.

Perhaps it was the close association with psychiatrists and psychologists that led many social workers to focus less on social or environmental factors and to become, like their colleagues, preoccupied with internal, psychological factors. Now, though, it appears that many social workers are moving away from psychoanalytic influences and returning to their earlier focus on the familial and social determinants of psychopathology.

The social work profession has been a leader in the use of supervised fieldwork as a learning device for students. Fieldwork placement is part of the program for the master's degree (usually the terminal degree for social workers), which typically requires two years. Compared to the training of clinical psychologists and psychiatrists, social work training is rather brief. As a result, the responsibilities of the social worker are generally not as great as those of the psychiatrist or clinical psychologist. Characteristic of social workers is their intense involvement with the everyday lives and stresses of their patients. They are more likely to visit the home, the factory, or the street—the places where their patients spend the bulk of their lives. Their role tends to be active, and they are less concerned with the abstract, theoretical generalizations that can be drawn from a particular case than they are with the practical matters of living.

Many psychiatric social workers are employed by public agencies of one sort or another. Some find their way into private practice, where their work in individual or family therapy is often indistinguishable from that of psychiatrists or clinical psychologists. Other social workers function as part of the mental health team (psychiatrist, clinical psychologist, and psychiatric social worker) in hospitals, social service agencies, or mental health clinics.

Currently, the field of social work appears to be growing tremendously. It is estimated that social workers now provide more than half of all the nation's mental health services, and social workers are likely to gain an even greater foothold in the mental health market in the future because they are a low-cost alternative to psychiatrists and psychologists (Clay, 1998). Enrollment in social work programs continues to increase, and the number of social workers is predicted to rise by 34% by the year 2005 (Clay, 1998).

School Psychologists. *School psychologists* work with educators and others to promote the intellectual, social, and emotional growth of school-age children. Toward this end, they may help to plan the learning environment. For example, they may generate programs to assist the development of children with special intellectual, emotional, or social needs. Often, they evaluate such children and recommend special programs, treatment, or placement if necessary. They also consult with teachers and school officials on issues of school policy or classroom management. Their work settings range from schools, nurseries, and day care centers to hospitals, clinics, and even penal institutions. A few are in private practice. There are a total of 45 APA-accredited programs in school psychology (*American Psychologist*, 1998), and it is estimated that fewer than 100 doctoral degrees in school psychology are awarded each year (Sayette, Mayne, & Norcross, 1998).

Rehabilitation Psychologists. In both research and practice, the focus of *rehabilitation psychologists* is on people who are physically or cognitively disabled. The disability may result from a birth defect or later illness or injury. Rehabilitation psychologists help individuals adjust to their disabilities and the physical, psychological, social, and environmental barriers that often accompany them. Their most frequent places of employment are in rehabilitation institutes and hospitals.

Health Psychologists. The field of health psychology has emerged in recent years and is growing rapidly (Brannon & Feist, 2000; Gatchel, Baum, & Krantz, 1989). *Health psychologists* are those who, through their research or practice, contribute to the promotion and maintenance of good health. They are also involved in the prevention and treatment of illness. They may design, execute, and study programs to help people stop smoking, manage stress, lose weight, or stay fit. Because this is an emerging field, those in it come from a variety of backgrounds, including clinical psychology, counseling psychology, social psychology, and others. Many health psychologists are employed in medical centers, but increasingly they are serving as consultants to business and industry—in any organization that recognizes the importance of keeping its employees or members well. As we will discuss in Chapter 3, this specialty is likely to profit most from the sweeping changes in health care. We discuss health psychology in greater detail in Chapter 17.

Psychiatric Nurses. In recent years, the roles of other mental health personnel have been expanding. We have long been aware of the role of psychiatric nurses. Because they spend many hours in close contact with patients, they are not only in a position to provide information about patients' hospital adjustment, but they can also play a crucial and sensitive role in fostering an appropriate therapeutic environment. Working in close collaboration with the psychiatrist or the clinical psychologist, they (along with those they supervise—attendants, nurse's aides, volunteers, and so on) implement therapeutic recommendations.

Others. Most well-staffed hospitals employ a variety of other therapeutic personnel, including occupational therapists, recreational therapists, horticultural therapists, and so on. By virtue of their training and experience, these people can play a vital adjunctive role in enhancing the adjustment patterns of patients. They can teach skills that will help patients in a variety of nonhospital settings. They can help make hospitalization a more tolerable experience, and they can provide outlets that increase the therapeutic value of institutions. Whether their role is to help put patients in touch with their feelings via art, music, gardening, or dancing, or to enhance patients' personal and social skills, the contributions of such therapeutic personnel are significant.

People who are trained to assist professional mental health workers are called *paraprofessionals*, and their role has expanded greatly in recent years. Volunteers are often provided short training sessions and then become the most visible personnel in crisis centers (both walk-in and telephone). Certain paraprofessional activities have become accepted practice. Research indi-

cates strongly that the efforts of paraprofessionals can effectively supplement the work of professionals (Christensen & Jacobson, 1994; Hattie, Sharpley, & Rogers, 1984). We will discuss this issue extensively in Chapter 16.

Now that we have briefly examined some of the other helping professions, let us turn to the work of the clinical psychologist.

The Clinical Psychologist

Trying to define clinical psychology in terms of the problems with which clinicians deal is hopeless. The number and kinds of problems are so extensive as to boggle the mind: depression, anxiety, psychosis, personality disorders, mental retardation, addictions, learning disabilities, juvenile delinquency, vocational problems, and sexual difficulties, to name but a few. Further, this list does not cover those individuals who seek out psychotherapy not because of current dysfunctional symptoms but as a way to better understand themselves.

Instead of defining clinical psychology in terms of problems or issues clinical psychologists are asked to address, we will try to give a picture of the field by reviewing the activities engaged in by clinical psychologists.

Activities of Clinical Psychologists

Much of our information about clinical activities comes from a series of studies conducted between 1973 and 1995. Each study involved a random sample of members of Division 12 (Division of Clinical Psychology) of the American Psychological Association (APA). Garfield and Kurtz (1976) examined more than 800 questionnaires collected in 1973. Norcross and Prochaska (1982) studied nearly 500 returns gathered in 1981; Norcross, Prochaska, and Gallagher (1989b) were able to analyze 579 questionnaires from 1986; and, finally, Norcross, Karg, and Prochaska (1997a, 1997b) surveyed 546 clinical psychologists in 1994–1995. The results of these four surveys are presented in Table 1-1.

■ **TABLE 1-1** Clinicians' Activities

Activity	Percentage involved in 1995	Mean percentage of time			
		1973	1981	1986	1995
Psychotherapy	84	31	35	35	37
Diagnosis/Assessment	74	10	13	16	15
Teaching	50	14	12	14	09
Clinical supervision	62	08	08	11	07
Research/Writing	47	07	08	15	10
Consultation	54	05*	07	11	07
Administration	52	13	13	16	11

*Garfield and Kurtz percentage is for "community consultation."
Source: Adapted from Norcross, Karg, & Prochaska (1997a).

From Table 1-1 it is apparent that psychotherapy of one sort or another is the most frequently engaged in activity and occupies the most time, as it has in all the cited surveys from 1973 to 1995. Diagnosis and assessment also continue as major activities. Research activity has grown over the years (to around 10% of the 1995 respondents' time), which is a bit surprising in light of the fact that 40% of the 1995 sample was employed full-time in private practice. Still, it is important to note that some clinical psychologists never publish a research paper and that only 10–15% of all clinicians produce 40–50% of all the work published by clinical psychologists (Norcross et al., 1989b, 1997b). Teaching is another relatively common activity among clinical psychologists. Unfortunately, time devoted to administration remains significant, perhaps reflecting the bureaucracy that is so prevalent in modern society. Let us now take a closer look at the six activities represented in Table 1-1.

Therapy/Intervention. It is clear from Table 1-1 that therapy is the activity that most frequently engages the typical clinician's efforts and to which the most time is devoted. The layperson often has an image of the therapy situation as one in which the client lies on a couch while the therapist, bearded and mysterious, sits behind with notepad and furrowed brow. Actually, therapy comes in many different sizes and shapes. A few therapists still use a couch, but more often the client sits in a chair adjacent to the therapist's desk. Most often therapy involves a one-to-one relationship, but today couple's therapy, family therapy, and group therapy are also very common. For example, a group of six or eight clients, all having trouble with alcohol use, may meet together with a therapist to work on their problems. Finally, sizable proportions of therapists are women, not men.

In some instances, therapy involves mainly a search for insight into the origins of one's problems or the purposes served by one's undesirable behavior. In other cases, therapy consists primarily of a relationship between client and therapist designed to produce an atmosphere of trust that will help dissolve the client's debilitating defenses. Other forms of therapy are cognitive-behavioral, in the sense that the client learns new and more satisfying ways of thinking and behaving. Sometimes the goals of therapy are sweeping, involving major changes in behavior. Other times patients desire help only with a troublesome fear that prevents them from achieving certain goals. Therapy varies, then, along many different dimensions.

Diagnosis/Assessment. All practicing clinicians engage in assessment of one form or another. Take, for example, the following cases:

A child who is failing the fourth grade is administered an intelligence test. Is there an intellectual deficit?

Personality tests are given to a client who is depressed and has lost all zest for life. Can the test results shed light on personality factors contributing to the depression?

It has been decided that a client will profit from therapy. But what form of therapy will be most suitable?

A father has been charged with child abuse. He is interviewed and tested to determine whether he suffers from a mental disorder that influences his judgment and impulse control.

Common to all these examples is the effort to better understand the individual so that a more informed decision can be made or the most desirable course of action selected. Assessment, whether through observation, testing, or interviewing, is a way of gathering information so that an important question can be answered or so that a problem can be solved. These questions or problems are virtually infinite in variety, as the foregoing examples suggest. Assessment has long been a critical part of the clinical psychologist's role. Indeed, for many years assessment, especially testing, was the chief element in the clinician's professional identity.

Teaching. Clinical psychologists who have full- or part-time academic appointments obviously devote a considerable amount of time to teaching. Those whose responsibilities are primarily in the area of graduate education teach courses in advanced psychopathology, psychological testing, interviewing, intervention, personality theory, experimental psychopathology, and so on. Some of them may also teach undergraduate courses such as introductory psychology, personality, abnormal psychology, introduction to clinical psychology, psychological testing, and

others. Even clinicians whose primary appointments are in clinics or hospitals or who operate a private practice sometimes teach evening courses at a nearby college or university or may even have part-time appointments in graduate programs.

Much of this teaching is of the familiar classroom-lecture type. But a considerable amount of teaching is also done on a one-to-one, supervisory basis. Clinical psychologists in clinical settings may also teach informal classes or do orientation work with other mental health personnel, such as nurses, aides, social workers, occupational therapists, and so on. In some cases, the clinician may go out into the community and lead workshops on various topics for police officers, volunteers, ministers, probation officers, and others.

Clinical Supervision. This activity is really another form of teaching. However, it typically involves more one-to-one teaching, small group approaches, and other less formal, non-classroom varieties of instruction. Whether in university, internship, or general clinical settings, clinical psychologists often spend significant portions of their time supervising students, interns, and others. Becoming skilled in the intricacies of therapy and assessment techniques requires more than just reading textbooks. It also involves seeing clients and then discussing their cases with a more experienced supervisor. In short, one learns by doing but under the controlled and secure conditions of a trainee–supervisor relationship. This kind of "practicum" teaching and supervision can occur both in university and internship settings, and in postdoctoral programs as well.

Research. Clinical psychology has grown out of an academic research tradition. As a result, when clinical training programs were first established after World War II, the scientist-practitioner model was adopted. This meant that, in contrast to other mental health workers such as psychiatrists or social workers, all clinicians were to be trained both as scientists and as practitioners.

Although this research emphasis may not be so prominent in some training programs as it once was, the fact remains that clinical psychologists are in a unique position both to evaluate research conducted by others and to conduct their own research. By virtue of their training in research, their extensive experience with people in distress, and their knowledge of both therapy and assessment, clinical psychologists have the ability both to consume and to produce new knowledge.

The range of research projects carried out by clinicians is enormous. Studies include searching for the causes of mental disorders, development and validation of assessment devices, evaluation of therapy techniques, and so on. To provide something of the flavor of these efforts, Figure 1-1 shows the table of contents of a fairly recent issue of the *Journal of Consulting and Clinical Psychology*, a major publication outlet for research by clinical psychologists.

Consultation. In both consultation and teaching, the goal is to increase the effectiveness of those to whom one's efforts are directed by imparting to them some degree of expertise. Consultation takes innumerable forms, in many different settings. For example, one might consult with a colleague who is having difficulty with a therapy case. Such consultation might be a one-shot affair with someone who simply needs help with one specific case. In other instances, however, a clinician might be retained on a relatively permanent basis to provide the staff of an agency with help. Perhaps, for example, our consulting clinician is an expert on the problems of drug addicts. By working with the staff, the consultant can increase the effectiveness of the entire agency. Consultation could come in the form of case-by-case advice, or the consultant might be asked to discuss general problems associated with drug addiction. Further, more police departments have begun using clinical psychologists as consultants in hostage negotiations (Fuselier, 1989). Finally, a growing number of clinical psychologists serve as consultants to physicians who deliver primary care services

(Haley et al., 1998; Pace, Chaney, Mullins, & Olson, 1995).

Consultation can run the gamut from clinical cases to matters of business, personnel, and profit. It can deal with individuals or entire organizations. Sometimes it is remedial; other times it is oriented toward prevention. Consulting, regardless of the setting in which it occurs or the particular purpose it has, is a significant activity of many clinical psychologists today. We discuss consultation in more detail in Chapter 16.

Administration. It has been said half-jokingly that no one in clinical psychology enjoys administrative work except masochists or those with obsessive-compulsive personalities. Nevertheless, nearly every clinical psychologist spends time on administrative tasks. For example, client records must be maintained, those infernal effort reports must be filled out each month, and research projects must be cleared by committees set up to safeguard the rights of human subjects. Clinical psychologists who work for agencies or institutions will likely serve on several committees: personnel, research, patient rights, or even the committee to select films for the patients' Friday night movies.

Some really hardy souls become full-time administrators. They do so for many reasons. Sometimes they are drafted by colleagues who regard them as skillful in human relations. Others may grow a bit weary with therapy or assessment and want a change. Or maybe they have the fantasy that administration is the route to power and wealth. In any event, good administrators are the ones who keep their organization running smoothly and efficiently. Being sensitive to the needs and problems of people in the organization and having the patience to sometimes suffer in silence are useful attributes of the good administrator. The ability to communicate well with those under supervision is also important, as is a knack for selecting the right people for the right jobs.

It would be difficult to list all the sorts of administrative posts held by clinical psychologists. However, here are a few examples: head of a

FIGURE 1-1 Sample table of contents from the *Journal of Consulting and Clinical Psychology*
Copyright 1999 by the American Psychological Association. Reprinted by permission.

August 1999   Volume 67, Number 4

Journal of
Consulting and Clinical Psychology
Copyright © 1999 by the American Psychological Association, Inc.

Regular Articles

TABLE 1-2 Employment Settings of Clinical Psychologists

Employment Site	1973 %	1981 %	1986 %	1995 %
Psychiatric hospital	08	08	09	05
General hospital	06	08	05	04
Outpatient clinic	05	05	04	04
Community mental health center	08	06	05	04
Medical school	08	07	07	09
Private practice	23	31	35	40
University, psychology	22	17	17	15
University, other	07	05	04	04
VA medical center	—	—	—	03
None	01	01	04	01
Other*	01	12	10	11

*This category includes professional schools, correctional facilities, managed care organizations, nursing homes, child and family services, rehabilitation centers, school systems, psychoanalytic institutes, health maintenance organizations, and so on.

Source: Adapted from Norcross, Karg, & Prochaska (1997a).

university psychology department, director of a Veterans Administration clinic, vice president of a consulting firm, director of the clinical training program, director of the psychological clinic in a university psychology department, chief psychologist in a state hospital, and director of a regional crisis center.

Employment Sites

Where are clinical psychologists employed? Data from the previously noted surveys will again help us answer this question. The results pertaining to work settings from the 1973 survey (Garfield & Kurtz, 1976) and the 1981, 1986, and 1995 surveys (Norcross & Prochaska, 1982a; Norcross, Prochaska, & Gallagher, 1989a; and Norcross et al., 1997a, respectively) are shown in Table 1-2. It is evident that private practice has grown steadily over the years and is now clearly the most frequent employment setting for clinical psychologists. University settings are the second most

common employment sites. Although not shown in Table 1-2, the data from Norcross et al. (1997b) indicate that of those clinicians whose primary job is that of a full-time university professor, 68% are engaged in some part-time form of private practice or supervision. From Tables 1-1 and 1-2, the diversity of both activities and work settings is very obvious. This is also evident in the increase over time in the numbers in the "Other" category in Table 1-2. This diversity is illustrated in the background and activities of the hypothetical clinician described in the next section.

A Week in the Life of Dr. Karen C.

Karen C. began her undergraduate career in journalism. However, following a course in general psychology, she decided to switch to psychology. After fulfilling the usual requirements for a psychology major (courses in psychobiology, statistics, cognitive psychology, history and systems, personality, social psychology, and so on), she applied to 11 graduate schools. With a strong grade point average and an equally strong set of scores on the Graduate Record Examination, she was accepted by four schools. She chose a large midwestern state university and later did her internship at a local state hospital.

Five years after enrolling, she was awarded the Ph.D. and began her career as a staff psychologist in a tri-county outpatient clinic. Four years later, we have a typical week in the life of Karen C.

Monday, Wednesday, Friday
8:00–9:00 A.M. Staff meeting. This period is devoted to a variety of activities, including discussion of cases, agency policy and problems, insurance questions, and other administrative business.

9:00–10:00 A.M. Psychotherapy. The current case is that of a moderately depressed 48-year-old woman who was recently divorced. Mrs. G. is showing gradual improvement, and the prospect of hospitalization seems to have passed. Dr. C. is using what might be termed an eclectic form of psychotherapy that is generally psychodynamic in flavor.

10:00–10:30 A.M. Psychotherapy. This patient, Sam F., is 19 years old. He has a record of arrests for shoplifting, truancy, and public intoxication. His intellectual potential is limited, and his learning history is quite deprived. The therapy employed might be described as behavioral in character. The focus is on enhancing Sam F.'s repertoire of social skills and decreasing the frequency of his maladaptive behaviors.

10:30 A.M.–12:00 noon This period is reserved for psychological testing, both for Dr. C.'s patients and for the patients of other therapists. Typically, intelligence tests, projective tests, and self-report tests are employed. Occasionally, neuropsychological assessment is also done.

1:00–2:00 P.M. Clinical supervision. The local university places several interns with Dr. C.'s agency. This period is devoted to supervising their psychotherapy and their diagnostic efforts. The supervision of two M.A.-level psychologists employed by the agency is also included here.

2:00–3:00 P.M. Psychotherapy. Bob S. is a university student. His major difficulty might be termed alienation. Dr. C. has tried a variety of therapeutic techniques, but nothing has seemed to work. Although the patient has been able to continue with his classes so far, the prospects of hospitalization seem to be increasing.

3:00–4:30 P.M. Group psychotherapy. This period is devoted to the treatment of a group of six male alcoholics with heterogeneous backgrounds. The treatment approach is largely supportive.

4:30–5:00 P.M. This time is typically devoted to report writing, administrative details, and so on.

Tuesday, Thursday
8:00–10:00 A.M. Dr. C. is engaged in a research project to determine whether certain psychological test responses (for example, from the MMPI-2) can be used to predict responsiveness to various forms of therapy. Dr. C. is using cases from her own agency along with cases from four other local clinics and institutions.

10:00 A.M.–12:00 noon Psychological testing.

1:00–3:00 P.M. Dr. C. serves as a consultant to the local school system. She serves four schools and meets with teachers to discuss their handling of specific problem children. She provides consultation for the school psychologist as well.

3:00–5:00 P.M. Dr. C. is advising a local institution for the mentally retarded on the establishment of a token economy. The goal is to upgrade the self-care habits of a group of moderately retarded children and young adults in the institution. It is hoped that the project can serve as a prototype demonstration for use throughout the institution.

7:00–8:30 P.M. Two evenings a week, Dr. C. teaches a course in abnormal psychology at the local university. It is a fully accredited course and enrolls both full- and part-time students.

Saturday
9:00–1:00 P.M. During this period, Dr. C. sees a series of patients in private practice. They are typically patients with a variety of complaints

■ **TABLE 1-3** **Wednesday at the University with Professor L.**

8:30–9:00 A.M.	Proofread test for Introduction to Clinical Psychology class
9:00–10:00 A.M.	Research meeting with two graduate students
10:00–11:30 A.M.	Teaching: Clinical practicum supervision
11:30 A.M.–12:30 P.M.	Jog at the track
12:30–1:00 P.M.	Brown bag lunch in the office (read journal articles)
1:00–2:00 P.M.	Office hour for undergraduate students
2:00–2:30 P.M.	Check mail and e-mail
2:30–4:00 P.M.	Attend meeting of the campus committee on computer use
4:00–5:00 P.M.	Work on a revision of a manuscript submitted earlier to a journal
7:00–9:00 P.M.	Teaching: Seminar on empirically supported psychological treatments
9:30–11:00 P.M.	Rest and rehabilitation

(for example, depression, anxiety). These patients are usually referred by local physicians and other professionals in the community who are aware of Dr. C.'s excellent work and reputation. Dr. C. also does some diagnostic testing on a referral basis during this time.

In contrast to Dr. C., a clinical psychologist who teaches at a major university might have a quite different schedule. Table 1-3 offers a glimpse of one such day for a new assistant professor.

Some Demographic Notes

Several demographic characteristics have been noted by Norcross et al. (1997a). First, in this survey of 546 randomly selected clinical psychologists from the APA Division 12 (Clinical Psychology) roster, roughly 28% were women. Only 7% of clinicians were members of racial minorities. Although these numbers seem low, they are roughly comparable to those published in 1993 by the APA Office of Demographic, Employment, and Educational Research (ODEER), suggesting the Norcross et al.'s sample was representative of Division 12 members. The mean age of the clinicians was 50 years old. The ten universities that produced the greatest number of clinical psychology doctorates in this sample were New York University, Pennsylvania State, Connecticut, Illinois, Iowa, Minnesota, Tennessee, Purdue, Ohio State, and Florida State.

As for primary *theoretical orientation*, 27% of the sample described themselves as eclectic/integrative, 24% as cognitive, 18% as psychodynamic, and 13% as behavioral. Table 1-4 presents the theoretical orientations of clinical psychologists in the Norcross et al. (1997a) survey, as well as those identified in four other surveys dating back to 1960. As can be seen, the percentage of clinicians adhering to a psychodynamic orientation has declined over the years, whereas the corresponding percentage for a cognitive orientation has increased dramatically. The popularity of the eclectic orientation, while still strong, has decreased somewhat in recent years.

Finally, although hardly a demographic feature, it is reassuring to note that of all the clinical psychologists sampled, only 9% expressed any dissatisfaction with their choice of clinical psychology as a career (Norcross et al., 1997b).

Research and the Scientific Tradition

Although clinical psychology is dedicated to the improvement of human welfare, it springs from a research tradition that emphasizes the quest for knowledge. This research tradition does not

■ TABLE 1-4 Theoretical Orientations of Clinical Psychologists

Orientation	1960 %	1973 %	1981 %	1986 %	1995 %
Behavioral	08	10	14	16	13
Cognitive	—	02	06	13	24
Eclectic/Integrative	36	55	31	29	27
Humanistic*	02	06	04	06	03
Interpersonal	—	—	—	—	04
Psychodynamic**	35	16	30	21	18
Rogerian	04	01	03	06	01
Sullivanian	10	03	02	02	01
Systems	—	—	04	04	04
Other	04	07	06	03	05

*Humanistic includes existential and Gestalt.

**Psychodynamic includes psychoanalytic and psychodynamic. The corresponding 1960 and 1973 figures are for psychoanalysis and neo-Freudian.

Source: Adapted from Norcross, Karg, & Prochaska, (1997a).

imply that every clinician ought to be heavily engaged in research or other scholarly pursuits. What it does suggest is that training in clinical psychology that incorporates courses and experience in research and statistical methods gives clinicians unique skills that help establish their professional identity. Such methodological training helps develop a capacity for evaluation and an attitude of caution and skepticism that permits clinical psychologists to become better, more perceptive diagnosticians and therapists, as well as researchers.

Art or Science?

Because clinical psychology deals with the problems of individuals, the focus of clinical psychology is often on individual differences rather than the commonalities among persons. Consider an example. Suppose that one of the authors is conducting an experiment on the effects of an attitude of personal control on problem solving. His goal is to develop certain principles that will indicate how a feeling of being in con-

trol of outcomes affects the ability to solve problems. Suppose, further, that he induces a feeling of control through verbal instructions. He instructs some subjects that they have much control and others that they have little. Several subjects may respond very differently from others in the same group. This, of course, increases the variance of the group and, statistically speaking, reduces the likelihood that significant differences between experimental groups will be found. As a result, the researcher will study ways to eliminate such variance. In searching for general principles of behavior (the so-called *nomothetic approach*), the research psychologist generally is less concerned with individual differences. The focus is on group differences that occur as a function of some experimental treatment or manipulation. The goal is the abstraction of general principles of behavior from the observation of many people.

The clinical approach, however, seeks the understanding of individual differences (often called the *idiographic approach*). Why is *this* patient so anxiety-ridden? Why is *this* patient unresponsive to certain reinforcements? This focus is perhaps responsible for the continuing debate over whether clinical psychology is an art or a science. For the more subjectively oriented clinician, it more often seems to be the former. Stated another way, there are clinicians who feel that when they make diagnostic judgments or therapeutic decisions, they do so largely on the basis of their own skill, experience, and subjective or intuitive awareness. Just as a person cannot be taught to paint a masterpiece, they believe, neither can one be taught to make highly sensitive and penetrating interpretations of a projective test or of a patient's report about a dream. Of course, the rudimentary elements of scoring a test or the basic mechanisms of therapy can be transmitted from one person to another. However, some believe that these other high-level skills cannot be taught.

Empirically oriented clinicians possess a more objective orientation. They argue that the answers lie in more research and in the objective application of the principles of human behavior to each case. Where subjectively oriented clinicians might seek the answer to a diagnostic problem in their own intuition, more empirically oriented clinicians may put their faith in the best possible statistical formula or actuarial prediction.

It is expected that through research and the development of general principles, a greater level of understanding of specific patients will be attained. At the same time, just as there are individual differences among patients, so there are individual differences among clinicians. Some are smarter, more experienced, or harder working than others. The application of general principles to individual cases is not easy. The discovery of the sameness within diversity is difficult; but so too is locating the unique within the homogeneous. Furthermore, seeing the relevance of laboratory or field research to a person in distress is an important and difficult task that requires its own brand of sensitivity and intelligence.

In the end, the art-versus-science dichotomy may be a "red herring." When making clinical decisions or predictions, *all* clinical psychologists should attend to relevant empirical re-search, recognize and overcome potential cultural biases, use reliable assessment methods, and perhaps even refuse to offer predictions or make decisions in some instances where reliability and validity of clinical judgment are poor (Garb, 1998). In this way, it is more likely that clinical judgment will be scientifically based, accurate, and useful. We will have more to say about these issues in Chapter 10.

Training: Toward a Clinical Identity

The preceding pages have provided a sketch of some of the activities, affiliations, and orientations of clinicians, touched upon the scientific tradition, and raised the issue of art versus science in clinical psychology. Now let us turn to a discussion of the unique background and skills that set clinical psychologists apart from other mental health professionals. None of this is set in stone, of course. The field is changing and, as always, there are disagreements among clinicians as to how to train students and in what direction the field should move. However, it is useful to remember that clinical psychology is but a specialized application of the more basic core of psychology (Matarazzo, 1987).

An Overview

The typical clinical psychologist completes a bachelor's degree and then five years of graduate work. The latter typically includes training in assessment, research, diagnosis, and therapeutic skills, along with an internship. Most often, this effort culminates in a Ph.D. (Doctor of Philosophy) degree from a university psychology department. In some instances, the degree awarded is the Psy.D. (Doctor of Psychology) either from a university department of psychology or from a training institution not affiliated with a university. There are also two-year programs that award the master's degree. Because of contemporary licensing laws that dictate who may practice independently as a psychologist, fewer individuals graduating from master's programs can achieve much in the way of professional independence. Many of them hope to transfer to Ph.D. or Psy.D. programs later and, indeed, some are quite successful in doing so (Quereshi & Kuchan, 1988). Past evidence suggests that subdoctoral clinicians are less in demand than doctoral-level clinicians, are paid less, and are perceived as less competent (Havens, Colliver, Dimond, & Wesley, 1982). In 1987, master's-level clinicians could be fully licensed to practice independently in psychology in only three states, while limited licensing was possible in 14 others (Dale, 1988). However, the number of master's degree programs and the number of master's degrees conferred appear to be growing. In 1994, three times as many master's degrees as doctoral degrees were awarded in psychology (B. Murray, 1995).

Master's-level training in clinical psychology has always been somewhat controversial. Master's-level psychologists claim that research indicates that master's-level clinicians are as effective as doctoral-level clinicians. The American Psychological Association, however, accepts the doctoral degree alone as the key to work as an independent professional. The presidents of the American Psychological Association continue to assert that a doctoral degree is a prerequisite for the title "psychologist" and that a doctoral degree should be required for those who wish to practice psychology independently (B. Murray, 1995). Nevertheless, master's-level clinicians continue to work in a variety of service-delivery settings. The increasing influence of managed care in the mental health care marketplace may lead to a resurgence of the popularity of master's programs in clinical psychology (Sleek, 1995a). In general, master's-level practitioners charge lower fees, making them an attractive alternative (in managed-care insurers' eyes) to doctoral-level clinicians. It will be interesting to see how this controversial issue unfolds as lobbying efforts to give master's-level clinicians "psychologist" status increase, and as increasing economic pressures come into play.

With this thumbnail sketch of training in clinical psychology, we can now examine the content of doctoral training more closely.

Clinical Training Programs

The predominant training philosophy in clinical psychology today is still the *scientist-practitioner model* (Raimy, 1950). We shall have a good deal more to say about this model in the next chapter, and in Chapter 3 we will discuss alternative training models for clinical psychologists as well. For the moment, however, a brief overview of the scientist-practitioner training model will be useful.

Training programs that emerged after World War II were based on the principle that the scientist and practitioner roles could be integrated. The goal was the creation of a unique profession. More recently, this training model has come under attack as (1) unrealistic and (2) unresponsive to the needs of students who aspire only to clinical practice. Nevertheless, a majority of clinical programs still subscribe to it in varying degrees. It is this model that differentiates clinical psychologists from the rest of the mental health pack.

A Sample Program. How does this model translate into an actual program that trains clinical psychologists? Table 1-5 presents a fairly typical program of study.

Several things should be said about the program outlined in Table 1-5. First, it is just one example. Some programs place less emphasis on research and more on clinical techniques. Some are structured so that one can complete all the work in four years, especially if summers can be devoted to coursework. In some programs the internship comes in the fourth year, often before the dissertation has been completed. A few schools still require competency in a foreign language, although many now allow the student to substitute courses in statistics or computer technology. It is also true that each school tends to have its own "personality." Some programs have a distinct cognitive-behavioral orientation, emphasizing such techniques as cognitive therapy for depression. Others have a psychodynamic flavor and emphasize projective testing. Faculty interests in some programs center on children, while in others the focus is on adults. Although

TABLE 1-5 Sample Ph.D. Program of Study: Scientist-Practitioner Model

Year 1	*Fall*	
	Statistics (Analysis of Variance)	
	Systems of Psychotherapy	
	Departmental Core Course: Social Psychology	
	Introduction to Data Analysis	
	M.A. Thesis Research	

Year 1 *Fall*
Statistics (Analysis of Variance)
Systems of Psychotherapy
Departmental Core Course: Social
 Psychology
Introduction to Data Analysis
M.A. Thesis Research

Year 1 *Winter*
Statistics (Regression)
Psychometrics (Test Construction)
Assessment (choose Adult or Child
 Assessment)
Introduction to Data Analysis
M.A. Thesis Research
Clinical Practicum

Year 2 *Fall*
Ethical and Professional Issues
Psychopathology
M.A. Thesis Research
Clinical Practicum

Year 2 *Winter*
Departmental Core Course: Functional
 Neuroscience
Elective: Family and Group Process
M.A. Thesis Research
Clinical Practicum

Year 3 *Fall*
Departmental Core Course: Cognitive
 Psychology
Elective: Experimental Psychopathology
Dissertation Research
Clinical Practicum

Year 3 *Winter*
Statistics (Latent Variables and Structural
 Equation Modeling)
Departmental Core Course: Developmen-
 tal Psychology
Dissertation Research
Clinical Practicum

Year 4 *Fall*
Outside Course: Psychological Anthropol-
 ogy
Dissertation Research
History and Systems of Psychology

Year 4 *Winter*
Outside Course: Violence in the Family
Dissertation Research

Year 5 *Fall and Winter*
Clinical Internship

*During the third year (usually in winter semester), students are expected to complete qualifying examinations.

there is diversity among clinical programs, there is a great deal of commonality as well. A student applying for graduate work should investigate such emphases so as to make informed choices.

Coursework. Clinical students normally must take a series of basic courses such as statistics and research design, biological foundations of behavior, social psychology, developmental psychology, and cognitive psychology. The exact number and content of these courses will vary somewhat from program to program. The intent is to give the student an understanding of the basics that underlie human behavior or that permit us to investigate that behavior. These courses provide a strong scientific foundation for the student's clinical training and give life to the sci-

entist-practitioner model in clinical psychology. Depending on the student's interests, several electives, advanced courses, and seminars in these same topics are often taken as well.

Clinical students also enroll in several courses that teach the fundamentals of clinical practice or deal with clinical topics at an advanced level. For example, there are often courses in psychopathology, theory and research in therapy, or principles of cognitive-behavioral interventions, or seminars in such topics as schizophrenia, methods of family and group therapy, community psychology, or neuropsychological assessment.

Practicum Work. Books and coursework are fine, but ultimately one must learn by doing. As a result, all programs seek to build the student's clinical skills through exposure to *clinical practica*. The dictionary defines a practicum as "work done by an advanced student that involves the practical application of previously studied theory." In many instances, the practicum will combine academic content with practical experience. Typically, there are practica or clinics in assessment (intelligence, neuropsychology, personality, and so on), therapy (psychodynamic treatment, cognitive-behavioral interventions), interviewing, and even methods of consulting with school officials, community agencies, or industry. Whatever the specific form or content of the practicum experience, it is a major vehicle for the acquisition of specific clinical skills. The student's practicum work is supervised by clinical faculty members or by clinicians in the community who have special skills. Most psychology departments that have clinical training programs also operate a *psychological clinic*. This clinic often provides assessment, therapy, and consulting services to university students, staff, and faculty, as well as to families of university personnel and to people in the surrounding community. Cases are accepted selectively in terms of their teaching value. Such a clinic may be staffed by a full-time secretary, a social worker, and clinical faculty.

Research. The implementation of the scientist-practitioner model requires that the student develop research competency. This is accomplished through courses in statistics, computer methods, and research methodology and also by active participation in research projects. There are differences among schools as to the extent of their commitment to the scientist-practitioner approach to training. Therefore, differences also exist among departments in the emphasis they place on research training and in the rewards they dispense to students for devotion to research. Most departments do, however, require the completion of a master's thesis (usually by the end of the second year). A dissertation reporting the results of an original research project is also required (by the end of either the fourth or fifth year, depending on the specific program). The dissertation is a more extensive project than the master's thesis, and it is designed to contribute significant new information to the field. Most programs continue to stress traditional experimental or correlational research for the dissertation.

Programs that emphasize the research commitment usually see to it that research experience is not confined to the thesis and dissertation. In one department, for example, each clinical student joins the research "team" of a faculty member. The team consists of from four to eight graduate students who are at varying year levels in the program. The team meets one evening per week for two or three hours. Research topics are discussed, and research projects are designed. Thesis and dissertation proposals may be discussed and defended. The more advanced students can provide guidance and also serve as role models for the younger students. In any case, the vigorous give-and-take of such meetings can go a long way toward building the research commitment.

The Qualifying Examination. Most clinical programs require students to pass a *qualifying examination*, sometimes called the preliminary examination or the comprehensive examination. Whatever its title, some students regard it as the most anxiety-provoking experience in their training. It is a written examination that takes different forms at different universities. In some cases three written examinations, each lasting four hours, are spaced over a week; others have a five-day examination. Some schools require an oral examination as well. In certain programs the tests cover all areas of psychology, whereas in others they are confined to the field of clinical psychology. Most often, these examinations are taken during the third year. Qualifying examinations serve a very useful function in ensuring the student's overall academic competency. A few programs, however, employ "innovative" alternatives. For example, students might prepare a research grant application or perhaps complete several integrative literature reviews of important topics in clinical psychology (for example, the etiology of schizophrenia).

The Internship. The *internship* is a vital part of any training program. It is the capstone of the student's previous experiences in clinical courses and practica and provides the experience that begins to consolidate the scientist-practitioner role. An internship of one sort or another is required of all students in clinical programs accredited by the APA. In the years immediately following World War II, the internship was most commonly taken during the third year of training. Now, however, so many programs are essentially five years in length that the internship most often seems to come at the end of graduate training. In a few instances, students may take half-time internships over a two-year period. Usually, an intern works at an independent facility off campus. However, some intern in such university facilities as counseling centers and medical schools. A total of 453 predoctoral internship sites were fully approved by the American Psychological Association in 1998; these "approved" internship programs are listed each year in the December issue of the *American Psychologist.*

The values of internship training are many. For example, it allows the student to work full-time in a professional setting. New skills can be acquired; older ones can be sharpened. Experience in a professional setting gives the student a real taste of the demands of professional life. Students are also exposed to clinical psychologists who may have ideas and orientations different from those of their university faculty. Thus, the experience can help break down any provincialism that may have crept into the student's university training. Exposure to different kinds of clients can likewise enhance the student's competency. Students encounter the clinical conditions that they have studied, and this experience can help stimulate research ideas. Ideally, the internship provides the opportunity to expand one's professional horizons and to integrate what one has learned at the university with the demands of the professional world. It becomes the final element in the three-dimensional world of academics, research, and experience.

Admission to Graduate Programs

The previous section described training in clinical psychology. But how does one get into graduate school in the first place? There are, of course, no guarantees, but the following pages should help answer some of the more frequently asked questions about admission to graduate training programs in clinical psychology.

Step 1: Know Your Program

To some degree or other, the purpose of graduate training is to challenge your intellect, open new vistas, and help you focus your aspirations. You should have a mental set receptive to new ideas. At the same time, you should be familiar with programs before you apply. Some have a psychodynamic orientation; others are cognitive-behavioral or perhaps eclectic. Some emphasize research; others are more practice-oriented. The guidebook survey by Sayette, Mayne, and Norcross (1998) provides some good information about clinical and research emphases of various programs.

There is no single authoritative source that will tell you everything you need to know about graduate programs in clinical psychology. However, the more sources you check, the more likely it is that you will be able to make informed decisions. Here are some possibilities:

1. Talk to your psychology faculty, especially those who are clinical psychologists. They will have both formal information as well as informal impressions through which you can sift to arrive at your own ideas.
2. The APA annually publishes a list of graduate programs. Called *Graduate Study in Psychology,* it contains a wealth of information on each school, including programs and degrees, addresses, application procedures, tuition charges, data on financial assistance, size of faculty, admission requirements, average test scores and GPAs of students admitted the previous year, and so on. Many psychology departments have a copy you can borrow, or you may purchase a copy from the APA.

3. Very often university libraries or psychology departments have copies of many catalogs from universities across the country. These are especially useful in discovering just what courses are offered, as well as the names of the faculty.

4. Once you know who is on the faculty at a given school, you can check the *APA Membership Directory* for additional information on faculty interests and background. Normally your psychology department office will have a copy of this directory.

5. A more laborious but sometimes more interesting strategy is to examine copies of journals that publish the research of clinical psychologists. This can give you an idea of who is active in research, the kind of research they do, and the programs with which they are affiliated. This is a "must" step for those applying to research-oriented clinical programs.

Once you have completed your preliminary examination of programs, you will probably want to write to several schools for more detailed information and application forms. A good time to do this is in September of the year preceding your planned enrollment. With this information in hand, you can further narrow your list of prospective schools.

Financing Your Education. Because of economic pressure and shifting priorities, both the federal government and state governments are providing less money to help students finance their graduate education. Historically, money has been available from four major sources:

1. Loan programs underwritten by the federal government allow students to borrow money at favorable interest rates and repay after leaving school. However, these loans have become increasingly difficult for graduate students to obtain as the federal government has begun to withdraw from the support of higher education.

2. Fellowships and scholarships are available in a number of programs. These are outright grants given to strong students to help them finance their training. Again, with the country's changing priorities, these grants are harder to get than formerly. Typically, the programs themselves nominate applicants for these awards, and such a nomination is accompanied by an offer of acceptance.

3. Research and teaching assistantships are frequently available. Research assistantships are often financed through research grants obtained by faculty members and require the student to work on a particular research project. Teaching assistantships may involve a variety of duties, from grading papers or leading discussion sessions to actual classroom teaching. Both kinds of assistantships normally require up to 20 hours of work per week.

4. Traineeships in clinical psychology are sometimes available, although again there have been cutbacks in recent years. These are usually financed by the federal government and are often outright grants to promising students.

Financing one's education is clearly becoming more difficult. On the one hand, a number of schools charge graduate assistants lower tuition rates, and students with fellowships or traineeships often pay no tuition at all. On the other hand, competition for all these forms of financial assistance is becoming increasingly keen. Information about financial matters will obviously be helpful in deciding where to apply for graduate study.

APA Accreditation. The APA maintains a Committee on Accreditation, which approves those programs that meet acceptable professional training standards. The list of approved schools is published each year in the December issue of the *American Psychologist*. The 1998 list contained 193 schools or sites with APA-approved programs in clinical psychology. This list can be found at web site 1-2 (see Web Sites of Interest at the end of this chapter).

When to Apply. Schools vary in their deadlines, although most range from January 1 to February 15. However, students are advised to check carefully to make sure there is not, for example, a

December deadline for a given school. Although master's-level programs sometimes have deadlines as late as August, it is best not to gamble, because many schools enforce their deadlines rigidly.

Number of Applications to Submit. There is no magic figure for the number of programs to which one should apply. A few students may apply to only a handful of programs and be accepted. Others may apply to 20 and be rejected by all of them. Obviously, the competition is fierce. Indeed, it has reached the point where the ratio of accepted applications to submitted ones is lower for clinical psychology programs offering a Ph.D. than for medical schools. It is not unusual for a school to receive 400 applications and accept fewer than 10.

The best strategy usually is to apply to as many schools as one can afford or for which can find the time and energy to prepare applications. Some schools have application fees as high as $50, although most are no higher than $25. A few charge nothing at all. Remember that official transcripts may cost as much as $5 and represent an added expense in the application process. Check with your school early on in the process to avoid surprises.

In view of all these considerations, it is best to rank-order the schools you are willing to attend. From this list select several at or near the top, several from the middle, and a few others from the bottom tier. Thus, you will not have put all your eggs in one very small basket. To a certain extent, too, being accepted is an unpredictable event. It is not unusual for a student to be rejected by a program that has a modest national reputation and accepted by one that is highly recognized. Each school's selection committee has a somewhat different set of biases and guidelines. Therefore, do not give up hope when that first letter of rejection arrives.

Step 2: Application Materials

Several elements comprise one's completed application package. The elements summarized below are typical.

Test Scores. Virtually every school requires applicants to submit test scores. The test most frequently required is the *Graduate Record Examination (GRE)*. In some cases the Miller Analogies Test (MAT) is required. Information about these tests is usually available from campus counseling centers or student personnel services as well as from your own psychology department. Additional information may be obtained by writing.

GRE: Graduate Record Examinations, Educational Testing Service, P.O. Box 6000, Princeton, NJ 08541-6000 (also: www.gre.org)

MAT: Psychological Corp., 304 East 4th St., New York, NY 10017

The GRE consists of questions that tap quantitative, verbal, and analytical abilities. In addition, there is a subject test in psychology. Some schools require the psychology subject test, while others do not. A computer-based GRE is offered year-round; the traditional paper-based GRE is offered less frequently. The paper-based GRE is being phased out.

The paper-based GRE is given in November, December (subject test only), and April. Because it takes up to six weeks for the results to be reported, most students choose the November date, which allows them to meet most schools' application deadlines. However, even this may be cutting it close. We recommend that you complete the GRE in the spring or summer before the fall you plan to apply. For the 1999–2000 academic year, the basic fee for the GRE test was $99, whereas the cost of the subject test was $130. See web site 1-8 for current information on the GRE, including schedules, fees, and sample items.

Transcripts. Most schools require transcripts detailing your work at each institution you have attended. The application form may have a space for you to indicate your grade point average. Transcripts will be mailed by the institution's office of student records to those schools you request. Usually, a fee is charged for the service (at the University of Missouri, for example, the fee is $5 per transcript).

Another point to consider is that some programs may require or strongly prefer coursework in certain areas. For example, a recent survey (Mayne, Norcross, & Sayette, 1994a) found that the following courses were either required or recommended by at least one-third of the 108 APA-accredited clinical psychology doctoral programs sampled: statistics (94%); experimental methods/research design (68%); abnormal psychology (51%); physiological psychology/biopsychology (33%). You will want to make sure that your transcript reflects that you have met any course requirements for a particular clinical program.

Letters of Recommendation. Three or four letters of recommendation are also required. The best persons to ask to write letters for you are professors who are familiar with your academic work and research experience. Letters from friends or relatives attesting to your high moral character are not very useful (even if they are truthful!). The best letters are those from psychology professors with whom you have worked—not just in class but on special topics or research projects. A letter from a professor who taught you in a class of 249 others and who can only remember (by consulting the grade book) that you received an "A" is not nearly as useful as one from a professor with whom you worked on an independent project. A letter from a professional for whom you worked in a mental-health-related job may also be quite helpful.

Unless you have specifically waived your right to see your letters of recommendation, the assumption by the readers of those letters will be that they are not confidential and that you have in fact seen them. It is often felt that such letters may be less frank and open in their assessment of your ability and potential than confidential statements. If you have doubts about how strong the letter of recommendation will be, you can always ask your potential reference for a candid assessment of your possibilities beforehand.

Personal Statement. Most application forms contain a section for a personal statement. This gives the selection committee a view of how you regard yourself in relation to clinical psychology. What are your motives? Why are you interested in clinical psychology? How did this interest develop? How have you prepared yourself? What are your career goals? Why are you interested in this particular clinical psychology program? These are just a few of the points often covered in such statements. They help to flesh out your application and also provide a glimpse of your verbal and writing abilities.

Experience. Evidence of quality research experience will usually be a definite plus and will give you a competitive edge. It suggests that you have had the interest and motivation to seek out something beyond routine courses or ordinary classroom experience. It indicates that you are involved and is usually taken as a positive sign of your potential for professional growth. In addition, such experience can be very helpful in your doctoral studies. For research-oriented programs, prior research experience is essential.

Practical experiences in mental health work can be helpful as well. Many students have been employed as aides in hospitals or as paraprofessionals in clinics, schools, community centers, crisis hotlines, and similar situations. Some have had practicum work associated with certain courses. Such experience suggests a greater level of sophistication—a sense that you already have some insight into what a career in the mental health field will be like. It also signifies something about your motivation.

Essential Qualifications

Students often ask about the minimum grade point average (GPA) required for admission or about the cutoff points for the GRE. These are difficult questions to answer, since programs vary considerably. Mayne et al.'s survey, however, did indicate that 90% of all doctoral programs in clinical psychology use GRE scores to screen applicants (Mayne et al., 1994a). Therefore, for better or for worse, it appears that admissions committees do place a great deal of emphasis on GRE scores. In general, those schools that receive very large numbers of applications tend to require high GPA levels and GRE scores. Research-oriented Ph.D. programs tend to prefer higher GRE scores and GPAs than do practice-oriented Ph.D. programs or Psy.D. programs (Mayne et al., 1994a). As might be expected from these survey results, Mayne et al. report that it is much harder to gain admission into a research-oriented Ph.D. program in clinical psychology (acceptance rate = 6% of applicants) than into a Psy.D. program in clinical psychology (acceptance rate = 23%).

Some selection committees are concerned more with the student's GPA over the last two years than with that of the entire four years. A GPA of less than 3.5 on a 4.0 scale is, however, likely to make admission difficult. In the case of schools with a strong reputation, a GPA of 3.7 may be the minimum. High GRE scores are important. However, a number of schools will tolerate more modest scores if there are other compensating factors such as a high GPA or particularly strong letters of recommendation.

The foregoing comments do not apply to master's programs in clinical psychology. There is not as much competition for admission to these programs and, as a result, the GPA and GRE scores need not be as high. At the same time, it should be noted that completing such a program does not inevitably enhance one's chances of being admitted to a Ph.D. program later. In summarizing these matters, one clinical director at a major university had this to say about admission qualifications:

> First, and most important, is a psychology undergraduate degree with a high grade point average. Incidentally, we prefer a science/math-based array of courses rather than a soft set of courses. Approximately a fourth of our students enter with M.A. degrees, but this does not help them. We generally find that most everyone gets A's in M.A.-level programs, and thus we end up going back to the undergraduate record. Second, letters of recommendation are exceedingly important. Such letters are most informative when they are authored by people who truly know the applicant. Third, additional research or therapy experience is a plus. Fourth, good GRE scores are desirable but not absolutely necessary. In this latter vein, we are much more prone to weigh the undergraduate performance and letters of recommendation. (Personal communication)

A Profession in Movement

Clinical psychology is a profession in flux and ferment. Although clinical psychology retains its basic mission of applying psychological principles to the problems of individuals, the methods and the professional framework through which it seeks to accomplish this mission are undergoing change. Whether such change is good or reflects a major identity crisis that bodes ill for the profession is unclear. But one thing is certain. This is an exciting time to be a clinical psychologist and to participate in the ongoing shaping of a profession.

Demographics

A recent demographic trend is important to note. Earlier in this chapter, we indicated that only approximately 25% of APA Division 12 (Clinical Psychology) members are women. However, this percentage is likely to increase dramatically in the future. Increasingly, more women than men are receiving their doctorates in psychology, and this is especially true for clinical psychology. Some have referred to this as the "feminization" of clinical psychology. What effect this change will have on the field is unclear. For example, it has been argued that the trend toward lower salaries for clinical psychologists in private practice may be directly related (Philipson, 1993). On the other hand, it is clear that an increased representation of women in clinical psychology will serve to greatly advance the field because it will bring a broader range of perspectives to problems encountered in both clinical practice and clinical research.

Training Models

Although the scientist-practitioner training model is still dominant, it is under fire. New models have emerged. Professional schools with no university affiliation have sprung up. New degree programs have been established within the structure of universities. For example, the *Doctor of Psychology (Psy.D.)* degree has become a more common alternative to traditional research-oriented Ph.D. degrees, with more than 500 Psy.D. degrees in clinical psychology awarded each year. The 1998 list of APA-accredited clinical programs that awarded the Psy.D. degree included 31 programs.

Others have called for a new model of training housed in university *professional schools*. Professional schools now award more than half of all doctorates in clinical psychology. L. H. Levy (1984) has outlined a charter for a new *human services psychology*. This would be a generic training program composed of all the specialties concerned with promoting human welfare through psychological principles, including clinical psychology, counseling psychology, school psychology, community psychology, health psychology, and other specialties. A training model that has gained some prominence over the past five years is the *clinical science model*. This model arose from concerns that clinical psychology, as currently practiced, is not firmly grounded in science. Programs that adhere to this model focus training on empirically supported approaches to assessment, prevention, and clinical intervention. Roughly 17% of clinical training programs identify themselves as clinical science training programs. This training model as well as others will be discussed in more detail in Chapter 3.

Clinical Practice

Despite the financial impact of managed care, recently trained clinical psychologists continue to go into private practice in large numbers. Issues of licensing and certification, participation in governmental health care programs, and other guild concerns seem to be preoccupying the clinical psychologist more and more. Paraprofessionals and subdoctoral mental health professionals are being employed with greater frequency in a variety of mental health settings. They are performing routine testing functions, assisting in group therapy, carrying out various administrative jobs in agencies, and so on. This trend has been reinforced by the fact that modern clinical psychologists seem less and less willing to invest their time in diagnostic testing. Where once we had traditional individual psychotherapy and some group psychotherapy, we now have brief therapy, cognitive-behavioral therapy, couples therapy, Gestalt therapy, family therapy, exposure therapy, rational-emotive therapy, and so on.

Some may find signs of the demise of clinical psychology in all of the foregoing; others may be excited by the sheer conflict of it all. But for the prospective student of clinical psychology, the current situation offers an unparalleled opportunity to participate in shaping the future of a profession.

A Tolerance for Ambiguity and a Thirst for New Knowledge

The orderly thing to do would be to conclude this chapter with a final, crisp definition of clinical psychology—one that would summarize and integrate our previous discussion and could readily be committed to memory. However, such a definition does not seem possible or even useful. The problem resides in the range, diversity, and patterning of the interests and activities of clinical psychologists. To encompass such diversity, a definition would have to be so lengthy or so general as to be essentially meaningless. For example, some feel that Resnick's (1991) definition presented at the beginning of this chapter is too broad and not specific to clinical psychology. Forty-five years ago, Shaffer and Lazarus, in their textbook of clinical psychology, commented, "Nowhere is there real agreement over the exact role which should be played by the clinical psychologist" (Shaffer & Lazarus, 1952,

p. 25). Little has occurred in the meantime to persuade us to reject their evaluation. It might be well, then, to mention an important characteristic of the clinical psychologist: the capacity to tolerate ambiguity.

Assailed by some as charlatans, adored by others as saviors, depressed at times by their lack of knowledge about human behavior, exhilarated at other times by the remarkable improvement in their patients, bombarded by the conflicting claims of success made by cognitive-behaviorists on the one hand and psychodynamic psychologists on the other, criticized by academicians as being too applied and by other mental health colleagues as being too abstract or scientific—is it any wonder that a tolerance for ambiguity can be a helpful quality for clinicians? For those students who want all the answers about human behavior, clinical psychology can be a very disturbing enterprise. But for those who wish to participate in a search for increasingly effective means to improve the human condition, it can be rewarding indeed.

Chapter Summary

Clinical psychology, as a field, is rather difficult to define in a precise way. The activities of clinical psychologists vary greatly, and there is some overlap with other mental health professions. In this chapter, we have presented the most current data available on the characteristics and activities of clinical psychologists within an historical context. The modern clinical psychologist typically spends a significant amount of the workweek engaged in direct clinical service, diagnosis/assessment, administration, and research/writing. Teaching, supervision, and consultation are also important roles. Clinical psychologists are employed in a wide range of settings, especially private practice, universities, and medical centers. According to surveys, most clinical psychologists are men, and the most frequently endorsed theoretical orientations are integrative/eclectic, cognitive, and psychodynamic. Above all, the field of clinical psychol-

ogy is strongly committed to the research tradition, with an emphasis on empirically supported approaches to assessment, prevention, and intervention. Finally, this chapter concludes with an overview of training in clinical psychology, including descriptions of the major components of graduate training as well as steps for gaining admission into a doctoral program in clinical psychology.

Key Terms

accreditation A designation bestowed by the American Psychological Association on psychological training programs that meet acceptable training standards.

clinical practicum A training experience designed to build specific clinical skills (in assessment, psychotherapy, etc.). Often, a practicum combines academic content, or theory, with practical experience.

clinical psychologist A member of a profession devoted to understanding and treating individuals affected by a variety of emotional, behavioral, and/or cognitive difficulties. Clinical psychologists may be involved in numerous activities, including psychotherapy, assessment and diagnosis, teaching, supervision, research, consultation, and administration.

clinical science A clinical psychology training model that emphasizes empirically supported approaches to assessment, prevention, and clinical intervention. This model arose from concerns that clinical psychology was not firmly grounded in science.

counseling psychologists Psychologists whose interests and activities overlap significantly with those of clinical psychologists. Traditionally, counseling psychologists have provided individual and group psychotherapy for normal or moderately maladjusted individuals and have offered educational and occupational counseling.

doctoral degree A degree that requires training beyond the master's degree. In clinical psychology, the doctoral degree is usually obtainable after four years of graduate training in assessment, diagnosis, psychotherapy, and research, plus a one-year internship.

Graduate Record Examination A test frequently required of applicants to graduate training programs. The GRE assesses quantitative, verbal, and analytical abilities. In addition, the GRE also offers subject tests for several disciplines, including psychology.

health psychologists Psychologists whose research or practical work focuses on the prevention of illness, the promotion and maintenance of good health, or the treatment of individuals with diagnosed medical conditions.

idiographic approach The approach that emphasizes individual differences over general behavioral principles. This approach is associated with subjectively oriented clinical practice.

internship An intensive clinical experience required of all clinical psychology students and usually occurring at the very end of their graduate training. Usually, internships last one year and involve full-time work at an independent facility.

master's degree An advanced degree, usually obtainable after two years of graduate work. Individuals with master's-level training in clinical psychology work in a variety of service-delivery settings but may be less likely to gain professional independence than individuals with doctoral degrees.

nomothetic approach The approach that examines or attempts to identify general principles of behavior, deemphasizing individual differences. This approach is associated with empirically oriented clinical practice.

paraprofessionals Individuals (such as crisis hotline workers) who have been trained to assist professional mental health workers.

professional schools Schools offering advanced training in psychology that emphasizes competency in assessment and psychotherapy over competency in research. Many professional schools are not affiliated with universities, and most award the Psy.D. degree.

Psy.D. degree An advanced degree in psychology that is emerging as an alternative to traditional research-oriented Ph.D. degrees.

psychiatric social workers Mental health professionals trained in psychiatric diagnosis and in individual and group psychotherapy. Compared to psychologists and psychiatrists, psychiatric social

workers' training is relatively brief, limited to a two-year master's degree. Social workers are intensely involved in the day-to-day lives of their patients and focus more on the social and environmental factors contributing to their patients' difficulties.

psychiatrist A physician with intensive training in the diagnosis and treatment of a variety of mental disorders. Because of their medical backgrounds, psychiatrists may prescribe medications for the alleviation of problematic behavior or psychological distress.

psychological clinic A clinic operated by a clinical psychology training program and staffed by clinical students, faculty, and others. The psychological clinic provides a setting for clinical students to gain practical experience by offering assessment, therapy, and consultation services to the public.

qualifying examination An examination required of all clinical psychology students, usually in their third year of training. The function of this exam is to ensure the student's academic competency.

rehabilitation psychologists Psychologists whose practice focuses upon individuals with physical or cognitive disabilities. Rehabilitation psychologists most often work in general or rehabilitation hospitals, and they help disabled individuals deal with the psychological, social, and environmental ramifications of their conditions.

school psychologists Psychologists who work with educators to promote the intellectual, social, and emotional growth of school-age children. Activities of school psychologists may include evaluating children with special needs, developing interventions or programs to address these needs, and consulting with teachers and administrators about issues of school policy.

scientist-practitioner model of training The predominant training philosophy in clinical psychology today. This model is based on the idea that clinical psychologists should integrate their roles of scientist and practitioner.

theoretical orientation This term refers to the theoretical framework that a psychologist relies on to conceptualize and treat clients' problems. Examples of such orientations include psychodynamic, cognitive, behavioral, interpersonal, systems, and eclectic/integrative.

Web Sites of Interest

To visit any of the web sites listed below, go to www.wadsworth.com and click on Links.

1-1   Accredited internship programs

1-2   Accredited doctoral training programs in clinical psychology

1-3   Financial aid resources

1-4   Getting into graduate school in psychology

1-5   Comparison of psychiatrists and psychologists

1-6   List of internship sites with web pages

1-7   Example of a clinical psychology program's web page (University of Missouri)

1-8   Graduate Record Examination (GRE) information

1-9   *U.S. News* rankings of clinical psychology programs

Historical Overview of Clinical Psychology

Reflection on the roots of clinical psychology can promote a better understanding of the field. This chapter provides a view of both the historical sweep of clinical psychology and some of the current issues that confront the field.

Historical Roots

Establishing a certain time period or designating a particular person as the beginning of clinical psychology can be arbitrary if not downright misleading. One can certainly go back to Greek philosophers such as Thales, Hippocrates, or Aristotle who, long before the birth of Christ, were speculating about human beings and the nature of thought, sensation, and pathology (Shaffer & Lazarus, 1952). Since these philosophers are cited as antecedents of nearly every profession, movement, or system of thought in Western society, their citation here does little, perhaps, except to affirm our honorable beginnings.

For the years prior to 1890, there is really very little in the history of clinical psychology to separate it from the history of abnormal psychology or, as Zilboorg and Henry (1941) termed it, "medical psychology." Reisman (1976) finds it more useful to search for the roots of modern clinical psychology in the reform movements of the nineteenth century, which ultimately resulted in improved care for the mentally ill. Such improvements, and the humanitarian impulses of those who encouraged them, fostered the faint beginnings of the mental health professions as we know them today (Hothersall, 1984). One of the major figures in this movement was Philippe Pinel, a French physician. Shocked by the senseless brutality that was the custom in nineteenth-century "mental hospitals," he managed to get himself appointed head of the asylum at Bicêtre, and later, Salpêtrière. He managed through kindness and humanity to accomplish much in a very difficult field. Whether Pinel's accomplishments should be regarded as personal achievements or as logical developments growing out of the philosophy of Rousseau and the idealism of the

French Revolution is unclear. In any event, his work was a milestone in the development of psychiatry, the mental health approach, and, ultimately, of clinical psychology.

At about the same time, an Englishman, William Tuke, was devoting himself to the establishment of what might be called a model hospital for the humane treatment of the sick and troubled. In America, Eli Todd was laboring long and successfully to develop a retreat in Hartford for the mentally ill. Like his European counterparts, Todd emphasized the role of civilized care, respect, and morality. Through his efforts, it became less fashionable to regard mental patients as incurable. The search for psychological antecedents to mental illness and an emphasis on treatment had begun to replace the routine harshness of custody.

Another American who had a profound effect on the mental health movement was Dorothea Dix. She campaigned for better facilities for the mentally ill. With determination and single-mindedness, Dix pushed, prodded, and cajoled until government officials responded. Using the force of logic, facts, public sentiment, and good old-fashioned lobbying, she wrought her will. And in 1848, New Jersey responded by building a hospital for the "insane"—the first in a procession of more than 30 states to do so.

Out of the efforts of such people, the groundwork was laid for a field of clinical psychology. However, it would be a mistake to evaluate these contributions apart from the social forces and ideas of the time. In the nineteenth century, philosophers and writers were proclaiming the dignity and equality of all. Governments were beginning to respond. Even science, which was just coming into its own, contributed to the movement. An atmosphere of "knowledge through experimentation" began to prevail. A feeling that people can predict, understand, and perhaps even control the human condition began to replace older wisdom. This ferment in science, literature, politics, government, and reform combined to produce the first clear and unmistakable signs of new professions in what would come to be referred to as "mental health."

FIGURE 2-1 Dorothea Dix traveled from state to state for 40 years campaigning for more humane treatment and better facilities for the insane and the mentally retarded. During the Civil War she was chief of hospital nurses for the Union forces.

The Bettmann Archive. © Bettman/CORBIS.

These short sketches represent some of the roots of clinical psychology. In the following pages, we will trace its development in the specific areas of diagnosis and assessment, intervention, research, and professional matters.

Diagnosis and Assessment

The Beginnings (1850–1899)

For many, the essence of clinical psychology has always been its emphasis on assessing differences among people. Much of that emphasis can be traced to Francis Galton, an Englishman. Galton devoted a great deal of effort to the application of quantitative methods to understanding differences among people. Pursuing his interests in sensory acuity, motor skills, and re-

action time, he established an anthropometric laboratory in 1882.

This tradition was furthered by the work of James McKeen Cattell, an American. Despite the disapproval of Wilhelm Wundt, in whose laboratory he assisted, Cattell turned his attention to reaction time differences among people. He believed, as did Galton, that this was a way of approaching the study of intelligence. In fact, he coined the term *mental tests* to describe his measures (Thorndike, 1997). Through the use of a battery of ten tests Cattell hoped to discover the constancy of mental processes, even predicting that such tests could be used in the selection and training of people as well as in the detection of disease. In this early work we can see the first halting steps of the testing movement.

A related trend of the same general period is illustrated by the diagnostic work of Emil Kraepelin in 1913. Few psychiatrists of the time could equal his professional stature. When Kraepelin divided mental illness into those types determined by exogenous factors (curable) and those caused by endogenous factors (incurable), he initiated a romance with classification schemes that persists even today. His descriptions and classifications of patients were heuristic and have served to stimulate an enormous amount of discussion about psychopathology.

The Advent of the Modern Era (1900–1919)

One of the major developments in this era was the rise of mental measurement or diagnostic psychological testing. The beginning may lie with Galton or Cattell, but the decisive impetus came from the work of Alfred Binet.

Binet was convinced that the key to the study of individual differences was the notion of norms and deviations from those norms. Following Binet's submission of a proposal to the minister of public instruction in Paris in 1904, a commission approached Binet and his collaborator Theodore Simon about developing a means of ensuring that children with cognitive limitations were properly educated (Thorndike, 1997).

In order to distinguish objectively among various degrees of limitations, the two men developed the 1908 Binet-Simon Scale. It is hard to overestimate the profound influence that this scale has exerted on the *measurement of intelligence*. Henry Goddard later introduced the Binet tests to America, and Lewis Terman produced an American revision in 1916.

Some progress was also being made in the area of *personality testing*. Carl Jung began using word-association methods around 1905 to attempt to uncover unconscious complexes. In 1910, the Kent-Rosanoff Free Association Test was published. Even though Galton had been experimenting with such techniques as early as 1879, these free-association tests marked a significant advance in diagnostic testing.

In 1904, Charles Spearman offered the concept of a general intelligence that he termed *g*. Edward Thorndike countered with a conceptualization that emphasized the importance of separate abilities. Whatever the truth, the great debate regarding the nature of intelligence was on—a debate that still rages today.

When the United States entered World War I in 1917, the need arose to screen and classify the hordes of military recruits who were being pressed into service. A committee of five members from the American Psychological Association (APA) was appointed by the Medical Department of the Army. Its chairman was Robert Yerkes. The committee was charged with the task of creating a system for classifying men according to their ability levels. It designed the Army Alpha test in 1917. This verbal scale was quickly followed by a nonverbal version, the Army Beta test. In a similar vein, Robert Woodworth developed his Psychoneurotic Inventory in 1917. This was perhaps the first questionnaire designed to reveal abnormal behavior. With the advent of such rough screening instruments as Woodworth's Personal Data Sheet and the Army Alpha and Beta, the group testing movement was on its way.

Between the Wars (1920–1939)

Between the two world wars, there was substantial progress in diagnostic psychological testing.

Pintner and Paterson introduced their nonverbal intelligence scale. In 1930, the Arthur Point Scale appeared, and in 1934 it was followed by the Cornell-Coxe test. In 1926, the Goodenough Draw-a-Man technique for measuring intelligence was published. The psychologist now had individual and group tests as well as verbal and nonverbal tests, and clinicians were using terms like "intelligence quotients."

Aptitude testing, epitomized by the Seashore tests of musical ability, was now with us. Interest tests had also made their appearance by this time. In 1927, the Strong Vocational Interest Blank came upon the scene, followed later by the Kuder Preference Record.

The continuing debate on theoretical issues in intelligence was further sparked in 1927 by Louis Thurstone's contribution based upon factor analysis. Spearman, Thorndike, and Thurstone had all now entered the intelligence arena, and each made important contributions. In 1928, Gesell's developmental scales were published, and in 1936, Doll's Vineland Social Maturity Scale appeared. Doll's scale approached behavior not strictly in terms of intelligence but in terms of an individual's social maturity or competence.

A major development in the intelligence testing movement occurred in 1939, when David Wechsler published the Wechsler-Bellevue test. Until then there had been no satisfactory individual measure of *adult* intelligence. Subsequent revisions of the Wechsler-Bellevue have served as the premier individual tests for adult intelligence.

Tests of intelligence, interests, and abilities were not the only testing developments in these years. The field of personality testing was also making great strides. Woodworth's Personal Data Sheet was followed in 1921 by the Pressey X-O Test for emotions and in 1923 by the Downey Will-Temperament Test. The Allport-Vernon Study of Values came along in 1931.

However, the big news was projective testing. Although some beginning progress had already been made through the word-association research of Galton, Jung, and Kent and Rosanoff, the watershed event for projective testing occurred in 1921, when Hermann Rorschach, a Swiss psychiatrist, published *Psychodiagnostik*. In this book, Rorschach described his use of inkblots to diagnose psychiatric patients. Rorschach's work suggested that when people respond to an ambiguous test stimulus, they will reveal something of their responses to real-life experiences.

It was not until 1937, when S. J. Beck and Bruno Klopfer published their separate manuals and scoring procedures, that the Rorschach method really caught on. Then, in 1939, L. K. Frank coined the term *projective techniques*. From that point on, a veritable flood of research publications, books, courses, and variations of projective techniques poured forth.

Another aspect of the projective movement is represented by the 1935 publication by Christiana Morgan and Henry Murray of the Thematic Apperception Test (TAT). This test requires the person to look at ambiguous pictures and then make up a story to describe the activities, thoughts, and feelings of the people in those pictures. The TAT remains a widely used projective device, probably second only to the Rorschach in popularity among projective tests. Then, in 1938, Lauretta Bender published her Bender-Gestalt test, which has also been used as a projective measure of personality.

World War II and Beyond (1940–Present)

Clinical psychology's success with intelligence tests was responsible for its subsequent movement into the arena of personality assessment. As clinicians moved beyond the settings of the public schools and the institutions for those with cognitive limitations and into penal institutions, mental hospitals, and clinics, referring physicians and psychiatrists gradually began to ask more complex questions. Questions such as "What is this patient's ability level?" began to evolve into more complicated questions that dealt with differential diagnosis. For example, "Is this patient's level of functioning a product of constitutional intellectual limitations, or is a 'disease process' such as schizophrenia eroding intellectual performance?" Because answering such questions involved more than simply identifying an IQ level, new methods of examining the patient's performance on intelligence tests

were developed. In many instances, the psychologist began to look at patterns of performance rather than just an overall score.

In 1943, the Minnesota Multiphasic Personality Inventory (MMPI) appeared (Hathaway, 1943). The MMPI was an objective self-report test whose major function, initially, seemed to be attaching psychiatric labels to patients. Although other tests such as the Rorschach were often being put to similar uses, the MMPI was unique in that no theoretical interpretation of scores or responses was necessary.

The decades of the 1940s and 1950s witnessed a growing sophistication in testing technology. Triggered by the development of the MMPI, debates over the relative effectiveness of clinical and statistical prediction arose (Meehl, 1954; Sarbin, 1943). Which was superior—the clinician's subjective impressions or hard, objective approaches based on crisp data such as test scores that were readily quantifiable? There were also sophisticated discussions of methods of validating tests and guarding against misleading test-taking attitudes on the part of test respondents (Cronbach, 1946; Cronbach & Meehl, 1955). Assessment had come a long way since the crude instruments of the World War I era. Indeed, during this period enough was known about constructing tests that APA could promulgate standards for their proper development (American Psychological Association, 1954).

In the aftermath of World War II, the importance of intelligence testing continued. In 1949, Wechsler published another individual test. This one, the Wechsler Intelligence Scale for Children, was to become a serious alternative to the Stanford-Binet. Later, in 1955, the Wechsler Adult Intelligence Scale (a revision of the Wechsler-Bellevue Scale) appeared. These tests marked the beginning of a whole series of subsequent revisions of children's and adult forms of the Wechsler scales.

The 1940s and 1950s saw an explosive growth of personality tests, especially projective tests. The Rorschach and the TAT continued in a preeminent position. However, many other measures were also published during these years

(Anderson & Anderson, 1951). Clinical psychologists were seen as experts in *psychodiagnosis*—the use and interpretation of psychological test scores as a basis for diagnostic formulation as well as treatment planning. However, a rift was growing within the profession as to whether objective or projective assessment measures were better suited to accurately describe personality and psychopathology. *Objective measures*, such as the MMPI and its revision, MMPI-2 (Butcher, Dahlstrom, Graham, Tellegen, & Kaemmer, 1989), are based on a nomothetic approach to assessment in which test scores are interpreted using empirically based rules involving the contrast between an obtained score and the average score obtained from a large representative sample. Responses from *projective measures*, in contrast, are often interpreted using an idiographic approach. The focus may be more on the individual, and often interpretations are guided as much by psychodynamic theory as they are by empirically supported rules. This rift between those who favor either objective or projective techniques continues to this day.

Surprisingly, however, the major challenger to personality testing came from outside these ranks. Beginning in the late 1950s, a movement termed *radical behaviorism* began to assert its influence. Those who adhered to this orientation held that only overt behavior can be measured and that it is neither useful nor desirable to infer the level or existence of personality traits from psychological test results; personality traits, according to the radical behaviorists, cannot be measured directly. Personality assessment came under attack, and clinical psychology programs in the 1960s took on much more of a behavioral bent. In 1968, Walter Mischel made a strong case that traits exist more in the minds of observers than in the behavior of the observed. Situations, and not some nebulous set of traits, were said to be responsible for the ways we behave. In tune with this view, the 1970s would witness the rise of *behavioral assessment*. Behaviors were understood within the context of the stimuli or situations that either preceded or followed them.

Did this, in turn, mark the death of personality assessment? Actually, it did not. A resurgence of interest in the 1980s and 1990s can be attributed to the presentation and coverage of a variety of *personality disorders* in the American diagnostic system for mental disorders, the introduction of a number of more contemporary and psychometrically sound personality inventories (for example, the Millon Clinical Multiaxial Inventory and the NEO-Personality Inventory), and several empirical demonstrations that personality traits *do* appear to be fairly stable across time and across situations (for example, Costa & McCrae, 1988; Epstein & O'Brien, 1985).

As we mentioned, the official American diagnostic classification system has influenced the clinical assessment field. The first edition of the American Psychiatric Association's *Diagnostic and Statistical Manual of Mental Disorders* (DSM-I) appeared in 1952. Revisions of this manual have appeared periodically, the most recent one in 1994 (DSM-IV). In addition to this diagnostic system's influence on the content of self-report inventories (new inventories were designed to measure the DSM mental disorders), it spurred the growth of another line of assessment tools—the *structured diagnostic interviews*. These interviews consist of a standard list of questions that are keyed to the diagnostic criteria for various disorders from the DSM. Clinicians (or researchers) who need to formulate a DSM diagnosis for a patient (or research participant) can use these interviews; it is no longer necessary to administer a psychological test and then infer a patient's diagnostic status from his or her test scores.

Interest in *neuropsychological assessment* has grown tremendously as well. Neuropsychological assessment is used to evaluate relative strengths and deficits of patients based on empirically established brain–behavior (test responses) relationships. Several devices were introduced to detect impaired brain functioning. In 1947, Halstead introduced an entire test battery to aid in the diagnosis of neuropsychological problems. Contemporary neuropsychological assessment typically involves one of two approaches. Some use a uniform group, or battery, of tests for all patients. Others use a small subset of tests initially, and then, based on the results of these initial tests, use additional tests to resolve and answer the referral

T I M E L I N E : Significant Events in Assessement

1882
Galton establishes anthropometric laboratory.

1890
Cattell coins the term *mental test*.

1904
Binet begins work on his intelligence scale.

1905
Jung begins using the word-association method.

1913
Kraepelin publishes work on diagnosis.

1914
Terman's American version of Binet scale.

1921
Rorschach's *Psychodiagnostics* is published.

1935
TAT is published.

1937
Term *projective techniques* is coined.

1939
Wechsler-Bellevue Intelligence Scale is published.

1943
MMPI is published.

1949
Halstead introduces neuropsychological test battery.

1952
DSM-I is published.

1968
DSM-II is published.

1970s
Rise of behavioral assessment.

1980
DSM-III is published.

1980s
Interest rises in personality assessment and computer-based test interpretations.

1987
DSM-III-R is published.

1990s
Managed health care impacts psychological assessment.

1994
DSM-IV is published.

| 1900 | 1920 | 1940 | 1960 | 1980 | 2000 |

questions. Some of the more popular neuropsychological test batteries include the Halstead-Reitan (Reitan, 1969) and the Luria-Nebraska Neuropsychological Battery (Golden, Purisch, & Hammeke, 1985). The field of neuropsychology is becoming increasingly sophisticated. Many neuropsychological tests are now computer-administered, more attention is being directed to identifying neuropsychological correlates of mental disorder, and test results are integral components of rehabilitation planning (Golden, Zillmer, & Spiers, 1992; Jones & Butters, 1991).

Finally, the rise and popularity of managed health care in the 1990s has had an impact on psychological assessment. Although we will discuss this trend in more detail in Chapter 3, it is worth highlighting here. Managed health care (including mental or behavioral health) developed in response to the rapidly increasing cost of health care. Third-party insurers (such as large companies) were attracted to managed health care because it controlled and reduced costs. Managed health care requires those who provide services to be more accountable and to be more efficient in service delivery. Clinical psychologists who are providers for various managed health care plans have become increasingly interested in using reliable and valid psychological measures or tests that (1) aid in treatment planning by identifying and accurately assessing problematic symptoms, (2) are sensitive to any changes or improvements in client functioning as a result of treatment, and (3) are relatively brief. These and other issues were the focus of a special section that appeared in the December 1997 issue of *Psychological Assessment* (Butcher, 1997).

A number of these assessment highlights are summarized in the timeline "Significant Events in Assessment" on page 37.

Interventions

The Beginnings (1850–1899)

Kraepelin's focus was on the classification of psychoses. But others were investigating new treatments for neurotic patients, such as suggestion and hypnosis. Specifically, Jean Charcot gained a widespread reputation for his investigations of hysterical patients. He was a master of the dramatic clinical demonstration with hypnotized patients. As a matter of fact, he believed that only hysterics could be hypnotized. However, he was probably investigating hypnosis rather than hysteria. Others, such as Hippolyte Bernheim and Pierre Janet, were critical of Charcot's work. Bernheim felt that the symptomatology of hysteria was nothing more than suggestibility. Janet, on the other hand, came to regard hysteria as a manifestation of a "split personality" and also as a kind of hereditary degeneration.

At about the same time, the momentous collaboration of Josef Breuer and Sigmund Freud began. In the early 1880s, Breuer was treating a young patient named "Anna O," who was diagnosed with hysteria. Anna O's treatment presented many challenges but also led to theoretical breakthroughs that would influence psychotherapy practice for years to come. Breuer discussed the case extensively with Freud, who became so interested that he went to Paris to learn all that Charcot could teach him about hysteria. To considerably shorten a long story, in 1895 Breuer and Freud published *Studies on Hysteria*. For a variety of reasons, the relationship between the two men subsequently became quite strained. But their collaboration served as the launching pad for *psychoanalysis*, the single most influential theoretical and treatment development in the history of psychiatry and clinical psychology.

The Advent of the Modern Era (1900–1919)

Reformers such as Clifford Beers have been important in the history of clinical psychology. Beers was hospitalized in the wake of severe depressions. While hospitalized, he passed into a manic phase and began recording his experiences in the hospital. When he was free of his manic-depressive symptoms, he was released. But this release did not weaken his resolve to write a book exposing the abuses in the hospital

FIGURE 2-2 Jean Charcot demonstrates hypnosis with a patient called "Wit." Although trained as a neurologist, Charcot employed a psychosocial approach in explaining hysteria.
The Bettmann Archive. © Bettman/CORBIS.

care of the mentally ill. He very much wanted to generate a public movement to rectify those abuses. In 1908, *A Mind That Found Itself* was published, and the mental hygiene movement in America was launched.

In 1900, shortly before Beers entered the hospital, Freud published *The Interpretation of Dreams*. With this event, the psychoanalytic movement was in full swing. Concepts such as the unconscious, the Oedipus complex, and the ego began their ascendance, and sexuality became the coin of the psychological realm. Freud's ideas were by no means an overnight success. Recognition was slow in coming, but converts did begin to beat a path to his door. Alfred Adler, Carl Jung, and others began to take notice. Freud published other books, and the list of converts grew still longer, including A. A.

Brill, Paul Federn, Otto Rank, Ernest Jones, Wilhelm Stekel, Sandor Ferenczi, and others.

Later in this chapter we will note Witmer's establishment of the first psychological clinic. Also important was William Healy's establishment of a child guidance clinic in Chicago in 1909. This clinic used a team approach involving psychiatrists, social workers, and psychologists. They directed their efforts toward what would now be labeled juvenile delinquents, rather than toward the learning problems of children that had earlier attracted Witmer's attention. Healy's approach was greatly influenced by Freudian concepts and methods. Such an approach ultimately had the effect of shifting clinical psychology's work with children in the dynamic direction of Freud rather than into an educational framework.

FIGURE 2-3 Clifford Beers wrote
A Mind That Found Itself, a chronicle of his
experiences while hospitalized as a mental
patient. His efforts were instrumental in
launching the mental hygiene movement.
The Bettman Archive. © Bettman/CORBIS.

In 1905, Joseph Pratt, an internist, and
Elwood Worcester, a psychologist, began to use a
method of supportive discussion among hospitalized mental patients. This was the forerunner
of a variety of group therapy methods that
gained prominence in the 1920s and 1930s.

Between the Wars (1920–1939)

The psychoanalysis of the early twentieth century was largely devoted to the treatment of
adults and was practiced almost exclusively by
analysts whose basic training was in medicine.
Freud, however, argued that psychoanalysts did
not need medical training. Despite Freud's protes-
tations (Freud, 1926/1959), the medical profession claimed exclusive rights to psychoanalytic
therapy, and in so doing made the subsequent
entry of psychologists into the therapy enterprise
quite difficult.

The eventual entry of psychologists into
therapeutic activities was a natural outgrowth of
their early work with children in various *guidance clinics.* At first, that work was largely confined to the evaluation of children's intellectual
abilities, and this, of course, involved consultations with parents and teachers. But it is hard to
separate intellectual functioning and school success from the larger psychological aspects of behavior. As a result, it was only natural that psychologists should begin to offer advice and make
recommendations beyond the narrow analysis of
abilities.

As psychologists looked for psychological
principles to aid them in their efforts, the work
of both Freud and Alfred Adler came to their attention. In particular, they were impressed by
Adler's work, which had a more commonsense
ring than Freud's. Moreover, Freud's emphasis
seemed to lie with adults and with the sexual antecedents of their problems, whereas Adler's
deemphasis of the role of sexuality in a person's
psychological economy and his concomitant
emphasis on the structure of family relationships
seemed much more congenial to American mental health professionals in the field. By the early
1930s, Adler's (1930) ideas were firmly en-
sconced in those American clinics that dealt
with children's problems.

A second trend that influenced early work
with children—*play therapy*—was more directly
derived from traditional Freudian principles.
Play therapy is essentially a technique that relies
on the curative powers of the release of anxiety
or hostility through expressive play. In 1928,
Anna Freud, the distinguished daughter of
Sigmund Freud, described a method of play
therapy derived from psychoanalytic principles.

Group therapy also began to attract attention. By the early 1930s, the works of both J. L.
Moreno and S. R. Slavson were having an impact. Another precursor of things to come was
the technique of "passive therapy" described by
Frederick Allen (1934). In this approach one can
see some of the first stirrings of what would be-

come client-centered therapy. But there were other straws in the wind too. In 1920, John Watson described the famous case of Albert and the white rat, in which a young boy was conditioned to develop a neurotic-like fear of white, furry objects (Watson & Rayner, 1920). A few years later, Mary Cover Jones (1924) showed how such fears could be removed through conditioning. Still later, J. Levy (1938) described "relationship therapy." These latter three events marked the beginnings of *behavior therapy*, a very popular and influential group of therapeutic methods used today.

World War II and Beyond (1940–Present)

World War II not only required enormous numbers of men, it also contributed to the emotional difficulties that developed in many of them. The military physicians and psychiatrists were too few in number to cope with the epidemic of these problems. As a result, psychologists began to fill the mental health breach. At first, role of psychologists was ancillary and often involved mainly group psychotherapy. But increasingly, they began to provide individual psychotherapy, performing well in both the short-term goal of returning men to combat and in the longer-term goal of rehabilitation. Psychologists' successful performance of these activities, along with their already demonstrated research and testing skills, produced a gradually increasing acceptance of psychologists as mental health professionals.

This wartime experience whetted the appetites of psychologists for greater responsibility in the mental health field. It is uncertain whether this increasing focus on psychotherapy stemmed from a desire to gain greater professional responsibility, an awareness that they possessed the skills to perform mental health tasks, an embryonic disenchantment with the ultimate utility of diagnostic work, or some combination of the three. However, the stage had been set.

An additional contributing factor to this chain of events was an outgrowth of the turmoil in Europe in the 1930s. The pressures of Nazi tyranny forced many European psychiatrists and psychologists to leave their homelands, and many of them ultimately settled in the United States. Through professional meetings, lectures, and other gatherings, the ideas of the Freudian movement generated excitement and also gained increasing credence in psychology. Partly as a result, clinical psychologists began to reduce their emphasis on the assessment of intelligence, ability testing, and the measurement of cognitive dysfunction and became increasingly interested in personality development and its description.

As intelligence testing receded in importance, psychotherapy and personality theory began to move into the foreground. A large part of the activity in these areas was psychoanalytic in character. However, in 1950, John Dollard and Neal Miller published their book *Personality and Psychotherapy,* which was a seminal attempt to translate the psychoanalysis of Freud into the language of learning theory. Indeed, psychoanalysis was such a dominant force of the time that when Carl Rogers published *Client-Centered Therapy* in 1951, his was the first major alternative to psychoanalytic therapy up to that point. Rogers' book was an enormously significant development that had extensive repercussions in the world of psychotherapy and research.

In 1946, Alexander and French published an influential book on briefer psychoanalytic interventions. Newer forms of therapy were beginning to proliferate. For example, Perls introduced Gestalt therapy (Perls, Hefferline, & Goodman, 1951), and Frankl (1953) talked about logotherapy and its relationship to existential theory. In 1958, Ackerman described family therapy, and in 1962, Ellis explained his rational-emotive therapy. About the same time, along came Berne's (1961) transactional analysis, or TA. Therapy had surely become a growth industry. There was no better indication of the importance of psychotherapy in the professional lives of clinicians than the effect of Eysenck's (1952) critique of therapy. His scathing report on the ineffectiveness of psychotherapy alarmed many and inspired others to conduct research designed to prove him wrong.

However, psychotherapy was not the whole story. The behaviorists were beginning to develop what they regarded as a more "hardheaded" brand of therapy. Andrew Salter (1949) wrote *Conditioned Reflex Therapy*, a pioneering work in what later evolved into desensitization methods. In 1953, B. F. Skinner furthered the behavioral therapy cause when he outlined the application of operant principles to therapeutic and social interventions. Then in 1958, Joseph Wolpe introduced systematic desensitization, a technique based on conditioning principles; the behavior therapy movement was now more firmly entrenched than ever. Albert Bandura (1969) set the stage for the cognitive-behavioral movement by demonstrating how behavior could be modified through the observation of others, or modeling.

Whereas psychoanalysis and psychodynamic psychotherapy were previously the dominant forces, behavior therapy was now gaining in popularity among clinical psychologists. Its appeal stemmed from its focus on observable (and measurable) behavior, the shorter length or treatment required, and the emphasis on the empirical evaluation of treatment outcome. Behavior therapy helped to stimulate the growth of psychotherapy research. Previously, only a select number of academics conducted studies of treatment efficacy. We now see many researchers and practitioners who use empirical methods to investigate the effectiveness of various treatment techniques.

Several other trends in intervention are noteworthy. First, the number of treatments employed by clinical psychologists has grown tremendously over the years. These range from cognitive-behavioral approaches that have empirical support to "trendier" approaches like "inner-child therapy" that have no empirical support. Some have estimated the number of therapies available at well over 400. Fortunately, not all of these are "therapies-of-the-month," and many have empirical support. Perhaps because of this startling array of therapeutic orientations and treatment choices, many clinical psychologists refer to themselves as *eclectics*.

These clinicians employ the techniques of more than one theoretical orientation, basing their selection on the particular problems presented by the individual client or patient. At the same time, many clinical psychologists are interested in integrating various approaches into one therapeutic modality, as well as identifying common factors that underlie different approaches to treatment (J. D. Frank, 1971).

Second, *brief* or *"time-effective" therapy* (Budman & Gurman, 1988) is becoming a preferred mode of psychotherapeutic intervention for several reasons. Many individuals cannot afford years of psychotherapy. Briefer forms of therapy have been shown to be equally as effective, if not more effective, than traditional psychotherapy. Further, managed care companies who control reimbursement for mental health treatment are often unwilling to reimburse clinicians for more than a handful of sessions. Along with the development of brief forms of therapy, *"manualized" forms of treatment* have been introduced into clinical work (Beck, Rush, Shaw, & Emery, 1979; Strupp & Binder, 1984). These manuals are useful for clinicians because they outline treatment goals for each session as well as techniques to be used, and typically the treatment "package" can be implemented and completed in 10 to 15 sessions or less. Further, they assist research aimed at determining the efficacy or effectiveness of psychological interventions. Currently, treatment manuals are available for a wide range of psychological problems, including depression, anxiety disorders, and personality disorders. We will highlight many of these treatments throughout this book.

Third, by the 1950s some clinicians had begun to be disenchanted with therapy methods that dealt with one patient at a time (or even ten patients at a time, as in group therapy). They sought a more "preventive" approach. Their search culminated in the rise of *community psychology* in the 1960s and *health psychology* in the 1980s. A growing number of clinical psychologists provide services related to the prevention of health problems, mental health problems, and injury. The area of prevention is often associated

T I M E L I N E : Significant Events in Intervention

1793
Pinel introduces humane care in French asylums.

1848
Dorothea Dix successfully lobbies for better facilities for the mentally ill in New Jersey.

1895
Breuer and Freud publish *Studies on Hysteria*

1900
Freud publishes *The Interpretation of Dreams*.

1908
Clifford Beers inaugurates mental hygiene movement.

1909
Healy founds a child guidance clinic in Chicago.

1920
Watson and Rayner describe the conditioning of fears.

1932
Moreno introduces group therapy.

1950
Dollard and Miller publish *Personality and Psychotherapy*.

1951
Rogers publishes *Client-Centered Therapy*.

1952
Eysenck publishes his critique of psychotherapy.

1953
Skinner outlines application of operant principles.

1958
Wolpe describes method of systematic desensitization.

1965
Conference in Swampscott, MA, gives birth to community psychology.

1980s
Rise of health psychology, increasing focus on
brief psychotherapy, increase in psychotherapy research.

1990s
Managed health care has tremendous impact
on psychological services.

1995
Lists of empirically supported treatment appear.

| 1800 | 1850 | 1900 | 1950 | 2000 |

with health psychology and will increasingly be in the spotlight in years to come as psychology is called upon by primary care physicians and managed care companies.

Finally, starting in 1995, lists of "empirically supported treatments" have been widely disseminated among clinical psychologists (for example, Task Force on Promotion and Dissemination of Psychological Procedures, 1995). The original list and subsequently revised lists have identified those interventions for commonly encountered clinical problems that have garnered empirical support through multiple outcome studies. We will discuss many of these interventions in later chapters.

A summary of the major historical events relevant to interventions is presented in the timeline "Significant Events in Intervention" on page 43.

Research

The Beginnings (1850–1899)

The academic research tradition in psychology owes much to the work of two men. Wilhelm Wundt, a German, is usually credited with establishing the first formal psychological laboratory in Leipzig in 1879. In that same decade, an American, William James, also established a laboratory, and in 1890 he published his classic text, *Principles of Psychology*. The works of both these men exemplify the scholarly tradition. Their influence is also clearly discernible in the scientist-practitioner model that has served the field of clinical psychology for so many years.

The Advent of the Modern Era (1900–1919)

During this period, Ivan Pavlov was lecturing on the conditioned reflex. His work on conditioning left an important legacy for clinical psychology. The notion of classical conditioning has become a central part of theory and research while also playing a significant role in a variety of therapeutic methods. Another important development

was research on intelligence testing. In 1905, Binet and Simon offered some evidence for the validity of their new test, and in 1916, Terman's research on the Binet-Simon test appeared. This was also the era of the development of the Army Alpha and Beta tests, described earlier.

Between the Wars (1920–1939)

Clinical research was still in its infancy. Much of the noteworthy work was in the area of test development—for example, the 1939 publication of the Wechsler-Bellevue test and all the personality testing work of the 1930s. On the academic research scene, both behaviorism and Gestalt psychology were prominent. Behaviorism taught clinicians the power of conditioning in the development and treatment of behavior disorders. Gestalt psychology emphasized the importance of understanding patients' unique perceptions as contributory to their problems.

World War II and Beyond (1940–Present)

By the mid-1960s, diagnosis and assessment had become less important for many clinicians. However, in the 1950s, you would hardly have predicted it. The journals were full of research studies dealing with both intelligence testing and personality assessment. Study after study dealt with various aspects of the Stanford-Binet and the Wechsler scales. Research on their validity and reliability, their use with various diagnostic groups, short forms, and implications for personality appeared in waves. The story was similar for projective tests. Literally hundreds of studies dealing with the Rorschach and TAT were published. Many of these studies also focused on issues of reliability and validity. Some observers attribute part of the subsequent decline in projective testing to the many negative validity studies that appeared during this time.

Another very important research development during these years was the emergence of studies on the process and effectiveness of psychotherapy. As noted previously, Eysenck's critique sent clinicians scrambling to shore up psychotherapy's image through solid research evidence. One of the real pioneers in therapy research was Carl Rogers (1951). His use of recordings to study the process of therapy opened windows to an activity that had long been shrouded in mystery. Rogers and Dymond (1954) reported controlled research findings on the counseling process.

Another research landmark of this era was the publication of Julian Rotter's *Social Learning and Clinical Psychology* in 1954. It presented not only a social learning theory but also a series of controlled studies that provided an empirical foundation for the theory. Research on the theory's implications for assessment and therapy was also included. The work provided a solid foundation upon which subsequent social learning theorists could build.

The 1950s also witnessed the explicit beginnings of the more behaviorally oriented forms of intervention. Joseph Wolpe's research in South Africa on animal and human learning convinced him that his work was relevant to human emotional problems and led him to develop the method of *systematic desensitization* (Wolpe, 1958). This behavioral method relies neither on insight, thought to be so necessary by the psychoanalysts, nor on growth potential, considered equally necessary by the client-centered school of therapy. Arnold Lazarus and Stanley Rachman were two others who helped facilitate this movement. Another influential figure in the behavioral research movement was Hans Eysenck, who coined the term "behavior therapy" and wrote an important book on the topic in 1960.

As noted earlier, beginning in the 1950s, the effectiveness of psychotherapy was being questioned. However, in 1977 Mary Smith and Gene Glass published a survey that supported the efficacy of therapy. This work laid the basis for a series of studies that has helped us better understand the way therapeutic methods affect patients. As noted previously, the field of *psychotherapy research* continues to grow to this day.

Other areas of research that have grown tremendously are diagnosis and classification, as well as psychological testing and measurement.

The publication of DSM-III (American Psychiatric Association, 1980) spurred an explosion of research aimed at evaluating the reliability, validity, and utility of specific criteria listed for the mental disorders included in this manual. Both psychiatry and psychology journals published numerous studies on the DSM-III criteria for syndromes such as schizophrenia, major depression, and antisocial personality disorder. In addition, more clinical psychologists began conducting research aimed at identifying the *etiological* (causal) factors associated with the development of various mental disorders. The factors investigated ranged from genetic predispositions to traumatic childhood events such as physical or sexual abuse.

Published research on psychological inventories, interviews, and rating scales has also increased. With the proliferation of psychological instruments available to both researchers and clinicians, the reliability and validity of these measures need to be evaluated empirically. Symptomatic of the growth of this research area is the "splitting" of a major clinical psychology journal, the *Journal of Consulting and Clinical Psychology (JCCP)*, in two. Now, in addition to *JCCP*, we have the journal *Psychological Assessment*, the primary outlet for research on psychological tests and measures used by clinical psychologists. It is important to note, however, that the research of clinical psychologists is published in many other high-quality journals besides these two. The following list indicates the range of journals that publish research important to the field:

Journal of Consulting and Clinical Psychology
Psychological Assessment
Clinical Psychology: Science and Practice
Journal of Abnormal Psychology
Psychological Bulletin
Behavior Therapy
Psychological Science
American Journal of Psychiatry
Archives of General Psychiatry
Professional Psychology: Research and Practice
Clinical Psychology Review

TIMELINE : Significant Events in Research

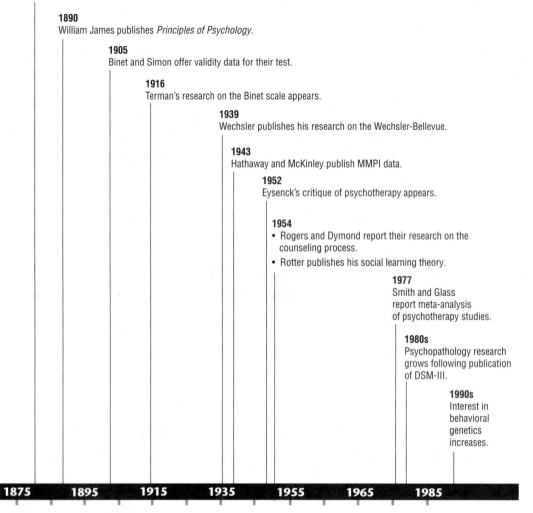

1879
Wundt establishes the first psychological lab in Leipzig.

1890
William James publishes *Principles of Psychology*.

1905
Binet and Simon offer validity data for their test.

1916
Terman's research on the Binet scale appears.

1939
Wechsler publishes his research on the Wechsler-Bellevue.

1943
Hathaway and McKinley publish MMPI data.

1952
Eysenck's critique of psychotherapy appears.

1954
• Rogers and Dymond report their research on the counseling process.
• Rotter publishes his social learning theory.

1977
Smith and Glass report meta-analysis of psychotherapy studies.

1980s
Psychopathology research grows following publication of DSM-III.

1990s
Interest in behavioral genetics increases.

1875   1895   1915   1935   1955   1965   1985

Finally, the decade of the 1990s has witnessed an increasing amount of interest among clinical psychologists in the field of behavioral genetics. Behavioral genetics is a research specialty in which both genetic and environmental influences on the development of behavior are evaluated. Behavioral geneticists have investigated these influences in a wide range of behaviors and individual differences, including intelligence, personality, and psychopathology. We will review this important field in later chapters.

Because research is such an important part of all clinical psychology, we will be discussing research methods, research on particular topics, and the historical context of research in these areas throughout this book. Many of the research highlights are mentioned in the timeline "Significant Events in Research" above.

The Profession

The Beginnings (1850–1899)

Two events of great significance in the development of clinical psychology as a profession occurred just as the nineteenth century was winding down. The first was the founding of the American Psychological Association (APA) in 1892, with G. Stanley Hall as its first president. Although the membership of the association was still fewer than 100 by the close of the nineteenth century, the profession had truly begun.

The birth of clinical psychology was not far behind. In 1896, Lightner Witmer established the first psychological clinic at the University of Pennsylvania. Many would date the real beginning of clinical psychology from this time (McReynolds, 1996).

Witmer's clinic was devoted to the treatment of children who were experiencing learning problems or who were disruptive in the classroom. In the very first issue of *The Psychological Clinic* in 1907, Witmer wrote:

> Children from the public schools of Philadelphia and adjacent cities have been brought to the laboratory by parents or teachers; these children had made themselves conspicuous because of an inability to progress in school work as rapidly as other children, or because of moral defects which rendered them difficult to manage under ordinary discipline.
>
> When brought to the psychological clinic, such children are given a physical and mental examination; if the result of this examination shows it to be desirable, they are then sent to specialists for the eye or ear, for the nose and throat, and for nervous diseases, one or all, as each case may require. The result of this conjoint medical and psychological examination is a diagnosis of the child's mental and physical condition and the recommendation of appropriate medical and pedagogical treatment. (Witmer, 1907, p. 1)

FIGURE 2-4 Lightner Witmer's development of the first psychological clinic began with the referral of a boy who showed an odd spelling problem. It ended by stimulating the establishment of a profession that was different from both education and medicine.
Brown Brothers.

In many ways, Witmer's influence on the field was historical rather than substantive. That is, he got the profession under way but really added little in the way of new theories or methods. It was he who named the field "clinical psychology," and he was the first to teach a specific course in clinical psychology. Further, it was Witmer who, in 1907, founded the first journal in clinical psychology, *The Psychological Clinic*—a journal that he edited and contributed articles to until it ceased publication in 1935. Although the manner in which clinical psychologists do things today may not have been much influenced by Witmer, the fact that they are doing them at all is due in no small measure to his efforts and foresight (McReynolds, 1987, 1996). Box 2-1 summarizes Witmer's seminal contributions to the field.

BOX 2-1

Lightner Witmer: The Founder of Clinical Psychology

Lightner Witmer (1867–1958) is credited with founding the field of clinical psychology. His contributions to the field include the following:

- In 1896, he established the first "psychological" clinic.
- In 1907, he proposed a new profession, clinical psychology;
- He served as founder and editor of the first journal in the field, *The Psychological Clinic.*
- He developed the first training program in clinical psychology (McReynolds, 1996).

In addition, Witmer's work influenced and anticipated future developments in clinical psychology, including an emphasis on children's academic problems, the use of active clinical interventions to improve individuals' lives, and collaboration with other professionals (such as physicians) in providing treatment (Routh, 1996).

The Advent of the Modern Era (1900–1919)

In the first decade of the twentieth century, only a very small number of psychologists could be found employed outside the universities. In 1906, Morton Prince began publishing the *Journal of Abnormal Psychology,* and in 1907 Witmer began publication of the *Psychological Clinic* (see Figure 2-5). With two journals of their own, applied clinicians could now begin to form their identity. This identity was further reinforced when, in 1909, Healy established the juvenile Psychopathic Institute in Chicago. The Iowa Psychological Clinic had been started in 1908, the same year that Goddard began offering psychological internships at the Vineland Training School in New Jersey. With its own journals, clinics, and internships, the profession of clinical psychology was beginning to take shape.

By 1910, there were 222 APA members, paying annual dues of one dollar. (In 1998, membership dues were $215, not including an additional $110 special assessment fee for licensed health care psychologists!) However, the focus of APA was on psychology as a science, not as a profession. At the same time, the public schools of the day were beginning to clamor for testing services,

and universities were beginning to respond with testing courses and studies of those with cognitive limitations. Finally, in 1919, the first Section of Clinical Psychology was created within the APA. Meanwhile, an ever-increasing number of psychological clinics were being established (for example, the organization by Healy in 1917 of the Judge Baker Foundation in Boston). However, World War I and the growth of the group testing movement did as much as anything to spur the development of the new profession.

Between the Wars (1920–1939)

The APA had long proclaimed that its mission was to further psychology as a science. However, by the close of the 1920s many clinically oriented psychologists were becoming uneasy and increasingly sought to gain recognition of their unique roles and interests from APA. In 1931, the Clinical Section of APA appointed a committee on training standards, and in 1935, the APA Committee on Standards of Training defined clinical psychology as "that art and technology which deals with the adjustment problems of human beings" (Reisman, 1976, p. 250). It is doubtful whether many clinicians even today would reject this definition.

FIGURE 2-5 Cover of the first issue of *The Psychological Clinic*

Vol. I, No. 1   March 15, 1907

THE PSYCHOLOGICAL CLINIC

*A Journal for the Study and Treatment
of Mental Retardation and Deviation*

Editor:
LIGHTNER WITMER, Ph.D.,
University of Pennsylvania.

Associate Editor: Associate Editor:
HERBERT STOTESBURY, Ph.D.,   JOSEPH COLLINS, M.D.,
The Temple College,   Post Graduate Medical College,
Philadelphia.   New York.

CONTENTS

	Page
CLINICAL PSYCHOLOGY. *Lightner Witmer*	1
AN INFANTILE STAMMER (BABY TALK) IN A BOY OF TWELVE YEARS. *Clara Harrison Town*, Resident Psychologist at Friends' Asylum for the Insane, Frankford	10
A JUVENILE DELINQUENT. *Edward A. Huntington*, Principal of Special School No. 3, Philadelphia	21
UNIVERSITY COURSES IN PSYCHOLOGY. *Lightner Witmer*	25
REVIEWS AND CRITICISM: "Child and Educational Psychology." The Psychological Bulletin, Vol. 3, No. 2, November 15, 1906, Edited by M. V. O'Shea	36
NEWS AND COMMENT	39

THE PSYCHOLOGICAL CLINIC PRESS
WEST PHILADELPHIA STATION, PHILADELPHIA, PA.

In 1936, Louttit published the first clinical psychology text, and in 1937 the *Journal of Consulting Psychology* was founded. Still published today as the *Journal of Consulting and Clinical Psychology (JCCP)*, it serves as a major publication outlet for the research of many clinicians. Such events signaled real growth for clinical psychology as a profession. Another trend also attested to the development of the field: Psychological tests were beginning to become financial winners. James McKeen Cattell founded the Psychological Corporation in 1921 to develop and market psychological tests (particularly those of interest to industry). The proceeds were to be used to stimulate psychological research. Thus, money began to invade the ivory tower. For example, a $75,000 gift enabled Morton Prince to establish the Harvard Psychological Clinic in 1927. Nevertheless, the clinical psychologists of the day were quite different in terms of both activities and training from those of today.

World War II and Beyond (1940–1969)

The process of absorbing large numbers of men into the U.S. military in the early 1940s generated many needs. One such need was for a large-scale screening program to weed out those who were unfit for military service. Psychologists had already begun to develop the rudiments of a testing technology that would assist in this task, and they also had expertise in research methods. These skills set them apart from their psychiatric colleagues. Both their technology and their research orientation served psychologists well in the establishment of a professional identity. More than 1700 psychologists served in World War II, and they returned to civilian life with increased confidence in their abilities and a determination to build a profession.

All of this was very important in affecting the federal government's response to the mental health problems facing the United States after World War II. To the Veterans Administration (VA) fell the enormous burden of providing care and rehabilitation for the thousands upon thousands of men and women who had suffered some form of emotional trauma from their military service. Without a marked increase in mental health professionals, there was no way that the VA could fulfill its mission and cope with the rising tide of patients that swept into its clinics and hospitals. The VA's solution was to increase the availability of mental health professionals by providing financial support for their training.

In the case of clinical psychology, the VA provided financially attractive internships for graduate students in approved university Ph.D. programs. Although not required to do so, many of these students chose to remain with the VA after completing their training. Through its programs, the VA played a chief role in upgrading and building the profession of clinical psychology. Its willingness to hire clinicians at salaries higher than could generally be obtained elsewhere raised the entire pay scale of the profession. Its need to deal with the psychological problems of adults resulted in a major shift in clinical psychologists' services from children to adults. At the same time, the VA came to expect clinical psychologists to conduct individual and group psychotherapy along with their accustomed psychodiagnostic activities. They also continued to serve in their familiar capacity as the research experts on mental health teams. When, in 1946, the VA initiated its program to train clinical psychologists, clinical training had secured a firm financial foundation. By 1949, 42 schools were offering the doctorate in clinical psychology, and large numbers of students of high quality were applying. The profession had attained public visibility.

The VA was not the only federal agency to promote the rise of clinical psychology. The aftermath of the war and the general increase in government activity also led to an attempt to ameliorate some of the mental health problems in the nation as a whole. The U.S. Public Health Service and the National Institute of Mental Health initiated support of clinical psychology graduate students working toward the Ph.D. and sponsored research and training programs designed to provide answers to the nation's mental health problems.

Further evidence of professional growth was the publication of the first *American Psychologist* in 1946. In 1945, Connecticut became the first state to pass a certification law for psychologists. During the following year, the American Board of Examiners in Professional Psychology (ABEPP) was established to certify the professional competence of clinicians holding the Ph.D. In 1949, the Educational Testing Service was started. The APA was now asserting that psychotherapy was an integral function of clinical psychologists—notwithstanding the opposition from the psychiatric profession. The APA was also assuming a more activist role. It was beginning to make recommendations for the training of clinical psychologists and also to certify clinical training programs. In 1953, it published *Ethical Standards,* a landmark achievement in the codification of ethical behavior for psychologists and a great step forward in the protection of the public. By the beginning of the 1950s, APA could claim more than 1000 members in its Clinical Division. In just a few years after World War II, the profession had made enormous strides.

In 1949, a conference on graduate education in clinical psychology was held in Boulder, Colorado. The Boulder Conference was a truly significant event in clinical psychology because it explicated the scientist-practitioner model for training clinical psychologists that has served as *the* principal guideline for training ever since. In succinct terms, this model asserts (1) clinical psychologists shall pursue their training in university departments; (2) they shall be trained as psychologists first and clinicians second; (3) they shall be required to serve a clinical internship; (4) they shall achieve competence in diagnosis, psychotherapy, and research; and (5) the culmination of their training shall be the Ph.D. degree, which involves an original research contribution to the field. By and large, this still serves as the training model, even though the scientist-practitioner model has always had its critics.

The 1950s witnessed a marked growth in the psychological profession. The membership of APA rose from 7250 in 1950 to 16,644 in 1959—

a phenomenal increase. In approximately the same period, federal research grants and contracts for psychological research rose from $11 million to more than $31 million.

The Growth of a Profession (1970–Present)

In the areas of assessment, intervention, and research, clinical psychology has become increasingly behavioral since the mid-1960s. The focus has shifted from a search for the traits or internal factors that lead people into a psychopathological condition to an analysis of the situational factors that control their behavior. In the late 1960s, the road to changing undesirable behavior began swerving sharply from psychotherapy (and the insight it was designed to produce) to conditioning and altered reinforcement contingencies. Research journals were full of articles describing new objective methods of assessing behavior and novel behavioral approaches to the treatment of everything from alcoholism, sexual dysfunctions, and lack of assertiveness to obesity, smoking, and loneliness. The key to everything lay not in patients' thoughts but in their behavior.

Some, of course, began to suspect that all this was an overreaction. Were traits really fictions that had no utility? Could behavioral analyses and methods address and cure everything? Many thought not, and by the mid-1970s, cognition had begun to creep back onto the scene. People now began talking about "cognitive behavior methods" (Goldfried & Davison, 1976). The cognitive-behavioral orientation to treatment is now among the most common.

At the same time, the field of community psychology, which had seemed poised in the 1960s to revolutionize clinical psychology, began to falter. Its promise seemed to many to be unfulfilled. Then in the 1980s, the preventive focus reappeared with the development of the field of health psychology. All these concepts, methods, and trends of the past 20 years constitute the major thrusts of this book and will be covered in detail in the ensuing chapters.

FIGURE 2-6 APA membership from 1937 to 1987

Adapted from "Report of the Executive Vice-president: 1987, " by L. D. Goodstein, American Psychologist, 1988, 43, 491–498. Copyright 1988 by the American Psychological Association, Reprinted by permission.

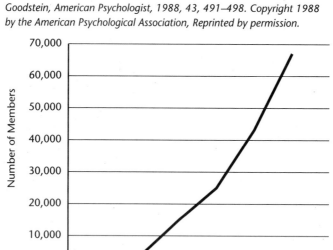

The 1970s and 1980s witnessed still further growth in the profession. In 1970, there were 81 fully approved graduate training programs in clinical psychology and well over 12,000 clinicians. As for APA itself, in 1892 there had been 42 members; by 1987, there were almost 67,000. This phenomenal growth is shown in Figure 2-6. By 1997, membership had grown to more than 83,000, and the operating budget that same year was about $64 million. Also, the Division of Clinical Psychology was the largest single unit in the APA. All 50 states, the District of Columbia, Puerto Rico, and several Canadian provinces either licensed or certified psychologists. Many clinical psychologists now have hospital privileges, and most can be reimbursed for their services by insurance and managed care companies. There has also been an increase in the number of clinical psychology graduate programs. Today, there are close to 200 doctoral training programs in clinical psychology with full APA approval.

The 1988 Schism

Within the APA there have always been conflicts, sometimes acrimonious, between clinicians and their scientific counterparts. Often, these conflicts placed the scientist-practitioner squarely in the middle. By 1988, the academic-scientific wing of the APA seems to have concluded that APA was under the control of the practitioners, who were using their power to promote their own interests. Scientific interests, they said, were being replaced by goals that were essentially guild-like. The APA seemed to be preoccupied with such professional issues as writing prescriptions, hospital privileges, reimbursement questions, licensing, legal actions against psychiatry, and so on. In short, many had come to feel that APA was no longer responsive to the academic-scientific needs of a significant number of its members. Indeed, former APA president Janet Spence charged that 90% of APA Council meetings were taken up by the professional interests of practicing clinicians.

Matters seemed to come to a head when, in 1988, a plan to reorganize APA so as to help heal the growing schism between the clinical wing and the academic-scientific wing failed by a 2-to-1 vote of the membership. The response of those disenchanted with APA was to form a new, separate organization. The *American Psychological So-*

T I M E L I N E : Significant Events in the Profession of Clinical Psychology

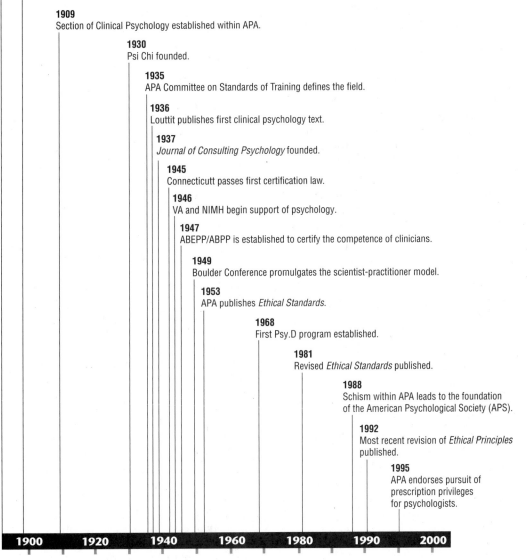

1892
American Psychological Association (APA) is founded.

1896
Witmer establishes the first "Psychological" Clinic.

1909
Section of Clinical Psychology established within APA.

1930
Psi Chi founded.

1935
APA Committee on Standards of Training defines the field.

1936
Louttit publishes first clinical psychology text.

1937
Journal of Consulting Psychology founded.

1945
Connecticutt passes first certification law.

1946
VA and NIMH begin support of psychology.

1947
ABEPP/ABPP is established to certify the competence of clinicians.

1949
Boulder Conference promulgates the scientist-practitioner model.

1953
APA publishes *Ethical Standards*.

1968
First Psy.D program established.

1981
Revised *Ethical Standards* published.

1988
Schism within APA leads to the foundation
of the American Psychological Society (APS).

1992
Most recent revision of *Ethical Principles*
published.

1995
APA endorses pursuit of
prescription privileges
for psychologists.

1900   **1920**   **1940**   **1960**   **1980**   **1990**   **2000**

ciety (APS) was founded in 1988, led by 22 former APA presidents who became founding members. The initial advisory board of APS read like a scientific "Who's Who." The first APS convention was held in June 1988 and by most accounts was a resounding success. This organization now has a newsletter, *The Observer,* a monthly *Employment Bulletin,* and two scientific journals, *Psychological Science* and *Current Directions in Psychological Science.* Today, the total APS membership exceeds 16,000. Approximately 13% of APS members identify themselves as clinical, counseling, or school psychologists. The professed goals of this new organization are to:

- Advance the discipline of psychology
- Preserve the scientific base of psychology
- Promote public understanding of psychological science and its applications
- Enhance the quality of education
- Encourage the "giving away" of psychology in the public interest

Many on both sides of the APA-APS split feel the break was tragic. They believe that it was unfortunate for both sides—that what the field needs is greater integration of the science of psychology and its practice. Unfortunately, the split may produce even less integration than now exists. Many believe that it will only hasten the day when APA becomes unabashedly a guild organization. Of course, many in the academic-scientist group and many who are traditional scientist-practitioners now belong to both APA and APS. Many scientific psychologists are exhilarated over the quick growth of APS. In any case, let us hope that both APA and APS remember their larger obligations to the public good.

Some of the highlights of these professional developments are summarized in the timeline "Significant Events in the Profession of Clinical Psychology" on page 53.

Today, the field of clinical psychology is challenged by a host of professional issues. In Chapter 3, we will discuss several of these in some detail. Briefly, they include the question of the optimal training model for contemporary clinical psychologists, the impact of the health care revolution and managed care on clinicians, and the current push for prescription privileges for clinical psychology. The way that these issues are resolved will greatly affect the field of clinical psychology for years to come.

Chapter Summary

Clinical psychology has changed, and it will certainly change even more. Witmer would scarcely recognize it. G. Stanley Hall, APA's first president, would doubtless be amazed at the things APA and APS are doing. However, though both training and practice are in a state of flux, certain constants remain. Clinical psychologists are still involved in assessment and treatment. They still have research contributions to make, and they are still concerned with their professional development. The goal that binds clinical psychologists together remains the same: to apply their knowledge and skill to the mental health needs of people everywhere.

Key Terms

American Psychological Society (APS) The professional psychological organization formed in 1988 when an academic-scientific contingent broke off from the APA. Goals of the APS include advancing the discipline of psychology, preserving its scientific base, and promoting public understanding of the field and its applications.

behavior therapy A popular or learning framework for treating disorders that is based on the principles of conditioning. Behavior therapy usually focuses on observable behavior and is typically of relatively brief duration.

behavioral assessment An approach to understanding and changing behavior by identifying the context in which it occurs (the situations or stimuli that either precede it or follow from it).

brief/time-effective therapy Generally speaking, therapy of 15 or fewer sessions' duration. Brief therapy has gained popularity in recent years due to the financial constraints imposed by managed care, as well as studies demonstrating that its effectiveness is on par with that of traditional psychotherapy.

community psychology A psychological specialty that focuses on the prevention and treatment of mental health problems, particularly among people that are traditionally underserved.

eclectics Clinicians that employ the techniques of more than one theoretical orientation. Which orientation is used in a given case is determined by the nature of the presenting problem.

etiological Causal. For example, an etiological factor for depression is believed to contribute to its onset.

g A term introduced by Charles Spearman to describe his concept of a general factor of intelligence.

guidance clinics Clinics devoted to the evaluation and treatment of children's intellectual and behavioral difficulties.

health psychology A psychological specialty that focuses on the prevention of illness, the promotion and maintenance of good health, and the psychological treatment of individuals with diagnosed medical conditions.

manualized treatment Treatment that is presented and described in a manual format (i.e., outlining the rationales, goals, and techniques that correspond to each phase of the treatment).

measurement of intelligence The use of tests to measure various mental capacities (e.g., the speed of mental processes, the ability to learn over trials).

mental tests The term coined by James McKeen Cattell to describe his measures of individual differences in reaction time. He believed that performance on these tests was associated with intelligence.

neuropsychological assessment An assessment approach—based on empirically established brain-behavior relationships—that evaluates a person's relative strengths and weaknesses across a number of areas (e.g., memory, speed of processing, and manual dexterity).

objective measures Psychological tests that draw conclusions about people's states or traits on the basis of their responses to unambiguous stimuli, such as rating scales or questionnaire items. Responses to objective measures are often interpreted using a nomothetic approach.

personality disorders Enduring and maladaptive patterns of experience and behavior that emerge by adolescence or young adulthood and persist through much of adulthood. Examples include the paranoid, antisocial, and dependent personality disorders.

personality testing The use of measures or techniques to provide insight into enduring characteristics or traits.

play therapy A technique, derived from traditional Freudian principles, that uses expressive play to help release anxiety or hostility. Proponents believe that such a release has a curative effect.

projective techniques Psychological testing techniques, such as the Rorschach or the Thematic Apperception Test, that use people's responses to ambiguous test stimuli to make judgments about their personality traits or their psychological state.

psychoanalysis A framework for understanding and treating mental illness based on the collaborative work of Breuer and Freud in the late 1800s.

psychodiagnosis The use and interpretation of psychological test scores for the purposes of diagnosis and treatment planning.

psychotherapy research Research that evaluates the effectiveness of therapy or certain therapy components. Psychotherapy research may be used to determine which intervention is more effective for treating a certain condition or which component of a particular therapy is most crucial for bringing about an observed change.

radical behaviorism A movement in psychology that began in the late 1950s and persisted through the 1960s. Proponents of this movement asserted that only overt behaviors could be measured, and even questioned the existence of personality traits.

scientist-practitioner model The principal model for clinical psychology training of the past 50 years (also referred to as the Boulder model). This model strives to produce professionals who can effectively integrate the roles of scientist and practitioner.

structured diagnostic interviews A class of assessment tools, all of which consist of questions keyed to diagnostic criteria. The term *structured* means that interviewers ask all interviewees the same questions in the same order, and score the answers in standard ways.

systematic desensitization A behavioral technique for the treatment of anxiety disorders in which patients practice relaxation while visualizing anxiety-provoking situations of increasing intensity.

Web Sites of Interest

To visit any of the web sites listed below, go to www.wadsworth.com and click on Links.

2-1   American Psychological Association

2-2   American Psychological Society

2-3   Society for a Science of Clinical Psychology

2-4   Classics in the History of Psychology

2-5   Daily Calendar of Events in the History of Psychology

2-6   Society of Clinical Psychology (Division 12 of the APA)

2-7   Web sites dedicated to specific individuals important in the history of psychology

2-8   Women in psychology

CHAPTER THREE

Current Issues in Clinical Psychology

In Chapter 2, we reviewed the history and development of the field of clinical psychology by examining important events in the areas of diagnosis and assessment, interventions and psychotherapy, research, and the profession. That review helped us to appreciate the roots of clinical psychology, as well as to put current activities in the appropriate historical context.

In this chapter, we discuss a variety of contemporary issues in clinical psychology: What are the best training models for a clinical psychologist? What is the best way to ensure professional competence? What are the issues that currently face clinical psychologists in private practice? How can clinical psychology maintain its independence and economic viability? How should clinical psychology respond to the increasing diversity of the population it serves? How will the health care revolution affect clinical psychologists? Should clinical psychologists pursue and obtain prescription privileges? What are contemporary ethical standards for clinical psychologists? We will begin with one of the most contentious of these issues—the appropriate training models for future clinical psychologists.

Models of Training in Clinical Psychology

The Scientist-Practitioner

The Training Model. In Chapter 2, we briefly discussed the landmark conference on graduate education in clinical psychology held in Boulder, Colorado, in 1949. Out of this conference arose the Boulder model or scientist-practitioner model of training. This model represents an attempt to "marry" science and clinical practice and remains the most popular training model for clinical psychologists even to this day.

It is useful to remember that clinical psychology began in universities as a branch of scientific psychology. It arose within the structure of colleges of arts and sciences, where teaching, research, and other scholarly efforts were the rewarded activities. Practitioner concerns were grafted onto this corpus, and the graft did not always take well. The goals of professionalism were not always the goals of one's dean or even of one's peers.

In the face of such conflict, some clinical psychology professors did carry out research and they did publish. But their critics (often graduate students or clinicians in the field) complained that much of the research was trivial, nonutilitarian, or just busywork whose only purpose was to gain financial rewards and titles. Worse, it seemed to professors that their own research detracted from their training of clinical students in the skills of the profession. Some students complained that they were learning too much about analysis of variance, theories of conditioning, or principles of physiological psychology and too little about psychotherapy and diagnostic testing.

These are the kinds of events and situations that led to demands for change. The Boulder model saw a profession comprised of skilled practitioners who could produce their own research as well as consume the research of others. The goal was to create a profession different from any that had gone before. The psychological clinician would practice with skill and sensitivity, but would also contribute to the body of clinical knowledge by understanding how to translate experience into testable hypotheses and how to test those hypotheses. The Boulder vision was of a systematic union between clinical skill and the logical empiricism of science. To separate the practitioner from the source of knowledge is to create someone who passively consumes information or "buys" techniques from a psychological huckster.

The scientist-practitioner model is less a quantitative breakdown of one's daily activities than it is a state of mind. No one ever intended to have all clinicians devote 50% of their time to their clinical practice and 50% to formal research. Some will be primarily researchers and others primarily clinicians. Although it is true that practicing clinicians do not do much in the way of research, this may be largely because their work settings do not permit it and not because they do not wish to do it.

The scientist-practitioner model is just as applicable to clinical researchers as it is to practicing clinicians. The former can only produce solid, meaningful research if they keep their clinical sensitivity and skills honed by continuing to see patients. Just as practitioners must not forsake their research training and interests, neither must researchers ignore their clinical foundation.

The Debate Goes On. A series of training conferences culminating in one at Salt Lake City, Utah, in 1987 have eroded any strict interpretation of the scientist-practitioner model. These conferences have recognized alternative routes to professional competence. Specifically, they have accepted approaches that deemphasize research experience in favor of more direct and extensive training in clinical skills.

The Boulder model has been durable, but the debate goes on. The mood of professionalism seems to grow every year. Increasingly, clinical psychologists are split into two groups—those interested primarily in clinical practice and those interested primarily in research. Moreover, many of those in practice show indifference to research (Barlow, 1981). Perhaps part of the problem stems from the failure to implement adequately the scientist-practitioner model. For example, Drabman (1985) describes students who arrive at their internship site without an adequate knowledge of how to administer, score, and interpret psychological tests. These students also sometimes show a surprising lack of experience with clinical populations. Although well versed in the nuts and bolts of research, they have little skill in the practical application of their knowledge. In a related vein, Goldfried (1984) has pointed out that, although research into the effectiveness of psychotherapy in *real* clinical settings is both exciting and needed, it is not always taught.

Many believe that the scientist-practitioner model has served us well and successfully. Still others conclude that it is a poor educational model that deserves the wrath of its critics. But the prospect of totally abandoning the Boulder model is worrisome to many. As Meltzoff (1984) put it:

> To train a new strain of purely applied psychologists who will be obliged to accept on faith what is handed down to them without being able to evaluate it or advance it, is the certain pathway to mediocrity. Research training conveys a mode of thought. It teaches how to be inquisitive and skeptical, how to think logically, how to formulate hypotheses and to test them, how to gather data rather than opinion, how to analyze those data and draw inferences from them, and how to make a balanced presentation of the findings. These are skills that help . . . professional psychologists to rise above the technician level. (p. 209)

The Doctor of Psychology (Psy.D.) Degree

The foregoing controversy was at least partially responsible for the emergence of Doctor of Psychology (Psy.D.) degrees. The special characteristics of such degrees are an emphasis on the development of clinical skills and a relative deemphasis on research competency. A master's thesis is not required, and the dissertation is usually a report on a professional subject rather than an original research contribution.

The first of these programs was developed at the University of Illinois in 1968 (D. R. Peterson, 1971), although that school has since closed its program. Subsequently, similar programs were developed at Rutgers, Baylor, and elsewhere. As Peterson (1968) envisioned them, Psy.D. programs are not substantially different from Ph.D. programs during the first two years of training. The real divergence begins with the third year. At that point, increasing experience in therapeutic practice and assessment becomes the rule. The fourth year continues the clinical emphasis with a series of internship assignments. More recently, Psy.D. programs have moved toward compressing formal coursework into the first year and expanding clinical experience by requiring such things as five-year practica. A good description and history of Psy.D. programs has been provided by McConnell (1984). In 1993, 544 of the 2,200 doctorates awarded in clinical psychology (24.5%) were Psy.D. degrees (ODEER, 1993). In 1998, there were 36 accredited doctoral programs in clinical psychology that offered the Psy.D.

Psy.D. programs have gained an increasing foothold in the profession. Snepp and Peterson (1988) even claim that students in Psy.D. and Ph.D. programs are essentially indistinguishable when it comes to being prepared for their internships. Research by Peterson, Eaton, Levine, and Snepp (1982) paints a portrait of Psy.D. practitioners who are satisfied with their careers and even more satisfied with their graduate training than are clinicians trained in traditional programs. They encounter few problems in becoming licensed and report that the Psy.D. degree is an advantage in competing for clinical positions. However, finding academic jobs is difficult for them. Further, when resources and incentives in the workplace permit, Ph.D. graduates engage in scholarly activities more often than do Psy.D. graduates (Barrom, Shadish, & Montgomery, 1988). One survey of graduates from one of the first Psy.D. programs to be established, at Baylor University (Hershey, Kopplin, & Cornell, 1991), found that the majority of graduates from this program (82%) identified themselves as practitioners, whereas few identified themselves as educators or researchers. Respondents were very satisfied with their graduate education and their career choice.

Professional Schools

Although the Psy.D. model represents a clear break with tradition, an even more radical innovation is the development of professional schools. Many of these schools have no affiliation with universities; they are autonomous, with their own financial and organizational framework. Often referred to as "free-standing" schools, most offer the Psy.D. (Peterson, Peterson, Abrams, & Stricker, 1997). Most schools emphasize clinical functions and generally have little or no research orientation in the traditional sense. Faculty are chiefly clinical in orientation and therefore are said to provide better role models for students. The first such free-standing professional school was the California School of Professional Psychology (Dorken, 1975). It was founded by the California State Psychological Association and offers several mental health degrees (Dorken & Cummings, 1977).

In 1987, there were 45 professional schools in operation, awarding several hundred of the 3000 yearly clinical doctorates (Strickland, 1988). By 1993, almost half (1,107 out of 2,220, or 49.9%) of the doctorates in clinical psychology were awarded by professional schools! Clearly, the proportion of doctorates in clinical psychology awarded by professional schools has increased dramatically. These programs tend to admit far more students than traditional, university-based scientist-practitioner programs. To cite one example, 6 students were admitted to one of the author's clinical program in 1997–1998, whereas a professional school in the same state admitted close to 100 students! Fewer than 1% of the students in this professional school were offered tuition fee waivers or assistantships/fellowships (Sayette et al., 1998).

Whether such schools ultimately will survive is still uncertain. One of their greatest problems is stability of funding. Many such institutions must depend on tuition as their chief source of funds, which does not generate enough money to make them financially secure. They often depend heavily on part-time faculty whose major employment is elsewhere—a shaky foundation for an academic structure. As one consequence, it is sometimes difficult for students to have the frequent and sustained contact with their professors that is so vital to a satisfactory educational experience. Although some professional schools are fully accredited by the APA, they are the exception rather than the rule. This is a major handicap that such schools will have to overcome if their graduates are to find professional acceptance everywhere. Recent conferences on training seem to suggest that both Ph.D. and Psy.D. programs have found secure niches and are here to stay. However, they continue to recommend that all doctoral programs be at or affiliated with regionally accredited universities (Belar & Perry, 1992; Fox & Barclay, 1989).

Clinical Scientist Model

Over the past decade, empirically oriented clinical psychologists have become increasingly concerned that clinical psychology, as currently practiced, is not well grounded in science. According to this view, many of the methods that practitioners employ in their treatment have not been demonstrated to be effective in controlled clinical studies. In some cases, empirical studies of these techniques have not been completed; in other cases, research that has been completed does not support continued use of the technique. Similarly, the use of assessment techniques that have not been shown to be reliable and valid and to lead to positive treatment outcome has been called into question.

The "call to action" for clinical scientists appeared in 1991, in the "Manifesto for a Science of Clinical Psychology" (McFall, 1991). In this document, McFall argued:

1. "Scientific clinical psychology is the only legitimate and acceptable form of clinical psychology" (p. 76).
2. "Psychological services should not be administered to the public (except under strict experimental control) until they have satisfied these four minimal criteria:
   a. The exact nature of the service must be described clearly.
   b. The claimed benefits of the service must be stated explicitly.
   c. These claimed benefits must be validated scientifically.
   d. Possible negative side effects that outweigh any benefits must be ruled out empirically" (p. 80).
3. "The primary and overriding objectives of doctoral training programs in clinical psychology must be to produce the most competent clinical scientists possible" (p. 84).

Like-minded clinical psychologists were urged to help build a *science* of clinical psychol-ogy by integrating scientific principles into their own clinical work, differentiating between scientifically valid techniques and pseudoscientific ones, and focusing graduate training on methods that produce *clinical scientists*—individuals that "think and function as scientists in every respect and setting in their professional lives" (McFall, 1991, p. 85).

This document has proved to be quite provocative. One outgrowth of this model of training is the newly formed *Academy of Psychological Clinical Science*. The academy consists of graduate programs that are committed to training in empirical methods of research and the integration of this training with clinical training. The academy is affiliated with the American Psychological Society (APS). As of 1999, it included 43 member programs. The primary goals of the academy are:

1. To foster the training of students for careers in clinical science research, who skillfully will produce and apply scientific knowledge.
2. To advance the full range of clinical science research and theory and their integration with other relevant sciences.
3. To foster the development of and access to resources and opportunities for training, research, funding, and careers in clinical science.
4. To foster the broad application of clinical science to human problems in responsible and innovative ways.
5. To foster the timely dissemination of clinical science to policy-making groups, psychologists and other scientists, practitioners, and consumers. (See web site 3-4.)

Essentially, a network of graduate programs that adhere to the clinical science model has developed. These programs share ideas, resources, and training innovations. Further, they collaborate on projects aimed at increasing grant funding from governmental agencies, addressing state licensing requirements for the practice of psychology, and increasing the visibility of clinical science programs in undergraduate education.

The ultimate success and influence of this new model of training remains to be seen.

PROFILE 3-1

Richard M. McFall, Ph.D.

Dr. McFall is a Professor of Psychology at Indiana University. He is an expert in the area of interpersonal competence, and his widely cited research has appeared in numerous journals and books read by clinical psychologists. In addition to his research pursuits, Dr. McFall has taught and trained many clinical psychologists through his roles as faculty member and Director of Clinical Training. Finally, Dr. McFall is recognized as influential in establishing the clinical science model of training. He served as the president of the Academy of Psychological Clinical Science from 1995 to 1998.

Dr. McFall was kind enough to respond to the following questions we posed:

What originally got you interested in the field of clinical psychology?

As an undergraduate at DePauw University, I was an art major until my junior year, when it occurred to me to ask my art professor what I might be able to do with a degree in art. Among other things, he suggested that I might become an account executive in advertising. He suggested that I take a psychology course to learn what motivated people to buy things. So, I went over to the psychology department. Of course, I had to take prerequisites (introductory, statistics, experimental, and so on) before

I could take the "good stuff," and before I knew it, I was a psychology major. At the start of my senior year, still intending to go into advertising, I took a clinical psychology course taught by John Exner (the world-famous Rorschach expert), devoted primarily to projective tests. Exner encouraged me to apply to graduate school in clinical psychology, and gave me a list of prospective graduate programs, all psychodynamically oriented. As I began filling out applications, my roommate's father, who happened to be a psychologist, visited campus. He suggested that I apply to Ohio State University (where he got his degree). I did, more or less as a "backup." OSU admitted me and offered a generous assistantship—more than any other program. Being financially independent and in debt, I accepted OSU's offer. As it turned out, the OSU clinical program was one of the best in the country at the time. It had a very strong scientific emphasis. I quickly learned that I had entered graduate school for illusory reasons; however, the research orientation of OSU's program was compelling, and I soon developed an interest in clinical psychology as a science.

Describe what activities you are involved in as a clinical psychologist.

First and foremost I am a teacher. For most of my career, I have taught Introduction to Clinical Psychology to advanced undergraduates and Clinical Psychology to first-year graduate students. My goal in both classes is to teach the students to think skeptically and critically about the problems that are the primary focus in clinical psychology. I also teach a clinical practicum for advanced doctoral students in which we review the empirical research evidence on the effectiveness of different methods of treating persons with obsessive-compulsive disorders (OCD); apply the best of the available methods to OCD clients in our own clinic; and evaluate the results of our interventions.

(continued)

Profile 3-1 *(continued)*

I also am an active researcher. The common theme of my research is interpersonal competence—how to define and measure it, how to predict and promote it, and the factors that lead to incompetence. Competence and psychopathology can be seen as opposite sides of the same coin. Psychopathology can be viewed as a lack of competence in one or more critical areas of functioning. To understand the etiology of psychopathology, then, clinical psychologists might want to understand the nature and origins of competence. My research draws heavily on the knowledge and methods of psychology as a whole, especially cognitive science and neuroscience. This means that I must be an active student of the discipline. Another facet of my professional life is my involvement in administrative and service roles. I have been director of the clinical training program at Indiana University; have been on the board of directors of the local community mental health center; have served on editorial boards of journals; and have been active in professional organizations at the national level. Virtually all of my professional efforts, in one way or another, are devoted to differentiating science from pseudoscience within clinical psychology, and to promoting clinical psychology as a science.

What are your particular areas of expertise or interest?

I've already described my content focus in research: interpersonal competence. In pursuing this interest, I have studied a variety of specific clinical problems and populations—including shy college men and women; nonassertive individuals; persons suffering from schizophrenia, depression, OCD, eating disorders, and addiction to tobacco; adolescent boys and girls identified as juvenile delinquents; and men who are sexually coercive toward women. My research across these problem areas has been characterized by an emphasis on conceptual and measurement issues. Recent work, in particular, has explored the use of concepts and methods adapted from cognitive science and neuroscience. My goal is to build better theoretical and quantitative models of clinically relevant phenomena.

What are the future trends you see for clinical psychology?

Clinical training programs that continue to have a strong "practice" focus (whether they identify themselves as Psy.D. programs or scientist-practitioner Ph.D. programs) are ignoring the dramatic changes currently taking place within the mental health field (increasingly called the behavioral health field). As health care in the United States shifts from the traditional fee-for-service model to the managed care model, clinical psychologists are losing their role as primary care providers. The reasons are obvious. Two to three social workers can be hired for the price of one psychologist. If the research evidence shows no difference in treatment outcome between doctoral-level clinical psychologists and master's-level social workers, then the cost-conscious managed care systems will hire social workers, rather than psychologists, to provide most mental health services. One feature distinguishes some doctoral-level clinical psychologists from most other mental health specialists, however; this is the psychologist's research training, or special preparation for the role of research scientist. Only those clinical training programs that have maintained and strengthened the Ph.D.'s traditional focus on scientific research training are preparing their students for a viable future in the changing mental health care field.

Combined Professional-Scientific Training Programs

A final alternative training model that we will discuss briefly involves a combined specialty in counseling, clinical, and school psychology. As outlined by Beutler and Fisher (1994), this training model assumes that (1) these specialties share a number of core areas of knowledge and (2) the actual practices of psychologists who graduate from each of these specialties are quite similar. The curriculum in these combined training programs focuses on core areas within psychology and exposes students to each subspecialty of counseling, clinical, and school psychology.

The combined training model emphasizes breadth rather than depth of psychological knowledge. However, this feature can also be seen as a potential weakness of the model. Graduates from this type of training program may not develop a specific subspecialty or area of expertise by the end of their doctoral training (Beutler & Fisher, 1994). Further, this model of training appears to be better suited for the future practitioner than for the future academician or clinical scientist (Beutler & Fisher, 1994). By the end of 1998, there were nine APA-accredited programs in combined professional-scientific psychology, one of which offers a Psy.D. degree.

Graduate Programs: Past and Future

In many ways, the changes in graduate training over the past 30 years have mirrored the marketplace for clinical psychologists (H. C. Ellis, 1992). Starting in the mid-1960s, a shift occurred from university-based academic jobs to jobs in private practice. Not surprisingly, complaints about the limitations of the scientist-practitioner model of training surfaced soon thereafter. These complaints focused primarily on the perceived inadequacy of the Boulder model of training for future practitioners. According to the critics, training in clinical skills was deficient, and faculty members were oblivious to the training needs of future practitioners.

Out of the Vail Training Conference in 1973 came an explicit endorsement of alternative training models to meet the needs of the future practitioner. The alternative Psy.D. degree and professional school model of training can be traced to the positions adopted by those attending this conference. Clearly, these alternative training programs are becoming increasingly influential, as indicated by the number of new doctorates they graduate. In addition, some have argued in support of designating any clinical psychologist who practices clinical work with a Psy.D. degree (Shapiro & Wiggins, 1994).

However, several recent trends may affect the viability and success of the various training models discussed here. First, some believe that there may be an oversupply of practice-oriented psychologists (Robiner, 1991). If true, this may ultimately affect the number of students entering and finishing graduate programs in clinical psychology. In recent years, there have been many more applicants for internship positions than slots available. The net result has been that some graduate students have not been able to secure an internship position. If the internship and job markets tighten, the programs that primarily train practitioners (professional schools, schools awarding the Psy.D. degree) will likely feel the brunt of this effect. This will be especially true for professional schools whose economic viability is heavily dependent on tuition fees and large numbers of students.

Second, the managed health care revolution in this country will likely affect the demand for clinical psychologists in the future, as well as the curriculum in training programs. More emphasis will be placed on coursework involving empirically supported brief psychological interventions and focal assessment. Training programs that do not employ faculty with expertise in these areas may produce graduates without the requisite skills to compete in the marketplace.

Finally, several authors (Robiner, 1991; Schneider, 1991) have noted that there may be an undersupply of academic and research-oriented clinical psychologists. If true, scientist-practitioner and clinical scientist programs may be in a better position to meet this need.

Professional Regulation

As clinical psychology grew and the number of its practitioners multiplied, issues of professional competence began to arise. How is the public to know who is well trained and who is not? Many people have neither the time, inclination, nor sophistication to distinguish the professional from the charlatan. Professional regulation, therefore, has attempted to protect the public interest by developing explicit standards of competence for clinical psychologists.

Certification. *Certification* is a relatively weak form of regulation in most cases. It guarantees that people cannot call themselves "psychologists" while offering services to the public for a fee unless they have been certified by a state board of examiners. Such certification often involves an examination, but sometimes it consists only of a review of the applicant's training and professional experience. Certification is an attempt to protect the public by restricting the use of the title "psychologist." Its weakness is that it does not prevent anyone (from the poorly trained to outright quacks) from offering psychological services to the public as long as the noncertified persons who offer such services do not use the title "psychologist" or the word "psychological" to describe themselves or their services. Some cynics have alleged that certification does more to protect psychologists than it does to protect the public.

Certification laws were often the result of effective psychiatric lobbying of state legislatures. Because many psychiatrists wanted to reserve psychotherapy as the special province of medicine, they resisted any law that would recognize the practice of psychotherapy by any nonmedical specialty. As a result, certification laws were the best regulation that psychologists could obtain.

Licensing. *Licensing* is a stronger form of legislation than certification. It not only specifies the nature of the title ("psychologist") and training required for licensure, it also usually defines what specific professional activities may be offered to the public for a fee. With certification, for example, individuals might call themselves "therapists" and then proceed to provide "psychotherapeutic" services with impunity. Many state licensing laws are designed to prevent such evasions by defining psychotherapy and specifically making it the province of psychiatry, clinical psychology, or other designated professions. However, determined charlatans are difficult to contain, and such persons may be very clever in disguising the true nature of their activities.

To help strengthen this system of oversight and consumer protection, the American Psychological Association developed a model act for the licensure of psychologists (for example, APA, 1987b). A more recent revision was published in 1992 by the American Association of State Psychology Boards (AASPB). States and provinces have used these guidelines to develop their own specific requirements for licensure in their jurisdictions. Although licensing laws vary from state to state (and province to province), there are several common requirements. These are summarized in Table 3-1.

Most states and provinces require applicants for licensure to sit for an examination. In addition, the licensing board usually examines the applicant's educational background and sometimes requires several years of supervised experience beyond the doctorate. Many states also have subsequent continuing education requirements. It appears that licensing boards are becoming increasingly restrictive, sometimes requiring specific courses, excluding master's candidates, and demanding degrees from APA-approved programs. They are also occasionally beginning to intrude into the activities of academic and research psychologists.

Licensing and certification remain topics of intense professional interest. Some insist that licensing standards should not be enforced until research demonstrates their utility and positive client outcomes can be shown to relate to the licensee's competence (Bernstein & Lecomte, 1981). Others have pointed out that certification and licensing are in no way valid measures of pro-

TABLE 3-1 Summary of Typical Requirements for Licensure

Education
A doctoral degree from an APA-accredited program in professional psychology (such as clinical) is required.

Experience
One to two years of supervised postdoctoral clinical experience is required.

Examinations
A candidate for licensure must pass (that is, score at or above a certain threshold score) the Examination for Professional Practice in Psychology (EPPP). In addition, some states and provinces require an oral or essay examination.

Administrative Requirements
Additional requirements include citizenship or residency, age, evidence of good moral character, and so on.

Specialties
Licensure to practice psychology is generic. However, psychologists must practice within the scope of their demonstrated competence, as indicated by their educational background and training.

fessional competence (Koocher, 1979). However, others suggest that licensing should be designed to ensure that the public will not be harmed, rather than to regulate levels of competence (Danish & Smyer, 1981). Kane (1982) reinforces this view, arguing that at the present time licensing examinations help provide safeguards against poor practice. Finally, some academic clinical psychologists are concerned that licensing requirements violate academic freedom because these requirements essentially dictate the coursework that is offered by clinical psychology programs. They argue that the faculty members involved in a clinical psychology training program have a better idea of what coursework is needed to produce well-trained clinical psychologists.

Despite these questions and problems, the regulation of professional practice seems here to stay. To date, it is the only method we have, imperfect though it is, to protect the public from

the poorly trained. Stewart and Stewart (1998) present an overview of trends in licensure requirements over the past ten years.

American Board of Professional Psychology (ABPP). Because of the failure of the individual states to take the lead, the American Board of Examiners in Professional Psychology was established as a separate corporation in 1947. In 1968, its name was shortened to *American Board of Professional Psychology (ABPP)*. ABPP offers certification of professional competence in the fields of behavioral psychology, clinical psychology, counseling psychology, family psychology, forensic psychology, health psychology, industrial and organizational psychology, school psychology, and clinical neuropsychology. An oral examination is administered, the candidate's handling of a case is observed, and the clinician is asked to submit records of his or her previous handling of cases.

Candidates for the ABPP examinations must have also had five years' postdoctoral experience. Overall, requirements are more rigorous than those involved in state certification or licensing. In essence, the public can be assured that such a clinician is someone who has submitted to the scrutiny of a panel of peers.

National Register. In recent years, insurance companies have increasingly extended their coverage to include mental health services. At the same time, clinical psychologists have gained recognition as competent providers of those services involving prevention, assessment, and therapy. In 1975, the first *National Register of Health Service Providers in Psychology* was published. The *Register* is a kind of self-certification, listing only those practitioners who are licensed or certified in their own states and who submit their names for inclusion and pay to be listed. Along with the increasing numbers of clinicians in private practice and their recognition as health care providers by insurance companies such as Blue Cross and Blue Shield, the *Register* is one more indication of the growing professionalization of clinical psychology.

Private Practice

Earlier we observed that substantial numbers of clinical psychologists work in private practice settings. This seems to be an ever-increasing trend, and it is mirrored in the aspirations of many students in clinical training. Their goal is essentially to open an office and hang out a shingle. This suggests that the physician is now serving as a role model for these aspiring clinicians—a model that does create certain hazards.

In the recent past, for example, the medical profession has experienced a great deal of criticism and the loss of its Good Samaritan image because it has appeared more concerned with economic privileges than with the welfare of patients. Doctors operate strong lobbies in the Congress and in state legislatures. They have gotten legislation passed that not only restricts entry by others into what they perceive as their professional arena but also protects them and their vested interests. The American Medical Association is often perceived not as the public's guardian but as the protector of the rights and advantages of the physician.

What alarms many psychologists is that clinical psychology seems to be moving in the same direction. The emphasis on restrictive legislation, diplomas, and political activism, and the deemphasis of research, strike many as misguided. They fear that what began as an honest and dedicated attempt to improve training, provide continuing professional growth, protect the public, and improve the common good will end in a selfish posture of vested interest. Obviously, private practice is not the only place where such trends can develop, but the danger exists. A larger social question is whether training clinicians for private practice is an economical, efficient response to the nation's mental health needs. Nevertheless, private practice, with all its concern about insurance coverage, professional rivalry with psychiatry, and statutory regulation, seems here to stay.

Traditional, fee-for-service private practice is a thing of the past (R. J. Resnick, 1997; Schneider, 1990); managed health care now dominates the scene. Private practice psychologists have felt the brunt of this change. However, training programs must ensure that future clinical psychologists are not sent out into the real world lacking the requisite skills and knowledge demanded by managed health care systems. Table 3-2 summarizes the conclusions of a recent American Psychological Association Working Group charged with identifying training needs for future practicing psychologists.

It may even be the case that, because of cost, today's Ph.D. clinicians will be replaced by tomorrow's master's-level mental health professionals! We will have more to say about the impact of managed care on the practice of clinical psychology later in this chapter.

TABLE 3-2 What Every Practicing Clinical Psychologist Needs to Know

In 1997, the American Psychological Association (APA) Working Group on the Implications of Changes in the Health Care Delivery System for the Education, Training, and Continuing Professional Education of Psychologists recommended mastery of the following:

1. Knowledge of new and evolving health care delivery systems such as managed care organizations (MCOs).

2. Sensitivity to ethical issues relevant to managed care settings, including confidentiality and informed consent.

3. Experience in multidisciplinary environments, such as medical settings.

4. Managed-care-relevant clinical skills, including brief interventions, treatment team approach, and focused assessment.

5. Expertise in "applied" research, such as program evaluation, cost effectiveness, and medical cost offset.

6. Management and business skills—for example, contracts, utilization review, marketing.

7. Technology such as computers, databases, and telemedicine.

Independence and Economics

Early opposition from the psychiatric profession prevented clinicians from engaging in the independent practice of psychotherapy. Eventually clinical psychology overcame the powerful psychiatric lobby that operated in most statehouses across the country and won the right to practice independently. Logic had finally prevailed; the psychiatric argument that psychotherapy is a form of medical intervention has faded into obscurity. Psychiatrists came to accept the new legal status accorded clinicians, and clinical psychologists began rushing into private practice to fill the voids in the mental health field. They have now become fully independent practitioners. R. J. Resnick (1997) provides a nice overview of the history of this struggle.

Indeed, one could now think of psychiatrists and clinical psychologists as competitors, and there is the rub. What had once been an ideological war now turned into an economic skirmish. Just as clinicians began settling into their newly found independence, more and more private and quasi-governmental health insurance plans became operative. Psychotherapy began to be included under these plans, and practitioners became eligible for reimbursement. People who previously could not have afforded therapy or were unwilling to pay for it were now covered. Very quickly the medical profession mounted campaigns to exclude clinical psychologists from reimbursement unless patients were referred to them by physicians. The old battle over independent practice had been lost earlier. The battleground now shifted to direct reimbursement of psychologists by insurance companies without a physician's involvement.

A good case example involved Blue Shield of Virginia (BSV). For a number of years BSV required psychologists to bill through a physician. There were repeated, futile attempts to obtain direct reimbursement of psychologists for their services rendered to BSV members. Eventually the Virginia Academy of Clinical Psychologists (VACP) brought antitrust action against BSV. The court ruled in favor of BSV. But on appeal a higher court reversed the decision and upheld the claim of VACP. All this court action began in 1978 and was not finally settled until 1982, when a federal court awarded VACP more than $405,000 for attorneys' fees. The outcome represented a significant victory for clinical psychologists in their quest to establish a fully independent profession that can compete in the marketplace on equal terms with psychiatry (Resnick, 1985).

A profession that began softly in hallowed halls of ivy now finds itself battling in the marketplace—less and less the scholar and more and more the entrepreneur. Today, practicing clinical psychologists enjoy reimbursement privileges from most insurance carriers, Medicare, and more than 30 Medicaid programs (Resnick, 1997).

The Health Care Revolution

The costs of health care have grown astronomically throughout many parts of the world. In the United States, these costs comprised only 4.5% of the gross national product in 1950; since then, they have ballooned to more than 14% of the gross domestic product, with a total cost exceeding $898 billion annually (Frank & VandenBos, 1994).

A few years ago, there was much talk of a national health insurance program in the United States. What we got instead was a profit-driven corporate health care industry that may well revolutionize all corners of health care (Zimet, 1989). This *managed care* approach to addressing health care needs targets the high cost not only of physical health services but of mental health services as well (often referred to as "behavioral health care"). Increasingly, insurance companies or other third-party payers are determining the amount of reimbursement for mental health services. Essentially, those that ultimately pay the bills (such as employers) have taken economic control away from practitioners (Cummings, 1995).

It is important to recognize that managed care exists on a continuum. In general terms, "managed care is an integrated approach to the financing and delivery of health care" (Bobbitt, Marques, & Trout, 1998, p. 54). The old, traditional, fee-for-service mental health care system was "unmanaged" in the sense that there was little control over which doctoral-level practitioners could be used, the amount paid for services, the quality of services, and the frequency of service utilization. Insurance plans become "more managed" as provider networks become more selective, as utilization of services is evaluated with regard to appropriateness and effectiveness, and as managed care organizations institute quality improvement programs (Bobbitt et al., 1998). These and other features are summarized in Table 3-3.

Although this health care revolution has been underway for more than two decades (Broskowski, 1991), its effects are now more salient. The focus is on cost containment, with corporations expanding into a kind of medical-industrial complex and emphasizing a marketplace mentality (Kiesler & Morton, 1988). By the end of 1997, 85% of Americans belonged to some kind of managed health care plan (Winslow, 1998). Thus, we can look for continued pressure on the independent practitioner. Brief, time-effective interventions are preferred, and practitioners are now being asked to demonstrate their effectiveness empirically and to document their efficiency in the provision of services (Cummings, 1995).

There are several models of managed care, all of which attempt to control costs and reduce use of services while at the same time ensuring their quality. We will briefly mention two major types of managed care systems: HMOs and PPOs. A *Health Maintenance Organization (HMO)* employs a restricted number of providers to serve those who enroll in the plan; costs for all services are fixed. A *Preferred Provider Organization (PPO)* has contracts with outside providers (at a discounted rate) to meet the needs of its membership; in exchange for the discounted rate, the providers theoretically receive an increased number of referrals.

These relatively new systems of service delivery are dictating new definitions of what consti-

---

TABLE 3-3 Common Features of a Managed Behavioral Health Care Organization

- Identified as a business entity or corporate structure

- Full range of clinical services is provided (or arranged)

- Credentialed provider network or staff delivery system

- Utilization and care management

- Management information systems (track membership, eligibility, and aggregate population data)

- Systematic quality management and improvement mechanisms

- Ability to assume financial risk, including the payment of insurance claims

Source: Adapted with permission from Bobbitt, B. L., Marques, C. C., & Trout, D. L. (1998). Managed behavioral health care: Current status, recent trends, and the role of psychology. *Clinical Psychology: Science and Practice, 5,* 53–66. Copyright 1998, American Psychological Association.

---

tutes psychological treatment as well as new modes of practice for clinical psychologists. Cummings (1995) recently discussed some of these "essential paradigm shifts": (1) Clients will be seen for a fewer number of sessions and a greater number of clients will be seen per year. (2) Treatment will be brief (fewer sessions) and it will be intermittent (clients may not be seen for consecutive weeks). (3) The therapist will serve as a catalyst for clients to make changes in their lives. (4) Most changes will occur outside of treatment. (5) Treatment will not be terminated ("You're cured"); rather, it will be interrupted after client progress is evident. (6) Community resources (for example, Alcoholics Anonymous, Parents Without Partners) will be used to a greater extent. (7) Most treatment will be delivered in a group format and will involve structured psychoeducational programs (such as stress management training). Each of these predicted changes is quite dramatic, and the net effect will be a style of psychological intervention that differs greatly from "traditional" psychotherapy.

In fact, managed care may directly affect the employment outlook for doctoral-level clinical psychologists who plan to make a career of clinical practice (Frank & VandenBos, 1994):

> Integrated managed care delivery systems will be characterized by reliance on primary care gatekeepers, clinical integration across the continuum of services provided to each patient, and sharing of financial risk by providers (capitated payment). Physician practice will shift toward primary care, and there will be an increase in the use of physician extenders, such as advanced practice nurses and physician assistants. A similar trend is likely in the mental health area, with greater use of master's level providers of all types. (p. 852)

Master's-level practitioners and paraprofessionals are much "cheaper" to use for the same services and, therefore, will be seen as more economically attractive to managed care companies (Cummings, 1995; Sleek, 1995a).

But the training of the scientist-practitioner or clinical scientist does offer some opportunities in this managed care environment. For example, clinical psychologists (1) have an empirical orientation that emphasizes the study of outcomes, which can help circumvent professional biases; (2) have skills different from those of physicians; (3) can bring an emphasis on preventing mental health problems in individuals and a focus on their wellness rather than their sickness; and (4) know about the effects of the environment on behavior (Kiesler & Morton, 1988). All of this can impress a profit-driven, corporate-directed system. However, we have not, to date, done a particularly good job of publicizing the demonstrated effectiveness of our psychological interventions (Barlow, 1994). Finally, perhaps tongue-in-cheek, some have suggested that clinical psychologists may actually benefit from managed care. These "hidden" benefits include increased technical assistance and education provided by the managed care

companies, increased opportunities for interdisciplinary collaboration, and "free" clinical supervision from case managers of managed care companies (Anonymous, 1995).

Broskowski (1995) has highlighted a number of implications for the training and careers of psychologists that follow from trends in health care reform. First, it is likely that the marketplace for independent practitioners (those in private practice) will continue to diminish in size. In contrast, the opportunities for clinical psychologists who specialize in health psychology will likely increase dramatically because these individuals, by virtue of their training, are better able to provide a broader range of services, including those related to medical care. Second, an increased focus on accountability and patient outcomes will open the doors for those clinical psychologists who have expertise in clinical and psychometric research. These individuals will be called upon to design and evaluate studies of patient outcome, patient satisfaction, and the effectiveness of various psychological interventions. Finally, training programs in clinical psychology need to place more emphasis on cost-effective psychological interventions, provide clinical training in managed care settings, and incorporate didactic instruction in applied health services research into their curricula. It is hoped that these suggestions will be heeded so that future clinical psychologists receive the training necessary to thrive in a managed care environment.

Bobbitt et al. (1998) offer the following summary view of future opportunities for clinical psychologists in a managed care world:

> Our vision for clinical psychology would be to continue forward with the development and dissemination of findings from psychological research, coupled with transformed training programs that emphasize the integration of clinical practice with administrative systems. . . . This application of science in a practical environment requires hands-on understanding of the administrative complexities involved in organized

health care. If psychology moves rapidly in the next few years and transforms training programs, it is possible that psychologists can be trained to play key roles—both as clinicians and as administrative leaders in the evolving managed care system. (p.64)

TABLE 3-4 Recent Developments Relevant to Behavioral Health Care

1. *Costs of health care are expected to rise again.* The recent trend of annual decreases in health care costs is expected to reverse itself. Specifically, health care costs are expected to double from $1.035 trillion in 1996 to $2.133 trillion in the year 2007 (McGinley, 1998). The one-time savings involved in shifting most Americans to managed care plans from fee-for-service have been realized. Increased costs in the future will be associated primarily with medical technology, physician services, and prescription drugs (McGinley, 1998).

2. *Psychotherapists are adopting novel approaches to managed care.* In order to maintain their autonomy, some psychotherapists are opting for self-review of their own costs. By formally serving as their own "watchdogs" and cost managers, groups of mental health professionals can avoid losing control over service delivery to the case managers of outside managed care organizations (Jeffrey, 1998). For example, therapists serve as their own "gatekeepers" by critically reviewing the number of sessions allotted to individual patients and evaluating quality of services internally.

3. *Clinical psychologists are delivering services based on a "case rate."* With case rates, a managed care company pays a clinical psychologist a flat fee (say, $300) for conducting up to ten sessions with a patient (Pollock, 1998). Clearly, the clinical psychologist has a financial incentive to use only a few treatment sessions. For example, a clinical psychologist who used only three sessions would receive about $100 per session, whereas one who used all ten allotted sessions would receive only $30 per session. Although the former would have a larger patient caseload, the reimbursement rate per session would be high. The latter clinician would have a caseload with fewer patients, but reimbursement rates per session would be significantly lower.

Prescription Privileges

A hotly debated current issue concerns the pursuit of *prescription privileges* for clinical psychologists. The American Psychological Association has recently endorsed this pursuit (Martin, 1995), as have several of its highest-ranking officials (see, for example, DeLeon & Wiggins, 1996; DeLeon, Fox, & Graham, 1991; Fox, 1988; Nickelson, 1995). Many others remain either neutral or adamantly opposed to obtaining prescription privileges (DeNelsky, 1991, 1996; Handler, 1988; Hayes & Heiby, 1996). The decision to pursue these privileges will have far-reaching implications for the role definition of clinical psychologists, the training they require, and their actual practice.

Background. As noted by Brentar and McNamara (1991), clinical psychologists in recent years have expanded their area of interest from mental health to health issues in general. This redefinition of clinical psychology as a field concerned with general health (including mental health) raises a number of interesting issues regarding how best to ensure that clinical psychologists can function autonomously and not be controlled or regulated by medical or other professions (Fox, 1982). Several advocates have argued that obtaining prescription privileges will ensure the autonomy of clinical psychologists as health service providers and will enable a continuity of care that is missing when a psychiatrist prescribes the patient's medications and a psychologist provides the same patient's psychotherapy. Further, DeLeon (1988) has argued that it is our professional and ethical duty to improve and broaden the services we offer so that society's needs can be met. Clinical psychologists with prescription privileges would be available to meet the needs of underserved populations (for example, rural residents, geriatric patients).

However, the pursuit of prescription privileges has been questioned on philosophical grounds. Handler (1988) has argued that the need for professional boundaries between clinical psychology and psychiatry dictates that we should not incorporate medical interventions

PROFILE 3-2

Patrick H. DeLeon, Ph.D., J.D.

Dr. DeLeon is a prominent clinical psychologist who serves as chief of staff for Senator Daniel K. Inouye (D-HI). Dr. DeLeon has been very active in the American Psychological Association (APA) as well. Over the years, he has served as president of the APA, as APA secretary, as a member of the APA Board of Directors, as chair of APA Board of Professional Affairs, and as president of the APA Divisions of Clinical Psychology (Division 12), Psychotherapy (Division 29), and Psychology and Law (Division 41).

Dr. DeLeon has been perhaps the most outspoken proponent of pursuing prescription privileges for psychologists. We asked him several questions about his background and activities.

Could you tell us a little about your background and interests?

I grew up in a family that was very politically active. Both of my parents were attorneys. My mother was one of the first female lawyers in Connecticut and the first elected female alderman in our hometown. I always knew I would become a lawyer. If I had not gone to graduate school first, I would undoubtedly have become an elected official. Working on Capitol Hill seems a "natural fit." Specifically, I began working for Senator Inouye the day that the Watergate hearings started—25-plus years ago.

At that time I was enrolled at the University of Hawaii School of Public Health and working for the State of Hawaii Division of Mental Health. The university required an internship, so I took the summer off, came to our nation's capital, and, except for a brief period to run a congressional campaign, have not left yet. Over the years, I have learned that many senior congressional staff have grown up in families that were very active in the political process. One learns from an early age to value public service. The political process and the public policy process become "natural"—personally meaningful and, in essence, a way of life.

Prior to working for Senator Inouye, I was a clinical psychologist with the State of Hawaii's Division of Mental Health. I first worked on an inpatient ward in our state hospital; then, as a result of the community mental health center movement, our inpatient and outpatient responsibilities were combined. I essentially functioned as deputy director of our center, clinically specializing in "dangerous" and "chronic" patients. Prior to that, my wife and I worked as Field Assessment Officers (FAOs) for the Peace Corps, staffing a Fiji and Philippines project. That was really interesting, especially the time we spent in the host countries.

What is the biggest challenge facing psychology today?

I think the biggest challenge we face today as a profession is an internal one—collectively appreciating the extent to which we really are one of the "learned professions" and, thus, that we have a societal obligation to provide effective and proactive leadership. Too many of us do not seem to appreciate that we really are one family. For example, an individual psychologist will gravitate to a high-level administrative position and then seem to act as if he or she is no longer a psychologist. Unlike organized medicine, which is always looking out for the future of their profession, far too few of us

(continued)

Profile 3-2 *(continued)*

go out of our way to systematically foster "growth" experiences for the next generation. We may talk about doing something, but it has been my observation that very little is actually accomplished. That is why, in my judgment, the establishment of the Committee for the American Psychological Association of Graduate Students (APAGS) is so important for the profession. APAGS currently has in excess of 40,000 members and represents the future of our profession. Somehow we have to reach out to them, particularly at the State Association level, and institutionally foster an entirely different "mind-set." If we can accomplish this, I am confident that we possess the expertise and creative ability to prosper, notwithstanding whatever might seem to be the daily crisis— managed care, budgetary constraints, and so on. Together, we will do extraordinarily well; as isolated individuals, it is hard to predict what will evolve.

In your opinion, why should clinical psychologists seek and obtain prescription privileges?

Summarized from DeLeon and Wiggins (1996):

- All objective evidence to date concerning the quality of care provided by non-

physician practitioners (such as nurses, physician assistants, optometrists) indicates that it is consistently high and cost-effective.
- It has been demonstrated that it is possible to successfully train nonphysicians to prescribe medications.
- Psychologists are interested in obtaining the psychopharmacological training and clinical experience necessary to prescribe in a competent manner.
- By obtaining prescription privileges, psychologists will also gain the legal authority to determine whether medications are necessary and appropriate (the ability to *not* prescribe).

In my view, psychologists will rely less on medication than physicians (this has been found in the pilot projects to date), and this should lead to a higher quality of care than is currently available.

(medications) into our treatment repertoire. Handler further asserts that it is clinical psychology's non-medication orientation that identifies it as a unique health profession and that is responsible for the field's appeal. DeNelsky (1991, 1996) notes that, even without prescription privileges, more and more psychologists have become providers of outpatient services, whereas the opposite trend is true for psychiatry. Following are some of the major arguments for and against prescription privileges.

Pros. A number of arguments have been made in favor of seeking prescription privileges; we

will briefly present several of the most commonly cited reasons. These arguments were discussed in a 1995 interview with the executive director of the Practice Directorate of the American Psychological Association (Nickelson, 1995) and have been emphasized by others advocating prescription privileges (for example, DeLeon & Wiggins, 1996).

First, having prescription privileges would enable clinical psychologists to provide a wider variety of treatments and to treat a wider range of clients or patients. Treatment involving medications would now be an option, and this would lead to more involvement by clinical psychologists in the treatment of conditions in which medications are the primary form of intervention (for example, schizophrenia).

A second advantage of having prescription privileges is the potential increase in efficiency and cost-effectiveness of care for those patients who need both psychological treatment and medication. These individuals often enlist more than one mental health professional (a psychiatrist for medications, a clinical psychologist for cognitive-behavioral treatment). A single mental health professional who could provide all forms of treatment might be desirable from both a practical and an economic standpoint.

There is also the belief that prescription privileges will give clinical psychologists a competitive advantage in the health care marketplace. The health care field is becoming increasingly competitive, and prescription privileges would provide an advantage to clinical psychologists over other health care professionals (such as social workers). Finally, some view obtaining prescription privileges as a natural progression in clinical psychology's quest to become a "full-fledged" health care profession, rather than just a mental health care profession.

Cons. Other clinical psychologists have voiced concerns about the possibility of obtaining prescription privileges (Brentar & McNamara, 1991; DeNelsky, 1991, 1996; Handler, 1988; Hayes & Heiby, 1996). These critics point out that prescription privileges may lead to a deemphasis of "psychological" forms of treatment because medications are often faster-acting and potentially more profitable than psychotherapy. Many fear that a conceptual shift may occur, with biological explanations of emotional conditions taking precedence over psychological ones.

The pursuit of prescription privileges may also damage clinical psychology's relationship with psychiatry and general medicine. Such conflict may result in financially expensive lawsuits. This new financial burden, as well as the legal fees necessary to modify current licensing laws, would come at the expense of existing programs. In addition, the granting of prescription privileges would likely lead to increases in

malpractice liability costs. In short, it may not be worth it.

Implications for Training. If clinical psychologists gain prescription privileges, this change will significantly affect the training of future clinical psychologists. In 1993, the Ad Hoc Task Force on Psychopharmacology of the American Psychological Association published its recommendations regarding competence criteria for training psychologists to provide services to those individuals who receive psychotropic medication (Smyer et al., 1993). This task force outlined the following three levels of competence and training in psychopharmacology. Note that only those who successfully complete Level 3 training would be qualified to prescribe.

Level 1: Basic Pharmacology Training. Competence at this level would include knowledge of the biological basis of neuropsychopharmacology and a mastery of the classes of medication used for treatment, as well as knowledge of substances that are abused (such as alcohol or cocaine). To achieve this level of training, a one-semester survey course in psychopharmacology is recommended.

Level 2: Collaborative Practice. Competence at this level, essentially enabling one to serve as a psychopharmacology consultant, would involve a more in-depth knowledge of psychopharmacology and drugs of abuse; competence in diagnostic assessment, physical assessment, drug interactions, and drug side effects; and practical (hands-on) training in psychopharmacology. Specifically, the committee recommended coursework in the areas listed above as well as supervised practical experience.

Level 3: Prescription Privileges. Competence must be demonstrated at this level in order to practice independently as a prescribing psychologist. The committee recommended a strong undergraduate background in biological sciences (including multiple courses in biology, chemistry, mathematics, and pharmacology), two years of graduate training in psychopharmacology (26 credit hours), and a postdoctoral psychopharmacology residency.

PROFILE 3-3

Elaine M. Heiby, Ph.D.

Dr. Heiby is a Professor of Psychology at the University of Hawaii. Her research interests include theories of self-control, emotional disorders, and adherence to health behaviors, and she has published extensively in these areas. Dr. Heiby is also known for her leadership among those who oppose seeking prescription privileges for psychologists. We had a chance to ask Dr. Heiby about her own background as well as her views regarding prescription privileges.

What originally got you interested in the field of clinical psychology?

When I entered graduate school in 1974, I intended to become an academic in a behavioral psychology program. This was an exciting time in behavioral psychology when the works of scientists like Wolpe, Staats, and Skinner were demonstrating the generalizability of basic laboratory principles to the understanding of complex human behavior and the alleviation of human suffering. I realized I wanted to contribute to the synthesis of behavioral principles and applied psychology. I also understood that clinical psychology was a growing profession with frighteningly few scientifically based guidelines for the selection of effective prevention and treatment programming. So I chose to complete doctoral training in both clinical and behavioral psychology, knowing that clinical training was essential to being able to concentrate my career on the integration of psychological science and practice.

Describe what activities you are involved in as a clinical psychologist.

I'm a professor in the Department of Psychology at the University of Hawaii at Manoa and am licensed. I teach two psychological assessment courses in our clinical program, serve as the Associate Director of Clinical Studies, supervise graduate and undergraduate clinical research, conduct several of my own research programs, and participate on the boards of organizations of psychologists. I had a small part-time psychotherapy practice for about ten years. Now my applied work is limited to consultations and serving as an expert witness. Consultations have included developing assessment and treatment protocols for behavioral health providers, conducting treatment outcome evaluations in mental health settings, and providing psychological assessments for family and criminal courts.

What are your particular areas of expertise or interest?

My interests include (a) developing integrative theories of self-control, emotional disorders (depression, anxiety, anger, and mania), and adherence to health behaviors; (b) construction of brief assessment devices, including measures of self-control and self-reinforcement skills and other behavioral competencies relevant to emotional disorders and adherence to health behaviors; and (c) applying chaos theory to the understanding of fitful and transitional emotional states.

What future trends do you see for clinical psychology?

I find this to be a very exciting time for clinical science and scientist-practitioners. The health care environment now requires evidence of cost-effective services. These market demands are congruent with the basic tenets of science that involve pursuit of parsimony and empirical support for predictions. Managed care can be rewarding for the scientist-practitioner whose approach involves the value that scientifically supported services are the most humane ones. Applied psychologists will be needed to train therapists in the most effective procedures, conduct prevention program and treatment outcome evaluations, provide direct services for the more difficult cases, and consult with medical providers, government agencies, businesses, and other organizations. Clinical scientists will find more grant monies to support research on the development of cost-effective assessment devices and treatment procedures. So I think that in the future, the scientifically trained clinical psychologists will find the most job opportunities and be the most satisfied with their work.

You have been an outspoken critic of the movement to seek and obtain prescription privileges for clinical psychologists. Why?

I believe psychology's plate is full. There are many unmet societal needs for effective psychological services. Psychologists are the only mental health service providers trained in the science of human behavior and positioned to make the most informed clinical decisions. Researchers have barely scraped the surface in understanding the psychological level of human adjustment and suffering. For psychol-

ogy to take on the task of medical training and practice, something else will have to give. At the training level, the undergraduate psychology major will include premedical courses that will probably not draw many of the students currently interested in the discipline. The graduate training would also be overhauled. Adding several years of medical training to clinical programs would necessarily have to come at the expense of psychology training. Applied psychologists would be less expert in the science of behavior, and there would be fewer psychology faculty conducting both basic and applied research.

Nevertheless, I believe there have been some positive effects of the prescription privileges proposal. Applied psychologists are being encouraged to become more competent in making recommendations to physicians and in evaluating the effectiveness of medical treatment. Researchers are being encouraged to synthesize clinical psychology and behavioral neuroscience. Greater collaboration and integrative research undoubtedly will promote comprehensive services and advance the science of psychology. In the long term, these changes may result in a hybrid discipline and profession that involves the current domains of psychological and medical sciences. At this point in time, however, I believe the attempt to legislatively transform psychology into a medical specialty is premature. Psychologists who want prescription privileges are free to seek training that is already available, such as in nursing, without reallocating resources away from psychology.

These recommendations, if implemented, would affect graduate training in clinical psychology in a number of ways. First, because of additional course requirements (for Levels 2 and 3), it would take longer to complete graduate school. In many cases, additional faculty would need to be hired to teach the new required

courses; most of these courses are not currently offered in clinical psychology graduate programs. Finally, applicants to clinical psychology graduate programs would likely be scrutinized more carefully to ensure that they have a strong background of undergraduate courses in the biological sciences. Perhaps not surprisingly, many directors of clinical training have serious concerns about the implementation of prescription training at the predoctoral level (Evans & Murphy, 1997).

Culturally Sensitive Mental Health Services

The United States Census Bureau projects that the population growth rate for non-Hispanic Whites between the years 1995 and 2050 (7.4%) will be the lowest of all major ethnic/racial groups in the United States. In contrast, it is projected that the Black population will increase 69.5%, the American Indian population 83.0%, the Hispanic population 258.3%, and the Asian American population 269.1%.

In an increasingly pluralistic society such as the United States, it is urgent that we develop mental health services that effectively serve the needs of cultural, racial, and ethnic minorities (Abe-Kim & Takeuchi, 1996; Shiang, Kjellander, Huang, & Bogumill, 1998; D. W. Sue, 1990). One can argue the point at almost any level: ethical (for example, Pedersen & Marsella, 1982), economic, and so on. But it is essential that we develop training programs that produce therapists who have learned to consider appropriate cultural factors in their clinical work with culturally diverse clients (Allison, Crawford, Echemendia, Robinson, & Knepp, 1994; Comas-Diaz, 1992; Lopez et al., 1989; Mio & Morris, 1990). For example, we must find ways to make successful treatments more available to Hispanics—treatments that are sensitive to the characteristic features of Hispanic culture (Rogler, Malgady, Costantino, & Blumenthal, 1987). Similar comments could be made in the case of Native Americans (Willis, 1989), African Americans (A. Jones, 1991), and Asian Americans (Shiang et al., 1998).

Toward this end, S. Sue (1998) has advocated that clinical psychologists and other mental health professionals must demonstrate *cultural competence*—a knowledge and appreciation of other cultural groups and the skills to be effective with members of these groups. Sue (1998) has identified three major characteristics of cultural competency:

- *Scientific-mindedness*. Clinicians must formulate and test hypotheses regarding the status of their culturally different clients; clinicians must not adhere to the "myth of sameness."
- *Dynamic sizing*. Clinicians must be skilled in knowing "when to generalize and be inclusive and when to individualize and be exclusive" (p. 446). This allows the clinician to avoid stereotypes but still appreciate the importance and influence of the culture in question.
- *Culture-specific expertise*. Clinicians must understand their own culture and perspectives, have knowledge of the cultural groups with whom they work, and if indicated, be able to use culturally informed interventions.

According to Sue (1998), these characteristics will be present to varying degrees in individual clinicians. Clinical psychologists must actively develop these skills in order to achieve cultural competence in their work with various groups of clients or patients.

Likewise, issues of gender have become prominent in recent years (for example, Good, Borst, & Wallace, 1994). We are hearing increasing numbers of reports about sexual exploitation of clients. From the days of Freud right up to the present, we seem to have trouble training therapists who are sensitized to the special life experiences of the opposite sex (Gilbert, 1987). In particular, many clinical psychologists (men and women alike) receive little training that focuses on the unique needs and experiences of women. In the future, we must train clinical psychologists to recognize and understand both gender differences and cultural diversity, and how these relate to the provision of mental health services. See web site 3-8 at the end of this chapter for a link to the American Psychological Association's Guidelines for Providers of Psychological Services to Diverse Populations.

Ethical Standards

One yardstick by which to measure the maturity of a profession is its commitment to a set of ethical standards. Psychology was a pioneer in the mental health field in establishing a formal code of ethics. The APA published a tentative code as early as 1951; in 1953, it formally published the *Ethical Standards of Psychologists* (APA, 1953). Revisions of these standards appeared in 1958, 1963, 1968, 1977, 1979, 1981, 1990, and 1992. In addition, the APA has published a casebook of ethical standards (APA, 1987a) and has formulated a statement of ethical principles involving psychological research with human subjects (APA, 1982). Standards for testing materials were developed (APA, 1966) and later updated (APA, 1985). Finally, a wide array of ethical issues have been discussed by Keith-Spiegel and Koocher (1985); Eyde et al. (1993); Bersoff (1995); and Koocher and Keith-Spiegel (1998).

The 1992 version of the *Ethical Principles of Psychologists and Conduct* presents six general principles as well as specific ethical standards relevant to various activities of clinical psychologists—assessment, intervention, therapy, forensic activities, and so on (APA, 1992). Web site 3-7 provides a link to the complete document online. The general principles include the following:

- Competence
- Integrity
- Professional and scientific responsibility
- Respect for people's rights and dignity
- Concerns for others' welfare
- Social responsibility

Although these general principles are not technically enforceable rules, they serve to guide psychologists' actions. The specific *ethical standards*, however, are enforceable rules of conduct. Acceptance of membership in the APA commits the member to adherence to these standards, several of which are discussed in the following sections. Of course, actual clinical practice and its day-to-day demands can generate ethical decisions and dilemmas that would tax the judgment of the wisest in the field. Also, changes in our culture over time can provide a shifting ground that challenges a clinical psychologist's judgment. Take, for instance, the example in Box 3-1.

Competence

Issues of *competence* have several important aspects (Pipes & Davenport, 1990). First, clinicians must always represent their training accurately. Thus, subdoctoral clinicians must never lead anyone to believe they possess the Ph.D. Simply ignoring the fact that someone keeps referring to such a person as "Doctor" will not suffice. If a clinician is trained as a counseling psychologist, that is how he or she must be presented—not as a clinical psychologist. Clinicians have an obligation to "actively" present themselves correctly with regard to training and all other aspects of competency. This also means that clinicians should not attempt treatment or assessment procedures for which they lack specific training or supervised experience. When there is any doubt about specific competencies, it is wise to seek out supervision from more experienced clinicians.

It is equally important that clinicians be sensitive to treatment or assessment issues that could be influenced by a patient's gender, ethnic or racial background, age, or sexual orientation. Finally, to the extent that clinicians have personal problems or sensitive spots in their own personality that could affect performance, they must guard against these problems' adversely influencing their encounters with patients. All aspects of competence are important, whether they involve knowledge, clinical skill, clinical judgment, or interpersonal skill (Overholser & Fine, 1990).

Confidentiality

Clinicians have a clear ethical duty to respect and protect the *confidentiality* of client information. Confidentiality is central to the client-psychologist relationship. When information is released

BOX 3-1

Clinicians Who Appear on Radio Psychology Call-In Shows or TV Talk Shows: Are They Ethical?

In 1953, the *Ethical Standards of Psychologists* (APA, 1953) stated:

> Principle 2.64-1. It is unethical to offer psychological services for the purpose of individual diagnosis, treatment, or advisement, either directly or indirectly, by means of public lectures or demonstrations, newspaper or magazine articles, radio or television programs, or similar media.

This idea, in 1953, was pretty clear and seemed to make good sense. Professional advice is an individual thing. It must be tailored to the individual, and there is no way a clinician can do this on the basis of a 3-minute conversation with a radio caller. But in 1953, there were relatively few radio call-in shows hosted by clinicians. By 1982, there were roughly 50 radio call-in shows hosted by mental health professionals (D. A. Levy, 1989). Now, there are surely many, many more. As in

all professions, some hosts are flip, comedic, and, in general, poor clinicians. Others seem quite skilled, concerned, and sincere while advising strongly that the caller seek professional help.

Aside from strong media ratings, there are probably valid reasons now for having good call-in shows. For many distressed or disadvantaged people, these shows may be their only route to help or support. The shows can also sensitize and educate other listeners, helping to prevent problems from developing or getting worse. For still others, these shows may provide the caller with that extra courage or understanding necessary to seek out professional services.

The 1992 APA revision of ethical standards reflects these points by now permitting "advice"—as opposed to "therapy"—on the air. Psychologists are allowed to provide advice or comment via radio or television programs as

without the client's consent, the trusting relationship can be irreparably harmed. Clinicians should be clear and open about matters of confidentiality and the conditions under which it could be breached. In today's climate, not all information is deemed "privileged." For example, third parties (such as insurance companies) may be paying for a client's therapy. They may demand periodic access to records for purposes of review. Sometimes school records that involve assessment data may be accessible to others outside the school system under certain conditions (for example, if they are subpoenaed by a court). More and more, clinicians are less certain of their ability to promise absolute confidentiality.

Another question is whether all information *should* be confidential. Take, for example, the fa-

mous 1976 *Tarasoff* case. The events leading up to this case began when a client at a university counseling center told his therapist that he planned to kill his girlfriend. The therapist informed the campus police of the client's intentions. The police promptly took the client into custody, but because the girlfriend was away on vacation, they decided to release him. Subsequently, the client did indeed kill his girlfriend. Later, the woman's parents sued the therapist, the police, and the university, arguing that these three parties were negligent in not informing them of the threat. The California Supreme Court eventually ruled in favor of the parents, holding that the therapist was legally remiss in not informing all appropriate persons so that violence could have been avoided. Such a deci-

long as "they take reasonable precautions to ensure that (1) statements are based on appropriate psychological literature and practice, (2) the statements are otherwise consistent with this Ethics Code, and (3) the recipients of the information are not encouraged to infer that a relationship has been established with them personally" (APA, 1992, p. 1604).

What does research tell us about the phenomenon of call-in programs? In one study, 368 patrons of shopping malls were surveyed, and another 122 persons who called one New York program were interviewed before and after they talked with the show's therapist (Bouhoutsos, Goodchilds, & Huddy, 1986). Half of the entire sample admitted to having listened to call-in shows, and these listeners considered the programs helpful and informative. Even those listeners who thought such programs *could* be harmful were generally enthusiastic about them. Although subject to several interpretations, callers reported feeling better after they called in. Many of the callers were people who had been in therapy, so these

shows do not seem to be a simple substitute for "real" therapy. Most listeners regarded advice given as helpful or educational. In another study done in Israel, subjects who received help from a clinic did have more favorable attitudes toward the help they received than did subjects who called in to a radio counseling show (Raviv, Raviv, & Yunovitz, 1989). D. A. Levy (1989) has found that responses of hosts to call-in shows are at least marginally helpful to the callers and provide a moderate amount of support both for callers and for listeners.

Recent evidence, then, suggests that these shows can be helpful to some people under some conditions. But do they fall within ethical guidelines? This is a difficult question because evidence suggests that the distinction between personal advice and therapeutic services dissolves when we analyze the verbal interactions on these programs (Henricks & Stiles, 1989). Further, some feel that the profession of psychology is damaged when psychologists go on one of the many sensationalistic television talk shows (Sleek, 1995b).

sion surely raises issues that would tax the judgment of nearly every clinician. What makes all this even more ambiguous is that the legal precedents differ in various states. Not only must clinicians decide when and whom to inform and under what circumstances, they must also try to determine whether the *Tarasoff* decision applies in their state. Despite the number of years since the *Tarasoff* case was adjudicated, confusion and uncertainty remain about when clinicians are obligated to break confidentiality and activate their "duty to protect."

Confidentiality involves numerous other complications. For example, what about working with children? Sometimes, adherence to strict rules of confidentiality could mean that parents cannot be integrated into the treatment

plan in a helpful way (Taylor & Adelman, 1989). Issues of confidentiality can also arise when clinicians are treating AIDS patients (Lamb, Clark, Drumheller, Frizzell, & Surrey, 1989; Knapp & VandeCreek, 1990; C. F. Morrison, 1989; Scott & Borodovsky, 1990; Totten, Lamb, & Reeder, 1990).

Apparently, the lay public believes in the principle and importance of confidentiality. But they also understand that confidences may be broken in cases of suspected child abuse, potential suicide or murder, and other potentially life-threatening situations. Most clinicians agree. However, only in situations where they have felt the need to consult with a colleague or have had a potentially dangerous client are most willing to consider disclosure without client consent.

Finally, it is worth noting that a 1996 Supreme Court ruling, *Jaffe v. Redmond*, provides for *privileged communication* between licensed mental health professionals and individual adult patients in psychotherapy. Therefore, at least in federal courts, a psychotherapy patient's consent is necessary before her or his psychotherapy records, communications, and document can be disclosed. Essentially, the Supreme Court's decision reinforces the view that privacy in psychotherapy is important. However, because this decision does not necessarily supercede state laws or state court decisions, clinical psychologists should become well acquainted with their state laws regarding confidentiality and privileged communication in psychotherapy. The *Jaffe v. Redmond* decision and its implications have been discussed extensively by DeBell and Jones (1997) and Knapp and VandeCreek (1997).

Client Welfare

Dual relationships pose many ethical questions regarding *client welfare*. Sexual activities with clients, employing a client, selling a product to a client, or even becoming friends with a client after the termination of therapy are all behaviors that can easily lead to exploitation of and harm to the client. Although perhaps not very common, such events are clearly troublesome to the profession (Borys & Pope, 1989). Sexual liaisons can be equally damaging in supervisory relationships (Bartell & Rubin, 1990).

The worst of these dual relationships are sexual intimacies between client and psychologist. Make no mistake, ethical principles condemn such behavior in no uncertain terms. What is alarming here is the dramatic increase in the number of complaints filed against psychologists for sexual improprieties (Gottlieb, Sell, & Schoenfeld, 1988). According to one survey, nearly 45% of clinicians felt that intimate relations with clients were unethical. But what is frightening is that more than 31% considered such relationships neither ethical nor unethical, and almost 24% regarded intimacies as only *somewhat* unethical (Akamatsu, 1988)! These statistics are disturbing and indicate the need for more emphasis in training programs on the harm produced by engaging in intimate relations with clients.

Another aspect of client welfare involves the clinician's willingness to terminate therapy when it is no longer helping the client. In one case referred to an ethics committee, a clinical psychologist had been treating a child continuously for more than two years and had informed the parent that two more years of therapy would be necessary. A review committee decided that the treatment was not consistent with the diagnosis and that there was no evidence of reasonable progress (APA, 1981).

Although these ethical principles do not explicitly require that clients be informed of their rights, this issue has received much attention recently (Pope, 1990). Relevant aspects of clients' rights include (Talbert & Pipes, 1988):

- The right to change therapists
- Possibilities of referral to other psychologists
- Mention of community services as another option
- Right to end therapy
- Risk of experiencing unpleasant emotions during therapy
- Risk of changes in personal relationships (for example, with a spouse)
- Limits of confidentiality
- Other risks, rights, and information

We shall return to this topic again in later chapters when we begin our discussion of therapy.

What types of ethical dilemmas do psychologists most frequently face? This question was addressed in a study by Pope and Vetter (1992). To assess the most commonly encountered "ethically troubling incidents," the authors surveyed a randomly selected sample of American Psychological Association members. Approximately 80% of the respondents indicated that they had encountered at least one such incident in the previous one or two years. The most frequently reported type of ethical dilemma involved confidentiality (breaching confidentiality because of actual or potential risks to third parties, suspected child abuse, or other reasons). Incidents involving blurred, dual, or conflictual relationships were the second most frequently reported (maintaining therapeutic boundaries with clients, personal versus professional relationships with clients). The third most frequently cited category of ethically troubling incidents involved payment sources, plans, settings, and methods (such as inadequate insurance coverage for clients with urgent needs). Other areas in which ethically troubling incidents arose included training and teaching dilemmas, forensic psychology, research, conduct of colleagues, sexual issues, assessment, questionable or harmful interventions, and competence.

Psychologists, whether laboratory researchers or practicing clinicians, are being increasingly scrutinized for evidence of ethical violations. Ethical issues in research or in practice are not always easy to resolve, nor are violations easy to monitor. But if clinical psychology is going to survive as a profession, it must find ways of ensuring adherence to the highest standards of conduct.

Chapter Summary

Many contemporary issues challenge the field of clinical psychology. First, several training models are available, each with different emphases and outcomes. The scientist-practitioner model is clearly the most popular one, but some have become disenchanted with this model and question whether a true integration of science and practice can be achieved. Several training models that emphasize the practice of clinical psychology (Psy.D. degree, professional schools) have become increasingly popular in recent years. Finally, the clinical scientist model of training represents an alternative model that emphasizes research and empirically supported approaches to assessment and intervention.

The professional regulation of clinical psychologists involves methods aimed at protecting the public interest and assuring competence. Certification and licensure occur at the state level and are attempts to make the public aware of those who are deemed to be well-trained and competent clinical psychologists. ABPP and membership in the National Register are more advanced forms of certification pursued by some clinical psychologists.

Although a large percentage of clinical psychologists work in private practice settings, changes in health care suggest that private practice, as we once knew it, will never be the same. Specifically, most Americans subscribe to managed care plans that, in general, limit the number of sessions, the rates of reimbursement, and the conditions that can receive (reimbursable) treatment. This "revolution" will affect the roles and activities of clinical psychologists in the future. Another hotly contested issue that is likely to affect clinical training in the future is the pursuit of prescription privileges. This pursuit may redefine the field and require a major overhaul of the doctoral training curriculum.

In this chapter, we have also explored the topics of cultural competence and cultural sensitivity. In an increasingly pluralistic society, clinical psychologists must be trained to develop mental health services that are appropriate and effective for various cultural groups. Finally, we have presented an overview of the ethical standards to which clinical psychologists are held accountable, including issues of competence, confidentiality, and client welfare.

Key Terms

Academy of Psychological Clinical Science An organization of clinical psychology programs and clinical psychology internship sites committed to the clinical scientist model of training. The academy is affiliated with the American Psychological Society (APS).

American Board of Professional Psychology (ABPP) An organization that offers certification of professional competence in many psychology specialties. ABPP certification may be sought after five years of postdoctoral experience and is granted on the basis of an oral examination, the observed handling of a case, and records from past cases.

certification A professional regulation that prohibits people from calling themselves psychologists while offering services to the public for a fee unless they have been certified by a state board of examiners.

client welfare An ethical principle that calls upon psychologists to respect the integrity of their clients and to guard the relationship from exploitation. This principle encompasses ethical standards such as avoiding entering into dual relationships with clients and discontinuing treatment when it is clear that the treatment is no longer beneficial.

clinical scientist model A training model that encourages rigorous training in empirical research methods and the integration of scientific principles into clinical practice.

combined professional-scientific training program A training model that offers a combined specialty in clinical, counseling, and school psychology.

competence An ethical principle that calls upon psychologists to recognize the boundaries of their professional expertise and to keep up to date on information relevant to the services they provide.

confidentiality An ethical principle that calls upon psychologists to respect and protect the information shared with them by clients, disclosing this information only when they have obtained the client's consent (except in extraordinary cases in which failing to disclose the information would place the client or others at clear risk for harm).

cultural competence A knowledge and appreciation of other cultural groups and the skills to be effective with members of these groups.

diversity The presence of differences, or variety (as in "cultural diversity").

Doctor of Psychology (Psy.D.) degree An advanced degree in psychology with a relative emphasis on clinical and assessment skills and a relative de-emphasis on research competency.

ethical standards As pertains to psychologists, enforceable rules of professional conduct identified by the APA.

health maintenance organization (HMO) A managed care system that employs a restricted number of providers to serve enrollees. In an HMO, costs for all services are fixed.

licensing A professional regulation that is more stringent than certification. It specifies not only the nature of the title and training required for licensure, but also the professional activities that may be offered for a fee.

managed care A profit-driven, corporate approach to health (and mental health) care that attempts to contain costs by controlling the length and frequency of service utilization, restricting the types of service provided and requiring documentation of treatment necessity and efficacy.

preferred provider organization (PPO) A managed care system that contracts with outside providers to provide services to members. These outside providers are reimbursed for their services at a discounted rate in return for an increased number of member referrals.

prescription privileges The legal ability to prescribe medication. There is currently a heated debate among clinical psychologists as to the desirability of obtaining this privilege.

professional schools Schools that offer advanced training in psychology that differs from that offered by traditional doctoral programs. In general, professional schools offer relatively little training in research, emphasizing instead training in assessment and psychotherapy.

scientist-practitioner model The predominant training model for clinical psychologists (also known as the Boulder model). This model strives to produce professionals who integrate the roles of scientist and practitioner (i.e., who practice psychotherapy with skill and sensitivity and conduct research on the hypotheses they have generated from their clinical observations).

Tarasoff case A landmark 1976 case in which the California Supreme Court ruled that a therapist was legally remiss for not informing all appropriate parties of a client's intention to harm. This case legally established a therapist's "duty to protect."

Web Sites of Interest

To visit any of the web sites listed below, go to www.wadsworth.com and click on Links.

3-1   American Board of Professional Psychology

3-2   Association of State and Provincial Psychology Boards

3-3   National Council of Schools and Programs of Professional Psychology

CHAPTER FOUR

Research Methods in Clinical Psychology

The scientist-practitioner model has long been the preeminent philosophy in training clinical psychologists. It is this training model that has enabled clinical psychologists to become the research experts on so many mental health teams. Regardless of whether clinical psychologists become active researchers or active consumers of research, methods of research are pivotal concerns of both groups. Even clinical psychologists who see clients full time in a private practice must have a knowledge and mastery of research methods. These skills enable them to critically evaluate different approaches to assessment and intervention, and ultimately choose the ones that are most likely to be useful and effective.

In this chapter, we present a brief overview of some of the principal methods, strategies, and issues in clinical research. Specific research questions (for example, therapy outcome studies) will be addressed at appropriate points later in the book. More comprehensive and technical discussions of research methods in clinical psychology may be found elsewhere (for example, Kazdin, 1992, 1998; Sher & Trull, 1996).

Introduction to Research

Someone once remarked that a major portion of clinical training consists of erasing students' misconceptions about the reasons people behave the way they do. For example, are the following statements true?

1. If patients talk about suicide, this means that they will not try it.
2. Ridding patients of symptoms without providing insight means that those symptoms will return later in another guise.
3. Projective tests prevent patients from successfully managing the impressions they wish to convey.
4. All a person needs in order to become a good therapist is a caring, empathic attitude.

All of these are common beliefs once held—and, for that matter, still held—by some people, clinicians and laypeople alike. Are they true? Probably not. Research employing the methods described in this chapter can shed light on these and many other issues.

Human behavior is terribly complex—so complex that theories to explain it abound. So many factors affect a given behavior at a given time in a given place that we must be skeptical about explanations that appear simple or inevitable. In fact, a healthy skepticism is a directing force behind the scientists' quest for knowledge or the clinicians' search for increasingly effective ways of serving their clients.

Because easy, simple, or traditional explanations are so often wrong or incomplete, increasingly sophisticated methods of generating satisfactory explanations for behavior have evolved. We now use better methods to make the kinds of systematic observations about behavior that can be publicly verified. These methods have changed over the years and will continue to change in the future; there are no inevitable or perfect scientific methods. But somehow ideas, hypotheses, or hunches must be stated clearly and precisely so that they can be tested by other observers. Only ideas that are stated in a manner that offers a clear opportunity for disproof are satisfactory ones.

Research has several purposes. First of all, it allows us to escape the realm of pure speculation or appeal to authority. For example, we do not just argue whether cognitive-behavior therapy works; we conduct the kind of research that will *demonstrate* its effectiveness or lack of it. Questions are settled in the forum of publicly verifiable and objective observation. Over the long haul, such procedures are better vehicles for settling issues than simple appeals to reason. These research procedures enable us to accumulate facts, establish the existence of relationships, identify causes and effects, and generate the principles behind those facts and relationships.

Research also helps us extend and modify our theories, as well as establish their parsimony and utility. There is an intimate relationship between theory and research. Theory stimulates and guides the research we do; but theories are also modified by the outcomes of research. For example, Aaron Beck, a pioneer in the study of depression, observed many years ago that depressed patients often exhibit personality features that could be categorized into one of two types: sociotropic (excessively socially dependent) and autonomous (excessively achievement oriented). Initially, Beck proposed that extreme sociotropy or extreme autonomy traits predispose a person to depression. However, subsequent research did not support this proposition. Investigators found that there were individuals who presented with rather extreme sociotropy or extreme autonomy, but who were not depressed. These results challenged Beck's initial theory, and led to a reformulation of how personality and depression may be related. The revised theory, labeled the congruency hypothesis, proposes that it is the interaction between personality style (sociotropic or autonomous) and the experience of thematically related negative life events that leads to depression (Beck, 1983). Specifically, this theory predicts that a highly sociotropic person who experiences relationship failures (negative events quite salient to a highly dependent person) will become depressed, whereas this is not necessarily true for a highly autonomous person (for whom these particular kinds of negative events are less relevant). In other words, negative life events must be *congruent* with one's personality style in order for depression to develop. In general, research results have been more supportive of Beck's revised theory (for example, Bartelstone & Trull, 1995; C. J. Robins, 1990).

This example serves to illustrate how research can inform our theories in a type of feedback-loop system. Of course, the ultimate reason for research is the enhancement of our ability to predict and understand the behavior, feelings, and thoughts of the people served by clinical psychologists. In the final analysis, only better research will enable us to intervene wisely and effectively on their behalf.

Methods

As noted earlier, there are many methods of research, each with its own advantages and limitations. Therefore, no method by itself will answer every question definitively. But together, a variety of methods can significantly extend our ability to understand and predict. We begin with an overview of the many forms of observation used by clinical scientists. We then summarize epidemiological and correlational approaches, longitudinal versus cross-sectional approaches, the classic experimental method, single-case designs, and finally, mixed designs.

Observation

The most basic and pervasive of all research methods is observation. Experimental, case study, and naturalistic approaches all involve making observations of what someone is doing or has done.

Unsystematic Observation. Casual observation does little by itself to establish a strong base of knowledge. However, it is through such observation that we develop hypotheses that can eventually be subjected to test. For example, suppose a clinician notes on several different occasions that when a patient struggles or has difficulty with a specific item on an achievement test, the effect seems to carry over to the next item and adversely affect performance. This observation leads the clinician to formulate the hypothesis that performance might be enhanced by making sure each failure item is followed by an easy item on which the patient will likely succeed. This should help build the patient's confidence and thus improve performance. To test this prediction, the clinician might administer an experimental version of the achievement test, in which difficult items are followed by easy items. It would then be relatively easy to develop a study that would test this hypothesis in a representative sample of clients.

Naturalistic Observation. Though carried out in real-life settings, *naturalistic observation* is more systematic and rigorous. It is neither casual nor free-wheeling, but carefully planned in advance. However, there is no real control exerted by the observer, who is pretty much at the mercy of freely flowing events. Frequently, observations are limited to a relatively few individuals or situations. Thus, it may be uncertain how far one can generalize to other people or other situations. It is also possible that in the midst of observing or recording responses, the observer may unwittingly interfere with or influence the events under study.

An example of a study using the naturalistic observation method might be an investigation of patient behavior in a psychiatric hospital. Perhaps a particular unit in this hospital is composed of patients who are scheduled to undergo electroconvulsive therapy (ECT) that day. The clinician's job is to focus on ten patients and observe each one for 2 minutes every half-hour. This observational study might yield interesting data about the reactions of patients prior to ECT. But with only ten patients from this particular hospital, can wide generalizations be made? Are these patients' reactions similar to those in other hospitals or other units where the overall atmosphere may be very different? Or were the patients aware of the observer's presence, and could they have altered their customary reactions in order to somehow impress him or her?

Investigators committed to more rigorous experimental methods sometimes condemn naturalistic observation as too uncontrolled. But this judgment may be too harsh. As with unsystematic observation, this method can serve as a rich source of hypotheses that can be subjected to careful scrutiny later. Naturalistic observations do get investigators closer to the real phenomena that interest them. Such observations avoid the artificiality and contrived nature of many experimental settings. For example, regardless of their feelings about psychodynamic theory, most acknowledge that Freud's clinical observation skills were extraordinary. Freud used his own powers of observation to construct one of the most influential and sweeping theories in the history of clinical psychology. It is important to recall that Freud had available no objective tests, no computer printouts, and no sophisticated experimental methods. What he did possess was the ability to observe, interpret, and generalize in an impressive fashion.

Controlled Observation. To deal in part with the foregoing criticisms of unsystematic and naturalistic observation, some clinical investigators employ *controlled observation*. While the research may be carried out in the field or in relatively natural settings, the investigator exerts some degree of control over the events. Controlled observation has a long history in clinical psychology. For example, it is one thing to have patients tell clinicians about their fears or check off items on a questionnaire. However, Bernstein, and Nietzel (1973) studied the nature of snake phobias by placing study participants in the presence of real snakes and then varying the distance between participant and snake. This controlled observation enabled them to gain some real insight into the nature of the participants' reactions. Controlled observation can also be used to assess communication patterns between couples or spouses. Instead of relying on distressed couples' self-reports of their communication problems, researchers may choose to actually observe communications styles in a controlled setting. Specifically, partners can be asked to discuss and attempt to resolve a moderate-sized relationship problem of their choosing (for example, partner spends too much money on unnecessary things) while researchers observe or videotape the interaction behind a one-way mirror. Although not a substitute for naturalistic observation of conflict and problem solving in the home, researchers have found this controlled observation method to be a useful and cost-effective means of assessing couples' interaction patterns.

Case Studies. The *case study method* involves the intensive study of a client or patient who is in treatment. Under the heading of case studies we include material from interviews, test responses, and treatment accounts. Such material might also include biographical and autobiographical data, letters, diaries, life-course information, medical histories, and so on. Case studies, then, involve the intensive study and description of one person. Such studies have long been prominent in the study of abnormal behavior and in the description of treatment methods. Their great

---

BOX 4-1

What Case Studies Can Tell Us about Phobias and Early Trauma

1. Specific phobias are unreasonable fears that are out of proportion to any real danger to the individual. Many learning theorists believe specific phobias are acquired through classical conditioning. As a prototypic experiment, these theorists often cite the classic Watson and Rayner (1920) study of Little Albert. Albert was conditioned to fear white rats by discovering that each time he began to play with one, a loud and unpleasant noise occurred. Over trials, Albert developed what appeared to be a full-blown phobia of rats and similar furry objects.

However, Davison and Neale (1998) have noted that despite what learning theory seems to teach us, clinical reports and histories fail to support the Little Albert model. While some specific phobias could develop in that manner, they usually occur without any prior frightening experiences in the situation. Individuals who fear elevators, snakes, or high places rarely report an early bad experience with such places or things. It is not clear that laboratory research on specific phobias is carried out in real-enough settings that researchers can say that the laboratory mimics real life.

2. Everybody "knows" that early childhood trauma is likely to predispose us to unhappiness and failure. Take the following example:

> A girl who is plain and lacks grace; whose mother favors her two younger brothers, whose mother nagged her, creating constant feelings of shame and estrangement; whose father left home when she was young; whose mother died when the girl was only 9, leaving her in the care of a grandmother; whose grandmother kept her away from other children and deprived her of most of her childhood; who was so lonely that her only pursuits were reading, daydreaming, and walking.

Such a person must be ripe for failure, emotional problems, or perhaps destined to become a social misfit (White, 1976). But as White asks wryly, who is it we are describing? It is none other than Eleanor Roosevelt, depicted by White as "the champion of the poor and the oppressed; ultimately [becoming] chairman [*sic*] of the committee which drew up the United Nations Declaration of Human Rights" (White, 1976, p. 522).

---

value resides in their richness as potential sources of understanding and as hypothesis generators. They can serve as excellent preludes to scientific investigation (see Box 4-1).

Over the years, many case studies have been influential in establishing our understanding of clinical phenomena. Following are some classic examples:

The Case of Dora (Freud, 1905/1953a) taught us about the concept of resistance in therapy.

The Case of Little Hans (Freud, 1909/1955) extended our understanding of the psychodynamics of phobias.

The Three Faces of Eve (Thigpen & Cleckley, 1957) outlined the anatomy of multiple personalities.

The Mask of Sanity (Cleckley, 1964) provided detailed accounts of the lives of psychopaths.

Cases in Behavior Modification (Ullman & Krasner, 1965) demonstrated the efficacy of behavioral treatments with single cases.

Nothing will ever likely supplant the case study as a way of helping clinicians to understand that unique patient who sits there before them. As Allport (1961) so compellingly argued, individuals must be studied individually. Case studies have been especially useful for (1) providing descriptions of rare or unusual phenomena or novel, distinctive methods of interviewing, assessing, or treating patients; (2) disconfirming "universally" known or accepted information; and (3) generating testable hypotheses (Davison & Neale, 1998). (See Box 4-2.)

There is, of course, a downside to case study methods. For example, it is difficult to use individual cases to develop universal laws or behavioral principles that apply to everyone. Likewise, one case study cannot lead to cause-effect conclusions because clinicians are not able to control important variables that have operated in that case. For example, one patient may benefit enormously from psychodynamic therapy for reasons that have less to do with the therapy method than with the personality characteristics of that patient. Only subsequent controlled research can pin down the exact causes of, or factors influencing, change.

Epidemiological Research

Epidemiology is the study of the incidence, prevalence, and distribution of illness or disease in a given population. Several terms are commonly used in epidemiology. *Incidence* refers to the rate of *new* cases of illness that develop within a given period of time, whereas *prevalence* refers to the overall rate of cases (old or new) within a given period of time. Incidence gives us some sense of whether the rate of new cases of the illness or disorder is on the increase (for example, is the rate of newly diagnosed AIDS cases increasing this year compared to last year?). Prevalence rates estimate what percentage of the target population is affected by the illness or disorder. For example, the lifetime prevalence rate of schizophrenia is estimated at 1%, suggesting that a member of the general population has a 1 chance in 100 of developing this disorder in his or her lifetime.

Historically, epidemiology has been most closely associated with medical research designed to help understand and control the major epidemic diseases, such as cholera and yellow fever. The simple counting of cases is central to this research method. The expectation is that analyzing the distribution of cases in a community or region and uncovering the distinguishing characteristics of the affected individuals or groups will teach us something about the causes of a particular disease and the methods by which it spreads. Epidemiological methods can also be quite important in identifying groups of individuals who are at risk.

A well-known example of epidemiological research is the study *Smoking and Health* (Surgeon General, 1964). That study linked cigarette smoking with lung cancer by the simple methods of counting and correlating. Although there was great debate as to whether smoking *caused* lung cancer, there were definite relationships and associations between smoking and lung cancer (for example, about 90% of lung cancer in males was associated with cigarette smoking, and the amount and duration of smoking were positively correlated with the probability of cancer). It is true that epidemiological research frequently suggests the possibility of multiple causation (several factors must be present before the disease occurs, or the greater the number of associated factors that are present, the greater the risk of the disease). It is equally true that obtained correlations *suggest* causes rather than definitively prove causation. However, the entire story of causation need not be known before preventive steps can be undertaken. Thus, we may not be sure that smoking causes lung cancer, or we may believe that some inherited predisposition interacts with smoking to produce cancer. Nevertheless, we know that groups of males who quit smoking reduce their risk of lung cancer.

As another example, in the field of mental illness, a number of studies have pointed out the relationship between schizophrenia and either socioeconomic class or factors of social disorganization (Faris & Dunham, 1939; Hollingshead & Redlich, 1958). Again, though such results hardly convey the essence of schizophrenia, they do tell us about major demographic factors that are associated with its prevalence. Armed with this information, clinicians can identify people whose potential vulnerability to schizophrenia is high, and can establish special programs that will provide early diagnostic evidence of its onset in such

Generating Hypotheses from Therapy

The case of Karl S. was first described by Phares (1976). Karl was an unmarried veteran referred to a Veterans Administration outpatient clinic. It did not take long for the therapist to realize that Karl's problems were not of the typical neurotic variety. No well-defined, classic "neurotic" symptoms were present. Karl was a bit anxious or, at times, depressed, but his main problem seemed to be a near total lack of interpersonal and social skills. He had no job, and he lived off his small government pension along with whatever support his mother could provide. Aside from his mother, with whom he lived, he rarely interacted with anyone except perhaps to buy cigarettes or get change from a disinterested bus driver. He certainly had no friends.

Therapy, then, became not an insight-oriented, uncovering process but a teaching process. The goals became teaching Karl to find work, enabling him to attend night school to learn a trade, and inculcating at least a few basic social skills. The focus was on how to find a job, keep a job, talk with a woman, and gain her interest. Hour after hour was spent on these tasks during the therapy.

But progress was slow. It was not that Karl failed to understand or was totally disinterested or even loath to try out newly learned skills. The difficulty was that even when Karl attempted a new behavior and was successful, that success seemed to have little effect on his subsequent behavior. This was strange indeed. Psychologists quickly learn that reinforcement strengthens the likelihood of the reinforced behavior in the future, given similar conditions. But not so with Karl. Reinforcement seemed to do little to raise his expectancies that the behavior would work again. Karl almost seemed to want to be the singular exception to a prime rule of learning theory—that reinforcement enhances habit strength!

The therapist and his consultants puzzled over this for months. For example, after applying for a job and getting it, Karl's confidence did not increase at all. Instead, he attributed his success to luck, not to his own efforts. Several other similar episodes followed. After much urging by the therapist, Karl asked a female co-worker for a date. She accepted. But again, Karl merely remarked on his good luck.

Eventually the therapist decided that perhaps Karl believed that the occurrence of reinforcement was outside his personal control. If so, the inability of success to increase his confidence began to make sense. He was not responding in defiance of learning theory. Instead, the therapist's conceptualization had been incomplete. Reinforcement will "stamp in" a behavior, but only when that behavior is seen as causally related to the subsequent reinforcement. Karl believed chance rather than personal skill was operative. And under chance conditions, reinforcement carries no implications for the future. Thus, the riddle of Karl's behavior seemed to have been solved. Or, at the very least, an important hypothesis had been formulated. In fact, a great deal of empirical research lay ahead. Only after several years of empirical research could the utility of the chance-versus-skill hypothesis be verified. This general research field came to be referred to as *internal-external control* (Rotter, 1966), or *locus of control*.

people, or treatment programs can be established that will be readily available to those who are at risk of developing schizophrenia.

Much epidemiological research is based on surveys or interviews. However, survey and interview data present a number of issues and potential problems. For example, how do we define a mental health problem, and having done so, where do we locate cases for counting? Checking only clinics and hospitals means ignoring other possible locales. These difficulties are magnified when we become interested in milder forms of dysfunction. In effect, we need objective methods of defining and measuring a problem. Further, we need survey procedures that will enable us to estimate the problem's true incidence or prevalence and not just to locate those cases that are already under treatment or that have identified themselves by seeking treatment. We need to sample residences (block by block, or area by area), not just clinics, hospitals, and agencies. Another potential problem with survey data is that respondents may get caught up in the need to say "the right thing." They may want to report only socially desirable things, and deny other, less socially desirable experiences. For example, respondents may be unwilling to admit to having experienced serious symptoms of psychopathology (such as auditory hallucinations) because they may be embarrassed.

In addition, some respondents may be asked to remember things from several years ago. Such *retrospective data* can be subject to all sorts of distortions, omissions, or embellishments. For example, one study (Henry, Moffitt, Caspi, Langley, & Silva, 1994) found that 18-year-olds who had been assessed on a regular basis from birth were not particularly accurate in their retrospective reports of certain types of childhood experiences (such as family conflict, their own depressive or anxious symptoms, or their own level of hyperactivity). These findings are noteworthy because clinical psychologists often request this type of retrospective information from clients or research participants. The point here is that we should attempt to assess our clients and research participants *at the time of interest* and not rely exclusively on retrospective reports.

Recently, several large-scale, methodologically sound epidemiological studies of mental disorder have been conducted. For example, Kessler et al. (1994) administered a structured diagnostic interview to a national probability sample in the United States in order to obtain estimates of the 12-month and lifetime prevalence of a variety of mental disorders. Some of these results appear in Table 4-1. Of particular interest are the differences in lifetime prevalence rates between men and women for some but not all disorders. Men are more likely than women to receive a diagnosis of substance use disorder or antisocial personality disorder, whereas mood and anxiety disorder disorders are more prevalent in women. From these data, one can conclude that men appear to be at greater risk for a variety of substance use disorders than women. Therefore, being a man is a *risk factor* for these disorders. Risk factors need not be limited to gender, but can involve other sociodemographic features as well (socioeconomic status, age, urban versus rural residence, and so on).

Correlational Methods

We have seen that epidemiology often relies on *correlational methods*; that is, it assesses the correlates (risk factors) of illness or disorder. We now focus more specifically on correlational methods. These techniques enable us to determine whether variable X is related to variable Y. For example, is a certain pattern of scores on an intelligence test related to specific psychiatric diagnostic categories? Are particular patient characteristics related to therapy outcomes? Is depression related to gender?

The Technique. In order to correlate two variables, we first obtain two sets of observations. For example, suppose that we administer two tests to 10 study participants. One test measures anxiety and the other a belief in external (rather than internal) control. These hypothetical data are shown in Table 4-2. When these data are correlated, the result is a *correlation coefficient*; in this case, it is +.76, indicating a strong positive relationship. As anxiety scores increase, so do scores on belief in external control, which means that anxiety and feelings of lack of control are positively related.

The *Pearson product-moment coefficient* is a commonly used index to determine the degree of relationship between two variables. This is

▮ TABLE 4-1 Lifetime Prevalence Rates for Selected DSM-III-R Mental Disorders

Disorder	Male %	Female %	Total%
Mood Disorders			
Major depressive episode	12.7	21.3	17.1
Manic episode	1.6	1.7	1.6
Dysthymia	4.8	8.0	6.4
Any mood disorder	14.7	23.9	19.3
Anxiety Disorders			
Panic disorder	2.0	5.0	3.5
Agoraphobia without panic disorder	3.5	7.0	5.3
Social phobia	11.1	15.5	13.3
Simple phobia	6.7	15.7	11.3
Generalized anxiety disorder	3.6	6.6	5.1
Any anxiety disorder	19.2	30.5	24.9
Substance Use Disorders			
Alcohol abuse without dependence	12.5	6.4	9.4
Alcohol dependence	20.1	8.2	14.1
Drug abuse without dependence	5.4	3.5	4.4
Drug dependence	9.2	5.9	7.5
Any substance abuse/dependence	35.4	17.9	26.6
Other Disorders			
Antisocial personality	5.8	1.2	3.5
Non-mood psychosis	0.6	0.8	0.7
ANY DISORDER	48.7	47.3	48.0

Source: Kessler, R. C., et al. (1994). Lifetime and 12-month prevalence of DSM-III-R psychiatric disorders in the United States: Results from the *National Comorbidity Survey. Archives of General Psychiatry, 51,* 8–19. Adapted with permission.

symbolized by *r*, which may vary anywhere from –1.00 to +1.00. An *r* of +1.00 denotes that the two variables are perfectly and positively related. An *r* of –1.00 indicates a perfect negative relationship. The *r* of +.76 from the data of Table 4-2 signifies a high but less than perfect relationship. A *scatter plot* of the data points for the two variables from Table 4-2 is shown in Figure 4-1. Each data point corresponds to one participant's scores on both anxiety and control. For example, the data point nearest the lower left corner represents Ralph's scores of 4 on anxiety and 2 on control. Figure 4-2 presents scatter plots for several correlations.

The more nearly perfect a relationship, the closer to a straight line the data points will be. As *r* approaches zero (no relationship), the data points are scattered in a nearly random fashion around a straight line.

The Question of Causality. As noted previously in the case of epidemiological research, correlational methods can founder on the question of cause and effect. No matter how logical it may appear, we cannot, on the basis of a correlation alone, assert that one variable has caused another. For example, suppose that an investigator discovers a correlation between being diagnosed with schizophrenia and having elevated levels of the neurotransmitter dopamine in the central nervous system. Does this mean that schizophrenia is caused by excessive levels of dopamine or, alternatively, that the experience of an episode of schizophrenia results in changes in

TABLE 4-2 Hypothetical Data for the Correlation between Anxiety and Control

Subject	Anxiety Score	Control Score
Ann	26	22
Jane	24	28
Tom	20	22
George	20	14
Esther	16	18
Nancy	12	22
Robert	12	6
Kevin	10	14
Lisa	6	12
Ralph	4	2

FIGURE 4-1 Scatter plot of data from Table 4-2

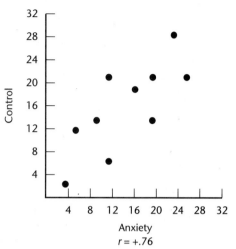

$r = +.76$

levels of dopamine? Maybe the real culprit is a third variable. For example, many patients with schizophrenia have a long history of taking psychoactive drugs (such as amphetamines); such long-term use could conceivably affect neurotransmitter levels. Therefore, the investigator must avoid assuming that one variable causes the other, because there is always the possibility that a third (unmeasured) variable is involved.

A classic example of the *third variable problem* is the observation that crime rates are significantly correlated with the number of churches and synagogues in a community. Does this mean that religion *causes* crime? No. The third variable that has been neglected in this example is population. Both the crime rate and the number of churches and synagogues are positively correlated with population, and they are correlated with each other because both increase as the population increases.

Correlational methods *can* demonstrate that a cause-effect hypothesis is invalid. If the expectation is that variable A causes variable B, we should at least be able to show they are correlated. Failure to find a significant relationship most certainly contradicts the hypothesis. Also, although causal inferences are not possible from

correlation coefficients, this is not to say that cause-effect relationships do not in fact exist. However, such relationships must be demonstrated through experimental methods (to be discussed later). There are research methods that can help vitiate the causation problem, such as matching participants on other variables that might be contributing to the obtained relationship or using longitudinal methods that study variables before a given disorder develops. But these are often cumbersome and expensive procedures, and thus are less frequently employed.

Sometimes we are forced to use correlational methods because we cannot either ethically or practically manipulate certain variables such as age, sex, marital status, or birth order. For example, we cannot ethically train someone to commit a homicide in order to study the effects of personality on violence. Certain things can *only* be studied by observing their occurrences; creating them is not an acceptable alternative.

Factor Analysis. Derived from the correlational strategy, *factor analysis* is a way of examining the interrelationships among a number of variables at the same time. This statistical method uses many separate correlations to determine which

FIGURE 4-2 Scatter plots showing several different magnitudes of relationships

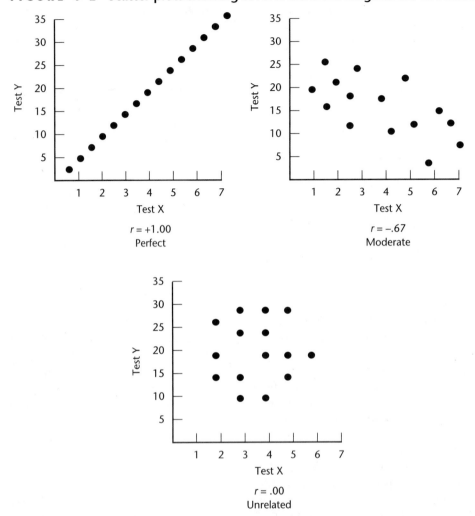

variables change in concert and, thus, can be considered functionally related. The idea is that when variables change together, they must have some element in common that underlies their relationship.

Consider the following example (Phares, 1991). Suppose we are trying to identify the basic elements of what is called "clinical skill." First, we ask a panel of judges to select 100 clinicians who are known to have excellent records in providing skilled services. Then, we administer a large number of tests that are believed to assess a variety of clinical skills and achievements. Let us suppose that we use the following seven tests:

A = IQ test

B = Mathematical achievement test

C = Test of spatial reasoning

D = Test of analytical reasoning

E = Measure of empathy

F = Measure of personal adjustment

G = Measure of altruism

TABLE 4-3 Hypothetical Correlation Matrix for Seven Tests

Test	A	B	C	D	E	F	G
A		.70	.80	.75	.15	.20	.10
B			.75	.70	.12	.10	.10
C				.70	.18	.15	.11
D					.12	.14	.12
E						.80	.85
F							.75

Source: From *Introduction to Personality,* 3rd ed., by E. J. Phares. Copyright © 1991 by HarperCollins. Reprinted by permission.

Next, we correlate each of these tests with every other test. This gives us a *correlation matrix,* in which the correlations between all possible pairs of tests are displayed. Such a matrix, with hypothetical correlations entered, is shown in Table 4-3.

When we look at the correlation matrix, an interesting pattern emerges. Measures A, B, C, and D all show a strong positive relationship (correlations range from .70 to .80). At the same time, E, F, and G also correlate highly with one another (correlations range from .75 to .85). But there is virtually no relationship between the group E, F, G and the group A, B, C, D (for example, the correlation between A and E is .15; between B and F, .10; and between D and G, .12). These patterns indicate that A, B, C, and D appear to be measuring a similar underlying dimension, or *factor.* Similarly, E, F, and G belong together, suggesting a second underlying dimension. In effect, factor analysis does statistically with large correlation matrices what was done here by inspection with correlations from seven measures. Were we to have had 200 measures, simple inspection would have been an impossible task.

From the previous example, it would appear that two factors or dimensions are involved. Let us call them X (derived from the correlations among A, B, C, and D) and Y (derived from E, F, and G). Together, these two factors account for the significant relationships in the matrix. Usu-

ally, these factors are then named. This is a highly inferential phase that can sometimes lead to communication problems. Sometimes names chosen convey information different from what was intended. However, in our example, where factor X involves A, B, C, and D, perhaps we could choose the name "intellectual ability." Factor Y is more difficult to name because it includes measures of empathy, adjustment, and altruism. Perhaps "healthy altruism" would be appropriate.

Factor analysis is an especially good way of helping organize in a coherent fashion the relationships that emerge from large arrays of data. As a way of identifying the basic elements of clinical skill (as in the example) or those of personality, factor analysis is not the ultimate answer. After all, what emerges from a factor analysis is determined by the nature of the measures included in the first place. What was not included in the sample battery of tests to study clinical skill could hardly be expected to turn up as factors!

Cross-sectional versus Longitudinal Approaches

Another way of classifying research studies is by considering whether the studies are cross-sectional or longitudinal in nature. A *cross-sectional design* is one that evaluates or compares individuals, perhaps of different age groups, at the

FIGURE 4-3 **Cross-sectional and longitudinal research designs**

Source: Diana Woodruff-Pak, Psychology and Aging, Copyright © 1988, p. 32. Reprinted by permission of Prentice-Hall, Englewood Cliffs, New Jersey.

Birthdate			Age		
1890	65	70	b 75	80	85
1895	60	65	70	75	80
1900	55	60	65	70	75
1905	50	55	60	65	70
1910	a 45	50	55	60	65
1915	40	45	50	55	60
1920	35	40	45	50	55
1925	30	35	40	45	50
Time of measurement	1955	1960	1965	1970	1975

same point in time. A *longitudinal design* follows the same subjects over time. The basic format of these two approaches is shown in Figure 4-3. In this example, row *a* illustrates the longitudinal design and column *b* the cross-sectional design.

Cross-sectional approaches are correlational, because the investigator cannot manipulate age nor can participants be assigned to different age groups. Because there are different participants in each age group, we cannot assume that the outcome of the study reflects age changes; it only reflects differences among the age groups employed. These differences could be due to the eras in which participants were raised rather than age per se. For example, a group of 65-year-olds might show up as more frugal than a group of 35-year-olds. Does this mean that advancing age promotes frugality? Perhaps. But it might simply reflect the historical circumstance that the 65-year-olds were raised during the Great Depression when money was very hard to come by.

Longitudinal studies are those in which we collect data on the same people over time. Such designs allow us to gain insight into how behavior or mental processes change with age. In the

interpretive sense, longitudinal studies enable investigators to better speculate about time-order relationships among factors that vary together. They also help eliminate the third variable problem that so often arises in correlational studies. For example, suppose we know that states of depression come and go over the years. If depression is responsible for the correlation between significant weight loss and decreased self-confidence, then both weight loss and decline in self-confidence should vary along with depressive states.

There are, of course, many variations in cross-sectional and longitudinal designs (Kausler, 1991). In the case of longitudinal studies, however, the main problems are practical ones. Such studies are costly to carry out, and they require great patience and continuity of leadership in the research program. Sometimes, too, researchers must live with design mistakes made years earlier or put up with outmoded research and assessment methods. Because longitudinal research is expensive in both time and money, it is not used as often as it should be. For these reasons, research in the developmental aspects of psychopathology has long suffered (Rotter, 1990; Wierson & Forehand, 1994). Still, it is to be hoped that there will be a return to those strategies that deal with psychopathology, treatment, or personality over extended periods of time, using a variety of measures (Phares, 1991). Too often, we have been captives of a cross-sectional methodology that sometimes seems to focus exclusively on 50-minute experiments. Such strategies have promoted a "snapshot" view of human behavior and personality that has done little to help us understand the coherence and organization of human behavior.

The Experimental Method

To determine cause-effect relationships among events, we must use experimental methods. Consider the following study, in which personal responsibility was studied in relation to several indicants of well-being (Langer & Rodin, 1976). Although this study was conducted some time ago, the design of the research nicely illustrates important features of the *experimental method*.

The study was carried out in a Connecticut nursing home with participants ranging in age from 65 to 90. The *experimental group* contained 47 subjects who were told that they would be encouraged to make a number of decisions. For example, rather than looking to the staff, they could decide on their own room arrangement, where they wished to meet visitors, how they wanted to spend their spare time, and so on. They were even encouraged to report their complaints to the staff. Each was also given a plant to personally care for. The *control group* consisted of 44 participants who were left with the distinct impression that all the foregoing matters would be decided by the staff. They were told how eager the staff was to care not only for them but even for their plants! The two groups were otherwise matched initially (one week before the instructions were given) on several variables, including health status, prior socioeconomic level, and psychological adjustment. Despite this matching, three weeks later, the two groups dif-

fered significantly on a variety of measures such as alertness, happiness, general well-being, frequency of attendance at movies, and engagement in group activities. Figure 4-4 shows the findings for self-reports of happiness before and after the instructions.

This study illustrates several features of a typical experimental study. The *experimental hypothesis* that elderly subjects would benefit from a sense of personal responsibility was developed both from observation of similar populations and from prior published research. An *independent variable* is one that is supposed to be under the control of the investigator. It is expected to have a causal effect on participants' behavior. The latter is referred to as the *dependent variable*. In this study, personal responsibility was the independent variable, and it was manipulated by the investigators through their instructions. The dependent variable was the participant's response (such as self-reported happiness) to felt responsibility or lack of it. Good experimental procedure was also followed by *matching* subjects on important variables that might have affected the outcome of the research (such as health status and adjustment). Sometimes, when matching is difficult, participants are *assigned randomly* to experimental and control groups. The idea is that the only significant feature different for the two groups should be the induced sense of personal responsibility. Hence, the higher happiness scores in the experimental group must have been *caused* by the instructions.

Between- and Within-Group Designs. In a *between-group design*, we have two separate sets of participants, each of which receives a different kind of treatment. Take, for example, a study of therapy effectiveness. In its simplest form, an experimental group (receiving some form of treatment) is compared to a control group (receiving no treatment at all). Ideally, patients would be randomly assigned to each group. Some set of measures (for example, level of anxiety, interview impressions, or test data) is taken from all patients in both groups prior to treatment (or no

FIGURE 4-4 Self-reports of happiness before and after experimental intervention

Source: Based on data from Langer & Rodin (1976).

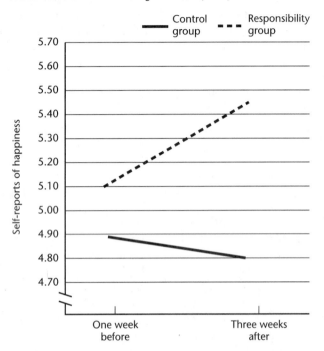

treatment), after treatment, and perhaps at a follow-up point six months or a year after treatment is concluded. Any differences between the two groups either at the conclusion of treatment or during the follow-up are assumed to be a function of the treatment that was received by the experimental group.

In a *within-group design*, comparisons might be made on the same patient at different points in time. To illustrate how this procedure works, suppose we are interested in the effects (such as level of distress) of being on a waiting list. We might decide to place every patient on a six-week waiting list but carry out a variety of assessment procedures before doing so (point A). Six weeks later, these patients would be reassessed just prior to beginning treatment (point B). At the conclusion of treatment (point C), the patients would be assessed for a third time, and they might also be followed up later (point D). Any changes taking place between points A and

B (while on the waiting list) could be compared to the changes that take place between point B and point C or D. These more complex analyses of changes would give us a better view of the efficacy of treatment relative to merely being on a waiting list.

There are many variations of the within-group design. However, a major advantage is that it requires fewer participants. Indeed, as we shall see later in the case of single-subject designs, we can determine whether or not a specific intervention has an effect merely by observing one participant.

Internal Validity. Sometimes it happens that an experiment is not *internally valid*. That is, we are not sure that the obtained outcome is really attributable to our manipulation of the independent variable. Some studies do not even include a control group for comparison with an experimental group. In this case, any observed changes could be the result of some other variable. For example, suppose in the nursing home experiment Langer and Rodin did not have a control group. Even though the experimental group showed increases in happiness, perhaps this was not at all due to feelings of responsibility. Maybe it was due to a new nursing home administrator hired in the midst of the study. Or maybe it was due to a change in dieticians that occurred over the course of the study. Without a control group that also experienced these other events, one can never be sure. In short, when extraneous variables are not controlled or cannot be shown to exist equally in experimental and control groups, these variables may *confound* the results.

We shall see later that sometimes in studies of therapy effectiveness, one group of patients receives a new form of therapy. A second group of patients is matched with the therapy group (or patients are randomly assigned to the two groups) and then assigned to a waiting list. The assumption is that the only difference between the waiting list subjects and the therapy subjects is that the latter received therapy and the former did not. Therefore, the study is internally valid. But is it really? Experience has shown that subjects who go on a waiting list do not always fail to receive help. Instead, they often seek help from a minister, wise counsel from a friend, or some other type of support. Thus, any improvement shown by the therapy group may be confounded by the extratherapy help received informally by subjects on the waiting list. Therefore, the fact that the therapy group improved no more than did the waiting list group does not mean that the therapy intervention was ineffective. It may only mean that both groups received some form of intervention.

Another factor that detracts from internal validity involves *expectations*. When either the investigator or the participant *expects* a certain outcome, that very outcome may be produced. It is not the experimental manipulation that causes the outcome; it is the expectations. This phenomenon is called a *placebo effect*. For example, people have been known to behave in a drunken manner when they believe that the situation

calls for such behavior even when they have not been drinking alcohol but only thought they were. Patients have been known to report that therapy has helped them when objectively they were not any better. Because the therapist has devoted so much time to them, they feel they must be better!

In other cases, experimenters have been known to unwittingly produce the very responses they expected to get. Perhaps they behaved in subtle ways that encouraged their patients to behave in the "proper" fashion. This is especially likely to happen when the experimenter knows who are experimental subjects and who are control subjects. Clinicians have been known on occasion to unconsciously give a patient a little extra time on a test item simply because they expected the patient to do well.

To avoid the effects of experimenter or participant expectations, studies commonly use a *double-blind procedure*. Here, neither participant nor experimenter knows what treatment or procedure is being used. For example, if an investigator is interested in studying the effects of two drugs, the person dispensing the drug does not know which is which. Nor can the participant tell, because the two kinds of pills are identical in size, shape, color, weight, texture, taste, and so on. But double-blind studies are not always as "blind" as we think they are (Margraf et al., 1991).

Matching, random assignment of participants to experimental and control groups, use of control groups, and double-blind procedures are all methods of helping ensure that experiments will display internal validity.

External Validity. When it is discovered that the results of an experiment cannot be generalized beyond the narrow and exact conditions of the experiment, the research does not show *external validity*. If the Langer and Rodin results apply only to that specific nursing home, they have a problem. In fact, most experimental research is done with the hope of generalizing the results beyond the confines of the immediate setting. Actually, it can be very difficult to determine the external validity of a given study. All too often, results produced in the laboratory cannot be reproduced in real-life settings. The worst mistake is merely to assume that because certain results were produced in situation A, they will automatically occur in situation B. Although laboratory experimental research usually allows better control of variables, its "artificial" nature may prevent wide generalization.

Analog Research. The question of generalization of results is particularly salient for *analog studies*—studies that are conducted in the laboratory, where control is easier to exert, but whose conditions are said to be "analogous" to real life. Most often they are used to highlight the nature of psychopathology or therapy. For example, when Watson and Rayner (1920) tried to show how Little Albert could learn to be phobic for white rats, they were constructing an analog of the way they thought real-life phobias were acquired (see Box 4-1). As another example, some researchers study the correlates and effects of depression by inducing depressive mood in nondepressed participants through the use of traditional mood induction techniques (such as reading text that has been shown to increase levels of dysphoria), or of slides and music that induce certain mood states (for example, Goodwin & Sher, 1993). These techniques presumably create a depressive state analogous to that seen in clinical depression.

In one sense, almost all experimental studies are analog studies. But when severe practical or ethical constraints prevent us from creating real-life conditions, we must turn to analog situations. The advantage of analog studies is that better internal validity is possible because of the superior control we can exert in the laboratory. The Achilles heel of the method is the degree of similarity between the analog and the real thing. For example, suppose we decide to study the role of failure in creating depression. We do not want to study real depressives for several reasons. First, it is difficult for us to get a large-enough sample of them who have similar backgrounds and who are equally depressed. Second, would it really be

ethical to subject such people to a strong, significant failure experience and thereby risk plunging them even deeper into depression? This, by the way, illustrates a real dilemma with analog research. If our experimental manipulations are really effective, they may be harmful (and therefore unethical). If they are mild, the research becomes trivial and has little external validity (Suomi, 1982). Given the foregoing ethical constraints and the fact that analog conditions will allow us to control the degree and kind of failure, the nature of the subjects, and so on, the use of analog studies can become an attractive alternative.

But when we use analog procedures, we may pay a price. For example, in the previous hypothetical experiment, how do we know that our participants are really the same as participants professionally diagnosed as depressed? Perhaps the participants are recruits from General Psychology classes whose only claim to being depressed is a score above some cutoff point on a questionnaire that purports to measure depression. They are not *clinical* cases of depression. In addition, we have no assurance that an experience of failure on a problem in a laboratory setting is at all the same as a "real" failure in a depressive's everyday life.

Some have urged the use of animals for research because they do not present some of the methodological problems that exist in research with humans. We can exert nearly perfect control over animals. We can control their diets, living conditions, and even genetic background. We can be so much more intrusive in the lives of animals. Because animals generally have shorter life spans, phenomena that may take years to study in humans can be studied in a few months with, say, rats. Further, there are a number of "naturally" occurring behavior disorders (for example, aggression, mood disorders, hyperactivity, eating disorders) commonly seen in veterinary practice that appear to be relevant to the field of psychopathology (Stein, Dodman, Borchelt, & Hollander, 1994). But again, exactly how similar is animal behavior to human behavior? Perhaps similar enough in certain instances, but in others, not at all. In the final analysis, analog research is important and can be quite enlightening. But we can never afford to completely relinquish our skepticism when we employ it.

A Closing Note. In closing this section on experimental methods, it should be noted that not everyone is enamored with these traditional approaches. For example, many years ago Cattell (1965) critiqued the so-called *bivariate* research strategy. This is a hallowed method, going all the way back to Pavlov and Wundt, in which only two variables are studied at once. The investigator manipulates an independent variable and then observes its effects on the dependent variable. For example, the experimenter induces in participants the belief that they lack personal control over the onset of electric shock (independent variable). The question is, what happens to the participant's anxiety level as measured by the galvanic skin response (dependent variable)? If the focus is on anxiety, it may become necessary to carry out thousands of such bivariate studies to determine how people become anxious. The experimenters must vary measures of anxiety, the nature of the stimulus, and the presence of pre-existing personality traits that may affect the nature of the participants' responses. If experimenters vary one condition at a time in study after study, they are left with a piecemeal view of the human being. Putting the results of all these bivariate studies together can be worse than trying to put Humpty Dumpty together again. And because the study is looking at anxiety in isolation from other variables, such as competency and adjustment, the results offer no sense of how these variables might affect anxiety.

As a consequence, some have advocated the use of a *multivariate* strategy. Here, the experimenters use a variety of measures on the same person but do not exert much in the way of control. They may use questionnaire data, life records, observation, and so on. Such data can be correlated and factor-analyzed. Because the method can focus on naturally occurring phenomena and can deal with many variables simultaneously, many regard it as a superior strategy. However, this method, like other correlational approaches, also has its limitations (Phares, 1991).

Single-Case Designs

Single-case designs are an outgrowth of behavioral and operant approaches. They bear similarities to both experimental and case study methods. For example, an experimenter measures a subject's behavior under several conditions and in this sense is employing a method akin to experimental techniques. But the focus is on the responses of *one* participant only. Such research usually begins by establishing a baseline. Here, a record is made of the participant's behavior prior to any intervention—for example, the number of anxiety attacks per week. After a reliable baseline has been established, an intervention is introduced. The effects of this intervention are then determined by comparing the baseline level of behavior with the postintervention level. Single-case designs are often used to study the effectiveness of a therapeutic method.

Single-case studies allow the experimenter to establish cause-effect relationships. More than that, they provide a method of studying clinical behavior (especially therapy methods) that does not require the withholding of treatment by assigning certain participants to control groups or waiting lists. Some have argued that such controlled procedures, although representing good science, are essentially unethical because they may deprive people of hope for relief. Even though the therapy to be used may be unproved—and even though some assert that, in the interests of the ultimate good of many people, science must deprive a few of the possibility of improvement—the specter of ethics still lurks in the background.

Another practical reason for using single-case designs is that it is often extremely difficult in clinical settings to find enough participants for matching or random assignment to control groups. Single-case studies reduce the numbers needed. Also, some have argued that most research (personality and clinical alike) generalizes

FIGURE 4-5 Robbie: The giving and withdrawal of reinforcement

Source: "Effects of Teacher Attention on Study Behavior," by R. V. Hall, D. Lund, and D. Jackson, Journal *of Applied Behavior Analysis, 1, 1968, 1–12. Copyright 1968 by the Society for the Experimental analysis of behavior. Reprinted by permission.*

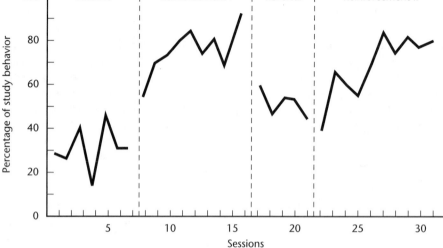

findings based on mean scores. Consequently, the results may not really apply to or characterize any one case (Lamiell, 1987). Single-case designs sidestep such problems.

The ABAB Design. The *ABAB design* permits measurement of a treatment's effectiveness by systematic observation of changes in the participant's behavior as treatment and no-treatment conditions alternate. It is called the ABAB design because the initial baseline period (A) is followed by a treatment period (B), a return to the baseline (A), and then a second treatment period (B).

A good illustration of the ABAB single-case approach is the study of Robbie (Hall, Lund, & Jackson, 1968). Robbie was a third grader who was very disruptive in the classroom. About 75% of his time was spent laughing, throwing things, and being a general nuisance. The rest of the time (25%), he studied. This baseline percentage of study time is shown in Figure 4-5. During the first treatment period (Reinforcement I), the teacher paid a lot of attention to Robbie, and his study behavior increased accordingly. During the reversal period, the teacher returned to her

former level of attention to Robbie, and his study behavior reverted to about the baseline level. When treatment was reintroduced (Reinforcement II), his behavior once again improved. The reversal period was inserted between the two treatment periods to enable the investigators to demonstrate a causal relationship between the teacher's behavior and Robbie's behavior.

One difficulty with the ABAB procedure is that withdrawing treatment could pose some ethical problems. However, the seriousness of this issue depends on the specific circumstances involved.

Multiple Baseline Designs. In some cases, it is impossible to use a reversal period. As we have noted, there may be ethical constraints. Also, in clinical research settings, therapists may be unwilling to have their clients reexperience situations that could reinstate the very behaviors they are seeking to eradicate. In such cases, investigators may use a *multiple baseline design*. Here, two or more behaviors are chosen for analysis. Perhaps an institutionalized patient has severe problems behaving in a responsible manner. He does not take care of his room, fails to follow good personal hygiene, or does not show up on time for work assignments. Baseline data are collected for his behavior in both personal and work settings. Next, immediate rewards are introduced whenever he behaves responsibly in personal settings but not in work settings. Then, after a prescribed period of time, measurements of behavior in both settings are once again collected. The last phase involves rewards for responsible behavior in both settings. If responsible behavior increases in the personal setting following reward but not in the work setting when there is no reward, it may be possible that some unknown and uncontrolled factor other than reward is operative. But if reward is then shown to enhance responsible behavior in the work setting also, it seems very unlikely that any factors other than reward are involved. The use of dual baselines gives investigators increased confidence in their manipulations.

A study by Moras, Telfer, and Barlow (1993) exemplifies a variant of the multiple baseline design. Their study is noteworthy for several reasons. First, they applied a single-case methodology to a treatment that is not primarily behavioral (unlike most applications of the single-case methodology). Second, they targeted a clinical condition that is common—coexisting generalized anxiety disorder and major depression—yet complex because of the myriad of presenting symptoms. Finally, they were able to test the hypothesis that each form of treatment used in the combined treatment (anxiety control treatment and interpersonal psychotherapy for depression) would affect specifically those symptoms for which the treatment was originally developed.

Box 4-3 presents Moras et al.'s (1993) descriptions of Case 2, a man in his 30s suffering from both generalized anxiety disorder and major depression, as well as his weekly scores on self-report measures of anxiety and depression throughout the treatment. As can be seen, Case 2's levels of anxiety (BAI scores) and depression (BDI scores) were elevated and clinically significant before treatment commenced (at baseline

weeks 1 and 2). Anxiety control treatment (ACT) was administered first for six sessions, followed by an assessment interview (Asmt). Next, interpersonal psychotherapy for depression (IDT) was administered for six sessions, followed by another assessment interview

Several features of the results for Case 2 are noteworthy. First, his anxiety scores did drop significantly over the course of ACT. However, so did his depression scores. Further, both depression and anxiety scores appeared to drop (although not as dramatically) during the IPT phase of treatment. Moras et al. concluded that this combined form of treatment (ACT and IPT) seems potentially efficacious for patients with generalized anxiety disorder and major depression. However, contrary to the original hypothesis, no evidence for differential and specific impact of ACT on anxiety symptoms and IPT on depressive symptoms was obtained.

This example illustrates nicely how the single-subject design can be used to document the efficacy of treatment (single or combined) for a commonly occurring clinical condition. Further, Moras et al., using a variant of the multiple baseline design, were able to test a hypothesis regarding the specificity of treatment effects.

Of course, all these single-subject designs, by definition, deal with one person. Can we generalize what has been shown to be true of one person to an entire population? As with case study methods, the external validity of the results or attempts to generalize about them can be problematic. But as long as we are interested in one specific person or are seeking evidence that will encourage us subsequently to initiate a full-blown traditional experimental study, the method has great merit.

Mixed Designs

Experimental and correlational techniques are sometimes combined into a *mixed design*. Here, participants who can be divided into specific populations (for example, schizophrenic versus normal) are assigned as groups to each experimental condition. In this way, variables such as

BOX 4-3

The Treatment of Mixed Anxiety and Depression

Moras, Telfer, and Barlow (1993, p. 414) provided the following description of Case 2:

> The patient was a man in his mid-30s who had three children (ranging in age from 4 to 12). He worked full time in a semiskilled position. His complaints were "breaking down easy and crying a lot," a "no care attitude," feeling nervous, and feeling like running from his job. When asked about relationships in his life, he said that he and his wife "seemed to be going their own

separate ways." However, he then quickly negated the statement by saying that they didn't seem to be growing apart; rather they seemed to be closer but more independent. The diagnosis based on two independent structured diagnostic interviews was co-principal Major Depression Episode (recurrent, moderate) 5 and GAD 5.

Below are the weekly scores produced by Case 2 on the Beck Anxiety Inventory (BAI) and Beck Depression Inventory (BDI).

Weekly changes in Beck Anxiety Inventory (BAI; Beck, Epstein, & Brown, 1988) and Beck Depression Inventory (BDI; Beck, Steer, & Garbin, 1988) scores for Case 2. (Ba1 = Baseline Week 1; Ba2 = Baseline Week 2; ACT = anxiety control treatment; Asmt = assessment week; IPT = Interpersonal Psychotherapy of Depression treatment)

Source: Moras, K., Telfer, L. A., & Barlow, D. H. (1993). Efficacy and specific effects data on new treatments: A case study strategy with mixed anxiety-depression. Journal of Consulting and Clinical Psychology, 61, 412–420. Copyright 1993 by the American Psychological Association.

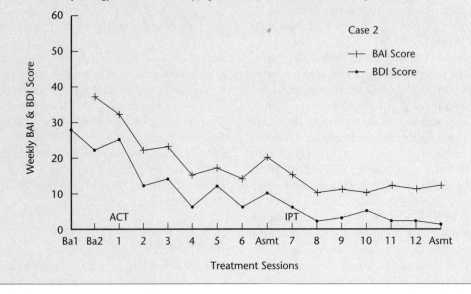

psychosis or normality are not manipulated or induced by the investigator. Instead, they are correlated with the experimental condition.

Davison and Neale (1998) provide an excellent hypothetical example of how mixed designs work. Suppose we decide to investigate the effi-

Figure 4-6 Effects of three treatments on patients whose problems vary in degree of severity
Source: From Abnormal Psychology, *7th ed., by G. C. Davison and J. M. Neale, p. 117. Copyright © 1998 by John Wiley & Sons, Inc. Reprinted by permission.*

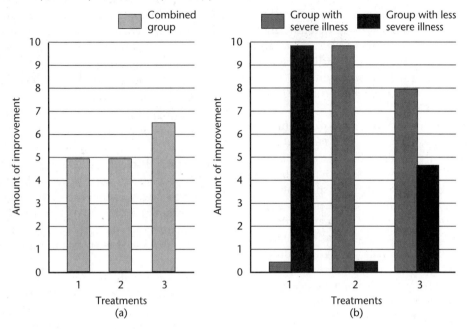

cacy of three forms of therapy (the experimental manipulation). We do this by identifying psychiatric patients who can be divided into two groups on the basis of the severity of their illness (the classificatory variable). Does effectiveness of treatment vary with severity of illness? The results of this hypothetical research are shown in Figure 4-6. Figure 4-6(b) presents data obtained when the patients were divided into two groups according to the severity of their illness. Figure 4-6(a) shows how confused we could become had patients not been divided into two groups. When all patients are combined, we find that treatment 3 produced the largest improvement, and we are mistakenly led to believe that this treatment is the best. But when we analyze the data according to severity of illness, treatment 3 is not the preferred one for either group of patients. Instead, as Figure 4-6(b) shows, for patients with less severe problems, treatment 1 is desirable, whereas for those with more severe problems, treatment 2 would be preferable.

Later in this book, it will become apparent that there is no "best" therapy for all problems and all people. There are only treatments that vary in their effectiveness for different kinds of psychological problems and different kinds of people. Mixed designs can help us discern what is best for whom. Of course, we must not forget that in mixed designs, one of the factors (for example, severity of illness) is not manipulated, and this raises the kinds of problems discussed earlier in the case of correlational methods (Davison & Neale, 1998).

Statistical versus Practical Significance

After a statistic (such as a correlation coefficient) has been calculated, it can be determined whether the obtained number is significant. Traditionally, if it is found that the obtained value (or a more extreme value) could be expected to occur by chance alone less than 5 times out of 100, it is deemed statistically significant. Such an obtained value is said to be significant at the .05 level, usually written as $p < .05$. The larger the correlation, the more likely it is to be significant. But when large numbers of participants are involved, even relatively small correlations can be significant. With 180 participants, a correlation of .19 will be significant; when only 30 participants are involved, a correlation of .30 would fail to be significant.

Therefore, it is important to distinguish between *statistical significance* and *practical significance* when interpreting statistical results. The correlation of .19 may be significant, but the magnitude of the relationship is still quite modest. For example, it might be true that in a study involving 5000 second-year graduate students in clinical psychology across the nation, there is a correlation of .15 between their GRE scores and faculty ratings of academic competence. Even though the relationship is not a chance one, the actual importance is rather small. Most of the variance in faculty ratings is due to factors other than GRE scores. In some cases, a correlation of .15 may be judged important, but in many instances, it is not. At the same time, we should remember that accepting significance levels of .05 as nonchance represents a kind of scientific tradition—it is not sacred. Other information may persuade us, in certain cases, that significance levels of .07 or .09, for example, should be taken seriously.

Research and Ethics

In Chapter 3, we discussed some of the ethical issues involved in the practice of clinical psychology. Research, too, involves important ethical considerations. Like patients, research participants have rights, and investigators have responsibilities to them.

In 1992, the American Psychological Association published an expanded and updated set of ethical standards for research with human participants (APA, 1992). We offer only a brief overview here. These standards require that investigators:

1. Plan research according to recognized standards of scientific competence and ethical principles

2. Implement safeguards for the welfare of participants, others that may be affected by the research, and animal subjects

3. Retain responsibility for ensuring ethical practices in research

4. Comply with pertinent federal and state law and regulations

5. Gain appropriate approval from host institutions or organizations before conducting research

6. Establish clear and fair agreements with their research participants so that the rights and obligations of each party are clarified

7. Obtain the informed consent of research participants, using language that is easily understandable to them, and document their consent

8. Take great care, in offering inducements for research participation, that the nature of the compensation (such as professional services) is made clear and that financial or other types of inducements are not be so excessive as to coerce participation

9. Use deception as part of their procedures only when it is not possible to use alternative methods

10. Protect participants from any mental and physical discomfort, harm, and danger that might arise during the research

11. Inform research participants of the anticipated use of the data and of the possibility of sharing the data with other investigators or any unanticipated future uses

12. Minimize the invasiveness of research procedures

13. Provide participants with information at the close of the research to erase any misconceptions that may have arisen

14. Treat animal subjects humanely and in accordance with federal, state, and local laws, as well as with professional standards

Several of these points require further comment.

BOX 4-4

Hot Topic   *Who Should Be Studied?*

For some time, clinical psychologists conducting research have been criticized for primarily using samples of convenience. Typically, the criticism has focused on the use of college undergraduates in analog research. However, over the past few decades, a great deal of concern has been expressed over the relative lack of research using women and/or ethnic minority participants. Specifically, some feel that too many studies use samples composed predominantly of white males. Some feel that the conclusions reached regarding psychological problems and their treatment may not be valid for women or for people of color.

Not only have these concerns heightened clinical scientists' awareness of these issues, but more formal requirements for those studies supported by United States government funds are now in place. The National Institutes of Health (NIH) now have a policy regarding the inclusion of women and members of minority groups in all studies involving human participants. Specifically, these groups must be represented in NIH-supported projects unless a clear and compelling rationale establishes that inclusion is inappropriate with respect to participants' health or to the purpose of the study. In this way, it is hoped that major research projects can address whether the general conclusions reached for men or for white participants also hold for women and for members of minority groups.

Informed Consent. Good ethical practice as well as legal requirements demand that participants give their formal *informed consent* (usually in writing) prior to their participation in research. Researchers inform the participants of any risks, discomforts, or limitations on confidentiality. Further, researchers inform the participants of any compensation for their participation. In the process, the researcher agrees to guarantee the participant's privacy, safety, and freedom to withdraw. Unless participants know the general purpose of the research and the procedures that will be used, they cannot fully exercise their rights. Box 4-5 presents an example of a consent form that was used in one of the author's research projects. Other consent forms from other investigators and other institutions will likely vary in the language that is used and, possibly, the points that are emphasized. However, most consent forms would be expected to contain the basic features in this example.

Confidentiality. Participants' individual data and responses should be confidential and guarded from public scrutiny. Instead of names, code numbers are typically used to protect anonymity. While the results of the research are usually open to the public, they are presented in such a way that no one can identify a specific participant's data. Finally, clinical psychologists must obtain consent before disclosing any confidential or personally identifiable information in the psychologist's writings, lectures, or presentations in any other public media (such as a television interview).

Deception. Sometimes, the purpose of the research or the meaning of a participant's responses is withheld. Such *deception* should be used only when the research is important and there is no alternative to the deception (in other words, when veridical information would compromise participants' data). Deception should

BOX 4-5

Sample Consent Form

Development of Personality Features
Consent Form
Code _____

Consent to Serve as a Participant in Research Study

I consent to participate in the study "Development of Personality Features" sponsored by the Psychology Department at the University of Missouri and conducted under the direction of Timothy J. Trull, Ph.D. This research project is aimed at assessing how personality features develop in young adults.

I understand that the study will involve the following procedures: (1) At Time 1 (study entry), I will be asked a number of questions, some of which may be extremely sensitive or upsetting, concerning various personal problems that I might have experienced as well as personal problems my biological parents may have experienced (e.g., depression, suicidal feelings, child abuse). I understand that I will also complete a computerized interview and will be given two interview questionnaires that allow the researcher to develop a psychological profile. I understand that these interviews will be audiotaped. Only project staff will have access to these audiotapes, and these tapes will be erased at the end of the project. For my participation at Time 1, which should take a total of about four hours, I will be compensated $35.00 for my time and efforts.

(2) At Time 2 (2 years later), I will be asked a number of questions, some of which may be extremely sensitive or upsetting, concerning various personal problems that I might have experienced as well as personal problems my biological parents may have experienced. I understand that I will also complete a computerized interview and will be given two interview questionnaires that allow the researcher to develop a psychological profile. For my participation at Time 2, which should take a total of about four hours, I will be compensated $35.00 for my time and efforts. Therefore, if I participate in all aspects of this study (i.e., at Time 1 and at Time 2) I will receive a total of $70.00. I also understand that I may be contacted at some point in the future and asked to provide follow-up information. I understand that I am under no obligation to participate at that time and I may at any time withdraw and request that I not be asked to participate in the future.

I give the project director permission to gain access to the following information from the University of Missouri–Columbia Office of Admissions and Registrar: high school rank and percentile, ACT scores, GPA at MU, standardized test scores at MU, and possibly some other information related to academic performance.

I understand that all possible steps have been taken to assure my privacy. I understand that the project staff will code the results of this research in such a manner that my identity will not be attached physically to the information I contribute. The key listing my identity and participant code number will be kept separate from the information in a locked file accessible only to the project staff. This key will be destroyed at the conclusion of the research project. Although the researchers do not know at this point when additional follow-ups may be attempted, the project will be concluded within 15 years time. I also understand that these identifiers will be preserved for the duration of the project unless I request otherwise. I understand that I may contact the project director at any time and request that all identifiers that link my identity to the information I have contributed be destroyed. If requested, all data I have contributed and all identifying information will be destroyed by the project director (Dr. Trull).

I realize that the purpose of this project is to examine the relations between certain variables in groups of individuals and not to evaluate the responses of a particular individual. I also understand that responding to some of the questions about personal problems, feelings, and behavior as well as about problems my biological parents may have experienced may cause discomfort because of their sensitive nature.

I understand that in the unlikely event that I am found to be suicidal or an imminent threat to someone else, the appropriate authorities will be contacted. Also, if I divulge information indicating that I am aware of possible ongoing child abuse or information raising the suspicion of ongoing child abuse, appropriate authorities will have to be notified. I understand that, although remote, it is possible that the information I contribute may be subject to subpoena.

I understand that participation is voluntary, that there is no penalty for refusal to participate, and that I am free to withdraw my consent and discontinue my participation before I complete the session. I also understand that I may refuse to answer any individual questions without penalty. In the event that I elect to discontinue participation, I understand that I will not receive any compensation and that any information I have contributed at any time to the study that is linked to me individually in any way will be destroyed. My name or any other identifiers also will be removed completely from the records.

If at any time I have questions about any procedures in this project, I understand that I may contact the project director, Timothy J. Trull, Ph.D., at 123-456-7890.

Name (Print): _____

Signature _____

Student Number _____

Date _____

never be used lightly. When it is used, extreme care must be taken that participants do not leave the research setting feeling exploited or disillusioned. It is important that careful debriefing be undertaken so that participants are told exactly why the deception was necessary. We do not want participants' levels of interpersonal trust to be shaken. Clearly, it is very important how we obtain informed consent when deception is involved.

An example of the need for deception in a study might be an experiment in which it is predicted that the viewing of gun magazines (or other materials associated with potential violence) will lead to increased scores on a ques-

tionnaire measuring hostility. All participants are told that the experiment is one focusing on short-term memory, and they will be completing a memory task on two occasions separated by a 15-minute waiting period during which they will be reading magazine articles. All participants first complete baseline measures (including the hostility questionnaire). Next, all participants complete a computer-administered memory task. During the waiting period, the experimental group is told to read selections from a gun magazine that is made available in the lab; the control group is told to read selections from a nature magazine (neutral with regard to violent imagery). All participants later complete the computer-administered memory task again. Finally, all participants complete the battery of self-report instruments a second time.

We are not so much interested in the viability of this hypothesis as we are in the need for some deception in the experiment. As you can see, to tell the participants the real purpose of the experiment would likely influence their responses to the questionnaires (especially to the one measuring hostility). Therefore, the investigator might need to introduce the experiment as one that is focusing on short-term memory.

Debriefing. Because participants have a right to know why researchers are interested in studying their behavior, a *debriefing* at the end of the research is mandatory. It should be explained to participants why the research is being carried out, why it is important, and what the results have been. In some cases, it is not possible to discuss results because the research is still in progress. But subjects can be told what kinds of results are expected and that they may return at a later date for a complete briefing if they wish.

Fraudulent Data. It hardly seems necessary to mention that investigators are under the strictest standards of honesty in reporting their data. Under no circumstances may they alter obtained data in any way. To do so can bring charges of fraud and create enormous legal, professional, and ethical problems for the investigator. Although the frequency of fraud in psychological research has so far been minimal, we must be on guard. There is no quicker way to lose the trust of the public than through fraudulent practices.

The complete APA Ethical Principles and Code of Conduct, including the principles relevant to conducting research, can be accessed through web site 4-1 at the end of this chapter.

Chapter Summary

Clinical psychologists use a wide variety of research methods to test theoretical propositions about human behavior. Research also leads to modification of theories in a type of feedback-loop system. Observational methods range from unsystematic and naturalistic observation, where little if any situational control can be exerted by the scientist, to more controlled forms of observation in which the researcher controls to some degree the situation in which the target behavior will be observed.

The case study method is a form of controlled observation that involves the intensive study and description of one person in treatment. Case studies document rare or unusual conditions or events, help disconfirm theories or explanations believed to apply to everyone, and facilitate the generation of hypotheses. However, case study methods typically do not result in universal laws or principles applicable to all and cannot lead to cause-effect conclusions.

Epidemiological methods are used to estimate the prevalence and incidence of a disorder or condition in the population. These methods also enable us to identify risk factors.

Correlational methods assess and quantify the relations between variables; this may stimulate ideas or theories about causal relations among variables. However, correlation is a necessary but not sufficient indicator of causation, which can only be established through experimental methods.

Cross-sectional designs involve an examination of participants at one point in time, whereas longitudinal designs evaluate the same participants over a period of time. Longitudinal studies allow scientists to evaluate time-order relationships among factors that vary together, and help address third variable explanations of observed relations. Unfortunately, longitudinal studies are time-intensive and expensive and are less frequently conducted than cross-sectional studies.

The experimental method is powerful because it enables scientists to evaluate cause-effect questions and to exert control over a number of potentially important factors that affect the behavior in question. Internal validity refers to the degree to which, based on the design of the experiment, we can be confident that the manipulation of the independent variable affected the dependent variable. External validity refers to the extent to which the results of the experiment are generalizable to other, preferably "real-world," conditions. In some instances, for practical or ethical reasons, it is not possible to conduct experiments on real-life problems. In these cases, analog studies may be used.

An important variant of the experimental and case study methods is the single-case design (for example, ABAB design, multiple baseline design). The mixed design combines features of the correlational and experimental methods and helps us evaluate which interventions are best for whom. Finally, a number of ethical considerations are involved in conducting research, including obtaining informed consent, assuring confidentiality, using deception appropriately, providing debriefing information, and protecting against fraud.

Key Terms

ABAB designs Single-case designs that observe systematic changes in the participant's behavior as the treatment and no-treatment conditions alternate. The initial baseline period is followed by a treatment period, a treatment reversal period, and a second treatment period.

analog study A study conducted in the laboratory under conditions that are purportedly analogous to real life.

between-group designs Designs in which two or more separate groups of participants each receive a different kind of treatment.

case study method A research method consisting of the intensive description or study of one person (usually a client or patient who is in treatment).

confidentiality In human subjects' research, confidentiality refers to the principle of protecting individual participants' data from public scrutiny.

confound A situation in which extraneous variables are not controlled or cannot be shown to exist equally in one's experimental and control groups. When there is a confound, one cannot attribute changes in the dependent variable to the manipulation of the independent variable.

control group The group in an experimental design that does not receive the treatment of interest. In the perfect experimental design, the experimental and control groups are similar on all variables except for the treatment variable.

controlled observation A research method similar to naturalistic observation, in which carefully planned observations are made in real-life settings, except that the investigator exerts a degree of control over the events being observed.

correlation coefficient A statistic (usually symbolized by r) that describes the relationship between two variables. r ranges between -1.00 and $+1.00$; its sign indicates the direction of the association, and its absolute value indicates the strength.

correlation matrix An array that displays the correlations between all possible pairs of variables in the array.

correlational methods Statistical methods that allow us to determine whether one variable is related to another. In general, correlational methods do not allow us to draw inferences about cause and effect.

cross-sectional design A research design that compares different groups of individuals at one point in time.

debriefing In human subjects' research, the legal requirement that researchers explain to participants the purpose, importance, and results of the research following their participation.

deception Deception is sometimes used in research when knowing the true purpose of a study would change the participants' responses or produce nonveridical data.

dependent variable The variable in an experimental design that is measured by the investigator.

double-blind procedure A procedure for circumventing the effects of experimenter or participant expectations. In a double-blind study, neither the participant nor the experimenter knows what treatment the participant is receiving until the very end of the study.

epidemiology The study of the incidence, prevalence, and distribution of illness or disease in a given population.

expectations What the investigator or the research participant anticipates about the experimental outcome.

experimental group The group in an experimental design that receives the treatment of interest.

experimental hypothesis The theory or proposal on which an experimental study is based. Often the hypothesis predicts the effects of the treatment administered.

experimental method A research strategy that allows the researcher to determine cause-and-effect relationships between variables or events.

external validity An experiment is considered externally valid to the extent that its results are generalizable beyond the narrow conditions of the study.

factor The hypothesized dimension underlying an interrelated set of variables.

factor analysis A statistical method for examining the interrelationships among a number of variables at the same time. This method uses many separate correlations to determine which variables change together and thus may have some underlying dimension in common.

fraudulent data Data that are fabricated, altered, or otherwise falsified by the experimenter.

incidence The rate of new cases of a disease or disorder that develop within a given period of time. Incidence figures allow us to determine whether the rate of new cases is stable or changing from one time period to the next.

independent variable The variable in an experimental design that is manipulated by the investigator.

informed consent In human subjects' research, the legal requirement that researchers inform potential participants about the general purpose of the study, the procedures that will be used, any risks, discomforts, or limitations on confidentiality, any compensation for participation, and their freedom to withdraw from the study at any point.

internally valid An experiment is considered internally valid to the extent that the change in the dependent variable is attributable to the manipulation of the independent variable.

longitudinal design A research design that compares the same group of individuals at two or more points in time.

matching A term used when research participants in the experimental and control groups are "matched" or similar on variables (e.g., age, sex) that may affect the outcome of the research.

mixed designs Research designs that combine both experimental and correlational methods. In this design, participants from naturally occurring groups of interest (e.g., people with panic disorder and people with social phobia) are assigned to each experimental treatment, allowing the experimenter to determine whether the effectiveness of the treatments varies by group classification.

multiple baseline designs Design used when it is not possible or ethical to employ a treatment reversal period. In this design, baselines are established for two (or more) behaviors, treatment is introduced for one behavior, and then treatment is introduced for the second behavior as well. By observing changes in each behavior from period to period, one may draw conclusions about the effectiveness of the treatments.

naturalistic observation A research method in which carefully planned observations are made in real-life settings.

placebo effect Describes the case where the expectations for the experimental manipulation cause the outcome, rather than (or in addition to) the manipulation itself.

prevalence The overall rate of cases (new or old) within a given period of time. Prevalence figures allow us to estimate what percentage of the target population is affected by the illness or disorder.

retrospective data Data based upon people's reports of past experiences and events.

risk factor A variable (e.g., demographic, environmental) that increases a person's risk of experiencing a particular disease or disorder over his or her lifetime.

scatterplot A visual representation of the relationship between two variables. The scatterplot consists of an *x*-axis (labeled to reflect one variable), a *y*-axis (labeled to reflect the other variable), and a number of data points, each corresponding to one person's scores on both variables.

single-case designs Designs that focus on the responses of only one participant. Usually, an intervention is introduced after a reliable baseline is established, and the effects of the intervention are determined by comparing the baseline and post-intervention levels of behavior.

statistical significance A term used to describe statistical values that would not be expected to occur solely on the basis of chance. By convention, a value is considered statistically significant if it would be expected to occur by chance alone fewer than five times out of 100.

third variable problem The possibility that a correlation between variables A and B is due to the influence of an unknown third variable, rather than to a causal relationship between A and B.

within-group designs Designs in which the same group of participants is compared at different points in time (say, before and after a treatment is administered).

Web Sites of Interest

To visit any of the web sites listed below, go to www.wadsworth.com and click on Links.

4-1   APA Ethical Principles and Code of Conduct

4-2   Research with Animals in Psychology

4-3   Guidelines for Ethical Conduct in the Care and Use of Animals

4-4   APA Guidelines for Providers of Psychological Services to Ethnic, Linguistic, and Culturally Diverse Populations

4-5   Research Methods Tutorials

CHAPTER FIVE

Diagnosis and Classification of Psychological Problems

FIGURE 5-1 In the nineteenth century people were treated for depression by spinning them in a rotating chair.
The Bettmann Archive. © Bettmann/CORBIS.

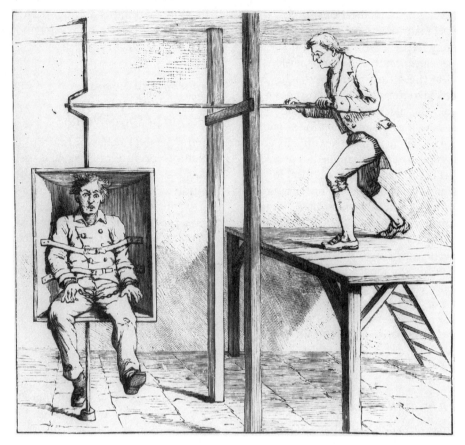

Clinical psychology is usually thought of as an applied field. Clinicians attempt to apply empirically supported psychological principles to problems of adjustment and abnormal behavior. Typically this involves finding successful ways of changing the behavior, thoughts, and feelings of clients. In this way, clinical psychologists lessen their clients' maladjustment or dysfunction or increase their levels of adjustment.

Before clinicians can formulate and administer interventions, however, they must first assess their clients' symptoms of psychopathology and levels of maladjustment. Interestingly, the precise definitions of these and related terms can be elusive. Further, the manner in which the terms are applied to clients is sometimes quite unsystematic.

Clinical psychology has moved beyond the primitive views that defined mental illness as possession by demons or spirits. Maladjustment is no longer considered a state of sin. The eighteenth and nineteenth centuries ushered in the notion that "insane" individuals are sick and require humane treatment. Even then, however, mental health practices could be bizarre, to say the least (see Figure 5-1). Clearly, clinical psychologists' contemporary views are considerably more sophisticated than those of their forebears. Yet many view current treatments such as electroconvulsive therapy (ECT) with some skepticism and concern. Still others may see the popularity of treatments using psychotropic medications (such as antipsychotic, antidepressant, antimanic, or antianxiety medications) as less than enlightened. Finally, many forms of "psychological treatment" (for example, primal scream therapy, age regression therapy) are questionable at best. All of these treatment approaches and views are linked to the ways clinical psychologists decide who needs assessment, treatment, or intervention, as well as the rationale for providing these services. These judgments are influenced by the labels or diagnoses often applied to people.

In this chapter, we will take a critical look at some of clinical psychology's definitions and labels. In this way, perhaps we can clarify some of the issues involved in their use.

To give you a better idea of the activities of clinical psychologists who specialize in abnormal behavior or psychopathology, we present a specific example in Profile 5-1. This profile describes the work of a *psychopathologist*, a scientist who studies the causes of mental disorders as well as the factors that influence the development of mental disorders.

What Is Abnormal Behavior?

Ask ten different people for a definition of abnormal behavior and you may get ten different answers. Some of the reasons that abnormal behavior is so difficult to define are (1) no single descriptive feature is shared by all forms of abnormal behavior, and no one criterion for "abnormality" is sufficient; and (2) no discrete boundary exists between normal and abnormal behavior. Many myths about abnormal behavior survive and flourish even in this age of enlightenment. For example, many individuals still equate abnormal behavior with (1) bizarre behavior, (2) dangerous behavior, or (3) shameful behavior.

In this section, we will examine in some detail three proposed definitions of abnormal behavior: (1) conformity to norms, (2) the experience of subjective distress, and (3) disability or dysfunction. We will discuss the pros and cons of each definition. Although each of these three definitions highlights an important part of our understanding of abnormal behavior, each definition, by itself, is incomplete.

Conformity to Norms: Statistical Infrequency or Violation of Social Norms

When a person's behavior tends to conform to prevailing social norms or when this particular behavior is frequently observed in other people, the individual is not likely to come to the attention of mental health professionals. However, when a person's behavior becomes patently deviant, outrageous, or otherwise nonconforming, then he or she is more likely to be categorized as "abnormal." Let us consider some examples.

The Case of Billy A.

Billy is now in the second grade. He is of average height and weight and manifests no physical problems. He is somewhat aggressive and tends to bully children smaller than himself. His birth was a normal one, and although he was a bit slow in learning to walk and talk, the deficit was not marked. The first grade was difficult for Billy, and his progress was slow. By the end of the school year, he was considerably behind the rest of the class. However, the school officials decided to pass him anyway. They reasoned that he was merely a bit slow in maturing and would "come around" shortly. They noted that his status as an only child, a pair of doting parents, a short attention span, and aggressiveness were all factors that combined to produce his poor school performance.

At the beginning of the second grade, Billy was administered a routine achievement test, on which he did very poorly. As a matter of school policy, he was referred to the school psychologist for individual testing and evaluation. Based on

PROFILE 5-1

Kenneth J. Sher, Ph.D.

A psychopathologist is a scientist who studies how mental disorders develop, as well as the causes (etiology) of mental disorders. A relatively small, but very productive, proportion of clinical psychologists who conduct research call themselves psychopathologists. Kenneth J. Sher is a prominent psychopathologist whose research focuses on the etiology and development of alcohol use disorders.

Dr. Sher is the Middlebush Professor of Psychology at the University of Missouri–Columbia. He has published well over 100 books, book chapters, or empirical articles on issues related to alcohol use disorders, methodology in psychopathology research, and personality-psychopathology relations. Dr. Sher has received multiple federal grants to support his research, and he has received numerous awards that acknowledge his scientific contributions.

Dr. Sher's empirical work has evaluated many theories of alcohol use (for example, tension reduction, self-awareness), as well as factors that influence the development of alcohol use disorders in "at-risk" subjects (biological offspring of fathers diagnosed with alcoholism). Dr. Sher is currently conducting a major prospective study that assesses "at-risk" subjects at regular intervals during their collegiate and young adult years. For example, one

of the studies from this large project found that children of alcoholics (COAs) reported a greater number of alcohol and drug problems, stronger alcohol expectancies, greater behavioral under-control, and lower academic achievement than control subjects who did not have a family history of alcoholism (Sher, Walitzer, Wood, & Brent, 1991). Data from the prospective phase of Dr. Sher's study will be used to evaluate a variety of theoretical models for how alcohol problems and other forms of psychopathology develop in children of alcoholics.

Dr. Sher responded to several questions we posed concerning his background and interests, as well as his predictions about future trends for clinical psychology and psychopathology research.

What originally got you interested in the field of clinical psychology?

I'm not really sure. Clinical psychology was the fourth and final focus of my undergraduate studies. I arrived at college with an interest in becoming a marine biologist. If the college had had any relevant courses when I arrived (it was in the middle of Ohio), I'd probably be a marine biologist today. After a brief stint as a communications major (focusing on broadcast media), I became a psychology major. At first, I was interested in becoming a cognitive psychologist because nothing seemed as fundamental a question as "What is thought?" and "How do we think?" However, I found the cognitive psychology of the time (early 1970s) to be overly behavioral and philosophically barren (a far cry from the current state of cognitive science).

My interest in clinical psychology gelled while working as a research assistant for Mardi Horowitz, an academic psychiatrist in San Francisco. There, I became convinced that much can be learned about human nature from an integrated research program including clinical studies (which help to describe phenomena), epidemiological investigations (which serve to establish the extent and course

(continued)

Profile 5-1 (continued)

of phenomena in the population), and laboratory research (which can help test specific hypotheses about underlying mechanisms). Horowitz told me that going into clinical psychology "would be the biggest mistake of my life"; he thought I should go to medical school, and my mother, of course, agreed. However, I've never once regretted my choice—although having a lab on a marine research vessel would have been nice too.

Describe what activities you are involved in as a clinical psychologist, as well as your areas of expertise.

I am primarily a researcher. I conduct both laboratory research on individual differences in alcohol effects and field studies of the course of substance use disorders in young adults. I am particularly interested in the interplay of the person and the environment and how risk for and protection from various "bad" outcomes unfold over time in the developing human. Much of my time is spent supervising graduate student research, analyzing data, writing, and peer review (both scholarly articles and grant reviews). I am also involved in a fair amount of administrative activities in the Psychology Department here. I'd say my main expertise is in clinical research methods, alcoholism, anxiety, and comorbidity research.

What are the future trends you see for clinical psychology?

I always think it is hazardous to guess the future, but it is clear that the role of the clinical psychologist as an independent health care provider is diminishing as a function of an oversupply of psychologists, competition from other mental health providers, and managed care. However, with challenges also come opportunities, and the changing mental health

scene could provide opportunities for clinical psychologists to have great influence in devising new treatment protocols, supervising treatment staff, and developing behavioral health policies. On the research front, clinical psychologists are uniquely trained to bridge multiple disciplines and can serve as leaders or important collaborators on a variety of research initiatives in basic research in psychopathology and health and in evaluating treatment outcomes.

What are the most promising areas for psychopathology research?

Psychopathology is poised to have a number of important new discoveries because of basic advances in allied disciplines. For example, recent developments in neuroimaging (PET, fMRI) provide the tools to better understand brain mechanisms underlying certain forms of abnormal thought and behavior. The molecular genetic revolution will permit us to discover genes that contribute to various behavior disorders and, by helping us understand how they work in the context of the environment, should tell us much about underlying biology as well as key environmental processes. At present, many psychologists are defensive about genetic research, fearing that it will trivialize or marginalize basic research on behavior. I hold the opposite view: Advances in genetics will permit us to refine our notions about the role of nongenetic influences on behavior. Also, dramatic advances in statistical methodology and an increased emphasis on the importance of prospective data will help us to better characterize psychopathology over the life course and will likely change our diagnostic system to one that views psychopathology more in the context of development.

the results of the Stanford-Binet Intelligence Scale, a Draw-a-Person Test, school records, and a social history taken from the parents, the psychologist concluded that Billy suffered from mental retardation. His IQ was 64 on the Stanford-Binet and was estimated to be 61 based on the Draw-a-Person Test. Further, a social maturity index derived from parental reports of his social behavior was quite low.

The Case of Martha L.

Martha seemed to have a normal childhood. She made adequate progress in school and caused few problems for her teachers or parents. Although she never made friends easily, she could not be described as withdrawn. Her medical history was negative. When Martha entered high school, changes began. She combed her hair in a very severe, plain style. She chose clothing that was quite ill fitting and almost like that worn 50 years ago. She wore neither makeup nor jewelry of any kind. Where before she would have been hard to distinguish from the other girls in her class, she now easily stood out.

Martha's schoolwork began to slip. She spent hours alone in her room reading the Bible. She also began slipping notes to other girls that commented on their immorality when she observed them holding hands with boys, giggling, dancing, and so on. She attended religious services constantly; sometimes on Sundays she went to services at five or six separate churches. She fasted frequently and decorated her walls at home with countless pictures of Christ, religious quotations, and crucifixes.

When Martha finally told her parents that she was going to join an obscure religious sect and travel about the country (in a state of poverty) to bring Christ's message to the country, they became concerned and took her to a psychiatrist. Shortly afterward, she was hospitalized. Her diagnosis varied, but it included such terms as schizophrenia, paranoid type; schizoid personality; and schizophrenia, undifferentiated type.

Both of these cases are examples of individuals commonly seen by clinical psychologists for evaluation or treatment. The feature that immediately characterizes both cases is that Billy's and Martha's behaviors violate norms. Billy may be considered abnormal because his IQ and school performance depart considerably from the mean. This aspect of deviance from the norm is very clear in Billy's case, because it can be described statistically and with numbers. Once this numerical categorization is accomplished, Billy's assignment to the deviant category is assured. Martha also came to people's attention because she is *different*. Her clothes, appearance, and interests do not conform to the norms typical of females in her culture.

Advantages of This Definition. The definition of abnormality in terms of statistical infrequency or violation of social norms is attractive for at least two reasons.

1. *Cutoff Points:* The statistical infrequency approach is appealing because it establishes *cutoff points* that are quantitative in nature. If the cutoff point on a scale is 80 and an individual scores a 75, the decision to label that individual's behavior as abnormal is relatively straightforward. This principle of statistical deviance is frequently used in the interpretation of psychological test scores. The test authors designate a cutoff point in the test manual, often based on statistical deviance from the mean score obtained by a "normal" sample of test-takers, and scores at or beyond the cutoff are considered "clinically significant" (that is, abnormal or deviant).

2. *Intuitive Appeal:* It may seem obvious to us that those behaviors we ourselves consider abnormal would be evaluated similarly by others. The struggle to define exactly what abnormal behavior is does not tend to bother us because, as a Supreme Court justice once said about pornography, we believe that we know it when we see it.

Problems with This Definition. Conformity criteria seem to play a subtle yet important role in our judgments of others. However, although we must systematically seek the determinants of the individual's nonconformity or deviance, we should resist the reflexive tendency to categorize every nonconformist behavior as evidence of mental health problems. Conformity criteria, in fact, have a number of problems.

1. *Choice of Cutoff Points:* Conformity-oriented definitions are limited by the difficulty of establishing agreed-upon cutoff points. As noted previously, a cutoff is very easy to use once it is established. However, very few guidelines are available for choosing the cutoff point. For example, in the case of Billy, is there something magical about an IQ of 64? Traditional practice sets the cutoff point at 70. Get an IQ below 70 and you may be diagnosed with mental retardation. But is a score of 69 all that different from a score of 72? Rationally justifying such arbitrary IQ cutoff points is difficult. This problem is equally salient in Martha's case. Are five crucifixes on the wall too many? Is attendance at three church services per week acceptable?

2. *The Number of Deviations:* Another difficulty with nonconformity standards is the number of behaviors that one must evidence in order to earn the label "deviant." In Martha's case, was it just the crucifixes, or was it the total behavioral configuration—crucifixes, clothes, makeup, withdrawal, fasting, and so on? Had Martha manifested only three categories of unusual behavior, would we still classify her as deviant?

3. *Cultural Relativity:* Martha's case, in particular, illustrates an additional point. Her behavior was not deviant in some absolute sense. Had she been a member of an exceptionally religious family that subscribed to radical religious beliefs and practices, she might never have been classified as maladjusted. In short, what is deviant for one group is not necessarily so for another. Thus, the notion of *cultural relativity* is important. Likewise, judgments can vary, depending on whether family, school authorities, or peers are making them. Such variability may contribute to considerable diagnostic unreliability, because even clinicians' judgments may be relative to those of the group or groups to which they belong.

Appearance or dress may violate social norms but does not necessarily indicate abnormality or psychopathology. *PhotoDisc*

Two other points about cultural relativity are also relevant. First, carrying cultural relativity notions to the extreme can place nearly every reference group beyond reproach. Cultures can be reduced to subcultures and subcultures to minicultures. If we are not careful, this reduction process can result in our judging nearly every behavior as healthy. Second, the elevation of conformity to a position of preeminence can be alarming. One is reminded that so-called nonconformists have made some of the most beneficial social contributions. It can also become very easy to remove those whose different or unusual behavior bothers society. Some years ago in Russia, political dissidents were often placed in mental hospitals. In America, it sometimes happens that 70-year-old Uncle Arthur's family is successful in hospitalizing him largely to obtain his power of attorney. His deviation is that, at

BOX 5-1

Hot Topic   *Culture and Psychopathology*

Culture may influence the manifestation, course, and treatment of psychopathology in many ways (Basic Behavioral Science Task Force of the National Advisory Mental Health Council, 1996):

- Although there are similarities across cultures in how emotions are expressed facially, the way emotions and bodily changes are experienced and interpreted varies across cultures.
- Race and ethnicity continue to appear to be risk factors for mental illness and psychosocial dysfunction.
- Racial and ethnic discrimination can produce chronic levels of stress that have mental health consequences.
- There is a substantial relationship between socioeconomic status (SES) and mental illness, and low SES may play a causal role in the onset and course of certain mental disorders.
- In the United States, the increase of women in the workforce may have important effects on marital relationships, parenting practices, and children's adjustment.

Therefore, clinical psychologists must consider cultural factors when evaluating a client or patient for abnormal behavior or psychopathology. As a reminder to clinicians, DSM-IV (the official diagnostic manual of mental disorders, discussed later in this chapter) provides three types of information relevant to cultural considerations:

- Cultural variations in the clinical presentations of the various mental disorders are discussed in the text.
- Culture-bound syndromes (for example, *koro* in East Asian countries) are described.
- An outline for "cultural formulation" is presented. The cultural formulation provides a systematic review of the individual's cultural identity, cultural explanations for the presenting problems, cultural factors related to the psychosocial environment, and potential cultural influences on the relationship between the individual and the clinician.

---

age 70, he is spending too much of the money that will eventually be inherited by the family. Finally, if all these points are not enough, *excessive* conformity has itself sometimes been the basis for judging persons abnormal.

Subjective Distress

We now shift the focus from the perceptions of the observer to the perceptions of the affected individual. Here the basic data are not observable deviations of behavior, but the subjective feelings and sense of well-being of the individual. Whether a person feels happy or sad,

tranquil or troubled, and fulfilled or barren are the crucial considerations. If the person is anxiety-ridden, then he or she is maladjusted, regardless of whether the anxiety seems to produce overt behaviors that are deviant in some way.

The Case of Cynthia S.

Cynthia has been married for 23 years. Her husband is a highly successful civil engineer. They have two children, one in high school and the other in college. There is nothing in Cynthia's history to suggest psychological problems. She is above average in intelligence, and she completed two years of college before marrying. Her friends all characterize her as devoted to her family. Of all her features, those that seem to describe her best include her strong sense of responsibility and a capacity to get things done. She has always been a "coper." She can continue to function effectively despite a great deal of personal stress and anxiety. She is a warm person, yet not one to wear her feelings or her troubles on her sleeve.

She recently enrolled in a night course at the local community college. In that course, the students were asked to write an "existential" account of their innermost selves. The psychologist who taught the course was surprised to find the following excerpts in Cynthia's account:

"In the morning, I often feel as if I cannot make it through the day. I frequently experience headaches and feel that I am getting sick. I am terribly frightened when I have to meet new people or serve as a hostess at a party. At times I feel a tremendous sense of sadness; whether this is because of my lack of personal identity, I don't know."

What surprised the instructor was that none of these expressed feelings were apparent from Cynthia's overt behavior. She appeared confident, reasonably assertive, competent, in good spirits, and outgoing.

The Case of Robert G.

In the course of a routine screening report for a promotion, Robert was interviewed by the personnel analyst in the accounting company for which he worked. A number of Robert's peers in the office were also questioned about him. In the course of these interviews, several things were established.

Robert was a very self-confident person. He seemed very sure of his goals and what he needed to do to achieve them. Although hardly a happy-go-lucky person, he was certainly content with his progress so far. He never expressed the anxieties and uncertainty that seemed typical of so many of his peers. There was nothing to

suggest any internal distress. Even his enemies conceded that Robert really "had it together."

These enemies began to be quite visible as the screening process moved along. Not many people in the office liked Robert. He tended to use people and was not above stepping on them now and then to keep his career moving. He was usually inconsiderate and frequently downright cruel. He was particularly insensitive to those below him. He loved ethnic humor and seemed to revel in his prejudices toward minority groups and those women who intruded into a "man's world." Even at home, his wife and son could have reported that they were kept in a constant turmoil because of his insensitive demands for their attention and services.

Cynthia and Robert are obviously two very different kinds of people. Cynthia's behavior is, in a sense, quite conforming. Her ability to cope would be cause for admiration by many. Yet she is unhappy and conflicted, and she experiences much anxiety. A clinical psychologist might not be surprised if she turned up in the consulting room. Her friends, however, would likely be shocked were they to learn that she had sought psychological help.

In contrast, many of Robert's friends, associates, and family members would be gratified if he were to seek help, since most of them have, at one time or another, described him as sick. But Robert is not at odds with himself. He sees nothing wrong with himself, and he would probably react negatively to any suggestion that he should seek therapy. Furthermore, his lack of motivation for therapy would probably make it an unprofitable venture.

Advantages of This Definition. Defining abnormal behavior in terms of *subjective distress* has some appeal. It seems reasonable to expect that individuals can assess whether they are experiencing emotional or behavioral problems and can share this information when asked to do so. Indeed, many methods of clinical assessment (for example, self-report inventories, clinical interviews) assume that the respondent is aware of his or her internal state and will respond to inquiries about personal distress in an honest manner. In some ways, this relieves the clinician of the burden of making an absolute judgment as to the respondent's degree of maladjustment.

Problems with This Definition. The question is whether Cynthia, Robert, or both are maladjusted. The judgment will depend upon one's criteria or values. From a strict standpoint of subjective report, Cynthia qualifies but Robert does not. This example suggests that labeling someone maladjusted is not very meaningful unless the basis for the judgment is specified and the behavioral manifestations are stated.

Not everyone whom we consider to be "disordered" reports subjective distress. For example, clinicians sometimes encounter individuals who may have little contact with reality yet profess inner tranquillity. Nonetheless, these individuals are institutionalized. Such examples remind us that subjective reports must yield at times to other criteria. Another problem concerns the amount of subjective distress necessary to be considered abnormal. All of us become aware of our own anxieties from time to time, so the total absence of such feelings cannot be the sole criterion of adjustment. How much anxiety is allowed, and for how long, before we acquire a label? Many would assert that the very fact of being alive and in an environment that can never wholly satisfy us will inevitably bring anxieties. Thus, as in the case of other criteria, using phenomenological reports is subject to limitations. There is a certain charm to the idea that if we want to know whether a person is maladjusted, we should ask that person, but there are obvious pitfalls in doing so.

Disability or Dysfunction

A third definition of abnormal behavior invokes the concept of *disability or dysfunction*. For behavior to be considered abnormal, it must create some degree of social (interpersonal) or occupational problems for the individual. Dysfunction in these two spheres is often quite apparent to both the individual and the clinician. For example, a lack of friendships or of relationships because of a lack of interpersonal contact would be considered indicative of social dysfunction, whereas the loss of one's job because of emotional problems (such as depression) would suggest occupational dysfunction.

The Case of Richard Z.

Richard was convinced by his wife to consult with a clinical psychologist. Previous contacts with psychiatrists had on one occasion resulted in a diagnosis of "hypochondriacal neurosis," and on another, a diagnosis of "passive aggressive personality." Richard has not worked in several years, even though he has a bachelor's degree in library science. He claims that he is unable to find employment because of his health. He reports a variety of physical symptoms, including dizziness, breathlessness, weakness, and "funny" sensations in the abdominal area. Making the rounds from physician to physician has enabled him to build an impressive stock of pills that he takes incessantly. None of his physicians, however, has been able to find anything physically wrong with him.

As a child, Richard was the apple of his mother's eye. She doted on him, praised him constantly, and generally reinforced the notion that he was someone special. His father disappeared about 18 months after Richard was born. His mother died six years ago, and he married shortly after that. Since then, his wife has supported both of them, thus enabling him to finish college. Only recently has she begun to accept the fact that something may be wrong with Richard.

The Case of Phyllis H.

Phyllis is a college student. She is in her sixth year of undergraduate study but has not yet obtained a degree. She has changed majors at least four times and has also had to withdraw from school on four occasions.

Her withdrawals from school have been associated with her drug habit. In two instances, her family placed her in a mental hospital; on two other occasions, she served short jail sentences following convictions on shoplifting charges. From time to time, Phyllis engages in prostitution to support her drug habit. Usually she can secure the money from her parents, who seem to have an uncanny knack for accepting her outrageous justifications. She has been diagnosed with "antisocial personality disorder" and with "drug dependence (cocaine)."

According to the disability/dysfunction definition, both of these cases would suggest the presence of abnormal behavior. Richard is completely dependent on his wife (social dysfunction), and this, coupled with his litany of somatic complaints and his inability to cope with stress, has left him unemployed (occupational dysfunction). Phyllis's drug habit has interfered with her occupational (in this case, school) functioning.

Advantages of This Definition. Perhaps the greatest advantage to adopting this definition of abnormal behavior is that relatively little inference is required. Problems in both the social and occupational sphere often *prompt* individuals to seek out treatment. It is often the case that individuals come to realize the extent of their emotional problems when these problems affect their family or social relationships as well as significantly affect their performance at either work or school.

Problems with This Definition. Who should establish the standards for social or occupational dysfunction? The patient, the therapist, friends, or the employer? In some ways, judgments regarding both social and occupational functioning are relative—not absolute—and involve a value-oriented standard. Although most of us may agree that having relationships and contributing to society as an employee or student are valuable characteristics, it is harder to agree on what specifically constitutes an adequate level of functioning in these spheres. In short, achieving

a reliable consensus about the nature of an individual's social relationships and contributions as a worker or student may be difficult. Recognizing this problem, psychopathologists have developed self-report inventories and special interviews to assess social and occupational functioning in a systematic and reliable way (see Goldman et al., 1992, for a review of these instruments).

To summarize, several criteria are used to define abnormal behavior. Each criterion has its advantages and disadvantages, and no one criterion can be used as a gold standard. Some subjectivity is involved in applying any of these criteria. As one of the authors has stated elsewhere,

> The inevitable conclusion . . . is that a definition of abnormality (maladjustment, pathology, etc.) is possible only with reference to a set of value judgments. To characterize someone as abnormal is to assert that he [sic] needs treatment. In short, someone has decided that the patient needs help in changing his behaviors—a relative, a court, or perhaps the patient himself. . . . Once someone decides that the patient needs treatment, then our psychiatrist or psychologist can deliver an opinion on how best to effect the desired changes. But the decision for treatment as a function of abnormality must be based on someone's value system—it does not reside in psychiatry or psychology. (Phares, 1967, p. 501)

Where Does This Leave Us?

As the previous discussion points out, all definitions of abnormal behavior have their strengths and weaknesses. These definitions can readily incorporate certain examples of abnormal behavior, but exceptions that do not fit these definitions are easy to provide. For example, all of us can think of an "abnormal behavior" that would not be classified as such if we adopted the subjective distress criterion (for example, spending sprees in mania), and we can think of a behavior that might be classified *incorrectly* as abnormal if we adopted the violation of norms definition (for example, an NFL all-star's athletic prowess).

It is also important to note that *abnormal behavior does not necessarily indicate mental illness*. Rather, the term *mental illness* refers to a large class of frequently observed syndromes that are comprised of certain abnormal behaviors or features. These abnormal behaviors/features tend to covary or occur together such that they often are present in the same individual. For example, major depression is a widely recognized mental illness whose features (such as depressed mood, sleep disturbance, appetite disturbance, and suicidal ideation) tend to co-occur in the same individual. However, an individual who manifested only one or two of these features of major depression would not receive this diagnosis and might not be considered mentally ill. One can manifest a wide variety of abnormal behaviors (as judged by any definition), and yet not receive a mental disorder diagnosis.

Mental Illness

Like abnormal behavior, the term *mental illness* or *mental disorder* is difficult to define. For any definition, exceptions come to mind. Nevertheless, it seems important to actually define mental illness rather than to assume that we all share the same implicit idea of what mental illness is.

The fourth edition of the *Diagnostic and Statistical Manual of Mental Disorders* (American Psychiatric Association, 1994), known as DSM-IV, the official diagnostic system for mental disorders in the United States, states that a mental disorder

> is conceptualized as a clinically significant behavioral or psychological syndrome or pattern that occurs in an individual and that is associated with present distress (e.g., a painful symptom) or disability (i.e., impairment in one or more important areas of functioning) or with a significantly increased risk of suffering, death, pain, disability, or an important loss of freedom. In addition, this syndrome or pattern must not be merely an expectable and culturally

sanctioned response to a particular event, for example, the death of a loved one. Whatever its original cause, it must currently be considered a manifestation of a behavioral, psychological, or biological dysfunction in the individual. Neither deviant behavior (e.g., religious, political, or sexual) nor conflicts that are primarily between the individual and society are mental disorders unless the deviance or conflict is a symptom of the dysfunction in the individual as described above. (pp. xxi–xxii)

Several aspects of this definition are important to note: (1) The *syndrome* (cluster of abnormal behaviors) must be associated with distress, disability, or increased risk of problems; (2) a mental disorder is considered to represent a dysfunction *within an individual*; and (3) not all deviant behaviors or conflicts with society are signs of mental disorder.

The astute reader has probably noticed that the DSM-IV definition of mental disorder incorporates the three definitions of abnormal behavior presented earlier in this chapter. On the one hand, the DSM-IV definition is more comprehensive than any one of the three individual definitions of abnormal behavior presented earlier. On the other hand, the DSM-IV definition is more restrictive because it focuses on syndromes, or clusters of abnormal behaviors, that are associated with distress, disability, or an increased risk for problems.

The Importance of Diagnosis

Before uncritically accepting this definition or taking for granted the utility of diagnosing and classifying individuals, we need to answer a basic question: Why should we use mental disorder diagnoses? *Diagnosis* is a type of expert-level categorization. Categorization is essential to our survival because it allows us to make important distinctions (for example, a mild cold versus viral pneumonia, a malignant versus a benign tumor). The diagnosis of mental disorders is an expert level of categorization used by mental health professionals that enables us to make important distinctions (for example, schizophrenia versus bipolar disorder with psychotic features).

There are at least four major advantages of diagnosis. First, and perhaps most important, a primary function of diagnosis is communication. A wealth of information can be conveyed in a single diagnostic term. For example, a patient with a diagnosis of paranoid schizophrenia was referred to one of the authors by a colleague in New York City. Immediately, without knowing anything else about the patient, a symptom pattern came to mind (delusions, auditory hallucinations, severe social/occupational dysfunction, continuous signs of the illness for at least 6 months). Diagnosis can be thought of as a "verbal shorthand" for representing features of a particular mental disorder. Using standardized diagnostic criteria (such as those that appear in the DSM-IV) ensures some degree of comparability with regard to mental disorder features among patients diagnosed in California, Missouri, Manhattan (New York), or Manhattan, Kansas.

Diagnostic systems for mental disorders are especially useful for communication because these classificatory systems are largely descriptive. That is, behaviors and symptoms that are characteristic of the various disorders are presented without any reference to theories regarding their causes. As a result, a diagnostician of nearly any theoretical persuasion can use them. If every psychologist used a different, theoretically based system of classification, a great number of communication problems would likely result.

Second, the use of diagnoses enables and promotes empirical research in psychopathology. Clinical psychologists define experimental groups in terms of individuals' diagnostic features, thus allowing comparisons between groups with regard to personality features, psychological test performance, or performance on an experimental task. Further, the way diagnostic constructs are defined and described will stimulate research on the disorders' individual criteria, on alternative criteria sets, and on the comorbidity (co-occurrence) between disorders.

Third, and in a related vein, research into the etiology, or causes, of abnormal behavior would

be almost impossible to conduct without a standardized diagnostic system. In order to investigate the importance of potential *etiological factors* for a given psychopathological syndrome, we must first assign subjects to groups whose members share diagnostic features. For example, several years ago it was hypothesized that the experience of childhood sexual abuse may predispose individuals to develop features of borderline personality disorder (BPD). The first empirical attempts to evaluate the veracity of this hypothesis involved assessing the prevalence of childhood sexual abuse in well-defined groups of subjects with borderline personality disorder as well as in non-borderline psychiatric controls. These initial studies indicated that childhood sexual abuse does occur quite frequently in BPD individuals and that these rates are significantly higher than those found in patients with other (non-BPD) mental disorder diagnoses. Before we could reach these types of conclusions, there had to be a reliable and systematic method of assigning subjects to the BPD category.

Finally, diagnoses are important because, at least in theory, they may suggest which mode of treatment is most likely to be effective. Indeed, this is a general goal of a classification system for mental disorders (Blashfield & Draguns, 1976). As Blashfield and Draguns (1976, p. 148) stated, "The final decision on the value of a psychiatric classification for prediction rests on an empirical evaluation of the utility of classification for treatment decisions." For example, a diagnosis of schizophrenia suggests to us that the administration of an antipsychotic medication is more likely to be effective than is a course of psychoanalytic psychotherapy. However, it is important to note one thing in passing. Although, in theory, the linkage between diagnosis and treatment would seem to justify the time involved in diagnostic assessment, often several treatments appear to be equally effective for an individual disorder.

In summary, diagnosis and classification of psychopathology serves many useful functions. Whether they are researchers or practitioners, contemporary clinical psychologists use some form of diagnostic scheme in their work. At this point, we turn to a brief description of classification systems that have been used to diagnose mental disorders over the years, and then we examine in more detail the features of the diagnostic classification system that is used most frequently in the United States, the DSM-IV.

Early Classification Systems

Classification systems for mental disorders have proliferated for many years. For example, the earliest reference to a depressive syndrome appeared as far back as 2600 B.C. (Menninger, 1963). Since that time, both the number of and breadth of classification systems have increased. To bring some measure of order out of this chaos, the Congress of Mental Science adopted a single classification system in 1889 in Paris. More recent attempts can be traced to the World Health Organization and its 1948 *International Statistical Classification of Diseases, Injuries, and Causes of Death,* which included a classification of abnormal behavior.

In 1952, the American Psychiatric Association published its own classification system in the *Diagnostic and Statistical Manual*, and this manual contained a glossary describing each of the diagnostic categories that were included. This first edition, known as DSM-I, was followed by revisions in 1968 (DSM-II), 1980 (DSM-III), and 1987 (DSM-III-R). Presently, the most widely used classification system is the previously mentioned American Psychiatric Association's *Diagnostic and Statistical Manual of Mental Disorders,* 4th edition (DSM-IV), which appeared in 1994. All of these manuals are embodiments of Emil Kraepelin's efforts in the late nineteenth century (see Figure 5-2). To illustrate how things have changed over the past 50 years, compare the British system in use in the late 1940s (see Table 5-1) with the DSM-IV system described in Table 5-2.

From the 1950s to the early 1960s, the enthusiasm for psychiatric diagnosis waned (Robins & Helzer, 1986). Diagnosis was said to be dehumanizing and to ignore individual variation. But diagnosis in psychiatry and psychology has

FIGURE 5-2 **Emil Kraepelin is generally regarded as the father of modern systems of psychiatric diagnosis and classification.**
Culver Pictures, Inc.

staged a comeback. The most revolutionary changes in our diagnostic system were introduced in DSM-III, published in 1980. These changes included the use of explicit diagnostic criteria for mental disorders, a multiaxial system of diagnosis, a descriptive approach to diagnosis that attempted to be neutral with regard to theories of etiology, and a greater emphasis on the clinical utility of the diagnostic system. Because these innovations have been retained in subsequent editions of the DSM (DSM-III-R and DSM-IV), they will be described in the following section.

DSM-IV

The fourth edition of the *Diagnostic and Statistical Manual of Mental Disorders* (DSM-IV) was published in 1994. Revisions to the previous diagnostic manual (DSM-III-R) were guided by a three-stage empirical process. First, 150 comprehensive reviews of the literature on important

TABLE 5-1 Classifications of Mental Disorders in Use by the Royal Medico-Psychological Association in the Late 1940s

PART I
A. Oligophrenia (amentia, mental deficiency)
   1. Idiocy
   2. Imbecility
   3. Feeblemindedness (moron)
   4. Moral deficiency
B. Neuroses and psychoneuroses
   1. Exhaustion states (including neurasthenia)
   2. Anxiety states
   3. Compulsions, obsessions and phobias
   4. Hysteria
   5. Mixed and other forms
C. Schizophrenic psychoses
   1. Dementia praecox
      a. Simple
      b. Hebephrenic
      c. Katatonic
      d. Paranoid
   2. Paraphrenia
   3. Other forms
D. Psychopathic constitution (including paranoia)
E. Affective psychoses:
   1. Manic-depressive psychosis (cyclothymia)
      a. Elation
      b. Depression
      c. Stupor
   2. Involutional melancholia
F. Confusional states
G. Epileptic psychoses
H. General paralysis
I. Other psychoses associated with organic brain disease
J. Dementia
K. Indeterminate types

Source: Adapted from Henderson & Gillespie (1950, pp. 20–21).

diagnostic issues were conducted. These literature reviews were both systematic and thorough. Results from these reviews led to recommendations for revisions and served to document the rationale and empirical support for the changes made in DSM-IV. Second, 40 major reanalyses of existing data sets were completed in cases where the literature reviews could not adequately re-solve the targeted diagnostic issue. Third, 12 DSM-IV field trials were conducted in order to assess the clinical utility and predictive power of alternative criteria sets for selected disorders (for example, antisocial personality disorder). In summary, the changes made in DSM-IV were based on empirical data to a much greater extent than was true in previous editions of the DSM. A condensed version of the DSM-IV appears in Table 5-2.

A complete DSM-IV diagnostic evaluation is a *multiaxial assessment*. Clients or patients are evaluated along five axes, or domains of information. Each of these axes/domains should aid in treatment planning and prediction of outcome. *Axis I* is used to indicate the presence of any of the clinical disorders or other relevant conditions, with the exception of the personality disorders and mental retardation. These two classes of diagnoses are coded on *Axis II*. *Axis III* is used to highlight any current medical condition that may be relevant to the conceptualization or treatment of an individual's Axis I or Axis II clinical disorder. Psychosocial and environmental problems relevant to diagnosis, treatment, and prognosis are indicated on *Axis IV*. Finally, a quantitative estimate (1 to 100) of an individual's overall level of functioning is provided on *Axis V*. Each of the five axes contributes important information about the patient, and together they provide a fairly comprehensive description of the patient's major problems, stressors, and level of functioning.

The Case of Michelle M.

Michelle M. was a 23-year-old woman who was admitted to an inpatient unit at a hospital following her sixth suicide attempt in two years. She told her ex-boyfriend (who had broken up with her a week earlier) that she had swallowed a bottle of aspirin, and he rushed her to the local emergency room. Michelle had a five-year history of multiple depressive symptoms that never abated; however, these had not been severe enough to necessitate hospitalization or treatment. They included dysphoric mood, poor

TABLE 5-2 A Condensed Version of the DSM-IV

Axis I: *Clinical Disorders or Other Conditions That May Be a Focus of Clinical Attention*
- Disorders usually first diagnosed in infancy, childhood, or adolescence (e.g., Pervasive Developmental Disorders)
- Delirium, Dementia, and Amnestic and Other Cognitive Disorders
- Mental Disorders Due to a General Medical Condition
- Substance-related Disorders (e.g., alcohol abuse; cocaine dependence)
- Schizophrenia and Other Psychotic Disorders
- Mood Disorders (e.g., Major Depression, Bipolar Disorder)
- Anxiety Disorders (e.g., Agoraphobia; Post-Traumatic Stress Disorder)
- Somatoform Disorders (e.g., Hypochondriasis)
- Factitious Disorders
- Dissociative Disorders (e.g., Dissociative Identity Disorder)
- Sexual and Gender Identity Disorders (e.g., Vaginismus; Fetishism)
- Eating Disorders (e.g., Anorexia Nervosa)
- Sleep Disorders (e.g., Narcolepsy)
- Impulse Control Disorders (e.g., Kleptomania)
- Adjustment Disorders
- Other conditions that may be a focus of clinical attention (e.g., Bereavement)

Axis II: *Personality Disorders and Mental Retardation*
- Personality Disorders (e.g., Borderline, Antisocial, Dependent, Paranoid)
- Mental Retardation

Axis III: *General Medical Conditions That Are Potentially Relevant to the Understanding or Management of the Individual's Mental Disorder*

Axis IV: *Psychosocial and Environmental Problems*
- Problems with primary support group
- Problems related to the social environment
- Educational problems
- Occupational problems
- Housing problems
- Economic problems
- Problems with access to heath care services
- Problems related to interaction with the legal system/crime
- Other psychosocial and environmental problems

Axis V: *Global Assessment of Functioning (GAF) Scale**

Code	Description
100 to 91	Superior functioning in a wide range of activities
81 to 90	Absent or minimal symptoms (e.g., mild anxiety before an exam), good functioning in all areas, interested and involved in a wide range of activities, socially effective, generally satisfied with life, no more than everyday problems or concerns (e.g., occasional argument).
71 to 80	If symptoms are present they are transient, expectable reactions to psychosocial stressors.
61 to 70	Some mild symptoms.
51 to 60	Moderate symptoms.
41 to 50	Serious symptoms (e.g., suicidal ideation, severe obsessional rituals, frequent shoplifting) OR any serious impairment in social, occupational, or school functioning (e.g., no friends, unable to keep a job).
31 to 40	Some impairment in reality testing or communication.
21 to 30	Behavior is considerably influenced by delusions or hallucinations.
11 to 20	Some danger of hurting self or others.
1 to 10	Persistent danger of severely hurting self or others (e.g., recurrent violence) OR persistent inability to maintain minimal personal hygiene OR serious suicidal act with clear expectation of death
0	Inadequate information

*Full descriptions are provided here only for Codes 90-81, 50-41, and 10-1.

Source: Adapted from American Psychiatric Association, *Diagnostic and Statistical Manual of Mental Disorders,* 4th edition. Washington, DC: American Psychiatric Association, 1994. Reprinted by permission.

appetite, low self-esteem, poor concentration, and feelings of hopelessness.

In addition, Michelle had a history of a number of rather severe problems that had been present since her teenage years. First, she had great difficulty controlling her emotions. She was prone to become intensely dysphoric, irritable, or anxious almost at a moment's notice. These intense negative affect states were often unpredictable and, although frequent, rarely lasted more than four or five hours. Michelle also reported a long history of impulsive behaviors, including polysubstance abuse, excessive promiscuity (an average of about 30 different sexual partners a year), and binge eating. Her anger was unpredictable and quite intense. For example, she once used a hammer to literally smash a wall to pieces following a bad grade on a test.

Michelle's relationships with her friends, boyfriends, and parents were intense and unstable. People who spent time with her frequently complained that she would often be angry with them and devalue them for no apparent reason. She also constantly reported an intense fear that others (including her parents) might abandon her. For example, she once clutched a friend's leg and was dragged out the door to her friend's car while Michelle tried to convince the friend to stay for dinner. In addition, she had attempted to leave home and attend college in nearby cities on four occasions. Each time, she returned home within a few weeks. Prior to her hospital admission, her words to her ex-boyfriend over the telephone were, "I want to end it all. No one loves me."

The DSM-IV diagnostic evaluation for Michelle M. is shown in Table 5-3.

Several features of this diagnostic formulation are noteworthy. First, Michelle has received multiple diagnoses on Axis I. This is allowed, and even encouraged, in the DSM-IV system because the goal is to describe the client's problems comprehensively. Second, note that her borderline personality disorder (BPD) diagnosis on Axis II is considered to be the *principal diagnosis*. This means that this condition is chiefly responsible

TABLE 5-3 Diagnostic Evaluation: Michelle M.

Axis I:	300.4	Dysthymic Disorder, early onset
	305.00	Alcohol Abuse
	305.20	Cannabis Abuse
	305.60	Cocaine Abuse
	305.30	Hallucinogen Abuse
Axis II:	301.83	Borderline Personality Disorder (PRINCIPAL DIAGNOSIS)
Axis III:	none	
Axis IV:	Problems with primary support group Educational problems	
Axis V:	GAF = 20 (Current)	

for her admission to the hospital and may be the focus of treatment. Finally, her *Global Assessment of Functioning (GAF)* score on Axis V indicates serious impairment—in this case, a danger of hurting herself.

General Issues in Classification

We have briefly described the DSM-IV to give the reader a general idea of what psychiatric classification entails. However, it is important to examine a number of broad issues related to classification in general, and to the DSM-IV specifically. Table 5-4 presents a summary of the eight major issues discussed below.

Categories versus Dimensions. Essentially, the mental disorder categories represent a typology. Based upon certain presenting symptoms or upon a particular history of symptoms, the patient is placed in a *category*. This approach has several potential limitations. First, in too many instances, it is easy to confuse such categorization with explanation. If one is not careful, there is a tendency to think "This patient is experiencing obsessions because she has obsessive-compulsive disorder" or "This person is acting psychotic because he has schizophrenia." When this

TABLE 5-4 General Issues in Classification

Categories versus Dimensions
Is the categorical model adopted in DSM-IV (that is, the disorder is either present or absent) really appropriate? Is a dimensional model preferable?

Bases of Categorization
Should there be multiple ways of making diagnostic judgments? Does this create too much heterogeneity within a diagnostic category?

Pragmatics of Classification
How do we decide whether a condition is included in the diagnostic manual?

Description
Are the features of the diagnostic categories adequately described? Are the diagnostic criteria specific and objective?

Reliability
Are diagnostic judgments reliable? Can different diagnosticians agree on the classification of an individual?

Validity
Can we make meaningful predictions based on our knowledge of an individual's diagnosis?

Bias
Are the features of the disorders in DSM-IV biased against particular individuals because of their gender, race, or SES background? Are diagnosticians biased in their interpretation or application of the diagnostic criteria?

Coverage
Do the DSM-IV diagnoses apply to the people who present for psychological or psychiatric treatment? Is the DSM-IV too narrow in its coverage, or is it too broad?

kind of thinking occurs, explanation has been supplanted by a circular form of description.

In addition, as noted earlier in this chapter, abnormal behavior is not qualitatively different from so-called normal behavior. Rather, these are endpoints of a continuous *dimension*. The difference between so-called normal behavior and psychotic behavior, for example, is one of degree rather than kind (Chapman & Chapman, 1985). Yet mental disorder diagnoses in terms of catego-

ries imply that individuals either have the disorder in question or they do not. This all-or-nothing type of thinking may be at odds with what we know about how symptoms of psychopathology are distributed in the population. For example, a categorical model of borderline personality disorder (BPD), as presented in the DSM-IV (that is, present versus absent), may not be appropriate because individuals differ only with respect to how many BPD symptoms they exhibit (a quantitative difference). In other words, the categorical model may misrepresent the true nature of the borderline construct (Trull, Widiger, & Guthrie, 1990). In fact, there may be relatively few diagnostic constructs that are truly categorical in nature.

Bases of Categorization. In order to classify psychiatric patients, one must use a wide assortment of methods and principles. In some cases, patients are classified almost solely on the basis of their current behavior or presenting symptoms. In other cases, the judgment is made almost entirely on the basis of history. In the case of major depression, for example, one individual may be diagnosed on the basis of a diagnostic interview conducted by a clinician; another may be classified because of a laboratory result, such as a "positive" dexamethasone suppression test (DST); still another may be diagnosed as a result of scores on a self-report measure of depression. Laboratory results provide the basis for some diagnoses of cognitive disorders (for example, vascular dementia), whereas other cognitive disorder diagnoses (such as delirium) are determined solely by behavioral observation. Thus, the diagnostic enterprise may be quite complicated for the clinician, requiring both knowledge of and access to a wide variety of diagnostic techniques. A major implication is that membership in any one diagnostic category is likely to be heterogeneous because there are multiple bases for a diagnosis.

Pragmatics of Classification. Psychiatric classification has always been accompanied by a certain degree of appeal to medical authority. But there is a concurrent democratic aspect to the system that is quite puzzling. For example, psychiatry for many years regarded homosexuality as a disease to be cured through psychiatric intervention. As a result of society's changing attitudes and other valid psychological reasons, homosexuality was dropped from the DSM system and is now regarded as an alternate lifestyle (see Spitzer, 1981). Only when homosexual individuals are disturbed by their sexual orientation or wish to change it do we encounter homosexuality in the DSM-IV (as an example under the category "sexual disorder not otherwise specified"). The issue here is not whether this decision was valid or not. The issue is how the decision to drop homosexuality from the DSM system was made. The demise of homosexuality as a disease entity occurred through a vote of the psychiatric membership.

This example also serves as a reminder that classification systems such as the DSM are crafted by committees. The members of such committees represent varying scientific, theoretical, professional, and even economic constituencies. Consequently, the final classification product adopted may represent a political document that reflects compromises that will make it acceptable to a heterogeneous professional clientele.

Description. Without doubt, the DSM-IV provides thorough descriptions of the diagnostic categories. For Axis I and II disorders, a detailed description of the symptoms of each diagnostic category is presented. As an example, Table 5-5 presents the DSM-IV diagnostic criteria for the eating disorder *bulimia nervosa*. The DSM also provides additional information for each diagnosis, including the age of onset, course, prevalence, complications, family patterns, cultural considerations, associated descriptive features and mental disorders, and associated laboratory findings. All this descriptive detail should enhance the system's reliability and validity.

Reliability. A scheme that cannot establish its reliability has serious problems. In this context, *reliability* refers to the consistency of diagnostic

---

TABLE 5-5 DSM-IV Criteria for Bulimia Nervosa

A. Recurrent episodes of binge eating. An episode of binge eating is characterized by both of the following:

(1) eating, in a discrete period of time (e.g., within any 2-hour period), an amount of food that is definitely larger than most people would eat during a similar period of time and under similar circumstances

(2) a sense of lack of control of eating during the episode (e.g., a feeling that one cannot stop eating or control what or how much one is eating)

B. Recurrent inappropriate compensatory behavior in order to prevent weight gain, such as self-induced vomiting; misuse of laxatives, diuretics, enemas, or other medications; fasting; or excessive exercise.

C. The binge eating and inappropriate compensatory behaviors both occur, on average, at least twice a week for 3 months.

D. Self-evaluation is unduly influenced by body shape and weight.

E. The disturbance does not occur exclusively during episodes of Anorexia Nervosa.

Specify Type

Purging Type: During the current episode of Bulimia Nervosa, the person has regularly engaged in self-induced vomiting or the misuse of laxatives, diuretics, or enemas.

Nonpurging Type: During the current episode of Bulimia Nervosa, the person has used other inappropriate compensatory behaviors, such as fasting or excessive exercise, but has not regularly engaged in self-induced vomiting or the misuse of laxatives, diuretics, or enemas.

Source: Reprinted from DSM-IV (American Psychiatric Association, 1994) with permission.

---

judgments across raters. One of the major changes seen in DSM-III (American Psychiatric Association, 1980)—the inclusion of specific and objective criteria for each disorder—reflected an attempt to increase the reliability of the diagnostic system. If Psychologist A and Psychologist B both observe the same patient but cannot agree on the diagnosis, then both their diagnoses are useless because we do not know which to accept. This is the very situation that plagued the American diagnostic systems for many years. For example, an early study illustrating the unreliability of previous diagnostic systems was carried out by Beck, Ward, Mendelson, Mock, and Erbaugh (1962). Two different psychiatrists each interviewed the same 153 newly admitted psychiatric patients. Overall agreement among these psychiatrists was only 54%. Some of the disagreements in diagnosis seemed to stem from inconsistencies in the information patients presented to the psychiatrists. For example, Patient A may have been relatively open with Psychiatrist F, but less so with Psychiatrist G. But much of the unreliability problem seemed to lie with the diagnosticians and/or the diagnostic system itself.

Certain pragmatic factors can also reduce reliability across diagnosticians. Sometimes it happens that a given institution will not admit patients who carry a certain diagnosis. Yet a mental health professional may feel strongly that the patient could benefit from admission (or perhaps has nowhere else to go). What should be done? The "humanitarian" choice often seems to be to alter a diagnosis, or at least to "fudge" a bit. The patient with alcohol dependence suddenly is diagnosed with something else. Similarly, an insurance company may reimburse a clinic for the treatment of patients with one diagnosis but not another. Or perhaps one diagnosis permits six therapy visits but another allows as many as 15 sessions. Therefore, a diagnosis may be intentionally or unintentionally manipulated.

These examples may lead us to believe that diagnostic unreliability is the rule and not the exception. However, Meehl (1977), for example, feels that psychiatric diagnosis is not nearly as unreliable as it is made out to be. Specifically, Meehl argues that if we confine ourselves to major diagnostic categories, require adequate clinical exposure to the patient, and study well-trained clinicians who take diagnosis seriously, then interclinician agreement will reach acceptable levels.

TABLE 5-6   SIDP-IV Questions Used to Assess a Dependent Personality Disorder Criterion

CRITERION 1-DEPEN: HAS DIFFICULTY MAKING EVERYDAY DECISIONS WITHOUT AN EXCESSIVE AMOUNT OF ADVICE AND REASSURANCE FROM OTHERS

Questions to Ask
Some people enjoy making decisions and other people prefer to have someone they trust tell them what to do. Which do you prefer?

Do you often turn to others for advice about everyday decisions like what to have for lunch or what clothes to buy?

Scoring
0 = not present
1 = subthreshold
2 = present
3 = strongly present

Source: Adapted from the *Structured Interview for DSM-IV Personality* (SIDP-IV; Pfohl, Blum, & Zimmerman, 1994). Copyright 1989, 1994. Used with permission.

The field of psychopathology has begun to address these concerns about reliability by developing *structured diagnostic interviews* that essentially "force" diagnosticians to assess individuals for the specific DSM criteria that appear in the diagnostic manual. For example, there are now several structured interviews that assess features of Axis I disorders, and a number of structured interviews for Axis II disorders exist as well. Interestingly, the overall level of diagnostic reliability reported in empirical studies has increased greatly following the introduction of these structured interviews. It is clear that adhering to the structure and format of these interviews has led to a significant increase in diagnostic reliability. Table 5-6 presents a brief section from a structured interview. We will discuss structured interviews in more detail in Chapter 6.

However, even with the use of structured interviews, reliability is not equally good across all categories. The presence versus absence of some disorders (for example, generalized anxiety disorder) may be particularly difficult to judge.

Further, there is some question as to whether or not busy clinicians will devote the time and effort necessary to systematically evaluate the relevant diagnostic criteria. Reliability coefficients never seem to be as high in routine, everyday work settings as they are in structured research studies.

Validity. Reliability will directly affect the validity of a diagnostic system. As long as diagnosticians fail to agree upon the proper classification of patients, we cannot demonstrate that the classification system has meaningful correlates—that is, has *validity*. Important correlates include prognosis, treatment outcome, ward management, etiology, and so on. And without predictive validity, classification becomes an intellectual exercise devoid of any really important utility. However, if we can demonstrate that categorization accurately indicates etiology, course of illness, or preferred kinds of treatment, then a valid basis for its use has been established.

The predominant method for establishing the validity of a diagnostic construct was outlined in a classic article by Robins and Guze (1970). They proposed that establishing the diagnostic validity of a syndrome is a five-stage process: (1) *clinical description*, including a description of characteristic features beyond the disorder's symptoms (such as demographic features); (2) *laboratory studies* (including psychological tests) to identify meaningful correlates of the diagnosis; (3) *delimitation from other disorders* to ensure some degree of homogeneity among diagnostic members; (4) *follow-up studies* to assess the test-retest reliability of a diagnosis; and (5) *family studies* to demonstrate that the proposed disorder tends to run in families, suggesting a hereditary component to the disorder. This particular five-stage method for establishing diagnostic validity remains quite influential even today. In fact, most contemporary research in psychopathology represents one or more of the validation stages outlined by Robins and Guze.

Bias. Ideally, a classification system will not be biased with respect to how diagnoses are as-

signed to individuals who have different backgrounds (for example, different gender, race, or SES). The validity and utility of a classification system would be called into question if the same cluster of behaviors resulted in a diagnosis for one individual but not for another individual. The two areas of potential bias that have received the most attention are sex bias (see, for example, Widiger & Spitzer, 1991) and racial bias (for example, Pavkov, Lewis, & Lyons, 1989).

Some critics have attacked the DSM system as a male-centered device that overestimates pathology in women (M. Kaplan, 1983); others deny this charge (Kass, Spitzer, & Williams, 1983). Widiger and Spitzer (1991) have presented a useful conceptual analysis of what constitutes *sex bias* in a diagnostic system. They argue that previous attempts to demonstrate diagnostic sex bias have been both conceptually and methodologically flawed. Further, some of the findings of earlier studies (for example, Broverman, Broverman, Clarkson, Rosenkrantz, & Vogel, 1970) have been grossly misinterpreted and misunderstood (see Widiger & Settle, 1987, for a demonstration of the flaws in the Broverman et al. study).

Widiger and Spitzer note that differential sex prevalence for a disorder does not in and of itself demonstrate diagnostic sex bias because, for example, it is conceivable that biological factors or cultural factors may make it more likely that men (or women) will exhibit the criteria for a certain diagnosis. For example, antisocial personality disorder is diagnosed much more frequently in men than in women, but this may be the result of biological differences (such as testosterone) or other factors that influence the two genders differentially (such as societal expectations for aggressiveness in men). However, Widiger and Spitzer did present evidence suggesting that clinicians may be biased in the way they *apply* diagnoses to men versus women, even in cases where the symptoms presented by men and women were exactly the same! Although this suggests that there may be some bias in the way clinicians interpret the diagnostic criteria (that is, clinicians may exhibit sex bias), it does not indicate sex bias within the diagnostic criteria. These results suggest the need for better training of diagnosticians rather than an overhaul of the diagnostic criteria.

Coverage. With close to 400 possible diagnoses, DSM-IV cannot be faulted for being too limited in its coverage of possible diagnostic conditions. It is likely that most conditions that bring individuals in for psychiatric or psychological treatment could be classified within the DSM-IV system. However, some may feel that DSM-IV errs in the opposite direction—that its scope is too broad. For example, a host of childhood developmental disorders are included as mental disorders. The child who is dyslexic, has speech problems such as stuttering, or has great difficulties with arithmetic is given a DSM-IV diagnosis. Many question the appropriateness or benefit of labeling these conditions as mental disorders.

Another example of the possible over-inclusiveness of the DSM-IV is the inclusion of "premenstrual dysphoric disorder" as a proposed diagnostic category. This diagnosis and its criteria appear in the appendix containing diagnostic criteria provided for further study. Many women objected strenuously to this diagnosis when it was first proposed because they argued that such a category could easily be used to discriminate against women in many arenas (such as employment). Controversial diagnoses like this one cause some to wonder whether the architects of the DSM have gone too far.

Additional Concerns. Although the previously described difficulties are real and fairly obvious, a number of indirect or subtle problems arise through the acceptance and use of diagnostic classification systems. For example, classifications tend to create the impression that mental disorders exist per se. Such terms as *disorder, symptom, condition,* and *suffering from* suggest that the patient is the victim of a disease process. The language of the system can eventually lead even astute observers toward a view that interprets learned reactions or person-environment encounters as disease processes.

In addition, if we are not careful, we may come to feel that classifying people is more satisfying than trying to relieve their problems. As we shall see later, therapy can be an uncertain, time-consuming process that is often fraught with failure. But pigeonholing can be immediately rewarding: it provides a sense of closure to the classifier. Like solving crossword puzzles, it may relieve tension without having any long-term positive social significance.

The system likewise caters to the public's desire to regard problems in living as medical problems that can be dealt with simply and easily by a pill, an injection, or a scalpel. Unfortunately, however, learning to solve psychological problems is hard work. The easier approach is to adopt a passive, dependent posture in which the patient is relieved of psychological pain by an omniscient doctor. Although such a view may be serviceable in dealing with strictly medical problems (but see Engel, 1977), it has dubious value at best in confronting the psychosocial problems of living.

A final indirect problem is that diagnosis can be harmful or even stigmatizing to the person who is labeled. In our society, diagnosis may close doors rather than open them for patients and ex-patients. Too often, diagnosis seems to obscure the real person; observers see labels, not the real people behind them. Thus, labels can damage relationships, prevent people from being hired or promoted, and, in extreme cases, even result in a loss of civil rights. Labels can even encourage some people to capitulate and assume the role of a "sick" person.

Other Classification Systems

A variety of attempts have been made to improve psychiatric classification. Many have used multivariate statistical methods, such as cluster analysis, to generate homogeneous categories. For example, Overall and Gorham (1962), working within the traditional psychiatric framework, developed the Brief Psychiatric Rating Scale (BPRS). This scale allows for the evaluation of symptoms in 16 relatively independent factor areas. Overall and Hollister (1982) have used cluster analysis and related numerical taxonomy methods to identify eight distinct phenomenological types in terms of BPRS profiles. Other systems have focused on psychotic behavior. For example, Lorr (1986) has helped in the development of a research-oriented interview procedure for assigning patients quantitative values on 12 dimensions (for example, paranoid projection, hostile belligerence). McReynolds (1989) has reviewed several other alternatives to the DSM classification system.

A relatively new alternative to the traditional diagnostic system for Axis II personality disorders is the *Five-Factor Model of personality (FFM)*. The FFM includes the personality dimensions of Neuroticism, Extraversion, Openness to Experience, Agreeableness, and Conscientiousness (Costa & McCrae, 1992). As Digman (1990) noted, a growing consensus regarding these five trait dimensions as a fairly comprehensive representation of adult personality has been evident in the psychological literature (see McCrae & John, 1992).

If the FFM is to be seen as a comprehensive account of normal and abnormal personality, then we would expect this model to be relevant to the personality disorders that are coded on Axis II. Personality disorders, by definition, involve inflexible and maladaptive personality traits. Studies that have explored the relationship between the FFM and Axis II disorders have obtained encouraging results (Costa & McCrae, 1990; Soldz, Budman, Demby, & Merry, 1993; Trull, 1992; Wiggins & Pincus, 1989). For example, Trull (1992) found that the FFM dimensions of Neuroticism, Extraversion, and Agreeableness were most apparent in the DSM-III-R conceptualizations of personality disorders in his clinical sample of outpatients.

Based on these and other findings, some have called for the use of the FFM as an alternative to DSM-IV's categorical classification system (Costa & Widiger, 1994). However, a number of issues must be addressed before converting over to a dimensional system such as the FFM: How is the maladaptivity of a personality trait assessed in these FFM personality measures? How does one determine cutoff points on a dimensional personality scale in order to decide the presence or absence of personality disorder? How can we take into account the context in which the maladaptive personality traits occur? (Costa & Widiger, 1994). Finally, there is the practical issue of training clinicians to use the FFM. To date, these issues have not been resolved, but it is likely that future research will shed some light on the viability of the FFM as a model of personality pathology. The interested reader might consider consulting McCrae and John (1992) for a good overview of the FFM, as well as Widiger (1991) for a survey of additional dimensional models of personality that were proposed for inclusion in the DSM-IV.

Causes of Abnormal Behavior and Mental Illness

Up to this point, we have discussed issues regarding the description and definition of abnormal behavior as well as the implications of diagnosing and classifying individuals. However, very little has been said about what factors may cause abnormal behavior and mental illness. Although we will discuss various *etiological models of psychopathology* in the chapters on intervention, it is useful to present these models briefly here in order to give the reader some idea of the predominant viewpoints.

Table 5-7 presents a brief overview of major models of psychopathology and the explanation of abnormal behavior offered by each. As can be seen, some of the etiological models are quite different in their perspective on abnormal behavior. These differences certainly have implications for how a clinician adhering to one of these viewpoints will conduct assessment and treatment. For example, a clinical psychologist subscribing to a cognitive theory of depression will probably use cognitively based assessment instruments to identify maladaptive cognitions, as well as cognitive-behavioral interventions to treat depression.

TABLE 5-7 Brief Description of Several Models of Psychopathology

Model	Explanation	Example of Abnormal Behavior
Biological	Processes in central nervous system (CNS) have gone awry	Schizophrenia is caused by an excess of dopaminergic activity.
Psychodynamic	Intrapsychic conflict	Specific phobia is due to the displacement of an intrapsychic conflict onto an external object that can then be avoided.
Learning	Learned the same way normal behavior is learned	Specific phobia is learned via classical conditioning.
Cognitive	Due to maladaptive cognitions	Depression results from negative views about oneself, the world, and the future.
Humanistic	Relative neglect of one's own self-view and overreliance on the appraisals of others when the two are incongruous	Generalized anxiety disorder reflects this overreliance and incongruity.

A more general model of etiology that can accommodate a variety of theoretical viewpoints (such as those in Table 5-7) is the diathesis-stress model of psychopathology (see Davison & Neale, 1998). The diathesis-stress model is not wedded to one school of thought and can incorporate biological, psychological, and environmental factors. A *diathesis* refers to a vulnerability or predisposition to possibly develop the disorder in question. A diathesis can be biological (for example, a genetic predisposition, a deficit or excess in neurotransmitter) or psychological (for example, maladaptive cognitive schema, maladaptive personality style). A diathesis is necessary but not sufficient to produce a mental disorder. What is required in addition to a diathesis is sufficient *environmental stress*. Stressors can be biological in nature (for example, poor nutrition) or psychological (for example, malignant family environment, traumatic life event). Both the diathesis and the stress are necessary to produce the disorder in question. Possessing the diathesis increases the likelihood of developing the disorder, but does not guarantee this outcome. Moreover, as may be apparent, the exact nature of the diathesis and stress necessary for developing a specific disorder is likely to vary from disorder to disorder. Finally, the interaction between the diathesis and stress is also likely to be disorder-specific (see, for example, Monroe & Simons, 1991).

Conclusion

Classification systems are necessary; otherwise, our experience and our consciousness become a chaotic array of events. By abstracting the similarities and the differences among the events of our experience, we can establish categories of varying width and purpose that allow us to generalize and predict.

Clinical psychology is very much concerned with the diagnosis, classification, and treatment of mental illness. The DSM-IV system, although clearly not perfect, will continue to be used by contemporary clinical psychologists in their research, consultation, and practice. All of us have, and will continue to have, some disagreement with the DSM-IV or any other diagnostic system. Diagnostic systems have their advantages and disadvantages, and the criteria for individual mental disorders are fallible (Widiger & Trull, 1991). The DSM-IV, like its predecessors, has been accused of being more useful for clinical research than for clinical practice. This is probably why clinicians often fail to use the diagnostic manual (Jampala, Sierles, & Taylor, 1988; Morey & Ochoa, 1989). However, we hope that the reader is convinced that diagnostic formulations are important because these formulations have communication value, have potential treatment implications, and facilitate psychopathology research.

Chapter Summary

Clinical psychologists engage in the diagnosis and classification of psychological problems. A single, all-encompassing definition of what constitutes "abnormality" is difficult to come by. In this chapter, we have reviewed the pros and cons of three frequently cited criteria for abnormal behavior: conformity to norms, subjective distress, and disability or dysfunction.

Mental illness refers to a large class of frequently observed syndromes that are comprised of co-occurring abnormal behaviors. The diagnosis of psychological problems or mental illness serves the function of communication, promotes research, and suggests treatment options. The DSM-IV is the official diagnostic system used in the United States (and other places as well).

Diagnostic classification systems should be practical, descriptive, reliable, valid, unbiased, and provide comprehensive coverage of frequently encountered clinical problems. Such diagnostic systems will advance the field by promoting psychopathology research, allowing us to investigate the causes and treatment of psychological problems.

Key Terms

Axis I The diagnostic axis of the DSM-IV that identifies all of the clinical disorders that are present, except for the personality disorders and mental retardation.

Axis II The diagnostic axis of the DSM-IV that indicates the presence of personality disorders or mental retardation.

Axis III The diagnostic axis of the DSM-IV that identifies current medical conditions that may be relevant to the conceptualization or treatment of the disorders diagnosed on Axes I and II.

Axis IV The diagnostic axis of the DSM-IV that specifies any psychosocial or environmental problems relevant to diagnosis, treatment, and prognosis.

Axis V The diagnostic axis of the DSM-IV that provides a numerical index of the individual's overall level of functioning.

categories Discrete classifications. Many of the mental disorders in the current diagnostic system are presented as categorical in nature, meaning that people are judged either to have the disorder or not to have it.

conformity to norms One of the three major definitions of abnormal behavior, this definition labels behavior as abnormal if it violates cultural norms.

cultural relativity In the context of conformity-oriented definitions of abnormal behavior, the fact that judgments about the abnormality of a particular behavior may vary from culture to culture or subculture to subculture.

cutoff points In the context of conformity-oriented definitions of abnormal behavior, the numerical values on a test or inventory that differentiate normal from abnormal performance.

diathesis In the diathesis-stress model of psychopathology, a vulnerability (e.g., genetic, psychological) to develop a particular disorder.

dimensions Continua. In a dimensional classification scheme, individuals may be seen as falling on any point of a continuum ranging from total absence of a disorder to its most severe manifestation.

disability or dysfunction One of the three major definitions of abnormal behavior, this definition labels behavior as abnormal if it creates social or occupational problems for the individual.

DSM-III The third edition of the *Diagnostic and Statistical Manual for Mental Disorders,* published in 1980. The DSM-III introduced revolutionary changes in the diagnostic system, including explicit, etiologically neutral diagnostic criteria and a multiaxial system of diagnosis.

DSM-IV The fourth (and current) edition of the *Diagnostic and Statistical Manual for Mental Disorders,* published in 1994.

environmental stress In the diathesis-stress model of psychopathology, a stressor (e.g., biological, psychological) that acts together with a diathesis to produce a given mental disorder.

etiological factors Causal factors.

etiological models of psychopathology Causal models of abnormal behavior and mental illness that also have implications for assessment and treatment. Major etiological models of psychopathology include the biological, psychodynamic, learning, and cognitive models.

Five-Factor Model of personality (FFM) A comprehensive model of personality that comprises the dimensions of Neuroticism, Extraversion, Openness, Agreeableness, and Conscientiousness, as well as the six facets belonging to each dimension.

Global Assessment of Functioning The score provided on Axis V that serves as an index of the person's overall level of functioning.

mental disorder A syndrome (cluster of abnormal behaviors) occurring within an individual that is associated with distress, disability, or increased risk of problems.

mental illness A large class of frequently observed syndromes that comprise certain abnormal behaviors or features.

multiaxial assessment The evaluation of patients along multiple domains of information. The DSM-IV calls for diagnosis along five separate axes, each of which aids in treatment planning and the prediction of outcome.

principal diagnosis The diagnosis that is chiefly responsible for a person's distress or disability and should be considered the focus of treatment.

psychopathologist A scientist who studies the causes of mental disorders as well as the factors that influence their development.

reliability In the context of diagnostic classification, the consistency of diagnostic judgments across raters.

sex bias In the context of diagnostic classification, sex bias would be demonstrated if the same cluster of behaviors resulted in a diagnosis for members of one sex, but not for the other. Although the current diagnostic criteria are not biased in and of themselves, clinicians may be biased in the way they apply these diagnoses to males and females.

structured diagnostic interviews A class of interviews that assesses for the specific criteria appearing in the diagnostic manual.

subjective distress One of the three major definitions of abnormal behavior, this definition labels as psychologically abnormal those people with a poor sense of well-being and/or a high level of subjective distress.

syndrome A group of symptoms that tends to occur together.

validity In the context of diagnostic classification, the extent to which diagnoses correlate with meaningful variables such as etiology, prognosis, and treatment outcome.

Web Sites of Interest

To visit any of the web sites listed below, go to www.wadsworth.com and click on Links.

5-1   Mental Health Net, Mental Disorders Symptoms and Treatment

5-2   National Alliance for the Mentally Ill

5-3   Links to Abnormal Psychology/Psychopathology web pages

PART 2

Clinical Assessment

CHAPTER SIX

The Assessment Interview

Assessment has long been an important activity of clinical psychologists. In the previous chapter, we touched on assessment in our discussion of the diagnosis of mental disorders. In this chapter, the focus will be on interviewing. Subsequent chapters will deal with the assessment of intelligence, personality and psychopathology, and behavior, along with the process of clinical judgment. Before we plunge into the specifics of interviewing, however, let us make a few general comments about assessment.

Assessment in Clinical Psychology

As we mentioned in Chapter 2, psychological assessment as an area of emphasis has seen its ups and downs. Abeles (1990) commented on the recent "rediscovery" of assessment. He observed that during the 1960s and 1970s, there seemed to be a decline in interest in psychological assessment. Therapy was the more glamorous enterprise, and assessment almost seemed to be somehow "unfair" to clients. It appeared that clinical psychology's historical commitment to assessment was waning. The prevailing attitude about assessment was "Let the technicians do it!"

But in the 1980s, something else began to happen. Students began to show an interest in specialization. They discovered forensic psychology (the application of psychology to legal issues), or they became intrigued by pediatric psychology, geriatrics, or even neuropsychology. But to become a specialist in such areas, one needs to know a great deal about assessment. You cannot answer a lawyer's questions about the competence of a defendant unless you have thoroughly assessed that individual through tests, interviews, or observations (Matarazzo, 1990). You cannot decide on issues of neurological insult versus mental disorder until you have assessed that client. As Abeles (1990) stated:

> It is my contention that one of the unique contributions of the clinical psychologist is the ability to provide assessment data. Providing assessments is again becoming a highly valued and respected part of clinical

psychology and in my opinion is coequal with intervention and psychotherapy as a vital activity of clinical psychology. Let us continue to rediscover assessment! (p. 4)

Definition and Purpose

Psychological assessment can be formally defined in many ways. *Clinical assessment* involves an evaluation of an individual's strengths and weaknesses, a conceptualization of the problem at hand (as well as possible etiological factors), and some prescription for alleviating the problem; all of these lead us to a better understanding of the client. Assessment is not something that is done once and then is forever finished. In many cases, it is an ongoing process—even an everyday process, as in psychotherapy. Whether the clinician is making decisions or solving problems, clinical assessment is the means to the end.

Intuitively, we all understand the purpose of diagnosis or assessment. Before physicians can prescribe a treatment, they must first understand the nature of the illness. Before plumbers can begin banging on pipes, they must first determine the character and location of the difficulty. What is true in medicine and plumbing is equally true in clinical psychology. Aside from a few cases involving pure luck, our capacity to solve clinical problems is directly related to our skill in defining them. Most of us can remember our parents' stern admonition: "Think before you act!" In a sense, this is the essence of the assessment or diagnostic process. To illustrate this idea, consider the following case.

The Case of Billy G.

Billy was in the third grade and having trouble. His teacher reported a number of classroom behavior problems. Billy was loud, talkative, and easily distracted. He was aggressive, and sometimes he struck the other children. His behavior was impulsive, erratic, and obviously hyperactive. He had become a totally disruptive force in the classroom.

Several conferences with the teacher finally convinced Billy's parents that the problem was not completely the school's responsibility. Indeed, much of Billy's behavior was mirrored at home, where he was equally difficult to control. His grades had plummeted in recent months, but his parents could not believe there was an intellectual problem. Therefore, it seemed to them that the explanation must lie in either physical or emotional factors.

Their first decision was to take Billy to their family physician. She could find nothing wrong physically and suggested that they have Billy see a neurologist. After a full neurological examination, including an electroencephalogram and an exhaustive behavioral and medical history, the neurologist could not arrive at a definitive diagnosis. There was no history of birth trauma, head injury, encephalitis, or risk factors for neurological disease. At the same time, a behavioral history compiled from teachers' reports, parental observations, and the neurologist's own observations confirmed the existence of a definite problem. The neurologist was leaning toward a diagnosis of attention-deficit/hyperactivity disorder (ADHD).

However, the neurologist was psychologically minded, and he felt that he detected a strained and somewhat hostile relationship between the parents. In the course of his conversations with the parents, he also learned that the husband was rarely home and seemed totally absorbed in his ambitions to advance in his job. The mother seemed to be reacting to her self-perceived neglect by becoming extremely active in community service and social functions. When Billy came home from school, she was almost always playing bridge, attending fund-raising activities, or shopping. It certainly seemed that neither parent had much time for Billy. In fact, only since Billy's problems had come to a head in school had the parents seemed aware of him at all.

Thus, the neurologist faced a diagnostic dilemma. Because stimulant medication (such as Ritalin) has often been effective with such cases, this might be the way to go. On the other hand, there certainly seemed to be a pattern of parental rejection that might have produced resentment in Billy. Therefore, the "hyperactivity" could be construed as an attempt to gain attention from the parents and parental surrogates (teachers). Such a formulation seemed to imply a recommendation of psychotherapy for the parents and for Billy as well.

The neurologist was concerned about making the wrong diagnosis. Medication has its side effects and might even exacerbate the problem. Further, if the problem were not ADHD, then Billy's behavioral reactions might become more established during the time wasted and psychotherapy might be more difficult. A diagnosis of ADHD might also create a greater unwillingness in the parents to accept their role in Billy's behavioral difficulties. On the other hand, suppose that the family went the psychotherapeutic route, only to learn later that the problem was treatable with medication. Then precious time would have been wasted, and perhaps avoidable physical harm would have occurred.

Thus, the assessment question became one of choosing between a behavioral or biological explanation for Billy's problems—each of which had very distinct treatment implications. Faced with this quandary, the neurologist decided to refer Billy to a clinical child psychologist, who could be expected to administer a variety of intelligence and personality tests, to interview the parents more thoroughly, and to observe Billy under a variety of conditions. The neurologist hoped that a psychological report, coupled with his own neurological findings, would allow him to arrive at a more informed diagnostic and treatment decision.

The Referral

The assessment process begins with a referral. Someone—a parent, a teacher, a psychiatrist, a judge, or perhaps a psychologist—poses a question about the patient. "Why is Johnny disobedient?" "Why can't Alice learn to read like the other children?" "Is the patient's impoverished behavioral repertoire a function of poor learning opportunities, or does this constriction represent an effort to avoid close relationships with other people who might be threatening?"

Clinicians thus begin with the *referral question*. It is important that they take pains to understand precisely what the question is or what the referral source is seeking. In some instances, the question may be impossible to answer; in others, the clinician may decide that a direct answer is inappropriate or that the question needs rephrasing. For example, the clinician may decide that the question "Is this patient capable of murder?" is unanswerable unless there is more information about the situation. Thus, the question might be rephrased to include probabilities with respect to certain kinds of situations. If parents want their child tested for the sole, often narcissistic, purpose of determining the child's IQ, the clinician might decide that providing such information would eventually do the child more harm than good. Most parents do not have the psychometric background to understand what the numerical IQ estimate means and are quite likely to misinterpret it. Thus, before accepting the referral in an instance of this kind, the clinical psychologist would be well advised to discuss matters with the parents.

What Influences How the Clinician Addresses the Referral Question?

The kinds of information sought are often heavily influenced by the clinician's theoretical commitments. For example, a psychodynamic clinician may be more likely to ask about early childhood experiences than a behavioral clinician. In other cases, the information obtained may be similar, but clinicians will make different inferences from it. For example, frequent headaches may suggest the presence of underlying hostility to a psychodynamic clinician but merely evidence of job stress to a behavioral clinician. For some clinicians, case history data are important because they aid in helping the client develop an anxiety hierarchy; for others, they are a way of confirming hypotheses about the client's needs and expectations.

Assessment, then, is not a completely standardized set of procedures. All clients are not given the same tests or asked the same questions. The purpose of assessment is not to discover the "true psychic essence" of the client but to describe that client in a way that is useful to the referral source—a way that will lead to the solution of a problem. Of course, this does not mean that one description is as good as another for a particular case. One clinician's cognitive-behavioral formulation of a case may involve a poor understanding of cognitive-behavioral theory. There are even instances in which certain cases seem to lend themselves more to a psychodynamic description than to a behavioral description. Because of the complexity of our subject matter and of the incomplete state of our knowledge, there is sometimes more than one good road to Rome.

The Interview

Almost all professions count interviewing as a chief technique for gathering data and making decisions. For politicians, consumers, psychiatrists, employers, or people in general, interviewing has always been a major tool. As with any activity that is engaged in frequently, people sometimes take interviewing for granted or believe that it involves no special skills; they can easily overestimate their understanding of the interview process. Although many people seem awed by the mystique of projective tests or impressed by the psychometric intricacies of objective tests, there is an easy yet deceptive familiarity to interviewing.

The *assessment interview* is at once the most basic and the most serviceable technique used by the clinical psychologist. In the hands of a skilled clinician, its wide range of application and adaptability make it a major instrument for clinical decision making, understanding, and prediction. But for all this, we must not lose sight of the fact that the clinical utility of the interview can be no greater than the skill and sensitivity of the clinician who uses it. In this section, we will discuss

Clinical psychologists frequently use interviews to assess their clients or patients.
© *CORBIS*

some basic features of the clinical interview, as well as the various interviewing skills and techniques that must be mastered.

General Characteristics of Interviews

An Interaction. An interview is an interaction between at least two persons. Each participant contributes to the process, and each influences the responses of the other. But this characterization falls short of defining the process. Ordinary conversation is interactional, but surely interviewing goes beyond that. Interviewing, like conversation, involves face-to-face verbal encounters or exchanges. However, a clinical interview is initiated with a goal or set of goals in mind. The interviewer approaches the interaction purposefully, bearing the responsibility for keeping the interview on track and moving toward the goal. Thus, the easy informality that often characterizes ordinary conversation is less evident. A good interview is one that is carefully planned, deliberately and skillfully executed, and goal oriented throughout.

Interviewing clearly takes many forms—from fact-finding to emotional release to cross-examination. However, all forms of professionally executed interviews are devoid of one feature that often characterizes normal conversation: Interviewers are not using the interchange to achieve either personal satisfaction or enhanced prestige. They are using it to elicit data, information, beliefs, or attitudes in the most skilled fashion possible.

Interviews versus Tests. In a sense, interviews occupy a position somewhere between ordinary conversation and tests. Interviews are more purposeful and organized than conversation, but sometimes less formalized or standardized than psychological tests. The exceptions are the structured diagnostic interviews, to be discussed later in this chapter. Structured interviews in some ways resemble standardized psychological tests. The hallmark of psychological testing is the collection of data under standardized conditions by means of explicit procedures. Most interviews, however, make provision for at least

BOX 6-1

Hot Topic   *Computer Interviewing: Are Clinicians Necessary?*

In recent years, use of *computer interviewing* has been growing. Computers have been used to take psychiatric histories, cover assessment of specific problems, do behavioral assessments, and assist in the diagnosis of mental disorders (First, 1994; Greist, 1998; Kobak, Greist, Jefferson, & Katzelnick, 1996). Such uses of the computer are said to have several advantages (Erdman, Klein, & Greist, 1985; First, 1994; Greist, 1998). For example, the computer always asks all the questions assigned, reliability is 100%, and for some patients at least, it is less uncomfortable and embarrassing to deal with an inanimate object than a live clinician. At the same time, computers are impersonal and, some might even say, dehumanizing. Then, too, only structured interviews can be employed; interviewer flexibility is not possible (First, 1994). For example, it is not possible to ask additional questions aimed at clarification when an interviewee's response is unclear. Also, the wording and order of questions cannot be tailored to meet the special needs of individual patients. Still, computer interviews have been shown to be useful in identifying target symptoms in clients (Farrell, Complair, & McCullough, 1987). There are computerized versions of diagnostic interviews as well. For example, the *Computerized Diagnostic Interview Schedule Revised* (Blouin, 1991), or CDISR, can be administered by a personal computer, and it assesses the presence and severity of symptoms related to more than 30 Axis I mental disorder diagnoses (for example, major depression, alcohol dependence, panic disorder). Studies comparing computer-administered and interviewer-administered versions of the DIS have been supportive (Blouin, Perez, & Blouin, 1988; Greist et al., 1987).

Finally, it is interesting to note that the use of computer-assisted interviews has been taken a step further. Recently, Baer et al. (1995) reported preliminary data on a fully automated

some flexibility. Thus, a unique characteristic of the interview method is the wider opportunity it provides for an individualized approach that will be effective in eliciting data from a particular person or patient. This flexibility represents both the strength and the weakness of many interviewing techniques. Although one can seek information in the way that seems most appropriate for Patient X, there is also a distinct potential for unreliability and error. We'll have more to say about threats to the reliability and validity of interview data later in this chapter.

The Art of Interviewing. Interviewing has often been regarded as an art. Except in the most structured, formal interviews, there is a degree of freedom to exercise one's skill and resourcefulness that is generally absent from other assessment procedures. When to probe, when to be silent, and when to be indirect or subtle are decisions that test the skill of the interviewer. With experience, one learns to respond to interviewee cues in a progressively more sensitive fashion that ultimately serves the purposes of the interview (Shea, 1998).

However, it is important to remember that a considerable amount of research on interviewing has been carried out. Consequently, there is a solid foundation of scientific research on interviewing. Practically, this means that novices do not need to rely solely on the slow and sometimes painful accumulation of experience in or-

telephone screening system that uses computerized digital voice recordings and touch-tone responses to assess community residents for symptoms of depression. In this study, a screening test was offered to community residents. When the toll-free number was called, a series of questions about a variety of depressive symptoms was administered to each caller. Callers answered the questions by selecting specified numbers on the telephone keypad, and there was an option to have the question repeated. All text was narrated by a professional actress and actor. Immediate feedback regarding the level of depression (no depression, minimal or mild depression, severe or extreme depression) was provided to each caller. Toll-free telephone numbers of selected health care professionals were provided to all callers whose responses indicated at least minimal levels of depression.

Do these new computer applications mean the clinician will soon be obsolete? First (1994), for one, thinks not. Although he acknowledges the various advantages of computer-assisted interview assessments, he cites several reasons why the computer cannot currently replace the clinician:

- Many nonverbal cues (such as facial expressions and vocal inflections) are not currently amenable to computer-based assessment.
- We do not currently have computer-based technology that can process unrestricted language (that is, free-form patient responses that are typed or submitted in response to computer queries).
- Only clinicians can encode and process information relevant to the course of a mental disorder or temporal sequencing of symptoms.
- Only clinicians are able to apply "clinical judgment"—the implicit threshold of clinical significance.

However, it is important to note that technological advances may someday make several of First's points moot, and, as we will discuss in Chapter 10, clinical judgment has its limitations as well.

der to polish their skill. They can profit from the study of a considerable body of research on interviewing that provides a scientific foundation for their art (Garb, 1998; Wiens, 1983).

Interviewing Essentials and Techniques

Many factors influence the productivity and utility of data obtained from interviews. Some involve the physical setting. Others are related to the nature of the patient. A mute or uncommunicative patient may not cooperate regardless of the level of the interviewer's skills. Few interviewers are effective with every patient. Several factors or skills, however, can increase the likelihood that interviews will be productive. Training

and supervised experience in interviewing are very important. Techniques that work well for one interviewer can be notably less effective for another; there is a crucial interaction between technique and interviewer. This is why gaining experience in a supervised setting is so important; it enables the interviewer to achieve some awareness of the nature of this interaction. Training, then, involves not just a simple memorization of rules but, rather, a growing knowledge of the relationships among rules, the concrete situation being confronted, and one's own impact in interview situations.

The Physical Arrangements. An interview can be conducted anywhere that two people can meet and interact. On some occasions, this happens by chance—an encounter with a patient on the street, for example. Usually, the clinician does not choose such a setting. But the needs of the patient, the degree of urgency in the situation, or even, in some instances, sheer coincidence may make an interview of sorts inevitable.

Obviously, certain physical arrangements are especially desirable for an interview. Two of the most important considerations are privacy and protection from interruptions. Nothing is more damaging to the continuity of an interview than a phone that rings relentlessly, a secretary's query, or an imperative knock on the door. Such interruptions are extremely disruptive. But even more important is the message they subtly convey—that the patient and his or her problems are of secondary importance. After all, secretaries do not knock on the door or put through a call if they have been instructed otherwise.

Because lack of privacy can lead to many deleterious outcomes, soundproofing is also very important. If noise from a hallway or an adjacent office intrudes, patients will probably assume that their own voices can also be heard outside. Few patients are likely to be open and responsive under such conditions.

The office or its furnishings can be as distracting as loud noises and external clamor. There are few rules in this area, and much depends on individual taste. However, many clinicians prefer offices that are fairly neutral, yet tasteful. In short, an office with furnishings that demand attention or seem to cry out for comment would not be ideal. The therapist-golfer need not turn the office into a shrine for those who chase par; the therapist with a penchant for antique cars would do well not to litter the desk with scale models of 1928 Fords. Somehow, there must be a middle ground between an office that is cold and forbidding through its very neutrality and one that is littered with obtrusive and distracting objects.

Note-Taking and Recording. All contacts with clients ultimately need to be documented. However, there is some debate over whether notes should be taken *during* an interview. Although there are few absolutes, in general, it would seem desirable to take occasional notes during an interview. A few key phrases jotted down will help the clinician's recall. Most clinicians have had the experience of feeling that the material in an interview is so important that there is no need to take notes—that the material will easily be remembered. However, after having seen a few additional patients, the clinician may not be able to recall much from the earlier interview. Therefore, a moderate amount of note-taking seems worthwhile. Most patients will not be troubled by it, and if one should be, the topic can be discussed. Occasionally a patient may comment that what is said must be really important since you are taking it down. Occasionally, too, a patient may request that the clinician not take notes while a certain topic is being discussed. Most patients probably expect a certain amount of note-taking.

However, any attempt at taking verbatim notes should be avoided (except when administering a structured interview, discussed below). One danger in taking verbatim notes is that this practice may prevent the clinician from attending fully to the essence of the patient's verbalizations. An overriding compulsion to get it all down can detract from a genuine understanding of the nuances and significance of the patient's remarks. In addition, excessive note-taking tends to prevent the clinician from observing the patient and from noting subtle changes of expression or slight changes in body position. Furthermore, a fully transcribed interview will have to be read in full later. The clinician must plow through 50 minutes of notes in order to extract the most important material, which may have taken up only 10 minutes of the interview.

With today's technology, it is easy to audiotape or videotape interviews. Under no circumstances should this be done without the patient's fully informed consent. In the vast majority of cases, a few minutes' explanation of the desirability of taping, with an accompanying assurance to the patient that the tape will be kept confidential (or released only to persons authorized by the patient), will result in complete cooperation. Because today's world is awash with audio and video recording, most patients are unlikely to object to it. By and large, patients are not even upset by a microphone and recorder that is in plain view. There may be a few passing moments of self-consciousness, but these quickly fade. Indeed, it may turn out that the clinician is more threatened by the recording than the patient, especially if the interview is likely to be examined or evaluated by superiors or consultants.

In some instances, it is desirable to videotape certain interviews. In the interests of research, of training interviewers or therapists, or of feedback to the patient as part of the therapeutic process, videotaping sometimes has great value. Like audio recording, it should be done openly, unobtrusively, and with the patient's informed consent.

Rapport

Perhaps the most essential ingredient of a good interview is a relationship between the clinician and the patient. The quality and nature of that relationship will vary, of course, depending on the purpose of the interview. These differences will undoubtedly affect the kind of relationship that develops during the contact.

Definition and Functions. *Rapport* is the word often used to characterize the relationship between patient and classification. Rapport involves a comfortable atmosphere and a mutual understanding of the purpose of the interview. Good rapport can be a primary instrument by which the clinician achieves the purposes of the interview. A cold, hostile, or adversarial relationship is not likely to be constructive. Although a positive atmosphere is certainly not the sole ingredient for a productive interview (a warm yet ill-prepared or slow-witted interviewer will not generate the best of interviews), it is usually a necessary one. Whatever skills the interviewer possesses will surely be rendered more effective in proportion to the interviewer's capacity to establish a positive relationship.

Patients approach most interviews with some degree of anxiety. They may be anxious lest they are discovered to be "crazy"; they may be fearful that what they state in the interview will be passed along to employers. Whatever the specific nature of these concerns, their presence is enough to reduce the interviewer's potential effectiveness.

Characteristics. Good rapport can be achieved in many ways—perhaps as many ways as there are clinicians. However, no bag of "rapport tricks" is likely to substitute for an attitude of acceptance, understanding, and respect for the integrity of the patient. Such an attitude does not require that the clinician like every patient. It does not require the clinician to befriend every patient. It does not require the clinician to master an agreed-upon set of behaviors guaranteed to produce instant rapport. It *does* require that patients not be prejudged based on the problems they seek help for. Attitudes of understanding, sincerity, acceptance, and empathy are not techniques; to regard them as such is to miss their true import. To ask to be taught how to appear sincere, accepting, and empathic is to confess the absence of these qualities.

When patients realize that the clinician is trying to understand their problems in order to help them, then a broad range of interviewer behavior becomes possible. Probing, confrontation, and interviewer assertiveness may be acceptable once rapport has been established. If the patient accepts the clinician's ultimate goal of helping, a state of mutual liking is not necessary. The patient will recognize that the clinician is not seeking personal satisfaction in the interview. Rapport is not, as is often thought by beginning students, a state wherein the clinician is always liked or always regarded as a great person. It is, rather, a relationship founded upon respect, mutual confidence, trust, and a certain degree of permissiveness. It is neither a prize bestowed by an awed client nor a popularity contest to be won by the clinician.

Some patients have had past experiences that will not easily permit them to accept even genuine overtures for a professional relationship. But in most cases, if the clinician perseveres in the proper role and maintains an attitude of respect as she or he searches for understanding, the relationship will develop. A common mistake of beginning interviewers in early interviews is to say something like "There, there, don't worry; I know exactly what you're feeling." Such comments may actually convince clients that the interviewer does not really know how they feel. After all, how could this stranger possibly know how I feel? Rapport will come, but it will come through quiet attitudes of respect, acceptance, and competence rather than through quick fixes.

Communication

In any interview, there must be communication. Whether we are helping persons in distress or assisting patients in realizing their potential, communication is our vehicle. The real problem is to identify those skills or techniques that will ensure maximum communication.

Beginning a Session. It is often useful to begin an assessment session with a casual conversation. A brief comment or question about difficulties in finding a parking space or even a banal comment on the weather may help establish the clinician as a real person and allay any fears the patient may have had as to whether he or she can ever relate to a "shrink." But whatever its specific content, a brief conversation designed to relax things before plunging into the patient's reasons for coming will usually facilitate a good interview.

Language. Of extreme importance is the use of language that the patient can understand. Some initial estimate of the patient's background, educational level, or general sophistication should be made. The kind of language employed should then reflect that judgment. It is offensive to speak to a 40-year-old woman with a master's degree in history as if she were an eighth grader. It is not necessary to infantilize people seeking help; asking for help need not imply that one has a diminished capacity to understand.

At the same time, it may be necessary to abandon psychological jargon in order to be understood by some patients. And it may well be that the depth of our understanding is questionable if we cannot communicate without resorting to four-syllable words. If we find ourselves unwittingly using grandiose language to extort admiration from patients, then something is wrong. Similarly, clinicians who try to use "teenage" language when interviewing a 15-year-old may wind up not only alienating the client but looking foolish in the process. In short, if your respect for the patient is intact, you generally need not reach for shallower techniques.

In a related vein, it is important to use words that will be interpreted by the patient as you mean them to be. Very often, for example, asking a mother how her son behaves is likely to prompt the response, "Oh, he's a good boy—he does just what I tell him." Sometimes we psychologists become so focused on concepts such as *behavior* that we forget what these words mean to most people.

It is also important to clarify the intended meaning of a word or term used by a client if there is any uncertainty or alternative interpretations. For example, a clinician should not assume he or she knows what a client means by the statement "She's abusive." It may indicate that the individual does not treat others particularly well, or it may indicate that the individual is physically abusive—something that warrants immediate intervention.

The Use of Questions. Maloney and Ward (1976) observed that the clinician's questions may become progressively more structured as the interview proceeds. They distinguish among several forms of questions, including open-ended, facilitative, clarifying, confronting, and direct questions. Each is designed in its own way to promote communication. And each is useful for a specific purpose or patient. Table 6-1 illustrates these types of questions.

■ TABLE 6-1 Five Types of Interview Questions

Type	Importance	Example
Open-ended	Gives patient responsibility and latitude for responding	"Would you tell me about your experiences in the Army?"
Facilitative	Encourages patient's flow of conversation	"Can you tell me a little more about that?"
Clarifying	Encourages clarity or amplification	"I guess this means you felt like . . . ?"
Confronting	Challenges inconsistencies or contradictions	"Before, when you said . . . ?"
Direct	Once rapport has been established and patient is taking responsibility for conversation, such questions can be efficient and useful.	"What did you say to your father when he criticized your choice?"

Source: Maloney & Ward (1976).

Silence. Perhaps nothing is more disturbing to a beginning interviewer than silence. However, silences can mean many things. The important thing is to assess the meaning and function of silence in the context of the specific interview. The clinician's response to silence should be reasoned and responsive to the goals of the interview rather than to personal needs or insecurities. Perhaps the client is organizing a thought or deciding which topic to discuss next. Perhaps the silence is indicative of some resistance. But it is as inappropriate to jump in and fill every momentary silence with chatter as it is to simply wait out the patient every time, regardless of the length of the silence. Whether the clinician ends a lengthy silence with a comment about the silence or decides to introduce a new line of inquiry, the response should facilitate communication and understanding and not be a desperate solution to an awkward moment.

Listening. If we are to communicate effectively in the clinician's role, our communication must reflect understanding and acceptance. We cannot hope to do this if we have not been listening. For it is by listening that we come to appreciate the information and emotions that the patient is conveying. If we are concerned about impressing the client, if we are insecure in our role, if we are guided by motivations other than the need to understand and accept, then we are not likely to be effective listeners. Many people, for example, when introduced to someone, cannot recall the name two minutes later. The most common reason for this is a failure to listen. They were distracted, preoccupied, or perhaps so concerned about their own appearance that they never really heard the name. It sometimes happens that therapists are so sure of an impression about the patient that they stop listening and thereby ignore important new data. The skilled clinician is one who has learned when to be an active listener.

Gratification of Self. The clinical interview is not the time or the place for clinicians to work out their own problems. Sometimes a clinician is professionally insecure or inexperienced. Sometimes the patient's problems, experiences, or conversation remind clinicians of their own problems or threaten their own values, attitudes, or adjustment. In one way or another, however, clinicians must resist the temptation to shift the focus to themselves. Rather, their focus must remain on the patient. This is obviously a matter of degree. None of us is so self-controlled that our thoughts never wander or our concentration never falters. However, the clinician-patient roles are definite and should not be confused.

In some instances, the patient will ask personal questions of the clinician. In general, clinicians should avoid discussing their personal lives or opinions. However, this advice must be tempered by awareness of the reasons for the question. Thus, a breezy opening question by a patient, such as "Say, what did you think of that basketball game last night?" does not have the same significance as the question "Do you think Freud was correct in his assessment of the importance of penis envy in women?" When a question seems to suggest something of importance about the patient's problems, it is usually best to deflect it or to turn it around so that you can pursue your clinical hypothesis. But if a question is trivial, innocent, or otherwise basically inconsequential, a failure to respond directly will probably be perceived as the worst kind of evasion.

The Impact of the Clinician. Some years ago, one of the authors worked in a clinic with several therapists. One therapist was a fifty-ish, matronly psychiatrist with a marked affinity for print housedresses. Another was a clinical psychologist—male, very youthful in appearance, quite thin, carefully dressed, and seemingly quite unsure of himself. It was inevitable that these two therapists would be perceived differently by their patients. The point is that each of us has a characteristic impact on others, both socially and professionally. As a result, the same behavior in different clinicians is unlikely to provoke the same response from a patient. The tall, well-muscled, athletic therapist may somewhat intimidate certain kinds of patients. The very feminine female interviewer may elicit responses in a client very different from those elicited by her male counterpart. Therefore, it behooves all clinicians to cultivate a degree of self-insight or at least a mental set to consider the possible effects of their own impact before attaching meaning to the behavior of their patients.

The Clinician's Values and Background. Nearly everyone accepts the notion that one's own values, background, and biases will affect one's perceptions. Unfortunately, we are usually more skilled at validating this notion in others than in ourselves. Therefore, clinicians must examine their own experiences and seek the bases for their own assumptions before making clinical judgments of others. What to the clinician may appear to be evidence of severe pathology may actually reflect the patient's culture. Take the following example:

A 48-year-old ethnic Chinese woman had been receiving antipsychotic and antidepressant medication for psychotic depression. On this regimen, the patient had lost even more weight and more hope and had become more immobilized. A critical element in this diagnosis of psychosis was the woman's belief that her deceased mother, who had appeared in her dreams, had traveled from the place of the dead to induce the patient's own death and to bring her to the next world. We interpreted this symptom not as a delusional belief but as a culturally consistent belief in a depressed woman who had recently begun to see her deceased mother in her dreams (a common harbinger of death in the dreams of some Asian patients). This patient responded well after the antipsychotic medication was discontinued, the antidepressant medication was reduced in dosage, and weekly psychotherapy was instituted. (Westermeyer, 1987, pp. 471–472)

This case illustrates how all the behavioral cues that clinicians typically rely upon may lose their meaning when applied to a patient from another culture. We begin to realize how much a clinician's ability to make sense of a patient's verbalizations is dependent upon a shared background. For example, some midwestern clinicians listening to Asian American patients may suddenly feel as if they have lost their own frame of reference. But in dealing with midwestern patients, how many times will those same clinicians mistakenly assume that their frames of reference are identical to those of their patients?

In other cases, gender differences can sometimes produce nearly the same effects. Gender-related factors can interact with a clinician's values and background. Then, everything from sheer ignorance to gender stereotypes can conspire to reduce the validity of the assessment interview. The answer seems to lie in making assessors more gender-aware (L. S. Brown, 1990; Good, Gilbert, & Scher, 1990). How does one become more gender aware? An expert in gender issues has made the following suggestions:

> Clinicians seeking to enhance their gender awareness might focus on three areas—their knowledge, attitudes, and behaviors. Knowledge is typically increased by reading (such as research and conceptual articles and books) or attending a course or seminar on gender issues. Attitudes are enhanced through experiences with people holding conceptions of gender that differ from one's own (such as people from differing cultures, religions, or sexual orientations), which serve to broaden our understanding of gender issues. Behaviors are improved through practice and feedback (with a supervisor that has expertise in gender-related issues).
> (G. Good, personal communication)

The Patient's Frame of Reference

If the clinician is going to be effective in achieving the goals of the interview, it is essential that he or she have an idea of how the patient views the first meeting. Only with such awareness can the patient's verbalizations and behaviors be placed in their proper context. By the same token, the establishment of rapport will be more difficult if the clinician is not sensitive to the patient's initial perceptions and expectations. A patient may have an entirely distorted notion of the clinic and even be ashamed of having to seek help.

Sometimes patients have been pressured into seeking help. A spouse has finally said, "Do it or we're through!" A sorority lays down an ultimatum that a member either "get therapy" or leave the house. Some patients present themselves at the clinic in order to placate employers. Whatever the reason, it will inevitably color the nature of interview behavior.

For many individuals, going to see a clinical psychologist arouses feelings of inadequacy. Some individuals will respond to this by "clamming up." Others will display a kind of bravura that says, "See, I'm not weak at all!" Still others may become competitive and imply that psychology is not all it's cracked up to be or suggest that it is really unlikely that the clinician has much to offer. In contrast, there are patients who start with a view of the clinician as a kind of savior. Although it is often quite reinforcing to be viewed as a miracle worker or a great healer, remember that the patient will probably reconsider this evaluation later. For example, a young inpatient diagnosed with borderline personality disorder once informed the entire inpatient unit that one of the authors was the best therapist in the hospital and maybe one of the best in all of clinical psychology. Imagine the author's chagrin when he witnessed, four days later, the same patient's announcement that the author was a horrible therapist and an embarrassment to his profession.

Some individuals seek help so that they will have someone to intercede on their behalf. They are looking for a "middleman" to help fight their battles with spouse, employer, police, and so on. For example, one of the author's first patients was an alcoholic who had been hospitalized off and on for more than 20 years. Despite his problems, he was quite charming and highly articulate. His major motivation was to manipulate the author into interceding with the ward psychiatrist to get him open-ward privileges and an occasional visit to town.

The Clinician's Frame of Reference

In a sense, the general dictum here, as in any endeavor, is "Be prepared." This implies that the clinician should have carefully gone over any existing records on the patient, checked the information provided by the person who arranged the appointment, and so on. Such a posture will ensure that the clinician knows as much as can be known at that point about the patient. Such preparation may also minimize spending interview time going over material that the patient may already have covered with other clinic staff.

In addition, the clinician should be perfectly clear about the purpose of the interview. Is it to evaluate the patient for hospitalization? Is the patient seeking information? If the interview is being conducted on a referral basis, the clinician should be quite sure that he or she understands what information is being requested by the referring person. It is always disconcerting to discover later that, as a clinician, you misinterpreted the reason for the interview.

Through it all, the clinician must remain focused. However, objectivity need not imply coldness or aloofness. Rather, it suggests that the clinician must be secure enough to maintain composure and not lose sight of the purposes of the interview. For example, if a client should become very angry and attack the clinician's ability, training, or good intentions, the clinician must remember that the first obligation is to understand. The clinician should be secure enough to distinguish between reality and the forces that drive the patient.

Depending on the purpose of the interview, the clinician should also be prepared to provide some closure for the client at the conclusion of the interview. That is, as the interview progresses, the clinician will be formulating hypotheses and recommendations. A confident but enigmatic smile at the close of the interview, coupled with a "We'll be in touch," will not suffice. The clinician should be prepared to make a referral, set up another appointment, and/or provide some feedback to the client.

Varieties of Interviews

Up to this point, we have reviewed various interviewing essentials and techniques that are relevant to the interviewing process, regardless of the type of interview. In this section, we will discuss several of the more common types of interviews that clinical psychologists conduct. It is important to note, however, that more than one of these interviews may be administered to the same client or patient. For example, the same patient may complete an intake-admission interview when admitted to a hospital, a case-history and mental status examination interview once on the hospital unit, and later a structured diagnostic interview by the treating clinician. With this in mind, let us now turn to a survey of some of the more commonly used types of interviews.

The many varieties of interviews have two primary distinguishing features. First, interviews differ in their purpose. For example, the purpose of one interview may be to evaluate a client who is presenting to an outpatient clinic for the first time (intake-admission interview), whereas the purpose of another interview may be to arrive at a DSM-IV diagnostic formulation (diagnostic interview). The second major distinguishing factor is whether an interview is unstructured (often labeled a "clinical interview") or structured. In unstructured interviews, clinicians are allowed to ask any questions that come to mind, in any order. In contrast, structured interviews require the clinician to ask, verbatim, a set of standardized questions in a specified sequence. We will have much more to say about structured versus unstructured interviews later in this chapter.

The same kinds of skills are required regardless of the purpose or type of interview. Rapport, good communication skills, appropriate follow-up questions, and good observational skills are all necessary, even when administering a structured interview. Also, it is well to bear in mind that any assessment interview may have strong therapeutic overtones. After all, patients' perceptions of the clinic, their motivation, and their expectations for help may all be shaped to a significant extent by their experiences in intake interviews or in diagnostic screening sessions.

We will organize our presentation in this section according to the purpose of an interview. However, it is important to keep in mind that structured and unstructured versions of all these interviews exist.

The Intake-Admission Interview

An *intake interview* generally has two purposes: (1) to determine why the patient has come to the clinic or hospital, and (2) to judge whether the agency's facilities, policies, and services will meet the needs and expectations of the patient. Many times, a psychiatric social worker conducts such interviews. Often, these talks are face-to-face, but there has been an increasing tendency to use telephone contacts prior to the initial interview. A skilled, sensitive telephone interviewer can obtain much of the information that has traditionally been gathered at the clinic. Under some conditions or in particular clinics, the intake interview may be conducted by the same person who later does the diagnostic interview or the test workup. An advantage of this procedure is that patients do not get shoved from pillar to post as they make the rounds from one type of interview to the next.

Another function of the initial interview is to inform the patient of such matters as the clinic's functions, fees, policies, procedures, and personnel. Patients are consumers and have every right to information regarding services and charges. Such concrete details can certainly influence patients' motivation for therapy and can often dispel some myths that might decrease their expectations for help.

Box 6-2 presents an example of an intake report based on an interview with a prospective client in a community-based outpatient clinic.

The Case-History Interview

In a *case-history interview*, as complete a personal and social history as possible is taken. The clinician is interested both in concrete facts, dates, and events and in the patient's feelings about them. It is important to note that a relentless pursuit of dates and names can sometimes obscure important data and create in the patient a set to respond in concrete terms. This mental set can sometimes impede progress in later interviews.

Basically, the purpose of a case history is to provide a broad background and context in which both the patient and the problem can be placed. Our diagnostic and therapeutic technol-ogy is not yet so advanced that specific behaviors, problems, or thoughts can always be understood in exactly the same way in every person. It is therefore essential that the patient's problems be placed in a proper historical-developmental context so that their diagnostic significance and their therapeutic implications can be more reliably determined.

The range of material covered in personal-social histories is quite broad. It covers both childhood and adulthood, and it includes educational, sexual, medical, parental-environmental, religious, and psychopathological matters. Although, as noted above, much of this material will be factual, it is extremely important to take note of how patients present the material—how they speak about it, the emotional reactions to the material, evasiveness or openness, and so on.

Although most patients, particularly competent adults, provide their own personal-social history, other knowledgeable adults can often furnish invaluable data and impressions. A spouse, an employer, a teacher, or a friend can be rich sources of information. Clinicians have never made as much use of such sources as they might, perhaps because such additional interviews are costly in time and effort. In addition, there are issues of confidentiality and trust. Even when the patient gives consent and helps recruit the informants, many clinicians fear that using them can impede the subsequent therapeutic relationship. Still, outside sources can often provide a picture of the patient that cannot be achieved in any other fashion. In the case of young children, persons who are mentally retarded, and persons who are incompetent, there are, of course, fewer barriers to the use of such sources.

Table 6-2 (page 160) presents a typical case-history outline.

Mental Status Examination Interview

A *mental status examination* is typically conducted to assess the presence of cognitive, emotional, or behavioral problems. The general areas covered in such interviews, along with excerpts from a sample report, are shown in Table 6-3 (page 161).

BOX 6-2

Sample Intake Report

Name: MORTON, Charles (fictitious name)

Age: 22

Sex: Male

Occupation: Student

Date of interview: June 1, 1998

Therapist: Luke Baldry, Ph.D. (fictitious name)

Identifying Information: The client is a 22-year-old white male who is presently a full-time student at a large midwestern university. Currently, he lives alone in an apartment and works part-time at a local grocery store.

Chief Complaint: The client presents to the clinic today complaining of "depression" that reportedly has become worse over the past two weeks.

History of Presenting Problem: The client reports that he has experienced symptoms of depression "off and on" for the past year. These symptoms include (1) depressed mood ("feeling sad"); (2) appetite disturbance but no significant weight loss; (3) sleep disturbance (early morning awakening); (4) fatigue; (5) feelings of worthlessness; and (6) difficulty concentrating. All of these symptoms have been present nearly every day over the past two weeks.

The client reports that about one year ago, a long-standing romantic relationship of four years ended. Following this breakup, the client reports, he became increasingly withdrawn and, in addition to some of the symptoms noted above, experienced several crying spells. Although his adjustment to this event became better as time progressed, the client reports that the breakup "shook" his confidence and led to a decrease in the number of social activities he engaged in. Further, he reports that he has not dated since.

Last semester, the client transferred to this university from a community college in another midwestern location. He reports that the move was difficult both emotionally and academically. Specifically, being away from his hometown, family, and friends has led him to feel more isolated and dysphoric. Further, his grades this past semester reportedly suffered. He reports that his grades dropped from A's in his previous school to C's at this university. Toward the end of this past semester (once his

A major limitation of mental status interviews has been their unreliability, because they are often highly unstructured in their execution. To address this problem, structured mental status examination interviews have been devised. Here, specific questions are asked to assess behavior in a variety of areas. As noted by Richard Rogers (1995), it is important for clinical psychologists to be familiar with the mental status examination because these interviews are one of the primary modes of clinical assessment for a variety of mental health professionals (including psychiatrists).

The Crisis Interview

Increasingly, clinicians have been functioning in novel settings, including storefront clinics and telephone hotlines specializing in advice or comfort to drug users, to parents fearful of abusing their children, or to persons who are just lonely. Many of the usual "rules" of interviewing or the usual categorizations of interviews are blurred in these instances. However, the basic principles remain. Take the example of a mother who, during the absence of her husband, became terrified that she would abuse her small son. The following telephone conversation ensued:

probable grades in his classes became apparent), he developed an increasing number of depressive symptoms.

Past Treatment History: The client reports that he has not previously sought out psychological or psychiatric treatment.

Medical History: No significant medical history was reported.

Substance Use/Abuse: The client denies any current symptoms of substance abuse or dependence. He has "tried" marijuana on three occasions in the past but denies current use. He reports drinking, on average, 3–4 cans of beer per week.

Medication: The client reports that he is not currently taking any medication.

Family History: Both of the client's biological parents are living, and he has one brother (age 20) and one sister (age 26). The client reports that his mother suffers from depression and has received outpatient treatment on numerous occasions. Further, he reports that his maternal grandfather was diagnosed with depression. No substance use problems among family members were noted.

Suicidal/Homicidal Ideation: The client denied any current or past suicidal or homicidal ideation, intent, or action.

Mental Status: The client was well-groomed, cooperative, and dressed appropriately. He was alert and oriented in all spheres. His mood and affect were dysphoric. His speech was clear, coherent, and goal-directed. Some attention and concentration difficulties were noted. Further, his immediate memory was mildly impaired. No evidence of formal thought disorder, delusions, hallucinations, or suicidal/homicidal ideation was found. His insight and judgment appear to be fair.

Diagnostic Impression

Axis I: 296.22, Major Depressive Disorder, Single Episode
Axis II: V71.09, No Diagnosis
Axis III: None
Axis IV: Problems related to the social environment
          Educational problems
Axis V: GAF = 55 (current)

Recommendations: Individual psychotherapy. Cognitive-behavioral treatment for depression.

Luke Baldry, Ph.D.
Licensed Clinical Psychologist

Mother: My God, help me. Is this the place . . . that . . . I mean, I need somebody. Tell me.

Volunteer: Yes, it is. Tell me what it is. Go ahead and talk.

Mother: I'm so nervous. I feel like I'll bust. Danny is crying, and my husband isn't here, and I've got to stop him. I can't stand it any longer.

Volunteer: OK, I think I understand. Are you alone?

Mother: Yes, but I can't handle it.

Volunteer: I know. And you're very upset. But I think we can talk it over. Where are you? What's your address?

Mother: I'm at home at 308 Park Place. I wish John would come home. I feel better when he's here. I just can't handle it. Nobody thought I should get married.

Volunteer: What do you think is wrong? Are you afraid of hurting Danny?

Mother: He won't stop crying. He's always crying. John doesn't know what it's like. I suppose he blames me—I know Mother does. (Starts crying uncontrollably.)

■ **TABLE 6-2** A Typical Case-History Outline

1. *Identifying data*, including name, sex, occupation, address, date and place of birth, religion, and education.

2. *Reason for coming* to the agency and expectations for service.

3. *Present situation*, such as description of daily behavior and any recent or impending changes.

4. *Family constellation* (family of orientation), including descriptions of mother, father, and other family members and the respondent's role in the family in which he or she grew up.

5. *Early recollections*, descriptions of earliest clear events and their surroundings.

6. *Birth and development*, including ages of walking and talking, problems compared with other children, and the person's view of his or her early experiences.

7. *Health*, including childhood and later diseases and injuries, problems with drugs or alcohol, and comparison of one's body with others.

8. *Education and training*, including subjects of special interest and achievement.

9. *Work record*, including reasons for changing jobs and attitudes toward work.

10. *Recreation and interests*, including volunteer work, reading, and the respondent's report of adequacy of self-expression and pleasures.

11. *Sexual development*, covering first awareness, kinds of sexual activities, and view of the adequacy of sexual expressions.

12. *Marital and family data*, covering major events and what led to them, and comparison of present family of birth and orientation.

13. *Self-description*, including strengths, weaknesses, and ideals.

14. *Choices and turning points in life*, a review of the respondent's most important decisions and changes, including the single most important happening.

15. *View of the future*, including what the subject would like to see happen next year and in five or ten years, and what is necessary for these events to happen.

16. *Any further material* the respondent may see as omitted from the history.

Source: Norman D. Sundberg, *Assessment of Persons,* © 1977, pp. 97–98. Reprinted by permission of Prentice Hall, Englewood Cliffs, New Jersey.

Volunteer: Look, that's all right. Take it easy. Where is John?

Mother: He's . . . he drives a truck. He won't be back till Thursday.

Volunteer: I think I understand . . . and I know this is hard for you. Have you talked with anybody about your feelings on these things?

Mother: No. Well, with Marge next door a little bit. She said she felt like that a few times. But . . . I don't know.

The volunteer in this situation kept on reinforcing the notion that she understood. The calm yet confident manner of the volunteer seemed to reassure the mother, who agreed to come in the next afternoon and to bring her son along with her.

Obviously, the purpose of the *crisis interview* is to meet problems as they occur and to provide an immediate resource. Their purpose is to deflect the potential for disaster and to encourage callers to enter into a relationship with the clinic or make a referral so that a longer-term solution

TABLE 6-3 **Mental Status Examination Interview of a 24-Year-Old Man Diagnosed with Schizophrenia**

General Outline of Mental Status Examination
- I. General Presentation: Appearance, Behavior, Attitude
- II. State of Consciousness: Alert, Hyperalert, Lethargic
- III. Attention and Concentration
- IV. Speech: Charity, Goal-directedness, Language deficits
- V. Orientation: To Person, Place, Time
- VI. Mood and Affect
- VII. Form of Thought; Formal Thought Disorder
- VIII. Thought Content: Preoccupations, Obsessions, Delusions
- IX. Ability to Think Abstractly
- X. Perceptions: Hallucinations
- XI. Memory: Immediate, Recent, Remote
- XII. Intellectual Functioning
- XIII. Insight and Judgment

* * * * * * * * * * * * * * * * *

The patient appeared disheveled and exhibited "odd" behavior throughout the interview. Although he appeared alert, some impairment in his attention and concentration was noted. Specifically, he experienced difficulty repeating a series of digits and performing simple calculations without the aid of pencil and paper. No language deficits were noted, although the patient's speech was at times difficult to understand and did not appear to be goal directed (not a response to the question posed). He was oriented to person and place, but was not oriented to time. Specifically, he was unsure of the month and day. He reported his mood as "fine"; his affect appeared to be blunted. He demonstrated some signs of formal thought disorder: tangentiality and loose associations. He denied suicidal ideation but did report his belief that he was being "framed by the FBI" for a crime he did not commit. When confronted with the fact that he was in a psychiatric hospital, not a prison, he stated that this was all part of an FBI "cover-up," so that he could be made to look "crazy." Although he denied hallucinations, his behavior suggested that, on occasion, he was responding to auditory hallucinations. For example, he stared off into space and began whispering on several occasions. His ability to abstract appeared to be impaired. For example, when asked how a baseball and an orange are alike, he responded, "They both are alive." The patient's immediate and recent memories were slightly impaired, although his remote memory was intact. It is estimated that he is of average intelligence. Currently, his insight and judgment appear to be poor.

can be worked out. Such interviewing requires training, sensitivity, and judgment. Asking the wrong question in a case-history interview may only result in a piece of misinformation. However, a caller who is asked a wrong question on the telephone may hang up. As clinical services begin to transcend the boundaries of the conventional clinic, there is a chance that they will be diluted by having to operate in situations that offer less opportunity for control. But the problems seem to be outweighed by the opportunity to intervene during real crises.

PROFILE 6-1

Thomas A. Widiger, Ph.D.

Dr. Thomas Widiger, a professor in the Psychology Department of the University of Kentucky, is perhaps best known for his work in the areas of classification and diagnosis of mental disorders. In his career, he has published close to 200 articles, books, or book chapters. As one of the few psychologists intimately involved in the latest revision of the diagnostic manual of mental disorders, Dr. Widiger served as Research Coordinator of DSM-IV. Dr. Widiger is the author of two semi-structured interviews, the *Personality Disorder Interview–IV*, or PDI-IV (Widiger, Mangine, Corbitt, Ellis, & Thomas, 1995), and the *Structured Interview for the Five Factor Model of Personality* (Trull & Widiger, 1997). We had the chance to ask Dr. Widiger a few questions about his background, his perspective on the field, and his thoughts on structured interviews.

What originally got you interested in the field of clinical psychology?

I suppose that what originally got me interested in clinical psychology was genetic dispositions and parental influences. However, my memory is that I was interested in why I was the way I was. Most of my friends who were in college were art majors, although one was pre-dental and another was pre-medicine (none were psychology majors). Those who did not attend college worked in the fields of auto mechanics and highway repair. For the first two years of college I majored in creative writing. I wanted to be a novelist.

However, I did recognize that it would be very difficult to make a reasonable living writing poetry and novels. In the second semester of my sophomore year, I took a course in abnormal psychology. I found it very interesting, rivaling even an English literature course that was taught by a very long-haired hippie who had students over to his house to discuss Vonnegut, Heller, and Castenada (the good old days). Clinical psychology was a field that was concerned with issues that were (or should be) of central importance to any individual's life—why you are the way you are and what you can do about it. Perhaps my interest was typical for a college-age student going through a normal period of identity confusion, or perhaps it reflected a concern with my own conflicts and struggles.

At the end of the semester, I asked the instructor to recommend some additional readings. I was attending a junior college, and this was the only advanced course in psychology that was offered. He recommended three books: Freud's *Interpretation of Dreams*, R. D. Laing's *Divided Self*, and Sandor Ferenczi's *Sex in Psychoanalysis*. I have no idea why he included Ferenczi's text along with Freud's and Laing's; one can only speculate. In any case, I was fascinated with the texts by Freud and Laing. I read them through voraciously, bought additional books by Freud, Laing, and others, and decided then to switch my major to clinical psychology.

Describe what activities you are involved in as a clinical psychologist.

My primary activity within clinical psychology is conducting and supervising research. I am fortunate to be assisted by many bright, motivated, and talented graduate students. Most of my studies are in collaboration with them. We meet regularly to discuss and generate new ideas for research, as well as to work out the nuts and bolts of ongoing projects. In my opinion, most (if not all) of the controversies and disputes within clinical psychology can be meaningfully informed, if not ultimately resolved, by empirical research, and I enjoy the challenge of trying to design and implement informative projects.

I also teach a number of graduate and undergraduate courses, including Abnormal Psychology, Psychopathology, History of Clinical Psychology, Ethical Issues in Clinical Psychology, and Personality. I try to emphasize current issues and controversies. Some of my more successful studies were generated in part through class discussions.

I am also an investigator for Kentucky's State Board of Psychology. Clinical psychologists within the state of Kentucky must be licensed by the State Board, and this Board receives complaints regarding fraudulent and unethical practices. I am usually investigating two or three psychologists at any particular point in time. This is difficult and time-consuming work, and always unpleasant (if not demoralizing), as there are no winners.

I also have a small private practice, confined to just one or two persons, usually undergraduate or graduate students enrolled within other departments of the university. I also supervise the psychotherapy provided by two or three graduate students within the Psychological Services Center, a small clinic operated by the University of Kentucky Department of Psychology. My own particular approach to psychotherapy is eclectic, although I emphasize in particular the cognitive-behavioral and psychodynamic (object-relational) perspective.

Outside of this, I garden, gamble, and wait for the college basketball season to begin.

What are your particular areas of expertise or interest?

My primary areas of interest are diagnosis, assessment, and classification, particularly dimensional versus categorical models of classification, gender differences and biases, and personality disorders. There are indeed specific etiologies and pathologies, but I believe that most instances of mental disorder are the result of a complex interaction over time of a number of biogenetic dispositions and environmental experiences. A demarcation between normal and abnormal functioning is meaningful but in many respects arbitrary. I do not consider persons with mental disorders to be qualitatively different from us ("I'm OK and you're not"). I have never met a person who I believe is without mental illness. This is perhaps a provocative remark, but perhaps it shouldn't be. We have no problem acknowledging that we have suffered from many physical disorders throughout our lives, and are probably currently suffering from a number of them. However, due in large part to the stigmatization of a mental disorder (the fear that we are not in fact "masters of our domain"), we somehow believe that we have never suffered from or never will suffer from a mental disorder ("I'm OK and you're OK"). Life can be extremely difficult, and our genetic dispositions and familial/social/cultural experiences will inevitably leave us with flaws, conflicts, dysregulations, irrationalities, and limitations that will significantly impair our ability to live a fully satisfying, meaningful, and enjoyable existence. Perhaps none of us is entirely psychologically healthy ("I'm not OK and neither are you").

What are the future trends you see for clinical psychology?

The future of clinical psychology is a good question. We appear to be in a significant time period for the profession. It may be very different 50 years from now, which is perhaps not surprising given that it was very different 50 years ago. My younger colleagues sometimes have the impression that this is an established profession that will successfully resist economic pressures to dissolve. In fact,

(continued)

Profile 6-1 *(continued)*

however, it is itself a young profession that came into existence largely in response to economic pressures.

What are the advantages of structured interviews, and what future developments do you see in this area of assessment?

Criticism is perhaps the lifeblood of scientific progress. The scientific documentation of the efficacy of psychotherapy developed in large part to address the charge that psychotherapy had no real or meaningful benefits. A comparable trend is occurring with respect to clinical assessment, including unstructured clinical interviews. Clinicians are having to defend the validity and credibility of their diagnoses and assessments to judges, lawyers, review boards, insurance companies, and so forth. Some of the attacks will have a self-serving (perhaps even unethical) motivation, but they must still be addressed.

One of the major innovations of the third edition of the American Psychiatric Association's (1980) *Diagnostic and Statistical Manual of Mental Disorders* (DSM-III) was the provision of relatively specific and explicit criteria sets to facilitate the obtainment of reliable clinical diagnoses. Prior to DSM-III, clinical diagnoses were so unreliable that there was no doubt that they lacked validity. If two clinicians provided different diagnoses, it is highly unlikely that both of them were correct. The relatively specific and explicit criteria sets in DSM-III has led to the obtainment of reliable diagnoses within research, which has in turn led to highly informative (and replicated) research concerning etiology, pathology, and treatment.

However, research has also indicated that unreliable diagnoses continue to be provided within applied clinical settings, largely because of the failure to conduct systematic and comprehensive assessments of the diagnostic criteria sets. There will be instances in which

there are valid reasons for not adhering to the DSM, but any such deviation should at least be acknowledged and documented. Unstructured clinical assessments in routine clinical practice do tend to be unsystematic, idiosyncratic, and unreliable. As a result, they fail to correlate meaningfully with external validators (that is, with valid indicators of etiology, pathology, and treatment); they often correlate with indicators of gender, ethnic, and other biased expectations or assumptions; and they often lack credibility when critiqued by an external review.

Semi-structured clinical interviews offer many advantages and benefits. They ensure that the interview will be systematic, comprehensive, and replicable. They minimize the occurrence of idiosyncratic biases and assumptions. They provide inquiries and probes that have been shown empirically to generate useful information. Reliable and valid diagnoses within clinical practice will be obtained if the interview is systematic, comprehensive, and objective. Semi-structured interviews should be used in forensic, disability, and other formal assessments, and should be part of initial intake assessments (along with self-report screening inventories). This is not to say that semi-structured interviews do not have limitations. They can be problematic to establishing rapport, and they will at times be superficial and inappropriately constraining. However, semi-structured interviewing can be incorporated into a clinical practice without suffering serious costs. Most graduate programs in clinical psychology devote a year of training to assessment. In the early years of the profession, none of this time appeared to be given to the importance of objective, systematic, and comprehensive clinical interviewing. However, this does appear to be changing. I do expect the assessment training of graduate students in clinical psychology in the future to give more attention to the value and techniques of semi-structured clinical interviews.

The Diagnostic Interview

As mentioned in Chapter 5, clinical psychologists evaluate patients according to DSM-IV criteria. Insurance companies, research protocols, or even court proceedings may require a *diagnostic evaluation*. How clinicians arrive at such a formulation, however, is for the most part left up to them. Historically, they used a clinical interview—a free-form unstructured interview whose content varied greatly from clinician to clinician. As might be expected, this interviewing method often results in unreliable ratings because two clinicians evaluating the same patient may arrive at different diagnostic formulations. Research on the reliability of diagnoses using unstructured clinical interviews has not supported this approach (for example, Matarazzo, 1983; Ward, Beck, Mendelson, Mock, & Erbauch, 1962).

Fortunately, things have changed. Researchers have developed structured diagnostic interviews that can be used by clinical psychologists in their research or clinical work. A *structured diagnostic interview* consists of a standard set of questions and follow-up probes that are asked in a specified sequence. The use of structured diagnostic interviews ensures that all patients or subjects are asked the same questions. This makes it more likely that two clinicians who evaluate the same patient will arrive at the same diagnostic formulation (high interrater reliability).

Several structured diagnostic interviews are available to clinical psychologists. Figure 6-1 presents a portion of the *Structured Clinical Interview for Axis I DSM-IV Disorders* (First, Spitzer, Gibbon, & Williams, 1995), known as the SCID-I. This section of the SCID-I assesses the presence of the DSM-IV criteria for "Specific Phobia." The questions the interviewer asks appear in the left-hand column, and the actual DSM-IV criteria for this disorder appear in the middle column.

Reliability and Validity of Interviews

As with any form of psychological assessment, it is important to evaluate the reliability and validity of interviews. The reliability of an interview is typically evaluated in terms of the level of agreement between at least two raters who evaluated the same patient or client. By agreement, we mean consensus on diagnoses assigned, on ratings of levels of personality traits, or on any other type of summary information derived from an interview. This is often referred to as *interrater reliability*. It can be quantified in many ways, including the *kappa coefficient* (Cohen, 1960) or the intraclass correlation coefficient (Shrout & Fleiss, 1979).

The validity of an interview concerns how well the interview measures what it intends to measure. For example, a demonstration that scores from a depression interview correlate highly with scores from a well-respected self-report measure of depression would suggest there is some degree of validity in the use of this interview's scores to assess depression. Evidence for an interview's *predictive validity* would be demonstrated if scores from this measure were significantly correlated with (and therefore "predicted") future events believed to be relevant to that construct. For example, if scores from our depression interview were highly correlated with poorer academic performance over the next two months, then we might say we have evidence supporting the predictive validity of our interview.

As should be apparent, both the reliability and validity of a measure, such as an interview, are a matter of degree. Scores from interviews, like those from psychological tests, are neither perfectly reliable nor perfectly valid. But the higher the reliability and validity, the more confident we are in our conclusions. Let us turn now to look more closely at reliability and validity issues regarding interviews.

Reliability

Standardized (structured) interviews with clear scoring instructions will be more reliable than unstructured interviews. The reason is that structured interviews reduce both information variance and criterion variance. *Information variance* refers to the variation in the questions that clinicians ask, the observations that are made during

FIGURE 6-1 Specific Phobia section of the *Structured Clinical Interview for Axis I DSM-IV Disorders* (SCID-I)

Source: From Structured Clinical Interview for Axis I DSM-IV Disorders by M. B. First, R. L. Spitzer, and J. B. W. Williams, pp. F16–F19. Copyright 1996 Biometrics Research. Reprinted by permission.

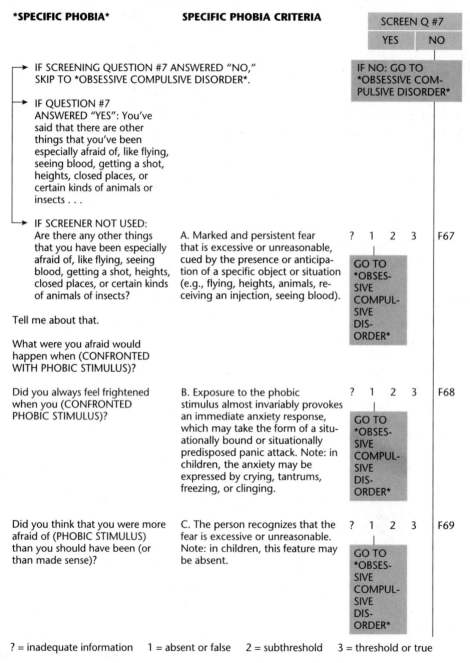

FIGURE 6-1 *(continued)*

Did you go out of your way to avoid (PHOBIC STIMULUS)?
 	
(Are there things you didn't do because of this fear, that you would otherwise have done?)
 	
    IF NO: How hard (is/was) it
    for you to (CONFRONT
    PHOBIC STIMULUS)?
	D. The phobic situation(s) is avoided or else endured with intense anxiety or distress.	? 1 2 3
		    |
		GO TO
		*OBSES-
		SIVE
		COMPUL-
		SIVE
		DIS-
		ORDER*
			F70

IF UNCLEAR WHETHER FEAR WAS CLINICALLY SIGNIFICANT: How much did (PHOBIA) interfere with your life?
 	
(Is there anything you've avoided because of being afraid of (PHOBIC STIMULUS)?
 	
    IF DOES NOT INTERFERE
    WITH LIFE: How much has the
    fact that you were afraid of
    (PHOBIC STIMULUS)
    bothered you?
	E. The avoidance, anxious anti-cipation, or distress in the feared situation interferes significantly with the person's normal routine, occupational (academic) function-ing, or with social activities or relationships with others, or there is marked distress about having the phobia.	? 1 2 3
		    |
		GO TO
		*OBSES-
		SIVE
		COMPUL-
		SIVE
		DIS-
		ORDER*
			F71

IF YOUNGER THAN AGE 18: How long have you had these fears?	F. For individuals under age 18 years, the duration is at least 6 months.	? 1 2 3 | GO TO *OBSES- SIVE COMPUL- SIVE DIS- ORDER*	F72
IF NOT ALREADY CLEAR: RETURN TO THIS ITEM AFTER COMPLETING SECTION ON PTSD AND OBSESSIVE-COMPULSIVE DISORDER.	G. The anxiety, panic attacks, or phobic avoidance associated with the specific object or situation are not better accounted for by another mental disorder, such as Obsessive-Compulsive Disorder (for example, fear of contamination), Posttraumatic Stress Disorder (for example, avoidance of stimuli associated with a severe stressor), Separation Anxiety Disorder (for example, avoidance of school), Social Phobia (for example, avoidance of social situations because of fear of embarrassment), Panic Disorder with Agoraphobia, or Agoraphobia without History of Panic Disorder.	? 1 2 3 | GO TO *OBSES- SIVE COMPUL- SIVE DIS- ORDER*	F73

? = inadequate information   1 = absent or false   2 = subthreshold   3 = threshold or true

FIGURE 6-1 *(continued)*

SPECIFIC PHOBIA CRITERIA   1   3   F74
A, B, C, D, E, F, AND G
ARE CODED "3"

GO TO *OBSESSIVE COMPULSIVE DISORDERS	SPE- CIFIC PHO- BIA

INDICATE TYPE:
(Check all that apply)

___ Animal Type (includes insects)   F75

___ Natural Environment Type (includes storms,   F76
heights, water)

___ Blood/Injection/Injury Type (includes   F77
seeing blood or injury or receiving an
injection or other invasive procedure)

___ Situational Type (includes public trans-   F78
portation, tunnels, bridges, elevators,
flying, driving, or enclosed places)

___ Other Type (for example, fear of situations   F79
that might lead to choking, vomiting, or
contracting an illness)
Specify: _____

SPECIFIC PHOBIA CHRONOLOGY

IF UNCLEAR: During the past   Has met criteria for Specific   ?   1   3   F80
month have you been bothered by   Phobia during past month
(SPECIFIC PHOBIA)?

INDICATE CURRENT SEVERITY: F81
1 – Mild: Few, if any, symptoms in excess of those required to make the diagnosis
    are present, and symptoms result in no more than minor impairments in social
    or occupational functioning.
2 – Moderate: Symptoms or functional impairment between "mild" and "severe"
    are present.
3 – Severe: Many symptoms in excess of those required to make the diagnosis or
    several symptoms that are particularly severe are present, or the symptoms re-
    sult in marked impairment in social or occupational functioning.

CONTINUE WITH *AGE AT ONSET*, BELOW.

? = inadequate information   1 = absent or false   2 = subthreshold   3 = threshold or true

FIGURE 6-1 *(continued)*

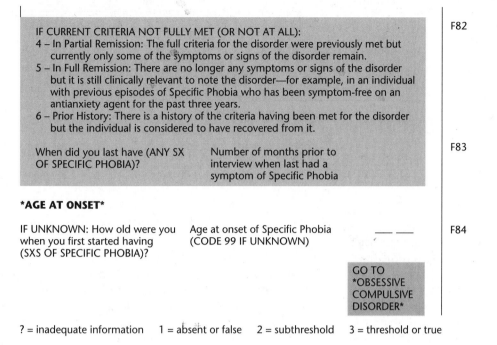

IF CURRENT CRITERIA NOT FULLY MET (OR NOT AT ALL):   F82
4 – In Partial Remission: The full criteria for the disorder were previously met but currently only some of the symptoms or signs of the disorder remain.
5 – In Full Remission: There are no longer any symptoms or signs of the disorder but it is still clinically relevant to note the disorder—for example, in an individual with previous episodes of Specific Phobia who has been symptom-free on an antianxiety agent for the past three years.
6 – Prior History: There is a history of the criteria having been met for the disorder but the individual is considered to have recovered from it.

| When did you last have (ANY SX OF SPECIFIC PHOBIA)? | Number of months prior to interview when last had a symptom of Specific Phobia | F83 |

AGE AT ONSET

| IF UNKNOWN: How old were you when you first started having (SXS OF SPECIFIC PHOBIA)? | Age at onset of Specific Phobia (CODE 99 IF UNKNOWN) | ___ ___ | F84 |

GO TO
*OBSESSIVE
COMPULSIVE
DISORDER*

? = inadequate information   1 = absent or false   2 = subthreshold   3 = threshold or true

the interview, and the method of integrating the information that is obtained (Rogers, 1995). *Criterion variance* refers to the variation in scoring thresholds among clinicians (Rogers, 1995). Clear-cut scoring guidelines make it more likely that two clinicians will score the same interviewee response in a similar way.

Because most of the research on the psychometric properties of interviews has focused on structured diagnostic interviews, we will discuss these in some detail. For many years, diagnostic interviews were considered quite unreliable (Matarazzo, 1983; Ward et al., 1962). However, several things changed. First, with the introduction of DSM-III (American Psychiatric Association, 1980), operational criteria were developed for most of the mental disorder diagnoses. This made it much easier to know what features to assess in order to rule in or rule out a particular mental disorder diagnosis. Second, and perhaps more important, several groups of investigators

developed structured interviews to systematically assess the various DSM criteria for mental disorders. Clearly, the reliability of the diagnostic information derived from structured interviews exceeds that obtained from unstructured interviews (Rogers, 1995).

As previously mentioned, the most common type of reliability assessed and reported for structured diagnostic interviews is interrater reliability. Another measure of reliability that is examined in structured diagnostic interviews, as well as other interviews, is *test-retest reliability*—the consistency of scores or diagnoses across time. We expect that, in general, individuals should receive similar scores or diagnoses when an interview is readministered. For example, a patient assigned a diagnosis of major depressive disorder based on a structured interview would be expected to receive the same diagnosis if reinterviewed (using the same structured interview) the next day.

■ **TABLE 6-4** Common Types of Reliability That Are Assessed in Order to Evaluate Interviews

Type of Reliability	Definition	Statistical Index
Interrater or interjudge reliability	Index of the degree of agreement between two or more raters or judges as to the level of a trait that is present or the presence/absence of a feature or diagnosis	Pearson's r Intraclass correlation Kappa
Test-retest reliability	Index of the consistency of interview scores across some period of time	Pearson's r Intraclass correlation

We expect the test-retest reliability of an interview to be quite high when the intervening time period between the initial testing and the retest is short (hours or a few days). However, when the intervening time period is long (months or years), test-retest reliability typically suffers. One reason—especially when assessing "current" mental disorder diagnoses—is that the psychological status of the patient may have changed. For example, the fact that a patient does not again receive a major depressive disorder diagnosis at 6-month retest is not necessarily an indictment of our structured interview. Because major depressive episodes can be of relatively short duration, our interview may be quite accurate in revealing no diagnosis at retest.

The point is that the level of test-retest reliability that is obtained must be interpreted in the context of the nature of the variable (a brief state or temporary syndrome versus a long-standing personality trait) as well as the length of the intervening time period between test and retest. When test-retest reliability is low, this may be due to a host of factors, including subjects' tendency to report fewer symptoms at retest, subjects' boredom or fatigue at retest, or the effect of variations in mood on the report of symptoms (Sher & Trull, 1996). Table 6-4 describes reliability indices for structured interviews.

Table 6-5 presents a hypothetical data set from a study assessing the reliability of alcoholism diagnoses derived from a structured interview. This example assesses interrater reliability (the level of agreement between two raters), but the calculations would be the same if one wanted to assess test-retest reliability. In that case, the data for Rater 2 would be replaced by data for Testing 2 (Retest).

As can be seen, the two raters evaluated the same 100 patients for the presence/absence of an alcoholism diagnosis, using a structured interview. These two raters agreed in 90% of the cases [(30 + 60)/100]. Agreement here refers to coming to the same conclusion—not just agreeing that the diagnosis is present, but also that the diagnosis is absent. Table 6-5 also presents the calculation for *kappa*—a chance-corrected index of agreement that is typically lower than overall agreement. The reason for this lower value is that raters will agree on the basis of chance alone in situations where the prevalence rate for a diagnosis is relatively high or relatively low. In the example shown in Table 6-5, we see that the diagnosis of alcoholism is relatively infrequent. Therefore, a rater who *always* judged the disorder to be absent would be correct (and likely to agree with another rater) in many cases. The kappa coefficient takes into account such instances of agreement based on chance alone and adjusts the agreement index (downward) accordingly. In general, a *kappa* value between .75 and 1.00 is considered to reflect excellent interrater agreement beyond chance (Cicchetti, 1994).

TABLE 6-5 Diagnostic Agreement between Two Raters

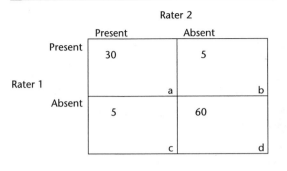

N = 100

Overall Agreement = a + d/N = .90

$$\text{Kappa} = \frac{(a+d/N)-[(a+b)(a+c)+(c+d)(b+d)]/N^2}{1-[(a+b)(a+c)+(c+d)(b+d)]/N^2}$$

$$= \frac{ad-bc}{ad-bc+N(b+c)/2}$$

$$= \frac{1775}{2275}$$

$$= .78$$

Validity

The validity of any type of psychological measure can take many forms. *Content validity* refers to the measure's comprehensiveness in assessing the variable of interest. In other words, does it do a good job of adequately measuring all important aspects of the construct of interest? For example, if an interview is designed to measure depression, then we would expect it to contain multiple questions assessing various emotional, cognitive, and physiological aspects of depression.

Criterion-related validity refers to the ability of a measure to predict (correlate with) scores on other relevant measures. These measures may be administered concurrently with the interview (concurrent validity) or at some point in the future (predictive validity). For example, an interview assessing conduct disorder in childhood may be said to have criterion-related validity to the extent that its scores correlate with measures of peer rejection and aggressive behavior.

Discriminant validity refers to the interview's ability to *not* correlate with measures that are not theoretically related to the construct being measured. For example, there is no theoretical reason why a specific phobia (of heights, for example) should be correlated with level of intelligence. Therefore, a demonstration that the two measures are not significantly correlated would indicate the specific phobia interview's discriminant validity.

Finally, the term *construct validity* is used to refer to all of these aspects of validity. Thus, many researchers describe the process of developing and validating a measure as a process of construct validation. Table 6-6 describes these validity indices.

In the case of structured diagnostic interviews, content validity is usually assumed, because these interviews were developed to measure the DSM criteria for specific mental disorders. That leaves the need for validation efforts aimed at establishing an interview's criterion-related, discriminant, and construct validity. Although some validation studies have been conducted, many more studies are needed. Let us take a popular structured diagnostic interview, the SCID, as an example. As noted by Rogers (1995), relatively few studies have attempted to demonstrate the criterion-related or discriminant validity of the SCID. Specifically, not many studies have compared SCID diagnoses and scores to those obtained from other diagnostic interviews, to clinical diagnoses, or to scores from self-report inventories.

Why is this the case? L. N. Robins (1985) has noted several difficulties associated with validating a structured diagnostic interview. Laboratory tests that validate mental disorder diagnoses are not available. Therefore, there is no "gold standard" to use as a comparison. Further, structured diagnostic interviews were developed at least partially because of a dissatisfaction with self-report inventories. Therefore, it does not seem appropriate or desirable to use a self-report inventory as a "gold standard." Any lack of agreement

TABLE 6-6 Common Types of Validity That Are Assessed in Order to Evaluate Interviews

Type of Validity	Definition
Content validity	The degree to which the interview items adequately measure the various aspects of the variable or construct.
Predictive validity	The degree to which interview scores can predict (correlate with) behavior or test scores that are observed or obtained at some point in the future.
Concurrent validity	The extent to which interview scores are correlated with a related, but independent, set of test/interview scores or behaviors.
Construct validity	The extent to which interview scores are correlated with other measures or behaviors in a logical and theoretically consistent way. This will involve a demonstration of both *convergent* and *discriminant* validity.

Note: Predictive and concurrent validity are both subtypes of criterion-related validity.

between a structured diagnostic interview and a self-report inventory may be more of an indictment against the validity of the self-report inventory than it is against the validity of the structured diagnostic interview. The same problem exists with using a "clinical impression" (based on an unstructured clinical interview) as a comparison. Some investigators have used a test-retest design to address the validity issue; however, this speaks more to the stability or reliability of interview scores than to the validity of the measure. Of course, we would expect that a valid measure would also be reliable. But the test-retest design does not directly address the validity question.

These points are well taken. We must realize that no infallible criterion measure exists for comparison purposes. In these situations, we conduct multiple validity studies, using a variety of criterion measures. Our confidence in the validity of our structured interview will increase as a function of the number of times we find that scores from our measure are highly associated with scores from alternative measures of the same or similar constructs *and* are not significantly related to scores from measures of constructs that, theoretically, should be unrelated to the diagnosis in question.

Suggestions for Improving Reliability and Validity

The following suggestions summarize some of the previous discussion; they should help improve both the reliability and validity of interviews.

1. *Whenever possible, use a structured interview.* A wide variety of structured interviews exist for conducting intake-admission, case-history, mental status examination, crisis, and diagnostic interviews.

2. *If a structured interview does not exist for your purpose, consider developing one.* Generate a standard set of questions to be used, develop a set of guidelines to score respondents' answers, administer this interview to a representative sample of subjects, and use the feedback from subjects and interviewers to modify the interview. If nothing else, completing this process will help you better understand what it is that you are attempting to assess and will help you become a better interviewer.

3. Whether you are using a structured interview or not, *certain interviewing skills are essential*: establishing rapport, being an effective communicator, being a good listener, knowing

when and how to ask additional questions, and being a good observer of nonverbal behavior.

4. *Be aware of the patient's motives and expectancies with regard to the interview.* For example, how strong are his or her needs for approval or social desirability?

5. *Be aware of your own expectations, biases, and cultural values.* Periodically, have someone else assess the reliability of the interviews you administer and score.

The Art and Science of Interviewing

Becoming a skilled interviewer requires practice. Without the opportunity to conduct real interviews, to make mistakes, or to discuss techniques and strategies with more experienced interviewers, a simple awareness of scientific investigations of interviewing will not confer great skill. What, then, are the functions of research on interviewing? A major one is to make clinicians more humble regarding their "intuitive skills." Research suggests, for example, that prior expectancies can color the interviewer's observations, that implicit theories of personality and psychopathology can influence the focus of an interview, and that the match or mismatch of interviewer and interviewee in terms of race, age, and gender may influence the course and outcome of the interview. Thus, a number of influences on the interview process have been identified.

Furthermore, if we never test our hypotheses, if we never assess the validity of our diagnoses, if we never check our reliability against someone else, or if we never measure the efficacy of a specific interview tactic, then we can easily develop an ill-placed confidence that will ultimately be hard on our patients. It may be true, as some cynics argue, that ten studies, all purporting to show that "mm-hmm" is no more effective than a nod of the head in expressing interviewer interest, still fail to disprove that in one specific or unique clinical interaction there may indeed be a difference. But such studies and many others like them will surely give us pause and encourage us to question our assumptions.

Although no single interview study will offer an unambiguous solution to an interview problem, such studies have a cumulative effect. Research can offer suggestions about improving the validity of our observations and tactics, shatter some timeworn illusions, and splinter a few clichés. By the sheer cumulative weight of its controlled, scientific approach, research can make interviewers more sensitive and effective. A clinician steeped in both the art and the science of interviewing will be more effective (though hardly more comfortable) than one who is conscious of only one of these dual aspects of interviewing.

Chapter Summary

Clinical assessment involves an evaluation of an individual's strengths and weaknesses, a conceptualization of the problem at hand, and some prescription for alleviating the problem. The interview is the most basic and most serviceable assessment technique used by clinical psychologists.

There are two primary distinguishing factors among interviews. First, interviews differ with regard to their purpose. In this chapter, we have discussed the intake-admission interview, the case-history interview, the mental status examination interview, the crisis interview, and the diagnostic interview. A second distinguishing feature concerns whether the interview is unstructured (often called a clinical interview) or structured. In contrast to unstructured interviews, structured interviews require the clinician to ask verbatim a set of standardized questions in a specified sequence.

Regardless of the type of interview or its purpose, certain skills are required, including rapport, good communication skills, appropriate follow-up questions, and good observational skills. As with any form of psychological assessment, it is important to evaluate the reliability and validity of interview scores. Finally, we have made several suggestions for improving the reliability and validity of interview scores.

Key Terms

assessment interview One of the most basic techniques employed by the clinical psychologist for the purpose of answering a referral question. If administered skillfully, the assessment interview can provide insight into the problem and inform clinical decision making.

case-history interview An interview conducted for the purpose of gaining a thorough understanding of the patient's background and the historical/developmental context in which a problem emerged.

clinical assessment An approach to assessment that involves an evaluation of an individual's strengths and weaknesses, a conceptualization of the problem at hand, and the generation of recommendations for alleviating the problem.

computer interviewing The use of computers for administering clinical interviews.

concurrent validity A form of criterion-related validity. The extent to which interview scores correlate with scores on other relevant measures administered at the same time.

construct validity The extent to which interview scores are correlated with other measures or behaviors in a logical and theoretically consistent way. In order to be construct valid, an interview must demonstrate all of the aspects of validity.

content validity The degree to which interview items adequately measure all aspects of the construct being measured.

crisis interview An interview conducted for the purposes of (1) defusing or problem-solving through the crisis at hand and (2) encouraging the individual to enter into a therapeutic relationship at the agency or elsewhere so that a longer-term solution can be worked out.

criterion-rated validity The extent to which interview scores predict (correlate with) scores on other relevant measures.

diagnostic interview An interview conducted for the purpose of arriving at a DSM-IV diagnostic formulation.

discriminant validity The extent to which interview scores do not correlate with measures that are not theoretically related to the construct being measured.

intake-admission interview An interview conducted for the purposes of (1) determining why the patient has come to an agency (e.g., clinic, hospital), (2) determining whether the agency can meet the patient's needs and expectations, and (3) informing the patient about the agency's policies and procedures.

interrater reliability The level of agreement between at least two raters who have evaluated the same patient independently. Agreement can refer to consensus on symptoms assigned, diagnoses assigned, and so on.

kappa coefficient A statistical index of interrater reliability computed to determine how reliably raters judge the presence or absence of a feature or diagnosis.

mental status examination interview An interview conducted to evaluate the patient for the presence of cognitive, emotional, or behavioral problems. In the MSE interview, the clinician assesses the patient in a number of areas, including (but not limited to) general presentation, quality of speech, thought content, memory, and judgment.

predictive validity A form of criterion-related validity. The extent to which interview scores correlate with scores on other relevant measures administered at some point in the future.

rapport A word often used to characterize the relationship between patient and clinician. In the context of the clinical interview, building good rapport involves establishing a comfortable atmosphere and sharing an understanding of the purpose of the interview.

referral question The question posed about the patient by the referral source (e.g., Why is a particular child earning poor grades?).

structured diagnostic interview A diagnostic interview that consists of a standard set of questions asked in a specified sequence. The questions may be keyed to the diagnostic criteria for a number of disorders.

test-retest reliability The consistency of interview scores over time. Generally, we expect individuals to receive similar diagnoses from one administration to the next if the interval between administrations is short.

unstructured interview An interview in which the clinician asks any questions that come to mind in any order.

The Assessment of Intelligence

The history of clinical psychology is inextricably tied to the assessment of intelligence. Without the success in this and related assessment enterprises, there might not have been a field of clinical psychology. As the years passed, however, clinicians became increasingly interested in the more "glamorous" aspects of the profession, such as therapy. Assessment began to take a back seat, and technicians started to become the assessors, as they had been prior to World War II (Tyler, 1976). However, as noted in the previous chapter, all this is beginning to change. Not only is the value of assessment being rediscovered, but intelligence tests in particular remain prominent in the clinician's arsenal of assessment devices (Watkins, Campbell, Nieberding, & Hallmark, 1995).

In this chapter, we provide some background relevant to the controversies over intellectual assessment, present major definitions and theories of intelligence, focus on the measurement of intelligence, and finally, discuss the appropriate interpretation of intelligence test scores.

FIGURE 7-1 Alfred Binet developed the first widely accepted test of intelligence. The test, which eventually became the Stanford-Binet, has undergone numerous revisions over the years.
The Bettmann Archive. © Bettmann/CORBIS.

Intelligence Testing: Yesterday and Today

Two important historical developments in the latter half of the nineteenth century greatly influenced the ultimate introduction of measures of intelligence (Thorndike, 1997). First, compulsory education in the United States and other countries resulted in a very diverse student body. Many students came from "uneducated" families or families that did not speak the native tongue. As a result, the failure rate in schools shot up dramatically. In order to preserve resources, there was pressure to identify those most likely to succeed in school. Second, psychological scientists believed, and ultimately demonstrated, that mental abilities could be measured. Although early attempts focused primarily on measures of sensory acuity and reaction time (for example, Francis Galton, James McKeen Cattell), the groundwork was laid in place.

Alfred Binet and his collaborator, Theodore Simon, became leaders in the intelligence testing movement when they devised the Binet-Simon test to identify individual differences in mental functioning (see Chapter 2). Binet's original purpose was to develop an objective method of identifying those truly lacking in academic ability (as opposed to those with behavior problems). Like others of the day, Binet and Simon regarded intelligence as a "faculty" that was inherited, although they also spoke of it as affected by training and opportunity. With the interest in quantifying intellectual performance and with the continuing growth of compulsory education in Europe and North America, intelligence testing became firmly entrenched (Thorndike, 1997).

Institutions such as schools, industries, military forces, and governments were, by their nature, interested in individual differences (such as levels of intelligence) that might affect performance in those settings; therefore, intelligence testing prospered (Herrnstein & Murray, 1994). For many years, the critical importance and widespread use of intelligence tests went largely unchallenged. However, by the end of the 1960s, everyone from psychologists to Ralph Nader seemed to be attacking the validity of these tests. Basically, the argument was that such tests discriminate through the inclusion of unfair items.

As a result of a lengthy civil rights suit (*Larry P. v. Wilson Riles*) begun in 1971, the California State Board of Education in 1975 imposed a moratorium on the use of intelligence tests to assess disabilities in African Americans. The court held that IQ testing is prejudicial to African American children and tends to place them, without real justification, in allegedly stigmatizing programs for cognitively impaired individuals. Others (for example, N. Lambert, 1981) have disputed the court's judgment, however. Some African Americans contemplated a court challenge of the ruling, claiming it assumed that African Americans would do poorly on the tests. Still others argued that IQ testing is not a social evil but the principal means by which we can right the wrongs imposed upon minorities by a devastating environment (Hebb, 1978).

Stephen Gould's (1981) popular book *The Mismeasure of Man* was a scathing critique of the intelligence testing movement and of the "reification" of the notion of intelligence. Essentially, Gould argued that theorists such as Spearman (see below) mistakenly accorded general intelligence, or *g*, the status of an true entity because of their misunderstanding of factor analytic techniques. Further, Gould contended that those arguing for the heritability of intelligence were in some cases mistaken and in other cases guilty of fraud. Gould's book was a huge success, and further intensified the attack on intelligence testing.

This rather heated debate has recently resurfaced with the publication of *The Bell Curve* (Herrnstein & Murray, 1994). In this book, Herrnstein and Murray review the concept of intelligence, recount the history of intelligence

testing, respond to many of the critiques offered by Gould (1981), and delve into public policy issues such as poverty, crime, welfare, and affirmative action. Box 7-1 briefly presents some of the more controversial aspects of this book. Whatever the outcome of all the controversy, it does illustrate that intellectual assessment is not an obscure academic activity; it is right there in the midst of contemporary social and public policy issues.

There is little question that intelligence tests have been misused at times in ways that have penalized minorities. There is also little doubt that some tests have contained certain items that have adversely affected the performance of some minorities. We should, therefore, do everything we can to develop better tests and to administer and interpret them in a sensitive fashion. However, banning tests seems an inappropriate cure that may ultimately harm the very people who need help.

The Concept of Intelligence

Two issues that have plagued psychologists from the beginning are still not resolved. First, exactly what is meant by the term *intelligence*? Second, how do we develop valid instruments for measuring it? In this section, we will address both questions. But first we need to review the psychometric concepts of reliability and validity.

Reliability and Validity

As we discussed in the previous chapter, all interviews and tests must demonstrate both reliability and validity in order to be useful. Tables 7-1 and 7-2 present brief definitions of the most common forms of reliability and validity that are used to evaluate psychological tests.

Reliability. With regard to psychological tests, reliability refers to the consistency with which individuals respond to test stimuli. There are several ways of evaluating reliability. First, there is *test-retest reliability*—the extent to which an in-

BOX 7-1

Hot Topic *The Bell Curve*

Perhaps no other book in recent times has generated as much controversy as Herrnstein and Murray's (1994) *The Bell Curve*. Briefly, Herrnstein and Murray argue that, over the past 30 years, the United States has become increasingly divided based on the cognitive or intellectual ability of its citizens. What has emerged is a class labeled the "cognitive elite" who are primarily concentrated in a small group of occupations (such as doctors, lawyers, professors) that essentially screen for high IQ. Although intelligence is a product of both genetic and environmental factors, our country's attempt to "equalize" the environment for all (that is, give everyone the same opportunities to succeed) ironically leads to a situation in which the genes we inherit are the primary source of individual differences. In a sense, Herrnstein and Murray contend, this will only serve to widen the gap between the haves and the have-nots in coming generations. The authors also present evidence supporting their position that cognitive ability/intelligence is the most important predictor of outcomes such as financial stability, success in college, welfare dependency, producing "illegitimate" children, and criminal behavior. They also review the data on ethnic/racial differences in IQ, and argue that efforts to raise IQ scores through educational programs or programs such as Head Start have not produced positive, long-term effects. Finally, Herrnstein and Murray provide a number of prescriptions for remedying the current disparity, including overhauling affirmative action policies for education and the workplace, as well as returning decision-making power to local governing bodies.

Most of the negative reaction to this book appears to be based on disagreement with the authors' prescriptions for social policy and, at times, appear to take the form of ad hominem arguments. In addition, some critics have taken issue with the methodology, analysis, and interpretation of some of the empirical studies cited and discussed in the book. On the other hand, a group of experts in the field of intelligence published a brief article in the *Wall Street Journal* (Arvey et al., 1994) that outlined "mainstream" conclusions among researchers on intelligence. Many of the points made in *The Bell Curve* are consistent with these conclusions. The experts, however, stopped short of prescribing social policy based on these conclusions.

dividual makes similar responses to the same test stimuli on repeated occasions. If each time we test a person we get different responses, the test data may not be very useful. In some instances, clients may remember on the second occasion their responses from the first time. Or they may develop a kind of "test-wiseness" from the first test that influences their scores the second time around. In still other cases, clients may rehearse between testing occasions or show practice effects. For all these reasons, another gauge of reliability is sometimes used—*equivalent-forms reliability*. Here, equivalent or parallel forms of a test are developed to avoid the preceding problems.

Sometimes it is too expensive (in time or money) to develop an equivalent form, or it is difficult or impossible to be sure the forms are really equivalent. Under such circumstances, or when retesting is not practical, assessing *split-half reliability* is a possibility. This means that a test is divided into halves (usually odd-numbered items versus even-numbered items), and participants'

TABLE 7-1 Common Types of Reliability That Are Assessed
in Order to Evaluate Psychological Tests

Type of Reliability	Definition	Statistical Index
Test-retest reliability	Index of the consistency of test scores across some period of time	Pearson's *r* Intraclass correlation
Equivalent forms reliability	Index of the consistency of test scores across time; not vulnerable to a "practice effect" (not repeating the same test)	Pearson's *r*
Split-half reliability	Index of the internal consistency of the test (do the items seem to be measuring the same variable or construct?)	Pearson's *r*
Internal consistency reliability	Preferred index of internal consistency, in which the average of all possible split-half correlations is computed	Cronbach's alpha Kuder-Richardson-20
Interrater or interjudge reliability	Index of the degree of agreement between two or more raters or judges as to the level of a trait that is present or the presence/absence of a feature or diagnosis	Pearson's *r* Intraclass correlation Kappa

TABLE 7-2 Common Types of Validity That Are Assessed
in Order to Evaluate Psychological Tests

Type of Validity	Definition
Content validity	The degree to which the test items adequately measure the various aspects of the variable or construct.
Predictive validity	The degree to which test scores can predict (correlate with) behavior or test scores that are observed or obtained at some point in the future.
Concurrent validity	The extent to which test scores are correlated with a related, but independent, set of test scores or behaviors.
Construct validity	The extent to which test scores are correlated with other measures or behaviors in a logical and theoretically consistent way. This will involve a demonstration of both convergent and discriminant validity.

Note: Predictive and concurrent validity are both subtypes of criterion-related validity.

scores on the two halves are compared. Split-half reliability also serves as one possible index of a test's *internal consistency*: Do the items on the test appear to be measuring the same thing? That is, are the items highly correlated with each other? The preferred method of assessing internal con-sistency reliability involves computing the aver-age of all possible split-half correlations for a given test (Cronbach's *alpha*).

Another aspect of reliability, *interrater* or *interjudge reliability*, was discussed in the previous chapter in the context of interview assessment.

The goal here is to demonstrate that independent observers can agree about their ratings or judgments of some particular aspect of the person's behavior.

Regardless of the particular kind of reliability in question, the goal is to demonstrate consistency in the data. A test must be able to provide evidence that the scores it yields are consistent over time and over examiners or are otherwise reliable (as in split-half or equivalent-forms reliability). Without reliability, consistency, or stability of measurement, a test cannot be valid. However, even though a test shows reliability, this does not automatically imply validity. For example, a test involving the ability to discriminate among weights may produce scores that are highly reliable over time, yet not be a valid measure of intelligence.

Validity. In general, *validity* refers to the extent to which an assessment technique measures what it is supposed to measure. Like reliability, there are several forms of validity. *Content validity* indicates the degree to which a group of test items actually covers the various aspects of the variable under study. For example, a test that purported to measure overall adjustment but that contained only items dealing with adjustment at work would not have content validity because it failed to include items dealing with adjustment at home, with friends, and in other contexts. *Predictive validity* is demonstrated when test scores accurately predict some behavior or event in the future. A test designed to predict school success is valid if scores today reflect the school achievement behavior of children two years hence. *Concurrent validity* involves relating today's test scores to a concurrent criterion (such as teachers' judgments of school success). Finally, *construct validity* is shown when test scores relate to other measures or behaviors in a logical, theoretically expected fashion. For example, suppose we have a test for alienation. Given the nature of alienation, a valid test of it might be expected to correlate with lack of vigor or even depression. If our test does that, our confidence in its construct validity is increased.

Definitions of Intelligence

Before dealing specifically with intelligence, we should distinguish among *ability*, *aptitude*, and *achievement*. As Sundberg (1977) explains it, "Ability is the currently available power to perform something and aptitude is the potential for performance after training. Both concepts have similarities with achievement, which is a measure of successful performance in the past" (p. 228). There can be considerable conceptual overlap between achievement and intelligence as measured on tests of intelligence. In one sense, intelligence tests are achievement tests, because they measure what one has learned (Anastasi, 1988). How the tests are used or how inferences are made from them determines whether they are tapping achievement or intelligence.

There is no universally accepted definition of intelligence. However, over the years, most have fallen into one of three classes:

1. Definitions that emphasize adjustment or adaptation to the environment—adaptability to new situations, the capacity to deal with a range of situations.
2. Definitions that focus on the ability to learn—on educability in the broad sense of the term.
3. Definitions that emphasize abstract thinking—the ability to use a wide range of symbols and concepts, the ability to use both verbal and numerical symbols.

To illustrate a little of the long-standing diversity of definitions, consider the following examples:

[Intelligence is] the aggregate or global capacity of the individual to act purposefully, to think rationally, and to deal effectively with his [sic] environment. (Wechsler, 1939, p. 3)

As a concept, intelligence refers to the whole class of cognitive behaviors which reflect an individual's capacity to solve problems with insight, to adapt himself [sic] to new situations, to think abstractly, and to profit from his experience. (Robinson & Robinson, 1965, p. 15)

Intelligence is expressed in terms of adaptive, goal-directed behavior. The subset of such behavior that is labeled "intelligent" seems to be determined in large part by cultural or societal norms. (Sternberg & Salter, 1982, p. 24)

Intelligence is a very general mental capability that, among other things, involves the ability to reason, plan, solve problems, think abstractly, comprehend complex ideas, learn quickly and learn from experience. It is not merely book learning, a narrow academic skill, or test-taking smarts. Rather, it reflects a broader and deeper capability for comprehending our surroundings—"catching on," "making sense" of things, or "figuring out" what to do. (Arvey et al., 1994)

The foregoing classes of and specific definitions of intelligence are not mutually exclusive. Furthermore, several of these definitions contain distinct overtones of both social values and motivational elements. Beyond this, however, many definitions of intelligence are so broad or general as to be nearly useless. In many ways, there is an overall sameness to tests of intelligence that belies their origins in diverse definitions. Thus, one begins to wonder whether definitions really make all that much difference or whether constructing IQ tests is just an atheoretical, pragmatic enterprise in which we generate items that we hope will correlate with some external criterion (such as school grades).

For some, the answer to all this ambiguity lies in "prototype" definitions. As Neisser (1979) has put it:

Our confidence that a person deserves to be called "intelligent" depends on that person's overall similarity to an imagined prototype, just as our confidence that some object is to be called "chair" depends on its similarity to prototypical chairs. There are no definitive criteria of intelligence, just as there are none for chairness; it is a fuzzy-edged concept to which many features are relevant. Two people may both be quite intelligent and yet have very few traits in common—they resemble the prototype along different dimensions. Thus, there is no such thing as chairness—resemblance is an external fact and not an internal essence. There can be no process-based definition of intelligence, because it is not a unitary quality. It is a resemblance between two individuals, one real and the other prototypical. (p. 185)

Theories of Intelligence

There have been many theoretical approaches to the understanding of intelligence. These include psychometric theories, developmental theories, neuropsychological theories, and information-processing theories (Kamphaus, 1993; Neisser et al., 1996). Over the years, there has been no dearth of either theories or controversies (Neisser et al., 1996; Weinberg, 1989). We present only a brief overview of several leading theories here.

Factor Analytic Approaches. Spearman (1927), the father of factor analysis, posited the existence of a *g* factor (general intelligence) and *s* factors (specific intelligence). The elements that tests have in common are represented by *g*, whereas the elements unique to a given test are *s* factors. Basically, however, Spearman's message, buttressed by factor analytic evidence, was that intelligence is a broad, generalized entity.

A number of individuals took issue with Spearman's contentions, including E. L. Thorndike and L. L. Thurstone. For example, Thurstone (1938) presented evidence (based on a factor analysis of 57 separate tests that had been administered to 240 participants) for a series of "group" factors rather than the almighty *g* factor. Ultimately, Thurstone described seven group factors, which he labeled number, word fluency, verbal meaning, perceptual speed, space, reasoning, and memory (Thurstone's *Primary Mental Abilities*). Unfortunately, Spearman and Thurstone were using different methods of factor extraction (principal components versus

FIGURE 7-2 **Model of a hierarchical organization of abilities.**
SOURCE: Adapted from The Structure of Human Abilities, *rev. ed., by P. E. Vernon, p. 22. Copyright ©
1960 by Methuen & Co., Ltd. Reprinted by permission.*

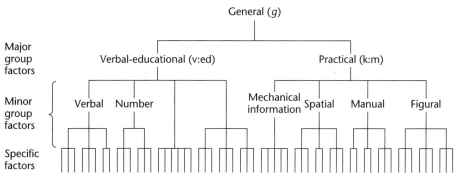

principal factors) and rotation, which often result in different solutions even when applied to
the same data set (Gould, 1981). Further, both
men appeared to be guilty of reifying the
factor(s) "discovered" by their respective analyses. The end result was an, at times, acrimonious
debate between Spearman and Thurstone, and
their respective followers.

Cattell's Theory. The work of R. B. Cattell
(1987) emphasizes the centrality of *g*. At the
same time, Cattell has offered a tentative list of
17 primary ability concepts. He has described
two important second-order factors that seem to
represent a partitioning of Spearman's *g* into two
components: *fluid ability* (the person's genetically based intellectual capacity) and *crystallized
ability* (the capacities, tapped by the usual standardized intelligence test, that can be attributed
to culture-based learning). Essentially, Cattell's
approach might be described as a hierarchical
model of intelligence. An example of this sort of
model is shown schematically in Figure 7-2.

Guilford's Theory. The views of Guilford
(1967) were quite different from those of
Cattell, Spearman, Thurstone, and most other
psychometricians. Guilford proposed a *Structure
of the Intellect (SOI) model* and then used a variety of statistical and factor analytic techniques
to test it. Whereas other psychometric ap-

proaches generally attempted to infer a model
from the data, Guilford used the model as a
guide in generating data.

Guilford reasoned that the components of
intelligence could be organized into three dimensions: operations, contents, and products.
The operations are cognition, memory, divergent
production (constructing logical alternatives),
convergent production (constructing logic-tight
arguments), and evaluation. The content dimension involves the areas of information in which
the operations are performed: figural, symbolic,
semantic, and behavioral. Finally, when a particular mental operation is applied to a specific
type of content, there are six possible products:
units, classes, systems, relations, transformations, and implications. If we contemplate all
possible combinations, we arrive at 120 separate
intellectual abilities. Perhaps the most widely
held reservation about Guilford's approach is
that it is a taxonomy or classification rather than
a theory.

Recent Developments. Traditionally, intelligence tests have been constructed to assess what
we know or can do. Recent approaches, however,
have begun to take on a highly cognitive or information-processing look. For example, some researchers try to describe a person's moment-by-
moment attempts to solve a problem—from the
moment a stimulus registers to the person's

verbal or motor response. This is a more dynamic view of intelligence than the older theories of mental components. Some of these researchers have focused on speed of information processing and others on strategies of processing. A number of levels of processing have been studied, including speed of processing, speed in making choices in response to stimuli, and speed with which individuals can extract various aspects of language from their long-term memory. But many problems and questions remain (Gardner, 1983). Is there a central processing mechanism for information? How do the processing elements change as the person develops? Are there general problem-solving skills, or merely skills specific to certain ability areas? Perhaps time will tell.

Gardner (1983) has described a theory of *multiple intelligences*. Human intellectual competence involves a set of problem-solving skills that enable the person to resolve problems or difficulties. Sometimes this results in the potential for acquiring new information. Gardner suggests that there is a family of six intelligences: linguistic, musical, logical-mathematical, spatial, bodily-kinesthetic, and personal. For example, the personal refers both to access to one's own feeling life and to the ability to notice and make distinctions among other individuals. A major criticism of Gardner's theory is that some of his proposed "intelligences" may be better conceptualized as "talents" than as forms of intelligence (Neisser et al., 1996). Nevertheless, Gardner's views have attracted a great deal of attention from psychologists and educators alike.

To cite another example of a theory of multiple forms of intelligence, Sternberg (1985, 1991) has proposed a *triarchic theory of intelligence*. He maintains that people function on the basis of three aspects of intelligence: componential, experiential, and contextual. This approach deemphasizes speed and accuracy of performance. Instead, the emphasis is on planning responses and monitoring them. The componential aspect refers to analytical thinking; high scores would characterize the person who is a good test-taker. The experiential aspect relates to creative thinking and characterizes the person

who can take separate elements of experience and combine them insightfully. Finally, the contextual aspect is seen in the person who is "street smart"—one who knows how to play the game and can successfully manipulate the environment. According to Sternberg, a person's performance is governed by these three aspects of intelligence. Other investigators are particularly interested in social competence as an aspect of intelligence (Sternberg & Wagner, 1986). However, whether all the foregoing can account for individual differences or is just a theory of cognition is debatable.

Although Spearman, Thurstone, and others may seem to have given way to Cattell, Guilford, Gardner, or Sternberg, clinicians' day-to-day use of tests suggests that they have not really outgrown the *g* factor of Spearman or the group factors of Thurstone. The whole notion of a single IQ score that can represent the individual's intelligence strongly implies that we are trying to discover how much *g* the person has. At the same time, however, most current intelligence tests are composed of subtests, so that the total IQ represents some average of subtest scores. This implies that, to some extent at least, we have also accepted Thurstone's group factors. We seem to want to identify and quantify how much intelligence the person has, yet we cannot escape the belief that intelligence is somehow patterned—that two people may have the same overall IQ score and still differ in specific abilities. Thus, it would appear that practicing clinicians think more in line with Spearman or Thurstone and are as yet little affected by the recent information-processing developments.

The IQ: Its Meaning and Its Correlates

The Intelligence Quotient (IQ)

Ratio IQ. Binet regarded the *mental age (MA)* as an index of mental performance. Each item successfully passed on a Binet test signified a certain number of months' credit. At the conclusion of the test, the items passed were added up and the

MA emerged. Thus, there was nothing magical about an MA; all it meant was that X number of items had been passed. Subsequently, Stern (1938) developed the concept of *intelligence quotient (IQ)* to circumvent several problems that had arisen in using the difference between the *chronological age (CA)* and the MA to express deviance. At first glance, two children, one with an MA of 4 years and a CA of 5 years and another with an MA of 14 years and a CA of 15 years, would seem to be equally deficient. However, this is not the case, because intellectual growth is much more rapid at younger age levels. Therefore, even though there is only a one-year discrepancy between the MA and the CA of both children, the younger child is actually more deviant than the older one. The IQ notion enables us to perform the following computation:

$$IQ = MA/CA \times 100$$

As a result, we find that our 15-year-old has an IQ of 93, whereas the 5-year-old has an IQ of 80. These differing scores better reflect the reality of more rapid intellectual growth at younger ages.

It should be noted that in measuring intelligence, we cannot be sure that we are dealing with equal-interval measurement. We cannot be sure that an IQ of 50 is really twice as much as an IQ of 25 or that our scale has an absolute zero point. We cannot add and subtract IQs. All we can do is state that a person with an IQ of 50 is brighter than a person with an IQ of 25. All of this should serve to remind us that IQs and MAs are merely scores.

Deviation IQ. Although initially appealing, the ratio IQ is significantly limited in its application to older age groups. The reason is that a consistent (even if very high) mental age (MA) score accompanied by an increasing chronological age (CA) score will result in a lower IQ. Thus, it may appear that IQ has decreased over time when, in fact, one's intellectual ability has been maintained.

To deal with this problem, Wechsler introduced the concept of *deviation IQ.* The assumption is made that intelligence is normally distributed throughout the population. A deviation IQ then involves a comparison of an individual's performance on an IQ test with that of his or her age peers. Thus, the same IQ score has a similar meaning, even if two individuals are markedly different in age (for example, a 22-year-old versus an 80-year-old). In both cases, an IQ of 100 indicates an average level of intellectual ability for that age group.

Correlates of the IQ

Whether intelligence tests are valid depends on how we define intelligence. If we are looking for some global entity that transcends school success or related achievements, the answer is probably no. But if we define intelligence mainly as a predictor of success in school, then the answer is likely to be yes.

Whether we define intelligence in terms of *g*, separate abilities, or hierarchical relationships among factors, society ultimately decides which abilities will be valued, rewarded, and nurtured. Perhaps this is why all intelligence tests seem so much alike. They are designed to predict what society values. Our society tends to reward verbal ability, reasoning, reading, information acquisition, analytic ability, and so on.

School Success. In general, IQs have been shown to relate substantially both to success in school and to achievement tests that measure what has been learned (Herrnstein & Murray, 1994; Kamphaus, 1993). The correlation between IQ scores and grades is about .50 (Neisser et al., 1996). It seems apparent that success in school is related to a host of variables, including motivation, teacher expectations, cultural background, attitudes of parents, and many others. We are then confronted with the very difficult clinical task of sorting out those variables. When success or failure in school occurs, is it because of intelligence, motivation, cultural background, or what? Any behavior is complexly determined by many variables other than just general or specific intelligence. However, the relationship between IQ scores and achievement is so high that many have suggested that intelligence tests might be best interpreted as a type of achievement test (Anastasi, 1988; Kaufman, 1990).

Occupational Status and Success. Because amount of education would seem to be, in general, a strong determinant of the kind of job one can obtain, it will come as no surprise to learn that IQ and occupational status are related. This seems to be true whether occupational status is defined in terms of income, rated prestige, or social prestige (Brody & Brody, 1976). Interestingly, however, intelligence scores also appear to be good predictors of job performance (Hunter & Hunter, 1984; Neisser et al., 1996); IQ scores outperform predictors such as biographical data, reference checks, education, and college grades. However, once entry to a profession has been gained, the degree of intelligence may not separate the more eminent from the less eminent (Matarazzo, 1972; Roe, 1953). Apparently, some minimum level of ability is necessary in order to achieve entry to or minimal performance in a given occupation (though this may be debatable). Once an individual gains entry, however, the degree of subsequent success may be more a function of nonintellectual factors.

Group Differences. Although most studies find few if any significant differences between males and females in overall IQ scores, significant differences between the sexes have been obtained for specific abilities (Neisser et al., 1996). Specifically, males tend to score significantly higher on measures of spatial ability and, after puberty, on measures of quantitative ability. Females tend to score significantly higher on measures of verbal ability (Neisser et al., 1996). Among racial/ethnic groups, Hispanic Americans and African Americans tend to obtain significantly lower IQ scores than do European Americans (Neisser et al., 1996). These findings, although consistent, have been the source of much controversy. Neisser et al. (1996) point out that although we do not know what causes these ethnic/racial differences, the size of the differences are within a range that could be accounted for by environ-

mental factors. More research is needed in this area to provide insight into the nature of these ethnic/racial differences. Despite the differences, however, IQ scores remain good predictors of school and college achievement among Hispanic Americans and African Americans.

Heredity and Stability of IQ Scores

Heritability of Intelligence. In contrast to the situation 30 or 40 years ago, almost all psychologists now acknowledge that intelligence is influenced, at least in part, by genetic factors (Neisser et al., 1996). The reason for this reversal of opinion is the large body of empirical evidence provided by *behavioral genetics* studies over the past several decades (McGue, Bouchard, Iacono, & Lykken, 1993). Box 7-2 presents a brief overview of the methods of behavioral genetics.

A landmark review by Bouchard and McGue (1981) summarizes many of these behavioral genetics studies of intelligence. Table 7-3 presents some of the data. As can be seen, similarity in intelligence appears to be a function of the amount of genetic material shared (monozygotic twins are more similar in intelligence than dizygotic twins or siblings). It is notable that this pattern also holds true for biological relatives reared apart. McGue, Bouchard, Iacono, and Lykken (1993) conclude:

> When taken in aggregate, twin, family, and adoption studies of IQ provide a demonstration of the existence of genetic influences on IQ as good as can be achieved in the behavioral sciences with nonexperimental methods. Without positing the existence of genetic influences, it simply is not possible to give a credible account for the consistently greater IQ similarity among monozygotic (MZ) twins than among like-sex dizygotic (DZ) twins, the significant IQ correlations among biological relatives even when they are reared apart, and the strong association between the magnitude of familial IQ correlation and the degree of genetic relatedness. (p. 60)

BOX 7-2

Behavioral Genetics

Behavioral genetics is a research specialty in which both genetic and environmental influences on the development of behavior are evaluated. Proteins are produced and regulated by genetic codes, and proteins interact with physiological intermediaries (hormones, neurotransmitters, structural properties of the nervous system) to produce behavior (Plomin, DeFries, & McClearn, 1990). The genetic makeup of an individual, referred to as the *genotype*, is fixed at birth. A person's genotype is passed down from the biological parents. The *phenotype* refers to observable characteristics of an individual, and a person's phenotype can change. Intelligence and even mental disorders are phenotypic characteristics that may change over time. The phenotype is a product of the genotype *and* the environment.

One of the most powerful (in the explanatory sense) research designs used in behavioral genetics is the twin method. This method involves comparing *monozygotic (MZ) twins*, who are genetically identical, with *dizygotic (DZ) twins*, who share only about 50% of their genetic material, on the behavior or characteristic of interest. The similarity among twin pairs is typically presented in the form of a *concordance rate* or *similarity index*. In its simplest form, a concordance rate is the percentage of instances across all twin pairs in which both twins exhibit similar behaviors or characteristics. A concordance rate or similarity index for the MZ twin sample that is significantly greater than that for the DZ twin sample suggests that genetic influences play an important role in the development of that set of behaviors or features.

Because MZ twins are identical and, if reared together, may be treated more similarly than DZ twins, one could argue that the higher concordance rate for MZ twins than DZ twins may have as much to do with environmental influences as genetic influences. An even more informative method used in behavioral genetic studies involves sampling MZ twins reared together (MZT), MZ twins reared apart (MZA), DZ twins reared together (DZT), and DZ twins reared apart (DZA). In this way, it is easier to separate out genetic and environmental influences. For example, the following findings would suggest genetic influences in the manifestation of the behaviors or features under study: (1) the concordance rates for MZT and MZA twins are significantly greater than those for DZT and DZA twins, respectively; (2) the concordance rate for MZA twins approaches that of MZT twins; and (3) the concordance rate of DZA twins approaches that of DZT twins. These findings would suggest that genetics plays an important role because similarity/concordance is a function of the amount of genetic material shared and being raised in different environments does not have an appreciable effect on similarity.

We have presented only a brief and rather simplistic overview of behavioral genetics. Interest in this field has waxed and waned over the years, and at times the field has been the target of attacks from a variety of groups (Plomin et al., 1990). However, it is important to keep several points in mind. First, concordance rates or similarity indices less than 100% (or 1.00) *necessarily* implicate environmental influences. Therefore, behavioral genetics methods are tools for identifying and quantifying environmental as well as genetic factors in behavior. Second, finding that a behavior or characteristic is genetically influenced does *not* mean that it is immutable or unchangeable. Genetics *and* the environment interact in complex ways to produce behavior.

▌TABLE 7-3 Average Familial IQ Correlations (R)

Relationship	Weighted Average Correlation	Number of Pairs
Reared-together biological relatives		
MZ twins	0.86	4,672
DZ twins	0.60	5,546
Siblings	0.47	26,473
Parent/offspring	0.42	8,433
Half-siblings	0.31	200
Cousins	0.15	1,176
Reared-apart biological relatives		
MZ twins	0.72	65
Siblings	0.24	203
Parent/offspring	0.22	814
Reared-together nonbiological relatives		
Siblings	0.32	714
Adoptive parent/offspring	0.19	1397

Note: MZ = monozygotic; DZ = dizygotic. Weighted average correlation was determined using sample-size-weighted average of *z* transformations.

SOURCE: Adapted from "Familial Studies of Intelligence: A Review" by T. J. Bouchard, Jr., and M. McGue, 1981, *Science*, *250*, p. 1056; copyright 1981 by the American Association for the Advancement of Science; adapted by permission.

Recent estimates of the percentage of IQ variance associated with genetic factors range from 51% (Chipeur, Rovine, & Plomin, 1990) to 81% (Pedersen, Plomin, Nesselroade, & McClearn, 1992). In general, it appears that IQ heritability estimates vary as a function of the age of the sample; these estimates are maximal in older age groups (McGue et al., 1993).

Given the evidence that intelligence scores are influenced by genetic factors, does this mean that IQ is not malleable? No. This is the source of much confusion and controversy. Recall that heritability estimates are *not* 100%. This suggests that the environment plays some role in the development of intelligence. As McGue et al. (1993) state, behavioral genetics studies of IQ "strongly implicate the existence of environ-

mental influences: The correlation among reared-together MZ twins is less than unity; biological relatives who were reared together are more similar than biological relatives who were reared apart; and there is a significant correlation between the IQs of nonbiologically related but reared-together relatives" (pp. 60–61).

Even if heritability estimates were 100%, this does not rule out the possibility that IQ scores may change. Some "genetically determined" traits, such as height, can be influenced by environmental circumstances, and genetic disorders can be controlled or even cured by environmental intervention (Kamphaus, 1993). Although some short-term gains or changes have been noted, in general the research examining the efficacy of psychosocial interventions for improving IQ scores has been mixed (Kamphaus, 1993;

BOX 7-3

The Concept of Heritability

The concept of evergreens in A vary in height. The degree to which they vary from each other is called the variance. What produces this variance? Some is probably due to genetics. To find out how much, we equate environmental conditions such as soil, water, and sunlight (indicated by different shadings of the ground). We now take a random group of seedlings chosen from A. We plant them in this equated environment (B) and wait patiently

until they mature. We note that the size variation in B is less than it was in A. This reflects the fact that environmental conditions in B are equal for all the trees so that any environmental sources of variance have been eliminated. The remaining variance in B is entirely produced by genetic factors. Therefore, the heritability of height for A is the variance in B (the variation attributable to genetic factors) divided by the variance in A (the total variation in the population).

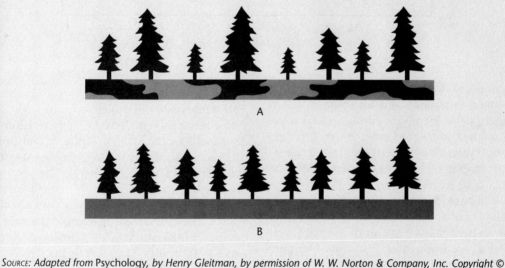

A

B

Source: Adapted from Psychology, *by Henry Gleitman, by permission of W. W. Norton & Company, Inc. Copyright ©️ 1981 by W. W. Norton & Company, Inc.*

Neisser et al., 1996). Despite these sometimes disappointing results, the general notion that favorable environments should be provided so as to allow individuals to realize their innate potential seems both plausible and a worthy goal (see Box 7-3).

In summary, genetic versus environmental influences are not either/or choices. Clearly, both play some role in the development and expression of intelligence. Behavioral geneticists

do not claim that environment plays no role in IQ; rather, their data clearly implicate environmental factors and should serve as a stimulus for more research on the nature and effect of these factors on the development of intelligence.

Stability of IQ Scores. As indicated earlier, one method of assessing the reliability of a measure is by computing a test-retest correlation. This gives us a sense of how stable scores are over

FIGURE 7-3 Graph depicting the relationship between age and stability

SOURCE: *Schuerger and Witt (1989). The temporal stability of individually tested intelligence.* Journal of Clinical Psychology, 45, p. 300. Reprinted by permission.

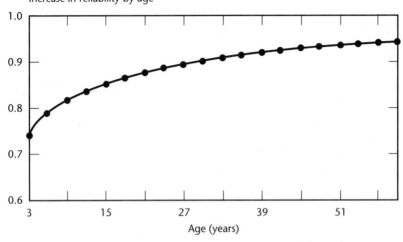

time. As noted by Schuerger and Witt (1989), IQ scores tend to be less stable for young children and more stable for adults. Further, and not too surprisingly, a longer test-retest interval (for example, 10 years versus 1 year) results in lower reliability/stability estimates. Figure 7-3 depicts stability of IQ scores as a function of age.

The implication of these findings is clear. Clinicians cannot assume that a single IQ test score will accurately characterize an individual's level of intelligence throughout his or her life span. IQ scores do tend to change, and this is especially true for young children. For this reason, clinicians often describe the individual's "present level of intellectual functioning" in their test reports. A variety of influences (such as illness or motivational and emotional changes) may affect an individual's score.

The Clinical Assessment of Intelligence

In this section, we will briefly describe several of the most frequently used intelligence tests for children and adults.

The Stanford-Binet Scales

For many years, the Binet scales were the preferred tests. They underwent many revisions after Binet's work in 1905. Terman's revision in 1916 was followed by the 1937 Revised Stanford-Binet (Terman & Merrill, 1937). The 1960 version of the Stanford-Binet (Terman & Merrill, 1960) gave way to a 1972 test kit with revised norms. The most recent revision of the scale appeared in 1986, the *Stanford-Binet Fourth Edition*, or SB-4 (Thorndike, Hagen, & Sattler, 1986).

Description. Until this latest revision, the Stanford-Binet was notable for being an age scale. It had 20 age levels, beginning at Year II and proceeding through Superior Adult Level III. Each level had six items. Each item passed was converted into one or two months of mental-age credit (depending upon whether it was located before or after Year Level V).

The 1986 version is radically different. It is based on a hierarchical model of intelligence. The *Stanford-Binet Fourth Edition* (SB-4) contains four general classes of items, and each class consists of several kinds of subtests:

FIGURE 7-4   The Stanford-Binet Intelligence Scale Fourth Edition (SB-4).
Photograph by courtesy of the Riverside Publishing Company, Itasca, Illinois.

1. *Verbal reasoning*: vocabulary, comprehension, absurdities, verbal relations
2. *Quantitative reasoning*: quantitative, number series, equation building
3. *Abstract/visual reasoning*: pattern analysis, copying, matrices, paper folding and cutting
4. *Short-term memory*: bead memory, memory for sentences, memory for digits, memory for objects

Each subtest is composed of items at varying levels of difficulty, from age 2 to adulthood. This revision uses an adaptive testing procedure called *multistage testing*. The examiner first gives the Vocabulary Test to determine the entry point (that is, which item to start with) for each remaining subtest. This initial estimate of ability provides a more appropriate entry or starting point on subsequent subtests, and is likely to result in more efficient testing, than relying exclusively on chronological age as a guide for a starting point. Thus, not all examinees of the same age are given the same items. Short forms or abbreviated versions of the SB-4 are discussed in

the manual; however, more research is needed on the equivalency of the full SB-4 and the abbreviated versions (Kamphaus, 1993).

Standardization. Final standardization of the SB-4 included 5013 participants. Using 1980 U.S. Census figures, participants were sampled according to geographic region, community size, ethnic group, age group, and gender. Socioeconomic status was considered as well.

Items were selected according to how well they seemed to measure the four listed classes. Items that led to unreliable scoring, showed ethnic or gender bias, or were not appropriate for a wide range of age groups were dropped.

Reliability and Validity. The SB-4 manual (Thorndike et al., 1986) indicates general support for the reliability of the composite score and subtest scores. Internal consistency reliabilities were basically in the .80s and .90s. Test-retest reliabilities for intervals of 2 to 8 months were (for preschoolers) mostly in the .70s, with a few in the .80s and .90s. But a few correlations for specific subtests were disappointingly low.

As for the validity of SB-4 composite scores, a variety of supportive evidence has been obtained (Laurent, Swerdlik, & Ryburn, 1992; Thorndike et al., 1986). For example, the correlation between SB-4 scores and scores on the 1972 Stanford-Binet was .81. Correlations between the SB-4 and several Wechsler scales (described next) were .83 for children, .80 for preschoolers, and .91 for adults. Correlations among subtests of the SB-4 and the Wechsler scales were also substantial. Therefore, using the criterion of relationship to other accepted tests of intelligence, the validity of the new Stanford-Binet is supported.

Finally, it was determined that the IQ scores of gifted children were significantly above the means of the standardization sample. Further, learning disabled and mentally retarded participants produced scores significantly below those of the standardization sample. All in all, the validity of the SB-4 looks promising. However, it should be noted that there has been only mixed support for the four factors originally proposed by the test authors to underlie SB-4 scores (Laurent et al., 1992).

The Wechsler Scales

Earlier versions of the Stanford-Binet had a number of disadvantages that led David Wechsler in 1939 to develop the Wechsler-Bellevue Intelligence Scale. This was a test designed for adults—one that would offer items whose content was more appropriate for and more motivating to adults than the school-oriented Binet. In contrast to the Stanford-Binet, whose items were arranged in age levels, the Wechsler-Bellevue Intelligence Scale grouped its items into subtests. For example, all arithmetic items were put into one subtest and arranged in order of increasing difficulty. In addition, there was a Performance Scale and a Verbal Scale (consisting of five and six subtests, respectively). A separate IQ for each scale could be calculated, along with a Full Scale IQ. The systematic inclusion of performance items helped remedy the overemphasis on verbal

FIGURE 7-5 David Wechsler published the Wechsler-Bellevue Intelligence Scale in 1939. Subsequent revisions of the adult and children's versions of this test have become the most widely used techniques to assess intellectual functioning.
Stock Montage.

skills that limited the utility of the earlier Stanford-Binet with special populations.

Wechsler used a deviation IQ concept. This approach, as we have seen, assumes that intelligence is normally distributed and compares individuals with their age peers. In effect, it compares the performance of a 15-year-old with that of other 15-year-olds. This method statistically establishes an IQ of 100 as the mean for each age group. As a result, an IQ of 100 means the same thing for any person, regardless of the person's age.

The WAIS-III

Description. A new version of the Wechsler-Bellevue, known as the Wechsler Adult Intelligent Scale (WAIS), first appeared in 1955. A revised edition (WAIS-R), was published in 1981. The most recent version, the *Wechsler Adult Intelligent Scale–Third Edition (WAIS-III)*, was introduced in 1997.

One major change introduced in the WAIS-III is the inclusion of *reversal items* in several subtests. On these subtests, all examinees begin with the same two basal items. If a perfect score on either basal item is not obtained, the preceding items are administered in reverse sequence until a perfect score is achieved for two consecutive items. The purpose of this change is to determine the examinee's ability level as efficiently as possible, without having to administer items markedly below that ability level. Another innovation is the WAIS-III's ability to provide *Index scores* in addition to IQ scores (Full Scale IQ, Verbal IQ, Performance IQ). By administering 13 subtests (excluding Object Assembly, an optional subtest; see below), the following four Index scores can be calculated: Verbal Comprehension, Perceptual Organization, Working Memory, and Processing Speed. These Index scores reflect the major ability factors that underlie the WAIS-III subtest scores. Thus, the Index scores provide a more detailed evaluation of the examinee's strengths and weaknesses across tasks.

Following are brief descriptions of the 14 WAIS-III subtests. The first seven constitute the Verbal subtests; the other seven are the Performance subtests.

1. *Vocabulary*. Here the examinee must define words that increase in difficulty. This is perhaps the best single verbal subtest. It correlates highly with Full Scale IQs, and some feel that it comes close to measuring what is usually termed *g*.
2. *Similarities*. This subtest consists of 19 items, for each of which the examinee must explain how two objects are alike. The subtest requires the basic ability to form abstractions and develop concepts.
3. *Arithmetic*. These 20 items are similar to arithmetic problems that appear in most school textbooks. The items are administered orally, and the examinee is not allowed to use paper and pencil.
4. *Digit Span*. This subtest is a measure of short-term memory and attention. Two sets of digits are read aloud by the examiner. For the first list, the examinee must repeat the digits in the order that they were read. For the second list, the digits must be repeated backward.
5. *Information*. These 28 items tap knowledge that one would be expected to have acquired as a result of everyday living and cultural interactions.
6. *Comprehension*. The 18 items of this subtest require the examinee to explain why certain procedures are followed, to interpret proverbs, and to determine what should be done in a given situation. The items measure common sense and practical judgment in solving a problem.
7. *Letter-Number Sequencing*. This new subtest consists of 7 items that assess working memory and attention. A combination of numbers and letters is read, and the examinee must first recall the numbers in ascending order, then the letters in alphabetical order. Each item consists of three trials of different combinations of numbers and letters. This is a supplementary subtest for IQ scores.
8. *Picture Completion*. This subtest consists of 25 colored cards, each showing a picture with a part missing. The examinee must identify the missing part. This requires concentration and the ability to note details and incongruities.
9. *Digit Symbol-Coding*. This code-substitution task requires the examinee to fill in the appropriate code in the blanks under a long series of numbers, using a key. The subtest requires the examinee to work in a direct, single-minded fashion.
10. *Block Design*. The examinee must assemble blocks to match the designs on a set of cards. The task involves visual-motor coordination and analytic synthesizing ability.

11. *Matrix Reasoning.* This new subtest consists of items that measure visual information processing and abstract reasoning skills.

12. *Picture Arrangement.* Several sets of pictures must be arranged in proper sequence to tell a coherent story. The subtest measures the ability to judge, anticipate, and plan ahead.

13. *Symbol Search.* This new subtest, consisting of 60 items, is similar to the WISC-III's Symbol Search subtest. The task is to indicate whether a stimulus symbol appears in the array that is present.

14. *Object Assembly.* Here five puzzles must be assembled. This subtest requires the ability to visualize a whole from its parts and to plan ahead, along with a certain degree of visual-motor coordination. Unlike in previous versions of the WAIS, this subtest is now optional.

Obtaining IQ Scores and Index Scores. Raw scores from each subtest are converted to *scaled scores*—standardized scores for a given age group. A number of IQ and Index Scores are then computed by adding together scaled scores from select subtests and converting these sums to IQ equivalents. Table 7-4 lists the WAIS-III subtests that are used to calculate each of the seven major IQ and Index scores: Verbal IQ, Performance IQ, Full Scale IQ, Verbal Comprehension, Perceptual Organization, Working Memory, and Processing Speed.

Standardization. The WAIS-III was standardized on a sample of 2450 adults, including equal numbers of men and women in each of 13 age groups ranging from age 16 to 89 years. The sample was stratified according to age, sex, race/ethnicity, education level, and geographic regions using 1995 U.S. Census Bureau data as a guide.

Reliability and Validity. The average Full Scale, Performance, and Verbal IQ reliability coefficients across age groups range from .94 to .98, and the average reliability coefficients across age groups for the Verbal Comprehension, Percep-

FIGURE 7-6 Simulated item from the WAIS-III Picture Completion Subtest.
Reproduced by permission of The Psychological Corporation.

tual Organization, Working Memory, and Processing Speed Index scores range from .88 to .96. Test-retest reliabilities over intervals of 2 to 12 weeks range from .67 to .94 across age groups for the various subtests.

Although it was introduced only recently, a wealth of data support the validity of WAIS-III scores (Psychological Corporation, 1997). Relevant subtest scores from other tests of cognitive ability (such as the WAIS-R and WISC-III) are significantly correlated with targeted subscale scores derived from the new WAIS-III. For example, the WAIS-III Working Memory Index is highly correlated with scales from other measures tapping attention and concentration, and the WAIS-III Verbal Comprehension Index and Verbal IQ Scale correlate significantly with scores from external measures of language fluency and language comprehension. Finally, as further support for the factorial validity of the WAIS-III, a series of exploratory and confirmatory factor analyses largely supported the predicted four factors of the WAIS-III (verbal comprehension, perceptual organization, working memory, and processing speed), as well as the predicted associations between the WAIS-III subtests and these factors.

TABLE 7-4 WAIS-III Subtests and Their Respective IQ or Index Scores

Subtest	Full Scale IQ	Verbal IQ	Performance IQ	Verbal Comprehension	Perceptual Organization	Working Memory	Processing Speed
Picture Completion	√		√		√		
Vocabulary	√	√		√			
Digit Symbol-Coding	√		√				√
Similarities	√	√		√			
Block Design	√		√		√		
Arithmetic	√	√				√	
Matrix Reasoning	√		√		√		
Digit Span	√	√				√	
Information	√	√		√			
Picture Arrangement	√		√				
Comprehension	√	√					
Symbol Search			O				√
Letter-Number Sequencing		O				√	
Object Assembly			O				

Note: √ indicates that scaled scores for the respective subtest are used to calculate that IQ Score or Index Score. O indicates that scaled scores for the respective subtest can be used in place of specified Performance or Verbal Subtests if they are not administered.

A Brief Case Report: Intellectual Evaluation

The following brief excerpt is from a report written by a clinical psychologist in response to a referral by a primary care physician, who requested that her patient be evaluated for cognitive limitations, especially in the area of short-term memory and attention. The patient reportedly had been experiencing difficulty at his new job as a forklift driver in a warehouse. Specifically, he was not meeting his quotas and was "forgetting" some of the tasks assigned to him. Here, we present only the WAIS-III test results and interpretation.

Patient: RYAN, Adam (fictitious name)

Age: 28; *Education*: High School Degree; *Marital Status*: Single

Test Behavior: Mr. Ryan was cooperative with all aspects of the testing, working diligently on all tasks that were presented. He did mention spontaneously that he was "getting in trouble" a lot because of his forgetfulness. It was also apparent that Mr. Ryan was distressed and bothered by his performance on several subtests requiring that he hold new information and then either repeat it back (Digit Span) or perform operations on the information (Arithmetic).

Intellectual Functioning: Based on his WAIS-III scores, Mr. Ryan is currently functioning in the Average range of intelligence, with a Full Scale IQ of 100. His Verbal IQ (100) and Performance IQ (100) scores were also in the Average range. An examination of subtest scores and Index scores, however, revealed a great deal of variability. A complete listing of his obtained scores appears below:

Verbal Subtests

Vocabulary	12
Similarities	13
Arithmetic	7
Digit Span	6
Information	11
Comprehension	12
(Letter-Number Sequencing)	(5)

Performance Subtests

Picture Completion	12
Digit Symbol-Coding	9
Block Design	10
Matrix Reasoning	10
Picture Arrangement	10
(Symbol Search)	(9)
(Object Assembly)	(10)

Composite Scores

Verbal IQ	100
Performance IQ	100
Full Scale IQ	100
Verbal Comprehension Index	110
Perceptual Organization Index	103
Working Memory Index	75
Processing Speed Index	93

Although his scores related to verbal comprehension, perceptual organization, and processing speed place him in the Average range of functioning, Mr. Ryan's scores reflective of working memory place him in the Borderline range of functioning. He demonstrated weaknesses on those subtests requiring attention, short-term memory, and the processing of new information.

This case example demonstrates how an overreliance on global IQ scores (Full Scale IQ, Verbal IQ, Performance IQ) can be misleading. Although Mr. Ryan's global scores were in the average range, a more in-depth examination of his individual subtest scores and Index scores suggests cognitive limitations. For this reason, it is important to calculate and interpret discrepancies among subtest scores, IQ scores, and Index scores in order to give a rich clinical picture of examinees' cognitive abilities.

The WISC-III

The Wechsler Intelligence Scale for Children (WISC) was first developed in 1949 and revised in 1974 (WISC-R). The latest version, the *Wechsler Intelligence Scale for Children–Third Edition (WISC-III)*, was published in 1991 (Wechsler,

1991). Appropriate for children ages 6 through 16 years, the WISC-III consists of 10 mandatory and 3 supplementary subtests. Like its predecessors, the WISC-III is in many ways a downward extension of the WAIS-R. Examples of items similar to those included on the WISC-III are shown in Figure 7-7.

Description. Like the WAIS-III, the WISC-III contains both Verbal and Performance subscales. The Verbal subtests are Information, Similarities, Arithmetic, Vocabulary, and Comprehension; Digit Span is the supplementary Verbal subtest. The Performance subtests are Picture Completion, Picture Arrangement, Block Design, Object Assembly, and Coding; Mazes and Symbol Search are the two supplementary Performance subtests. Verbal and Performance IQs are calculated, as is an overall Full Scale IQ.

Several new WISC-III features are noteworthy. The Symbol Search optional subtest is new; Picture Completion is now the first subtest to be administered to examinees; and improvements in subtest content, administration, and scoring have been incorporated into the WISC-III (Wechsler, 1991).

Standardization. Normative data for the WISC-III were obtained from a standardization sample of 2200 cases representative of the U.S. population of children. Using 1988 U.S. Census Bureau data, cases were selected to represent the U.S. population of children proportionally by race/ethnicity, geographic region, and parent education. The sample included 200 children (100 girls and 100 boys) in each of 11 age groups (ages 6 to 16 years).

Reliability and Validity. Wechsler (1991) reported that the average (across age groups) split-half reliabilities for the Verbal, Performance, and Full Scale of the WISC-III were .95, .91, and .96, respectively. The average split-half reliabilities for the individual subtests ranged from .69 to .87. The test-retest reliabilities (median interval between testings = 23 days) across three different age groups were fairly high, with the exception

of the Mazes subtest (Wechsler, 1991); this subtest's scores are likely to be unstable over time. As for validity, WISC-III scores are highly correlated with scores from other measures of intelligence (the WISC-R, WAIS-R, and SB-4). Further, scores from the WISC-R, and presumably the WISC-III, have been shown to be predictive of academic achievement.

Finally, several factor analytic studies have been conducted using WISC-III scores. Previous factor analyses of WISC-R scores suggested a three-factor structure: Verbal Comprehension, Perceptual Organization, and Freedom from Distractibility. However, results supporting this third factor have been mixed (Wechsler, 1991). Interestingly, factor analyses reported in the WISC-III manual suggest a four-factor solution for WISC-III scores: Verbal Comprehension, Perceptual Organization, Freedom from Distractibility, and Processing Speed. The last two factors are quite different from those identified using the WISC-R. To date, the validity and utility of these two factors remain to be demonstrated (Kamphaus, 1993).

The Clinical Use of Intelligence Tests

In the preceding sections we have described several of the more commonly used intelligence tests. It is time to take a closer look at how such tests are used in the clinical setting.

The Estimation of General Intellectual Level. The most obvious use of an intelligence test is as a means for arriving at an estimate of the patient's general intellectual level. Often the goal is the determination of how much general intelligence (g) a given person possesses. Often, the question is stated a bit differently—for example, What is the patient's intellectual potential? Posing the question in this way suggests that perhaps the person is not functioning as well as his or her potential would indicate. The potential can form a baseline against which to measure current achievements, thus providing information about the patient's current level of functioning.

FIGURE 7-7 Examples of items similar to those on the WISC-III.

Art courtesy of The Psychological Corporation.

Information (30 questions)

How many legs do you have?
What must you do to make water freeze?
Who discovered the North Pole?
What is the capital of France?

Similarities (19 questions)

In what way are pencil and crayon alike?
In what way are tea and coffee alike?
In what way are inch and mile alike?
In what way are binoculars and microscope alike?

Arithmetic (24 questions)

If I have one piece of candy and get another one, how many pieces will I have?
At 12 cents each, how much will 4 bars of soap cost?
If a suit sells for 1/2 of the regular price, what is the cost of a $120 suit?

Vocabulary (30 words)

ball   summer   poem   obstreperous

Comprehension (18 questions)

Why do we wear shoes?
What is the thing to do if you see someone dropping his packages?
In what two ways is a lamp better than a candle?

Digit Span (15 items; 8 in Digits Forward, 7 in Digits Backward)

The task is to repeat digits presented by the examiner in a forward direction in one part (2 to 9 digits in length; example: 1–8) and in a backward direction in the other part (2 to 8 digits in length; example: 3–9–1).

Picture Completion (30 items)

The task it to identify the essential missing part of the picture, such as (a) a car without a wheel, (b) a dog without a leg, and (c) a telephone without numbers on the dial (see below).

Coding (59 items in Coding A and 119 items in Coding B)

The task is to copy symbols from a key (see below).

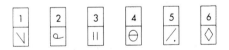

Picture Arrangement (14 items)

The task is to arrange a series of pictures into a meaningful sequence (see below).

Block Design (12 items)

The task is to reproduce stimulus designs using four of nine blocks (see below).

Object Assembly (5 items)

The task is to arrange pieces into a meaningful object (see below).

FIGURE 7-7 Examples of items similar to those on the WISC-III *(continued)*
Art courtesy of The Psychological Corporation.

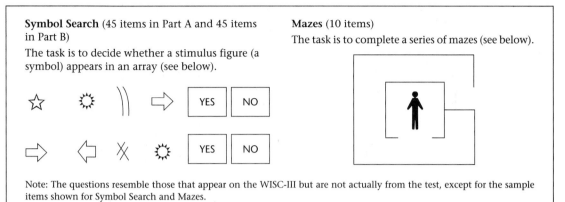

Symbol Search (45 items in Part A and 45 items in Part B)

The task is to decide whether a stimulus figure (a symbol) appears in an array (see below).

Mazes (10 items)

The task is to complete a series of mazes (see below).

Note: The questions resemble those that appear on the WISC-III but are not actually from the test, except for the sample items shown for Symbol Search and Mazes.

Many pitfalls and fallacies are associated with the pursuit of these goals. The following is an example.

The Case of Harold

Harold was being routinely evaluated prior to transfer to a special class for advanced junior high school students. Rather surprisingly, his Full Scale WISC-III IQ turned out to be 107. This score was in the average range but below the cutoff point for admission to the class. It was also considerably below what his teachers had estimated, based on his classroom performance. A closer look at his subtest scores revealed that his performances on Block Design, Coding, and Object Assembly were significantly below those on the other subtests. A follow-up interview with Harold was quite revealing. Since early childhood, he had suffered from muscular weakness in both arms and hands. This weakness prevented him from making fine, quick motor responses. However, he had developed a number of clever compensations to prevent others from guessing his limitation. For example, what had appeared to be slow, deliberate, even confused responses on Block Design were really not that at all. He was feigning confusion in order to mask his difficulty with fine motor functions. Clearly, then, Harold's IQ score had been unduly affected by a motor weakness that had nothing to do with his ability to perform intellectually.

This example is but the tip of the iceberg. It does suggest, however, that obtaining an IQ is not the end of a clinician's task—it is only the beginning. The IQ score must be interpreted. Only through knowledge of the patient's learning history and by observations made during the testing situation can that score be placed in an appropriate interpretive context and adequately evaluated (Oakland & Glutting, 1990).

Prediction of Academic Success. As mentioned previously, there are data that demonstrate a relationship between intelligence test scores and school success (Herrnstein & Murray, 1994; Kamphaus, 1993; Neisser et al., 1996). To the extent that intelligence should logically reflect the capacity to do well in school, we are justified in expecting intelligence tests to predict school success. Not everyone would equate intelligence with scholastic aptitude, but the fact remains that a major function of intelligence tests is to predict school performance. One must remember, however, that intelligence and academic success are not conceptually identical.

The Appraisal of Style. As we have noted, what is important is not only whether the client succeeds or fails on particular test items but also how that success or failure occurs. One of the major values of individual intelligence tests is that they permit us to observe the client or patient at work. Such observations can help us greatly in interpreting an IQ. For example, did this child do as well as possible? Was there failure-avoidance? Did the child struggle with most items, or was there easy success? Was the child unmotivated, and could this have detracted from the child's performance? Such questions and the ensuing interpretations breathe life into an otherwise inert IQ score.

The following simulated questions from the WAIS-III and a hypothetical patient's responses to them are examples of the data that can be obtained beyond the sheer correctness or incorrectness of a response.

Query: Who wrote *Paradise Lost*? (Information subtest)

Answer: Probably a Catholic. But since the Pope began changing things around, they retitled it.

Query: What is the advantage of keeping money in a bank? (Comprehension subtest)

Answer: There isn't. There's so damn many crooks. But they'll get theirs someday.

Query: In what ways are a lion and a tiger alike? (Similarities subtest)

Answer: Well, now, that's a long story. Do they look alike? They really can't breed together, you know.*

Some clinicians have ventured considerably beyond making a few limited personality inferences that would inject some added meaning into IQs and have based mental disorder diagnoses on the Stanford-Binet and Wechsler scales.

---

*These simulated items were provided courtesy of The Psychological Corporation, New York. The answers are based on responses to actual items.

They believed that by examining patterns of scores (known as intertest scatter), they could apply diagnostic labels to patients (such as schizophrenia or depression). Over the years, however, studies purporting to show the validity of these interpretations of intertest scatter could rarely be replicated. Thus, diagnoses cannot be reliably inferred from patterns of test performance (Piedmont, Sokolove, & Fleming, 1989).

Some Final Observations and Conclusions

In the preceding pages, we have discussed definitions and theories of intelligence, descriptions of intelligence tests, and the uses of intelligence tests. We can now make some general concluding statements.

An Abstraction. Because the IQ does not signify that a person will perform in all situations at a constant level, we talk about "present functioning" rather than innate potential. Many would argue that intelligence, like an attitude, is not a thing. Rather, it is an abstraction that may enable clinicians to accurately predict certain behaviors. A clinician who observes that Charles gets A's in class, is highly regarded by his instructors, and solves problems faster than his peers will probably conclude that Charles is intelligent. To reach that conclusion, the clinician will have abstracted a common element of Charles's behavior in several situations The clinician can now use that abstraction to predict that Charles will again be successful in related future situations. However, despite the notion that intelligence is an abstraction rather than an entity located in a specific region of the brain, and despite the difficulties in distinguishing between what people cannot do and what they choose not to do, most people tend to believe that a "true" IQ exists and that intelligence tests are the best way to assess it.

The Role of the Situation. Over the years, research has demonstrated the role of situational factors and examiner effects on vulnerable groups such as patients, young children, minorities, and others (for example, Masling, 1960; Sattler, 1970). The age, socioeconomic status, professional level, and even appearance of the examiner can play a role, as can similar qualities in the person being tested (Babad, Mann, & Mar-Hayim, 1975). Some critics have also claimed that African American children get lower IQ scores when tested by white examiners (Sattler, 1970). Other research seems less clear on this point (for example, Sattler & Gwynne, 1982). The examiner's expectations about a person's abilities can also have an effect—the so-called self-fulfilling prophecy (Rosenthal, 1966). Coaching, practice, and the overall test sophistication of the examinee may also affect scores (Anastasi, 1988).

As Flaugher (1978) argues, however, it is a mistake to believe that a test that is unbiased or free of situational effects will automatically result in the same performance level for all groups. A child from a background where standard English is not used may well have trouble coping with the highly verbal nature of some intelligence tests. Such children may show lower test scores than will other children. Although one should be wary of inferring too much about native ability from such scores, the fact remains that the scores may reflect what will later happen in school. The less verbal children may achieve lower grades just as they received lower IQ scores, and for the same reasons. As Green (1978) indicates, ethnic differences in average test scores do not so much reflect test bias as different cultural backgrounds. We will have more to say about the issue of test bias in Chapter 8 (Personality Assessment).

Generality versus Specificity of Measurement. Given all the caveats, qualifications, and disclaimers, the reader may wonder why clinical psychologists use general tests of intelligence at all. In many ways, this question can be reduced to cost-benefit terms. If one is especially pressed for time, or if the diagnostic issues do not revolve specifically around intellectual matters, then one would probably be better advised either to skip such general tests or to use a short form.

However, it is important to recognize exactly what a general test of intellectual functioning, such as a Stanford-Binet or a Wechsler, can do. It can provide a broad, general index of intellectual functioning across a range of situations. Because the Full Scale IQ is a general index, it may predict moderately well to many diverse situations that depend significantly upon intellectual skills. However, it may not predict to any specific situation at an acceptable level. Thus, if the goal is solely to predict scholastic success in Situation Y, then one would be better advised to use a more specific measure than a Wechsler test, or at least to use a Wechsler test whose subtests contain elements similar to the performance one hopes to predict. Often, however, the clinician may need a basis for choosing remedial or clinical options. With standardized procedures, the clinical psychologist can compare the patient with similar persons who have performed in the same situation.

Chapter Summary

The assessment of intelligence has a long history in clinical psychology. Compulsory education and psychologists' ability to measure mental abilities contributed to the development and success of the field of intelligence testing. However, by the end of the 1960s, the validity of these tests was being challenged. To this day, there are many controversies about how intelligence is defined and how it is measured. Contemporary clinical psychologists appear to believe in both a general factor of intelligence, *g*, and specific abilities that underlie the general intelligence factor. Intelligence scores are correlated with school success, occupational status, and job performance. In addition, there are group differences in intelligence test scores between males and females and among ethnic/racial groups. Although intelligence test scores are influenced by genetic factors, environment does play some role in the development of intelligence. IQ scores are more stable for adults than they are for children.

We have discussed three major intelligence tests in use today. The Stanford-Binet Fourth Edition is used to assess children, adolescents, and adults, the Wechsler Adult Intelligence Scale–Third Edition to assess adolescents and adults, and the Wechsler Intelligence Scale for Children–Third Edition to assess children. Intelligence test results are used to quantify overall levels of general intelligence, as well as specific cognitive abilities. This versatility allows clinical psychologists to use intelligence test scores for a variety of prediction tasks (such as school achievement).

Key Terms

behavioral genetics A research specialty that evaluates both genetic and environmental influences on the development of behavior.

chronological age What we commonly refer to as age; years of life.

concordance rate An index of similarity between individuals. The simplest form of concordance rate is the percentage of instances in which two individuals exhibit similar behaviors or characteristics.

concurrent validity The extent to which test scores correlate with scores on other relevant measures administered at the same time.

construct validity The extent to which test scores correlate with other measures or behaviors in a logical and theoretically consistent way. Construct validity requires a demonstration of all aspects of validity.

content validity The degree to which test items adequately measure all aspects of the construct of interest.

crystallized ability One of two higher-order factors of intelligence conceived by Cattell. Crystallized ability refers to the intellectual capacities obtained through culture-based learning.

deviation IQ A concept introduced by Wechsler to address problems observed when applying the ratio IQ to older individuals. An individual's performance on an IQ test is compared to that of her or his age peers.

dizygotic (DZ) twins Fraternal twins, or twins that share about 50% of their genetic material.

equivalent-forms reliability The extent to which an individual obtains similar scores on equivalent, or parallel, forms of the same test.

fluid ability One of two higher-order factors of intelligence conceived by Cattell. Fluid ability refers to a person's genetically based intellectual capacity.

genotype The genetic makeup of an individual.

g The term introduced by Charles Spearman to describe his concept of a general intelligence.

index scores Scores that correspond to the major ability factors that underlie the WAIS-III subtest scores (i.e., Verbal Comprehension, Perceptual Organization, Working Memory, and Processing Speed).

intelligence quotient A term developed by Stern in 1938 to address problems with using the difference between chronological age and mental age to represent deviance. Typically, a deviation IQ score is used.

intelligence There is no universally accepted definition of intelligence. However, many definitions of intelligence emphasize the ability to think abstractly, the ability to learn, and the ability to adapt to the environment.

internal consistency reliability The extent to which the items of a test "hang together" (most often assessed by computing Cronbach's alpha).

interrater reliability The level of agreement between two or more raters who have evaluated the same individual independently. Agreement can refer to consensus on behaviors, attributes, and so on.

mental age A term introduced by Binet as an index of mental performance. This idea was based on the notion that individuals of a certain age should have mastered certain abilities.

monozygotic (MZ) twins Identical twins, or twins that share 100% of their genetic material.

phenotype The observable characteristics of an individual. The phenotype is a product of both the genotype and the environment.

predictive validity The extent to which test scores correlate with scores on other relevant measures administered at some point in the future.

Primary Mental Abilities Seven factors of intelligence derived by Thurstone on the basis of his factor analytic work: number, word fluency, verbal meaning, perceptual speed, space, reasoning, and memory.

reversal items A feature on several subtests of the WAIS-III that allows the examiner to determine the examinee's ability level without having to administer items markedly below that ability level.

split-half reliability The extent to which an individual's scores on one-half of a test (e.g., the even-numbered items) are similar to his or her scores on the other half (e.g., the odd-numbered items).

stability of IQ scores The similarity of IQ scores measured at different points in time. Based upon test-retest correlations, IQ scores tend to be less stable for young children than for adults.

Stanford-Binet Fourth Edition (SB-4) An intelligence test based on a hierarchical model of intelligence. The SB-4 contains four general classes of items (verbal reasoning, quantitative reasoning, abstract/visual reasoning, short-term memory), each of which consists of several subtests.

Structure of the Intellect Model A model proposed and tested by Guilford that asserts that the components of intelligence may be organized into three dimensions: operations (e.g., memory), contents (e.g., symbolic), and products (e.g., relations). In Guilford's scheme, a particular mental operation is applied to a specific type of content, resulting in a product.

test-retest reliability The extent to which an individual makes similar responses to the same test stimuli on repeated occasions.

theory of multiple intelligences A theory forwarded by Gardner that posits the existence of six intelligences: linguistic, musical, logical-mathematical, spatial, bodily-kinesthetic, and personal.

triarchic theory of intelligence A theory proposed by Sternberg that maintains that people function on the basis of three aspects of intelligence: componential (refers to analytical thinking), experiential (creative thinking), and contextual ("street smarts," or the ability to successfully manipulate one's environment).

twins reared apart MZ or DZ twins separated from each other shortly after birth; such twins share genetic material but not specific environmental influences.

twins reared together MZ or DZ twins reared in the same family environment; such twins share both genetic material and specific environmental influences. Comparing the concordance rates of twins reared apart and twins reared together can help tease apart the genetic and environmental influences on a particular behavior or characteristic.

validity The extent to which an assessment technique measures what it is supposed to measure. There are several forms of validity.

Wechsler Adult Intelligence Scale–Third Edition (WAIS-III) An adult intelligence test comprised of both a Verbal Scale and a Performance Scale, each of which consists of several subtests. The WAIS-III yields a Verbal IQ, a Performance IQ, and a Full-Scale IQ, in addition to Index scores.

Wechsler Intelligence Scale for Children–Third Edition (WISC-III) An intelligence test designed for children between the ages of 6 and 16. Like the WAIS-III, the WISC-III contains both Verbal and Performance subscales and yields a Verbal IQ, a Performance IQ, and a Full-Scale IQ.

Web Sites of Interest

To visit any of the web sites listed below, go to www.wadsworth.com and click on Links.

7-1 Intelligence: Knowns and Unknowns

7-2 Task Force Report of the American Psychological Association

7-3 Update on APA's revised *Standards for Educational and Psychological Testing*

7-4 APA's Science Directorate Testing and Assessment Web Page

CHAPTER EIGHT

Personality Assessment

For years it has been popular to bemoan the sorry state of psychological testing. Supposedly, "no one" uses such tests any longer. Many academics argue that testing in general—and projective testing in particular—is invalid. Except perhaps for the MMPI-2, they say, objective tests are also out of style. Others advise that textbooks such as this one should drastically reduce the coverage of personality assessment. There is only one thing wrong with the foregoing claims and advice: They do not reflect the real world of clinical practice. In fact, psychological assessment continues to be a high-profile activity of today's practicing clinician (see, for example, Butcher, 1995a). Results from surveys of clinicians reinforce the conclusion that projective tests, the Wechsler scales, and the Minnesota

Multiphasic Personality Inventory continue to be highly popular and that many clinicians do depend on psychological tests (Watkins, Campbell, Nieberding, & Hallmark, 1995). As we shall see later in this book, testing in such specialty areas as forensic psychology, pediatric psychology, neuropsychological assessment, and health psychology actually seems to be on the upswing. Even in the case of projective testing (the favorite "whipping boy" of many who claim that testing is a dying field), the usage trends remain fairly strong.

Perhaps, then, the reports of the demise of personality assessment are a bit exaggerated (Exner, 1995). Table 8-1 gives an idea of the kinds of tests in use today and the frequency of their use. This table presents a rank-ordering of

TABLE 8-1 Top Twenty Assessment Procedures Used by Clinical Psychologists

Test or Procedure	Percentage of Clinical Psychologists*
Clinical Interview	95
Wechsler Adult Intelligence Scale–Revised (WAIS-R)	93
Minnesota Multiphasic Personality Inventory–2 (MMPI-2)	85
Sentence Completion Methods	84
Thematic Apperception Test (TAT)	82
Rorschach	82
Bender-Gestalt	80
Projective Drawings	80
Beck Depression Inventory	71
Wechsler Intelligence Scale for Children–III (WISC-III)	69
Wide Range Achievement Test–Revised (WRAT-R)	68
Wechsler Memory Scale–Revised	65
Peabody Picture Vocabulary Test–Revised (PPVT-R)	50
Millon Clinical Multiaxial Inventory–II (MCMI-II)	49
WPPSI-R	44
Children's Apperception Test	42
Vineland Social Maturity Scale	42
Millon Adolescent Personality Inventory	40
Strong Interest Inventory	39
Stanford-Binet Intelligence Scale	38

*Percentage of clinical psychologists who indicated that they used test or procedure at least "occasionally."
Source: Adapted from Watkins et al. (1995), Table 4, p. 57.

the top 20 assessment procedures used by a randomly selected sample of clinical psychologists (Watkins et al., 1995).

However, there are other important considerations besides frequency of usage. Personality assessment measures must show high levels of reliability and validity in order to be useful to clinical psychologists. A long history of relatively uncritical use of certain personality measures does not justify their use today. Therefore, in this chapter, we will not only describe some of the more popular objective and projective personality measures, but we will critically evaluate their psychometric properties as well.

Objective Tests

We will begin our survey of personality assessment with an examination of objective tests. *Objective personality measures* involve the administration of a standard set of questions or statements, to which the examinee responds using a fixed set of options. Many objective tests use a true/false or yes/no response format; others provide a dimensional scale (for example, 0 = strong disagree; 1 = disagree; 2 = neutral; 3 = agree; 4 = strongly agree). Objective tests have both advantages and disadvantages, discussed below.

Some Advantages. Objective tests of personality or self-report inventories have had a central role in the development of clinical psychology (Goldberg, 1971; R. I. Watson, 1959). The historical role of inventories, as well as their current prominence, is due in large part to their obvious advantages. First of all, they are economical. After only brief instructions, large groups can be tested simultaneously, or a single patient can complete an inventory alone. Even computer scoring and interpretation of these tests are possible. Second, scoring and administration are relatively simple and objective. This, in turn, tends to make interpretation easier and seems to require less interpretive skill on the part of the clinician. Often a simple score along a single dimension (such as adjustment-maladjustment) or on a single trait (such as dependency or psych-

Objective paper-and-pencil tests are economical, easy to administer, and easy to score.
Photodisc

opathy) is possible. This apparent simplicity obviously attracts many clinicians. However, as we shall see, rarely does such simple interpretation culminate in the validity claimed for it. In fact, this apparent simplicity can frequently lead to rather widespread misuse by ill-trained testers. A final attraction of self-report inventories, particularly for clinicians who are disenchanted with the problems inherent in projective tests, is their apparent objectivity and reliability.

Of course, as is so often the case, in the process of achieving the foregoing advantages and economies, clinical psychology seems to have traded one set of problems for another. Whether the trade-off is worthwhile is ultimately determined by one's values and one's theoretical orientation.

Some Disadvantages. The items of many inventories are often behavioral in nature. That is, the questions or statements concern behaviors that may (or may not) characterize the respondent. Those interested in identifying motives or dynamics may glean little understanding through such items. For example, although two individuals may endorse the same behavioral item ("I have trouble getting to sleep"), they may do so for entirely different reasons. Of course, for clinicians who tend to pay little attention to mediating variables such as motives or cognitions, this is a virtue rather than a defect.

Some inventories contain a mixture of items dealing with behaviors, cognitions, and needs. Yet inventories often provide a single, overall score—which may reflect various combinations of these behaviors, cognitions, and needs. Therefore, two individuals who achieve the same score may actually be quite different, even in reference to the personality trait or construct in question. Thus, the same score on a measure may have several alternative interpretations.

Other difficulties involve the transparent meaning of some inventories' questions, which can obviously facilitate faking on the part of some patients. Some tests tend to depend heavily on the patient's self-knowledge. In addition, the forced-choice approach prevents individuals from qualifying or elaborating their responses, so that some additional information may be lost or distorted. In other instances, the limited understanding or even the limited reading ability of some individuals may lead them to misinterpret questions (a misinterpretation not necessarily attributable to personality determinants) or to answer questions in a random fashion.

Methods of Test Construction for Objective Tests

Now that we have some appreciation of the advantages and limitations of objective tests, it is instructive to turn our attention to the various methods of test construction used in developing these tests. Over the years, a variety of strategies for constructing self-report inventories have been proposed.

Content Validation. The most straightforward approach to measurement is for clinicians to decide what it is they wish to assess and then to simply ask the patient for that information. For example, the Woodworth Personal Data Sheet used in World War I was a kind of standardized psychiatric interview. Content was determined by surveying the psychiatric literature to identify the major manifestations of "neuroses" and "psychoses." Items were then constructed that would tap those manifestations. Consequently, if the domain of neurosis or psychosis (as defined by the psychiatric literature) were adequately sampled, then the test could be assumed to be valid. "Do you sleep well at night?" "Do you get angry easily?" and "Are you easily insulted?" were considered good items if they related to what prevailing psychiatric opinion regarded as maladjustment.

Ensuring content validity, however, involves much more than simply deciding what you want to assess and then making up some items that appear to do the job. Rather, more sophisticated *content validation* methods involve (1) carefully defining all relevant aspects of the variable you are attempting to measure; (2) consulting experts before generating items; (3) using judges to assess each potential item's relevance to the variable of interest; and (4) using psychometric analyses to evaluate each item before you include it in your measure (Haynes, Richard, & Kubany, 1995; Nunnally & Bernstein, 1994).

However, as Wiggins (1973) observes, several potential problems are inherent in the content validity approach to test construction. First, can clinicians assume that every patient interprets a given item in exactly the same way? Second, can patients accurately report their own behavior or emotions? Third, will patients be honest, or will they attempt to place themselves in a good light (or even a bad light at times)? Fourth, can clinicians assume that the "experts" can be counted on to define the essence of the concept they are trying to measure? Most of these seem to be general problems for the majority of inventories, regardless of whether they depend on content sampling to establish their validity.

Empirical Criterion Keying. In an attempt to help remedy the foregoing difficulties, the *empirical criterion keying* approach was developed. The most prominent example of this general method is the original Minnesota Multiphasic Personality Inventory (MMPI). In this approach, no assumptions are made as to whether a patient is telling the truth or the response really corresponds to behavior or feelings. What is important is that certain patients describe themselves in certain ways. As Meehl (1945) put it, "Thus if a hypochondriac says that he [sic] has 'many headaches' the fact of interest is that he says this" (p. 9).

The important assumption inherent in this approach is that members of a particular diagnostic group will tend to respond in the same way. Consequently, it is not necessary to select test items in a rational, theoretical fashion. All that is required is to show on an empirical basis that the members of a given diagnostic group respond to a given item in a similar fashion. For example, if, in contrast to nonclinical respondents, most individuals diagnosed with psychopathy agree with the item "I grew up in a house that had three steps on the front porch," then that item is a good one because it is endorsed by members of the psychopathic group. Thus, independent of an item's surface content, the test response becomes a "sign" of one's diagnostic status. The utility of an item is thus determined solely by the extent to which it discriminates among known groups. The test response is not necessarily a *sample* of behavior, because the content of the item may not be directly associated with the symptoms that characterize members of that diagnostic group.

Of course, the criterion keying method has its problems. Foremost is the difficulty of interpreting the meaning of a score. For example, suppose that some patients diagnosed with schizophrenia are answering items intended to place them somewhere along the adjusted-maladjusted dimension. Suppose also that most of these patients happen to come from less educated families than do the participants in a comparison group. When these patients with schizo-phrenia endorse the item "I almost never read books," that endorsement may reflect their poor educational background rather than their psychopathology. Although demonstrating that the test can discriminate among various patient groups is one aspect of establishing the validity of a test, the sole use of the empirical criterion keying method to select items for a test is not recommended (Clark & Watson, 1995).

Factor Analysis. These days, the majority of test developers use a factor analytic (or internal consistency) approach to test construction (Clark & Watson, 1995; Floyd & Widaman, 1995). The Guilford Inventories (Guilford, 1959) are excellent historical examples of a *factor analytic approach*. Here, the idea is to examine the intercorrelations among the individual items from many existing personality inventories. Succeeding factor analyses will then reduce or "purify" scales thought to reflect basic dimensions of personality. The *exploratory* factor analytic approach is atheoretical. One begins by capturing a universe of items and then proceeds to reduce them to basic elements—personality, adjustment, diagnostic affiliation, or whatever—hoping to arrive at the core traits and dimensions of personality. *Confirmatory* factor analytic approaches are more theory-driven, seeking to confirm a hypothesized factor structure (based on theoretical predictions) for the test items (Floyd & Widaman, 1995). Although a detailed explanation of confirmatory factor analysis procedures is beyond the scope of this book, we anticipate that an increasing number of clinical psychologists will employ confirmatory factor analysis in the development and evaluation of objective assessment measures.

The strength of the factor analytic approach to test construction is the emphasis on an empirical demonstration that items purporting to measure a variable or dimension of personality are highly related to one another. However, a limitation of this approach is that it does not in and of itself demonstrate that these items are actually measuring the variable of interest; we only know that the items tend to be measuring the same "thing."

TABLE 8-2 Strategies for Determining the Validity
of Inventory Item "I Wish I Could Be Happier"

Strategy	Item Is Valid If
Content validity	"Authorities" assert that the item is representative of the syndrome of depression.
Empirical criterion keying	This item discriminates between depressed and nondepressed groups.
Factor analysis	The item has been shown through factor analysis to be significantly related to a homogeneous and independent cluster of items that purport to measure depression.
Construct validity	The item measures the depression construct as theoretically defined (depression involves a negative view of oneself—in this case, seeing oneself as unhappy).

Construct Validity Approach. This approach combines many aspects of the content validity, empirical criterion keying, and factor analytic approaches (Clark & Watson, 1995). In this approach, scales are developed to measure specific concepts from a given theory. In the case of personality assessment, the intent is to develop measures anchored in a theory of personality. Validation is achieved when it can be said that a given scale measures the theoretical construct in question. The selection of items is based on the extent to which they reflect the theoretical construct under study. Item analysis, factor analysis, and other procedures are used to ensure that a homogeneous scale is developed. Construct validity for the scale is then determined by demonstrating, through a series of theory-based studies, that those who achieve certain scores on the scale behave in nontest situations in a fashion that could be predicted from their scale score. Because of its comprehensiveness, the *construct validity approach* to test construction is both the most desirable and the most labor intensive. In fact, establishing the construct validity of a test is a never-ending process, with empirical feedback used to refine both the theory and the personality measure (Smith & McCarthy, 1995).

To summarize and illustrate, Table 8-2 outlines the validity of an item that purports to measure depression according to each of the four test-construction strategies just discussed. We

now turn to a discussion of several of the major objective personality measures available to clinical psychologists.

The MMPI and the MMPI-2

The MMPI was long the best example of the empirical keying approach to test construction. More than 50 years after its publication by Hathaway and McKinley in 1943, it is still considered the preeminent self-report inventory. The MMPI has been used for virtually every predictive purpose imaginable, ranging from likelihood of episodes of psychosis to marriage suitability. What is even more staggering, Graham (1990) estimates that more than 10,000 studies on the MMPI have been published. Despite all its success over the years, it was decided that the MMPI needed updating and restandardization. The result was the new *MMPI-2* (Butcher, Dahlstrom, Graham, Tellegen, & Kaemmer, 1989).

Description: MMPI. When Hathaway and McKinley developed the MMPI, their basic purpose was to identify the psychiatric diagnoses of individuals. Items were assembled from previously published tests of personality, from case histories, and from clinical experience. This pool of items was administered to nonclinical individuals (more than 700 visitors to University of Minnesota hospitals) and psychiatric patients

▌ TABLE 8-3 Simulated MMPI Items

Clinical Scales	Simulated Items (Answered True)
Hypochondriasis (Hs) (Excessive concern with bodily functions)	"At times I get strong cramps in my intestines."
Depression (D) (Pessimism, hopelessness, slowing of action and thought)	"I am often very tense on the job."
Hysteria (Hy) (Unconscious use of physical and mental problems to avoid conflicts or responsibility)	"Sometimes there is a feeling like something is pressing in on my head."
Psychopathic Deviate (Pd) (Disregard of social custom, shallow emotions, inability to profit from experience)	"I wish I could do over some of the things I have done."
Masculinity-Femininity (Mf) (Items differentiating between traditional sex roles)	"I used to like to do the dances in gym class."
Paranoia (Pa) (Abnormal suspiciousness, delusions of grandeur or persecution)	"It distresses me that people have the wrong ideas about me."
Psychasthenia (Pt) (Obsessions, compulsiveness, fears, guilt, indecisiveness)	"The things that run through my head sometimes are horrible."
Schizophrenia (Sc) (Bizarre, unusual thoughts or behavior, withdrawal, hallucinations, delusions)	"There are those out there who want to get me."
Hypomania (Ma) (Emotional excitement, flight of ideas, overactivity)	"Sometimes I think so fast I can't keep up."
Social Introversion (Si) (Shyness, disinterest in others, insecurity)	"I give up too easily when discussing things with others."

Source: Copyright 1943, renewed 1967 by the University of Minnesota, Published by The Psychological Corporation, New York, NY. All rights reserved. Reproduced by permission.

(more than 800). The following psychiatric categories were used: hypochondriasis (Hs), depression (D), hysteria (Hy), psychopathic deviate (Pd), paranoia (Pa), psychasthenia (Pt), schizophrenia (Sc), and hypomania (Ma). Two additional scales, masculinity-femininity (Mf) and social introversion (Si) were added later. It is important to note that these scale names reflect a diagnostic classification system that was used in the 1940s and 1950s but is now antiquated. To translate all these diagnostic labels into more meaningful terms, refer to Table 8-3.

The original MMPI was composed of 550 items to which the patient answers "True," "False," or "Cannot Say." Only those items that differentiated a given clinical group from a nonclinical group were included. For example, items were retained if they distinguished individuals with depression from nonclinical individuals, or individuals with schizophrenia from nonclinical individuals, or individuals with psychopathic features from nonclinical individuals. No attempt was made to select items that differentiated one diagnostic category from another.

As a result, some items tend to be highly correlated with each other, and the same item may appear in several different scales.

There was an individual form of the test in which the items were printed on cards; here the individual separated the cards according to the Yes–No–Cannot Say categories. There was also a group form with items printed in a test booklet; here the answers were marked on an answer sheet. Although the test was originally designed for people age 16 and older, the MMPI has actually been used with individuals considerably younger. The test was machine scored or hand scored. Indeed, it was possible to completely administer, score, and interpret the MMPI by computer (Dunn, Lushene, & O'Neil, 1972).

Description: MMPI-2. The original MMPI standardization sample had been criticized for many years as unrepresentative of the general U.S. population. Participants came largely from the Minneapolis area. All were white, with an average of eight years' education; they were typically 35 years old, married, and from small towns. The language of many of the items had become obsolete, and some items contained sexist language. Other items made inappropriate references to Christian religious beliefs and sometimes seemed to overemphasize sexual, bowel, and bladder functions. Several items even had poor grammar and punctuation. Finally, many people felt the items did not adequately address behaviors such as suicide or drug use. All in all, the time seemed ripe for revision (Graham, 1990).

For restandardization, all 550 items were retained, but 82 were rewritten (though most changes were slight). The original meaning of items was preserved, but the language was made more contemporary. In addition, 154 new items were added to the item pool, bringing the total to 704 items. After adjustments, the final version of the MMPI-2 now includes 567 of the larger pool of 704 items. However, only the first 370 items in the test booklet are administered when only the traditional validity and clinical scales are of interest.

Participants for the restandardization sample came from Minnesota, Ohio, North Carolina, Washington, Pennsylvania, Virginia, and California, and the sample was based on U.S. Census data from 1980. The final sample contained 1138 men and 1462 women. The racial composition was as follows: White, 81%; African American, 12%; Hispanic, 3%; American Indian, 3%; Asian American, 1%. Participants ranged in age from 18 to 85 years and in formal education from 3 years or less to 20 years or more. About 3% of the men and 6% of the women reported being in treatment for mental health problems at the time of testing.

The authors of the MMPI-2 state that it can be used with individuals who are at least 13 years old and/or can read at an eighth-grade level. It can be administered individually or in groups. Unlike the MMPI, the MMPI-2 has only one booklet form. It can be computer-scored and non-English-language versions of the test are available. Finally, a version of the MMPI-2 specifically developed for adolescents (MMPI-A; Butcher et al., 1992) is also available.

Validity Scales. A potential problem with self-report inventories, including the MMPI-2, is their susceptibility to distortion through various test-taking attitudes or response sets. For example, some respondents may wish to place themselves in a favorable light; others may "fake bad" to increase the likelihood of receiving aid, sympathy, or perhaps a discharge from military service; still others have a seeming need to agree with almost any item regardless of its content. Obviously, if the clinician is not aware of these response styles in a given patient, the test interpretation can be in gross error.

To help detect malingering ("faking bad"), other response sets or test-taking attitudes, and carelessness or misunderstanding, the MMPI-2 continues to incorporate the traditional four *validity scales* that were included in the original MMPI.

1. *? (Cannot Say) Scale.* This is the number of items left unanswered.

PROFILE 8-1

Yossef S. Ben-Porth, Ph.D.

Dr. Yossef Ben-Porath is an Associate Professor of Psychology at Kent State University who specializes in psychological assessment, particularly the use of the MMPI-2 and MMPI-A in clinical and forensic settings. In addition, he studies the use of computers in psychological assessment and how individuals cope with various forms of stress. Dr. Ben-Porath is the author of numerous articles, book chapters, and books on psychological assessment, and he frequently leads workshops on the clinical applications of the MMPI-2 and MMPI-A. Finally, he currently serves as an Associate Editor for the journal *Psychological Assessment*, and he is the Associate Director of Clinical Training at Kent State University. We had a chance to ask Dr. Ben-Porath several questions concerning his background, activities, and predictions for the future.

What originally got you interested in clinical psychology?

I became interested in clinical psychology as an undergraduate psychology major at the University of Haifa in Israel. Course work in abnormal and personality psychology piqued my interest, and opportunities to become involved in research projects in this area led to my decision to pursue graduate training in clinical psychology. One of my undergraduate professors, Dr. Moshe Almagor, had recently earned his Ph.D. at the University of Minnesota and was doing research in the area of clinical personality assessment. I found this research intriguing because of its applied nature and its implications for clinical practice. Eventually, I too received my graduate training in clinical psychology at the University of Minnesota.

Describe what activities you are involved in as a clinical psychologist.

My primary activities as a clinical psychologist are related to my duties as a faculty member in the Department of Psychology at Kent State University. At Kent, I teach various psychology undergraduate and graduate classes, I supervise the research activities of students ranging from undergraduate students doing honors research to graduate students working on their doctoral dissertations, and I conduct my own research. I also supervise the assessment and community field placement components of our clinical psychology graduate students. I serve as associate editor of a research journal, *Psychological Assessment*. This involves sending articles that researchers would like to publish in the journal for review by experts in the area and deciding, based on their evaluations, which articles to recommend for publication in the journal. I also conduct continuing education workshops for practicing psychologists in different parts of the country and sometimes in other countries as well. In addition to my university work, I have a part-time clinical practice in forensic psychology. My clinical activities involve conducting various court-ordered evaluations, including examinations of defendants' competence to stand trial and pleas of not guilty by reason of insanity, and commitment evaluations.

What are your particular areas of expertise or interest?

My primary interest is in clinical assessment. My area of expertise is in use of the MMPI-2 and MMPI-A in applied psychological assessment. My research is designed to provide empirical data to guide psychologists who use these instruments in a variety of applied settings. Specific applications of these tests include identification of malingering and expansion of the database on traits, symptoms, and behaviors that are associated with certain scores on the instruments. I am also interested in examining whether it is necessary to interpret the test differently in various settings, such as inpatient and outpatient mental health centers, or forensic and correctional settings.

What are the trends you see for clinical psychology?

The primary trend I see for clinical psychology is a movement away from direct clinical service delivery. Cost-containment pressures of managed care, coupled with the absence of clear empirical evidence that doctoral-level clinical psychologists are more effective than less costly service deliverers such as master's level counselors and social workers, will likely result in fewer clinical psychologists' working as full-time therapists in either community agencies or private practices. Instead, clinical psychologists will be called upon increasingly to apply their training and expertise in research to assist in program development and evaluation. Specifically, clinical psychologists will

become involved in developing methods to identify treatment needs and to evaluate treatment progress and outcome at the agencies or organizations that employ them. In addition, clinical psychologists will likely become increasingly involved in forensic practice that requires the highest possible level of training and expertise.

What are some future trends you see in MMPI-2 research?

The most exciting trend I foresee for MMPI-2 research and application is the increasing incorporation of computer technology in administration, scoring, and interpretation of the test. Presently, computer software exists to accomplish all three of these tasks. However, most testing with the MMPI-2 is still conducted by paper and pencil and most interpretation is done by individual clinical psychologists. When a computer is used to administer the test, it serves as a proxy for the conventional test booklet. In the future, the MMPI-2 will be administered adaptively in a manner that reduces the number of items to those that are necessary to answer specific assessment questions posed by the psychologist. Computers will become essential in MMPI-2 interpretation because of the ever-increasing volume of data that must be considered in generating an empirically based test interpretation.

---

2. *F (Infrequency) Scale.* These 60 items were seldom answered in the scored direction by the standardization group. A high F score may suggest deviant response sets, markedly aberrant behavior, or other hypotheses about extra test characteristics or behaviors.

3. *L (Lie) Scale.* This includes 15 items whose endorsement places the respondent in a very positive light. In reality, however, it is unlikely that the items would be truthfully so endorsed. For example, "I like everyone I meet."

4. *K (Defensiveness) Scale.* These 30 items suggest defensiveness in admitting certain problems.

These items purportedly detect "faking good," but they are more subtle than either L or F items. For example, "Criticism from others never bothers me."

In addition to the four traditional validity scales, three "new" validity scales can be scored from the MMPI-2.

5. F_b *(Back-page Infrequency) Scale.* These 40 items occurring near the end of the MMPI-2 are infrequently endorsed.

6. *VRIN (Variable Response Inconsistency) Scale.* This consists of 67 pairs of items with either

similar or opposite content. High VRIN scores suggest random responding to MMPI-2 items.

7. *TRIN (True Response Inconsistency) Scale.* This consists of 23 item pairs that are opposite in content. High TRIN scores suggest a tendency to give "True" responses indiscriminately; low TRIN scores suggest a tendency to give "False" responses indiscriminately.

These seven MMPI-2 validity scales provide a means for understanding the test respondent's motivations and test-taking attitudes. For example, attempts to present oneself in an overly favorable light will likely be detected by the L (Lie) or K (Defensiveness) scale (Baer, Wetter, & Berry, 1992), whereas the tendency to exaggerate one's problems or symptoms usually results in elevations on the F (Infrequency) and F_b (Back-page Infrequency) scales (Berry, Baer, & Harris, 1991; Rogers, Bagby, & Chakraborty, 1993; Wetter, Baer, Berry, Smith, & Larsen, 1992; Wetter, Baer, Berry, Robison, & Sumpter, 1993). Finally, the VRIN and TRIN scales are useful indicators of random responding or answering true (or false) to most items, respectively (Berry et al., 1992; Tellegen & Ben-Porath, 1992).

Short Forms. Over the years, a variety of short forms of the MMPI have appeared. Such scales typically shorten the MMPI to considerably less than the traditional 550 items. Although economies in screening or rapid classification may be achieved by their use, some loss in interpretive power can also be expected. Controversies such as those between Butcher, Kendall, and Hoffman (1980), who urge caution in the use of MMPI short forms, and Newmark, Woody, Finch, and Ziff (1980), who press for the utility of certain short forms, are still unresolved. As for the MMPI-2, both Butcher, Dahlstrom, Graham, Tellegen, and Kaemmer (1989) and Butcher, Graham, and Ben-Porath (1995) continue to question the use of short forms.

Interpretation through Patterns: Profile Analysis. Because the original scales were developed to predict psychiatric categorization, the initial use of the MMPI depended on simple interpretations based on elevated scale scores. That is, if an Sc scale score was significantly elevated, this suggested a diagnosis of schizophrenia. However, clinical experience quickly taught that such compartmentalized interpretations were gross oversimplifications. Some nonclinical respondents achieve high Sc scores, and so do other diagnostic groups.

Interpretation has now shifted to an examination of patterns, or "profiles," of scores. For example, individuals who produce elevations on the first three clinical scales (Hs, D, Hy) tend to present with somatic complaints and depressive symptoms and often receive somatoform, anxiety, or depressive disorder diagnoses. Elevations on scales 6 (Pa) and 8 (Sc) suggest extreme suspiciousness and potential psychotic thought processes; these characteristics are found among individuals diagnosed with paranoid schizophrenia.

Interpretation through Content. Lest the reader conclude that only diagnostic labels can result from the analysis of a profile, consider the following excerpt from a pretherapy workup based on the MMPI-2 profile shown in Figure 8-1 (Butcher, 1990):

> Ed approached the testing in a frank and open manner, producing a valid MMPI-2 profile. . . . He related a number of psychological adjustment problems and seemingly was seeking help in overcoming them. The MMPI-2 clinical profile highlights a number of problems and symptoms that Ed was experiencing at the time of his first treatment session. He reported being depressed and anxious about his situation and related feeling tense, lonely, and insecure. He appeared to be having great difficulty concentrating on his work and was indecisive. He had no zest for life and was preoccupied with his inability to accomplish personal goals. The relatively high score on the psychopathic deviate scale (Pd) reflects rebellious attitudes and family conflict (the Harris-Lingoes Family Problems Scale, Pd1,

FIGURE 8-1   The Case of Ed: A pretreatment MMPI-2 clinical profile

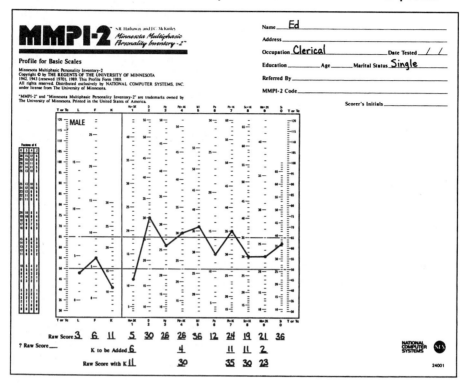

was T = 69). He appeared to be a somewhat passive young man who reported being shy and isolated. (p. 12)

Thus, a major change and improvement in the clinical use of the MMPI and MMPI-2 has been the shift away from differential psychiatric diagnosis based on the evaluation of a single score to a more sophisticated profile analysis of scale scores considered as measures of personality traits.

For the MMPI-2, a variety of content scales have been developed as well (Butcher, Graham, Williams, & Ben-Porath, 1990). For example, certain items can help identify fears, health concerns, cynicism, the Type A personality, and so on. Such scales enable the clinician to move beyond simple diagnostic labels to a more dynamic level of interpretation. Take the following example from Graham (1990):

Family Problems (FAM)
High scores on the FAM indicate persons who

1. Describe considerable discord in their current families and/or families of origin
2. Describe their families as lacking in love, understanding, and support
3. Resent the demands and advice of their families
4. Feel angry and hostile toward their families
5. See marital relationships as involving unhappiness and lack of affection (p. 137)

Supplementary Scales. In addition to the standard validity scales, the clinical scales, and the content scales, the MMPI-2 item pool has been used to develop numerous other scales. Many years ago, Dahlstrom, Welsh, and Dahlstrom (1972, 1975) noted 450 MMPI supplementary scales, ranging from Dominance and Suspiciousness to Success in Basketball! For the MMPI-2, 12 supplemental scales have been developed so far. A few examples are Anxiety, Repression, Ego Strength, Dominance, and Social Responsibility. It is likely that many more supplemental scales will be developed in the future (Butcher et al., 1995).

A Summary Evaluation of the MMPI and MMPI-2

Screening. Many clinicians are attracted to the MMPI-2 because of its screening capabilities. When information about the severity of a patient's problems is needed, and when the clinician must generate hypotheses about a patient's diagnostic status, the MMPI-2 can be a valuable asset. Therefore, when groups of patients are being screened, it can be both useful and efficient as an aid to mental disorder diagnosis or as a hypothesis generator. The MMPI-2, however, is quite long. For many screening purposes, such a time-intensive self-report inventory may be unnecessary. For example, if a clinician simply wants to screen new clients for depression, a much shorter inventory than the MMPI-2 might be more desirable. The MMPI-2 items measure a wide range of symptoms, only a minority of which are related to depression. The comprehensiveness of the MMPI-2 is both a strength and a weakness.

The Question of Personality Dynamics. The MMPI-2 is *atheoretical* (Butcher, 1995c; Helmes & Reddon, 1993). For those clinicians who are psychodynamically oriented or who seek an understanding of their patients through the subtle interplay of general personality characteristics and situational determinants, the MMPI-2 may not be the instrument of choice. The MMPI-2 is primarily a measure of various symptoms of psychopathology. Although the features tapped by MMPI-2 items may suggest certain personality traits or styles, it was not developed with personality constructs in mind. Does it help with personality description, psychotherapy planning, or the host of other predictions that the clinician must confront in day-to-day interactions with the patient? Many would question the MMPI-2's contribution to ongoing clinical decisions once the initial diagnostic category has been selected. However, Butcher (1990, 1995c) would argue that the MMPI-2 is a valuable aid in planning and evaluating the effects of treatment.

Reliability and Validity. As noted earlier, there have been more than 10,000 published studies of the MMPI. Aside from the comments already made, the authors of this textbook do not have the temerity to "briefly" summarize this voluminous research. However, something of the flavor of MMPI research is contained in the following remarks.

When the MMPI "is used in the manner for which it was designed and validated, its psychometric properties are likely to be adequate for either clinical or research purposes" (Parker, Hanson, & Hunsley, 1988, p. 373). However, there may be some debate about those exact purposes. In any case, Parker, Hanson, and Hunsley's meta-analysis pronounced the reliability, stability, and validity of the MMPI to be acceptable, particularly when there is a theoretical or empirical rationale for the MMPI. A recent reanalysis of these meta-analytic data for the MMPI supported this conclusion (Garb, Florio, & Grove, 1998). The ultimate question, then, is not whether the MMPI-2 is valid. Rather, for what specific purposes is it valid?

There are many instances when specific scales may not seem to work all that well. For example, research on the original MMPI MacAndrew Scale (a scale designed to classify individuals with alcohol problems) was surveyed by Gottesman and Prescott (1989). The data were so weak that Gottesman and Prescott called for a suspension of the use of the scale.

Two other issues related to the validity of MMPI-2 scores are important as well. Although presented in the context of developing "new"

MMPI-2 supplemental scales, Butcher et al. (1995) noted the necessity of establishing the *incremental validity* of a scale as well as the *validity of cutoff scores (thresholds)*. Incremental validity is supported if scale scores provide information about a person's behavior, personality features, or psychopathology features that is not provided by other measures. Do MMPI-2 scores convey information relevant to psychopathology or personality that cannot be provided by other measures? This issue of incremental validity tends to be neglected for all psychological tests, including the MMPI-2.

As for the validity of cutoff scores, it is important to keep in mind that the optimal cutoff score (in terms of maximizing correct decisions as to which patients have the disorder or trait in question, given their scores on the measure) will vary, depending on the nature of the population of patients sampled. The cutoff scores provided in test manuals were derived for a certain population, which may or may not be similar to the population of patients with which a clinician is working. MMPI-2 cutoffs (*T* score of 65 or greater) were derived using the distribution of scores from the normative sample. Therefore, these cutoffs may or may not be appropriate in certain clinical contexts.

Personnel Selection and Bias. Recent developments in our society have also created problems for the MMPI-2. Lack of trust in our social institutions and the concerns of minorities have both been reflected in criticisms of the test. For example, the MMPI-2 has often been lauded for its empirical criterion keying approach, which works well for those who understand it. But what about people who know nothing of criterion keying or psychometrics but want to work for Corporation X? Suppose that these individuals fail to get a job after taking an MMPI-2. What shall we tell them when they demand to know what items such as "I used to keep a diary" or "My sex life is satisfactory" have to do with hiring? For the person who is seeking therapy, a test such as the MMPI-2 may be acceptable. However, for one who takes the test in a personnel setting, it may be regarded as an invasion of privacy (Butcher, 1971).

Given the nature of the original sample that the MMPI was validated on, questions have been raised as to whether the instrument may be "biased" against certain ethnic and racial groups. This has been a rather contentious debate over the years (for example, Gynther, 1972; Gynther & Green, 1980; Pritchard & Rosenblatt, 1980). Some studies have found significant differences in scores between racial groups, whereas others have not. It is important to keep in mind, however, that a significant difference between mean scores for groups of people does *not*, in and of itself, indicate test bias. Rather, *test bias* refers to a situation in which different decisions or predictions are made for members of two groups even when they obtain the same score (Anastasi, 1988). We will return to the general issue of test bias later in this chapter. To our knowledge, there have been very few published studies that evaluate the possibility of test bias for the MMPI-2. It is encouraging that, to date, these few studies have not found evidence suggesting that the use of the MMPI-2 for certain purposes results in bias against certain ethnic or racial groups (for example, Timbrook & Graham, 1994).

Concerns about the MMPI-2. The reasons that prompted the revision of the MMPI were, in the main, laudable. Without doubt, though, some clinicians seem to be nervous about the MMPI-2. Some of these concerns are likely to diminish as clinical psychologists become more familiar with the revision. Nevertheless, here is a sample of the complaints and reservations that have been voiced about the MMPI-2:

1. The normative sample, compared to U.S. Census Bureau data, is too highly educated. Only 5% of MMPI-2 normative respondents have less than a college education, and 45% of the normal respondents in the sample are college educated! Schooling can account for much of the variance in the scores of psychiatric patients.

2. Is all the old MMPI research applicable to the new MMPI-2?

3. Were "unnecessary" revisions made?
4. Criteria for the inclusion of "normal" respondents are puzzling.
5. Some respondents who are administered both versions of the test show psychological problems on one version but not on the other.
6. Scores are generally lower on the MMPI-2 compared to the MMPI.
7. Validity of the new content scales is unclear.
8. Many scales on the MMPI-2 are somewhat unreliable over time.
9. Internal consistency of several MMPI-2 scales is quite low.
10. There remains too much item overlap among the scales, making study results hard to interpret.

Despite these limitations and concerns, the MMPI and MMPI-2 remain the "benchmarks" for self-report inventories measuring psychopathology or personality. It is likely that the MMPI-2 will enjoy the same success as its predecessor. However, as is true for any instrument, it is important that clinical psychologists appreciate the potential limitations as well as the strengths of this popular measure.

The Revised NEO-Personality Inventory

Description. The *Revised NEO-Personality Inventory (NEO-PI-R)* (Costa & McCrae, 1992) is a self-report measure of personality features that comprise an influential model of personality known as the *Five-Factor Model (FFM)* (Goldberg, 1993). The FFM has evolved over the past four decades (Digman, 1990), and has roots in both the lexical tradition (the analysis of trait adjectives found in English and other languages) and the factor analytic tradition in personality research. As operationalized by the NEO-PI-R, the five factors or *domains* are Neuroticism, Extraversion, Openness to Experience, Agreeableness, and Conscientiousness. Each domain has six *facets* or subscales—personality traits that represent various aspects of each domain. Table 8-4 presents the facets that represent each domain.

The NEO-PI-R consists of 240 items (8 items for each of the 30 facets, or 48 items for each of the 5 domains). Individuals rate each of the 240 statements on a 5-point scale (strongly disagree, disagree, neutral, agree, strongly agree). Research that led to development of the NEO-PI-R began in the 1970s. At that time, there was no clear consensus regarding which personality model or system provided the most useful and comprehensive description of personality features. Costa and McCrae became convinced that there was more agreement among the various competing personality models regarding higher-order dimensions (such as Neuroticism or Extraversion) than there was for the lower-level traits that comprise these (the facets of each dimension). For this reason, Costa and McCrae adopted a "top-down" approach in constructing their inventory. They began by selecting those higher-order factors or dimensions of personality believed to be of greatest import and utility (based on reviews of the literature as well as their own empirical research). They then identified those traits, or facets, that comprised each major dimension. The original version of their instrument assessed only three of the five factors (Neuroticism, Extraversion, and Openness); the NEO-PI-R assesses all five domains of the FFM and includes facet scales for each.

The NEO-PI-R was developed using a rational-empirical test construction strategy that emphasized construct validity. Each personality trait to be included was identified, defined, and then analyzed so that items measuring various aspects of the trait could be generated. Final item selection was based on empirical performance; that is, the most reliable and valid items were retained. In addition, factor analyses were performed to ensure that items loaded on their respective factors.

Approximately half of the NEO-PI-R items are reverse-scored; that is, lower scores are more indicative of the trait in question. This was done to address a potential acquiescence (or nay-saying) bias that may present problems for inventories in which all or most items are keyed in the same direction. In such inventories, high scores

■ TABLE 8-4 Domains and Facets of Personality Measured by the NEO-PI-R

Domain	Facets
Neuroticism	Anxiety, Hostility, Depression, Self-Consciousness, Impulsiveness, Vulnerability
Extraversion	Warmth, Gregariousness, Assertiveness, Activity, Excitement Seeking, Positive Emotions
Openness to Experience	Fantasy, Aesthetics, Feelings, Actions, Ideas, Values
Agreeableness	Trust, Straightforwardness, Altruism, Compliance, Modesty, Tender-Mindedness
Conscientiousness	Competence, Order, Dutifulness, Achievement Striving, Self-Discipline, Deliberation

may be due either to acquiescence or to the actual level of the trait in question, so that interpretation of a high score is problematic. One of the more controversial aspects of the NEO-PI-R is its lack of a validity scale (or set of scales) to evaluate respondents' test-taking approaches. Instead, the NEO-PI-R has three individual items that assess the validity of responses. One item asks respondents to indicate if they have responded to the items in an honest and accurate manner, another asks if they have answered all items, and the last assesses whether responses have been placed in the correct spaces.

Norms. Adult norms are based on a total of 500 men and 500 women drawn from several samples of community residents. The normative sample closely approximates U.S. Census Bureau projections for 1995 in the distribution of age and racial groups. The NEO-PI-R manual presents normative data for college students as well.

Reliability and Stability. NEO-PI-R scores show excellent levels of both internal consistency and test-retest reliability. Internal consistency coefficients range from .86 to .92 for the domain scales and from .56 to .81 for the facet scales. A recent study of clinical outpatients reported six-month test-retest reliability coefficients that ranged from .76 to .84 for the domain scores (Trull, Useda, Costa, & McCrae, 1995). Test-retest

reliability has been impressively high over time periods as long as six years.

Factor Structure. Factor analyses have, in general, supported the hypothesized five-factor structure of the NEO-PI-R. This is true whether individual item scores or facet scores were used in the analyses (Costa & McCrae, 1992).

Validity. The NEO-PI-R manual (Costa & McCrae, 1992) presents a variety of evidence attesting to the validity of the instrument's scores. Domain and facet scores from the NEO-PI-R have been shown to relate in predictable ways to personality trait scores from a variety of personality measures, peer reports, and adjective checklists.

Clinical Applications. Although the NEO-PI-R was developed from a model of "normal" personality, investigators have begun to assess this instrument's usefulness in clinical samples. Because Axis II personality disorders involve, by definition, maladaptive personality traits (that is, extreme variants of personality traits that are common in all individuals), these disorders represent an obvious application for FFM instruments such as the NEO-PI-R. Several studies have supported the utility of NEO-PI in characterizing personality disorders (for example, Schroeder, Wormworth, & Livesley, 1992; Trull, 1992; Trull et al., 1995). Further, investigators are now beginning to evaluate the utility of FFM instruments such as the NEO-PI-R in assessing personality characteristics of individuals with Axis I mood, anxiety, and substance use disorders (Trull & Sher, 1994). Taken together, these studies suggest that the NEO-PI-R and related instruments hold some promise in the area of clinical assessment.

Alternate Forms. A 60-item short form of the NEO-PI-R, known as the NEO-Five Factor Inventory (NEO-FFI), may be useful in situations where a relatively short measure of the five major personality dimensions is desired; the NEO-FFI does not contain facet scales. Another version of the NEO-PI-R, known as Form R, is used for observer ratings. It contains the 240 items of the self-report version, reworded to reflect the gender of the target person being rated. Form R scores can be used to validate or supplement self-report scores (Costa & McCrae, 1992).

NEO-PI-R Case Illustration

Bruehl (1994) presents a case study of a 45-year-old, white, divorced woman who received an Axis I diagnosis of Major Depressive Disorder and an Axis II diagnosis of Borderline Personality Disorder. "Betty" presented for treatment because of her concerns over parenting her daughter, who had recently been arrested for drug possession and suspended from high school. Betty had a history of sexual abuse in childhood, of poor family and peer relationships, of physical abuse in adulthood, and of intense and labile emotions. Table 8-5 presents the results of her NEO-PI-R administration.

As can be seen, Betty produced elevations on all Neuroticism facets, scored in the low range on several Extraversion and Agreeableness facets, and produced several elevations on Openness facets. Several interpretive statements regarding Betty's NEO-PI-R scores illustrate how these scores can be useful in understanding a client and in treatment planning.

. . . Betty's elevated Neuroticism and low Agreeableness were consistent with what would be expected based on the DSM-III-R criteria for BDL [Borderline Personality Disorder].

. . . The strength of the psychotherapeutic relationship was slow to develop because of Betty's low levels of Warmth and Trust . . .

. . . The transference issues observed in therapy related primarily to Betty's low Trust and high Hostility. As might be expected given her low Straightforwardness, she expressed her anger and lack of trust passively . . .

. . . Betty's low Compliance suggested that it was important to watch for control issues in therapy. On the few occasions when therapeutic "homework" assignments were attempted and agreed on, Betty failed to complete them . . .

. . . Her low Compliance seemed to interact with her low Trust and high Hostility to cause interpersonal difficulties in therapy. These same issues were responsible for her problems in previous intimate relationships with close friends, family members, and husbands . . .

. . . Information provided by the NEO-PI-R also suggested strengths that improved treatment progress. Betty's high level of Openness to Ideas did reflect in part pathological aspects, but it also reflected an ability to be more cognitively flexible . . . she was very open to looking at her problems in different ways and considering alternative ways for understanding and addressing these problems. (Bruehl, 1994, pp. 195–196)

Limitations of the NEO-PI-R Recently, several authors have suggested limitations of the NEO-PI-R in clinical assessment (Ben-Porath & Waller, 1992; Block, 1995; Tellegen, 1993). First, the NEO-PI-R has been criticized for its relative lack of validity items. In contrast to the MMPI-2 and other self-report measures, the NEO-PI-R does not devote a number of test items to assessing

TABLE 8-5 Revised NEO Personality Inventory Personality Profile for "Betty"

Scale	Range	Clinical Implications
Neuroticism	Very high	
Anxiety	High	Nervous/ruminative
Angry Hostility	Very high	Rageful/bitter
Depression	Very high	Gloomy/despondent
Self-Consciousness	High	Insecure/ashamed
Impulsiveness	High	Spontaneous/unpredictable
Vulnerability	High	Overwhelmed/defenseless
Extraversion	Low	
Warmth	Low	Cold
Gregariousness	Low	Shy/withdrawn
Assertiveness	Average	
Activity	Average	
Excitement Seeking	High	Adventurous
Positive Emotions	Low	Placid/disinterested
Openness	High	
Fantasy	Very high	Imaginative/dissociative
Aesthetics	Average	
Feelings	Average	
Actions	Average	
Ideas	High	Cognitively flexible
Values	High	Open-minded
Agreeableness	Low	
Trust	Low	Cynical/suspicious
Straightforwardness	Low	Deceptive/manipulative
Altruism	Average	
Compliance	Low	Aggressive/oppositional
Modesty	Average	
Tender-Mindedness	Average	
Conscientiousness	Average	
Competence	High	Perfectionistic
Order	Average	
Dutifulness	Low	Unreliable/irresponsible
Achievement Striving	High	Driven
Self-Discipline	Average	
Deliberation	Low	Hasty

Source: Bruehl, 1994.

response styles that may influence interpretations of the obtained scores. Second, the use of the NEO-PI-R for clinical diagnostic purposes remains to be demonstrated. Although the initial studies that have shown associations between NEO-PI-R scores and mental disorder diagnoses are encouraging, the NEO-PI-R may not be especially well suited for the general purpose of clinical diagnosis because its development was guided by a model of "normal" personality. Third, too little research has been conducted on the use of the NEO-PI-R in treatment planning to warrant the routine use of this measure in clinical settings at this time. Finally, several psychometric criticisms have been leveled at the NEO-PI-R, including the intercorrelation among certain domain scores and the placement of certain facets within particular domains (for example, the placement of Impulsiveness and Hostility within the Neuroticism domain). In summary, although promising, the utility of the NEO-PI-R in routine clinical assessment remains to be demonstrated.

Projective Tests

Projective techniques have a long and rich history. William Shakespeare wrote about the projective qualities of clouds, and William Stern used clouds as test stimuli before Rorschach and his inkblots. Sir Francis Galton (1879) suggested word-association methods, and Kraepelin made use of them. Binet and Henri (1896) experimented with pictures as projective devices. Alfred Adler asked patients to recall their first memory, which is also a kind of projective approach.

However, the real impetus for projective techniques can be traced to Hermann Rorschach's classic 1921 monograph, in which he described the use of inkblots as a method for the differential diagnosis of psychopathology. Later in the 1920s, David Levy brought the inkblot test to America, and it was not long before Beck, Klopfer, and Hertz all began teaching Rorschach courses. In 1935, Morgan and Murray introduced the Thematic Apperception Test (TAT), and in 1938 Murray carefully described the process of projection. The term *projective* really came into popular use following L. K. Frank's widely discussed 1939 paper on projective methods.

The Nature of Projective Tests

For some, the definition of a projective test resides in Freudian notions regarding the nature of ego defenses and unconscious processes. However, these do not seem to be essential characteristics. Over the years, many definitions have been offered (Anderson & Anderson, 1951; Lindzey, 1961; Murstein, 1963; Semenoff, 1976; Wiggins, 1973; Zubin, Eron, & Schumer, 1965). Perhaps the easiest solution is a pragmatic one that comes from consulting the English and English (1958) psychological dictionary, which defines a projective technique as "a procedure for discovering a person's characteristic modes of behavior by observing his [sic] behavior in response to a situation that does not elicit or compel a particular response."

Projective techniques, taken as a whole, tend to have the following distinguishing characteristics (Rotter, 1954):

1. In response to an unstructured or ambiguous stimulus, examinees are *forced to impose their own structure* and, in so doing, reveal something of themselves (such as needs, wishes, or conflicts).

2. The stimulus material is *unstructured*. This is a very tenuous criterion, even though it is widely assumed to reflect the essence of projective techniques. For example, if 70% of all examinees perceive Card V on the Rorschach as a bat, then we can hardly say that the stimulus is unstructured. Thus, whether a test is projective or not depends on the kinds of responses that the individual is encouraged to give and on how those responses are used. The instructions are the important element. If a patient is asked to classify the people in a set of TAT cards as men or

women, then there is a great deal of structure—the test is far from ambiguous. However, if the patient is asked what the people on the card are saying, the task has suddenly become quite ambiguous indeed.

3. The method is *indirect*. To some degree or other, examinees are not aware of the purposes of the test; at least, the purposes are disguised. Although patients may know that the test has something to do with adjustment-maladjustment, they are not usually aware in detail of the significance of their responses. There is no attempt to ask patients directly about their needs or troubles; the route is indirect, and the hope is that this very indirectness will make it more difficult for patients to censor the data they provide.

4. There is *freedom of response*. Whereas questionnaire methods may allow only for a "yes" or a "no," projectives permit a nearly infinite range of responses.

5. Response interpretation deals with *more variables*. Since the range of possible responses is so broad, the clinician can make interpretations along multiple dimensions (needs, adjustment, diagnostic category, ego defenses, and so on). Many objective tests, in contrast, provide but a single score (such as degree of psychological distress), or scores on a fixed number of dimensions or scales.

Measurement and Standardization

The contrasts between objective tests and projective tests are striking. The former, by their very nature, lend themselves to an actuarial interpretive approach. Norms, reliability, and even validity seem easier to manage. The projectives, by their very nature, seem to resist psychometric evaluation. Indeed, some clinicians reject even the suggestion that a test such as the Rorschach should be subjected to the indignities of psychometrics; they would see this as an assault upon their intuitive art. In this section, we offer several general observations about the difficulties involved in evaluating the psychometric properties of projective tests.

Standardization. Should projective techniques be standardized? There are surely many reasons for doing so. Such standardization would facilitate communication and would also serve as a check against the biases and the interpretive zeal of some clinicians. Furthermore, the enthusiastic proponents of projectives usually act as if they have norms (implicit though these may be), so that there seems to be no good reason *not* to attempt the standardization of those norms. Of course, research problems with projectives can be formidable.

The dissenters argue that interpretations from projectives cannot be standardized. Every person is unique, and any normative descriptions will inevitably be misleading. There are so many interacting variables that standardized interpretive approaches would surely destroy the holistic nature of projective tests. After all, they say, interpretation is an art.

Reliability. Even the determination of reliability turns out not to be simple. For example, it is surely too much to expect an individual to produce, word for word, exactly the same TAT story on two different occasions. Yet how many differences between two stories are permissible? Of course, one can bypass test responses altogether and deal only with the reliability of the personality interpretations made by clinicians. However, this may confound the reliability of the test with the reliability of the judge. Also, test-retest reliability may be affected by psychological changes in the individual—particularly when dealing with patient populations. It is true that clinicians can opt for establishing reliability through the use of alternate forms. However, how do they decide that alternate forms for TAT cards or inkblots are equivalent? Even split-half reliability is difficult to ascertain because of the difficulty of demonstrating the equivalence of the two halves of each test.

Validity. Because projectives have been used for such a multiplicity of purposes, there is little point in asking general questions: Is the TAT valid? Is the Rorschach a good personality test?

The questions must be more specific: Does the TAT predict aggression in situation A? Does score X from the Rorschach correlate with clinical judgments of anxiety?

With these issues in mind, we turn now to a discussion of several of the more popular projective tests.

The Rorschach

Although the origins of the *Rorschach* lie in Europe, its subsequent development and elaboration occurred in the United States (Exner, 1993). Disenchantment with objective inventories probably facilitated this development (Shneidman, 1965). However, the general rise of the psychodynamic, psychoanalytic movement and the emigration of many of its adherents from Europe to the United States in the 1930s were also important.

What has confused many and perhaps impeded efforts to demonstrate reliability and validity is the fact that there are several different general Rorschach approaches. For example, in the past, Klopfer, Beck, Hertz, Piotrowski, and Rapaport each offered Rorschach systems (Exner, 1993). The systems differ in the manner in which they administer, score, and interpret the results of the test, and in the instructions they provide to examinees. This has created many problems in interpreting the results of research studies and in generalizing from one study to another. In addition, Exner and Exner (1972) discovered that 22% of the clinicians they surveyed did not formally score the Rorschach at all, and 75% reported that when they did use a scoring scheme, it was a highly idiosyncratic one. However, it is now virtually a requirement for research publication that Rorschach protocols be scored in a systematic fashion and that adequate interscorer agreement be demonstrated (Weiner, 1991). At a minimum, we expect that Rorschach responses should be scored similarly by independent raters.

Description. The Rorschach consists of ten cards on which are printed inkblots that are

FIGURE 8-2 Inkblot similar to those employed by Rorschach

symmetrical from right to left. Five of the ten cards are black and white (with shades of gray), and the other five are colored. A simulated Rorschach card is shown in Figure 8-2.

Administration. There are various techniques for administering the Rorschach. However, for many clinicians, the process goes something like this. The clinician hands the patient the first card and says, "Tell me what you see—what it might be for you. There are no right or wrong answers. Just tell me what it looks like to you." All of the subsequent cards are administered in order. The clinician takes down verbatim everything the patient says. Some clinicians also record the length of time it takes the patient to make the first response to each card, as well as the total time spent on each card. Some patients produce many responses per card, others very few. The clinician also notes the position of the card as each response is given (right side up, upside down, or sideways). All spontaneous remarks or exclamations are also recorded.

Following this phase, the clinician moves to what is called the Inquiry. Here the patient is reminded of all previous responses, one by one, and asked what it was that prompted each response. The patient is also asked to indicate for each card the exact location of the various responses. This is also a time when the patient may elaborate or clarify responses.

Scoring. Although Rorschach scoring schemes vary, most employ three major determinants. *Location* refers to the area of the card to which the patient responded—the whole blot, a large detail, a small detail, white space, and so on. *Content* refers to the nature of the object seen (an animal, a person, a rock, fog, clothing, and so on). *Determinants* refer to those aspects of the card that prompted the patient's response (the form of the blot, its color, texture, apparent movement, shading, and so on). Some systems also score Popular responses and Original responses (often based on the relative frequency of certain responses in the general population). Currently, Exner's Comprehensive System of scoring is the most frequently used (Exner, 1974, 1993). Although the specifics of this scoring system are beyond the scope of this chapter (a total of 54 indices are calculated in Exner's Structural Summary), a number of resources are available that provide details on the Comprehensive System (including Exner, 1991, 1993).

The actual scoring of the Rorschach involves such things as compiling the number of determinants, computing their percentages based on the total number of responses, and computing the ratio of one set of responses to another set (for example, computing the total number of movement responses divided by the number of color responses). Indeed, the layperson is often surprised to learn that orthodox scoring of the Rorschach is much more concerned with the formal determinants than with the actual content of the responses. However, many contemporary clinicians do not bother with formal scoring at all, preferring to rely on the informal notation of determinants. Furthermore, these clinicians tend to make heavy use of content in their interpretations. Case illustrations 1 and 2 (at the bottom of the page and following) may help provide an idea of what is involved in the administration and scoring of a Rorschach.

Rorschach Case Illustration 2

The following unscored set of responses was provided by a 42-year-old woman who was diagnosed by a psychiatrist as "anxiety reaction, chronic, severe" following a traumatic accident in her home. It is important to note that this diagnosis was arrived at by an examination of all the data available and not by use of the Rorschach alone.

Card I	Bat. (Anything else?) It's on a web.
Card II	A couple of bears.
Card III	I don't know. (See anything at all?) A couple of little birds.

Rorschach Case Illustration 1

The examinee is an 18-year-old "normal" male college student.

	Response	*Inquiry*	*Scoring*
Card I	Looks like a crab or a sea animal of some kind	Claws make it look like a crab.	D F+ A (large detail, good form, animal object)
Card VIII	A flower of some kind. Possibly an iris.	The petals have that shape. And the colors of it, I guess.	W FC P1 (whole card, form predominant over color, plant)

PROFILE 8-2

John E. Exner, Jr., Ph.D.

Dr. John Exner is Professor Emeritus of Psychology at Long Island University and Executive Director of the Rorschach Research Foundation (Rorschach Workshops). Dr. Exner is perhaps best known for his development of the *Comprehensive System* of Rorschach scoring and interpretation. This is the most widely used scoring and interpretive system today. He has published numerous books, articles, and book chapters on Rorschach assessment techniques. In addition to being named a Fellow of prestigious organizations such as the American Psychological Association and the American Psychological Society, he has been honored with Distinguished Contribution awards from the Society for Personality Assessment and the American Psychological Association. Dr. Exner provided the following responses to questions about his own background as well as future trends in assessment.

What originally got you interested in clinical psychology?

My original interest in clinical psychology was probably prompted by an abnormal psychol-ogy course that I took during the first semester of my third undergraduate year. At that time, I was a "dual" major in pre-law and psychology.

Describe what activities you are involved in as a clinical psychologist.

Currently, I am semi-retired and devote most of my work effort to research on issues of personality assessment and individual differences.

What are your particular areas of expertise or interest?

Personality assessment, treatment planning, and treatment evaluation.

What are the future trends you see for clinical psychology?

I find it very difficult to predict much of the future for clinical psychology, although I do believe that it will gradually be marked by much more research concerning treatment efficacy as related to individual differences.

What are some future trends you see in Rorschach research?

I believe that Rorschach research will probably focus more extensively on three major areas, (1) the development of information concerning the stimulus features of the blots; (2) concern for response styles in establishing or extending interpretive guidelines of Rorschach data; and (3) the study of Rorschach variables to detect various characteristics of personality that have no direct relationship to psychopathology, such as friendliness, idealism, or ambition.

Card IV	Looks like a bearskin of some kind, stretched out.
Card V	A butterfly.
Card VI	The middle looks like a lampstand or a pipestand.
Card VII	Looks like an island. (Anything else?) A ship in port. A vessel of some kind.
Card VIII	A couple bears climbing a tree. (Anything else?) No.
Card IX	I don't know what that looks like.
Card X	Looks like something I've seen in the bottom of the ocean. A crawfish.

An excerpt from the clinician's report observed: "On the Rorschach, the patient's performance was constricted and conforming. Her responses seemed to be influenced by anxiety factors. There was a noticeable tendency for her to avoid the threatening aspects of the test (lack of structure) by giving only a few responses and then making them into popular or conforming ones. Her tendency to respond to the test in terms of animals or inanimate objects suggests some disturbance in social relationships or else a potential for withdrawal."

As we observed earlier, Rorschach interpretation can be a complex process. For example, a patient's overuse of form may suggest conformity. Poor form, coupled with unusual responses, may hint at psychosis. Color is said to relate to emotionality, and if it is not accompanied by good form it may often indicate impulsivity. Extensive use of white spaces has been interpreted as indicative of oppositional or even psychopathic qualities. Use of the whole blot points to a tendency to be concerned with integration and to be well organized. Extensive use of details is thought to be correlated with compulsivity or obsessional tendencies. But content is also important. Seeing small animals might mean passivity. Responses of blood, claws, teeth, or similar images, could suggest hostility and aggression. Even turning a card over and examining the back might lead to an interpretation of suspiciousness. However, it is important that the reader treat these as examples of poten-

tial interpretations or hypotheses and not as successfully validated facts!

We will conclude our discussion of the Rorschach with some general evaluative comments. As previously mentioned, the most comprehensive approach to scoring has been developed by Exner (1974, 1993). His system incorporates elements from the scoring systems of other clinicians. Exner and his associates have offered a substantial amount of psychometric data, evidence of stable test-retest reliability, and construct validity studies. It is a promising, research-based approach that warrants careful attention from clinicians who choose to use the Rorschach. However, it is also important to note that many of the reliability and validity studies cited by Exner have been challenged (Wood, Nezworski, & Stejskal, 1996). Below, we discuss current perspectives on the reliability and validity of Rorschach scores.

Reliability and Validity. Research-oriented clinical psychologists have questioned the reliability of Rorschach scores for years. As we mentioned previously, at the most basic level one should be confident that Rorschach responses can be scored reliably across raters. If the same Rorschach responses cannot be scored similarly by different raters using the same scoring system, then it is hard to imagine that the instrument would have much utility in clinical prediction situations. Unfortunately, the extent to which Rorschach scoring systems meet acceptable standards for this most basic and straightforward form of reliability remains contentious. For example, in a recent rather heated exchange, Meyer (1997a, 1997b) reported that evidence indicates "excellent" interrater reliability for Exner's scoring system, while Wood, Nezworski, and Stejskal (1997) remained unconvinced by his new reliability analyses and results.

Although interscorer reliability is important to address, we must also evaluate the consistency of an individual's scores across time or test conditions, as well as the reliability of interpretations of scores. Weiner (1995) argues that frequent retests (even on a daily basis) are possible because "the basic structure and thematic focus of their Rorschach data tends to remain the same" (p. 335). However, we are not aware of a large body of empirical studies that support the stability of Rorschach summary scores. The limited available evidence does tend to support the stability over time of summary scores believed to reflect trait-like dispositions (Meyer, 1997a), but more evidence is needed to address this question.

Of crucial importance is the reliability of clinicians' interpretations. This important but relatively neglected type of reliability is crucial for measures like the Rorschach. It is quite probable that two clinicians trained together over several years can achieve reliability in their interpretations. However, what about two clinicians with no common training? The proliferation of formal scoring schemes, coupled with the tendency of so many clinicians to use freewheeling interpretive approaches, makes the calculation of this type of reliability difficult.

As for validity of Rorschach scores and interpretations, there have been many testimonials over the years. When skilled, experienced clinicians speak highly of an instrument, those in the field listen. But at some point, these testimonials must give way to hard evidence. From the vast Rorschach literature, it is apparent that the test is not equally valid for all purposes. In a very real sense, the problem is not one of determining whether the Rorschach is valid, but of differentiating the conditions under which it is useful from those under which it is not. For many years, a procedure involving interpretation of a Rorschach with almost no other information about the patient was used to assess Rorschach validity. Even when Rorschach response protocols are submitted for analysis in this manner, however, identifying cues are often present. For example, the Rorschach protocols of 10-year-olds may be combined in one study with those of 60-year-olds. Sometimes the protocols are sent to former teachers or to friends, so that there may be a higher than usual level of agreement. Just knowing that the protocols came from Hospital X may provide important cues about the nature of the patients.

Other studies have used a matching technique—specifically, the matching of Rorschach protocols with case histories—to assess the validity of Rorschach interpretations. However, there are also problems with these studies. Correct matching may be a function of one or two strikingly deviant variables. Consequently, what has really been validated? There have even been instances in which the person who had administered the Rorschach was subsequently asked to match it with the correct case history. Thus, a correct match may have been determined by the recall of patient characteristics observed during the testing.

Despite the questions raised about the validity of the Rorschach, several surveys have placed the Rorschach in a favorable light (for example, Atkinson, 1986; Parker, 1983; Parker et al., 1988). For example, Parker et al. (1988), in a broad survey of Rorschach studies, found the average validity coefficient across a variety of Rorschach scales to be .41. Also, both interjudge reliability and test-retest reliability were in the mid-.80s. Still, many remain critical of the quality of the individual studies that have been cited as supporting the validity of Rorschach scores (for example, Wood et al., 1996). Perhaps most important, a recent reanalysis of the studies included in Parker et al.'s (1988) meta-analysis arrived at a different conclusion. Garb, Florio, and Grove (1998), using data from the same studies reviewed by Parker et al., reported significantly lower validity estimates for Rorschach scores (validity coefficient of .29 versus previous estimate of .41). Further, the revised, corrected estimate of Rorschach validity was significantly lower than that of the MMPI (.48). These findings, in addition to findings that fail to support the incremental validity of Rorschach scores (Archer & Krishnamurthy, 1997; Garb, 1984, 1998), led the authors to "recommend that less emphasis be placed on training in the use of the Rorschach" (p. 404). It remains to be seen whether clinical psychology programs will heed this call.

The debate over the utility of the Rorschach in clinical assessment continues (Meyer, 1999). Advocates (Stricker & Gold, 1999; Viglione, 1999) argue that the Rorschach is useful when the focus is on the unconscious functioning and problem-solving styles of individuals. However, critics remain skeptical of the clinical utility of Rorschach scores (Hunsley & Bailey, 1999) or their incremental validity (Dawes, 1999).

Rorschach Inkblot "Method." Recently, Weiner (1994) has argued that the Rorschach is best conceptualized as a *method* of data collection, not a test.

> The Rorschach is not a test because it does not test anything. A test is intended to measure whether something is present or not and in what quantity. . . . But with the Rorschach, which has traditionally been classified as a test of personality, we do not measure whether people have a personality or how much personality they have. (p. 499)

Several implications follow. First, Weiner argues that data generated from the Rorschach method can be interpreted from a variety of theoretical positions. These data suggest how the respondent typically solves problems or makes decisions (cognitive structuring processes) as well as the meanings that are assigned to these perceptions (associational processes). Weiner calls this an "integrationist" view of the Rorschach, because the method provides data relevant to both the structure and dynamics of personality. According to Weiner, a second, practical implication is that viewing the Rorschach as a method allows one to fully use all aspects of the data that are generated, resulting in a more thorough diagnostic evaluation.

The influence and utility of this reconceptualization remains to be seen. In any case, empirical data supporting the utility and incremental validity of data generated by the Rorschach "method" are still necessary before its routine use in clinical settings can be advocated.

The Thematic Apperception Test

The *Thematic Apperception Test (TAT)* was introduced by Morgan and Murray in 1935. It purports to reveal patients' basic personality characteristics through the interpretation of their imaginative productions in response to a series of pictures. Although the test is designed to reveal central conflicts, attitudes, goals, and repressed material, it actually produces material that is a collage of these plus situational influences, cultural stereotypes, trivia, and so on. The clinician's job is to separate the wheat from the chaff.

Most clinicians use the TAT as a method of inferring psychological needs (achievement, affiliation, dependency, power, sex, and so on) and of disclosing how the patient interacts with the environment. In contrast to the Rorschach, the TAT is used to infer the content of personality and the mode of social interactions. With a TAT, clinicians are likely to make specific judgments, such as "This patient is hostile toward authority figures, yet seeks their affection and approval." The TAT is less likely to be used to assess the degree of maladjustment than to reveal the locus of problems, the nature of needs, or the quality of interpersonal relationships.

Description. There are 31 TAT cards (one is a blank card); most depict people in a variety of situations, but a few contain only objects. Some are said to be useful for boys and men, some for girls and women, and some for both genders. Murray suggested that 20 of the 31 cards be selected for a given examinee. As a test, the TAT does not appear to be as ambiguous or unstructured as the Rorschach. However, though the figures in the pictures may clearly be people, it is not always clear what their gender is, exactly who they are, what they are doing, or what they are thinking. Figure 8-3 illustrates one of the TAT cards.

Administration. In practice, clinicians typically select somewhere between 6 and 12 cards for administration to a given patient. Although the exact instructions used will vary from clinician to clinician, they go something like this: "Now, I want you to make up a story about each of these pictures. Tell me who the people are, what they are doing, what they are thinking or feeling, what led up to the scene, and how it will turn out. OK?" The patient's productions are

FIGURE 8-3 **Card 12F of the TAT**

transcribed verbatim by the clinician (or sometimes tape-recorded). In some instances, patients may be asked to write out their stories, but this can result in shorter than normal stories.

Scoring. Many scoring schemes have been proposed over the years (Exner, 1983; Shneidman, 1951, 1965). It seems that most clinicians have chosen to accept the judgment that quantified scoring schemes cause clinically useful evidence to be distorted or lost and use such schemes only for research purposes. Interestingly, the TAT has never been as soundly criticized as has the Rorschach. This may be partially due to the fact that there has never been much interest in or emphasis on scoring the TAT; it is hard to carry out empirical studies that fail to support underutilized scoring schemes.

The following examples illustrate several TAT themes and the interpretations or analyses made from them. They are verbatim responses from the same 42-year-old woman described in Case Illustration 2 of the Rorschach section.

TAT Case Illustration

Card 3BM	Looks like a little boy crying for something he can't have. (Why is he crying?) Probably because he can't go somewhere. (How will it turn out?) Probably sit there and sob hisself [sic] to sleep.
Card 3GF	Looks like her boyfriend might have let her down. She hurt his feelings. He's closed the door on her. (What did he say?) I don't know.
Card 9GF	Girl looks like somebody's run off and left her. She's ready for a dance. Maid is watching to see where she goes. (Why run off?) Probably because she wasn't ready in time.
Card 10	Looks like there's sorrow here. Grieving about something. (About what?) Looks like maybe one of the children's passed away.
Card 13MF	Looks like his wife might have passed away and he feels there's nothing more to do.
Card 20	Looks like a man that's ready to rob something. Hiding behind a high fence of some kind. Has his hand in his pocket with a gun ready to shoot if anybody comes out.

An excerpt from the clinician's report offers this analysis. "The TAT produced responses that were uniformly indicative of unhappiness, threat, misfortune, or lack of control over environmental forces. None of the test responses were indicative of satisfaction, happy endings, and so on. In this test, as in the Rorschach, impoverished and constricted responses are evident which probably indicate anxiety and depression. . . . In summary, the test results point to an individual who is anxious and, at the same time, depressed. Feelings of insecurity, inadequacy, and lack of control over environmental forces are apparent, as are unhappiness and apprehension. These factors result in a constriction of performance that is largely oriented toward avoiding threat and that hampers sufficient mobilization of energy to perform at an optimal level."

Lindzey, Bradford, Tejessy, and Davids (1959) compiled a dictionary of interpretive generalizations that might be made from TAT stories, based on a survey of nearly 200 publications. The sheer volume of possible TAT interpretations from the various story cues is tremendous. This highlights the difficulty of assessing TAT validity—namely, validity with respect to what? Following are a few of the interpretive generalizations culled from the literature by Lindzey et al.:

> Paranoid symptomatology indicated by: Stereotyped phrases used throughout a record. (Rapaport, 1946, p. 449)

> Anxiety indicated by: . . . plots emphasizing sudden physical accidents and emotional trauma, such as loss of wife, mother, sweetheart, job, a house burning down, or a stock crash. (Rotter, 1946, p. 88)

> Dependency in adolescents indicated by . . . three or more references to one or more members of the family. (Symonds, 1949, p. 87)

> Patients with sexual problems may: . . . avoid the picture on the wall in Picture #4 or refuse to discuss the nude female in Picture #13. (Stein, 1948, p. 42)

Unfortunately, these propositions have received relatively little research attention. Further, we are not aware of any research suggesting that information obtained from the TAT is significantly related to treatment outcome. Given the TAT's purported ability to identify interpersonal styles that might influence choices regarding the therapist's treatment approach, this is somewhat surprising.

Reliability and Validity. As with the Rorschach, let us conclude this section with a summary evaluation of the TAT. It is very difficult to evaluate the reliability and validity of the TAT in any formal sense. There are so many variations in instructions, methods of administration, number of cards used, and type of scoring scheme (if any) that hard conclusions are virtually impossible. The same methodological issues arise when studying reliability. For example, personality changes may obscure any conclusions about test-retest reliability, or there may be uncertainty about equivalent forms when trying to assess alternate-forms reliability. It is possible to investigate theme reliability, but since one cannot expect word-for-word similarity from one occasion to the next, one is usually studying the reliability of judges' interpretations. When there is an explicit, theoretically derived set of scoring instructions (for example, B. J. Fitzgerald, 1958), interjudge agreement can reach acceptable proportions. Interjudge reliability can also be achieved when quantitative ratings are involved (Harrison, 1965). But broad, global interpretations can present problems.

Some attempts have been made to establish the validity of the TAT. Methods have included (1) comparison of TAT interpretations with case data or with therapist evaluations of the patient; (2) matching techniques and analyses of protocols with no additional knowledge about the patient; (3) comparisons between clinical diagnoses derived from the TAT and psychiatrists' judgments; and (4) establishment of the validity of certain general principles of interpretation (for example, the tendency of the person to identify with the hero of the story, or the probability that unusual themes are more significant than common ones).

The typical clinical use of the TAT suggests that it remains basically a subjective instrument. Although it is possible to identify general principles of interpretation, these can serve only as guides—not as exact prescriptions for interpretation. Adequate interpretation depends upon some knowledge of the patient's background. As the clinician examines the test protocol, attention must be paid to the frequency with which thematic elements occur, the unusualness of stories, the manner in which plots are developed, misrecognitions, the choice of words, identifications with plot characters, and so on. The clinician will want to look closely at the nature of the TAT heroes or heroines and at their needs and goals. The environmental presses are also important, as is the general emotional ambiance of the themes.

Sentence Completion Techniques

A very durable and serviceable, yet simple, technique is the *sentence completion method*. The most widely used and best-known of the many versions is the Rotter Incomplete Sentences Blank (Rotter & Rafferty, 1950; Rotter, 1954). The *Incomplete Sentences Blank (ISB)* consists of 40 sentence stems—for example, "I like . . . ," "What annoys me . . . ," I wish . . . ," and "Most girls . . . ." Each of the completions can be scored along a 7-point scale to provide a general index of adjustment-maladjustment (for example, Jessor, Liverant, & Opochinsky, 1963). The ISB has great versatility, and scoring schemes for a variety of variables have been developed (for example, Fitzgerald, 1958).

The ISB has several advantages. The scoring is objective and reliable, due in part to extensive scoring examples provided in the manual. The ISB can be used easily and economically, and it appears to be a good screening device. Although it can be scored objectively, it also allows considerable freedom of response. Thus, the ISB falls somewhere between the two extremes of the objective-projective dimension. It represents a fairly direct approach to measurement that does not require the degree of training that is necessary, for example, to score the Rorschach. Some clinicians may be disturbed by the ISB's relative lack of disguise. Perhaps because of this, the ISB does not typically provide information that could not be gleaned from a reasonably extensive interview. In many ways, then, the ISB provides a cognitive and behavioral picture of the patient rather than a "deep, psychodynamic" picture.

Illusory Correlation

The interpretation of projective test responses depends heavily on the psychodiagnostician's experience. Observations are accumulated regarding the presence of certain test responses that supposedly occur in connection with certain personality characteristics. As a result, the clinician "learns" to associate these test responses with specific personality characteristics. They become "signs" of these underlying personality characteristics. However, a great deal of research evidence fails to support the meaningfulness of many of these diagnostic signs. Little and Shneidman (1959) found, for example, that eminent clinicians performed only slightly better than chance in making valid statements about patients on the basis of their test responses. Chapman and Chapman (1969) believe that one reason for this poor performance lies in the tendency to rely on *illusory correlations* between test responses and personality characteristics. Chapman and Chapman found that in the case of the Rorschach, clinicians tended to focus on test responses that have a high associative value with male homosexuality. Thus, when they observed such test responses of males as "This looks like a man bending over" or "This is an anal opening," they quickly but mistakenly assumed they had evidence for the presence of homosexual tendencies. At the same time, they overlooked valid signs that had low associative strength, such as threatening animals or animals that are humanized (such as a headless monster or a woman with butterfly wings). Although the "diagnosis" of homosexuality is not relevant to the practice of contemporary clinical psychology because ho-

mosexuality is not considered a mental disorder (as it was in DSM-II, 1968), the important point is that illusory correlation based on associative strength can introduce a powerful source of error.

Incremental Utility

As mentioned in the discussion of the MMPI-2, incremental validity refers to the degree to which a procedure adds to the prediction obtainable from other sources (Meehl & Rosen, 1955; Sechrest, 1963).

For an assessment procedure to be of real value, it must tell clinicians something of importance that they cannot get from merely inspecting the *base rates* (prevalence rates) for the population of interest. If a clinician in a state school for those who suffer from mental retardation reports via the WISC-III that a certain patient should be given a diagnosis of mental retardation, this hardly comes as a surprise, because we already know that 98% of the institutional populace suffers from mental retardation. If, however, the test can tell the clinician something about the patient's patterning of abilities that will assist in planning vocational training, then some incremental validity may be ascribed to the testing procedure. Discovering from a Rorschach that a 70-year-old widower "seems to be grappling with intense feelings of loneliness" hardly represents a breakthrough in incremental validity, even though the statement may be entirely true. Asserting that the TAT themes of a patient with schizophrenia reveal adjustment difficulties or that the Rorschach responses of a patient known to be depressed are suggestive of dysphoria and sadness adds little if anything to existing knowledge, even though it may appear that something correct and profound has been said. Finally, it should be noted that a given assessment instrument must demonstrate incremental validity over other, more economical measures (such as short self-report inventories) in order to justify its use. Otherwise, the extra effort for the same information wastes the clinician's and the patient's time.

The Use and Abuse of Testing

Ours has long been a test-oriented society. Whether the question concerns personnel selection, intellectual assessment, or measuring the "real me," many people turn to tests. Some consult popular magazines (and now the Internet!) for these tests, others consult skilled clinicians, but the abiding curiosity and the inflated set of expectations about tests seem constant. And quite often, such high expectations lead to abuse.

Testing is big business. Psychological, educational, and personnel corporations sell many thousands of tests each year. So many of our lives are touched in so many ways by assessment procedures that we have become accustomed to them and hardly notice them. Admission to college, employment, discharge from military service, imprisonment, adoption, therapeutic planning, computer dating, and special classes all may depend on test performance. Any enterprise that becomes so large and affects such large numbers of people invites careful scrutiny.

Protections. The APA's (1992) ethical standards require that psychologists use only techniques or procedures that lie within their competence. These ethical standards, the growth of state certification and licensing boards, and the certification of professional competence offered by the American Board of Professional Psychology all combine to increase the probability that the public's interests will be protected.

In addition, the purchase of testing materials is generally restricted by the publisher to individuals or institutions that can demonstrate their competence in administering, scoring, and interpreting tests. In effect, then, the sale of tests is not open but is dependent upon the user's qualifications. However, neither professional guidelines nor publishers' restrictions are totally successful. Tests still sometimes find their way into the hands of unscrupulous individuals. Ethical standards are not always sufficient either.

The marketers for each test bear some responsibility as well. Normative data and instructions for administration and scoring should be included in *every* test manual. All in all, enough data should be included to enable the user to evaluate the reliability and validity of the test.

The Question of Privacy. Most people assume that they have the right to reveal as little or as much as they like about their attitudes, feelings, fears, or aspirations. Of course, with subtle or indirect assessment procedures, an examinee cannot always judge with complete certainty whether a given response is desirable. But whatever the nature of a test, the individual has the right to a full explanation of its purposes and of the use to which the results will be put.

The examinee must be given only tests relevant to the purposes of the evaluation. If an MMPI-2 or a Rorschach is included in a personnel-selection battery, it is the psychologist's responsibility to explain the relevance of the test to the individual. Informed consent to the entire assessment process should be obtained, and individuals should be fully informed of their options. This applies even to those who have initiated the contact (as by voluntarily seeking clinical services).

The Question of Confidentiality. Issues of trust and confidentiality loom large in our society. The proliferation of computer processing facilities and huge data banks makes it very easy for one government agency to gain access to personal records that are in the files of another agency or a company. Credit card agencies, the FBI, the CIA, the IRS, and other organizations create a climate in which no one's records or past seem to be confidential or inviolable. Although information revealed to psychiatrists and clinical psychologists is typically regarded as privileged, there are continuing assaults on the right to withhold such information. For example, the *Tarasoff* decision of the California Supreme Court makes it clear that information provided by a patient in the course of therapy cannot remain privileged if that information indicates that the patient may be dangerous. If the "sanctity" of the therapy room is less than unassailable, it is certain that personnel records, school records, and other test repositories are even more vulnerable. Clinical psychologists employed in industrial settings are also unable to ensure absolutely the privacy of test results. Clinicians can become caught in the middle of tugs of war between union and management over grievance claims. It sometimes happens also that when people are treated under insurance or medical assistance programs, their diagnoses are entered into computer records to which many companies may obtain access.

When an individual is tested, every effort should be made to explain the purposes of the testing, the use to which the results will be put, and the people or institutions that will have access to the results. If the individual gives informed consent, the testing can proceed. However, if it subsequently becomes desirable to release the results to someone else, the individual's consent must be obtained. It is clear that not all clients wish to have their mental health records released, and even when they sign consent forms, they often seem to do so either out of a fear that they will be denied services or out of sheer obedience to authority (C. E. Rosen, 1977).

The Question of Discrimination. Since the rise of the civil rights movement, most people have become increasingly aware of the ways in which society has both knowingly and unknowingly discriminated against minorities. Within psychology, attacks have recently centered on the ways in which tests discriminate against minorities. For example, the original standardization of the Stanford-Binet contained no African American samples. Since then, many tests have been published whose attempts to include racially unbiased samples have been questioned. It is often charged that most psychological tests are really designed for white middle-class populations and that other groups are handicapped by being tested with devices that are inappropriate for them.

Sometimes the minority group member's lack of exposure to tests and test situations may be a major source of the problem. Such inexperi-

ence, inadequate motivation, and discomfort in the presence of an examiner from another race all may affect test performance. Often, too, test materials are prepared or embedded in a racially unfair context. For example, the TAT cards may all depict white characters, or the items on an intelligence test may not be especially familiar to an African American child. The problem here is that the test items themselves, the manner in which they are presented, or the circumstances surrounding a test may work to the disadvantage of the minority individual.

Test Bias. It is important to remember that significant differences between mean scores on a test for different groups do not in and of themselves indicate test bias or discrimination. Rather, test bias or discrimination is a *validity* issue. That is, if it can be demonstrated that the validity of a test (in predicting criterion characteristics or performance, for example) varies significantly across groups, then a case can be made that the test is "biased" for that purpose. In other words, a test is biased to the extent that it predicts more accurately for one group than for another group.

An example can illustrate these considerations. Let us assume that one of the authors developed a personality inventory measuring the trait "hostility." As part of the standardization project for this test, the author discovered that men scored significantly higher than women on this test. Doe this indicate that the test is biased? Not necessarily. The author found, in a series of validity studies, that the relationship (correlation) between hostility inventory scores and the number of *verbal* fights over the succeeding two months was quite similar for both men and women. In other words, the predictive validity coefficients for the two groups were comparable; similar hostility scores "meant" the same thing (predicted a comparable number of verbal fights) for men and women. On the other hand, it is quite possible that the strength of the correlation between hostility scores and *physical* fights over the next two months is significantly greater for men than for women. In this case, the use of the test to predict physical aggression in women would be biased if these predictions were based on the known association between hostility scores and physical fights found in men.

Several general points should be clear. First, differences in mean scores do not necessarily indicate test bias. In the previous example, there may be good reasons why men score higher on average than women on a measure of hostility (for example, hormonal differences or other biological factors may lead to higher levels of hostility for men). In fact, to find no difference in mean scores might call into question the validity of the test in this case. Second, the pronouncement of a test as "valid," although frequently seen in the clinical psychology literature, is incorrect. Tests may be valid (and not biased) for some purposes but not for others. Finally, one can "overcome" test bias by using different (and more appropriate) prediction equations for the different groups. In other words, bias comes into play when the clinical psychologist makes predictions based on empirical associations that are characteristic of another group (such as men) but not of the group of interest (such as women). The goal is to investigate the possibility of differential validity and, if found, to use the appropriate prediction equation for that group.

Computer-Based Assessment. Computers have been used for years to score tests and to generate psychological profiles. Now they are also used to administer and interpret responses to clinical interviews, IQ tests, self-report inventories, and even projective tests. The reasons given for using computers include cutting costs, enhancing clients' attention and motivation, and standardizing procedures across clinicians. Clearly computers have great potential, but they also contain the seeds of definite problems (Burke & Normand, 1987). To begin with, there needs to be greater acceptance of computers by professionals. Beyond that, more attention must be devoted to the feelings and reactions of clients upon whom these procedures are imposed. Important issues of reliability and validity (for example, Gottesman & Prescott, 1989), as well as

proper feedback to clients, have yet to be settled. Finally, the field needs better overall professional standards for such testing. It is important to remember that computer systems can easily be misused, either by those who are poorly trained or by those who endow computers with a sagacity that transcends the quality and utility of the information programmed into them.

Numerous efforts have been made to computerize the scoring and interpretation of the MMPI in particular (Honaker, 1988; Kleinmuntz, 1972; Dahlstrom et al., 1972). The approaches are mainly descriptive and most often useful for screening. But programs exist to generate highly interpretive statements as well (for example, Dahlstrom et al., 1972). However, not everyone believes that computerized and conventional usages of the MMPI yield comparable results (Buros, 1972; Honaker, 1988).

The use of *computer-based test interpretations (CBTIs)* is a controversial issue (for example, Bloom, 1992; Fowler & Butcher, 1986; Matarazzo, 1986). Guidelines have been proposed as to how best to evaluate the reliability and validity of CBTIs (Moreland, 1985; Snyder, Widiger, & Hoover, 1990), as well as how best to use CBTIs in clinical work (Butcher, 1995b). Butcher (1990, 1995b), for example, has outlined seven steps in providing MMPI-2 feedback to clients.

1. Provide historical information about the MMPI-2.
2. Briefly describe how the MMPI-2 scales were developed, as well as the vastness of the empirical literature on the MMPI/MMPI-2.
3. Briefly describe the validity scales and what they indicate about the client's approach to the testing.
4. Describe the clinical hypotheses that have been generated based on the MMPI-2 profile, couching this in terms of how the client presented him- or herself and how she or he is viewing the problems (if any) at this time.
5. Discuss any significant elevations on the content scales, because what these items measure is intuitively apparent.
6. Invite the client to ask questions about his or her scores, and clarify any confusing issues.

7. Discuss how the client feels the test results fit or do not fit her or his experience. (adapted from Butcher, 1995b, p. 82)

Interestingly, results from a recent study (Finn & Tonsager, 1992) suggest that MMPI-2 test feedback may actually serve as a type of clinical intervention. In this study, one group of student clients at a university counseling center received MMPI-2 test feedback while they were on a waiting list at the clinic; a second group did not take the MMPI-2. The first group showed improvement on measures of both psychopathology symptoms and self-esteem, whereas the control group did not. Although it is possible that the "therapeutic effect" observed may be attributable just to taking the MMPI-2 (that is, not necessarily the feedback), future research in this area seems warranted. This study is laudable because it attempted to demonstrate the clinical utility of the MMPI-2.

Ultimately, the success of any clinical assessment instrument will depend on whether the information provided by the test is useful for planning, conducting, and evaluating treatment.

Chapter Summary

Clinical psychologists frequently engage in personality assessment. However, the utility of even the most popular measures continues to be questioned. The managed care environment has placed even more pressure on personality testing advocates to justify the use of popular measures.

In this chapter, we have discussed several test construction strategies and concluded that the construct validity approach should be adopted when developing a measure. We have also reviewed several objective and projective personality assessment techniques. The MMPI-2 is the major objective personality test, and a wealth of data supports its use in clinical assessment. Although several concerns have been expressed about this newest version, in general it has been widely accepted and represents perhaps the most important measure in the field. Among projective techniques, we focused most of our discussion on the Rorschach. In many respects, clinical psychologists' allegiance to this test divides the field along the lines of believers versus nonbelievers. Academic clinical psychologists tend to be highly critical of the Rorschach, and the acrimonious debate over its legitimacy and merits rages on.

We have concluded with a discussion of the use and abuse of testing. The American Psychological Association is finalizing a new version of its *Standards for Educational and Psychological Testing* (for the most recent draft version, see web site 8-5 at the end of the chapter). These new, revised standards will continue to promote the ethical use of tests. Issues of protection, privacy, confidentiality, discrimination, and test bias must be considered by clinical psychologists involved in the development and use of personality tests. Finally, we have discussed the contemporary trend of computer-based testing and interpretation. It is likely that technological advances will continue to influence the way psychological tests are developed, administered, and interpreted.

Key Terms

base rates Prevalence rates.

computer assessment The use of computers to administer (and possibly interpret) responses to clinical interviews, IQ tests, self-report inventories, and so on.

computer-based test interpretations (CBTIs) The interpretive profiles generated by computer scoring programs for various psychological tests. The use of such profiles has been the subject of intense debate.

construct validity approach An approach to test construction in which scales are developed based upon a specific theory, refined using factor analysis and other procedures, and validated by showing (through empirical study) that individuals who achieve certain scores behave in ways that could be predicted by their scores.

content validation The process by which one ensures that a test will adequately measure all aspects of the construct of interest. Methods of content validation include carefully defining all relevant aspects of the construct, consulting experts, having judges assess the relevance of each potential item, and evaluating the psychometric properties of each potential item.

empirical criterion keying An approach to test development that emphasizes the selection of items that discriminate between normal individuals and members of different diagnostic groups, regardless of whether the items appear theoretically relevant to the diagnoses of interest.

factor analysis A statistical method often used in test construction to determine whether potential items are or are not highly related to each other.

Five-Factor Model (FFM) A comprehensive model of personality that comprises the dimensions of Neuroticism, Extraversion, Openness, Agreeableness, and Conscientiousness, as well as six facets belonging to each dimension.

illusory correlation In the context of projective testing, the phenomenon by which certain test responses become associated with specific personality characteristics. These responses come to be viewed as signs of the trait in question and may be given undue weight when interpreting the test.

Incomplete Sentences Blank (ISB) The best known and most widely used of the sentence completion techniques, consisting of 40 sentence stems.

incremental validity The extent to which a scale score provides information about a person's behavior, personality features, or psychopathology features that is not provided by other measures.

MMPI-2 A measure of psychopathology that was developed using the empirical criterion keying approach. The MMPI-2 consists of 567 true-false items and provides scores on ten clinical scales, seven validity scales, and several content and supplementary scales. Interpretation of the MMPI-2 is usually based upon an analysis of the entire profile, rather than on selected scores. Like the MMPI before it, the MMPI-2 has been used for many different purposes across multiple settings, and it remains one of the primary self-report inventories of personality and psychopathology.

NEO-PI-R A self-report measure of the FFM that consists of 240 statements, each of which is rated on a five-point scale. This test yields scores on all five domains of the FFM (Neuroticism, Extraversion, Openness, Agreeableness, and Conscientious-

ness) as well as the six facets corresponding to each domain.

objective personality measures Personality assessment tools in which the examinee responds to a standard set of questions or statements using a fixed set of options (e.g., true or false, dimensional ratings).

projective techniques Psychological testing techniques that use people's responses to ambiguous test stimuli to make judgments about their adjustment/maladjustment. Proponents believe that examinees "project" themselves onto the stimuli, thus revealing unconscious aspects of themselves.

Rorschach A projective technique that interprets people's responses to a series of ten inkblots.

sentence completion method A simple projective technique in which people are asked to complete, in writing, a number of sentence stems (e.g., "I often believe . . .").

test bias The situation in which different decisions or predictions are made for members of two groups, even when they obtain the same score on an instrument.

Thematic Apperception Test A projective technique that purports to reveal patients' personality characteristics by interpreting the stories they produce in response to a series of pictures.

validity of cutoff scores (thresholds) The extent to which a particular cutoff score accurately classifies people as either possessing or not possessing the disorder or trait in question.

validity scales Test scales that attempt to shed light on the respondent's test-taking attitudes and motivations (e.g., to present themselves in an overly favorable light, to exaggerate their problems or symptoms, to engage in random responding).

Web Sites of Interest

To visit any of the web sites listed below, go to www.wadsworth.com and click on Links.

8-1   Frequently Asked Questions (FAQ) on Psychological Tests

8-2   APA Statement on the Use of Secure Psychological Tests in the Education of Graduate and Undergraduate Psychology Students

CHAPTER NINE

Behavioral Assessment

FOCUS QUESTIONS

1. Why is behavioral assessment an ongoing process?

2. What are the major differences between behavioral assessment and traditional assessment?

3. What factors affect the reliability and validity of observations?

4. What is the SORC model, and how is it applied to clinical problems?

5. What is the importance of cognitive variables in behavioral assessment?

In the traditional view, personality is a system of constructs that greatly influences behavior. Whether the construct is ego, expectancy, trait, paranoia, or growth potential, this view is concerned with relatively stable personal characteristics that contribute to behavior. It follows, then, that to understand or predict behavior one must assess those underlying variables. This is, of course, an oversimplification that masks a good deal of disagreement, because the underlying constructs that are important to a psychoanalytic clinician are likely to be quite different from those that are important to a social learning theorist.

Behavior therapists and assessors, however, do not look at personality in the traditional fashion. They see personality more in terms of behavioral tendencies in specific situations. The focus shifts from a search for underlying personality characteristics to one that looks for the interaction between behaviors and situations. This kind of conceptualization leads some to view personality much like a set of abilities (Wallace, 1966). For such people, personality becomes a set of abilities or skills rather than a constellation of predispositions (such as needs or traits) that convey the essence of the person. Aggression and dependency are skills, much as riding a bicycle is a skill. The focus turns to adjectival properties rather than to nouns. For example, behavior therapists are interested in aggressive behavior, not aggression.

The Behavioral Tradition

Before we examine specific methods of *behavioral assessment*, let us consider three broad ways in which it differs from traditional assessment.

Sample versus Sign

In traditional assessment, a description of the situation is much less important than the identification of the more enduring personality characteristics. In behavioral assessment, the paramount issue is how well the assessment device samples the behaviors and situations in which

the clinician is interested. How well the test is disguised or how deeply into the recesses of personality it reaches become irrelevant questions. Years ago, Goldfried (1976) described the difference between a *sign* and a *sample* orientation to testing:

> When test responses are viewed as a sample, one assumes that they parallel the way in which a person is likely to behave in a nontest situation. Thus, if a person responds aggressively on a test, one assumes that this aggression also occurs in other situations as well. When test responses are viewed as signs, an inference is made that the performance is an indirect or symbolic manifestation of some other characteristic. An example is a predominance of Vista responses on the Rorschach, in which the individual reports that his [sic] percepts are viewed as if they were seen from a distance. In interpreting such a response, one does not typically conclude that the individual is in great need of optometric care, but rather that such responses presumably indicate the person's ability for self-evaluation and insight. For the most part, traditional assessment has employed a sign as opposed to sample approach to test interpretation. In the case of behavioral assessment only the sample approach makes sense. (pp. 283–284)

Functional Analysis

Another central feature of behavioral assessment is traceable to Skinner's (1953) notion of *functional analysis*. This means that exact analyses are made of the stimuli that precede a behavior and the consequences that follow it. Assessing the manner in which variations in stimulus conditions and outcomes are related to behavior changes makes possible a more precise understanding of the causes of behavior (Haynes & O'Brien, 1990). The major thesis is that behaviors are learned and maintained because of consequences that follow them. Thus, to change an undesirable behavior, the clinician must (1) identify the stimulus conditions that precipitate it and (2) determine the reinforcements that follow. Once these two sets of factors are assessed, the clinician is in a position to modify the behavior by manipulating the stimuli and/or reinforcements involved.

Crucial to a functional analysis is careful and precise description. The behavior of concern must be described in observable, measurable terms so that its rate of occurrence can be recorded reliably. With equal precision, the conditions that control it must also be specified. Both *antecedent conditions* and *consequent events* are thus carefully elaborated. Such events as time, place, and people present when the behavior occurs are recorded, along with the specific outcomes that follow the behavior of concern.

Suppose, for example, that a child is aggressively disruptive in the classroom. Traditional assessment might well be directed toward analyzing the needs that the child is trying to satisfy. The hope is that once these needs are identified, they can be modified, and the undesirable behavior eliminated. A behavioral assessment would ignore such hypothesized internal determinants as "needs" and focus instead on the target—aggressive behavior. It might be discovered that the child usually takes objects (such as a pencil) from another child (that is, behaves aggressively) when the teacher is paying attention to others in the classroom. When the aggressiveness occurs, the teacher almost invariably turns her attention to the disruptive child. A functional analysis, then, reveals that lack of attention (*stimulus*) is followed by taking a pencil from another child (*behavior*), which in turn is followed by attention (*consequence*). Once this pattern of relationships is established, steps can be taken to change it and thereby modify the undesirable behavior. As an example, the child might be put in a room alone following the disruptive behavior. This treatment would be expected to alter the behavior, because it is no longer followed by consequences that the child finds reinforcing. This scenario may not seem much different from what many parents would do intuitively. The difference, however, resides in the care and precision with which relationships are identified and in the exact specification of the target behaviors. Table 9-1 summarizes a number of differences between traditional and behavioral approaches to assessment.

Most behavioral therapists have broadened the method of functional analysis to include "organismic" variables as well. *Organismic variables* include physical, physiological, or cognitive characteristics of the individual that are important for both the conceptualization of the client's problem and the ultimate treatment that is administered. For example, it may be important to assess attitudes and beliefs that are characteristic of individuals who are prone to experience depressive episodes because of their purported relationship to depression as well as their suitability as targets for intervention. A useful model for conceptualizing a clinical problem from a behavioral perspective is the *SORC model* (Kanfer & Phillips, 1970):

S = stimulus or antecedent conditions that bring on the problematic behavior

O = organismic variables related to the problematic behavior

R = response or problematic behavior

C = consequences of the problematic behavior

Behavioral clinicians use this model to guide and inform them regarding the information needed to fully describe the problem and, ultimately, the interventions that may be prescribed.

Behavioral Assessment as an Ongoing Process

As pointed out by Peterson and Sobell (1994), behavioral assessment in a clinical context (like most good assessment) is not a one-shot evaluation performed before treatment is initiated. Rather, is an ongoing process that occurs before, during, and after treatment. Behavioral assessment is important because it informs the initial selection of treatment strategies, provides a means of feedback regarding the efficacy of the treatment strategies employed as they are enacted in the treatment process, allows evaluation

TABLE 9-1 Differences between Behavioral and Traditional Approaches to Assessment

	Behavioral	Traditional
I. Assumptions		
1. Conception of personality	Personality constructs used, if at all, mainly to summarize specific behavior patterns	Personality as a reflection of enduring underlying states or traits
2. Causes of behavior	Maintaining conditions sought in current environment	Intrapsychic (within the individual)
II. Implications		
1. Role of behavior	Important as a sample of person's repertoire in specific situation	Behavior assumes importance only insofar as it indexes underlying causes
2. Role of history	Relatively unimportant except, for example, to provide a retrospective baseline	Crucial in that present conditions seen as a product of the past
3. Consistency of behavior	Behavior thought to be specific to the situation	Behavior expected to be consistent across time and settings
III. Uses of data	To describe target behaviors and maintaining conditions	To describe personality functioning and etiology
	To select the appropriate treatment	To diagnose or classify
	To evaluate and revise treatment	To make prognosis; to predict
IV. Other characteristics		
1. Level of inferences	Low	Medium to high
2. Comparisons	More emphasis on intra-individual or idiographic	More emphasis on inter-individual or nomothetic
3. Methods of assessment	More emphasis on direct methods (e.g., observations of behavior in natural environment)	More emphasis on indirect methods (e.g., interviews and self-reports)
4. Timing of assessment	More ongoing; prior, during, and after treatment	Pre- and perhaps post-treatment, or strictly to diagnose
5. Scope of assessment	Specific measures and of more variables (e.g., of target behaviors in various situations, of side effects, context, strengths as well as deficiencies)	More global measures (e.g., of cure, or improvement) but only of the individual

Source: Adapted from "Some Relationships Between Behavioral and Traditional Assessment," by D. P. Hartmann, B. L. Roper, and D. C. Bradford, *Journal of Behavioral Assessment*, 1979, *1*, 4. Copyright © 1979 by Plenum Publishing Corporation. Reprinted by permission.

of the overall effectiveness of treatment once completed, and highlights situational factors that may lead to recurrence of the problematic behavior(s).

Figure 9-1 illustrates behavioral assessment at various stages of treatment (Peterson & Sobell, 1994). First, diagnostic formulations provide descriptions of maladaptive behaviors, or potential

FIGURE 9-1 Model of the role of behavioral assessment within behavior therapy

Source: Peterson, L., & Sobell, L. C. (1994). Introduction to the state-of-the art review series: Research contributions to clinical assessment. Behavior Therapy, 25, 523–531. *Reprinted with permission.*

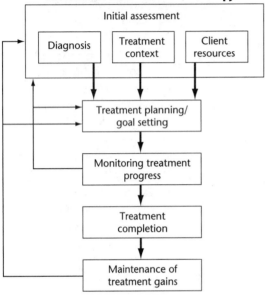

Iterative Model: The Role of Assessment within Behavior Therapy

Initial assessment

Diagnosis — Treatment context — Client resources

Treatment planning/goal setting

Monitoring treatment progress

Treatment completion

Maintenance of treatment gains

targets for intervention. Second, the patient's context or environment (social support system, physical environment) is important to assess because of the relevance to treatment planning and the setting of realistic treatment goals. An evaluation of client resources, such as skills, level of motivation, beliefs, and expectations, is also important. As noted by Peterson and Sobell (1994), the initial assessments of diagnosis/maladaptive behaviors, treatment context, and client resources will naturally lead to a data-based initial treatment plan. This plan involves collaborative (patient and therapist) goal setting as well as mutually agreed upon criteria to indicate improvement. Formal assessments of treatment progress serve as ongoing feedback as well as avenues for building the patient's self-efficacy as progress is made. Assessment following completion of treatment provides objective data regard-

ing the patient's end-state functioning, which can then be compared to data from the pretreatment assessment. Finally, thorough assessment throughout all these stages will provide information regarding the likelihood of symptom recurrence, including identification of "high-risk" environments that may lead to relapse.

Peterson and Sobell (1994) argue that this model of behavioral assessment has great potential to bridge the often wide gap between behavioral research and clinical practice. As we shall discuss in Chapter 14, the field of behavior therapy is unique in its emphasis on data-based decision making throughout all phases of treatment. Therefore, behavioral assessment is not a luxury, but a necessity.

With these notions in mind, we now turn to an examination of some of the more common behavioral assessment methods.

Interviews

Obviously, one cannot begin a functional analysis or develop a program of behavioral treatment before one has at least a general notion of what the problem is. To develop such notions, the behavioral clinician is likely to turn to that old standby, the interview—the clinician's best and most durable friend. During *behavioral interviews*, the clinician attempts to gain a general impression of the presenting problem and of the variables that seem to be maintaining the problem behavior (Goldfried & Davison, 1994). Other information sought includes relevant historical data and an assessment of the patient's strengths and of past attempts to cope with the problem. Also of interest are the patient's expectations regarding therapy. Finally, when feasible, some initial establishment and communication of therapeutic goals by the clinician can be helpful. However, the basic goal of the interview is to identify specific problem behaviors, situational factors that maintain the problem behavior, and the consequences that result from the problem behavior. It should also be noted that the use of structured diagnostic interviews (see Chapter 6) is increasing among behavioral clinicians, who

PROFILE 9-1

Stephen N. Haynes, Ph.D.

Dr. Stephen N. Haynes is a Professor of Psychology at the University of Hawaii, where he previously served as Director of the Clinical Psychology program. Dr. Haynes is an internationally recognized expert in behavioral assessment, psychological test development and evaluation, and health psychology. In addition to publishing more than 100 articles and book chapters, Dr. Haynes has authored several books on these topics. Currently, Dr. Haynes serves as editor of the journal *Psychological Assessment*, and he is on the editorial board of other major clinical psychology journals as well.

Dr. Haynes provided the following responses to our questions about his background, interests, and viewpoints.

What originally got you interested in the field of clinical psychology?

My commitment to psychology as a career occurred in Kalamazoo, Michigan, on a clear, crisp spring day during my sophomore year in high school. I was drawn to questions about my environment when I was in high school. I contemplated air flow around falling leaves, why water circled during its drain exits, and why girls behaved the way they did. In the spring semester of my sophomore year, I encountered Ms. Mountjoy, a new teacher

who taught a one-semester course in psychology. We had intriguing and hilarious discussions of sex, how people learned and remembered things, and how they formed attitudes and cried. We were able to make Ms. Mountjoy blush almost daily. Psychology was a fascinating application of science, and it was the most interesting and fun thing I did in high school. It was a Tuesday morning in April of that sophomore year that I decided that clinical psychology was something I could make a career of.

Describe what activities you are involved in as a clinical psychologist.

My current scholarly activities mostly involve research in clinical psychopathology and clinical assessment. I am involved in psychopathology research on the causes of sleep disorders in persons who have experienced trauma (such as sexual assault or war trauma), on the effects of chronic pain on sleep, mood, and social interactions, on the psychosocial correlates of cardiovascular disorders, and on the triggers of migraine headaches.

My assessment research involves the development of assessment instruments to measure important personal and social problems. The valid measurement of these problems is a necessary antecedent to good research and treatment. Current research projects involve measurement of the responses of persons who have experienced traumatic life events, the areas of satisfaction and dissatisfaction of married persons, physical abuse of wives by husbands, dating aggression among high-school students, and parent-child interactions in families with children with learning disabilities.

The best aspect of my research is that it occurs in collaboration with many excellent and fun colleagues and graduate and undergraduate students. Many of the projects are directed by graduate students and are often used as their theses and dissertations. Typically,

(continued)

Profile 9-1 *(continued)*

each graduate student functions as a principal investigator and has a team of undergraduates working for him/her.

I also teach behavioral assessment courses to graduate students. We learn behavioral interviewing, observation, self-monitoring, and psychophysiological assessment. In these courses, we study scientific principles of psychological assessment and apply these principles to the evaluation of families who are having significant troubles with their children. The goal of the assessment is to specify the problems in the family and, most important, identify the causes of these troubles so that they can be treated.

I also enjoy editing and writing. I am editor of *Psychological Assessment*. We review about 320 manuscripts a year. It is a humbling experience, in that I am continually confronted with the limits of my knowledge and the impressive expertise of many assessment scholars and reviewers. I just finished a book with William O'Brien on behavioral assessment to be published by Plenum Press.

I don't do private therapy, but I do work with the family court system as a volunteer guardian for abused/neglected children. This mostly involves the use of behavioral assessment methods in the community—home observations, school observations, interviews—in order to make judgments about the safety and best placement of children.

I also work with many other excellent professionals in the community to help them develop measurement strategies and designs for their clinical research.

What are your particular areas of expertise or interest?

As I noted above, the areas in which I feel competent continue to shrink as I encounter the expertise of others. I would say that I am mildly to moderately familiar with methods of

developing and evaluating assessment instruments, principles of clinical judgment derived from assessment information (such as functional analysis), measurement principles, and research designs, including single-subject time-series designs. The content areas that I am most familiar with include health psychology (sleep disorders, cardiovascular disorders, chronic pain), experimental psychopathology, and marital distress.

What are the future trends you see for clinical psychology?

There are many; most are based on the advancement of the scientific aspects of clinical psychology. The advancement of the field will be associated with continued research and a scholarly approach to clinical psychology, particularly clinical assessment, as well as changes in the methods of service delivery. Trends include:

1. An increasing emphasis on empirically validated treatments and the use of empirically validated assessment instruments.
2. An emphasis on clinical case formulation to select the best treatments.
3. An emphasis on ongoing evaluation of treatment outcome (time-series measurements), using valid measures.
4. In assessment, increasing use of alternative assessment strategies, such as hand-held computers, computerized interviews, analog clinical observations, and specifically focused questionnaires.

The focus of the discipline is also likely to change:

1. An emphasis on the Ph.D. as a clinical supervisor and administrator.
2. A reduction in the number of expensive Psy.D. programs because of decreased payoff for the Psy.D. in private practice.

What future trends do you see in behavioral assessment?

1. Continued integration with mainstream psychology. Note that most articles in the *Journal of Consulting and Clinical Psychology* use some form of behavioral assessment method now, compared to approximately 0% in the 1960s.
2. Increasing use of computer technology—for example, ambulatory monitoring, hand-held computers for self-monitoring, instrumentation in other ways (such as monitoring medication use or exercise).
3. Increasing use of analog clinic assessment—observation of parent-child interac-

tions, marital interactions, social skills of abusive spouses.
4. More cost-efficient assessment: use of above procedures with less time involvement.
5. Increased understanding of sources of error in measurement and ways to control for measurement errors; a continued emphasis on a scholarly, empirically grounded approach to psychological assessment.
6. Increasing sophistication in the functional analysis of clients (clinical case formulation) and matching treatments to the functional analysis.

view the symptoms of mental disorders as problematic behaviors targeted for intervention (Morrison, 1988).

Observation Methods

Naturalistic Observation

To assess and understand behavior, one must first know what one is dealing with. It comes as no surprise, then, that behavioral assessment employs *observation* as a primary technique. A clinician can try to understand a phobic's fear of heights, a student's avoidance of evaluation settings, or anyone's tendency to overeat. These people could be interviewed or assessed with self-report inventories. But many clinicians would argue that unless those people are directly observed in their natural environments, true understanding will be incomplete. To determine the frequency, strength, and pervasiveness of the problem behavior or the factors that are maintaining it, behavioral clinicians advocate direct observation.

Of course, all this is easier said than done. Practically speaking, it is difficult and expensive to maintain trained observers and have them available. This is especially true in the case of

adults who are being treated on an outpatient basis. It is relatively easier to accomplish with children or those with cognitive limitations. It is likewise easier to make observations in a sheltered or institutional setting. In some cases, it is possible to use observers who are characteristically part of the person's environment (such as spouse, parent, teacher, friend, or nurse). In certain instances, as we shall see later, it is even possible to have the client do some self-observation. Of course, there is the ever-present question of ethics. Clinical psychologists must take pains to make sure that people are not observed without their knowledge or that friends and associates of the client are not unwittingly drawn into the observational net in a way that compromises their dignity and right to privacy.

For all these reasons, naturalistic observation has never been used in clinical practice as much as it might be. Indeed, observation is still more prominent in research than in clinical practice. However, one need not be a diehard proponent of the behavioral approach to concede the importance of observational data. It is not unlikely that clinicians of many different persuasions have arrived at incomplete pictures of their clients. After all, they may never see them except during the 50-minute therapy hour or through the prism of objective or projective test data. But because of the cumbersome nature of many observational procedures, for years most clinicians opted for the simpler and seemingly more efficient methods of traditional assessment.

Naturalistic observation is hardly a new idea. McReynolds (1975) traced the roots of naturalistic observation to the ancient civilizations of Greece and China. About 50 years ago, Barker and Wright (1951) described their systematic and detailed recordings of the behavior of a 7-year-old over one day (a major effort that took an entire book). Beyond this, all of us recognize instantly that our own informal assessments of friends and associates are heavily influenced by observations of their naturally occurring behavior. But observation, like testing, is useful only when steps are taken to ensure its reliability and validity. As we pursue these topics, the reader may notice that a number of the factors that affect the reliability and validity of observations are basically the same as those discussed in connection with the interview (see Chapter 6).

Examples of Naturalistic Observation

Over the years, many forms of naturalistic observation have been used for specific settings. These settings have included classrooms, playgrounds, general and psychiatric hospitals, home environments, institutions for those with mental retardation, and therapy sessions in outpatient clinics. Again, it is important to note that many of the systems employed in these settings have been most widely used for research purposes. But most of them are adaptable for clinical use.

Home Observation. Because experiences in the family or home have such pervasive effects on adjustment, it is not surprising that a number of assessment procedures have been developed for behaviors occurring in this setting. One of the best known systems for *home observation* is the Behavioral Coding System (BCS) developed by Patterson (1977) and his colleagues (Jones, Reid, & Patterson, 1975). This observational system was designed for use in the homes of predelinquent boys who exhibit problems in the areas of

aggressiveness and noncompliance. Trained observers spend one or two hours in the homes of such boys, observing and recording family interactions. Usually the observations are made immediately before or during dinner. Observers are not allowed to interact with family members (although occasionally they may talk with them before or after the observations to gain better acceptance of the procedure). Each family member is observed for two 5-minute periods during each observational occasion. Observations are made of behaviors in 28 categories, and every 6 seconds during the period a given family member is being observed, the observer notes whether these behaviors have or have not occurred. Figure 9-2 shows a sample BCS coding sheet. The 6-second subintervals are shown within each row of the sheet, and each row represents a 30-second interval. Among the 28 categories rated are

HU (Humiliate): Makes fun of, shames, or embarrasses the individual intentionally.

CO (Compliance): A person immediately does what is asked of him or her.

WH (Whine): A person states something in a slurring, nasal, high-pitched, falsetto voice.

In a recent study, Patterson and Forgatch (1995) reported observational data—in this case, the sum of multiple categories of aversive behavior (such as yelling, humiliating, destructiveness)—coded from home interactions between 67 children and their respective families. All these children had been referred for treatment because of antisocial behavior problems. Interestingly, Patterson and Forgatch (1995) found that children's aversive behavior scores at treatment termination significantly predicted future arrests over the two-year follow-up period. In contrast, no teacher, mother, or father rating of the children at termination significantly predicted arrests. Thus, in this study, the predictive value of naturalistic observation (over more traditional ratings by parents or teachers) was demonstrated.

School Observation. Clinical child psychologists must often deal with behavior problems that take place in the school setting; some chil-

FIGURE 9-2 A blank sample coding sheet for the BCS
SOURCE: From "Naturalistic Observation in Clinical Assessment," by R. R. Jones, J. B. Reid, and G. R. Patterson. In P. McReynolds (Ed.), Advances in Psychological Assessment, Vol. 3, p. 56. Copyright © 1975 by Jossey-Bass, Inc. Reprinted by permission.

BLANK SAMPLE CODING SHEET FOR THE BCS

Family Number _____

ID Number _____

BEHAVIOR CODING SHEET

Phase _____

Subject _____ Observer _____ Date _____ No._____

AP	Approval	HU	Humiliate	PP	Positive physical contact
AT	Attention	IG	Ignore		
CM	Command	LA	Laugh	RC	Receive
CN	Command (negative)	NC	Noncompliance	SS	Self-stimulation
		NE	Negativism	TA	Talk
CO	Compliance	NO	Normative	TE	Tease
CR	Cry	NR	No response	TH	Touching, handling
DI	Disapproval	PL	Play		
DP	Dependency	PN	Negative physical contact	WH	Whine
DS	Destructiveness			WK	Work
HR	High rate			YE	Yell

1				
2				
• • •				
10				

Description _____

---

dren are disruptive in class, overly aggressive on the playground, generally fearful, cling to the teacher, will not concentrate, and so on. Although the verbal reports of parents and teachers are useful, the most direct assessment procedure is actually to observe the problem behavior in its natural habitat. Several coding systems have been developed over the years for use in *school observation.*

An example of a behavioral observation system used in school settings is Achenbach's (1994) Direct Observation Form (DOF) of the Child Behavior checklist. The DOF is used to assess problem behaviors that may be observed in school classrooms or other settings (Achenbach, 1994). It consists of 96 problem items, as well as an open-ended item that allows assessors to indicate problem behaviors not covered by these items. Assessors are instructed to rate each item according to its frequency, duration, and intensity within a 10-minute observation period. It is recommended that three to six 10-minute observation periods be completed, so that scores can be averaged across occasions (Achenbach, 1994). In this way, a more reliable and stable estimate of the child's level of behavior problems in the classroom can be obtained. Table 9-2 provides sample items from the DOF.

TABLE 9-2 Sample Items from the Direct Observation Form (DOF) of the Child Behavior Checklist

Externalizing Behavior Problems

1. Argues

2. Defiant or talks back to staff

3. Cruelty, bullying, or meanness

4. Disturbs other children

5. Physically attacks people

6. Disrupts group activities

Internalizing Behavior Problem

1. Nervous movements or twitching

2. Apathetic, unmotivated, or won't try

3. Shy or timid behavior

4. Stares blankly

5. Unhappy, sad, or depressed

6. Withdrawn, doesn't get involved with others

Note: All items are rated on a scale of 0 to 3 for the specified observation period. 0 = not observed; 1 = very slight or ambiguous occurrence; 2 = definite occurrence with mild to moderate intensity and less than 3 minutes duration; 3 = definite occurrence with severe intensity or greater than 3 minutes duration.

Source: Copyright 1986. T. M. Achenbach; Center for Children, Youth, and Families; University of Vermont, 1 South Prospect Street, Burlington, VT 05401. Reprinted with permission.

Hospital Observation. Observation techniques have long been used in such settings as psychiatric hospitals and institutions for those with mental retardation. The sheltered characteristics of these settings have made careful observation of behavior much more feasible than in more open, uncontrolled environments.

An example of a *hospital observation* device is the Time Sample Behavioral Checklist (TSBC) developed by Gordon Paul and his associates (Mariotto & Paul, 1974). It is a time-sample behavioral checklist that can be used with chronic psychiatric patients. By time-sample is meant that observations are made at regular intervals for a given patient. Observers make a single 2-second observation of the patient once every waking hour. Thus, a daily behavioral profile can be constructed on each patient. Interobserver reliability for this checklist has typically been

quite high, and such scales as the TSBC are helpful in providing a comprehensive behavioral picture of the patient. For example, using the TSBC, Menditto et al. (1996) documented how a combination of a relatively new antipsychotic medication (clozapine) and a structured social learning program (Paul & Lentz, 1977) helped significantly decrease the frequency of inappropriate behaviors and aggressive acts over a 6-month period in a sample of chronically mentally ill patients on an inpatient unit.

Controlled Observation

Naturalistic observation has a great deal of intuitive appeal. It provides a picture of how individuals actually behave that is unfiltered by self-reports, inferences, or other potentially contaminating variables. However, this is easier said than done. Sometimes the specific kind of behavior in which clinicians are interested does not occur naturally very often. Much time and resources can be wasted waiting for the right behavior or situation to happen. The assessment of responsibility-taking, for example, may require day after day of expensive observation before the right situation arises. Then, just as the clinician is about to start recording, some unexpected "other" figure in the environment may step in to spoil the situation by subtly changing its whole character. Furthermore, in free-flowing, spontaneous situations, the client may move away so that conversations cannot be overheard, or the entire scene may move down the hall too quickly to be followed. In short, naturalistic settings often put clinicians at the mercy of events that can sometimes overwhelm opportunities for careful, objective assessment. As a way of handling these problems, clinicians sometimes use *controlled observation.*

For many years, researchers have used techniques to elicit controlled samples of behavior (Lanyon & Goodstein, 1982). These are really *situational tests* that put individuals in situations more or less similar to those of real life. Direct observations are then made of how the individuals react. In a sense, this is a kind of work-sample approach in which the behavioral test situation and the criterion behavior to be predicted are quite similar. This should reduce errors in prediction, as contrasted, for example, to psychological tests whose stimuli are far removed from the predictive situations.

Studies in Honesty and Deceit. Early arrivals on this scene were the studies of Hartshorne and May and their associates (1928, 1929, 1930). Although Hartshorne and May were oriented principally toward research, the approaches they used have found direct application in the assessment field. Because Hartshorne and May viewed personality or character in habit-response terms, they attempted to measure it by directly sampling behavior. For example, if one wants to assess children's honesty, why not do so by confronting them with situations where cheating is

possible and then observe their responses? This is exactly what Hartshorne and May did in assessing such behaviors as cheating, lying, and stealing. Using a series of ingenious natural settings, they were able to execute their research under disguised yet highly controlled conditions. Of particular interest were data that suggested that children's deceitful behavior was highly situation-specific and should not be construed as reflecting a generalized trait.

Response to Stress. During World War II, the urgent demand for highly trained and resourceful military intelligence personnel led to the development of a series of situational stress tests. Instead of using personality tests to assess the manner in which the individual might handle disruptive or emotionally stressful situations, the U.S. Office of Strategic Services used assigned tasks (OSS Assessment Staff, 1948). Through both objective records and qualitative observation by trained staff, the assessment of reaction to stress was undertaken. Although the demands of war did not provide many good opportunities for the strict validation of OSS assessment techniques, they did provide an excellent model of what is possible in assessment. A sample OSS task is the following:

> A large cube had to be constructed out of pegs, poles, and blocks. Since the job could not be done by one person alone, two helpers were provided—but the task had to be completed in 10 minutes. The helpers were actually stooges who interfered, were passive, made impractical suggestions, and the like. They ridiculed the candidate and generally frustrated him terribly. In fact, no candidate was ever successful in assembling the cube.

Somewhat related techniques were used in selecting candidates for the British Civil Service (Vernon, 1950). Although stress was not incorporated into the British procedures, the tasks on which candidates worked prior to their selection were based on careful job analyses. L. V. Gordon (1967) has evaluated several work-sample

■ **TABLE 9-3** Sample Codes and Definitions from the Interaction Behavior Code (IBC)

Negative Behavior

1. *Yelling*—raising the volume of one's voice in an angry manner.

2. *Name-calling*—applying a name to the other person that connotes something negative. Must be a noun.

3. *Mind-reading*—stating or attributing beliefs to the other person.

Positive Behavior

1. *Making suggestions*—offering solutions and possible ideas (without demanding) of things that can be done differently in the future.

2. *Asking what the other would like*—attempting to find out what the other person wants, expects, or prefers.

3. *Compromise*—modifying original intentions or preferences, willingness to do so.

Each code is rated according to whether it occurred during the time frame of interest.

Source: Reprinted with permission of author, Dr. Ronald J. Prinz.

approaches to assessment used in the prediction of the performance of Peace Corps trainees.

Parent-Adolescent Conflict. In order to more accurately assess the nature and degree of parent-adolescent conflict, Prinz and Kent (1978) developed the Interaction Behavior Code (IBC) system. Using the IBC, several raters review and rate audiotaped discussions of families attempting to resolve a problem about which they disagree. Items are rated separately for each family member according to the behavior's presence or absence during the discussion (or for some items, the degree to which they are present). Summary scores are calculated by averaging scores (across raters) for negative behaviors and positive behaviors. Table 9-3 presents a sample of the codes and definitions from the IBC.

For the strict behaviorist, of course, the preceding techniques represent a mixture of observation and inference. When ratings of leadership, stress level, or ingenuity are made, what is really happening is that observers are inferring something from behavior. They are not just compiling lists of behaviors or checking off occurrences.

Controlled Performance Techniques

As seen in the OSS assessment studies, contrived situations allow one to observe behavior under conditions that offer potential for control and standardization. A more exotic example is the case in which A. A. Lazarus (1961) assessed claustrophobic behavior by placing a patient in a closed room that was made progressively smaller by moving a screen. Similarly, Bandura (1969) has used films to expose people to a graduated series of anxiety-provoking stimuli.

A series of assessment procedures using *controlled performance techniques* to study chronic snake phobias illustrates several approaches to this kind of measurement (Bandura, Adams, & Beyer, 1977):

Behavioral avoidance. The test of avoidance behavior consisted of a series of 29 performance tasks requiring increasingly more threatening interactions with a red-tailed boa constrictor. Subjects were instructed to approach a glass cage containing the snake, to look down at it, to touch and hold the snake with gloved and then bare hands, to let it loose in the room and then return it to

Clinical psychologists can use various assessment devices to observe and rate the degree of conflict between parents and adolescents.
© *CORBIS*

the cage, to hold it within 12 cm of their faces, and finally to tolerate the snake crawling in their laps while they held their hands passively at their sides. . . . Those who could not enter the room containing the snake received a score of 0; subjects who did enter were asked to perform the various tasks in the graded series. To control for any possible influence of expressive cues from the tester, she stood behind the subject and read aloud the tasks to be performed. . . . The avoidance score was the number of snake-interaction tasks the subject performed successfully.

Fear arousal accompanying approach responses. In addition to the measurement of performance capabilities, the degree of fear

aroused by each approach response was assessed. During the behavioral test, subjects rated orally, on a IQ-interval scale, the intensity of fear they experienced when each snake approach task was described to them and again while they were performing the corresponding behavior. (pp. 127–128)

It is especially important that the demand characteristics of the situation be carefully examined. Behavior in these stressful situations may not be at all typical of a patient's real-life behavior. The presence of the clinician, combined with a trusting attitude that such a clinician will not permit harm to come to the patient, may significantly distort the reality of the situation.

In some cases, psychophysiological assessment procedures have been employed for both clinical and research purposes (Sturgis & Gramling, 1988). *Psychophysiological measures* are used to assess unobtrusively central nervous system, autonomic nervous system, or skeletomotor activity (Tomarken, 1995). These measures have been used in the assessment of a host of clinical conditions, including anxiety, stress, and schizophrenia. Clinical psychologists typically use psychophysiological measures to complement other, more traditional forms of assessment. The advantage of psychophysiological measures is that they may assess processes (such as emotional responsivity) that are not directly assessed by self-report or behavioral measures, and they tend to be more sensitive measures of these processes than alternative measures (Tomarken, 1995). Examples of psychophysiological measures include event-related potentials (ERPs), electromyographic (EMG) activity, electroencephalographic (EEG) activity, and electrodermal activity (EDA). Although these measures do offer some advantages to the clinician, they are still subject to the same psychometric considerations of reliability and validity as other, more traditional clinical assessment techniques (Tomarken, 1995).

Self-Monitoring

In the previous discussion of naturalistic observation, the observational procedures were designed for use by trained staff: clinicians, research assistants, teachers, nurses, ward attendants, and others. But such procedures are often expensive in both time and money. Furthermore, it is necessary in most cases to rely on time-sampling or otherwise limit the extent of the observations. When dealing with individual clients, it is often impractical or too expensive to observe them as they move freely about in their daily activities. Therefore, clinicians have been relying increasingly on *self-monitoring*, in which individuals observe and record their own behaviors, thoughts, and emotions (Ciminero, Calhoun, & Adams, 1986; Mahoney, 1977b).

In effect, clients are asked to maintain behavioral logs or diaries over some predetermined time period. Such a log can provide a running record of the frequency, intensity, and duration of certain target behaviors, along with the stimulus conditions that accompanied them and the consequences that followed. Such data are especially useful in telling both clinician and client how often the behavior in question occurs. In addition, it can provide an index of change as a result of therapy (for example, by comparing baseline frequency with frequency after six weeks of therapy). Also, it can help focus the client's attention on undesirable behavior and thus aid in reducing it. Finally, clients can come to realize the connections between environmental stimuli, the consequences of their behavior, and the behavior itself.

Of course, there are problems with self-monitoring. Some clients may be inaccurate or may purposely distort their observations or recordings for various reasons. Others may simply resist the whole procedure. Despite these obvious difficulties, self-monitoring has become a useful and efficient technique. It can provide a great deal of information at very low cost. However, self-monitoring is usually effective as a change agent only in conjunction with a larger program of therapeutic intervention.

A variety of monitoring aids has been developed. Some clients are provided with small counters or stopwatches, depending upon what is to be monitored. Small file-sized or wallet-sized cards have been developed upon which clients can quickly and unobtrusively record their data. At a more informal level, some clients are simply encouraged to make entries in a diary. Such aids are especially useful when assessing or treating such problems as obesity, smoking, lack of assertiveness, and alcoholism. These aids can help reinforce the notion that one's problems can be reduced to specific behaviors. Thus, a client who started with global complaints of an ephemeral nature can begin to see that "not feeling good about myself" really involves inability to stand up for one's rights in specific circumstances, speaking without thinking, or whatever. An example of a self-monitoring log—in this case, a dysfunctional thought record—is shown in Figure 9-3.

FIGURE 9-3 An Example of a Dysfunctional Thought Record

SOURCE: Beck, J. S. (1995). Cognitive Therapy: Basics and Beyond. New York: Guilford. Reprinted with permission.

Directions: When you notice your mood getting worse, ask yourself, "What's going through my mind right now?" and as soon as possible jot down the thought or mental image in the Automatic Thought column.

Date/time	Situation	Automatic thought(s)	Emotion(s)	Adaptive response	Outcome
	1. What actual event or stream of thoughts, or daydreams or recollection led to the unpleasant emotion? 2. What (if any) distressing physical sensations did you have?	1. What thought(s) and/or image(s) went through your mind? 2. How much did you believe each one at the time?	1. What emotion(s) (sad/anxious/angry/etc.) did you feel at the time? 2. How intense (0–100%) was the emotion?	1. (optional) What cognitive distortion did you make? 2. Use questions at bottom to compose a response to the automatic thought(s). 3. How much do you believe each response?	1. How much do you now believe each automatic thought? 2. What emotion(s) do you feel now? How intense (0–100%) is the emotion? 3. What will you do (or did you do)?
Friday 2/25 10 A.M.	Talking on the phone with Donna.	She must not like me any more. 90%	Sad 80%		
Tuesday 2/27 12 P.M.	Studying for my exam.	I'll never learn this. 100%	Sad 95%		
Thursday 2/29 5 P.M.	Thinking about my economics class tomorrow.	I might get called on and I won't give a good answer. 80%	Anxious 80%		
	Noticing my heart beating fast and my trouble concentrating.	What's wrong with me?	Anxious 80%		

Questions to help compose an alternative response: (1) What is the evidence that the automatic thought is true? Not true? (2) Is there an alternative explanation? (3) What's the worst that could happen? Could I live through it? What's the best that could happen? What's the most realistic outcome? (4) What's the effect of my believing the automatic thought? What could be the effect of my changing my thinking? (5) What should I do about it? (6) If _____ [friend's name] was in the situation and had this thought, what would I tell him/her?

The dysfunctional thought record (DTR) is completed by the client and provides the client and therapist with a record of the client's automatic thoughts that are related to dysphoria or depression (J. S. Beck, 1995). This DTR can help the therapist and client target certain thoughts and reactions for change in a cognitive-behavioral treatment for depression. The client is instructed to complete the DTR when she or he notices a change in mood. The situation, automatic thought(s), and associated emotions are specified. The final two columns of the DTR can be filled out in the therapy session and serve as a therapeutic intervention. In this way, clients are taught to recognize, evaluate, and modify these automatic dysfunctional thoughts.

Variables Affecting Reliability of Observations

Whether their data come from interviewing, testing, or observation, clinicians must be assured that the data are reliable. In the case of observation, clinicians must have confidence that different observers will produce basically the same ratings and scores. For example, when an observer of interactions in the home returns with ratings of a spouse's behavior as "low in empathy," what assurance does the clinician have that someone else rating the same behavior in the same circumstances would have made the same report? Many factors can affect the reliability of observations. The following is a good sample of these factors.

Complexity of Target Behavior. Obviously, the more complex the behavior to be observed, the greater the opportunity for unreliability. Behavioral assessment typically focuses on less complex, lower-level behaviors (Haynes, 1998). Observations about what a person eats for breakfast (lower-level behavior) are likely to be more reliable than those centering on interpersonal behavior (higher-level, more complex behavior). This applies to self-monitoring as well. Unless specific agreed-upon behaviors are designated, the observer has an enormous range of behavior upon which to concentrate. Thus, to identify an

instance of interpersonal aggression, one observer might react to sarcasm while another would fail to include it and focus instead on clear, physical acts.

Training Observers. There is no substitute for the careful and systematic training of observers (Foster, Bell-Dolan, & Burge, 1988; Tryon, 1998). For example, observers who are sent into psychiatric hospitals to study patient behaviors and then make diagnostic ratings must be carefully prepared in advance. It is necessary to brief them extensively on just what the definition of, say, depression is, what specific behaviors represent depression, and so on. Their goal should not be to "please" their supervisor by coming up (consciously or unconsciously) with data "helpful" to the project. Nor should they protect one another by talking over their ratings and then "agreeing to agree."

Occasionally there are instances of *observer drift*, in which observers who work closely together subtly, without awareness, begin to drift away from other observers in their ratings. Although reliability among the drifting observers may be acceptable, it is only so because, over time, they have begun to shift their definitions of target behaviors (Kent & Foster, 1977). Occasionally, too, observers are not as careful in their observations when they feel they are on their own as when they expect to be monitored or checked (Reid, 1970). To guard against observer drift, regularly scheduled reliability checks (by an independent rater) should be conducted and feedback provided to raters.

Variables Affecting Validity of Observations

At this point, it seems unnecessary to reiterate the importance of validity. We have encountered the concept before in our discussions of both interviewing and testing; it is no less critical in the case of observation. But here, issues of validity can be deceptive. It seems obvious in interviewing that what patients tell the interviewer may not correspond to their actual behavior in noninterview settings. Or in the case of projective tests, there may be validity questions about inferring aggression from Rorschach responses that involve vicious animals, blood, or large teeth. After all, percepts are not the same as "real" behavior. But in the case of observation, things seem much clearer. When a child is observed to bully his peers unmercifully and these observations are corroborated by reports from teachers, there would seem to be little question of the validity of the observers' data. Aggression is aggression! However, things are not always so simple, as the following discussion will illustrate.

Content Validity. A behavioral observation schema should include the behaviors that are deemed important for the research or clinical purposes at hand. Usually the investigator or clinician who develops the system also determines whether or not the system shows content validity. But this process is almost circular, in the sense that a system is valid if the clinician decides that it is valid. In developing the Behavioral Coding System (BCS), Jones et al. (1975) circumvented this problem by organizing several categories of noxious behaviors in children and then submitting them for ratings. By using mothers' ratings, they were able to confirm their own a priori clinical judgments as to whether or not certain deviant behaviors were in fact noxious or aversive.

Concurrent Validity. Another way to approach the validity of observations is to ask whether one's obtained observational ratings correspond to what others (such as teachers, spouse, friends) are observing in the same time frame. For example, do observational ratings of children's aggression on the playground made by trained observers agree with the ratings made by the children's peers? In short, do the children perceive each other's aggression in the same way that observers do?

Construct Validity. Observational systems are usually derived from some implicit or explicit theoretical framework. For example, the BCS of Jones et al. (1975) was derived from a social learning framework that sees aggression as the re-

sult of learning in the family. When the rewards for aggression are substantial, aggression will occur. When such rewards are no longer contingent on the behavior, aggression should subside. Therefore, the construct validity of the BCS could be demonstrated by showing that children's aggressive behavior declines from a baseline point after clinical treatment, with clinical treatment defined as rearranging the social contingencies in the family in a way that ought to reduce the incidence of observed aggression.

Mechanics of Rating. It is important that a *unit of analysis* be specified (Tryon, 1998). A unit of analysis is the length of time observations will be made, along with the type and number of responses to be considered. For example, it might be decided that every physical movement or gesture will be recorded for 1 minute every 4 minutes. The total observational time might consist of a 20-minute recess period for kindergarten children. This means that every 4 minutes the child would be observed for 1 minute and all physical movements recorded. These movements would then be coded or rated for the variable under study (such as aggression, problem solving, or dependency).

In addition to the units of analysis chosen, the specific form that the ratings will take must also be decided. One could decide to record behaviors along a dimension of *intensity*: How strong was the aggressive behavior? One might also include a *duration* record: How long did the behavior last? Or one might use a simple *frequency* count: How many times in a designated period did the behavior under study occur?

Beyond this, a scoring procedure must be developed. Such procedures can range from making check marks on a sheet of paper attached to a clipboard to the use of counters, stopwatches, timers, and even laptop computers. All raters, of course, will employ the same procedure.

Observer Error. No one is perfect. Observers must be monitored from time to time to ensure the accuracy of their reports. Sometimes they simply miss things or else believe they have observed things that never really happened. A child's yell may be accidentally attributed to the wrong child. Or perhaps the yell is coded as verbal aggression when actually it represented a kind of camaraderie. In other cases, it may not be error so much as bias. For some reason, an observer may not like a person in a family being observed. That observer may then be prone to provide a less than flattering rating for that person whenever the opportunity arises. It sometimes happens that a person being observed does something early in the observational sequence—solving a problem quickly, perhaps, or making an intelligent remark—that the observer reacts to. The result is a kind of halo effect, so that later the observer is more likely to assign favorable ratings to that person. Whatever the nature of the potential bias or error, it is important to hold careful training sessions for observers in advance, along with periodic review sessions, to help keep these sources of trouble in check.

Reactivity. Another factor affecting the validity of observations is called *reactivity*. Patients or study participants sometimes react to the fact that they are being observed by changing the way they behave. The talkative person suddenly becomes quiet. The complaining spouse suddenly becomes the epitome of self-sacrifice. Sometimes an individual may even feel the need to apologize for the dog by saying, "He never does that when he is alone with us." In any case, reactivity can severely hamper the validity of observations because it makes the observed behavior unrepresentative of what normally occurs. The real danger of reactivity is that the observer may not recognize its presence. If observed behavior is not a true sample, this affects the extent to which one can generalize from this instance of behavior. Then, too, observers may unwittingly interfere with or influence the very behavior they are sent to observe. In the case of sexual dysfunction, for example, Conte (1986) has noted that behavioral ratings are so intrusive that clinicians usually have to rely on self-report methods.

Ecological Validity. One of the biggest problems in psychology (and one that has never been fully resolved) is what Brunswik (1947) referred to many years ago as *ecological validity*. The basic question is whether or not clinicians do obtain really representative samples of behavior. Is the client's behavior today typical, or is it the product of some uncharacteristic stimulus? Such a question goes beyond simple reactivity. It asks whether or not observers have a large-enough sample to assure that their observations will be truly representative. It is doubtful that any one piece of behavior will be typical of a given client. This being so, is the sample of 4 or 10 or 20 instances the proper number? All areas of psychology have long grappled with this problem. Is one experiment on altruism a good-enough sample of all possible situations to allow psychologists to make generalizations about it? Are responses to three TAT cards enough of a sample to permit sweeping generalizations about the client's need structure? Are observations of hospitalized patients about to undergo surgery general enough to suggest how these patients might react to other stressful situations?

Suggestions for Improving Reliability and Validity of Observations

The following suggestions are offered as ways to improve the reliability and validity of observational procedures. Like similar suggestions made for interviews (see Chapter 6), they often cannot be fully implemented in clinical situations. Nevertheless, an awareness of these points may help focus the clinician's attention in directions that will improve the validity of observations.

1. Decide on target behaviors that are both relevant and comprehensive. Specify direct and observable behaviors that can be defined objectively.
2. In specifying these behaviors, work as much as possible from an explicit theoretical framework that will help define the behaviors of interest.
3. Employ trained observers whose reliability has been established and who are familiar with the objective, standardized observational format to be used.

4. Make sure that the observational format is strictly specified, including the units of analysis, the form in which observers' ratings will be made, the exact observational procedures, the scoring scheme, and the observational schedule to be followed.

5. Be aware of such potential sources of error in the observations as bias and fluctuations in concentration.

6. Consider the possibility of reactivity on the part of those being observed and the general influence of awareness that they are being observed.

7. Finally, give careful consideration to issues of how representative the observations really are and how much one can generalize from them to behavior in other settings.

Contemporary Trends in Data Acquisition

Haynes (1998) has recently outlined several ways in which technological advances have begun to change the face of behavioral assessment methods that involve observation. First, the availability of laptop and hand-held computers facilitates the coding of observational data by assessors. Second, hand-held computers can be assigned to clients so that clients can provide real-time self-monitoring data. One advantage of using hand-held computers is that they can be programmed to prompt clients to respond to queries at specified times of the day or night. Finally, data from either laptop or hand-held computers can be loaded onto other computers that have greater processing and memory capacity so that observations can be aggregated, scored, and analyzed. It is clear that behavioral assessors will continue to capitalize on future technological advances.

Role-Playing Methods

Role-playing is another technique that has been used in behavioral assessment for many years. Rotter and Wickens (1948) suggested this procedure for behavioral assessment many years ago. Goldfried (1976) catalogs several instances in

which role-playing has been used, particularly in the area of assertiveness training. Goldfried and Davison (1994) also discuss role-playing or *behavioral rehearsal* as a means of training new response patterns. Although role-playing is an old clinical technique, behavioral assessors have carried out few systematic studies on the methodological problems inherent in the technique as a means of assessment—among them, demand characteristics, standardization of procedures, rater halo effects, and sampling problems involved in role selections.

Role-playing has been widely used in the assessment of social skills and assertiveness. In a study of social skills in shy men, for example, Twentyman and McFall (1975) developed six social behavior situations that required the individual to play a role. Participants were instructed to respond aloud as they would were they actually in the situation described to them. For example:

> You are on a break at your job. You see a girl [sic] who is about your age at the canteen. She works in another part of the store, and consequently you don't know her very well. You would like to talk to her. What would you say? (p. 386)

Once the individual began speaking, a trained female assistant responded to his efforts. The conversation continued until the participant terminated the conversation or 3 minutes had gone by.

McFall and Lillesand (1971) also used role playing in assessing assertiveness. Individuals were asked to respond aloud to nine prerecorded stimuli. For example:

> *Narrator:* A person you do not know very well is going home for the weekend. He, or she, has some books which are due at the library and asks if you would take them back so they won't be overdue. From where you live it is a twenty-five minute walk to the library, the books are heavy, and you hadn't planned on going near the library that weekend. What do you say? (Subject responds aloud.) (p. 315)

Obviously, role-playing techniques are not new. They have been used as therapeutic devices for many years (for example, Kelly, 1955; Moreno, 1946). The behaviorally oriented clinician is interested in role-playing techniques because they provide a simple, efficient means of sampling the client's behavioral skills and deficits. However, we cannot assume that the behavioral skills developed in the therapy room are practiced consistently in the real world.

Inventories and Checklists

Behavioral clinicians have used a variety of self-report techniques to identify behaviors, emotional responses, and perceptions of the environment. The Fear Survey Schedule (Geer, 1965; Lang & Lazovik, 1963) has been widely used. It consists of 51 potentially fear-arousing situations and requires the patient to rate the degree of fear each situation arouses. Other frequently used self-report inventories include the Rathus Assertiveness Schedule (Rathus, 1973), the Beck Depression Inventory (Beck, 1972), the Youth Self Report (Achenbach, 1991), and the Marital Conflict Form (Weiss & Margolin, 1977).

Notably absent from this brief and partial listing of inventories are instruments that have a psychiatric diagnostic orientation. Historically, this has been a conscious omission on the part of behavioral assessors, who generally found little merit in psychiatric classification (Follette & Hayes, 1992). Their tests were more oriented toward the assessment of specific behavioral deficits, behavioral inappropriateness, and behavioral assets (Sundberg, 1977). The focus of behavioral inventories is, in short, behavior. Clients are asked about specific actions, feelings, or thoughts that minimize the necessity for them to make inferences about what their own behavior really means.

Inventories have also been developed that assess the person's perception of the social environment (Insel & Moos, 1974). The scales that Moos and his colleagues have developed attempt to assess environments in terms of the opportunities they provide for relationships, personal growth, and systems maintenance and change. There are separate scales for several environments, including work, family, classrooms, wards, and others.

Cognitive Behavioral Assessment

As we shall see in later chapters, behavioral approaches have become increasingly cognitively oriented (Goldfried & Davison, 1994; Meichenbaum, 1977). Cognitions along with behaviors are becoming the subject of intense study, as they relate to the development of a pathological situation, its maintenance, and changes in it (Kendall & Hollon, 1981). Central to this type of *cognitive behavioral assessment* is the notion that the client's cognitions and thoughts (from self-images to self-statements) play an important role in behavior (Brewin, 1988). Indeed, Meichenbaum (1977) advocates a *cognitive-functional approach*. In essence, this means that a functional analysis of the client's thinking processes must be made in order to plan an intervention strategy. A careful inventory of cognitive strategies must be undertaken to determine which cognitions (or lack of them) are aiding or interfering with adequate performance, and under what circumstances.

As Parks and Hollon (1988) note, a number of methods and procedures are available for assessing cognitive functioning. For example, clients can be instructed to "think aloud," or verbalize immediate thoughts; they can report their thoughts and feelings in reaction to prerecorded conversations of various types (such as stressful, social-evaluative situations); they can complete rating scales whose items target adaptive and maladaptive cognitions that may have occurred in the past; and they can list thoughts that occur in reaction to specific stimuli (such as topics or problems) that are presented.

A good example comes from work in which a task analysis of assertive behavior was made (Schwartz & Gottman, 1976). Cognitive self-statements as they relate to assertion situations were assessed by means of the Assertiveness Self-

Statement Test (ASST). This is a 34-item questionnaire, with 17 positive self-statements that would make it easier to refuse a request and 17 negative self-statements that would make it harder. For example:

> *Positive*: I was thinking that I am perfectly free to say no; I was thinking that this request is an unreasonable one.

> *Negative*: I was worried about what the other person would think of me if I refused; I was thinking that the other person might be hurt or insulted if I refused. (Schwartz & Gottman, 1976, p. 913)

Through such assessment, it becomes clearer exactly what role is being played by self-statements in the maintenance of problems such as lack of assertiveness.

Similar procedures can be applied to such problems as overeating, depression, and shyness. For example, to assess agoraphobics' fear of fear, Chambless, Caputo, Bright, and Gallagher (1984) have developed a scale comprising thoughts about negative consequences as one experiences anxiety. Another example of cognitive assessment comes from the work of Seligman et al. (1988). Using the Attributional Style Questionnaire, they found that healthier explanations for events occurred in depressive patients following a course of cognitive therapy.

Methods that assess multiple cognitive constructs at the same time are also available (Linscott & DiGiuseppe, 1998). For example, Davison, Robins, and Johnson (1983) have used a method in which participants listen to an audiotape that presents several problem situations. Every 10 or 15 seconds, the tape pauses so that the participants can report whatever is in their minds at that point. Results from numerous studies suggest that the method uncovers how people think about both difficult and innocuous situations (Davison & Neale, 1998), and it reveals cognitions related to a variety of conditions including depression, anxiety, family conflict, and aggression (Linscott & DiGiuseppe, 1998).

Concluding Comments

The field of behavioral assessment's use of more systematic and precise methods of evaluation is laudable. Behavioral assessors operationalize the clinical problem by specifying the behaviors targeted for intervention. Further, multiple assessments of these behaviors before, during, and following treatment are conducted. Finally, assessment results are used to inform or modify treatment. This is in contrast to "traditional" assessment in which, too often, assessment occurs only once, either before or in the beginning stages of treatment. In addition, it is often not clear how these assessment results influence treatment.

The precision and comprehensiveness of behavioral assessment methods, however, appear to be both a strength and a weakness. Many of these techniques have proved to be impractical in clinical settings. Some of the natural observation methods, as well as the psychophysiological methods of assessment, are quite time-intensive and expensive. Therefore, behavioral clinicians have begun to incorporate less time-intensive methods and measures into their assessments. For example, it is now quite common to administer some type of self-report inventory as part of the behavioral assessment battery. Granted, these inventories contain items of a more cognitive or behavioral nature than those found in traditional self-report inventories. However, all these measures assume that a patient's self-report conveys an accurate representation of his or her behavior or cognitive processes. Early behaviorists placed little faith in these types of self-report inventories.

Another interesting development in this field is the seeming acceptance of the *Diagnostic and Statistical Manual of Mental Disorders* (DSM) diagnostic classification scheme. Behavioral assessors, in general, now concede that such a diagnostic formulation may be useful as one component of the overall assessment. Diagnoses must be supplemented with data from more traditional behavioral methods. It was not so long ago, however, that behavioral clinicians not only ignored mental disorder diagnostic information, but attacked the legitimacy and utility of this source of information. Of course, there are still some radical behaviorists who maintain this rather anachronistic perspective on mental disorder diagnoses. They are in the minority, however.

Why the change of heart for most behaviorists? A multitude of explanations are plausible, but several possibilities stand out. First, the criteria for the various mental disorders have become increasingly objective and behavioral. Second, behavioral clinicians have discovered some degree of utility in using diagnostic labels. These diagnoses describe constellations of maladaptive behaviors that can be targeted for intervention, and may also help the clinician anticipate which other symptoms (other than the target behaviors) may change as a result of treatment. These predictions are based on the established covariation patterns among the disorder's symptoms. For example, increasing the amount of social interaction engaged in by a depressed patient may also result in fewer reports of depressed mood. Although more research is needed regarding the covariation among problematic behaviors (Kazdin, 1985), the criteria sets (symptom lists) for mental disorders at least give us initial hypotheses about what behaviors may or may not change as a result of treatment.

Finally, it is noteworthy that cognitive phenomena and processes are now considered to be more legitimate subjects for behavioral assessment and behavioral intervention. In behavioral assessment, not only are behaviors, antecedent/stimulus conditions, and consequences sampled, but so are "organismic" variables (Goldfried & Davison, 1994). These organismic variables may include a variety of physiological factors, but many cognitive variables are assessed as well. In particular, client expectations are regarded as important. The client's expectations concerning the nature and meaning of the presenting problem, the minimal standards of success that the client sets, and the client's expectations from behavior therapy are just a few of the variables that are assessed in contemporary behavioral assessment. Behavior therapists appear to have found

that an overly rigid adherence to learning models that do not incorporate organismic variables is too constraining.

However, this does not leave the door wide open for *any* kind of physiological or cognitive measure. Rather, these measures and methods must satisfy the same rigorous standards set forth for the more traditional behavioral methods. Validity must be demonstrated, not assumed. For example, a cognitive measure purported to be related to panic disorder (such as beliefs of "uncontrollability") must be correlated with other behavioral measures of panic disorder symptoms, and changes in these beliefs should result in some improvement in other panic disorder symptoms and lead to better outcome in the future. Through these and other procedures, the concurrent and predictive validity of a measure can be established as well as its treatment utility (Hayes, Nelson, & Jarrett, 1987; Kazdin, 1985).

Chapter Summary

Behavioral assessment differs from traditional assessment in several fundamental ways. Behavioral assessment emphasizes direct assessments (naturalistic observations) of problematic behavior, antecedent (situational) conditions, and consequences (reinforcement). By conducting such a functional analysis, clinicians can obtain a more precise understanding of the context and causes of behavior. It is also important to note that behavioral assessment is an ongoing process, occurring at all points throughout treatment.

We have surveyed some of the more common behavioral assessment methods. Behavioral interviews are used to obtain a general picture of the presenting problem and of the variables that seem to be maintaining the problematic behavior. Observation methods provide the clinician with an actual sample (rather than a self-report) of the problematic behavior. Observations can be made in naturalistic conditions (as behavior typically and spontaneously occurs) or under more controlled conditions (in simulated or contrived situations or conditions). Behavioral assessors may also have clients self-monitor ("self-observe") their own behaviors, thoughts, and emotions. A variety of factors can affect both the reliability and validity of observations, including the complexity of the behavior to be observed, how observers are trained and monitored, the unit of analysis chosen, the behavioral coding system that is used, reactivity to being observed, and the representativeness of the observations.

Finally, we have discussed the use of role playing or behavioral rehearsal, of behavior-based inventories or checklists, and of more cognitively focused assessments. The future of behavioral assessment is likely to include more cognitive and psychophysiological assessment methods, and to take advantage of technological advances (such as computer-assisted data acquisition methods) in order to make behavioral assessment more precise, valid, and efficient.

Key Terms

antecedent conditions Stimulus conditions, or conditions that lead up to the behavior of interest.

behavioral assessment An assessment approach that focuses on the interactions between situations and behaviors for the purpose of effecting behavioral change.

behavioral interviews Interviews conducted for the purpose of identifying a problem behavior, the situational factors that maintain the behavior, and the consequences that result from the behavior.

behavioral rehearsal Role playing. The term *behavioral rehearsal* is usually used in cases where the patient is trying to develop a new response pattern.

cognitive behavioral assessment An assessment approach recognizing that the person's thoughts or cognitions play an important role in behavior.

cognitive-functional approach An assessment approach that calls for the functional analysis of the client's thinking processes. In this approach, the clinician completes a careful analysis of the person's cognitions, how they are aiding or interfering with performance, and under what situations this is occurring.

consequent events Outcomes, or events that follow from the behavior of interest.

controlled observation An observational method in which the clinician exerts a certain amount of purposeful control over the events being observed. Controlled observation may be preferred in situations where a behavior does not occur very often on its own or where normal events are likely to draw the patient outside the observer's range.

controlled performance technique An assessment procedure in which the clinician places individuals in carefully controlled performance situations and collects data on their performance/behaviors, their emotional reactions (subjectively rated), and/or various psychophysiological indices.

ecological validity In the context of behavioral assessment, the extent to which the behaviors analyzed or observed are representative of a person's typical behavior.

functional analysis A central feature of behavioral assessment. In a functional analysis, careful analyses are made of the stimuli preceding a behavior and the consequences following from it, in order to gain a precise understanding of the causes of the behavior.

home observation Observation that is carried out in the patient's home by trained observers using an appropriate observational rating system.

hospital observation Observation that is carried out in psychiatric hospitals or institutions using an observational device designed for that purpose.

observation A primary technique of behavioral assessment. Observation is often used to gain a better understanding of the frequency, strength, and pervasiveness of the problem behavior, as well as the factors that are maintaining it.

observer drift A phenomenon in which observers who work closely together subtly, and without awareness, begin to drift away from other observers in their ratings.

organismic variables Physical, physiological, or cognitive characteristics of the client that are important for both the conceptualization of the client's problem and the formulation of effective treatments.

reactivity In the context of observation, reactivity refers to the phenomenon in which individuals respond to the fact that they are being observed by changing their behavior.

role playing A technique in which patients are directed to respond the way they would typically respond if they were in a given situation. The situation may be described to them, or an assistant may actually act the part of another person.

sample Behavioral assessment uses a "sample" orientation to testing—that is, the goal is to gather examples that are representative of the situations and behaviors of interest.

school observation Behavioral observation that is conducted in the school setting. As with home observation, trained observers rate the patient using an appropriate observational system.

self-monitoring An observational technique in which individuals observe and record their own behaviors, thoughts, or emotions (including information on timing, frequency, intensity, and duration).

sign Traditional assessment uses a "sign" approach to testing—that is, the goal is to identify marks of underlying characteristics.

situational test A controlled observation technique in which the clinician places individuals in situations more or less similar to those of real life and then observes their reactions directly.

SORC model A model for conceptualizing clinical problems from a behavioral perspective. In this model, S = the stimulus or antecedent conditions that bring on the problematic behavior, O = the organismic variables related to the behavior, R = the response or the behavior itself, and C = the consequences of the behavior.

unit of analysis In the context of observation, the unit of analysis refers to the length of time observations will be made and the type and number of responses that will be rated.

Web Sites of Interest

To visit any of the web sites listed below, go to www.wadsworth.com and click on Links.

9-1   Association for Advancement of Behavior Therapy (AABT)

9-2   Association for Behavior Analysis (ABA)

9-3   Division of the Experimental Analysis of Behavior (Division 25 of the APA)

9-4   Behavior Analysis Resources

Clinical Judgment

As scientific and objective as clinical psychology has tried to become, it is still virtually impossible to evaluate its diagnostic and assessment techniques apart from the clinician involved. The very title of this chapter, "Clinical Judgment," is enough to suggest that clinicians use inferential processes that are often far from objective. The process, accuracy, and communication of clinical judgment are still very often extremely personalized phenomena.

In this chapter, we will examine some of the means by which the clinician puts together assessment data and arrives at particular conclusions. In addition, we will discuss the accuracy of clinical judgments and impressions. Finally, we will examine briefly the method by which the results of assessment are typically communicated—the clinical report.

Process and Accuracy

Our discussion of clinical judgment will begin with its basic element—interpretation.

Interpretation

It is hard to disagree with L. H. Levy's (1963) statement that "Interpretation is the most important single activity engaged in by the clinician" (p. viii). Interpretation is an inferential process (Nisbett & Ross, 1980) that takes up where assessment leaves off. The interviews have been completed; the psychological tests have been administered. Now, what does it all mean, and what decisions are to be made?

At the very least, *clinical interpretation* or judgment is a complex process. It involves stimuli—an MMPI-2 profile, an IQ score, a gesture, a sound. It also involves the clinician's response. "Is this patient psychotic?" "Is the patient's behavior expressive of a low expectancy for success?" Or even "What is the patient like?" It also involves the characteristics of clinicians—their cognitive structures and theoretical orientations. Finally, situational variables enter into the process. These can include everything from

the type and range of patients to the constraints that the demands of the setting place on predictions. For example, a clinician in a university mental health center may make a range of judgments—from hospitalization to psychotherapy to just dropping out of school—whereas a clinician in a prison setting may be limited to many fewer options.

The Theoretical Framework. As we have mentioned throughout this book, clinical psychologists strive to discover the etiology, or origins, of psychological problems and to understand patients so that they can be helped. Clinical problems can be conceptualized in a variety of ways (for example, psychodynamic, behavioral, cognitive). The kinds of interpretations made by a Freudian are vastly different from those made by a behavioral clinician. Two clinicians may each observe that a child persistently attempts to sleep in his mother's bed. For the Freudian, this becomes a sign of an unresolved Oedipus complex. For the behaviorist, the interpretation may be in terms of reinforcement. Indeed, one way in which clinicians can evaluate interpretations is by examining their consistency with the theory from which they are derived. The number of interpretations that can be made from a set of observations, interview responses, or test data is both awesome and bewildering. By adopting a particular theoretical perspective, clinicians can evaluate interpretations and inferences according to their theoretical consistency and can also generate additional hypotheses.

Samples, Signs, and Correlates. As noted in Chapter 9, patient data can be viewed in several ways. First, one can view such data as *samples*. Observations, test scores, test responses, or other data are seen as samples of a larger pool of information that could be obtained outside the consulting room. For example, when a patient does poorly on the Wechsler Memory Scale, this could be regarded as a sample of nontest behavior (memory problems).

A second way in which patient data can be interpreted is as *signs* of some underlying state,

Clinical psychologists must collect, integrate, and interpret data from multiple sources.
PhotoDisc

condition, or determinant. Aside from radical behaviorists, many clinicians will seek to infer from observations of the patient's behavior and test responses a variety of underlying determinants. For some clinicians, the underlying determinant might be anxiety; for others, ego strength; and for still others, expectancies. But in every case, the observation is seen as something that signifies underlying determinants. For example, poor form quality in a patient's Rorschach responses is often interpreted as a sign of poor reality testing (psychosis).

A third view of patient data emphasizes their status as *correlates* of other things. Once the anxious behavior, the flat affect, or the inability to concentrate have been noted in a depressed patient, the clinician might predict an associated decline in sexual activity, in social relationships, in willingness to seek employment, and so on. In effect, then, assessment data can be interpreted to suggest behavioral, attitudinal, or emotional correlates.

Levels of Interpretation. Whether clinicians view clinical data as samples, signs, or correlates, they are making inferences that will enable them to go from those clinical data to recommendations, reports, or predictions. Sundberg, Tyler, and Taplin (1973) have described three levels of inferences or interpretations, as shown in Figure 10-1.

Level I interpretations generally involve little in the way of inference and certainly nothing in the way of a sign approach. From input to output, there are practically no intervening steps. For example, if it is known on the basis of past experience that students who sit in the front row of a class almost always get A's or B's, then clinicians can go directly from seat number to grade prediction without any necessity for intervening attributions of intelligence scores, previous courses, and so on. This simple yet efficient approach can dispense with high-level clinicians who make exotic inferences prior to their predictions; it can be handled by technicians,

FIGURE 10-1 Levels of interpretation

Source: From N. D. Sundberg, L. E. Tyler, and J. R. Taplin, Clinical Psychology: Expanding Horizons *(2d ed.), © 1973, p. 143. Reprinted by permission of Prentice-Hall, Englewood Cliffs, NJ.*

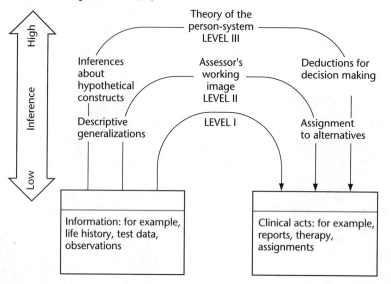

computers, or machines. Level I interpretations can often be used with large populations if the prime purpose is screening and if predicting the outcome for a specific person is relatively unimportant. A college entrance exam is a case in point. Here a single test score may predict with considerable accuracy the academic performance of 1,000 freshmen. Although that single score may be erroneous as a predictor for student X, a certain degree of error can easily be tolerated if one is interested primarily in the number who are likely to graduate.

Level II interpretations involve two kinds of inferences. The clinician may observe a patient and then conclude that the observed behavior generally characterizes the patient. Sundberg et al. (1973) call this first kind of inference *descriptive generalization*. In effect, the clinician goes from a few behavioral instances to a broader generalization—still at the descriptive level. Thus, for a patient who fidgets, smokes three cigarettes during the interview, and stammers, the clinician may make a descriptive generalization—interview tension. If it turns out later that the patient has trouble relaxing at home, cannot

sit through meetings at the office, and is very worried about paying off the mortgage, the clinician may go to a broader descriptive generalization. The second kind of inference is a *hypothetical construct* that suggests an inner state and takes the clinician a bit beyond descriptive generalizations. When clinicians begin to make generalizations and, particularly, to impute inner determinants to the patient, they are moving directly into clinical interpretation as it is often used.

Level III interpretations take clinicians beyond Level II primarily by being more inclusive and better integrated. At this level, they attempt to achieve a consistent, broad understanding of the "individual in situation." Clinicians will draw an integrated picture of the patient's developmental, social, and physiological determinants that involves a highly articulated theoretical system of hypotheses and deductions. For example, a preponderance of "blood" responses on the Rorschach might be interpreted as a sign of underlying aggression that may lead to future impulsive outbursts or loss of control (Rapaport, 1946).

Theory and Interpretation

Currently, clinicians may be assigned to three very broad interpretive classes. First, there are the behavioral clinicians. As we have seen, the strict behaviorist avoids making inferences about underlying states and instead concentrates on the behavior of the patient. The behavioral clinician typically seeks patient data based on personal observation or on direct reports from the patient or from other observers. These data are regarded as samples. Interpretation is largely at Levels I and II, although more recently some behavioral clinicians have begun to show an interest in Level III interpretation.

A second group of clinicians pride themselves on being empirical and objective. In particular, these clinicians are likely to use objective tests to predict to relatively specific criteria. For example, will scores from tests A, B, and C predict success in college, therapy outcome, or aggressive outbursts? This *psychometric approach* to interpretation, as we shall see a bit later, is especially useful when the criteria being predicted are crisp and well articulated. In general, this approach uses data as correlates of something else—for example, a score at the 95th percentile on test X may be related to recidivism in prisoners. The psychometrically oriented clinician is most concerned with standardized tests and their norms, regression equations, or actuarial tables, and tends to employ Level I and II interpretations.

A third group of clinicians is more comfortable with a *psychodynamic approach*. This has long been a popular orientation in clinical psychology. Although current clinicians often seem to opt for a more objective behavioral or psychometric approach, there is still more of the psychodynamicist in many of them than they might like to admit. The psychodynamic approach strives to identify inner states or determinants. Data from projective tests, unstructured clinical interviews, and other sources are viewed as signs of an underlying state. Interpretation tends to be pitched at Level III. A broad, often highly impressionistic picture of the patient is drawn, although in many instances subtle normative assertions are made.

Quantitative versus Subjective Approaches

Quietly embedded in the preceding discussion are two distinct approaches to clinical judgment and interpretation. First is the *quantitative or statistical approach*, which emphasizes objectivity and is presumably free from fuzzy thinking. Second is the *subjective or clinical approach*, which adherents claim is the only method to offer truly useful interpretations and predictions.

The Quantitative, Statistical Approach. Perhaps the simplest form of quantitative prediction that clinicians can use involves assigning scores to the various characteristics of their patients. This enables clinicians to determine the correlation between any two characteristics. For example, suppose that after several years of practice, a clinician begins to suspect a direct relationship between early termination of therapy and patients' needs for independence. The clinician might attempt to verify this hypothesis by correlating "need for independence" scores from a self-report inventory with the length of time that patients remain in therapy. Should the correlation turn out to be substantially above .50, the clinician could use need for independence scores to make interpretations and predictions regarding the duration of therapy.

Of course, more often than not, one cannot base important predictions on a single score or attribute. The conclusion of therapy is more often a complex event that has a number of determinants. Consequently, the clinician might want to obtain scores on several other variables, such as ego strength, the experience of the therapist, marital satisfaction, and interpersonal trust. A multivariate prediction model could then be constructed and tested. A particular caution to bear in mind, however, is that even though a multiple correlation from such an analysis may turn out to be quite high, it may well be much lower when applied to a new sample. This is especially true if the original sample is small and the number of predictors is large. Further, the sample on which the initial study is carried out may not be representative of therapy patients in general. What is true in Kansas may not be true in California; what is true for psychoanalytic therapy may not be true for behavior therapy. Therefore, clinicians have to be sure that they have correctly weighted various predictor scores before they can generalize very far. They must cross-validate their prediction models using other samples.

These statistical techniques permit a mechanical application that does not involve clinical decision making at all once the formulas have been established. The feature that distinguishes these statistical approaches from clinical approaches is that the former (no matter what their complex mathematical development), once established, can be routinely applied by a clerk or a computer.

The quantitative, statistical approach, then, requires that the clinician keep careful records of test data, observations, and related material so that clinical interpretations and judgments can be quantified. Such careful recordkeeping will permit the clinician to go beyond informal impressions based on previous experience. With adequate records on large enough samples, the relations among a host of variables can be assessed. Whether clinicians are evaluating their own performance or the performance of an entire clinic, or are relating certain patient characteristics to various diagnostic or therapeutic outcomes, quantified data can play a facilitating role. Such data enable clinicians to evaluate their judgment, interpretations, and performance.

The Subjective, Clinical Approach. The clinical approach is much more subjective, experiential, and intuitive. Here, subjective weights based on experience suffice. The emphasis is on the application of judgment to the individual case. The classical notion is that "clinical intuition" is not readily amenable to analysis and quantification. It is a private process in which clinicians themselves are sometimes unable to identify the cues in a patient's test responses or verbalizations that led them to a given conclusion or judgment.

Once, for example, in the course of a Rorschach administration, a patient said, "This looks like a Christmas tree." What did this mean? Perhaps nothing. Or perhaps it indicated a career in forestry. Or perhaps it suggested an underlying sadness or depression in a person with few friends or family with whom to enjoy the approaching holiday season. In this case, the last interpretation was later supported by the patient during a discussion of his family background. The clinical student who had made the correct interpretation in a training exercise explained her reasoning as follows: "It was near the Christmas season; there were several references in the TAT to remote family figures; I remembered how I always seem to become a little sad during Christmas; it suddenly popped into my head, and I just knew with complete certainty that it was true—it simply felt right!"

This example illustrates several things about clinical interpretation. First, such interpretation involves a sensitive capacity to integrate material. The astute clinical psychologist pays attention to the wide range of events that characterize the patient's behavior, history, other test responses, and so on. A clinician must function a bit like the detective who takes in everything at the scene of the crime and then makes a series of inductive or deductive generalizations that link these observations together. In addition, there is often a willingness in the clinician to see a bit of him- or herself in the patient—a kind of assumed similarity that enables the clinician to utilize his or her own experience in interpreting the behavior and feelings of another.

Unfortunately, the presentation of this example has been one-sided. Little has been made of the clinical student who believed that the Christmas tree suggested an interest in forestry. Therefore, we may make two additional observations. First, there are individual differences in clinical sensitivity. Second, for every instance of brilliant and sensitive clinical inference, there probably lurks in the unrecalled recesses of memory an equally impressive misinterpretation.

Clinical interpretation, then, involves the sensitive integration of many sources of data into a coherent picture of the patient. It also fulfills a hypothesis-generating function that is best served by guidance from a well-articulated theory of personality. But it behooves responsible clinicians to make every effort to articulate the cues involved in their judgments and to explicate the manner in which they make the leap from cues to conclusions. It is not enough to be good clinicians. There is also a responsibility to pass on these skills to others.

The Case for a Statistical Approach

A quantitative, statistical approach to clinical judgment is particularly effective when the outcome or event to be predicted is known and specific. Indeed, in such cases, additional clinical data of an impressionistic nature usually add little. This is especially true when dealing with fairly large numbers of persons and when the percentage of correct predictions is more important than the correct prediction of the performance of any one individual. As noted earlier, were the task solely one of predicting the grades of an incoming class of college freshmen, the clinician would be well advised to use the objective data of high school grades and ability test scores. Because good grades in college can generally be predicted from ability and its previous effective use, more ubiquitous and subtle personality factors may add little.

Many of the failings in purely subjective, clinical approaches result from the tendency to depend on vague criteria. Too often, a clinician will make the following judgment: The patient, based upon MMPI-2 Scale 7 scores, will benefit from psychotherapy. This vague statement contains no explicit referents. What constitutes benefit? Will the conclusion that the patient has or has not benefited from therapy be based on the patient's own assertions or on the therapist's judgment? The loose conceptualization of the foregoing prediction precludes an empirical test. But suppose that the clinician explicitly defined the outcome as, say, remaining in rational-emotive therapy for 12 months, coupled with a therapy success rating of 7 or higher (on a 10-point scale) by an outside observer? Then it might be possible to develop a formula based on objective interview or test criteria that would successfully predict to a defined universe of therapists.

Clinical terms are often used loosely and without explicit meaning. For example, Grayson and Tolman (1950) long ago showed that psychologists and psychiatrists ascribe marked variations in meaning to such concepts as aggression and compulsion. An objective, statistical approach forces greater specification of meaning that should eventually lead to more specific predictions that could be represented in formulas. This would attenuate much of the unreliability of judgment inherent in more intuitive approaches.

Another reason for adopting the statistical approach is that so many clinical descriptions seem applicable to everyone. As noted in a previous chapter, personality descriptions should show incremental utility—they must reveal something beyond what everyone knew before the assessment began. More precisely, clinicians must develop descriptions of their patients that are meaningful and will lead to explicit predictions. Too often, however, clinicians make interpretations that seem valid but in actuality characterize everybody. This is known as the *Barnum effect*—a notion that goes back to a report distributed by D. G. Paterson that was later cited by Meehl (1956). Barnum statements appear to be self-descriptive but, in reality, describe almost everyone and are not very discriminative. For example, who would deny the personal relevance of the following statements?

> At times I am unsure of my sexual maturity.
>
> I am not always as confident as most people think I am.
>
> Often I keep my real feelings to myself unless I am around people I like.

Box 10-1 discusses the Barnum effect in more detail.

By moving toward quantification, the statistical approach could eliminate much of the unreliability in clinical judgment. Objectively derived formulas, explicit norms, weighted predictors and regression equations, and carefully stated descriptions and predictions could combine to

BOX 10-1

An Example of a "Barnum Effect": Purported Characteristics of Adult Children of Alcoholics (ACOAs)

Logue, Sher, and Frensch (1992) examined whether the apparent widespread acceptance of personality descriptions of ACOAs was due, at least in part, to a Barnum effect. Barnum-like statements apply to most everyone, and therefore appear to be self-descriptive. In reality, however, they are descriptive of people in general and lack both a discriminative ability and clinical utility.

Authors of several popular books on ACOAs have proposed that parental alcoholism produces negative effects on the family, leading to a host of problems in children of alcoholics once they become adults. These include feelings of guilt, shame, insecurity, low self-esteem, and powerlessness, as well as problems coping with emotions and intimate relationships. Logue et al. hypothesized that these descriptors have gained popularity because they not only describe ACOAs but also tend to be descriptive of people in general.

Two groups of undergraduates (ACOAs and non-ACOAs) were asked to rate personality

profiles as to how self-descriptive they were. These profiles consisted of six personality statements (for example, "In times of crisis, you need to take care of others.") There were two personality profile types: (1) ACOA personality profile, consisting of personality statements drawn from the ACOA literature; and (2) Barnum personality profile, consisting of personality statements drawn from several existing personality inventories and used in previous Barnum research. These profiles were matched on overall level of social desirability (assessed through an independent sample). Briefly, results of the Logue et al. study indicated that ACOA profiles were rated as highly self-descriptive by both ACOA participants and non-ACOA participants. The authors concluded that these popular personality descriptors appear to have a Barnum-like quality and, therefore, lack validity as specific descriptors of ACOA individuals.

---

replace the fallibilities of clinical judgment with a mechanical procedure that will minimize errors.

Why, then, do not more clinical psychologists adopt the statistical approach? There are probably many reasons why some people find statistical approaches distasteful. Dawes (1979) describes three such reasons.

Take a situation in which a student is denied admittance to graduate school because of the application of such empirical predictors such as GPA and Graduate Record Examination (GRE) test scores. First, Dawes notes, some will argue with such predictors on technical grounds. They claim that the indices are short term and rather

unprofound. The plea "I just know I could succeed if they would only give me a chance" is less an argument than an expression of hope. The antistatistical argument often claims that there are expert judges "out there somewhere" who could do as well or even better than formulas. But, somehow, these experts never seem to be produced!

Second, this approach may be rejected for psychological reasons. Many persons easily remember those instances in which their intuition was right but conveniently forget those occasions when it was wrong. To take another example, a clinician may unconsciously work harder with a client for whom the clinician has predicted success in therapy. A positive outcome will then prove to the clinician that his or her clinical hunch was right!

Third, there are ethical sources of resistance. Some people have the idea that reducing an applicant to a set of numbers is unfair or dehumanizing. Dawes (1979) discusses this argument:

> No matter how psychologically uncompelling or distasteful we may find their results to be, no matter how ethically uncomfortable we may feel at "reducing people to mere numbers," the fact remains that our clients are people who deserve to be treated in the best manner possible. If that means—as it appears at present—that selection, diagnosis, and prognosis should be based on nothing more than the addition of a few numbers representing values or important attributes, so be it. To do otherwise is cheating the people we serve. (p. 581)

The Case for a Clinical Approach

The difficulty with a statistical approach that relies on prediction models or regression equations is that clinical psychologists would need a multitude of them in order to function as clinicians. The field currently does not have well-established, cross-validated formulas to predict therapy outcomes, make interpretations during the course of a therapy session, or recommend a special class rather than institutionalization. Should the clinician suggest bibliotherapy, a hobby, a marriage counselor, a trial separation, or what? The busy, harried clinician does not have available a regression equation for even important decisions, let alone the pedestrian judgments that must continually be made. It was Meehl (1957) who long ago said, "Mostly we will use our heads, because there just aren't any formulas" (p. 273). Unfortunately, the situation has not changed much over the past 40 years.

Of course, when specific outcomes are to be predicted and the clinician has enough time to develop good formulas, the clinician can easily be outperformed by those formulas. We will re-

view this evidence shortly. However, even here, the clinician's judgment can add something in some instances—especially when the sample is relatively homogeneous. Suppose, for instance, that the formula for selecting students for graduate training depends solely on Graduate Record Examination scores and undergraduate grades. The formula would probably do quite well in selecting from an initial, heterogeneous sample of applicants those who will do well. However, from that point on, clinical judgments regarding motivation or personality features may be quite helpful in further discriminating among those selected. That is, the final sample is so selective that previous grades and test scores may not be very discriminating. Clinical inferences may become useful after the initial screening because they provide extra data that relate to success in training. Holding large amounts of data in our heads and integrating them are not what we humans excel at (Dawes, 1979). Clinicians should use computers and formulas for that and save their own mental powers for what they do excel at—selecting what to look at and deciding what to do with the results.

Another important contribution involves the clinician's function as a data gatherer. For example, it may turn out to be important to know about certain patient characteristics for purposes of prediction. However, it may not be possible to uncover those characteristics without extensive interviewing or some in-depth interpretation based on test results. As a further example, several facets of a patient's life history data may suggest to a sensitive clinician that the patient could be prone toward making violent sexual assaults on women. Although clinical psychology does not have a reliable regression equation to predict such assaults, the data uncovered by an astute clinician could be important. Thus, at present, certain data may be discoverable only through extensive clinical investigation. Predictive formulas work best when test data are available. Sometimes, however, tests of the right sort simply do not exist. When dealing with rare events (such as suicide), the frequency of occurrence is so low that clinicians cannot develop adequate equations for them. But rare or not, such events are important, and they must be dealt with by clinical judgment.

Finally, many people who would argue that the power to predict specific outcomes is not the only goal of science—that understanding and describing phenomena are the overriding goals. Although there may be some validity to this argument, all too frequently it can become a rationalization for using vague terminology and applying equally vague criteria, as noted above. The counterargument would assert that when description and understanding are couched in explicit terms, with clear-cut referents and criteria, then prediction will be a natural by-product.

Comparing Clinical and Actuarial Approaches

Over the years, many studies have compared the relative accuracy of clinical and actuarial methods. Let us now examine some of that work.

Comparison Studies. Sarbin (1943) contrasted the prediction of academic success for college freshmen made by a clerk employing a regression equation with the predictions made by several counselors. The regression equation predictors were aptitude test scores and high school rank. The counselors had available to them the two preceding sources of data (but without their mathematical weighting), vocational interest scores, interview data, and biographical data. Sarbin (1943) found that the counselors were no better than the regression equation in their predictions, even though they had the benefit of much more information.

Meehl (1954) surveyed a number of the studies available on clinical versus statistical prediction and concluded that in "all but one . . . the predictions made actuarially [statistically] were either approximately equal or superior to those made by a clinician" (p. 119). In a later survey of additional research, Meehl (1965) reaffirmed his earlier conclusions. However, Meehl (1954) also observed that, in several studies, statistical predictions were made on the same data from

which the regression equations were developed. In short, the formulas were not cross-validated. As noted earlier, such formulas frequently show a marked reduction in efficiency when they are applied to samples different from those used in their derivation.

Sawyer (1966) regarded data collected by interview or observation as clinical data. He viewed inventory, biographical, or clerically obtained data as statistical or mechanical. Having considered the methodological problems and the equivocal results of the studies he examined, Sawyer concluded that in combining data the mechanical mode is superior to the clinical mode. However, he also concluded that the clinical method is useful in the data collection process. The clinical method can provide an assessment of characteristics that would not normally be assessed by more mechanical techniques of data collection. But once the data (from whatever source) are collected, they can best be combined by statistical approaches.

An example of an individual study comparing clinical and statistical prediction may help further illustrate the nature of this controversy.

One of the most frequently cited studies of clinical versus statistical prediction was reported by Goldberg (1965). In this study, 13 Ph.D.-level staff members and 16 predoctoral trainees were asked to make judgments regarding the diagnostic status of more than 800 patients, based on these patients' MMPI scores. These judgments were made without any contact with the patient or any additional information on the patient. Each judge simply examined the MMPI profile (scores) for each patient and then predicted whether the patient was "psychotic" or "neurotic." These judgments constituted clinical predictions because it was left up to each judge as to how she or he used the MMPI information to formulate a diagnosis.

In contrast, statistical predictions involved the application of a variety of algorithms, in which MMPI scale scores were combined (added or subtracted) in some manner and previously established cutoff scores for psychosis versus neurosis were used. In addition, some statistical

■ **TABLE 10-1** Accuracy of Clinical versus Statistical Predictions in Goldberg's (1965) Study

Source of Prediction	Average Accuracy Percentage (n = 861)
Clinicians	
13 Ph.D.-level staff	62 (range = 59 to 65)
16 Trainees	61 (range = 55 to 67)
29 Total judges	62 (range = 55 to 67)
Statistical Indices	
(L + Pa + Sc) – (Hy + Pt)	70
Two point code rules	67
Sc – (Hs + D + Hy)	67
(Pt – Sc)	65
High point code rules	66
(Hy – Pa)	61
Pa – (Hs + D + Hy)	62
(Hs – Sc)	61
(Pd + Pa) – (Hs + Hy)	63

Source: Adapted from Goldberg (1965).

predictions involved the application of specified decision rules based on MMPI high point codes or other psychometric signs. A total of 65 different quantitatively based rules were considered.

What were these clinical and statistical predictions compared to in order to assess their accuracy? In this study, the criterion diagnosis was the psychotic versus neurotic diagnosis provided by each patient's hospital or clinic. Thus, the accuracy of each clinician's and each statistical algorithm's prediction was determined by assessing the agreement between predictions and the actual criterion diagnoses across all cases.

Table 10-1 presents selected results from this study. Not all of the statistical indices used are presented in this table, but it should serve to give the reader a general impression of the results. First, judges (clinical prediction) were correct, on average, in 62% of the cases. It is noteworthy that the trainees' accuracy rate was comparable to that of doctoral-level clinicians with more years of clinical experience. Second, a number (14 in all) of statistical indices (statistical prediction) were comparable to or outperformed the judges with regard to overall accuracy of pre-

diction. Several diagnostic decision rules based on simple linear combinations of MMPI scale scores (for example, Pt – Sc) outperformed the clinicians.

A variety of additional, updated reviews of the studies pitting clinical versus statistical prediction have uniformly demonstrated the superiority of statistical procedures (for example, Dawes, 1979, 1994; Dawes, Faust, & Meehl, 1989; Garb, 1998; Goldberg, 1991; Kleinmuntz, 1990; Meehl, 1986; Wiggins, 1973). As stated by Meehl (1986):

There is no controversy in social science that shows such a large body of qualitatively diverse studies coming out so uniformly in the same direction as this one. When you are pushing 90 investigations [this number is dramatically higher as of 2001], predicting everything from the outcome of football games to the diagnosis of liver disease, and when you can hardly come up with a half dozen studies showing even a weak tendency in favor of the clinician, it is time to draw a practical conclusion. (pp. 373–374)

FIGURE 10-2 Paul Meehl is widely recognized as a major proponent of the actuarial or statistical approach to prediction.

Courtesy of Paul Meehl.

Objections to These Findings. Dawes (1994) has outlined several of the major objections to the large body of evidence supporting the superiority of statistical prediction, along with responses to each objection. First, critics argue that several of the individual studies reviewed contained research design flaws that may have affected the findings. Dawes (1994) refers to this an "argument from a vacuum"—a possibility is raised, but there is no empirical demonstration supporting the possibility. Although every study has its limitations, it is difficult to imagine that the opposite conclusion (clinical prediction is superior) is warranted when practically all of the studies support statistical prediction.

The second objection concerns the expertise of the judges/clinicians in these studies. Perhaps they were not "true" experts, and a study employing expert clinicians would demonstrate the superiority of clinical judgment. Although a wide variety of judges/clinicians were used in these studies, a number of studies employed recognized "experts"—clinicians with many years of experience performing the predictive task in question. There were a few instances in which an individual clinician performed as well as the statistical formula, but this was more the exception than the rule. Thus, there is no compelling empirical evidence that "expert" clinicians are superior.

A third objection is that the predictive tasks were not representative of prediction situations facing clinicians (that is, not ecologically valid). A clinician's diagnosis may not be based only on the MMPI-2, for example, but also on an interview with the patient. Dawes (1994) argues, however, that the predictive tasks are components of what may go on in clinical practice—clinicians purportedly use the MMPI-2 information to make predictions. Further, several of the studies demonstrate that additional information (such as interview material) obtained and used in the judge's clinical prediction may actually result in less accurate predictions than would be the case if the clinician had simply "stuck with" the statistical formula that was available.

Dawes (1994) goes on to suggest that much of the negative reaction to the findings is a function of our human need to believe in a high degree of predictability in the world. This appears to be both a cognitive and an emotional need. People have a built-in tendency to both seek and see order in the world, and a lack of predictability in the world is likely to result in some degree of discomfort or emotional distress. However, the need for predictability does not prove its existence.

Bias in Clinical Judgment. Clinical judgment suffers when bias of any kind intrudes into the decision-making process. Bias exists when accuracy of clinical judgment or prediction varies as a function of some client or patient characteristic, not simply when judgments differ according to client characteristics (Garb, 1997, 1998). For example, finding that a higher percentage of women than men are judged to suffer from major depression would not indicate a bias against women. However, finding that a higher percentage of women than men are given this diagnosis when the same symptoms are presented would indicate bias.

Garb (1997) recently reviewed the empirical evidence for race bias, social class bias, and gender bias in clinical judgment. Interestingly, he found that many conventionally held beliefs about these types of bias were not supported. For example, there was little support for the beliefs that (1) lower-socioeconomic-class patients are judged to be more seriously disturbed than those from higher socioeconomic classes or (2) women patients are judged to be more disturbed or dysfunctional than men patients. However, there was strong evidence to support the existence of several other types of biases: (1) Black and Hispanic patients who have psychotic mood disorders are more likely to be misdiagnosed with schizophrenia than are similar White patients. (2) Even when presenting the same constellation of symptoms, men are more likely to be diagnosed as antisocial and women are more likely to be diagnosed as histrionic. (3) Middle-class patients are more likely to be referred for psychotherapy than lower-class patients. (4) Black patients are more likely to be prescribed antipsychotic medications than members of other racial groups, even when the Black patients are not more psychotic.

Garb (1997) made the following recommendations to help clinicians overcome these and other biases: (1) Be aware of and sensitive to the biases that have been documented in the literature. (2) Attend to the diagnostic criteria in diagnostic manuals. (3) Whenever possible, use statistical prediction rules instead of clinical judgment or prediction.

Experience and Training. Faust (1986) has reported:

> To whom do these studies of low judgment performance apply? The answer is not that

they apply to hacks or novices alone. There is limited evidence—in fact, almost none—that experts or those with exhaustive experience perform significantly better than "regulars" or "relative beginners." (p. 420)

To date, empirical evidence does not support the position that increased clinical experience results in increased accuracy in prediction (Dawes, 1994; Garb, 1989, 1998). This seems to fly in the face of conventional wisdom. Why is it that we do not see evidence for the effect of clinical experience in clinical psychology and other mental health fields? There are several possibilities (Dawes, 1994). First, the accuracy of predictions is limited by the available measures and methods that are used as aids in the prediction process. If scores from psychological tests, for example, are not strongly correlated with the criterion of interest (that is, highly valid), then it is unlikely one could ever observe an effect for clinical experience. The accuracy of predictions will remain modest at best and will not depend on how "clinically experienced" the clinician is. Second, we often cannot define precisely what we are trying to predict (for example, "abusive personality"), and no gold standards for our criteria exist to enable us to assess objectively the accuracy of our predictions. As a result, true feedback is impossible, and diagnosticians are not able to profit from experience. Third, we tend to remember our accurate predictions and to forget our inaccurate ones. Therefore, more experience in the prediction process does not necessarily lead to increased accuracy because the feedback that is incorporated is incomplete.

As for the virtue of receiving specific types of professional training, there is not much evidence to suggest that one profession is superior to another in making accurate diagnostic judgments. For example, even in differentiating psychological symptoms that are masking medical disorders from those without underlying medical disorders, medical and nonmedical practitioners did not differ in their accuracy (Sanchez & Kahn, 1991).

All of this research is somewhat sobering for the field of clinical psychology. However, it is our professional responsibility to be aware of the limits of our predictive ability and not to promote the "myth of experience." One thing is sure. Clinicians will continue to make decisions—they have no choice. The important thing is to ensure that clinical psychologists are as well prepared as they can be, as well as to train clinical psychologists to use the best available measures and techniques for a given prediction situation.

Conclusions

Given the current state of affairs, the following conclusions regarding the relative strengths of clinical and actuarial methods seem warranted.

The clinical approach is especially valuable when:

1. *Information is needed about areas or events for which no adequate tests are available.* In this case, the research fails to offer any evidence that the data-gathering function of the clinician can be replaced by a machine.
2. *Rare, unusual events of a highly individualized nature are to be predicted or judged.* Regression equations or other formulas cannot be developed to handle such events, and clinical judgment is the only recourse.
3. *The clinical judgments involve instances for which no statistical equations have been developed.* The vast majority of instances, in effect, fall into this category. The day-to-day decisions of the clinician are such that the availability of a useful equation would itself be a rare and unusual event.
4. *The role of unforeseen circumstances could negate the efficiency of a formula.* For example, a formula might very easily outstrip the performance of a clinician in predicting suitability for hospital discharge. In the role of data gatherer, however, the clinician might unearth important data from a patient that would negate an otherwise perfectly logical statistical prediction.

The statistical approach is especially valuable when:

1. *The outcome to be predicted is objective and specific.* For example, the statistical approach will be especially effective in predicting grades, successful discharge, vocational success, and similar objective outcomes.
2. *The outcomes for large, heterogeneous samples are involved, and interest in the individual case is minimal.* Having a statistical formula to predict how many of 50,000 men will receive dishonorable discharges from the Army will be highly useful to the Army, though less so for the clinician who is dealing with Private Smith.
3. *There is reason to be particularly concerned about human judgmental error or bias.* Fatigue, boredom, bias, and a host of other human failings can be responsible for clinical error. Often, such effects are random and unpredictable. Formulas, equations, and computers never become tired, bored, or biased.

Much of the controversy over clinical versus statistical methods has been heated. Each camp seems to scorn the other. If a formula appears to do better than intuition, clinicians become threatened and react defensively. Similarly, some researchers view all clinicians as nothing but second-rate adding machines when it comes to making predictions. Such reactions do little to resolve anything but instead freeze both factions into positions that prevent either from accepting the strengths of the other.

The most useful position would seem to be one that integrates the two approaches. The sensible clinician will use every regression equation, objective test score, or statistical method that shows promise of working for a specific task. Such a clinician will fully understand that clinical data gathering, hypothesis formation, and even intuition will never be totally supplanted by a formula.

By the same token, the clinician can take comfort from the fact that even regression equations must spring from somewhere. Just as someone must program a computer, so too must someone decide which kinds of data should be quantified and submitted for statistical analysis.

PROFILE 10-1

Howard N. Garb, Ph.D.

Dr. Howard Garb is a clinical psychologist at the Pittsburgh V. A. Health System. Dr. Garb is especially noteworthy because he is both a highly respected researcher and a full-time clinician. Dr. Garb has published numerous research articles and chapters, as well a book on psychological assessment and clinical judgment. Dr. Garb's recent book, *Studying the Clinician: Judgment Research and Psychological Assessment*, has received widespread praise for its thoroughness and comprehensiveness. In his clinical work, Dr. Garb serves as coordinator for an anxiety and adjustment disorders clinic, and he supervises psychology interns.

We asked Dr. Garb a few questions about his background and his views on clinical psychology.

What originally got you interested in the field of clinical psychology?

I decided to become a clinical psychologist by the time I was 16. Many of the relatives on my mother's side of the family were mental health professionals. In fact, I am a third-generation mental health professional. In contrast, my father's brother died in a mental health hospital as a young man. He died because of the inappropriate use of shock treatment—an occurrence that was not unknown in the

1940s. I decided to become a clinical psychologist because I enjoyed reading and thinking about psychology and because I could think of no more meaningful work.

Describe what activities you are involved in as a clinical psychologist.

As a clinical psychologist at the Pittsburgh V. A. Health Care System, I see clients for interviews, for psychological testing, and for individual and group therapy. I am also on the hospital psychiatric emergency team. People often ask me how I am able to do research while I carry a full clinical load. My response is that if one wants to do research, one should be willing to work 70–80 hours a week. After seeing clients for 40 hours a week, I am able to find time for research.

What are your particular areas of expertise or interest?

My general area of expertise is psychological assessment. I am especially interested in the validity of psychological tests, the validity of judgments and decisions made by mental health professionals, the cognitive processes of clinicians, and the use of computers for making judgments and decisions.

What are the future trends you see for clinical psychology?

Computers will become increasingly important in psychological assessment, just as they will become increasingly important for society in general. Eventually, computers will be used to describe personality traits, make diagnoses, predict behaviors, and make treatment decisions. However, before computers transform psychological assessment, it is important that we understand how, and how well, clinicians make judgments. It is important to understand something before one tries to change it.

(continued)

Profile 10-1 *(continued)*

What are the major lessons clinical psychologists should learn from studies of clinical judgment?

There are many lessons to learn from studies on clinical judgment. Clinicians should attend to empirical research, be aware of and overcome cultural biases, be wary of some judgment tasks because they are too difficult (such as describing defense mechanisms or making causal judgments), be systematic and comprehensive when conducting interviews, attend to diagnostic criteria when making diagnoses,

make use of psychological tests and behavioral assessment methods, consider alternatives when making judgments, decrease reliance on memory, and follow legal and ethical principles.

Results on clinical judgment are neither all positive nor all negative. Clinicians may be unhappy when the results of a study are negative. However, only by examining ourselves critically can progress be made in clinical practice.

Someone must initially select the tests and the test items. Although formulas can be applied mechanically, their initial development depends on the clinical psychologist.

Improving Judgment and Interpretation

In this chapter, and in preceding chapters on interviewing and assessment, we have discussed a variety of factors that can reduce the efficiency and validity of clinical predictions and interpretation. One cannot presume to lay down a series of prescriptions that will lead inevitably to perfect performance. Let us, however, call attention to several factors that are important to keep in mind as one moves from data to interpretation to prediction. Although the performance of clinicians has not been good, there are ways of making improvements (Faust, 1986; Garb, 1998).

Information Processing

As clinicians process assessment information, they are often bombarded with tremendous amounts of data. In many instances, this information can be difficult to integrate because of its volume and complexity. Clinicians must guard against the tendency to oversimplify. It is easy

for them to overreact to a few "eye-catching" bits of information and to ignore other data that do not fit into the picture they are trying to paint. Whether the pressure comes from an overload of information or from a need to be consistent in inferences about the patient, clinicians must be able to tolerate the ambiguity and complexity that arise from patients who are inherently complex.

The Reading-In Syndrome

We commented in an earlier chapter that clinicians sometimes tend to overinterpret. They often inject meaning into remarks and actions that are best regarded as less than deeply meaningful. Because clinicians are set to make such observations, they can easily react to minimal cues as evidence of psychopathology. What is really amazing is that the world gets along with so many "sick" people out there. It is so easy to emphasize the negative rather than the positive that clinicians can readily make dire predictions or interpretations that fail to take the person's assets into account. Garb (1998) points out that clinicians who do evaluate clients' strengths and assets in addition to assessing pathology and dysfunction are less likely to pronounce clients as maladjusted or impaired.

Validation and Records

Too often, clinicians make interpretations or predictions without following them up. If clinicians fail to record their interpretations and predictions, it becomes too easy to remember only the correct ones. Taking pains to compare the clinician's view with that of professional colleagues, relatives, or others who know the patient can also help to refine interpretive skills.

Vague Reports, Concepts, and Criteria

One of the most pervasive obstacles to valid clinical judgment is the tendency to use vague concepts and poorly defined criteria. This process, of course, culminates in psychological reports that are equally vague. Under these conditions, it can be very difficult to determine whether clinicians' predictions and judgments were correct (which may be why some of them use such shadowy terminology!). To combat this problem, Garb (1998) recommends that clinicians use structured interviews, structured rating scales, objective personality tests, and behavioral assessment methods to inform their clinical judgment and predictions.

The Effects of Predictions

Sometimes predictions turn out to be in error not because they were based on faulty inferences but because the predictions themselves influenced the behavioral situation. For example, a prediction that a patient would have difficulty adjusting at home after release from the hospital may have been correct. However, the patient's relatives may have accepted the prediction as a challenge and therefore provided an environment that was more conducive to the patient's adjustment than it would have been in the absence of the prediction. Thus, the very act of having made a judgment may serve to alter the clinician's own behavior or that of others.

Prediction to Unknown Situations

Clinical inferences and predictions are likely to be in error when clinicians are not clear about the situations to which they are predicting. Inferring aggression from the TAT is one thing; relating it to specific situations is another. Furthermore, no matter how careful and correct clinicians are, an extraneous event can negate an otherwise perfectly valid prediction. Take the following example from the OSS assessment program:

> One high-ranking OSS officer, while operating abroad, received a letter from a friend of his in America informing him that his wife had run off with the local garage man, leaving no message or address. As a result the officer's morale, which had formerly been high, dropped to zero. The assessment staff could predict that a small percentage of men would have to cope with a profoundly depressing or disquieting event of this sort, but, again, it was not possible to guess which of the assessees would be thus afflicted. (OSS Assessment Staff, 1948, p. 454)

Common sense should suggest that to accurately predict a person's behavior, the clinician must consider the environment in which that behavior will take place. This is also a tenet of behavioral assessment. However, clinicians are frequently asked to make predictions based on only imprecise and vague information regarding the situation in which their patient will be living or working.

In a hospital setting, a clinician may be requested to provide a prerelease workup on a given psychiatric patient. But the information available to the clinician will too often cover only general background, with supplementary descriptions of individual differences. Investigators such as Chase (1975), Ekehammar (1974), Megargee (1970), Mischel (1968), and Moos (1975) all agree that such data are subject to a ceiling effect that will allow correlations of no better than .30 to .40 between the data and subsequent behavior. To say the least, correlations of that magnitude leave a great deal to be desired. Therefore, personality data alone are likely to be insufficient in many prediction situations.

Fallacious Prediction Principles

In some instances, intuitive predictions can lead clinicians into error because they ignore the logic of statistical prediction. Intuitive predictions often ignore base rates, fail to consider regression effects, and assume that highly correlated predictors will yield higher validity (Garb, 1998; Kahneman & Tversky, 1973). For example, suppose that a clinician is assessing a patient by collecting samples of behavior in a variety of situations. Even though observations reveal an extremely aggressive person, the clinician should not be surprised to learn that eventually the person behaves in a nonaggressive fashion. Regression concepts should lead one to expect that exceptionally tall parents will have a shorter child, that brilliant students sometimes do poorly, and so on.

In addition, clinicians' own confidence can sometimes be misleading. For example, Kahneman and Tversky (1973) showed that individuals are more confident when they are predicting from correlated tests. More specifically, although clinicians are often more confident of their inferences when they stem from a combination of the Rorschach, the TAT, and the MMPI rather than from a single test, M. Golden (1964) could find no evidence to support this confidence. The reliability and validity of clinical interpretations did not increase as a function of increasing amounts of test data. One should always seek to corroborate one's inferences, but it would be a mistake to believe that the validity of inferences is inevitably correlated with the size of the test battery.

The Influence of Stereotyped Beliefs

Sometimes clinicians seem to interpret data in terms of *stereotyped beliefs* (Chapman & Chapman, 1967). For example, Golding and Rorer (1972) found that certain clinicians believed that anal responses on the Rorschach indicated homosexuality, and they were extremely resistant to changing their preconceptions even in the face of intensive training to the contrary. Such research is a reminder that clinicians must constantly be on guard against any tendency to believe that certain diagnostic signs are inevitably valid indicators of certain characteristics.

Another example comes from a survey of the effects of clients' socioeconomic status on clinicians' judgments (Sutton & Kessler, 1986). A sample of 242 respondents read case histories identical in all respects except that the client was placed in different socioeconomic classes. When the client was described as an unemployed welfare recipient with a seventh-grade education, clinicians predicted a poorer prognosis and were less likely to recommend insight therapy.

"Why I Do Not Attend Case Conferences"

In an engaging paper, Meehl (1977) lists a variety of reasons why he gave up attending case conferences. He catalogs a number of fallacies that often surface at such meetings. Most of them are entirely relevant to the interpretive process generally. The following synopsis of a few of Meehl's examples provides something of their general flavor:

- *Sick-sick fallacy*: the tendency to perceive people very unlike ourselves as being sick. There is a tendency to interpret behavior very unlike our own as maladjusted, and it is easier to see pathology in such clients.
- *Me-too fallacy*: denying the diagnostic significance of an event in the patient's life because it has also happened to us. Some of us are narcissistic or defensive enough to believe we are paragons of mental health. Therefore, the more our patients are like ourselves, the less likely we are to detect problems.
- *Uncle George's pancakes fallacy*: "There is nothing wrong with that; my Uncle George did not like to throw away leftover pancakes either." This is perhaps an extension of the previous fallacy. Things that we do (and by extension, things that those close to us do) could not be maladjusted; therefore, those like us cannot be maladjusted either.
- *Multiple Napoleons fallacy*: There was only one Napoleon, despite how strongly a psychotic patient may feel that he or she is also

Napoleon. An objection to interpreting such a patient's belief as pathological is buttressed by the remark, "Well, it may not be real to us, but it's real to him (or her)!" Further, "Everything is real to the person doing the perceiving. In fact, our percepts are our reality." If this argument were invoked consistently, nothing could possibly be pathological. Even the patient with paranoid schizophrenia who believes aliens are living in his nasal passages would be normal since, after all, this is reality for him.

■ *Understanding it makes it normal fallacy*: the idea that understanding a patient's beliefs or behaviors strips them of their significance. This trap is very easy for clinicians to fall into. Even the most deviant and curious behavior can somehow begin to seem acceptable once we convince ourselves that we know the reasons for its occurrence. This may not be unlike the reasoning of those who excuse the criminal's behavior because they understand the motives and poor childhood experiences involved.

Communication: The Clinical Report

To this point, we have discussed the process of clinical judgment in assessment. The clinician has completed the interview, administered the tests, and read the case history. The tests have been scored, and hypotheses and impressions have been developed. The time has come to write the report. This is the communication phase of the assessment process.

Appelbaum (1970) has characterized the role of the assessor as sociologist, politician, diplomat, group dynamicist, salesperson, artist, and yes, even psychologist. As a sociologist, the assessor must assay the local mores to aid in the acceptance of the report and to direct the report to those most likely to implement it. In some instances, this may mean interacting directly with hospital personnel to convince them of the validity of the report and to encourage them to act on it. These interactions may involve ward attendants, nurses, psychiatrists, and others. Such persuasion may at times seem more suitable for a politician or a diplomat than for a clinician.

One should not accept the role of clinical huckster. However, there are certainly times when reports will have to serve the function of convincing reluctant others. Not everyone is willing to regard the clinician as a purveyor of wisdom and unadulterated truth. Ideally, of course, the evidence for clinicians' conclusions and the tightness of their arguments will be reasons enough for accepting their descriptions and recommendations.

There is no single "best format" for a report. The nature of the referral, the audience to which the report is directed, the kinds of assessment procedures used, and the theoretical persuasion of the clinician are just a few of the considerations that may affect the presentation of a clinical report. What one says to a psychiatrist is likely to be couched in language different from that directed to a school official. The feedback provided to the parents of a mentally retarded child must be presented differently from the feedback given to a professional colleague. In Table 10-2, we present a sample outline of a psychological test report (Beutler, 1995).

The Referral Source

The major responsibility of the report is to address the *referral question*. The test report should carefully and explicitly answer the questions that prompted the assessment in the first place. If the referral questions cannot be answered or if they are somehow inappropriate, this should be stated in the report and the reasons given for this judgment. In some (perhaps most) instances, contradictions will be inherent in the assessment data. Although the clinician must make every effort to resolve such contradictions and present a unified view of the patient, there are instances in which such resolution is not possible. In those instances, the contradictions should be described. Distortion in the service of consistency is not a desirable alternative.

■ **TABLE 10-2** Sample Outline of Psychological Report

I. Identifying information
   A. Name of patient
   B. Sex
   C. Age
   D. Ethnicity
   E. Date of evaluation
   F. Referring clinician

II. Referral question

III. Assessment procedures

IV. Background
   A. Information relevant to clarifying the referral question
   B. A statement of the probable reliability/validity of conclusions

V. Summary of impressions and findings
   A. Cognitive level
      ■ Current intellectual and cognitive functioning (ideation, intelligence, memory, perception)
      ■ Degree (amount of) impairment compared to premorbid level
      ■ Probable cause of impairment

      (By end of this subsection, referrer should know whether the patient has a thought disorder, mental retardation, organicity.)

   B. Affective and mood levels
      ■ Mood, affect at present—compare this with premorbid levels
      ■ Degree of disturbance (mild, moderate, severe)
      ■ Chronic versus acute nature of disturbance
      ■ Lability—how well can the person modulate, control affect with his/her cognitive resources?

      (By end of this subsection, referrer should know whether there is a mood disturbance, what the patient's affects are, and how well controlled his/her emotions are.)

   C. Interpersonal-intrapersonal level
      ■ Primary interpersonal and intrapersonal conflicts, and their significance
      ■ Interpersonal and intrapersonal coping strategies (including major defenses)
      ■ Formulation of personality

VI. Diagnostic impressions
   A. Series of impressions about cognitive and affective functioning, *or*
   B. The most probable diagnoses

VII. Recommendations
   A. Assessment of risk, need for confinement, medication
   B. Duration, modality, frequency of treatment

Source: Beutler (1995), p. 36. Reprinted with permission.

There are often secondary readers of clinical reports. For example, although the primary report may be sent to the referring person (a psychiatrist, another clinician, or an agency), a secondary reader may be an agency administrator, a program evaluator, or a research psychologist. In specific circumstances it may be necessary or even desirable to prepare a special report for such people. In any event, a clinical report does not always serve an exclusively clinical or direct helping function. It can also be useful in assisting an agency to evaluate the effect of its programs. It can likewise be useful from the standpoint of psychological research. Information in clinical reports can often be helpful in validating tests or the interpretations and predictions made from tests. Such data can sometimes provide a baseline against which to compare subsequent change in the patient as a function of various forms of intervention.

Aids to Communication

The function of a report is communication. The following are some suggestions for enhancing that function.

Language. One should not resort to jargon or to a boring and detailed test-by-test account of patient responses. Again, it is important to recall the nature of the referral source. In general, it is probably best to write in a style and language that can be understood by the intelligent layperson. Of course, what is jargon or excessively technical is partly in the eye of the beholder. A considerable amount of technical language can be tolerated in a report sent to a professional colleague whom one knows. On the other hand, technical jargon has no place in a report that is going to a parent. The terms *intertest scatter* and *Erlebnistypus* may be all right for another clinician, but they should not appear in a report sent to a junior high school counselor.

Individualized Reports. We observed earlier in this chapter the importance of avoiding the Barnum effect, and it is well to repeat the point here. The distinctive (be it current characteristics, development, or learning history) is preferred over the general. To say "Jack is insecure" hardly distinguishes him from 90% of all psychotherapy patients. To say that Jack's insecurity stems from a history of living with several different relatives as a child and that it will become particularly acute whenever he must make a decision that will take him away (even temporarily) from wife and home is considerably more

meaningful. In this case, a general characteristic has been distinctly qualified by both antecedent and subsequent conditions.

The Level of Detail. The question often arises as to how detailed a report ought to be. Again, the answer depends largely on the audience. In general, however, it seems desirable to include a mix of abstract generalities, specific behavioral illustrations, and some testing detail. For example, in reporting depressive tendencies, a few illustrations of the test responses that led to the inference would be in order. A few of the relevant behavioral observations that were made during testing could also be quite helpful. A certain amount of detail can give readers the feeling that they can evaluate the clinician's conclusions and interpretations. The exclusive use of abstract generalities places the reader at the mercy of the author's inferential processes.

A Case Illustration of a Clinical Report

To illustrate several of the points that this chapter has made regarding clinical judgment and communication, let us consider a specific clinical case report (Corbishley & Yost, 1995, pp. 322–340).

Identifying Information
Name: Antonio Ramirez
Date of birth: 7/4/62
Sex: Male
Dates of examination: 8/22/94, 8/23/94

Referral Question
Antonio Ramirez, a 32-year-old Latino male, is a sergeant with the Detroit, Michigan, Police Department, currently working as a narcotics officer. In the past few weeks, he has exhibited signs of stress but has refused to take sick leave, claiming that there is nothing wrong. He was referred by his commanding officer for psychological assessment to determine the extent to which recent events in Mr. Ramirez's life may have affected his ability to continue with his present duties.

Assessment Procedures

Mr. Ramirez's personnel file and the referring physician's report were reviewed, and Mr. Ramirez reluctantly agreed to allow his wife, Donna, to be interviewed. On August 22, 1994, Mrs. Ramirez was interviewed for 1 hour while her husband took the Minnesota Multiphasic Personality Inventory–2 (MMPI-2). He complained of headache and blurred vision, which he claimed prevented further assessment that day. He returned the next day for a 1-hour interview, after which he completed the Rorschach and the Wechsler Adult Intelligence Scale–Revised (WAIS-R).

Background

Mr. Ramirez is currently living with his wife of 8 years, a 6-year-old daughter, and a 4-year-old son. He has been employed by the Detroit Police Department since 1984 and has a satisfactory record. In general his health is good, and he expresses satisfaction with his job and marriage. His social life is limited, which he attributes to the fact that as a police officer he is viewed with unease by potential friends, and also to the unpredictable hours he must work.

He has good relationships with his siblings but sees them rarely, as they all live in distant parts of the country. He has no hobbies and spends his limited spare time at home, occasionally playing with his children, but primarily maintaining his house and yard. His relationship with his wife is by his report close, but he says they rarely discuss feelings and he would not burden her with his worries. His wife describes him as a good husband, faithful, even-tempered, and a loving father, but she says he takes life too seriously, and would like him to learn to have more fun.

Mr. Ramirez was raised by his mother in considerable poverty, his father having died in an industrial accident when Antonio was 8 years old. He remembers his father as "stern, but you knew he loved you." He describes his mother as "always worn out, always sad." At the time of his father's death, there were three younger children, ages 5 years, 3 years, and 6 months. Mr. Ramirez early took on the role of family supporter, working after school and on weekends to add to the family income, and helping to discipline his younger siblings. He remembers his development years as "not much fun, a lot of struggling to survive."

At school he was an isolate because of his work schedule and also because he was determined to complete his education, and thus had no time for "fooling with the guys." He learned to fight in self-defense when necessary, to pursue his own course, and to persist at whatever he tried. His sexual development was unremarkable. Since his mother seemed already to be burdened and since he had no close friends, he learned to keep problems and feelings to himself. After 2 years of college he entered the police academy, attracted by the discipline and structure of the organization and the opportunity to defend the public. On the police force he acquired a reputation for being fair, even-tempered, tough, and completely dependable, but not an easy person to get close to—indeed, almost frightening in his self-sufficiency.

In the last 3 months, he has experienced a number of disturbing events. His partner was wounded during a raid; Mr. Ramirez himself was shot at, though not injured, while making a routine traffic check; his wife was attacked, though not raped or physically harmed, on the way home from work one evening; and he was the first on the scene to discover two children under the age of 5 beaten to death in a "crack" house.

This accumulation of violence appears to have affected Mr. Ramirez in several ways. He has had several uncharacteristic outbursts of temper at minor frustrations; on one occasion, to the distress of his fellow officers, he fired his police weapon with insufficient provocation. Somatic symptoms include a 15-pound weight loss over the past 2 months, and (according to his wife) restless sleep and nightmares several times a week. In addition, he has become irrationally overprotective of his family, refusing to let the children visit friends' houses, and angrily demanding that his wife stop work. At work he appears jumpy and distractible, to an extent that has become a concern to his fellow officers. When doing work requiring close attention, he has, on several occasions, developed a headache. Several of his written reports, usually meticulously completed, have contained careless errors and omissions. He has refused to discuss any of these incidents or their impact with his partner, his immediate supervisor, or the police-appointed physician.

When asked about these unusual behaviors, Mr. Ramirez denied that he had changed and claimed that people were exaggerating. On probing, he admitted that sometimes, when he is involved in unrelated daily activities, he gets flashbacks (especially to the scene with the dead children), but claimed that they neither upset him nor made him lose concentration. He attributed his weight loss and restless sleep to the hot summer weather, and insisted throughout the assessment process that he is "fine," that the events of the past months are just part of his job and of life, and that he is capable of continuing to work as before.

Reliability and Validity of Conclusions
At various points in the evaluation, Mr. Ramirez became agitated and appeared irritated; he jokingly accused the examiner of trying to make him remember "things best forgotten." In unstructured situations (the Rorschach), he produced fewer responses as the test proceeded. It is likely that his high level of arousal affected the validity of his responses to unstructured materials. He had fewer complaints regarding structured materials (the MMPI-2), but indices of validity indicate an effort to present himself in a favorable light and to deny pathology. During intellectually challenging tasks (the WAIS-R), he appeared to try hard and was minimally distracted.

All external evidence indicates that Mr. Ramirez's behavior over the past few weeks represents a considerable departure from premorbid levels of functioning, despite his denials. The re-

sults of procedures should therefore be interpreted in the light of objective information from external sources.

Summary of Impressions and Findings
On both days of assessment, Mr. Ramirez arrived punctually, in full uniform and meticulously groomed. Whether standing or sitting, he held himself rigidly and made little movement, as if at attention. He made eye contact infrequently and briefly, and spoke in a clear, quite loud, monotone voice, often pausing before speaking, and rarely expanding upon his answers without prompting. Even when he spoke of his inner experiences, he gave the impression of a person making a formal report to a superior. Only while he was responding to unstructured material was there a sense that his responses were spontaneous.

Intellectually, this man is functioning within the "bright normal" range of intelligence, but at a considerably lower level than previous assessment has indicated. In normal circumstances, he thinks carefully and logically (though unimaginatively), and is capable of sustained intellectual efforts. At the present time, he is easily distracted by intense inner experiences. Strong affect and mental images of unpleasant recent events appear to intrude on his problem-solving efforts and reduce his cognitive efficiency. Thus, his concentration and memory are somewhat impaired; recognizing this, he makes halting and ineffective efforts to overcome and compensate. These efforts produce increased physical tension, which may account for his somatic symptoms. It is likely that his reality testing is somewhat impaired under conditions of high stress, especially the stress of perceived threats to his sense of competence or to the welfare of others; under these conditions, his cognitive controls may be insufficient to prevent his becoming overwhelmed by internal or external stimuli. There is no evidence of a thought disorder, and it is likely that he can return to premorbid levels of functioning if he receives appropriate treatment.

Mr. Ramirez's mood is normally bland, almost stoic, with mild expression of emotions appropriate to the situation. He rarely exhibits anger, and, indeed, generally manages his affective experiences so as to avoid arousing strong feelings in himself. He is, however, capable of great emotional intensity, the expression of which he views as weakness, both in himself and in others. His greatest fear is the loss of self-control, since he believes such control to be the prime means of attaining satisfaction in life. Typically, he maintains control over his emotions by avoidance, withdrawal, and denial—even at home, where he feels less need to protect himself. He attempts to prevent both his wife and his children from expressing intense or prolonged affect, both positive and negative. He is experienced by others as emotionally insulated, but not cold or threatening.

Currently, he is reacting with unusual intensity to mild stimuli, and there are indications that he is experiencing acute dysphoria, with barely suppressed rage and frustration. It is apparent that his normal controls over affect are becoming less effective, though he continues to deny either the existence of strong emotion or his own inability to contain it. Since, as a police officer, he must work in daily contact with situations that are bound to elicit unpleasant emotions, and since he will never be able to completely protect his family from all harm, it is likely that his emotions will intensify and that his control will weaken further. A breakdown of control may manifest itself in more severe somatic complaints or in hostile and aggressive action, or in both. It is clear that Mr. Ramirez's current method of dealing with recently encountered stresses is increasingly ineffective.

Mr. Ramirez is generally conforming and conventional, with a need for structure and a strong sense of morality, loyalty, and responsibility to others. He performs best, and experiences a strong sense of competence and self-confidence, in situations where both role and task are clear. He has a need to be—and to be seen as—strong, effective, and in control. To this end, he is planful, vigilant, persistent, and determined, setting goals for himself and pursuing them in an organized manner. When difficulties arise, he tackles them immediately, directly, and actively, and is impatient with ambiguous resolutions to problems. On the other hand, he demonstrates a lack of flexibility and a tendency to be dogmatic and domineering, especially with those he views as inferior or in need of his protection. Because of his confidence and competence, others tend to trust, rely on, and respect him, but they find him emotionally distant and hard to know. Because of these attitudes and behaviors, Mr. Ramirez is, in general, a highly competent police officer.

In his personal life, both his single-minded pursuit of goals and his refusal to acknowledge intense affect make for a rather joyless and dogged existence. His need to avoid appearing vulnerable and his tendency to enjoy solitary pursuits keep him from an active social life, and he experiences considerable discomfort in what appear to him to be purposeless social occasions. Only in his most intimate relationships is he able to relax to some degree—for example, when playing with his children. He has a strong sense of the importance of family, and generally adheres to a traditional view of the male's role as provider and protector. Thus, the recent attack on his wife was experienced by Mr. Ramirez as a severe and multifaceted threat, calling for immediate action. Because he had no control over the situation and has no way to control future, similar situations, Mr. Ramirez feels helpless and vulnerable to a degree that is extremely difficult for him to tolerate.

Diagnostic Impressions
This man's premorbid functioning is likely to have been characterized by mild social phobia, a tendency to restrict affective experiences and expression, and a somewhat rigid personality structure. However, it is likely that he was generally effective in daily living, with stable work and personal relationships. Recent changes in his affect, behavior, and cognitive functioning appear directly related to several severe psychosocial stressors. He reexperiences these events; avoids stimuli associated with the events; and suffers from loss of interest in significant activities, poor concentration, exaggerated startle response, and

intense irritability. These symptoms having persisted for at least 1 month. A diagnosis of Post-Traumatic Stress Disorder is warranted.

Axis I   309.89, Post-Traumatic Stress Disorder
Axis II   No diagnosis on Axis II
Axis III   None
Axis IV   Psychosocial stressors: Injury of partner; wife attacked; discovery of dead children in "crack" house Severity: 4–5 (acute events)
Axis V   Global Assessment of Functioning (GAF): Current, 53; highest past year, 75

Recommendations

Mr. Ramirez's responses to his environment are increasingly atypical and therefore unpredictable. His current assignment requires self-discipline and cool judgment, which he may no longer be able to produce reliably at premorbid levels. Furthermore, he has apparently almost no insight into his condition, is experiencing anger, and is capable of acting aggressively. It is recommended, therefore, that he be relieved of those duties that involve direct confrontation with violence or danger to himself or to others, with return to active duty contingent upon psychological change.

It is further recommended that Mr. Ramirez seek behavioral psychotherapy—in a group, if possible—that takes a self-management approach. His defensiveness, self-sufficiency, assumption of a conventional male role, and resistance to psychological material indicate that he is unlikely to be a good candidate for insight-oriented psychotherapy, which he would be likely to see as evidence of personal failure. However, it is essential that he learn to modify his need to control every aspect of life, especially if he wishes to continue his present career path. The behavioral/self-management approach seems most likely to present the process of self-examination and change in an acceptable light.

Some Comments on the Antonio Ramirez Report. The primary function of a report is communication. It should not be an ego trip for the writer. In general, the report on Antonio Ramirez could be read and understood by a layperson; it included little of a technical nature. However, some of the language used (for example, "intense inner experiences," "reality testing") may only be familiar to other mental health professionals.

Another positive feature is the level of detail. The report begins with some background material, along with references to the patient's accounts of his behavior and feelings. It also includes some behavioral observations by the clinician. It then moves to a discussion of test responses and some inferences from them. Following that, several integrative statements are made.

At the same time, occasional examples of Barnum statements are apparent in the report—for example, "It is likely that his reality testing is somewhat impaired under conditions of high stress." There were also occasional predictions or statements that were somewhat vague. For example, how would one validate the prediction "It is likely that he can return to premorbid levels of functioning if he receives appropriate treatment." In many cases, it is unclear what test data were used to support the stated interpretations and predictions. Were these based on MMPI-2, WAIS-R, or Rorschach results? What specific test scores from any or all of these measures were used as the basis for these statements?

Despite these few critical comments, we want to emphasize that this report has many more strengths than it has limitations. Reports will vary with regard to structure, style, and language. What is most important, however, is that the test report contribute to an increased understanding of the patient so that the appropriate course of action/treatment can be undertaken. After all, that is the primary goal of psychological assessment.

Chapter Summary

Clinicians are an integral part of diagnosis and assessment. Clinicians make important decisions as to what data are gathered, how they are gathered, and how they are interpreted. Data can be viewed as a sample of behavior, as a sign of some underlying condition, or as a correlate of other behavioral or emotional constructs. Likewise, interpretations can take many forms, ranging from the more straightforward and less inferential to the highly complex and highly inferential variety.

Clinical psychology has for some time debated the merits of clinical (subjective) versus statistical (objective, quantitative) prediction. Research clearly supports the statistical approach to clinical prediction. Although intuitively appealing, clinical prediction is subject to a variety of biases (such as race, social class, and gender), may lead to unwarranted overconfidence, and is characterized by unreliability and validity problems. However, objective decision rules and statistical algorithms are not available for most of the prediction tasks that face clinicians. Therefore, clinical judgment and clinical prediction are often required.

We offer a number of recommendations to improve the reliability and validity of clinical judgments: (1) Consider all available information, and do not ignore inconsistent data. (2) Consider clients' or patients' strengths and assets as well as pathology and dysfunction. (3) Document all predictions, try to evaluate their accuracy, and use this information as feedback. (4) Use only structured interviews, structured rating scales, objective personality tests, and behavioral assessment methods to gather data. (5) Consider the client's situation and environment before making predictions. (6) Consider base rates and regression effects. (7) Do not let one's level of confidence influence prediction. (8) Be aware of and guard against stereotyped beliefs and illusory correlations.

The clinical report serves as the major form of communication to convey the findings from a clinician's assessment and evaluation. The report should address the referral questions, using language that is tailored to the person or persons who will be reading the report. Finally, the report should contain information that is detailed and specific to the client and should avoid vague, Barnum-like statements.

Key Terms

Barnum effect A term applied in cases where statements that appear to be valid self-descriptions in actuality characterize almost everybody.

clinical interpretation A complex, inferential process in which the clinician considers the information at hand (e.g., interview data, test results) to conceptualize the problem and determine a course of action.

clinical or subjective approach An approach to clinical judgment and interpretation that is largely intuitive and experiential. Clinical or subjective interpretation requires that the clinician be sensitive to information from a wide range of sources and make a series of inductive or deductive generalizations to link the observations and predict the outcome.

correlates Related variables. Clinicians employing a correlational orientation to patient data focus on the presumed behavioral, attitudinal, or emotional correlates of specific results.

quantitative or statistical approach An approach to clinical judgment and interpretation that uses formulas and statistical models (already derived) to make predictions about clinical outcomes. Once the formulas have been established, this approach involves no clinical decision making at all.

referral question The question about the patient that prompted the assessment.

samples Specimens of behavior. One orientation to patient data views these data as samples of a larger pool of information about the patient.

signs Markers of underlying characteristics. One orientation to patient data regards these data as signs of some underlying state or trait.

stereotyped beliefs Fixed beliefs (e.g., about certain diagnostic signs, about certain demographically defined groups) that may influence clinical judgment.

PART 3

Clinical Interventions

CHAPTER ELEVEN

Psychological Interventions

In this chapter, we will provide a general description of psychotherapy, describe its major features, discuss issues about its effectiveness, and present an introduction to psychotherapy research. The focus will be on a broad overview of some of the major features shared by different methods of clinical intervention. These interventions go by many different names: psychoanalysis, cognitive therapy, group therapy, family therapy, behavior therapy, existential therapy, and on and on. In some ways, each has a set of unique defining characteristics or is directed toward specific kinds of problems. In subsequent chapters, we will focus on these defining characteristics. Here, however, our attention will be directed toward shared features rather than differences.

Introduction

Intervention Defined

In a most general way, *psychological intervention* is a method of inducing changes in a person's behavior, thoughts, or feelings. Although the same might also be said for a TV commercial or the efforts of teachers and close friends, psychotherapy involves intervention in the context of a professional relationship—a relationship sought by the client or the client's guardians. In some cases, therapy is undertaken to solve a specific problem or to improve the individual's capacity to deal with existing behaviors, feelings, or thoughts that are debilitating. In other cases, the focus may be more on the prevention of problems than on remedying an existing condition. In still other instances, the focus is less on solving or preventing problems than it is on increasing the person's ability to take pleasure in life or to achieve some latent potential.

Over the years, many definitions of the intervention process have been offered. As often as not, the terms *intervention* and *psychotherapy* have been used interchangeably. A rather typical general definition of psychotherapy was provided years ago by Wolberg (1967):

> Psychotherapy is a form of treatment for problems of an emotional nature in which a trained person deliberately establishes a professional relationship with a patient with the object of removing, modifying or retarding existing symptoms, of mediating disturbed patterns of behavior, and of promoting positive personality growth and development. (p. 3)

Wolberg's definition includes such words as *symptoms* and *treatment*, and his subsequent elaboration of the definition gives it a distinctly medical flavor. Yet, overall, the definition is not much different from one offered by a more psychologically oriented clinician (Rotter, 1971a, p. 79): "Psychotherapy . . . is planned activity of the psychologist, the purpose of which is to accomplish changes in the individual that make his [sic] life adjustment potentially happier, more constructive, or both." J. D. Frank (1982) elaborates this general theme as follows:

> Psychotherapy is a planned, emotionally charged, confiding interaction between a trained, socially sanctioned healer and a sufferer. During this interaction the healer seeks to relieve the sufferer's distress and disability through symbolic communications, primarily words but also sometimes bodily activities. The healer may or may not involve the patient's relatives and others in the healing rituals. Psychotherapy also often includes helping the patient to accept and endure suffering as an inevitable aspect of life that can be used as an opportunity for personal growth. (p. 10)

Granted, such definitions are rather broad. Practitioners of such specific approaches as psychoanalysis, rational-emotive therapy, client-centered counseling, cognitive therapy, Gestalt therapy, and other forms of psychological treatment will rightly note that such definitions hardly convey the essence of their unique "brand" of therapy.

Does Psychotherapy Help?

Before we describe in more detail the goals and features of psychotherapy, a general question needs to be addressed. Does psychotherapy work? Both advocates (for example, Lambert & Bergin, 1994) and critics (for example, Dawes, 1994) agree that empirical evidence supports the efficacy of psychotherapy. Of course, this does not mean that everyone benefits from psychotherapy. Rather, on average, individuals who seek out and receive psychotherapy achieve some degree of relief. For example, a frequently cited meta-analytic review of more than 475 psychotherapy outcome studies reported that the *average* person receiving psychological treatment is functioning better than 80% of those not receiving treatment (Smith, Glass, & Miller, 1980). We will discuss this study and other reviews of psychotherapy outcomes in a later section focusing on psychotherapy research methods.

At this point, however, a recent large-scale survey on the benefits of psychotherapy deserves mention. The November 1995 issue of *Consumer Reports* ("Mental Health," 1995) summarized the results of a survey of 4,000 readers who had sought treatment for a psychological problem from a mental health professional, family doctor, or self-help group during the years 1991–1994. Most of the respondents were well educated, their median age was 46 years, and about half were women. Of this sample, 43% described their emotional state at the time that treatment was sought as "very poor" ("I barely managed to deal with things") or "fairly poor" ("Life was usually pretty tough"). The 4,000 respondents presented for treatment of a wide range of problems, including depression, anxiety, panic, phobias, marital or sexual problems, alcohol or drug problems, and problems with children. The major findings were as follows:

1. Psychotherapy resulted in some improvement for the majority of respondents. Those who felt the worst before treatment began reported the most improvement.
2. As for which types of mental health professionals were most helpful, psychiatrists, psychologists, and social workers all received high marks. All appeared to be equally effective even after controlling for severity and type of psychological problem.

3. Respondents who received psychotherapy alone improved as much as those who received psychotherapy plus medication as part of their treatment.
4. In this survey, longer treatment (more sessions) was related to more improvement.

These findings are both interesting and provocative. This survey, however, is limited in a number of respects such that we must be cautious in our generalizations. For example, few respondents reported severe psychopathology (such as schizophrenia), and reports were both retrospective and based solely on the clients' self-reports. In addition, the percentage of potential respondents who returned the survey was relatively low, raising the possibility of an unrepresentative sample. Further, readers of this publication may not be particularly representative of the general U.S. population. Despite these limitations, the *Consumer Reports* survey provides some support for the contention that psychotherapy works. Further, it represents the largest study to date that has assessed "the effectiveness of psychotherapy as it is actually performed in the field with the population that actually seeks it, and it is the most extensive, carefully done study to do this" (Seligman, 1995, p. 971).

What Problems Are Amenable to Change?

Are all concerns, worries, problematic behaviors, and psychopathological symptoms responsive to psychological interventions? Probably not. Despite the proliferation of pop psychology antidotes and almost charlatanesque claims to the contrary, it appears that some conditions that clients present with are difficult to change, whereas other conditions are quite amenable to change. In an intriguing guide to self-improvement, Seligman (1994) reviewed the empirical research on the treatment of a wide variety of "problems" in order to compile a list of "what you can change and what you can't." Table 11-1 summarizes some of his findings.

Why are some problems amenable to change, whereas others are not? Seligman (1994) invokes

▮ TABLE 11-1 What You Can Change and What You Can't

Problem/Condition	Changeability
Panic disorder	Curable
Specific phobias	Almost curable
Sexual dysfunctions	Marked relief possible
Social phobia	Moderate relief possible
Agoraphobia	Moderate relief possible
Depression	Moderate relief possible
Obsessive-compulsive disorder	Moderate/mild relief possible
Anger	Mild/moderate relief possible
Everyday anxiety	Mild/moderate relief possible
Alcoholism	Mild relief possible
Overweight	Temporary change only
Posttraumatic stress disorder	Marginal relief only

Source: Adapted from Seligman (1994). Used with permission.

the concept of *depth of a problem* to explain the "changeability" of a variety of conditions or behaviors. The level of depth of a problem depends on whether it is innate/biologically determined, whether it is difficult to disconfirm the belief underlying it, and whether the belief underlying the problem is "powerful" in the sense that it is relatively general and can explain many of the facts of the world. For example, transsexuality is probably unchangeable ("deep") because "It is biologically laid down in gestation. It is virtually undisconfirmable and pervades all of life" (Seligman, 1994, p. 247)" On the other hand, a specific phobia of spiders is not "deep" because spider phobias per se are not inherited, they can be disconfirmed, and the underlying belief (spiders are dangerous) is not powerful because it explains only spiders.

Seligman's (1994) review, analysis, and theory help us to make some sense out of why certain psychological problems seem relatively intractable whereas others can be alleviated with appropriate treatment. Another attractive feature of this book is Seligman's critical, empirically based evaluation of various popular treatments for specific disorders. We will return to this issue in later chapters.

Features Common to Many Therapies

The apparent diversity among psychotherapies can sometimes lead us to overlook the marked similarities among them. One reason is that the purveyor of a new brand of psychotherapy must emphasize the special features of the new product. Bringing forth a minor variation of an old therapeutic theme would be unlikely to capture anyone's interest. Yet most psychotherapies have a great deal in common—a commonality that in many respects outweighs the diversity.

Hundreds of "brands" of psychotherapy have been identified. Some are effective, whereas others probably are not. Unfortunately, not all of these forms of psychological intervention have been subjected to empirical scrutiny. Of those that have received research attention, however,

PROFILE 11-1
Martin E. P. Seligman, Ph.D.

Martin E. P. Seligman is the Fox Leadership Professor of Psychology at the University of Pennsylvania. He is a leading authority on learned helplessness, explanatory style, and optimism and pessimism. He has published 15 books and more than 150 scholarly articles on motivation and personality. Over the last 30 years of his research career, he has received support from the National Institute of Mental Health, the National Institute of Aging, the National Science Foundation, the Guggenheim Foundation, and the MacArthur Foundation; in 1991, he won the coveted Merit Award from the National Institute of Mental Health. His colleagues have recognized his achievements by presenting him with prizes such as the Zubin Award of the Society for Research in Psychopathology, the William James Fellow Award of the American Psychological Society, and two Distinguished Scientific Contribution Awards from the American Psychological Association. Dr. Seligman recently served as president of the American Psychological Association.

The central theme of Dr. Seligman's work has been recognizing our explanatory style—what we say to ourselves when we experience setbacks—and how it influences our lives. He has identified effective techniques to transform negative thoughts and unlearn helplessness and to rise above pessimism and the depression that may accompany these negative thoughts. With years of research behind him, he has demonstrated how we can boost our moods, and immune systems, with healthful thoughts. In *What You Can Change and What You Can't* (Seligman, 1994), he pinpoints what techniques and therapies will work best to effect change, and also identifies what conditions we should stop trying to change. His most recent book, *The Optimistic Child* (Seligman, Reivich, Jaycox, & Gillham, 1995), presents research he and his colleagues have done to show how depression in children can be prevented. They propose a program that parents and educators can use to identify the danger signs of pessimism in children and teach them the skills of thinking optimistically.

there is only limited evidence that one approach or technique is more effective than others. As Lambert and Bergin (1994) note, one implication of therapeutic equivalence is that the positive changes effected by psychological treatment may actually be the result of a set of *common factors* that cuts across various theoretical and therapeutic boundaries. Lambert and Bergin (1994) provide a list of common factors categorized according to a sequential process that they believe is associated with positive outcome.

Briefly, they propose that *supportive factors* (for example, positive relationship, trust) lay the groundwork for changes in clients' beliefs and attitudes (*learning factors*—for example, cognitive learning, insight), which then lead to behavioral change (*action factors*—for example, mastery, taking risks). Although a detailed discussion of each of the common factors, such as those listed in Table 11-2, is beyond the scope of this book, it may be instructive to discuss some of them briefly.

TABLE 11-2 Common Factors of Psychotherapy Associated with Positive Outcome

Support Factors	Learning Factors	Action Factors
Catharsis	Advice	Behavioral regulation
Identification with therapist	Affective experiencing	Cognitive mastery
Mitigation of isolation	Assimilation of problematic experiences	Encouragement of facing fears
Positive relationship	Changing expectations for personal effectiveness	Mastery efforts
Reassurance	Cognitive learning	Modeling
Release of tension	Corrective emotional experience	Practice
Structure	Exploration of internal frame of reference	Reality testing
Therapeutic alliance	Feedback	Success experience
Therapist/client active participation	Insight	Taking risks
Therapist expertness	Rationale	Working through
Therapist warmth, respect, empathy, acceptance, genuineness		
Trust		

Source: Lambert and Bergin (1994)

The Expert Role. It is assumed that the therapist brings to the therapy situation something more than acceptance, warmth, respect, and interest. These personal qualities are not sufficient for certification as a clinical psychologist. Conventional wisdom seems to suggest that all one needs in order to conduct psychotherapy is an unflagging interest in others. In fact, however, this is not enough.

In all forms of psychotherapy, patients have a right to expect that they are seeing not only a warm human being but a competent one as well. Competence can only come from a long, arduous period of training. Some may be quick to reply that the assumption of an *expert role* introduces an authoritarian element into the relationship, implying that the patient and the therapist are not equal, and thus destroying the mutual respect that should exist between them. However, mutual understanding and mutual acceptance of the different roles to be played would seem sufficient to guarantee the maintenance of mutual re-

spect. Therapists are, of course, no better than patients, and they cannot lay claim to any superior consideration in the cosmic scheme of things. However, this kind of equality need not deny the importance of training, knowledge, and experience that will assist therapists in their efforts to resolve the patient's problems.

The Release of Emotions/Catharsis. Some have stated that psychotherapy without anger, anxiety, or tears is no psychotherapy at all. Psychotherapy is an emotional experience. The conviction of most psychotherapists is so strong on this point that they would seriously question whether a patient who, session after session, maintains a calm, cool, detached, or intellectual demeanor is really benefiting. The problems that bring a person to psychotherapy are typically important ones. Consequently, they are likely to have important antecedents.

The release of emotions, or *catharsis* as it is sometimes termed, is a vital part of most psychotherapies. Its depth and intensity will vary, depending on the nature and severity of the problem and on the particular stage in therapy. But the psychotherapist must be prepared to deal with emotional expression and to use it to bring about change. Although some forms of psychotherapy certainly place more reliance on emotional expression than do others, a new brand of therapy is likely to be criticized if it seems to neglect this important facet. On the other hand, there are clearly some forms of psychotherapy (such as anger management) in which catharsis is not likely to be a desirable goal. In these cases, the goal may be to gain better control over the expression of one's emotions.

Relationship/Therapeutic Alliance. For some, the nature of the relationship or *therapeutic alliance* between patient and therapist is the single element most responsible for the success of psychotherapy. Although not all therapists would elevate the relationship to the status of the primary "curative" agent, almost all therapists would attest to the unique importance of the relationship. Where else can patients find an accepting, nonjudgmental atmosphere in which to discuss their innermost urges, secrets, and disappointments? Discussions of this kind with a friend or relative always seem to contain an implicit aura of evaluation and often lead to unforeseen complications because the other person has a personal stake in the matters discussed. Friends can easily be threatened by such discussions because the content of the discussions has the potential to disturb the basis for the relationship. Can a husband discuss his dependency anxieties with his wife, whose perception of her role may be disturbed by such revelations? Can a son reveal his fear of failure to a father who has been boastful of the son's achievements? Can a daughter tell her mother that she wants to give up her role as housewife in favor of a career without seeming to question her mother's values?

In psychotherapy, all of this is possible. The effective therapist is someone who can be accepting, nonjudgmental, objective, insightful, and professional all at the same time. These lavish adjectives scarcely fit all therapists all of the time. Nevertheless, the general ability of therapists to rise above their personal needs and to respond with professional skill in a nonjudgmental atmosphere of confidentiality, understanding, and warmth is probably a major reason for the success and persistence of psychotherapy in our society.

Anxiety Reduction/Release of Tension. Initially, it is important that the anxiety accompanying the patient's problems in living be reduced enough to permit examination of the factors responsible for the problems. The essential conditions of psychotherapy—including the nature of the relationship, the qualifications of the therapist, confidentiality, and privacy—combine to provide a reassurance and a sense of security that can lower the patient's anxiety and permit the patient to contemplate his or her experiences systematically.

In instances in which the anxiety level is extremely high, some patients may require, on medical advice, antianxiety medications to help deal with the situation. However, it is important that such medications be regarded as a temporary tool rather than a permanent solution. Some clients may experience side effects to medications, and medications may actually interfere with some forms of psychological treatment (such as exposure-based therapies) in which the goal is to increase anxiety levels in the face of certain stimuli so that habituation will occur. We will have more to say about these exposure treatments in Chapter 14.

Interpretation/Insight. Many nonprofessionals erroneously view psychotherapy as a rather straightforward process in which a person presents a problem, the therapist asks the person to describe his or her childhood experiences, the therapist offers a series of interpretations as to the real meaning of those childhood experiences, and the person then achieves *insight*. With the sudden, explosive force of revelation, this insight strikes home. A brief period of wonderment follows, as the problem falls away like melting snow. In conclusion, the patient walks away from the consulting room, framed in the light from the setting sun, assured that relief and everlasting joy have been attained. This, of course, is a scenario from a bad movie or from the fantasies of a beginning therapist.

There is, however, an element of reality in the foregoing scenario. A broad band of psychotherapies does attach importance to patients' childhood experiences, though such psychotherapies vary in the degree of importance they attach to them, the amount of related information they seek, and their view of the effects generated by the experiences. Similarly, *interpretation* is a very common component of psychotherapy. But again, the extent of its use, the kinds and the timing of the interpretations, and the importance attributed to those interpretations vary with the school of psychotherapy. But regardless of terminology, an important element in many forms of psychotherapy is the attempt to get the patient to view past experience in a different light.

The importance attached to insight has eroded over the years. Once it was naively thought that insight into the nature and origin of one's problems would somehow automatically propel the patient into a higher level of adjustment. Most psychotherapists no longer cling to this simple belief. Insight is still viewed as important, but it is recognized that significant behavioral change can be brought about by other means. Insight may be seen as a facilitator of psychological growth and improvement, but not as something that by itself will inevitably bring about such changes. Indeed, waiting for insight to free one from problems can be a delaying tactic used by some patients to avoid taking the responsibility for initiating changes in their lives.

Building Competence/Mastery. In one sense, a goal of most therapies is to make the client a more competent and effective human being. All of the foregoing features of psychotherapy will facilitate the achievement of greater effectiveness and satisfaction. But beyond such elements as the therapeutic relationship and anxiety re-

duction, some forms of therapy have other features that are also applicable here. For example, therapy can be a setting in which the client learns new things and corrects faulty ways of thinking. At times, some forms of therapy will take on distinct teaching overtones. The client may be "tutored" on more effective ways to find a job, or sexual information may be provided to help alleviate past sexual difficulties and promote a better sexual adjustment in the future. Therapy, then, can be more than just exorcising old psychological demons; it can also be a learning experience in the direct sense of the word. Bandura (1989) has emphasized the importance of feelings of self-efficacy in promoting a higher performance level in the individual. In short, those persons who experience a sense of *mastery*—who feel confident, expect to do well, or just feel good about themselves—are more likely to function in an effective fashion.

Nonspecific Factors. Call it faith, hope, or expectations for increased competence, successful therapy tends to be associated with such *nonspecific factors* (Kazdin, 1979). Numerous factors can conspire to promote such expectancies. First of all, there is often a mystique to therapy—at least in the eyes of the general public. Patients often come to therapy fully expecting to participate in a process almost guaranteed to promote mental health. Therapists often encourage such beliefs, knowing full well that a believing, motivated client is more likely to show progress than a cynical, recalcitrant one. Finally, nearly every therapist is committed to a theory of therapeutic change. Whether it be an operant theory, a theory of the unconscious, or a belief in growth potential, its ubiquitous presence in the therapist's explanations of how therapy works can ignite a confidence that can help alleviate the client's earlier feelings of despair. Although successful therapy can almost always be characterized as having rekindled the patient's hope, faith, and morale (J. D. Frank, 1973), it seems unlikely that therapy can be reduced to nothing more than what some have disparagingly referred to as a placebo effect. The expectations of the client help make even more effective the specific techniques applied in therapy. The successes of such techniques then act to further increase the client's expectations.

In Frank's (1982) description of psychotherapy, he notes that therapy involves a rationale, conceptual scheme, or myth that provides a plausible explanation for the patient's difficulties and also prescribes a ritual for restoring equilibrium. Such explanations and rituals can, as Frank points out, provide the patient with a face-saving reason to abandon a symptom when ready to do so. To cease complaining or give up a cherished symptom without a good reason would imply that it was trivial. So, whatever we call it—nonspecific factor, placebo effect, or faith—it becomes an important element in the therapy process.

Nature of Specific Therapeutic Variables

It would be pleasant if psychotherapy were a simple routine in which the therapist makes a diagnosis, conveys it to the patient, gives a lecture or two, and presto, the patient is cured. Unfortunately, things do not work that way. Indeed, it is often necessary to spend considerable time correcting patients' expectations that they will be given a simple psychological prescription. Because psychotherapy is an active, dynamic process, passivity and lack of motivation can be obstacles. A number of factors involving the nature of the patient, the therapist, and the patient-therapist interaction affect the process of therapy in important ways. Often their effects are felt over and above the specific mode of therapy employed.

The Patient or Client

Are there specific or general patient characteristics that influence the outcomes of therapy? Such a deceptively simple question really has no answer other than "It depends." The reason is that the outcomes of therapy are exceedingly complex events that are not shaped by patient characteristics alone. They are also determined by therapist qualities and skills, the kinds of therapeutic procedures employed, the circumstances and environment of patients, and so on. Eventually, the field will have to identify specifically which kinds of patients benefit from which procedures, under which circumstances, and by which therapists (Kiesler, 1966; Paul, 1967).

With the foregoing caveat firmly in mind, we can proceed to discuss some of the more prominent patient variables that have been related to outcomes in traditional therapies.

The Degree of the Patient's Distress. A broad generalization often made by clinicians is that the persons who need therapy the least are the persons who will receive the greatest benefit from it. A more sophisticated version of this relationship is reflected in Truax and Carkhuff's (1967) distinction between patients' feelings of disturbance and their overt behavioral disturbance. This distinction implies to many clinicians that a good prognosis may be expected for a patient who is experiencing distress or anxiety but is functioning well behaviorally.

At best, however, the research data are contradictory and inconsistent (which, again, probably reflects the impossibility of coming to a simple conclusion without considering many other factors). For example, one group of studies finds that greater initial distress is associated with greater improvement (for example, Stone, Frank, Nash, & Imber, 1961). Another group of studies (for example, Barron, 1953) finds exactly the reverse. To complicate matters further, Miller and Gross (1973) contend that the relationship between improvement and the initial disturbance is curvilinear; that is, patients with little disturbance or extreme disturbance show poorer outcomes than do moderately disturbed patients. Summarizing research in this area, Garfield (1994) concludes that, although mixed findings across studies temper one's degree of confidence in general conclusions, more recent studies seem to find with some consistency that individuals who are more severely disturbed have poorer outcomes.

Intelligence. In general, psychotherapy requires a reasonable level of intelligence (Garfield, 1994). This is not to say that persons who suffer from mental retardation do not, under certain conditions, benefit from counseling or from the opportunity to talk about their difficulties. Nevertheless, other things being equal, brighter individuals seem better able to handle the demands of psychotherapy.

This is so for several reasons. First, psychotherapy is a verbal process. It requires patients to articulate their problems, to frame them in words. Second, psychotherapy requires patients to establish connections among events. Patients must have the capacity to see relationships between prior events and current problems, and ultimately they must be able to connect their current feelings with a variety of events whose relationship to those feelings may at first seem improbable. Finally, to enable connections among events to be made, psychotherapy requires a degree of introspection. Since traditional psychotherapy has always emphasized the inner determinants of behavior, it follows that a patient who finds it difficult to look inward may have problems in adjusting to the process.

However, behavioral forms of therapy have often been used with considerable success with individuals suffering from cognitive limitations. A variety of behavior modification approaches are quite feasible, especially when goals involve specific behavioral changes rather than insight. In such populations, improved social abilities, self-care skills, and other skills can be developed with a focus on behavior rather than cognitions. As a generalization, when behavioral deficits are the problem, behavioral techniques are frequently the preferred ones.

Age. Other things being equal, younger patients have long been considered the best bets for therapy. Younger patients are presumably more flexible or less "set in their ways." Perhaps younger patients are better able to make the appropriate connections because they are closer to their childhood years, or perhaps they have been reinforced for negative behaviors less often than their older counterparts. In any event, the notion that younger persons do better in therapy is quite prevalent among clinicians. Research evidence supporting the contention that older clients have a poorer prognosis, however, is weak at best (Smith et al., 1980; Garfield, 1994).

It is best to consider not age alone, but rather the specific characteristics of the prospective patient. It often happens that a 55-year-old will be an active, open, introspective person who can really benefit from therapy. In short, denial of therapy to an elderly person can be construed as a form of ageism in some instances! Research supports the efficacy of various forms of both cognitive-behavioral and psychodynamic treatment with older adults (Gallagher-Thompson & Thompson, 1995; Scogin & McElreath, 1994).

Motivation. Psychotherapy is sometimes a lengthy process. It demands much from a patient. It can be fraught with anxiety, setbacks, and periods of a seeming absence of progress. If psychotherapy is to be successful, it will force the patient to examine corners of the mind that have long remained unscrutinized. It may demand that the patient engage in new behaviors that will provoke anxiety. As was noted previously, psychotherapy is not a passive process in which insights are fed to the patient. Instead, the patient must actively seek insights. Typically, the search is not easy. For these and other reasons, successful psychotherapy seems to require motivation.

At some level, the patient must want psychotherapy (though there are times during psychotherapy when even highly motivated patients want out). It follows, then, that psychotherapy is a voluntary process. One cannot be forced into it. When people are forced, either openly or subtly, to become patients, they rarely profit from the experience. Therapy is not likely to be of much benefit to the prisoner who seeks therapy to impress a parole board; to the college student who, following a marijuana charge, is given the option of reporting to a counseling center or facing the prospect of jail; or to the person who undergoes therapy to protect an insurance claim.

Despite the conventional wisdom that cites client motivation as a necessary condition for positive change, research support is mixed (Garfield, 1994). One methodological problem concerns how best to assess client motivation. Studies vary widely in how they attempt to measure motivation. For example, Yoken and Berman (1987) used client payment for services as an index of client motivation. Finding relatively little difference in outcome between those clients who paid the standard fees for services and those whose fees were waived, Yoken and Berman (1987) concluded that motivation appears to be unrelated to outcome. The lack of definitive findings, however, may simply reflect the difficulty researchers have experienced in defining and measuring client motivation.

Openness. Most therapists intuitively attach a better prognosis to patients who seem to show some respect for and optimism about the utility of psychotherapy. They are relieved when patients are willing to see their problems in psychological rather than medical terms. Such persons can be more easily "taught to be good psychotherapy patients," in contrast to patients who view their difficulties as symptoms that can be cured by an omniscient, authoritative therapist while they passively await the outcome. Thus, a kind of "openness" to the therapeutic process (Strupp & Bergin, 1969) appears to make the patient a better bet for therapy.

Gender. In the present climate, there are several prominent issues related to gender. One is the relationship between the outcome of therapy and the gender of the patient. Research does not support the view that biological sex of the client is significantly related to outcome in psychotherapy (Garfield, 1994).

A second, more volatile issue is whether sexism operates in therapy and whether, for example, male therapists exploit female patients. Stricker (1977) suggests that this issue often serves as a platform for extremists on both sides: Those at the feminist end of the spectrum claim exploitation, and the male chauvinists deny that

it exists. Research into the question of whether therapists and counselors are guilty of gender bias and stereotyping is highly inconsistent (Barak & Fisher, 1989). Many, however, are confident in suggesting that clinical psychologists should do a better job of educating clinical students regarding gender issues (for example, Gilbert, 1987). Good, Gilbert, and Scher (1990) have even recommended a brand of psychotherapy called Gender Aware Therapy (GAT). GAT integrates feminist psychotherapy and knowledge of gender into a treatment approach for both women and men. This approach, which focuses on exploring unique gender-related experiences, may be appropriate for a variety of issues faced by women (such as career development and eating disorders) and men (such as depression and sexual dysfunction). Finally, although sex of the client has not been reliably linked to outcome, it is probably true that sex or gender of the therapist may be especially important to consider in certain cases. For example, women rape victims may feel much more comfortable talking to women psychotherapists than to men psychotherapists.

Feminist Therapy. For many years, therapy was a male-dominated enterprise. The special problems facing women were poorly addressed and poorly understood by male therapists. New treatment models were needed to deal with the disorders prevalent among women (Hare-Mustin, 1983). What was needed, many felt, was a *feminist therapy*—a therapy that would recognize the manner in which women have been oppressed by society through the ages (Ballou & Gabalac, 1985; Rosewater & Walker, 1985).

Feminist therapy grew out of the women's movement and has been quite visible since the early 1970s. It acknowledges that many of the personal problems of women arise out of the social position women are forced to adopt. It points to the failure of the psychiatric and psychological establishment to see the oppression of women as a prime factor in their development of personal distress. The feminist approach views the relationship between therapist and patient in terms of equality rather than power versus subordination. Feminists, in short, do not take kindly to the "power of expertise." This form of therapy also requires a frank admission of the values of both therapist and client and the development of specific contracts with regard to the therapy process itself.

Feminist therapists tend to be especially attuned to specific emotional problems experienced by women: anger and its expression, learned helplessness and depression, autonomy and dependency, and sexuality. Also important are concrete issues such as work, finances, and family choices. Particularly critical are issues of personal freedom and choice and a willingness to consider life alternatives that depart from traditional sex-role expectations (Brody, 1987; Sturdivant, 1980).

Race, Ethnicity, and Social Class. For years, debate has raged over the effectiveness of therapy for ethnic minority patients—especially when they are treated by white therapists. It does appear that many therapeutic techniques have been designed and developed for white, middle- and upper-class patients. Too few procedures seem to take into account the particular cultural background and expectations of patients. Banks (1972) has suggested that greater rapport and self-exploration may occur when both therapist and patient are of the same race. Others have reached the same conclusion regarding social class, background, values, and experience and have proposed that conventional therapies be abandoned in favor of more supportive techniques. Still, two decades of research have seemingly failed to show conclusively that ethnic minorities achieve differential treatment outcomes (Sue, 1988; Sue, Zane, & Young, 1994).

It was Schofield (1964) who described the psychotherapist's belief in the ideal patient as the YAVIS syndrome (young, attractive, verbal, intelligent, and successful). However, numerous reviews of existing research have concluded that there appears to be virtually no relationship between social class and outcome (Garfield, 1994). What has not been examined in great detail is whether patients and therapists should be matched according to social class or whether some forms of psychotherapy are more effective than others for patients from lower socioeconomic levels.

When there is a significant difference between the social class or the values of the patient and those of the therapist, some researchers have found that the patient's willingness to remain in therapy may suffer (Pettit, Pettit, & Welkowitz, 1974). Some (R. G. Hunt, 1960; Lorion, 1974; Magaro, 1969) have also suggested that traditional forms of therapy are inappropriate for patients from lower socioeconomic levels. Others (Orne & Wender, 1968; Terestman, Miller, & Weber, 1974), however, maintain that special efforts to build a therapeutic relationship can overcome the difficulties encountered when therapist and patient differ in background. Heitler (1976) has reviewed not only the difficulties encountered in offering traditional therapy to unsophisticated patients, but also the methods devised to prepare such patients for so-called expressive psychotherapy. For example, Goldstein (1973) has described a "psychotherapy for the poor," in which he adapts the language and methods of psychotherapy to these patients while making heavy use of such techniques as modeling, role-playing, and related behavioral procedures.

Few would disagree, however, that *cultural sensitivity* on the part of the therapist is very important. The field needs to develop culturally sensitive mental health services (Rogler, Malgady, Constantino, & Blumenthal, 1987; Sue et al., 1994). Clinicians also need to develop a kind of cognitive empathy, or what Scott and Borodovsky (1990) have referred to as cultural role taking in their work with ethnic minorities. In the final analysis, it is imperative that clinical psychology develop culturally sensitive therapists who can work effectively with culturally diverse populations (Lopez et al., 1989; Paniagua, 1998).

Therapists' Reactions to Patients. In the best of all worlds, it would not make any difference whether or not the patient was an engaging per-

BOX 11-1

Hot Topic *Cultural Competence*

Increasingly, clinical psychologists are providing services to members of nonwhite, multicultural groups. Clinicians must consider a number of factors when assessing and treating clients from an ethnic or socioeconomic group different from their own. Paniagua (1998) provides a number of general guidelines and considerations:

1. *Acculturation.* This refers to "the degree of integration of new cultural patterns into the original cultural patterns" (Paniagua, 1998, p. 8). Acculturation can be internal (for example, moving from one region of the United States to another) or external (moving to a new country). Clinicians can estimate the level of acculturation exhibited by a client by administering brief scales that assess variables such as language preference, preferred racial group with which to socialize, and generation (Paniagua, 1998).
2. *Language Barriers.* Although it is ideal to avoid the use of a translator if at all possible, in some cases a translator is necessary. Paniagua (1998) suggests that translators should share the client's cultural background, should have a background in mental health, should develop some rapport with the client ahead of time, and should use a sequential mode of translation (rather than concurrent translation). The use of friends, relatives, and bilingual children as translators should be avoided, and the level of acculturation of the translator should also be considered.

3. *Overdiagnosis.* Clinicians must guard against inaccurately viewing behaviors of members of multicultural groups as pathological simply because these are unfamiliar or unusual.
4. *Extended Family.* Clinicians should rely on the client's definition of extended family (which may include nonbiological members) before enlisting others to aid in the client's treatment.
5. *Type of Theory.* Directive, active, and structured therapies are generally preferred by African Americans, American Indians, Hispanics, and Asian Americans. Individual therapy should precede any family or marital therapy in those instances where acculturation appears to play a major role in the presenting problems.
6. *Amount of Data Collected.* Clinicians should avoid collecting massive amounts of data early in the assessment or treatment process. Members of multicultural groups may view this as a sign of incompetence and gross unfamiliarity with their respective cultures. Data should be gathered gradually across multiple sessions.
7. *Definition of "Therapist."* It is important to understand the client's definition of the term *therapist.* The term may be equated with "physician," "medicine man/woman," or "folk healer." Therefore, it may be necessary to modify unwarranted expectations.

son who elicited positive responses from others. A therapist should be able to work with elegant effectiveness regardless of her or his positive or negative reactions to the patient. As we saw earlier, however, therapists are far from perfect creatures; they are indeed affected by the personal qualities of other persons. Fortunately, the understanding and self-control of therapists in

The outcome of psychotherapy is influenced by a number of variables, including client characteristics, therapist qualities and skills, the problems for which relief is sought, and the therapeutic procedures that are used.
PhotoDisc

their professional relations with patients exceed the understanding and self-control of many laypersons in their social and interpersonal relationships. Nevertheless, there is some evidence to suggest that patients who receive higher global ratings of attractiveness (for example, Nash et al., 1965) or to whom the therapist can relate better (for example, Isaacs & Haggard, 1966) tend to have better outcomes in therapy (Garfield, 1994). Also, in at least one study, therapists were less inclined to treat hypothetical patients whom they did not like as compared to those they liked (Lehman & Salovey, 1990).

The Therapist

It will hardly come as a shock to learn that certain therapist characteristics may affect the process of therapy. Having a specific theoretical or therapeutic orientation does not override the role of personality, warmth, or sensitivity. Freud very early recognized the potential effects of the

psychoanalyst's personality on the process of psychoanalysis. To "prevent" such personal factors from affecting the process, he recommended that analysts undergo periodic analyses so that they could learn to recognize and control them. In a sense, Rogers turned to the other side of the same coin and made therapist qualities such as acceptance and warmth the cornerstones of therapy. Although Freud may have emphasized the negative and Rogers the positive, they both set the stage for an understanding of the role of therapist variables in the process of therapy. Unfortunately, although nearly everyone agrees that therapist variables are important, there is much less agreement on specifics. How therapist characteristics contribute to therapy outcome has become an important research area (Beutler, Machado, & Neufeldt, 1994).

Sex, Age, and Ethnicity. In a recent comprehensive review of therapist features that may influence psychotherapy outcome, Beutler et al.

(1994) report that the available research evidence suggests that therapist age is not related to outcome, that female versus male therapists do not appear to produce significantly better therapeutic effects, and that patient-therapist similarity with regard to ethnicity does not necessarily result in better outcome. Beutler et al. acknowledge that these conclusions may run counter to prevailing sociopolitical opinions. At the same time, they assert that existing research in this area suffers from a number of methodological problems. These therapist variables may interact with client characteristics, setting for treatment, and modality of treatment. Again, the solution seems to be for therapists to become more sensitized to age, gender, and racial identity issues in relation to themselves as well as to the patient.

Personality. In discussing therapist variables, Strupp and Bergin (1969) made two points worth noting. First, even though the evidence shows that the therapist's personality is a potent force, other factors in combination largely determine therapy outcomes. Second, research in this area has taken a back seat as behavioral therapies have gained in popularity. However, as behavior therapists attend increasingly to factors other than techniques or mechanics, it is likely that they will "rediscover" the importance of therapist characteristics and begin to integrate those characteristics into their research and practice.

Is there a set of personality traits that the "ideal" therapist should possess? Krasner (1963), with tongue in cheek, suggested that the research literature would depict the ideal therapist as

> mature, well-adjusted, sympathetic, tolerant, patient, kindly, tactful, nonjudgmental, accepting, permissive, non-critical, warm, likable, interested in human beings, respectful, cherishing and working for a democratic kind of interpersonal relationship with all people, free of racial and religious bigotry, having a worthwhile goal in life, friendly, encouraging, optimistic, strong, intelligent, wise, curious, creative, artistic, scientifically oriented, competent, trustworthy, a model for the patient to follow, resourceful,

emotionally sensitive, self-aware, insightful of his own problems, spontaneous, having a sense of humor, feeling personally secure, mature about sex, growing and maturing with life's experiences, having a high frustration tolerance, self-confident, relaxed, objective, self-analytic, aware of his own prejudices, non-obsequious, humble, skeptical but not pessimistic or self-deprecatory . . . dependable, consistent, open, honest, frank, technically sophisticated, professionally dedicated, and charming. (pp. 16–17)

Certainly no human being, let alone a therapist, could possibly possess all of these traits (even allowing for overlap in terms). Therefore, as Goldstein, Heller, and Sechrest (1966) point out, it is doubtful whether the concept of the "ideal therapist" is very useful. Any study that is confined to a single trait or a small group of traits seems to make a great deal of sense. Taking all the traits together makes the message much less coherent.

Beutler et al. (1994) note that the influence of therapist personality traits on outcome has not received adequate research attention. Of those traits that have been studied, the greatest amount of attention has been focused on dominance/dogmatism, locus of perceived control, and cognitive processing style. General conclusions are difficult to draw, however, because each of these variables appears to affect outcome differentially depending on client traits and type of therapy (Beutler et al., 1994). For example, Hall and Malony (1983) reported that high levels of dominance in a therapist resulted in better outcome in cases where the therapist and client were culturally similar, but low-dominance therapists were more effective with culturally dissimilar clients.

Empathy, Warmth, and Genuineness. Swenson (1971) has suggested that a major factor that differentiates successful from unsuccessful therapists is their interest in people and their commitment to the patient. In a similar vein, Brunink and Schroeder (1979) found that expert therapists of several different theoretical persuasions were similar in their communication of empathy.

The attention to empathy, along with the related notions of warmth and genuineness, grew out of Carl Rogers' (1951) system of client-centered therapy. He described these variables as necessary and sufficient conditions for therapeutic change (Rogers, 1957). Some research evidence has seemed to point to a relationship between these three qualities and successful outcomes in therapy (Truax & Carkhuff, 1967; Truax & Mitchell, 1971). However, in a careful review of research on therapeutic outcomes as they relate to therapist empathy, regard, and genuineness, Lambert, DeJulio, and Stein (1978) could find only modest support for the Rogerian hypothesis. Strupp and Bergin (1969) seem to regard empathy, warmth, and genuineness as necessary but not sufficient conditions for good therapy outcomes. In more recent years, these three qualities have been regarded more as trainable and learnable skills. According to Bergin and Suinn (1975), "It is clearer now that these variables are not as prepotent as once believed; but their presence and influence is ubiquitous, even showing up strongly in behavior therapies" (p. 52). In the case of empathy, however, some have found that less effective therapists tend to score lower on empathy than do their more effective peers (Lafferty, Beutler, & Crago, 1989).

It has also been argued (Beutler et al., 1994; Gurman, 1977) that these three features reflect not only qualities of the therapist but also qualities of the therapeutic relationship. Viewed this way, these features can be considered indicators of the quality of the therapeutic alliance. Studies have consistently demonstrated that the nature and strength of the working relationship between therapist and patient is a major contributor to positive outcome (Beutler et al., 1994).

Freedom from Personal Problems. Does personal therapy lead to greater effectiveness as a therapist? In a survey of 749 practicing therapists who were APA members, 44% responded regarding their own personal problems. Of this group, 18% reported that they had never received any form of personal therapy (Guy, Stark, & Poelstra, 1988). But more than 44% reported experiencing personal distress in the past three years, and almost 37% said that it decreased the quality of patient care (Guy, Poelstra, & Stark, 1989). Further, out of 562 licensed psychologists, more than a third reported high levels of both emotional exhaustion and depersonalization—what is often called "burnout" (Ackerley, Burnell, Holder, & Kurdek, 1988).

Although therapists need not be paragons of adjustment, it is unlikely that a therapist beset with emotional problems can be as effective as one would like. It is important that therapists recognize areas in their own lives that are tender. The tendency to become angry or anxious when certain topics arise or the inability to handle a client's questions without becoming defensive is a signal that something is amiss. In short, self-awareness is an important quality in the therapist (I. B. Weiner, 1975). Therapists must be able to look at their patients with objectivity and not become entangled in their personal dynamics. Nor is the therapy room a place for the gratification of one's own emotional needs (Bugental, 1964; Singer, 1965).

In some instances, the therapist may find it necessary to undergo personal therapy in order to resolve emotional problems. However, whether undergoing personal therapy makes the therapist more effective has long been argued. Unfortunately, the actual research evidence (Beutler et al., 1994) is less than definitive. This is not surprising when one considers the complexity of the therapy process. Nevertheless, it would not seem necessary for all therapists to undergo treatment as a qualification for conducting therapy.

Sexual Exploitation. In Chapter 3, it was noted in no uncertain terms that sexual intimacies between patient and therapist are to be condemned unequivocally. Unfortunately, there are still too many examples of victimization of women by their male therapists, and an increasing number of cases of women being victimized by female therapists. Many questions about this kind of unethical conduct, what kinds of behaviors are appropriate on the part of the therapist, what patients should do in response, and with whom they can lodge complaints have been discussed in detail (Committee on Women in Psychology, 1989). Too often, women do not complain to the proper authorities because they lack knowledge about the complaint process (Vinson, 1987). Concrete suggestions are available, however, to help women file complaints (Gottlieb, 1990). Even the act of touching clients or other nonerotic physical contacts are sensitive issues that need to be addressed in training programs and by ethics committees. One wonders whose needs are being met by such contact (Holub & Lee, 1990).

Experience and Professional Identification.
Conventional wisdom suggests that the more experienced a psychotherapist, the more effective she or he will be with patients. Although this is intuitively appealing, the bulk of research evidence has not supported this position (Beutler et al., 1994; Smith et al., 1980). Not only does there appear to be no consistent relationship between therapist experience and positive outcome, but several studies suggest that *paraprofessionals* trained specifically to conduct psychotherapy produce outcomes equivalent to, or even sometimes exceeding, those produced by trained psychotherapists (Berman & Norton, 1985; Durlak, 1981; Hattie, Sharpley, & Rogers, 1984; Weisz, Weiss, Alicke, & Klotz, 1987). Lambert and Bergin (1994) argue that the jury is still out on this issue because the studies that have been conducted to date are flawed. However, the research that is available is somewhat sobering. Like all of us, Lambert and Bergin (1994) wonder why more studies supporting the superiority of experience and professional training have not appeared.

Does one profession turn out better therapists than others? Over the years, there have been many running feuds over which profession is best equipped to carry out proper therapy. For a long time, psychiatrists actively sought to prevent clinical psychologists from conducting therapy in the absence of psychiatric supervi-

sion. Their main argument was often reducible to one of medical omniscience and was never based on solid research, and clinical psychologists gradually freed themselves from this psychiatric domination. But old animosities and fights over territorial prerogatives fade slowly. Indeed, with the availability of federal funds to pay for health costs and with insurance coverage being broadened to include psychotherapy, economic competition has once again kindled these territorial fights between psychiatry and clinical psychology.

In fact, no real evidence supports the argument that one profession boasts superior therapists (be they clinical psychologists, psychiatric social workers, psychiatrists, or psychoanalysts). In the *Consumer Reports* study ("Mental Health," 1995), people who saw a mental health professional rather than a family physician for their psychological problems reported greater progress and more satisfaction with their treatment. However, psychologists, psychiatrists, and social workers all received similarly high satisfaction ratings from consumers. Thus, at this point in time, data do not seem to support the superiority of one mental health profession over others in terms of effectiveness and client satisfaction.

To this point, we have surveyed a variety of patient and therapist variables that are commonly assumed to be related to outcome in psychotherapy. As noted in our discussion, many of these assumptions are unsupported by psychotherapy research findings. Table 11-3 lists some common assumptions about psychotherapy outcome that currently have little or no empirical support.

Course of Clinical Intervention

There are so many forms of intervention, along with so many different kinds of problems, that it is impossible to describe with precision a sequence of procedures that will apply equally well to every case. Nevertheless, it may be useful to examine the overall sequence of therapeutic progress as described by Hokanson (1983).

TABLE 11-3 Common but Unfounded Assumptions Regarding the Relationship between Patient/Client and Therapist Variables and Psychotherapy Outcome

Assumption	Evidence
1. Patients who are the least disturbed/distressed benefit from psychotherapy the most.	Results inconclusive (Garfield, 1994)
2. Older patients have worse outcomes.	No strong support for this assumption (Garfield, 1994; Smith et al., 1980)
3. Only highly motivated patients achieve good outcomes.	Mixed support (Garfield, 1994)
4. Women patients achieve better outcomes.	Biological sex appears unrelated to outcome (Sue et al., 1994)
5. Ethnic minority patients achieve worse outcomes.	No support for this assumption (Sue et al., 1994)
6. Patients of high socioeconomic status achieve better outcomes.	No relationship between social class and outcome (Garfield, 1994)
7. Older therapists produce better outcomes.	No relationship between therapist age and outcome (Beutler et al., 1994)
8. Women therapists produce better outcomes.	Mixed support (Beutler et al., 1994)
9. Therapists matched with patients according to their ethnicity produce better outcomes.	Evidence is equivocal (Beutler et al., 1994)
10. Therapists who have undergone their own personal therapy produce better outcomes.	Mixed results (Beutler et al., 1994)
11. More experienced therapists produce better outcomes.	No relationship between therapist experience and outcome (Beutler et al., 1994; Smith et al., 1980)

Initial Contact

When clients first contact the clinic or enter the clinician's office, they often do not know exactly what to expect. Some will be anxious; others, perhaps, suspicious. Some do not clearly understand the differences between medical treatment and psychotherapy. Others may be embarrassed or feel inadequate because they are seeking help. The first order of business, then, is for someone to explain generally what the clinic is all about and the kind of help that can be given. This is an important step that can have a significant bearing on the client's attitude and willingness to cooperate. Whether this initial contact is made by a therapist, a social worker, a psychological technician, or someone else, it is important that the contact be handled with skill and sensitivity.

Once the client's reasons for coming have been discussed, the next step in the general se-

quence can be explained. It may be useful at this point to discuss several specific issues. Who are the professional staff, and what are their qualifications? What about the matter of fees? Are the contacts confidential, and if not, exactly who will have access to information? If there are medical complications, how will these problems be integrated with therapy contacts? Does it seem reasonable to proceed with the client, or does a referral to another agency or professional seem more appropriate? These and other questions must be dealt with up front.

Assessment

Once it has been mutually agreed that the client can likely profit from continued contact with the clinic, one or more appointments can be arranged for an assessment of the client's problems.

As we have already seen in preceding chapters, a variety of assessment procedures may be followed, depending on the exact nature of the client's problem, the orientation of the professional staff, and other factors. Often there is an intake interview, which may consist largely of compiling a case history. Other information may be gathered by administering various psychological tests. Sometimes arrangements are made to interview a spouse, family members, or friends. In some instances, too, it may be considered desirable to have the client systematically record self-observations of behavior, thoughts, or feelings in different situations.

For some clients, consultations with other professionals may be desirable. A neurological workup may be necessary, or a medical examination may be scheduled to rule out nonpsychological factors. For some clients whose problems are related to economic problems or unemployment, additional consultation with social workers or job counselors may be appropriate.

After all the information has been compiled and analyzed, a preliminary integration is attempted. What is desirable here is not a simple diagnostic label but a comprehensive construction of the client's problems in light of all the psychological, environmental, and medical data available. This initial conceptualization of the client will provide guidelines for the specific therapeutic interventions to be undertaken. As therapy proceeds, changes in the conceptualization of the client will likely occur, and therapeutic goals and techniques may well change somewhat as a result. Assessment is an ongoing process that does not cease with the second or third interview.

The Goals of Treatment

As soon as the assessment data are integrated, the therapist and client can begin to discuss more systematically the nature of the problems and what can be done about them. Some therapists describe this phase as a period of negotiation over the goals of treatment. Others suggest that client and therapist enter into a "contract" in which the therapist agrees to alleviate a specified set of the client's problems and to do it in the most effective way possible. Naturally, no one can absolutely promise a perfect cure or resolution of all problems. Clients, in turn, will state their desires and intentions. In effect, their contract usually covers such matters as the goals of therapy, length of therapy, frequency of meetings, cost, general format of therapy, and the client's responsibilities.

Again, it is important to understand that various features of the contract may be modified as time goes on. One must deal with clients in terms of what they are prepared to accept now. An especially anxious or defensive client may be willing to accept only a limited set of goals or procedures. As therapy proceeds, that client may become more open and comfortable and thus better able to accept an expanded set of goals. Then, too, additional information about the client may surface during therapy, with the result that some modifications may be necessary. Some clients will want to expand their goals for treatment as they gain more confidence and trust in the therapist. Discussion of goals and methods must be handled with discretion, sensitivity, and skill. Therapists must try to take clients only where they are psychologically prepared to go. Moving too fast or setting up grandiose treatment objectives can frighten or alienate certain clients. It is usually desirable to proceed with enough subtlety and skill so that clients feel they are the ones who are establishing or modifying the goals.

Hokanson (1983) uses a classification of therapy goals in terms of *crisis management, behavior change, corrective emotional experience*, and *insight and change*. Table 11-4 illustrates these goals. In the most general sense, the goal of psychotherapy is to improve the patient's level of psychosocial adjustment and to increase the patient's capacity for achieving satisfactions from life.

Implementing Treatment

After the initial goals are established, the therapist decides on the specific form of treatment. It may be client-centered, cognitive, behavioral, or psychoanalytic. The treatment may be very

■ **TABLE 11-4** The Nature of Goals and Therapy According to Hokanson

Therapeutic Goal	Examples of Problems	Treatment Procedures
Crisis management	Incipient psychotic episode; poorly planned, impulsive actions; explosive acting-out behavior	Supportive therapy; emergency consultation in psychiatric hospital; crisis work in community
Behavior change	Habits and behaviors of long standing that create health problems for patient	Behavior therapy; self-regulation techniques
Corrective emotional experience	Broadly based maladaptive "way of life" stemming from persistent negative interpersonal experiences	Relationship therapy
Insight and change	Symptoms or distress for which client can find no suitable explanation	Psychoanalytic therapy; client-centered therapy; existential analysis; Gestalt therapies; other therapies

circumscribed and deal only with a specific phobia, or it may involve a broader approach to the client's personality style. All of this must be carefully described to the client in terms of how it relates to the client's problems, the length of time involved, and perhaps even the difficulties and trying times that may lie ahead. Exactly what is expected of the client will be detailed as well—free association, "homework" assignments, self-monitoring, or whatever. Inherent in all of this is the issue of informed consent. Just as participants in research have a right to know what will happen, so do therapy patients have the right to know what will happen in therapy. Box 11-2 provides an outline of the information to which outpatients should have access.

Termination, Evaluation, and Follow-up

It is certainly to be hoped that a client will not be in psychotherapy her or his entire life. As the therapist begins to believe the client is able to handle his or her problems independently, discussions of termination are initiated. Sometimes termination is a gradual process in which meetings are reduced, for example, from once a week to once a month. As termination approaches, it is important that it be discussed in detail and the

client's feelings and attitudes thoroughly aired and dealt with. Clients do sometimes terminate suddenly, in some cases before the therapist feels it is appropriate. Whenever possible, however, it is important to find the time to discuss at least briefly the client's feelings about leaving the support of therapy and the possibility of returning later for additional sessions if necessary. In other instances, the termination is forced because the therapist must leave the clinic, which can precipitate numerous client reactions. Many therapists find that "booster sessions" scheduled months after termination—perhaps 6 months and then one year later—can be quite helpful. These booster sessions are used to review the client's progress, to address new problems or issues that have arisen in the interim, and to solidify the gains that have been made.

It is important to evaluate with clients the progress they have made. Therapists should also compile data and make notes on progress in order to evaluate the quality of their own efforts or the agency's services and continue to improve services to clients. The most reliable data, of course, will come from formally designed research projects (described in the following section). However, clinicians and individual agencies owe it to themselves and their clients to evaluate the success of their own efforts.

BOX 11-2

Information Patients Have a Right to Know

Handelsman and Galvin (1988) have prepared a consent form for potential patients that sets forth the questions they are entitled to ask their therapists. Some research has shown that forms such as this can enhance patients' first impressions of their therapists (Handelsman, 1990).

When you come for therapy, you are buying a service. Therefore, you need information to make a good decision. Below are some questions you might want to ask. We've talked about some of them. You are entitled to ask me any of these questions, if you want to know. If you don't understand my answers, ask me again.

I. Therapy
  A. How does your kind of therapy work?
  B. What are the possible risks involved? (like divorce, depression)
  C. What percentage of clients improve? In what ways?
  D. What percentage of clients get worse?
  E. What percentage of clients improve or get worse without this therapy?
  F. About how long will it take?
  G. What should I do if I feel therapy isn't working?
  H. Will I have to take any tests? What kind?

II. Alternatives
  A. What other types of therapy or help are there? (like support groups)
  B. How often do they work?
  C. What are the risks of these other approaches?

III. Appointments
  A. How are appointments scheduled?
  B. How long are sessions? Do I have to pay more for longer ones?
  C. How can I reach you in an emergency?
  D. If you are not available, who is there I can talk to?
  E. What happens if the weather is bad, or I'm sick?

IV. Confidentiality
  A. What kind of records do you keep?

Who has access to them? (insurance companies, supervisors)
  B. Under what conditions are you allowed to tell others about the things we discuss? (suicidal or homicidal threats, child abuse, court cases, insurance companies, supervisors)
  C. Do other members of my family, or of the group, have access to information?

V. Money
  A. What is your fee?
  B. How do I need to pay? At the session, monthly, etc.?
  C. Do I need to pay for missed sessions?
  D. Do I need to pay for telephone calls or letters?
  E. What are your policies about raising fees? (For example, how many times have you raised them in the past two years?)
  F. If I lose my source of income, can my fee be lowered?
  G. If I do not pay my fee, will you take me to small claims court? Do you use a collection agency or lawyer? Under what circumstances?

VI. General
  A. What is your training and experience? Are you licensed? Supervised? Board certified?
  B. Who do I talk to if I have a complaint about therapy that we can't work out? (e.g., Supervisor, State Board of Psychologist Examiners, APA ethics committee)

The contract [or brochure, or our conversation] dealt with most of these questions. I will be happy to explain them, and to answer other questions you have. This will help make your decision a good one. You can keep this information. Please read it carefully at home. We will also look this over from time to time.

Source: From "Facilitating Informed Consent for Outpatient Psychotherapy: A Suggested Written Format," by M. M. Handelsman and M. D. Galvin, *Professional Psychology: Research and Practice*, 1988, *19*, 223–225. Copyright 1988 by the American Psychological Association. Reprinted by permission.

BOX 11-3

Eysenck's Bombshell

In arriving at his conclusions about the efficacy of psychotherapy, Eysenck considered statistical outcome data from more than 7000 patients. These patients included 5 psychoanalytic groups and 14 groups who had undergone "eclectic" therapy. As control data, Eysenck used the discharge rate among hospitalized patients from New York State hospitals and the amount of improvement that occurred in individuals who were seeking insurance settlements and were receiving medical treatment from general practitioners.

Basically, Eysenck claimed that 72% of the patients who had received only custodial or medical care had improved, whereas only 44% of the patients who had received psychoanalytic treatment and only 66% of the patients who had received eclectic therapy showed improvement. Thus, a smaller percentage of psychotherapy patients than of control patients showed improvement.

Although some have argued for the validity of Eysenck's conclusions (for example, Rachman, 1973; Truax & Carkhuff, 1967), others have vehemently disagreed (for example, Bergin, 1971; deCharms, Levy, & Wertheimer, 1954). The criticisms have centered on Eysenck's failure to match participants in the treatment and control groups. In fact, there really was no control group in the classic sense, and there certainly was no matching for education, social class, personality structure, expectations about therapy, or other relevant factors. Also, there was little evidence that physicians and psychiatrists were using the same standards for improvement. Finally, there is a question about how Eysenck calculated his improvement rates. For example, Bergin (1971) argued that the improvement rate for custodial and medical care groups was really 30% rather than 72%, as calculated by Eysenck.

Psychotherapy Research

In this last section, we will briefly review the methods of psychotherapy research, the results of several major outcome studies, and the recent trends in psychotherapy research. More extensive reviews and books on methods of psychotherapy research are available for the interested reader (for example, Bergin & Garfield, 1994; Kazdin, 1994).

For many years, the prevailing philosophy seemed to be that therapy probably benefited many patients, and at the very least was not harmful to the others, so why worry? But over the years, some did worry. For example, Cartwright (1956), Bergin (1971), and Hadley and Strupp (1977) called attention to the likelihood of deterioration effects in some psychotherapy patients and the need, therefore, to study outcomes in therapy. Although not everyone believes that therapy patients are at greater risk for psychological deterioration than similar individuals not in treatment, there still may be danger for some individuals (Bergin, 1980; Lambert & Bergin, 1994; Mays & Franks, 1985).

The work that really stood the psychotherapy establishment on its ear was Eysenck's (1952) report declaring in no uncertain terms that the research evidence failed to support the claim that psychotherapy with neurotics was more effective than no therapy at all (see Box 11-3). Investigators took this and related work (Eysenck, 1965, 1966) as a challenge. Consequently, the significance of Eysenck's work lies less in the validity of his conclusions (which many deemed flawed) than in the attack he made on the field's complacency.

As we mentioned earlier in this chapter, the evidence concerning the efficacy of psychotherapy is now considerably more favorable. Still, an undercurrent of suspicion remains (Dawes, 1994). To better understand the nature of therapeutic change, we will consider issues of research design and method, the results of outcome studies, and the process of change itself.

Issues in Psychotherapy Research

It is not enough to collect 25 patients undergoing psychoanalytic therapy, administer before-and-after measures of adjustment, determine that positive changes have occurred after six months, and then conclude that psychoanalytic treatment is effective. Would a comparable group of patients without therapy have shown improvement? Would a similar group undergoing systematic desensitization have improved as much? Was the improvement due to the psychoanalytic procedures employed, or was the crucial factor the mere presence of a warm, interested person who listened? The simple design suggested in our example does not permit answering any of these important questions.

As with many psychological experiments (see Chapter 4), studies that seek to investigate the effectiveness of psychotherapy typically employ an experimental group and a control group of patients. The experimental group, or *treatment group*, receives the treatment that is being investigated, whereas the *control group* does not. Control groups can take many forms. In a *waiting list control group*, patients' treatment is delayed until after the study is completed; in an *attention only control group*, patients meet regularly with a clinician, but no "active" treatment is administered. As much as possible, patients in the treatment and control groups are matched on variables that might be related to outcome, such as gender, age, diagnostic status, and severity of symptoms before the study began, before they are randomly assigned to groups. Assessments of *patient functioning* (symptoms of psychopathology) are conducted in parallel fashion for both treatment and control participants. At the very least, assessments are obtained at the beginning of the

study, at treatment completion, and possibly at some period of time after treatment is terminated (follow-up). This design allows a comparison of the two groups at treatment completion and follow-up, as well as an evaluation of the amount of change (if any) within each group.

Following are some of the research considerations that help shape the meaning and generality of research findings on therapeutic outcomes.

1. What is the sample? Are the patients voluntary, or were they subtly or overtly coerced into therapy (for example, prisoners versus private-practice patients). Were the therapists experienced, or were they neophytes? Were they psychoanalysts, or were they behaviorists? Were the patients "real" patients, or were they recruited by a newspaper ad requesting paid volunteers for an analog study on the "treatment of snake phobias"? Undoubtedly, the answer to each of these questions (and others like them) will determine how researchers can interpret their results. There are no absolute findings, only findings relative to the sample and to the conditions of the given study.

2. What relevant patient variables were controlled? Unfortunately, one cannot hope to provide a control group that is exactly the same as the treatment group. This being the case, how close did the study come to controlling relevant factors? If the waiting list or attention only control group was not identical with the patient group, in what ways did it differ? Were the presenting complaints of the patient group all basically alike, or was there diversity? Was the control group similar to the treatment group with respect to demographic factors, personality, knowledge about therapy, and expectations for help?

3. What were the *outcome measures*? Were the outcome measures identical for every patient and control, or were they "tailored" to meet the idiosyncratic situation (goals, hopes, and expectations) of each patient? Was a single outcome measure used, or were multiple measures employed? Were the measures nonreactive or unobtrusive, or were they

measures that, by their very character, might reflect things other than what they were supposed to be measuring? Unfortunately, there is currently no consensus about which outcome measures should be used in psychotherapy research studies. This makes comparisons across studies more difficult.

4. What was the general nature of the study? The effects of therapy can be evaluated in a variety of ways. So far we have concentrated on experimental studies. Other methods include case studies, clinical surveys, correlational studies, and analog studies. Each type has characteristic strengths and weaknesses. For example, a case study can offer a richness of detail and a fountain of hypotheses that may be far more valuable than an experimental study or an analog study. But a case study has an *N* of 1, and how far can one generalize from one patient? Analog studies offer great potential for controlling relevant variables, avoiding ethical problems with no-treatment groups, and collecting a satisfactory number of participants. But how close to reality is an analog study? As we have had occasion to remark before, each method offers unique advantages and characteristic limitations. How researchers choose to proceed must be determined by what they seek to learn and what they can tolerate in the way of limitations. Perhaps the best hope is that numerous good investigators will decide to follow diverse research paths.

Comparative Studies

Therapy research has become increasingly sophisticated since Eysenck's critique. More and more studies do not just assess outcomes but also compare two or more techniques in terms of efficacy. However, several critics have questioned whether some designs are powerful enough (have enough study participants) to detect differences between alternative treatments (Kazdin & Bass, 1989).

The Temple University Study. A major comparative study was conducted by Sloane, Staples, Cristol, Yorkston, and Whipple (1975a, 1975b). More than 90 outpatient neurotics were assigned to (1) behavior therapy, (2) short-term psychoanalytically oriented therapy, or (3) a minimal treatment waiting list. The groups were matched in terms of sex and severity of symptoms; otherwise, assignment was random. Treatment was carried out by three behavior therapists and three analysts, all of whom were highly trained and experienced. Before and after measurements included psychological tests, a target symptoms technique (a measure oriented toward individualized treatment criteria), a standard interview, informants' reports (people who had known the patients for an average of 12 years), and ratings by the therapist, the patient, and an independent rater. The reader will note that these procedures correspond closely to several of the recommendations made earlier in the methodology section of this chapter.

All three groups had improved at a 4-month posttesting point. However, the psychoanalytic therapy (PT) and behavior therapy (BT) groups improved more than did the waiting list (W) group. The independent rater could find no differences with respect to improvement in target symptoms between the BT and PT groups. General estimates, such as improvement in work or social situations, also failed to discriminate between the PT and BT groups. The rater's global outcome assessment indicated that 80% of both the BT group and the PT group improved, whereas only 48% of the W group did. For general adjustment, 93% of the BT group and 77% of both the PT group and the W group showed improvement. Although the comparative change between the BT group and the PT group varied depending on the specific criterion, in general there was a slight trend in favor of the BT group. There was no evidence of deterioration effects, and all three groups maintained their improvement after one year. It should be noted, however, that there was a trend for the improvement to continue and for patients in the W group to approach or equal those in the BT and PT groups. This could suggest that what therapy does is accelerate change, rather than produce more change, as compared to no treatment. Psy-

TABLE 11-5 Average Effect Size ($\overline{ES}$) and Percentile Equivalent for Select Forms of Psychological Intervention

Type of Therapy	$\overline{ES}$	Percentile Equivalent
Psychodynamic	0.69	75%
Client-centered	0.62	73%
Gestalt	0.64	74%
Rational-emotive therapy (RET)	0.68	75%
Non-RET cognitive therapies	2.38	99%
Systematic densensitization	1.05	85%
Behavior modification	0.73	77%
Cognitive-behavioral therapy	1.13	87%
Undifferentiated counseling	0.28	61%
All forms of psychological intervention	0.85	80%

Note: Percentile equivalent indicates the percentage of those not receiving treatment whose outcome is exceeded by those receiving the treatment in question.
Source: Adapted from Smith, Glass, and Miller (1980).

choanalysts produced better outcomes with less disturbed patients, whereas the level of patient disturbance made no difference for behavior therapists. This suggests that behavior therapy may have greater versatility, perhaps because of the greater flexibility and eclecticism of the techniques employed by behavior therapists.

Meta-analyses. In 1977, Smith and Glass published a review of nearly 400 psychotherapy outcome studies. Their verdict was that the evidence is convincing in showing the effectiveness of psychotherapy. What is unique about their review is their use of a method called *meta-analysis*. Using this method, they analyzed all therapy studies that dealt with at least one therapy group and one control group, or with two therapy groups, and averaged the effects of therapy across all these studies. In their analysis, they defined *effect size* as the mean difference between treated and control participants' scores on relevant outcome measures, divided by the standard deviation of the control group.

Earlier, we mentioned the meta-analysis of Smith et al. (1980). Their survey included 475 studies involving 25,000 patients treated by

some 78 therapies for an average of 16 sessions. Outcome comparisons showed effect sizes that averaged .85 standard deviations. As previously mentioned, this means "the average person who receives therapy is better off at the end of it than 80% of the persons who do not" (Smith et al., 1980, p. 87). Using a somewhat stricter definition of therapy and removing "placebo therapy" and "undifferentiated counseling" from the data, the average effect size increased from .85 to .93 of a standard deviation unit. This figure would be analogous to reducing an illness or death rate from 66% to 34%! Table 11-5 presents a summary of Smith et al.'s findings for several major forms of psychotherapy.

A number of investigators have supported the general utility of meta-analysis procedures and have thereby corroborated the Smith and Glass conclusions on the efficacy of psychotherapy (for example, Fiske, 1983; Landman & Dawes, 1982; Shapiro & Shapiro, 1982, 1983). These meta-analytic studies, however, do have some problems (Parloff, London, & Wolfe, 1986). Major clinical conditions (such as depression and alcoholism) are underrepresented in these studies, while others (for example, phobias) are overrepresented. Therapists tend to be novice clinicians or psychiatric residents, and therapies are too often short-term behavioral interventions. Some critics are skeptical of meta-analysis methods. For example, Wilson and Rachman (1983) are concerned about Smith and Glass's tendency to lump together for analysis studies that vary significantly in their quality and methodological sophistication.

On balance, it would appear that meta-analysis has served to strengthen the case for the effectiveness of psychotherapy. However, meta-analysis has by no means solved all the problems in this area. Anyone who thinks that sophisticated statistical analysis can ever really substitute for carefully designed research is in for a rude shock. As Wilson and Rachman (1983) put it, "A failure to recognize the problems with meta-analysis threatens to perpetuate the impression that statistical techniques can make acceptable poor quality data that distort therapeutic process and outcome" (p. 54).

Process Research

So far, we have focused on the outcomes of therapeutic intervention, along with many of the patient and therapist variables that may affect those outcomes. Other investigators, however, have addressed the specific events that occur during therapy in the course of the interaction between therapist and patient. This is called *process research*. The Rogerians were pioneers in this area and commonly conducted studies relating, for example, the amount of therapist talk in a given session to client spontaneity or the effects of therapist clarifications and restatements on the client's taking responsibility for the progress in a given session.

For a long time, therapy investigators were split into two camps (Beutler, 1990)—those who did process research and those who did outcome research. Those who focused on outcomes criticized process research as failing to show that processes internal to therapy were correlated with outcome and, therefore, as not worthy of serious consideration. Indeed, it sometimes

seemed as if the process was misleading in predicting outcomes.

But process-oriented researchers felt there ought to be relationships between outcome and the processes that occur during therapy (Strupp, 1971). One way of doing this kind of research is to film or tape actual therapy sessions. This kind of research has increasingly begun to show substantive relationships between what happens during therapy and ultimate outcome (Garfield, 1990; Marmar, 1990). For example, Windholz and Silberschatz (1988) found that by examining audiotapes they could show that active involvement in the therapy process was a significant predictor of therapy outcomes for outpatients ranging in age from 20 to 85.

A simple example of process research is a study by Lassen (1973) that investigated the effects of physical distance on anxiety and communication in an initial psychiatric interview. Interviews between the patient and the therapist were conducted at distances of 3 feet, 6 feet, and 9 feet. Several results emerged: (1) The Speech Disturbance Ratio (a measure of anxiety) increased with increasing distance. (2) Patients reported that they were not as well understood when the distances were larger. (3) Patients talked more about their anxieties and fears and reported themselves as having been more open at 6 feet. Such a study certainly does not turn the therapy field around. But carefully building many such studies one upon the other can increase our understanding of what it is in therapy that affects what.

Another example of process research is the work on communication and speech interactions (Matarazzo & Wiens, 1972). This kind of research has investigated formal properties of utterances, including their duration and frequency, as well as interruptions, the proportions of patient-therapist talk, and other variables. Other research combines process and outcome features. For example, Staples, Sloane, Whipple, Cristol, and Yorkston (1976) found that patients showing greater total speech time and longer speech durations in therapy evidenced more improvement.

More recently, Hill (1990) has reviewed a variety of studies of process variables. Therapist variables include verbal responses, facilitative behavior (for example, empathy), and tendency to give advice, provide information, or offer interpretations. Client process variables include degree of involvement, nature of client statements, presence of emotions during therapy, and identification of "good" moments in therapy that seem to portend improvement.

Recent Trends

Focus of Psychotherapy Research. Asking whether therapy is effective is no longer a very good strategy. The question is too broad. A more useful approach is to consider specific therapies applied to specific patients in specific ways. Most studies now focus on the effectiveness of certain treatments with specific psychological problems (Barlow, 1996; Nathan, 1998). For example, Gortner, Gollan, Dobson, and Jacobson (1998) studied patients with major depression, and McLean, Woody, Taylor, and Koch (1998) investigated the efficacy of cognitive-behavioral therapy in panic disorder patients with and without comorbid major depression. Kazdin and Crowley (1997) examined the effectiveness of cognitive treatment of antisocial children, and Craske, Rowe, Lewin, and Noriega-Dimitri (1997) examined which component of cognitive-behavioral treatment for panic disorder with agoraphobia (interoceptive exposure versus breathing retraining) was most effective.

In addition, more and more studies now evaluate the effects of psychotherapy versus medication. Given the increasing frequency with which many psychiatrists and family physicians prescribe medications for psychological problems, the unwillingness of the health care bureaucracy to pay for "interminable" therapy, and the growing interest of some clinical psychologists in prescribing medications (see Chapter 1), such research is gaining in importance. In any event, we need to conduct studies that can accurately assess how medications and psycho-

therapy compare and how they may interact (for example, Elkin, Gibbons, Shea, & Shaw, 1996; Jacobson & Hollon, 1996; Klein, 1996).

Practice Guidelines. Increasingly, clinical psychologists are being held accountable for the services they provide. Insurers and managed care companies no longer give clinicians free rein as to the interventions they employ and the pace at which treatment is administered. In order to maintain control over the psychotherapy enterprise, several professional organizations have become increasingly active in developing *practice guidelines* (Nathan, 1998). Practice guidelines recommend specific forms of intervention for specific psychological problems or disorders, and they have a common goal of "detailed specification of methods and procedures to ensure effective treatment for each disorder" (Nathan & Gorman, 1998, p. 12).

Exemplifying this trend, the Division of Clinical Psychology of the American Psychological Association published a list of *empirically validated treatments (EVTs)* in 1995 (Task Force on Promotion and Dissemination of Psychological Procedures, 1995). Using standard criteria, this APA Task Force developed lists of well-established and probably efficacious treatments for a number of psychological problems. Table 11-6 presents the most up-to-date list of well-established EVTs for a variety of conditions (Chambless et al., 1998). We will discuss several of these forms of psychological intervention in subsequent chapters.

It is important to note, however, that these lists are not without controversy. Garfield (1996), for example, argues that (1) the lists are premature, and much more research needs to be conducted before such a publication; (2) the term "empirically validated" is misleading, suggesting that other interventions not on the list are useless or harmful; (3) the EVTs lack external validity because they do not represent psychotherapy as it is typically conducted outside the research laboratory; and (4) these regimented EVTs ignore the importance of both therapist and patient variables in outcome (assuming "one size fits all") and fly in the face of evidence

■ **TABLE 11-6** Examples of "Well-Established" Empirically Validated Treatments (EVTs)

Anxiety and Stress Problems
Cognitive behavior therapy for panic disorder (with and without agoraphobia)

Cognitive behavior therapy for generalized anxiety disorder

Exposure treatment for agoraphobia

Exposure/guided mastery for specific phobia

Exposure and response prevention for obsessive-compulsive disorder

Stress inoculation training for coping with stressors

Depression
Behavior therapy for depression

Cognitive therapy for depression

Interpersonal therapy for depression

Health Problems
Behavior therapy for headache

Multi-component cognitive behavior therapy for pain associated with rheumatic disease

Multi-component cognitive behavior therapy with relapse prevention for smoking cessation

Cognitive behavior therapy for bulimia

Childhood Problems
Behavior modification for enuresis

Parent training programs for children with oppositional behavior

Marital Problems
Behavioral marital therapy

Source: Adapted from Chambless et al. (1998). Update on empirically validated therapies, II. *The Clinical Psychologist, 51,* 3–16. Adapted with permission of the Division of Clinical Psychology, American Psychological Association.

suggesting the lack of superiority of one form of treatment over others.

Garfield's (1996) criticisms are important for the field to consider, and several clinical psychologists who conduct psychotherapy research have responded. Barlow (1996), Chambless (1996), and others disagree that the publication of the EVTs was premature. First, they point out that the efficacy of the treatments on these lists is well supported. Although it is important to conduct additional research and modify the lists as appropriate, delaying publication would put psychological interventions at risk because other professional organizations (such as psychiatry) have published their own practice guidelines, and managed care companies are beginning to incorporate these lists in their own guidelines (Barlow, 1996). Second, many agree with Garfield that "empirically supported" may be a better descriptor for these treatments; however, a change in terms has not been made for fear that it would only lead to more confusion (Chambless, 1996). Third, the effectiveness of "therapy-as-usual" has not been adequately studied (Barlow, 1996). However, we do know that, on average, patients who receive one of the EVTs function significantly better than those in control groups. Finally, although intuitively appealing, Garfield's (1996) statements regarding the importance of patient and therapist variables to clinical outcome should be seen as working hypotheses, not empirically demonstrated facts (Barlow, 1996; Chambless, 1996).

Manualized Treatment. A related, hotly debated issue is whether manual-based treatments should be used in clinical practice. Treatment manuals were originally developed by psychotherapy researchers in order to ensure that treatment protocols were standardized across patients. However, *manualized treatment* has also been used outside the research context in clinical practice. Some have criticized manual-based treatment for "undermining" the clinical judgment of clinicians, for not being tailored to patients with multiple problems (comorbid conditions), and for ignoring therapist effects on outcome (Davison & Lazarus, 1995; Garfield, 1996; Wilson, 1998).

In addressing these and other criticisms, Wilson (1998) points out that manual-based treatment has greater clinical utility than it is given credit for. The psychological testing and clinical judgment literature suggests that clinical judgment and clinical prediction are limited and are likely to be outperformed by an empirically supported manualized treatment that prescribes for the therapist the methods of intervention for a given problem. Second, there are no data to support the position that manual-based treatments are inferior to treatment-as-usual with regard to comorbid psychological problems (Wilson, 1998). In fact, manual-based treatments might be used to treat comorbid problems sequentially or concurrently. Third, Wilson (1998) argues that manual-based treatments actually encourage clinical innovation because they help identify those patients who do not seem to respond to "first-choice" treatments. It then becomes possible and necessary to modify protocols in order to treat these individuals successfully. Finally, Wilson (1998) points out that manual-based treatments, like other forms of treatment, require clinical skill and a positive therapeutic alliance. He does acknowledge that treatment manuals need to become more "therapist friendly" and suggests providing more practical guidelines as well as more discussions of commonly encountered problems in implementing the treatment.

We would like to highlight a few additional advantages of manual-based treatment. This form of treatment is more focused, often more engaging from the patient's perspective, and easier to teach, supervise, and monitor (Wilson, 1998). Finally, the clinicians who master manual-based treatments will be much more attractive to managed care companies because these treatments are recognized as efficacious and efficient (Marques, 1998; Strosahl, 1998). Marques (1998) predicts that clinicians will be required to use manual-based treatment protocols to maintain their provider status for managed care organizations. For all of these reasons, it is important that clinical psychology trainees receive thorough training in manual-based empirically supported treatments (Calhoun, Moras, Pilkonis, & Rehm, 1998). Table 11-7 presents a preliminary set of guidelines for training in empirically supported treatments.

Some General Conclusions

A generalization about the effectiveness of psychotherapy seems to be emerging. However, there is little evidence to suggest that one form of therapy is in any sense uniquely effective for all problems. J. D. Frank's (1979) conclusions about psychotherapy several decades ago also seen to characterize current thinking:

1. Nearly all forms of psychotherapy are somewhat more effective than unplanned or informal help.
2. One form of therapy has typically not been shown to be more effective than another for all conditions.
3. Clients who show initial improvement tend to maintain it.
4. Characteristics of the client, the therapist, and their interaction may be more important than therapeutic technique.

◼ **TABLE 11-7 Guidelines for Training in Empirically Supported Treatments (ESTs)**

1. Include videotapes that illustrate the conduct of the central components of the EST in the training program.

2. Rely mainly on audio- or videotapes of therapy sessions for supervision, rather than on trainees' self-reports.

3. Use adherence measures developed for the EST to systematically and frequently evaluate each trainee's progress.

4. Training material that illustrates common errors in the implementation of central components of an EST are efficient training aids.

5. Group supervision using audiotapes of sessions may be more efficient than individual supervision in terms of rate of learning.

6. Expect to provide supervision on a minimum of three to four prototypical cases for the EST, plus a minimum of four more nonprototypic cases to develop minimally adequate skill performing it.

7. Include instruction in ongoing evaluation of a patient's response to the EST.

Source: Adapted from Calhoun, K. S., Moras, K., Pilkonis, P. A., & Rehm, L. P. (1998). Empirically supported treatments: Implications for training. *Journal of Consulting and Clinical Psychology, 66,* 151–162.

This last point is important because it suggests that, given the equal effectiveness of various forms of therapy, the field should turn its attention to those elements that are common to all forms of therapy. Not all agree with this conclusion, however. Telch (1981), for one, argues that the more potent the therapeutic technique being used, the less important are therapist or client characteristics. As an example, Telch notes that evidence strongly suggests that systematic desensitization is highly effective with patients with phobias. Yet for those who have trouble using mental imagery, desensitization may prove ineffective, and modeling may be the technique of choice. Lazarus (1980) also argues that specific therapies are indicated for specific problems. At the same time, however, he seems to suggest that various nonspecific factors play an important role in improvement. For example, regardless of whether the therapist is using desensitization, modeling, or the quest for insight, the result may be an increased sense of self-efficacy on the part of the patient that, in turn, facilitates change.

Perhaps the safest course is to pursue a two-front assault. Careful research should be designed to help us predict which therapy will best work for a given problem. Lists of empirically supported treatments for common psychological problems should continue to be updated and expanded. At the same time, effort should also be devoted to investigating the factors common to all therapies and the manner in which they operate. Research might also focus on the effects of matching patients and therapists in terms of relevant characteristics. However, in the final analysis, therapist competence may be more critical than the simple matching of patients and therapists along lines of race, class, or sex.

Therapy is an intermittent process that occurs, for example, once a week. Thus, it is only a small part of a client's ongoing life. Other, concurrent experiences may be as important or even more important in determining whether or not improvement occurs. Also, what happens in therapy may interact with other experiences in complex ways. Others may begin to react differently to the client, and these changed reactions may reinforce or counteract changes induced by therapy. Changes in the client may threaten family members, who then quietly conspire to sabotage treatment. The whole process is so complex and interactive that it is difficult for research to show what factors in therapy are related to client change or lack of it (J. D. Frank, 1982).

Perhaps the greatest reality limitation of all is suggested by Barlow's (1981) charge that many clinical psychologists simply do not pay attention to outcome research. They continue doing what they have always done without full realization of the difficulties in making valid inferences from their experiences with single cases (Kazdin, 1981). Persons (1995) discusses how deficits in training and the perceived inaccessibility of resources have caused clinicians to delay adopting empirically supported treatment techniques. However, Chambless et al. (1996) has said it best:

> Psychology is a science. Seeking to help those in need, clinical psychology draws its strength and uniqueness from the ethic of scientific validation. Whatever interventions that mysticism, authority, commercialism, politics, custom, convenience, or carelessness might dictate, clinical psychologists focus on what works. They bear a fundamental ethical responsibility to use where possible interventions that work and to subject any intervention they use to scientific scrutiny. (p. 10)

Clinical psychologists must learn more about the specifics of the effectiveness of various forms of therapy and routinely implement this knowledge. They are under both ethical and scientific imperatives to do so.

Chapter Summary

Clinical psychologists use psychological interventions to induce changes in a person's behavior, thoughts, or feelings. Psychotherapy is a form of intervention that occurs in a professional context whose aim is to solve psychological problems, improve coping and functioning, prevent future problems, or increase life satisfaction. Evidence suggests that psychotherapy is effective, especially for certain types of psychological problems. However, no one form of psychotherapy or intervention is superior for all problems.

Certain features or characteristics are common to all forms of therapy, including the expert role of the therapist, the relationship or therapeutic alliance, the building of competence, the release of anxiety or tension, and the expectation of change. Although specific characteristics of the patient and of the therapist may influence outcome, such relationships appear to be multidimensional and complex. Interestingly, many commonly held beliefs regarding the relationships between patient and therapist factors and psychotherapy outcome are not supported by research.

Psychotherapy research is aimed at assessing whether or not certain interventions are effective with specific client populations, what factors seem related to change, and how such change can be brought about. More recent studies examine whether a specific therapy is effective with patients with specific psychological problems (such as specific DSM-IV diagnoses). In addition, clinical psychologists have begun to examine more thoroughly the relative benefits of psychotherapy versus medication for certain conditions, and of combined therapy/medication treatments. Finally, research has helped to shape practice guidelines that incorporate empirically supported treatments. In the future, clinical psychologists are likely to be using manual-based treatments with increasing frequency.

Key Terms

attention-only control group A control group whose members meet regularly with a clinician but receive no "active" treatment.

behavior change A general therapeutic goal that may involve extinguishing or decreasing the frequency of an undesired behavior and/or increasing the frequency of a desired behavior.

catharsis The release of emotions.

common factors A set of features that characterize many therapy orientations and that may be the source of the positive changes effected by psychological treatment.

control group In psychotherapy research, the group that does not receive the treatment under investigation.

corrective emotional experience A general therapeutic goal, typically accompanied by an emotional reaction, in which the client changes his or her assumptions about others and learns new ways of relating to others by virtue of the fact that the therapist does not "react" to the client's hostility, dependency, and so on in the same way that others have tended to react.

crisis management A general therapeutic goal that involves calming or de-escalating individuals in a crisis situation, helping them to problem solve, and/or providing them with support.

depth of a problem The changeability of a condition or behavior. (The "deeper" the condition, the less changeable it is perceived to be.)

effect size The size of the treatment effect (determined statistically).

empirically validated treatments (EVTs) Treatments for various psychological conditions that have been shown through careful empirical study to be either "well established" or "probably efficacious." A list of EVTs is updated and published periodically by the APA's Division of Clinical Psychology.

expert role The therapist's demonstration of competence (i.e., knowledge and experience).

feminist therapy A psychotherapy orientation that deals with the emotional difficulties and disorders experienced by women and acknowledges that many of the difficulties that women experience arise from the social position they are forced to adopt.

gender bias In the context of psychotherapy, gender bias is demonstrated if the same treatment results in differential outcomes for males and females. Although there is no good evidence linking biological sex with treatment outcome, clinicians need to appreciate how issues specific to the client's sex may affect his or her adjustment, perspective, and/or approach to therapy.

insight In the context of psychotherapy, the achievement of understanding into the nature and origins of one's problems.

interpretation In the context of psychotherapy, the therapist's conceptualization of the meaning behind the patient's experiences or behaviors.

manualized treatment Psychotherapeutic treatment that is presented and described in a standardized, manual format (i.e., outlining the rationales, goals, and techniques that correspond to each phase of the treatment).

mastery The acquisition of a high level of knowledge or skill. One goal of psychotherapy may be for the patient to develop competence/mastery in a particular area.

meta-analysis A method of research in which one compiles all studies relevant to a topic or question and combines the results statistically.

nonspecific factors Factors that are not specific to any particular therapy orientation yet contribute to a positive treatment outcome (e.g., the expectation that one will improve).

outcome measures In psychotherapy research, indicators of patient functioning following treatment, used to gauge the treatment effectiveness.

paraprofessionals Individuals without advanced education in psychology who have been trained to assist professional mental health workers.

patient functioning How well a patient is getting along across a number of domains (e.g., psychological, social/interpersonal, occupational).

process research Research that investigates the specific events that occur in the course of the interaction between therapist and patient. Some therapy processes have been shown to relate to treatment outcome.

psychological intervention A method of inducing changes in a person's behavior, thoughts, or feelings.

therapeutic alliance The relationship between therapist and patient. The forging of a strong therapeutic alliance is believed to be of primary importance for therapeutic change.

treatment group In psychotherapy research, the group that receives the treatment under investigation.

waiting-list control group A control group whose members receive treatment only after the study is completed.

Web Sites of Interest

To visit any of the web sites listed below, go to www.wadsworth.com and click on Links.

11-1 Links to a variety of documents concerning empirically supported treatments (lists, manual references)

11-2 Link to Seligman (1995) article about the *Consumer Reports* study

11-3 Gateway to a number of links to issues concerning managed care

11-4 Gateway to a number of links to issues concerning psychotherapy

11-5 *Prevention and Treatment*, an electronic journal devoted to research on interventions

CHAPTER TWELVE

Psychotherapy: The Psychodynamic Perspective

The psychodynamic approach to therapy focuses on unconscious motives and conflicts in the search for the roots of behavior. It likewise depends heavily on the analysis of past experience. The epitome of this perspective resides in the original psychoanalytic theory and therapy of Sigmund Freud (see Box 12-1).

Without question, psychoanalytic theory represents one of the most sweeping contributions to the field of personality. What began as a halting flow of controversial ideas based on a few neurotic Viennese patients was transformed into a torrent that changed the face of personality theory and clinical practice. Hardly an area of modern life remains untouched by Freudian thought. It influences art, literature, and motion pictures as well as our textbooks. Such words and phrases as *ego*, *unconscious*, *death wish*, and *Freudian slip* have become a part of our everyday language.

What is true in our culture at large is no less true for therapeutic interventions. Although psychoanalytic therapy is sometimes regarded as an anachronism, it is still widely practiced by clinical psychologists (Norcross, Karg-Bray, & Prochaska, 1997a). In fact, almost every form of therapy that relies on verbal transactions between therapist and patient owes some debt to psychoanalysis—both as a theory and as a therapy. Whether it be existential therapy, cognitive-behavioral therapy, or family therapy, psychoanalytic influences are clearly evident, even though they are not always formally acknowledged.

Psychoanalysis: The Beginnings

In 1885, Freud was awarded a grant to study in Paris with the famous Jean Charcot. Charcot was noted for his work with hysterics. Hysteria then was viewed as a "female" disorder most often marked by paralysis, blindness, and deafness. Such symptoms suggested a neurological basis, yet no organic cause could be found. Earlier, Charcot had discovered that some hysterical patients would, while under hypnosis, relinquish

their symptoms and sometimes recall the traumatic experiences that had caused them. It is likely that such recall under hypnosis helped stimulate Freud's thinking about the nature of the unconscious. In any event, Freud was greatly impressed by Charcot's work and, upon his return to Vienna, explained it to his physician friends. Many were quite skeptical about the benefits of hypnosis, but Freud nevertheless began to use it in his neurological practice.

Anna O.

A few years earlier, Freud had been fascinated by Josef Breuer's work with a young "hysterical" patient called Anna 0. She presented many classic hysterical symptoms, apparently precipitated by the death of her father. Breuer had been treating her using hypnosis, and during one trance she told him about the first appearance of one of her symptoms. What was extraordinary, however, was that when she came out of the trance, the symptom had disappeared! Breuer quickly realized that he had stumbled onto something very important, so he repeated the same procedures over a period of time. He was quite successful, but then a complication arose. Anna began to develop a strong emotional attachment to Breuer. The intensity of this reaction, coupled with a remarkable session in which Anna began showing hysterical labor pains, convinced Breuer that he should abandon the case. The jealousy of Breuer's wife may also have played a part in his decision.

These events, with which Freud was familiar, undoubtedly helped prompt his initial theories about the unconscious, the "talking cure," catharsis, transference, and moral anxiety. He treated many of his patients with hypnosis. However, not all patients were good candidates for hypnotic procedures. Others were easily hypnotized but showed a disconcerting tendency not to remember what had transpired during the trance, which destroyed most of the advantages of hypnosis. An example was Elisabeth, a patient Freud saw in 1892. He asked her, while she was fully awake, to concentrate on her ailment and

BOX 12-1

A Brief Biography of Sigmund Freud

Sigmund Freud was born in Austria (in an area that later became part of Czechoslovakia) on May 6, 1856. Most of his childhood was spent in Vienna. He was the oldest of seven children. After a classical education, he began medical studies at the University of Vienna and received an M.D. degree in 1881. After a short period in research, he began a private practice, even though such work did not greatly interest him. At least three things helped him make this decision. First, he knew that as a Jew he stood little chance of advancement in a research-academic environment rife with anti-Semitic feelings. Second, his research efforts did not seem likely to produce much income. Third, he had fallen in love with Martha Bernays. Just as it does today, marriage required money, and Freud had very little. Consequently, he decided to open a practice as a neurologist. His marriage to Martha produced six children, one of whom, Anna, became a famous psychoanalyst herself.

Around this time, Freud began a brief but very productive collaboration with Josef Breuer, a renowned physician in Vienna. Together they sought an explanation for Breuer's discovery of the "talking cure," a method by which a patient's neurotic problems are alleviated just by talking about them. In 1895, Breuer and Freud published *Studies on Hysteria*, a landmark psychiatric treatise. A bit later, the two men had a falling out, for reasons not completely clear. Some suggest the problem was a disagreement over money, whereas others believed it had to do with Breuer's alarm over Freud's growing emphasis on sexual factors as a cause of hysteria.

Freud's most acclaimed work, *The Interpretation of Dreams*, appeared in 1900, capping a

remarkably productive decade of work. As the twentieth century dawned, his professional stature was growing, and his work had begun to attract a dedicated band of followers. Several of these converts later left the orthodox Freudian camp to develop their own psycho-analytic theories. Notable among these were Alfred Adler, Carl Jung, and Otto Rank. Freud became a truly international figure when, in 1909, he was invited to lecture at Clark University in the United States.

Many books and papers followed. But so did Nazi harassment in the 1930s. They burned his books and turned him into a choice anti-Semitic target. Finally, he was allowed to emigrate to England. In his declining years, he suffered from cancer of the jaw, experiencing great pain and undergoing about 32 operations. A heavy cigar smoker, he periodically gave up cigars, but never completely. He died in England in September 1939.

Photo-Researchers

to remember when it began. He asked her to lie on a couch as he pressed his hand against her forehead. Subsequently, Freud found that placing his hand on patients' foreheads and asking them to remember events surrounding the origin of the symptom was just as effective as hypnosis. He soon gave up placing his hand on patients' foreheads and simply asked them to talk about whatever came to their minds. This was the beginning of what came to be known as the method of free association.

The Freudian View: A Brief Review

A major assumption of Freudian theory, *psychic determinism*, holds that everything we do has meaning and purpose and is goal directed. Such a view enables the psychoanalyst to utilize an exceptionally large amount of data in searching for the roots of the patient's behavior and problems. The mundane behavior, the bizarre behavior, the dream, and the slip of the tongue all have significance and meaning.

To account for many aspects of human behavior, Freud also assumed the existence of *unconscious motivation*. His use of this assumption was more extensive than that of any previous theorist, and it allowed him to explain much that had previously resisted explanation. The analyst first of all assumes that healthy behavior is behavior for which the person understands the motivation. The important causes of disturbed behavior are unconscious. Therefore, it follows that the goal of therapy is to make the unconscious conscious.

The Instincts. The energy that makes the human machine function is provided by two sets of instincts: the *life instincts (Eros)* and the *death instincts (Thanatos)*. The life instincts are the basis for all the positive and constructive aspects of behavior; they include such bodily urges as sex, hunger, and thirst as well as the creative components of culture, such as art, music, and literature. But all these activities can serve destructive ends as well. When this happens, the death instincts are responsible. In practice, modern ana-

lysts pay scant attention to death instincts. However, Freud found them necessary to account for the dark side of human behavior (the compulsively self-destructive behavior of the neurotic, our inability to avoid wars, and so on). In any event, for Freud the ultimate explanation for all behavior was an instinctual one, even though the instincts he posited are unobservable, cannot be measured, and often seem better able to explain events after they occur than before.

The Structure. Psychoanalysis views personality as composed of three basic structures: the id, the ego, and the superego. The *id* represents the deep, inaccessible portion of the personality. We gain information about it through the analysis of dreams and various forms of neurotic behavior. The id has no commerce with the external world—it is the true psychic reality. Within the id reside the instinctual urges, with their desire for immediate gratification. The id is without values, ethics, or logic. Its essential purpose is to attain the unhampered gratification of urges whose origin resides in the somatic processes. Its goal, then, is to achieve a state free from all tension or, if that is unattainable, to keep the level as low as possible.

The id is said to obey the *pleasure principle*, trying to discharge tension as quickly as tension reaches it. To do this, it uses a *primary process* kind of thinking, expending energy immediately in motor activity (for example, a swelling of the bladder that results in immediate urination). Later, the id replaces this aspect of the primary process by another form. It manufactures a mental image of whatever will lessen the tension (for example, hunger results in a mental representation of food). Dreaming is regarded as an excellent example of this form of the primary process. Of course, this primary process cannot provide real gratifications, such as food. Because of this inability, a second process develops, bringing into play the second component of personality—the ego.

The *ego* is the executive of the personality. It is an organized, rational system that uses perception, learning, memory, and so on, in the service of need satisfaction. It arises out of the inadequacies of the id in serving and preserving the organism. It operates according to the *reality principle*, deferring the gratification of instinctual urges until a suitable object and mode are discovered. To do this, it employs the *secondary process*—a process that involves learning, memory, planning, judgment, and so on. In essence, the role of the ego is to mediate the demands of the id, the superego, and the real world in a way that will provide satisfaction to the organism and at the same time prevent it from being destroyed by the real world.

The third component of the personality is the *superego*. It develops from the ego during childhood, arising specifically out of the resolution of the *Oedipus complex* (the child's sexual attraction to the parent of the opposite sex). It represents the ideals and values of society as they are conveyed to the child through the words and deeds of the parents. These ideals and values are also conveyed via rewards and punishments. Behavior that is punished typically becomes incorporated into the individual's *conscience*, whereas rewarded behavior generally becomes a part of the *ego ideal*. Thus, within the superego, the conscience eventually serves the purpose of punishing individuals by making them feel guilty or worthless, whereas the rewards of the ego ideal are experienced as pride and a sense of worthiness. In general, the role of the superego is to block unacceptable id impulses, to pressure the ego to serve the ends of morality rather than expediency, and to generate strivings toward perfection.

The Psychosexual Stages. Like many other theorists, Freud considered childhood to be of paramount importance in shaping the character and personality of the individual. He believed that each person goes through a series of developmental stages. Termed *psychosexual stages*, each is marked by the involvement of a particular erogenous zone of the body (especially during the first five years). The *oral stage*, which lasts about a year, is a period in which the mouth is the chief means of reaching satisfaction. It is followed by the *anal stage*, in which attention becomes centered on defecation and urination; this stage may span the period from 6 months to 3 years of age. Next is the *phallic stage* (from 3 to 7 years of age), during which the sexual organs become the prime source of gratification. Following these so-called pregenital stages, the child enters the *latency stage*, which is characterized by a lack of overt sexual activity and, indeed, by an almost negative orientation toward anything sexual. This stage may extend from about the age of 5 until 12 or so. Following the onset of adolescence, the *genital stage* begins. Ideally, this stage will culminate in a mature expression of sexuality, assuming that the sexual impulses have been handled successfully by the ego.

When the child experiences difficulties at any stage, these difficulties may be expressed in symptoms of maladjustment, especially when the troubles are severe. Either excessive frustration or overindulgence at any psychosexual stage will lead to problems. The particular stage at which excessive gratification or frustration is encountered will determine the specific nature of the symptoms. Thus, obsessive-compulsive symptoms signify that the individual failed to successfully negotiate the anal stage, whereas excessive dependency needs in an adult suggest the influence of the oral stage. Freud believed that all people manifest a particular character formation, which may not always be particularly neurotic but nonetheless does represent perpetuations of original childish impulses, either as sublimations of these impulses or as reaction formations against them. Examples would include an oral character's food fads or puristic speech patterns, an anal character's prudishness or dislike of dirt, and a phallic character's excessive modesty.

Anxiety. The circumstances that give rise to the formation of the ego, and later the superego, produce a painful affective experience called *anxiety*. Exaggerated responses of the heart, the lungs, and other internal organs are perceived and experienced as anxiety. There are three general classes of anxiety. The first is *reality anxiety*—

anxiety based on a real danger from the outside world. *Neurotic anxiety* stems from a fear that one's id impulses will be expressed unchecked and thus lead to trouble from the environment. *Moral anxiety* arises from a fear that one will not conform to the standards of the conscience. What identifies and defines these anxieties is the source rather than the quality of the anxiety experience. The essential function of anxiety is to serve as a warning signal to the ego that certain steps must be initiated to quell the danger and thus protect the organism.

The Ego Defenses. We have already observed that the ego uses the secondary process of memory, judgment, and learning to solve problems and stave off environmental threats. But such measures are less serviceable when threats arise from within the person. When one fears the wrath of the superego or the unleashed lusts of the id, where does one turn? The answer lies in the *ego defenses*, or as they are sometimes called, *defense mechanisms*. Nowhere was the genius of Freud more evident than in his ability to abstract the defense mechanisms from the often disconnected and illogical verbalizations of his patients. These mechanisms are generally regarded as pathological because they divert psychic energy from more constructive activities and at the same time distort reality. All the defense mechanisms operate actively and involuntarily, without the person's awareness.

The basic ego defense is *repression*. This can be described as the banishment from consciousness of highly threatening sexual or aggressive material. In some instances, the process operates by preventing the offending impulse from reaching consciousness in the first place. *Fixation* occurs when the frustration and anxiety of the next psychosexual stage are so great that the individual remains at his or her present level of psychosexual development. *Regression* involves a return to a stage that earlier provided a great deal of gratification; this may occur following extensive frustration. *Reaction formation* is said to occur when an unconscious impulse is consciously expressed by its behavioral opposite. Thus, "I

hate you" is expressed as "I love you." *Projection* is revealed when one's unconscious feelings are attributed not to oneself but to another. Thus, the feeling "I hate you" is transformed into "You hate me."

From Theory to Practice

As mentioned earlier, Breuer's experiences with Anna O. had led to the discovery of the "talking cure." This, in turn, became transformed into free association during Freud's work with Elisabeth. *Free association* meant simply that the patient was to say everything and anything that came to mind regardless of how irrelevant, silly, dull, or revolting it might seem. Freud also realized that Anna had transferred onto Breuer many of her feelings that really applied to significant males in her life. This notion of *transference* would eventually become a valuable diagnostic tool during therapy for understanding the nature of the patient's problems—especially the unconscious ones.

Through hypnosis, Freud learned that patients could relive traumatic events associated with the onset of the hysterical symptom. In some cases, this reliving served to release formerly bottled-up energy. This became known as *catharsis*—a release of energy that often had important therapeutic benefits. In his work with Elisabeth, Freud also witnessed *resistance*—a general reluctance to discuss, remember, or think about events that are particularly troubling or threatening. He viewed this as a kind of defense, but later he also analyzed it as repression—the involuntary banishing of a thought or impulse to the unconscious. The *unconscious*, of course, is the area of the mind inaccessible to conscious thought.

The Role of Insight

The ultimate goal of psychoanalytic intervention is the removal of debilitating neurotic problems. But the unswerving credo of the traditional psychoanalytic therapist is that, ultimately, the only final and effective way of doing this is to help the patient achieve *insight*. What does insight mean?

FIGURE 12-1 Freud's consulting room.
The Bettman Archive. © CORBIS.

It means total understanding of the unconscious determinants of those irrational feelings, thoughts, or behaviors that are producing one's personal misery. Once these unconscious reasons are fully confronted and understood, the need for neurotic defenses and symptoms will disappear. All of the specific techniques described later in this chapter have as their ultimate purpose the facilitation of insight.

An analysis culminating in insight is slow, tedious, and often very lengthy. An orthodox analysis is not measured in weeks or months but in years. This is so because the patient is not simply informed, for example, that unconscious feelings of hostility and competitiveness toward a long-departed father are causing present outbursts against friends, a boss, or coworkers. At an intellectual level, the patient may readily concede this interpretation. But the unconscious is not likely to be much affected by such sterile information. The patient must actually experience the unconscious hostility. This may happen through the transference process; early experiences associated with the father may be relived as competition with the therapist begins to occur. The analyst begins to seem like that father of years gone by, and all the old reactions start flooding back. As the therapist comes to stand for someone else (the father), old emotions are reexperienced and then reevaluated. From this comes a deeper insight.

The true meaning of this insight is then brought into the patient's consciousness by the *working-through process*. This refers to a careful and repeated examination of how one's conflicts and defenses have operated in many different areas of life. Little may be accomplished by a simple interpretation that one's passivity and helplessness are really an unconscious form of aggression. Once the basis for the interpretation is firmly laid, it must be repeated time and time again. The patient must be confronted with the insight as it applies to relations with a spouse, a friend, or a supervisor, and, yes, even as it affects reactions to the therapist. Patients must be helped to work through all aspects of their lives with this insight. This is not unlike learning a principle in a physics class. The principle only begins to take on real life and importance when one sees that it applies not just in a laboratory but everywhere—in automobile engines, house construction, baseball, and so on. So it is with insight. It comes alive when it becomes painfully clear in example after example how it has affected one's life and relationships. It is due in part to this extensive working-through period that traditional psychoanalysis takes so long—three to five therapy sessions per week for three to five years, and sometimes much longer.

Techniques of Psychodynamic Psychotherapy

The analyst regards the symptoms of neurosis as signs of conflict among the id, ego, superego, and the demands of reality. A phobia, an undesirable character trait, and excessive reliance on defense mechanisms are all signs of a deeper problem. The symptom, then, indicates an unconscious problem that needs resolution. Obviously, if patients could resolve their problems alone, they would not need therapy. But the very nature of unconscious problems and defenses makes self-healing exceedingly difficult. To dissolve defenses and confront the unconscious in a therapeutic relationship is the whole purpose of psychoanalysis. Over the years, many variations in techniques have been developed. However, in nearly all these variations, the basic emphasis is on the dissolution of repressions through the reanalysis of previous experience. The fundamental goal remains freedom from the oppression of the unconscious through insight.

Free Association

A cardinal rule in psychoanalysis is that the patient must say anything and everything that comes to mind. This is not as easy for the patient as it may appear to be at first glance. It requires the patient to stop censoring or screening thoughts that are ridiculous, aggressive, embarrassing, or sexual. All our lives we learn to exercise conscious control over such thoughts to protect both ourselves and others. According to Freud, however, if the therapist is to release patients from the tyranny of their unconscious and thereby free them from their symptoms and other undesirable behavior, then such an uncensored train of free associations is essential. From it, the patient and the therapist can begin to discover the long-hidden bases of the patient's problems.

Traditionally, the psychoanalyst sits behind the patient, who reclines on a couch. In this position, the analyst is not in the patient's line of vision and will not be as likely to hinder the associative stream. Another reason for sitting behind the client is that having patients stare at you six or more hours a day can be rather fatiguing for the analyst. The purpose of the couch is to help the patient relax and make it easier to free-associate.

The psychoanalyst assumes that one association will lead to another. As the process contin-

ues, one gets closer and closer to unconscious thoughts and urges. Any single set of associations may not be terribly clear. But over many sessions, patterns of associations start to emerge, and the analyst can begin to make sense out of them through their repetitive themes. In one sense, free associations are not really "free" at all. They are outgrowths of unconscious forces that determine the direction of one's associations. Often, but not always, these associations lead to early childhood memories and problems. Such memories of long-forgotten experiences give the analyst clues to the structure of personality and its development.

Analysis of Dreams

A related technique is the *analysis of dreams*. Dreams are thought to reveal the nature of the unconscious because they are regarded as heavily laden with unconscious wishes, albeit in symbolic form. Dreams are seen as symbolic wish fulfillments that often provide, like free associations, important clues to childhood wishes and feelings. During sleep, one's customary defenses are relaxed and symbolic material may surface. Of course, censorship by the ego is not totally removed during sleep, or the material from the id would become so threatening that the person would quickly awaken. In a sense, dreams are a way for people to have their cake and eat it too. The material of the dream is important enough to provide some gratification to the id but not usually so threatening as to terrorize the ego. However, in some cases this scenario is not applicable, and traumatizing dreams do occur.

The *manifest content* of a dream is what actually happens during the dream. For example, the manifest content of a dream may be that one is confronted with two large, delicious-looking ice cream cones. The *latent content* of a dream is its symbolic meaning. In the preceding example, perhaps there is a message about the need for oral gratification or a longing to return to the mother's breast.

In order to get at the latent content, the patient is often encouraged to free-associate to a dream with the hope of gaining insight into its

BOX 12-2

Freud's Self-Analysis

To support his notion that people are motivated by sexual wishes that go all the way back to their childhood, Freud drew upon the results of his own self-analysis.

Freud's father died in 1896. This disturbed Freud a great deal, even though his father was old and ill. In fact, Freud became extremely anxious and depressed, so much so that his work was severely hampered. He became so disturbed at his own reactions that he decided to embark upon a detailed self-analysis, drawing on his dreams, associations, and behavior.

One childhood dream in particular seemed important. This was a dream Freud remembered having when he was 7 or 8 years old. Thirty years later, he interpreted it. In his dream, he saw his "beloved mother, with a peculiarly calm, sleeping countenance, carried

into the room and laid on the bed by two (or three) persons with birds' beaks" (Freud, 1938, p. 522). His free associations led him to the idea of death and to an expression on his grandfather's face shortly before his death. This was a composite dream, then, combining elements of both his mother and grandfather. From here his associations took him to the idea of a dying father. Freud then realized to his dismay that unconsciously he had harbored as a child hostile wishes toward his father. Additional associations (for example, the German slang word for sexual intercourse was derived from the German word for bird) led him inevitably to the conclusion that his childhood sexual urges were directed toward his mother. So it was that the unconscious Oedipal strivings he had interpreted so often in his patients were equally true for him.

meaning. Normally, the manifest content is an amalgam of displacement, condensation, substitution, symbolization, or lack of logic. It is not easy to cut through all this and find the latent meaning. Free association will help in this search, but the meaning of one dream alone is not always apparent. The real meaning of a dream in the life of an individual may only become apparent from the analysis of a whole series of dreams. Another problem is that patients often distort the actual content of a dream as they retell it during the analytic session. Thus, not only does the analyst have to delve deeply to find the symbolic meaning, but there is the added burden of the patient's waking defenses that strive to thwart the goal of understanding. For many analysts, dreams do not provide inevitable, final clues to the patient's dynamics; rather, they are clues that help the analyst formulate hypotheses that can be validated or in-

validated with further information. An example of how dreams and free associations go hand in hand is shown in a brief description of Freud's self-analysis (Box 12-2).

Psychopathology of Everyday Life

Another important method for gaining access to the unconscious is illustrated by Freud's (1901/1960) sensitive analysis of the "psychopathology of everyday life." In the Freudian view, everything is determined; there are no accidents. The slip of the tongue and the forgotten appointment are not simple mistakes. Rather, they represent the conscious expression of an unconscious wish. These little mistakes of everyday life are like dreams in the sense that sexual and aggressive urges receive partial gratification even though they interfere with our lives in minor ways. When the patient makes such mistakes in therapy or recounts during therapy mistakes made outside the therapy room, the therapist is provided additional data by which to assess the patient's problems. In some instances, the meaning of the mistake is not readily apparent, and the patient may be asked to free-associate to the mistake. These associations, coupled with the therapist's interpretation, can help provide the patient with added insight.

Resistance

During the course of psychotherapy, the patient will attempt to ward off efforts to dissolve neurotic methods of resolving problems. This characteristic defense, mentioned earlier, is called resistance. Patients are typically loath to give up behaviors that have been working, even though these behaviors may cause great distress—the distress, in fact, that led the patients to seek help in the first place. In addition, patients find painful subjects difficult to contemplate or discuss. For example, a male patient who has always feared his father or has felt that he did not measure up to his father's standards may not wish to discuss or even recall matters related to his father. Although a certain amount of resistance is to be expected from most patients, when the resistance becomes sufficient to retard the progress of therapy, it must be recognized and dealt with by the therapist.

Resistance takes many forms. Patients may begin to talk less, to pause longer, or to report that their minds are blank. Lengthy silences are also frequent. Sometimes a patient may repeatedly talk around a point or endlessly repeat the same material. Therapy may become an arena for discussing such problems as unemployment or taxes—weighty issues, but hardly the ones that brought the patient to therapy. Some patients may intellectualize about the relative merits of primal screaming versus nude marathons or even the effect of Freud's boyhood on the subsequent development of psychoanalysis. If the patient knows that the therapist has a penchant for dreams, then the therapist may be deluged with dream material. In some instances, the

patient's feelings or ideas about the therapist may begin to dominate the sessions. This can be very flattering until the therapist realizes that this interest is just a way of avoiding the real problems. Another form of resistance is the tendency to omit or censor certain information.

Resistance is also evidenced when a patient repeatedly comes late, cancels appointments without good reason, forgets meetings, and so on. The therapist may also begin to notice that a variety of "real" events in the patient's life seem to be conspiring against the sessions. For example, the patient may start to miss sessions because of a succession of physical illnesses or may constantly ask to change appointment times in order to meet one daily crisis after another.

Nearly anything can become a form of resistance. As the patient's defenses are addressed, there is sometimes an intensification of symptoms. But the opposite can also occur, so that an actual "flight into health" occurs—the patient gets better. It is almost as if, in the first instance, the patient is saying, "Don't make me confront these things, I'm getting worse." In the second instance, the patient is saying, "See, I don't need to deal with these matters, I'm getting better." Another method is "acting out." Here the patient attempts to escape the anxiety generated in therapy by indulging in irrational acts or engaging in potentially dangerous behavior. For example, a patient suddenly takes up mountain climbing or begins to use cocaine or heroin. Still other patients flee into "intellectualization." Experiences or memories become stripped of their emotional content and are dissected calmly and rationally. Everything becomes cold and detached. Losing one's job becomes an occasion for an elaborate, intellectual discussion of economic conditions or the shift to high technology. Feelings are ignored, and the experience is handled by a flight into rationality.

In one form or another, resistance goes on throughout the course of therapy. In one sense, it is an impediment to the swift resolution of neurotic conflicts. But in another sense, it is the central task in therapy. The resistance that goes on in therapy probably mirrors what has happened in real life. If resistance during therapy can be analyzed and the patient made to understand its true function, then such defenses will not be as likely to operate outside the therapist's office. The following is an example of how one therapist met the problem of resistance.

A Case Illustration of Resistance

The wife of a minister has been seen for several months. In the previous session, a series of interpretations were made regarding her tendency to see her husband rather than herself as completely responsible for their unsatisfactory sexual adjustment.

Therapist: You don't seem very responsive today.

Patient: I don't have much on my mind.

Therapist: You seem almost impatient.

Patient: I was just thinking what a stupid little office this is. It's so oppressive.

Therapist: That's strange. You never commented on it till now.

Patient: I never thought about it until now.

There is a long silence during which the patient glances at her watch twice. Finally, the therapist breaks the silence.

Therapist: I wonder if all this has anything to do with what we discussed last time.

Patient: I just knew you were going to say that. Well, I don't think so because I can't recall what it was we talked about.

Therapist: Is that right? (Smiling)

Patient: Well . . . as a matter of fact . . . well, I think it is my husband's fault. He can be so aggressive. With other people he seems so patient and understanding, but . . .

The session continues, and further exploration into the patient's sexual attitudes is made.

Transference

A key phenomenon in psychoanalytic therapy, as we have seen, is transference. To one degree or another, transference is operative in most individual forms of verbal psychotherapy. It occurs when the patient reacts to the therapist as if the latter represented some important figure out of childhood. Both positive and negative feelings can be transferred. In short, conflicts and problems that originated in childhood are reinstated in the therapy room. This provides not only important clues as to the nature of the patient's problems but also an opportunity for the therapist to interpret the transference in an immediate and vital situation. Many characteristics of the psychoanalytic session—the patient is seated on a couch facing away from the analyst, the analyst does not give advice or reveal personal information—serve to encourage the establishment of transference.

Positive transference is often responsible for what appears to be rapid improvement at the beginning stages of therapy. Being in a safe, secure relationship with a knowledgeable authority can produce rapid but superficial improvement. Later, as the patient's defenses are challenged, this improvement is likely to fade, and marked negative transference may intrude.

Transference can take many forms. It may be reflected in comments about the therapist's clothing or office furnishings. It may take the form of direct comments of admiration, dislike, love, or anger. It may assume the guise of an attack on the efficacy of psychotherapy or a helpless, dependent posture. The important point is that these reactions do not reflect current realities but have their roots in childhood. It is all too easy to view every reaction of the patient as a manifestation of transference. However, the truly sensitive therapist is one who can separate reactions that have some support in reality from reactions that are neurotic in character.

Basically, both positive and negative transferences are forms of resistance. Through interpretation, the patient is helped to recognize the irrational nature and origins of transference feelings. With repeated interpretation and analysis, the patient can begin to gain control over such reactions in the therapy room and learn to generalize such control to the real world as well.

Interpretation

Interpretation is the cornerstone of nearly every form of dynamic psychotherapy. Although the content may vary significantly, depending on the therapist's theoretical affiliation, the act of interpreting is perhaps the most common technique among all forms of psychotherapy. From the psychoanalyst's perspective, *interpretation* is the method by which the unconscious meaning of thoughts and behavior is revealed. In a broader sense, however, interpretation is a process by which the patient can be induced to view thoughts, behavior, feelings, or wishes in a different manner. It is a method calculated to free the patient from the shackles of old ways of seeing things—ways that have led to the patient's current problems in living. It is a prime method for bringing about insight. Of course, significant insight or behavioral change rarely comes from a single interpretation. Rather, it is a slow, repetitive process in which the essential meaning behind certain behaviors, thoughts, and feelings is repeatedly pointed out to the patient in one context after another.

The following case study illustrates the interpretive process.

A Case Illustration of Interpretation

This exchange occurred during the 15th session of psychotherapy with the 27-year-old wife of a college professor. In previous sessions, she had described how inadequate their sexual relationship was. In more recent sessions, she had also begun to discuss how much she and her husband shared the belief that theirs was a frank, open, and communicative relationship. Sometime before the present session, the patient had taken a two-day trip to attend a convention in a neighboring city. On the first day of the convention, she met a man and promptly went to bed with him. Afterward, she was several days late with her period. This convinced her that she was pregnant. Suspecting that emotional factors might have delayed her period, her therapist suggested that she hold off telling her husband

until she was sure. She disregarded this suggestion, and proceeded to tell her husband everything. The very next day, her period began.

Patient: Well, I told Dick everything. God, was I upset.

Therapist: Then what happened?

Patient: He took it better than I thought he would. He was really understanding. Not so much forgiving, just calm and understanding. And now I'm not even pregnant. Can you beat that? But I think it really solidified our relationship and we can go on from here.

Therapist: Did you expect Dick to be so understanding?

Patient: I'm not sure I knew what to expect. I suppose I thought he would be upset as hell, but what else could I do? I know the episode at the convention was silly. But I just had to find out whether it was still possible to really enjoy sex.

Therapist: Was it?

Patient: Yes, it really was. Now I know it, and in a way I feel great.

Therapist: And now Dick knows it, and in a way he doesn't feel so great. That could well be the reason you were so eager to tell him everything.

In this case study, the therapist used his final remarks to encourage understanding on the part of the patient. By calling attention to the possibility that the patient's behavior might have been a way of hurting her husband, the therapist was seeking to get the patient to reexamine her views of herself, her relationship with her husband, and her motives. His interpretation was directed to a central part of the patient's problems. It is important to emphasize that interpretations are not sprinkled about like confetti. Rather, they are limited to important life areas—those that relate directly to the problems that the therapist is trying to resolve.

It is best to offer an interpretation when it is already close to the patient's awareness. In addition, an interpretation should be offered when it will arouse enough anxiety to engage the patient's serious contemplation but not so much anxiety that the patient will reject it. Although therapists have sometimes been known to make interpretations as shots in the dark, it is generally wise to be reasonably sure of one's target before firing the salvo. Being wrong, offering an interpretation too soon, or providing an interpretation that is beyond what the patient is ready to accept is likely to be counterproductive. As Colby (1951) put it, "Like pushing a playground swing at the height of its arc for optimum momentum, the best-timed interpretations are given when the patient, already close to it himself [sic], requires only a nudge to help him see the hitherto unseen" (p. 91).

As a general rule, small dosages are best. Therefore, rather than prepare one grand interpretation that will subsume all the major aspects of the patient's conflicts, it is advisable to approach matters gradually over a period of time. One can gradually move from questions to clarifications to interpretations. This will allow the patient to integrate each step. In making interpretations, it is important to build on what the patient has said previously, using the patient's own comments and descriptions to build the interpretive case.

It can be difficult to determine whether a specific interpretation has been effective. Sometimes the patient's response (for example, a surprised exclamation, flushing, saying "My God, I never thought of it that way!") will suggest that the target has been hit. But at other times patients may be entirely noncommittal, only to remark some sessions later how true the therapist's comment was. In any event, the real test of the utility of an interpretation is more likely to come from the subsequent course of the sessions. Even a patient's overt acceptance can sometimes be nothing more than a way of diverting the therapist or erecting a defense.

A classic psychoanalytic interpretation is designed to open up the patient to new ways of viewing things and, ultimately, to neutralize unconscious conflicts and defenses. In doing this, the therapist makes use of free associations,

dream material, behavior that indicates resistance and transference, and so on. Interpretations can vary a great deal in terms of their complexity and their incisiveness. Sometimes they are designed to cut right to the heart of a patient's unconscious conflicts. But in other cases, they may be little more than comments or questions designed to move the patient ever so slightly in the direction of insight. Perhaps they should be labeled as verbal interventions rather than interpretations. But all have the potential for altering how a patient thinks or feels. These verbal interventions might be considered as a dimension in terms of how directly they seek to lead the patient to a fresh way of viewing things.

Psychoanalytic Alternatives

Psychoanalytic theory underwent considerable modification by the neo-Freudians, Alfred Adler, Carl Jung, Otto Rank, the ego analysts, and others. The seminal contributions of Freud remained, but the emphases often changed. Jung made much more of dreams and symbolic processes. Rank elevated the birth trauma to a preeminent position. Adler and the neo-Freudians stressed the importance of culture, learning, and social relationships instead of instinctual forces.

Such variations would be expected to influence the methods of therapy. However, these changes often did little to alter the critical roles of free association, dream analysis, interpretation, transference, and resistance. The supreme role of insight was little changed. Insight came about through traditional psychoanalytic methods, but now it was the insight of Horney or Fromm or Sullivan. The neurotic symptom was seen as rooted not only in repressed sexual or aggressive urges; it now became the outgrowth of a fear of being alone or of the insecurity that goes along with the adult role. In most of these early variants of psychoanalysis, interpretation remained the essential therapeutic ingredient. What distinguished these variants was often the content of the interpretation—the different ways in which unconscious material was construed by the analyst.

Over the years, enough changes have been made in traditional psychoanalysis that those who no longer practice the strict Freudian techniques are often said to be practicing "psychoanalytically oriented" therapy. These changes involve many factors. In some cases, the number of analytic sessions is reduced from five per week to three, and the entire treatment process may last but a year and a half (Alexander & French, 1946). The therapist is no longer inevitably seated behind the patient's couch but now often sits at a desk, with the patient seated in a facing chair. Perhaps the easiest way to characterize these and other modifications is to say that greater flexibility has been introduced. Although basic Freudian tenets are still observed, the overall context is not so rigid. For example, free association is no longer absolutely required by these psychoanalytically oriented therapists. The importance of dreams may be downplayed somewhat. Drugs and even hypnosis may be used.

For many years, the therapy room was like an inner sanctum. The therapist talked with the patient and no one else. Now, family members or a spouse are often consulted, or sometimes therapy is conducted with the family as a unit. There tends to be much less emphasis on the past (childhood) and a more active confrontation with the present. Even the nature of the clientele has changed a bit. Clinics or institutes now provide some therapeutic services to aging clients, minority group clients, and others who have not traditionally received psychoanalytic treatment. They have tried to open up therapy to nontraditional populations. Again, none of this is meant to be a denial of Freudian principles; rather, it is a demonstration that traditional Freudian treatment procedures are not the only therapeutic techniques that can be deduced from Freudian psychoanalytic theory.

Ego Analysis

The *ego analysis* movement, originating from within the framework of traditional psychoanalysis rather than as a splinter group, held that classical psychoanalysis overemphasized unconscious and instinctual determinants at the ex-

pense of ego processes. This group of theorists accepted the role of the ego in mediating the conflict between the id and the real world but believed that the ego also performed other extremely important functions. They emphasized the adaptive, "conflict-free" functions of the ego, including memory, learning, and perception. These theorists include Hartmann (1939), Anna Freud (1946a), Kris (1950), Erikson (1956), and Rapaport (1953).

Ego-analytic psychotherapy has not departed from the usual therapy methods except in degree. In a sense, the ego analysts seem to prefer reeducative goals rather than the reconstructive goals of orthodox psychoanalysis. The exploration of infantile experience and the induction of a transference neurosis seem to be less common in ego-analytic therapy than in classical psychoanalysis. Ego-analytic therapy focuses more on contemporary problems in living than on a massive examination and reinstatement of the past. Also, the therapist must understand not only the neurotic aspects of the patient's personality but also the effective parts and how they interact with those neurotic trends.

The ego-analytic approach has also tended to emphasize the importance of building the patient's trust through "reparenting" in the therapy relationship. This approach sometimes even views transference as an impediment to therapy and works toward building adaptive defenses in the patient (Blanck & Blanck, 1974).

Other Contemporary Developments

In particular, the work of Horney, Sullivan, and Adler has been important in giving a new spin to psychoanalysis. Likewise, ego psychology and theories of object relations have encouraged an emphasis on the manner in which the patient relates to other people, rather than on conflicts among instinctual forces. For example, object relations theorists see the need to form relationships with others as a primary influence on human behavior. Therefore, these theorists focus more on the role of love and hate, as well as autonomy and dependency, in the development of the self. In the self psychology of Kohut (1977), the central task of maturation is not the successful negotiation of the psychosexual stages but the development of an integrated self.

Discussions of changes in psychoanalytic therapies emphasize a shift in the therapeutic focus to the "here and now" and to the interpersonal exchanges that occur within it (Henry, Strupp, Schacht, & Gaston, 1994). Strupp and Binder (1984) have synthesized some of the more critical developmental changes in psychoanalytic practice. They emphasize a movement away from the recovery of childhood memories and their analysis toward a focus on the corrective emotional experiences that occur through the agency of the therapeutic relationship. The transference relationship as it occurs now helps provide the means for constructive changes in interpersonal relations outside the therapy room.

Brief Psychodynamic Psychotherapy

Perhaps the chief practical thrust of recent years in psychodynamic therapy has been the development of brief methods (Goldfried, Greenberg, & Marmar, 1990; Koss, Butcher, & Strupp, 1986). Many of these brief therapies retain their psychodynamic identity even as they are employed in emergency, crisis-oriented situations. This allows the therapist to capitalize on the patient's heightened motivation and also to depend on the transference relationship (Goldfried et al., 1990).

Although it would be nice to believe that theory and/or research considerations have dictated the shift toward briefer psychotherapies, this is not entirely the case. An important driving force has been the increasing focus on cost containment in health care systems (Cummings, 1986). Insurers have been cutting the number of visits for which they will reimburse therapists. Cost containment has also provided indirect competition from psychiatrists, who frequently prescribe medications rather than psychotherapy. The net effect has been a turn to *brief psychotherapy* to remain economically competitive.

There are now several hundred different brands of brief therapy. In fact, the widespread availability of these treatments has diminished

the exclusive role of psychiatrists and brought many nonmedical therapists into the arena. Not all of these briefer therapies could be labeled psychodynamic, as we shall see in later chapters. In some cases, briefer therapies are highly similar to crisis intervention techniques. Finally, many forms of brief psychotherapy are quite eclectic in their approach (Garfield, 1989).

Although some define 25 sessions as the upper limit of brief therapy (Butcher & Koss, 1978), others indicate that the range can be from one session (Bloom, 1981) to 40 or 50 (Sifneos, 1972). However, the issue seems less the number of sessions than the rationing of time allotted to therapy (Budman & Gurman, 1983) and the state of mind in patient and therapist alike. Table 12-1 presents some of the value contrasts between long-term and short-term therapists.

Events move rapidly in crisis-oriented therapy. Thus, the quest for insight is not the leisurely process that it is in traditional forms of psychotherapy. The entire working-through process is accelerated. The ultimate goal is not reconstruction of the personality, but the development of a benign cycle of functioning and the better handling of day-to-day problems in living. Transference is encouraged, but mainly as a means of ensuring that the therapist will be perceived as helpful, competent, and active.

Specific techniques in brief therapy are numerous. However, the maintenance of a clear and specific focus on realistic goals is important. Usually, the level of therapist activity is high, and both therapist and patient are keenly aware of the element of time. The therapist is likely to use homework assignments for the patient and to involve relatives or significant others in the treatment plan. Supportive activities outside therapy are likely to be used as well (for example, exercise, Overeaters Anonymous). There tends to be a great deal of flexibility in treatment activities that take brief therapy beyond the strict psychodynamic perspective.

Research evidence attests to the efficacy of brief forms of psychotherapy across a number of clinical conditions (Koss & Shiang, 1994), and evidence suggests that brief psychodynamic

PROFILE 12-1

Hans H. Strupp, Ph.D.

Dr. Hans Strupp is a Distinguished Professor Emeritus at Vanderbilt University. Dr. Strupp is an expert in the areas of psychotherapy research and psychodynamic psychotherapy. He has published more than 200 articles, book chapters, or books, and is considered one of the most influential "pioneers" of psychotherapy research. Dr. Strupp has received numerous awards, including the American Psychological Association Distinguished Scientific Contribution Award, the Society for Psychotherapy Research Distinguished Career Contribution Award, and the American Psychological Association Distinguished Professional Contributions to Knowledge Award.

Dr. Strupp is perhaps best known for his groundbreaking research on the process of psychotherapy, and in particular psychodynamic psychotherapy. For example, in the "Vanderbilt I" study, Dr. Strupp and colleagues investigated whether trained professional therapists would produce significantly better results than untrained (in psychotherapy) college professors in the treatment of college

students with moderately severe anxiety, depression, and social withdrawal. As expected, psychotherapy was significantly more beneficial than no treatment. However, the surprising finding was that, in general, those treated by college professors had similar outcomes to those treated by professional therapists. Supplementary analyses revealed that professional therapists were most effective with patients who were highly motivated for psychotherapy, able to form a good relationship with the therapist early in treatment, and did not have a long-standing history of interpersonal problems.

Dr. Strupp's subsequent research has focused on the therapeutic alliance and how it influences outcome, individual differences in both patients and therapists that influence outcome, brief and manualized forms of psychodynamic psychotherapy, and the training of psychotherapists. His research is well regarded by scientists and practitioners alike because he conducts empirical investigations of clinically relevant topics. Dr. Strupp strongly believes that clinical practice and clinical science can be complementary, with each informing the other.

> Research should lead to modifications in practice, which should then be subjected to further investigative scrutiny . . . if the field [of psychotherapy research] is to advance, it must rely increasingly on empirical research and resist authoritarian and doctrinaire pronouncements, which have remained rampant. (Strupp, 1990, p. 318)

For a poignant, revealing, and interesting glimpse into the various influences on Dr. Strupp's life and career, we highly recommend "Reflections on My Career in Clinical Psychology" (Strupp, 1990).

■ TABLE 12-1 Comparative Values in Long-Term versus Short-Term Therapy

Long-Term Therapist	Short-Term Therapist
1. Seeks change in basic character.	Prefers pragmatism, parsimony, and least radical intervention and does not believe in notion of "cure."
2. Believes that significant psychological change is unlikely in everyday life.	Maintains an adult-development perspective from which significant psychological change is viewed as inevitable.
3. Sees presenting problems as reflecting more basic pathology.	Emphasizes patient's strengths and resources; presenting problems are taken seriously (although not necessarily at face value).
4. Wants to "be there" as patient makes significant changes.	Accepts that many changes will occur "after therapy" and will not be observable to the therapist.
5. Sees therapy as having a "timeless" quality and is patient and willing to wait for change.	Does not accept the timelessness of some models of therapy.
6. Unconsciously recognizes the fiscal convenience of maintaining long-term patients.	Fiscal issues are often muted either by the nature of the therapist's practice or by the organizational structure for reimbursement.
7. Views psychotherapy as almost always benign and useful.	Views psychotherapy as being sometimes useful and sometimes harmful.
8. Sees patient's being in therapy as the most important part of patient's life.	Sees being in the world as more important than being in therapy.

Source: Adapted from "The Practice of Brief Therapy," by S. H. Budman and A. S. Gurman, *Professional Psychology Research and Practice,* 1983, *14,* 277–292. Copyright 1983 by the American Psychological Association. Reprinted by permission.

psychotherapy may be as effective as traditional time-unlimited psychoanalysis (Koss, Butcher, & Strupp, 1986). Two recent meta-analyses are noteworthy. Svartberg and Stiles (1991) found that brief psychodynamic psychotherapy was superior to no treatment but somewhat inferior in its effects compared to other forms of brief treatment, especially cognitive-behavioral treatment. Although Crits-Christoph (1992) also examined the effects of brief psychodynamic psychotherapy, his meta-analysis only included studies that used a treatment manual as part of the research protocol. Crits-Christoph (1992) found that brief psychodynamic psychotherapy was clearly superior to no treatment and, in contrast to Svartberg and Stiles (1991), that brief psychodynamic psychotherapy was approximately equivalent in its effects to alternative psychological treatments.

Interpersonal Psychotherapy: An Empirically Supported Treatment

A particular form of brief therapy that is psychodynamic in flavor deserves mention. It has received a great deal of attention from psychotherapy researchers, and it has been highlighted in several practice guidelines. *Interpersonal psychotherapy,* or *IPT* (Klerman, Weissman, Rounsaville, & Chevron, 1984) is a brief, insight-oriented approach that has been applied primarily to depressive disorders, although it has been modified for use in the treatment of other disorders (such as substance abuse and bulimia) as well. When used to treat depression, IPT involves thorough assessment of depressive symptoms, targeting a major problem area (such as delayed grief, role transitions or disputes, or interpersonal deficits), and alleviating depressive symptoms by improving relationships with

BOX 12-3

Features of Interpersonal Psychotherapy (IPT)

IPT is a brief form of psychodynamic psycho-therapy that has been used in numerous research studies. It is one of the treatments cited as examples of empirically validated/supported treatments by the Division 12 Task Force of the American Psychological Association. Weissman and Markowitz (1998) discuss the primary features of IPT.

Focus

IPT focuses on the connection between onset of clinical problems and current interpersonal problems (with friends, partners, relatives). Current social problems are addressed, not enduring personality traits or styles.

Length

Typically 12–16 weeks.

Role of the IPT Therapist

IPT therapists are active, nonneutral, and supportive. They use realism and optimism to counter patients' typically negative and pessimistic outlook. Therapists emphasize the possibility for change and highlight options that may effect positive change.

Phases of Treatment

1. *First phase* (up to 3 sessions): This includes a diagnostic evaluation and psychiatric his-

tory, an interpersonal functioning assessment, and patient education about the nature of the clinical condition (such as depression). The therapist provides a clinical formulation of the patient's difficulties by linking symptoms to current interpersonal problems, issues, and situations.

2. *Second phase*: Depending on which interpersonal problem area has been chosen (for example, grief, role disputes, role transition, interpersonal deficits), specific strategies and goals are pursued. For example, treatment focusing on role disputes would aim to help the patient explore the problematic relationships, the nature of the problems, and the options for resolving them. If an impasse has been reached in a relationship, the therapist helps the patient find ways to circumvent whatever is hindering progress or to end the relationship.

3. *Third phase* (last 2–3 sessions): The patient's progress and mastery experiences are reinforced and consolidated. The IPT therapist reinforces the patient's sense of confidence and autonomy. Methods of dealing with a recurrence of clinical symptoms are discussed.

others (as by improving communication skills and social skills). IPT has been shown to be effective in treating acute depressive episodes and in preventing or delaying the recurrence of depressive episodes (Weissman & Markowitz, 1994). Box 12-3 outlines the major features and characteristics of IPT.

Summary Evaluation of Psychodynamic Psychotherapy

In this section, we will review the available empirical evaluations and offer some general observations about those psychotherapeutic practices that trace their origins to the psychoanalytic method.

Does Psychodynamic Psychotherapy Work?

What evidence is there that the psychodynamic approach is effective? In the previous chapter, we mentioned the widely cited meta-analytic study by Smith, Glass, and Miller (1980) that examined the effectiveness of psychotherapy. In addition to examining the effects of psychotherapy in general, these authors also reported effects separately for different types of psychological intervention. They found that the average patient who had received psychodynamic psychotherapy was functioning better than 75% of those who had received no treatment. Two recent meta-analyses of studies examining the effectiveness of brief psychodynamic psychotherapy have produced conflicting results, with one supporting the efficacy of brief psychodynamic treatment (Crits-Christoph, 1992) but the other not (Svartberg & Stiles, 1991). Based on these and other results, we offer the tentative conclusion that there appears to be at least modest support for the effectiveness of psychodynamic psychotherapy. However, a number of thorny methodological issues plague research on psychodynamic therapy (for example, appropriate outcome measures, length of treatment), and additional investigations are warranted.

Interpretation and Insight

A wide range of current psychotherapies depend to a greater or lesser extent on the patient's achieving insight through therapist interpretation. Psychoanalysis seems to retain its total commitment to insight as the supreme means for solving problems in living. When understanding is complete enough, it is believed that the patients' symptoms will be ameliorated, or even disappear entirely.

This emphasis on the pursuit of understanding has great appeal to many people. For example, although many people who are sad may seek the therapeutic goal of happiness, most of them are not content just to become happy—they also want to know why they are sad. The commitment of psychoanalysis and its psycho-

therapeutic heirs to insight and understanding is their greatest asset, but it also contains the seeds of their failures. Especially in the case of psychoanalysis, reconstruction of the personality through insight and understanding can lead to a nearly interminable and sometimes exhausting examination of the past and analysis of motives. Although one can hardly fault psychoanalysis for teaching the importance of the past in shaping the present, there can be too much of a good thing. At times, it almost seems that the patient can use the need for understanding and the pursuit of the past as reasons not to come to grips with current problems. The endless analysis of conflicts and motives and of their childhood origins can easily replace the need to find solutions and behavioral alternatives to problems in living. Although learning the reasons for one's problems may be important (and ultimately efficient if one is to attain generalized rather than piecemeal solutions), the failure to emphasize alternative ways of behaving can be a major shortcoming of traditional psychoanalysis.

Psychoanalysis often appears to involve a tacit assumption that more adaptive behavior will occur automatically once insight is achieved by the working-through process—that behavioral change will surely follow insight. However, the evidence for this assumption is exceedingly sparse. In fact, it has been argued for some time that the true course of events follows a reverse pattern—that insight is brought about by behavioral change (Alexander & French, 1946).

One of the chief methods used by psychodynamic clinicians to facilitate patient insight is the interpretation of transference. A recent review of empirical studies that examined transference interpretation in psychodynamic psychotherapy (W. P. Henry et al., 1994) offers the following general conclusions:

1. The frequency of interpretations made is not related to better outcome. Indeed, some studies have found that a higher frequency of interpretation is related to poorer outcome.

2. Transference interpretations do not result in a greater degree of affective experience in the patient as compared with other types of in-

terpretations or other types of interventions. When followed by affective responses, however, transference interpretations appear to be related to positive outcome.

3. Interpretations by the therapist are more likely to result in defensive responding on the part of the patient than are other types of interventions. Frequent transference interpretations may damage the therapeutic relationship.

4. Clinicians' accuracy of interpretations may be lower than was previously believed.

The authors summarize: "The available findings challenge some dearly held beliefs. In short, transference interpretations do not seem uniquely effective, may pose greater process risks, and may be counter-therapeutic under certain conditions" (W. P. Henry et al., 1994, p. 479).

This is not to say that transference interpretations are always harmful and should be avoided. Rather, the existing research suggests that the relationship between interpretation and outcome is a complex one that is likely to depend on factors such as patient characteristics, clinician interpersonal style, timing of interpretations, and accuracy of interpretations (W. P. Henry et al., 1994).

Curative Factors

What, then, seems to be responsible for positive outcomes following psychodynamic psychotherapy? The empirical evidence points to the quality and strength of the therapeutic alliance (W. P. Henry et al., 1994). Although the quality of the therapeutic alliance is related to outcome across a number of therapeutic modalities (for example, client-centered, cognitive-behavioral), it is interesting to note that the importance of the clinician-patient relationship was recognized by Freud (1912/1966). Although various definitions of the therapeutic alliance have been proposed, this term is generally used to refer to the patient's affective bond to the therapist. A positive relationship or strong bond facilitates self-examination by the patient and permits interpretation. Presumably, a strong therapeutic

alliance makes it less likely that a patient will react defensively to interpretations by the clinician. Research evidence suggests a direct link between alliance and outcome, whether short-term or long-term psychodynamic treatments are examined and regardless of the particular outcome measure used (W. P. Henry et al., 1994).

The Lack of Emphasis on Behavior

The stereotypic practitioner of psychoanalytic psychotherapy plays a relatively passive role except for interpretation. The failure to deal with behavior, to make suggestions, or to adopt a generally more activist posture would seem to prolong psychotherapy unnecessarily. For example, it may be true that a male patient's unhappy heterosexual adjustment or lack of skills with women stems from unconscious generalizations from past unfavorable comparisons with a dominant brother. But simple insight into the childhood origins of the problem does not provide the skills that are lacking. The patient's expectations for success in establishing relationships with women will continue to be low and a source of anxiety until a heterosexual behavioral repertoire is established. An active therapist who not only provides interpretations that will lead to insight but also guides the patient into new learning situations seems more likely to achieve lasting solutions to the patient's problems than does a therapist who relies solely on insight (or solely on behavior, for that matter).

It seems clear that a major reason for the rapid rise of the behavioral therapies was the failure of so many psychotherapists to deal directly with the specific problems of the patient. The approach inevitably seemed to be one of relegating the presenting problem to the status of a "symptom of something deeper." The therapist then began working with that "something deeper" while clinging to the abiding belief that once the patient understood it, the symptom or deficit would disappear. Unfortunately, things did not work out that way often enough. In any case, more and more therapists are trying to foster both insight and behavioral alternatives in their patients.

The Economics of Psychotherapy

By its very nature (reconstruction of the personality), psychoanalysis is a long and costly procedure. Its course over three to five years and the long and costly preparation of its practitioners ensure that it will be an expensive undertaking. Consequently, it has become a therapy for the affluent—for those who have both the money and the time to pursue the resolution of their neuroses. Moreover, the procedures of psychoanalysis are such that only relatively intelligent, sophisticated, and educated groups are likely to be able to accept the therapeutic demands it makes. For all these reasons, only a small portion of those in need of psychotherapy are likely to be reached by traditional psychoanalysis. The poor, the undereducated, minority groups, older populations, the severely disturbed, and those beset by reality burdens of living for which they are woefully unprepared will in all likelihood not become psychoanalytic patients.

For these reasons alone, many regard psychoanalysis as a failure. It is inherently incapable of putting even a dent in the mental health problems of the nation. Yet, for persons who have the necessary personal qualities and financial resources, psychoanalysis has been helpful, particularly for those whose problems can best be met through the development of understanding.

Psychoanalytic techniques seem to have helped many patients, and as a theory of therapy, psychoanalysis undergirds many forms of psychotherapy. Yet many clinicians still question whether, after all these years, there is really much in the way of definitive research evidence for its effectiveness. These sentiments are echoed by Wolpe (1981). Although hardly unbiased, Wolpe is particularly critical of a method that can allow patients to remain so long in therapy, often with little evidence of improvement. Wolpe cites examples offered by Schmideberg (1970). In one case, a 54-year-old man had been in psychoanalysis for 30 years without noticeable improvement. A woman who began psychoanalysis with no specific symptoms later developed agoraphobia and after 12 years of therapy was worse than when she began. Admittedly, nearly every brand of therapy contains its share of horror stories. But

lengthy therapy combined with little improvement does raise questions.

It is encouraging, however, that brief forms of psychodynamic psychotherapy have been developed. Crits-Christoph's (1992) meta-analysis indicates that brief psychodynamic treatments that incorporate the use of manuals show stronger treatment effects (versus psychodynamic treatments that do not use manuals) and in some cases may be equivalent to other forms of brief psychological treatment. In addition to providing encouragement to psychodynamically oriented clinicians, this finding should serve to impel them toward mastery and use of manual-based, empirically supported brief psychodynamic treatments, such as interpersonal psychotherapy (Markowitz, 1998). This approach is both scientifically defensible and appealing to managed care companies.

Chapter Summary

The psychodynamic approach to therapy evolved from the work of Sigmund Freud. It focuses on the analysis of past experience and emphasizes unconscious motives and conflicts in the search for the roots of behavior. Even today, a significant percentage of clinical psychologists identify their therapeutic orientation as psychodynamic. According to this viewpoint, psychological problems result from the conflicting demands of the id, ego, superego, and reality. Techniques of psychodynamic psychotherapy are aimed at uncovering unconscious conflicts and motivation. For example, dreams are analyzed, as are free associations and the nature of the transference.

Psychoanalytic theory and therapy have been modified considerably over the years by neo-Freudians, ego-analysts, and others. Brief psychodynamic psychotherapy is also an important development. Here, the length of treatment is much shorter, and the focus is more on the here and now. Interpersonal psychotherapy is a form of brief psychodynamic therapy that has good empirical support for treating depression and other conditions.

Research evidence suggests that traditional forms of psychodynamic psychotherapy are moderately effective and that brief, manual-based forms are more effective. The major curative factor appears to be the quality and strength of the therapeutic alliance. Research evidence and the managed care environment should lead more and more psychodynamic clinicians to use brief, manual-based forms of psychodynamic psychotherapy.

Key Terms

anal stage The psychosexual stage that extends from about 6 months to 3 years of age, during which the child focuses on urination and defecation as means of satisfaction.

analysis of dreams A psychoanalytic technique that attempts to shed light on unconscious material. Because dreams are regarded as heavily laden with unconscious wishes in symbolic form, the analysis of dreams is believed to provide important clues to these wishes.

brief psychotherapy Psychotherapy of relatively brief duration that has grown in popularity due in large part to the cost-containment measures imposed by health-care systems. Many brief therapies have retained a psychodynamic identity.

catharsis The release of psychic energy (achieved by reliving traumatic events) believed by psychoanalysts to have important therapeutic benefits.

death instincts (Thanatos) The innate drives that are responsible for all of the negative or destructive aspects of behavior.

defense mechanisms Strategies used by the ego to stave off threats originating internally, from one's id or superego. (Also referred to as ego defenses.)

ego The organized, rational component of the personality. The ego uses perception, learning, planning, and so forth to satisfy the needs of the organism while at the same time preserving its place in the world.

ego analysis An alternative to traditional psychoanalysis that is characterized by relative deemphases on the role of the unconscious and the exploration of childhood experience, and relative emphases on the adaptive functions of the ego (e.g., perception, learning, memory) and the exploration of contemporary problems in living.

fixation The defense mechanism that occurs when the frustration and anxiety of the next psychosexual stage cause the individual to be arrested at his or her current level of psychosexual development.

free association A cardinal rule of psychoanalysis in which patients are required to say anything and everything that comes to mind. Over time, free association is believed to shed light on unconscious thoughts and urges.

genital stage The psychosexual stage that follows the onset of adolescence and ideally culminates in a mature expression of sexuality.

id The deep, inaccessible portion of the personality that contains the instinctual urges. The id is without order, logic, or morals and operates solely to gratify the instinctual urges.

insight In psychoanalytic psychotherapy, insight refers to a complete understanding of the unconscious determinants of one's irrational and problematic thoughts, feelings, or behaviors.

interpersonal psychotherapy (IPT) A brief, insight-oriented therapy that is psychodynamic in tone. IPT has been applied primarily to the treatment of depression and is considered a "well-established" EVT for this disorder.

interpretation A method in which the psychoanalyst reveals the unconscious meanings of the patient's thoughts and behaviors, thus helping the patient to achieve insight. Interpretation is the cornerstone of nearly every form of dynamic psychotherapy.

latency stage The psychosexual stage that extends from about 5 to 12 years of age, during which the child is characterized by a lack of overt sexual activity (and perhaps even a negative orientation toward anything sexual).

latent content The symbolic meaning of a dream's events.

life instincts (Eros) The innate drives that are responsible for all of the positive or constructive aspects of behavior.

manifest content What actually happens during a dream.

moral anxiety Anxiety that arises from the concern that a person will act in a way that conflicts with the standards of his or her conscience.

neurotic anxiety Anxiety that stems from the fear that a person's id impulses will be expressed unchecked, thus resulting in trouble.

Oedipus complex The phase in which a child feels sexual attraction for the parent of the opposite sex and feelings of hostility toward the parent of the same sex. The superego emerges from the resolution of this complex.

oral stage The psychosexual stage spanning about the first year of life, during which the mouth is the chief source of pleasure and satisfaction.

phallic stage The psychosexual stage that extends from about 3 to 7 years of age, during which the sexual organs become the primary source of gratification.

pleasure principle The rule of conduct by which one seeks pleasure and avoids pain. The id operates according to the pleasure principle.

primary process The irrational and impulsive type of thinking that characterizes the id.

projection The defense mechanism that occurs when a person attributes his or her unconscious feelings to someone else.

psychic determinism A major assumption of Freudian theory that holds that everything one does has meaning and is goal directed.

psychosexual stages A series of developmental stages posited by Freud, each of which is marked by the involvement of a particular erogenous zone of the body.

reaction formation The defense mechanism that occurs when an unconscious impulse is consciously expressed by its behavioral opposite.

reality anxiety Anxiety that arises from the presence of a real danger in the outside world.

reality principle The rule of conduct by which one defers the gratification of instinctual urges until a suitable object and mode of satisfaction are discovered. The ego operates according to the reality principle.

regression The defense mechanism that occurs when extensive frustration causes a person to return to a stage that once provided a great deal of gratification.

repression The most basic defense mechanism. Repression serves to keep highly threatening sexual or aggressive material out of conscious awareness, often involuntarily.

resistance Any attempt by the patient to ward off the therapist's efforts to dissolve his or her neurotic methods for resolving problems.

secondary process The rational and self-preservative type of thinking that characterizes the ego.

superego The component of the personality that represents the ideals and values of society as they are conveyed to the child through the words and deeds of his or her parents. The role of the superego is to block unacceptable id impulses and to pressure the ego to serve the ends of morality rather than those of expediency.

talking cure Discovered by Breuer, "talking cure" refers to the use of techniques that encourage patient talking as a way of addressing and alleviating neurotic symptoms.

therapeutic alliance The bond between patient and therapist. A strong therapeutic alliance is believed to contribute significantly to a positive therapeutic outcome.

transference A key phenomenon in psychoanalytic therapy in which the patient reacts to the therapist as if the therapist represented an important figure from the patient's past.

unconscious motivation Motivation that resides outside of conscious awareness. Freud posited the existence of unconscious motivation and asserted that it was responsible, in large part, for disturbed behavior.

unconscious The portion of the mind that is not accessible to awareness.

working-through process A careful and repeated examination of how one's conflicts and defenses have operated in many areas of one's life. It is through this process that an insight achieves true, full meaning for the patient.

Web Sites of Interest

To visit any of the web sites listed below, go to www.wadsworth.com and click on Links.

12-1 American Psychoanalytic Association

12-2 Online Preview of the Exhibition "Sigmund Freud: Conflict and Culture"

12-3 Sigmund Freud on the Internet

12-4 Burying Freud: Online debate between Freud critics and supporters

CHAPTER THIRTEEN

Psychotherapy: Phenomenological and Humanistic-Existential Perspectives

Traditional psychotherapy traces its origins to a psychoanalytic point of view that regards both pathology and the inability to achieve one's potential as failures in understanding the past. These failures are seen as rooted in the unacknowledged role of inner forces or even instincts. Through therapy, one can learn to understand all this, and the ensuing insight will set one free—free from the misery of problems, symptoms, and the failure to live a productive, meaningful life.

For many years, the foregoing views dominated psychotherapy. In the early 1940s, however, a serious alternative to psychoanalytic psychotherapy began to appear. An approach known as *nondirective counseling*—later to become *client-centered therapy*—was taking shape under the guidance of Carl Rogers (see Box 13-1).

Client-Centered Therapy

The perspective of Carl Rogers is almost the diametric opposite of psychoanalysis; yet the two points of view do share a few characteristics. Both theories developed out of therapeutic encounters with people who had problems. As a result, neither perspective can be totally understood without an appreciation of the ways in which it relates to therapy.

Origins

The full extent of Rogers' contribution becomes apparent if one recalls the personality-therapy world of the late 1930s. Psychoanalysis, both as theory and practice, was the dominant force. The theories of psychologists such as Gordon Allport and Kurt Lewin were attracting some attention, but the real spotlight was on those theories that had a close association with treatment—which meant psychoanalysis or at least some close derivative of it. This attention seemed to increase as many prominent psychoanalysts fled Europe and settled in the United States.

At this time, Carl Rogers was an obscure clinical psychologist in Rochester, New York, struggling with the clinical problems of disturbed children. Like most therapists of the day, Rogers had been heavily exposed to psychoanalytic thinking. After completing his Ph.D. at Columbia University, he began work at a child guidance clinic in Rochester. There, he came in touch with the will therapy of Otto Rank and the relationship therapy of Jessie Taft. Rank believed that patients should be allowed free opportunity to exert their wills and to dominate the therapist. Taft, a social worker, brought Rank's notions to America, emphasizing the relationship between the therapist and the patient. Indeed, Taft regarded this relationship as more important than any intellectual explanations of the patient's problems. Consequently, the therapeutic situation was made a very permissive one.

Rogers found these views highly congenial. They were consonant both with his religious beliefs and with his democratic convictions regarding the nature of human relationships in society. A belief that no person has the right to run another person's life found subsequent expression in his therapeutic notions of permissiveness, acceptance, and the refusal to give advice.

The Phenomenological World

Rogers' theory of personality developed mainly out of therapeutic encounters with patients and from certain philosophic notions about the nature of people. Furthermore, client-centered therapy anchors itself in phenomenological theory (Combs & Snygg, 1959; Rogers, 1951).

Phenomenology teaches that behavior is totally determined by the phenomenal field of the person. The phenomenal field is everything experienced by the person at any given point in time. Therefore, to understand people's behavior, one must know something about their phenomenal field—that is, what the world is like for them. A difficulty, however, is that one must make inferences regarding this field from the person's behavior. Those inferences, in turn, can be used to predict or understand the behavior in question. There is a real potential here for circularity if the therapist is not careful. For example, a therapist observes that George is behaving nervously prior to a test, infers that George must be

BOX 13-1

A Brief Biography of Carl Rogers

Courtesy of Natalie Rogers

Born in Oak Park, Illinois, on January 8, 1902, Carl Rogers was the fourth of six children and grew up in a financially secure family. When Rogers was 12, his father, a civil engineer and contractor, moved the family to a farm outside Chicago. His parents maintained a devout, almost dogmatic set of religious beliefs, and the family became a tight little unit—perhaps in part because of those beliefs. Rogers had few friends and spent much of his time alone reading. He was an outstanding student in high school, but was not really a part of the social scene.

He went to the University of Wisconsin in 1919 to major in agriculture. He was very active in campus religious affairs, especially during his first two years, even attending a religious conference in Peking, China, during this period. He was so impressed by the cultural and religious diversity he encountered on this trip that his traditionalist family and religious views were shaken. As a result, his fundamentalist orientation began to change noticeably. He graduated from the university with a degree in history in 1924.

He married Helen Elliott, with whom he had two children. Moving to New York City, he attended Union Theological Seminary for two years. However, a growing religious skepticism coupled with a desire to help others more directly led him to transfer to Columbia University and pursue training in clinical psychology. He was awarded the Ph.D. in 1931. He moved on to Rochester, New York, where he became a staff psychologist in a child guidance clinic.

The beginnings of Rogers' methods are clearly visible in his book *The Clinical Treatment of the Problem Child*, which was published in 1939. When he moved to Ohio State University in 1940, Rogers began to develop his approach to psychotherapy in earnest (Rogers, 1942). In 1945, he moved to the University of Chicago and began a period of intensive research as he developed a theoretical structure to buttress his therapeutic practices. During this period, the term "client-centered" began to supplant the older "nondirective" label (Rogers, 1951). Then, in 1957, Rogers accepted a position at the University of Wisconsin in order to extend his ideas about psychotherapy to more extreme populations, such as hospitalized schizophrenics (Rogers, Gendlin, Kiesler, & Truax, 1967). From 1968 until his death in February 1987, Rogers was a resident fellow at the Center for Studies of the Person in La Jolla, California.

Rogers published numerous books (several of which are cited in the References at the end of this book). His autobiography, written in 1967, is included in *A History of Psychology in Autobiography* (Vol. 5). An autobiographical paper, "In Retrospect: Forty-Six Years," appeared in the *American Psychologist* in 1974. *A Way of Being*, published in 1980, provides some insight into the changes that occurred in his thinking over the years. A sensitive and revealing portrait of Rogers—both as a psychologist and as a person—has been offered by Gendlin (1988).

experiencing threat from the test, and then proceeds to account for his nervousness by attributing it to the threat. Such an observation is both the basis for the inference and the object of the explanation.

A very important concept within phenomenological theory is the *phenomenal self*—that part of the phenomenal field that the person experiences as the "I." Obviously, this is not an objective experience. In addition, phenomenological theory states that the basic human urge is to preserve and enhance the phenomenal self. In a sense, then, self-esteem becomes the fountainhead of behavior.

Problems in adjustment arise when the phenomenal self is threatened. However, what is a threat for one person is not necessarily a threat for another. In essence, a person will experience threat whenever he or she perceives that the phenomenal self is in danger. Thus, a man who perceives himself as being very attractive to women may become anxious if he is rejected by a woman, because this represents a threat to his self-concept. Faced with such a threat, the man may adopt a variety of defensive postures. For example, he may rationalize his failure, or he may narrow his perceptual field. The truly adjusted person is one who can integrate all experiences into the phenomenal field, not just the experiences that are immediately consistent with the self-concept. For example, a well-adjusted student who fails an exam will not claim unfairness or physical illness (assuming that these claims are unjustified). Rather, the student will integrate this experience by perhaps revising the self-concept. For example, "Maybe I am not as good in biochemistry as I thought. But then again, I do quite well in other areas, and I have good social skills. So clearly this doesn't diminish me as a person." Or "I did fail, but with more effort I think I can do it. But if not, I will try other things that will bring a sense of fulfillment or contribution."

Theoretical Propositions

Early on, Rogers (1951) formulated a series of propositions that set the tone for a client-centered view of personality. He stated that individuals exist in a world of experience of which they are the center. This experience can only be known by the person. Therefore, the person is the best source of information about the self. These views have led members of the client-centered movement to rely heavily on self-reports, rather than on inferences from test data or related observations, as the primary source of information. Because people react to the perceptual field as it is experienced and perceived, their perceptual field is reality. Therefore, objective knowledge about stimuli is not enough to predict behavior. The clinician must know something about the person's awareness of those stimuli. The psychology of objectivity is rejected in favor of the inner world of experience as reported by the person.

The basic human tendency is toward maintaining and enhancing the experiencing self, or *self-actualization*. This is what produces the forward movement of life—a force upon which the therapist will rely heavily in therapeutic contacts with the client. But this forward movement can occur only when the choices of life are clearly perceived and adequately symbolized.

Behavior is fundamentally a set of goal-directed attempts by the organism to satisfy experienced needs. All needs can ultimately be subsumed under the single urge of enhancement of the phenomenal self. All of this would seem to imply a kind of learning theory, but it is difficult to find any learning concepts in Rogers' theoretical expositions.

A crucial concept is the *self*, the awareness of one's being and functioning. The structure of the self is formed out of interactions with the environment, and in particular out of evaluations of the person by others. The self is an organized, fluid, and yet consistent pattern of perceptions of the characteristics and relationships of the I or the Me, along with the values attached to them. During the life of the individual, a variety of experiences occur. Following an experience, three possibilities present themselves: (1) the experience can be symbolized or organized into some relationship with the self; (2) the experience can be ignored because its relevance to the self is not perceived; or (3) the experience can be denied symbolization or distorted because it is inconsistent with the structure of the self.

Under certain conditions, experiences that are inconsistent with the self may be examined and perceived, and the structure of the self revised to assimilate them. The principal condition is a complete absence of threat to the self. This, in effect, states the rationale for the warm, accepting, permissive, and nonjudgmental atmosphere that is the cardinal condition in client-centered therapy.

Theory of Therapy

As Rogers (1959) put it, psychotherapy is the "releasing of an already existing capacity in a potentially competent individual, not the expert manipulation of a more or less passive personality" (p. 221). This is the so-called *growth potential* on which the client-centered therapist relies so heavily. All people possess such a potential; the trick is to release it. In client-centered therapy, presumably the release is effected, thus permitting one's self-actualizing tendencies to gain ascendance over previously internalized factors that restricted one's acceptance of personal worth. The three therapist characteristics that precipitate all of this are (1) accurate, empathic understanding; (2) unconditional positive regard; and (3) genuineness or congruence. These three variables were discussed briefly in Chapter 11, where it was observed that research evidence does not accord them as much power as did Rogers (see, for example, Greenberg, Elliott, & Lietaer, 1994).

Empathy. To convey *empathy* is to transmit to the client a sense of being understood. The empathic therapist conveys a kind of sensitivity to the needs, feelings, and circumstances of the client. Exceptionally empathic therapists can assume the attitudes of clients and, as it were, climb behind their eyeballs and see the world as they do. The client must come to know that the therapist is making every effort to understand correctly. When the client realizes this, the basis is laid for a therapeutic relationship. Empathy can never be total, of course—and a good thing,

too. A measure of objective detachment must always be maintained; otherwise, the therapist would have the same problems as the client. Nevertheless, the empathic therapist can convey or communicate to clients a sense of understanding and appreciation of their needs or plight. And clients can find this attitude tremendously reassuring, more so than any words or any exclamations of interest. For the attitude of empathy is not stated; it is conveyed by its very existence.

Perhaps Rogers' (1946) own words will convey something of this attitude of understanding and empathy:

> We have come to recognize that if we can provide understanding of the way the client seems to himself [sic] at this moment, he can do the rest. The therapist must lay aside his [sic] preoccupation with diagnosis and his diagnostic shrewdness, must discard his tendency to make professional evaluations, must cease his endeavors to formulate an accurate prognosis, must give up the temptation subtly to guide the individual, and must concentrate on one purpose only; that of providing deep understanding and acceptance of the attitudes consciously held at this moment by the client as he explores step by step into the dangerous areas which he has been denying to consciousness.
>
> This type of relationship can exist only if the counselor is deeply and genuinely able to adopt these attitudes. Client-centered counseling, if it is to be effective, cannot be a trick or a tool. It is not a subtle way of guiding the client while pretending to let him guide himself. To be effective, it must be genuine (pp. 420–421).

Unconditional Positive Regard. In most relationships, with parents, friends, a spouse, or others, clients have learned that approval and acceptance are conditional upon meeting certain stipulations. Parents accept children if they are obedient. An employer is accepting if employees are prompt and efficient. Spouses require that their partners be interested and loving. But in therapy, there must be no conditions. Acceptance is given without hidden clauses or subtle disclaimers. *Unconditional positive regard* is nothing more and nothing less than a respect for the client as a human being. The therapist must lay aside all preconceived notions and be able to care about the client, be accepting, and above all, convey that here is someone who has faith and trust in the client's ability and strength to achieve that inner potential. These qualities, coupled with a complete lack of evaluative judgments on the part of the therapist, will go a long way toward creating an atmosphere in which the client is free to give up debilitating defenses and can, in the absence of threat, begin to grow as a person.

Exhibiting these qualities with someone the therapist finds pleasing and in tune with his or her own background and values is relatively easy. The true test of the therapist's unconditional positive regard comes with clients whose behaviors and attitudes really challenge the therapist's beliefs. The bigot, the unmotivated or lazy, or the client who describes an incestuous experience with his niece can force a real test of the therapist's tolerance and acceptance. But just as every citizen is entitled to vote, so is every client worthy of unconditional positive regard, according to Rogers.

Congruence. At first glance, *congruence*—or *genuineness,* as it is sometimes called—would seem to contradict the qualities of empathy and positive regard. Congruent therapists are those who express the behaviors, feelings, or attitudes that the client stimulates in them. One does not smile if one is angry. If the client's remarks are upsetting, the therapist does not hide behind a mask of calm (Rogers, 1961). Rogers believed that in the long run clients would respond favorably to this honesty and congruence, knowing that here was a real person dedicated to their welfare. This can be most reassuring and can stimulate a sense of personal worth and a desire to come to grips with one's latent potential.

Attitude versus Technique. In many ways, the core of client-centered therapy seems to reside more in stated values and attitudes toward people than in any specific methods. To that extent, client-centered therapy is a state of mind rather than a set of techniques. The client-centered therapist seeks to become nondirective by relinquishing any procedures that point to the therapist as an expert who will diagnose the client's ills and recommend the proper measures for their alleviation.

In fact, client-centered therapists will argue that such "prescriptions" are unnecessary, because the release of clients' resources or potential will resolve the problems in question. Given therapist congruence, unconditional positive regard, and accurate empathic understanding, clients will discover their own capacity for growth and self-direction. In contrast to the psychoanalysts, Rogers saw people not as destructive, but as possessed of a constructive force reaching toward health and self-fulfillment. In addition, the Rogerians forgo an emphasis on the past in favor of an awareness of current experience. For the interpretations of the activist psychoanalytic therapist they substitute the quiet, listening therapist whose caring facilitates the client's own discovery of inner strength and valid personal experience.

There are also distinct differences between client-centered therapy and the behavioral approaches (discussed in the following chapter). Rogerians declare that inner experiences are the paramount data and that to ignore those experiences is to ignore the basic data of the human being. Whereas behavioral approaches sometimes seem to focus on manipulating or controlling the environment to effect change, the client-centered therapist relies on change that emanates from within—a release of inner potential.

The Therapeutic Process

It almost seems easier to describe client-centered therapy in terms of what does *not* take place. A long series of "don'ts" includes giving information or advice, using reassurance or persuasion, asking questions, offering interpretations, and making criticisms. Perhaps the major activities of the therapist are the recognition and clarification of the feelings associated with the client's statements. For example, Greenberg et al. (1994) reports that approximately 75% of all client-centered therapists' responses were "reflections" of what the client had said. Comments are also made that convey to the client the therapist's total and unconditional acceptance. Occasionally the therapist will find it necessary to explain the respective roles of the client and the therapist. Called *structuring*, this too includes the element of acceptance.

Typically, neither reassurance nor interpretation is used. It is assumed that the recognition of feeling and the accompanying acceptance are themselves reassuring. Reassurance is also conveyed by the therapist's tone of voice, choice of words, facial expression, and general demeanor. Providing interpretation and giving advice or information are avoided because these imply that the therapist knows what is best for the client. In some instances, it may be necessary to refer the client to a source of information. In general, however, the idea is to place the responsibility for therapeutic progress on the client's shoulders rather than on those of the therapist. Similarly, to interpret is to tell clients why they behaved in a given fashion. Interpretation means that the therapist has preempted responsibility for progress rather than waiting for clients to arrive at their own explanations.

In the case of acceptance, this is less a technique than an all-pervasive attitude. The durable belief is that the client is capable of reaching a satisfactory solution to problems in living. Acceptance provides the atmosphere in which the client's potential for growth and self-actualization can be asserted. By responding to the client's feelings and then accepting them, the therapist provides a warmth that leads to the feeling of being understood.

Client-centered therapy sessions are usually scheduled once a week. More frequent sessions, extra sessions, and phone calls are discouraged because these can lead to a dependency that will stifle any sense of growth.

The general sequence or process of therapy has been described by Rogers as involving a series of seven stages that the client undergoes (Meador & Rogers, 1984). We present a highly condensed version here.

First stage: Unwillingness to reveal self; own feelings not recognized; rigid constructs; close relationships perceived as dangerous.

Second stage: Feelings sometimes described, but person is still remote from own personal experience; still externalizes heavily, but begins to show some recognition that problems and conflicts exist.

Third stage: Description of past feelings as unacceptable; freer flow of expressions of self; begins to question validity of own constructs; incipient recognition that problems are inside rather than outside the individual.

Fourth stage: Free description of personal feelings as owned by the self; dim recognition that long-denied feelings may break into the present; loosening of personal constructs; some expression of self-responsibility; begins to risk relating to others on a feeling basis.

Fifth stage: Free expression of feelings and acceptance of them; previously denied feelings, although fearsome, are clearly in awareness; recognition of conflicts between intellect and emotions; acceptance of personal responsibility for problems; a desire to be what one is.

Sixth stage: Acceptance of feelings without need for denial; a vivid, releasing sense of experience; willingness to risk being oneself in relationships with others; trusts others to be accepting.

Seventh stage: Individual now comfortable with experiencing self; experiences new feelings; little incongruency; ability to check validity of experience.

Diagnosis

In general, diagnosis or assessment is deemphasized or avoided in client-centered therapy. Most Rogerians believe that formal assessment is not only unnecessary but actually detrimental. According to these Rogerians, assessment places the psychologist in a superior, authoritative role that can impede the development of autonomy and self-actualization. The abandonment of assessment seems to imply that client-centered therapy is so potent and effective a method that it works on all clients, regardless of their problems or of the particular circumstances in which they find themselves. Needless to say, the utility of this assumption has not yet been adequately demonstrated (Greenberg et al., 1994).

A Case Illustration of Client-Centered Therapy

The following case example illustrates some of the features of client-centered counseling that have been discussed. The client was a 20-year-old sophomore who was being seen in a university counseling center. His initial complaint involved a generalized feeling of unworthiness. As the sessions moved along, he began to focus specifically on his feelings of intellectual inadequacy. Even though his college grade point average in a demanding curriculum was 3.3, he was constantly absorbed by a sense of inferiority. He frequently compared himself (always unfavorably) to an older brother who had recently completed medical school and was the source of much parental pride. The following exchange took place in the 15th session.

Client: Well, it happened again yesterday. I got back that exam in American Lit.

Therapist: I see.

Client: Just like before. I got an "A" all right—me and eight others. But on the third question the instructor wrote a comment that I could have been a little clearer or else could have given more detail. The same old crap. I got an "A" all right, but it's pretty damn clear that I'm like a machine that can generate correct answers without ever understanding. That's it. I memorize, but there's no spark, no creativity. Boy!

Therapist: What else can you tell me about the exam?

Client: Well, it was like we talked about before. I'm doing OK, but I just don't feel like I really measure up. I remember my brother bringing home a paper in high school. It was a "C," but the instructor said John had real potential. I just don't think I've got it.

Therapist: Even though you got an "A" you are not satisfied.

Client: That's right. Never satisfied. I could get 42 "A+s" and never feel good. I hate myself!

Therapist: M-hm.

Client: Sometimes I'm so ridiculous.

Therapist: You feel silly because of the way you react. Is that right?

Client: I should put it aside, think about other things. But I don't, and then I feel silly when I don't.

Therapist: You're silly because you feel dissatisfied and silly because you don't just forget it.

Client: I know I should be satisfied with an "A." Other guys would be. They'd be glad to get an "A."

Therapist: M-hm.

Client: But I can't. No wonder the folks are so proud of John. He got decent grades, and he was satisfied—not like me. It's a wonder they don't get fed up with my moping around.

Therapist: So even with good grades your unhappiness is enough to turn people off.

Client: Sure. But somehow I've got to get rid of this defeatist attitude. I've got to think about the good side.

Therapist: M-hm.

Client: A lot of times I've tried to forget my lack of potential. Just go on and plug along.

Therapist: Yeah. I guess you really felt people put you down because of this lack of potential?

Client: Boy, did they! Especially my folks. They never really said so, but I could tell from the way they acted.

Therapist: M-hm.

Client: They'd say that John really has a head on his shoulders, or (pause) . . . he can think his way out of anything.

Therapist: And this made you feel sort of worthless—not hearing things like that about yourself.

Client: That's right.

Therapist: M-hm.

Intense feelings were expressed in this session. The client felt worthless and inferior to his brother. Despite an outstanding college record, he continued to find ways to prove that he was intellectually unacceptable. The therapist did not attempt to contradict him or to prove him wrong; nor did he make reassuring comments. Rather, he accepted the client's statements and the feelings they conveyed.

What is important in client-centered therapy is the feelings, not whether they are wrong or whether they stem from an earlier unhealthy home situation. The therapist accepts the feelings in a manner that transmits neither approval nor disapproval—just understanding. It is the understanding and the occasional clarifications that permit the client to move ever closer to a careful examination of himself and of what he can do to change matters. Only in an atmosphere of acceptance can this potential for growth be cultivated and released. The foregoing case illustration also highlights the empathic statements made by the therapist, often summarizing, almost inferentially, what the client was feeling. The therapist, then, does more than just accept the client's feelings. By rephrasing and inferring, the therapist reminds the client of what he or she must be feeling.

Over the years, like any movement, client-centered therapy has evolved and changed. Both the method and the theory have been modified and extended. A brief summary of these developments can be found in Greenberg et al. (1994).

Other Applications

The client-centered approach was developed primarily in the counseling psychotherapy context, and this remains its chief application. However, the movement has found other applications as well. For example, the client-centered orientation is frequently used in human relations training. The emphasis on relationship, acceptance, and warmth is often an integral part of training programs for those who seek to work in crisis centers, for paraprofessionals who engage in counseling, and for volunteers in charitable organizations or agencies. Thus, whether one is dealing with professionals such as physicians and nurses, psychological technicians, or Peace Corps volunteers, their training in human relationships often contains a heavy dose of the client-centered philosophy. When the client-centered approach is applied to problems outside the therapy room, it is often called the *person-centered approach.*

As we shall see in Chapter 15, small groups, encounter groups, and personal growth groups make use of the client-centered framework. Often, these groups are established to reduce tension between factions in conflict, such as blacks and whites, labor and management, or students and faculty. In some instances, institutions such as churches, businesses, and school systems use the client-centered approach to foster improved human relations or changes in institutional functioning and goals.

Some Concluding Remarks

The Positive. The client-centered approach has had many salutary effects. It provided a serious alternative to the traditional psychoanalytic forms of therapy. In so doing, it offered an alternative focus on self-determination and inner directedness rather than on the biological urges and instincts of the Freudian view. The becoming, evolving person replaced the victim of personal history. Freedom to choose was substituted for a mechanistically determined set of behaviors.

Rogers demonstrated that it is not necessary to dig up the past in order to conduct psychotherapy. Emphasis was placed on the relationship between the client and the therapist, and the application of "techniques" became secondary. Even the word *client* suggests something of importance. The role of the passive patient in the context of the physician's demand for authority was replaced by that of the client who actively seeks to experience choice, equality, and freedom.

The general ahistorical stance of the Rogerians also led to a form of therapy much shorter than the often interminable psychoanalysis. The move away from lengthy resolutions of transference relationships, the detailed reconstruction of the past, and cathartic experiences considerably shortened the therapeutic process. In addition, the less active role played by the therapist required less training. Given the mental health needs of the nation, any therapeutic discipline that can provide personnel faster and more economically is to be seriously considered. However, it is possible that client-centered therapy has become a double-edged sword. Some feel that the client-centered, humanistic axis has produced a whole generation of pseudotherapists whose lack of training can never be fully offset by their enthusiasm and "authenticity."

A contribution of major proportions was Rogers' emphasis on research. He was responsible for the first concerted efforts to carry out research on the therapeutic process. It was he who first employed recordings of therapy sessions to study the process and to investigate its effectiveness. The use of recordings is now a staple ingredient of training and research. Prior to Rogers, the sanctity of the therapy room was guarded with a vengeance. Rogers opened up therapy and made it an object of study rather than a subject of mystery. In making available recordings and transcripts of his own therapy sessions, he exhibited a degree of courage unusual for its time (though it may be commonplace today).

In addition to the pioneering efforts of Rogers and others in the recording and transcription of interviews, significant efforts were made to investigate the outcomes of therapy. For example, Rogers and his colleagues developed indices of therapeutic outcome based on client ratings of their present and their ideal self-concept, along with various indicators of improvement gleaned from counseling sessions, such as the ratio of client to therapist talk and the responsibility for talk (for example, Cartwright, 1956; Rogers & Dymond, 1954; Rogers, Gendlin, Kiesler, & Truax, 1967; W. U. Snyder, 1961; Truax & Carkhuff, 1967; Truax & Mitchell, 1971).

As noted in Chapter 11, meta-analyses of studies including a client-centered treatment condition have indicated an effect size of 0.62, indicating that a client who received this form of therapy was functioning (on average) better than 73% of those who did not receive treatment. To investigate whether this finding characterized "newer" research (1978 to 1992) on client-centered therapy, Greenberg et al. (1994) conducted another meta-analysis. It is noteworthy that they could identify only eight studies conducted during this time period that investigated the effectiveness of client-centered therapy and also included a control group. The average effect size across these studies was .88; on average, a client in these studies was functioning better than 81% of those not receiving treatment. Greenberg et al. were also able to evaluate the relative effectiveness of client-centered therapy compared to other forms of psychological treatment. Of the seven relevant comparisons, in only one instance did client-centered therapy outperform another treatment (in this case, short-term dynamic therapy; A. E. Meyer, 1981). In summary, research evidence suggests that client-centered therapy is effective, but no more effective than any other psychological treatment.

The Negative. There is, however, another side of the coin. Client-centered therapists repeatedly argue that their efforts do not change clients. Instead, they say, the client's inner potential for growth is released. Whether this view is based on conviction or modesty, it seems to be incomplete. Therapy is a stimulus (the particular character of which is greatly affected by the therapist) that sets many reactions into motion. Whether those reactions are deemed positive, negative, or neutral, they seem in large measure to be attributable to the stimuli and the methods of the therapist.

Client-centered therapists claim that in order to understand clients, one must climb behind their eyeballs to experience the same phenomenological world. But how does one do that? With intuition? How does one ever completely shed the idiosyncratic bias of a personal framework? Critics would argue that avoiding assessment and giving the past short shrift actually impair the therapist's ability to understand and enter into the client's perceptual framework.

Client-centered therapy seems to involve only one technique, or rather one attitude: empathy, acceptance, and unconditional positive regard. Thus, every client is treated in exactly the same way. The therapist need not assess the client in order to choose the most effective therapy or the specific technique to fit the unique characteristics of that client. Thus, a good case could be made for the contention that client-centered therapy is really technique centered!

There is also an abiding faith that the client knows best. The movement's emphasis on democracy, freedom of choice, and the indisputable supremacy of the client's inner potential leads to condemnation of therapist "interference" through interpretation, advice, or expressed values. In many cases, however, the severity of the client's problems or the deviant quality of the client's values would seem to dictate the use of a more active and directing set of procedures. One might well have reason to doubt the wisdom and resources of a psychopathic or schizophrenic client. Even if it were true (though this is probably not a testable proposition) that, given unlimited time or optimum circumstances, each client could make the right decisions or reach the proper conclusions, it seems a very inefficient to operate. Client-centered therapists seem to be seeking to change the client (though claiming not to do so) without collecting enough diagnostic and/or histori-

cal data to do so efficiently. Their emphasis on verbal reports by the client places them at the mercy of information that is often defensive, distorted, and incomplete.

Much of the research on the effectiveness of client-centered therapy has relied on internal criteria. That is, clients are said to be improving when they take more responsibility for the conversation during the therapy session or talk proportionately more than the therapist. Others would argue, however, that the real criteria for improvement must come from outside the therapy room (through observation, reports by peers and spouse, and so on). Without validation from such external sources, it is possible that any client changes observed within the therapy room represent adjustments to the demands of the situation rather than changes that will generalize beyond the confines of therapy.

Very often, descriptions of client-centered treatment philosophies and procedures are unique and involve a great deal of undefined terminology. Such words as *being, becoming, actualizing,* and *congruency* are not clearly defined or seem to carry a surplus of meaning that is difficult to communicate reliably. At other times, there is a grandiosity of language that seems out of keeping with the modesty that appears elsewhere. For example, Rogers (1951) says, "Therapy is the essence of life" (p. x).

Although some may simply chalk this up to jargon, there is nevertheless a marked tendency for Rogerians to use language that is emotionally tinged in such a way as to almost serve a propaganda function. Such words as *nondirective* and *client-centered* not only seem to convey something distinctly positive, but by implication also seem to depict other approaches as directive or therapist-centered. A terminology that includes words such as *freedom, democratic, genuine, warm,* and *authentic* is likely to put advocates of other approaches at an immediate disadvantage. Before such advocates can explain what their approaches really are, they may have to answer implicit charges of being authoritarian, technique-centered, controlling, and without common humanistic values.

Finally, the client-centered approach grew and came of age on college campuses. The clients of the 1940s and 1950s were college students who were being seen at campus counseling centers. As often as not, the therapists trained in the Rogerian tradition in these centers became staff members at other college counseling centers. It is worth noting that, compared with people in the general population, college students as a group are brighter, better educated, and less severely maladjusted when they do develop problems, and they have a stronger arsenal of coping methods. The so-called nondirective, client-centered methods would probably be more effective with such a population than with, for example, those with psychosis, poor verbal skills, or from a limited educational background.

The Humanistic-Existential Movement

The strands of phenomenology, humanism, and existentialism in psychology are inextricably woven together. In the preceding section, we have seen the importance that Rogers attached to immediate experience. This is basic phenomenology. At the same time, client-centered approaches stress the worth, uniqueness, and dignity of the client. This is basic humanism. Before we proceed to discuss existential therapies, logotherapy, and Gestalt therapy, let us pause to acknowledge the humanistic tradition that pervades those therapies.

Humanism

Although humanistic psychology is a fairly recent development, its origins extend far back into philosophy and the history of psychology. When one speaks of *humanism*, one thinks of psychologists such as Allport, Goldstein, James, Murray, and Rogers. The values that humanism contributes to psychology are not rooted in the determinism of either psychoanalysis or behaviorism. From a humanist perspective, people are

not products of the past, the unconscious, or the environment. Rather, they exercise free choice in the pursuit of their inner potential and self-actualization. They are not fragmented patchworks of cognitions, feelings, and aspirations; rather, they are unified, whole, and unique beings. To understand is to appreciate those qualities, and this understanding can only be achieved by an awareness of the person's experience. So-called scientific constructs based on norms, experiments, or data must give way to intuition and empathy. The emphasis is not on sickness, deviations, or diagnostic labels, but on positive striving, self-actualization, freedom, and naturalness. Bugental (1965), Buhler (1971), Buhler and Allen (1971), Jourard (1971), and Maslow (1962) have addressed various aspects of these values. In one form or another, humanism is expressed as a resistance to the positivistic determinism of science and as an active embrace of the essential humanity of people.

Existential Therapy

Existential psychology rejects the mechanistic views of the Freudians and instead sees people as engaged in a search for meaning. At a time when so many people are troubled by the massive problems of a technological society and seek to repair their alienated modes of living, existentialism has gained great popularity. It seems to promise the restoration of meaning to life, an increased spiritual awakening, and individual growth that will bring freedom from the conventional shackles created by a conformist society (Bugental, 1978).

Hardly a unified movement that speaks with a single voice, the existential view actually turns out to be many views. Its roots lie deep in the philosophies of Kierkegaard, Heidegger, Tillich, Sartre, Jaspers, and others. When we discuss the psychological applications of existentialism, such names as Binswanger, Boss, Gendlin, Frankl, May, and Laing come to mind. Philosophically, existentialism springs from the same sources as does phenomenology (MacLeod, 1964; Van Kaam, 1966).

PROFILE 13-1

Leslie S. Greenberg, Ph.D.

Dr. Leslie S. Greenberg is a Professor of Psychology at York University in Toronto, Canada. He specializes in psychotherapy research, and he has become a leader in conceptualizing and studying experiential psychotherapy. This psychotherapeutic approach which comes out of the humanistic-existential tradition, emphasizes the client's own experience or phenomenology, the client's potential for change or growth, and the value of the therapeutic relationship and emotional validation. Dr. Greenberg is the author of 12 books and more than 100 book chapters or articles, and he has received numerous honors and awards for his work in the field, including an Early Career Award from the Society for Psychotherapy Research. Dr. Greenberg responded to several questions regarding his views of the field as well as his predictions for the future of clinical psychology and of experiential psychotherapy.

What originally got you interested in the field of clinical psychology?

I came from a master's degree in engineering in 1970 into psychology, as I was seeking greater social and personal relevance. I completed my Bachelor's of Engineering in South Africa, where I had gone into engineering rather than physics because I liked working with people and thought that engineering would lead more to managing and working with people. I was involved in anti-apartheid

student politics in South Africa, and when I came to Canada in the 1960s, I was not happy in engineering and was much more interested in people. I also saw psychology as a way of becoming more involved in the issues of the era—personal growth and changing society.

Describe what activities you are involved in as a clinical psychologist.

I teach counseling and psychotherapy, and engage in research on the process of change and the role of emotion in this process. I supervise students' clinical practice in the research studies that I do. I have a private practice in which I see individuals and couples. I write.

What are your particular areas of expertise or interest?

I specialize in psychotherapy research, focusing most specifically on the process of change and on experiential and integrative methods of intervention. I am particularly concerned with bringing emotion back into psychotherapy, as I see it as central in functioning and in change.

What are the future trends you see for clinical psychology?

I believe that eventually there will be a single area of study, mental health, integrating the various disciplines—clinical psychology, social work, psychiatry (maybe), and nursing—and the different levels of intervention—biological, psychological, social, and so on—plus an end to schools of therapy and the school wars.

What are some future trends you see for experiential/humanistic-existential therapy?

I see experiential therapy as overcoming its heritage of being seen as involving "just" listening, being based on the view of people as having an actualizing tendency that is an inner guide to health, and that simply getting in

(continued)

Profile 13-1 *(continued)*

touch with one's feelings will lead to health. Although there is some truth in all these statements, I see these as becoming more differentiated and modified as our understanding of functioning increases. Experiential therapy will develop theoretically beyond its original statements into a more sophisticated view of human functioning, based on emotion and constructivist theory and research. It will offer a process view of functioning and therapy, offering more detail on in-session states that are amenable to particular types of intervention and how change in these states occurs. I also see experiential therapy as becoming more research based. Ultimately, it will become integrated into a non-school-based approach offering an understanding of in-session process.

The existentialists make a number of assertions about human nature (Kobasa & Maddi, 1977; Maddi, 1989). Basic to all is a fundamental human characteristic: the search for meaning (Binswanger, 1963; Boss, 1963). That search is carried out through imagination, symbolization, and judgment. All of this occurs in a matrix of participation in society. From the standpoint of both their physical environment and their biological environment, people function in a social context.

A crucial facet of personality is decision making, which involves the world of both facts and possibilities. Thus, personality is not just what one is—a biological, social, and psychological being—but also what one might become. Many existentialists believe that decision making involves a set of inevitable choices. One can choose the present (the status quo), which represents lack of change and a commitment to the past. That choice will lead to guilt and remorse over missed opportunities. But one can also choose alliance with the future. That choice propels the person into the future with an anxiety that stems from one's inability to predict and control the unknown. Such experiences of guilt and anxiety are not learned, but are part of the essence of living. It requires courage to choose the future and suffer the inevitable anxieties that this choice entails. A person can find that courage by having faith in self and by recognizing that choosing the past will inevitably lead to a guilt that is even more terrifying than anxiety.

The Goals of Therapy. The ultimate goal of existential psychotherapy is to help the individual reach a point at which awareness and decision making can be exercised responsibly. The exercise of cognitive abilities will allow for the achievement of higher states of love, intimacy, and constructive social behavior. Through therapy, one must learn to accept responsibility for one's own decisions and to tolerate the anxiety that accumulates as one moves toward change. This involves self-trust and also a capacity to accept those things in life that are unchangeable or inevitable.

Techniques. Existential therapy does not emphasize techniques. Too often, techniques imply that the client is an object to which those techniques are applied. Instead, the emphasis is on understanding and on experiencing the client as a unique essence. Therapy is an encounter that should enable the client to come closer to experience. By experiencing self, the client can learn to attach meaning and value to life. Sometimes the therapist will confront the client with questions—questions that force the client to examine the reasons for failure to search for meaning in life. For example, a client who repeatedly complains that his job is not very fulfilling may be asked why he does not search for other employment or return to school for more training. Such questions may force the client to examine his orientation toward the past more closely, and this, in turn, creates feelings of guilt and a sense of emptiness. Gendlin (1969, 1981) discusses focusing as a means of reaching the pre-conceptual, felt sense. This is achieved by having clients focus on the concretely felt bodily sense of what is troubling them. Silences are encouraged to help accomplish this. However, very few research studies have been published that evaluate the effectiveness of focusing in treating clients; its efficacy, therefore, remains to be established (Greenberg et al., 1994).

Logotherapy

One of the most widely known forms of existential therapy is *logotherapy*. This technique encourages the client to find meaning in what appears to be a callous, uncaring, and meaningless world. Viktor Frankl developed the technique. His early ideas were shaped by the Freudian influence. However, he moved on to an existential framework as he tried to find ways of dealing with experiences in Nazi concentration camps. He lost his mother, father, brother, and wife to the Nazi Holocaust and was himself driven to the brink of death (Frankl, 1963). It seemed to him that the persons who could not survive these camps were those who possessed only the conventional meanings of life to sustain them. But such conventional meanings could not come to grips with the realities of the Nazi atrocities. Therefore, what was required was a personal meaning for existence. From his wartime experiences and the existential insights that he felt permitted him to survive, Frankl developed logotherapy (the therapy of meaning). Many of his ideas are expressed in a series of books (Frankl, 1963, 1965, 1967). Frankl's views about personality and his ideas about the goals of therapy are generally quite consonant with our previous discussion of existentialism. However, it is not always clear that logotherapy techniques bear any close or rational relationship to the theory.

Logotherapy is designed not to replace but to complement more traditional psychotherapy. However, when the essence of a particular emotional problem seems to involve agonizing over the meaning or the futility of life, Frankl regards logotherapy as the specific therapy of choice. Logotherapy then strives to inculcate a sense of the client's own responsibility and obligations to life (once the latter's meaning has been unfolded). Frankl makes much of responsibility, regarding it as more important than historical events in the client's life. What is crucial is the meaning of the present and the outlook for the future.

In particular, two techniques described by Frankl (1960) have gained considerable exposure. *Paradoxical intention* is a popular technique in which the client is told to consciously attempt to perform the very behavior or response that is the object of anxiety and concern. Fear is thus replaced by a paradoxical wish. For example, suppose that a client complains that she is fearful of blushing when she speaks before a group. She would be instructed to try to blush on such occasions. According to Frankl, the paradoxical fact is that she will usually be unable to blush when she tries to do what she fears she will do. Typically, the therapist tries to handle all of this in a light tone. For example, in the case of a client fearful of trembling before his instructor, Frankl (1965) instructs the client to say to himself: "Oh, here is the instructor! Now I'll show him what a good trembler I am—I'll really show him how nicely I can tremble" (p. 226). This procedure resembles those of implosive therapy, which is discussed in Chapter 14. Some evidence suggests the effectiveness of these techniques (Shoham-Salomon & Rosenthal, 1987).

The second technique, *de-reflection*, instructs the client to ignore a troublesome behavior or symptom. Many clients are exquisitely attuned to their own responses and bodily reactions. De-reflection attempts to divert the client's attention to more constructive activities and reflections.

Gestalt Therapy

In *Gestalt therapy*, the emphasis is on present experience and on the immediate awareness of emotion and action. "Being in touch" with one's feelings replaces the search for the origins of behavior. Existential problems expressed by a failure to find meaning in life have arisen in a technological society that separates people from themselves. The "unreality" of computers and plastic credit cards has overwhelmed the true meaning of life, which can only be found in the immediate experience of emotions. Gestalt therapy promises to restore the proper balance.

A Movement of Heterogeneity. Frederick (Fritz) Perls is the figure most closely identified with the development of the Gestalt therapy movement. Perls's initial grounding was in medicine and psychoanalysis. He left Germany in 1934, after the Nazis came to power, and settled in South Africa, where he established a psychoanalytic institute. As time went on, however, he began to move away from the tenets of psychoanalysis and toward the development of what was to become Gestalt therapy. In 1946, Perls emigrated to the United States. He died in 1970.

Gestalt therapy is really a heterogeneous mix of techniques and ideas. Gestalt therapists do not agree among themselves, and at times seem to revel in their lack of agreement. Their goal does not seem to be the construction of a monolithic theory of therapy, but rather to express through their therapy their own sense of uniqueness and their interpretation of life. Even the contribution of Perls himself was hardly a model of consistency. Some of his major works—*Ego, Hunger, and Aggression* (Perls, 1947), *Gestalt Therapy* (Perls, Hefferline, & Goodman, 1951), *Gestalt Therapy Verbatim* (Perls, 1969a), and *In and Out the Garbage Pail* (Perls, 1969b)—express a variety of notions. Kempler (1973) provides an account of Gestalt therapy theory, as does Smith (1976). Adding to the confusion is the fact that Gestalt therapy does not really have very much to do with the Gestalt principles of Wertheimer, Koffka, Kohler, or Lewin. The connections are more superficial than substantive.

Basic Notions. Central to Gestalt therapy is the conceptualization of the person as an organized whole, not as a disjointed collection of emotions, cognitions, and behaviors. Also running through

FIGURE 13-1 "Fritz" Perls, the colorful founder of Gestalt therapy as well as of several Gestalt institutes in Cleveland, New York, and Los Angeles. He was also associated with the Esalen Institute at Big Sur, California.
© Esalen Institute/Photo by Paul Herbert.

accounts of Gestalt therapy is the admonition that individuals must develop an awareness not only of themselves but also of the ways in which they defeat themselves. This awareness is reached through the expression of what one is feeling *now*, on a moment-to-moment basis. Whatever is impeding progress toward a higher plane of adjustment must be experienced so that it, too, becomes a part of awareness. Presumably, the person's inner potential is capable of overcoming problems in adjustment. But first there must be awareness both of the obstacles to improved adjustment and of that potential itself.

The therapist becomes a catalytic agent who facilitates the client's awareness of how inner potential is being deflected from expression. Thus, the therapist does not give the client reasons for the ineffective use of potential or tell the client how it all got started. Instead, the therapist shows the client where the responsibility for more effective experiences resides—in the client. The emphasis is on momentary awareness, not on the recovery of memories or repressed impulses. However, though Perls rejected many features of psychoanalysis, his approach is really an amalgam of existentialism and psychoanalysis. For example, he seems to readily accept the importance of traditional psychoanalytic insights regarding the nature of motivation and defense.

The Now. For Perls, reality is now, behavior is now, and experience is now. To seek answers in the past is to deal with what no longer exists. Therapy is now, and it must deal with and encourage the client's awareness of that now. One's capacity for growth can only be realized by attacking anything that threatens to divert awareness from the now. As Perls (1970) put it, "To me, nothing exists except the now. Now = experience = awareness = reality. The past is no more and the future not yet. Only the *now* exists" (p. 14).

For the Gestalt therapist, anxiety is the gap between now and later (a preoccupation with what the future may bring). Being preoccupied with the past also creates a host of negative emotions. A focus on either the past or the future leads to an immobilization of the individual in the present. During therapy, the patient is required to repeat, "Now I am aware. . . ." Or the therapist will frequently ask, "What are you aware of now?" The role of the therapist is to constantly call the patient's attention to present feelings, thoughts, and experiencing. However, the therapist does not interpret, because it is assumed that awareness of the now has its own curative powers. That awareness will enable the patient to integrate the formerly disavowed aspects of his or her personality.

Nonverbal Behavior. In order to probe the patient's defenses and expose the games being played, the therapist often pays close attention to nonverbal behavior. The patient may say one thing but suggest the opposite through various cues. Take the following example:

Therapist: How are you feeling?

Patient: I'm calm; I feel good.

Therapist: You are, really?

Patient: Oh yes.

Therapist: Why are you sitting so stiff, like a ramrod?

Patient: I'm not!

Therapist: Check yourself. See your legs, feel your back against the chair?

Patient: I see what you mean.

Therapist: Let the stiffness talk. What is it telling you?

Patient: I'm afraid to let go—I feel like I'm trying to control myself.

By paying attention to nonverbal cues, the therapist was able to cut right through to a significant experience. The therapist then used the posture cue to get to feelings that existed now and helped the patient get in touch with them.

Dreams. The psychoanalyst asks the patient to associate to various elements of dreams. The Gestalt therapist, in contrast, attempts to get the patient to relive the dream now, in the therapy room. This even means acting out the dream. According to the Gestalt therapist, interpretation leads only to an intellectualized insight. In Gestalt therapy, the patient discovers the inner self by confronting the dream experience directly. The dream conveys messages or even epitomizes the conflicting sides of the self. A dream is a kind of condensed reflection of the individual's own existence and the ways used to avoid facing oneself. By playing the part of various persons or objects in the dream, the individual can learn to recognize and identify the alienated parts of the self and then integrate them.

Topdog-Underdog. When conflicts involve opposing aspects of the personality, the patient may be asked to take each part in a dialogue. The opposing parts are usually analogous to Freud's superego and id. The topdog is the superego and contains the introjected "shoulds" of the personality (parental dictates and the like). The underdog is similar to the id. It is primitive, evasive, and constantly disrupts the efforts of the topdog. By playing both roles in a dialogue, the patient can integrate these two conflicting aspects of the self.

The Defenses. In Gestalt therapy, the aim is to expose the games clients play and the defenses behind which they hide. Perls explains neurotic behavior in terms of layers. In the first layer, the client plays games, avoids facing the self, and in general is not an authentic person. Gestalt therapy forces one to experience and become aware of these shams. But this awareness is threatening, because it leads to an experience of the very fears that the shams helped evade. Genuine behavior is threatening because such behavior could lead to terrible consequences (or so the client hypothesizes). Indeed, as environmental supports are also exposed, the client really becomes terrified, feeling that the inner capacity for growth is not equal to the relinquishing of neurotic defenses in favor of honest, independent behavior. Finally, however, the client becomes aware of the hollowness that the anxieties, phobias, or doubts are producing. Such awareness propels the person into an experience of aliveness, wholeness, and authenticity.

Responsibility. Of great importance in Gestalt therapy is getting clients to accept responsibility for their own actions and feelings. These belong to the client, and the client cannot deny them, escape them, or blame them on something or someone else. In summary, if one had to extract from Gestalt therapy expositions the four most descriptive words, they might be *awareness*, *experience*, *now*, and *responsibility*.

The Rules. The "rules" of Gestalt therapy (Levitsky & Perls, 1970) include the following:

1. Communication is in the present tense (looking backward or forward is discouraged).
2. Communication is between equals (one talks with, not at).
3. One uses "I" language rather than "it" language (to encourage the acceptance of responsibility).
4. The client continually focuses on immediate experience (for example, the therapist will ask, "How does it feel to describe the hostility?" "Tell me what you are feeling at this moment").
5. There is no gossip (talking about someone else).
6. Questions are discouraged (because questions are often quiet ways of stating opinions rather than seeking information).

Gestalt Games. The Gestaltists have received much attention for the so-called games they have developed (Levitsky & Perls, 1970). For example, clients are taught to add the phrase "and I take responsibility for that" when describing something about themselves. Thus, "I am not a very happy person . . . and I take responsibility for that." Another game involves getting the client to repeat again and again (and louder and louder) some phrase or remark that the therapist deems important. Often various aspects of role-playing are employed. To what extent any positive effects from these games are generalized beyond the therapy room has not yet been established empirically.

Moral Precepts. The "moral precepts" (or rules for patients to live by) of Gestalt therapy are described by Naranjo (1970):

1. Live now. (Be concerned not with the past or the future but with the present.)
2. Live here. (Be concerned with what is present, not with what is absent.)
3. Stop imagining. (Experience only the real.)
4. Stop unnecessary thinking. (Be oriented toward hearing, seeing, smelling, tasting, and touching.)
5. Express directly. (Do not explain, judge, or manipulate.)

6. Be aware of both the pleasant and the un-pleasant.
7. Reject all "shoulds" and "oughts" that are not your own.
8. Take complete responsibility for your actions, thoughts, and feelings.
9. Surrender to being what you really are.

Concluding Comments. As indicated in Chapter 11, Smith et al. (1980) reported an effect size of 0.64 for Gestalt therapies, based on a large meta-analysis of relevant studies. The average client who received Gestalt therapy in these studies was functioning better than 74% of those not receiving treatment. Unfortunately, very little research on Gestalt therapy has been published since this review. Of those studies that have appeared more recently, none suggests that Gestalt therapy is more effective than other forms of treatment, and some suggest that it may be less effective (Greenberg et al., 1994). One reason we know relatively little about the effectiveness of Gestalt therapy is that most Gestalt therapists are vehemently opposed to the idea of research. For reasons that are not always clear, evaluation research is seen almost as an anti-humanistic endeavor.

Gestalt therapy took root in America in an era of social turmoil and alienation. As a result, its most suitable clientele may turn out to be young, well-educated people whose problems center on personal estrangement and alienation. Therapists who have a Gestalt orientation sometimes seem to do especially well with overly intellectualized, college-educated people who have lost touch with their feelings and immediate experience. It will certainly not be an antidote suitable for all patients—no therapy is. However, it remains to be seen whether Gestalt therapy will become more than a flashy solution and whether it will be able to address itself successfully to the problems in living that a wide range of patients bring to therapy. By dealing only with the present, Gestalt therapy runs the danger of becoming a short-lived solution that replaces the search for meaning with a hedonism that can be quite attractive to some whose brush with a powerful, technocratic society has left

them inhibited and overcontrolled. At the same time, Gestalt therapy has already demonstrated a staying power greater than many expected.

Summary Evaluation of Phenomenological and Humanistic-Existential Therapies

As we have mentioned throughout this chapter, surprisingly few empirically sound studies have been conducted to evaluate the effectiveness of client-centered, Gestalt, and other existential therapies. This is somewhat ironic in light of Carl Rogers' pioneering role in psychotherapy research. Although some believe that this state of affairs is changing (Greenberg et al., 1994), the relative lack of well-controlled outcome studies makes an evaluation of the effectiveness of these therapies difficult. Based on this limited database, it does appear that these therapies are modestly effective—but, again, no more so than any other form of treatment. More research is clearly needed, especially studies investigating the clinical conditions for which these approaches are most appropriate.

The general phenomenological and humanistic-existential therapies presented in this chapter, like all therapeutic approaches, offer a mixed bag of contributions and problems. The reader will recall that several of the following points were made earlier with regard specifically to Rogerian approaches.

Contributions

Let us begin with an enumeration of some of the chief contributions of the phenomenological and humanistic-existential perspectives.

Experience. By stressing the importance of inner experience and awareness, these therapies have helped reaffirm the view that clinicians must rely on something more than the sheer quantification or enumeration of stimulus/environment conditions. Human experiences run the gamut from knowing to joy to agony, and clinical psychologists can ill afford to ignore them in either their theories or their therapies. The phenomenological-humanistic-existential axis has brought them in touch once more with the essential data of experience and awareness.

Choices. The phenomenological and humanistic-existential therapies also are reminders that humans are more than just concatenations of instincts, urges, and habits. We are not simply automatons that respond to stimuli. We make choices, we decide, we change, we examine ourselves, and yes, we even invent such words as *existential* and *humanistic*. Human beings are not only the objects of study; they are also the initiators of study. For perhaps too many years, psychology has tried to deny its essential human qualities by slavishly following the paths of the biologists and the physicists. Although the controversy over free will versus determinism is unlikely to be resolved soon, there does seem to be a growing recognition that a simple deterministic view of the individual can be sterile and unproductive.

The Present. By emphasizing the present, phenomenologists have helped the field to cast aside the view that positive change can only be achieved by insight into the past or by some enlightened awareness of the true nature of the unconscious. By exercising choice and responsibility, we can all mold the present and thereby escape the constrictions of the past.

The Relationship. Many of the therapies described in this chapter have attached great value to the therapeutic relationship. These therapies often represent a triumph of relationship over technique. Conventional therapies had long recommended a detached therapist who exercised benign interest and cool skill. Whether the newly prescribed role is one of passive yet unconditional positive regard, acceptance, or jumping in feet first to "have an encounter" with the patient, things have certainly changed. The nature of the therapeutic relationship is obviously of crucial importance, and may indeed be a major contributor to the success or failure of any

brand of therapy. With this recognition, the therapeutic relationship is no longer considered a given or an unobtrusive backdrop. It has become a major part of the foreground, thanks in part to phenomenologists and to humanistic-existential therapists.

Growth. For many years, the emphasis in therapy has been on psychopathology, sickness, or behavioral deficits. However, the humanists and the existentialists have brought an emphasis on positive growth. They look not so much for sickness as for self-actualizing tendencies or growth potential. They seek not to contain pathology but to liberate awareness, feeling, being, peak experiences, and freedom. This is heady language that may sometimes exhilarate to the point of confusion. But it does point out an essential emphasis on the positive rather than a sometimes depressing and stultifying emphasis on the negative. Thus, the goal has become not just the healing of psychopathology, but personal growth. Many institutes, growth centers, encounter groups, and weekend retreats have sprung up to serve those who feel the need for experiences that will expand their awareness and heighten their authenticity as human beings.

Problems

Now we can turn to the problem side of the coin as we evaluate the phenomenological and humanistic-existential approaches.

Prejudicial Language. The general humanistic movement, like the more specific client-centered approach, can sometimes be accused of using language prejudicially. The constant use of words such as *humanistic, acceptance, freedom, self-fulfillment, growth,* and *authentic* seems to suggest by implication that all other approaches preach inhumanity, rejection, authoritarianism, emptiness, and phoniness. Yet nearly all psychoanalysts, psychiatrists, behaviorists, cognitive therapists, and eclectic psychotherapists are accepting persons who care a great deal; who are interested, involved, and permissive; and who try to do the best job possible to help their patients experience richer and more fulfilling lives. In short, not all the attributes that are said to be at the core of the humanistic movement are its private domain.

Emphasis on Feelings. The reliance on subjective experience and feelings binds the clinician to a source of data that can be unreliable, biased, or self-serving, and devoid of the most human of all qualities—reason. The real issue is whether feelings or transcendental awareness, unleavened by sober analysis, reason, and insight, can lead the individual into a durable adjustment that will increase both personal satisfactions and social contributions. It seems evident now that most individuals cannot work their way out of problems and private terrors solely by the application of cold analysis and reason. But it does not seem likely that trips into what can be a quagmire of subjectivity will enable them to do so either. Perhaps the lesson here is that any single method or route is likely to be incomplete and therefore less than successful. Human beings think, act, feel, experience, look to the past for guidance, and are pulled into the future by their aspirations. Any approach that focuses on behavior alone, or experience alone, or insight alone ignores much that is a central part of the human being. When such single-edged approaches work (at least for a while), it is probably because they confront individuals with an aspect of themselves that they had long ignored. For example, an inhibited, overintellectual, repressed patient may find great joy and happiness as she works herself through an "emotional now," guided by a sensitive therapist. However, any long-term abandonment of intellect and reason is likely to lead to other problems.

Anti-intellectualism. At times, the humanistic-existential movement strikes a vigorous anti-intellectual and anti-scientific pose that rejects the possibility that any meaningful contributions can be made by science. To the extent that psychotherapy had become tied to a science that was too behavioral, or too insight oriented, or too rooted in a sterile scientific method, this pose has helped return many clinical psychologists to important facets of the human organism. But complete rejection of science, the past, the unconscious, the role of insight, or the modification of behavior through planned consequences seems to be a narrow and dangerous course. Although the fervor of those who urge such a course can be compelling and contagious, it seems likely that, ultimately, unchecked fervor will be no more convincing than, for example, the unbridled operationalism of psychological science.

Phenomenal Field. Another problem is whether one person can ever completely know the nature of another person's subjective experience. Phenomenology instructs that a person's behavior is determined by his or her phenomenal field as it exists at any moment in time. This places the therapist in the position of having to know the patient's inner world of experience in order to understand or predict. Yet how do clinicians climb into that world? How do they escape from the past experiences that have shaped their own perceptions? How do clinicians gain an unbiased appreciation of the patient's phenomenal awareness? It almost seems that the phenomenological viewpoint demands something of clinicians that, given all humans' very imperfect and biased nature, it is impossible for them to achieve.

The problem is not with an empathic attempt to get close to the patient's experience or to "try to put oneself in the patient's shoes." It is always useful to search one's own experience in order to better relate to the patient's feelings or predicaments (while recognizing the ever-present danger of bias). The problem lies in the exclusive reliance on the clinician's exact knowledge of the patient's inner experience in order to operate as a clinician.

Assessment. In many of the humanistic-existential approaches, there is a total disregard for assessment and diagnosis. This disregard is reinforced by the belief that assessment interferes with or destroys the empathic relationship. Assessment is seen as impinging on the freedom and dignity of the individual. It is believed to thwart the self-actualizing potential of the client by imposing a conceptualization from the therapist.

Many will agree that diagnosis is not always necessary in its more full-blown manifestations. Indeed, the humanistic-existential movement has rendered a real service by pointing out some of clinical psychology's diagnostic excesses and by suggesting that too often diagnostic emphasis is on pathology rather than the growth potential or strengths of patients. It is all too true that diagnosis has often become a search for weaknesses rather than strengths and assets.

But if clinical psychologists were to totally reject assessment, where would this leave them? With the patient's verbal report perhaps—with all its potential for distortion and incompleteness. Faith in patients' abilities to solve their problems through getting in touch with their own feelings may work well with intelligent, introspective, sophisticated young persons who are not terribly disturbed. But what about the patient who is psychotic or the patient who is burdened with psychosomatic problems? And how does one deal with the nonverbal person who has only a minimal education and has never learned to look inward? Does the clinician ignore assessment in the case of the person who is having adjustment problems and may also suffer from mental retardation? No one condones diagnoses that are nothing more than mindless labeling. But the prohibition against all assessment seems to assure that therapists will remain more ignorant than they need be.

Technique-Centered. Perhaps many humanistic-existential clinicians disregard assessment in part because they treat every patient alike. Many of these clinicians seem to have an abiding faith that every troubled soul can be rescued by acceptance, positive regard, and the assertion of responsibility for self. If that is so, then diagnosis does indeed become superfluous. But if this is the case, then the charge of many humanistic

existentialists that psychoanalysis or behavior therapies are technique centered can be turned against them as well. To the extent that everyone who enters the therapy room is seen as having the same basic problem, with the "cure" always the same, then such approaches are, in a sense, themselves technique centered. Increasingly, however, clinicians seem to be recognizing the need to develop data that will allow them to select from among several treatment possibilities the one most suitable for a given patient. Such recognition should enhance the role of diagnosis in the future.

Lack of Research. As we mentioned previously, relatively little empirical research is conducted on client-centered or phenomenological/existential psychotherapy compared to other major modes of treatment. This is likely to be problematic for several reasons. First, in this age of managed care and of the sophisticated consumer, modes of treatment that are not supported empirically will likely be shunned or ignored. For example, it is hard to imagine that a managed behavioral health care company would be willing to reimburse a provider who cannot provide an empirically supported rationale for the choice of client-centered treatment or who refuses to set objective goals for treatment. Second, it is likely that training programs will emphasize these forms of treatment less in order to focus more on empirically supported treatments that are frequently evaluated in the empirical literature and that are preferred by managed care organizations. Finally, the relative dearth of research may give the impression that these treatments are primarily of historical interest and not relevant to contemporary clinical practice. As noted by Norcross et al. (1997a), the humanistic and Rogerian orientations are among the least frequently endorsed by contemporary clinical psychologists (3% and 1% of clinical psychologist surveyed, respectively). Proponents of these orientations should take these trends seriously and consider how the deemphasis of empirical research may be affecting professional and public perception.

Obscure Language. A final problem for many who seek to understand what it is that the humanistic-existential movement offers has to do with the language used. Part of this difficulty lies in the lack of cohesiveness within the movement. There are so many thematic variations that the language readily becomes vague and ill defined. But beyond this, there is often a wild, undisciplined quality to the writing that almost assures that variable meanings will be applied. The terminology is so vague that almost any interpretation is possible. It is almost as if the language has taken on a life of its own. In fact, it is possible to string together words in such a way that they sound exactly like a profound discourse in humanistic-existential psychology even though the writer does not have the foggiest notion of what they mean. It is very like the comedian who can imitate speaking in a foreign language without ever using real words—only some characteristic sounds and emphases are necessary.

From Maslow, Perls, Bugental, Boss, Binswanger, Rogers, and others we find such phrases and terms as "internal silence," "from here-to-there rhythmic awareness exercises," "meta-needs," "peak experiences," "Dasein," "authenticity," "I-process," "being," "encounter," and "sick point." Granted that every theory seems to contain its share of neologisms and jargon, but the humanistic-existentialist movement seems to be especially well endowed with such terms. The language does serve to underline the movement's conscious divorce from any alliance with science. But in "humanizing" its language, the movement may also have erected barriers against the more widespread acceptance of the really important elements of its contributions.

Chapter Summary

The best example of a phenomenological and humanistic-existential approach to psychotherapy is perhaps Carl Rogers' client-centered therapy. This mode of treatment developed from Rogers' reaction to traditional, psychoanalytic perspectives on psychopathology and on psychological health. Instead of adopting such a deterministic and, to some degree, pessimistic perspective, Rogers' views emphasized the client's own phenomenological world and experience and the client's inherent tendency toward self-actualization. Client-centered therapists seek to facilitate the client's growth potential by providing empathic understanding, unconditional positive regard, and genuineness. Diagnosis, formal assessment, and therapeutic "techniques" are generally eschewed. Humanistic-existential approaches are similar to client-centered therapy in that they emphasize the client's free will, inner potential, and ability to get in touch with her or his emotions.

These forms of treatment have made several noteworthy contributions to the field of psychotherapy. Clients' internal experience, feelings, free will, and growth potential have been brought to the forefront. Demonstrating the importance of the therapeutic relationship and of rapport is another major contribution. However, these forms of therapy also present some problems. The sometimes prejudicial language used implies that other approaches are insensitive and harmful. Feelings seem to be overemphasized, and behavior underemphasized. Obscure and jargony language is often used, and there is a strong bias against empirical research and formal assessment. How these forms of treatment will be modified, or if they will even survive in their present form, remains to be see. A number of trends (such as managed behavioral health care) pose threats to the popularity and utility of these forms of psychotherapy.

Key Terms

client-centered therapy A psychotherapy developed by Carl Rogers that emphasizes the importance of the client's perceptions of his or her experience and recognizes an inherent human tendency toward developing one's capacities. This therapy orientation seeks to facilitate the client's growth potential.

congruence One of the three therapist characteristics considered essential for client-centered work (also referred to as genuineness). Congruence refers to the honest expression by the therapist of the behaviors, feelings, and attitudes that have been stimulated by the client.

de-reflection A technique described by Frankl in which the client is instructed to ignore a troublesome behavior or symptom in order to divert his or her attention to more constructive thoughts or activities.

empathy One of the three therapist characteristics considered essential for client-centered work. Empathy refers to sensitivity to the needs, feelings, and circumstances of clients so that they feel understood.

existential psychology An orientation to psychology that views people as engaged in a search for meaning.

Gestalt games "Games" developed by the gestaltists to emphasize the "rules" of Gestalt therapy. Often these games may involve making prescribed verbalizations or engaging in various role plays.

growth potential A capacity for competence that all individuals possess. The goal of client-centered therapy is to release this capacity.

humanism An approach to psychology that views individuals as unified, whole, and unique beings who exercise free choice and strive to develop their inner potentials.

logotherapy (Literally, "the therapy of meaning.") A widely known form of existential therapy developed by Victor Frankl that encourages the client (1) to find meaning in what appears to be a callous, uncaring, and meaningless world and (2) to develop a sense of responsibility for his or her life.

moral precepts In Gestalt therapy, moral precepts are rules for patients to live by (e.g., live now, express directly, reject all "shoulds" and "oughts" that are not your own, take complete responsibility for your actions).

paradoxical intention A technique described by Frankl in which the client is told to consciously attempt to perform the very behavior or response that is the object of anxiety or concern. The paradox is that the person will usually be unable to do what he or she fears doing when he or she tries to do it intentionally.

person-centered approach A term that refers to the client-centered approach when it is applied to problems or situations outside of the therapy room (e.g., volunteer training, the training of medical professionals).

phenomenal self The part of the phenomenal field that the person experiences as "me." According to phenomenological theory, humans have a basic urge to preserve and enhance the phenomenal self.

phenomenology A philosophical/theoretical approach that asserts that an individual's behavior is completely determined by his or her phenomenal field, or everything that is experienced by the person at any given point in time.

self The awareness of one's being and functioning as separate and distinct from all else.

self-actualization The basic human tendency toward maintaining and enhancing the self.

unconditional positive regard One of the three therapist characteristics considered essential for client-centered work. Unconditional positive regard refers to complete acceptance of and respect for the client as a human being, without conditions or requirements.

Web Sites of Interest

To visit any of the web sites listed below, go to www.wadsworth.com and click on Links.

13-1   Center for the Studies of the Person

13-2   Carl Rogers Biography

13-3   Gestalt Therapy Page

13-4   Gestalt Organizations

CHAPTER FOURTEEN

Psychotherapy: Behavioral and Cognitive-Behavioral Perspectives

FOCUS QUESTIONS

1. What features best characterize a behavioral approach to clinical problems?

2. What are the major features of the following forms of behavior therapy: systematic desensitization, exposure therapy, behavioral rehearsal, contingency management, aversion therapy?

3. How have behavioral and cognitive perspectives been integrated into a cognitive-behavioral viewpoint?

4. What are the major features of the following forms of cognitive-behavioral therapy: modeling, rational restructuring, cognitive therapy?

5. What are the strengths and limitations of behavior therapy?

CHAPTER OUTLINE

Origins of the Behavioral Approach
Definition
A Brief History

Traditional Techniques of Behavior Therapy
The Relationship
Broad Spectrum of Treatment
Systematic Desensitization
Exposure Therapy
Behavior Rehearsal
Contingency Management
Aversion Therapy

Cognitive-Behavioral Therapy
Background
Modeling
Rational Restructuring
Stress Inoculation Training
Beck's Cognitive Therapy

An Evaluation of Behavior Therapy
Strengths
Criticisms
The Future

CHAPTER SUMMARY
KEY TERMS
WEB SITES OF INTEREST

Behavioral and cognitive-behavioral therapies, often together referred to as *behavior therapy* (Goldfried & Davison, 1994), have become a major force in clinical psychology. A constant flow of books provides wide-ranging discussions of the theory, technique, and application of an extensive variety of these methods. Lists of empirically supported treatments (see Chapter 11) include many treatments that fall under the broad rubric of behavior therapy. Behavior therapy has truly come of age and is now a force with which to be reckoned.

Origins of the Behavioral Approach

We will begin our discussion of behavior therapy with the question of definitions and then move into a brief presentation of this treatment's historical roots.

Definition

The diversity of behavioral approaches to therapy makes a satisfactory definition almost impossible. Some definitions are couched largely in the terminology of operant conditioning (Skinner, 1971). Others are clothed in the style of classical conditioning (Wolpe, 1958). For still others, the emphasis is on general principles of learning (Ullman & Krasner, 1969) or may even have strikingly cognitive overtones (Meichenbaum, 1977). In light of this diversity, Goldfried and Davison (1994) were moved to comment:

> We believe that behavior therapy is more appropriately construed as reflecting a general orientation to clinical work that aligns itself philosophically with an experimental approach to the study of human behavior. The assumption basic to this particular orientation is that the problematic behaviors seen within the clinical setting can best be understood in light of those principles derived from a wide variety of psychological experimentation, and that these principles have implications for

behavior change within the clinical setting. (pp. 3–4)

Traditionally, the behavioral approach allies itself with (1) a scientific emphasis and (2) a deemphasis of the role of inferred variables. The behaviorists are likely to trace their origins to the "science" of Skinner or Pavlov rather than the "mentalism" of Freud. The focus is on stimuli and responses rather than variables that are presumed to mediate them. However, as we shall see later in this chapter, behavior therapy over the years has broadened its scope to include techniques that address cognitive and other mediational processes (Goldfried & Davison, 1994). Nevertheless, it is instructive to review behavior therapy's historical roots.

A Brief History

We begin by presenting the groundbreaking work of Watson and Rayner (1920), who conducted the widely cited laboratory study of Albert and the laboratory rat. This study was, in effect, a demonstration of how a "neurosis" can develop in a child. In the tradition of Pavlovian conditioning, Albert was given a laboratory rat to play with. But each time the rat was introduced, a loud noise was introduced simultaneously. After a few such trials, the rat (previously a neutral stimulus) elicited a fearful response that also generalized to similar furry objects.

Mary Cover Jones (1924) demonstrated how such learned fears can be removed. A 3-year-old boy, Peter, was afraid of rabbits, rats, and other such objects. To eradicate the fear, Jones brought a caged rabbit closer and closer as the boy was eating. The feared object thus became associated with food, and after a few months Peter's fear of the rabbit disappeared entirely. It is important, however, to recall Jones's admonition that the fear of the rabbit must not be so intense that the child will develop an aversion to food. Watson's conditioning of fears and Jones's "reconditioning" of them were direct antecedents of the development of Wolpe's (1958) therapy by reciprocal inhibition, which arrived on the scene some 30 years later.

As the foregoing experiences of Albert and Peter suggest, the major theoretical underpinnings of the behavior therapy movement were Pavlovian conditioning and Hullian learning theory. In the 1950s, Joseph Wolpe and Arnold Lazarus in South Africa and Hans Eysenck at Maudsley Hospital in London began to apply the results of animal research to the acquisition and elimination of anxiety in humans. Wolpe began to experiment with the reduction of fears in humans by having patients, while in a state of heightened relaxation, imagine the situations in which their fears occurred. Wolpe's technique of *systematic desensitization*, like Jones's reconditioning work, provided a practical demonstration of how principles of learning could be applied in the clinical setting. In his work on conditioned reflex therapy, Salter (1949) also attempted to develop a method of therapy that was derived from the Pavlovian tradition.

It is important to note that these investigators did not merely introduce new techniques. They also argued vigorously that their techniques were derived from the framework of a systematic experimental science. In addition, they took pains to point out that their demonstrations of the origins and treatment of neurotic fears proved that it was unnecessary to subscribe to the "mentalistic demonology" of Freudianism or to the "psychiatric pigeonholing" practiced by Kraepelinians.

At about the same time that Wolpe, Lazarus, and Eysenck were developing their conditioning procedures, the operant tradition was beginning to have an impact. Skinner and his colleagues (Lindsley & Skinner, 1954; Skinner, 1953) were demonstrating that the behavior of hospitalized psychotic patients could be modified by operant procedures. By establishing controlled environments to ensure that certain responses of the patient would be followed by specific consequences, significant behavioral changes were produced.

At first, there was a radical quality to behavior therapy. The inner world of the patient was largely ignored in the rush to focus on behavior. Whether in reaction to the mentalism of psychoanalysis or out of an overly provincial view of what should be the subject matter of science, the early behavior therapists studiously avoided anything of a cognitive nature. However, in 1954, Julian Rotter published his book *Social Learning and Clinical Psychology*. In it he demonstrated convincingly that a motivation-reinforcement approach to psychology could be coupled with a cognitive-expectancy approach. Thus, behavior was regarded as being determined both by the value of reinforcements and by the expectancy that such reinforcements would occur following the behavior in question. What is more, Rotter's novel views were supported by a series of laboratory studies that left no doubt that one could be clinical, oriented toward both learning theory and cognitive theory, and scientifically respectable, all at the same time. Also significant in this context was the application of Albert Bandura's (1969) social learning contributions to the modification of behavior. It was theorists such as Rotter and Bandura who led the way to the current cognitive emphasis, giving behavior therapy a more wideranging and serviceable character (Goldfried & Davison, 1994; Meichenbaum, 1977; Thorpe & Olson, 1997).

It is important to point out that the "mentalism" of psychoanalysis or other psychodynamic approaches is not the same as the "cognitive processes" concepts that are used today. Freud's references to thinking processes were never defined operationally. They were vague notions incapable of objective measurement, poorly anchored either to antecedent conditions or consequent outcomes. More often than not, Freud viewed thinking processes as irrational, distorting processes rather than problem-solving processes. For Freud, mentalism seemed to function largely in the service of the reified ego, id, and superego—little people who ran about the mind distorting, projecting, condemning, or figuring out ways of fooling one another. In contrast, current notions of cognition emphasize such concepts as expectancies, cognitive schemas, or

memory processes. These are concepts that can be measured and quantified. They can be objectively defined in ways that lead to reliable understanding among separate investigators. We will have more to say about cognitive-behavioral treatments later in this chapter.

Traditional Techniques of Behavior Therapy

Before we discuss specific behavior therapy techniques, let us note both the importance of the therapeutic relationship and the tendency of modern behavior therapists to use multiple techniques with the same patient.

The Relationship

In their explanation of the success of their therapeutic methods, many behavior therapists seem to ignore the relationship as a contributing factor. Yet in Wolpe's (1958) accounts of systematic desensitization, we find that the therapist is exhorted to adopt an attitude of acceptance toward patients, to explain their difficulties to them, and to make clear to them the behavioral rationale for treatment. In fact, there are data that indicate clients perceive relationship factors to be very important to successful behavior therapy outcome, similar to clients' perceptions concerning other forms of psychotherapy (Sloane, Staples, Cristol, Yorkston, & Whipple, 1975a). There are several reasons why behavior therapy clients

mentoring of graduate and postdoctoral students, clinical training of graduate and postdoctoral students, and providing direct clinical services. I have been an active researcher throughout my career and pride myself on being a scientist-practitioner. I also have held or currently hold several administrative positions. These include Internship Director, Clinic Director, and Director of Clinical Training. I also have been active in organized psychology, serving in a number of capacities. Finally, I have been a participant at the national level in bodies charged with making research funding decisions.

What are your particular areas of expertise or interest?

My particular areas of interest include anxiety disorders in adults and children, behavior therapy, and behavioral assessment.

What are the future trends you see for clinical psychology?

I do not have much to say about the future trends of clinical psychology. The one thing that appears to be happening is that clinical psychologists appear to be more and more interested in general health as opposed to just mental health. Also, the growing numbers of clinical psychologists trained in professional schools likely will change the image of clinical psychology in the eyes of other professions as well as of the public in general. Unfortunately, I fear this change will not be a positive one.

What are some future trends you see for cognitive-behavioral therapy?

Here, too, it is difficult to say what the future trends will be for cognitive-behavioral therapy. Not much is happening at this juncture. Attempts to integrate cognitive approaches with behavioral ones do not appear to have resulted in improvement in treatment outcome in most cases. In fact, we have yet to see serious cognitive models examined in the clinical area. Perhaps this is something that we can look forward to seeing in the future.

---

might view the therapeutic relationship as positive and at least partially responsible for changes made. Behavior therapists may be experienced as more open and accepting of the client's problems (rather than viewing problems as indicative of unconscious processes); treatment is collaborative and more "educational" in style; and interventions are clearly linked to the problematic behaviors that have been targeted for change by the client and therapist (Thorpe & Olson, 1997).

None of this is meant to suggest that behavior therapy can be reduced to "nothing more" than subtle relationship factors. What is suggested, however, is that one can never afford to ignore aspects of the relationship as contributors to successful therapeutic intervention. After all, it is through the therapy relationship that the patient's expectations of help can be nurtured so that behavioral therapy will be accepted as a viable alternative (Goldfried & Davison, 1994). Stated differently, behavior therapy is not going to be successful if the patient expects it to fail or is otherwise antagonistic toward it. Behavior therapists have sometimes been said to be cold and mechanistic in their approach to patients. This is probably more myth or stereotype than fact. Indeed, Sloane et al. (1975a) found that behavior therapists were generally warmer and more empathic than other psychotherapists!

Broad Spectrum of Treatment

Behavior therapists use a variety of specific techniques—not only for different patients but for the same patient at different points in the overall treatment process. Lazarus (1971a) refers to this as *broad spectrum behavior therapy*. As specific techniques are described in the following pages, the reader should realize that each can serve a specific purpose but that, in reality, they are complementary. For example, a woman who has trouble coping with a domineering husband may undergo assertiveness training to learn specific behaviors. But when she uses these behaviors, other sets of fears about their relationship may begin to worry her. Therefore, she may also require therapeutic sessions that will help her restructure her beliefs about the marriage that are illogical and tend to perpetuate her submissive behavior. She might also participate in modeling or observational learning to help her cope.

In addition, it is important to recall from Chapter 9 that a comprehensive behavioral assessment is conducted before behavioral treatments or techniques are selected and implemented. For example, a functional analysis of the presenting problem helps to identify (1) the stimulus or antecedent conditions that bring on the problematic behavior; (2) the organismic variables (such as cognitive biases) that are related to the problematic behavior; (3) the exact description of the problem; and (4) the consequences of the problematic behavior. By completing such a detailed analysis, behavior and cognitive-behavioral therapists can prescribe appropriate treatments.

Systematic Desensitization

This technique is typically applied when a patient has the capacity to respond adequately to a particular situation (or class of situations), yet reacts with anxiety, fear, or avoidance. Basically, systematic desensitization is a technique to reduce anxiety. Developed by Salter (1949) and Wolpe (1958), it is based on *reciprocal inhibition*—the apparently simple principle that one cannot be relaxed and anxious simultaneously. The idea is to teach patients to relax and then, while they are in the relaxed state, to introduce a gradually increasing series of anxiety-producing stimuli. Eventually, the patient becomes desensitized to the feared stimuli by virtue of having experienced them in a relaxed state. Systematic desensitization has been shown to be efficacious for animal phobias, public speaking anxiety, and social anxiety (Chambless et al., 1998).

Technique and Procedures. Systematic desensitization begins with the collection of a history of the patient's problem. This includes information both about specific precipitating conditions and about developmental factors. Collecting a history may require several interviews, and it often includes the administration of questionnaires. The principal reason for all of this is to pinpoint the locus of the patient's anxiety. It is also part of assessment to determine whether systematic desensitization is the proper treatment. In a patient with adequate coping potential who nevertheless reacts to certain situations with severe anxiety, desensitization is often appropriate. On the other hand, if a patient lacks certain skills and then becomes anxious in situations that require those skills, desensitization could be inappropriate and counterproductive. For example, if a man becomes seriously anxious in social situations that involve dancing, it would seem more efficient to see that he learns to dance rather than desensitize him to what is, in fact, a behavioral deficit.

Next, the problem is explained to the patient. This explanation is normally elaborated to include examples from the patient's life and to cover the manner in which the patient acquired and maintains the anxieties. Following this, the rationale for systematic desensitization is also explained. The explanations and the illustrations should be in language that the patient can understand—free from scientific jargon. In a sense, the clinician uses this phase to "sell" the patient on the efficacy of systematic desensitization. It should be added that the entire process of interviewing, assessment, and explanation is conducted with warmth, acceptance, and understanding.

The next two phases involve training in *relaxation* and the establishment of an *anxiety hierarchy*. While work is begun on the anxiety hierarchy, training in relaxation is also started.

Relaxation. Behavior therapists frequently use the progressive relaxation methods of Jacobson (1938). The patient is first taught to tense and relax particular muscle groups and then to distinguish between sensations of relaxation and tensing. The instructions for relaxation can easily be taped and played at home for practice. Generally, about six sessions are devoted to relaxation training. In some instances, hypnosis may be used to induce relaxation. In other instances, the patient may be asked to imagine relaxing scenes. And in still other instances, breathing exercises are used to enhance relaxation.

The Anxiety Hierarchy. In discussions about specific problems, the situations in which they occur, and their development, the patient and the therapist work together to construct a hierarchy. The recurrent themes in the patient's difficulties and anxieties are isolated and then ordered in terms of their power to induce anxiety (from situations that provoke very low levels of anxiety through situations that precipitate extreme anxiety reactions). A typical anxiety hierarchy consists of 20 to 25 items in approximately equal intervals from low through moderate to extreme. The following anxiety hierarchy was that of a 24-year-old female student who experienced severe examination anxiety (Wolpe, 1973):

1. Four days before an examination.
2. Three days before an examination.
3. Two days before an examination.
4. One day before an examination.
5. The night before an examination.
6. The examination paper lies face down before her.
7. Awaiting the distribution of examination papers.
8. Before the unopened doors of the examination room.
9. In the process of answering an examination paper.
10. On the way to the university on the day of the examination. (p. 116)

This hierarchy illustrates two points. First, it is organized largely along spatial-temporal lines. Second, the items are not exactly organized in a logical fashion. One might expect item 10 (the most anxiety-provoking item) to be placed near the middle of the hierarchy. This suggests how idiosyncratic hierarchies can be—after all, it is the patient's anxiety, not the clinician's!

In the desensitization procedure, the patient is asked to imagine the weakest item in the hierarchy (the item that provokes the least anxiety) while being completely relaxed. The therapist describes the scene, and the patient imagines (for about 10 seconds) being in the scene. The therapist moves the patient up the hierarchy gradually (between two and five items per session). However, if at any time the level of anxiety begins to increase, the patient is instructed to signal, whereupon the therapist requests that the patient stop visualizing that scene. The therapist then helps the patient to relax once more. After a few minutes, the procedure can be started again. Ideally, over a period of several sessions, the patient will be able to imagine the highest item in the hierarchy without discomfort. A typical example of the instructions given to a male patient during desensitization is provided by Goldfried and Davison (1994):

> (*The client has been relaxing on his own in the reclining chair.*) OK, now just keep relaxing like that, nice and calm and comfortable. You may find it helpful to imagine a scene that is personally calm and relaxing, something we'll refer to as your pleasant scene.... Fine. Now, you recall that 0 to 100 scale we've been using in your relaxation practice, where 0 indicates complete relaxation and 100 maximum tension. Tell me approximately where you'd place yourself on that scale.... (*Therapist is advised to look for a rating that reflects considerable calm and relaxation, often in the range of 15 to 25.*)
>
> Fine. Soon I shall ask you to imagine a scene. After you hear the description of the situation, please imagine it as vividly as you can, through your own eyes, as if you were actually there. Try to include all the details in the scene. While you're visualizing the situation, you may continue feeling as relaxed as you are now. If so, that's good.

FIGURE 14-1 Joseph Wolpe has been primarily identified with the development of systematic desensitization as a method of reducing neurotic anxiety.

Courtesy of Joseph Wolpe.

After 5, 10, or 15 seconds, I'll ask you to stop imagining the scene and return to your pleasant image and to just relax. But if you begin to feel even the slightest increase in anxiety or tension, please signal this to me by raising your left forefinger. When you do this, I'll step in and ask you to stop imagining the situation and then will help you get relaxed once more. It's important that you indicate tension to me in this way, as we want to maximize your being exposed to fearful situations without feeling anxious. OK? Do you have any questions? . . . Fine, we'll have ample opportunity afterwards to discuss things in full. (pp. 124–125)[1]

---

[1]From *Clinical Behavior Therapy* (Expanded Edition) by M. R. Goldfried & G. C. Davison (1994). Reprinted by permission.

A Case Illustration of Systematic Desensitization

In order to select the most useful hierarchy, one must determine exactly what is prompting the patient's anxiety reactions. To illustrate the importance of selecting the appropriate hierarchy, let us consider the following example, in which it appeared at first that the problem was essentially a simple matter of a woman's discomfort when eating in a restaurant with her husband's business associates.

Therapist: Can you tell me what it is about these business dinners that upsets you? For instance, are they formal, and are you on the spot as a sort of reluctant hostess having to entertain people who do not really mean anything to you?

Patient: I guess so.

Therapist: Don't let me put words in your mouth. Think carefully. Picture yourself in the situation right now. Imagine that you are at a restaurant with your husband and his colleagues, and tell me what associations and feelings you have.

Patient: (Closes her eyes) It makes me angry and I don't see why I have to be subjected to it.

Therapist: What does your husband say?

Patient: Oh, Herb says it brings in more business.

Therapist: How often do these business dinners arise?

Patient: About once a month.

Therapist: How do they come about?

Patient: How do you mean?

Therapist: I mean how does Herb let you know about them?

Patient: Oh, he comes home and says, "Honey, is it all right if we take the Ryans and two other couples to the Red Goblet a week from Friday?" And I usually say, "Why bother to ask?"

Therapist: So a verbal battle ensues and by the time the dinner date is reached, you and

Herb have been at each other's throats for about two weeks and a thoroughly tense atmosphere prevails.

Patient: Well, I resent it.

Therapist: Why?

Patient: What do you mean?

Therapist: You know what I mean. What is really behind all this resentment?

Patient: I simply don't like dining with the Ryans and the Millers and the rest of those money grabbers.

Therapist: Wait, let's go back. You said that you have only felt this way since Herb went into the marketing field last year.

Patient: Well, let me explain. He used to work for my dad, and when he died about two years ago, Herb took over the business.

Therapist: Let me guess. Was your father in charge of the marketing setup before he died?

Patient: What has that got to do with it?

Therapist: (Remains silent)

Patient: Oh for heaven's sake! You think I resent Herb because he's taken over my dad's position.

Therapist: Well?

Patient: Well, it never struck me that way before.

As the interview progressed, it became obvious that we were not dealing with a specific "sensitivity to dining in a restaurant with husband and his business associates," but to a basic resentment concerning the patient's feelings that her husband was "less of a man than her father" . . . and desensitization was directed toward a death-of-father dimension.[2]

Rationale. Although Wolpe's explanation for the success of systematic desensitization is based on the principle of *counterconditioning* (the substitution of relaxation for anxiety), others are not

---

[2]From *Behavior Therapy and Beyond*, by A. A. Lazarus, pp. 99–100. Copyright © 1971 by McGraw-Hill, Inc. Reprinted by permission.

so sure (Davison & Wilson, 1973). Some have argued that the operative process is really *extinction*. That is, when the patient repeatedly visualizes anxiety-generating situations but without ensuing bad experiences, the anxiety responses are eventually extinguished (Wilson & Davison, 1971). Alternatively, Mathews (1971) argues on behalf of a *habituation* hypothesis. Emmelkamp (1982) has reviewed the empirical support for these and other theoretical explanations.

The standard method of desensitization is to present scenes in a graduated ascending fashion in order to avoid premature arousal of anxiety that would disrupt the procedure. However, some clinicians have found that presenting the hierarchy in the reverse order (most anxiety-provoking items first) is also effective in reducing various phobias. Richardson and Suinn (1973) also report positive results when participants are exposed only to the three highest hierarchy scenes.

Systematic desensitization involves a number of components. The instructions suggest that a positive outcome is likely. Consequently, the patient's expectations for improvement may affect the process. Another crucial element may be positive reinforcement from the therapist following the patient's reports of lessened anxiety, improvement outside the consulting room, or the successful completion of anxiety hierarchies. For example, Leitenberg, Agras, Barlow, and Oliveau (1969) observed that, with snake phobias, the effects of systematic desensitization are best when the therapist uses reinforcing comments, such as "Good," "Excellent," and "You're doing fine," when participants (1) visualize a scene without reporting anxiety, (2) complete a hierarchy item, and (3) report progress in approaching a snake during practice. Goldfried (1971) argues that systematic desensitization is far from a passive process that is applied to patients to reduce their fears. Rather, it represents the acquisition of a skill that the patients can use to reduce their own fear. In that sense, Goldfried regards systematic desensitization as training in self-control. From a cognitive viewpoint, Valins and Ray (1967) explain the effectiveness of systematic desensitization in terms of patients' belief that they are relaxed. Others, such as Sullivan and Denney (1977), emphasize the importance of getting the patient to expect improvement.

All of the foregoing suggests that systematic desensitization is hardly the simple mechanical or conditioning process that it was once thought to be. A number of relationship variables seem implicated, as well as beliefs or expectations on the part of the patient. In general, systematic desensitization has proven to be a moderately effective form of psychological intervention for a variety of clinical conditions. As might be expected, research suggests that it is most effective when used to treat anxiety disorders, particularly specific phobias, social anxiety, public speaking anxiety, and generalized anxiety disorder (Chambless et al., 1998; Emmelkamp, 1994).

Exposure Therapy

The term *exposure therapy* is used to describe a behavior therapy technique that is a refinement of a set of procedures originally known as flooding or implosion. The roots of exposure therapy can be traced to Masserman (1943), who studied anxiety reactions and avoidance behaviors in cats (Kazdin, 1978). Masserman's studies involved inducing "neurotic behaviors" in cats by administering shock under certain environmental conditions. He subsequently discovered that the avoidance behavior could be extinguished if the cats were forced to remain in the situation in which they had previously been shocked (that is, no escape or avoidance was possible). These findings were the basis for developing anxiety treatments for humans. There is empirical support for the efficacy of exposure treatments for specific phobias, panic disorder, agoraphobia, social phobia, posttraumatic stress disorder, and obsessive-compulsive disorder (Chambless et al., 1998; Emmelkamp, 1994).

In exposure therapy, patients expose themselves to those stimuli or situations that were previously feared and avoided. The "exposure" can be in real life (in vivo) or in fantasy (in imagino). In the latter version, patients are asked to imagine themselves in the presence of the feared stimulus (such as a spider) or in the anxi-

ety-provoking situation (such as speaking in front of an audience). Several researchers suggest that certain features must be present in exposure treatments in order for the patient to achieve maximum benefit (Barlow & Cerny, 1988):

1. Exposure should be of long rather than short duration.
2. Exposure should be repeated until all fear/anxiety is eliminated.
3. Exposure should be graduated, starting with low-anxiety stimuli/situations and progressing to high-anxiety stimuli/situations.
4. Patients must attend to the feared stimulus and interact with it as much as possible.
5. Exposure must provoke anxiety.

Like other behavioral therapies we describe in this chapter, exposure treatment can be used as a self-contained treatment or as one component of a multimodal treatment. For example, Barlow and Cerny (1988) describe a psychological treatment for panic disorder that includes relaxation, cognitive restructuring, and exposure components. What is especially ingenious about their version of exposure treatment is that they have patients expose themselves to *interoceptive cues*—internal physiological stimuli such as rapid breathing and dizziness. This modification was necessary because individuals suffering from panic disorder typically report that their panic attacks are unpredictable and "come out of the blue." In such cases, no external anxiety-provoking stimulus or situation is apparent. In contrast, individuals with other, non-panic anxiety disorders report acute anxiety primarily in the face of certain external stimuli or situations.

How do clinicians convince patients that completing tasks that increase levels of anxiety will ultimately be helpful? To illustrate the rationale that is presented for exposure treatment, Box 14-1 provides the introduction that is used in Barlow and Cerny's (1988) psychological treatment for panic disorder.

Craske, Rowe, Lewin, and Noriega-Dimitri (1997) recently compared the effectiveness of two forms of treatment for panic disorder with agoraphobia—one that included interoceptive exposure and one that incorporated breathing

BOX 14-1

Rationale for Exposure Therapy

As you may recall from our earlier meetings, we feel that panic attacks are essentially "false alarms" issued by the body in response to a cue or signal that you have learned to associate with danger or threat. The problem, of course, is that these panic alarms are, in fact, false. Nevertheless, the fear associated with the panic attacks is quite real. Just as false alarms are learned phenomena, the treatment for them also involves planned relearning experiences. The term we use to describe these corrective learning experiences is *exposure therapy*.

The basic logic of exposure therapy is quite simple. Exposing yourself to those situations and cues that have been associated with anxiety and panic attacks provides you with the opportunity to learn at least three things: (1) You will learn that anxiety and panic symptoms can be controlled using the relaxation and cognitive coping techniques that you have been learning. In fact, you will learn that you are able not only to reduce those troublesome symptoms, but also actually to bring them on at will. (2) You will learn that there is no basis for the fear associated with your panic attacks. (3) And, finally, you will learn to break the association between the cues that signal your fears and panic attacks and teach yourself new ways of responding during graduated exposure to those panic-associated cues.

At the present time, we do not fully understand the exact mechanisms that explain how this new learning takes place, but we do know that exposure therapy is highly effective in treating anxiety disorders. Let me emphasize that it is the new learning that takes place during exposure trials that is the critical element in therapy. The exposure to panic-associated cues merely provides the opportunity for that learning to occur. Therefore, passive exposure to these same cues—that is, unplanned exposures during which no corrective learning takes place—is not sufficient to bring about therapeutic changes in your behavior. During the exposure trials we encourage you to deal directly with your anxiety and fear and to take an active part in the new learning process.

Because you will be exposing yourself to these anxiety-provoking cues, you should anticipate that initially you may become more anxious and perhaps notice an increase in panic attacks. However, as you know, in most cases, anxiety and panic attacks are self-limiting—that is, in most situations the anxiety and/or panic symptoms will subside. The anxiety and fear itself, of course, may be quite unpleasant.

In order to minimize the amount of unpleasantness you will have to experience, we will develop together a graduated hierarchy of anxiety-provoking cues and work through that hierarchy from the least to the most anxiety-provoking situations. Nevertheless, it will be necessary for you to tolerate some anxiety, at least initially. As you learn to deal more effectively with anxiety and panic symptoms and to eliminate "false alarms," you should notice substantial reductions in the number and perhaps the intensity of your panic attacks.

There are three ways that you can expose yourself to panic-provoking cues. First, you can imagine yourself experiencing the panic-provoking situation or cues. Imaginal exposure provides not only an exposure trial under controlled and low-arousal conditions, but it also allows you rather easily to plan and practice your management skills in imagination so that you will be prepared to take advantage of in vivo exposures. Second, you can expose yourself to certain panic-provoking cues here in the office. We will explore ways to induce those bodily sensations that have come to signal the possibility of a false alarm. And, finally, you will be exposing yourself to actual situations in your daily life. Today, we will begin with imagery training and hierarchy development.

Source: Barlow, D. H., & Cerny, J. A. (1988). Psychological Treatment of Panic (pp. 155–156). New York: Guilford. Reprinted with permission.

retraining instead of interoceptive exposure. Although both forms of treatment were effective, results indicated that panic disorder patients who received the interoceptive exposure component reported less impairment and fewer panic attacks at posttreatment and at follow-up. Thus, the addition of the interoceptive exposure component had some beneficial effects.

In order to provide another example of an exposure-based empirically supported treatment, Box 14-2 presents an overview of the treatment *exposure plus response prevention* for obsessive-compulsive disorder.

Behavior Rehearsal

Included under this broad heading are a variety of techniques whose aim is to enlarge the patient's repertoire of coping behaviors. Clearly, *behavior rehearsal* is not a new concept; it has been around in one form or another for many years. For example, Moreno (1947) developed psychodrama, a form of role playing, to help solve patients' problems, and Kelly (1955) used fixed-role therapy. However, it is important to note that such forms of role playing or behavior rehearsal have purposes that depart from behavioral goals. For Moreno, role playing provided a therapeutic release of emotions that was also diagnostic in identifying the causes of the patient's problems. For Kelly, role playing was a method of altering the patient's cognitive structure. Again, we are reminded that specific therapeutic techniques are not the exclusive province of one theoretical frame of reference. Different theorists may use similar techniques for vastly different reasons.

The Technique. According to Goldfried and Davison (1994), the use of behavior rehearsal involves four stages. The first stage is to prepare the patient by explaining the necessity for acquiring new behaviors, getting the patient to accept behavior rehearsal as a useful device, and reducing any initial anxiety over the prospect of role playing. The second stage involves the selection of target situations. At this point, many therapists will draw up a hierarchy of role-playing or rehearsal situations. This hierarchy

should relate directly to those situations in which the patient has been having difficulty. A sample hierarchy of target situations (ranked in order of the increasingly complex behavioral skills required) might be as follows:

1. You ask a secretary for information about a class.
2. You ask a student in class about last week's assignment.
3. After class, you approach the instructor with a question about the lecture.
4. You go to the instructor's office and engage her in conversation about a certain point.
5. You purposely engage another student, who you know disagrees with you, in a minor debate about some issue.

The third stage is the actual behavior rehearsal. Moving up the hierarchy, the patient plays the appropriate roles, with the therapist providing both coaching and feedback regarding the adequacy of the patient's performance. Sometimes videotaped replays are used as an aid. In other instances, the therapist (or a therapeutic aide) exchanges roles with the patient in order to provide an appropriate model. When patients develop proficiency in one target situation, they move up the hierarchy.

The final stage is the patient's actual utilization of newly acquired skills in real-life situations. After such in vivo experiences, the patient and the therapist discuss the patient's performance and feelings about the experiences. Sometimes patients are asked to keep written records describing the situations they were in, their behavior, and its consequences.

Assertiveness Training. One application of behavioral rehearsal is *assertiveness training*. Wolpe regarded assertive responses as an example of how reciprocal inhibition works. That is, it is impossible to behave assertively and to be passive simultaneously. Situations that once evoked anxiety will no longer do so because the assertive behavior inhibits the anxiety.

Originally, assertiveness training was designed as a treatment for persons whose anxiety seemed to stem from their timid mode of coping

BOX 14-2

Behavior Therapy for Obsessive Compulsive Disorder

Obsessive-compulsive disorder (OCD) is an Axis I disorder characterized by recurrent intrusive thoughts, impulses, or images (obsessions) that generate great anxiety and distress. Repetitive behavior or ritualistic mental acts aimed at counteracting obsessions or otherwise preventing or reducing anxiety often are present as well (American Psychiatric Association, 1994). Once thought to be largely intractable, research results over the past few decades indicate that a particular form of behavior therapy, exposure plus response prevention, can be particularly effective in treating OCD symptoms.

As noted by Foa (1996), this treatment is based on the assumption that obsessions produce marked anxiety and distress, while compulsions serve to reduce this anxiety. Further, even though compulsions temporarily reduce anxiety, obsessional anxiety is maintained because no habituation develops. Compulsive behavior continues because it is reinforced by the reduction in anxiety. Exposure plus response prevention aims to disrupt this pattern by (1) exposing the patient to those situations that lead to obsessional distress and (2) prevent the patient from engaging in compulsive behaviors that are typically emitted in the face of this distress. In this way, it is hoped that (1) habituation to the obsessional thoughts, images, or impulses will develop (and, thus, the level of anxiety produced by these will be reduced), and (2) compulsive behaviors will no longer be reinforced because they will be prevented.

Foa (1996) provides an overview of a typical exposure plus response prevention treatment for OCD:

1. Fifteen 2-hour exposure sessions are conducted over the course of three weeks.
2. During these sessions, patients are "exposed" to the situations or objects that seem to trigger the obsessions. For example, a patient who obsesses about dirt and germs might be asked to rub newspaper print all over his arms and face.
3. In addition, patients are asked to imagine that the tragic consequences they anticipate occurring if they do not engage in compulsive behavior *did* occur. In this way, patients can begin thinking about these "catastrophes" without being markedly fearful.
4. Homework is assigned and involves repeating these exposure experiences.
5. At the same time that exposure is introduced, the therapist ensures that ritualistic compulsions that typically occur in the face of the obsessional fear do not occur. For example, the patient who obsesses about dirt and germs and engages in excessive hand washing or showering would not be allowed to engage in these behaviors. At a later point in time, "normal" hand washing and showering will be introduced.
6. Finally, a maintenance phase of treatment involves about ten office visits or phone calls aimed at encouraging the patient and reinforcing the therapeutic gains.

with situations (Wolpe, 1958; Wolpe & Lazarus, 1966). A variety of assertiveness training programs have been developed specifically for individuals seeking to overcome destructive passivity. But assertiveness training has also been used

in treating sexual problems, depression, and marital conflicts. It is important to note that cognitive self-statements (for example, "I was thinking that I am perfectly free to say no") may enhance the effects of assertiveness training. In fact, many procedures can be used to increase assertiveness. Behavior rehearsal is perhaps the most obvious one.

Lack of assertiveness may stem from a variety of sources. In some cases, the cause may be a simple lack of information, in which case the treatment might center largely on information giving. In other instances, a kind of anticipatory anxiety may prevent persons from behaving assertively. In such cases, the treatment may involve desensitization. Yet other individuals may have unrealistic (negative) expectations about what will ensue if they become assertive. Some clinicians would deal with such expectations through interpretation or rational-emotive techniques. Similar techniques might be applied to patients who feel that assertiveness is wrong. Finally, there are patients whose lack of assertiveness involves a behavioral deficit—they do not know how to behave assertively. For such patients, behavior rehearsal, modeling, and related procedures would be used.

Assertiveness training is not the same as trying to teach people to be aggressive. It is really a method of training people to express how they feel without trampling on the rights of others in the process (Wolpe & Lazarus, 1966). Take the spectator at a basketball game who cannot see because the person in front constantly jumps up. To react by saying "If you don't sit down, I'm going to knock you down" is aggressive. But saying "Please, I wish you would sit down; I just can't see anything" is an assertive response. Indeed, assertiveness training has been useful in teaching overly aggressive persons gentler and more effective ways of meeting their needs.

Contingency Management

A variety of Skinnerian or operant techniques are all referred to as *contingency management* procedures. They share the common goal of controlling behavior by manipulating its consequences.

Techniques. Contingency management can take many forms, of which the following are just a few examples.

1. *Shaping*: A desired behavior is developed by first rewarding any behavior that approximates it. Gradually, through selective reinforcement of behavior more and more closely resembling the desired behavior, the final behavior is shaped. This technique is sometimes called *successive approximation*.
2. *Time-out*: Undesirable behavior is extinguished by removing the person temporarily from a situation in which that behavior is reinforced. A child who disrupts the class is removed so that the disruptive behavior cannot be reinforced by the attention of others.
3. *Contingency contracting*: A formal agreement or contract is struck between therapist and patient, specifying the consequences of certain behaviors on the part of both.
4. *"Grandma's rule"*: The basic idea is akin to Grandma's exhortation, "First you work, then you play!" It means that a desired activity is reinforced by allowing the individual the privilege of engaging in a more attractive behavior. For example, the child is allowed to play ball after the music lesson is completed. This method is sometimes referred to as the *Premack principle* (Premack, 1959).

Token Economies. The operant approach is most commonly used in environments in which a therapist or other institutional staff can exert significant control over the reinforcement contingencies relative to patient behavior. The principles of operant conditioning are especially apparent in *token economy* programs that are designed to modify the behavior of institutionalized populations, such as those with mental retardation or chronic mental illness (Kazdin, 1977; Liberman, 1972). Such programs can make an institution a more livable place that ultimately is more conducive to therapeutic gains. Many of the social skills that are "shaped" will also facilitate a smoother transition to a noninstitutional setting.

In establishing a token economy, there are three major considerations (Krasner, 1971). First, there must be a clear and careful specification of the desirable behaviors that will be reinforced.

Second, a clearly defined reinforcer (or medium of exchange—for example, colored poker chips, cards, or coins) must be decided upon. Third, backup reinforcers are established. These may be special privileges or other things desired by the patient. Thus, two tokens, each worth 10 points, might be exchanged for permission to watch TV an extra hour, or one token worth 5 points might be exchanged for a small piece of candy. It goes without saying that a token economy also requires a fairly elaborate system of record keeping and a staff that is very observant and committed to the importance of the program.

Token economies are used to promote desired behavior through the control of reinforcements. Whether the desired behavior is increased neatness, greater social participation, or improved job performance, the probability of its occurrence can be enhanced by the award of tokens of varying value. But why use tokens at all? Why not reinforce proper bedmaking directly? The reason is essentially that the effect of reinforcement is greater if the reinforcement occurs immediately after the behavior occurs. If the reward of attending a movie occurs ten hours after a patient sweeps out his or her room, it is not likely to be nearly so effective as a token given immediately. That token will come to signify reward and will assume much of the effectiveness of the backup reward for which it may be exchanged.

Aversion Therapy

One of the most controversial of all treatments is *aversion therapy*. Actually, this is not a single therapy but a series of different procedures applied to behaviors regarded as undesirable. These applications are based on the apparently simple principle that when a response is followed by an unpleasant consequence (such as punishment or pain), its strength will diminish. As Wolpe (1973) put it, "Aversion therapy consists, operationally, of administering an aversive stimulus to inhibit an unwanted emotional response, thereby diminishing its habit strength" (p. 216). An unpleasant stimulus is placed in temporal contigu-

ity with the undesirable behavior. The idea is that a permanent association between the undesirable behavior and the unpleasant stimulus will be forged, and conditioning will take place.

Such techniques may appear to be recent additions to scientific and clinical repertoires. However, a little reflection will remind us that they have been around for eons, often in the form of such unsophisticated practices as spanking, "Go to your room," and "No TV tonight for you." Modern aversive therapy techniques differ from these examples in at least two important ways. First, the presentation of the aversive agent is done systematically. The temporal contiguity is very carefully monitored. Second, the punishment is consistently applied. The punishment applied by parents is often highly inconsistent. Sometimes the undesirable behavior of the child is immediately punished. But very often, the parent forgets or is distracted, too tired, or whatever to respond. As a result, the child learns that sometimes the behavior is ignored, and thus extinction fails to occur. As formal clinical procedures, these techniques have been applied most often to help patients develop increased self-control. They have been used to cope with problems of obesity, smoking, alcoholism, and sexual deviations.

Aversive Agents. Among the aversive agents that have been used most frequently are electrical stimulation and drugs. For example, strong emetic drugs have been used aversively for many years (see, for example, Voegtlin & Lemere, 1942), especially in the treatment of alcoholism. The patient is given a drug that produces nausea or vomiting and then takes a drink (or the drug may be mixed with the drink). The patient soon becomes ill. This combination of alcohol and emetic is given for a week to ten days. Eventually, just the sight of a drink is sufficient to induce nausea and discomfort.

Wolpe (1973) has described a variety of other aversive agents, including holding one's breath, stale cigarette smoke, vile-smelling solutions of asafetida, intense illumination, white noise, and shame. Clearly, the range of potential aversive agents is limited only by the imagination of resourceful therapists.

Covert Sensitization. Cautela (1967) developed a set of procedures, known as *covert sensitization,* that rely on imagery rather than the actual use of punishment, drugs, or stimulation. Patients are asked to imagine themselves engaging in the behaviors they wish to eliminate. Once they have the undesired behaviors clearly in mind, they are instructed to imagine extremely aversive events. Some of the instructions are vivid to say the least. A rather mild example from the treatment of a case of overeating should suffice: "As you touch the fork, you can feel food particles inching up your throat. You're just about to vomit" (Cautela, 1967, p. 462). The ensuing descriptions become more graphic.

Other Techniques. Other behavior therapy techniques, while technically considered forms of aversion therapy or punishment, are less extreme than the administration of aversive agents or covert sensitization. For example, *response cost* is a technique in which positive reinforcers (such as tokens in a token economy system) are removed following an undesired response (such as a temper tantrum) made by a patient (Thorpe & Olson, 1997). Another example is a technique called *overcorrection.* Here, the idea is that having the patient or client "overcorrect" the consequences of an act will make the behavior less likely to recur (Thorpe & Olson, 1997). For example, an adolescent who has used a marker to write "Screw you, Dad" on a bedroom wall might be required to apply a fresh coat of paint to all the walls of the bedroom.

Second Thoughts. Prominent behaviorists (such as Skinner) have questioned the effectiveness of punishment in influencing and controlling behavior, and many clinicians have deemphasized aversion methods in their behavioral therapy approaches. Lazarus (1971a), for example, stated that the building of better response repertoires and the reduction of anxiety produce longer-lasting results than do aversion techniques. Thus, it may turn out that, in the long run, it is more efficient to deal with a sexual fetish by reducing the patient's fear of heterosexual behaviors through behavior rehearsal than by punishing him each time he visualizes a pair of women's shoes.

Many critics, both within and without the behavior therapy movement, have been highly critical of aversion therapy. The concentration on punishment and the use of what are sometimes terrifying stimuli often seem totally incompatible with human dignity. Whether or not patients present themselves voluntarily for treatment is beside the point. Such techniques as inducing vomiting, using a curare-like drug so that the patient will experience the sensation of suffocating, or injecting stale smoke into the nostrils seem better relegated to the status of torture than dignified as treatment.

Others, however, maintain that aversive techniques, used in a sensitive fashion by reputable professionals, have real merit. Most often, aversive techniques are used after everything else has failed. Furthermore, patients are not dragged kicking and screaming into the situation. Usually, the procedures are applied to people who have seriously debilitating problems (alcoholism, excessive smoking, sexual deviations) and who are in despair because nothing else has worked. Such people voluntarily undertake aversion therapy as the lesser evil—in the same spirit, perhaps, that one submits yearly to that terrifying torture at the hands of a friendly dentist. The debate goes on!

Cognitive-Behavioral Therapy

Background

Not too long ago, a chapter on behavior therapy was largely dominated by terms and concepts such as *behavior modification, systematic desensitization, operant, shaping, token economies,* and *aversive conditioning.* But this is no longer true. We now find coverage of concepts and terms such as *cognitive-behavior modification, cognitive restructuring, stress inoculation,* and *rational restructuring.*

The change signifies a cognitive orientation in behavior therapy that has overtaken the field in recent years (Hollon & Beck, 1994).

A cognitive perspective on clinical problems emphasizes the role of thinking in the etiology and maintenance of problems. *Cognitive-behavioral therapy* seeks to modify or change patterns of thinking that are believed to contribute to a patient's problems. These techniques have a great deal of empirical support (Smith et al., 1980; Hollon & Beck, 1994) and are seen as among the most effective of all psychological interventions. For example, cognitive-behavioral treatments dominate the most recent list of examples of empirically supported treatments (Chambless et al., 1998).

The Move toward Cognitive-Behavioral Therapy. In reflecting upon these cognitive trends, apparent even two decades ago, Mahoney (1977a) observed:

> Despite their long history of often bitter rivalry, behaviorists and cognitive psychologists appear to be cautiously easing into the same theoretical bed. This rather startling flirtation is not, of course, without its detractors. A few behaviorists seem to be viewing it as a softheaded fling with mentalism that they hope will pass. Likewise, some cognitive psychologists have viewed the merger with suspicion. (p. 5)

Although several effective treatments based on traditional behavioral learning principles had been developed, by the early 1970s it was clear that a number of frequently encountered clinical conditions (such as depression) were not so easily addressed by treatments based on classical or operant conditioning (Thorpe & Olson, 1997). In a sense, the present blending of behavioral and cognitive methods was stimulated by the limitations of both psychodynamics and radical behaviorism. This blending was also facilitated by the presence of several theoretical models that incorporated cognitive variables along with the scientific and experimental rigor so precious to behaviorists.

The Role of Social Learning Theory. In particular, Rotter's social learning theory (Rotter, 1954; Rotter, Chance, & Phares, 1972) helped bridge the chasm between traditional psychodynamic clinical practice and learning theory. It was a theory that explained behavior as a joint product of both reinforcement and expectancies. People choose to behave in the way they do because the behavior chosen is expected to lead to a goal or outcome of some value.

The presence of such a social learning theory did at least two things for the development of behavior therapy. First, it produced a number of clinicians (and influenced others) who were ready to accept newer behavioral techniques and were equipped with a theoretical point of view that could facilitate the modification of those techniques along more cognitive lines. Second, the theory, being both cognitive and motivational, was capable of blending the older psychodynamically derived therapeutic procedures with the newer behavioral and cognitive approaches. By its very presence, then, social learning theory facilitated a fusion of approaches that is still in progress. In evaluating the relevance of this social learning theory for the practice of both traditional psychotherapy and behavior therapy, consider the following implications discussed by Rotter (1970):

1. Psychotherapy is regarded as a learning situation, and the role of the therapist is to enable the patient to achieve planned changes in observable behavior and thinking.
2. A problem-solving framework is a useful way in which to view most patients' difficulties.
3. Most often, the role of the therapist is to guide the teaming process so that not only are inadequate behaviors and attitudes weakened but more satisfying and constructive behaviors are learned.
4. It is often necessary to change unrealistic expectancies; in so doing, one must realize how it was that certain behaviors and expectancies arose and how prior experience was misapplied or overgeneralized by the patient.

5. In therapy, the patient must learn to be concerned with the feelings, expectations, motives, and needs of others.
6. New experiences or different ones in real life can often be much more effective than those that occur only during the therapy situation.
7. In general, therapy is a kind of social interaction.

Another highly significant contribution that has facilitated the cognitive swing in behavior therapy has been the work of Bandura (1969). Bandura demonstrated the importance of vicarious learning and the role of cognitive mediators in both affect and performance. Bandura's (1977a) emphasis on the ways in which various treatment procedures increase the patient's sense of self-efficacy is a further step toward unifying the behavioral and cognitive realms. In his proposed model, Bandura argues that expectations of personal efficacy arise from the patient's actual accomplishments, verbal persuasion, vicarious experience, and physiological states. Various forms of therapy are seen as particularly productive in leading patients to an increased belief in their personal efficacy.

Social learning theorists such as Rotter, Bandura, and others highlighted the idea that learning is an active not a passive process. That is, a host of personal characteristics and cognitive processes influence behavior, sometimes independently of stimuli, situations, or reinforcers. Therefore, attempts were made to better investigate these "new" influences on behavior, and treatments that focused on these mediating, cognitive, and personal factors were developed. In this section, we describe a number of different cognitive-behavioral treatment approaches.

Modeling

Bandura (1969, 1971) has advocated the use of *modeling*, or observational learning, as a means of altering behavior patterns, particularly in children. Imitation, modeling, or observation are much more efficient techniques for learning than is a simple reliance on punishment for in-

correct responses and reward for correct ones. A new skill or a new set of behaviors can be learned more efficiently by observing another person. Seeing others perform a behavior can also help eliminate or reduce associated fears and anxieties. Finally, through observation one can learn to use behaviors that are already part of the behavioral repertoire.

Perhaps the most widespread use of modeling has been to eliminate unrealistic fears (Bandura, Adams, & Beyer, 1977; Bandura, Jeffrey, & Wright, 1974). Phobias (especially snake phobias) have been the principal means both of demonstrating and of investigating modeling techniques. In participant modeling, for example, the patient observes the therapist or model holding a snake, allowing the snake to crawl over the body, and so on. Next, in guided participation, the patient is exhorted to try out a series of similar activities, graded according to their potential for producing anxiety. Illustrative of this general approach is a study of nonorgasmic women treated by a self-administered masturbation-training program over a six-week period. The general techniques, used in two different treatment conditions, were described by McMullen and Rosen (1979) as follows:

> *Videotape modeling procedure.* A series of six 20-minute videotape sequences were prepared specifically for the study. The tapes featured a coping model, an actress portraying a nonorgasmic woman who learns over the course of the six sessions to stimulate herself to orgasm and then to transfer her ability to sexual intercourse with her partner. Content of the tapes included self-exploration, self-stimulation, and finally, an explicit representation of reaching orgasm through intercourse with a partner.

> *Written instructions.* The videotaped scripts were excerpted in the form of written booklets, which pretesting indicated were of equivalent content to the videotapes. The same procedure was followed for these subjects, in that they were required to come in once a week to read the appropriate

booklet over the six weeks of the training program. Booklets were also read in private, and approximately the same amount of time was spent by these subjects in the clinic. (p. 914)

As noted by Thorpe and Olson (1997), observational learning is best and most efficient when the following four conditions are met:

1. Patients attend to the model. Incentives may be helpful to facilitate attention.
2. Patients retain the information provided by the model. It may be helpful to use imagery techniques or verbal coding strategies to help patients organize and retain the information provided.
3. Patients must perform the modeled behavior. It is important that the behavior be mimicked and practiced to facilitate learning and behavior change.
4. Finally, patients must be motivated to use the behavior that is modeled. It is suggested that reinforcing consequences be used to increase the likelihood that the modeled behavior will be used.

Rational Restructuring

Drawing on the work of Albert Ellis (1962), Goldfried and Davison (1994) accept the notion that much maladaptive behavior is determined by the ways in which people construe their world or by the assumptions they make about it. If this is true, it follows that the behavior therapist must help patients learn to label situations more realistically so that they can ultimately attain greater satisfactions. To facilitate this *rational restructuring* of events, the therapist may sometimes use argument or discussion in an attempt to get patients to see the irrationality of their beliefs. In addition to providing patients with a rational analysis of their problems, the therapist may attempt to teach them to "modify their internal sentences." That is, patients may be taught that when they begin to feel upset in real situations, they should pause and ask themselves what they are telling themselves about

those situations. In other instances, the therapist may have patients in the therapy room imagine particular problem situations. All of this may be combined with behavior rehearsal, in vivo assignments, modeling, and so on. Thus, rational restructuring is not a self-contained, theoretically derived procedure, but an eclectic series of techniques that can be tailored to suit the particular demands of the patient's situation.

A good example of rational restructuring is Ellis's (1962) *rational-emotive therapy (RET)*. Ellis was clearly a pioneer in what has become cognitive behavior therapy. RET aims to change behavior by altering the way the patient thinks about things. Conventional wisdom often suggests that events cause (lead directly to) emotional and behavioral problems. According to Ellis, however, all behavior, whether maladjusted or otherwise, is determined not by events but by the person's interpretation of those events. In the ABCs of RET, Ellis argues that it is *beliefs* (B) about *activating* events or situations (A) that determine the problematic emotional or behavioral *consequences* (C). He sees psychoanalytic therapy, with its extreme reliance on insight, as inefficient; the origins of irrational thinking are not nearly so important as the messages that people give to themselves.

In a sense, the basic goal of RET is to make people confront their own illogical thinking. Ellis tries to get the client to use common sense. The therapist becomes an active and directive teacher. Box 14-3 presents some of the more common irrational ideas believed by Ellis to influence many people. Reviews of the empirical literature suggest that RET is an effective psychological intervention (Smith et al., 1980). However, more detailed investigation of the components of RET that lead to change in clinical status have has been called for (Haaga & Davison, 1993).

Stress Inoculation Training

Based on his own research, which indicated that patients could use self-talk or self-instruction to modify their behavior and that therapists could, in effect, train patients to change their self-talk,

BOX 14-3

Common "Irrational" Ideas

The 12 irrational ideas that Ellis (1977) believes are very common in the thinking of many people are listed below. While most of us share this kind of thinking, *extreme* reliance on such beliefs can be debilitating.

1. The idea that you must, yes, must have sincere love and approval almost all the time from all the people you find significant.
2. The idea that you must prove yourself thoroughly competent, adequate, and achieving; or that you must at least have real competence or talent at something important.
3. The idea that people who harm you or commit misdeeds rate as generally bad, wicked, or villainous individuals, and that you should severely blame, damn, and punish them for their sins.
4. The idea that life proves awful, terrible, horrible, or catastrophic when things do not go the way you would like them to go.
5. The idea that emotional misery comes from external pressures and that you have little ability to control your feelings or rid yourself of depression and hostility.
6. The idea that if something seems dangerous or fearsome, you must become terribly occupied with and upset about it.
7. The idea that you will find it easier to avoid facing many of life's difficulties and self-responsibilities than to undertake some rewarding forms of self-discipline.
8. The idea that your past remains all-important and that, because something once strongly influenced your life, it has to keep determining your feelings and behavior today.
9. The idea that people and things should turn out better than they do; and that you have to view it as awful and horrible if you do not quickly find good solutions to life's hassles.
10. The idea that you can achieve happiness by inertia and inaction or by passively and uncommittedly "enjoying yourself."
11. The idea that you must have a high degree of order or certainty to feel comfortable; or that you need some supernatural power on which to rely.
12. The idea that you give yourself a global rating as a human and that your general worth and self-acceptance depend upon the goodness of your performance and the degree that people approve of you.

Source: From "A Basic Clinical Theory of Rational-Emotive Therapy," by A. Ellis, p. 10. In A. Ellis and R. Grieger (Eds.), Handbook of Rational-Emotive Therapy. *Copyright © 1977 by Springer Publishing Company, Inc., New York 10012. Used by permission.*

Meichenbaum (1977) developed *stress inoculation training (SIT)*. SIT aims to prevent problems from developing by "inoculating" individuals to ongoing and future stressors (Meichenbaum, 1996). It is designed to help individuals develop new coping skills and make full use of the coping strategies that are already in place (Meichenbaum, 1996). SIT for coping with stressors appears on the most recent list of examples of empirically supported treatments (Chambless et al., 1998). SIT proceeds in three overlapping phases (Meichenbaum, 1996):

1. *Conceptualization phase*: First, the client is educated with regard to how certain thinking or appraisal patterns lead to stress, other

negative emotions, and dysfunctional behavior. The client is taught how to identify potential threats or stressors and how to cope with them.

2. *Skill acquisition and rehearsal phase*: The client practices coping skills (for example, emotional self-regulation, cognitive restructuring, using support systems) in the clinic and then gradually out in the "real world" as he or she is confronted with the stressors.

3. *Application phase*: Additional opportunities arise for the client to apply a wide variety of coping skills across a range of stressful conditions. In order to consolidate these skills, the client may be asked to help others who are experiencing similar problems. Further "inoculation" procedures, including relapse prevention and booster sessions, are incorporated during the follow-up period.

To give one concrete example, Novaco (1977) describes the application of stress inoculation procedures to deal with the anger problems of depressed patients on acute psychiatric wards. In essence, the procedures involve the cognitive preparation of such patients, the acquisition and rehearsal of the necessary skills, and practice in the application of those skills. To cognitively prepare patients, they are given instructional manuals describing the nature and functions of anxiety, including a discussion of situations in which anger is a problem, what causes anger, and how anger can be regulated. The components of this cognitive preparation include identifying persons and situations that precipitate anger, learning to differentiate between anger and aggression, discriminating between justified and unnecessary anger, and recognizing early signs of tension and arousal in a provocation sequence.

Beck's Cognitive Therapy

Aaron Beck has been a pioneer in the development of cognitive-behavioral treatments for a variety of clinical problems (Beck, 1991). This model of intervention entails the use of both cognitive and behavioral techniques to modify dysfunctional thinking patterns that character-

ize the problem or disorder in question (Beck, 1993). For example, depressed individuals are believed to harbor negative/pessimistic beliefs about themselves, their world, and their future. Thus, a depressed 45-year-old man might be prone to be highly self-critical (and often feel guilty, even when it is not appropriate), to view the world as generally unsupportive and unfair, and not to hold much hope that things will improve in the future. The following *cognitive therapy (CT)* techniques might be used in the treatment of his depression (Beck, Rush, Shaw, & Emery, 1979):

1. Scheduling activities to counteract his relative inactivity and tendency to focus on his depressive feelings.
2. Increasing the rates of pleasurable activities as well as of those in which some degree of mastery is experienced.
3. Cognitive rehearsal: Have the patient imagine each successive step leading to the completion of an important task (such as attending an exercise class), so that potential impediments can be identified, anticipated, and addressed.
4. Assertiveness training and role playing.
5. Identifying automatic thoughts that occur before or during dysphoric episodes (for example, "I can't do anything right").
6. Examining the reality or accuracy of these thoughts by gently challenging their validity ("So you don't think there is *anything* you can do right?").
7. Teaching the patient to reattribute the "blame" for negative consequences to the appropriate source. Depressed patients have a tendency to blame themselves for negative outcomes, even when they are not to blame.
8. Helping the patient search for alternative solutions to his problems instead of resigning himself to their insolubility.

This is an abbreviated, illustrative sample of the techniques used in Beck's cognitive therapy of depression. Box 14-4 presents the major features of cognitive therapy for depression. It is worth repeating that cognitive therapy has proven to be one of the most effective techniques

BOX 14-4

Features of Cognitive Therapy for Depression

Aaron Beck's cognitive therapy for depression is an empirically supported treatment (Chambless et al., 1998) that is active, structured, and time-limited. It is characterized by the following features (Butler & Beck, 1996).

Focus

CT focuses on the connection between thinking patterns/styles, emotions, and behavior.

Length

Typically 14–16 sessions. Many patients show a remission of symptoms in 8–12 sessions.

Role of the CT Therapist

The CT therapist is an active, supportive collaborator. Through psychoeducation, guided discovery, Socratic questioning, role playing, and behavioral experiments, patients are helped to address and change maladaptive ways of thinking that lead to or maintain depression and other negative affects.

Structure of a Typical Session

Mood symptoms are checked, an agenda for the session is set, the previous session is summarized, homework assignments are reviewed, issues on the agenda are discussed, new homework is assigned, and the current session is summarized and evaluated by both therapist and patient.

Phases of Treatment

In the first phase (about eight sessions), the cognitive model is introduced, skills are acquired, and some mastery is achieved. Reduction in depressive symptoms occurs.

In the remaining sessions, dysfunctional beliefs that may lead to relapse (for example, "This good feeling won't last") are evaluated and modified, relapse prevention skills are taught, and termination issues are discussed.

---

available for treating depression (Chambless et al., 1998; Dobson, 1989; Hollon & Beck, 1994). In addition, cognitive therapy has been adapted for use with patients suffering from anxiety disorders (Beck & Emery, 1985), eating disorders (Fairburn et al., 1991), and personality disorders (Beck, Freeman, & Associates, 1990), to cite but a few examples. Empirical studies suggest that it may be an especially effective form of intervention for a broad range of clinical problems (Hollon & Beck, 1994; Smith et al., 1980)

An Evaluation of Behavior Therapy

Proponents of behavior therapy see their progress as tangible evidence of what can be accom-

plished when the mentalistic, subjective, and nonscientific "mumbo jumbo" of psychodynamics or phenomenology is cast aside. Critics, on the other hand, see behavior therapy as superficial, pretentiously scientific, and even dehumanizing in its mechanistic attempts to change human behavior. Indeed, these criticisms reflect many of the "myths" about behavior therapy (Goldfried & Davison, 1994). In any case, more clinical psychologists describe their orientation as cognitive or behavioral than any other orientation (Norcross et al., 1997a).

We will now examine some of the strengths and limitations of the behavioral and cognitive-behavioral approaches, and then close with a summary of some of the challenges ahead.

Strengths

In many ways, behavior therapy has changed the fields of psychotherapy and clinical psychology (Wilson, 1997). Below, we discuss several major ways that behavior therapy has had an impact.

Effectiveness. As mentioned throughout this chapter, there is ample evidence that a wide variety of behavioral and cognitive-behavioral therapies are effective (Chambless et al., 1998; Emmelkamp, 1994; Hollon & Beck, 1994; Smith et al., 1980). In fact, behavior therapy appears to be the treatment of choice for many disorders (Wilson, 1997). The reader may recall the results of the Smith et al. (1980) meta-analysis presented in Chapter 11 (see Table 11-5). The separate effect sizes calculated for RET, non-RET cognitive therapies, systematic desensitization, behavior modification, and cognitive-behavioral therapy indicated that, on average, a client who received any of these forms of behavior therapy was functioning better than at least 75% of those who did not receive any treatment. More recent meta-analyses have reached similar conclusions across a range of disorders. Further, the majority of meta-analytic studies that have compared the effectiveness of behavioral or cognitive-behavioral techniques with that of other forms of psychotherapy (such as psychodynamic or client-centered) have found a small but consistent superiority for behavioral and cognitive-behavioral methods (Dobson, 1989; Dush, Hirt, & Schroeder, 1983; Nicholson & Berman, 1983; Robinson, Berman, & Neimeyer, 1990; Shapiro & Shapiro, 1982; Svartberg & Stiles, 1991). Clearly, these are important treatment techniques for a clinician to master.

Efficiency. The behavior therapy movement also brought with it a series of techniques that were shorter and more efficient. The interminable number of 50-minute psychotherapy hours was replaced by a much shorter series of consultations that focused on the patient's specific complaints. A series of equally specific procedures was applied, and the entire process terminated when the patient's complaints no longer existed. Gone was the everlasting "rooting out" of underlying pathology, the exhaustive sorting out of the patient's history, and the lengthy quest for insight. In their place came an emphasis on the present and a pragmatism that was signaled by the use of specific techniques for specific problems. Because of its efficiency, behavior therapy may be especially well suited for the managed care environment (Wilson, 1997).

In fact, some behavioral techniques can be implemented by technicians who are trained to work under the supervision of a doctoral-level clinician. Thus, not every component of behavior therapy needs to be executed by Ph.D. personnel. Behavior therapy programs (for example, token economies) should be set up by trained professionals, but their day-to-day execution can be put in the hands of technicians, paraprofessionals, nurses, and others. This constitutes a considerable savings in mental health personnel and enables a larger patient population to be reached than can be treated by the in-depth, one-on-one procedures of an exclusively psychodynamic approach.

An Array of Empirically Supported Techniques. Behavior therapy has evolved to the point that it includes a broad array of techniques, from systematic desensitization to cognitive restructuring (Wilson, 1997). Unless a behavior therapist is unalterably committed to a single set of procedures, this broad spectrum demands that choices be made. To increase the probability of making the correct choice, the therapist is likely to gather information that will best match technique with patient (Peterson & Sobell, 1994). If assessment eventually recaptures its position of prominence in the list of the clinician's preferred activities, it will be due in no small measure to the behavior therapist's desire for information to guide the therapeutic decision-making process.

Judith S. Beck, Ph.D.

Dr. Judith S. Beck is the director of the Beck Institute for Cognitive Therapy and Research and a Clinical Assistant Professor at the University of Pennsylvania School of Medicine. Dr. Beck is an expert in cognitive therapy, and she travels around the country and the world training practitioners in the theory and practice of this approach for psychological problems. In addition to her teaching and administrative roles, Dr. Beck conducts and publishes research in the areas of cognitive assessment and cognitive treatment. Dr. Beck has also authored or coauthored a number of publications for the general public concerning cognitive therapy and depression. Dr. Beck gave us some background information about herself, as well as her impressions regarding the future of clinical psychology and of cognitive therapy.

What originally got you interested in the field of psychology?

I had always been interested in working with children and decided early on I wanted to be a teacher. In fact, my degrees are in education and educational psychology. Initially, I taught students with learning disabilities, then supervised special education teachers. I then became interested in the work of Aaron T. Beck, M.D., who is my father and the "father" of cognitive therapy. Midway through my doctoral program, I decided I should learn more about his field of expertise. I was skeptical at first that I could ever be a good

psychologist, because I did not realize that counseling skills could be learned; they did not have to be inborn or intuitive, the way my teaching skills had been. Taking psychology courses and doing practica demonstrated to me that many of the skills I had learned and refined as a teacher (and later as a supervisor), served me in good stead.

Coming full circle, one of my favorite professional activities today is teaching students and professionals in mental health fields, and occasionally in education as well.

Describe what activities you are involved in as a psychologist.

As the director of a nonprofit psychotherapy center whose missions include clinical care, education, and research, my activities are quite varied. I spend a great deal of time in administration. I supervise our clinical staff, psychologists and other mental health professionals in our extramural and visitor training programs. I do a significant amount of teaching of cognitive therapy, nationally and internationally, in courses, conferences, and workshops.

In addition, I treat a small caseload of patients with a variety of outpatient psychiatric disorders. I am involved in several research grants as a consultant or principal investigator. I publish articles and chapters and am currently working on a second book, which teaches clinicians how to conceptualize, plan treatment, and work with patients who have challenging disorders. I am on the board of several community and professional organizations, including one to credential mental health professionals as cognitive therapists.

As a clinical assistant professor of psychology in psychiatry at the University of Pennsylvania, I develop and teach courses in cognitive therapy, supervise third- and fourth-year psychiatric residents, and teach graduate-level psychology students and psychiatric nurses.

What are your particular areas of expertise or interest?

My major expertise is cognitive therapy. One area I have concentrated on is the cognitive conceptualization of patients, especially those with personality disorders. I have developed a structured format to help clinicians make data-based hypotheses about how patients, as a result of adverse childhood experiences (and genetic predisposition), develop rigid, global, negative beliefs about themselves, other people, and their worlds, and how these beliefs have affected their information processing, perceptions, emotional reactions, and behavior throughout their lives.

Connected with this interest is teaching clinicians to use cognitive conceptualization as a guide in forming and maintaining a sound therapeutic alliance, in developing treatment plans, and in varying the structure, interventions, and expectations for patients with complex problems and disorders who do not respond to standard cognitive therapy.

I also continue to develop more effective strategies to teach and supervise students and professionals. For example, I structure teaching and supervision sessions in the same way that I structure therapy. Also, I have developed instruments for patients to evaluate therapists, for supervisors to evaluate therapists (and for therapists to evaluate supervisors).

I have coauthored a scale measuring personality-related beliefs and am involved in developing self-administered scales for children that assess symptoms of depression, anxiety, anger, disordered conduct, and low self-esteem.

What are the future trends you see for clinical psychology?

One trend will be in devising and refining instruments to diagnose patients and assess their symptoms more accurately. Future scales will likely include more cognitive items in addition to the traditional emotional, behavioral, and biological symptoms. More scales will be developed to identify and measure relevant beliefs that underlie specific problems and diagnoses. Clinical psychologists will increasingly focus on measuring outcomes to assess efficacy of treatment.

I believe that master's-level clinicians, social

workers, and primary care physicians will provide treatment for straightforward cases of depression and anxiety. Clinical psychologists, who are more highly trained and have specific expertise, will be asked primarily to care for patients with more complex problems, and they will increasingly utilize empirically based treatments. Behavioral health care organizations will ultimately ration care that psychologists provide on a more rational basis that recognizes the severity and comorbidity of various diagnoses.

What are some future trends you see in cognitive therapy?

One trend is the application of cognitive therapy to a wider variety of psychiatric disorders. Recent outcome studies, for example, have demonstrated the efficacy of cognitive therapy for substance abuse, eating disorders, personality disorders, and as an adjunctive treatment for bipolar disorder and schizophrenia, to name a few. Cognitive therapy will also continue to be refined for the treatment of a variety of medical illnesses: post–heart attack patients who are depressed, diabetics who do not follow their treatment regimen, patients with stress-induced or stress-exacerbated conditions.

Clinicians will also continue to expand the delivery of cognitive therapy to patients (and their families) in a variety of settings: in inpatient and partial hospitalization programs, outpatient clinics, in the offices of primary care providers and specialists, rehab centers, nursing homes, and schools. Cognitive therapists who are clinical psychologists will do more widespread teaching of psychiatrists, psychiatric nurses, social workers, counselors, primary care physicians, and other adjunctive therapists whose efficacy can be enhanced by incorporating cognitive techniques into their practice.

Finally, cognitive therapy teachers and supervisors will refine methods to take advantage of evolving technology for distance learning programs, dissemination of information, forums for discussion via the Internet, and interactive multimedia computer programs.

Behavior therapy is a very active collection of procedures. It involves assessment, planning, decisions, and techniques. In some ways, it may be construed as a complex technology. A technology cannot be passively allowed to happen to a patient. It is something that must be guided with care and foresight and with great attention to detail. It is not a process that permits the therapist to wait until the patient shows up on Thursday before thinking about the case. The therapist cannot play everything by ear. If a therapist is using aversion procedures, the time relationship between the onset of the stimulus and the onset of punishment may need strict supervision. Token economies are not haphazard regimens that can be left to creative, on-the-spot decision making. Everything must be worked out carefully in advance. It is important to decide whether the patient has a behavioral deficit rather than a "pure" anxiety problem, because the therapeutic implications are vastly different in the two cases.

None of this is meant to imply that every psychodynamically oriented psychotherapist fails to think about cases between therapy sessions or always makes up strategy spontaneously along the way. Yet the nature of traditional psychotherapy renders it vulnerable to such problems of passivity. It is even possible that the active, vigorous quality of behavioral methods and the analogous attitude that this forces upon the therapist may be responsible for a measure of patient improvement beyond that caused by the specific procedures employed. An active therapist may be reassuring, exciting, or encouraging to some patients (in contrast to a passive, contemplative, noncommittal psychotherapist who often has little to say or suggest).

It is also worth repeating that behavior therapy is the undisputed leader in "manualizing" its treatments so that empirically supported techniques can be administered in a standardized fashion. Not only does this facilitate conducting research and providing effective treatment, but it also facilitates the training of future clinical psychologists to administer these effective treatments.

Symptom Substitution. As much as anything, behavior therapies will have a secure and valued position in the history of psychology because they helped lay to rest the hallowed notion of *symptom substitution*. They not only demonstrated that there are alternatives to the psychodynamic view of pathology, but they also effectively attacked the medical model of pathology and its cherished notions of illnesses and symptoms. After years of research and clinical experience, it is now clear that not every patient's complaint can be labeled as a symptom of some underlying psychic illness—an illness that will surely return in the form of another symptom if the present one is removed without attending to the underlying pathology. Attacking a patient's anxieties directly will not necessarily force the anxieties to return in another guise. This demonstration not only lent credibility to the behavioral movement; it also chipped away at the credibility of those psychiatric and psychodynamic orientations that had so stoutly defended the symptom substitution notion. As a result, the avenue was opened for the development of specific techniques for dealing with specific patient complaints. However, these remarks should be tempered by a recognition that direct onslaughts on the patient's stated problem may not always be the most efficient route. As we noted earlier in this chapter, it may turn out that a specific anxiety is being sustained by something not immediately obvious (Lazarus, 1971a).

Breadth of Application. A contribution of major proportions has been the extension of the range of applicability of therapy. Traditional psychotherapy had been reserved for the middle and upper classes who had the time and money to devote to their psychological woes and for articulate, relatively sophisticated college students with well-developed repertoires of coping behaviors who were attending colleges or universities that made counseling services available to them at little if any cost. Behavior therapy has changed all that.

Now, even financially strapped individuals with mental retardation or a chronic mental illness can be helped by therapy. Such persons may not be raised to the level of independent functioning, but with the advent of operant procedures and token economies, their institutional adjustment can often be significantly improved.

Not only the institutionalized have benefited from behavioral techniques. Patients at lower socioeconomic levels with limited sophistication and verbal skills can also experience anxieties and phobias or lack necessary problem-solving skills. In cases where lengthy verbal psychotherapies that were highly dependent on insight, symbolism, or the release of some inner potential were likely to fail, a broad band of behavior therapies seems to offer real hope.

Scientist-Practitioner and Clinical Scientist. For those who support the scientist-practitioner or clinical scientist model of clinical psychology, behavior therapy is a field that seems to encourage a blending of the two roles. The behavioral tradition springs from a heritage that is experimental and oriented toward research. Many of the specific techniques of behavior therapy have developed directly from the experimental laboratory. Sometimes even the language of behavior therapy is straight out of the experimental research journals. In behavior therapy, there is an easy communication between the researcher and the clinician, and very often the same person alternates comfortably between the two roles. Such rapport increases the likelihood that advances in the laboratory will be reflected in new therapeutic techniques and, conversely, that clinical experience will serve a vital role in determining the kind of research and evaluation that is carried out.

Criticisms

Many of the customary criticisms of behavior therapy lost their force once the field assumed its cognitive stance. As noted before, Goldfried and Davison (1994) use the term *behavior therapy* more broadly to include both strictly behavioral and cognitive techniques that derive from principles established empirically in the laboratory

that have clinical applications. However, the degree of association between laboratory-based principles and behavior therapy techniques is the subject of much debate.

Linking Practice to Science. For some years, the behavioral movement rode the crest of a wave of scientific respectability. Many behaviorists, especially the radical variety, seemed to be clamoring for preferred status by claiming that behavior therapy rested on the sturdy, established scientific principles of learning theory. Psychodynamic approaches, by contrast, were said to be crude extrapolations from a mentalism only slightly removed from witchcraft. At times, the sheer repetition of claims of being scientifically based or experimentally derived seems to have deluded the more ardent adherents of behavior therapy into overestimating their "science." But not all behavioral methods are based on strong experimental evidence; many have grown out of clinical experience (Wilson, 1997). Moreover, many things that behavioral therapists do can be equally well explained by nonbehavioral points of view (Goldfried & Davison, 1994).

Dehumanizing. Among the more durable characterizations of the behavioral movement are "sterile," "mechanistic," and "dehumanizing." To demonstrate that there is real labeling bias operating here, Woolfolk, Woolfolk, and Wilson (1977) asked two groups of undergraduates to view identical videotapes of a teacher using reinforcement methods. The first group was told that the tape illustrated behavior modification; for the second group, the tape was labeled as an illustration of humanistic education. A subsequent questionnaire revealed that when the tape was described in humanistic terms, the teacher on the tape received significantly better ratings and the teaching method depicted was seen as significantly more likely to promote learning and emotional growth.

The use of mechanistic-sounding terms such as *response*, *stimulus*, *reinforcement*, and *operant* need not imply that either the therapist or the method is detached, sterile, or dehumanizing. The systematic use of learning principles and the examination of animal analogues for simple illustrations to highlight the nature of human learning should not lead to a facile inference that behavior therapists are cold, manipulating robots whose interests lie more in their learning principles than in their clients. It is to be hoped that with the increasing cognitive orientation, such erroneous images will begin to fade.

Although nothing inherent in behavior therapy should lead one to conclude that it is necessarily dehumanizing, its early history provided a few unfortunate episodes and a considerable stridency of rhetoric. We have already commented on the use of aversion techniques that to many seemed more akin to sadism than therapy. In addition, many early behaviorists seemed to be so obsessed with their principles and their technology that common sense seemed to be the chief casualty. Their sometimes naive attacks on psychodynamics and their zealous overconfidence in technology often played right into the hands of their critics and only served to make life more difficult for their successors. In the final analysis, no technology or set of principles is going to permit clinicians the luxury of giving up their clinical sensitivity.

Inner Growth. Behavior therapy has also been criticized as ameliorative but not productive of any inner growth. It has been said to relieve symptoms or provide a few skills while failing to offer fulfilling creative experiences. Although it may alter behavior, it falls short of promoting understanding. It leaves out the inner person, values, responsibility, and motives. Again, though not completely off the mark, such criticisms are less appropriate for the newer cognitive emphasis in behavior therapy, an emphasis that does deal with mediating variables such as expectancies and self-concepts—as long as these are objectively describable and are inferred from specific stimuli and responses.

Nonspecific Problems. For some years, critics of behavior therapy have complained that it does not deal adequately with problems that are vague or existential in character. A good, crisp snake phobia can readily be handled by relaxation, systematic desensitization, or modeling. But what about the depressed, unfulfilled housewife who faces an empty home now that her family is grown? And what about a vague, ill-defined sense of anxiety or depression? In short, do the techniques that handle specific anxieties or behavioral deficits also resolve moral dilemmas or the sense of meaninglessness? The answer is not clear. As early as 1964, Grossberg recognized this limitation of behavior therapy when he commented, "A review of this literature revealed that behavior therapies have been applied to many neurotic and psychotic disorders, and have been most successful with disorders involving specific maladaptive behaviors" (p. 73).

It is in part because of these limitations that behavioral therapy has begun to transform itself into a more cognitive, yes, even more psychodynamic and humanistic enterprise (Goldfried & Davison, 1994). And if it maintains its rapport with learning theory, objectivity, and scientific investigation as it moves gingerly toward this more cognitive, dynamic, and humanistic stance, it may yet have the best of all worlds.

Mental Processes. Although few behavior therapists can be said to embrace the unconscious, only the radical behaviorists still insist on the absolute rejection of all so-called mental processes. Likewise, not many behavioral clinicians are likely to recommend an exhaustive reconstruction of the patient's past (especially the psychosexuality of childhood). But this is not to argue that past learning experiences have not led to the patient's current predicament. Indeed they have. Any sensitive behavioral clinician will devote time to understanding what those learning experiences were all about. By so doing, the clinician can better distinguish between behavioral deficits and problems and can better understand how to structure present learning experiences so as to enable patients to better cope with their problems.

Manipulation and Control. One of the most volatile, emotion-laden criticisms of behavior therapy centers on the issue of manipulation and control. The argument seems to be that behavior therapies represent insidious and often direct assaults on the patient's capacity to make decisions, assume responsibility, and maintain dignity and integrity. But patients typically seek professional assistance voluntarily, thereby acknowledging their need for help and guidance in altering their lives. Thus, the patient does have the opportunity to accept or reject the procedures offered (though this defense may not apply as well in institutional settings). Further, many behavior therapy techniques are aimed at helping patients establish skills that will lead to greater self-direction and self-control (Goldfried & Davison, 1994).

Generalization. A particularly damaging criticism of several forms of behavior therapy concerns their effectiveness in settings other than those in which they are conducted. In other words, do the effects of behavior therapy programs generalize beyond the situations in which they are practiced? Again, in the interests of evenhandedness, it should be pointed out that most forms of psychotherapy are subject to the same question. For example, some patients show a marked improvement or adjustment in the psychotherapy situation even though this adjustment fails to generalize to nontherapy settings.

It is the operant approaches (token economies and related behavioral management programs) that have been most suspect here. Such programs always seem to work best where a great deal of control over the life of the patient is possible. They may seem quite effective in institutions for those with mental retardation or chronic mental illness, as well as certain classroom settings and experimental living arrangements. In these settings, trained personnel are available to observe behavior or issue tokens, making it relatively easy to maintain the appropriate contingencies between behavior and reinforcement. However, when individuals leave such a sheltered environment, it becomes clear that although certain desired behaviors were maintained by the operant procedures, little was learned that would generalize to a noncontrolled setting. There are many practical problems in establishing behavior modification programs in natural settings, let alone getting their effects to generalize beyond the institution.

Other techniques, such as aversion therapies, suffer from similar problems. For example, one of the authors once knew an alcoholic who was able to conquer his drinking problem with the help of Antabuse and a very controlled hospital environment. This patient knew full well that with the medication in his system, he would become violently ill if he drank. However, upon his release from the hospital, he soon encountered several stressful situations. He had learned the connection between drinking and becoming ill, but unfortunately he had also learned that if he stopped taking the Antabuse and waited awhile he could drink with impunity—which he did.

The foregoing kinds of experiences have led many to characterize behavioral treatment techniques as superficial, simplistic, or supportive methods that produce little of lasting value. Such critics argue that the benefits of these techniques are largely confined to institutional settings in which behavioral management is important and do not generalize to unsupervised situations in which self-control and independence are at a premium. Indeed, some have gone so far as to argue that the use of external incentives to maintain certain desired behaviors actually serves to undermine the person's "real" interest in the activity in question (Condry, 1977). That is, in their efforts to induce people to emit certain behaviors, therapists actually destroy whatever intrinsic motivation they might have developed for the activity. This, in turn, assures that the behavior will drop out once the extrinsic motivators have been withdrawn. Sophisticated behavior therapists are, however, not insensitive to this problem. They will often "fade" or gradually reduce the frequency of certain reinforcers as they prepare the client for settings in which immediate reinforcement (or any reinforcement at all) is not possible.

Theoretical Chaos. A final problem with behavior therapy may be its potential for theoretical chaos. At present, it is an amalgam of techniques—some from the operant tradition, others from a classical conditioning base, and still others that are heavily cognitive in nature. Without an integrating theoretical framework, individual clinicians may find themselves flailing about in a morass of competing techniques, each claiming to be forms of behavior therapy. What is needed is a systematic theoretical position that will incorporate the techniques, classify them, and help the clinician decide when and under what conditions to use one technique rather than another. Such a theoretical framework would be infinitely more efficient than multiple rules of thumb.

The Future

Recently, Wilson (1997) reflected on behavior therapy's past and highlighted some of the challenges for the future. Wilson noted the need for wider dissemination and adoption of behavior therapy; given its strong empirical support, it is somewhat surprising that these techniques are not more widely used. Interestingly, behavior therapy has had substantially less influence outside of clinical psychology (for example, in the fields of psychiatry and social work). Perhaps what is needed are better methods to train mental health professionals (within and outside of clinical psychology) in behavior therapy techniques as well as more effective treatments for a broader range of clinical problems. Finally, Wilson (1997) is concerned that behavior therapy remain firmly linked to advances in psychological science:

> To fulfill its original promise of linking clinical practice to advances in scientific research, behavior therapy must be responsive to developments both in experimental psychology and biology. Dramatic breakthroughs in genetics and neuroscience have already revolutionized the biological sciences, and progress will likely continue to unlock the secrets of the brain. A better

understanding of the role of brain mechanisms in the development and maintenance of clinical disorders, and in the modification of these disorders via both pharmacological and behavioral methods, will arguably improve our theories of behavior change. (p. 454)

Chapter Summary

Behavior therapy is based on the assumption that clinical problems should be addressed using assessment and treatment techniques that have empirical support and are supported by established principles from experimental psychology. Although procedures derived from classical and operant conditioning initially dominated this approach, behavior therapy has been broadened to include procedures that draw from learning theories based on observational learning and cognitive processes.

Traditional behavioral treatments include systematic desensitization, exposure therapy, behavior rehearsal, contingency management, and aversion therapy. These treatments have documented efficacy, and several are the treatments of choice for certain clinical problems (for example, systematic desensitization for phobias, exposure plus response prevention for obsessive-compulsive disorder). Cognitive-behavioral treatments emphasize the roles of thinking, expectations, and beliefs in the etiology and maintenance of clinical problems. Examples of cognitive-behavioral techniques include modeling, rational restructuring, stress inoculation training, and cognitive therapy. The most recent list of examples of empirically supported treatments is dominated by cognitive-behavioral and traditional behavioral techniques.

Behavior therapy has had a positive impact on the field because of its wide range of effective and efficient treatments. It has been the leader in manualizing treatments, facilitating research, training, and practice. In many ways, it is the ideal therapeutic orientation choice for scientist-practitioners and clinical scientists. There are, however, several limitations and challenges that lie ahead. At times, the link between behavior therapy techniques and scientific, experimental evidence has not been as strong as has been claimed. Further, many myths still plague the field, including that behavior therapy is dehumanizing and overly controlling. For the future, there is a need for wider dissemination of behavior therapy techniques, better training both within and outside of clinical psychology, and more attention to the incorporation of advances in psychological science.

Key Terms

anxiety hierarchy In systematic desensitization, a list of situations that precipitate anxiety reactions, ordered from lowest to highest severity. Oftentimes items may be organized according to their spatial or temporal distance from the feared stimulus.

assertiveness training Using behavioral rehearsal and other techniques to train people to express their needs effectively without infringing upon the rights of others.

aversion therapy A controversial type of treatment in which an undesired behavior is followed consistently by an unpleasant consequence, thus decreasing the strength of the behavior over time.

behavioral rehearsal A general technique for expanding the patient's repertoire of coping behaviors. Successful behavioral rehearsal involves explaining to the patient the necessity of acquiring the new behaviors, selecting the target situations, conducting the rehearsal and providing feedback, and having the patient apply the newly acquired skills in real-life situations.

behavior therapy A framework for treating disorders that is based upon the principles of conditioning or learning. The behavioral approach is scientific in nature, and de-emphasizes the role of inferred (i.e., unobservable) variables on behavior.

cognitive-behavioral therapy A therapy framework that emphasizes the role of thinking in the etiology and maintenance of problems. Cognitive-behavioral techniques attempt to modify the patterns of thinking that are believed to contribute to a patient's problems and may also employ the principles of conditioning and learning to modify problematic behaviors.

cognitive therapy A mode of therapy pioneered by Beck that focuses on the connection between thinking patterns, emotions, and behavior, and uses both cognitive and behavioral techniques to modify the dysfunctional thinking patterns that characterize a disorder. Cognitive therapy is active, structured, and time limited, and has been adapted for the treatment of several disorders.

contingency contracting A contingency management technique in which the therapist and patient draw up a contract that specifies the behaviors that are desired and undesired, as well as the consequences of engaging or failing to engage in these behaviors.

contingency management Any one of a variety of operant conditioning techniques that attempts to control a behavior by manipulating its consequences.

counterconditioning The principle of substituting relaxation for an anxiety response.

covert sensitization A form of aversion therapy in which patients are directed to imagine themselves engaging in an undesired behavior, and then are instructed to imagine extremely aversive events occurring once they have the undesired behavior clearly in mind.

exposure plus response prevention A behavioral technique often used for the treatment of OCD. In this technique, the patient is exposed to the situation that spurs his or her obsession (e.g., touching a doorknob) and is prevented from engaging in the compulsive behavior that relieves the obsession (e.g., repeated handwashing). Ultimately, the patient will habituate to his or her obsession and his or her compulsive behavior will be extinguished.

exposure therapy A behavioral technique for reducing anxiety in which patients expose themselves (in real life or in fantasy) to stimuli or situations that are feared or avoided. In order to be effective, the exposure must provoke anxiety, must be of sufficient duration, and must be repeated until all anxiety is eliminated.

extinction The elimination of an undesired response (e.g., behavioral, emotional).

habituation The elimination of a response that comes about from the repeated and/or prolonged presentation of the provoking stimulus.

interoceptive cues Internal physiological stimuli (such as dizziness or nausea).

modeling Also known as observational learning, modeling refers to learning a new skill or set of behaviors by observing another person perform these skills/behaviors.

overcorrection A form of aversion therapy in which the client is made to "overcorrect" for the consequences of his or her undesired behavior.

Premack principle Also known as "Grandma's rule," this term refers to the contingency management technique in which a behavior is reinforced by allowing the individual to engage in a more attractive activity once the target behavior is completed.

rational-emotive therapy (RET) A therapy pioneered by Ellis in which patients are forced to confront and correct their own illogical thinking. In Ellis's scheme, a person's beliefs about events, rather than the events themselves, determine the problematic emotional or behavioral consequences.

rational restructuring An eclectic set of techniques that teaches individuals to examine their assumptions about situations or the world in general, and alter their ideas to be more realistic or rational.

relaxation A state of lowered anxiety, stress, and physiological arousal. Relaxation may be induced by tensing and then relaxing various muscle groups, or via breathing exercises, imagery exercises, or hypnosis.

response cost A form of aversion therapy in which positive reinforcers are removed following an undesired behavior.

shaping A contingency management technique in which a behavior is developed by first rewarding any behavior that approximates it, and then by selectively reinforcing behaviors that more and more resemble the target behavior.

stress-inoculation training A technique developed by Meichenbaum that attempts to prevent problems by "inoculating" patients to ongoing and future stressors. SIT involves educating patients about how certain appraisal patterns lead to stress, teaching them to identify and cope with potential stressors, rehearsing these coping skills in the therapy setting, and consolidating these skills by applying them across a range of real-life, stressful situations.

successive approximation Another term for shaping.

symptom substitution The notion that if a symptom is removed without attending to the underlying pathology of an illness, another symptom will emerge to take its place.

systematic desensitization A behavioral technique for reducing anxiety in which patients practice relaxation while visualizing anxiety-provoking situations of increasing intensity. In this way, the patient becomes "desensitized" to the feared stimulus.

time-out A contingency management technique in which a person is removed temporarily from the situation that is reinforcing the undesired behavior.

token economy A system in which desired behaviors are promoted through the strict control of reinforcements. Establishing such a system requires specifying the immediate reinforcers for each behavior, as well as the backup reinforcers for which patients can exchange their immediate reinforcers.

Web Sites of Interest

To visit any of these web sites listed below, go to www.wadsworth.com and click on Links.

14-1 Links to a variety of documents concerning empirically supported treatments

14-2 Association for the Advancement of Behavior Therapy (AABT)

14-3 The Beck Institute for Cognitive Therapy and Research

14-4 International Association for Cognitive Psychotherapy

14-5 Albert Ellis Institute. This web site includes a link through which you can submit a question to Dr. Ellis and view previous questions and answers.

CHAPTER FIFTEEN

Group Therapy, Family Therapy, and Couples Therapy

One could argue that most of the problems that bring patients to therapy are acquired and maintained in a social context. It is very likely that current emotional and behavioral problems have been influenced, to some degree, by past interpersonal dysfunction. A marital conflict, by definition, involves two people. An unassertive salesperson manifests his or her problem in interactions with customers. Therefore, inasmuch as the strands of human misery are woven so tightly into the fabric of social relationships, should we not consider forms of therapy that take place in a group or dyadic setting?

In addition, proponents maintain, group and family therapies are more economical. Seeing patients individually for therapy is, they argue, simply not a rational response to the mental health needs of society. The economics of health care has led many insurers to demand more efficient and less costly forms of mental health treatment. Whatever the reasons, a variety of methods for treating a number of patients at one time, including group therapy, family therapy, and couples therapy, have become increasingly popular. In this chapter, we will discuss group therapy, family therapy, and couples therapy in some detail.

Group Therapy

A Historical Perspective

For many years, group therapy was practiced as a method of choice by only a handful of dedicated therapists. Others used it primarily because their caseload was so heavy that group therapy was the only means by which they could deal with the overload. Still other therapists used group therapy as a supplementary technique. During individual therapy, for example, a therapist might work toward getting a patient to achieve insight into his pathological need to derogate women; then, during a group session, other members of the group might reinforce the therapist's interpretation through their reactions to the patient. Instead of being seen as a second choice or supplementary form of treatment,

however, group methods have now achieved considerably more visibility and respectability.

One of the earliest formal uses of group methods was Joseph H. Pratt's work with tubercular patients in 1905. This was an inspirational approach that used lectures and group discussion to help lift the spirits of depressed patients and promote their cooperation with the medical regimen. A major figure in the group movement was J. L. Moreno, who began to develop some group methods in Vienna in the early 1900s and, in 1925, introduced his psychodrama to the United States. Moreno also used the term *group therapy*. Trigant Burrow was a psychoanalyst who used the related term *group analysis* to describe his procedures (Rosenbaum, 1965). In the 1930s, Slavson encouraged adolescent patients to work through their problems with controlled play. His procedures were based on psychoanalytic concepts. These and other figures have been identified as pioneers of the group movement (American Group Psychotherapy Association, 1971; Lubin, 1976).

As was true for clinical psychology generally, it was the aftermath of World War II that really brought group methods to center stage. As we have observed before, the large number of war veterans sharply increased the demand for counseling and therapy. The limitations of the existing agency and hospital facilities made it necessary to use group methods to cope with the immediate demand. Once these methods had gained a foothold in the terrain of pragmatism, respectability was but a short distance away. As a result, nearly every school or approach to individual psychotherapy now has its group counterpart. There are group therapies based on psychoanalytic principles, Gestalt therapy principles, behavior therapy principles, and many other types as well.

Approaches to Group Therapy

Different approaches to group therapy have emanated from different theoretical origins, and the descriptions of group therapy are couched in a variety of theoretical languages. However, as we saw with individual psychotherapy, experienced group therapists of the same theoretical persuasion often use quite different methods. Because of this poor fit between what therapists do and where they come from theoretically, it is difficult to evaluate the similarities and differences among approaches and, indeed, to describe in any coherent way the methods used in a particular approach. Nevertheless, the following approaches seem fairly typical of the general group therapy movement.

Psychoanalytic Group Therapy. Most forms of psychoanalytic group therapy are basically psychoanalytic therapy carried out in a group setting. Although there are obvious differences from individual psychotherapy (for example, multiple transference effects, modified therapist-patient transference, and influences from one member to another), the focus is still on phenomena such as free association, transference, interpretation of resistance, and working through. Although one can hardly argue that group processes do not exist, their role is viewed as secondary to that of individual processes. The group becomes a vehicle through which the individual can express and eventually understand the operation of unconscious forces and defenses and thereby reach a higher level of adjustment.

Wolf (1975) has emphasized that psychoanalysis can occur in groups as well as on the individual couch. Wolf believes that the dynamics of the group are secondary to the individual analysis and that the role of the therapist is key. In contrast to individual psychotherapy, group therapy can permit a deeper analytic experience because individuals can "lean" on the group and thus increase their anxiety tolerance. In addition, group members react to one another, to the therapist, and to relationships of authority and intimacy. By observing how others in the group communicate with one another, by participating in a situation in which the individual is not the sole object of the therapist's attention, and by both receiving help from others and giving help to them, the individual can achieve an analysis that is more effective than it might be in the individual therapy setting.

Typically, Wolf's groups consist of eight to ten members (equal numbers of men and women) who meet for 90 minutes three times a week. Sometimes the group meets once or twice a week without the therapist so as to facilitate the working through of transference relationships. Patients often free-associate to their feelings about other members, report dreams, and analyze resistance and transference feelings toward both the therapist and other group members. The following excerpts illustrate *psychoanalytical group psychotherapy*.

A Case Illustration of Psychoanalytic Group Therapy

This particular group consists of three men (A, B, C), three women (X, Y, Z), and the therapist. The therapist is a psychoanalytically oriented psychiatrist. The meeting place is the therapist's office. He arranges chairs in a circle, seating himself behind his desk. He knows each of the members, having had them in individual treatment for from several to several hundred sessions. The group is to meet twice weekly, for an hour at a time, and is "closed"—that is, no new members will be permitted during the life of the group. Below, we present excerpts from the first and the tenth group sessions. The members do not know one another when the first session begins.

Session 1

Therapist: This is our first session in an experience that I hope will be helpful to each of you. None of you know each other, and I would like to introduce you. To my right is Mr. A. . . .

Now that we are through with introductions, I would like to explain how I think we should operate, and make some remarks that I hope will help us in getting the greatest value out of group psychotherapy.

Each of you has been in individual therapy with me. But we are starting here afresh.

I will not reveal in the group any information that I may have about you that I have obtained prior to today. In general, the same rules will hold as in individual therapy—that is to say, you will speak about whatever may be in your mind, and I will try to tell you whatever I see in your statements. You may try to analyze one another if you wish. I expect that each of you will respect each other's confidences. While I cannot give you any guarantees about the other members, I know each of you rather well, and I have every confidence in the integrity of each of you. But at the same time you will do well to use your good judgment on what to talk about.

I don't expect to talk in the future as much as I will today in the first session, but let me continue a bit more with some further information. First, psychotherapy is psychotherapy, no matter in which mode it is found. Essentially, it is a problem of self-understanding, learning what unconscious motives excite us to behavior. We want to attain insight, so that we will understand what is behind our behavior and our reactions. The goal of psychotherapy is increased satisfaction with ourselves and greater improvement in social behavior. Second, you may be somewhat suspicious about this method, and you think, as I know from talks with each of you, that it may be difficult for you to reveal yourself to others. I think you all share this feeling. However, if you will be able to defer judgment and share in the discussions, you may find that the group method will be valuable and more useful than you believe now. Third, the experience of being in the group per se may not be of value, unless you participate. As trite as this may seem, you will probably get no more out of the situation than you put in. And finally, we may experience all sorts of positive and negative attitudes about one another. These transferences are an essential part of psychotherapy, and you should not be upset if you go through these experiences.

I think that I have said enough, but let me conclude by saying that I am very optimistic about the potentialities of what we are doing, and that I have great hopes we shall all benefit. And so, let us now start.

Session 10

Therapist: Well, I guess we are all here and ought to begin. I wonder how things have been going with Miss Z? She seemed to be right in the midst of a problem when we stopped last session.

A: I was wondering about that too. I hoped that she was able to make out.

Z: Well, I thought quite a lot about what we discussed, and I am glad to say that I think I made progress. I realized that I was fighting with my mother because of resentment I had to her, and that I really did not love her as much as I thought. Then, it came to me, I was really too dependent on her and it would be much healthier if I were able to deal more realistically with her. After all, it wasn't good for her, either.

Y: Then you think you really don't love your mother?

Z: I wouldn't say that. What I think is true is that I am overly dependent on her, and that my resentment of her was really a resentment of myself because, because . . . no one really loves me. [Begins to cry]

X: I feel that Z is wrong. People can love her, just anybody can be loved, but in order to be loved, you have to love others.

A: Even in this group, Z seems to keep aloof and won't let others get too close to her.

Z: It is as though my mother and I formed a combination against the whole world. My father left her, and so she depended on me, and I was frightened of the world by her, and so the two of us were alone together, and I had little to do with anyone else. It is a pretty bad situation.

Therapist: Let us try to understand this. I think you are touching something of great value.

Both you and your mother formed a cabal against the world. I think you resent her complete possession of you. But now you are aware that it isn't only love you have for your mother, but also hatred. However, you begin to understand how you came to depend on your mother, and also how she came to depend on you. Finally, you are able to see how you have been emotionally enslaved by her. But it must be difficult to experience such emotions, and you must feel alone.[1]

Psychodrama. This is a form of role playing that was developed by Moreno (1946, 1959). The patients act out roles much as if they were in a play. This acting is said to bring about a degree of emotional relief (catharsis) and spontaneity that heightens insight and self-understanding. Patients may be asked to play themselves or another role. At times, they may be asked to switch roles in the midst of a dramatization. The drama may involve an event from the patient's past or an upcoming event toward which the patient looks with trepidation.

In general, *psychodrama* involves a patient, a stage on which the drama is played, a director or therapist, "auxiliary egos" (other patients, therapeutic aides, and others), and an audience. The director assigns the patient a role, and the supporting cast is made up of the auxiliary egos. The audience can provide acceptance and understanding, and may even participate contemporaneously.

Moreno contended that acting out a situation, listening to the responses of the auxiliary egos, and sensing the reactions of the audience lead to a deeper kind of catharsis and self-understanding. He believed that this is much more effective than simply "talking" to a therapist. Particularly for patients who are inhibited or lack social skills, psychodrama can lead to improved

---

[1]From *Methods of Group Psychotherapy*, by R. J. Corsini, pp. 160–161, 163–164. Copyright © 1957 by McGraw-Hill, Inc. Reprinted by permission of the author.

levels of self-expression and to the development of heightened social skills.

Transactional Analysis. Eric Berne (1961) was the developer of and the dynamic force behind *transactional analysis (TA)*. TA is essentially a process in which the interactions among the various aspects of the people in the group are analyzed. Analyses often focus on three chief "ego states" within each person: the Child ego state, the Parent ego state, and the Adult ego state. Each state is composed of positive and negative features. The positive Child is spontaneous, uninhibited, and creative. The negative Child is fearful, overly emotional, or full of guilt. On the positive side, the Parent state may be characterized as supportive, loving, or understanding. The negative Parent is punishing and quick to condemn. The Adult ego state is less oriented toward feelings and emotions and is more involved with logic, planning, or information gathering. But the Adult can be reasonable (positive) or nonspontaneous (negative).

Depending on how a person was raised, he or she will manifest various aspects of these positive and negative characteristics. A child who was oversupervised or overregulated by the parents might develop an inhibited or guilt-ridden ego state. As a result, if a person in the TA group setting discusses sex in a pompous, authoritative way, and the inhibited person is then asked to respond, she or he may be unable to do so or may respond under great tension. The therapist might then point out how each person is playing negative roles (either Child, Adult, or Parent). One person is playing a negative Parent role by being pompous and authoritative. The other person is responding in a negative Child fashion by being inhibited and tense. Repeated analyses of the interactions among group members reveal the ego states that they typically employ. These analyses lead the patients toward more rational, appropriate ways of thinking that are closer to the Adult ego state (positive).

The units that are analyzed are *transactions*—the stimuli and responses that are active between ego states in two or more people at any given moment. A transactional analysis involves the determination of which ego states are operative in a given transaction between people.

Another aspect of TA is the emphasis on *games* (Berne, 1964). Games are behaviors that people frequently use to avoid getting too close to other people. Such games are orderly transactions that contain ulterior motives. In TA group therapy, much effort is devoted to discovering and analyzing how the members play games with one another. Berne tends to believe that pseudo-intimacy rather than authentic intimacy characterizes TA groups. The games members play tend to cover their real feelings and beliefs. He sees one function of the therapist as that of a teacher who, through questions, interpretation, and even confrontation, tries to bring patients to the point where they can choose between games and more satisfying behavior. In a few instances, TA principles have also been used at an institutional level. For example, Jesness (1975) describes a TA program to rehabilitate institutionalized juvenile delinquents.

TA tends to be a swift-moving, action-oriented approach. There is an emphasis on the present, a sense of grappling with immediate problems, that makes it attractive to many patients and therapists. TA has an aura of responsibility, of learning how to choose between options, and this can be a desirable alternative to more traditional forms of group therapy that often appear to lumber along at an agonizingly slow pace. There is also a conceptual simplicity to the whole scheme that seems to make it understandable and perhaps more acceptable to patient and professional alike.

Yet this very simplicity, coupled with the zeal and entrepreneurship of some TA practitioners, has led to a popularization that can be dangerous. Critics argue that human problems are complex events that cannot easily be translated into games and that any gains from such procedures are therefore likely to be short-lived. Certainly there is little in the research literature to calm such fears, since TA therapists rarely produce research.

Gestalt Groups. *Gestalt group therapy* is difficult to categorize. Like psychoanalytic group therapy, it is oriented toward the experience of the individual patient. At the same time, its emphasis on resident seminars, weekend retreats, brief workshops, and general popularization give it a distinct flavor of the encounter movement (for example, Rogers, 1970). These features may have stemmed in part from the strong and at times flamboyant nature of Fritz Perls (the leader of the Gestalt movement), coupled with the considerable publicity that was given the Esalen Institute in Big Sur, California.

As we saw in Chapter 13, Gestalt therapy focuses on leading the patient to an awareness of the "now" and an appreciation of one's being in the world. In group therapy, this is achieved by concentrating on one member at a time. The therapist focuses on the patient, while the other group members serve as observers. This has been dubbed the "hot seat" approach. Patients are asked to experience their feelings and behavior—to lose their minds and find their senses. Other members of the group are not just passive observers; they may be called on to say how they regard the person in the hot seat. At times there are bits of role playing, the reporting of dreams, and dialogues between patients (Perls, 1973). But regardless of whether a member is an observer or in the hot seat, there tends to be intense involvement in the proceedings. As with TA methods, the popularization of the procedures, the lack of research on the results, and the emotionality involved all make it difficult to assess the effectiveness of Gestalt group therapy and to determine whether its effects generalize beyond the specific situation or weekend.

Behavior Therapy Groups. *Group behavior therapy* seems to have grown out of considerations of efficiency rather than any feeling that the dynamics of the group interaction would be especially valuable (Lazarus, 1975; Rose, 1991). It is entirely feasible to conduct desensitization sessions, model interpersonal skills, or use cognitive restructuring interventions in a group setting

(Rose, 1991). For example, it is possible to teach patients in a group setting how to relax, and it is equally possible to establish common anxiety hierarchies simultaneously with several patients. Where such procedures are feasible, it is certainly efficient to use them.

Behavioral and cognitive-behavioral groups are usually time limited (for example, 12 sessions) and are comprised of patients with similar problems. As in most behavior therapy treatments, these group members complete a number of assessment instruments before, during, and after treatment in order to monitor progress. Rose (1991) provides a number of examples of how reinforcement, modeling, problem solving, and cognitive interventions are implemented in behavior therapy groups. Research has supported the efficacy of behavioral and cognitive-behavioral group interventions for the treatment of depression, social skills deficits, pain, agoraphobia, and other conditions (Rose, 1991).

One kind of group behavior therapy that was not established mainly for efficiency is assertiveness training. Here, a group approach is usually the treatment of choice. Groups provide nonassertive individuals with an excellent environment in which to confront their problems, reduce their fear of being assertive, and learn acceptable methods of self-expression. Such groups typically involve direct teaching, with the therapist describing the group's goals and the problems that nonassertiveness can generate for people. Assertiveness training groups are usually also characterized by such features as cooperative problem solving, honesty, and acceptance among group members. Group members are provided with opportunities to comment and to criticize the manner in which they present themselves. New assertiveness skills are demonstrated and practiced, and homework assignments are often given, followed by group discussion of their success.

Time-Limited Group Therapy. The final example of a group approach that we will discuss is *time-limited group therapy* (Budman & Gurman,

1988). This contemporary model is appealing because of its efficiency, and it is likely to guide group interventions in the age of managed care. These groups typically meet on a weekly basis for a predetermined number of sessions (for example, eight sessions for a group consisting of members who are dealing with a life crisis). As described by Budman and Gurman (1988), time-limited groups are characterized by four central features:

1. *Pregroup preparation and screening.* A 1-hour pregroup workshop is used to evaluate and screen potential group members. This screening makes it more likely that, once the actual group begins, the group can "hit the ground running" and that group members have the requisite skills to contribute to the group and thus to benefit.

2. Establishing and maintaining a *working focus* in the group. The working focus is defined as a particular concern, problem, or issue that is shared by all group members (for example, problems with intimacy). The focus is introduced in the first group session. For example:

> As I've mentioned to all of you previously, this is a young adult group that will have as its central theme problems of intimacy. Members of this group have all, in one way or another, been struggling with these issues recently. Experience indicates that a short-term group like this one can be a very useful vehicle for helping people with such difficulties. Obviously, you all have other concerns as well as those related to intimacy. To the degree that it is possible, we will talk about some of these too. However, because of our limited time working together, we will need to remain focused for the most part on intimacy concerns. (Budman & Gurman, 1988, p. 269)

3. *Group cohesion.* Theorists and researchers are convinced that group cohesion (the degree to which group members are involved in the

process, trust each other, cooperate, focus, and express compassion) is an important determinant of outcome.

4. *Reactions to time limits.* Because these groups are time limited, group members may experience feelings related to life stage, to prior losses, and to frustration that more has not been accomplished in the group.

Budman and Gurman (1988) also analyze the different stages of the group (starting the group, early group development, termination, follow-up), because each stage presents the therapist with different challenges. For example, the termination stage is often characterized by the expression of sadness, and some group members may push for the therapist to extend the number of sessions. In this stage, the therapist's job is to review the positive changes in the group and in each individual (in reference to the working focus) and to have group members express their thoughts and feelings about what it will be like without the group. Budman and Gurman (1988) recommend a follow-up session (6 to 12 months after termination) to maintain the positive changes that took place and to demonstrate the changes group members have made on their own in the interim.

Box 15-1 describes the application of this approach to patients with personality disorders.

The Arrangements

Because of the wide variety of group approaches used by clinicians, it may be somewhat misleading to give a general description of the arrangements for group therapy. Despite the diversity of techniques, however, there are some general similarities. For example, most groups consist of five to ten patients who meet with the therapist at least once a week for 90-minute to two-hour sessions. The members are often seated in a circle, so that members can all see each other. Sometimes they are seated around a table, sometimes not.

The composition of the group may vary, depending both on the therapist's convictions and on practical considerations. Some therapists feel strongly that a heterogeneous group is best—one that includes women and men with a variety of problems, backgrounds, and personalities. Other therapists feel that homogeneous groups are best—groups composed, for example, exclusively of alcoholics or patients with phobias. They believe that homogeneity makes for greater efficiency, quicker understanding, and mutual acceptance (for example, Budman & Gurman, 1988). In institutional settings with large numbers of patients, it is relatively easy to establish homogeneous groups. In private practice, however, the therapist may have no alternative except to use heterogeneous groups. Most therapists agree that certain kinds of patients must generally be excluded. These include those with severe cognitive limitations, the grossly psychotic, and persons who are especially prone to disrupt the group process (for example, those who monopolize group discussions or are extremely antagonistic).

In some instances, the therapist sees all group members concurrently on an individual basis. In others, the therapist sees the patients only at group therapy meetings. At times, some therapists like to use a cotherapist (often a therapist of the opposite sex who will add another dimension to such processes as transference). Some groups meet occasionally without a therapist. Whatever the exact format, the role of the group leader is critical. In some groups, there are prohibitions against extracurricular fraternizing; other therapists feel that such prohibitions are unrealistic. Open groups admit a new member whenever someone leaves the group; closed groups admit no new members once the group has begun to function. Issues of confidentiality in group therapy can be important. In explaining the arrangements and "rules" of the group to group members, the therapist may find it necessary to state that though it is hoped that all members will maintain the confidentiality of the sessions, no final guarantees can be offered (see the case illustration earlier in the chapter).

BOX 15-1

Time-Effective Group Psychotherapy for Patients with Personality Disorders

Budman et al. (1996) discussed how group psychotherapy can be particularly effective and useful for a group of patients that are often seen as among the most difficult to treat—those with Axis II personality disorders. Group therapy offers special advantages with these patients:

- The patients' social/interpersonal behavior can be observed directly (for example, being hostile and critical of others).
- Group members can provide on-the-spot feedback regarding the adaptive and maladaptive aspects of a patient's interpersonal behavior (for example, "When you said that I don't know what I am talking about, I felt hurt and angry at you").
- Patients have a chance to modify their interpersonal behavior in a group setting.
- Peer pressure may encourage the individual group member to decrease problematic behaviors (for example, verbally lashing out at others) and to increase more adaptive responses (for example, telling another member that she or he felt hurt by a particular comment).
- The group essentially serves as "a social microcosm of the 'real-world'" (Budman et al., 1996, p. 331).

A number of other features are noteworthy. Budman et al.'s (1996) time-effective group psychotherapy (1) has an interpersonal focus;

(2) requires the therapist/leader to actively facilitate the group process (for example, "jump-starting" the group, setting limits on actions that are destructive to the group); (3) is time limited in order to encourage change; (4) encourages patient responsibility, goal setting, and monitoring of progress toward the goals; (5) uses homework assignments to encourage change; and (6) uses session summaries to tie together group process, recurring themes, and individual progress.

Group members are evaluated for appropriateness based on an extensive screening (via an individual session with the group leader) and a pregroup workshop in which all prospective members meet to introduce themselves, to complete small-group tasks (for example, role-playing problematic interpersonal behaviors and then alternative behaviors), and to complete a whole-group exercise (for example, planning a party). In this way, the group leader can assess each prospective member's appropriateness for the group: Does he respond well to limit setting? Does she use feedback appropriately? Is he able to engage with other group members?

Budman et al. (1996) report that such a treatment is likely to lead to better affective control, the development of better coping skills, and improved interpersonal behavior in patients with personality disorders.

The Curative Factors

The diversity of group approaches is apparent. Yet underlying all of them are common threads that speak to the utility of group therapy. Yalom (1975) has specified a set of *curative factors* that seems to define the essence of what these group methods offer:

1. *Imparting information.* Group members can receive advice and guidance not just from the therapist but also from other group members.
2. *Instilling hope.* Observing others who have successfully grappled with problems helps to instill hope—a necessary ingredient for any successful therapy experience.
3. *Universality.* Listening to others, one discovers that he or she has the same problems, fears, and concerns. Knowing that one is not alone can be highly rewarding.
4. *Altruism.* In the beginning, a group member often feels useless and demoralized. As it becomes apparent that one can help others in the group, a feeling of greater self-value and competence emerges.
5. *Interpersonal learning.* Interacting with others in the group can teach one about interpersonal relationships, social skills, sensitivity to others, resolution of conflicts, and so on.
6. *Imitative behavior.* Watching and listening to others can lead to the modeling of more useful behaviors. Group members learn from one another.
7. *Corrective recapitulation of the primary family.* The group context can help clients understand and resolve problems related to family members. The effects of past family experiences can be dissolved by learning that maladaptive coping methods will not work in the present group situation.
8. *Catharsis.* Learning how to express feelings about others in the group in an honest, open way builds a capacity for mutual trust and understanding.
9. *Group cohesiveness.* Group members become a tightly knit little group that enhances self-esteem through group acceptance.

Does Group Therapy Work?

Reviews of the research literature assessing the effectiveness of group psychotherapy consistently conclude that group treatment is more effective than no treatment (for example, Bednar & Kaul, 1994). However, group treatments do not appear to be any more effective than other forms of psychotherapy. The major advantage of group therapy is that it is more efficient and more economical, especially the time-limited group treatments.

Unfortunately, research on group therapy has not advanced much beyond answering the general question of overall effectiveness (Bednar & Kaul, 1994; Riva & Smith, 1997). Although theorists such as Yalom have proposed a variety of "curative factors" or other variables that may influence outcome in group treatment (for example, group leadership style, the necessity of pregroup training), relatively few studies have been conducted that critically examine the effect of these factors. The studies that have been completed are plagued with a number of conceptual and methodological problems. Clearly, more research investigating the process of group psychotherapy and the proposed curative factors is needed in order to better understand why and how group therapy works (Bednar & Kaul, 1994; Rose, 1991).

The Future of Group Therapy

Despite the economy and efficiency of group treatments, they appear to be underutilized. One major reason is that clients and therapists alike tend to view group therapy as a second-choice form of treatment. Fewer clients are referred for group therapy as compared with other forms of treatment, and even those who are referred may not follow through and join a group.

Managed behavioral health care is likely to make group therapy a more viable option in the future (Steenbarger & Budman, 1996). Group therapy is attractive to therapists and managed care organizations because it can save staff time (and ultimately money) in the care of less severely disturbed patients (MacKenzie, 1994), and it offers an alternative to inpatient treatment in some cases (Steenbarger & Budman, 1996). However, to take advantage of these opportunities, group therapists need to better educate the public and health care professionals about this mode of treatment, aggressively lobby governments

PROFILE 15-1

Simon H. Budman, Ph.D.

Dr. Simon H. Budman is the founder and president of Innovative Training Systems, a private company that provides consultation, training, and products to health care providers and institutions. Dr. Budman has held numerous academic and hospital appointments as well, and he has been intimately involved in implementing managed behavioral health care at several institutions. Dr. Budman is well known for his work in the areas of time-effective (time-limited) treatment, group psychotherapy, and psychotherapy research. He has authored more than 100 books, chapters, and articles, as well as several videotapes used in training health care professionals. Dr. Budman has received more than 25 federal grants to support his research in substance abuse, eating disorders, smoking cessation, and many other areas. We asked Dr. Budman several questions about his background, his interests and expertise, and his predictions for the field of clinical psychology and for group psychotherapy.

What originally interested you in the field of clinical psychology?

I had planned to be a physician from the time I was in elementary school. This was mostly based on my experiences with the two local doctors in the town in which I grew up. This was during the 1950s, when doctors still made house calls and had no high-tech tools and

little more than penicillin at their disposal. Also, there was no managed care, nor productivity pressures on most of them. An important part of a doctor's intervention at that time was talking to people! I naively believed that this was what being a doctor was about. Entering college in the 1960s as a premed student, I was quickly disillusioned to find that my courses had more to do with biology and chemistry than with people and their behaviors. I quickly quit premed as a major and wandered through a half-dozen other possibilities before a college career counselor told me about clinical psychology and introduced me to a psychologist at the counseling center. My love for psychology was immediate. It had all of the components and more that I thought would exist in medicine, but didn't. I have never had a day of regret since that time about my career choice.

Describe what activities you are involved in as a clinical psychologist.

I started out doing mostly direct clinical work in individual, group, and family therapy (all of which I still do.) Over the years, however, my activities changed and diversified. I began to do clinical research shortly after graduate school and have done, and continue to do, numerous clinical trials. I also do extensive training, clinical consulting, and organizational consulting. At present, I am the president of a company that does consulting and training and develops new health care products. In this role, I do a lot of administration, research, marketing, business development, and training. A large part of my time is now spent developing multimedia health care programs and health-related web sites, writing grants, raising money for the company, and working with teams of psychologists, programmers, businesspeople, and so on. I would never have imagined, even ten years ago, the types of things I would be doing that are related (both directly and indirectly) to my psychology training.

(continued)

Profile 15-1 *(continued)*

What are your particular areas of expertise or interest?

At present, I am most interested in population-based health interventions, preventive behavioral health care, behavioral oncology, substance abuse treatment and prevention, and the use of computers, the Internet, and multimedia technology in health care. I have written or cowritten video programs and multimedia games for teens.

What are the future trends you see for clinical psychology?

I think that the future is grave unless clinical psychology is flexible and can "reinvent" itself. Social workers, nurses, and master's-level counselors will do more of the outpatient and inpatient therapy that goes on in this country. Jobs for clinical psychologists will become scarcer than they are already. Incomes will go

down. I foresee a grim future, unless psychologists learn unique skills such as how to intervene with populations of people and how to use new technologies in support of such interventions. Although I believe that there will always be a need for clinical psychologists to provide direct clinical care, there is currently a glut of providers in this country who can offer such services. Clinical psychology will look very different ten years from now than it does today. If it doesn't reinvent itself, it will blend in with and be indistinct from the other behavioral health professions.

What are some future trends for group therapy?

I think that more services will be provided in the context of groups. It is cost-effective, and the outcomes look favorable when compared with individual treatment.

and managed behavioral health care companies to financially support group therapy as a service, and better educate themselves about managed care and the health care needs that remain unfulfilled (Steenbarger & Budman, 1996).

Family Therapy and Couples Therapy

Generally, when a member of a family develops a problem, everyone in the family is affected. Increasingly, families are going into therapy as units in an attempt to fathom the nature of their difficulties and the means by which to deal with them. Family and couples therapy is a burgeoning field, as indicated by the numerous handbooks and overviews of the field that appear every year. Further evidence of this interest is the special sections on the treatment of families and

couples that appear frequently in clinical journals such as the *Journal of Consulting and Clinical Psychology.*

Many years ago, a number of psychotherapists recognized that therapy for a child was often just an excuse to get the parents into the clinic for "therapeutic" interviews. For example, it was not unusual to schedule therapy for the child twice a week. During that time, the child would finger-paint, engage in expressive play, or do other things that were assumed to have cathartic, therapeutic value. However, many clinicians recognized intuitively that it made little sense to work with a child two hours a week and then send the child back to an unchanged home environment—the environment that may have contributed to the development of the problem in the first place. Consequently, it became common practice to talk with the parents during the time that the child was in the clinic playroom.

Indeed, many clinicians came to believe that those interviews were more responsible than the playroom experiences for improvements in the child's behavior. Such clinical experiences paved the way for the development of the *family therapy* movement.

The Development of Family Therapy

Fruzzetti and Jacobson (1991) trace the origins of family therapy to the nineteenth-century social work movement. However, family therapy did not immediately gain prominence. It was not until the mid-twentieth century that family therapy became a popular form of treatment. Some of the delay had to do with the long-standing dominance of psychoanalysis. The perspectives of behaviorism and humanism paved the way for an alternative treatment like family therapy to become a viable option for clinicians. The problems of individuals were conceptualized in systemic terms, as a manifestation of some type of family dysfunction. This new perspective on clinical problems was most evident in some of the conceptualizations of severe mental disorders such as schizophrenia.

In trying to understand schizophrenia, a Palo Alto research group (Bateson, Jackson, Haley, Satir, and others) approached the problem from a communication point of view. To influence one family member, one must deal with the entire family system (Jackson & Weakland, 1961). Related to the idea of the family as a unit is the concept of the *double bind* (Bateson, Jackson, Haley, & Weakland, 1956). For example, a child might be told by a father, "Always stand up for your rights, no matter who, no matter what!" But the same father tells the same child, "Never question my authority; I am your father, and what I say goes!" The contradiction inherent in the two messages ensures that no matter what the child does in relation to the father, it will be wrong. According to the Bateson group, the contradiction, the father's failure to admit that there is a contradiction, and the lack of support from other family members can provide fertile soil for the development of schizophrenia. Actually,

there is very little empirical support for the double-bind theory of schizophrenia. Indeed, there has been a failure even to establish such communications as reliable phenomena. But the hypothesis was a remarkably fertile one, because it nourished much of the Palo Alto family therapy work. This illustrates the point that the value of concepts and research does not reside exclusively in their rightness or wrongness. Their heuristic value—that is, the extent to which they stimulate new work, new ideas, or new procedures—is also important.

Theodore Lidz and his research team also emphasized the family in the etiology of schizophrenia (Lidz, Cornelison, Fleck, & Terry, 1957a, 1957b). When marriage partners fail to meet each other's psychological and emotional needs, one partner may form a pathological alliance with the child, ultimately precipitating the child's schizophrenia. Bowen's (1960) observation of schizophrenic patients who lived together with their parents in a hospital ward for sustained periods led to the conclusion that the entire family unit was pathogenic, not just the patient. Ackerman (1958, 1966) reached similar conclusions. This work is important not because it explained the etiology of schizophrenia (it did not), but because such work and that of Satir (1967a), Haley (1971), Jackson (1957), and Bell (1961) gave impetus and direction to the family therapy movement—a movement rich in technique, theory, and history.

The Concept of Communication

From the time of its origins in the work on schizophrenia, family therapy has emphasized *communication*. Pathology has typically been seen as a failure of communication among family members. This communication focus can be seen in what many regard as the central concept in family therapy—*general systems theory*. Family therapy deals with the relationship between the individual family member and the family system. The family is conceived of as a system, which family therapy seeks to alter in some important way. The emphasis is not on the person's overt pathological symptoms or dysfunction or on purported intrapsychic conflicts. An overactive id, for example, is not considered the cause of sexual problems. Rather, the individual experiences problems because of a lack of information. Therapy is a process of correcting this lack of information or changing the manner of feedback. The therapist achieves positive change, not from an awareness of the patient's intrapsychic conflicts, but by using feedback that alters the way the system functions. Others, such as Bowen (1960), see communication as something that is subsumed under a larger system of relationships.

Ackerman (1958, 1960, 1966) occupies a position midway between the individual or intrapsychic approach to pathology and the systems approach that characterizes the communication theorists. He believes that there is a constant interchange among the patient, the family, and society. Full understanding of the patient requires an appreciation of this interchange. Although Ackerman attaches great importance to the communication process in the family system, he also regards the content of that communication as extremely important.

Forms and Methods

There is no clear, consensual definition of what constitutes family therapy. Indeed, there is not even a consensus on who should conduct it. The general procedures of family therapy are carried on by psychologists, psychiatrists, social workers, counselors, and others. Family therapists and counselors are trained in several different programs, including clinical psychology, counseling psychology, psychiatry, social work, family and child development, and education. All of this, of course, makes for considerable confusion and some squabbling over professional credentials. Some therapists use family therapy as only one of several techniques; others are exclusively family therapists. With so little agreement as to who is qualified to conduct family therapy, is it any wonder that the specific techniques employed (which actually seem to have much in common) are given such distinctive titles? Thus,

we have *family therapy, behavioral family therapy, conjoint family therapy, concurrent family therapy, collaborative family therapy, network family therapy, structural family therapy, multiple family therapy,* and on and on. Theoretical approaches range from the systemic, to the psychodynamic, to the behavioral, and on to those that purport to integrate various theoretical practices.

The Goals. Most family therapists share the primary goal of improving communication within the family and deemphasize the problems of the individual in favor of treating the problems of the family as a whole. However, once we get beyond such general statements, there seems to be some disarray of purposes and goals. For example, many therapists who talk about the family system still seem to view family therapy as a kind of context in which to solve an individual's problems. Seeing the family together becomes a technique (perhaps a more efficient one) for inducing changes in the individual patient. Other family therapists are devoted to the philosophy that regarding the family as a unit and working with it as such will enhance that unit. Although this may benefit the individual members, the real focus is on the family. As in most enterprises, the largest number of family therapists falls somewhere between the two extremes.

Some General Characteristics. Certain aspects of family therapy differentiate it from the customary individual therapy. For example, family members have a shared frame of reference, a common history, and a shared language of connotations that may be foreign to the therapist. The therapist has to learn the family roles and something about the family's idiosyncratic subculture. This information is used to enhance communication or to confront family members. At the same time, the therapist must remain detached and not become overly identified with one faction of the family at the expense of another. This can be a difficult and delicate task, for often family members will attempt to use the therapist in their power struggles or in their defenses against open communication.

A history and assessment process is a typical part of family therapy. The presenting problem must be stated and understood. It may be that a son is a delinquent or a daughter is sexually promiscuous. It is often interesting and diagnostically important to see how different family members construe the same problem in quite divergent ways. Usually a family history will be taken. This, too, can have ramifications. When the family problem is placed in the larger context of information about the parents' origins and their early life and marriage, children can often attain improved communication and understanding. Laying out the entire panorama of family history—its extended members and their goals, aspirations, fears, and frailties—can lead to deeper understanding, empathy, and tolerance. This larger context can promote a shared frame of reference that was not possible earlier. A child can begin to learn what it meant for the mother to relinquish her own aspirations in favor of the family, what it meant for the father to experience abuse from his own father. In the controlled setting of the family therapy room, the parents may, at the same time, remember (via the current experience of their children) what it was like to encounter peer pressure.

Conjoint Family Therapy

In *conjoint family therapy*, the entire family is seen at the same time by one therapist. In some varieties of this approach, the therapist plays a rather passive, nondirective role. In other varieties, the therapist is an active force, directing the conversation, assigning tasks to various family members, imparting direct instruction regarding human relations, and so on.

Satir (1967a, 1967b) regarded the family therapist as a resource person who observes the family process in action and then becomes a model of communication to the family through clear, crisp communication. Thus, Satir viewed the therapist as a teacher, a resource person, and a communicator. Such a therapist illustrates to family members how they can communicate better and thereby bring about more satisfying relationships. The following excerpts from Satir (1967a) clarify the interaction process for a family.

A Case Illustration of Conjoint Family Therapy

Therapist: (to husband) I notice your brow is wrinkled, Ralph. Does that mean you are angry at this moment?

Husband: I did not know that my brow was wrinkled.

Therapist: Sometimes a person looks or sounds in a way of which he is not aware. As far as you can tell, what were you thinking and feeling just now?

Husband: I was thinking over what she [his wife] said.

Therapist: What thing that she said were you thinking about?

Husband: When she said that when she was talking so loud, she wished I would tell her.

Therapist: What were you thinking about that?

Husband: I never thought about telling her. I thought she would get mad.

Therapist: Ah, then maybe that wrinkle meant you were puzzled because your wife was hoping you would do something and you did not know she had this hope? Do you suppose that by your wrinkled brow you were signaling that you were puzzled?

Husband: Yeah, I guess so.

Therapist: As far as you know, have you ever been in that same spot before, that is, where you were puzzled by something Alice said or did?

Husband: Hell, yes, lots of times.

Therapist: Have you ever told Alice you were puzzled when you were?

Wife: He never says anything.

Therapist: (smiling, to Alice) Just a minute, Alice, let me hear what Ralph's idea is of what he does. Ralph, how do you think you have let Alice know when you are puzzled?

Husband: I think she knows.

Therapist: Well, let's see. Suppose you ask Alice if she knows.

Husband: This is silly.

Therapist: (smiling) I suppose it might seem so in this situation, because Alice is right here and certainly has heard what your question is. She knows what it is. I have the suspicion, though, that neither you nor Alice are very sure about what the other expects, and I think you have not developed ways to find out. Alice, let's go back to when I commented on Ralph's wrinkled brow. Did you happen to notice it, too?

Wife: (complaining) Yes, he always looks like that.

Therapist: What kind of message did you get from that wrinkled brow?

Wife: He don't want to be here. He don't care. He never talks. Just looks at television or he isn't home.

Therapist: I'm curious. Do you mean that when Ralph has a wrinkled brow that you take this as Ralph's way of saying, "I don't love you, Alice. I don't care about you, Alice"?

Wife: (exasperated and tearfully) I don't know.

Therapist: Well, maybe the two of you have not yet worked out crystal-clear ways of giving your love and value messages to each other. Everyone needs crystal-clear ways of giving their value messages. (to son) What do you know, Jim, about how you give your value messages to your parents?

Son: I don't know what you mean.

Therapist: Well, how do you let your mother, for instance, know that you like her, when you are feeling that way. Everyone feels different ways at different times. When you are feeling glad your mother is around, how do you let her know?

Son: I do what she tells me to do. Work and stuff.

Therapist: I see, so when you do your work at home, you mean this for a message to your mother that you're glad she is around.

Son: Not exactly.

Therapist: You mean you are giving a different message then. Well, Alice, did you take this message from Jim to be a love message? (to Jim) What do you do to give your father a message that you like him?

Son: (after a pause) I can't think of nothing.

Therapist: Let me put it another way. What do you know crystal-clear that you could do that would bring a smile on your father's face?

Son: I could get better grades in school.

Therapist: Let's check this out and see if you are perceiving clearly. Do you, Alice, get a love message from Jim when he works around the house?

Wife: I s'pose—he doesn't do very much.

Therapist: So from where you sit, Alice, you don't get many love messages from Jim. Tell me, Alice, does Jim have any other ways that he might not now be thinking about that he has that say to you that he is glad you are around?

Wife: (softly) The other day he told me I looked nice.

Therapist: What about you, Ralph, does Jim perceive correctly that if he got better grades you would smile?

Husband: I don't imagine I will be smiling for some time.

Therapist: I hear that you don't think he is getting good grades, but would you smile if he did?

Husband: Sure, hell, I would be glad.

Therapist: As you think about it, how do you suppose you would show it?

Wife: You never know if you ever please him.

Therapist: We have already discovered that you and Ralph have not yet developed crystal-clear ways of showing value feelings toward one another. Maybe you, Alice, are now observing this between Jim and Ralph. What do you think, Ralph? Do you suppose it would be hard for Jim to find out when he has pleased you?[2]

In conjoint and other forms of family therapy, there are five basic modes of communication (Satir, 1975): placating (always agreeing, no matter what is going on); blaming (a person's way of showing how much he or she can criticize another and thus throw his or her weight around); super-reasonable (especially characteristic of teachers, whose words may come out "super-reasonable" but may bear no relationship to how they feel); irrelevant (the words are completely unrelated to what is going on); congruent (the words relate to what is real). These modes of communication provide, in a sense, the essence of communication and feeling. They do not negate the role of cognitions, but they do place the emphasis where Satir believed it belongs.

Other Varieties of Family Therapy

There are many other versions of family therapy. The following are a sample of the more commonly encountered versions.

Concurrent Family Therapy. In *concurrent family therapy*, one therapist sees all family members, but in individual sessions. The overall goals are the same as those in conjoint therapy. In some instances, the therapist may conduct traditional psychotherapy with the principal patient but also occasionally see other members of the family. As a matter of fact, it is perhaps unfortunate that the last variation is not used more often as a part of traditional psychotherapy. Because it is often the case that an individual patient's problems can be understood better and dealt with better in collaboration with significant others in

the patient's life, the use of such arrangements should facilitate the therapeutic process.

Collaborative Family Therapy. In *collaborative family therapy*, each family member sees a different therapist. The therapists then get together to discuss their patients and the family as a whole. As we saw earlier, the use of this approach with child patients was one of the factors that stimulated the early growth of family therapy. In a variation of this general approach, cotherapists are sometimes assigned to work with the same family. That is, two or more therapists meet with the family unit.

Behavioral Approaches to Family Therapy. Some clinicians (for example, Liberman, 1970; Patterson, 1971) have viewed family relations in terms of reinforcement contingencies. The role of the therapist is to generate a behavioral analysis of family problems. This analysis helps identify the behaviors whose frequency should be increased or decreased as well as the rewards that are maintaining undesirable behaviors or that will enhance desired behaviors. *Behavioral family therapy* then becomes a process of inducing family members to dispense the appropriate reinforcements to one another for the desired behaviors. Indeed, some therapists (Stuart, 1969) even have family members use tokens for this purpose. For example, a husband might earn four tokens if he does not watch Sunday football on TV and instead takes his wife for a drive in the country. Of course, it must be made clear in advance exactly what these tokens may be exchanged for later!

Given the recent developments in cognitive-behavioral therapy, it is not surprising that this approach has found its way into the family therapy enterprise. Similar to cognitive-behavioral therapy for the individual, the family "version" involves teaching individual family members to self-monitor problematic behaviors and patterns of thinking, to develop new skills (communication, problem resolution, negotiation, managing conflict), and to challenge interpretations of family events and reframe these inter-

[2]Virginia Satir, *Conjoint Family Therapy*, 2nd ed., 1967, pp. 97–100. Science and Behavior Books, Inc. Palo Alto, CA. USA 1-415-965-0954.

pretations if necessary (Carlson, Sperry, & Lewis, 1997; Epstein, Schlesinger, & Dryden, 1988).

Other Forms. In network family group therapy (Speck & Attneave, 1971), the therapist works with the entire "network" of important persons in the patient's life (neighbors, employers, friends, family, and so on). Obviously, such therapy requires a high degree of cooperation on the part of interested persons.

Multiple impact therapy (MacGregor, Ritchie, Serrano, & Schuster, 1964) involves two days of very intensive work with the entire family on the part of a clinic team of professionals. Working in sessions with individual family members, the team examines the marriage, the role of authority, the views of the children regarding the family, and other factors. Typically, a six-month follow-up is conducted to assess the family's progress.

In multiple-family therapy (Strelnick, 1977) several couples or families meet as a group with a therapist. The notion is that sharing experiences will enable each couple or family to help the other couples or families. This is a sort of cross between family therapy and group therapy.

Another approach is typified by the Homebuilders program developed in Tacoma, Washington (Kinney, Madsen, Fleming, & Haapala, 1977). In this program, a therapist who is on call 24 hours a day will enter the home of a family in crisis to help prevent the removal of family members to alternative living situations (such as institutionalization). The therapist can remain within the home as long as is required within a six-week period.

Structural family therapy (Minuchin, 1974) is oriented toward the resolution of immediate problems while stressing the manner in which authority is arranged in the family. Matters concerning the development of the marriage and the family are also emphasized.

When Family Therapy?

There are no hard-and-fast rules as to when family therapy is appropriate and when it is not.

Most often, family therapy is begun with an adolescent as the principal patient. Perhaps the patient's problems are so tied up with the family that family therapy is really the only sensible course. Perhaps the family has impeded therapeutic progress in the past or has resisted the therapist's advice. It is hoped that involving the entire family in the therapy network can dissolve some of this resistance.

In other cases, the patient's problems (or sometimes even the patient's improvement in therapy!) have so involved or threatened the fabric of the family that it seems wise to treat the family as a whole. Sometimes, family crises, such as the death of a family member, propel the entire family unit into pathology almost as one. In some families, there are conflicts over values. For example, an adolescent who begins to take drugs or becomes totally absorbed in a cult or a different religion may disrupt the entire family by seeming to undermine its values. In such instances, family therapy may be a logical recourse.

Finally, significant marital or sexual problems may be resolved best by a form of family therapy. It can, of course, be difficult to determine whether individual, family, or couples therapy should be undertaken as a way of working out such problems. However, family therapy or couples counseling would seem appropriate when the problems do not seem to stem from deep-seated emotional conflicts but from matters that can be dealt with educationally, including misguided attitudes, poor knowledge about sexuality, or lack of communication.

However, family therapy is not a cure-all, and it is not always appropriate. It sometimes happens that a family is so disrupted that such intervention would clearly be doomed to fail. It may also happen that one or more family members will simply refuse to cooperate. In some instances, it quickly becomes clear that a given family member is so disturbed, so uncooperative, or so disruptive that the entire process of family therapy would be poisoned by his or her presence.

Since family therapy involves several people, one must sometimes consider its possible use in cost-benefit terms. Although family therapy might benefit the identified patient of the group, the process could have malignant consequences for some of the other members. Like individual patients, some families simply do not possess the psychological strength or resources to cope with the threatening material that may come out in family therapy sessions. Deciding when to use family therapy and when not to is often a difficult matter that requires careful assessment and a great deal of clinical sensitivity.

Couples Therapy

Although we use the term *couples therapy*, this approach is not limited to married couples, but can be provided to unmarried couples, same-sex couples, and others. There are many issues that bring couples in to consult with a clinician. In one sense, couples therapy can be construed as a form of family therapy. For example, when a husband and wife are seen together and the focus of treatment is on the marital relationship rather than on the problems of the individuals, a form of family therapy seems to be involved.

Although the couples therapy movement, like the family therapy movement, owes much to interpersonal theorists such as Sullivan, Horney, and Fromm, the development of couples therapy as a discipline can be attributed to pragmatic concerns (Fruzzetti & Jacobson, 1991). Essentially, a wide variety of professionals (including doctors and lawyers), in the course of carrying out their normal professional duties, became increasingly involved in attempting to resolve marital conflicts. Fruzzetti and Jacobson (1991) note the remarkable growth of couples therapy since the 1960s. Today, the most popular forms of couples therapy are behavioral marital therapy, cognitive couples therapy, emotionally focused couples therapy, sex therapy, and insight-oriented (psychodynamic) couples therapy. To give the reader a flavor of what techniques are used in couples therapy, we will briefly describe behavioral marital therapy (Jacobson & Margolin, 1979; Stuart, 1980; Weiss, Hops, & Patterson, 1973) and emotionally focused couples therapy (Johnson, Hunsley, Greenberg, & Schindler, 1999).

Behavioral Marital Therapy. The beginnings of *behavioral marital therapy (BMT)* are often traced to the work of Richard Stuart (1969). (Again, despite the use of the term *marital*, BMT does not require that the partners to be married.) Stuart's treatment of marital dysfunction involved the application of reinforcement principles to couple's interactions. A major component of his treatment was a technique called *contingency contracting*; spouses were trained to modify their own behavior in order to effect a specific desired change in their mate's behavior.

Over the years, BMT has broadened to include a number of additional techniques. *Support-understanding techniques* aim to increase positive behaviors emitted by partners, increase collaboration within the couple, and increase positive feelings in each partner. For example, each partner generates a list of behaviors that, if produced by his or her mate, will bring pleasure. Next, each partner agrees to perform three of the behaviors from her or his partner's list before the next session. *Problem-solving techniques* involve training couples in positive communication skills so that effective decision making and negotiating are possible. For example, couples are given a list of basic rules of positive communication skills, and then "practice" these skills within the session. The clinician intervenes if she or he thinks it will be helpful (for example, clarifying the appropriate communication skills, modeling alternative ways to communicate that are more positive). These and other BMT strategies are described in more detail in a number of sources (for example, Gottman, Notarius, Gonso, & Markman, 1976; Jacobson & Margolin, 1979; Stuart, 1980).

Emotionally Focused Couples Therapy. *Emotionally focused couples therapy (EFT)* is a brief treatment that seeks to change partners' problematic interaction styles and emotional responses so that a stronger and more secure emotional bond can be established (Johnson et al.,

---

BOX 15-2

The Nine Steps of Emotionally Focused Couples Therapy (EFT)

Cycle De-escalation

Step 1. Assessment—creating an alliance and explicating the core issues in the couple's conflict using an attachment perspective.

Step 2. Identifying the problem interactional cycle that maintains attachment insecurity and relationship distress.

Step 3. Accessing the unacknowledged emotions underlying interactional positions.

Step 4. Reframing the problem in terms of the cycle, the underlying emotions, and attachment needs.

Changing Interactional Positions

Step 5. Promoting identification with disowned needs and aspects of self and integrating these into relationship interactions.

Step 6. Promoting acceptance of the partner's new construction of experience in the relationship and new responses.

Step 7. Facilitating the expression of specific needs and wants and creating emotional engagement.

Consolidation/Integration

Step 8. Facilitating the emergence of new solutions to old problematic relationship issues.

Step 9. Consolidating new positions and new cycles of attachment behavior. (p. 70)

Source: Johnson, S. M., Hunsley, J., Greenberg, L., & Schindler, D. (1999). Emotionally focused couples therapy: Status and challenges. Clinical Psychology: Science and Practice, 6, 67–79. Copyright 1999, American Psychological Association. Reprinted with permission.

1999). This treatment approach assumes that negative affect and associated destructive interactional styles create marital distress. Further, it is believed that a more secure attachment to one's partner is necessary to stabilize a dyadic relationship.

Johnson et al. (1999) have outlined the nine treatment steps in EFT (see Box 15-2). The first four steps involve assessment of the couple and attempts to interrupt the cycle of negative interactions. The next three steps involve helping create new, more adaptive interactional styles that meet partners' needs. Finally, the last two steps of EFT involve the consolidation of changes made.

Through these steps, partners are better able to recognize their own emotional and bonding needs, and to modify the way they interact with each other. In this way, they can ensure that these needs are more likely to be met and that destructive interactional patterns are minimized.

Are Family Therapy and Couples Therapy Effective?

As with other forms of psychotherapy, it is important to evaluate the empirical evidence that speaks to the efficacy of different forms of family and couples therapy. Before presenting these data, however, it is important to note that the measurement of outcome in family and couples therapy is complex because of the multiple perspectives that must be considered (different family members, both spouses). As in individual psychotherapy research, self-report measures,

TABLE 15-1 Average Effect Size (ES) and Percentile Equivalent for Selected Forms of Family Therapy and Couples Therapy

Type of Therapy	Mean ES	Percentile Equivalent[*]
Any Type of Family Therapy	0.47	68%
Behavioral/Psychoeducational	0.44	67%
Systemic	0.25	60%
Humanistic	0.29	61%
Eclectic	0.55	71%
Any Type of Couples Therapy	0.60	73%
Behavioral/Psychoeducational	0.74	77%
Systemic	0.62	73%
Humanistic	0.12	55%
Eclectic	0.63	74%

*Percentile equivalent indicates the percentage of those not receiving treatment whose outcome is exceeded by those receiving the treatment in question.

Source: Adapted from Shadish et al. (1993) with permission.

ratings by others (such as the therapist), and observational ratings are used extensively in family and couples therapy research.

Family Therapy. Despite the popularity of family therapy in clinical practice, relatively few well-controlled empirical studies have been conducted to evaluate its effectiveness. A recent meta-analysis of this literature (Shadish et al., 1993) computed only 44 effect sizes from published articles and unpublished dissertations (years 1963–1988) that evaluated the efficacy of family therapy. The average effect size for any form of family therapy was .47, indicating that the average treated client was functioning better than 68% of those individuals not receiving treatment. Shadish et al. also reported average effect sizes separately for various types of family therapy. Eclectic (combinations of orientations) and behavioral/psychoeductional treatments were most effective, whereas humanistic and systemic approaches were least effective. These data are shown in Table 15-1.

Although the Shadish et al. meta-analysis gives us a sense of the overall efficacy of family

therapy across modalities and target populations, a more recent meta-analytic study provides data on the efficacy of family therapy for specific disorders in a particular family member. Baucom, Shoham, Mueser, Daiuto, and Stickle (1998) report that family treatment appears to be helpful in treating two particular psychological disorders. Specifically, family-assisted exposure plus response prevention treatment for obsessive-compulsive disorder (see Chapter 14) was superior to the traditional form of treatment without a family member assisting (Mehta, 1990). However, this finding needs to be replicated. Family therapy has also been shown to be efficacious for a second psychological disorder, schizophrenia. Baucom et al. (1998) report that behavioral, supportive, and family systems forms of family therapy provided for at least nine months to the families of patients with schizophrenia appear efficacious in reducing relapse rates for the disorder. Relapse rates for patients with schizophrenia typically range between 50% and 75%, but the relapse rates for patients whose families received treatment were typically 35% or less.

Couples Therapy. In addition to the data on family therapy, Table 15-1 presents Shadish et al.'s (1993) meta-analytic results for couples therapy. First, it should be noted that even fewer studies and effect sizes were available to evaluate couples therapy than family therapy. As can be seen in Table 15-1, the average effect size for any form of couples therapy was .60, somewhat higher than for family therapy. Shadish et al. found great variability in the effectiveness of different forms of couples therapy; humanistic couples therapy appeared to be much less effective than other forms.

Baucom et al. (1998) provide additional information on the efficacy of different forms of couples therapy. They concur that behavioral marital therapy (BMT) is efficacious, noting that data suggest that between one-third and two-thirds of those couples who receive BMT are likely to be similar to nondistressed couples (based on their scores on outcome measures of relationship functioning) by the end of treatment. In addition, Baucom et al. report that the available evidence suggests that emotionally focused couples therapy (EFT) is also an effective form of treatment, especially with mildly to moderately distressed couples, and that EFT was superior to BMT in at least one study (Johnson & Greenberg, 1985). Finally, Baucom et al. note that cognitive, cognitive-behavioral, and insight-oriented forms of couples therapy appear promising in their effects to date and should be investigated further.

In summary, reviews of the empirical literature by Shadish et al., Baucom et al., and others (for example, Alexander, Holtzworth-Munroe, & Jameson, 1994; Hahlweg & Markman, 1988; Hazelrigg, Cooper, & Borduin, 1987) suggest that, in general, these treatments appear to be at least modestly effective. Some variation in effectiveness among types of treatment was apparent, with humanistic versions of both family and couples treatment consistently showing weaker effects. Further, both couples and family therapy may be useful in the treatment of specific psychological disorders in individual partners or family members (Baucom et al., 1998).

Special Problems

Family therapy and couples therapy would seem to pose some special problems for the clinician. For example, the expression of strong emotions, negative feelings, and hostility in the group setting could threaten the unity of the family and shake the foundations of parental authority and respect. However, it is questionable just how serious such potentialities really are. Families and couples that seek therapy are families and couples in trouble, and it is improbable that problems involving lack of parental respect and hostility, for example, were absent prior to therapy. When such problems arise in therapy, they can be worked through by the sensitive therapist. Indeed, their resolution may be the basis on which improvement in family relations occurs. The discussion of such issues in therapy may make for some stormy sessions and some equally stormy confrontations at home. But in the long run, this may be beneficial.

It has also been pointed out that individual therapy tends to disrupt families more than does family therapy (R. V. Fitzgerald, 1973). In individual therapy, a patient may decide, for example, that the "personal growth" he or she has achieved makes it impossible to continue living with a spouse who has not attained comparable growth. It is sometimes true that individual therapy exposes a great deal of incompatibility of needs among family members or partners that was not obvious before. In such instances, a family breakup may ensue. In one study of the effects of one partner's psychotherapy on the other partner (Brody & Farber, 1989), several findings stand out. The nontherapy partners believed their therapy partners were more open, empathic, and communicative as a result of the therapy. At the same time, they experienced feelings of exclusion, resentment, and inadequacy because of their partner's relationship with a therapist. Most also did not appreciate the cost of their partner's therapy. All in all, it was clear that therapy initiated a process of change in the relationship. Couples therapy is known to sometimes precipitate divorce (Alexander et al., 1994). This happens frequently enough that the possibility of divorce is sometimes listed as a risk on couples therapy contracts and consent forms. In some cases, dissolution of the relationship may in fact be the best outcome.

Another issue that can be thorny is identifying who the real patient is. When a therapist recommends that an entire family be seen along with the patient who was originally referred individually, the situation is fairly clear. But at times, another member of the family may subsequently appear to be even more disturbed than the original patient. In any case, for therapists committed to the view that the client is "the family," such situations can pose problems in communication that must be clarified. Depending on one's theoretical orientation, seeing one person as the patient and the remainder of the family as the backdrop can be a problem. Problem or not, however, how the therapy situation is being structured must be clearly understood.

In summary, we may ask, as does Margolin (1982), "Who is the client? How is confidential information handled? Does each family member have an equal right to refuse treatment? What is the role of the therapist's values vis-à-vis conflicting values of family members?" (p. 788). These are complex and controversial questions. Basically, they center around ethical issues. If family problems are the focus, then what is family health, and who decides what a "good" family really is (Huber & Baruth, 1987)? Perhaps, as Constantine (1986) argues, there are many forms of "normal" family functioning. And what about the "sexism" in so many marriages and relationships that often subtly fuels the development of problems (Goodrich, Rampage, Ellman, & Halstead, 1988)? These and many other special issues can arise whenever family or couples therapy is undertaken.

Chapter Summary

Over the years, group, family, and couples therapies have become more viable treatment options. Group therapy developed primarily out of the necessity of managing heavy caseloads. However, some clinicians came to view group therapy as a treatment of choice. Unlike its predecessors, contemporary group therapy is typically time limited (meeting for a predetermined number of sessions) and focused in the present. Managed behavioral health care is likely to increase the use of contemporary versions of group therapy by clinicians. These groups are efficient and economical for clinicians, managed behavioral health care organizations, and clients. Unfortunately, from a research perspective, we know relatively little about group therapy other than it is more effective than no treatment but no more effective than other forms of psychotherapy. Again, its main attraction is its economy and efficiency.

The origins of family therapy can be traced back to the nineteenth-century social work movement. Problems of individuals came to be conceptualized in systemic terms, as a manifestation of some type of family dysfunction. As with group therapy, many forms of family therapy exist. They are distinguished by their methods and techniques, as well as by their underlying theoretical orientation (for example, behavioral). Marital therapy, the traditional name for couples therapy, is a misnomer because there is no requirement that participants be married or of different sexes. The two most frequently studied forms of couples therapy are behavioral marital therapy (BMT) and emotionally focused couples therapy (EFT).

There is evidence to suggest that several forms of family and couples therapies are efficacious. Among family therapies, eclectic and behavioral/psychoeducational treatments for obsessive-compulsive disorder and schizophrenia in a family member appear useful. Among the varieties of couples therapy, research most strongly supports the use of BMT and EFT.

Finally, it is important to take note of the many special problems and issues associated with group, family, and couples therapy. Further, because so many perspectives are involved, research is more complicated in these areas of intervention.

Key Terms

behavioral family therapy An approach to family therapy that views family relations in terms of reinforcement contingencies. Here, the therapist's role is to generate a behavioral analysis of family problems and induce family members to reinforce each other so as to increase the frequency of desired behaviors. A more cognitively focused therapist might teach individual family members to self-monitor problematic behaviors and patterns of thinking and to challenge their interpretations of family events.

behavioral marital therapy (BMT) A form of couples therapy that applies principles of reinforcement to a couple's interactions. Major components of BMT include contingency contracting, support-understanding techniques, and problem-solving techniques.

behavior therapy groups An approach in which patients with similar problems (e.g., depression, agoraphobia, pain) are treated as a group using standard behavioral or cognitive-behavioral methods. In behavior therapy groups, little attention is generally given to group dynamics.

collaborative family therapy A form of family therapy where each family member sees a different therapist, and the therapists meet periodically to discuss their patients and the family as a whole. A variation of this approach involves having co-therapists work with the same family.

communication The verbal or nonverbal exchange of information about facts, thoughts, or feelings.

concurrent family therapy A form of family therapy in which one therapist sees all family members in individual sessions. In some cases, the therapist may conduct traditional psychotherapy with the principal patient but also occasionally see other members of the family.

conjoint family therapy A form of family therapy in which one therapist meets with the entire family at the same time.

contingency contracting In BMT, a technique in which spouses are trained to modify their own behavior in order to bring about a specific desired change in the behavior of their mate.

couples therapy A form of psychotherapy in which a couple (married, unmarried, or same-sex) meets with one or more therapists to work on any number of issues.

curative factors in group therapy The commonalities among diverse group therapy approaches proposed by Yalom to be the source of the positive treatment effect. These factors include imparting information, instilling hope, universality, altruism, interpersonal learning, imitative behavior, corrective recapitulation of the primary family, catharsis, and group cohesiveness.

double-bind A case in which an individual is told two contradictory messages by an important figure in his or her life, such that every response he or she makes with regard to that figure is wrong. At one time, double-bind situations were believed to contribute to the development of schizophrenia.

emotionally focused couples therapy (EFT) A form of couples therapy that is based on the assumption that marital distress results from negative affect and destructive interactional styles. The interventions of EFT attempt to change partners' problematic interactional styles and emotional responses so that a stronger and more secure emotional bond can be established.

family therapy A form of psychotherapy in which several members of a family are seen by the therapist in addition to the identified patient. This therapy modality is based on the idea that everyone in a family is affected when one member develops a problem, and that the home environment may have contributed to the development of the problem in the first place. Although there are a variety of theoretical family approaches, most share the primary goal of improving communication within the family.

general systems theory An important concept in family therapy that conceives of the family as a system, and believes that "pathology" is best reduced by altering the way that the system functions.

Gestalt groups A group approach in which the therapist focuses on one patient at a time and asks that person to experience his or her feelings and behaviors while the other group members are asked to observe or provide feedback to the person in the "hot seat."

group therapy A form of psychotherapy in which one or more therapists treat a number of patients at the same time. Generally speaking, most groups consist of 5-10 patients who meet with the therapist at least once a week for 90-minute to 2-hour sessions. However, groups may differ greatly in their theoretical orientations, their rules and exclusions, and whether they are viewed as primary or supplemental modes of treatment.

problem-solving techniques In BMT, training couples in positive communication skills in order to enhance the effectiveness of decision-making and negotiation.

psychoanalytic group psychotherapy Generally speaking, psychoanalytic therapy carried out in a group setting. Here, group dynamics are considered secondary to individual processes, and the group acts as a vehicle through which the individual may obtain insight into his or her unconscious forces and defenses.

psychodrama A form of role playing developed by Moreno in which one patient in a group acts out a role assigned by the therapist, other patients serve as the supporting cast of "auxiliary egos," and yet other patients serve as the audience. The idea is that by listening to the responses of the auxiliary egos and the reactions of the audience, the patient in the primary role will experience catharsis and self-understanding.

support-understanding techniques In BMT, techniques that aim to increase partners' positive feelings, positive behaviors, and the degree of collaboration between them.

time-limited group therapy A group approach to brief therapy forwarded by Budman and Gurman in which patients meet weekly for a predetermined number of sessions. Four central characteristics include pregroup screening and preparation, the establishment and maintenance of a working focus, group cohesion, and member reactions to the time limits of the group.

transactional analysis A group method developed by Berne that focuses upon the "ego states"—Child, Parent, or Adult—that are evident based on patients' transactions with other group members, as well as the valence (positive or negative) of these ego states, and helps patients adopt ways of thinking that are more characteristic of the positive Adult ego state. Another emphasis in TA is on identifying the games that patients employ in order to avoid getting too close to others, and helping them to adopt more satisfying behaviors.

Web Sites of Interest

To visit any of the web sites listed below, go to www.wadsworth.com and click on Links.

15-1 American Association for Marriage and Family Therapy

15-2 Association for Specialists in Group Work

15-3 International Association of Group Psychotherapy

Specialties in
Clinical Psychology

CHAPTER SIXTEEN

Community Psychology

At least since the appearance of psychoanalysis, the helping professions have sought to alleviate problems by one form of therapy or another. Some approaches have emphasized insight; others have sought to change behavior more directly. Whatever the differences in approaches, their basic common focus has been on the individual who has already developed psychological problems. By and large, clinical psychology has been a psychology of the individual.

At the theoretical level, therapists have long accepted the idea that all behavior (pathological or otherwise) is a joint product of situational and personal factors. Yet in their day-to-day therapeutic efforts, the emphasis of clinicians was generally on one-to-one therapy of some sort. The troubled individual engaged the help of an expert, and by this act he or she submitted to the role of patient. The clinician treated; the patient responded. However, given the rate of mental health problems in the world today, some have questioned whether this general approach is a reasonable one. For them, a relatively newer approach, *community psychology*, shows great promise for addressing mental health problems.

Perspectives and History

Let us begin by trying to identify exactly what community psychology is. Then we can move to those events that gave rise to the movement. Table 16-1 presents a set of principles that characterize community psychology, including assumptions regarding the causes of problems, the variety of levels of analysis that can be used to define a problem, where community psychology is practiced, how services are planned, the emphasis on prevention, and the willingness to "give psychology away" by consulting with self-help programs and nonpsychologists. We will discuss each of these basic principles at various points throughout this chapter.

▌ **T A B L E 1 6 - 1** Principles of Community Psychology

What "causes" problems?
Problems develop due to an interaction over time between the individual, social setting, and systems (e.g., organizations); these exert a mutual influence on each other.

How are problems defined?
Problems can be defined at many levels, but particular emphasis is placed on analysis at the level of the organization and the community or neighborhood.

Where is community psychology practiced?
Community psychology is typically not practiced in clinics, but rather out in the field or in the social context of interest.

How are services planned?
Rather than providing services only for those who seek help, community psychologists proactively assess the needs and risks in a community.

What is the emphasis in community psychology interventions?
An emphasis is placed on prevention of problems rather than treatment of existing problems.

Who is qualified to intervene?
Attempts are made to share psychology with others via consultation; actual interventions are often carried out through self-help programs or through trained non-psychologists/non-professionals.

Source: Adapted from Orford (1992), p. 4.

The Community Psychology Perspective

Community psychology has been described as an approach to mental health that emphasizes the role of environmental forces in creating and alleviating problems (Zax & Specter, 1974). Rappaport (1977) finds it more useful to talk about community psychology in terms of a perspective than to attempt a formal definition. The major aspects of this perspective are cultural relativity, diversity, and ecology (the fit between persons and the environment).

This perspective implies several things. First, community psychologists should not be concerned exclusively with inadequate environments or persons. Rather, they should direct their attention to the fit between environments and persons—a fit that may or may not be good. Second, community psychologists should emphasize the creation of alternatives through identifying and developing the resources and strengths of people and communities. Thus, the focus is on action directed toward the competencies of persons and environments rather than their deficits. Third, the community psychologist is likely to believe that differences among people and communities are desirable. Societal resources, therefore, should not be allocated according to one standard of competence. The community psychologist does not become identified with a single social norm or value, but instead looks to the promotion of diversity.

In Rappaport's (1977) view, three sets of concerns define the community psychology perspective: human resource development, political activity, and science. In many ways, these are antagonistic elements. Political activists are often impatient and deride more traditional clinicians as bringing society too little too late. Clinicians, in turn, often criticize activists as unprofessional and overly concerned with hawking their own visions of the world. Both groups often regard scientists as too far removed from real problems to know what is going on in the world (the "ivory tower" syndrome). The scientists, in turn, are appalled by activists and clinicians alike; both are seen as shockingly willing to act on the basis of unvalidated hunches and lack of data or, worst of all, without a viable theory to guide them. However, true societal changes vis-à-vis mental health will require the cooperation of each of these "camps." For example, scientists must provide data to support and direct the efforts of clinicians and political activists, and political activists must assist with funding for scientists so that they can conduct the research that is needed. After all, each camp has the common goal of improved well-being and mental health for individuals, communities, and the larger society.

Whatever else community psychology may be, it is not a field that emphasizes an individual disease or individual treatment model (Iscoe, 1982). The focus is preventive rather than curative. Further, individuals and community organizations are encouraged to take control of and master their own problems (via empowerment) so that traditional professional intervention will not be necessary (Orford, 1992).

Chronology and Catalyzing Events

In 1955, the U.S. Congress passed legislation creating the Joint Commission on Mental Health and Illness. Its report encouraged the development of a community mental health concept and urged a reduction in the population of mental hospitals. Based on the premise that psychological distress and the development of mental disorders were influenced by adverse environmental conditions, President Kennedy called for a "bold new approach" to *prevent* mental disorder. The so-called Kennedy Bill of 1963 funded the construction of mental health centers. Their aims were to promote the early detection of mental health problems, treat acute disorders, and establish comprehensive delivery systems of services that would prevent the "warehousing" of chronic patients in mental hospitals (Bloom, 1973). The American Psychological Association endorsed the desirability of community residents' participating in all these decisions (Smith & Hobbs, 1966) and helped focus attention on the concept of community approaches and participation.

FIGURE 16-1 President John F. Kennedy and President Lyndon B. Johnson were instrumental in providing the political leadership to get the community psychology movement underway.
Library of Congress.

A conference held in 1965 is regarded by many as the "official" birth of community psychology (Zax & Specter, 1974). At Swampscott, Massachusetts, a group of psychologists set out to review the status of the field and to plot a future course of development for the place of psychology in the community mental health movement.

Shortly after this conference, the Division of Community Psychology was organized within the American Psychological Association. Soon *The Community Mental Health Journal* and the *American Journal of Community Psychology* began publication. Textbooks began to appear, including Zax and Specter (1974), Heller and Monahan (1977), Rappaport (1977), Mann (1978), Heller, Price, Reinharz, Riger, and Wandersman (1984), and more recently, Orford (1992), Duffy and Wong (1996), and Levine and Perkins (1997). Reviews began to appear regularly in the *Annual Review of Psychology*, and handbooks have been published (for example, Rappaport & Seidman, in press; Schulberg & Killelea, 1982). Courses in community psychology and programs of gradu-

ate training have been established, and there are even books now on the history of community mental health.

To flesh out the foregoing chronology, it will be helpful to pinpoint several issues or concerns that have catalyzed the emergence of community psychology.

Treatment Facilities. Although the mental hospital population in the United States peaked at about 500,000 in the mid-1950s, socially oriented clinicians continued to press for alternatives to the costly, inefficient, and often largely custodial hospitalization of patients. Three factors combined at about this time to markedly reduce the population of mental hospitals: the advent of psychotropic medications, a more liberal discharge philosophy, and better treatment in mental hospitals. But as more patients were being discharged, often under heavy medication, and as patients who formerly would have been hospitalized were no longer admitted, the need for better community treatment and supportive services became evident. In some ways a cause but in other ways an effect of these events, the community philosophy was beginning to gain a foothold.

A problem with many mental hospitals was their lack of trained therapists. Regarded by laypersons as a realistic means for solving difficult emotional problems, hospitalization itself often created nearly as many problems as it alleviated. Over the years, mental hospitals (particularly those run by the states) too often became warehouses or custodial bins. Care was often marginal and sometimes downright inhumane. Professional staff was severely lacking in numbers and sometimes in quality. Indeed, many still argue (and have demonstrated empirically) that hospitalization is not an especially effective treatment strategy.

Personnel Shortage. Even as more clinical psychologists and psychiatrists were trained, demands for their services outstripped their increase in numbers. Many of the newcomers were entering private practice, and others were being diverted into teaching or research. In any event, the supply of trained professionals for service in hospitals and clinics was hardly keeping pace with the demand. A number of trends (Albee, 1959, 1968; Arnhoff, 1968) all seemed to coalesce to produce critical shortages of hospital and clinic personnel. To grapple with these shortages, it became imperative that new sources of personnel be sought, that more effective use be made of professional time, and that new models of coping with human problems be developed. Albee (1959, 1968) predicted that it would be literally impossible to train enough mental health professionals to meet existing and future needs, and recommended that prevention be pursued as a strategy.

Questions about Psychotherapy. In the 1950s, people began to question not just the efficiency of psychotherapy but also its effectiveness. Some began to wonder if it was not just intrapsychic factors that created problems, but the interaction between person and society. At the same time, because psychotherapy was expensive and more and more clinicians and psychiatrists were going into private practice, economic factors were pushing therapy beyond the reach of the poor and disadvantaged. The relationship between mental illness and social class had been documented by Hollingshead and Redlich (1958). Now, it seemed, there was also a relationship between social class and the availability of psychotherapy.

Medical Models and Roles. Throughout this book, we have commented on the widespread role of the medical model and some of the discontent with it. The 1960s ushered in a climate in which institutional prerogatives and traditionalist beliefs came under attack. That climate produced listeners who were more willing to accept attacks on traditional views about mental illness. All of this contributed to an increased tendency to look for the social-community antecedents of problems in living, rather than internal biological or psychological etiological agents.

The general activism of the 1960s also catalyzed the long-standing discontent of many clinicians with a role that relegated them to waiting passively for society's casualties to walk in the door. Would not an activist role that took mental health services to the people be more consonant with a social-community model? If so, such a role would also provide a measure of autonomy from the dominance of the medical profession. We must not overstate these developments, however. After all, a major current trend in clinical psychology has been a headlong rush into private practice. Such behavior is hardly a rejection of the medical model or an acceptance of the social-community approach.

The Environment. Another force that helped shape the community psychology movement was a greater awareness of the importance of social and environmental factors in determining people's behavior and problems. Poverty, discrimination, pollution, and crowding were being recognized as potent factors. Providing people with choices and enhancing their well-being required that psychologists pay attention to these factors—that they go beyond a reflexive consideration of the early childhood determinants of people's personalities. The emotional problems of large numbers of people may be influenced by poverty, unemployment, job discrimination, racism, diminished educational opportunities, sexism, and other social factors. Such influences are hardly the ones proposed by psychoanalytic and other theories that seek answers in internal dynamics.

The Tenor of the Times. Perhaps as much as anything, the sociopolitical events that saturated the 1960s gave sustenance to the community approach. The school desegregation ordered by the Supreme Court in 1954 and the rise of the civil rights movement pointed to discrimination in all its malignant forms and raised the consciousness of the entire country. For the first time, many began to understand what social repression does to the minds and emotions of its victims. At the same time, civil rights activists proved that protests, rallies, pressure, and occasionally even logic could have an effect. The lessons of this era were not lost on some of the persons who later became advocates of a community approach to mental health.

Key Concepts

To this point, we have tried to sketch an overall perspective and chronology of community psychology. In the process, we have alluded to several important concepts. Now, following the analysis of Rappaport (1977), we will take a closer look at some of these concepts.

The Concept of Community Mental Health

The 1955 Joint Commission on Mental Health and Illness made several basic recommendations that set the tone for the subsequent development of community psychology—a tone that still resonates in accord with political and financial pressures across the nation. These recom-

mendations were (1) more and better research into mental health phenomena; (2) a broadened definition of who may provide mental health services; (3) that mental health services should be made available in the community; (4) that an awareness should be fostered that mental illness can stem from social factors (such as ostracism and isolation); and (5) that the federal government should support these recommendations financially.

In 1963, federal funds were provided to help in the construction and staffing of comprehensive mental health centers across the United States. To qualify for these funds, a *community mental health center* had to provide five essential services: (1) inpatient care; (2) outpatient care; (3) partial hospitalization (for example, the patient works during the day but returns to the hospital at night); (4) round-the-clock emergency service; and (5) consultation services to a variety of professional, educational, and service personnel in the community. Beyond these required services, it was hoped that the mental health centers would also provide (1) diagnostic services, (2) rehabilitation services, (3) research, (4) training, and (5) evaluation. But despite Hobbs's (1964) description of a "third revolution" in mental health, the medical model still prevailed (perhaps because psychiatrists remained at the top of the administrative hierarchy), and there seemed to be a continuing neglect of minority patients, poverty-stricken individuals, and even children.

In a highly influential paper, Smith and Hobbs (1966) argued that community control of mental health care and services was essential. They saw the role of prevention as paramount. This implied early detection and work with schools, police departments, social service agencies, businesses, and other organizations. The idea of personal deficit was replaced by the view that the social system had failed to provide an appropriate environment. A community mental health center, then, must not merely set about remedying individual deficits, but must do everything it could to enable the system to function better. Consultation was given prominence, as was the development of new community resources. Going beyond Smith and Hobbs, some even argued that the center should be the central coordinator of all social systems in the community. The goal was to reach those who needed services, and in particular those who were so often excluded from services (the poor, the indigent, minorities). New methods to meet mental health needs were encouraged (such as crisis intervention and group treatment). Advocacy of social action programs to improve housing, employment, and opportunity took precedence over the one-to-one therapy session. The role of the therapist was replaced by that of the social change agent.

Many of the foregoing antecedents had an idealistic tone. Nevertheless, in the 1960s, many community centers became operational. Some approximated the hopes of Smith and Hobbs. Others were more in the mold of older clinical approaches even though they used a community language. Some have been smooth-running enterprises, but others have created community tensions and controversy. For many reasons (including cutbacks in federal funding beginning in 1968), the goal of establishing 2000 centers by 1975 was not realized. In fact, by 1974, only 540 centers had been established with funds from the Community Mental Health Centers Act. Despite the recommendations of President Carter's Commission on Mental Health in 1978 that more emphasis should be placed on "serving the underserved" (children, elderly, ethnic minorities, and rural inhabitants), fewer funds were appropriated specifically for community mental health centers over the subsequent years. State and local governments failed to fill the financial gaps. Today, there are about 1500 community mental health centers nationwide, still well short of the goal set several decades ago.

The Concept of Prevention

The idea of *prevention* is the guiding principle that has long been at the heart of public health programs in this country. Basically, the principle asserts that, in the long run, preventive activities will be more efficient and effective than individual treatment administered after the onset of diseases or problems (Felner, Jason, Moritsugu, & Farber, 1983). That such approaches can work is graphically illustrated by Price, Cowen, Lorion, and Ramos-McKay (1988). Their book, *Fourteen Ounces of Prevention*, describes 14 model prevention programs for children, adolescents, or adults. Box 16-1 presents an overview of one of these programs that targets preschool children from low-income families.

Prevention programs for adults have been developed and implemented as well. Box 16-2 presents an overview of the JOBS program, a program designed to assist adults who have recently lost their employment.

Primary Prevention. This type of prevention represents the most radical departure from the traditional ways of coping with mental health problems. The essence of the notion of *primary prevention* can be seen in Caplan's (1964) emphasis on "counteracting harmful circumstances before they have had a chance to produce illness" (p. 26). Albee (1986) points out, however, that the complexity of human problems often requires preventive strategies that depend on social change and redistribution of power. For many in society, this is not a highly palatable prospect. Some examples of primary prevention include programs to reduce job discrimination, enhance school curricula, improve housing, teach parenting skills, and provide help to children from single-parent homes. Also grouped under this heading are genetic counseling, Head Start, prenatal care for disadvantaged women, Meals on Wheels, and school lunch programs. Box 16-3 presents the results of a recent meta-analysis evaluating the efficacy of primary prevention mental health programs for children and adolescents (Durlak & Wells, 1997).

Secondary Prevention. This involves programs that promote the early identification of mental health problems and prompt treatment of problems at an early stage so that mental disorders do not develop. The basic idea of *secondary prevention* is to attack problems while they are still

BOX 16-1

Prevention: The High/Scope Perry Preschool Program

The High/Scope Perry Preschool Program (HSPPP) was initiated in 1962 to help children who were deemed at risk for school failure, and its curriculum is used today by thousands of early childhood instructors (Schweinhart & Weikart, 1988). Based on the rationale that childhood poverty often leads to school failure, which in turn results in adult poverty and social problems (such as crime), the HSPPP targeted 3- and 4-year-olds from families of low socioeconomic status (SES) for intervention. These interventions were characterized by

1. A developmentally appropriate curriculum, based on Piaget's views of children as active and self-initiating learners
2. Classroom enrollment limits with adequate adult supervision (at least two adults who had training in early childhood development)
3. Supervisory support of staff and frequent in-service training opportunities
4. Emphasis on parental involvement in each child's education
5. Sensitivity to the needs of children and their families (Schweinhart & Weikart, 1988)

The 58 children, ages 3 to 4, in the Perry Preschool study intervention group attended the program for two years, which included classroom instruction five mornings a week for seven months a year and home visits by the teacher once a week. Outcome data were also collected from a control group of 65 children matched on IQ, sex, and SES. The major findings from this study can be summarized as follows (Schweinhart & Weikart, 1988):

1. Program participants demonstrated better academic achievement throughout elementary and secondary school, were rated by teachers as more socially and emotionally mature, and endorsed more favorable attitudes toward high school.
2. Program participants as a group obtained more and better jobs, and received higher wages by age 19. Further, they were more likely to be self-supporting, less likely to have dropped out of high school, less likely to be arrested, and more likely to have enrolled in college or vocational school.
3. A cost-benefit analysis of the program indicated significant benefits to society and to the taxpayer. For every dollar invested in the two-year program, three dollars in savings were returned. For example, the program resulted in a reduction of costs for special classes, welfare, and crime.

---

manageable, before they become resistant to intervention (Caplan, 1961; Sanford, 1965). Often this approach suggests the screening of large numbers of people. These people are not seeking help, and they may not even appear to be at risk. Such screening may be carried out by a variety of community service personnel, including physicians, teachers, clergy, police, court officials, social workers, and others. Early assessment is followed, of course, by appropriate referrals.

An example of secondary prevention is the early detection and treatment of those individuals with potentially damaging drinking problems (Alden, 1988). A further example is the Rochester Primary Mental Health Project pioneered by Emory Cowen, which began in 1957. The project systematically screens primary-grade children for risk of school maladjustment. The development of early detection and prevention programs in several states has been described

BOX 16-2

The JOBS Program

Loss of employment can lead to a number of problems, including depression, substance abuse, health problems, family conflict, suicide, and financial strain (Caplan, Vinokur, & Price, 1997). Programs that help individuals manage this difficult transition and assist them in obtaining new employment would clearly be beneficial. Caplan et al. (1997) provide an overview and evaluation of such an intervention—the JOBS program.

The JOBS program is administered in a group format and involves multiple 3.5-hour sessions over the course of one or two weeks. The program focuses on (1) training participants to seek reemployment effectively (for example, training in behavioral skills such as interviewing effectively); (2) increasing the self-confidence of job seekers; and (3) stress inoculation training for coping with barriers to reemployment and setbacks. Studies have

shown that JOBS program participants who were still unemployed at follow-up demonstrated higher levels of self-confidence about their job-seeking ability and a greater sense of self-efficacy than did those who did not participate and remained unemployed. Further, among those at greater risk for depression, JOBS participants demonstrated lower levels of depressive symptoms at follow-up. Additional outcomes are also noteworthy. JOBS participants found reemployment sooner and were more likely to obtain better (that is, in their field of interest) and more stable jobs than those who did not participate. Finally, the JOBS program appears to be cost effective. Economic projections suggest that the program's costs are offset by participants' lifetime earning payouts to federal and state governments (through taxes).

BOX 16-3

Primary Prevention Mental Health Programs for Children and Adolescents

Durlak and Wells (1997) recently published a meta-analytic review of 177 primary prevention programs designed to prevent behavioral, emotional, and social problems in children and adolescents. Durlak and Wells found that these programs, on average, produced meaningful positive effects such that the average participant in a primary prevention program showed better (more adaptive) outcome than 59% to 82% of those in a control group. Most intervention programs not only reduced

problems, but they also significantly increased competencies across a number of affective/emotional, cognitive, academic, and behavioral domains. Finally, Durlak and Wells found that, in general, in those studies that collected follow-up data, these effects were durable over time. This study demonstrates that a wide range of primary prevention programs do work—that is, the mental health of children and adolescents improves significantly as a result of these programs.

by Cowen, Hightower, Johnson, Sarno, and Weissberg (1989).

Tertiary Prevention. The goal of *tertiary prevention* is to reduce the duration and the negative effects of mental disorders after their occurrence. Thus, tertiary prevention differs from primary and secondary prevention in that its aim is not to reduce the rate of new cases of mental disorder, but to lessen the effects of mental disorder once diagnosed.

A major focus of many tertiary programs is rehabilitation. This can range from increasing vocational competence to enhancing the client's self-concept. The methods used may be counseling, job training, and the like. Whether the purpose of a program is to teach better independent living skills to those with mental retardation or to restore the social skills of a recently discharged patient with a diagnosis of schizophrenia, the goal is the prevention of additional problems. Although their language is a bit different, tertiary preventive programs are not very different from person-oriented programs based on a deficit philosophy. However, it is important to remember that all forms of prevention are distinguished by their attempts to reduce the rates of, or problems associated with, mental disorder on a community-wide (or population-wide) basis.

Alternative Models of Prevention. Although the traditional primary-secondary-tertiary prevention model (Caplan, 1964) is the one that is most commonly cited, alternative classification frameworks have been proposed (Orford, 1992). As one example, we will briefly discuss a framework for preventing mental disorder proposed in the 1994 Institute of Medicine (IOM) report, *Reducing Risks for Mental Disorders*. This model, adopting terms proposed by R. Gordon (1983, 1987), classifies prevention intervention into one of three types. *Universal preventive interventions* target the entire population; these interventions may be costly because they are given to everyone. *Selective preventive interventions* target individuals or subgroups of the population that have a higher than average likelihood of developing the disorder in question (either in the near or distant future). These targeted individuals are identified on the basis of biological, psychological, or social risk factors that have been shown to be associated with disorder development. Finally, *indicated preventive interventions* target "high-risk" individuals, identified by their manifestation of subthreshold symptoms of the disorder or by biological markers indicating a predisposition to develop the disorder.

The value of this model is that it places prevention, treatment of mental disorder, and maintenance on a continuum representing the full range of interventions for mental disorders. Prevention occurs before a disorder develops; treatment is administered to those who meet (or are close to meeting) diagnostic criteria for a disorder; and maintenance involves interventions for individuals with a diagnosis of mental disorder whose illness continues to warrant attention (IOM, 1994). Figure 16-2 depicts the IOM's conceptualization of the intervention spectrum for mental disorders.

Prevention Research. Planning, developing, and evaluating prevention programs is a multistage process requiring years of community psychologists' time. To guide prevention researchers, the IOM (1994) recommends a series of steps focusing on the conceptualization, design, implementation, and evaluation of prevention intervention research programs. Figure 16-3 depicts these steps. First, the problem or disorder to be addressed by the program must be clearly specified, along with its prevalence, incidence, and costs to society. Next, risk and protective factors relevant to the problem or disorder are identified, and the existing research on the prevention or treatment of the condition is reviewed. Third, pilot studies to evaluate the efficacy of the planned intervention are designed and conducted. The fourth step involves planning and carrying out large-scale trials of the intervention program. Finally, assuming that the trials yield encouraging results, the program is implemented in the community, and its effectiveness is again assessed. As can be seen from Figure 16-3, this last step does

FIGURE 16-2 Prevention on a continuum of services addressing mental health needs

Source: IOM (1994). Summary: Reducing risks for mental disorders. Washington, DC: National Academy Press, p. 8. Reprinted with permission.

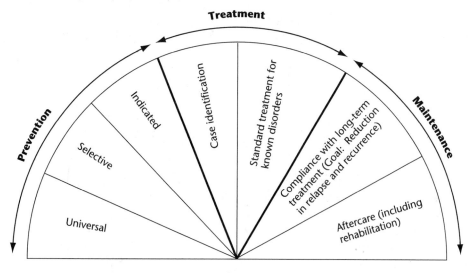

not mark the end of the process. Rather, information regarding the effectiveness of the intervention in the community (does it lead to decreases in the incidence of the problem or disorder?) leads to modification of the intervention, and the steps are repeated. In this way, prevention programs are refined with the ultimate goal of improving their effectiveness.

Empowerment

In their discussion of poverty, Gurin and Gurin (1970) emphasize the importance of a low expectancy of attaining valued goals and an expectancy of powerlessness. These notions are closely related to the social learning concept of locus of control (Phares, 1976; Rotter, 1966). As Rappaport (1977) notes:

> What is important about this variable for community psychology is its connection to the sociological idea of power and its converse, alienation. Locus of control is one of the few variables in social science that may be shown to have a consistent relation-

ship that ties research across levels of analysis. (p. 101)

For Rappaport (1981), a major goal of community psychology is the prevention of feelings of powerlessness. It is not easy to accomplish this goal of *empowerment*, and community psychologists have not been as conspicuously successful here as they would have liked (Heller, 1990). Gesten and Jason (1987) question whether any unique methods have been developed out of the empowerment concept. Still, Rappaport (1981) initially argued that strategies to enhance people's sense that they control their own destinies are preferable even to prevention or treatment approaches. Examples of attempts to enhance feelings of control range from reducing child and spouse abuse, to eradicating exploitation of women, migrant workers, and the elderly, to decreasing bias against the disabled and the mentally ill.

Although he initially pitted empowerment and prevention approaches against each other, it appears that Rappaport (1987) has more recently tempered his position. He now allows for the

444

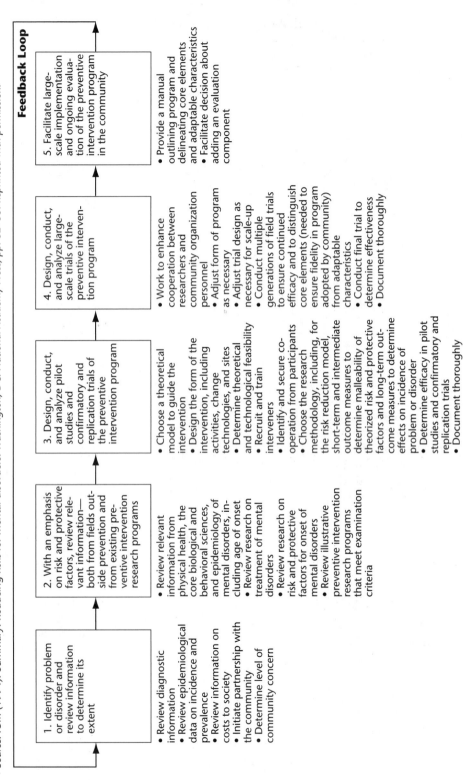

FIGURE 16-3 **Recommended steps for designing, implementing, and evaluating prevention programs**

Source: IOM (1994). Summary: Reducing risks for mental disorders. Washington, DC: National Academy Press, pp. 32–33. Reprinted with permission.

Feedback Loop

1. Identify problem or disorder and review information to determine its extent

- Review diagnostic information
- Review epidemiological data on incidence and prevalence
- Review information on costs to society
- Initiate partnership with the community
- Determine level of community concern

2. With an emphasis on risk and protective factors, review relevant information—both from fields outside prevention and from existing preventive intervention research programs

- Review relevant information from physical health, the core biological and behavioral sciences, and epidemiology of mental disorders, including age of onset
- Review research on treatment of mental disorders
- Review research on risk and protective factors for onset of mental disorders
- Review illustrative preventive intervention research programs that meet examination criteria

3. Design, conduct, and analyze pilot studies and confirmatory and replication trials of the preventive intervention program

- Choose a theoretical model to guide the intervention
- Design the form of the intervention, including activities, change technologies, and sites
- Determine theoretical and technological feasibility
- Recruit and train interveners
- Identify and secure cooperation from participants
- Choose the research methodology, including, for the risk reduction model, short-term and intermediate outcome measures to determine malleability of theorized risk and protective factors and long-term outcome measures to determine effects on incidence of problem or disorder
- Determine efficacy in pilot studies and confirmatory and replication trials
- Document thoroughly

4. Design, conduct, and analyze large-scale trials of the preventive intervention program

- Work to enhance cooperation between researchers and community organization personnel
- Adjust form of program as necessary
- Adjust trial design as necessary for scale-up
- Conduct multiple generations of field trials to ensure continued efficacy and to distinguish core elements (needed to ensure fidelity in program adopted by community) from adaptable characteristics
- Conduct final trial to determine effectiveness
- Document thoroughly

5. Facilitate large-scale implementation and ongoing evaluation of the preventive intervention program in the community

- Provide a manual outlining program and delineating core elements and adaptable characteristics
- Facilitate decision about adding an evaluation component

possibility that prevention interventions may be consistent with (rather than diametrically opposed to) empowerment. However, for this possibility to be realized, preventive interventions must be collaborative and delivered in a manner that avoids the paternalistic style that characterizes some traditional therapist-client interactions (Felner et al., 1983).

Social Intervention Concepts

The conventional strategy of intervention has always implied that one achieves good health exclusively through one's own efforts, and that when those efforts fail and ill health occurs, one visits a comprehensive mental health center for clinical help. But the community psychologist seeks to restructure roles and social organizations. For example, to reduce the problems created by crime and delinquency, community psychologists seek to change social institutions and organizations to make advantages and resources available to potential criminals and delinquents.

Inherent in such social intervention strategies is the idea that when individuals are given the necessary resources or alternatives, they will solve their problems themselves. Also inherent is the belief that people have competencies and strengths. When the environment is changed or when people are allowed to exert power to make their own decisions, these strengths and competencies will be evident. This emphasis on competencies rather than deficits allows the community psychologist to move toward creating a proper person-environment fit, rather than changing the affected people so that they will fit the appropriate environment as determined by majority values.

Blaming the Victim. Particularly illustrative of the notions that have given rise to the strategy of social intervention is the contrast between blaming the victim and blaming the system. In a highly influential book, Ryan (1971) argued that society sees the economically disadvantaged, school dropouts, drug addicts, or the unemployed as individual failures whose healing will require remedial reading programs, drug counseling, and so on. According to Ryan, society misses the real message, which is bad social environments. Their problems are not clinical; they are community-social.

Why are we so prone to place responsibility on individuals who are disadvantaged rather than on society or the environment? Caplan and Nelson (1973) cite several reasons:

- Such explanations free the government and cultural institutions from blame.
- Institutions, therefore, cannot be held responsible for "solving" the problem.
- Placing responsibility on the individual gives a degree of legitimacy to attempts to intervene at the person level (as is common in traditional clinical psychology).

Caplan and Nelson (as well as others) hope to highlight these factors, which may serve to influence how we conceptualize the cause(s) of social problems. As a result, we may be better able to resist the temptation to "blame the victim" when it is not justified.

The Focus on Intervention Strategies. One way of contrasting traditional clinical and community orientations is by focusing on intervention strategies. Such strategies, according to Heller, Price, Reinharz, Riger, and Wandersman (1984), can vary along two dimensions: theoretical (deficit versus competence) and ecological (the individual, the organization, or the community). Table 16-2 summarizes the way these dimensions operate.

Methods of Intervention and Change

We now shift our attention to methods of intervention. Here our focus will be on patterns of service delivery.

Consultation

What is *consultation*? Orford (1992) offers the following definition:

TABLE 16-2 Strategies for Change as Determined by Theoretical Orientation and Level of Analysis

Theoretical Orientation	Level of Analysis		
	Individual	Organizational	Community
Deficit	Somatic therapies to correct biochemical or physiological imbalance	Group psychotherapy or sensitivity training to correct interpersonal problems	Institutionalization or special facilities built for the handicapped or emotionally disturbed
Competency	Most forms of behavior therapy, particularly skill training	Training and consultation to increase job competencies of organization members	Creating new settings and alternative programs
	Prevention programs for high-risk persons	Prevention programs to reduce organizational stress and increase coping	Community-wide prevention programs to reduce environmental stress and increase citizen competencies

Source: Adapted from *Psychology and Community Change: Challenges of the Future,* by K. Heller, R. H. Price, S. Reinharz, S. Riger, and A. Wanderman. Copyright © 1984 by Kenneth Heller. Reprinted by permission of the publisher, Brooks/Cole Publishing Company, a division of Wadsworth, Inc.

Consultation is the process whereby an individual (the consultee) who has responsibility for providing a service to others (the clients) voluntarily consults another person (the consultant) who is believed to possess some special expertise which will help the consultee provide a better service to his or her clients. (p. 139)

In a world short of mental health personnel, the basic advantage of consultation is that its effects are multiplied like the ripples from a stone thrown into a pond. Using individual techniques of intervention, the mental health specialist can reach only a very limited number of clients. But by consulting with other service providers, such as teachers, police, and ministers, he or she can reach many more clients indirectly (Orford, 1992).

Consultation can be viewed from several orientations, each springing from a somewhat different historical perspective (Brown & Schulte, 1987; Heller, Price, Reinharz, Riger, & Wanderman, 1984; Nietzel, Winett, MacDonald, & Davidson, 1977; Orford, 1992). First, there is mental health consultation. This grew out of the psychoanalytic and psychodynamic tradition. It was often practiced in rural or underdeveloped areas where there was a shortage of mental health personnel. Consultation became a way of using existing community personnel (such as teachers or ministers) to help solve the mental health problems of such areas. A second orientation developed out of the behavioral tradition. In order to implement the technology of behavior modification that had been so successful in laboratory settings, it was necessary to move into real-life situations. To do that, people in the patient's environment (such as home or school) had to be trained to properly dispense reinforcements for the desired behavior. Consultation became a way of providing such training. The third orientation is an organizational one that emphasizes consultation to industry. Specialists work with management or work group leaders to improve morale, job satisfaction, and productivity or to reduce inefficiency, absenteeism, alcoholism, or other problems.

Types of Mental Health Consultation. Approaches to mental health consultation can be classified in many ways. Perhaps the most widely accepted classification is Caplan's (1970). It includes the following categories:

1. *Client-centered case consultation.* Here the focus is on helping a specific client or patient to solve a current problem. For example, a clinician might be asked to consult with a colleague on a diagnostic problem involving a specific patient.
2. *Consultee-centered case consultation.* In this instance, the aim is to help the consultee enhance the skills that he or she needs in order to deal with future cases. For example, a teacher might be advised on how to selectively reinforce behavior in order to reduce classroom disturbances.
3. *Program-centered administrative consultation.* The notion here is to assist in the administration or management of a specific program. For instance, a consultant might be hired to set up an "early warning system" in the schools to detect potential cases of maladjustment.
4. *Consultee-centered administrative consultation.* Here the aim is to improve the skills of an administrator in the hope that this will enable her or him to function better in the future. For example, a sensitivity group consisting of administrators might be monitored by a consultant in order to help enhance the administrators' communication skills.

Techniques and Phases. Several general techniques can enhance the effectiveness of the consulting process. In most cases, the consultation process will pass through the following phases:

1. *The entry or preparatory phase.* In the initial phase, the exact nature of the consultant relationship and mutual obligations are worked out.
2. *The beginning or warming-up phase.* In this phase, the working relationship is established.
3. *The alternative action phase.* This phase encompasses the development of specific, alter-native solutions and strategies of problem solving.
4. *Termination.* When it is mutually agreed that further consultation is unnecessary, termination follows.

Unfortunately, community mental health centers have had difficulty providing consultation services, especially to schools and community agencies; the budgetary support has just not been there (Iscoe & Harris, 1984). What is particularly troubling about this state of affairs is that there is empirical support for the efficacy of consultation (Duffy & Wong, 1996; Medway & Updike, 1985; Orford, 1992).

Community Alternatives to Hospitalization

As noted earlier in this chapter, the nation's mental hospitals have long been objects of criticism. Despite the fact that there is a core of "undischargeable" patients, there are alternatives to our current hospital system—alternatives that will provide environments geared to the goal of enabling patients to resume a responsible place in society.

Examples of alternatives include the community lodge (Fairweather, Sanders, Maynard, & Cressler, 1969). This is akin to a halfway house where formerly chronic, hospitalized patients can learn independent living skills. The Mendota Program (Marx, Test, & Stein, 1973) was a pioneering attempt to help formerly "undischargeable" patients find jobs, learn cooking and shopping skills, and so on. Finally, there is the growing popularity of day hospitals that are often more effective and less expensive than traditional 24-hour hospitalization.

Crisis Intervention

The basic goal of *crisis intervention* is to reach people in an acute state of stress and to provide them with enough support to prevent them from becoming the chronically mentally ill of the future. Persons in crisis are often in a uniquely "reachable" state that can pave the way for future long-term interventions.

Crisis intervention requires the relinquishing of traditional procedures and prerogatives. For example, crisis intervention centers must be close to the communities they serve. Clients should not have to travel 20 miles to reach an office or wade through 15 secretaries once they reach it. Obviously, there must be immediate service. Walk-in centers or phone services must be available all day and all night, and appointments should not be required. Staff members must be prepared to leave their office—to go with police or to visit homes. Finally, crises tend to obliterate customary professional roles, pecking orders, and prerogatives. There is typically no time for discussion of whether a paraprofessional received an A or a B in abnormal psychology, or for a visit from an expert consultant. This is not to suggest that training has no place. However, crisis intervention requires a versatility and flexibility that are not often found in traditional clinics or hospitals.

Early crisis programs were often built largely around telephone answering services. However, it soon became apparent that such services were too slow. Consequently, the emphasis is now on 24-hour services staffed by workers who personally take calls. Current interventions emphasize follow-up both to check on the well-being of the client and to assess the adequacy of the services provided by the agency to which the client was referred. Current intervention procedures also encourage face-to-face contact rather than the earlier overreliance on the telephone. Emerging interventions even include temporary shelter (such as for battered women and their children), transportation, and follow-up services and consultation to survivors of suicides.

One of the earliest applications of the crisis philosophy was the establishment of suicide prevention centers (Shneidman & Farberow, 1965). An illustrative example is McGee's (1974) development of the Suicide and Crisis Intervention Service (SCIS) in Gainesville, Florida. The policy of SCIS was simply "to respond to every request to participate in the solution of any human problem whenever and wherever it occurs" (McGee,

1974, p. 181, italics deleted). The attitude of the SCIS was that people in crisis were neither sick nor mentally ill. Thus, the service was not necessarily either a medical one or a mental health one. People in crisis were to be given immediate, active, and aggressive services. SCIS regarded people in crisis as the responsibility of the community and felt that, as citizens, they had a right to expect such a community service. In contrast to many community health organizations that are often at least subtly immersed in intrapsychic concepts, the SCIS-type crisis center is organized with the idea of community control. It is staffed largely by neighborhood volunteers, and it is geared toward the specific characteristics of the immediate community.

Are these interventions really helpful? Although studies on crisis intervention proliferated in the 1970s, we still do not have a definitive answer. Much depends on the questions asked. For example, Decker and Stubblebine (1972) found that psychiatric hospitalizations were reduced when crisis intervention procedures were used. Yet when Gottschalk, Fox, and Bates (1973) compared crisis patients with patients who had been randomly assigned to a waiting list, they could find no differences in several indices of psychiatric improvement. Other reports (Getz, Fujita, & Allen, 1975; Huessy, 1972; Maris & Connor, 1973) are much more optimistic. There are obviously many problems in obtaining controls in crisis intervention research. Thus, little can be said with certainty at this point. Not all research shows the efficacy of crisis intervention (Kelly, Snowden, & Munoz, 1977). However, others argue that additional preventive measures could well reduce the number of deaths from suicide (Dew, Bromet, Brent, & Greenhouse, 1987).

Clearly, crisis interventions can help reduce distress. For example, when a teacher commits suicide, interventions must be undertaken to at least try to reduce students' shock (Kneisel & Richards, 1988). When a school bus collides with a train, the survivors must be helped to cope (Klingman, 1987). Under such circumstances, the community cannot wait for the ideal study to demonstrate the utility of an intervention.

Intervention in Early Childhood

Public health workers and mental health workers have long been aware of the educational disadvantages experienced by the poor. Of great concern is the fear that early deprivation in crucial developmental periods will mark the child for life. Impoverished preschool environments and experiences may almost guarantee that the child will do poorly in school and thus become vulnerable to a wide variety of mental health, legal, and social problems. But if successful preschool interventions can be developed, then a truly preventive course of action will have been taken.

Head Start Programs. We have already discussed the High/Scope Perry Preschool Program in Box 16-1. However, probably the best-known early childhood program is *Head Start*. In the mid-1960s, President Johnson created the Office of Economic Opportunity (OEO). Head Start was one of the programs targeted specifically for disadvantaged children. It was designed to prepare preschool children from disadvantaged backgrounds for elementary school. Head Start programs are locally controlled but required to conform to general federal guidelines. Local programs vary in number of hours of attendance, number of months (summer versus the entire year), background of teachers, and so on. The specific techniques used also vary, but basic learning skills are usually stressed. Physical and medical needs are also addressed, as are general school preparation and adjustment.

Evaluation. How effective are these early childhood programs? Gomby, Larner, Stevenson, Lewit, and Behrman (1995) find it useful to distinguish between child-focused programs and family-focused programs. In the former case, interventions are administered directly to the child; in the latter case, family members (such as parents) receive the intervention or training.

Participation in a child-focused program results in an average IQ gain of about 8 points immediately after program completion (although these relative gains dissipate over time), makes it less likely that the child will be placed in special

education or retained in grade, and makes it more likely that the child will graduate from high school (Barnett, 1995; Gomby et al., 1995). Positive social outcomes resulting from program participation have also been reported, including fewer contacts with the criminal justice system, fewer out-of-wedlock births, and higher average earnings than nonparticipants (Gomby et al., 1995; Yoshikawa, 1995).

Although family-focused programs appear to have more impact on parents' behaviors than do child-focused programs, it is not clear how much positive impact they have on children (Gomby et al., 1995; Yoshikawa, 1995). Not only is the focus of the intervention different, but so is its intensity and frequency. In the case of family-focused interventions, services may be rendered only once a week.

Self-Help

Not all help comes from professionals. Informal groups of helpers can provide valuable support that may stave off the need for professional intervention. What is more, such nonprofessional *self-help groups* as Alcoholics Anonymous, Parents without Partners, Le Leche League, Al-Anon, and many others can be incorporated as an effective part of treatment by a referring professional.

What needs do self-help groups meet? Orford (1992) discussed eight primary functions of self-help groups: (1) they provide emotional support to members; (2) they provide role models—individuals who have faced and conquered problems that group members are dealing with; (3) they provide ways of understanding members' problems; (4) they provide important and relevant information; (5) they provide new ideas about how to cope with existing problems; (6) they give members the opportunity to help other members; (7) they provide social companionship; and (8) they give members an increased sense of mastery and control over their problems.

Clearly, self-help groups serve several important functions for group members. However, research suggests that professionals should be available to serve as consultants to these groups

PROFILE 16-1

David DuBois, Ph.D.

Dr. David DuBois is an Associate Professor of Psychology at the University of Missouri. He received his B.S. in Psychology and Economics from Oberlin College and his Ph.D. in Clinical Psychology from the University of Illinois. Dr. DuBois specializes in clinical child psychology and community psychology. His community psychology research focuses on primary prevention of mental health problems in children and adolescents. Dr. DuBois is the author of numerous articles on self-esteem in childhood and adolescence, risk and resiliency among high-risk and economically disadvantaged youth, and school-based and community-based prevention programs for children, adolescents, and families. In addition to his scholarly pursuits, Dr. DuBois is an active member of his community and serves as a consultant to public schools, community mentoring programs, and community support services.

Dr. DuBois responded to several questions we posed concerning his background, his interests, and his assessment of the field of community psychology.

What originally got you interested in the field of clinical psychology?

There are two primary reasons that I became interested in the field of clinical psychology. First, as a young person, I found myself deeply concerned about the welfare of others and interested in doing whatever I could to make some small but significant difference in the world around me for the better. This all sounds a bit clichéd, I'll admit, but those are the sincere feelings I had then and still have now. Second, I also developed, at a relatively young age, a fascination with science—that is, the excitement of developing and then testing theories about why things work the way they do. Putting two and two together, in college I quickly found myself becoming interested specifically in the science of why people think, feel, and behave as they do and how this can lead not just to greater understanding but also (and this was of critical importance to me) to increased happiness and more positive lives for others out there in the "real" world when new knowledge is applied in ways that are useful. There are many ways, of course, to help the world become a better place through our careers, but I seemed to have some aptitude and natural ability for psychology. Fueled by my own values and the encouragement I received from various instructors, it therefore was not long before I was focused intently on pursuing a career in clinical psychology.

Describe what activity you are involved in as a clinical psychologist.

Currently, I spend most of my time conducting basic and applied research. I also teach a wide range of both undergraduate and graduate-level classes in psychology. I am a licensed psychologist and, in this role, I provide assessment and therapy services, on a limited basis, primarily for children and adolescents. In addition, I occasionally am asked to consult with schools and other agencies in the community about mental health issues. Finally, a new and exciting challenge that I have taken on in the past year is to do a weekly "ask the expert" segment on child mental health issues for a local television station. The common thread, for me, throughout all of these activities is research. So, if I am not actually doing research myself, I am likely, when teaching, for example, to be sharing the findings of some of the latest and most exciting studies with students or, even better yet, helping them learn how to conduct their own investigations. Similarly, when providing therapy or serving as a consultant, I am always looking for ways that research knowledge and methods can be used to both document and improve the effectiveness of services.

What are your particular areas of expertise or interest?

My particular areas of expertise are clinical child psychology and primary prevention. Essentially, I am interested in discovering the factors and experiences that make it less likely that children and adolescents will develop significant mental health–related problems either while growing up or later in adulthood. Of equal importance for me, though, is then translating this knowledge into programs and interventions that, once evaluated and shown to be effective, can be disseminated for use on a wide-scale basis. My current research focuses specifically on self-esteem as a factor that can be influential in a wide range of mental health issues for young people, ranging from depression and suicidal tendencies to behavioral problems such as delinquency and substance use. I also am investigating mentoring programs for youth, such as Big Brothers/Big Sisters, and the factors that lead them to be more or less successful in reaching their prevention goals.

What are the future trends you see for clinical psychology?

The most important future trend that I see for clinical psychology is an increasing emphasis on its scientific and research foundations. Whether it is providing therapy services in the clinic or prevention programs out in the community, the single characteristic that most clearly distinguishes clinical psychologists from other mental health professionals is their specialized set of skills for using research to guide and direct their activities toward greater effectiveness. In the era of managed care and growing competition for program funding, we can and should use this distinctive strength of the field to more firmly establish a niche for ourselves as having uniquely valued contributions to make to both the treatment and prevention of mental disorders.

What are some future trends you see in community psychology?

Community psychology will have much to offer in the coming years as the search for strategies to deal effectively and economically with mental health problems intensifies. Although not necessarily developed originally with cost concerns primarily in mind, innovations such as the use of paraprofessional helpers and mutual support groups can be expected to become a more prominent part of the landscape of traditional mental health treatment as they are increasingly viewed as viable and economical alternatives to an exclusive reliance on delivery of services by mental health professionals. To the extent that they can be shown to have a favorable cost-benefit ratio, preventive interventions also are likely to enjoy an increasingly broad base of support that includes not only social activists but also the CEOs of managed care companies! With growing demands on our society to deal effectively with issues of cultural diversity, community psychology also will be in a position to make a valuable contribution to ensuring that individuals and groups from differing backgrounds can work and live together in ways that promote positive mental health and well-being.

in order for the groups to be maximally effective. Professionals should not control the group, but a total lack of involvement on the part of a community psychologist does not appear to be helpful either (Orford, 1992). Certain organizational features appear to be correlated with the appraisal of group success, including a certain degree of order and rules to govern the group as well as the capability and knowledge of group leaders (Maton, 1988), and a community psychologist can play an invaluable indirect role by serving as a consultant to group leaders.

Paraprofessionals

One of the more visible features of the community movement is its use of laypersons who have received no formal clinical training, or *paraprofessionals,* as therapists. The use of paraprofessionals in the mental health field has been growing, but this trend has generated controversy. In reviewing 42 studies, Durlak (1979) concluded that professional education, training, and experience are not prerequisites for becoming an effective helping person. However, Nietzel and Fisher (1981) took issue with this conclusion and urged caution in interpreting the results of many of the studies reviewed by Durlak. They argued that many of the studies included in the Durlak review were methodologically flawed, and objected to Durlak's definitions of "professional" and "paraprofessional." With these and other criticisms in mind, Hattie, Sharpley, and Rogers (1984) reanalyzed the studies included in the Durlak review. Results from their meta-analysis concurred with those of Durlak. The overall results favored paraprofessionals, especially those who were more experienced and received greater amounts of training. More recent summaries have also argued that the available evidence suggests that paraprofessionals may be as effective as (and in some cases more effective than) professionals (for example, Christensen & Jacobson, 1994).

Besides effectiveness, there is also the issue of access to those who can provide help. Like it or not, most individuals who are in need of mental health services do not seek out mental health professionals. Instead, informal "therapy" takes place in many contexts and is provided by a variety of laypersons. For example, in an interesting and provocative set of studies, Cowen (1982) investigated the "helping behavior" of hairdressers and bartenders. Results indicated that a small but significant proportion of their customers raised moderate to serious personal problems, and both hairdressers and bartenders attempted a range of interventions (for example, just listening, trying to be supportive and sympathetic, presenting alternatives). Many community psychologists view these and other studies as evidence supporting the idea that consultation programs might be aimed at laypersons who naturally come into contact with individuals with mental health needs. These needs might not otherwise be addressed because the target individuals are not likely to seek out help from a mental health professional.

Although it hardly seems wise to argue that professionally trained clinical psychologists are unnecessary, it certainly appears that there is a vital role for paraprofessionals in the mental health field today. Clinical psychologists are needed, at the very least, to serve as consultants. Further, research may ultimately indicate that certain types of mental health problems respond better to services provided by a mental health professional. To date, however, the research questions addressed (for example, are paraprofessionals effective overall?) have been too broad to shed light on this issue.

Concluding Comments

In a relatively short time, the community emphasis has become a force that has led clinical psychologists to reexamine many of their old assumptions. But there are important questions that must be confronted as we conclude our discussion of this field.

Questions of Effectiveness

Years ago, Cowen (1967, 1973, 1978) raised the question of how much the community movement has accomplished beyond that accomplished by more traditional mental health approaches. The question was whether excitement and rhetoric had masked what was really very little substantive change. For example, Cowen (1973) could find relatively few research reports in the *Community Mental Health Journal* that provided concrete data. The papers also notably failed to address issues of prevention—a notion central to the community approach. Rappaport (1977) stated that no evidence really existed that U.S. communities had shown improved mental health. He even went so far as to suggest that the community mental health movement's greatest accomplishment may have been that it opened up new careers for persons who were formerly not part of the movement.

Although for years there was more rhetoric than implementation with regard to prevention programs (Iscoe & Harris, 1984), intervention is one of the cornerstones of the community movement. The question remains, however, whether the field really knows enough about the causes of mental health problems to mount large-scale, successful preventive programs. Fortunately, recent reports evaluating the effectiveness of a wide range of prevention programs lead us to a state of cautious optimism (for example, Durlak & Wells, 1997; Felner, DuBois, & Adan, 1991; IOM, 1994). Whereas many early reports regarding the efficacy of prevention programs were disappointing, community psychologists were able to learn from these failures and incorporate changes into new programs (Felner et al., 1991). For example, increased focus was placed on modifying psychological processes underlying various mental disorders, and interventions were designed to be more intensive and to extend over longer periods of time. The recent Institute of Medicine (IOM, 1994) report on preventing mental illness presented a group of 39 exemplary intervention programs (with demonstrated effectiveness) that targeted infants, preschoolers, elementary-age children, adolescents, adults, or the elderly.

Issues remain, to be sure. For example, there are questions regarding how intervention programs should be disseminated and by whom, how the programs are to be maintained over time (funding issues), and the need to train more researchers who are qualified to design, implement, and evaluate preventive interventions (IOM, 1994; Orford, 1992). The IOM report estimates that only about ten new prevention experts are produced a year; training programs and financial support are needed to increase this woefully low number.

Values, Power, and Civil Rights

Clearly, the community movement seeks to bring about social change and the reorganization of social institutions. The goal of such changes is undoubtedly laudable—better mental health for all. In case the reader had not noticed, this last statement almost sounds as if it might have been made by a candidate for public office. Indeed, some have argued that if community professionals want to bring about social change, they should run for political office. Those who take this position say that social change (especially when it is accomplished by public funds) is a political phenomenon and should be mandated by the public.

Obviously, there is much to be said on both sides. There is danger in adopting the narrow role of the patient's advocate rather than the broader role of advocate for the larger community. Adopting the narrow role may cause the real bases of patients' problems to be ignored. But there is also great danger in becoming a political advocate. It is hoped that the individual practitioner and the community-oriented advocate will each carefully examine the potential for both harm and good that is inherent in their positions.

The Training of Community Psychologists

At present, many have difficulty in understanding exactly what a community psychologist is. Perhaps because of its multidisciplinary orientation, community psychology has yet to develop an adequate or identifiable theoretical framework apart from those of other disciplines. This, at times, makes for role confusion. The community psychologist is part sociologist, part political scientist, part psychotherapist, part ombudsman, but lacks a specific identity. This ambiguity makes it difficult to design appropriate training programs.

Fortunately, there are some guidelines for training. The recent IOM report (1994) recommends that future prevention research specialists should have a solid background in a relevant discipline (such as nursing, sociology, social work, public health, epidemiology, medicine, or clinical/community psychology). Training in the design of interventions and the empirical evaluations of interventions is essential. Finally, practicum or internship-like training in prevention is also recommended. Educational requirements for prevention field specialists (those that actually carry out the interventions) are less stringent. Often, a bachelor's degree in a relevant field (such as psychology) is sufficient.

Given the increasing cultural and ethnic diversity in the United States, it is also important for community psychologists to receive training in how diversity issues may impact their work. For example, a knowledge of and sensitivity to cultural and ethnic differences will inform the following activities and roles of a prevention researcher (IOM, 1994):

1. Developing relationships with community leaders and organizations
2. Conceptualizing and identifying potential risk factors, mechanisms, and antecedents of problems or disorders
3. Developing interventions that will have maximum effect, and deciding how these should be disseminated and delivered to the target population
4. Determining the content and format of evaluation instruments

In order to achieve "cultural competence" (Cross, Bazron, Dennis, & Isaacs, 1989; Isaacs & Benjamin, 1991), community psychologists need to garner relevant professional experience with a variety of cultural and ethnic populations and to receive supervision from those who have expertise in designing, implementing, and evaluating interventions for individuals from these cultural and ethnic groups (IOM, 1994).

The Age of Managed Care

With its emphasis on prevention of mental health problems as well as initial reports indicating the cost-effectiveness of prevention efforts (see Box 16-1), community psychology is likely to play a primary role in designing and implementing interventions that will be recommended and financially supported by managed care companies.

However, the level of financial support for prevention efforts from the managed care industry will be related to the field's ability to continue to document the cost-effectiveness of these forms of intervention. In general, several factors influence the cost-effectiveness of a prevention program: cost of the intervention, frequency of the intervention necessary for the "effect," personnel costs, length of time necessary for an adequate trial, and the ability of prevention specialists to efficiently and accurately identify and enlist at-risk individuals (IOM, 1994). These are complex considerations that can only be addressed by systematic, and often time-consuming, prevention studies.

In addition to prevention programs, several other programs often associated with community psychology may be used to reduce the costs of mental health services, including crisis intervention, community alternatives to hospitalization, and self-help groups. Finally, it is likely that community psychologists will be called upon as consultants in order to tap their expertise in planning and implementing interventions.

The Future of Prevention

Given the compelling rationale of prevention and, more recently, the documented effectiveness of preventive efforts, it may seem puzzling that more resources are not dedicated to these forms of intervention. In a classic but still highly relevant article, Cowen (1983) described a number of barriers and resistances to the prevention movement. To cite just a few examples, those outside the field may remain skeptical because (1) the social and environmental focus of preventive interventions differs philosophically from the traditional focus on individual variables practiced by many clinical psychologists; (2) prevention, in a sense, must compete with more established forms of intervention (such as one-on-one psychotherapy); and (3) preventive programs may appear to be impractical and too costly (Cowen, 1983; Davison & Neale, 1998). In addition, the prevention field itself has served as an "enemy from within" (Cowen, 1983) by being less than precise with its terminology, being slow to document the effectiveness of preventive interventions, and neglecting to coordinate efforts across programs (for example, Hawkins & Catalano, 1992).

It is hoped that these issues can be adequately addressed in the future so that the interventions characteristic of community psychology will be more widely used. Perhaps in the future we should begin to focus as much on psychological wellness and health as on psychopathology and treatment of mental disorders (Cowen, 1991). If so, we will grasp the importance of such concepts as competence, resilience, prevention, modification of social systems, and empowerment.

Chapter Summary

Community psychology is an approach to mental health that emphasizes the role of environmental and societal forces in creating and alleviating problems. The focus is on prevention of problems rather than cure, and both individuals and the community are encouraged to take control of and master their own problems so that professional intervention is not necessary. A number of influences led to the development of the community psychology field, including the creation of the Joint Commission on Mental Health and Illness in 1955; the 1963 Kennedy Bill, which funded the construction of community mental health centers; deinstitutionalization; a shortage of mental health professionals; and a number of sociopolitical events in the 1960s.

Several concepts are central to community psychology. The concept of community mental health refers to the conviction that communities are responsible for their members, and that com-

munity mental health services should provide services to prevent problems and help the community and its systems function better. Community psychologists focus on prevention because it is believed that, in the long run, prevention initiatives will be more efficient and effective than individual treatment administered after the onset of problems. Community psychologists also focus on strategies to increase levels of empowerment—that is, to enhance individuals' sense that they control their own destinies. Finally, community psychologists seek to make positive changes by restructuring roles and social institutions. Increasing positive alternatives and resources for individuals makes it more likely that individuals will succeed and that a good person-environment fit will be realized.

Community psychologists frequently serve as consultants to mental health professionals, teachers, ministers, and other community personnel by lending their advice and expertise. Additional types of services offered by or orchestrated by community psychologists include crisis intervention, intervention in childhood and adolescence, self-help groups, and the enlistment of paraprofessionals to provide services to community members.

The future of community psychology looks bright. Many prevention programs have been shown to be effective and cost efficient, and consultation appears to be effective as well. There have been calls for more community psychologists and prevention field specialists to be trained in the future. Finally, it is likely that more and more interventions and programs designed and implemented by community psychologists will be recommended and financially supported by managed care companies in the future.

Key Terms

client-centered case consultation A type of mental health consultation that focuses on helping to solve a current problem with a specific client.

community mental health A movement arising in the 1950s that viewed mental health problems as emerging from failures in the social system. This movement called for community control of mental health services and strong focuses on prevention, early detection, and the provision of services to populations who had traditionally been under-served.

community psychology A psychological approach that emphasizes the role of environmental forces in creating and alleviating problems. Community psychology is preventative rather than remedial in orientation. Furthermore, it attends to the fit between the person and the environment (rather than the inadequacies of either) and focuses upon identifying and developing the strengths and resources of people and communities.

consultation The act by which a person who provides services to others (or oversees the provision of services) enlists the help of an expert for the purpose of improving these services.

consultee-centered administrative consultation A type of mental health consultation that focuses on helping an administrator enhance his or her skills so that he or she will be able to function more effectively in the future.

consultee-centered case consultation A type of mental health consultation that focuses on helping the consultee enhance the skills he or she will need to deal effectively with future cases.

crisis intervention A model of intervention that involves reaching people in acute states of stress and providing them with enough support to prevent larger problems from developing. This model requires flexibility and versatility, and traditional procedures and professional roles are often relinquished.

empowerment Providing individuals with the sense that they are in control of their own destinies, or enhancing existing feelings of control.

Head Start programs Primary prevention, early childhood programs designed to prepare preschool children from disadvantaged backgrounds for elementary school by focusing upon their basic learning skills, among other things.

indicated preventive interventions Preventive interventions that target people at high risk for developing the disorder (as determined by the presence of subthreshold symptoms or biological markers indicating a predisposition for developing the disorder).

paraprofessionals Persons with no formal clinical training who have been trained to assist professional mental health workers. The use of paraprofessionals has been growing in community psychology and in the mental health field as a whole, and the results of meta-analyses suggest that paraprofessionals may be as effective (or in some cases even more effective) than professionals.

prevention The principle that, in the long run, preventive activities will be more efficient and effective than individual treatment administered after the onset of disease or problems.

primary prevention Correcting negative conditions before significant problems emerge as a consequence of these conditions. The application of this prevention model often necessitates a degree of social change.

program-centered administrative consultation A type of mental health consultation that focuses on helping with the institution or management of a specific program.

secondary prevention Detecting and correcting problems early, while they are still amenable to intervention. This prevention model often entails screening large numbers of people, including people who are not seeking help and may not even appear to be at risk.

selective preventive interventions Preventive interventions that target individuals or subgroups of the population with a higher-than-average chance for developing the disorder in question (as determined by the presence of certain biological, psychological, or social risk factors).

self-help groups Informal groups that provide support for individuals facing specific problems and may stave off the need for professional intervention. Functions of self-help groups include providing important and relevant information to members, providing role models (individuals who have successfully confronted the problem at hand), providing emotional support and ideas for coping, and giving members an increased sense of mastery and control over their problems.

tertiary prevention Reducing the duration and negative effects of problems after they have occurred. This prevention model most often involves rehabilitation.

universal preventive interventions Preventive interventions that target the entire population.

Web Sites of Interest

To visit any of the web sites listed below, go to www.wadsworth.com and click on Links.

16-1 Society for Community Research and Action (Division 27 of the American Psychological Association)

16-2 Community Psychology Net

16-3 Prevention Science Clearinghouse

16-4 Society for Prevention Research

16-5 The Future of Children (links to prevention articles)

16-6 Community Psychology Graduate Programs

CHAPTER SEVENTEEN

Health Psychology and Behavioral Medicine

It seems that everyone realizes now that lifestyle affects our health and sense of well-being. Most health problems in the United States are related to chronic diseases (such as heart disease, cancer, and stroke), and these diseases are often associated with behavior or lifestyle choices (such as smoking or overeating) made by individuals (Brannon & Feist, 2000; P. L. Rice, 1998). The costs of medical care have skyrocketed to more than 14% of the gross domestic product (GDP), or more than $898 billion annually (Frank & VandenBos, 1994). The potential financial burden associated with health problems has led many to reevaluate their lifestyles and behavior. There has also been a shift in perception. Health has become associated with positive well-being rather than simply the absence of disease (Brannon & Feist, 2000; Rice, 1998). These trends, as well as others, have led Americans to focus much more intensely on behaviors and lifestyles that promote health and prevent disease.

Psychology, as a science of behavior, has much to contribute to the field of health, and health psychology has become a fast-growing specialty in clinical psychology. One clue that an emerging field has indeed been recognized is the appearance of textbooks and handbooks detailing that field. General textbooks on health psychology are now prevalent (for example, Brannon & Feist, 2000; Rice, 1998; S. E. Taylor, 1999), as are specialized textbooks on clinical health psychology (Belar & Deardorff, 1995; Camic & Knight, 1998), women and health (Blechman & Brownell, 1998), and pediatric health psychology (Goreczny & Hersen, 1999). In addition, several specialty journals (including *Health Psychology* and *Journal of Behavioral Medicine*) report on research in these fields. Finally, a separate division of the American Psychological Association (Division 38) has been established as a way to publicize and advance the contributions of health psychologists.

History and Perspectives

Although a variety of overlapping subdisciplines focus on health-related issues, we will focus primarily on two areas of psychology: behavioral medicine and health psychology. Recognition that mind and body are inextricably linked has been around since at least early Greek civilization. However, it was not until the late 1970s that definitions of behavioral medicine and health psychology began to crystallize.

Definitions

Although a variety of definitions have been offered over the years (for example, N. E. Miller, 1983; Schwartz & Weiss, 1977), *behavioral medicine* basically refers to the integration of the behavioral sciences with the practice and science of medicine. Matarazzo (1980) uses the term to refer to the broad interdisciplinary field of scientific investigation, education, and practice that is concerned with health, illness, and related physiological dysfunctions.

Health psychology is a specialty area within psychology. It is a more discipline-specific term, referring to psychology's primary role as a science and profession in behavioral medicine. It includes health-related practice, research, and teaching by many kinds of psychologists—social, industrial, physiological, and others. Health psychology has been specifically defined as

> the aggregate of the specific educational, scientific, and professional contributions of the discipline of psychology to the promotion and maintenance of health, the prevention and treatment of illness, and the identification of etiologic and diagnostic correlates of health, illness and related dysfunction. (Matarazzo, 1980, p. 815)

This definition was later amended to include psychologists' roles as formulators of health care policy and contributors to the health care system (see, for example, DeLeon, Frank, & Wedding, 1995). A recent definition of health psychology that incorporates these new roles has been offered by Brannon and Feist (2000), who state that health psychology "includes psychology's contributions to the enhancement of health, the prevention and treatment of illness, the identification of health risk factors, the improvement of the health care system, and the shaping of public opinion with regard to health" (p. 14).

History

As noted by Rice (1998), two major perspectives have influenced our views of health and illness. First is the biomedical tradition, which developed over time as people sought to gain knowledge through experience and observation. Early attempts were rather crude (for example, the discovery of the benefits of acupuncture, Hippocrates' humoral theory of disease and treatment), but later biomedical scientists focused on anatomy, "germ theory," and ultimately genetics in their attempt to define and understand illness and disease. This Western tendency to focus solely on biological factors and to adopt a reductionistic approach is not without its limitations, however (Rice, 1998). For example, critics argue that we still do not know what causes disease; rather, we have simply discovered another malfunction at a smaller level of analysis (for example, at the DNA level). Biomedical research may be so enamored with somatic correlates (such as abnormal physical processes and biochemical imbalances) that psychosocial variables are often ignored. Finally, this tradition reinforces the mind-body dualism perspective, one that is both outdated and limited in its utility. This is not to say that the biomedical tradition has been unimportant or irrelevant to medicine, science, and psychology. Rather, a strict biomedical viewpoint is at times too narrow because it cannot adequately account for widely encountered forms of illness and disease.

A second major influence on our views of health and illness is the psychosocial perspective (Rice, 1998). For centuries, medical literature has recognized that psychological and social processes may either cause or influence illness and disease. By the 1940s, this broad generalization had coalesced into the field of *psychosomatic medicine*. Psychosomatic medicine is based on the assumption that certain illnesses and disease

states are caused by psychological factors. Researchers (for example, Alexander, 1950) identified several "psychosomatic" diseases, including peptic ulcers, essential hypertension, and bronchial asthma. All illnesses were divided into those caused by "organic" or physical factors and those caused by psychological factors. Some who adopted this perspective believed that each psychosomatic illness had a different, specific underlying unconscious conflict predisposing the person to that disorder. For example, repressed hostility was believed to result in rheumatoid arthritis. Although initially appealing, these ideas (and psychosomatic medicine in general) began to founder as it became apparent that such specific psychogenic factors were not very predictive; most empirical studies did not support the theories. In fact, psychosocial factors are involved in all diseases, but these factors may not necessarily have a primary causal role.

Psychosomatic medicine was largely the province of psychiatrists and physicians. However, behavioral psychologists began to extend the range of their therapy methods to the so-called medical disorders. Problems such as obesity and smoking came under the scrutiny of psychologists as well. Then came a rapid increase in the use of biofeedback (discussed later in this chapter) to help patients control or modify certain physiological responses.

Another set of factors was slow to develop but ultimately had a strong impact. By the 1960s, many major infectious diseases had been conquered. The helping professions began to turn their attention to two of the biggest killers: cardiovascular diseases and cancer. Behaviors such as overeating, smoking, and drinking were increasingly identified as major correlates of these diseases. The spotlight began to shine not just on the disease process itself, but also on the associated behaviors whose reduction or elimination might reduce individuals' vulnerability to disease.

During the 1960s, stressful life events began to be implicated as specific risk factors for illness (for example, Holmes & Rahe, 1967). The examination of how stressful major life events affect health led to an examination of the health consequences of daily hassles, which can also prove stressful (for example, R. S. Lazarus, 1984). A related line of research demonstrated how personality and behavioral style can influence health. The impetus came from two cardiologists who were impressed with a common constellation of traits and behaviors shared by many who suffered from coronary heart disease. The so-called Type A personality (Friedman & Rosenman, 1974) is characterized by hostility, competitiveness, and being time driven. Although subsequent research has failed to support a direct link between Type A personality and heart disease (Brannon & Feist, 2000; Rice, 1998), the hypothesis stimulated research in health psychology and served to focus attention on other behavioral risk factors for coronary heart disease (such as smoking and lack of exercise), as well as on prevention efforts.

The recognition that both psychological and social factors influence illness and health is the basis of an influential perspective known as the *biopsychosocial model* (Engel, 1977). In many ways, this model can be viewed as an integration of the biomedical and psychosocial perspectives. As the name implies, the biopsychosocial model holds that illness and health are a function of biological, psychological, and social influences. Biological influences can include genetic predispositions, nutritional deficiencies, and biochemical imbalances. Psychological influences can include the individual's behaviors, emotions, and cognitions. Finally, social influences can include friends, family members, home environment, and life events. This biopsychosocial model represents how health psychologists conceptualize problems and plan interventions.

Many other factors were important in the development of the field of health psychology. The tremendous cost of health care has already been noted, along with the fact that infectious diseases were no longer the principal culprits. A large portion of health care costs are directly traceable to human behaviors and lifestyles that result in injuries, accidents, poisonings, or violence. Lifestyle choices such as alcohol and drug abuse, smoking, and dietary patterns contribute to a variety of illnesses and diseases.

The foregoing are just a few of the more prominent factors in the development of the health psychology field. We turn now to a discussion of how stress, lifestyle and behavior, personality, social support, and health are linked. These links form the basis of the field of health psychology.

Linking Stress, Lifestyle and Behavior, Personality, Social Support, and Health

What are the processes by which psychological and social factors influence health and disease?

Stress and Health. Although the term *stress* is frequently used, it is not often precisely defined (Brannon & Feist, 2000). Some use the term to refer to a quality of an external stimulus (such as a stressful interview), others to refer to a response to a stimulus (the interview caused stress), and still others believe stress results from an interaction between stimulus and response (stress resulted because the interview was challenging and I was not prepared). Most contemporary health psychologists adopt this third, interactionist viewpoint, seeing stress as a process that involves an environmental event (a stressor), its appraisal by the individual (is it challenging or threatening?), the various responses of the organism (physiological, emotional, cognitive, behavioral), and the reevaluations that occur as a result of these responses and changes in the stressor (Rice, 1998). This transactional model of stress is depicted in Figure 17-1. These and other psychosocial stimuli may contribute to a stress process that can then directly affect the hormonal system, the autonomic system, and the immune system.

The physiological effect of stress on the body involves a complex chain of events (Brannon & Feist, 2000), illustrated in Figure 17-2. Stress causes the sympathetic nervous system, a system responsible for mobilizing body resources in urgent situations, to stimulate the adrenal medulla of the adrenal gland. This results in the produc-

FIGURE 17-1 The stress process: an interactionist view

Source: Rice, P. L. (1998). Health psychology. *Pacific Grove, CA: Brooks/Cole. Page 177. Used with permission.*

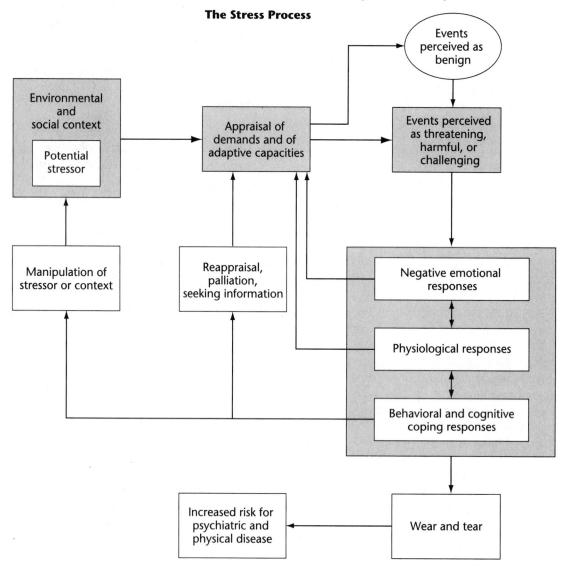

The Stress Process

tion of the catecholamines epinephrine and norepinephrine, whose effects on the body include increased heart rate, respiration, blood flow, and muscle strength. Stress also causes the pituitary gland (a structure connected to the hypothalmus in the forebrain) to release adreno-corticotropic hormone (ACTH), and ACTH stimulates the adrenal cortex of the adrenal gland to secrete glucocorticoids. The most im-

portant glucocorticoid where stress is concerned is cortisol. Cortisol is a hormone that, like epinephrine and norepinephrine, mobilizes the body's resources. Cortisol serves primarily to increase energy level and decrease inflammation. The latter function is particularly useful if injuries are sustained in an urgent situation.

Although responses of the body to stress can be helpful, severe stress and prolonged activa-

FIGURE 17-2 Physiological effects of stress

Source: Brannon, L., & Feist, J. (2000). Health psychology: An introduction to behavior and health (4th edition). Pacific Grove, CA: Brooks/Cole. Page 116. Used with permission.

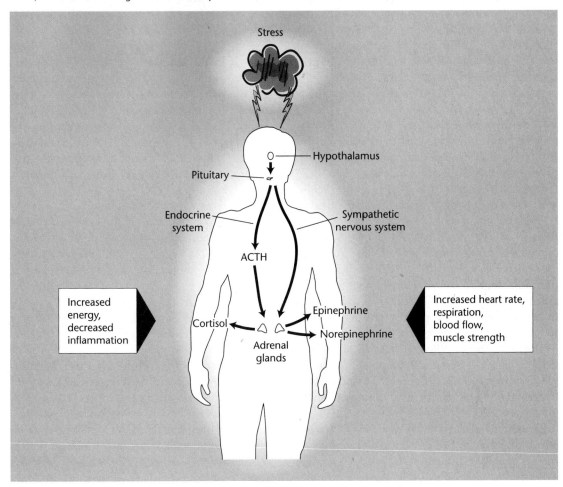

tion of these systems can have adverse effects on body organs, mental functions, and the immune system. For example, stress can affect the immune system so that it cannot effectively destroy viruses, bacteria, tumors, and irregular cells. More than two decades ago, Ader and Cohen (1975) presented evidence suggesting that the nervous system and the immune system interact and are interdependent by demonstrating that immune system responses in rats could be classically conditioned. This initial report eventually led to a number of studies investigat-

ing the relationship between physiological factors (such as reactions to stress) and immune system response (Brannon & Feist, 2000). Currently it remains unclear whether immunosuppression is a direct effect of stress or whether it is simply part of the body's response to stressful events (Brannon & Feist, 2000). In any case, stress does appear to be an important (though not the only) influence on health and illness.

Behavior and Health. Behaviors, habits, and lifestyles can affect both health and disease.

Everything from smoking, excessive drinking, or poor diet to deficient hygiene practices have been implicated. Such behaviors are often deeply rooted in cultural values or personal needs and expectations. In any event, they are not easily changed. Later in this chapter, we will discuss in more detail several behaviors or lifestyle choices that have been linked to health. These include cigarette smoking, alcohol abuse and dependence, and weight control.

Cognitive variables may influence our decisions about adopting healthy or unhealthy behaviors. To cite one example, many health psychologists have focused on the variable self-efficacy. Self-efficacy, discussed in earlier chapters, refers to "people's beliefs about their capabilities to exercise control over events that affect their lives" (Bandura, 1989, p. 1175). Self-efficacy is relevant to a number of topics addressed by health psychologists, including major theories of health-related behavior change (Maddux, Brawley, & Boykin, 1995). This construct plays a major role in the most prominent social cognitive models of health behavior, including the health belief model (Rosenstock, 1974; Rosenstock, Strecher, & Becker, 1988), protection motivation theory (R. W. Rogers, 1975; Sturges & Rogers, 1996), and the theory of planned behavior (Ajzen, 1985, 1988).

Protection motivation theory (PMT), for example, posits that behavior is a function of threat appraisal (an evaluation of factors that will affect the likelihood of engaging in the behavior, such as perceived vulnerability and perceived potential for harm) and coping appraisal (an evaluation of one's ability to avoid or cope with negative outcome). Coping appraisal is influenced by one's self-efficacy or belief that one can implement the appropriate coping behavior or strategy (Maddux et al., 1995). An example that applies PMT to a real-life health decision may be instructive. Janey, an adolescent girl faced with a decision about whether or not to start smoking cigarettes, according to PMT, would engage in threat appraisal and coping appraisal. Threat appraisal might involve evaluating the dangers of smoking (such as lung cancer)

as well as the likelihood of her own vulnerability to this outcome. To the extent that she does not perceive the danger to be severe or immediate to herself, Janey might be more likely to start smoking. Coping appraisal is also relevant. This process might involve Janey's evaluation of how likely it is that she could refrain from smoking (the recommended coping strategy). To the extent that Janey believes she will not be able to refrain from smoking (for example, because all her friends smoke), it becomes more likely that she will engage in this behavior. Thus, the cognitive variable self-efficacy can play a prominent role in behavior and lifestyle choices that ultimately influence health.

Problems can also arise from the ways in which people respond to illness. Some people may be unable or unwilling to appreciate the severity of their illness and fail to seek timely medical help. When they do get medical advice, they may fail to heed it. All of these behaviors can indirectly foster adverse outcomes. We will discuss medical treatment compliance later in this chapter.

Personality Factors. Both directly and indirectly, personality characteristics can affect health and illness in many ways (Friedman & Booth-Kewley, 1987): (1) personality features may result from disease processes; (2) personality features may lead to unhealthy behaviors; (3) personality may directly affect disease through physiological mechanisms; (4) a third, underlying biological variable may relate to both personality and disease; and (5) several causes and feedback loops may affect the relationship between personality and disease.

Perhaps the most widely studied association between a personality trait and illness is that between Type A behavior and coronary heart disease. As mentioned previously, the notion of a possible link between personality or coping style and adverse health consequences, specifically coronary heart disease, was proposed by two cardiologists (Friedman & Rosenman, 1974). They identified a set of discriminating personality characteristics and behaviors and proposed that these constitute a *Type A behavior pattern.* Glass (1977) describes Type A individuals as those who tend to

Perceive time passing quickly

Show a deteriorating performance on tasks that require delayed responding

Work near maximum capacity even when there is no time deadline

Arrive early for appointments

Become aggressive and hostile when frustrated

Report less fatigue and fewer physical symptoms

Are intensely motivated to master their physical and social environments and to maintain control

Table 17-1 provides some examples of interview questions that are used to identify Type A individuals.

A number of early studies suggested a relationship between Type A behavior and coronary heart disease. However, these findings were often misinterpreted as indicating that Type A individuals are likely to develop coronary heart disease (Davison & Neale, 1998). More recent studies do not show as strong a relationship between Type A behavior and heart disease as was once thought (Smith, 1992), and it is clear that the vast majority of Type A individuals do not develop coronary heart disease (CHD). However, Type A individuals are at relatively greater risk for CHD. More recent studies suggest that the anger-hostility component of the Type A pattern does a better job of predicting coronary heart disease than the more global Type A categorization (Guyll & Contrada, 1998; Smith, 1992).

In an important methodological and conceptual analysis of the research examining hostility and health, Smith (1992) presented several theoretical models that might explain the link between hostility and health. The *psychophysiological reactivity model* posits that hostile individuals experience larger increases in heart rate, blood pressure, and stress-related hormones in re-

---

TABLE 17-1 Selected Items from the Behavior Pattern Interview

4. Does your job carry heavy responsibility?
   a. Is there any time when you feel particularly rushed or under pressure?
   b. When you are under pressure, does it bother you?

6. When you get angry or upset, do people around you know about it? How do you show it?

12. When you are in your automobile, and there is a car in your lane going far too slowly for you, what do you do about it? Would you mutter and complain to yourself? Would anyone riding with you know that you were annoyed?

14. If you make a date with someone for, oh, two o'clock in the afternoon, for example, would you be there on time ?
   a. If you are kept waiting, do you resent it?
   b. Would you say anything about it?

17. Do you eat rapidly? Do you walk rapidly? After you've finished eating, do you like to sit around the table and chat, or do you like to get up and get going?

19. How do you feel about waiting in lines: Bank lines, or supermarket lines? Post office lines?

Source: From "The Interview Methods of Assessment of the Coronary-prone Behavior Pattern," by R. H. Rosenman, pp. 68–69. In T. M. Dembroski, S. M. Weiss, J. L. Shields, S. G. Haynes, and M. Feinleib (Eds.), *Coronary-prone Behavior,* Copyright © 1978 by Springer-Verlag. Reprinted by permission.

---

sponse to potential stressors. Increased psychophysiological reactivity is believed to encourage the development of coronary artery disease and the symptoms of coronary heart disease. The *psychosocial vulnerability model* proposes that hostile individuals are more likely to experience a more stressful psychosocial environment because they have higher levels of mistrust and are scanning their environments for possible future mistreatment. A *transactional model* reflects a combination and integration of the psychophysiological and psychosocial models. This integrative model proposes that those high in hostility *create* potentially stressful situations in their lives because of their general mistrust and their subsequent actions.

Finally, the *health behavior model*, unlike the previous models, does not assume that the physiological aspects of stress are the crucial link between hostility and health. Rather, the health behavior model proposes that hostile individuals tend to engage in poor health habits (such as smoking, excessive drinking of alcohol, poor exercise habits) and thus are more susceptible to coronary heart disease. This parsimonious explanation of the findings of an association between hostility and coronary heart disease needs to be evaluated further in future studies.

Social Support and Health. A topic attracting increased research interest is social support and its effects on health and well-being. *Social support* refers not only to the number of social relationships, but also to the quality of those relationships (can you confide in your friends and family members?) The basic idea is that interpersonal ties can actually promote health. They insulate people from harm when they encounter stress, decrease susceptibility to illness, and help people comply with and maintain treatment regimens. Social support is, in many ways, a kind of coping assistance. A number of studies have indicated that better health outcomes are positively related to social support (for example, Berkman, Leo-Summers, & Horwitz, 1992; Berkman, Vaccarino, & Seeman, 1993; Cohen & Herbert, 1996; House, Landis, & Umberson, 1988; Williams et al., 1992). For example, Williams et al. (1992) followed approximately 1400 patients with coronary artery disease for an average of 9 years, and found that patients who rated higher on measures of social support (for example, married, able to confide in spouses) exhibited significantly lower rates of mortality over the follow-up period. This relation held even after controlling for demographic variables and medical risk factors. This study and others suggest that social support may act as a type of "buffer" against adverse health outcomes.

The relationships among social support, stress, and health may depend on a number of factors, including race, gender, and culture. For example, women (on average) seem to benefit more from social support than do men; this may be because women tend to have more emotionally intimate relationships (Brannon & Feist, 2000). Preliminary data also suggest that whites may benefit from social support more than non-whites (Brannon & Feist, 2000). However, the reason for this is not clear, and the possibility of race and ethnic differences needs further study. Clearly, the relationship between social support and health is complex.

Range of Applications

A full description of all the problems to which health psychology has addressed itself is beyond the scope of this chapter. A partial list culled from recent accounts would include the following:

Smoking

Alcohol abuse

Obesity

Type A personality

Hypertension

Cardiac arrhythmia

Raynaud's disease

Alzheimer's disease

Acquired immune deficiency syndrome (AIDS)

Cystic fibrosis

Anorexia nervosa

Chronic vomiting

Encopresis-fecal incontinence

Ulcers

Irritable bowel syndrome

Spasmodic torticollis

Tics

Cerebral palsy

Cerebrovascular accidents

Epilepsy

Asthma

Neurodermatitis

Psoriasis

Prurigo nodularis

Hyperhidrosis

Chronic pain

Headaches

Insomnia

Diabetes

Dysmenorrhea

Dental disorders

Cancer

Spinal cord injuries

Sexual dysfunction

In the pages that follow, we will deal with several of these disorders, especially as they illustrate methods of intervention and prevention. Box 17-1 suggests some of the issues that are within the province of health psychology and behavioral medicine, especially as applied to the problem of human immunodeficiency virus (HIV) infection and acquired immune deficiency syndrome (AIDS).

Methods of Intervention

In essence, health psychology and behavioral medicine apply behavioral and cognitive-behavioral methods of assessment and treatment. We will present brief overviews of general classes of interventions used (respondent methods, operant methods, cognitive-behavioral methods, and biofeedback), and then present a few examples of how these techniques are used by health psychologists.

Respondent Methods

Over time, a neutral stimulus (conditioned stimulus) that is paired with a naturally eliciting stimulus (unconditioned stimulus) may itself become capable of eliciting a particular response.

This is the classic Pavlovian paradigm. Emotional reactions may, for example, become associated with formerly neutral, innocuous stimuli. This process may then produce conditioned emotional reactions that, if chronic, can produce such persistent tissue changes as ulcers, neurodermatitis, or essential hypertension. These kinds of symptoms have been treated by health psychologists in various ways. In the case of respondent techniques, extinction or systematic desensitization interventions are commonly used.

In *extinction*, a conditioned emotional reaction is eliminated by creating a situation in which the conditioned stimuli are no longer associated with the environmental stimuli that generated the behavior. This approach can be used, for example, to eliminate children's fears of visiting the dentist. The child is brought to the dentist's office, familiarized with the office personnel, allowed to meet other children who have successfully negotiated the terrors of dentistry, and so on. In short, the child's emotional reactions are extinguished because, over time, less anxiety is aroused in the dentist's office. A variation would be exposure techniques, described in Chapter 14. Instead of the gradual approach just described, the child, under professional supervision, would be forced to remain in the "terrifying situation," the anxiety would peak and then rapidly diminish, and the child would thereby learn that the anxiety was needless. The result is extinction of the anxiety responses.

Systematic desensitization is a good example of counterconditioning (see Chapter 14). If the patient can be taught to relax in the face of anxiety-provoking stimuli, the anxiety diminishes. Relaxation techniques are designed to enable individuals to produce a state of lowered arousal through their own efforts. As a preliminary step, patients are usually taught the basic behavioral principles related to their symptoms and how therapy relates to the implementation of these principles. For example, a patient whose stressful lifestyle has led to some physical problems would be taught the relationship between lifestyle and illness by means of a fairly extensive

BOX 17-1

Hot Topic   *The Role of Health Psychology in the Future: Acquired Immunodeficiency Syndrome (AIDS)*

Chesney (1993) has illustrated the challenges that will likely confront the fields of health psychology and behavioral medicine in the future by using the epidemic spread of human immunodeficiency virus (HIV) infection and the subsequent lethal condition of AIDS as an example. It is estimated that millions of Americans are infected with HIV. Further, an estimated 270,841 persons are living with AIDS, and this number has been increasing each year (Centers for Disease Control and Prevention, 1998). Because there currently is no cure for AIDS nor any vaccine for HIV, prevention of high-risk behavior is paramount (Chesney, 1993). Further, those who are infected with the virus and become symptomatic are in need of psychological treatment focusing on coping with AIDS. Chesney (1993) outlines five trends in medicine that are relevant to HIV infection and AIDS, as well as to other conditions that are within the province of health psychology and behavioral medicine:

1. *Early identification of those who are at risk.* With regard to HIV infection, this involves encouraging voluntary testing, counseling following the dissemination of test results, and decreasing (and hopefully stopping) high-risk behavior (such as unprotected sex and sharing of needles).

2. *Expectation of successful behavior change programs.* In order to stop the spread of HIV, behavior must be changed. In addition, "relapse" in this case (for example, engaging in unprotected sex) may have potentially lethal consequences. It is important to maintain behavior change by incorporating factors that have been empirically shown to lead to non-high-risk behavior.

3. *Growing population of those dealing with chronic disease.* Along with a trend toward a "graying" of America and a related increase in the prevalence of chronic diseases that characteristically plague older adults, the number of Americans who will have AIDS in the near future will drastically increase the need for health-related services. Specifically, health psychologists will increasingly be called on to assist in teaching coping skills to patients as well as their primary caregivers.

4. *Broadening perspectives.* Health psychologists will need to incorporate community and public health perspectives in addition to focusing on the individual patient. For example, community-based media campaigns and community-based interventions are necessary to combat the spread of HIV and other precursors to chronic disease.

5. *Addressing health problems on a global scale.* We must keep in mind that illnesses and diseases affect people around the world, and these must be addressed in all nations. For example, J. M. Mann (1991) reported that the World Health Organization estimates that 30 to 40 million people (adults and children) will be infected with HIV by the year 2000.

Finally, a type of paradox should be mentioned. As medications that improve length of survival for AIDS patients become more readily available, the fear associated with AIDS and HIV infection has begun to subside. An unintended consequence has been that risky behaviors (such as unprotected sex) have increased, especially among adolescents and young adults. Therefore, a challenge for health psychology and other fields is to educate the public and implement interventions that will serve to decrease the frequency of high-risk behaviors, especially within the younger age groups.

verbal explanation (or reading material). Following this, a thorough psychophysiological assessment might be conducted, using recording equipment, self-ratings of tension, and the therapist's own observation.

Next, patients are taught to self-monitor. For example, they might be trained in how and when to record the presence of headaches. They would be taught to record data on the presence of environmental stimuli that precede the headache, their own response to the headache, and the consequences that follow from the symptoms.

Finally, patients receive specific training in relaxation. Chapter 14 provides detailed information on relaxation training. Positive expectancies for a good outcome are engendered, and the physical conditions are arranged so that relaxation will be easy to achieve (assuming a comfortable position, loosening tight clothing, adjusting lighting). Regular practice in the therapist's office is followed by practice at home.

How effective are relaxation techniques in treating problems addressed by health psychologists? Relaxation appears to be effective in treating hypertension, tension headaches, and anxiety (Brannon & Feist, 2000). When combined with guided imagery—a technique in which patients bring images of peaceful and calm situations to consciousness—relaxation has also proven effective for treating burn pain and the nausea and anxiety associated with chemotherapy (Brannon & Feist, 2000).

Operant Methods

Learned responses may be either maintained or eliminated through the consequences they bring about. As we discussed in Chapter 14, behaviors that are reinforced tend to recur, whereas behaviors that are not reinforced or are punished tend to decrease in frequency.

Operant conditioning can be used in health psychology and behavioral medicine either to increase behaviors said to lead toward health or to decrease those said to contribute to health problems. For example, health psychologists have used operant methods in addressing pain behaviors (Brannon & Feist, 2000). From an op-

erant perspective, many of the behaviors displayed by pain patients (complaining, moaning, and the like) have been initiated and maintained because of positive reinforcement. Family members and medical staff may have paid more attention to the patient following these behaviors. Additional reinforcers might include sympathy, time off from work, or fewer expectations from the family. To change these pain behaviors, family members and medical staff may be trained to reinforce more desirable behaviors (such as attempts to become more physically active) and to ignore less desirable behaviors (such as constant complaining). Research suggests that these approaches to pain behaviors do show some success, as indicated by increased physical activity and decreased intake of pain medication (Brannon & Feist, 2000).

Finally, health psychologists may use *contingency contracting*. In this method, the therapist and patient draw up a formal agreement or contract that specifies the behaviors that are expected as well as the consequences for certain behaviors. For example, patients may be reinforced for participating more in physical therapy, taking their medication, or reducing their number of somatic complaints. Reinforcement may take the form of tokens that can be exchanged for something of value to the patient.

Cognitive-Behavioral Strategies

Health psychologists use a variety of cognitive techniques. These techniques may be used alone or in concert with other strategies, such as relaxation or biofeedback. Some of these methods, such as rational restructuring and stress inoculation training, were discussed in Chapter 14. All of these methods emphasize the role of thinking in the etiology and maintenance of problems. Cognitive-behavioral interventions seek to change or modify cognitions and perceptions that are believed to be related to a patient's problem.

The list of "well established" empirically validated treatments presented in Chapter 11 contains several cognitive-behavioral treatments for stress or other health problems. In Chapter 14, we discussed stress inoculation training (SIT) for coping with various stressors. This approach is used by health psychologists for a wide variety of patients (such as chronic pain patients). Other effective cognitive-behavioral treatments for health problems include those for headache, pain, smoking cessation, and bulimia.

Cognitive-behavioral therapy is a major component of a treatment for chronic headaches (Blanchard & Andrasik, 1985). Blanchard and Andrasik's treatment begins with a psychoeducational component, in which the following points are emphasized to the headache sufferer: (1) tension, anxiety, and worry can cause headache; (2) headache is a signal from the body that the person is not effectively coping with stress; (3) any situation can lead to stress—our interpretations and beliefs about a situation determine whether or not it produces stress; and (4) there are some common beliefs or expectations that may lead to stress and headache. In the treatment, patients are taught to monitor their thinking processes via a *self-monitoring record* whenever tension, worry, or anxiousness occurs. A sample self-monitoring record for events associated with headaches is shown in Figure 17-3. For each situation, patients list the cues that trigger tension and anxiety, the physical sensations, their thoughts right before the onset of the tension, a rating of their emotions, and their behavioral responses to the episode (such as withdrawal or attack).

The therapist uses these data to tailor specific interventions. First, attempts are made to connect situations, the patient's thoughts, and the emotional and behavioral responses. The therapist emphasizes that the patient's thoughts are a crucial link in the process that produces headaches and that these thought patterns can be modified. The patient's "maladaptive" thoughts, expectancies, and beliefs (those associated with stress and headache) are examined closely and their validity challenged. For example, a professor may report that thoughts regarding inadequacy ("I'm never going to get this chapter written") typically precede the experience of tension and anxiety that leads to headache. The therapist might challenge these thoughts ("Is it

really true that you have never finished any articles or chapters?") and train the professor to disrupt the situation→thought→tension headache chain by using alternative thinking and coping strategies (repeating, internally, more adaptive thoughts such as "This task is difficult but I will get it done, just as I have been able to do in the past"). Finally, as the patient is able to implement these alternative ways of thinking and coping in real-life situations and achieves some success, the therapist reinforces progress through praise.

Biofeedback

Biofeedback has become enormously popular and, for some, has become almost synonymous with behavioral medicine itself. Under certain conditions, patients can learn to modify or control physiological processes, such as heart rate, blood pressure, and brain waves.

Biofeedback encompasses a wide array of procedures. Basically, however, some aspect of the patient's physiological functioning (such as heart rate or blood pressure) is monitored by an apparatus that feeds the information back to the patient in the form of an auditory, tactile, or visual signal. The idea is for the patient to then modify that signal by changing the physiological function. Thus, a patient experiencing severe headaches might have electrodes placed on the forehead. The electrodes pick up tiny muscle contractions in that region of the head, which are amplified and transformed into tones. The tones vary as the muscular activity changes. The patient's task is to voluntarily reduce or eliminate the tone, thus signifying a reduction of muscular tension and a corresponding reduction in the headache.

Biofeedback has been shown to be effective for a number of different problems (Brannon & Feist, 2000). For example, biofeedback has been used successfully in clinical studies to reduce headache pain, lower muscle tension, and reduce low back pain. However, several caveats must be acknowledged. First, in some cases, the effects of biofeedback are not superior to the effects

FIGURE 17-3 Example of a self-monitoring record for situations associated with tension headache

TIME	SITUATION	PHYSICAL SENSATIONS	THOUGHTS	FEELING (0–100)	BEHAVIOR
8:00 a.m.	Breakfast, husband says I look "scattered"		Worry about getting to work on time. (If I'm late, Mr. ___ will notice.)	Anxiety (25) Hurt (20)	Rush through breakfast, leave dishes in sink
10:00 a.m.	Given too many technical letters to type	Upset stomach from coffee, tense muscles	Everybody assumes I'm superwoman. No one takes account of other demands on my time.	Anxiety (30) Annoyance (20)	Rushed typing, curt on telephone, take extra long break to calm down
12:00 noon	Jerry (fellow employee and supervisor) asks me to lunch. Talks suggestively about recent divorce.	Lightheaded, tingling sensations in head and face, nausea	Jerry is on the make. I don't like fending him off—so why am I here? Am I seductive?	Anxiety (50) Awkwardness (40) Is that a feeling?	Try to offer sympathy but resent ulterior motive. Probably curt.
2:00 p.m.	Spencer gives me a long report with 5 tables to be done by 5 p.m.	Headache—back of neck	F___ him—he didn't even ask what else I had to do. Fantasize Spencer stuck in elevator. No time to relax.	Anger (60) Anxiety (60)	Typing report—distractedly
4:00 p.m.	Report completed	Headache worsening, nausea	If I could quit ruminating and was more organized, I would get more work done.	Anger (40) Anxiety (50)	Give report for correction. Complain to Susan. Type letters.

Source: From Holroyd, K. A., & Andrasik, F. (1982). A cognitive-behavioral approach to recurrent tension and migraine headache. In P. E. Kendell (Ed.), Advances in cognitive-behavioral research and therapy (Vol. 1). New York: Academic Press. Used with permission.

obtained from relaxation. This is important because biofeedback requires expensive equipment and trained personnel. Thus, the cost of this treatment is much higher than some alternatives, like relaxation. Second, because biofeedback and relaxation are often included in the same treatment package, it is sometimes hard to separate the effects of one from the other. However, some studies have separated the effects of the two and reported that biofeedback may provide unique positive effects, especially for those who do not respond to relaxation techniques (Lehrer, Carr, Sargunaraj, & Woolfolk, 1994).

Still, many critics remain uncomfortable about the scientific status of biofeedback. Some are suspicious because of the cultish, faddish, or evangelistic pronouncements of some of its practitioners. In some cases, biofeedback seems to operate largely as a placebo. Although supporters point to the many clinical reports of its efficacy, others have made the harsh judgment that "there is absolutely no convincing evidence that biofeedback is an essential or specific technique for the treatment of any condition" (Roberts, 1985, p. 940).

Biofeedback may not, by itself, lead to optimal therapeutic gains. When it is effective, it is usually part of a larger package that also includes relaxation or cognitive strategies; if removed from such a package, it may lose its effectiveness. However, it may serve as an example to the patient that self-regulation in life is possible. It may be that biofeedback works better in the clinic than in the research laboratory because the clinic places the biofeedback machine in a larger context of an understanding clinical relationship and additional therapeutic techniques. At the very least, biofeedback appears to be a useful technique to teach patients to become more aware of their bodily signals and of what these may mean.

Prevention of Health Problems

Nearly everyone agrees that a few simple behaviors, if widely practiced, would dramatically reduce the toll of human misery and the torrent of dollars pouring into the health care system. These include reducing our consumption of salt and fatty foods, driving carefully and using seat belts, exercising regularly, avoiding cigarettes, and decreasing stress. But giving advice and having people take it are two very different things. Therefore, psychologists, other behavioral specialists, and medical professionals have mounted research programs to learn how to treat and also prevent a variety of potentially harmful human behaviors. In this section, we will discuss prevention efforts in several important areas related to health: cigarette smoking, alcohol abuse, and weight control.

Cigarette Smoking

Increased awareness of the dangers of cigarette smoking has led to a steady decline since the mid-1960s in the percentage of Americans who are habitual smokers (Brannon & Feist, 2000). However, rates of smoking differ according to gender, level of education, and income. One disconcerting trend is that the rate of smoking for women has shown much less of a decline than that for men (Centers for Disease Control and Prevention, 1994). In fact, among white-collar workers, the smoking rate for women now exceeds that for men.

Cigarette smoking has been linked to an increased risk of cardiovascular disease and cancer, the two leading causes of death in the United States. Even though smoking increases one's chances of premature death from diseases such as coronary heart disease, cancers of the respiratory tract, emphysema, and bronchitis, people still smoke. Why? Possible reasons include tension control, social pressure, rebelliousness, the addictive nature of nicotine, and genetically influenced personality traits such as extraversion (Brannon & Feist, 2000; Krantz, Grunberg, & Baum, 1985). Tension control and social pressure are thought to be reasons for initiation of smoking, whereas rebelliousness, addiction, and personality are seen primarily as maintaining factors.

A variety of techniques have been used to induce people to stop smoking, including educational programs, aversion therapy (such as rapid smoking), behavioral contracts, acupuncture, cognitive therapy, and group support (Brannon & Feist, 2000). Relapse rates are high (70–80%), however, and research findings about which cessation approach is best are conflicting. Most smokers who do quit, do so on their own.

The best approach seems to be to prevent the habit from starting in the first place. Unfortunately, education alone (such as warning messages on packages) does not appear to deter young people from smoking (Brannon & Feist, 2000). What appears to be more effective is focusing on immediate rather than delayed negative consequences, teaching coping skills, and increasing feelings of self-efficacy.

One of the early encouraging multiple-component prevention programs aimed at children and teenagers was based on social learning principles and used peer role models (R. I. Evans, 1976). Videotaped presentations, peer modelings, discussion groups, role playing, monitoring smoking, and checking repeatedly on attitudes and knowledge about smoking were all used with elementary school children. Such an approach seems superior to those used with adolescents that focus on long-term negative effects from smoking. The trick seems to be to focus on immediate negative consequences (for example, from peers) rather than delayed ones (such as emphysema). Programs similar to Evans's in Houston have been undertaken in other states. Other prevention programs that use student rather than adult models to encourage teenagers not to smoke have been successful as well (for example, Murray, Richards, Luepker, & Johnson, 1987). Programs that teach refusal skills (practicing responding to audiotaped offers of cigarettes) also seem to reduce rates of smoking (Elder et al., 1993).

Alcohol Abuse and Dependence

It is estimated that about 70% of men and 50% of women in the United States consume alcoholic beverages (United States Department of Health and Human Services, 1993). Although some studies have suggested positive health ben-

efits from alcohol for light or moderate drinkers, consumption of alcohol has also been associated with a number of negative outcomes. Heavy alcohol use has been associated with increased risk for liver or neurological damage, certain forms of cancer, cardiovascular problems, fetal alcohol syndrome, physical aggression, suicide, motor vehicle accidents, and violence (USDHHS, 1997). This extensive list of alcohol-related problems has made the treatment and prevention of alcohol abuse and alcohol dependence (alcoholism) a high priority.

Over the years, many treatment approaches have been applied to problem drinkers; most of these treatments preach total abstinence. These have ranged from medical treatments and medications such as disulfiram (Antabuse) and naltrexone to traditional psychotherapy and group supportive strategies such as Alcoholics Anonymous. However, alcoholism is a problem that has been extremely resistant to virtually all intervention, and the relapse rate is high.

Another, more controversial, approach to the treatment of alcohol problems is *controlled drinking* (Sobell & Sobell, 1978). As the name implies, this approach has as its goal light to moderate (but controlled) drinking. Clients are taught to develop alternative coping responses (other than drinking) and to closely monitor alcohol intake. The field is divided as to the merits of this approach, but research does suggest that controlled drinking is a viable treatment option for some alcoholics (USDHHS, 1997). Many alcohol treatment programs also incorporate *relapse prevention* training (Marlatt & Gordon, 1985). The majority of clients treated for alcohol problems have a relapse episode soon after treatment is terminated. Rather than see this as a failure (a sign that total relapse is imminent), clients are taught coping skills and behaviors they can use in "high-risk" situations to make total relapse less likely.

Alcohol abuse and dependence are complex problems that will probably require multimodal treatment strategies. Because of the difficulties with secondary and tertiary approaches to treatment or prevention, more and more professionals have turned to primary prevention to forestall the development of problem drinking. For both

Beth E. Meyerowitz, Ph.D.

Dr. Beth Meyerowitz is a Professor of Psychology in the Department of Psychology at the University of Southern California and an Associate Professor of Preventive Medicine at the University of Southern California School of Medicine. Dr. Meyerowitz is an expert on quality-of-life issues and coping among cancer patients and their family members. Among her many honors and accomplishments, she serves as a panel member of the Health Behavior and Prevention Review Committee for the National Institute of Mental Health, she is a reviewer for a number of prominent journals in clinical psychology, and she has received several awards for her undergraduate teaching. Dr. Meyerowitz has published numerous articles and book chapters in her field and has obtained several federal grants to fund her research.

Dr. Meyerowitz responded to several questions we posed concerning her background and interests, and she offered her views on the future of clinical psychology and health psychology.

What originally got you interested in the field of clinical psychology?

Looking back, I realize that I became interested in clinical psychology when I was 14 years old. During that summer, I was a volunteer counselor at a day camp for children with cerebral palsy. I greatly enjoyed playing with and teaching the children, but mostly I found that I was fascinated by trying to understand the experience of these severely disabled children and their families. I was especially intrigued by the fact that some families seemed to cope so well, even in the face of what seemed to me to be overwhelming difficulties. How was it that some individuals, when faced with chronic problems over which they had little control, could appear to be happy and well adjusted? Throughout high school and college, I volunteered to work in different clinical settings. In each of these settings, I found myself wondering how some people managed to fare so well, whereas others faced ongoing distress and disruption in their lives. By the time I applied to graduate school, I knew that I wanted to focus on research about how psychologically "normal" individuals react to and cope with chronically stressful situations.

Describe what activities you are involved in as a clinical psychologist.

As a clinical psychologist in a university psychology department, my primary activities are teaching, research, and administration. My classroom teaching includes undergraduate courses in Introduction to Clinical Psychology and Human Sexuality and graduate seminars in Introduction to Clinical Interviewing, Human Sexuality, and Health Psychology. I also spend a lot of time with undergraduate and graduate students supervising research projects. My research activities involve planning and designing studies, developing collaborations with physicians and patient groups, writing grant proposals, overseeing data collection, analyzing research results, giving talks, and writing journal articles. In addition to my research and teaching, I am involved with a number of organizations and committees both at the university level and nationally. I also review grants for NIH and several foreign governments, review articles for psychological and medical journals, and serve as a licensing examiner for the State of California. One of the things that I like best about being an academic clinical psychologist is that I am able to engage in a wide variety of interesting activities.

What are your particular areas of expertise or interest?

My research focuses primarily on quality of life and coping among patients and family members following the diagnosis of chronic illness, particularly cancer. I am interested in understanding the common reactions to diagnosis and treatment across quality-of-life domains including emotional, cognitive, social, physical, and functional changes. What can patients, their families, and their health care providers expect at different stages of the disease? What person, social, contextual, or medical factors predict who will adjust quickly and who will have ongoing problems? What are the psychological mechanisms through which these factors play a role in adjustment? What are the processes through which many individuals find benefit and meaning in adversity? Recently, my colleagues and I have been developing and testing brief psychosocial interventions designed to improve quality of life and to enhance coping skills in patients with early-stage cancer and their partners. I also have been interested in issues of culture and ethnicity, which I investigate through research projects in Italy and with diverse populations in the United States.

What are the future trends you see for clinical psychology?

I believe that the most exciting possibilities for the future of clinical psychology lie in our expertise as clinical researchers. Clinical psychologists are involved in broadening the traditional boundaries of research and expanding methodologies to address a wide range of clinically relevant questions. We will be called upon to design research that is responsive to societal needs, as well as being firmly based on sound theory and methodology. Because research is a transportable skill, research activities can be housed in community settings through establishing scientist-community links. I also expect that clinical psychologists will need to defend their role as service providers, in light of increasing demands to document those areas in which Ph.D.-level training is essential to optimal performance. Psychologists with doctoral degrees might be called on to develop effective treatments and psychometrically sound assessment tools to determine which treatments are best suited for which individuals. Cost-effectiveness will need to be taken into account in a variety of clinical domains.

What are some future trends you see in health psychology?

Health psychology and behavioral medicine are relatively new fields of study, which have received dramatically increased focus over the past three decades. As such, the field is wide open for development in numerous exciting directions. For example, we are learning a lot about the importance of psychological factors in causing illness, through the impact of stress and isolation on immunologic and hormonal functioning. In addition, health psychologists should continue to develop theories and interventions designed to increase healthy behaviors and decrease risky behaviors. After all, much of the premature death in industrial countries is related to individual failure to adopt guidelines for healthy living. Research in both of these areas needs to be extended to underserved populations, with a focus on identifying the role of culture in influencing health and quality-of-life outcomes. Research on culture also should include investigation of the culture of the health care system and of ways to make health care more "user friendly" for patients and their families. A comprehensive understanding will require considering health-related behaviors and quality of life within the context of the individual's ongoing life, rather than as separate and isolated domains. With this information, psychologists can continue to develop novel approaches to primary, secondary, and tertiary prevention. I anticipate that as researchers develop behavioral and psychosocial interventions that are effective and easily integrated into ongoing health care delivery, these interventions will gradually become components of standard care. To the extent that psychologists can demonstrate the money-saving benefits of health psychology and behavioral medicine, insurers will be more likely to begin reimbursing for such services.

drinking and drug abuse, programs similar to those designed to prevent adolescents from smoking are being developed. Often these programs are implemented through health-education courses in high school or media campaigns. School-based prevention programs typically involve one or more of the following components: affective education (building self-esteem, increase decision-making skills); life skills (communication skills, assertiveness training); resistance training (learn to resist pressures to drink alcohol); and correction of erroneous perceptions about peer norms (USDHHS, 1997). Current research evidence suggests that programs that incorporate peer resistance training and correction of misperceptions regarding peer norms show the most promise (USDHHS, 1997).

Obesity

Behavioral treatments for obesity have been more common than for any other condition. One reason for this emphasis is that obesity is associated with such medical disorders as diabetes, hypertension, cardiovascular disease, and certain cancers (Brannon & Feist, 2000). It is also a socially stigmatizing condition that impairs the self-concept and inhibits functioning in a wide array of social settings. Often problems of weight can be traced to childhood: 10–25% of all children are obese, and 80% of these individuals become obese adults (Stunkard, 1979).

Although it is clear that obesity has a genetic component (Meyer & Stunkard, 1993), causes of obesity undoubtedly represent complex interactions among biological, social, and behavioral factors, and exact mechanisms are difficult to pin down. Traditional medical and dietary methods of treatment have not been very effective; obese individuals lose weight but then quickly regain it. Furthermore, the dropout rate may be high in traditional weight-control programs. Most behavior modification programs include components aimed at restricting certain types of foods, teaching when and under what conditions to eat, encouraging regular exercise, and maintaining modified eating patterns after the program has ended.

Again, however, early prevention may be the best and safest road to weight control. An excellent example of such an approach is the Stanford Adolescent Obesity Project (Coates & Thoresen, 1981). A variety of strategies were used with adolescents in the hope that control at this age would lead to prevention in adulthood. The strategies used were self-observation, cue elimination, and social and family support. These interventions were noticeably more effective when parents were involved. Many investigators are also exploring the possibility of using peer group discussion. A recent ten-year outcome study of a family-based behavioral treatment for childhood obesity suggests that early intervention in childhood can effect important and lasting changes in weight control (Epstein, Valoski, Wing, & McCurley, 1994).

Other Applications

Treatment and preventive initiatives must be supplemented with techniques that encourage patients to cope with medical procedures and to follow medical advice.

Coping with Medical Procedures

The prospect of facing surgery, a visit to the dentist, or a variety of medical examinations has been enough to strike fear into the heart of even the strongest. Faced with such procedures, many patients delay their visits or even forgo them entirely. Health psychologists specializing in behavioral medicine have developed interventions to help patients deal with the stress surrounding such procedures.

Medical Examinations and Procedures. Some medical examinations or procedures are especially stressful. Without them, however, the patient may not be properly diagnosed and may miss out on a health-saving intervention. A good example is sigmoidoscopy, a fairly common procedure designed to examine the mucous lining of the bowel to discover the presence of any pathological growths in the last ten inches of the colon. This, in turn, can aid in the early detection and prevention of colon cancer. For many patients, however, the procedure is very stressful. It involves inserting a scope into the colon, with some stretching of the bowel. Although all of this is not very painful or dangerous, it does unnerve many people, and they perceive it as a humiliating procedure. Interventions have been developed that help patients cope with the stress of this and other procedures. For example, brief instructions might be given to prepare the patient for what to expect.

What kind of information is most likely to help patients cope with stressful medical procedures? Often a distinction is made between *procedural information* (descriptions of what will occur) and *sensory information* (descriptions of the sensations that will be felt). Reviews of relevant studies indicate that although procedural preparation was superior to sensory preparation in reducing negative affect, pain reports, and other distress, combined procedural-sensory preparation was the most effective method (for example, Suls & Wan, 1989).

In addition to informational interventions, evidence supports the use of behavioral interventions in certain situations as well. For example, venipunctures are common in the course of cancer treatment, and this procedure can be quite distressing to children undergoing cancer treatment, their parents, and nurses who perform the procedure (Manne et al., 1990). Manne et al. developed a behavioral intervention to reduce the level of distress associated with the procedure. Its components include attentional distraction (using a party blower during the procedure), pacing of breathing, positive reinforcement (for example, receiving stickers if the child cooperates), and parent coaching. The researchers found that this intervention package markedly reduced children's behavioral distress, parents' anxiety, and parents' ratings of child pain. Interestingly, however, this treatment did not significantly reduce children's self-reported pain.

Preparation for Surgery. A sizable amount of research has been done on ways to improve psychological preparation for surgery. Similar to

those used to prepare patients for medical examinations and procedures, interventions include (1) relaxation strategies, (2) basic information about the procedures to be used, (3) information concerning the bodily sensations experienced during the procedures, and (4) cognitive coping skills (Brannon & Feist, 2000). For example, Wilson (1981) carried out a well-controlled study in which intensive training in relaxation was provided. In a sample of 700 patients undergoing either cholecystectomy (removal of the gall bladder) or abdominal hysterectomy, this relaxation intervention not only reduced hospital stays but improved both self-reports and physiological data.

Another technique was used with children about to undergo surgery. It was found that a film showing a *coping model* significantly reduced the children's emotional reactions during their time in the hospital (Melamed & Siegel, 1975). The model on the film was shown coping successfully with the procedure. Those who saw the film prior to surgery were less anxious before their operation and showed fewer behavior problems afterward. In general, the most effective modeling interventions involve models who (1) are undergoing the same procedure as the target, (2) appear initially anxious about the procedure, and (3) successfully cope with the anxiety and the procedure (Brannon & Feist, 2000).

Compliance with Regimens

Despite the availability of intervention strategies, the fact remains that many individuals do not comply with program interventions or else do not maintain their new behavior over any significant period of time. It is estimated that the rate of noncompliance with medical or health advice is approximately 50% (Brannon & Feist, 2000). Truly successful program strategies must generate both compliance and long-term maintenance. Both behavioral and psychosocial factors must be considered.

In general, purported predictors of patient compliance can be broken down into four categories: illness/disease characteristics, personal characteristics of the patient, cultural norms, and practitioner-patient interaction (Brannon & Feist, 2000). Table 17-2 summarizes research findings concerning the relationship between a variety of factors and patient compliance.

Educational and instructional methods have not been particularly helpful in improving compliance, but behavioral interventions have proved more successful (Brannon & Feist, 2000). DiMatteo and DiNicola (1982) recommend several general strategies to improve patient compliance:

1. The use of prompts as reminders (for example, taking medicine before each meal, telephone calls from providers).
2. Tailoring the treatment regimen to the patient's schedule and lifestyle.
3. Using written contracts that promise a reward to the patient for complying with treatment guidelines.

Health Psychology: Prospects for the Future

Health psychology is a growing field, and more psychologists are entering it every year. Therefore, it may now be time for the field to take a look at itself and decide how best to train health psychologists and structure programs to achieve training goals (Belar, 1997). In this last section, we will discuss several health care trends, training issues for future health psychologists, and important issues for the field of health psychology to address in the future.

Health Care Trends

By the end of 1997, 85% of Americans belonged to some kind of managed health care plan (Winslow, 1998). In managed care systems, containing costs is a high priority. In previous chapters, we have noted the great impact managed care has had and will have on clinical psychologists. The impact on health psychologists will be even greater because these specialists often work in medical centers or primary care settings. Health psychologists, by virtue of their training,

are well suited to provide interventions that will serve to cut the costs of medical care (Belar, 1997; Friedman, Sobel, Myers, Caudill, & Benson, 1995). As business and industry realize the costs they must absorb from employees whose habits and lifestyles create absenteeism, inefficiency, and turnover, it is expected they will use the skills of health psychologists more often.

Although there appears to be an ever-increasing need for clinical psychologists specializing in health or behavioral medicine, it should also be noted that currently there appears to be a surplus of mental health professionals. For example, Frank and Ross (1995) estimate that there are approximately 32.8 social workers, 22.8 psychologists, 13.1 psychiatrists, and 4.3 psychiatric nurses for every 100,000 Americans (a total of 73 mental health professionals per 100,000). The problem lies in the overlapping definitions of each discipline; all claim to assess and treat similar problems. As the economic stakes become higher, it is likely that these disciplines' self-definitions will incorporate concepts and issues once thought to be uniquely characteristic of health psychology and behavioral medicine. Frank and Ross (1995) call for more coordination of health workforce planning at the national level.

> Clearly defining and establishing psychology's role in health care also requires efforts at delineating psychology's unique contributions amid an increasing supply of other health-related professions . . . efforts to establish clear professional boundaries and identities among the various health care groups should be based on dialogue, coordination, and cooperation to ensure that the health care needs of the population are met by qualified, ethical, and competent professionals. (p. 524)

Training Issues

A major source of health psychologists continues to be clinical psychology programs. The scientist-practitioner and clinical scientist models adopted by most clinical psychology programs

TABLE 17-2 Summary of Findings Relating Disease/Illness Characteristics, Personal Characteristics of the Patient, Cultural Norms, and Practitioner-Patient Interaction Factors to Adherence

Predictors	Findings
I. Disease Characteristics	
1. Severity of medication's side effects	No relationship
2. Severity of illness	
(as seen by the physician)	No relationship
(as seen by the patient)	Positive relationship
3. Duration of treatment	Negative relationship
4. Complexity of treatment	Complexity leads to non-adherence, as does number of doses over 3
II. Personal Characteristics	
1. Age	
Adults	
(exercise up to 6 months)	Positive relationship
(exercise after 6 months)	No relationship
(cancer screening)	Curvilinear relationship
(hypertensive medication)	Positive relationship
(diabetes)	Positive relationship
(heart disease)	Positive relationship
Adolescents	
(diabetes)	Negative relationship
(diabetes)	Negative relationship
2. Gender	
(exercise)	Men and women equal
(hypertensive medication)	Men and women equal
(diet)	Women more compliant
(medication)	Women more compliant
3. Social support	Positive relationship
(hemodialysis regimen)	Positive relationship
(appointment keeping)	Positive relationship
4. Emotional support	
(diabetes)	Positive relationship
(heart regimen)	Emotional support better predictor than marriage
5. Personality traits	
(personality disorder)	No relationship
(obsessive-compulsive)	Positive relationship
(cynical hostility)	Negative relationship
6. Personal beliefs	
(avoidance coping)	Negative relationship
(personal control)	Positive relationship
III. Cultural Norms	
(diabetic & hypertensive patients in Zimbabwe)	Cultural beliefs predict compliance
(physician's knowledge of Hispanic culture)	Positive relationship
IV. Practitioner/Patient Interaction	
1. Verbal communication	
(emotional information)	Negative relationship
(physician disinterest)	Negative relationship
2. Practitioner's personal qualities	
(friendliness)	Predicts compliance
(gender)	Female doctors provide more information
(communication skills)	Positive relationship

Source: Brannon & Feist (2000), *Health psychology: An introduction to behavior and health* (4th ed.), pp. 98–99. Pacific Grove, CA: Brooks/Cole. Reprinted with permission.

enable them to train clinicians well suited for health psychology. Until recently, no other psychology specialty offered the combination of academic, scientific, professional, and hospital experiences required for work in medical settings. At the same time, Stroebe and Stroebe (1995) make a case for the background of social psychologists. Again, the roles of methodology, quantitative analysis, and research design are emphasized. Other psychology subspecialties are also well represented in health psychology. Many of the people cited in this chapter are experimental or physiological psychologists—not just clinicians or social psychologists.

For the most part, health psychology is still a kind of ad hoc appendage to doctoral programs in psychology. The student enters a clinical, social, or experimental program and then, in addition to the core experience, does some specialized research or takes a practicum or two in a health-related topic. Perhaps this is augmented by an internship at a health care site. But essentially, the health experiences are grafted onto an already existing program in clinical psychology or some other related discipline.

Many people are now calling for health psychology to be a standard, core training component for all professional psychologists (for example, Frank & Ross, 1995). Because of the importance of health issues and the broadening of the definition of clinical and professional psychology, training in areas such as psychopharmacology, neuropsychology, and psychoneuroimmunology is considered essential. Further, future health psychologists must be trained so that they can design and conduct studies to empirically evaluate health outcomes. Currently, some clinical psychology graduate programs offer "tracks" in health psychology or behavioral medicine, but this is the exception rather than the rule. In any case, curricular recommendations for health psychology training continue to be offered (Brannon & Feist, 2000). Several web sites listed at the end of this chapter are good starting points for those interested in training models and opportunities for health psychologists.

Other Challenges

Any newly emerging field has problems in defining the roles of its members; health psychology is no exception. Years ago, S. E. Taylor (1984) identified several of these problems. One problem is simply role ambiguity. No one is totally prepared to say just what a health psychologist should do—especially in a practical work setting. Health psychologists may actually find themselves without psychology colleagues or role models in the health setting, which only adds to their confusion. Second, issues of status also arise. In health settings, the physician is clearly at the top of the heap. Sometimes the psychologist enjoys much less status in a medical center setting than, for example, in an academic setting. Furthermore, the psychologist and the health care professional may have competing goals. The latter may be interested only in identifying immediate ways of helping the patient. The psychologist may be more tentative and contemplative while thinking about research, theoretical models, and interventions.

As one way of establishing their identity and presence in settings traditionally dominated by physicians, health psychologists need to document the cost-effectiveness of their interventions (Friedman et al., 1995). In this era of health care reform, insurance companies and government agencies are scrupulously examining ways to drive down the cost of health care. Given the many successful and cost-efficient interventions performed by those specializing in health psychology and behavioral medicine, ask Friedman et al. (1995), why haven't these interventions been integrated to a greater extent into our health care system? They suggest several possible reasons:

1. Many of the data supporting the role of health psychology are unknown to physicians.
2. Biological origins of diseases and illnesses have been emphasized, causing many to overlook the possible benefits of psychosocial explanations and behavioral interventions.
3. Patients may be resistant to psychological interventions (and explanations).

BOX 17-2

Ethnicity and Cancer Outcomes

An examination of the incidence and mortality rates of common forms of cancer among different ethnic groups reveals a number of striking differences (Meyerowitz, Richardson, Hudson, & Leedham, 1998). In general, African Americans have the highest incidence rates and mortality rates overall, whereas Latinos, Chinese Americans, and Native Americans have the lowest rates. However, incidence and mortality rates also vary according to gender and to anatomical site of the cancer. Thus, it is difficult to come to any general conclusions that focus on broad ethnic labels. Meyerowitz et al. (1998) make a strong case for going beyond ethnic categories in trying to better understand cancer incidence and mortality. For example, they found that significant associations between ethnicity and cancer screening and follow-up could be accounted for by variables such as income, knowledge of cancer and screening procedures, access to health care, and doctor recommendation. Further, they reported that the relation between ethnicity and survival

could be accounted for by socioeconomic status, knowledge of cancer and its treatment, access to adequate treatment, and adherence to treatment.

These findings are important for several reasons. First, they show that broad generalizations regarding ethnicity and health may be somewhat misleading, in that the relation between ethnicity and illness may be primarily due to other variables that are associated with ethnicity. This suggests that researchers need to dig deeper when they find ethnic differences in order to provide a better theoretical explanation for the outcome of interest. Second, the variables identified by Meyerowitz et al. (1998) are more psychologically meaningful and can be targeted for intervention. For example, their findings suggest that free screenings and follow-ups, more information on cancer and screening procedures, and better health care access would induce more individuals to participate in screenings, thus improving the chances of early detection and successful treatment.

4. Clinical health psychology and behavioral medicine are still confused with traditional, long-term psychotherapy.

Clearly, physicians, insurance companies, the federal government, and the general public need to be educated regarding the role of health psychologists, as well as the potential financial and clinical benefits of their interventions.

Another challenge for the field concerns ethnicity and health. The health profiles (such as life expectancy and health status) of various ethnic minority populations in the United States appear to differ greatly from one another, and more research is needed on health-promoting and

health-damaging behaviors among members of these groups (N. B. Anderson, 1995). Informative articles reporting on the health status of African Americans, Asian Americans, and Hispanic Americans (Flack et al., 1995), behavioral risk factors related to chronic diseases in ethnic minorities (Meyers, Kagawa-Singer, Kumanyika, Lex, & Markides, 1995), and the use of health care systems by ethnic minorities (Penn, Snehendu, Kramer, Skinner, & Zambrana, 1995) have recently appeared in a special issue of *Health Psychology*. These reports and others point out the need to further assess the relations between behavior and health in special populations. (See, for example, Box 17-2.)

It is easy to become carried away with the enthusiasm generated by an exciting new field. This has been true in virtually every area of clinical psychology so far. However, there is still a gap between the field's promise and its accomplishments. As any experienced clinician will tell you, it is very hard to change human behavior over the long haul. Nevertheless, health psychology most assuredly deserves our enthusiasm as well as our caution. Many people are optimistic about the future of health psychology, given the pressing demands of improved health care. In fact, Belar (1997) and others believe that health psychology is uniquely suited to be *the* specialty for the professional practice of psychology in the twenty-first century.

Chapter Summary

Health psychology is an increasingly popular specialty that includes psychology's contributions to health promotion, to prevention and treatment of health problems, and to the health care system. Most health psychologists adhere to a biopsychosocial model of health and illness, a model that integrates the more traditional biomedical model and the psychosocial model. The links between stress, lifestyle and behavior, personality, social support, and health form the basis of the field of health psychology. The stress process has physiological, emotional, behavioral, and cognitive effects that may make one more vulnerable to illness. Behaviors and lifestyle choices can also have a major impact on health. Further, personality and coping styles have also been associated with illness. Finally, social support can influence one's vulnerability to adverse health outcomes.

Health psychologists address a wide range of problems through assessment, intervention, and prevention initiatives. Most interventions are behavioral or cognitive-behavioral in nature and include techniques such as systematic desensitization, operant conditioning, stress inoculation training, and biofeedback. Specific interventions for chronic headache, cigarette smoking, alcohol abuse, obesity, coping with medical procedures, and treatment compliance were discussed.

The prospects for health psychology look bright. There is an increasing need for better and more efficient interventions to cut health care costs. Further, data support the role of health psychologists in health care.

Key Terms

behavioral medicine A broad, interdisciplinary field of research, education, and practice that integrates the behavioral sciences with the discipline of medicine.

biofeedback A wide array of procedures through which a patient learns to modify or control certain physiological processes. Usually the physiological process of interest is monitored by an apparatus and the information is fed back to the patient in the form of an auditory, tactile, or visual signal. The patient then attempts to modify the signal (and thus change the physiological response) using a variety of techniques.

biopsychosocial model A theoretical model that holds that health and illness are a function of biological (e.g., genetic predispositions, nutritional deficiencies), psychological (e.g., the individual's cognitions and emotions), and social (e.g., friends and family, life events) influences.

cognitive-behavioral strategies Techniques that emphasize the role of thinking in the etiology and maintenance of problems, and attempt to modify the patterns of thinking that are believed to contribute to a patient's problem. Several cognitive-behavioral treatments for stress or other health problems appear on the current list of empirically validated psychological treatments.

contingency contracting An operant method in which a therapist and patient draw up a formal agreement that specifies the behaviors that are desired or undesired, as well as the consequences for engaging or failing to engage in these behaviors.

controlled drinking A controversial approach to the treatment of alcohol problems that has as its goal light to moderate drinking. Clients are taught to monitor their alcohol intake closely, and to develop coping responses that do not involve drinking.

coping appraisal In Protection Motivation Theory, the evaluation of one's ability to successfully avoid or cope with negative outcomes. If one concludes that one is unlikely to cope effectively (by refraining from an undesired behavior), one will be more likely to engage in the behavior.

coping model An individual who demonstrates effective coping in a stressful situation (e.g., preparing for a medical procedure or surgery). Observing or playing a tape of such a model may be useful for individuals who are about to experience similar procedures.

extinction The elimination of an undesired conditioned response by creating a situation in which the conditioned stimulus is no longer associated with the environmental stimulus that initially generated the response.

health behavior model A theoretical model that proposes that the relationship between a hostile predisposition and health is mediated by the performance (or lack of performance) of health behaviors, rather than by the physiological aspects of stress.

health psychology A specialty area within psychology that applies the tools of the discipline to the prevention of illness, the enhancement and maintenance of health, the identification of the correlates of illness and health, the treatment of individuals in the health care system, and the formulation of health care policy.

operant conditioning The principle whereby behaviors that are reinforced tend to recur whereas behaviors that are not reinforced or are punished tend to decrease in frequency.

prevention In health psychology, the idea that by performing a few simple behaviors consistently (e.g., exercising, avoiding smoking, using seat belts), people may dramatically reduce their risk for health problems and may significantly reduce health care costs.

procedural information Descriptions of what will actually occur when one undergoes a stressful medical procedure.

Protection Motivation Theory A model of health behavior that posits that behavior is a function of both threat appraisal and coping appraisal.

psychosomatic medicine A field (popular in the 1940s and 1950s but currently out of vogue) that is based on the assumption that certain illnesses and disease states are caused by psychological factors. Some adherents believed that each "psychosomatic" illness corresponded to a specific unconscious conflict that predisposed the patient to that illness.

relapse prevention A range of strategies for preventing relapse, usually in the context of treating the addictive behaviors. Patients are directed to anticipate problem situations and are taught coping skills to navigate their way through these situations without engaging in the undesired behavior. Or, in the event of a lapse, patients are taught how to respond so as to prevent a total relapse.

relaxation A state of lowered anxiety, stress, and physiological arousal. Relaxation may be induced in a number of ways, and it appears to be effective in the treatment of a number of health concerns.

self-efficacy People's beliefs about their capacity to control or gain mastery over the events that affect them. This construct plays a prominent role in most social-cognitive models of health behavior.

self-monitoring record A record often employed in cognitive-behavioral treatments on which individuals monitor the occurrence of a certain emotional response, including the situation that triggered it, the strength of the emotions, any physical or behavioral reactions, and their thinking processes at the time. By examining the data collected, the therapist may draw connections between certain situations and the patient's thoughts, emotions, and behaviors, and may ultimately tailor specific treatment interventions.

sensory information Descriptions of the sensations that will be encountered when one undergoes a stressful medical procedure.

social support A term that refers to the number and quality of one's social relationships. A number of studies have shown that social support is positively associated with better health outcomes.

sympathetic nervous system The portion of the nervous system that is responsible for mobilizing body resources in urgent situations. Prolonged sympathetic activation can have adverse effects on body organs, mental functions, and the immune system.

systematic desensitization A respondent method for reducing anxiety in which patients practice relaxation while visualizing anxiety-provoking situations of increasing intensity. This technique is based on the principle that one cannot be relaxed and anxious simultaneously.

threat appraisal In Protection Motivation Theory, the evaluation of negative factors (such as the potential for harm) that affect the likelihood of engaging in a particular behavior. If one concludes that there is little immediate threat to oneself, one will be more likely to engage in the behavior.

transactional model of stress A model that views stress as a process that involves an environmental event, its appraisal (as threatening or benign) by the individual, the individual's physiological, emotional, cognitive, and behavioral responses to the event, and the reappraisal of the event that occurs secondary to the person's responses, as well as to changes in the stressor.

Type A Behavior pattern A personality pattern that has been associated with increased risk for coronary heart disease. Among other things, Type A individuals exhibit a great sense of time urgency, work near maximum capacity even when there is no time deadline, become aggressive and hostile when frustrated, and are motivated to master their environments and to maintain control.

Web Sites of Interest

To visit any of the web sites listed below, go to www.wadsworth.com and click on Links.

17-1 Division 38 of the American Psychological Association (Health Psychology)

17-2 Guide to Internships in Health Psychology

17-3 Major rotations

17-4 Minor rotations

17-5 Postdoctoral Training Programs in Health Psychology

17-6 Centers for Disease Control and Prevention

17-7 Society of Behavioral Medicine

17-8 Health Psychology and Rehabilitation

Neuropsychology

A very important growth area in clinical psychology over the past several decades has been the field of neuropsychology. This growth has been reflected in (1) increases in membership in professional neuropsychological associations; (2) the number of training programs that offer neuropsychology courses; and (3) the many papers, books, and journals now being published on neuropsychological topics. As the field moves into its "early adulthood," the primary challenge appears to be health care reform (Meier, 1997). The number of jobs available to clinical neuropsychologists is no longer unlimited, and the clinical services offered by neuropsychologists will need to be provided at lower cost and higher effectiveness (Meier, 1997). Let us begin, however, by taking a step back in order to get a better sense of how this field developed as well as the roles of neuropsychologists.

Perspectives and History

As the term would suggest, neuropsychologists have a foot in both the psychological and neurological domains. While some have received their basic training in clinical psychology, others have been trained by neurologists.

Definitions

What is *neuropsychology*? Most simply, it can be defined as the study of the relation between brain function and behavior (Golden, Zillmer, & Spiers, 1992). It deals with the understanding, assessment, and treatment of behaviors directly related to the functioning of the brain (Golden, 1984). *Neuropsychological assessment* is a noninvasive method of describing brain functioning based on a patient's performance on standardized tests that have been shown to be accurate and sensitive indicators of brain-behavior relationships (Golden et al., 1992). The neuropsychologist

> may address issues of cerebral [brain] lesion lateralizations, localization, and cerebral lesion progress. Neuropsychological evaluations have also provided useful information

about the impact of a patient's limitations on educational, social, or vocational adjustment. Since many patients with neurological disorders, such as degenerative diseases, cerebrovascular accident, or multiple sclerosis, vary widely in the rate at which the illness progresses or improves, the most meaningful way to assess patients for the severity of their condition is to assess their behavior objectively via neuropsychological assessment procedures. (Golden et al., 1992, p. 19)

Roles of Neuropsychologists

Neuropsychologists function in a number of different roles (Golden et al., 1992). First, neuropsychologists are often called on by neurologists or other physicians to help establish or rule out particular diagnoses. For example, a patient may present with a number of symptoms that may have either a neurological or an emotional basis. Neuropsychological test results may help clarify the diagnosis in this situation. Second, because of an emphasis on functional systems of the brain (see below), neuropsychologists can often make predictions regarding the prognosis for recovery. A third major role involves intervention and rehabilitation. Information provided by neuropsychologists often has important implications for treatment; test results provide guidance as to which domains of functioning may support rehabilitative efforts. Finally, neuropsychologists may be asked to evaluate patients with mental disorders in order to help predict the course of illness (based on, for example, the degree of cognitive impairment present) as well as to help tailor treatment strategies to patients' strengths and weaknesses (Keefe, 1995).

With these definitions and descriptions of the roles of neuropsychologists in mind, we now turn to a brief history of the field.

History of Neuropsychology

Theories of Brain Functioning. As in most areas of psychology, the historical roots of neuropsychology extend about as far back in time as we are inclined to look. Some authors point to

PROFILE 18-1

Brick Johnstone, Ph.D.

Dr. Brick Johnstone is an Associate Professor in the Department of Physical Medicine and Rehabilitation at the University of Missouri Hospital and Clinics. He is the Director of the Division of Clinical Health Psychology and Neuropsychology and is also certified by the American Board of Clinical Neuropsychology. Dr. Johnstone's research focuses on neuropsychological assessment, training in clinical neuropsychology, and health care reform. We asked Dr. Johnstone about his background and interests, as well as his take on the future of clinical psychology and neuropsychology.

What originally got you interested in the field of clinical psychology?

I became interested in clinical psychology as an undergraduate at Duke University, through both academic coursework and clinical practica. I developed a strong interest in psychopathology based on an abnormal psychology course I took, as well as volunteer activities I engaged in at Butner State Hospital. Coursework in cognitive and perceptual psychology led to my long-term interest in brain functioning, and eventually in neuropsychology. Finally, as an undergraduate, I was able to participate as a research assistant on a study determining psychometric correlates of

popularity in children, which led to my interest in psychological research.

Describe what activities you are involved in as a clinical psychologist.

I currently serve as the Director of the Division of Clinical Health Psychology and Neuropsychology in the University of Missouri–Columbia Department of Physical Medicine and Rehabilitation. Although I have administrative and research duties, my primary interest is clinical. I am board certified as a neuropsychologist, but view myself as a clinical psychologist who specializes in brain dysfunction. Although I work with a special needs population, the skills I employ are those I was taught in graduate school. My assessment of patients is based primarily on a detailed clinical interview and behavioral observations, and secondarily on objective test data. My treatment of patients with brain dysfunction is based on all the behavioral treatment methods I learned in my clinical psychology graduate program at the University of Georgia.

Consistent with trends suggesting that clinical psychologists will need to develop administrative skills in the future, I am also the administrator for a division of seven psychologists, six postdoctoral fellows, two interns, and numerous staff members. Unfortunately, my graduate training did not prepare me for many of the financial and political issues we face today, and it is my hope that our graduate programs can do a better job of educating our future students in these areas. My research focus has been on demonstrating the functional utility of neuropsychological evaluations. I am currently the primary investigator (PI) for one of 17 national Traumatic Brain Injury Model Systems Centers, and it is important to note that 12 of the 17 PIs for these grants are psychologists. Opportunities for clinical psychologists to expand in numerous areas of health care and health policy are extraordinary.

(continued)

Profile 18-1 *(continued)*

What are your particular areas of expertise or interest?

My main area of expertise is neuropsychology. In graduate school, I completed a summer externship at the Kansas City V.A. Hospital in neuropsychology, even though I had never even administered a WAIS before that. That experience solidified my interest in working with individuals with brain dysfunction. My clinical and research interests involve making neuropsychological evaluations more functionally relevant. As a result of historical factors, the specialty of neuropsychology evolved primarily to assist with diagnosing various disorders and identify brain-behavior relationships. However, with the advent of sophisticated neuroradiological techniques, neuropsychology needs to become more functionally relevant and focus on practical treatment strategies for individuals with brain injury and their families. I have learned much regarding rehabilitation psychology from my colleagues in the Department of Physical Medicine and Rehabilitation, and it is my goal to improve neuropsychological treatments for individuals with brain dysfunction and update training guidelines for neuropsychologists to include better training in rehabilitation and disability issues.

What are the future trends you see for clinical psychology?

It is always entertaining to project the future of psychology, particularly given the potential growth opportunities as well as stressors related to managed care. On the positive side, clinical psychologists continue to expand their expertise into areas outside of traditional mental health. At my current setting, clinical psychologists are primary investigators on Robert Wood Johnson Foundation grants focusing on (1) developing Medicaid managed care programs for individuals with disabilities and (2) investigating the impact of managed care on children with disabilities in rural settings. Other psychologists in our division are primary investigators on

grants investigating the use of telemedicine applications for individuals with traumatic brain injury in rural settings, and one colleague is the only psychologist who is a PI for one of 17 national Spinal Cord Injury Model Systems. In addition, many medical school psychologists are identifying numerous medical populations that can benefit from psychological services (including those with systemic illnesses, infectious diseases, and cardiovascular diseases).

Managed care trends have had positive effects in that they have forced all health care professionals to better demonstrate the effectiveness of our services. However, because we have not demonstrated that psychologists can provide superior and less expensive services than social workers and licensed professional counselors, there is a good chance that clinical positions for psychologists will decrease in the future. As president of the Missouri Psychological Association, I have learned that the future of clinical psychology rests on our shoulders, including our ability to advocate for our profession and demonstrate our value to others. If we do not do it for ourselves, no one else will.

What are some future trends you see in neuropsychology?

I see the specialty of neuropsychology diverging in two directions. The first will be toward an experimental focus, with more research identifying specific brain-behavior relationships. Sophisticated neuroradiological techniques will allow us to gain a much better understanding of how the brain works. On the other hand, I foresee clinical neuropsychology focusing on the development of rehabilitation-based assessment and treatment. In the future, most individuals who are referred for neuropsychology evaluations will have known etiologies for their difficulties. Therefore, clinical neuropsychologists will need to develop specific treatment recommendations to assist individuals in their daily functions, at home, work, or school.

the Edwin Smith Surgical Papyrus, a document thought to date between 1700 and 3000 B.C., which discusses localization of function in the brain (Walsh & Darby, 1999). Others suggest that it all began when Pythagoras said that human reasoning occurs in the brain. Others are partial to the second century A.D.. when Galen, the Roman physician, argued that the mind was located in the brain, not in the heart as Aristotle had claimed.

However, the most significant early base for neuropsychology seems to have been laid in the nineteenth century (Hartlage, 1987). Researchers then were beginning to understand that damage to specific cortical areas was related to impaired function of certain adaptive behaviors. The earliest signs of this understanding came with Franz Gall and his now discredited phrenology. Gall believed that certain individual differences in intelligence and personality (such as reading skills) could be measured by noting the bumps and indentations of the skull. Thus, the size of a given area of the brain determines the person's corresponding psychological capacity. This was the first popularization of the notion of *localization of function*. Localization achieved much greater credibility with Paul Broca's surgical work in 1861. Observations from two autopsies of patients who had lost their powers of expressive speech convinced Broca that he had found the location of motor speech. Within the next 30 to 40 years, many books presented maps of the brain that located each major function (Golden, 1984).

Others, such as Pierre Flourens, would surgically destroy certain areas of the brains of animals and then note any consequent behavioral losses. Such work led Flourens and later, in the early twentieth century, Karl Lashley to argue for the concept of *equipotentiality*. That is, although there certainly is localization of brain function, the cortex really functions as a whole rather than as isolated units. In particular, higher intellectual functioning is mediated by the brain as a whole, and any brain injury will impair these higher functions. Yet there is the ability of one area of the cortex to substitute for the damaged area.

Both the localization and equipotentiality theories presented some problems, however. Localizationalists could not explain why lesions in very different parts of the brain produced the same deficit or impairment, whereas those adhering to the equipotentiality theory could not account for the observation that some patients with very small lesions manifested marked, specific behavioral deficits (Golden et al., 1992). An alternative theory that integrates these two perspectives is the *functional model*. First proposed by the neurologist Jackson and later adapted by the Soviet neuropsychologist Luria, the functional model holds that areas of the brain interact with each other to produce behavior. Behavior "is conceived of as being the result of several functions or systems of the brain areas, rather than the result of unitary or discrete brain areas. A disruption at any stage is sufficient to immobilize a given functional system" (Golden et al., 1992). The importance of this formulation is that it can account for many of the clinical findings that are inconsistent with previous theories. According to the functional model, the nature of the behavioral deficit will depend on which functional system (such as arousal, perception, or planning behavior) has been affected, as well as the localization of the damage within that functional system. Finally, through a process called reorganization, recovery from brain damage is sometimes possible.

Neuropsychological Assessment. With regard to specific psychological assessment instruments, neurology was for a long time bewitched by notions of mass action of brain functioning. These ideas tended to make localization of function a secondary goal of diagnosis, and brain damage was often viewed as a unitary phenomenon. The psychological tests used (for example, the Benton Visual Retention Test and the Graham-Kendall Memory-for-Designs Test) were oriented toward the simple assessment of the presence or absence of brain damage. Information about specific test correlates of specific brain lesions was not collected very efficiently.

Neuropsychology as a field began to grow immediately after World War II, because of (1) the large numbers of head injuries in the War and (2) the development of the field of clinical psychology itself (Hartlage, 1987). An important development of the postwar period was the work of Ward Halstead. By observing people with brain damage in natural settings, Halstead was able to identify certain specific characteristics of their behavior. Next, he tried to assess these characteristics by administering a variety of psychological tests to these patients. Through factor analysis, he settled on ten measures that ultimately comprised his test battery. Later, Ralph Reitan, a graduate student of Halstead's, refined the battery by eliminating two tests and adding several others. Subsequently, Reitan and his colleagues could relate test responses to such discrete aspects of brain lesions as lateralized motor deficits. This work culminated in the Halstead-Reitan Neuropsychological Test Battery. By 1980 the Luria-Nebraska Neuropsychological Battery had been developed, and it is now frequently used as an alternative to the Halstead-Reitan Battery. We'll have more to say about these and other neuropsychological tests in a later section.

An additional historical development deserves mention here. Contemporary clinical neuropsychologists have increasingly adopted a flexible battery approach to assessment. Flexible batteries allow each assessment to be tailored to the individual, based on the clinical presentation and on the hypotheses of the neuropsychologist. Standard batteries, such as the Halstead-Reitan and the Luria-Nebraska, may be too time consuming and are not easily modified to accommodate specific clinical situations. We will compare the standard battery and flexible battery approaches later in this chapter.

The Brain: Structure, Function, and Impairment

Before proceeding, it will be helpful to review some important aspects of the brain. This will, of necessity, be a brief excursion. More extensive accounts can be found elsewhere (for example, Golden et al., 1992; Walsh & Darby, 1999).

Structure and Function

The brain consists of two hemispheres. The *left hemisphere* controls the right side of the body and is thought to be more involved in language functions, logical inference, and detail analysis in almost all right-handed individuals and a good many left-handers as well. The *right hemisphere* controls the left side of the body. It is more involved in visual-spatial skills, creativity, musical activities, and perception of direction. But, again, note that some left-handers may reverse this hemispheric pattern. The two hemispheres communicate with one another via the corpus callosum, which helps to coordinate and integrate our complex behavior.

Each cerebral hemisphere has four lobes: the frontal, temporal, parietal, and occipital lobes (see Figure 18-1). The *frontal lobes* are the most recently developed parts of the brain. They enable us to observe and compare our behavior and the reactions of others to it in order to obtain the feedback necessary to alter our behavior to achieve valued goals. Also associated with the frontal lobes are executive functions—formulating, planning, and carrying out goal-directed initiatives. Finally, emotional modulation—the ability to monitor and control one's emotional state—is also associated with frontal lobe functioning.

The *temporal lobes* mediate linguistic expression, reception, and analysis. They are also involved in auditory processing of tones, sounds, rhythms, and meanings that are nonlanguage in nature. The *parietal lobes* are related to tactile and kinesthetic perception, understanding, spatial perception, and some language understanding and processing. They are also involved in body awareness. The *occipital lobes* are mainly oriented toward visual processing and some aspects of visually mediated memory. Motor coordination, as well as the control of equilibrium and muscle tone, are associated with the *cerebellum*.

Antecedents or Causes of Brain Damage

What causes brain damage? There are a number of possibilities.

FIGURE 18-1 **The cerebral cortex**

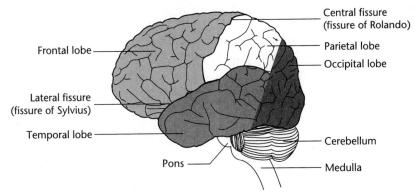

Trauma. It is estimated that head injuries occur in more than 2 million Americans every year (Smith, Barth, Diamond, & Giuliano, 1997). Incidents producing these injuries range from automobile accidents to falls off a stepladder. The outcomes are wide-ranging, and the nature of the head injury (such as closed versus open/penetrating) may have implications as well. Although most head injuries are considered mild, a substantial percentage of cases require hospitalization. Head trauma is the leading cause of death and disability in young Americans (R. J. Smith et al., 1997).

The major effects of head trauma can be categorized as concussions, contusions, and lacerations. *Concussions* (jarring of the brain) usually result in momentary disruptions of brain function, although permanent damage is uncommon (unless there are repeated concussions, as might be the case in football, soccer, or boxing, for example). *Contusions* refer to cases in which the brain has been shifted from its normal position and pressed against the skull. As a result, brain tissue is bruised. Outcomes can often be severe and may be followed by comas and deliriums. *Lacerations* involve actual ruptures and destruction of brain tissue. They can be caused by bullets or flying objects, for example. These lacerations are, of course, exceedingly serious forms of damage.

Cerebrovascular Accidents. The blockage or rupture of cerebral blood vessels is often termed a "stroke." This is a very common cause of brain

damage in adults, and stroke is one of the leading causes of death in the United States (and other countries). Although primarily occurring in the elderly, stroke is also one of the most common causes of death in middle-aged adults (Mora & Bornstein, 1997). In *occlusions*, a blood clot blocks the vessel that feeds a particular area of the brain. This can result in *aphasia* (language impairment), *apraxia* (inability to perform certain voluntary movements), or *agnosia* (disturbed sensory perception). In the case of a *cerebral hemorrhage*, the blood vessel ruptures and the blood escapes onto brain tissue and either damages or destroys it. The exact symptoms that ensue depend on the site of the accident and its severity. In very severe cases, death is the outcome. Those who survive often show paralysis, speech problems, memory and judgment difficulties, and so on.

It is very important to get stroke patients to the hospital immediately. Medications that essentially dissolve occlusions ("clot-busting" medications) can limit the permanent damage from occlusive strokes. In addition, new medications are being developed that prevent the cascade of chemical reactions responsible for neuronal damage or even death (for example, tissue plasminogen activator, tPA; Fagan et al., 1998). Therefore, in many cases, prompt action can be of major benefit.

Tumors. Brain *tumors* may grow outside the brain, within the brain, or result from metastatic cells spread by body fluids from some other organ of the body, such as the lung or the breast (R. A. Berg, 1997). Initial signs of brain tumors are often quite subtle and can include headaches, vision problems, gradually developing problems in judgment, and so on. As the tumor grows, so does the variety of other symptoms (such as poor memory, affect problems, or motor coordination). Tumors can be removed surgically, but the surgery itself can result in more brain damage. Some tumors are inoperable or located in areas too dangerous to operate on. In such cases, radiation treatments are often used.

Degenerative Disease. This group of disorders is characterized by a degeneration of neurons in the central nervous system (Allen, Sprenkel, Heyman, Schramke, & Heffron, 1997). Common *degenerative diseases* include Huntington's chorea, Parkinson's disease, and Alzheimer's disease and other dementia. Alzheimer's disease is the most common degenerative disease (age of onset is typically 65 years old or older), followed by Parkinson's disease (age of onset 50 to 60 years old), and finally Huntington's chorea (age of onset 30 to 50 years old). In all three cases, there is progressive cerebral degeneration along with other symptoms in the motor areas. Eventually, patients in these categories show severe disturbances in many behavioral areas, including motor, speech, language, memory, and judgment difficulties.

Nutritional Deficiencies. Malnutrition can ultimately produce neurological and psychological disorders. They are most often observed in cases of Korsakoff's psychosis (resulting from nutritional problems brought about by poor eating habits common in longtime alcoholics), pellagra (niacin/vitamin B-3 deficiency), and beriberi (thiamin/vitamin B-1 deficiency).

Toxic Disorders. A variety of metals, toxins, gases, and even plants can be absorbed through the skin. In some instances, the result is a toxic or poisonous effect that produces brain damage. A very common symptom associated with these disorders is *delirium* (disruption of consciousness).

Chronic Alcohol Abuse. Chronic exposure to alcohol often results in tolerance for and dependence on the substance. Tolerance and dependence appear to have neurological correlates, including, for example, changes in neurotransmitter sensitivity and shrinkage in brain tissue.

Several regions of the brain seem especially vulnerable to damage from chronic exposure to alcohol (U.S. Department of Health and Human Services, 1997). We will highlight only a few of the most consistent findings here. The limbic system is a network of structures within the brain associated with memory formation, emotional regulation, and sensory integration. Studies of alcoholics have indicated deficits in these areas of functioning. The diencephalon is a region near the center of the brain that includes the mammillary bodies of the hypothalamus. Studies suggest shrinkage or lesions in these areas as a result of chronic alcohol exposure, and memory deficits in alcoholics are consistent with these findings. Several studies have also reported findings that suggest alcoholics evidence atrophy of the cerebral cortex. Finally, damage to the cerebellum, responsible for motor coordination, is also well documented. A history of accidental falls or automobile accidents may suggest neurological damage resulting from alcohol abuse/dependence. Figure 18-2 depicts these brain regions that have been implicated in studies of the effects of alcoholism on the brain.

Consequences and Symptoms of Neurological Damage

Brain injury or trauma can produce a variety of cognitive and behavioral symptoms. Unfortunately for the diagnostician, many of these symptoms may also occur in connection with traditional mental disorders. Moreover, patients' responses to neurological impairment may give rise to psychological and emotional reactions. For example, an individual with neurological damage may become depressed over the inability to manage certain daily tasks. This, in turn, can easily obscure the process of differential diagnosis. These difficulties aside, several common

FIGURE 18-2 Brain structures affected by chronic alcohol abuse

Source: Courtesy of the U.S. Department of Health and Human Services. The Ninth Special Report to the U.S. Congress on Alcohol and Health, 1997, p. 150.

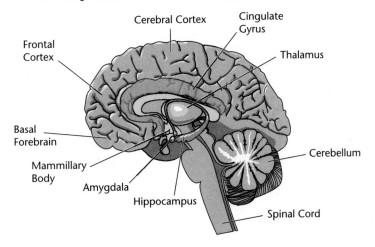

symptoms associated with neurological damage are listed below. However, each of these may occur in every disorder, and there is considerable variation among patients with the same disorder.

1. *Impaired orientation*: inability, for example, to say who one is, name the day of the week, or know about one's surroundings.
2. *Impaired memory*: patient forgets events, especially recent ones, sometimes confabulates or invents memories to fill the gaps, and may show impaired ability to learn and retain new information.
3. *Impaired intellectual functions*: comprehension, speech production, calculation, and general knowledge may be affected (for example, cannot define simple words, name the U.S. president, or add figures).
4. *Impaired judgment*: patient has trouble with decisions (for example, cannot decide about lunch, when to go to bed, and so on).
5. *Shallow and labile affect*: person laughs or weeps too easily and often inappropriately; shifts from joy to tears to anger, for example, very rapidly.
6. *Loss of emotional and mental resilience*: patient may function reasonably well under normal circumstances, but stress (for example, fatigue, mental demands, emotional upset) may result in deterioration of judgment, emotional reactions, and similar problems.
7. *Frontal lobe syndrome*: a group of personality characteristics often follow the destruction of frontal-lobe tissue through surgery, tumor, or injury. Typical symptoms are impaired impulse control, poor social judgment and planning ability, lack of concern over the consequences of one's actions, apathy and indifference, some suspiciousness, and temper tantrums. Box 18-1 illustrates the personality changes that can follow such injuries.

Brain-Behavior Relationships

Before describing specific assessment techniques, we should review at least briefly some basic ways of looking at brain-behavior relationships.

We observed earlier that in the second half of the nineteenth century, localization of function became a popular view. The idea that specific areas of the brain control specific behaviors is still an important operating principle among neuropsychologists. Such a principle means that in assessing brain damage, a chief concern is *where* the injury is located in the brain. Extent of an injury is important only to the degree that larger

BOX 18-1

Personality Changes Following Brain Injury: A Case Example

A young Vietnam veteran lost the entire right frontal portion of his brain in a land mine explosion. His mother and wife described him as having been a quietly pleasant, conscientious, and diligent sawmill worker before entering the service. When he returned home, all of his speech functions and most of his thinking abilities were intact. He was completely free of anxiety and thus without a worry in the world. He had become very easygoing, self-indulgent, and lacking in general drive and sensitivity to others. His wife was unable to get him to share her concerns when the baby had a fever or the rent was due. Not only did she have to handle all the finances, carry all the family and home responsibilities, and do all the

planning; but she also had to see that her husband went to work on time and that he didn't drink up his paycheck or spend it in a foolish spending spree before getting home on Friday night. For several years, it was touch and go as to whether the wife could stand the strain of a truly carefree husband much longer. She finally left him after he stopped working altogether and began a pattern of monthly drinking binges that left little of his rather considerable compensation checks.

Source: From Neuropsychological Assessment, *3rd edition, by Muriel Deutsch Lezak, p. 42. Copyright © 1995 by Oxford University Press, Inc. Reprinted by permission.*

injuries tend to involve more areas of the brain (Golden, 1984). Indeed, some tumors may produce intracranial pressure that impairs areas located far from the tumor itself. The basic idea, however, is that same-sized lesions in different regions of the brain will produce different behavior deficits (Krech, 1962).

But according to equipotential theory, all areas of the brain contribute equally to overall intellectual functioning (Krech, 1962). Location of injury is secondary to the amount of brain injury. Thus, all injuries are alike except in degree. Equipotentialists tend to emphasize deficits in abstract, symbolic abilities, which are thought to accompany all forms of brain damage and to produce rigid, concrete attitudes toward problem solving (see Goldstein & Scheerer, 1941). Such views have led to the development of tests that attempt to identify the basic deficit common to all cases of brain damage. Unfortunately, such tests have not worked well enough for everyday clinical use (Golden, 1981).

Many investigators have been unable to accept either localization or equipotentiality completely. Thus, alternatives such as the one proposed by Hughlings Jackson (Luria, 1973) have become prominent. Although, according to Jackson, very basic skills can be localized, the observable behavior is really a complex amalgamation of numerous basic skills, so the brain as an integrated whole is involved. This functional model of the brain subsumes both localization and equipotential theory. Further, according to Luria (1973), very complex behaviors involve complex functional systems in the brain that override any simple area locations. Because our ability to abstract is a complex intellectual skill, for example, it involves many systems of the brain.

Brain damage can have many effects, involving visual perception, auditory perception, kinesthetic perception, voluntary motor coordination and functioning, memory, language, conceptual behavior, attention, or emotional reactions. Often clinicians are called upon to determine the presence of *intellectual deterioration*. This goes beyond the measurement of present functioning because it involves an implicit or explicit comparison to a prior level. Generally speaking, intellectual deterioration may be of two broad types: (1) a decline resulting from psychological factors (psychosis, lack of motivation, emotional problems, the wish to defraud an insurance company, and so on); and (2) a decline stemming from brain injury. Of course, assessment would be a good deal easier if the clinician had available a series of tests taken by the patient prior to injury or illness. Such premorbid data would provide a kind of baseline against which to compare present performance. Unfortunately, clinical psychologists seldom seem to have such data on the patients they most need to diagnose. They are left to infer patients' previous level of functioning from case history information on education, occupation, and other variables. Over the years, clinicians have used such signs of premorbid functioning in a rather intuitive fashion, without much empirical evidence for their validity. However, all these methods are imperfect (Matarazzo, 1990).

Methods of Neuropsychological Assessment

Assessment is a complex affair that involves many issues in addition to those already discussed. Let us consider a few of the more important ones (Golden et al., 1992).

Major Approaches

Should a standard test or test battery be administered to all patients referred for a neuropsychological workup, or should the test(s) be chosen on the basis of clinical judgment, the nature of the referral, or the clinician's special skills and proclivities? The first approach is sometimes termed the *standard battery* or *fixed battery* approach. It has the advantages of evaluating patients for all basic neuropsychological abilities,

accumulating a standard database for all patients over time, and allowing for the identification of important patterns of scores. Major disadvantages include the time and expense involved, the potential for patient fatigue, and the inflexibility of this approach in that assessments are not tailored to individual patients.

The second approach is called the *flexible approach* or the *hypothesis-testing approach*. Here, each assessment is tailored to the individual patient, with the neuropsychologist choosing tests based on her or his hypotheses about the case. In some cases, a test may be altered in the way it is administered to the patient so that additional hypotheses can be tested. Some argue that the individualized approach is a sensitive one that capitalizes on the clinician's best impressions. Others suggest that if a clinician picks the wrong test(s), it may result in a poor assessment. Also, the individualized approach hampers the systematic collection of data from specific tests on specific kinds of patients. Of course, some clinicians combine these two strategies by using one or more standard screening devices and then going to other specific tests, depending on the outcome of the initial screening.

Interpretation of Neuropsychological Test Results

Golden et al. (1992) note a number of ways in which neuropsychologists interpret test data. First, a patient's level of performance may be interpreted in the context of normative data. For example, does a patient's score fall significantly below the mean score for the appropriate reference group, suggesting some impairment in this area of functioning? Second, some calculate *difference scores* between two tests for a patient; certain levels of difference suggest impairment. Third, *pathognomonic* signs of brain damage (such as failing to draw the left half of a picture) may be noted and interpreted. Fourth, a *pattern analysis* of scores may be undertaken; certain patterns of scores on tests have been reliably associated with specific neurological injuries or impairments. Finally, a number of statistical formulas that weight test scores differentially may be available for certain diagnostic decisions.

A final point about interpretation has to do with the desirability of making qualitative evaluations of patients' responses. Should neuropsychologists depend on qualitative testing or quantitative methods that reduce the results to numerical values? Is the *way* a patient responds the important datum, or is it the scored responses that are critical? Many neuropsychologists probably combine the two approaches, which need not be mutually exclusive. Whether a patient scores zero points for barely missing the proper reconstruction of a block design task or for pushing the blocks off the examiner's table in anger is likely to be significant for the patient's ultimate diagnosis. Although the point value obtained (zero) is the same in both cases, consideration and analysis of the quality or nature of the patient's response helps the neuropsychologist in her or his case conceptualization.

Neurodiagnostic Procedures

By now it may have occurred to the reader that the medical field already has a variety of *neurodiagnostic procedures*. They include the traditional neurological examination performed by the neurologist, spinal taps, X rays, electroencephalograms (EEGs), computerized axial tomography (CAT) scans, positron emission tomography (PET) scans, and the more recent nuclear magnetic resonance imaging (NMR or MRI) technique. These are indeed valuable means for locating the presence of damage and disease. But not all of these procedures work equally well in diagnosing impairment. Likewise, these techniques sometimes produce evidence of abnormalities in the absence of actual brain damage. Finally, some of these procedures pose risks for the patient. Spinal taps can be painful and sometimes harmful; we all know about the dangers of too many X rays.

Still, the neurologist's diagnostic procedures search directly for evidence of brain damage. In addition to these standard forms of neurodiagnostic procedure, several other imaging methods are available that provide a better sense of the "working" brain (Bigler, Porter, & Lowry, 1997). Single photon emission computed tomography (SPECT) imaging is based on cerebral blood flow and this provides a "picture" of how the brain is working. As another example, functional MR imaging (fMRI) also assesses blood flow changes in the brain. Both of these newer alternative neurodiagnostic procedures hold some promise in clinical neuropsychology because they are perhaps more likely to provide information on how different areas of the brain are working.

Many of these neurodiagnostic procedures are quite expensive, and some are invasive. Therefore, it may be helpful to use neuropsychological tests as screening measures, the results of which may indicate whether more expensive neurodiagnostic tests are indicated. Next, we will consider some specific neuropsychological assessment devices and batteries.

Testing Areas of Cognitive Functioning

Many tests are available for assessing a wide range of cognitive and behavioral functioning. In this section, we discuss only a handful of the areas of functioning assessed by neuropsychologists. Further, because of space constraints (entire books on neuropsychological assessment are available), we will only give a few tests as examples.

Intellectual Functioning. A number of techniques have been used over the years to assess levels of intellectual functioning. To estimate level of intellectual ability, many neuropsychologists use the WAIS-III (see Chapter 7) and subtests from a modified version of the WAIS-R, called the WAIS-R-NI (Kaplan, Fine, Morris, & Delis, 1991). The modifications include, for example, changes in administration (such as allowing the patient to continue on a subtest despite consecutive incorrect answers) and additional subtest items. Because of these modifications, it is believed that the WAIS-R-NI provides more information regarding the patient's cognitive strategies (R. M. Anderson, 1994).

FIGURE 18-3 The Wisconsin Card Sorting Test

Source: From Lezak, M. D. (1995). Neuropsychological assessment (3rd ed.). New York: Oxford. Page 621. Used with permission.

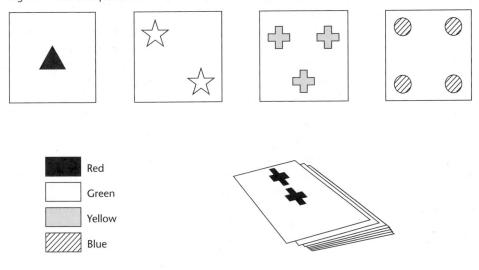

If it is not possible to administer the entire WAIS-III, certain individual subtests may be used—most commonly, the Information subtest, Comprehension subtest, and Vocabulary subtest. These subtests are believed to be least affected by brain trauma or injury and thus can also provide estimates of premorbid intelligence. This is important because often no preinjury test data are available to serve as a baseline against which to compare present functioning.

Abstract Reasoning. For many years, clinicians observed that patients diagnosed with schizophrenia or those deemed cognitively impaired seemed to find it difficult to think in an abstract or conceptual fashion. Such patients seemed to approach tasks in a highly concrete manner. Some of the more commonly used tests to assess abstract reasoning abilities include the Similarities subtest of the WAIS-III (see Chapter 7) and the Wisconsin Card Sorting Test, or WCST (Heaton, 1981). The Similarities subtest requires the patient to produce a description of how two objects are alike. The WCST consists of decks of cards that differ according to the shapes im-

printed, the colors of the shapes, and the number of shapes on each card (see Figure 18-3). The patient is asked to place each card under the appropriate stimulus card according to a principle (same color, same shapes, same number of shapes) deduced from the examiner's feedback ("that's right" or "that's wrong"). At various points during the test, the examiner changes principles; this can only be detected from the examiner's feedback regarding the correctness of the sorting of the next card.

Memory. Brain damage is often marked by memory loss. To test for such loss, Wechsler (1945) developed the Wechsler Memory Scale, or WMS. The Wechsler Memory Scale–III, or WMS-III (Wechsler, 1997b), is the most recent revision of the WMS. The WMS-III was developed in conjunction with the WAIS-III (Wechsler, 1997a), because clinicians often measure intellectual ability and memory concurrently. WMS-III subtest scores are combined into eight primary indexes that assess a range of memory functioning: Auditory Immediate, Visual Immediate, Immediate Memory, Auditory Delayed, Visual Delayed,

Auditory Recognition Delayed, General Memory, and Working Memory. Four supplementary Auditory Process Composites can also be calculated. These are used to assess memory processes when stimuli are presented auditorily. In addition to interpretations based on single subscale and single index scores, patterns of discrepancy between index scores are also informative. For example, problems with retention of previously learned material might be indicated by relatively higher immediate versus delayed index scores (Psychological Corporation, 1997). Another example that incorporates intelligence test scores is a pattern of scores in which relatively lower Working Memory and Immediate Memory index scores occur in the context of relatively higher intelligence scores. This pattern suggests that some impairment in attention is affecting the patient's ability to initially learn the material (Psychological Corporation, 1997).

Two additional tests also assess memory loss. On these tests, the patient must demonstrate spatial perception and perceptual-motor coordination as well as recall. The Benton Visual Retention Test (Benton, 1963) is basically a test of memory for designs. Ten cards are presented for 10 seconds each. After a card is withdrawn, the patient must draw the design from memory. There are several variants of this procedure. Scoring instructions and some normative data are available (for example, Benton, 1974). The Rey-Osterrieth Complex Figure Test (Lezak, 1995) is used by many neuropsychologists to assess visual-spatial memory. Patients first copy a complex figure, then draw it from memory immediately, and then draw it again after a specified period of time. Thus, this test can assess how the figure was initially processed (immediate copy), and comparisons can be made between subsequent copies under different recall conditions (Kramer & Delis, 1997). Further, because the figure is characterized by both larger configural features (for example, a large triangle) and smaller internal details (dots, small hash marks), differentiations can be made between those with right versus left hemisphere damage (Lezak, 1995). Different scoring systems and normative data across a broad range of ages are available (Kramer & Delis, 1997). Figure 18-4 presents the Rey-Osterrieth Complex Figure.

Visual-Perceptual Processing. Visual-spatial skills are necessary for a broad range of activities, including reading a map, parallel parking a car, and throwing a baseball from the outfield to a base (Caplan & Romans, 1997). In addition to the Rey-Osterrieth Complex Figure Test, many neuropsychologists seeking to assess visual-spatial skills examine performance on certain WAIS-III subtests, such as the Block Design subtest. Several specialized tests of these skills are also available. For example, the Judgment of Line Orientation Test (Benton, Hamsher, Varney, & Spreen, 1983) requires examinees to indicate the pair of lines on a response card that "match" (lie in the same orientation as) the two lines on the stimulus card. Figure 18-5 provides examples of items from this test.

Language Functioning. Various forms of brain injury or trauma can affect either the production or comprehension of language. Tests that require patients to repeat words, phrases, and sentences can assess articulation difficulties and paraphasias (word substitutions); naming tests can help diagnose anomias (impaired naming). Language comprehension can be assessed using the Receptive Speech Scale of the Luria-Nebraska (described in the following section). This subtest requires patients to respond to verbal commands (as by pointing to named body parts or objects or responding to simple commands). Speech and language pathologists do an excellent job of comprehensively assessing language dysfunction, and the neuropsychologist may choose to refer patients to these health professionals if a screening test indicates suspected problems in language production or comprehension.

Test Batteries

Let us now examine two commonly used neuropsychological test batteries: the Halstead-Reitan and the Luria-Nebraska.

FIGURE 18-4 **Rey-Osterrieth Complex Figure**
Source: From Lezak, M. D. (1995). Neuropsychological assessment (3rd ed.). New York: Oxford. Page 570. Used with permission.

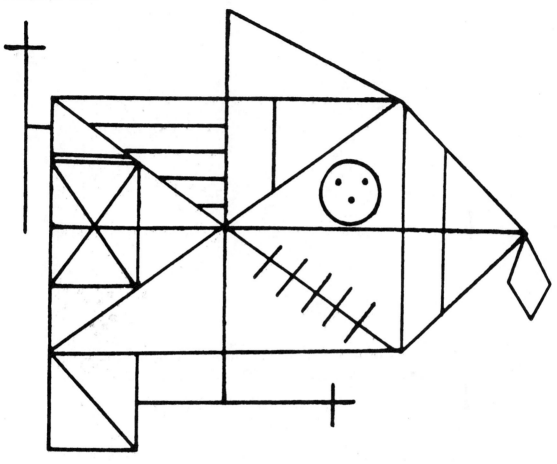

The Halstead-Reitan Battery. To counter the criticism that single tests for brain dysfunction were too limited in their scope to provide definitive answers, the *Halstead-Reitan Neuropsychological Battery* was developed (Halstead, 1947; Reitan & Davison, 1974). This is now undoubtedly the most widely used test battery. The battery, as generally used, consists of several measures: the Category Test, the Seashore Rhythm Test, the Finger Oscillation Test, the Speech-Sounds Perception Test, the Tactile Performance Test, the Trail-Making Test, the Strength of Grip Test, the Sensory-Perceptual Examination, the Finger Localization Test, the Fingertip Number Writing

Perception Test, the Tactile Form Recognition Test, and the Aphasia Screening Test. These tests may be supplemented by the MMPI-2 and the WAIS-III. The scale can be used with people aged 15 years and older; other versions can be used with children ages 9 to 14 and 5 to 8. Reitan and Wolfson (1993) provide a detailed description of the battery.

The Halstead-Reitan battery is used to provide information about the probable localization of lesions and whether they appear to be of gradual or sudden onset. It also suggests something about specific psychological deficits that a therapist should note. The battery can take more

FIGURE 18-5 Sample items from the Judgment of Line Orientation Test

Source: Lezak, M. D. (1995). Neuropsychological assessment (3rd ed.) New York: Oxford. Page 400. Used with permission.

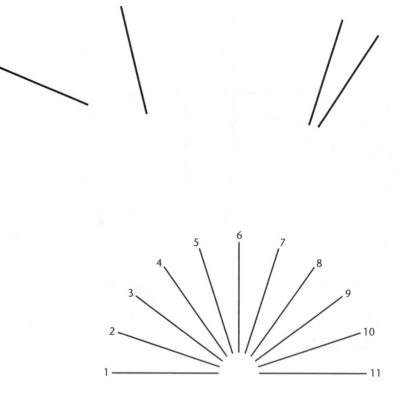

than 6 hours to administer. Many clinics have trained technicians to do this work, so that clinicians are not bogged down in lengthy procedures of administration and can concentrate instead on the complexities of interpretation.

Both the validity and the reliability of the Halstead-Reitan are supported by a number of studies across a wide range of age groups (G. Goldstein, 1997). The major weaknesses of the test battery are its length, cumbersomeness, and relative neglect of certain areas of functioning, such as memory (Goldstein, 1997). A brief case report summary based on the Halstead-Reitan and other tests is shown in Box 18-2.

The Luria-Nebraska Battery. As an alternative to the Halstead-Reitan, the *Luria-Nebraska battery* consists of 269 separate tasks comprising 11 subtests: motor functions, rhythm functions, tactile functions, visual functions, receptive speech, expressive speech, writing functions, reading skills, arithmetic skills, memory, and intellectual processes. Studies assessing the battery's reliability and diagnostic validity have been supportive (for example, Golden, Hammeke, & Purisch, 1978; Golden, Purisch, & Hammeke, 1985). The Luria-Nebraska shows substantial agreement with results obtained from the Halstead-Reitan method (Goldstein & Shelly, 1984; Kane, Parsons, Goldstein, & Moses, 1987; Sears, Hirt, & Hall, 1984). A children's version performed as well as the WISC-R in discriminating psychiatric and neurological cases (Carr, Sweet, & Rossini, 1986) and was also able to reliably diagnose attention deficit disorders in children (Lahey, Hynd, Stone, Piacentini, & Frick, 1989).

BOX 18-2

A Brief Neuropsychological Report Based on Halstead-Reitan and Other Information

Name: Mr. Y.
Date of Birth: 8-29-26
Occupation: Retired Air Force Pilot–USAF
Education: 18 Years (Master's Degree)

Referral Information

Mr. Y. is a 57-year-old white male who is retired from the United States Air Force. For the past several years he has noticed a decline in his perception, mechanical abilities, reaction time, driving abilities, and ability to read and produce cursive handwriting. He reports that the symptoms have been especially pronounced over the past two to three years. Dr. ——— requested a neuropsychological evaluation in order to evaluate the presence and/or extent of organic impairment.

Summary and Recommendations

1. Neuropsychological assessment reveals severe impairment in several areas of functioning, such as severe constructional difficulties and problems on all tasks requiring nonverbal and visual-spatial abilities, including memory for visual information. These areas of deficit point to a pathological process in the right parietal-occipital area of the brain. The possibility of major structural damage in this area should be investigated thoroughly.
2. Mr. Y.'s verbal abilities as well as verbal memory have been preserved and are, in general, in the superior range.
3. Personality assessment reveals that Mr. Y. is suffering from a moderate depression accompanied by worry and rumination. This appears to be of a rather long standing nature rather than being an acute emotional reaction.
4. The patient's neuropsychological deficits cannot be attributed to his depression.
5. In light of our findings, a careful review of the patient's capabilities both at work and at home should be made with him and his wife.
6. As this information is worked through, supportive psychotherapy would be helpful.
7. A current neurological reevaluation is recommended.

Source: From "Overview of the Halstead-Reitan Battery," by O. A. Parsons, pp. 179–180. In T. Incagndi, G. Goldstein, and C. J. Golden (Eds.), Clinical Application of Neuropsychological Test Batteries. Copyright © 1986 by Plenum Publishing Corporation. Reprinted by permission.

The main advantage of the Luria-Nebraska is that it takes only about 2.5 hours to complete, compared with the 6 hours sometimes required to complete the Halstead-Reitan battery. However, some clinical neuropsychologists believe that the Luria-Nebraska is limited because of its standardization and rationale (Goldstein, 1997). Specifically, many of the reliability and validity studies are based on small numbers of patients, and some critics feel that the Luria-Nebraska does not adequately translate A. R. Luria's theories and methods into a neuropsychological assessment instrument

Variables That Affect Performance on Neuropsychological Tests

A number of patient variables may influence neuropsychological test scores (Anderson, 1994; Golden et al., 1992). Because test scores differ according to the biological sex, age, and educational level of the patient, appropriate norms should be used in interpretation. In addition, test scores will be influenced by handedness, by premorbid ability (before brain trauma or injury), by the chronicity of the neurological condition, and by the presence of other (nonneurological) physical conditions (for example, a peripheral arm injury might affect performance on the Strength of Grip test of the Halstead-Reitan battery). Finally, motivational variables (arousal, level of cooperation) will also affect scores. For example, a patient who is taking medication that has a sedative effect will probably not be able to perform optimally.

A motivational variable that deserves additional comment is *malingering*. Detecting faking or malingering on psychological tests can be difficult for even the most astute clinician. There is controversy about how often malingering occurs in neuropsychological assessment. Recognizing that it may occur and improving clinicians' abilities to detect it are both very important, especially given the clinician's growing presence as an expert witness in court cases of various kinds (see Chapter 19). Several approaches have been suggested to address malingering on neuropsychological tests, ranging from the development and use of an objective malingering index (Reitan & Wolfson, 1996) to the use of strategies to evaluate test scores (R. Rogers, Harrell, & Liff, 1993). For example, Rogers et al. (1993) suggest that failure of very easy test items, differential performance on difficult versus easy test items, and below chance performance on alternative-choice test items should raise suspicions of malingering.

Intervention and Rehabilitation

Issues of neurological impairment usually revolve around two principal questions. First, what is the nature of the deterioration or damage? For example, is it a perceptual loss or a cognitive loss? Second, is there any real brain damage that can account in some way for the patient's behavior? More specifically, is the damage permanent,

or can recovery be expected after an acute phase? Is the damage focal or diffused throughout the brain? In general, focal damage results in more specific, limited effects on behavior, whereas diffuse damage can cause wide effects. Referral sources often need to know whether the damage will be progressive (as in diffuse brain involvement or in damage caused by disease) or nonprogressive (as is often true in the case of strokes or head traumas). Answers provided by clinical neuropsychologists significantly affect the kinds of rehabilitation programs designed for various patients.

Rehabilitation is becoming one of the major functions of neuropsychologists (Golden et al., 1992). The neuropsychologist is often thrust into the role of coordinating the cognitive and behavioral treatment of patients who have shown cognitive and behavioral impairment as a result of brain dysfunction or injury. First, a thorough assessment of the patient's strengths and deficits is conducted; this may include not only neuropsychological test results but also observations from other staff members, such as nurses, physicians, and physical therapists. A program of rehabilitation is then developed that will be maximally beneficial to the patient, given her or his deficits, as well as one that will be efficient in the sense of requiring a minimum amount of staff time and supervision (Golden et al., 1992).

As noted by Golden et al. (1992), rehabilitation can take place through spontaneous recovery of functioning. However, the neuropsychologist and the rehabilitation team are more likely to be involved when rehabilitation is to be accomplished by having the patient "relearn" via developmentally older and intact functional systems, the development of new functional systems, or changing the environment to ensure the best quality of life possible. In this last case, the judgment may be that it will not be possible to develop alternative or new functional systems that will significantly lessen the level of cognitive or behavioral impairment.

In the case of developing alternative or new functional systems, rehabilitation tasks are formulated to "treat" the patient's deficits. Golden et al. (1992, pp. 214–215) offer the following general guidelines for formulating this type of rehabilitation task:

1. It should include the impaired skill that one is trying to reformulate. All other skill requirements in the task should be in areas with which the subject has little or no trouble.
2. The therapist should be able to vary the task in difficulty from a level that would be simple for the patient to a level representing normal performance.
3. The task should be quantifiable, so that progress can be objectively stated.
4. The task should provide immediate feedback to the patient.
5. The number of errors made by the patient should be controlled.

Golden et al. (1992) give examples of rehabilitation programs for various cognitive and behavioral deficits. For example, verbal memory impairment might be treated by administering simple memory problems (those involving one unit of information) to the patient and then, later, more complex tasks (for example, a problem requiring the memorization of six or seven units of information). The complexity of the task can be varied further by, for example, using unrelated words or decreasing the time of exposure to the stimulus words.

Concluding Remarks

Training

Without doubt, neuropsychology as a specialty area within clinical psychology is dynamic and exciting. At the same time, however, the procedures in this subfield have become so sophisticated that specialty training is necessary.

Some clinical psychologists do not feel very comfortable doing neuropsychological assessment, nor are they qualified. Their training in such assessment is often limited, as is their knowledge of brain-behavior relationships. As Lezak (1995) has pointed out, the success of any neuropsychological assessment will depend on how well examiners understand not only normal brain-behavior relationships but also the psychological effects of brain dysfunction. Therefore, experts are needed. Reitan and Davison (1974) some time ago remarked on the necessity for developing a new field of clinical neuropsychology. Clinical neuropsychology is now a specialty that is formally recognized by both the American Psychological Association and the Canadian Psychological Association.

The September 1997, the *Houston Conference* convened leaders involved in the training of future clinical neuropsychologists. Guidelines for the graduate (doctoral) internship and postdoctoral training of future clinical neuropsychologists were offered. Briefly, these guidelines recommend a Ph.D. from a graduate program with a specialty track in clinical neuropsychology. As a required knowledge base, the Houston Conference recommended (1) a generic psychology core (statistics, learning, social psychology, physiological psychology, developmental psychology, history); (2) a generic clinical core (psychopathology, psychometrics, assessment, intervention, ethics); (3) neurosciences and basic human and animal neuropsychology (functional neuroanatomy, neurodiagnostic techniques, neurochemistry, neuropsychology of behavior); and (4) specific clinical neuropsychological training (research design in neuropsychology, specialized neuropsychological assessment techniques, specialized neuropsychological intervention techniques). Further, the conference recommended that skills be acquired in assessment, treatment and interventions, consultation, research, and teaching and supervision. Knowledge and skills in these areas can be acquired and mastered through coursework, supervised experience, internship experience, and a required two-year residency/postdoctoral training. Those completing such a rigorous training experience in clinical neuropsychology should, at the end of their training, be able to demonstrate advanced skill in neuropsychological assessment, treatment, and consultation, and should be eligible for board certification in clinical neuropsychology by the American Board of Professional Psychology.

The Future

In the future, neuropsychology may hope for the development of increasingly more sophisticated individual tests and batteries. Better assessment devices and procedures, including enhanced provisions for planning, therapy, and rehabilitation for patients with brain dysfunction, are highly desirable. Assessment obviously means more than pinning labels on people; it is meant to enable clinicians to help the patient adjust to the future (Johnstone & Frank, 1995). In particular, then, the field must concern itself more with predicting and facilitating recovery from brain injury. Fortunately, this is exactly what is beginning to happen. Training procedures that help foster rehabilitation, tests that predict the extent and rate of recovery, and general information on the course of debilitating injury can offer hope and structure to patients and their families. Even bad news, offered sensitively and constructively, can facilitate adjustment.

Johnstone and Frank (1995) have urged more neuropsychologists to shift their focus to rehabilitation. Although the need for rehabilitation services has increased in recent years, relatively few neuropsychologists have received specific training in rehabilitation. Moreover, traditional neuropsychological tests have not generally been used (or adapted) to provide information that is clinically useful to rehabilitation specialists. Johnstone and Frank argue, for example, that many important cognitive abilities (such as attention, executive functions, and memory) are poorly understood and poorly measured. In their view, neuropsychological test results need to be clearly tied (via empirical research) to real-world functions, so that rehabilitation can address deficits or impairments that, if improved, will lead to positive outcome. If heeded, these suggestions will likely affect research, training, and clinical applications in the field of neuropsychology.

Changes in the way that health care is delivered and reimbursed will also have a great impact on the field of neuropsychology. K. M. Adams (1996) has discussed many of the ways that managed health care will affect present and future neuropsychologists. First, neuropsychological assessment may no longer be routinely conducted when brain-behavior issues are raised, nor is it likely that it will be routinely reimbursed. Rather, neuropsychological assessment is likely to be seen by managed care companies as a luxury—to be conducted only when absolutely necessary. Adams also predicts that the marketplace for neuropsychologists will likely shrink, and that neuropsychologists will be called upon to document their utility. If true, this tightening of the job market will stand in sharp contrast to the wealth of job opportunities in neuropsychology that has been characteristic of the past decade. Finally, Adams cites the need to educate insurance companies, physicians, and hospital administrators as to what neuropsychologists do, how they can be helpful, and how their examination and rehabilitation procedures are cost effective.

Chapter Summary

The field of neuropsychology has witnessed tremendous growth over the past several decades. Neuropsychology is the study of the relations between brain function and behavior. Neuropsychologists are called on to consult with neurologists or other physicians in order to assess functioning, to make predictions regarding prognosis and course, and to plan interventions and rehabilitation. Models of brain functioning have evolved from localization of function to equipotentiality and, finally, to the functional model. The functional model holds that different areas of the brain interact to produce behavior, and that behavior is a result of several different functional systems of brain areas.

We have briefly reviewed the major structures of the brain, a number of antecedents or causes of brain damage, and various consequences of neurological damage. Neuropsychological assessment involves the use of noninvasive standardized testing methods that are sensitive to various forms of brain functioning. A critical distinction is that between the standard (or fixed) battery approach, in which a standard set of tests is given to all patients regardless of the clinical picture, and the flexible (or hypothesis-testing) approach, in which only selected tests are administered. Major areas of functioning that are targeted by neuropsychologists include intellectual functioning, abstract reasoning, memory, visual-perceptual processing, and language functioning. Neurodiagnostic tests may also be used to diagnose problems. A clinical neuropsychologist's evaluation can then be used to formulate and implement a plan of intervention or rehabilitation tailored to the individual patient. The program of rehabilitation should be maximally beneficial to the patient and efficient in terms of staff time and supervision.

Specialty training in clinical neuropsychology is necessary because of the complexity and sophistication of the procedures involved. Most graduate programs are not able to devote sufficient time, coursework, and practicum experience to the study of brain-behavior relationships. Therefore, an integrated model for the training of clinical neuropsychologists has been adopted that includes predoctoral, internship, and postdoctoral experiences. Many challenges lie ahead for the field, including the need for more sophisticated and more economical assessment and rehabilitative techniques, as well as a tightening in the job market as a result of managed care.

Key Terms

agnosia Impairment in one's sensory perception.

aphasia Impairment in one's language ability.

apraxia Impairment in one's ability to perform certain voluntary movements.

cerebellum A subcortical structure that is associated with motor coordination and the control of muscle tone, posture, and equilibrium.

cerebral hemorrhage A situation in which a blood vessel ruptures and the blood escapes onto brain tissue, either damaging or destroying it. The symptoms of a hemorrhage are determined by its site and severity.

concussions Jarring of the brain sufficient to result in a momentary disruptions of brain function. A single concussion usually does not cause permanent damage, but repeated ones may.

contusions Bruises. In the brain, contusions result when the brain has been shifted from its normal position and pressed against the skull. Brain contusions may be severe and may result in delirious or comatose states.

degenerative disease A group of disorders—such as Alzheimer's disease, Parkinson's disease, and Huntington's chorea—that result from the degeneration of neurons in the central nervous system. These disorders are characterized by progressive cerebral degeneration and disturbance in several behaviors or functions.

delirium A disruption of consciousness often caused by exposure to toxins.

difference scores A method for interpreting neuropsychological test data that focuses upon the difference between a patient's scores on two separate tests. Difference scores above a certain level are suggestive of impairment.

equipotentiality The notion that the cortex functions as a whole, and that all areas of the brain contribute equally to overall intellectual functioning. On the basis of this perspective, when one area of cortex is damaged, the functions of that area may be assumed by another area of cortex.

flexible approach or hypothesis-testing approach In this approach, the neuropsychologist selects the tests to be administered to each patient based on his or her hypotheses about the case and may even alter the administration of one or more tests.

frontal lobes The most recently developed part of the human brain. The frontal lobes are associated with executive functions such as formulating, planning, and carrying out goal-directed behavior, monitoring and controlling behavior, and modulating emotions.

functional model A theory that integrates the localization-of-function and equipotentiality perspectives. This theory holds that any behavior is due to the interaction of several brain systems, and that the nature of a behavioral deficit will depend on which functional system is affected as well as the localization of damage within that functional system.

Halstead-Reitan battery The most widely used neuropsychological test battery. The Halstead-Reitan consists of several measures and is used to provide data about specific deficits, the probable localization of lesions, and whether lesions appear to be of gradual or sudden onset. Although the reliability and validity of this battery have been supported, a significant disadvantage is the time required for administration.

Houston Conference A conference on clinical neuropsychology training that convened in September 1997. As a result of this conference, specific guidelines were offered for the graduate training, predoctoral internship, and postdoctoral training of future clinical neuropsychologists.

lacerations Cuts, tears, or ruptures. Lacerations of brain tissue may occur when the skull has been breached by a bullet or other object.

left hemisphere The hemisphere of the brain that controls the right side of the body and for most people is more involved in the language functions, logical inference, and detail analysis.

localization of function The idea that certain portions of the brain are responsible for specific functions or behaviors.

Luria-Nebraska battery A neuropsychological test battery that assesses abilities over 11 subtest groupings. Studies have supported the reliability and diagnostic validity of the battery, which takes less time to administer than the Halstead-Reitan.

neurodiagnostic procedures Procedures (such as spinal taps, CAT scans, and functional MRIs) for detecting the presence and location of brain damage. These procedures vary in their expense, their sensitivity, their invasiveness, and the risk they pose to the patient.

neuropsychological assessment The assessment of brain functioning based on a person's performance on noninvasive, standardized tests that are believed to be accurate and sensitive indicators of brain-behavior relationships.

neuropsychology The study of the relationship between brain function and behavior. Neuropsychologists study, assess and/or treat behaviors directly related to the functioning of the brain.

occipital lobes The portion of the cortex that is involved with visual processing and some aspects of visually mediated memory.

occlusions Blockages in blood vessels caused by clots. The vessels serving particular areas of the brain may become occluded, resulting in one type of "stroke."

parietal lobes The portion of the cortex related to tactile and kinesthetic perception and understanding, spatial perception, and some language comprehension and processing.

pathognomonic Indicative of a specific disease or condition. One method for interpreting neuropsychological test data notes and draws inferences about pathognomonic signs.

pattern analysis A method of neuropsychological test interpretation in which the basic pattern of scores on tests is examined to see whether it matches a pattern that has been reliably associated with a specific neurological injury or impairment.

rehabilitation In the context of neuropsychology, the treatment of patients with cognitive and behavioral impairment due to brain dysfunction or injury. Rehabilitation may involve helping the patient "relearn" skills and/or changing the patient's environment in order to best compensate for the impairment. Rehabilitation planning/coordination is a major function of neuropsychologists.

right hemisphere The hemisphere of the brain that controls the left side of the body and for most people is more involved in visual-spatial skills, the perception of direction, creativity, and musical activities.

standard battery Also known as the "fixed battery" approach. In this approach, all referred patients are administered the same set of neuropsychological tests.

temporal lobes The portion of the cortex that mediates linguistic expression, reception, and analysis, and is involved in processing tones, sounds, rhythms, and meanings that are nonlanguage in nature.

tumors Abnormal tissue growths that may grow inside or outside the brain or spread to the brain from other areas of the body. Symptoms are usually subtle at first and become more noticeable as the tumor grows and exerts pressure on surrounding areas of the brain.

Web Sites of Interest

To visit any of the web sites listed below, go to www.wadsworth.com and click on Links.

18-1 Division 40 of APA—Clinical Neuro-psychology

18-2 Training Programs in Clinical Neuro-psychology

18-3 Neuropsychology Central

18-4 The Whole Brain Atlas

CHAPTER NINETEEN

Forensic Psychology

Because clinical psychologists are said to be "experts" in human behavior, it is not surprising that some of them would begin to specialize in the application of psychological knowledge to the problems that face judges, attorneys, police officials, and indeed anyone who must face or deal with issues related to civil, criminal, or administrative justice—victims and violators alike. This domain of clinical psychology, now called *forensic psychology*, underwent a highly visible growth spurt in the 1970s, and it continues to thrive (Melton, Huss, & Tomkins, 1999). It has gained all the trappings of a significant subspecialty: graduate training programs, professional organizations and boards, an APA division (Division 41—The American Psychology-Law Society), and journals and textbooks. Many of these entities are distinctly interdisciplinary and span the fields of both law and psychology. However, the success and popularity of the field of forensic psychology has also invited some harsh criticism (Hagen, 1997; Huber, 1993).

Perspectives and History

Let us begin our description of the field by defining it, briefly tracing its history, and then discussing a few professional matters.

Definitions

Forensic psychology involves "the application of the methods, theories, and concepts of psychology to the legal system" (Wrightsman, Nietzel, & Fortune, 1998, p. 499). Just how broad these applications are is illustrated in Table 19-1, which lists several examples. A variety of settings and clients may be involved, including children as well as adults. All manner of institutions, including corporations, government agencies, universities, hospitals and clinics, and correctional facilities may be involved as clients or objects of testimony.

History

In 1908, Hugo von Munsterberg published his book *On the Witness Stand* (see Box 19-1). Despite

■ **TABLE 19-1** **Areas of Testimony and Expertise of Forensic Psychologists**

Commitment to mental hospitals

Child custody issues

Psychological damages suffered as the result of another's negligence

Release from involuntary confinement

Determination of the need for a conservator due to incapacity

Predicting dangerousness

Rights of mentally disabled person in an institution

Competency to stand trial

Criminal responsibility (insanity defense)

Determination of disability for Social Security claims

Workers' Compensation claims

Conditions affecting accuracy of eyewitness testimony

Advice to attorneys regarding factors that will affect jurors' behavior

Extent to which advertising claims are misleading

Battered woman syndrome

Rape trauma syndrome

Accuracy of eyewitness identification

Sexual harassment

Police psychology

Jury selection

Offender treatment programs

Criminal profiling

this notable event, psychology had relatively little direct influence on the law until 1954—the year the Supreme Court finally paid attention to the social sciences in the *Brown* v. *Board of Education* desegregation case. Then, in 1962, Judge Bazelon, writing for the majority on the United States Court of Appeals for the District of Columbia Circuit, held for the first time that psychologists who were appropriately qualified could testify in court as experts on mental disorder (*Jenkins* v. *United States*, 1962). Finally, the forensic psychologist was about to appear on the

BOX 19-1

Munsterberg on Trial

Munsterberg (1908) complained that no one (teacher, artist, businessman, physician, minister, politician, or soldier) could be as resistant as an attorney to the idea that psychologists might be of help. He charged that lawyers, judges, and even members of juries seemed to think that all they needed in order to function correctly was common sense.

Professor John Wigmore (1909), an eminent professor of law at Northwestern University, considered Munsterberg's claims the height of arrogance. Reflecting the feelings of many attorneys, Wigmore wrote a clever yet scathing parody in response. He sketched a fictional libel suit filed against Munsterberg, accusing him of overstating what psychology had to offer, ignoring the many disagreements among psychologists themselves, and failing to understand the difference between laboratory results and the realities of legal requirements.

The "suit" was filed in "Windyville" in "Wundt County." Munsterberg's attorneys were named "R. E. Search, Si Kist, and X. Perry Ment." "Judge Wiseman" heard the case against Munsterberg and his claim that "lawyers are obdurate."

Of course, the proceedings went against Munsterberg. After only a few minutes of whispered consultation, the jury agreed on the verdict and found for the plaintiffs. Munsterberg was fined one dollar in damages. All in all, Wigmore's attack was so clever and devastating that it took 25 years for psychologists to once again be considered fit as expert witnesses. In fact, however, shortly before his death some 30 years later, Wigmore softened his critique. He asserted that courts should be ready to use any methods that psychologists themselves agree are sound, accurate, and practical. Now, of course, Wigmore's change of heart is reflected in everyday court procedures. But it may well be true that had Munsterberg been a little more restrained in his original claims, the entire Munsterberg-Wigmore episode would never have occurred.

scene, even though psychiatrists had enjoyed the privilege of providing expert testimony for many years. Today, psychologists regularly testify as experts in virtually every area of criminal, civil, family, and administrative law. In addition, they serve as consultants to agencies and individuals throughout the legal system.

Of course, the foregoing thumbnail sketch of forensic history from Munsterberg to Bazelon leaves out many details and controversies. Even before Munsterberg, William Stern reported in 1901 that he was studying the "correctness" of recollection—an early precursor of today's research on eyewitness testimony. And even Freud, in a 1906 speech to some Austrian judges, claimed that psychology has real applications to the law. Later, John Watson also asserted that the law and psychology have common interests.

Lest the reader think that forensic psychology marched inexorably toward professional respectability, it would be well to note that not everyone thought psychology had much to offer the legal system. Even Munsterberg was hardly without critics. Because he tended to promote the role of psychology before he had much empirical data to back his claims, many dismissed his book out of hand. In a 1931 address, Lewis Terman noted "that Munsterberg's error was in exaggerating the importance of psychology's contributions based on research then at hand. He went on to suggest that in light of significant scientific advances the ultimate significance of psychology for the legal profession could not be overestimated" (Blau, 1998, p. 3). Box 19-1 illustrates just how harsh some members of the legal community could be regarding Munsterberg's thesis. Certainly into the 1950s, before Judge Bazelon's ruling took hold, judges as often as not failed to qualify psychologists as experts in the courtroom.

The standoff between psychology and law has been characterized by Loh (1984) as a phase during which psychologists wanted to contribute to the legal system but attorneys were having none of it. In the 1930s, psychology was primarily applied to a critique of legal doctrine and decisions. In the 1950s, psychologists were mainly occupied in trying to serve as expert witnesses, and in the 1970s and 1980s, as consultants on matters pertaining to juror behavior (Loh, 1984).

Now, as noted at the outset, forensic psychology has arrived at a point where there are specialists in psycholegal research, interdisciplinary training programs are commonplace, and numerous specialty books are being published. The many journals in this area include *Law and Human Behavior, Criminal Justice Journal, Law and Psychology Review, Criminal Justice and Behavior, Behavioral Sciences and the Law, American Journal of Forensic Psychology*, and *Psychology, Public Policy, and Law*.

Professional Issues

For some years, many were concerned that forensic psychologists lacked status and recognition in the eyes of their peers in other specialties (for example, Kurke, 1980). The establishment of the American Board of Forensic Psychology in 1978, to help the public identify qualified practitioners and to promote the discipline, has served to allay some of these concerns. Nevertheless, professional matters such as certification and licensing have long been issues of importance to forensic psychologists.

Training. Some years ago, Poythress (1979) observed that forensic training should give students a familiarity with legal tests and concepts,

proper assessment, knowledge of relevant literature, and an orientation to the courtroom. To accomplish these goals, he recommended that students interested in forensic psychology be required to complete an introductory survey of the field, topical seminars in forensic psychology, and a field placement in a forensic setting. In addition to being well trained in clinical psychology more generally, clinical psychologists specializing in forensic psychology must gain expertise in the law, so that their testimony, consultation, and research are well informed. Increasingly, academic departments are offering forensic courses. A 1994 brochure from Division 41 of the American Psychological Association (American Psychology-Law Society) identified six universities offering joint degree (J.D. and Ph.D. or Psy.D.) programs in psychology and law; (2) four universities offering Ph.D. programs with specialization in the areas of psychology and law, criminal justice, and corrections; and three programs offering doctorates in forensic psychology. In addition, several master's programs with a focus on forensic psychology are available, as are postdoctoral training opportunities. Each year, the number and kinds of programs continue to grow. Web site 19-2 at the end of this chapter presents the most up-to-date information on training opportunities.

Ethics and Standards. All of the ethical principles and guidelines explored in previous chapters are relevant here as well. In addition, it has been recommended that the forensic scientist follow the code of the American Academy of Forensic Sciences (Blau, 1998). This code stresses (1) completeness and accuracy in stating one's professional qualifications, (2) technical and scientific accuracy and honesty in reports and testimony, and (3) impartiality. As a further resource, Division 41 (American Psychology-Law Society) of APA has developed a set of *Specialty Guidelines for Forensic Psychologists* (Committee on Ethical Guidelines for Forensic Psychologists, 1991) that elaborate on APA's *Ethical Principles of Psychologists* as they apply to the practice of forensic psychology (see web site 19-4). Still, as we will

> **TABLE 19-2** **Standards for Financial Arrangements Applicable to the Expert Witness**
>
> 1. The psychologist should never accept a fee contingent upon the outcome of a case.
>
> 2. The fee structure and details of reimbursement should be established between the psychologist and the retaining attorney during the initial consultation. The understanding should be in writing between the two parties.
>
> 3. All outstanding fees should be paid before the psychologist testifies.
>
> 4. Misunderstandings or disagreements about fees should be resolved before proceeding in the case.
>
> 5. Psychologists who testify regularly as expert witnesses should devote some portion of their professional time to pro bono publico* cases.
>
> ---
>
> *Cases without compensation for the purpose of advancing a social cause or representing someone who cannot otherwise afford it.
> *Source:* Blau (1998), p. 402.

discuss later in this chapter, the ethical issues encountered by forensic psychologists in the adversarial legal system can be formidable (Wrightsman et al., 1998). Finally, Blau (1998) has proposed several very explicit guidelines for the expert witness activities of psychologists. They involve matters of work quality, competence and decorum, and financial arrangements. Blau's standards for financial arrangements are presented in Table 19-2.

Issues of ethics and standards will weigh heavily in any professional arena that allows for so many role conflicts, biases, distortions, and subjectivity. Forensic psychology is just such an arena.

Some Major Activities of Forensic Psychologists

The growth of forensic psychology has thrust the psychologist into many different roles. We will focus on eight such roles, beginning with the forensic psychologist as expert witness.

The Expert Witness

Consider the following scenario:

Ms. Ferris, an employee of the Diego Pan Company, was working at her desk on April 28, 1999. Her supervisor, a Mr. Smith, stopped by her desk. He had a history of telling dirty jokes in her presence, commenting on her physical attributes, and asking about her dating activities. This day, however, he explicitly propositioned her and made it clear that if she wanted to advance in the company, and indeed even remain employed, she had better agree to have sexual relations with him. She refused. Two weeks later, she was fired. Subsequently, she filed sexual harassment charges against Mr. Smith and also sought damages for emotional suffering.

Dr. Miller, a clinical psychologist, was retained by Ms. Ferris's attorney. He conducted extensive interviews with Ms. Ferris and several of her coworkers. He also administered several tests. Mr. Wright, a coworker, had inadvertently overheard the April 28 conversation between Ms. Ferris and her supervisor and had also previously observed some of the alleged sexual harassment.

During the trial, Mr. Wright served as a witness, testifying to the facts with reference to his own observations. Dr. Miller testified as to his opinions and inferences about emotional damage that were within the scope of his training and experience. This illustrates the basic difference between a lay witness and an *expert witness*. The former may testify only to events witnessed. The latter may offer opinions and inferences. This goes beyond merely stating a conclusion. The expert witness must help the court understand and evaluate evidence or determine a fact at issue (Gutheil, 1998).

Qualifications. An expert witness can be anyone who can provide information that, by its uniqueness in relation to some science, profession, training, or experience, is unlikely to be known to the average juror (Blau, 1998; Wrightsman et al., 1998). Initially, the court will decide whether the expert witness may, in fact, claim expert status. Often, in the case of physicians, psychologists, or psychiatrists, a license is taken as evidence of competence. But if opposing counsel objects to the witness's claim to be an expert, further evidence will typically be presented regarding competence. Ultimately, it is up to the judge to decide (Blau, 1998). In general, the bases of clinical psychological expertise include (1) education, formal training, and subsequent learning; (2) relevant experience, including positions held; (3) research and publications; (4) knowledge and application of scientific principles; and (5) use of special tests and measurements (Maloney, 1985). What is accepted as evidence will vary from jurisdiction to jurisdiction.

A 1993 decision by the United States Supreme Court, *Daubert* v. *Merrell Dow*, established what many thought would be a more liberal standard for the admissibility of an expert's evidence. Briefly, the standard was changed from "general acceptance" in the relevant scientific community (the *Frye* v. *U.S.*, 1923, standard) to one of "relevance and validity" as determined by the trial judge. In other words, the burden now falls on the judge to determine what expert evidence is admissible (Bartol & Bartol, 1994). Although this new standard was intended to be more liberal and flexible, in many cases *Daubert* has resulted in more restrictive criteria for the admissibility of expert testimony. Trial judges have used the *Daubert* decision to exclude various kinds of social science evidence as "not scientific enough," even though it would have been admissible under *Frye*. Indeed, the field of forensic psychology continues to debate whether *Daubert* promotes science in expert testimony, confuses judges and juries, or opens the door for dubious theories and findings (Hess, 1999).

Given the *Daubert* ruling, Rotgers and Barrett (1996) have offered the following guidelines to assist clinical psychologists who testify as expert witnesses:

- Use theoretically and psychometrically adequate data-gathering instruments.
- Draw conclusions using scientifically validated theoretical positions.
- Weigh and qualify testimony on the basis of the adequacy of theory and empirical research on the question being addressed.
- Be prepared to defend the scientific status of your data-gathering methods during the process of qualification as an expert witness.

Rotgers and Barrett (1996) encourage expert witnesses to readily acknowledge to the court the limitations of scientific knowledge in any area about which they are asked to testify.

Topics for Expert Testimony. We have already seen from Table 19-1 how wide the range of topics suitable for expert testimony really is. This list is by no means exhaustive, and additional areas for expert psychological opinion exist (Wrightsman et al., 1998). However, experts are not allowed to state opinions that are the legal prerogative of the jury. Thus, an expert may testify about the manner in which early child abuse might predispose the victim to later be aggressive toward others, but it is up to the jury to decide whether this is true in a particular case. Therefore, expert witnesses are prevented from providing "ultimate opinion" testimony (Wrightsman et al., 1998).

Testifying. Regardless of the topic, testifying in court can be a harrowing experience for the expert witness. Anxiety and self-doubt are common as the expert is tugged at by attorneys on both sides of the issue. Just as the neuropsychologist rarely gets the easy cases to diagnose, the behavioral expert in court rarely testifies about simple matters. Publicity, sensationalism, and the adversarial legal process are companions not calculated to make the life of the expert witness an easy one.

An important prelude to testifying is pretrial preparation. This can sometimes involve many hours of study, interviewing, testing, and conferences, depending on the case. The expert may be asked to testify by the court or by counsel for either a defendant or a plaintiff.

Cross-Examination. Consider the following two gems that illustrate what cross-examination can be like (Schwitzgebel & Schwitzgebel, 1980, p. 243):

> "Good morning, doctor. I see you are here on behalf of an accused killer (or 'your fellow psychologists') again. How are you today?"

> "Doctor, were you paid to perform your examination? [Yes] How much? [$200 an hour.] How many hours did you spend in all? [20 hours.] That's $4,000, isn't it, doctor? [Yes] And in your opinion the patient was insane on the night of January 26, 1975? [Yes] That's all, doctor."

Other, equally provocative questions that have been asked of psychologists serving as expert witnesses include the following:

> "Isn't it true that most of your experiments are done with rats?"

> "You are not a real doctor, are you?"

> "You can't tell what's going on up here, can you?" (Opposing attorney points to his head.)

Several authors (for example, Blau, 1998; Brodsky, 1991; Schwitzgebel & Schwitzgebel, 1980) provide numerous hints about how the expert witness should behave in the courtroom, even to the point of appropriate dress. Schwitzgebel and Schwitzgebel (1980) summarize their recommended strategies for coping with cross-examination as follows:

> Be prepared.

> Be honest.

> Admit weaknesses.

> Talk in personally meaningful terms.

> Listen carefully to the wording of questions.

> Take time to think.

Criminal Cases

For generations, society has grappled with questions of how best to deal with people who have committed criminal acts but who were so disturbed at the time that it is debatable whether they were personally responsible. Also difficult are decisions as to whether an accused person is really competent to understand the trial proceedings and thus to cooperate in his or her own defense.

The Insanity Plea. If the accused is judged to have been sane at the time of the alleged crime, then conviction will bring with it imprisonment, fines, or probation. But the individual adjudged insane at the time of the alleged crime will, if convicted, be regarded as not responsible and thereby held for treatment rather than punishment. However, despite popular conceptions to the contrary, the *insanity plea* is seldom successful (Wrightsman et al., 1998). The defendant is typically assumed to be responsible. Thus, an insanity plea places the burden of its proof on the accused. In most states and in the District of Columbia, the *burden of proof* is on the defense; the defendant must prove that she or he was insane at the time of the criminal offense (Ogloff, 1991). It should be noted that insanity is a legal term, not a medical, psychiatric, or psychological one. The legal system assumes that people make premeditated and rational choices. Therefore, to behave irrationally is evidence of insanity. But most psychologists would not agree that all normal behavior is rationally chosen. The deterministic view of science creates problems for such a simple notion.

So, then, how is it decided that the accused was insane? Although standards vary from state to state, one of three standards typically prevails. The oldest standard is the *M'Naghten rule*, promulgated in England in 1843. It states that a successful insanity defense must prove that the person committed the unlawful act while "labouring under such a defect of reason, from disease of the mind, as not to know the nature and quality of the act he [sic] was doing; or, if he did know it, that he did not know he was doing what was wrong."

The second standard is the idea of an "irresistible impulse." According to this test, although the person might have known the moral or legal ramifications of the act, it was impossible for the individual to resist the impulse—it was irresistible (Schwitzgebel & Schwitzgebel, 1980). The third standard is that the defendant is not responsible for a criminal act if it was the result of mental disease or defect such that substantial capacity to appreciate the criminality of the act or to conform to the law was lacking. This is the so-called *ALI standard* of the American Law Institute. The ALI standard is viewed as the most liberal or expansive in that criminal responsibility can be excused if mental illness causes a lack of substantial capacity to understand what one is doing (a cognitive deficit) *or* an inability to control one's behavior (a volitional deficit) (Ogloff, 1991).

The famous *Hinckley* case (attempted assassination of President Reagan) changed the judicial scene in the United States. Its first impact was to encourage a return to the M'Naghten rule where cognitive factors rather than volitional ones are paramount. Its second impact is seen in the Supreme Court's ruling that it is constitutional to automatically and indefinitely confine someone who is acquitted of a crime as the result of an insanity plea (Simon & Aaronson, 1988). Third, the verdict "guilty but mentally ill" was introduced into the defense statutes of several states as well as the federal government. Finally, more states began to place the burden of proving the defendant's insanity on the defense, rather than requiring the prosecution to prove the defendant's sanity (Ogloff, 1991).

To conduct an evaluation for criminal insanity, the psychologist must address three questions: (1) Does the person have a mental disorder or defect? (2) What is the person's present mental status? (3) What was the person's mental status at the time of the alleged crime? (Maloney, 1985). In the process, the psychologist will assess many factors, including the defendant's history and that of the defendant's family, intellectual status, neuropsychological factors, competency to stand trial, reading skills, personality, and measures of faking or malingering (Blau, 1998).

Competency to Stand Trial. For this question, the issue is the defendant's state of mind at the time of the trial, not when the offense was allegedly committed. A defendant may have been insane when the crime was committed but later be competent to stand trial. The reverse is also possible. In fact, issues of *competency to stand trial* are raised much more often than the insanity defense. In answering questions of competency, three basic issues commonly come to the fore (Maloney, 1985): (1) Can the person appreciate the nature of the charges, and can that person report factually on his or her behavior at the time of the alleged crime? (2) Can the person cooperate in a reasonable way with counsel? (3) Can the person appreciate the proceedings of the court? In most instances, the evaluation factors noted in the previous paragraph will apply here as well.

Civil Cases

A very large number of civil issues engage the attention of forensic psychologists, running the gamut from trademark litigation to class action suits. Two areas that are especially important for clinical psychologists are (1) commitment to and release from mental institutions and (2) domestic issues such as child custody disputes. Let us focus on these areas as examples of activity in the civil arena.

Commitment to Mental Institutions. Picture this scenario. Not too long ago, a disheveled man in his late 30s entered a restaurant and began haranguing customers as they approached the cashier to pay their checks. He was incoherent, but it

PROFILE 19-1

Lawrence S. Wrightsman, Jr., Ph.D.

Dr. Lawrence Wrightsman is a Professor of Social Psychology at the University of Kansas who specializes in forensic psychology. He is the author or coauthor of 40 books and more than 70 articles and book chapters. In addition to authoring one of the leading forensic psychology textbooks, Dr. Wrightsman maintains an active research program that focuses on judicial decision making, the comparison of judge and jury verdicts, and police interrogations and jurors' reactions to confessions. Dr. Wrightsman has received many awards and honors, including a 1998 Distinguished Career

Award from the American Psychology-Law Society (American Psychological Association, Division 41).

Dr. Wrightsman provided responses to several questions we posed concerning his background and assessment of the field of forensic psychology.

What originally got you interested in the field of forensic psychology?

I was trained as a social psychologist and around the mid-1970s began doing research on psychology-and-law topics (as a number of social psychologists did at that time). I have always been intrigued with the courtroom and the jury trial—two versions of the truth always zealously and usually sincerely portrayed, but only one can be true.

From the early 1980s to the present, I have taught courses on psychology and the law, jury behavior, judicial decision making, and similar topics. About five years ago, I noticed undergraduate students were increasingly coming into my office, wanting to become "forensic psychologists." This term was just beginning to surface in the public consciousness, mainly as a result of the movie *Silence of the Lambs*. Suddenly, young people wanted to be criminal profilers like Jodie Foster was in the movie.

was possible to pick out the obscenities and references to God that peppered his remarks. He did this for about five minutes, whereupon the manager appeared and unceremoniously escorted him to the door. Outside, he continued his tirade while pacing back and forth before the door. He repeatedly accosted customers and tried to make them listen to him. The manager finally called the police. After a brief interrogation, they "helped" him into the patrol car and subsequently deposited him in the emergency ward of the local psychiatric hospital.

This and related scenarios are repeated thousands of times, day after day, across the nation. After an examination (sometimes a rather cursory one), the individual may be involuntarily detained for hours or days, depending on particular state laws. But in a few states, even emergency detentions require judicial consent.

Hospitalization that occurs against the will of the individual is referred to as *involuntary commitment*. Some authors, such as Szasz (1970), have argued strenuously that involuntary hospitalization is a dangerous and often misused

So, I began to explore just what was "forensic psychology." I began to teach a graduate-level course on the topic (which draws 40–50 students every time it is offered). The term remains vague and controversial; I prefer to think of it as any application of psychological concepts or findings to the legal system, but others want to restrict it to clinical/practitioner activities. I am currently completing a forensic psychology textbook (for Brooks/Cole–Wadsworth), which will be the first of its kind. So I suppose I am a "forensic psychologist," although I am not a clinical psychologist and hence am not eligible for ABEPP or similar fellow status.

Describe what activities you are involved in as a forensic psychologist.

In addition to teaching, I am occasionally involved in trial consultation. For example, I carry out change-of-venue surveys when a criminal defendant claims that pretrial publicity in the local area means that he/she cannot get a fair trial there. I also serve as an expert witness, especially on the accuracy of eyewitness identification or the validity of confessions. (These are topics that I believe reflect "forensic psychology," although the basis for the testimony comes from experimental, not clinical, psychology.)

What are your particular areas of expertise or interest?

As I indicated, any topic dealing with an application of psychology to the courtroom. Recently, I analyzed a number of the amicus briefs submitted by the American Psychological Association to the Supreme Court.

What are some future trends you see in forensic psychology?

Currently, there is more demand from students than there are programs. Fewer than ten schools offer a program clearly labeled as Forensic Psychology, and some of these are too new to be accredited by APA. One freestanding professional school now offers such a program, and I expect others to follow.

The issue remains, should forensic psychology seek specialty status by APA, as clinical, school, and counseling psychology have done? And if it does, should it be only clinical-practitioner based, or is there room for the experimental psychologist who serves as an expert witness or a survey consultant? The field is struggling over this issue right now.

power that has been repeatedly exercised by psychiatrists and others to maintain control over those who will not conform to certain social dictates. The permissible length of involuntary commitment typically varies from one day to three weeks or so, depending on the jurisdiction. After that, a hearing must be held to decide whether detention should continue.

In a *voluntary commitment*, the individual agrees to admission and may leave at any time. Some hospitals require patients to sign a form stating that their leaving is "against medical advice." Others demand that such patients indicate their intention to leave several days in advance. This enables the hospital to initiate commitment proceedings if the patient is believed to be dangerous to self or others or so disturbed as not to be responsible. It should be noted that "voluntary" admission is often not as voluntary as it might appear at first glance. Most often there is strong pressure from relatives, friends, police, court authorities, or mental health personnel.

For the court to commit someone, a hearing must be held to determine whether the person involved meets the criteria laid out by law and whether treatment will be helpful. Most often these criteria refer to a person who (1) is dangerous to self or others, (2) is so disturbed or disabled as to be incapable of making responsible decisions about self-care and hospitalization, or (3) requires treatment or care in a hospital. An additional criterion is that no less restrictive alternative (other than hospitalization) is available or feasible. But above all, the person must be determined to be mentally ill.

Literally anyone can petition the court for an examination of someone he or she believes requires commitment. Usually it is family or friends, or sometimes the police or welfare officials, who act as petitioners. If the court agrees, an order is issued and the person is required to submit to a professional examination. Such an examination should be based on personal observations of the individual by professionals and not just on what others have reported. Common matters to note are general appearance, clarity of thinking, presence of delusions or hallucinations, how well the patient understands the complaints, the person's use of drugs or alcohol, employment status, intelligence, prior history of mental and criminal problems, and kindred factors (Schwitzgebel & Schwitzgebel, 1980).

Domestic Issues. Many domestic issues these days require intervention by the courts. Child custody, parental fitness, visitation rights, child abuse, juvenile misbehavior, and adoption are but a few of these issues. As an example, we will discuss the issue of child custody.

Because divorce has become so prevalent in our society in recent years, it is only natural that problems of child custody have proliferated as well. The fact that marital roles and norms have likewise changed also complicates matters. Increasingly, fathers have assumed child care responsibilities and mothers are now commonly employed outside the home. These and other factors have made custodial questions much more complex than before.

Today, the doctrine of the "best interests of the child" always takes precedence in custody

disputes. To better articulate exactly what standards are involved here, the Michigan Child Custody Act of 1970 established the following factors that are typically relied upon by the courts in making custodial decisions:

1. The love, affection, and other emotional ties existing between the competing parties and the child.
2. The capacity and disposition of competing parties to give the child love, affection, and guidance, and continuation of educating and raising the child in his [sic] religion or creed, if any.
3. The capacity and disposition of competing parties to provide the child with food, clothing, medical care, or other remedial care recognized and permitted under the laws of this state in lieu of medical care or other material needs.
4. The length of time the child has lived in a stable satisfactory environment and desirability of maintaining continuity.
5. The permanence, as a family unit, of the existing or proposed custodial home.
6. The moral fitness of the competing parties.
7. The home, school, and community record of the child.
8. The mental and physical health of the competing parties.
9. The reasonable preference of the child, if the court deems the child to be of sufficient age to express preference.
10. Any other factor considered by the court to be relevant to a particular child custody dispute.

Although 150 years ago children of divorce were automatically awarded to the father and 50 years ago almost always awarded to the mother, such reflexive decisions no longer hold today. The present norm is *joint custody*, which rests on the belief that children should maintain ties with both parents. In fact, many divorces culminate in informal joint custody decisions by the divorced couple; a formal ruling by the court never occurs. When the court does issue an order for joint custody, this probably means that a dispute of some sort has arisen between competing parties. In the final analysis, however, the only way joint custody can really work is when competing parents set aside their animosity and anger toward each other and act in concert and with sensitivity to the best interests of the child.

Joint custody, however, may not always be in the best interest of the child. Specifically, joint custody may be contraindicated in situations where parents have an emotionally charged, conflictual relationship (Wrightsman et al., 1998). In these instances, legal custody may be granted to one parent, while the other parent is granted visitation rights (Wrightsman et al., 1998).

In doing a child custody evaluation, the psychologist must remember that the critical element is a system of past, present, and future relationships among father, mother, children, and sometimes other relatives. Maloney (1985) has discussed both procedural and content issues relevant to the psychologist's preparation of reports on the evaluation of families facing custody problems. He has also listed some basic questions in child custody disputes that must be addressed in reports:

1. Does any of the major parties in the child custody suit have a mental illness? How is such an illness manifested in terms of injuring or affecting the rights of others? Can the mental illness be defined in terms of interpersonal or relationship terms?
2. If a mental illness does exist, is it of such a type that would jeopardize the health, welfare, and safety of the children?
3. If such an illness does exist and it poses a danger to the children or spouse, is it treatable or remediable by drugs or other forms of psychological/psychiatric treatment?
4. Regardless of whether the illness is treatable or remediable, is it of such severity that it would make the other parent a better custodian?
5. If both parents are suffering from mental illness, which one would be better qualified to deal with the children? Would it be more

appropriate to take the children away from both parents?
6. What effect might the mental illness have on the right of children to visit their mentally ill parents? What effect would the deprivation of visitation of the parents have on the children?
7. Are there ways that the examiner can suggest of controlling visitation or denying visitation if such recommendations are pertinent?
8. If the child were to be placed with a parent with homosexual or heterosexual promiscuity tendencies, how would the child be affected? (The judge goes on to spell out several other specific questions relating to the issue of placing children with parents with sexual problems.)
9. Who could best fill the emotional needs of the children? What is the basis for this judgment? What is the least detrimental alternative to this judgment, and what basis can be cited for this?
10. Do you recommend family counseling?*

The foregoing questions were based on a specific case, but they do have relatively general implications.

The ultimate goal of all the previous factors and questions is identifying a situation in which the best interests of the child are served. Other specific issues, such as changes in previously established custody arrangements or visitation rights, follow the same overriding principle.

Rights of Patients

The rights of hospitalized mental patients have come under increasing judicial scrutiny. We hear talk of the "hospitalized consumer" (Ladkin & Levine, 1976), arguments for the necessity for mental patient advisory boards (J. K.

---

*Reprinted with permission of The Free Press, a division of Macmillan, Inc. from *A Clinician's Guide to Forensic Psychological Assessment*, by Michael P. Maloney. Copyright © 1985 by The Free Press.

Morrison, 1976), and even a clients' bill of rights (Noll, 1974).

Beginning in the early 1970s, courts have held that patients who are involuntarily hospitalized have a constitutional right to individualized treatment that offers them a realistic chance for "cure," or at least improvement (Schwitzgebel & Schwitzgebel, 1980). The courts have been less attentive to the rights of voluntary patients because it is assumed they can leave the hospital if they so choose.

Additional rights and standards involve the physical environment (dayrooms, lavatories, dining rooms, and so on), personal clothing, and personal activities (opportunities for physical exercise, regular outdoor opportunities, or social activities). In addition, involuntary labor is prohibited, and when labor is undertaken voluntarily, appropriate wages must be paid. Although many states recognize patients' rights to correspondence and visitation, institutional personnel often have wide discretion in controlling visits (except by lawyers, physicians, or clergy). Statutes have also generally asserted the patient's right to dignity and privacy. In practice, however, these rights tend to be subject to wide interpretation and discretion. Indeed, as observed earlier, statutes and court orders are one thing; their actual implementation in practice is another.

A controversial and complex issue is the right to refuse treatment or medication Wrightsman et al., 1998). The question is one of informed consent. Not every involuntarily hospitalized patient is mentally incompetent, and such individuals have the right to decide their own fate. But what about patients who are incompetent? How does one protect the rights of the competent while also ensuring that the incompetent can experience the benefits of treatment? These are truly complex problems. In Box 19-2, we can see that related issues also tax our good judgment in the case of prison inmates.

Predicting Dangerousness

As we saw in Chapter 3, the *Tarasoff* case resulted in a California court decision that therapists have a duty to protect potential victims from their pa-

tients' violent behavior. Beyond that, many would agree that, by law or moral imperative, we all have the obligation to protect others from those who are deemed dangerous. But how accurately can psychologists or anyone else actually predict dangerous behavior? The reality is that to truly protect against those individuals who are dangerous, we would have to fish with a very large net—a net that would snare large numbers of individuals who would never actually commit a violent act. After all, the incidence of violence relative to the total population is quite low—so low that in order to protect against the truly dangerous, it would be necessary to confine many who are not (Rappaport, 1977). But, as Livermore, Malmquist, and Meehl (1968) put it, "If, in the criminal law, it is better that ten guilty men go free than one innocent man suffer, how can we say in the civil commitment area that it is better that 54 harmless people be incarcerated lest one dangerous man be free?" (p. 84).

According to Monahan (1976), violent acts are highly overpredicted. But many people seem willing to sacrifice many to protect society from one. There are undoubtedly many reasons why people tend to see danger when none exists (Monahan, 1976). But as much as anything, it is probably the television program or news story that describes how a mental patient was released only to kill someone, sexually abuse a child, or otherwise behave so as to lead the lay public to question the competency (and often the common sense) of the psychiatrist or psychologist involved in the release decision. All this leads to the conclusion that predicting dangerousness is very, very difficult. Although it is perhaps true that all of us have the potential to commit dangerous acts, given the right conditions, the fact remains that unless someone has previously behaved in a dangerous fashion, the ability to accurately predict such behavior is extremely limited (Shah, 1978).

Difficult though such predictions are, psychological evaluation for this purpose may constitute the largest single category of evaluation requested of the clinician by the criminal justice system (Blau, 1998). These evaluations are used for many decisions, ranging from holding a pris-

BOX 19-2

Recent Legal Controversies

A recent case, *Perry* v. *Louisiana* (1989), raised the issue of whether state officials may forcibly administer psychotropic medications to a death row inmate in order to render him mentally competent for his own execution. A macabre yet real-life question!

Who should decide whether prison inmates may be administered antipsychotic drugs against their will? This question was argued before the U.S. Supreme Court in the case of *Washington* v. *Harper* (1990). Harper was a convicted robber who initially accepted the medication voluntarily. Later, he refused. A prison administrative committee concluded that Harper was both mentally ill and dangerous, and they authorized the antipsychotic medication. Harper then filed a suit, which ultimately reached the Supreme Court. During oral arguments, several justices asked questions such as the following:

- Is it permissible to medicate an objecting inmate just to make the prison environment safer?
- As a ward of the state, how can a convicted criminal be presumed competent to make medication decisions?
- Why can't a dangerous inmate, even though competent, be medicated against his will?
- Because an inmate's competency may fluctuate over time, would not frequent judicial review be required for a given inmate? And would not such frequent review be an onerous burden to the court?

Ultimately, the Supreme Court ruled that a mentally ill prisoner could not be medicated without his or her consent unless there was a consensus of professional opinion that safety would otherwise be compromised.

---

oner without bail, to granting work-release status to hospitalized defendants, to invoking special sentencing options for violent offenders (Shah, 1978). As noted by Wrightsman et al. (1998), research suggests that the following types of predictions of violent behavior are likely to be the most accurate:

1. Predictions for the near, short-term future
2. Predictions for the same setting or circumstances that the clinician already has historical data on
3. Predictions based on the clinician's knowledge of the individual's past history of violent behavior
4. Predictions for individuals from groups with relatively high base rates of violent behavior

Because of the tremendous implications for public policy, to say nothing of human values, much more research is needed in this broad area of forensic psychology.

Psychological Treatment

In the case of prisoners, legally established rights to psychological treatment or rehabilitation are still somewhat in a state of flux (Schwitzgebel & Schwitzgebel, 1980). Such persons have the right to medical treatment, and juvenile prisoners generally have the right to both psychological and medical treatment. When the right to psychological treatment for adult prisoners is recognized, it is most often for severely mentally disturbed individuals. Some experts are reluctant to promote treatment rights for prisoners because they believe that sometimes punishment and deprivation occur under the label of "treatment" or perhaps "behavior modification."

We have already observed that people have a right to refuse treatment, especially in the case of very intrusive forms such as psychosurgery or electroconvulsive therapy (ECT). But this right is most apparent in instances where the therapy may be considered punishing or manipulative.

In such instances, the state must show a compelling interest that will override the prisoner's refusal. Because of the ambiguities and potential for violations of human rights, many correctional institutions now have committees to protect the rights of prisoners. Such committees typically include a majority of members who are not affiliated with the institution.

There are wider forensic treatment implications, however. In criminal cases, therapy may focus on restoring an incompetent person to a state of mental competency. Or therapy may be undertaken to provide emotional support for one who faces imprisonment. For criminal offenders, the focus is often on personality problems, sexual behavior, and aggressiveness. Sometimes therapy is conducted while the person is incarcerated, but other times it is on an outpatient basis as a condition of parole or probation. The forms of therapy employed include both individual and group methods that involve everything from insight-oriented and supportive methods to behavioral techniques, biofeedback, and cognitive approaches. One of the major problems for the forensic clinician is the knowledge that testimony may be required later in court. What the court wants, what the client's attorney will permit, what is best for the client, and what the clinician sees as most desirable may conflict and lead to many problems. In child custody issues, the treatment problems and conflicts among parents and child may be especially difficult and poignant. They can often lead to real professional dilemmas. For example, to best help the child, the parents should undergo therapy themselves, but sometimes one or both will refuse to do so.

Consultation

Another common activity of forensic psychologists is consultation. Of course, many of the activities discussed previously also involve some manner of consultation. In this section, we focus on several additional aspects of consultation.

Jury Selection. A consulting psychologist may work with attorneys in the process of *jury selection*. The legal term *voir dire* is used to refer to that part of a trial in which a jury is impaneled. During this phase, attorneys have the opportunity to discover biases in potential jurors; to obtain information for *peremptory challenges* (a set number of challenges allowed each side in a trial to remove jurors thought to be biased against a given side); to ingratiate themselves with jurors or get them to identify with a given side; or to indoctrinate jurors so they will be receptive to an attorney's presentation of the case. All this is designed to give an attorney an edge. The consulting psychologist will work with attorneys to help them in a variety of ways to achieve better jury selection or deselection. Table 19-3 summarizes the goals and techniques of jury consultation.

Jury Shadowing. Another form of consultation is *jury shadowing*. Here the jury consultant hires analogous jurors (that is, individuals similar to those actually serving on the jury) and monitors their reactions to the actual testimony as it is presented at the trial. In this way, the consultant and attorneys can anticipate the reactions and impressions of the actual jurors and prepare a better informed courtroom strategy.

Public Opinion Surveys. Public opinion surveys have been used in many ways over the years. In a trademark suit, for example, an attorney might hire a psychological consultant to determine the public's recognition of some company name or symbol. One way to do this is through a survey. In other cases, an opinion survey might be administered to a representative sample of people from the same geographical area in which the trial will be held, asking for their opinions about a certain case and about the trial tactics planned by the attorney. In a sense, this survey allows the trial attorney to pretest the significant trial issues and to hone the proposed method of presenting evidence. Another use of surveys is to determine whether a change in venue (location) for the trial might be in order. Attitudes in the community about the trial, and particularly toward the defendant, can be elicited to help convince the court to change the location and also to help in the jury selection process (Nietzel & Dillehay, 1986).

TABLE 19-3 Goals and Techniques of Jury Consultation

Stage of Consultation	Goals	Techniques
Stage I: Voir dire preparation.	Learn about the case.	Hold planning sessions with attorneys.
	Educate attorneys about contributions that consultants can make.	Review media, interview client, observe courtroom procedures.
	Develop instruments.	If necessary, develop juror questionnaires, survey questionnaires, trial simulations, and interviews with key informants.
	Formulate initial theory of jury selection.	Analyze data from above and propose theory of jury selections that is integrated with attorneys' theory of case.
Stage II: Improving voir dire conditions.	Structure voir dire in a manner that improves chances to uncover juror bias and to identify juror prejudice.	Provide affidavits, expert testimony on: change of venue; individual, sequestered, attorney-conducted voir dire; struck vs. "as you go" system; and composition challenge.
	Improve voir dire skills of attorney.	Preparations of voir dire topics and training of attorneys in interviewing techniques.
Stage III: Juror deselection.	Develop final theory of jury selection.	Coordinate pretrial data with in-court observation of *venire* persons.
	Impanel a jury as favorably disposed toward client and theory of case as possible.	Develop rating system to identify jurors for peremptory challenge by juror experience, intelligence, sentiment, and social influence.

Source: From *Psychological Consultation in the Courtroom*, by M. T. Nietzel and R. C. Dillehay, p. 24. Copyright © 1986 by Pergamon Press. Reprinted by permission.

Witness Preparation. It would be unethical for the consultant to work with a witness in any way designed to encourage any alteration in the facts of testimony. Although the line is a very thin one, the idea of *witness preparation* is to help witnesses present their testimony better, without changing the facts to which their testimony is directed. Because this is such a delicate matter, some consultants will not work with witnesses in criminal proceedings—only in civil cases. Nietzel and Dillehay (1986) have discussed many aspects of witness preparation, including the manner in which facts are presented, associated emotions on the part of the witness, preparation for the sheer experience of being a witness in a courtroom, cross-examination, appearance, and threats by the opposing attorney to the credibility of the witness.

Convincing the Jury. Finally, consultants can often help attorneys in the way they present their cases and evidence (within the allowable constraints of the judicial system) to jurors. Consultants can assist attorneys in predicting how jurors will respond to certain kinds of evidence or methods of presentation, especially in opening and closing arguments. In effect, the beliefs, feelings, and behavior of jurors are the targets here. The consultants then help attorneys find the very best way to present their cases.

Research and Forensic Psychology

In a real sense, virtually all research in psychology is relevant to some forensic issue. For example, research on the genetic components of schizophrenia may be very important in a mental competency hearing. The nature of prejudice or the basic elements of the persuasive process are as germane to the attorney as they are to the social psychologist. Consumer research may have direct application to a product liability suit. And recently, research on attributions and interpersonal relationships has been applied to the law on searches and seizures (Kagehiro, 1990). However, several research areas have become particularly identified with forensic psychology, and we have chosen to sample two of them here.

Eyewitness Testimony. Nothing can be so dramatic or damaging as an eyewitness who identifies the person accused of a crime. Such *eyewitness testimony* has been a powerful factor in the conviction of countless individuals over the years (Cutler & Penrod, 1995). But such testimony has all too often convicted the innocent as well as the guilty (Loftus, 1979). The reason, put simply, is that eyewitness testimony is often unreliable and inaccurate. A case in point occurred in 1979 in Wilmington, Delaware. A Catholic priest was put on trial because a citizen told police that the priest looked very much like an artist's sketch of a robber being circulated by the police. Later, seven eyewitnesses to the robbery positively identified the priest as the robber. The trial was halted, however, when another man confessed to the crime. What had happened with these eyewitnesses? Apparently, before showing pictures of suspects to the witnesses, the police had quietly revealed that the robber might be a priest. And the priest's picture was the only one with the subject wearing a clerical collar!

Over the years, Loftus and her colleagues have conducted a number of experiments that together show that eyewitnesses' memory can easily be distorted by subsequent information. For example, Loftus, Miller, and Burns (1978) had subjects view a series of color slides of an auto accident. Half the subjects were shown a series in which there was a stop sign present; the other half saw a yield sign. Afterward, subjects answered questions about the slides. The critical question asked whether a particular sign (either stop or yield) was present. For half the subjects, the sign asked about was consistent with what subjects had seen earlier; for the other half, it was inconsistent. Still later, the subjects were shown 15 slides and were asked to pick out the one they had seen before. Interestingly, subjects whose question was consistent with the sign they had actually seen chose the correct slide 75% of the time, whereas those in the inconsistent group made the correct choice only 41% of the time.

It is clear that people often make inferences on the basis of their expectations. Also, as Loftus (1979) points out, an eyewitness to an accident or crime is almost always questioned prior to the trial. In these conversations, something may easily be said to alter the witness's recollection. It is the role of the forensic psychologist to help identify the conditions in a specific case that might produce distortions in veridical testimony.

Experience has taught us that eyewitnesses to events all too often cannot agree among themselves. They differ in their descriptions of subjects' height, weight, hair color, clothing, and even race. A dramatic illustration of this axiom was provided by Buckhout (1975), who staged a demonstration as part of a television program. Viewers watched a staged purse-snatching episode that lasted but 12 seconds. Following this, viewers saw a police lineup of six men that, the viewers were told, might include the assailant. Viewers could call in and render their judgments. What happened? More than 2000 callers responded, and 1800 of them were mistaken! Of course, none of the foregoing is meant to suggest that eyewitnesses are never correct. But it does suggest that caution should be exercised in accepting accounts uncritically. At the very least, our legal system can use improvement in its procedures for identifying suspects (Loftus, 1983; Wells, 1995). Factors of perception, stress levels, information storage, identification procedures, and even unconscious integrative processes all need further study (Horowitz & Willging, 1984). Also important are prior experiences and conditioning, along with personal biases and stereotypes (Buckhout, 1980).

In response to the concerns over false eyewitness identification, a subcommittee was appointed by the American Psychology-Law Society (Division 41 of the American Psychological Association) to review scientific evidence in this area and to formulate recommendations (Wells et al., 1998). Web site 19-5 at the end of this chapter provides a link to the subcommittee's report. Briefly, the subcommittee made the following recommendations:

- The person who conducts the lineup or photospread in the case should not know the identity of the suspect.
- Eyewitnesses should be told that a suspect in the case may or may not be in the lineup or photospread and that the person conducting the lineup or photospread does not know which person (if any) is the suspect in the case.
- The suspect in a lineup or a photospread should not stand out (in appearance or dress) as being different from the others.
- The eyewitness's confidence in the identification should be assessed at the time of the identification and prior to any feedback.

In this way, it is hoped that eyewitness identification errors will be reduced (Wells et al., 1998).

Jury Behavior. The better we understand the conditions that affect how juries think and reach decisions, the better our judicial system will be. A great deal of research has been done on just how jurors make sense out of evidence and process information, how they respond to instructions from the bench, and how they react to certain kinds of arguments (Kassin & Wrightsman, 1988; Wrightsman et al., 1998). Let us consider several examples.

Jurors are often confused by instructions from the judge. Severance and Loftus (1982) modified the pattern of instructions given to the jury. They wrote instructions in active rather than passive sentences and made the messages short and concise. In addition, they gave abstract notions such as "reasonable doubt" greater elaboration than usual. The result was a more accurate application of the law by jurors than is usually the case.

Even such a simple condition as the order in which the judge's instructions are presented can have an effect on jurors. For example, Kassin and Wrightsman (1979) used mock jurors who watched a videotaped trial. They found that informing jurors as to the requirements of proof before presenting the evidence rather than after had definite effects. Jurors under the former condition were more likely to hold to the dictum of presumed innocence than were jurors under the latter condition.

There are also many conditions that may bias jury decisions. For example, an individual may be charged with several instances of a crime. Sometimes, these instances are joined into one indictment; in other cases, the defendant is tried separately for each instance. Greene and Loftus (1981) discovered that when charges are joined into one indictment, the jury is more likely to hand down harsher verdicts than when the charges are tried separately.

Much research on jury behavior has been simulated. That is, real juries in real situations are not studied. Instead, subjects are placed in jury-like settings to study their behavior. It has been found that mock jurors who were exposed to a voir dire process were less prejudiced than jurors who did not have this experience (Padawer-Singer & Barton, 1975). Also, pretrial publicity colored those same mock jurors' understanding of the case. Likewise, Garcia and Griffitt (1978) found that the testimony of "likable" witnesses had a greater impact on mock jurors than did testimony from "dislikable" witnesses. Of course, the problem with simulated jury studies is that it is unclear how far one can generalize from them to real trials and real jurors (Kassin & Wrightsman, 1988). But simulations provide a flexible method that allows researchers to exert greater control over conditions and variables.

Chapter Summary

Forensic psychology is concerned with the application of psychological methods, theories, and concepts to the legal system. Although Hugo von Munsterberg's 1908 book proclaimed that psychology had much to offer to the legal system, little influence was observed until the 1950s. Today, the influence and popularity of forensic psychology is apparent; many journals, books, and specialty training programs exist. However, forensic psychologists are a target of harsh criticism as well.

In this chapter, we have discussed eight activities of the forensic psychologist. Forensic psychologists may serve as expert witnesses or as consultants for both criminal and civil cases. Forensic psychologists may also be called on to represent hospitalized patients' rights or to evaluate and predict whether a patient is likely to be a danger to self or to others. Forensic psychologists also serve as consultants regarding jury selection and witness preparation. Finally, forensic psychologists may conduct research on important issues such as eyewitness testimony and jury behavior.

Key Terms

ALI standard The most liberal standard for determining the insanity of a defendant. This standard attests that the defendant is not responsible for an unlawful act if it resulted from a mental disease or defect such that he or she lacked substantial capacity either to appreciate the criminality of the act (a cognitive deficit) or to conform to the law (a volitional deficit).

burden of proof The obligation to establish the truth of an assertion in a court of law. In the case of the insanity plea, the burden of proof is usually on the defense.

competency to stand trial The defendant's state of mind at the time of trial. In order to be deemed competent, it must be shown that the defendant appreciates the nature of the charges and can report on his or her behavior at the time of the alleged offense, has a basic understanding of the court proceedings, and is capable of cooperating with his or her attorney.

expert witness An individual who, by his or her unique profession, training, or experience, is called on to help the court understand and evaluate evidence or offer opinions and inferences on an issue.

eyewitness testimony Testimony given by an individual that has witnessed part or all of an event (e.g., a crime, an accident). Eyewitness testimony is often inaccurate, unreliable, and distorted by subsequent information. One role of forensic psychologists is to help identify the conditions in a specific case that might produce distortions in testimony.

forensic psychology A psychology subspecialty that focuses upon applying psychological concepts and methods to questions/problems arising within the context of the legal system. Forensic psychologists may be called upon to provide expertise on matters of child custody, jury selection, the prediction of dangerousness, etc.

insanity plea The assertion of someone accused of a crime that he or she was not "sane" or rational at the time of the alleged crime. If this plea is successful, an individual is regarded as not responsible for his or her actions and is held for treatment rather than punishment.

joint custody An arrangement in which both parents share in the custody of a child following divorce. Many "joint custody" arrangements are determined informally by the parents; formal court orders tend to be issued only in cases where the parties could arrive at no satisfactory agreement on their own.

jury selection A process in which attorneys for the prosecution and defense choose jurors for a case from a larger pool of possible jurors. Forensic psychologists may be consulted to assist attorneys with jury selection (e.g., to come up with a theory for jury selection, to improve the voir dire skills of the attorney).

jury shadowing The process of hiring individuals similar to those who are serving on a given jury and monitoring their reactions to the testimony as it is presented at the trial. The reactions of the shadow jurors are used to anticipate the reactions of the actual jurors and may serve as the basis for a shift in courtroom strategy.

M'Naghten rule The oldest standard for determining the insanity of a defendant. The M'Naghten rule requires the defense to prove that at the time of the unlawful act, the defendant's reasoning was so impaired by "a disease of the mind" that he or she either did not appreciate what he or she was doing or did not comprehend that it was wrong.

peremptory challenges A set number of challenges allowed each side (prosecution and defense) during voir dire in order to remove jurors suspected of bias against that side.

voir dire A legal term that refers to that part of the trial in which a jury is impaneled, or selected.

voluntary commitment The circumstance in which the individual agrees to be admitted to a psychiatric hospital and is permitted to leave at any time.

witness preparation Helping witnesses present their testimony more effectively without changing the facts to which their testimony is directed. Forensic psychologists may be consulted to assist with many aspects of witness preparation (e.g., preparing them for the sheer experience of being a witness in the courtroom; making recommendations as to their appearance, the manner in which they present facts, etc.)

Web Sites of Interest

To visit any of the web sites listed below, go to www.wadsworth.com and click on Links.

19-1 American Psychological Association Division 41: The American Psychology-Law Society

19-2 Careers and Training in Psychology and Law

19-3 Links to Graduate Programs in Psychology and Law

19-4 Ethical Guidelines for Forensic Psychologists

19-5 Eyewitness Identification Procedures: Recommendations for lineups and photo-spreads

Pediatric and Clinical Child Psychology

It has been estimated that at least 8 million children in the United States need mental health services (Roberts, 1994). For years, the mental health needs of children and adolescents have not been adequately met. Unfortunately, this trend is likely to continue into the next century (Culbertson, 1993). Projections of demographic changes for the United States between 1990 and 2025 suggest that although the overall population growth rate is expected to decline for some groups (such as European Americans), the rates for groups whose mental health needs are currently underserved (such as African American and Hispanic American children and adolescents) are expected to climb dramatically (Lewit & Baker, 1994). Two subfields of clinical psychology, pediatric psychology and clinical child psychology, are uniquely qualified to address these needs.

Definitions, History, and Perspectives

Before touching on historical aspects of these child specialties, we should first discuss the distinction between clinical child psychology and pediatric psychology.

Definitions

The distinctions between pediatric psychologists and clinical child psychologists are somewhat blurred at best. However, in *clinical child psychology*, a common activity over the years has been work with children and adolescents once psychopathological symptoms have developed. This work has often been conducted either in private practice settings or in outpatient clinic settings in the context of the traditional team of psychologist, psychiatrist, and social worker, along with some collaboration with pediatricians.

In contrast, *pediatric psychology* (or child health psychology, as it is often called) has been described as clinical child psychology conducted in medical settings, including hospitals, developmental clinics, or medical group practice

(Routh, 1988). Pediatric psychologists frequently intervene before psychopathology develops (or at least at an earlier stage of the disorder), and their referrals often come from pediatricians (Pruitt & Elliott, 1992). Specifically, Roberts, Maddux, and Wright (1984) have defined pediatric psychology as

> a field of research and practice [that] has been concerned with a wide variety of topics in the relationship between the psychological and physical well-being of children, including behavioral and emotional concomitants of disease and illness, the role of psychology in pediatric medicine, and the promotion of health and prevention of illness among healthy children. (pp. 56–57)

Even though the overlap is considerable, surveys of pediatric and clinical child psychologists reveal several differences between the two (see, for example, Kaufman, Holden, & Walker, 1989). First, pediatric clinicians are characterized by a behavioral orientation, with a related tendency to use short-term, immediate intervention strategies. In contrast, clinical child psychologists are more diverse in their orientations (psychodynamic and family/systems orientations are more common among clinical child specialists). Second, pediatric psychologists tend to place greater emphasis on medical and biological issues in their approaches to training, research, and service delivery. Their interests in health psychology and behavioral medicine (see Chapter 17), as well as their consultations with pediatricians, are distinguishing features. Clinical child specialists tend to place greater emphasis on training in assessment, developmental processes, and family therapy.

Because of the increased relevance of pediatric psychology to clinical psychologists of the twenty-first century, we will focus a fair amount of our discussion in this chapter on this emerging specialty. Before reviewing the major activities of pediatric and clinical child psychologists, however, it is important to survey briefly the history of these specialties and to discuss the developmental perspective adopted by these psychologists.

PROFILE 20-1

Lizette Peterson, Ph.D.

Dr. Lizette Peterson is a Professor of Psychology at the University of Missouri who specializes in pediatric psychology, prevention of child abuse and neglect, and injury prevention. Dr. Peterson has received awards for her scientific contributions from the American Psychological Association, the University of Missouri, and the Society for Pediatric Psychology. She was honored with the Frederick A. Middlebush Endowed Chair at the University of Missouri, and she currently holds the Byler Distinguished Professorship at the same institution. Dr. Peterson is one of the most prolific clinical psychologists in the field, with more than 150 published books, book chapters, or articles. In addition, she has received funds from multiple sources (including the National Institutes of Health) to support her research projects. Finally, Dr. Peterson provides psychological services to children, adolescents, and adults, and serves as a consultant to physicians and other medical personnel.

Dr. Peterson responded to questions we posed concerning her background, interests, and views on the field.

What originally got you interested in the field of clinical psychology?

A fabulous psychologist (Grayson Osborn) who taught a class in child psychology. He later let me work in his lab and gave me a lot of one-on-one attention.

Describe what activities you are involved in as a clinical psychologist.

You name it. I have two research grants, advise several graduate and undergraduate students, serve on six editorial boards, and serve on nearly 20 master's, comprehensive exam, and dissertation committees.

What are your particular areas of expertise or interest?

Broadly, clinical psychology. Specifically, pediatric psychology with emphasis on prevention of child abuse and unintentional injury.

What are the future trends you see for clinical psychology?

Clinicians in practice must rethink how they perform therapy. Researchers and teachers must think divergently, be more applied, and do a better job of disseminating information.

What are some future trends you see in pediatric and clinical child psychology?

More multidisciplinary work, greater specialization, and more innovative work for a wider age range (especially toddlers).

History

The history of clinical child psychology goes back to at least 1896, when Witmer stimulated the profession of clinical psychology by starting the first psychological clinic. As noted in Chapter 2, this clinic was devoted to treating children who were having learning problems or were disruptive in the classroom.

The scientific study of childhood psychopathology can probably be dated to the early 1900s. For a long time, children were not recognized as being very different from adults in terms of their

TABLE 20-1 Examples of Problems Commonly Addressed by Pediatric Psychologists

Problems	Examples
Negative behaviors	Tantrums, crying
Toileting	Enuresis, toilet training
Developmental delays	Speech, overactivity
School	Reading, dislikes school
Sleeping	Nightmares, resists bedtime
Personality	Poor self-control, stealing
Sibling/peers	No friends, fighting
Divorce, separation, adoption	Visiting schedule, custody
Infant management	Feeding, colic
Family problems	Discipline, child abuse
Sex-related	Poor identification, no same-sex friends
Food/eating	Picky eater, obesity
Specific fears	Dogs, trucks
Specific bad habits	Thumb-sucking, tics

Source: Roberts (1986), p. 20.

needs and abilities. They were pretty much regarded as miniature adults. By the late 1800s and early 1900s, however, several developments occurred to increase the focus on children (Ollendick & Hersen, 1998). These developments included the identification and care of those with mental retardation, the development of intelligence testing, the formulation of psychoanalysis and behaviorism, the child study movement, and the emergence of child guidance clinics.

Even the classification of childhood disorders has changed greatly, especially in the past 30 years (Davison & Neale, 1998). Both the DSM-I and the DSM-II regarded childhood problems as downward extensions of adult disorders. However, starting with the DSM-III and continuing today with DSM-IV, we now have diagnostic categories specifically relevant to children. Currently, there are 43 specific diagnoses contained in ten groups (American Psychiatric Association, 1994). We will have more to say about diagnostic classification issues later in this chapter.

The foregoing trends have culminated in what is now referred to as clinical child psychology. Indeed, the field is essentially oriented toward assessment, treatment, and prevention of a variety of problems.

Pediatric psychology evolved as a specialty when it became apparent that neither pediatrics nor clinical child psychology could handle all the problems presented in childhood (Roberts, 1986). Many "well-child" visits to pediatricians require mainly support and counseling rather than medical interventions. Often at issue are matters relevant to all child psychologists, including child rearing, behavioral management problems, or questions about academic performance. When these problems reflect the psychological-behavioral accompaniments of physical illness, handicap, or medical procedures, the pediatric psychologist typically has more relevant expertise than a traditional clinical child psychologist. Table 20-1 suggests the variety of cases seen by pediatric psychologists.

By 1966, some 300 psychologists were working in pediatric settings in the United States (Routh, 1988). At about the same time, Wright (1967), recognizing the "marriage" between

FIGURE 20-1 **An overview of development and examples of associated problems**
Source: Mash, E. J., & Wolfe, D. A. (1999). Abnormal Child Psychology. *Pacific Grove, CA: Brooks/Cole/Wadsworth. Page 33.*

Approximate Age	Normal Achievements	Areas of Common Behavior Problems	Clinical Disorders
 0–2	Eating, sleeping, attachment	Stubbornness, temper, toileting	Mental retardation, feeding disorders, autistic disorder
 2–5	Language, toileting, self-care skills, self-control, peer relationships	Arguing, demanding attention, disobedience, fears, overactivity, resisting bedtime	Speech and language disorders, problems stemming from child abuse and neglect, some anxiety disorders, such as phobias
 6–11	Academic skills and rules, rule-governed games, simple responsibilities	Arguing, inability to concentrate, self-consciousness, showing off	ADHD, learning disorders, school phobia, conduct problems
 12–20	Relations with opposite sex, personal identity, separation from family, increased responsibilities	Arguing, bragging	Anorexia, bulimia, delinquency, suicide attempts, drug and alcohol abuse, schizophrenia, depression

pediatrics and psychology, called for a new specialty—pediatric psychology. Soon, the Society of Pediatric Psychology was formed. This society now has close to 1200 members, and in 1999 became an official division of the American Psychological Association (Division 54).

A Developmental Perspective

Those who work with children and adolescents recognize the importance of a developmental viewpoint. From a developmental perspective, psychological problems in children and adolescents result from some deviation in one or more areas of development (cognitive, biological, physical, emotional, behavioral, social) when compared with same age peers (Mash & Wolfe, 1999). At the same time, however, it is important to recognize that (1) development is an active, dynamic process that is best assessed over time; (2) similar developmental problems may lead to different outcomes (clinical disorders); (3) different developmental problems may lead to the

same outcome; (4) developmental processes and failures may interact; and (5) developmental processes and the environment are interdependent—each influences the other such that they cannot be viewed separately, in isolation (Mash & Wolfe, 1999). Figure 20-1 presents a general overview of developmental periods, with examples of typical achievements, problems, and clinical disorders commonly associated with each developmental stage.

Pediatric and clinical child psychologists go beyond simply viewing children and adolescents as miniature adults. Instead, children and adolescents are assessed and treated within the context of the developmental and environmental challenges with which these individuals are faced. The age of children, stage of development across spheres of functioning (cognitive, emotional, social), and their family and social situations, must be considered as one tries to conceptualize their problems and prescribe treatment. Indeed, failing to take into account the developmental stage of the child will lead to inaccurate

■ **TABLE 20-2** **Characteristics of Resilient Children and Adolescents**

Source	Characteristic
Individual	Good intellectual functioning
	Appealing, sociable, easygoing disposition
	Self-efficacy, self-confidence, high self-esteem
	Talents
	Faith
Family	Close relationship to caring parental figure
	Authoritative parenting: warmth, structure, high expectations
	Socioeconomic advantages
	Connections to extended supportive family networks
Extrafamilial context	Bonds to prosocial adults outside the family
	Connections to prosocial organizations
	Attending effective schools

Source: Masten & Coatsworth (1998), p. 212.

assessments and inappropriate treatments. For example, bedwetting is a problem at age 12, but not at age 2. The prognostic implications of a behavior such as temper tantrums will be different for toddlers than for adolescents. These developmental considerations help the pediatric or clinical child psychologist decide whether a problem is indeed present, how severe it is, how to conceptualize it, and what kind of intervention to recommend.

Resilience

Why do some children, even though faced with what seems to be incredible adversity, seem to adapt well with few noticeable problems? The term *resilience* refers to qualities in individuals that are associated with their ability to overcome adversity and achieve good developmental outcomes (Masten & Coatsworth, 1998). Psychologists have become increasingly interested in studying factors that are associated with resiliency, especially among children who are at risk for negative outcomes due to unfavorable environments (war, violence in the home, poverty). Table 20-2 presents a summary of characteristics

(of the individual, of the family, and of influences outside the family) associated with resilience in children and adolescents.

It is worth emphasizing that these factors have only been shown to be associated with good outcome; they are not necessarily causal (Masten & Coatsworth, 1998). Still, the theme that comes through is that factors promoting strong attachments or bonds between child and parent and those indicating the capacity for good problem-solving skills seem to help buffer the individual against adverse circumstances. As for practical applications, studies of resilience and competence can lead to interventions aimed at preventing or eliminating risk factors, building or improving resources, and enhancing relationships or processes such as self-efficacy and self-regulation (Masten & Coatsworth, 1998).

Major Activities

Now that we have reviewed definitions and perspectives important to the field, we can turn to a discussion of the many diverse and still evolving activities in which pediatric and clinical child psychologists are involved. To simplify matters a bit, we will group these activities under the headings of assessment, intervention, prevention, and consultation. First, however, we will consider several general issues relevant to all these types of activities.

General Issues

Epidemiology. It is important to have some idea of how common various problems are across age groups and other segments of the population. For example, between the ages of 1 and 2 years, feeding and sleeping problems are very common. Hyperactivity and conduct disorders occur more frequently in boys than in girls. Even behaviors that might seem to indicate the presence of a mental disorder occur commonly in nonclinical groups (S. B. Campbell, 1989). To properly understand and diagnose, the field must have information on how behaviors change over time, how they covary with one another, and how behaviors are distributed throughout the community (Yule, 1989).

The Situation. As noted throughout this text, behavior is often situation-specific. A child may be quiet and withdrawn at home but not with peers. Another child may be compliant with authority figures but hostile with other children. This is not to say that general dispositional factors are unimportant. Rather, to adequately conceptualize a child's problem (or presumed problem), those who work with the child must pay attention to the interaction between factors in the child's environment and generalized personality characteristics.

Who Is the Client? In our earlier discussion of family therapy (see Chapter 15), we noted that it is sometimes difficult to determine exactly who in the group is the real patient. That observation is equally true in the context of this chapter. In many instances, the most effective treatment is directed at the parents, because they are largely in control of the child. Furthermore, children do not refer themselves for assessment or therapy. They are referred by parents, physicians, teachers, or even court authorities. As Campbell (1989) puts it, "The first task of the clinician working with children and families is to determine whether a problem actually exists. Intolerance, ignorance, and misconceptions on the part of adults often lead to referral" (p. 7). For example, in a large epidemiological study of psychopathology in children, Shepherd, Oppenheim, and Mitchell (1971) compared children being seen in clinics with others matched in terms of severity of symptoms but whose parents had not sought help. The main factor differentiating the two groups was maternal perceptions of the problem as being serious. Clearly, parental concern, tolerance, and skill in managing children play a large part in defining childhood problem behavior.

Diagnosis and Classification of Problems. Because we have already covered the DSM-IV in Chapter 5, only a few points with respect to children will be noted here. First, the classification of childhood disorders has been of more interest to clinical child specialists than to pediatric psychologists because the former have historically had to deal more often with psychiatric cases. Second, the DSM-IV incorporates the growing interest in childhood disorders. There are ten major groups of disorders that are usually first diagnosed in infancy, childhood, or adolescence. These groups, with diagnostic examples from each, are listed in Table 20-3. It is important to note two things. First, all of the disorders in Table 20-3 except the subtypes of mental retardation are coded on Axis I. Second, children and adolescents *can* receive diagnoses that are not listed in Table 20-3 (for example, major depressive disorder, dysthymic disorder, or bulimia nervosa). Often, however, diagnostic criteria or thresholds are modified so that they are more appropriate for children or adolescents. For example, to obtain a dysthymic disorder diagnosis, a child or adolescent can present with an irritable (versus depressed) mood, and the duration of all symptoms can be only one year (versus two years for adults).

TABLE 20-3 DSM-IV Disorders Usually First Diagnosed in Infancy, Childhood, or Adolescence

Group	Diagnostic Examples
Mental Retardation	Mild, Moderate, or Severe Mental Retardation
Learning Disorders	Reading Disorder, Mathematics Disorder
Motor Skills Disorder	Developmental Coordination Disorder
Communication Disorders	Expressive Language Disorder, Stuttering
Pervasive Developmental Disorders	Autistic Disorder, Asperger's Disorder
Attention Deficit and Disruptive Behavior Disorders	Attention Deficit/Hyperactivity Disorder, Conduct Disorder
Feeding and Eating Disorders of Infancy	Pica, Rumination Disorder or Early Childhood
Tic Disorders	Tourette's Disorder, Transient Tic Disorder
Elimination Disorders	Encopresis, Enuresis
Other Disorders of Infancy, Childhood	Separation Anxiety Disorder, Selective Mutism or Adolescence

Source: DSM-IV (APA, 1994). Copyright 1994 by the American Psychiatric Association. Reprinted by permission.

In order to give the reader a better sense of what kinds of behaviors and problems are included in a diagnostic criteria set for a DSM-IV childhood disorder, Table 20-4 presents the diagnostic criteria for Conduct Disorder. *Conduct disorder* is one of the most frequently encountered diagnoses in inpatient and outpatient settings that treat children and adolescents. Further, as will be seen throughout this chapter, a number of assessment and treatment approaches have been developed to address the behavior problems that comprise this disorder.

Often, psychological problems experienced by children and adolescents are subdivided into internalizing disorders and externalizing disorders. *Internalizing disorders* are characterized by symptoms of anxiety, depression, shyness, and social withdrawal. Examples of internalizing disorders are mood disorders (such as major depressive disorder) and anxiety disorders (such as separation anxiety disorder). *Externalizing disorders* are characterized by aggressive behaviors, impulsive behaviors, and conduct problems. Examples of externalizing disorders are conduct

disorder (see Table 20-4) and attention deficit/hyperactivity disorder. A variety of assessment methods and techniques—including interviews, behavioral observations, questionnaires and checklists, intelligence and achievement tests, and neuropsychological tests—can be used to identify these types of problems in children and adolescents. We discuss assessment in more detail in the next section.

Assessment

Assessment with children and adolescents differs in several important ways from that with adults. In contrast to adults, children and adolescents rarely seek out treatment on their own. Further, with children and adolescents, it is almost always necessary to seek information from other people besides the child: parents, teachers, social workers, school psychologists, physicians, and others. Although parental consent is required, it is also important to obtain the child's permission to seek information from these other sources. This will help a great deal in building an atmosphere

■ **TABLE 20-4 Diagnostic Criteria for Conduct Disorder**

A. A repetitive and persistent pattern of behavior in which the basic right of others or major age-appropriate societal norms or rules are violated, as manifested by the presence of three (or more) of the following criteria in the past 12 months, with at least one criterion present in the past 6 months:

Aggression to people and animals
1. often bullies, threatens, or intimidates others
2. often initiates physical fights
3. has used a weapon that can cause serious physical harm to others (e.g., a bat, brick, broken bottle, knife, gun)
4. has been physically cruel to people
5. has been physically cruel to animals
6. has stolen while confronting a victim (e.g., mugging, purse snatching, extortion, armed robbery)
7. has forced someone into sexual activity

Destruction of property
8. has deliberately engaged in fire setting with the intention of causing serious damage
9. has deliberately destroyed others' property (other than by fire setting)

Deceitfulness or theft
10. has broken into someone else's house, building, or car
11. often lies to obtain goods or favors or to avoid obligations (i.e., "cons" others)
12. has stolen items of nontrivial value without confronting a victim (e.g., shoplifting, but without breaking and entering; forgery)

Serious violations of rules
13. often stays out at night despite parental prohibitions, beginning before age 13 years
14. has run away from home overnight at least twice living in parental or parental surrogate home (or once without returning for a lengthy period)
15. is often truant from school, beginning before age 13 years

B. The disturbance in behavior causes clinically significant impairment in social, academic, or occupational functioning.

C. If the individual is age 18 years or older, criteria are not met for Antisocial Personality Disorder.

Specify type based on age at onset:

   Childhood-Onset Type: onset of at least one criterion characteristic of Conduct Disorder prior to age 10 years

   Adolescent-Onset Type: absence of any criteria characteristic of Conduct Disorder prior to age 10 years

Specify severity:

   Mild: few if any conduct problems in excess of those required to make the diagnosis *and* conduct problems cause only minor harm to others

   Moderate: number of conduct problems and effect on others intermediate between mild" and "severe"

   Severe: many conduct problems in excess of those required to make the diagnosis *or* conduct problems cause considerable harm to others

Source: American Psychiatric Association (1994). *Diagnostic and Statistical Manual of Mental Disorders* (4th edition). Washington, DC: Author, pp. 90–91. Reprinted with permission.

of trust and respect. Finally, children and adolescents know less about the roles of mental health professionals and thus may harbor resistance or even fear.

The issue of multiple sources of information in child and adolescent assessment warrants further comment. It should be recognized that these multiple sources of information may not always agree with one another. For example, some have suggested that depressed mothers tend to exaggerate the nature and severity of a child's problems compared to other informants (Richters & Pellegrini, 1992). Although more recent evidence has challenged this claim (Tarullo, Richardson, Radke-Yarrow, & Martinez, 1995), there is currently no consensus as to how a clinician or researcher should integrate discrepant diagnostic information (Sher & Trull, 1996). This problem is compounded in the area of clinical child psychology, where multiple sources of data are tapped routinely. Fortunately, researchers are now beginning to investigate how best to integrate assessment data from multiple informants (for example, Piacentini, Cohen, & Cohen, 1992).

When assessing children or adolescents, it is very important to estimate the nature and severity of the problem early on. The complaint may be as specific as vomiting or fear of walking to school, or as general as a "depression" or lack of interest in schoolwork. The examiner will want to learn why help is being sought, how long the problem has existed, and what other steps have been taken to resolve the problem. From all the sources available, a case history will then be generated in order to gain an understanding of exactly how the problem has developed. Again, all this is done to determine the nature of the problem and how best to deal with it.

For most problems, a comprehensive assessment will generally include information from multiple informants (self, parent, peer, teacher) and from multiple assessment methods (self-report scales, behavior checklists, interviews, intelligence or ability tests). In the sections that follow, we will present several issues associated with some of the most common methods of assessment used by clinical child and pediatric psychologists.

Interviewing. In Chapter 6, we dealt extensively with the interview process; that material is entirely relevant here. In the interest of brevity, this section will focus on interviewing just the parents and the child. Clinical child and pediatric psychologists interview parents to (1) elicit information about behavior, events, and situations; (2) gauge parental feelings and emotions; and (3) establish the basis for subsequent therapeutic relationships (Yule, 1989). Interviews with children and adolescents allow them to "tell their own story." The psychologist asks questions aimed at the individual's perception of self, perception of others, and perception of the existence and nature of the problem.

When interviewing children, it is important to remember that they have not always been told why help is being sought, or they may understand only imperfectly what they have been told. Just being in a clinic without understanding why, or without having been allowed to decide on treatment for themselves, can be very anxiety provoking for children (or anyone else). Therefore, it is important to find out how the child feels and what the child understands as the real purpose for the visit. As much as possible, the clinician must set a reassuring tone for the interview and then, within the limits of the child's understanding, explain what will take place. In some cases, for example, it may be necessary to stress that the child will be going home after the visit to the clinic or that the specific diagnostic procedures will not hurt.

It can be very difficult to interview children. They cannot always communicate their feelings and thoughts in any precise way. Equally important, children can be highly suggestible or fearful. Consequently, they may tell the examiner what they think he or she wants to hear or what others have told them. They may be so intimidated or nervous that they get their stories mixed up. The length of an interview with a

■ **TABLE 20-5** Tips for Interviewing Children

General Communication Skills

1. Use descriptive statements (for example, "You look happy today").

2. Use reflective statements to help increase the amount of verbal interchange.

3. Use praise.

4. Avoid critical statements.

5. Use open-ended questions (those that cannot be answered with a simple yes or no).

6. Use sentences and words that are age appropriate.

Conducting the Interview

1. Introduce self to parent(s) and child.

2. Provide information about the plan for the session to both the child and parent(s).

3. Provide structure for the child to ease her or his potential anxiety (for example, "Here, why don't we start by drawing some pictures?").

4. Use an organizational format to gather information that focuses on the child's (1) environment (peer relations, school, family); (2) self (wishes, interests, fears); and (3) presenting problems(s).

5. In wrapping up the interview, it is important to summarize for the child, to reinforce the child for his or her efforts, to ask for any additional information the child might want to offer, and to provide the child with information about what the interviewer plans to do from here on out.

Source: Adapted from Kanfer, R., Eyberg, S. M., & Krahn, G. L. (1992). Interviewing strategies in child assessment. In C. E. Walker & M. C. Roberts (Eds.), *Handbook of clinical child psychology* (2nd ed.). New York: Wiley.

child may depend on factors such as age or intellectual level. Kanfer, Eyberg, and Krahn (1992) have provided some good tips on interviewing children. Table 20-5 presents a summary of their suggestions.

A number of structured diagnostic interviews are available for assessing children and adolescents for both internalizing disorders (Silverman & Serafini, 1998) and externalizing disorders (Franz & Gross, 1998). These include the Diagnostic Interview Schedule for Children, or DISC (Costello, Edelbrock, Dulcan, Kalas, & Klaric, 1984); the Child Assessment Schedule, or CAS (Hodges, Kline, Fitch, McKnew, & Cytryn, 1981); and the Diagnostic Interview for Children and Adolescents–Revised, or DICA-R (Kaplan & Reich, 1991). These interviews are available in both child and parent (informant) versions. These structured interviews have the advantage of being standardized (all children are asked the same questions), more comprehensive in cover-

age, and more reliable than unstructured clinical interviews. They are particularly useful in situations where there is a question of differential diagnosis.

Behavioral Observations. As noted in Chapter 6, it is helpful to make behavioral observations during the interview. In addition, whenever possible, direct observations of the child at home and school should be undertaken (see Chapter 9). A variety of observational methods are available. For example, there are naturalistic, analogue, participant, and self-observational techniques for use with children, and a variety of coding systems are available for rating behavior (La Greca & Stone, 1992). As is true with all behavioral observations, child and pediatric psychologists need to keep in mind issues such as reliability of observations, reactivity to observation, and the validity of the observational data (La Greca & Stone, 1992).

In Chapter 9, we provided several examples of observational methods and systems used in the assessment of children and adolescents. One of these was the Behavioral Coding System (BCS) developed and used by Patterson (1971) and colleagues (Jones, Reid & Patterson, 1975; Patterson & Forgatch, 1995). The BCS was designed for use in the homes of predelinquent boys with aggression and noncompliance problems. Trained observers spend one to two hours in the home observing and recording family interactions, using the BCS coding system (see Figure 9-2 in Chapter 9 for a sample BCS coding sheet). Recently, Patterson and Forgatch (1995) reported that children's aversive behavior scores (derived from the BCS) predicted future arrests over a two-year follow-up period.

Another commonly used observational system, also discussed in Chapter 9, is Achenbach's (1994) Direct Observation Form (DOF) of the Child Behavior Checklist. The DOF is used to assess problem behaviors that may be observed in classroom or other settings. Observers rate each problem behavior item (96 in all) according to its frequency, duration, and intensity over a specified observation period (for example, 10 minutes). Table 9-2 (in Chapter 9) provides sample items from the DOF.

Intelligence Tests. When questions of intellectual achievement, academic deficits, or the development of an educational plan for the child are involved, intelligence tests are often used. The most frequently used tests are the Wechsler Intelligence Scale for Children, Third Edition (WISC-III), the Kaufman Assessment Battery for Children (K-ABC), the Wechsler Preschool and Primary Scale of Intelligence–Revised (WPPSI-R), the Stanford-Binet Intelligence Scale, Fourth Edition, and the Peabody Picture Vocabulary Test–Revised. These and other measures are well suited for test batteries assessing learning disabilities, mental retardation, neurological dysfunction, or pervasive developmental disorders in children (Sattler, 1992).

We discussed the WISC-III in Chapter 7, so we will only make a few additional comments

here. The WISC-III consists of ten mandatory and three supplementary subtests. There are Verbal subtests (Information, Similarities, Arithmetic, Vocabulary, and Comprehension) and Performance subtests (Picture Completion, Picture Arrangement, Block Design, Object Assembly, and Coding). As with other measures of intelligence, WISC-III scores can be used to estimate an individual's overall level of intelligence (Full Scale IQ), abilities in certain areas of functioning (Verbal IQ, Performance IQ), or levels of functioning in even more specific areas (Verbal Comprehension, Perceptual Organization, Freedom from Distractibility, Processing Speed). In practice, the WISC-III is often used as part of a battery of tests, including achievement tests, to evaluate whether a particular learning disability may be present. Figure 7-7 (in Chapter 7) presents examples of items similar to those in the WISC-III.

Achievement Tests. These tests are used to assess past learning, particularly that associated with training or school programs. They can address a variety of different academic subjects, from reading to arithmetic. Three widely used screening devices are the Peabody Individual Achievement Test–Revised, the Woodcock-Johnson Psychoeducational Battery, and the Wide Range Achievement Test–3 (WRAT-3). Other commonly used test batteries are the Iowa Tests of Basic Skills, the SRA Achievement Series, the Stanford Achievement Test, and the Metropolitan Achievement Tests Survey Battery.

Projective Tests. Although the use of projective tests with children is somewhat controversial, some clinicians argue that they can be useful when a more dynamic picture of personality is required (for example, Levitt & French, 1992). One argument for the use of projective techniques in the assessment of children and adolescents is that the ambiguity of the stimuli in these tests or their use of animals as subject matter may be less threatening for those youngsters whose anxiety level is high. Both the TAT and the Rorschach are often used, as well as the

Children's Apperception Test, Incomplete Sentences Blank, and Draw-A-Person Test. As we mentioned in Chapter 8, however, clinicians who use projective techniques must consider the reliability and validity of their interpretations and guard against falling prey to interpretive errors based on illusory correlations.

Questionnaires and Checklists. Many scales, checklists, and questionnaires can be administered to adults, who are asked to respond in terms of their observations and inferences about the child's behavior and problems. Parents, teachers, and others who are in frequent contact with the child can provide information at general or very specific levels, and in terms of personality characteristics. Frequently used measures include the Personality Inventory for Children, the Child Behavior Checklist, the Teacher's Report Form, the Revised Behavior Problem Checklist, and the Conners Rating Scales.

The Child Behavior Checklist, or CBCL (Achenbach, 1994), is one of the most frequently used measures for assessing behavior problems in children and adolescents. Major strengths of the CBCL are its strong psychometric properties, its comprehensive coverage of problems, and its clinical utility. For these reasons, the CBCL is used by clinicians and researchers alike. Several scores can be calculated from the CBCL. First, there is an overall problem score that gives the psychologist some idea of the significance of the individual's overall behavior problems. In addition, eight syndrome scores are calculated: Withdrawn, Somatic Complaints, Anxious/Depressed, Social Problems, Thought Problems, Attention Problems, Delinquent Behavior, and Aggressive Behavior. Finally, an overall Internalizing Problem score and an overall Externalizing Problem score (each comprised of specific syndrome scores) can be calculated. Figure 20-2 presents a sample profile of CBCL scores for Felicia, a 13-year-old girl referred by her parents because of depression, school refusal, social withdrawal, and sleep problems (Mash & Wolfe, 1999). As can be seen, Felicia's mother (who completed the check-list) is primarily concerned about her daughter's social withdrawal, anxiety and depression, somatic complaints, and social problems

Occasionally, self-report measures are administered directly to children when it is felt they are capable of understanding directions and reporting properly on their feelings, thoughts, or behavior. Examples are the Children's Depression Inventory (said to be readable for first-grade children), the Perceived Competence Scales, and for adolescents, the MMPI-2 and the Youth Self-Report test. McConaughy (1992) provides an overview of these and other questionnaires and checklists.

Neuropsychological Assessment. The recent growth of child neuropsychology as a specialty can be attributed to an increased focus on neurodevelopmental disorders following passage of the Education for All Handicapped Children Act (Public Law 94-142, Federal Register, 1976), as well as advances in medical care that have decreased mortality from devastating diseases but increased the need for comprehensive assessment of their neurological effects on surviving children (Hooper & Hynd, 1993). Current research areas for child neuropsychologists include assessing the neurophysiological correlates of conduct disorder (Lahey, Hart, Pliska, Applegate, & McBurnett, 1993), of inattention/overactivity (McBurnett et al., 1993), of aggression/defiance (McBurnett et al., 1993), of anxiety disorders (Kusché, Cook, & Greenberg, 1993), and a host of medical conditions (for example, R. T. Brown et al., 1993; Taylor, Barry, & Schatschneider, 1993; Wills, 1993).

Many of the issues, questions, and methods of neuropsychological assessment were touched upon in Chapter 18. Tests often used with children include the Reitan-Indiana Battery, the Halstead Neuropsychological Battery for Children, the WISC-III, and the Luria-Nebraska Neuropsychological Battery.

Cognitive Assessment. Increasingly in this field we have come to realize that many behavioral, emotional, and even medical problems in chil-

FIGURE 20-2 Child Behavior Checklist (CBCL) profile for Felicia, a depressed and withdrawn 15-year-old

Source: Mash, E. J., & Wolfe, D. A. (1999). Abnormal Child Psychology. Pacific Grove, CA: Brooks/Cole–Wadsworth. Page 112.

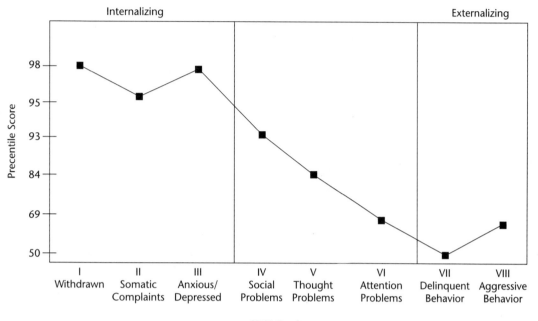

dren are mediated by cognitive factors. For example, children with medical problems often do not understand the facts of their own condition nor do they appreciate the prescribed treatment. This can have an important impact on their recovery. Likewise, the child's self-efficacy can influence a host of reactions to medical problems and treatments. Finally, the child's cognitive appraisal can be vital in affecting behavior and feelings. For example, children's levels of stress or their responses to treatment may be partially controlled by the manner in which they process information. It is critical that clinical and pediatric child psychologists be able to understand and measure these cognitive variables.

To give the reader a flavor of what these cognitive instruments target, we will briefly describe two cognitive measures that are used in child and adolescent assessment. The *Coping Questionnaire* (CQ) (Kendall, 1994) assesses children's coping in the face of anxiety-provoking situations. Three

situations are rated, and these are chosen by the evaluator and the child (e.g., sleeping in my own room, meeting new kids). There are both child and parent versions of this measure. Another measure, the *Negative Affectivity Self-Statement Questionnaire* (NASSQ) (Ronan, Kendall, & Rowe, 1994), assesses thoughts and self-statements the child experiences in the face of anxiety and depression (negative affectivity). Each child rates 70 thoughts as to their frequency over the prior week. Both the CQ and NASSQ can be used in the treatment of childhood anxiety disorders. For example, Levin, Ashmore-Callahan, Kendall, and Ichii (1996) demonstrated how the CQ and NASSQ assessments are integrated into a cognitive-behavioral treatment for separation anxiety disorder in children.

Family Assessment. To a large extent, children's problems are embedded in the overall family context. The child is shaped by the family, and the family in turn is shaped by the child. Therefore, to understand the child's problems and intervene appropriately, one must also understand the family system. A variety of assessment devices exist for this purpose. Several commonly used measures of family functioning are the Family Environment Scale, or FES (Moos & Moos, 1981); the Family Adaptability and Cohesion Evaluation Scales, or FACES III (Olson, Portner, & Lavee, 1985); and the Family Assessment Measure, or FAM (Skinner, Steinhauer, & Santa-Barbara, 1983).

A recent trend has been to combine existing family measures in a data collection and then retain only those items that demonstrate good reliability and validity to serve as a final composite measure of various aspects of family functioning (for example, Gondoli & Jacob, 1993; Tolan, Gorman-Smith, Huesmann, & Zelli, 1997). For example, Tolan et al. (1997) administered several measures of family functioning, including the FACES III and FAM, to a sample of urban youth and their primary caretaking parent (usually the mother). The authors identified six major scales comprised of items from the family measures. These scales were labeled Beliefs about Family (purpose and development), Cohesion, Shared Deviant Beliefs, Support, Organization, and Communication. Additional confirmatory factor analyses identified three major underlying dimensions: Cohesion (the degree of family closeness and dependability, support, and clear communication), Family Beliefs (expectations about the purpose of the family and about child development), and Structure (extent to which the family is organized, and predictability regarding expectations and roles). Tolan et al. found that scores on these three major dimensions were significantly related to child functioning—in this case, aggression and depression.

Interventions

In Chapters 11–15 of this book, we covered a variety of treatment approaches. In the case of children, the approaches are equally diverse and generally similar to those used with adults. However, child therapy is also different, for at least two reasons already noted. Children do not typically refer themselves for treatment, nor do they possess the same capacity for introspection and self-report as do most adults.

Kazdin (1988) has conservatively estimated that more than 230 therapeutic techniques are used in treating children or adolescents. If anything, this number has grown. The majority of these treatments have not been subjected to empirical investigation regarding their efficacy and effectiveness (Kazdin & Weisz, 1998). First, we will briefly discuss some of the more commonly used approaches. Then, we will examine the research support for interventions in general, as well as for specific treatments for specific problems.

Psychoanalytically Oriented Therapy. Although psychoanalytically oriented treatments are frequently used in the treatment of children and adolescents, modification of traditional techniques is often necessary. Children are unlikely to understand or be able to adhere to the strict requirements of an orthodox analysis in the same way that adults can. They usually cannot deal with the highly verbal, abstract, and introspective nature of the process. Children who have particularly weak egos or are living in extremely threatening home situations with unsupportive parents are not often good candidates for psychoanalytic procedures.

Modified psychoanalytic approaches, however have been widely applied to children. Although Anna Freud (1946b) believed that children in therapy must achieve insight into their troubled feelings and defenses, other less traditional analysts have proceeded differently (Tuma, 1989). The frequency of meetings is usually reduced to once or twice per week. The approach is more symptom-oriented and is designed to teach the child that certain behaviors are really defenses against anxiety. All of this may help the child to negotiate a certain developmental stage rather than "cure" a fixation, for example. In general, the differences in approaches are in degree rather than kind. For example, daydreams rather than nocturnal dreams might be solicited. In a greater departure, play rather than direct verbalization may be used as a communication vehicle, as we will see in the next section.

Play Therapy. Rather than use dreams or free associations, some therapists have chosen to study the psychic life of the child through play—either of a free or a structured variety. The child is brought to a playroom containing a variety of materials such as a sandbox, clay, puppets, dolls, and toys of all kinds. How children play, what objects they choose, and the nature of their verbalizations as they play can all be revealing, cathartic, and therapeutic. Sometimes the therapist enters into the play and makes comments and suggestions or otherwise guides the child toward certain conflict or problem areas. The nature of children's play may convey how they relate to significant other figures in their lives, how they handle their anxieties, and so on. In essence, play becomes a substitute for verbalization.

An example of *play therapy* is Solomon's (1955) approach. He brings the child into a room with a table on which has been placed a number of dolls. He selects one and then asks the child what to do with it. Sometimes the dolls are arrayed to represent the child's family. As the child arranges the dolls and plays, the therapist interprets what the child is doing, which then facilitates the expression of feelings on the part of the child. Concrete family experiences, wishes, and even unconscious urges may be expressed in the process. In general, however, play therapy has evolved into a rather eclectic, amorphous set of techniques and procedures.

Play therapy is no longer associated solely with a psychodynamic orientation, but has also been used with a cognitive-behavioral approach (Knell, 1998). Although children may not be able to process the verbal subtleties that characterize cognitive therapy for adults, Knell (1998) argues that cognitive-behavioral play therapy can effect cognitive and behavioral changes in children through techniques such as modeling

adaptive coping skills, indirectly communicating cognitive change through play, and providing opportunities (again through play) for the child to reenact problem situations and gain some mastery over them. For example, Knell (1998) discussed how cognitive-behavioral play therapy was used in the case of an almost- 5-year-old girl with separation anxiety:

> The child would cry inconsolably, and cling to her mother whenever any separation was imminent. During PT [play therapy], the child was encouraged to express her feelings about separation fears through pictures, stories, and puppet play. In the latter, the therapist helped the child experiment with a puppet's fear of being left at school, by guiding the child through a series of discussions. These discussions included generating a list of the puppet's fears (e.g., fear that his mom would not return), as well as lists of positive coping statements (e.g., "I can think of something happy"; "I can think about my mom, who will be coming back"). The therapist, through the "voice" of the puppet, modeled adaptive coping skills for the child, and as therapy progressed, the child began to incorporate these skills into her stories, puppet play, and eventually into her own coping behavior at school. (p. 30)

Behavior Therapy. Behavioral techniques (reviewed in Chapter 14) have overtaken psychodynamic methods as the treatment of choice for childhood problems. For children, it has always seemed evident that their problems are the direct outgrowth of environmental factors or the people who are in control of various aspects of the child's life. Either respondent principles (behavior is acquired through classical conditioning) or operant principles (behavior is maintained by its consequences) seem ideally suited to account for many childhood behaviors. Moreover, these principles can easily be applied by parents and teachers as part of the therapeutic plan. Most of these procedures, whether systematic desensitization, aversion therapy, or contingency management techniques, are highly efficient in comparison to older, more traditional psychodynamic methods. Changes that once took months or even years to occur can be achieved in 20 or fewer sessions. Parents and teachers can be trained to enhance the effectiveness of the techniques and to help ensure that changes will generalize outside the therapist's office.

Parent management training involves a set of therapeutic procedures that are designed to "train" parents to modify a child or adolescent's behavior at home. Parents master basic learning principles (contingency management, reinforcement) and then implement them at home. Enlisting parents in the treatment process makes it more likely that behavior change will be effected in the child or adolescent. For example, Barkley (1987) has developed a program for teaching child management skills to parents of children who are defiant and noncompliant. Table 20-6 presents a handout from this program that instructs parents on how to give effective commands.

Behavioral Pediatrics. Clinical child psychologists and pediatric psychologists can also contribute a great deal to the management of children during their stay in the hospital. This includes help in preparing children for particular medical procedures and in assisting the child and family in coping later with their medical problems. Techniques used here range from behavioral rehearsal and stress inoculation to various methods of cognitive reappraisal. Whether the problem is a simple fear of needles or the stress and pain associated with repeated changing of bandages for burn patients, behavioral methods can be helpful. The management of pain and headaches and ensuring compliance with medical regimens are also important provinces of *behavioral pediatrics.*

Cognitive-Behavioral Therapy. In recent years, cognitive-behavioral therapy has increasingly been applied to problems such as impulsivity, hyperactivity, anxiety, depression, and conduct disorders. The basic idea is to improve problem solving and enhance planning and delay of gratification. Through internal assessments and self-statements, children are taught to bring their previously distressing or problematic behavior under rational control. The vehicle through which this is accomplished is the alteration of cognitions, and the ultimate goal is the creation of a new, more adaptive "coping template" (Kendall, 1993).

Group and Family Therapy. Many of the approaches outlined in Chapter 15 as group or family therapy are applicable to the problems of children and adolescents. Many of these problems are learned and even nourished in the family setting; to relieve them often requires the cooperation and understanding of the family unit. Because children are so much influenced by and are the product of their families, in some cases it only makes good sense to treat the entire family. However, the relatively modest evidence for the overall efficacy of family therapy (see Table 15-1) suggests that family therapy might be used selectively in those cases or disorders in which there is evidence supporting its effectiveness. For example, recent reviews suggest that certain forms of family therapy effectively treat anxiety disorders and conduct disorders in children and adolescents (Brestan & Eyberg, 1998; Ollendick & King, 1998; see Table 20-8, below).

As for group therapy, a recent meta-analysis indicated that, overall, group treatments for children and adolescents were more effective than wait-list and placebo control groups (Hoag & Burlingame, 1997). The overall effect size across treatments averaged .61, indicating that, on average, a child or adolescent who received one of these treatments was better off than 73% of those in the control groups. Although the small number of studies sampled by Hoag and Burlingame (1997) precluded adequate tests of the efficacy of different types of group treatment and different types of clinical problems addressed, it seems likely that some forms of group treatment for specific clinical problems (for example, cognitive-behavioral group treatment for depression) are more effective.

■ **TABLE 20-6** Handout for Parents of Defiant/Noncompliant Children

Parent Handout:
How to Give Effective Commands

In our work with many behavior problem children, we have noticed that if parents simply change the way they give commands to their children, they can often achieve significant improvements in the child's compliance. When you are about to give a command or instruction to your child, be sure that you do the following:

1. *Make sure you mean it!* That is, never give a command that you do not intend to see followed up to its completion. When you make a request, plan on backing it up with appropriate consequences, either positive or negative, to show that you mean what you have said.

2. *Do not present the command as a question or favor.* State the command simply, directly, and in a businesslike tone of voice.

3. *Do not give too many commands at once.* Most children are able to follow only one or two instructions at a time. For now, try giving only one specific instruction at a time. If a task you want your child to do is complicated, then break it down into smaller steps and give only one step at a time.

4. *Make sure the child is paying attention to you.* Be sure that you have eye contact with the child. If necessary, gently turn the child's face toward yours to ensure that he or she is listening and watching when the command is given.

5. *Reduce all distractions before giving the command.* A very common mistake that parents make is to try to give instructions while a television, stereo, or video game is on. Parents cannot expect children to attend to them when something more entertaining is going on in the room. Either turn off these distractions yourself or tell the child to turn them off before giving the command.

6. *Ask the child to repeat the command.* This need not be done with each request, but it can be done if you are not sure your child heard or understood the command. Also, for children with a short attention span, having them repeat the command appears to increase the likelihood they will follow it through.

7. *Make up chore cards.* If your child is old enough to have jobs to do about the home, then you may find it useful to make up a chore card for each job. This can simply be a three-by-five file card. Listed on it are the steps involved in correctly doing that chore. Then, when you want your child to do the chore, simply hand the child the card and state that this is what you want done. Of course, this is only for children who are old enough to read. These cards can greatly reduce the amount of arguing that occurs over whether a child has done a job or chore properly. You might also indicate on the card how much time the chore should take and then set your kitchen timer for this time period so the child knows exactly when it is to be done.

If you follow these seven steps, you will find some improvement in your child's compliance with your requests. When used with the other methods your therapist will teach you, remarkable improvements can occur in how *well* your child *listens* and behaves.

Source: Barkley (1987). *Defiant Children: Parent-Teacher Assignments.* New York: Guilford, page 43. Used with permission.

TABLE 20-7 Average Effect Size ($\overline{ES}$) and Percentile Equivalent for Psychological Interventions Used to Treat Children and Adolescents

Meta-analysis Study	$\overline{ES}$	Percentile Equivalent*
Casey & Berman (1985)	0.71	76%
Weisz et al. (1987)	0.79	79%
Kazdin, Bass, Ayers, & Rodgers (1990), no-treatment control	0.88	81%
Kazdin et al. (1990), active control	0.77	78%
Weisz, Weiss, et al. (1995)	0.71	76%

*Percentile equivalent indicates the percentage of those not receiving treatment whose outcome is exceeded by those receiving the treatment in question.

Psychopharmacological Treatment. Medications may be used as adjuncts to psychotherapy in the treatment of the child. The medications most frequently used are those that treat attention deficit/hyperactivity disorder, or ADHD (Pelham & Hinshaw, 1992). The most frequently prescribed medication for ADHD is the psychostimulant methylphenidate (Ritalin). Although studies have demonstrated the positive effects of Ritalin in treating ADHD symptoms, not all children and adolescents have a positive response (Pelham & Hinshaw, 1992). The costs, in the form of side effects, may outweigh the benefits, and there have been few demonstrations of long-term benefit in the form of improved prognosis (Pelham & Hinshaw, 1992). These same points apply to other forms of medication that are used to treat the range of clinical problems presented by children and adolescents.

Are Psychological Interventions for Children and Adolescents Effective?

We have described several of the more commonly used psychological interventions for children and adolescents. How effective are these interventions? Recent reviews of the treatment outcome literature agree that, in general, psychological interventions for children and adolescents are effective (for example, Peterson & Bell-Dolan, 1995; Weisz, Donenberg, Han, & Weiss,

1995). This conclusion is based on the converging results of several major meta-analyses of the treatment outcome literature. Table 20-7 summarizes the results of four major meta-analytic studies.

The effect size estimates across these studies are quite consistent and are comparable to those reported for the psychological treatment of adults (Weisz, Weiss, et al., 1995). Taken together, these meta-analytic results suggest that the average child or adolescent client who receives psychological treatment is functioning better than more than 75% of those who do not receive treatment.

Although these findings are encouraging, more outcome research is necessary for several reasons. First, a disproportionately greater number of treatment outcome studies have been conducted on adult than on child or adolescent patients. This relative paucity of child and adolescent outcome studies prohibits more fine-grained analyses aimed at comparing the effectiveness of competing forms of treatment for the same clinical problem (for example, cognitive-behavioral versus play therapy for childhood depression), as well as analyses identifying patient or therapist variables that may moderate treatment effects. In addition, there is some preliminary evidence suggesting that more naturalistic "clinic therapy" is less effective than "research therapy" (Weisz, Donenberg, et al., 1995). Because the published literature typically reports on studies using recruited (not clinic-referred) patients, narrow (not broad or multiple) problem focus in treatment, brief and time-limited treatments, and primarily behavioral treatments, generalization from the meta-analytic results to situations involving psychotherapy as it is usually conducted may be problematic. For example, a recent study specifically designed to test whether child psychotherapy, as typically delivered in clinics, was effective failed to find evidence for its superiority over a control condition (Weiss, Catron, Harris, & Phung, 1999).

Future research on psychological interventions for children and adolescents should attend to these and other methodological issues (Kazdin & Weisz, 1998; Peterson & Bell-Dolan, 1995; Weisz, Donenberg, et al., 1995). Further, these results suggest that efforts should be directed toward developing and implementing effective treatments in traditional clinic settings (Kazdin & Weisz, 1998; Weiss et al., 1999).

Aside from the general question of whether or not interventions for children and adolescents are effective, it is of considerable interest to evaluate the merits of specific psychological interventions for specific problems treated by clinical child and pediatric psychologists. The reader may recall that in Chapter 11 we presented information on empirically supported treatments for a number of problems treated by psychologists (see Table 11-6). Few interventions for children or adolescents appeared on that list. Partly in response to this movement to evaluate the empirical support for psychological interventions, clinical child and pediatric psychologists have begun to systematically evaluate their respective research literatures in order to identify interventions for these populations that have empirical support.

We have summarized the findings from recent reviews of both the clinical child and pediatric psychology intervention literature in Tables 20-8 and 20-9, respectively. As can be seen, a number of empirically supported psychological interventions have been identified for problems such as depression, phobia, anxiety disorder,

conduct disorder, and attention deficit/hyperactivity disorder (see Table 20-8). Almost all of these interventions are behavioral or cognitive-behavioral in orientation. Similarly, behavioral and cognitive-behavioral treatments dominate the list of empirically supported treatments in pediatric psychology (Table 20-9). These treatments target problems such as recurrent headache, recurrent abdominal pain, medical procedure–related pain, pediatric obesity, emotionally triggered asthma, and side effects from cancer chemotherapy.

In summary, the research literature suggests that, in general, psychological treatments for childhood and adolescent problems are effective. Further, recent reviews have identified specific interventions for specific child and adolescent problems that have empirical support.

Prevention

Taking a page from the book of community psychology (see Chapter 16), clinical child and pediatric psychologists have been especially concerned about the prevention of childhood problems. Of course, prevention and treatment are activities that blend and merge. Recall from Chapter 16 that primary prevention is defined as counteracting problems before they have a chance to develop, and secondary prevention involves the prompt treatment of problems in order to minimize their impact. Certainly, the clinical child or pediatric psychologist wants to either prevent problems before they occur or at least identify the problems before they get out of control. In any case, the stance of either the pediatric or clinical child psychologist is a proactive one (Peterson, Zink, & Farmer, 1992).

In the context of pediatric practice, Roberts (1986) likes to use the term *anticipatory guidance*—the use of counseling and education in advance of difficulties. For example, parents may be counseled about "childproofing" their home at various stages of the child's development. This could cover almost anything from covering electrical outlets to blocking off stairways. At a more psychological level, it may involve providing

■ **TABLE 20-8** Examples of Psychosocial Interventions for Children and Adolescents That Have Empirical Support for Their Efficacy

Problem	Treatment	Review Citation
Depression (child)	Cognitive-behavioral therapy	Kaslow & Thompson (1998)
Depression (adolescent)	Cognitive-behavioral therapy	Kaslow & Thompson (1998)
Phobias	Systematic desensitization	Ollendick & King (1998)
	Modeling (filmed and live)	Ollendick & King (1998)
	Operant conditioning (reinforced practice)	Ollendick & King (1998)
	Cognitive-behavioral therapy	Ollendick & King (1998)
Anxiety disorders	Cognitive-behavioral therapy (CBT)	Ollendick & King (1998)
	CBT and family anxiety management	Ollendick & King (1998)
Conduct disorder	Parent training program (Patterson)	Brestan & Eyberg (1998)
	Videotape modeling parent training	Brestan & Eyberg (1998)
	Anger control training with stress inoculation	Brestan & Eyberg (1998)
	Assertiveness training	Brestan & Eyberg (1998)
	Delinquency prevention program	Brestan & Eyberg (1998)
	Multisystemic therapy	Brestan & Eyberg (1998)
	Parent-child interaction therapy	Brestan & Eyberg (1998)
	Parent training	Brestan & Eyberg (1998)
	Problem-solving skills training	Brestan & Eyberg (1998)
	Rational-emotive therapy	Brestan & Eyberg (1998)
	Time-out plus signal seat treatment	Brestan & Eyberg (1998)
Attention deficit / hyperactivity disorder	Behavioral parent training	Pelham, Wheeler, & Chronis (1998)
	Behavior modification in the classroom	Pelham, Wheeler, & Chronis (1998)

Note: Treatments cited here met criteria for "well-established" or "probably efficacious" treatments according to the guidelines in Task Force on Promotion and Dissemination of Psychological Procedures (1995). See Chapter 11 for more details.

information on preparing the child for the birth of a sibling or the death of a grandparent. In the case of a child with cystic fibrosis, it might take the form of counseling the youngster on how to respond to teasing from peers prompted by the physical limitations imposed by the disease.

One of the tenets of community psychology has always been the identification of people at risk for the development of subsequent problems. One example is the child who is hospitalized. As we discussed earlier in the context of behavioral pediatrics, there is much that can be done for these children. Programs have been designed to provide information to hospitalized children, to encourage emotional expression in such children, to offer them coping strategies, or

■ **TABLE 20-9** **Examples of Empirically Supported Treatments in Pediatric Psychology**

Problem	Treatment	Review Citation
Recurrent headache	Relaxation/self-hypnosis	Holden, Deichmann, & Levy (1999)
	Thermal biofeedback	Holden, Deichmann, & Levy (1999)
Recurrent abdominal pain	Cognitive-behavioral therapy	Janicke & Finney (1999)
Medical procedure–related pain	Cognitive-behavioral therapy	Powers (1999)
Pediatric obesity	Behavior modification	Jelalian & Saelens (1999)
Emotionally triggered asthma	EMG biofeedback	McQuaid & Nassau (1999)
	Relaxation	McQuaid & Nassau (1999)
Cancer chemotherapy side effects	Imagery with suggestion	McQuaid & Nassau (1999)
	Distraction with relaxation	McQuaid & Nassau (1999)

to just help build trusting relationships. In addition, as mentioned in Chapter 17, numerous films and videotapes also have been developed to help children cope with medical interventions.

To aid in the prevention of physical problems, safety programs directed toward children have addressed issues that range from crossing the street safely to avoiding abduction or molestation. Programs to train so-called latchkey children have also been developed. Research suggests that specific recommendations and pediatric counseling with parents will increase the use of safety car seats. More recently, attempts have been made to integrate child injury and child abuse/neglect research because similar interventions may be used to prevent harm in both domains (Peterson & Brown, 1994). Table 20-10 presents a model of an intervention sequence aimed at preventing child abuse/neglect in children from high-risk families (Peterson & Brown, 1994). These are but a brief sampling of the many approaches to prevention that characterize pediatric psychology today.

Lest the reader think that only pediatric psychologists (and not clinical child psychologists) concern themselves with prevention, it is worth recalling some of the research that was presented in Chapter 16. As described in Box 16-3, a meta-analysis by Durlak and Wells (1997) of 177 primary prevention programs designed to prevent mental health problems in children and adolescents indicated that, on average, these intervention programs were effective in reducing problems, and the effects were durable over time. Most of these interventions did not occur in a medical setting. Thus, prevention is not the sole province of pediatric psychologists; clinical child psychologists are becoming increasingly more involved as well. Examples of prevention programs outside of medical settings include an early intervention and prevention program to reduce anxiety disorders in 7- to 14-year-olds who were at risk for these problems (Dadds et al., 1999) and the Children of Divorce Intervention Program (Pedro-Carroll, 1997) aimed at improving the adjustment of children and adolescents to divorce.

Consultation

Consultation-liaison relationships have long been typical in the professional lives of pediatric psychologists. Drotar (1995) and Roberts (1986) have described the consultation process at some length, and we will discuss the models they highlight in this section. Although the focus here will be on the pediatric psychologist, many points apply equally to clinical child psychologists.

TABLE 20-10	**Proposed Treatment Plan for Prevention of Child Abuse/Neglect in Children from High-Risk Families**

Session	Content Areas
1	Introduction: Orientation to format, goals, *reimbursement, meeting,* and getting acquainted
2	I. Base problem solving (that is, recognize and define typical life problems, list a goal, evolve options, input plan, evaluate outcome)
	II. Positive parenting: enjoying the child
3–4	1. Reemphasize normative development and how to enjoy the child's unfolding abilities
	2. Reciprocal activities: child-led play and mutual reinforcement
	3. Seeing the world through the child's eyes
	III. Parenting skills
5–6	A. General skills
	1. Defining behaviors and goals
	2. Recognizing developmentally appropriate goals
	3. Identifying antecedents and consequences
	4. Identifying rewards
	5. Identifying a reasonable level of control
7	B. Request skills
	1. How to make requests to ensure compliance (alpha commands)
	2. Reasonable requests
8–9	C. Response reduction
	1. Ignoring
	2. Reward the absence of negative behaviors
	3. Time-out
	4. Getting past the "testing the limits" phase
10	D. Response increasing
	1. Use of praise
	2. Explicit rewards: appropriate rewards, token economy
	IV. Extending parenting
11	A. Child safety
	1. Discipline and abuse: How discipline can slip into abuse, outcomes of abuse
	2. Responsibility for selecting nonabusive care agents
	3. Other kinds of injury "child proofing"
	4. Supervision
	5. Child as precious to mother: work to protect
12	B. Meeting the challenges of parenting: How to maintain parenting skills and other changes without group
13–14	V. Anger management
	A. Seeing oneself through the child's eyes
	1. Recalling one's own parents and parental anger
	2. Characterization of how being the focus of anger feels
	B. Neurolinguistic programming
	1. Anger as feeling, color, or state
	2. Power to alter that state
15	C. Behavioral treatment
	1. Relaxation
	2. Becoming aware of anger triggers
	3. Safety valves
	4. Self-esteem
	D. Successful parenting as anger reducing
16	VI. Open house and review

Source: From "Integrating Child Injury and Abuse-Neglect Research: Common Histories, Etiologies, and Solutions," by L. Peterson and D. Brown, 1994, *Psychological Bulletin, 116,* 293–315. Copyright © 1994 by the American Psychological Association. Reprinted with permission.

Because of the problems presented in the pediatric setting, consultation has become an integral part of the psychologist's role. Consultation occurs with parents, pediatricians, medical staff, school systems, welfare agencies, juvenile court systems, and other health or service agencies. The subjects of consultation may range from psychiatric, psychosomatic, or developmental problems to any kind of illness-related difficulties common to health care settings. In particular, pediatric psychologists consult with pediatricians, who call upon the psychologist much as they might consult with other specialists such as cardiologists or oncologists. Because pediatricians encounter such a wide range of both well and ill children (probably more than any other specialist during the early stages of development), they often face problems for which they have little training, knowledge, or interest in treating. Hence, they may turn to the psychologist.

Consultation may occur in hospital practice or in outpatient settings. It may involve requests for immediate and very brief help or for long-term interventions. Requests may come in the form of hallway chats and quick telephone calls or in the shape of case workups and written reports. Some interventions are directly with the child; others involve work with the family or with the pediatrician's staff. Indeed, several models of consultation have been offered (for example, Drotar, 1995). Let us consider them now.

Independent Functions Model. Here, the psychologist functions as a specialist and independently carries out diagnostic and treatment activities on patients referred by the pediatrician (or other professional). On the surface, this seems relatively noncollaborative. However, information is exchanged between parties both before and after the patient is seen. This model has several advantages (Drotar, 1995). Medical professionals, such as pediatricians, find it familiar and comfortable. Further, the model is efficient and cost effective. However, the limited contact may lead to less comprehensive consultations and fewer training opportunities (Drotar, 1995).

Indirect Consultation Model. In this case, the pediatrician retains chief responsibility for patient management. The psychologist has, at best, limited contact with the actual patient and makes a contribution through analysis of information provided by the pediatrician (or other specialist). This kind of consultation is especially characteristic of medical center settings where teaching is a major function. Often the role of the psychologist is an educational or supervisory one, especially when pediatric residents are involved. This kind of consultation may involve (1) brief contacts, such as phone calls or informal hallway consultations); (2) presentation of information in seminars, conferences, workshops, or in-service training for other professionals; or (3) situations where another professional carries out specific behavioral or psychosocial interventions recommended by the psychologist. For example, the psychologist may develop specific guidelines and give them to the pediatrician, who either implements them or else supervises parents who do the actual intervention. These guidelines may involve how to handle problems such as temper tantrums, bedwetting, mealtime problems, or general behavioral management. Roberts (1986) has provided a list of sample guidelines or protocols for the assessment and treatment of childhood problems.

As noted by Drotar (1995), indirect consultation is more likely to be well received and effective if the focus is on clinical relevance and if there are practical applications that follow. However, there are some limitations and drawbacks as well (Drotar, 1995). This model can be very time-consuming and may be seen as a detractor from time spent on direct clinical service. Further, pediatricians and other medical personnel often want immediate solutions, to which complex clinical problems do not always lend themselves.

Collaborative Team Model. A third model represents what most consider true collaboration. Here, pediatrician, psychologist, nurse, or others work together and share the responsibility and decision making. This might be referred to as "conjoint case management." In this instance, the professionals involved act as functional equals. Of course, such a model is not often possible in nonteaching/nonresearch settings for several practical and financial reasons. However, such a model is especially appropriate for those cases that clearly involve both medical and psychological features. Effective collaborative team consultation evolves over time among those who have worked closely together, who respect each other's viewpoint, and who offer expertise that complements what other team members possess (Drotar, 1995). The biggest challenge is for team members to learn from each other, develop new professional skills, and maintain their own professional identities (Drotar, 1995).

Training

Issues of training in both clinical child and pediatric psychology have come to the forefront in recent years. This is due in part to the growing interest in health and medical issues and in the developing collaboration between medicine and psychology.

Roberts et al. (1998) recently presented a training model for psychologists who will provide services for children and adolescents. These recommendations apply to those seeking to become either clinical child psychologists or pediatric psychologists, although in both cases some additional specialized training might be required. Roberts et al. (1998) listed their recommendations by topic area.

1. *Life span developmental psychology*: Trainees should obtain knowledge and expertise in developmental processes (social, cognitive, emotional, behavioral, physical) and how these processes may influence assessment, diagnosis, treatment, and outcome.
2. *Life span developmental psychopathology*: Trainees must be exposed to information about mental, emotional, and developmental disorders and abnormal development.
3. *Child, adolescent, and family assessment methods*: Trainees should learn to administer and interpret assessments (intellectual,

personality, behavioral, family, sociocultural context) commonly used with children and adolescents. Trainees should focus on assessments with empirical support and appreciate how assessments can be influenced by ethnic or cultural background, or disability.
4. *Intervention strategies*: Trainees should be exposed to leading child/adolescent, parent, family, and school and community interventions, as well as the research literature on their effectiveness.
5. *Research methods and systems evaluations*: Trainees should be familiar with research methods so that critical evaluations of assessments, treatments, and services are possible. Further, trainees should be able to conduct research on important topics.
6. *Professional, ethical, and legal issues*: Trainees must be familiar with issues that pertain to children, adolescents, and families. These issues include child abuse reporting, custody, confidentiality, duty to protect, and relevant state and federal laws.
7. *Issues of diversity*: Trainees must appreciate the role of ethnicity and culture and how diverse beliefs and expectations affect assessment, intervention, and the interaction between service delivery systems and children or adolescents and their families.
8. *Multiple disciplines and service delivery systems*: Services for children and adolescents have become more interdisciplinary in nature and involve different service delivery systems. Trainees should be exposed to other disciplines (pediatrics and family practice, social work) and how professionals from these disciplines seek to address problems.
9. *Prevention, family support, and health promotion*: Trainees should have expertise in other forms of intervention that improve quality of life and can help prevent future problems.
10. *Social issues affecting children, adolescents, and families*: A number of social circumstances (natural disasters, abuse and neglect, vio-

lence) can greatly impact the well-being of children, adolescents, and their families. Trainees should have knowledge and appreciation of these potential adversities.

11. *Specialized experience in assessment, intervention, and consultation*: Trainees should acquire a broad range of applied experiences with a diverse selection of children, adolescents, and their families. This means working in several different settings (such as medical hospitals, public-sector mental health agencies).

Roberts et al. (1998) believe that training in these areas should occur through didactic coursework, observation in an applied or research setting, and supervised service delivery. These experiences can be obtained at the predoctoral, internship, and postdoctoral phases of training.

Regarding specialized training in pediatric psychology, Drotar (1998) notes that the needs of pediatric psychology trainees are complex. At a minimum, pediatric psychologists must learn to consult and collaborate with physicians, to recognize and manage the clinical problems that are typically encountered in pediatric settings, to teach primary care providers about principles of behavior and development, and to engage in interdisciplinary research. These training goals may be attained through didactic coursework, observation of pediatric psychologists in these situations, and hands-on experience in the field.

The Future of Clinical Child and Pediatric Psychology

What lies ahead for clinical child and pediatric psychology? In closing, we note several trends and issues that will confront these specialties as they enter the twenty-first century.

1. *Issues related to ethnicity, race, or culture.* As the population of the United States becomes increasingly diverse, clinicians and researchers alike must commit themselves to providing their services to children and adolescents from underrepresented groups (Culbertson, 1993). Demographic trends suggest a great shortage of professionals to meet the needs of these children and adolescents. Training programs need to provide the instruction and experience necessary to adequately prepare future child clinical and pediatric psychologists to meet these needs.

2. *Research.* As previously mentioned, more research is needed on commonly used interventions for children and adolescents. More research that evaluates the role of ethnicity, race, and culture in the treatment of children and adolescents is crucial as well. Foster and Martinez (1995) provide a nice overview of conceptual and methodological issues that need to be considered in this line of research. What do the experts predict will be the most important research areas in the future? Table 20-11 presents the results from a survey of both pediatric and clinical child psychologists.

3. *Innovative treatment models.* Traditional interventions (one-on-one therapy) may not be the most practical or effective in the treatment of children or adolescents. Recently, a task force report made the following recommendations regarding mental health services for children, adolescents, and their families (Henggeler, 1994):

   a. Reduce the use of inpatient services and residential treatment and increase the use of home- and community-based services.

   b. Train providers in the delivery of cost-effective services and increase provider accountability.

   c. Increase the integration of services (mental health, education, primary care).

   d. Provide flexible, individualized services and elicit the support of families.

4. *Increased focus on injury prevention and prevention of child abuse/neglect.* Injury is the leading cause of death among children, and the safety and health of children is receiving more attention from psychologists and laypersons alike. The boundary between unintentional/inadvertent injury and injury

TABLE 20-11 Rankings of Important Research Trends for the Future

Rank	Pediatric Experts	Clinical Child Experts
1	Chronic illness	Sexual abuse
2	Prevention	Childhood depression/suicide
3	Cost/benefit interventions	Developmental psychopathology
4	Treatment effectiveness	Prevention
5	Medical compliance	Treatment of conduct disorders
6	Neuropsychology	Custody and alternative living arrangements
7	Patenting issues	Parenting influences on development
8	Early intervention with children at risk	Diagnostic systems for children
9	Research strategies	Therapy effectiveness
10	Child abuse and neglect	Child neuropsychology

Source: From "Future Directions in Pediatric and Clinical Child Psychology," by K. L. Kaufman, E. W. Holden, and C. E. Walker, *Professional Psychology: Research and Practice*, 1989, *20*, 148–152. Copyright 1989 by the American Psychological Association. Reprinted by permission.

resulting from neglect or abuse is often blurred (Peterson & Brown, 1994). Increasingly, psychologists are developing and applying interventions aimed at both caregivers and children (Peterson & Roberts, 1992), and this trend is likely to continue.

Chapter Summary

Pediatric psychologists focus more on the relationship between psychological and physical well-being of children and adolescents, tend to be more behavioral in orientation, place more emphasis on medical and biological issues, and are more likely to consult with pediatricians and other physicians than their clinical child psychologist colleagues. However, there is a great deal of overlap as well. Both pediatric and clinical child psychologists adopt a developmental perspective on problems, engage in a variety of assessment activities (interviewing, behavioral observations, psychological testing), treat a diverse range of problems, and are involved in prevention initiatives as well.

In addition to a general description of the roles and activities of pediatric and clinical child psychologists, this chapter has focused on the evidence for the efficacy of specific interventions for specific problems encountered by both clinical child and pediatric psychologists. We have also provided an overview of training models for these psychologists. Finally, we have highlighted several important themes to be addressed by clinical child and pediatric psychologists in the future. These include issues of ethnic, racial, and cultural diversity; important areas for future research, including interventions, sexual abuse, prevention, and medical problems; innovative treatment models; and prevention of injury, abuse, and neglect.

Key Terms

achievement tests Tests that assess past learning across a variety of different subjects, particularly learning that is associated with training or academic programs.

behavioral observation A method in which an individual is observed directly in order to gain a better understanding of the problem behavior, as well as the factors that are maintaining it. Children and adolescents may be observed using naturalistic, analogue, participant, or self-observational strategies, and a variety of coding systems are available to rate their behavior in the home or classroom setting.

behavioral pediatrics The application of cognitive and/or behavioral techniques to problems encountered by children in medical settings (preparing for medical procedures, managing pain, complying with treatment regimens, etc.).

behavior therapy A popular framework for treating disorders that is based upon respondent or operant principles. Behavioral techniques are usually the treatment of choice for childhood problems because they account for so many childhood behaviors, are efficient, and may be applied easily by both parents and teachers.

clinical child psychology A branch of psychology that deals with assessing and treating children and adolescents following the development of psychopathological symptoms. Often this work is conducted in private practice settings or in outpatient clinic settings. Although there is much overlap between the subspecialties, clinical child psychologists are often more diverse in their theoretical orientations than pediatric psychologists, and they tend to place a greater emphasis on training in assessment, developmental processes, and family therapy.

cognitive assessment In clinical child psychology and pediatric psychology, assessing the cognitive factors that may mediate a child's behavioral, emotional, or medical problems. For instance, a child's sense of self-efficacy or lack of understanding about a problem or treatment may have an important impact on the child's stress level or the success of the treatment.

cognitive-behavioral therapy A therapy framework that emphasizes the role of thinking in the etiology and maintenance of problems. By teaching children to alter their cognitions through internal assessments and self-statements, the therapy aims to improve the child's problem solving and planning, help him or her to delay gratification, and bring any problematic behaviors under rational control.

conduct disorder A disorder in which a child or adolescent repetitively and persistently violates either the basic rights of others or major societal norms or rules.

consultation The act by which a person who provides services to others enlists the help of an expert for the purpose of improving these services. Various health, social, and legal service agencies consult with clinical child psychologists and pediatric psychologists about psychiatric, developmental, psychosomatic, or other illness-related difficulties.

externalizing disorders Childhood disorders (such as conduct disorder and attention-deficit/hyperactivity disorder) that are characterized by conduct problems or aggressive or impulsive behaviors.

family therapy A form of psychotherapy in which several members of a family are seen by the therapist in addition to the identified patient. Family therapy is based on the idea that many of the problems exhibited by children or adolescents are learned or even reinforced in the family setting, such that alleviating these problems requires the cooperation of the entire family unit.

family systems assessment An assessment focus based on the idea that a child's problems are embedded in the overall family context, such that understanding and treating the child's problems appropriately requires that one understand the family system as well.

intelligence tests Tests that measure one's general mental capacity or a range of abilities. In clinical child psychology and pediatric psychology, intelligence tests are used to answer questions involving intellectual ability, academic deficits, or the development of an individualized educational plan.

internalizing disorders Childhood disorders (such as the mood or anxiety disorders) that are characterized by symptoms of anxiety, depression, shyness, and social withdrawal.

neuropsychological assessment An assessment approach, based on empirically established brain-behavior relationships, that evaluates a person's relative strengths and weaknesses across a number of areas. Child neuropsychology has grown as a specialty in recent years due to an increased focus on neurodevelopmental disorders as well as decreased mortality from devastating conditions.

parent management training A set of therapeutic procedures that teaches parents how to modify a child or adolescent's behavior at home using behavioral techniques such as contingency management.

pediatric psychology (Also known as child health psychology.) A branch of psychology that deals with treating children and adolescents prior to or early in the development of psychopathology. Pediatric psychology referrals often come from pediatricians, and the work is frequently performed in medical settings. Compared to clinical child psychology, pediatric psychologists tend to use short-term, immediate intervention strategies and tend to place a greater emphasis on medical and biological issues in their approaches to research and treatment.

play therapy An eclectic set of techniques that uses expressive play as a substitute for or supplement to verbalizations. The way that children play, the objects they choose, and the nature of any verbalizations they make as they play can be revealing, cathartic, and/or therapeutic.

prevention The principle that, in the long run, preventive activities will be more efficient and effective than individual treatment administered after the onset of disease or problems. Both pediatric and clinical child psychology focus upon the prevention of childhood problems by (for instance) providing education, establishing safety programs, and identifying and proactively treating children at risk.

projective tests Psychological testing techniques that use people's responses to ambiguous stimuli to make judgments about their personality traits or psychological state. Among children with high anxiety levels, projective tests may be less threatening than objective tests.

psychoanalytically oriented therapy In clinical child psychology and pediatric psychology, the modification of the psychoanalytic approach to account for children's inability to adhere to the traditional requirements of analysis or to deal with the highly abstract nature of analysis-as-usual. In general, this approach teaches children that certain behaviors are really defenses against anxiety and helps them to successfully negotiate their developmental stage.

questionnaires and checklists Objective measures of behavior or personality. In the context of child assessment, adults who are in frequent contact with the child are often asked to complete scales, checklists, or questionnaires based upon their observations of the child's behaviors. In cases where the child is believed capable of providing a reliable report, an objective measure may be administered directly to him or her.

resilience A term that refers to characteristics of the person, the family, or the extrafamilial environment (e.g., sociability, socioeconomic advantages, close and caring relationships with prosocial adults outside the family) that are associated with an individual's ability to overcome adversity and achieve good outcomes.

structured diagnostic interviews A class of interviews that assess for the criteria occurring in the diagnostic manual by asking all interviewees the same questions in the same specified sequence. A number of structured diagnostic interviews are available for assessing children and adolescents for both the internalizing and externalizing disorders.

Web Sites of Interest

To visit any of the web sites listed below, go to www.wadsworth.com and click on Links.

20-1 The Society of Pediatric Psychology (Division 54)

20-2 Clinical Child Psychology (Division 53)

20-3 The Future of Children

20-4 APA Guidelines for providers of Psychological Services to Ethnic, Linguistic, and Culturally Diverse Populations

20-5 Psychological Testing of Language Minority and Culturally Different Children

20-6 Prevention Science Clearinghouse

20-7 Society for Prevention Research

APPENDIX

Web Sites of Interest

For updated links to any of the web sites listed below, go to www.wadsworth.com and click on Links.

1-1 Accredited internship programs
http://www.apa.org/ed/intern.html

1-2 Accredited doctoral training programs in clinical psychology
http://www.apa.org/ed/clin.html

1-3 Financial aid resources
www.apa.org/ppo/fineduc.html

1-4 Getting into graduate school in psychology
www.apa.org/ed/getin.html

1-5 Comparison of psychiatrists and psychologists
www.psych.org/pub_pol_adv/difference.html

1-6 List of internship sites with web pages
http://35.8.37.170/w05doctweb.html

1-7 Example of a clinical psychology program's web page (University of Missouri)
web.missouri.edu/~psywww/clinical.htm

1-8 Graduate Record Examination (GRE) information
www.gre.org

1-9 *U.S. News* rankings of clinical psychology programs
www.usnews.com/usnews/edu/beyond/gradrank/gbpsysp1.htm

2-1 American Psychological Association
www.apa.org

2-2 American Psychological Society
www.psychologicalscience.org

2-3 Society for a Science of Clinical Psychology
www.sscp.psych.ndsu.nodak.edu

2-4 Classics in the History of Psychology
www.yorku.ca/dept/psych/classics

2-5 Daily Calendar of Events in the History of Psychology
www.cwu.edu/~warren/calendar/datepick.html

2-6 Society of Clinical Psychology (Division 12 of the APA)
www.apa.org/divisions/div12/homepage.html

2-7 Webs sites dedicated to specific individuals important in the history of psychology
www.yorku.ca/dept/psych/orgs/individ.htm

2-8 Women in psychology
www.webster.edu/~woolflm/women.html

3-1 American Board of Professional Psychology
www.biof.com/americanpsychology.html

3-2 Association of State and Provincial Psychology Boards
www.asppb.org

3-3 National Council of Schools and Programs of Professional Psychology
www.am.org/ncspp

3-4 Academy of Psychological Clinical Science
www.arizona.edu/~psych/apcs/apcs.html

3-5 National Register of Health Services Providers in Psychology
www.nationalregister.com/newmenu.html

3-6 Example of Licensure Requirements: Missouri
www.mopsych.org/legal/licensing.htm

3-7 American Psychological Association Ethical Principles of Psychologists and Code of Conduct
www.apa.org/ethics/code.html

3-8 APA Guidelines for Providers of Psychological Services to Ethnic, Linguistic, and Culturally Diverse Populations
www.apa.org/pi/oema/guide.html

4-1 APA Ethical Principles and Code of Conduct
www.apa.org/ethics/code.html

4-2 Research with Animals in Psychology
www.apa.org/science/animal2.html

4-3 Guidelines for Ethical Conduct in the Care and Use of Animals
www.apa.org/science/anguide.html

4-4 APA Guidelines for Providers of Psychological Services to Ethnic, Linguistic, and Culturally Diverse Populations
www.apa.org/pi/guide.html

4-5 Research Methods Tutorials
http://trochim.human.cornell.edu/tutorial/tutorial.htm

5-1 Mental Health Net, Mental Disorders Symptoms and Treatment
www.cmhc.com/disorders/

5-2 National Alliance for the Mentally Ill
www.nami.org

5-3 Links to Abnormal Psychology/Psychopathology web pages
www.yorku.ca/faculty/academic/rmuller/

7-1 Intelligence: Knowns and Unknowns
www.apa.org/releases/intell.html

7-2 Task Force Report of the American Psychological Association
www.apa.org/releases/intell.html

7-3 Update on APA's revised *Standards for Educational and Psychological Testing*
www.apa.org/science/standards.html

7-4 APA's Science Directorate Testing and Assessment Web Page
www.apa.org/science/testing.html

8-1 Frequently Asked Questions (FAQ) on Psychological Tests
www.apa.org/science/test.html

8-2 APA Statement on the Use of Secure Psychological Tests in the Education of Graduate and Undergraduate Psychology Students
www.apa.org/science/coft.html

8-3 Psychological Testing of Language Minority and Culturally Different Children
www.apa.org/pi/oema/psych.htlm

8-4 Psychologists and APA staff give guidance on when to use psychological tests for job screening
www.apa.org/monitor/nov95/medexams.html

8-5 Update on APA's revised *Standards for Educational and Psychological Testing*
www.apa.org/science/standards.html

8-6 APA's Science Directorate Testing and Assessment Web Page
www.apa.org/science/testing.html

8-7 Test Locator and Reviews of Tests
www.unl.edu/buros/

9-1 Association for Advancement of Behavior Therapy (AABT)
http://www.aabt.org

9-2 Association for Behavior Analysis (ABA)
www.wmich.edu/aba/

9-3 Division of the Experimental Analysis of Behavior (Div. 25 of the APA)
www.apa.org/divisions/div25/

9-4 Behavior Analysis Resources
http://typhoon.coedu.usf.edu/behavior/index.html

11-1 Links to a variety of documents concerning empirically supported treatments (lists, manual references)
www.sscp.psych.ndsu.nodak.edu/est_docs/tf_docs.htm

11-2 Link to Seligman (1995) article about the *Consumer Reports* study
http://mentalhelp.net/articles/seligm.htm

11-3 Gateway to a number of links to issues concerning managed care
www.apa.org/concept/managed.html

11-4 Gateway to a number of links to issues concerning psychotherapy
www.apa.org/concept/therapy.html

11-5 *Prevention and Treatment*, an electronic journal devoted to research on interventions
http://journals.apa.org/prevention/

12-1 American Psychoanalytic Association
www.apsa.org

12-2 Online Preview of the Exhibition, "Sigmund Freud: Conflict and Culture"
http://lcweb.loc.gov/exhibits/freud/preview.html

12-3 Sigmund Freud on the Internet
http://plaza.interport.net/nypsan/
freudarc.html

12-4 Burying Freud – Online debate between
Freud critics and supporters
www.shef.ac.uk/uni/projects/gpp/
burying_freud.html

13-1 Center for the Studies of the Person
www.centerfortheperson.org

13-2 Carl Rogers Biography
http://oprf.com/Rogers/

13-3 Gestalt Therapy Page
www.gestalt.org/index.htm

13-4 Gestalt Organizations
www.sonoma.edu/people/daniels/
gestaltorg.html

14-1 Links to a variety of documents concerning
empirically supported treatments
www.sscp.psych.ndsu.nodak.edu/est_docs/
tf_docs.htm

14-2 Association for the Advancement of Behavior
Therapy (AABT)
www.aabt.org

14-3 The Beck Institute for Cognitive Therapy
and Research
www.beckinstitute.org

14-4 International Association for Cognitive
Psychotherapy
http://iacp.asu.edu

14-5 Albert Ellis Institute. This web site includes a
link through which you can submit a
question to Dr. Ellis and view previous
questions and answers.
www.rebt.org/index.html

15-1 American Association for Marriage and
Family Therapy
www.aamft.org

15-2 Association for Specialists in Group Work
http://coe.colstat.edu/asgw/

15-3 International Association of Group
Psychotherapy
www.psych.mcgill.ca/labs/iagp/IAGP.html

16-1 Society for Community Research and Action
(Division 27 of the American Psychological
Association)
www.apa.org/divisions/div27

16-2 Community Psychology Net
www.cmmtypsych.net

16-3 Prevention Science Clearinghouse
www.oslc.org/ecpn/psc97.html

16-4 Society for Prevention Research
www.oslc.org/spr/sprhome.html

16-5 The Future of Children (links to prevention
articles)
www.futureofchildren.org

16-6 Community Psychology Graduate Programs
www.msu.edu/user/lounsbu1/cpdcra.html

17-1 Division 38 of the American Psychological
Association (Health Psychology)
www.apa.org/divisions/div38

17-2 Guide to Internships in Health Psychology
www.apa.org/divisions/div38/9899pdrip/
new/preface.html

17-3 Major rotations
www.apa.org/divisions/div38/9899pdrip/
new/preface.html

17-4 Minor rotations
www.apa.org.divisions/div38/9899pdrip/
minor.html

17-5 Postdoctoral Training Programs in Health
Psychology
www.apa.org/divisions/div38/pdoc/
contents.html

17-6 Centers for Disease Control and Prevention
www.cdc.gov

17-7 Society of Behavioral Medicine
www.sbmweb.org

17-8 Health Psychology and Rehabilitation
www.healthpsych.com

18-1 Division 40 of APA—Clinical Neuropsychology
www.div40.org

18-2 Training Programs in Clinical Neuropsychology
www.swets.nl/sps/ntp/ntphome.html

18-3 Neuropsychology Central
www.neuropsychologycentral.com

18-4 The Whole Brain Atlas
www.med.harvard.edu/AANLIB/home.html

19-1 American Psychological Association
Division 41: The American Psychology-
Law Society
www.unl.edu/ap-ls/

19-2 Careers and Training in Psychology and Law
www.unl.edu/ap-ls/careers.htm

19-3 Links to Graduate Programs in Psychology
and Law
www.unl.edu/ap-ls/gradp.htm

19-4 Ethical Guidelines for Forensic Psychologists
www.unl.edu/ap-ls/foren.pdf

(You will need Adobe Acrobat to view the
file—free download at www.adobe.co.uk/
products/acrobat/download/readstep.html)

19-5 Eyewitness Identification Procedures:
Recommendations for lineups and
photospreads
www.unl.edu/ap-ls/whiteeye.html

20-1 The Society of Pediatric Psychology
(Division 54)
www.apa.org/divisions/div54/

20-2 Clinical Child Psychology (Division 53)
www.psy.fsu.edu/~clinical_child

20-3 The Future of Children
www.futureofchildren.org

20-4 APA Guidelines for providers of Psychological Services to Ethnic, Linguistic, and
Culturally Diverse Populations
www.apa.org/pi/oema/guide.html

20-5 Psychological Testing of Language Minority
and Culturally Different Children
www.apa.org/pi/oema/psych.html

20-6 Prevention Science Clearinghouse
www.oslc.org/ecpn/psc97.html

20-7 Society for Prevention Research
www.oslc.org/spr/sprhome.html

REFERENCES

Abe-Kim, J. S., & Takeuchi, D. (1996). Cultural competence and quality of care: Issues for mental health service delivery in managed care. *Clinical Psychology: Science and Practice, 3,* 273–295.

Abel, E. L. (1981). Behavioral teratology of alcohol. *Psychological Bulletin, 90,* 564–581.

Abeles, N. (1990). Rediscovering psychological assessment. *Clinical Psychologist, 10,* 3–4.

Achenbach, T. M. (1991). *Manual for the Youth Self-Report and 1991 Profile.* Burlington: University of Vermont, Department of Psychiatry.

Achenbach, T. M. (1994). Child behavior checklist and related instruments. In M. E. Maruish (Ed.), *The use of psychological testing for treatment planning and outcome assessment* (pp. 517–549). Hillsdale, NJ: Erlbaum.

Ackerley, G. D., Burnell, J., Holder, D. C., & Kurdek, L. A. (1988). Burnout among licensed psychologists. *Professional Psychology: Research and Practice, 19,* 624–631.

Ackerman, N. W. (1958). *The psychodynamics of family life.* New York: Basic Books.

Ackerman, N. W. (1960). Family focused therapy of schizophrenia. In S. Scher & H. Davis (Eds.), *The outpatient treatment of schizophrenia.* New York: Grune and Stratton.

Ackerman, N. W. (1966). *Treating the troubled family.* New York: Basic Books.

Adams, H. E., & Frye, R. L. (1964). Psychotherapeutic techniques as conditioned reinforcers in a structured interview. *Psychological Reports, 14,*163–166.

Adams, K. M. (1996). President's message: "May you live in interesting times" Chinese proverb. *Division of Clinical Neuropsychology: Newsletter 40, 14,* 2–5, 10.

Adams, K. M., & Heaton, R. K. (1985). Automated interpretation of neuropsychological test data. *Journal of Consulting and Clinical Psychology, 53,* 790–802.

Ader, R., & Cohen, N. (1975). Behaviorally conditioned immuno-suppression. *Psychosomatic Medicine, 37,* 333–340.

Adler, A. (1924). *The practice and theory of individual psychology.* New York: Harcourt Brace Jovanovich.

Adler, A. (1930). *Guiding the child on the principles of individual psychology.* New York: Greenberg.

Adler, A. (1939). *Social Interest: A challenge to mankind.* New York: Putnam.

Ajzen, I. (1985). From intentions to actions: A theory of planned behavior. In J. Kuhl & J. Beckman (Eds.), *Action control: From cognition to behavior* (pp. 11–39). Heidelberg: Springer.

Ajzen, I. (1988). *Attitudes, personality, and behavior.* Chicago: Dorsey Press.

Akamatsu, T. J. (1988). Intimate relationships with former clients: National survey of attitudes and behavior among practitioners. *Professional Psychology: Research and Practice, 19,* 454–458.

Albee, G. W. (1959). *Mental health manpower trends.* New York: Basic Books.

Albee, G. W. (1968). Conceptual models and manpower requirements in psychology. *American Psychologist, 23,* 317–320.

Albee, G. W. (1969). Emerging concepts of mental illness and models of treatment: The psychological points of view. *American Journal of Psychiatry, 125,* 870–876.

Albee, G. W. (1970). The uncertain future of psychology. *American Psychologist, 25,* 1071–1080.

Albee, G. W. (1982). Preventing psychopathology and promoting human potential. *American Psychologist, 37,* 1043–1050.

Albee, G. W. (1986). Toward a just society: Lessons from observations on the primary prevention of psychopathology. *American Psychologist, 41,* 891–898.

Alden, L. E. (1988). Behavioral self-management controlled-drinking strategies in a context of secondary prevention. *Journal of Consulting and Clinical Psychology, 56,* 280–286.

Alexander, F. (1950). *Psychosomatic medicine.* New York: Norton.

Alexander, F., & French, T. M. (1946). *Psychoanalytic therapy.* New York: Ronald Press.

Alexander, J. F., Holtzworth-Munroe, A., & Jameson, P. (1994). The process and outcome of marital and family therapy: Research review and evaluation. In A. E. Bergin & S. L. Garfield (Eds.), *Handbook of psychotherapy and behavior change* (4th ed.) (pp. 595–630). New York: Wiley.

Allen, D. N., Sprenkel, D. G., Heyman, R. A., Schramke, C. J., & Heffron, N. E. (1997). Evaluation of demyelinating and degenerative disorders. In G. Goldstein, P. D. Nussbaum, & S. R. Beers (Eds.), *Neuropsychology* (pp. 187–208). New York: Plenum Press.

Allen, F. H. (1934). Therapeutic work with children. *American Journal of Orthopsychiatry, 4,* 193–202.

Allison, K. W., Crawford, I., Echemendia, R., Robinson, L., & Knepp, D. (1994). Human diversity and professional competence: Training in clinical and counseling psychology revisited. *American Psychologist, 49,* 792–796.

Allport, G. W. (1937). *Personality: A psychological interpretation.* New York: Holt, Rinehart and Winston.

Allport, G. W. (1961). *Pattern and growth in personality.* New York: Holt, Rinehart and Winston.

American Association of State Psychology Boards. (1992). *Model act for licensure of psychologists.* Montgomery, AL: Author.

American Association on Mental Deficiency. (1974). *Adaptive Behavior Scale: Manual.* Washington, DC: AAMD.

American Group Psychotherapy Association. Committee on History. (1971). A brief history of the American Group Psychotherapy Association, 1943–1968. *International Journal of Group Psychotherapy, 21,* 406–435.

American Psychiatric Association. (1952). *Diagnostic and statistical manual of mental disorders.* Washington, DC: Author.

American Psychiatric Association. (1968). *Diagnostic and statistical manual of mental disorders* (2nd ed.). Washington, DC: Author.

American Psychiatric Association. (1980). *Diagnostic and statistical manual of mental disorders* (3rd ed.). Washington, DC: Author.

American Psychiatric Association. (1987). *Diagnostic and statistical manual of mental disorders* (3rd ed. rev.). Washington, DC: Author.

American Psychiatric Association. (1994). *Diagnostic and statistical manual of mental disorders* (4th ed.). Washington, DC: Author.

American Psychological Association. (1953). *Ethical standards of psychologists.* Washington, DC: Author.

American Psychological Association. (1954). *Technical recommendations for psychological tests and diagnostic techniques.* Washington, DC: Author.

American Psychological Association. (1966). *Standards for educational and psychological tests and manuals.* Washington, DC: Author.

American Psychological Association. (1973). *Ethical principles in the conduct of research with human participants.* Washington, DC: Author.

American Psychological Association. (1981). Ethical principles of psychologists. *American Psychologist, 36,* 633–638.

American Psychological Association. (1982). *Ethical principles in the conduct of research with human subjects.* Washington, DC: Author.

American Psychological Association. (1985). *Standards for educational and psychological tests.* Washington, DC: Author.

American Psychological Association. (1987a). *Casebook on ethical principles of psychologists* (rev. ed.). Washington, DC: Author.

American Psychological Association. (1987b). Model act for state licensure of psychologists. *American Psychologist, 42,* 696–703.

American Psychological Association. (1990). Ethical principles of psychologists (amended June 2, 1990). *American Psychologist, 45,* 390–395.

American Psychological Association. (1992). Ethical principles of psychologists and code of conduct. *American Psychologist, 47,* 1597–1611.

American Psychological Association. (1997). *Final report of the American Psychological Association Working Group on the Implications of Changes in the Health Care Delivery System for the Education, Training, and Continuing Professional Education of Psychologists: Discussion of knowledge and skills and selected readings.* Washington, DC: Author.

American Psychological Association. (1998). Accredited doctoral programs in professional psychology: 1998. *American Psychologist, 53,* 1324–1335.

Anastasi, A. (1988). *Psychological testing* (6th ed.). New York: Macmillan.

Anderson, H. H., & Anderson, G. L. (Eds.). (1951). *An introduction to projective techniques.* Englewood Cliffs, NJ: Prentice-Hall.

Anderson, N. B. (1995). Behavioral and sociocultural perspectives on ethnicity and health: Introduction to the special issue. *Health Psychology, 14,* 589–591.

Anderson, R.M., Jr. (1994). *Practitioner's guide to clinical neuropsychology.* New York: Plenum Press.

Angoff, W. W. (1988). The nature-nurture debate, aptitudes, and group differences. *American Psychologist, 43,* 713–720.

Anonymous. (1995). Hidden benefits of managed care. *Professional Psychology: Research and Practice, 26,* 235–237.

Ansbacher, H. L., & Ansbacher, R. R. (1956). *The individual psychology of Alfred Adler.* New York: Basic Books.

Appelbaum, S. A. (1970). Science and persuasion in the psychological test report. *Journal of Consulting and Clinical Psychology, 35,* 349–355.

Appelbaum, S. A. (1977). The refusal to take one's medicine. *Bulletin of the Menninger Clinic, 41,* 511–521.

Archer, R. P., & Krishnamurthy, R. (1997). MMPI-A and Rorschach indices related to depression and conduct disorder: An evaluation of the incremental validity hypothesis. *Journal of Personality Assessment, 69,* 517–533.

Arnhoff, F. N. (1968). Realities and mental health manpower. *Mental Hygiene, 52,* 181–189.

Arvey, R. D., et al. (1994, December 13). Mainstream science on intelligence. *The Wall Street Journal,* p. A18.

Atkinson, L. (1986). The comparative validities of the Rorschach and MMPI: A meta-analysis. *Canadian Psychology, 27,* 238–247.

Atthowe, J. M., Jr., & Krasner, L. (1968). A preliminary report of the application of contingent reinforcement procedures (token economy) on a "chronic psychiatric ward." *Journal of Abnormal Psychology, 73,* 37–43.

Ayllon, T., & Azrin, N. (1968). *The token economy: A motivational system for therapy and rehabilitation.* New York: Appleton-Century-Crofts.

Babad, E. Y., Mann, M., & Mar-Hayim, M. (1975). Bias in scoring the WISC subtests. *Journal of Consulting and Clinical Psychology, 43,* 268.

Bach, G. R. (1966). The marathon group: Intensive practice of intimate interaction. *Psychological Reports, 18,* 995–1002.

Baer, L., Jacobs, D. G., Cukor, P., O'Laughlen, J., Coyle, J. T., & Magruder, K. M. (1995). Automated telephone screening survey for depression. *Journal of the American Medical Association, 273,* 1943–1944.

Baer, R., Wetter, M., & Berry, T. (1992). Detection of under reporting of psychopathology on the MMPI: A meta-analysis. *Clinical Psychology Review, 12,* 509–525.

Ballou, M., & Gabalac, N. W. (1985). *A feminist position on mental health.* Springfield, IL: Charles C Thomas.

Bandura, A. (1969). *Principles of behavior modification.* New York: Holt, Rinehart and Winston.

Bandura, A. (1971). Psychotherapy based upon modeling principles. In A. E. Bergin & S. L. Garfield (Eds.), *Handbook of psychotherapy and behavior change: An empirical analysis.* New York: Wiley.

Bandura, A. (1974). Behavior theories and models of man. *American Psychologist, 29,* 859–869.

Bandura, A. (1977a). Self-efficacy: Toward a unifying theory of behavioral change. *Psychological Review, 84,* 191–215.

Bandura, A. (1977b). *Social learning theory.* Englewood Cliffs, NJ: Prentice-Hall.

Bandura, A. (1978). The self-system in reciprocal determinism. *American Psychologist, 33,* 344–358.

Bandura, A. (1986). *Social foundations of thought and action: A social cognitive theory.* Englewood Cliffs, NJ: Prentice-Hall.

Bandura, A. (1989). Human agency in cognitive theory. *American Psychologist, 44,* 1175–1184.

Bandura, A., Adams, N. E., & Beyer, J. (1977). Cognitive processes mediating behavioral change. *Journal of Personality and Social Psychology, 35,* 125–139.

Bandura, A., Jeffrey, R. W., & Wright, C. L. (1974). Efficacy of participant modeling as a function of response induction aids. *Journal of Abnormal Psychology, 83,* 56–64.

Bandura, A., & Walters, R. (1963). *Social learning and personality development.* New York: Holt, Rinehart and Winston.

Bangert-Drowns, R. L. (1986). Review of developments in meta-analytic method. *Psychological Bulletin, 99,* 388–399

Banks, W. M. (1972). The differential effects of race and social class in helping. *Journal of Clinical Psychology, 28,* 90–92.

Barak, A., & Fisher, W. A. (1989). Counselor and therapist gender bias? More questions than answers. *Professional Psychology: Research and Practice, 20,* 377–383.

Barker, R. G., & Wright, H. F. (1951). *One boy's day.* New York: Harper and Row.

Barker, S. L., Funk, S. C., & Houston, B. K. (1988). Psychological treatment versus nonspecific factors: A meta-analysis of conditions that engender comparable expectations for improvement. *Clinical Psychology Review, 8,* 579–594.

Barkley, R. A. (1987). *Defiant children: Parent-teacher assignments.* New York: Guilford Press.

Barlow, D. H. (1977). Assessment of sexual behavior. In A. R. Ciminero, K. S. Calhoun, & H. E. Adams (Eds.), *Handbook of behavioral assessment,* New York: Wiley.

Barlow, D. H. (1981). On the relation of clinical research to clinical practice: Current issues, new directions. *Journal of Consulting and Clinical Psychology, 49,* 147–155.

Barlow, D. H. (1994). Psychological interventions in the era of managed competition. *Clinical Psychology: Science and Practice, 1,* 109–122.

Barlow, D. H. (1996). The effectiveness of psychotherapy: Science and policy. *Clinical Psychology: Science and Practice, 3,* 236–240.

Barlow, D. H., & Cerny, J. A. (1988). *Psychological treatment of panic.* New York: Guilford Press.

Barnett, W. S. (1995). Long-term effects of early childhood programs on cognitive and school outcomes. In R. E. Behrman (Ed.), *The Future of Children: Long-term outcomes of early childhood programs* (Vol. 5, no. 3, pp. 25–50). Los Altos, CA: The Center for the Future of Children.

Barrom, C. P., Shadish, W. R., Jr., & Montgomery, L. M. (1988). PhDs, PsyDs, and real-world constraints on scholarly activity: Another look at the Boulder model. *Professional Psychology: Research and Practice, 19,* 93–101.

Barron, F. (1953). Some test correlates of response to psychotherapy. *Journal of Consulting Psychology, 17,* 235–241.

Bartell, P. A., & Rubin, L. J. (1990). Dangerous liaisons: Sexual intimacies in supervision. *Professional Psychology: Research and Practice, 21,* 442–450.

Bartelstone, J. H., & Trull, T. J. (1995). Personality, life events, and depression. *Journal of Personality Assessment, 64,* 279–294.

Bartol, C. R., & Bartol, A. M. (1994). *Psychology and law: Research and application* (2nd ed.). Pacific Grove, CA: Brooks/Cole.

Basic Behavioral Science Task Force of the National Advisory Mental Health Council. (1996). Basic behavioral science research for mental health: Sociocultural and environmental processes. *American Psychologist, 51,* 722–731.

Bateson, G., Jackson, D. D., Haley, J., & Weakland, J. H. (1956). Toward a theory of schizophrenia. *Behavioral Science, 1*, 251–264.

Baucom, D. H., Shoham, V., Mueser, K. T., Daiuto, A. D., & Stickle, T. R. (1998). Empirically supported couple and family interventions for marital distress and adult mental health problems. *Journal of Consulting and Clinical Psychology, 66*, 53–88.

Baum, A., Fleming, R., & Singer, J. (1982). Stress at Three Mile Island: Applying psychological impact analysis. In C. Beckman (Ed.), *Applied social psychology annual* (Vol. 3). Newbury Park, CA: Sage.

Baum, A., & Singer, J. E. (Eds.). (1987). *Handbook of psychology and health: Vol. 5. Stress.* Hillsdale, NJ: Erlbaum.

Bayley, N. (1955). On the growth of intelligence. *American Psychologist, 10*, 805–818.

Bayley, N. (1969). *Manual for the Bayley Scales of Infant Development.* New York: Psychological Corporation.

Beck, A. T. (1972). *Depression: Causes and treatment.* Philadelphia: University of Pennsylvania Press.

Beck, A. T. (1983). Cognitive therapy of depression: New perspectives. In P. J. Clayton & J. E. Barrett (Eds.), *Treatment of depression: Old controversies and new approaches* (pp. 265–290). New York: Raven.

Beck, A. T. (1991). Cognitive therapy: A 30-year retrospective. *American Psychologist, 46*, 368–375.

Beck, A. T. (1993). Cognitive therapy: Past, present, and future. *Journal of Consulting and Clinical Psychology, 61*, 194–198.

Beck, A. T., & Emery, G. (1985). *Anxiety disorders and phobias.* New York: Basic Books.

Beck, A. T., Freeman, A., & Associates. (1990). *Cognitive therapy of personality disorders.* New York: Guilford Press.

Beck, A. T., Rush, A. J., Shaw, B. F., & Emery, G. (1979). *Cognitive therapy of depression.* New York: Guilford Press.

Beck, A. T., Ward, C. H., Mendelson, M., Mock, J. E., & Erbaugh, J. K. (1962). Reliability of psychiatric diagnoses: II. A study of consistency of clinical judgments and ratings. *American Journal of Psychiatry, 119*, 351–357.

Beck, J. S. (1995). *Cognitive therapy: Basics and beyond.* New York: Guilford Press.

Bednar, R. L., & Kaul, T. J. (1994). Experiential group research: Can the canon fire? In A. E. Bergin & S. L. Garfield (Eds.), *Handbook of psychotherapy and behavior change* (4th ed.) (pp. 631–663). New York: Wiley.

Beers, C. W. (1908). *A mind that found itself.* New York: Longmans, Green.

Belar, C. D. (1997). Clinical health psychology: A specialty for the 21st century. *Health Psychology, 16*, 411–416.

Belar, C. D., & Deardorf, W. W. (1995). *Clinical health psychology in medical settings: A practitioner's guidebook.* Washington, DC: American Psychological Association.

Belar, C. D., & Perry, N. W. (1992). National conference on scientist-practitioner education and training for the professional practice of psychology. *American Psychologist, 47*, 71–75.

Bell, J. E. (1961). *Family group therapy* (no. 64). Washington, DC: U.S. Department of Health, Education, and Welfare.

Bellack, A. S., & Hersen, M. (Eds.). (1988). *Behavioral assessment: A practical handbook* (3rd ed.). Oxford, England: Pergamon Press.

Bellak, L. (1954). *The Thematic Apperception Test and the Children's Apperception Test.* New York: Grune and Stratton.

Benne, K. D. (1964). History of the T-group in the laboratory setting. In L. P. Bradford, J. R. Gibb, & K. D. Benne (Eds.), *T-group theory and the laboratory method.* New York: Wiley.

Ben-Porath, Y. S., & Waller, N. G. (1992). "Normal" personality inventories in clinical assessment: General requirements and the potential for using the NEO Personality Inventory. *Psychological Assessment, 4*, 14–19.

Benton, A. L. (1963). *The revised visual retention test* (3rd ed.). New York: Psychological Corporation.

Benton, A. L. (1974). *Revised visual retention test* (4th ed.). New York: Psychological Corporation.

Benton, A. L., Hamsher, K., Varney, N., & Spreen, O. (1983). *Contributions to neuropsychological assessment.* New York: Oxford University Press.

Berg, I. A. (1954). The clinical interview and the case record. In L. A. Pennington & I. A. Berg (Eds.), *An introduction to clinical psychology.* New York: Ronald Press.

Berg, R. A. (1997). Evaluation of neoplastic processes. In G. Goldstein, P. D. Nussbaum, & S. R. Beers (Eds.), *Neuropsychology* (pp. 169–247). New York: Plenum Press.

Bergin, A. E. (1971). The evaluation of therapeutic outcomes. In A. E. Bergin & S. L. Garfield (Eds.), *Handbook of psychotherapy and behavior change.* New York: Wiley.

Bergin, A. E. (1980). Negative effects revisited: A reply. *Professional Psychology, 11*, 93–100.

Bergin, A. E., & Garfield, S. L. (1994). *Handbook of psychotherapy and behavior change* (4th ed.). New York: Wiley.

Bergin, A. E., & Suinn, R. M. (1975). Individual psychotherapy and behavior therapy. In M. R. Rosenzweig & L. W. Porter (Eds.), *Annual review of psychology.* Palo Alto, CA: Annual Reviews.

Berkman, L. F., Leo-Summers, L., & Horwitz, R. I. (1992). Emotional support and survival after myocardial infarction: A prospective, population-based study of the elderly. *Annals of Internal Medicine, 117*, 1003–1009.

Berkman, L. F., Vaccarino, V., & Seeman, T. (1993). Gender differences in cardiovascular morbidity and mortality: The contribution of social networks and social support. *Annals of Behavioral Medicine, 15,* 112–118.

Berman, J. S., & Norton, N. L. (1985). Does professional training make a therapist more effective? *Psychological Bulletin, 98,* 401–407.

Berne, E. (1961). *Transactional analysis in psychotherapy.* New York: Grove Press.

Beme, E. (1964). *Games people play.* New York: Grove Press.

Bernstein, B. L., & Lecomte, C. (1981). Licensure in psychology: Alternative directions. *Professional Psychology, 12,* 200–208.

Bernstein, D. A., & Nietzel, M. T. (1973). Procedural variation in behavioral avoidance tests. *Journal of Consulting and Clinical Psychology, 41,* 165–174.

Berry, D., Baer, R., & Harris, M. (1991). Detection of malingering on the MMPI: A meta-analysis. *Clinical Psychology Review, 11,* 585–598.

Berry, D., Wetter, M., Baer, R., Larsen, L., Clark, C., & Monroe, K. (1992). MMPI-2 random responding indices: Validation using a self-report methodology. *Psychological Assessment, 4,* 340–345.

Bersoff, D. N. (1995). *Ethical conflicts in psychology.* Washington, DC: American Psychological Association.

Bertelson, A. D., Marks, P. A., & May, G. D. (1982). MMPI and race: A controlled study. *Journal of Consulting and Clinical Psychology, 50,* 316–318.

Beutler, L. E. (1990). Introduction to the special series on advances in psychotherapy process research. *Journal of Consulting and Clinical Psychology, 58,* 263–264.

Beutler, L. E. (1995). Integrating and communicating findings. In L. E. Beutler & M. R. Berren (Eds.), *Integrative assessment of adult personality* (pp. 25–64). New York: Guilford Press.

Beutler, L. E., & Fisher, D. (1994). Combined specialty training in counseling, clinical, and school psychology: An idea whose time has come. *Professional Psychology: Research and Practice, 25,* 62–69.

Beutler, L. E., Machado, P. P. P., & Neufeldt, S. A. (1994). Therapist variables. In A. E. Bergin & S. L. Garfield (Eds.), *Handbook of psychotherapy and behavior change* (4th ed.) (pp. 229–269). New York: Wiley.

Bevan, W. (1982). Human welfare and national policy: A conversation with Stuart Eisenstat. *American Psychologist, 37,* 1128–1135.

Bigler, E. D. (1990). Neuropsychology and malingering: Comment on Faust, Hart, and Guilmette (1988). *Journal of Consulting and Clinical Psychology, 58,* 244–247.

Bigler, E. D., Porter, S. S., & Lowry, C. M. (1997). Neuroimaging: Interface with clinical neuropsychology. In M. E. Maruish & J. A. Moses (Eds.), *Clinical neuropsychology: Theoretical foundations for practitioners* (pp. 163–218). Mahwah, NJ: LEA.

Binet, A., & Henri, V. (1896). Psychologie individuelle. *Annee Psychologie, 3,* 296–332.

Binswanger, L. (1958). The existential school of thought. In R. May, E. Angel, & H. F. Ellenberger (Eds.), *Existence.* New York: Basic Books.

Binswanger, L. (1963). *Being-in-the-world: Selected papers of Ludwig Binswanger.* New York: Basic Books.

Birdwhistell, R. L. (1970). *Kinesics and context: Essays on body motion communication.* Philadelphia: University of Pennsylvania Press.

Blanchard, E. B., & Andrasik, F. (1985). *Management of chronic headaches: A psychological approach.* New York: Pergamon Press.

Blanck, G., & Blanck, R. (1974). *Ego psychology: Theory and practice.* New York: Columbia University Press.

Blashfield, R. K., & Draguns, J. G. (1976). Evaluative criteria for psychiatric classification. *Journal of Abnormal Psychology, 85,* 140–150.

Blau, T. H. (1998). *The psychologist as expert witness* (2nd ed.). New York: Wiley.

Blechman, E. A., & Brownell, K. D. (1998). *Behavioral medicine and women: A comprehensive handbook.* New York: Guilford Press.

Block, J. (1995). A contrarian view of the five-factor approach to personality description. *Psychological Bulletin, 117,* 187–215.

Bloom, B. L. (1968). The evaluation of primary prevention programs. In L. M. Roberts, N. S. Greenfield, & M. H. Miller (Eds.), *Comprehensive mental health: The challenge of evaluation.* Madison: University of Wisconsin Press.

Bloom, B. L. (1972). Mental health program evaluation. In S. E. Golann & C. Eisdorfer (Eds.), *Handbook of community mental health.* New York: Appleton-Century-Crofts.

Bloom, B. L. (1973). *Community mental health: A historical and critical analysis.* Morristown, NJ: General Learning Press.

Bloom, B. L. (1981). Focused single-session therapy: Initial development and evaluation. In S. H. Budman (Ed.), *Forms of brief therapy.* New York: Guilford Press.

Bloom, B. L. (1992). Computer-assisted psychological intervention: A review and commentary. *Clinical Psychology Review, 12,* 169–197.

Blouin, A. G. (1991). *Computerized Diagnostic Interview Schedule (Revised) DSM-III-R. Version 2.0* [computer program]. Ontario, Canada: C-DIS Management Group.

Blouin, A. G., Perez, E. L., & Blouin, J. H. (1988). Computerized administration of the Diagnostic Interview Schedule. *Psychiatry Research, 23,* 335–344.

Blum, G. S. (1950). *The Blacky Pictures and manual.* New York: Psychological Corporation.

Blum, G. S. (1968). Assessment of psychodynamic variables by the Blacky Pictures. In P. McReynolds (Ed.), *Advances in psychological assessment* (Vol. 1). Palo Alto, CA: Science and Behavior Books.

Bobbitt, B. L., Marques, C. C., & Trout, D. L. (1998). Managed behavioral health care: Current status, recent trends, and the role of psychology. *Clinical Psychology: Science and Practice, 5,* 53–66.

Boice, R. (1983). Observational skills. *Psychological Bulletin, 93,* 3–29.

Bolgar, H. (1965). The case study method. In B. B. Wolman (Ed.), *Handbook of clinical psychology.* New York: McGraw-Hill.

Borkovec, T. D. (1972). Effects of expectancy on the outcome of systematic desensitization and implosive treatments for analogue anxiety. *Behavior Therapy, 3,* 29–40.

Borkovec, T. D., Weerts, T. C., & Bernstein, D. A. (1977). Assessment of anxiety. In A. R. Ciminero, K. S. Calhoun, & H. E. Adams (Eds.), *Handbook of behavioral assessment.* New York: Wiley.

Bornstein, P. H., & Bornstein, M. T. (1986). *Marital therapy: A behavioral-communications approach.* New York: Pergamon Press.

Borys, D. S., & Pope, K. S. (1989). Dual relationships between therapist and client: A national study of psychologists, psychiatrists, and social workers. *Professional Psychology: Research and Practice, 20,* 283–293.

Boss, M. (1958). *The analysis of dreams.* New York: Philosophical Library.

Boss, M. (1963). *Psychoanalysis and Daseinanalysis.* New York: Basic Books.

Bouchard, T. J., Jr., & McGue, M. (1981). Familial studies of intelligence: A review. *Science, 212,* 1055–1059.

Bouhoutsos, J. C., Goodchilds, J. D., & Huddy, L. (1986). Media psychology: An empirical study of radio call-in psychology programs. *Professional Psychology: Research and Practice, 17,* 408–414.

Bowen, M. (1960). A family concept of schizophrenia. In D. D. Jackson (Ed.), *Etiology of schizophrenia.* New York: Basic Books.

Bowen, M. (1971). The use of family therapy in clinical practice. In J. Haley (Ed.), *Changing families.* New York: Grune and Stratton.

Bowers, T. G., & Clum, G. A. (1988). Relative contribution of specific and nonspecific treatment effects: Meta-analysis of placebo-controlled behavior therapy research. *Psychological Bulletin, 103,* 315–323.

Boyd-Franklin, N. (1989). *Black families in therapy: A multi-systems approach.* New York: Guilford Press.

Brannon, L., & Feist, J. (2000). *Health psychology: An introduction to behavior and health* (4th ed.). Belmont, CA: Wadsworth/Thomson Learning.

Breger, L., & McGaugh, J. L. (1965). Critique and reformulation of "learning theory" approaches to psychotherapy and neurosis. *Psychological Bulletin, 63,* 338–358.

Brentar, J., & McNamara, J. R. (1991). The right to prescribe medication: Considerations for professional psychology. *Professional Psychology: Research and Practice, 22,* 179–187.

Bresler, C. (1988). Health promotion in the community: Development of a curriculum for predoctoral clinical psychologists. *Professional Psychology: Research and Practice, 19,* 87–92.

Brestan, E. V., & Eyberg, S. M. (1998). Effective psychosocial treatments of conduct-disordered children and adolescents: 29 years, 82 studies, and 5,272 kids. *Journal of Clinical Child Psychology, 27,* 180–189.

Breuer, J., & Freud, S. (1955). *Studies on hysteria: Standard edition* (Vol. 2). London: Hogarth Press. (First German edition published 1895)

Brewin, C. R. (1988). *Cognitive foundations of clinical psychology.* London: Erlbaum.

Brewin, C. R. (1989). Cognitive change processes in psychotherapy. *Psychological Review, 96,* 379–394.

Brodsky, S. L. (1991). *Testifying in court: Guidelines and maxims for the expert witness.* Washington, DC: American Psychological Association.

Brody, C. (Ed.). (1987). *Women's therapy groups: Paradigms of feminist treatment.* New York: Springer.

Brody, E. B., & Brody, N. (1976). *Intelligence: Nature, determinants, and consequences.* New York: Academic Press.

Brody, E. M., & Farber, B. A. (1989). Effects of psychotherapy on significant others. *Professional Psychology: Research and Practice, 20,* 116–122.

Brody, N. (1990). Behavior therapy versus placebo: Comment on Bowers and Clum's meta-analysis. *Psychological Bulletin, 107,* 106–109.

Brom, D., Kleber, R. J., & Defares, P. B. (1989). Brief psychotherapy for posttraumatic stress disorders. *Journal of Consulting and Clinical Psychology, 57,* 607–612.

Broskowski, A. (1991). Current mental health care environments: Why managed care is necessary. *Professional Psychology: Research and Practice, 22,* 6–14.

Broskowski, A. T. (1995). The evolution of health care: Implications for the training and careers of psychologists. *Professional Psychology: Research and Practice, 26,* 156–162.

Broverman, I., Broverman, D., Clarkson, F., Rosenkrantz, P., & Vogel, S. (1970). Sex-role stereotypes and clinical judgments of mental health. *Journal of Consulting and Clinical Psychology, 34,* 1–7.

Brown, D., & Schulte, A. C. (1987). A social learning model of consultation. *Professional Psychology: Research and Practice, 18,* 283–287.

Brown, J. F. (1940). *The psychodynamics of abnormal behavior*. New York: McGraw-Hill.

Brown, L. S. (1990). Taking account of gender in the clinical assessment interview. *Professional Psychology: Research and Practice, 21,* 12–17.

Brown, R. T., Buchanan, I., Doepke, K., Eckman, J. R., Baldwin, K., Goonan, B., & Schoenherr, S. (1993). Cognitive and academic functioning in children with sickle-cell disease. *Journal of Clinical Child Psychology, 22,* 207–218.

Bruehl, S. (1994). A case of borderline personality disorder. In P. T. Costa, Jr., & T. A. Widiger (Eds.), *Personality disorders and the five-factor model of personality* (pp. 189–198). Washington, DC: American Psychological Association.

Brunink, S. A., & Schroeder, H. E. (1979). Verbal therapeutic behavior of expert psychoanalytically oriented, Gestalt, and behavior therapists. *Journal of Consulting and Clinical Psychology, 47,* 567–574.

Brunswik, E. (1947). *Systematic and representative design of psychological experiments with results in physical and social perception*. Berkeley: University of California Press.

Bryant, F. B., & Veroff, J. (1982). The structure of psychological well-being: A socio-historical analysis. *Journal of Personality and Social Psychology, 43,* 653–673.

Buck, J. N. (1948). The H-T-P Technique: A qualitative and quantitative scoring manual. *Journal of Clinical Psychology, 4,* 319–396.

Buckhout, R. (1975). Nearly 2000 witnesses can be wrong. *Social Action and the Law, 2,* 7.

Buckhout, R. (1980). Eyewitness identification and psychology in the courtroom. In G. Cooke (Ed.), *The role of the forensic psychologist*. Springfield, IL: Charles C Thomas.

Budman, S. H., Cooley, S., Demby, A., Koppenaal, G., Koslof, J., & Powers, T. (1996). A model of time-effective group psychotherapy for patients with personality disorders: The clinical model. *International Journal of Group Psychotherapy, 46,* 329–355.

Budman, S. H., & Gurman, A. S. (1983). The practice of brief therapy. *Professional Psychology: Research and Practice, 14,* 277–292.

Budman, S. H., & Gurman, A. S. (1988). *Theory and practice of brief therapy*. New York: Guilford Press.

Bugental, J. F. T. (1964). The person who is the psychotherapist. *Journal of Consulting Psychology, 28,* 272–277.

Bugental, J. F. T. (1965). *The search for authenticity*. New York: Holt, Rinehart and Winston.

Bugental, J. F. T. (1978). *Psychotherapy and process: The fundamentals of an existential-humanistic approach*. Reading, MA: Addison-Wesley.

Buhler, C. (1971). Basic theoretical concepts of humanistic psychology. *American Psychologist, 26,* 378–386.

Buhler, C., & Allen, M. (1971). *Introduction to humanistic psychology*. Pacific Grove, CA: Brooks/Cole.

Burke, M. J., & Normand, J. (1987). Computerized psychological testing: Overview and critique. *Professional Psychology: Research and Practice, 18,* 42–51.

Buros, O. K. (Ed.). (1972). *Seventh mental measurements yearbook*. Highland Park, NJ: Gryphon Press.

Butcher, J. N. (1971). *Objective personality assessment*. Morristown, NJ: General Learning Press.

Butcher, J. N. (1990). *MMPI-2 in psychological treatment*. New York: Oxford University Press.

Butcher, J. N. (1995a). *Clinical personality assessment: Practical approaches*. New York: Oxford University Press.

Butcher, J. N. (1995b). How to use computer-based reports. In J. N. Butcher (Ed.), *Clinical personality assessment: Practical approaches* (pp. 78–94). New York: Oxford University Press.

Butcher, J. N. (1995c). Interpretation of the MMPI-2. In L. E. Beutler & M. R. Berren (Eds.), *Integrative assessment of adult personality* (pp. 206–239). New York: Guilford Press.

Butcher, J. N. (1997). Introduction to the Special Section on Assessment in Psychological Treatment: A necessary step for effective intervention. *Psychological Assessment, 9,* 331–333.

Butcher, J. N., Dahlstrom, W. G., Graham, J. R., Tellegen, A., & Kaemmer, B. (1989). *Minnesota Multiphasic Personality Inventory MMPI-2: Manual for administration and scoring*. Minneapolis: University of Minnesota Press.

Butcher, J. N., Graham, J. R., & Ben-Porath, Y. S. (1995). Methodological problems and issues in MMPI, MMPI-2, and MMPI-A research. *Psychological Assessment, 7,* 320–329.

Butcher, J. N., Graham, J. R., Williams, C. L., & Ben-Porath, Y. S. (1990). *Development and use of the MMPI-2 content scales*. Minneapolis: University of Minnesota Press.

Butcher, J. N., & Hostetler, K. (1990). Abbreviating MMPI item administration: What can be learned from the MMPI for the MMPI-2? *Psychological Assessment: A Journal of Consulting and Clinical Psychology, 2,* 12–21.

Butcher, J. N., Kendall, P. C., & Hoffman, N. (1980). MMPI short forms: Caution. *Journal of Consulting and Clinical Psychology, 48,* 275–278.

Butcher, J. N., & Koss, M. P. (1978). Research on brief and crisis-oriented therapies. In S. L. Garfield & A. E. Bergin (Eds.), *Handbook of psychotherapy and behavior change* (2nd ed.). New York: Wiley.

Butcher, J. N., Williams, C. L., Graham, J. R., Archer, R., Tellegen, A., Ben-Porath, Y. S., & Kaemmer, B. (1992). *Minnesota Multiphasic Personality Inventory–Adolescent (MMPI-A): Manual for administration, scoring, and interpretation*. Minneapolis: University of Minnesota Press.

Butler, A. C., & Beck, A. T. (1996). Cognitive therapy for depression. *Clinical Psychologist, 49,* 6–7.

Butler, R. N., & Lewis, M. I. *(1982). Aging and mental health* (3rd ed.). St. Louis: C. V. Mosby.

Cahalan, D., Tamulonis, V., & Verner, H. W. (1947). Interviewer bias involved in certain types of opinion survey questions. *International Journal of Opinion and Attitude Research, 1,* 63–77.

Calhoun, K. S., Moras, K., Pilkonis, P. A., & Rehm, L. P. (1998). Empirically supported treatments: Implications for training. *Journal of Consulting and Clinical Psychology, 66,* 151–162.

Camic, P. M., & Knight, S. J. (1998). *Clinical handbook of health psychology: A practical guide to effective interventions.* Seattle: Hogrefe & Huber.

Campbell, D. T., & Stanley, J. C. (1963). Experimental designs for research on teaching. In N. L. Gage (Ed.), *Handbook of research on teaching.* Chicago: Rand McNally.

Campbell, M., Green, W. H., & Deutsch, S. I. (1985). *Child and adolescent psychopharmacology* (Vol. 2). Newbury Park, CA: Sage.

Campbell, S. B. (1989). Developmental perspectives. In T. H. Ollendick & M. Hersen (Eds.), *Handbook of child psychopathology* (2nd ed.). New York: Plenum Press.

Cannell, C. F., & Kahn, R. L. (1968). Interviewing. In G. Lindzey & E. Aronson (Eds.), *The handbook of social psychology* (2nd ed.). Reading, MA: Addison-Wesley.

Caplan, G. (Ed.). (1961). *Prevention of mental disorders in children. New* York: Basic Books.

Caplan, B. M., & Romans, S. (1997). Assessment of spatial abilities. In G. Goldstein, P. D. Nussbaum, & S. R. Beers (Eds.), *Neuropsychology* (pp. 379–419). New York: Plenum Press.

Caplan, G. (1964). *Principles of preventive psychiatry.* New York: Basic Books.

Caplan, G. (1970). *The theory and practice of mental health consultation.* New York: Basic Books.

Caplan, N., & Nelson, S. D. (1973). On being useful: The nature and consequences of psychological research on social problems. *American Psychologist, 28,* 199–211.

Caplan, R. D., Vinokur, A. D., & Price, R. H. (1997). From job loss to reemployment: Field experiments in prevention-focused coping. In G. W. Albee & T. P. Gullotta (Eds.), *Primary prevention works* (pp. 341–379). Thousand Oaks, CA: Sage.

Carlson, J., Sperry, L., & Lewis, J. A. (1997). *Family therapy: Ensuring treatment efficacy.* Pacific Grove, CA: Brooks/Cole.

Carlson, R. E. (1972, May). *The current status of judgmental techniques in industry.* Paper presented at the symposium Alternatives to Paper and Pencil Personnel Testing, University of Pittsburgh.

Carr, M. A., Sweet, J. J., & Rossini, E. (1986). Diagnostic validity of the Luria-Nebraska Neuropsychological Test Battery–Children's Revision. *Journal of Consulting and Clinical Psychology, 54,* 354–358.

Cartwright, D. S. (1956). Note on "Changes in psychoneurotic patients with and without psychotherapy." *Journal of Consulting Psychology, 20,* 403–404.

Cartwright, D. S., Kirtner, W. L., & Fiske, D. W. (1963). Method factors in changes associated with psychotherapy. *Journal of Abnormal and Social Psychology, 66,* 164–175.

Casey, R. J., & Berman, J. S. (1985). The outcome of psychotherapy with children. *Psychological Bulletin, 98,* 388–400.

Casriel, D. (1971). The dynamics of Synanon. In R. W. Siroka, E. K. Siroka, & G. A. Schloss (Eds.), *Sensitivity training and group encounter.* New York: Grosset and Dunlap.

Cattell, P. (1947). *The measurement of intelligence of infants and young children.* New York: Psychological Corporation.

Cattell, R. B. (1965). *The scientific analysis of personality.* Baltimore: Penguin.

Cattell, R. B. (1987). *Intelligence: Its structure, growth and action.* Amsterdam: North-Holland.

Cautela, J. R. (1967). Covert sensitization. *Psychological Reports, 20,* 459–468.

Cavaness, W. (1977). Incidence of cranial cerebral trauma in the United States. *Transamerican Neurological Association, 102,* 136–138.

Centers for Disease Control and Prevention. (1994, November 18). Surveillance for selected tobacco use behaviors: United States, 1900–1994. *CDC surveillance summaries. Morbidity and Mortality Weekly Report, 43,* Number SS3.

Centers for Disease Control and Prevention. (1998, December). *HIV/AIDS Surveillance Report, 10*(2), 1–43.

Chambless, D. L. (1996). In defense of dissemination of empirically supported psychological interventions. *Clinical Psychology: Science and Practice, 3,* 230–235.

Chambless, D. L., Baker, M., Baucom, D. H., Beutler, L. E., Calhoun, K. S., Crits-Christoph, P., Dauito, A., DeRubeis, R., Detweiler, J., Haaga, D. A. F., Johnson, S. B., McCurry, S., Mueser, K. T., Pope, K. S., Sanderson, W. C., Shoham, V., Stickle, T., Williams, D., & Woody, S. R. (1998). Update on empirically validated therapies: II. *The Clinical Psychologist, 51,* 3–16.

Chambless, D. L., Caputo, G. C., Bright, P., & Gallagher, R. (1984). Assessment of fear in agoraphobics: The body sensations questionnaire and the agoraphobic cognitions questionnaire. *Journal of Consulting and Clinical Psychology, 52,* 1090–1097.

Chambless, D. L., Sanderson, W. C, Shoham, V., Bennett Johnson, S., Pope. K. S., Crits-Christoph, P., Baker, M., Johnson, B., Woody, S. R., Sue, S., Beutler, L., Williams, D. A., & McCurry, S. (1996).

An update on empirically validated therapies. *Clinical Psychologist, 49,* 5–18.

Chapman, L. J., & Chapman, J. P. (1967). Genesis of popular but erroneous psychodiagnostic observations. *Journal of Abnormal Psychology, 72,* 193–204.

Chapman, L. J., & Chapman, J. P. (1969). Illusory correlation as an obstacle to the use of valid psychodiagnostic signs. *Journal of Abnormal Psychology, 74,* 271–280.

Chapman, L. J., & Chapman, J. P. (1985). Psychosis proneness. In M. Alpert (Ed.), *Controversies in schizophrenia* (pp. 157–174). New York: Guilford Press.

Chase, M. (1975). The impact of correctional programs: Absconding. In R. Moos (Ed.), *Evaluating correctional and community environments.* New York: Wiley.

Chesney, M.A. (1993). Health psychology in the 21st century: Acquired immunodeficiency syndrome as a harbinger of things to come. *Health Psychology, 12,* 259–268.

Chipeur, H. M., Rovine, M., & Plomin, R. (1990). LISREL modelling: Genetic and environmental influences on IQ revisited. *Intelligence, 14,* 11–29.

Chodorkoff, B. (1954). Self-perception, perceptual defense, and adjustment. *Journal of Abnormal and Social Psychology, 49,* 508–512.

Christensen, A., & Jacobson, N. S. (1994). Who (or what) can do psychotherapy? The status and challenge of nonprofessional therapies. *Psychological Science, 5,* 8–14.

Cicchetti, D. V. (1994). Guidelines, criteria, and rules of thumb for evaluating normed and standardized instruments in psychology. *Psychological Assessment, 6,* 284–290.

Ciminero, A. R., Calhoun, K. S., & Adams, H. E. (Eds.). (1986). *Handbook of behavioral assessment.* New York: Wiley-Interscience.

Clark, L. A., & Watson, D. (1995). Constructing validity: Basic issues in objective scale development. *Psychological Assessment, 7,* 309–319.

Clark, M. M. (1986). Personal therapy: A review of empirical research. *Professional Psychology: Research and Practice, 17,* 541–543.

Clay, R. A. (1998). Mental health professions vie for position in the next decade. *APA Monitor, 29*(9), 20–21.

Cleckley, H. (1964). *The mask of sanity* (4th ed.). St. Louis, MO: Mosby.

Clum, G. A., & Bowers, T. G. (1990). Behavior therapy better than placebo treatments: Fact or artifact? *Psychological Bulletin, 107,* 110–113.

Coates, T. J., & Thoresen, C. E. (1981). Treating obesity in children and adolescents: Is there any hope? In J. M. Ferguson & C. B. Taylor (Eds.), *The comprehensive handbook of behavioral medicine* (Vol. 2). New York: Spectrum.

Cohen, J. (1960). A coefficient of agreement for nominal scales. *Educational and Psychological Measurement, 20,* 37–46.

Cohen, S., & Herbert, T. B. (1996). Health psychology: Psychological factors and physical disease from the perspective of human psychoneuroimmunology. *Annual Review of Psychology, 47,* 113–142.

Colby, K. M. (1951). *A primer for psychotherapists.* New York: Ronald Press.

Comas-Diaz, L. (1992). The future of psychotherapy with ethnic minorities. *Psychotherapy, 29,* 88–94.

Combs, A. W., & Snygg, D. (1959). *Individual behavior.* New York: Harper and Row.

Committee on Ethical Guidelines for Forensic Psychologists. (1991). Specialty guidelines for forensic psychologists. *Law and Human Behavior, 15,* 655–665.

Committee on Women in Psychology. (1989). If sex enters into the psychotherapy relationship. *Professional Psychology: Research and Practice, 20,* 112–115.

Condry, J. (1977). Enemies of exploration: Self-initiated versus other-initiated learning. *American Psychologist, 35,* 459–477.

Constantine, L. L. (1986). *Family paradigms: The practice of theory in family planning.* New York: Guilford Press.

Conte, H. R. (1986). Multivariate assessment of sexual dysfunction. *Journal of Consulting and Clinical Psychology, 54,* 149–157.

Corbishley, M. A., & Yost, E. B. (1995). Integrative assessment: A workbook. In L. E. Beutler & M. R. Berren (Eds.), *Integrative assessment of adult personality* (pp. 320–402). New York: Guilford Press.

Corsini, R. J. (1957). *Methods of group psychotherapy.* New York: McGraw-Hill.

Costa, P. T., Jr., & McCrae, R. R. (1988). Personality in adulthood: A six-year longitudinal study of self-reports and spouse ratings on the NEO Personality Inventory. *Journal of Personality and Social Psychology, 54,* 853–863.

Costa, P. T., Jr., & McCrae, R. R. (1990). Personality disorders and the five-factor model of personality. *Journal of Personality Disorders, 4,* 362–371.

Costa, P. T., Jr., & McCrae, R. R. (1992). *Revised NEO Personality Inventory (NEO-PI-R) and NEO Five Factor Inventory (NEO-FFI): Professional manual.* Odessa, FL: Psychological Assessment Resources.

Costa, P. T., Jr., & Widiger, T. A. (1994). *Personality disorders and the five-factor model of personality.* Washington, DC: American Psychological Association.

Costello, A. J., Edelbrock, C. S., Dulcan, M. K., Kalas, R., & Klaric, S. H. (1984). *Report on the NIMH Diagnostic Interview Schedule for Children (DIS-C).* Washington, DC: National Institute of Mental Health.

Cousins, N. (1976). Anatomy of an illness (as perceived by the patient). *New England Journal of Medicine, 195,* 1458–1463.

Cowen, E. L. (1967). An overview and directions for future work. In E. L. Cowen, E. A. Gardner, & M. Zax (Eds.), *Emergent approaches to mental health problems.* New York: Appleton-Century-Crofts.

Cowen, E. L. (1973). Social and community intervention. In P. H. Mussen & M. R. Rosenzweig (Eds.), *Annual review of psychology.* Palo Alto, CA: Annual Reviews.

Cowen, E. L. (1978). Some problems in community program evaluation research. *Journal of Consulting and Clinical Psychology, 46,* 792–805.

Cowen, E. L. (1982). Help is where you find it: Four informal helping groups. *American Psychologist, 37,* 385–395.

Cowen, E.L. (1983). Primary prevention in mental health: Past, present, and future. In R. D. Felner, L. A. Jason, J. N. Moritsugu, & S. S. Farber (Eds.), *Preventive psychology: Theory, research, and practice* (pp. 11–30). New York: Pergamon Press.

Cowen, E. L. (1991). In pursuit of wellness. *American Psychologist, 46,* 404–408.

Cowen, E. L., Hightower, A. D., Johnson, D. B., Sarno, M., & Weissberg, R. P. (1989). State-level dissemination of a program for early detection and prevention of school maladjustment. *Professional Psychology: Research and Practice, 20,* 309–314.

Craske, M. G., Rowe, M., Lewin, M., & Noriega-Dimitri, R. (1997). Interoceptive exposure versus breathing retraining within cognitive-behavioural therapy for panic disorder with agoraphobia. *British Journal of Clinical Psychology, 36,* 85–99.

Crits-Christoph, P. (1992). The efficacy of brief dynamic psychotherapy: A meta-analysis. *American Journal of Psychiatry, 149,* 151–158.

Crits-Christoph, P., Cooper, A., & Luborsky, L. (1988). The accuracy of therapists' interpretation and the outcome of dynamic psychotherapy. *Journal of Consulting and Clinical Psychology, 56,* 490–495.

Crits-Christoph, P., & Mintz, J. (1991). Implications of therapist effects for the design and analysis of comparative studies of psychotherapies. *Journal of Consulting and Clinical Psychology, 59,* 20–26.

Crockett, D., Clark, C., & Klonoff, H. (1987). Introduction: An overview of neuropsychology. In S. B. Filskov & T. J. Boll (Eds.), *Handbook of clinical neuropsychology.* New York: Wiley.

Cronbach, L. J. (1946). Response sets and test validity. *Educational and Psychological Measurement, 6,* 475–494.

Cronbach, L. J., & Meehl, P. E. (1955). Construct validity in psychological tests. *Psychological Bulletin, 52,* 281–302.

Cross, D. G., Sheehan, P. W., & Khan, J. A. (1982). Short- and long-term follow-up of clients receiving insight-oriented therapy and behavior therapy. *Journal of Consulting and Clinical Psychology, 50,* 103–112.

Cross, T. L., Bazron, B. J., Dennis, K. W., & Isaacs, M. R. (1989). *Toward a cultural competent system of care* (Vol. I). Washington, DC: Georgetown University Child Development Center.

Crow, W. J. (1957). The effect of training upon accuracy and variability in interpersonal perception. *Journal of Abnormal and Social Psychology, 55,* 355–359.

Culbertson, J. L. (1993). Clinical child psychology in the 1990s: Broadening our scope. *Journal of Clinical Child Psychology, 22,* 116–122.

Cummings, N. A. (1986). The dismantling of our health system: Strategies for the survival of psychological practice. *American Psychologist, 41,* 426–431.

Cummings, N. A. (1995). Impact of managed care on employment and training: A primer for survival. *Professional Psychology: Research and Practice, 26,* 10–15.

Curran, W. J. (1986). Ethical perspectives: Formal codes and standards. In W. J. Curran, A. L. McGarry, & S. A. Shah (Eds.), *Forensic psychiatry and psychology.* Philadelphia: F. A. Davis.

Cutler, B. L., & Penrod, S. D. (1995). *Mistaken identification: The eyewitness, psychology, and the law.* New York: Cambridge University Press.

Dadds, M. R., Holland, D. E., Laurens, K. R., Mullins, M., Barrett, P. M., & Spence, S. H. (1999). Early intervention and prevention of anxiety disorders in children: Results at 2-year follow-up. *Journal of Consulting and Clinical Psychology, 67,* 145–150.

Dahlstrom, W. G., Welsh, G. S., & Dahlstrom, L. E. (1972). *An MMPI handbook: Vol. 1. Clinical interpretation* (rev. ed.). Minneapolis: University of Minnesota Press.

Dahlstrom, W. G., Welsh, G. S., & Dahlstrom, L. E. (1975). *An MMPI handbook: Vol. 2. Research developments and applications.* Minneapolis: University of Minnesota Press.

Dale, R. H. I. (1988). State psychological associations, licensing criteria, and the "master's issue." *Professional Psychology: Research and Practice, 19,* 589–593.

D'Amato, R. C., Dean, R. S., & Holloway, A. F. (1987). A decade of employment trends in neuropsychology. *Professional Psychology: Research and Practice, 18,* 653–655.

Dana, R. H. (1988). Culturally diverse groups and MMPI interpretation. *Professional Psychology: Research and Practice, 19,* 490–495.

Dance, K. A., & Neufeld, R. W. J. (1988). Aptitude-treatment interaction research in the clinical setting: A review of attempts to dispel the "patient uniformity" myth. *Psychological Bulletin, 104,* 192–213.

Danish, S. J., & Smyer, M. A. (1981). Unintended consequences of requiring a license to help. *American Psychologist, 36,* 13–21.

Davison, G. C., & Lazarus, A. A. (1995). The dialectics of science and practice. In S. C. Hayes, V. M. Follette, R. M. Dawes, & K. E. Grady (Eds.), *Scientific standards of psychological practice: Issues and recommendations* (pp. 95–120). Reno, NV: Context Press.

Davison, G. C., & Neale, J. M. (1998). *Abnormal psychology* (7th ed.). New York: Wiley.

Davison, G. C., Robins, C., & Johnson, M. K. (1983). Articulated thoughts during simulated situations: A paradigm for studying cognition in emotion and behavior. *Cognitive Therapy and Research, 1,* 17–40.

Davison, G. C., & Stuart, R. B. (1975). Behavior therapy and civil liberties. *American Psychologist, 30,* 755–769.

Davison, G. C., & Wilson, G. T. (1973). Processes of fear reduction in systematic desensitization: Cognitive and social reinforcement factors in humans. *Behavior Therapy, 4,* 1–21.

Dawes, R. M. (1979). The robust beauty of improper linear models in decision making. *American Psychologist, 34,* 571–582.

Dawes, R. M. (1994). *House of cards: Psychology and psychotherapy built on myth.* New York: Free Press.

Dawes, R. M. (1999). Two methods for studying the incremental validity of a Rorschach variable. *Psychological Assessment, 11,* 297–302.

Dawes, R. M., Faust, D., & Meehl, P. E. (1989). Clinical versus actuarial judgment. *Science, 243,* 1668–1674.

DeBell, C., & Jones, R. D. (1997). Privileged communication at last: An overview of *Jaffe* v. *Redmond. Professional Psychology: Research and Practice, 28,* 559–566.

deCharms, R., Levy, J., & Wertheimer, M. (1954). A note on attempted evaluations of psychotherapy. *Journal of Clinical Psychology, 10,* 233–235.

Decker, J. B., & Stubblebine, J. M. (1972). Crisis intervention and prevention and psychiatric disability: A follow-up study. *American Journal of Psychiatry, 129,* 725–729.

DeLeon, P. H. (1988). Public policy and public service: Our professional duty. *American Psychologist, 43,* 309–315.

DeLeon, P. H., Fox, R. E., & Graham, S. R. (1991). Prescription privileges: Psychology's next frontier? *American Psychologist, 46,* 384–393.

DeLeon, P. H., Frank, R. G., & Wedding, D. (1995). Health policy and public policy: The political process. *Health Psychology, 14,* 493–499.

DeLeon, P. H., & Wiggins, J. G. (1996). Prescription privileges for psychologists. *American Psychologist, 51,* 225–229.

DeNelsky, G. Y. (1991). Prescription privileges for psychologists: The case against. *Professional Psychology: Research and Practice, 22,* 188–193.

DeNelsky, G. Y. (1996). The case against prescription privileges for psychologists. *American Psychologist, 51,* 207–212.

DeNelsky, G. Y., & Boat, B. W. (1986). A coping skills model of psychological diagnosis and treatment.

Professional Psychology: Research and Practice, 17, 322–330.

Dew, M. A., Bromet, E. J., Brent, D., & Greenhouse, J. B. (1987). A quantitative literature review of the effectiveness of suicide prevention centers. *Journal of Consulting and Clinical Psychology, 55,* 239–244.

Dicken, C., Bryson, R., & Kass, N. (1977). Companionship therapy: A replication in experimental community psychology. *Journal of Consulting and Clinical Psychology, 45,* 637–646.

Digman, J. M. (1990). Personality structure: Emergence of the five-factor model. *Annual Review of Psychology, 41,* 417–470.

DiLoreto, A. O. (1971). *Comparative psychotherapy: An experimental analysis.* Chicago: Aldine-Atherton.

DiMatteo, M. R., & DiNicola, D. D. (1982). *Achieving patient compliance: The psychology of the medical practitioner's role.* New York: Pergamon Press.

Dittmann, A. T. (1963). Kinesic research and therapeutic processes. In P. Knapp (Ed.), *Expression of the emotions in man.* New York: International Universities Press.

Dobson, K. S. (1989). A meta-analysis of the efficacy of cognitive therapy for depression. *Journal of Consulting and Clinical Psychology, 57,* 414–419.

Dohrenwend, B. P., & Dohrenwend, B. S. (1969). *Social status and psychological disorders.* New York: Wiley.

Doll, E. A. (1965). *Vineland Social Maturity Scale: Manual of directions* (rev. ed.). Minneapolis: American Guidance Service.

Dollard, J., & Miller, N. E. (1950). *Personality and psychotherapy.* New York: McGraw-Hill.

Dorken, H. (1975). Private professional sector innovations in higher education: The California School of Professional Psychology. *Journal of Community Psychology, 3,* 15–21.

Dorken, H., & Cummings, N. A. (1977). A school of psychology as innovation in professional education: The California School of Professional Psychology. *Professional Psychology, 8,* 129–148.

Dougherty, F. E. (1976). Patient-therapist matching for prediction of optimal and minimal outcome. *Journal of Consulting and Clinical Psychology, 44,* 889–897.

Drabman, R. S. (1985). Graduate training of scientist practitioner-oriented clinical psychologists: Where we can improve. *Professional Psychology: Research and Practice, 16,* 623–633.

Drotar, D. (1995). *Consulting with pediatricians: Psychological perspectives.* New York: Plenum Press.

Drotar, D. (1998). Training students for careers in medical settings: A graduate program in pediatric psychology. *Professional Psychology: Research and Practice, 29,* 402–404.

Druckman, D., Rozelle, R. M., & Baxter, J. C. (1982). *Nonverbal communication: Survey, theory, and research.* Newbury Park, CA: Sage.

Dublin, J. E. (1976). Gestalt therapy, existential-Gestalt therapy and/versus "Perlsism." In E. W. L. Smith (Ed.), *The growing edge of Gestalt therapy*. New York: Brunner/Mazel.

Duffy, K. G., & Wong, F. Y. (1996). *Community psychology*. Boston: Allyn and Bacon.

Dunn, L. M. (1959). *Peabody Picture Vocabulary Test Manual*. Minneapolis: American Guidance Service.

Dunn, L. M. (1965). *Expanded manual for the Peabody Picture Vocabulary Test*. Minneapolis: American Guidance Service.

Dunn, T. G., Lushene, R. E., & O'Neil, H. F., Jr. (1972). Complete automation of the MMPI and a study of its response latencies. *Journal of Consulting and Clinical Psychology, 39*, 381–387.

Durlak, J. A. (1979). Comparative effectiveness of paraprofessional and professional helpers. *Psychological Bulletin, 86*, 80–92.

Durlak, J. A. (1981). Evaluating comparative studies of paraprofessional and professional helpers: A reply to Nietzel and Fisher. *Psychological Bulletin, 89*, 566–569.

Durlak, J. A., & Wells, A. M. (1997). Primary prevention mental health programs for children and adolescents: A meta-analytic review. *American Journal of Community Psychology, 25*, 115–152.

Dush, D. M., Hirt, M. L., & Schroeder, H. E. (1983). Self-statement modification with adults: A meta-analysis. *Journal of Consulting and Clinical Psychology, 94*, 408–442.

Edelstein, B. A., & Berler, E. S. (1987). Interviewing and report writing. In C. L. Frame & J. L. Matson (Eds.), *Handbook of assessment in child psychopathology*. New York: Plenum Press.

Edwards, A. L., & Cronbach, L. J. (1952). Experimental design for research in psychotherapy. *Journal of Clinical Psychology, 8*, 51–59.

Ekehammar, B. (1974). Interactionism in personality from a historical perspective. *Psychological Bulletin, 81*, 1026–1048.

Ekman, P., & Friesen, W. V. (1969). The repertoire of nonverbal behavior: Categories, origins, usage, and coding. *Semiotica, 1*, 49–98.

Elder, J. P., Wildey, M., de Moor, C., Sallis, J. F., Jr., Eckhardt, L., Edwards, C., Erickson, A., Golbeck, A., Hovell, M., Johnston, D., Levitz, M. D., Molgaard, C., Young, R., Vito, D., & Woodruff, S. I. (1993). The long-term prevention of tobacco use among junior high school students: Classroom and telephone interventions. *American Journal of Public Health, 83*, 1239–1244.

Elkin, I., Gibbons, R. D., Shea, M. T., & Shaw, B. F. (1996). Science is not a trial (but it can sometimes be a tribulation). *Journal of Consulting and Clinical Psychology, 64*, 92–103.

Elliott, C. H. (1983). Behavioral medicine: Background and implications. In C. E. Walker (Ed.), *The handbook of clinical psychology: Theory, research, and practice* (Vol. 2). Pacific Grove, CA: Brooks/Cole.

Ellis, A. (1962). *Reason and emotion in psychotherapy*. New York: Lyle Stuart.

Ellis, A. (1977). A basic clinical theory of rational-emotive therapy. In A. Ellis & R. Grieger (Eds.), *Handbook of rational-emotive therapy*. New York: Springer.

Ellis, H. C. (1992). Graduate education in psychology: Past, present, and future. *American Psychologist, 47*, 570–576.

Emmelkamp, P. M. G. (1982). *Phobic and obsessive-compulsive disorders: Theory, research, and practice*. New York: Plenum Press.

Emmelkamp, P. M. G. (1994). Behavior therapy with adults. In A. E. Bergin & S. L. Garfield (Eds.), *Handbook of psychotherapy and behavior change* (4th ed.) (pp. 379–427). New York: Wiley.

Endler, N. S., & Okada, M. (1975). A multidimensional measure of trait anxiety: The S-R Inventory of General Trait Anxiousness. *Journal of Consulting and Clinical Psychology, 43*, 319–329.

Engel, G. L. (1977). The need for a new medical model: A challenge for biomedicine. *Science, 196*, 129–136.

English, H. B., & English, A. C. (1958). *A comprehensive dictionary of psychological and psychoanalytic terms*. New York: Longmans, Green.

Enright, J. B. (1970). Synanon: A challenge to middle-class views of mental health. In D. Adelson & B. L. Kadis (Eds.), *Community psychology and mental health*. Scranton, PA: Chandler.

Epstein, L. H., Valoski, A., Wing, R. R., & McCurley, J. (1994). Ten-year outcomes of behavioral family-based treatment for childhood obesity. *Health Psychology, 13*, 373–383.

Epstein, N., Schlesinger, S. E., & Dryden, W. (Eds.). (1988). *Cognitive behavioral therapy with families*. New York: Brunner/Mazel.

Epstein, S., & O'Brien, E. J. (1985). The person-situation debate in historical perspective. *Psychological Bulletin, 98*, 513–537.

Epting, F. R. (1984). *Personal construct counseling and psychotherapy*. Chichester, England: Wiley.

Erdman, H. P., Klein, M. H., & Greist, J. H. (1985). Direct patient computer interviewing. *Journal of Consulting and Clinical Psychology, 53*, 760–773.

Erikson, E. H. (1956). The problem of ego identity. *Journal of the American Psychoanalytic Association, 4*, 56–121.

Erikson, E. H. (1963). *Childhood and society* (2nd ed.). New York: Norton.

Erlich, J., & Riesman, D. (1961). Age and authority in the interview. *Public Opinion Quarterly, 25*, 39–56.

Evans, G. D., & Murphy, M. J. (1997). The practicality of predoctoral prescription training for psychologists: A survey of Directors of Clinical Training. *Professional Psychology: Research and Practice, 28*, 113–117.

Evans, R. I. (1976). Smoking in children: Developing a social psychological strategy of deterrence. *Preventive Medicine, 5,* 122–127.

Exner, J. E., Jr. (1974). *The Rorschach: A comprehensive system.* New York: Wiley.

Exner, J. E., Jr. (1983). Rorschach assessment. In I. B. Weiner (Ed.), *Clinical methods in psychology* (2nd ed.). New York: Wiley-Interscience.

Exner, J. E., Jr. (1991). *The Rorschach: A comprehensive system: Vol. 2. Interpretation* (2nd ed.). New York: Wiley.

Exner, J. E., Jr. (1993). *The Rorschach: A comprehensive system: Vol. 1. Basic foundations* (3rd ed.). New York: Wiley.

Exner, J. E., Jr. (1995). Why use personality tests? A brief historical view. In J. N. Butcher (Ed.), *Clinical personality assessment: Practical approaches* (pp. 10–18). New York: Oxford University Press.

Exner, J. E., Jr., & Exner, D. E. (1972). How clinicians use the Rorschach. *Journal of Personality Assessment, 36,* 402–408.

Eyde, L. D., Robertson, G. J. Krug, S. E., Moreland, K. L, Robertson, A. G., Shewan, C. M., Harrison, P. L., Porch, B. E., & Hammer, A. L. (1993). *Responsible test use: Case studies for assessing human behavior.* Washington, DC: American Psychological Association.

Eysenck, H. J. (1952). The effects of psychotherapy: An evaluation. *Journal of Consulting Psychology, 16,* 319–324.

Eysenck, H. J. (1965). The effects of psychotherapy. *International Journal of Psychiatry, 1,* 99–142.

Eysenck, H. J. (1966). *The effects of psychotherapy.* New York: International Science Press.

Fagan, S. C., Morgenstern, L. B., Petitta, A., Ward, R. E., Tilley, B. C., Marler, J. R., Levine, S. R., Broderick, J. P., Kwiatkowski, T. G., Frankel, M., Brott, T. G., & Walker, M. D. (1998). Cost-effectiveness of tissue plasminogen activator for acute ischemic stroke. NINDS rt-PA Stroke Study Group. *Neurology, 50,* 883–890.

Fairburn, C. G., Jones, R., Peveler, R. C., Carr, S. J., Solomon, R. A., O'Connor, M. E., Burton, J., & Hope, R. A. (1991). Three psychological treatments for bulimia nervosa: A comparative trial. *Archives of General Psychiatry, 48,* 463–469.

Fairweather, G. W. (1967). *Methods in experimental social innovation.* New York: Wiley.

Fairweather, G. W., Sanders, D. H., Maynard, H., & Cressler, D. L. (1969). *Community life for the mentally ill: An alternative to institutional care.* Chicago: Aldine-Atherton.

Farber, I. E. (1975). Sane and insane: Constructions and misconstructions. *Journal of Abnormal Psychology, 84,* 589–620.

Faris, R., & Dunham, H. (1939). *Mental disorders in urban areas.* Chicago: University of Chicago Press.

Farrell, A. D. (1989). Impact of computers on professional practice: A survey of current practices and attitudes. *Professional Psychology: Research and Practice, 20,* 172–178.

Farrell, A. D., Complair, P. S., & McCullough, L. (1987). Identification of target complaints by computer interview: Evaluation of the computerized assessment system for psychotherapy evaluation and research. *Journal of Consulting and Clinical Psychology, 55,* 691–700.

Faust, D. (1986). Research on human judgment and its application to clinical practice. *Professional Psychology: Research and Practice, 17,* 420–430.

Faust, D., Hart, K., & Guilmette, T. J. (1988). Pediatric malingering: The capacity of children to fake believable deficits on neuropsychological testing. *Journal of Consulting and Clinical Psychology, 56,* 578–582.

Faust, D., Hart, K., Guilmette, T. J., & Arkes, H. R. (1988). Neuropsychologists' capacity to detect adolescent malingerers. *Professional Psychology: Research and Practice, 19,* 508–515.

Felner, R. D., DuBois, D., & Adan, A. (1991). Community-based intervention and prevention: Conceptual underpinnings and progress towards a science of community intervention and evaluation. In C. E. Walker (Ed.), *Clinical psychology: Historical and research foundations* (pp. 459–510). New York: Plenum Press.

Felner, R. D., Jason, L. A., Moritsugu, J. N., & Farber, S. S. (Eds.). (1983). *Preventive psychology: Theory, research, and practice.* New York: Pergamon Press.

Fenichel, O. (1945). *The psychoanalytic theory of neurosis.* New York: Norton.

Fiedler, F. E. (1950). A comparison of therapeutic relationships in psychoanalytic, nondirective, and Adlerian therapy. *Journal of Consulting Psychology, 14,* 436–445.

Fiedler, F. E. (1951). Factor analyses of psychoanalytic, nondirective, and Adlerian therapeutic relationships. *Journal of Consulting Psychology, 15,* 32–38.

Finn, S. E., & Tonsager, M. E. (1992). Therapeutic effects of providing MMPI-2 test feedback to college students awaiting therapy. *Psychological Assessment, 4,* 278–287.

First, M. B. (1994). Computer-assisted assessment of DSM-III-R diagnoses. *Psychiatric Annals, 24*(1), 25–29.

First, M. B., Spitzer, R. L., Gibbon, M., & Williams, J. B. W. (1995). *Structured Clinical Interview for DSM-IV Axis I Disorders–Patient Edition (SCID-I/P, Version 2.0).* New York: Biometrics Research Department, New York State Psychiatric Institute.

Fiske, D. W. (1983). The meta-analytic revolution in outcome research. *Journal of Consulting and Clinical Psychology, 51,* 71–75.

Fitzgerald, B. J. (1958). Some relationships among projective tests, interview, and sociometric measures of dependent behavior. *Journal of Abnormal and Social Psychology, 56,* 199–204.

Fitzgerald, L. F., & Osipow, S. H. (1988). We have seen the future, but is it us? The vocational aspirations of graduate students in counseling psychology. *Professional Psychology: Research and Practice, 19,* 575–583.

Fitzgerald, R. V. (1973). *Conjoint marital therapy.* New York: Jason Aronson.

Flack, J. M., Amaro, H., Jenkins, W., Kunitz, S., Levy, J., Mixon, M., & Yu, E. (1995). Panel I: Epidemiology of minority health. *Health Psychology, 14,* 592–600.

Flaugher, R. L. (1978). The many definitions of test bias. *American Psychologist, 33,* 671–679.

Floyd, F. J., & Widaman, K. F. (1995). Factor analysis in the development and refinement of clinical assessment instruments. *Psychological Assessment, 7,* 286–299.

Flynn, J. R. (1987). Massive IQ gains in 14 nations: What IQ tests really measure. *Psychological Bulletin, 101,* 171–191.

Foa, E. B. (1996). The efficacy of behavioral therapy with obsessive-compulsives. *Clinical Psychologist, 49,* 19–22.

Follette, W. C., & Hayes, S. C. (1992). Behavioral assessment in the DSM era. *Behavioral Assessment, 14,* 293–295.

Forer, B. R. (1959). Psychological test reporting: A problem in communication between psychologists and psychiatrists. *Journal of Nervous and Mental Disease, 129,* 83–86.

Foster, A. (1951). Writing psychological reports. *Journal of Clinical Psychology, 7,* 195.

Foster, S. L., Bell-Dolan, D. J., & Burge, D. A. (1988). Behavioral observation. In A. S. Bellack & M. Hersen (Eds.), *Behavioral assessment: A practical handbook* (pp. 119–160). New York: Pergamon Press.

Foster, S. L., & Martinez, C. R., Jr. (1995). Ethnicity: Conceptual and methodological issues in child clinical research. *Journal of Clinical Child Psychology, 24,* 214–226.

Fowler, R. D., & Butcher, J. N. (1986). Critique of Matarazzo's view on computerized testing: All sigma and no meaning. *American Psychologist, 41,* 94–96.

Fox, R. E. (1982). The need for a reorientation of clinical psychology. *American Psychologist, 37,* 1051–1057.

Fox, R. E. (1988). Prescription privileges: Their implications for the practice of psychology. *Psychotherapy, 25,* 501–507.

Fox, R. E., & Barclay, A. (1989). Let a thousand flowers bloom: Or, weed the garden? *American Psychologist, 44,* 55–59.

Frank, G. H. (1976). Measures of intelligence and conceptual thinking. In I. B. Weiner (Ed.), *Clinical methods in psychology.* New York: Wiley-Interscience.

Frank, J. D. (1959a). The dynamics of the psychotherapeutic relationship. *Psychiatry, 22,* 17–39.

Frank, J. D. (1959b). Problems of controls in psychotherapy as exemplified by the psychotherapy research project of the Phipps Psychiatric Clinic. In E. A. Rubinstein & M. B. Parloff (Eds.), *Research in psychotherapy.* Washington, DC: American Psychological Association.

Frank, J. D. (1971). Therapeutic factors in psychotherapy. *American Journal of Psychotherapy, 25,* 350–361.

Frank, J. D. (1973). *Persuasion and healing* (rev. ed.). Baltimore: Johns Hopkins University Press.

Frank, J. D. (1979). The present status of outcome studies. *Journal of Consulting and Clinical Psychology, 47,* 310–316.

Frank, J. D. (1982). Therapeutic components shared by all psychotherapies. In J. H. Harvey & M. M. Parks (Eds.), *The Master Lecture Series: Vol. 1. Psychotherapy research and behavior change.* Washington, DC: American Psychological Association.

Frank, L. K. (1939). Projective methods for the study of personality. *Journal of Psychology, 8,* 389–413.

Frank, R. G., & Ross, M. J. (1995). The changing workforce: The role of health psychology. *Health Psychology, 14,* 519–525.

Frank, R. G., & VandenBos, G. R. (1994). Health care reform: The 1993–1994 evolution. *American Psychologist, 49,* 851–854.

Frankl, V. E. (1953). Logos and existence in psychotherapy. *American Journal of Psychotherapy, 7,* 8–15.

Frankl, V. E. (1960). Paradoxical intention: A logotherapeutic technique. *American Journal of Psychotherapy, 14,* 520–535.

Frankl, V. E. (1963). *Man's search for meaning* (rev. ed.). New York: Washington Square Press.

Frankl, V. E. (1965). *The doctor and the soul* (2nd ed.). New York: Knopf.

Frankl, V. E. (1967). *Psychotherapy and existentialism: Selected papers on logotherapy.* New York: Washington Square Press.

Franz, D., & Gross, A. M. (1998). Assessment of child behavior problems: Externalizing disorders. In A. S. Bellack & M. Hersen (Eds.), *Behavioral assessment: A practical handbook* (4th ed.) (pp. 361–377). Boston: Allyn & Bacon.

Freud, A. (1928). *Technique of child analysis.* New York: Nervous and Mental Disease Publishing.

Freud, A. (1946a). *The ego and the mechanisms of defense.* New York: International Universities Press. (Originally published 1936)

Freud, A. (1946b). *The psychoanalytic treatment of children.* New York: International Universities Press.

Freud, S. (1938). *The basic writings of Sigmund Freud.* New York: Modern Library.

Freud, S. (1953a). Fragments of an analysis of a case of hysteria. In *Standard edition* (Vol. 7). London: Hogarth Press. (Originally published 1905)

Freud, S. (1953b). *The interpretation of dreams. Standard edition* (Vols. 4 and 5). London: Hogarth Press. (Originally published 1900)

Freud, S. (1955). Analysis of a phobia in a five-year-old boy. In *Standard edition* (Vol. 10). London: Hogarth Press. (Originally published 1909)

Freud, S. (1959). The question of lay analysis. In *Standard edition* (Vol. 20). London: Hogarth Press. (Originally published 1926)

Freud, S. (1960). Psychopathology of everyday life. In *Standard edition* (Vol. 6). London: Hogarth Press. (Originally published 1901)

Freud, S. (1966). The dynamics of transference. In *Standard edition* (Vol. 12). London: Hogarth Press. (Originally published 1912)

Freud, S. (1967). On narcissism. In *Standard edition* (Vol. 14). London: Hogarth Press. (Originally published 1914)

Friedman, H. S., & Booth-Kewley, S. (1987). The "disease-prone personality": A meta-analytic view of the construct. *American Psychologist, 42,* 539–555.

Friedman, M., & Rosenman, R. H. (1974). *Type A behavior and your heart.* New York: Knopf.

Friedman, R., Sobel, D., Myers, P., Caudill, M., & Benson, H. (1995). Behavioral medicine, clinical health psychology, and cost offset. *Health Psychology, 14,* 509–518.

Fromm, E. (1941). *Escape from freedom.* New York: Holt, Rinehart and Winston.

Fromm, E. (1947). *Man for himself.* New York: Holt, Rinehart and Winston.

Fromm-Reichman, F. (1949). Recent advances in psychoanalytic therapy. In P. Mullahy (Ed.), *A study of interpersonal relations.* New York: Hermitage Press.

Fruzzetti, A. E., & Jacobson, N. S. (1991). Marital and family therapy. In M. Hersen, A. E. Kazdin, & A. Bellack (Eds.), *The clinical psychology handbook* (2nd ed.) (pp. 643–666). New York: Pergamon Press.

Fuselier, G. D. (1989). Hostage negotiation consultant: Emerging role for the clinical psychologist. *Professional Psychology: Research and Practice, 19,* 175–179.

Galanter, M. (1980). Young adult social drinkers: Another group at risk? *Alcoholism: Clinical and Experimental Research, 4,* 241–242.

Gallagher-Thompson, D., & Thompson, L. W. (1995). Efficacy of psychotherapeutic interventions with older adults. *Clinical Psychologist, 48,* 24–30.

Galton, F. (1879). Psychometric experiments. *Brain, 2,* 149–162.

Gamble, K. R. (1972). The Holtzman Inkblot Technique: A review. *Psychological Bulletin, 77,* 172–194.

Garb, H. N. (1984). The incremental validity of information used in personality assessment. *Clinical Psychology Review, 4,* 641–655.

Garb, H. N. (1988). Comment on "The study of clinical judgment: An ecological approach." *Clinical Psychology Review, 8,* 441–444.

Garb, H. N. (1989). Clinical judgment, clinical training, and professional experience. *Psychological Bulletin, 105,* 387–396.

Garb, H. N. (1997). Race bias, social class bias, and gender bias in clinical judgment. *Clinical Psychology: Science and Practice, 4,* 99–120.

Garb, H. N. (1998). *Studying the clinician: Judgment research and psychological assessment.* Washington, DC: American Psychological Association.

Garb, H. N., Florio, C. M., & Grove, W. M. (1998). The validity of the Rorschach and the Minnesota Multiphasic Personality Inventory: Results from meta-analyses. *Psychological Science, 9,* 402–404.

Garcia, L. T., & Griffitt, W. (1978). Impact of testimonial evidence as a function of witness characteristics. *Bulletin of the Psychonomic Society, 11,* 37–40.

Gardner, H. (1983). *Frames of mind: The theory of multiple intelligences.* New York: Basic Books.

Garfield, S. L. (1978). Research on client variables in psychotherapy. In S. L. Garfield & A. E. Bergin (Eds.), *Handbook of psychotherapy and behavior change: An empirical analysis* (2nd ed.). New York: Wiley.

Garfield, S. L. (1989). *The practice of brief psychotherapy.* Elmsford, NY: Pergamon Press.

Garfield, S. L. (1990). Issues and methods in psychotherapy process research. *Journal of Consulting and Clinical Psychology, 58,* 273–280.

Garfield, S. L. (1994). Research on client variables in psychotherapy. In A. E. Bergin & S. L. Garfield (Eds.), *Handbook of psychotherapy and behavior change* (4th ed.) (pp. 190–228). New York: Wiley.

Garfield, S. L. (1996). Some problems associated with "validated" forms of psychotherapy. *Clinical Psychology: Science and Practice, 3,* 218–229.

Garfield, S. L., & Bergin, A. E. (1971). Personal therapy, outcome, and some therapist variables. *Psychotherapy: Theory, Research, and Practice, 8,* 251–253.

Garfield, S. L., & Kurtz, R. (1976). Clinical psychologists in the 1970s. *American Psychologist, 31,* 1–9.

Gatchel, R. J., Baum, A., & Krantz, D. S. (1989). *An introduction to health psychology* (2nd ed.). New York: Random House.

Geer, J. H. (1965). The development of a scale to measure fear. *Behavior Research and Therapy, 3,* 45–53.

Gendlin, E. T. (1969). Focusing. *Psychotherapy: Theory, Research, and Practice, 6*(1).

Gendlin, E. T. (1981). *Focusing* (2nd ed.). New York: Bantam Books.

Gendlin, E. T. (1988). Carl Rogers (1902–1987). *American Psychologist, 43,* 127–128.

Gesten, E. L., & Jason, L. A. (1987). Social and community interventions. In M. R. Rosenzweig & L. W. Porter (Eds.), *Annual review of psychology*. Palo Alto, CA: Annual Reviews.

Gettinger, M., & Kratochwill, T. R. (1987). Behavioral assessment. In C. L. Frame & J. L. Matson (Eds.), *Handbook of assessment in childhood psychopathology*. New York: Plenum Press.

Getz, W. L., Fujita, B. N., & Allen, D. (1975). The use of paraprofessionals in crisis intervention: Evaluation of an innovative program. *American Journal of Community Psychology, 3,* 135–144.

Gibb, J. R. (1970). The effects of human relations training. In A. E. Bergin & S. L. Garfield (Eds.), *Handbook of psychotherapy and behavior change*. New York: Wiley.

Gilbert, L. A. (1987). Educating about gender and sexuality issues in graduate training: Introduction. *Professional Psychology: Research and Practice, 18,* 554.

Glass, D. C. (1977). *Behavior patterns, stress, and coronary disease*. Hillsdale, NJ: Erlbaum.

Gleitman, H. (1981). *Psychology*. New York: Norton.

Gochman, S. I., Allgood, B. A., & Geer, C. R. (1982). A look at today's behavior therapists. *Professional Psychology, 13,* 605–609.

Goldberg, L. R. (1959). The effectiveness of clinicians' judgments: The diagnosis of organic brain damage from the Bender-Gestalt Test. *Journal of Consulting Psychology, 23,* 25–33.

Goldberg, L. R. (1965). Diagnosticians versus diagnostic signs: The diagnosis of psychosis versus neurosis from the MMPI. *Psychological Monographs, 79*(9, Whole No. 602).

Goldberg, L. R. (1968). Seer over sign: The first good example? *Journal of Experimental Research in Personality, 3,* 168–171.

Goldberg, L. R. (1971). A historical survey of personality scales and inventories. In P. McReynolds (Ed.), *Advances in psychological assessment* (Vol. 2). Palo Alto, CA: Science and Behavior Books.

Goldberg, L. R. (1991). Human mind versus regression equation: Five contrasts. In D. Cicchetti & W. M. Grove (Eds.), *Thinking clearly about psychology* (Vol. 1, pp. 173–184). Minneapolis: University of Minnesota Press.

Goldberg, L. R. (1993). The structure of phenotypic personality traits. *American Psychologist, 48,* 26–34.

Golden, C. J. (1981). *Diagnosis and rehabilitation in clinical neuropsychology*. Springfield, IL: Charles C Thomas.

Golden, C. J. (1984). Neuropsychology. In R. J. Corsini (Ed.). *Encyclopedia of psychology*. New York: Wiley-Interscience.

Golden, C. J., Hammeke, T. A., & Purisch, A. O. (1978). Diagnostic validity of a standardized neuropsychological battery derived from Luria's neuropsychological tests. *Journal of Consulting and Clinical Psychology, 46,* 1258–1265.

Golden, C. J., & Kuperman, S. K. (1980). Graduate training in clinical neuropsychology. *Professional Psychology, 11,* 55–63.

Golden, C. J., Purisch, A. O., & Hammeke, T. A. (1985). *Luria-Nebaraska Neuropsychological Battery: Forms I and II Manual*. Los Angeles: Western Psychological Services.

Golden, C. J., Zillmer, E., & Spiers, M. (1992). *Neuropsychological assessment and intervention*. Springfield, IL: Charles C Thomas.

Golden, M. (1964). Some effects of combining psychological tests on clinical inferences. *Journal of Consulting Psychology, 28,* 440–446.

Goldfried, M. R. (1971). Systematic desensitization as training in self-control. *Journal of Consulting and Clinical Psychology, 37,* 228–234.

Goldfried, M. R. (1976). Behavioral assessment. In I. B. Weiner (Ed.), *Clinical methods in psychology*. New York: Wiley-Interscience.

Goldfried, M. R. (1984). Training the clinician as scientist professional. *Professional Psychology: Research and Practice, 15,* 477–481.

Goldfried, M. R., & Davison, G. C. (1976). *Clinical behavior therapy*. New York: Holt, Rinehart and Winston.

Goldfried, M. R., & Davison, G. C. (1994). *Clinical behavior therapy: Expanded edition*. New York: Wiley.

Goldfried, M. R., Greenberg, L. S., & Marmar, C. (1990). Individual psychotherapy: Process and outcome. In M. R. Rosenzweig & L. W. Porter (Eds.), *Annual review of psychology*. Palo Alto, CA: Annual Reviews.

Goldfried, M. R., & Kent, R. N. (1972). Traditional versus behavioral personality assessment: A comparison of methodological and theoretical assumptions. *Psychological Bulletin, 77,* 409–420.

Goldfried, M. R., Stricker, G., & Weiner, I. B. (1971). *Rorschach handbook of clinical and research applications*. Englewood Cliffs, NJ: Prentice-Hall.

Golding, S. L., & Rorer, L. G. (1972). Illusory correlation and subjective judgment. *Journal of Abnormal Psychology, 80,* 249–260.

Goldman, H. H., Skodol, A. E., & Lave, T. R. (1992). Revising Axis V for DSM-IV: A review of measures of social functioning. *American Journal of Psychiatry, 149,* 1148–1156.

Goldstein, A. P. (1962). *Therapist-patient expectancies in psychotherapy*. New York: Pergamon Press.

Goldstein, A. P. (1973). *Structured learning therapy: Toward a psychotherapy for the poor*. New York: Academic Press.

Goldstein, A. P., Heller, K., & Sechrest, L. B. (1966). *Psychotherapy and the psychology of behavior change*. New York: Wiley.

Goldstein, A. P., & Wolpe, J. (1972). Behavior therapy in groups. In H. I. Kaplan & B. J. Sadock (Eds.), *New models for group therapy*. New York: Dutton.

Goldstein, G. (1997). Neuropsychological assessment of adults. In G. Goldstein, P. D. Nussbaum, & S. R. Beers (Eds.), *Neuropsychology* (pp. 63–81). New York: Plenum Press.

Goldstein, G., & Shelly, C. (1984). Discriminative validity of various intelligence and neuropsychological tests. *Journal of Consulting and Clinical Psychology, 52*, 383–389.

Goldstein, K., & Scheerer, M. (1941). Abstract and concrete behavior. *Psychological Monographs, 53*(2).

Gomby, D. S., Larner, M. B., Stevenson, C. S., Lewit, E. M., & Behrman, R. E. (1995). Long-term outcomes of early childhood programs: Analysis and recommendations. In R. E. Behrman (Ed.), *The future of children: Long-term outcomes of early childhood programs* (Vol. 5, No. 3, pp. 6–24). Los Altos, CA: Center for the Future of Children.

Gondoli, D. M., & Jacob, T. (1993). Factor structure within and across three family assessment procedures. *Journal of Family Psychology, 6*, 278–289.

Good, G. E., Borst, T. S., & Wallace, D. L. (1994). Masculinity research: A review and critique. *Applied and Preventive Psychology, 3*, 3–14.

Good, G. E., Gilbert, L. A., & Scher, M. (1990). Gender aware therapy: A synthesis of feminist therapy and knowledge about gender. *Journal of Counseling and Development, 68*, 376–380.

Goodenough, F. L. (1926). *Measurement of intelligence by drawing*. Yonkers, NY: World Book.

Goodman, G. (1972). *Companionship therapy: Studies in structured intimacy*. San Francisco: Jossey-Bass.

Goodrich, T. J., Rampage, C., Ellman, B., & Halstead, K. (1988). *Feminist family therapy: A casebook*. New York: Norton.

Goodstein, L. D. (1988). Report of the Executive Vice President: 1987. *American Psychologist, 43*, 491–498.

Goodwin. A. H., & Sher, K. J. (1993). Effects of induced mood on diagnostic interviewing: Evidence for a mood and memory effect. *Psychological Assessment, 5*, 197–202.

Gordon, L. V. (1967). Clinical, psychometric, and work sample approaches in the prediction of success in Peace Corps training. *Journal of Applied Psychology, 51*, 111–119.

Gordon, R. (1983). An operational classification of disease prevention. *Public Health Reports, 98*, 107–109.

Gordon, R. (1987). An operational classification of disease prevention. In J. A. Steinberg & M. M. Silverman (Eds.), *Preventing mental disorders* (pp. 20–26). Rockville, MD: Department of Health and Human Services.

Goreczny, A. J., & Hersen, M. (1999). *Handbook of pediatric and health psychology*. Boston: Allyn & Bacon.

Gortner, E. T., Gollan, J. K., Dobson, K. S., & Jacobson, N. S. (1998). Cognitive-behavioral treatment for depression: Relapse prevention. *Journal of Consulting and Clinical Psychology, 66*, 377–384.

Gottesman, I. I. (1963). Genetic aspects of intelligent behavior. In N. Ellis (Ed.), *Handbook of mental deficiency: Psychological theory and research*. New York: McGraw-Hill.

Gottesman, I. I., & Prescott, C. A. (1989). Abuses of the MacAndrew MMPI Alcoholism Scale: A critical review. *Clinical Psychology Review, 9*, 223–242.

Gottlieb, M. C. (1990). Accusation of sexual misconduct: Assisting in the complaint process. *Professional Psychology: Research and Practice, 21*, 455–461.

Gottlieb, M. C., Sell, J. M., & Schoenfeld, L. S. (1988). Social/romantic relationships with present and former clients: State licensing board actions. *Professional Psychology: Research and Practice, 19*, 459–462.

Gottman, J. Notarius, C., Gonso, J., & Markman, H. (1976). *A couple's guide to communication*. Champaign, IL: Research Press.

Gottschalk, L. A., Fox, R. A., & Bates, D. E. (1973). A study of prediction and outcome in a mental health crisis clinic. *American Journal of Psychiatry, 130*, 1107–1111.

Gould, S. J. (1981). *The mismeasure of man*. New York: Norton.

Graham, J. R. (1990). *MMPI-2: Assessing personality and psychopathology*. New York: Oxford University Press.

Grant, I., & Adams, K. (Eds.). (1986). *Neuropsychological assessment of neuropsychiatric disorders*. New York: Oxford University Press.

Grayson, H. M., & Tolman, R. S. (1950). A semantic study of concepts of clinical psychologists and psychiatrists. *Journal of Abnormal and Social Psychology, 45*, 216–231.

Green, B. F., Jr. (1978). In defense of measurement. *American Psychologist, 33*, 664–670.

Greenberg, L., Elliott, R., & Lietaer, G. (1994). Research on experiential psychotherapies. In A. E. Bergin & S. L. Garfield (Eds.), *Handbook of psychotherapy and behavior change* (4th ed.) (pp. 509–539). New York: Wiley.

Greene, E., & Loftus, E. F. (1981). *When crimes are joined at trial: Institutionalized prejudice*. Paper presented at American Psychology-Law Society, Boston.

Greist, J. H. (1998). The computer as clinician assistant: Assessment made simple. *Psychiatric Services, 49*(4), 467–468, 472.

Greist, J. H., Klein, M. H., Erdman, H. P., Bires, J. K., Bass, S. M., Machtinger, P. E., & Kresge, D. G. (1987). Comparison of computer- and interview-administered versions of the Diagnostic Interview Schedule. *Hospital and Community Psychiatry, 38*, 1304–1311.

Grossberg, J. M. (1964). Behavior therapy: A review. *Psychological Bulletin, 62*, 73–88.

Guilford, J. P. (1959). *Personality.* New York: McGraw-Hill.

Guilford, J. P. (1967). *The nature of human intelligence.* New York: McGraw-Hill.

Gurin, G., & Gurin, P. (1970). Expectancy theory in the study of poverty. *Journal of Social Issues, 26,* 83–104.

Gurman, A. S. (1973). The effects and effectiveness of marital therapy: A review of outcome research. *Family Process, 12,* 145–170.

Gurman, A. S. (1977). Therapist and patient factors influencing the patient's perception of facilitative therapeutic conditions. *Psychiatry, 40,* 16–24.

Gutheil, T. G. (1998). *The psychiatrist as expert witness.* Washington, DC: American Psychiatric Press.

Guy, J. D., Poelstra, P. L., & Stark, M. J. (1989). Personal distress and therapeutic effectiveness: National survey of psychologists practicing psychotherapy. *Professional Psychology: Research and Practice, 20,* 48–50.

Guy, J. D., Stark, M. J., & Poelstra, P. L. (1988). Personal therapy for psychotherapists before and after entering professional practice. *Professional Psychology: Research and Practice, 19,* 474–476.

Guyll, M., & Contrada, R. J. (1998). Trait hostility and ambulatory cardiovascular activity: Responses to social interaction. *Health Psychology, 17,* 30–39.

Gynther, M. D. (1972). White norms and black MMPIs: A prescription for discrimination. *Psychological Bulletin, 78,* 386–402.

Gynther, M. D., & Green, S. B. (1980). Accuracy may make a difference, but does a difference make for accuracy? A response to Pritchard and Rosenblatt. *Journal of Consulting and Clinical Psychology, 48,* 268–272.

Gynther, M. D., & Gynther, R. A. (1976). Personality inventories. In I. B. Weiner (Ed.), *Clinical methods in psychology.* New York: Wiley-Interscience.

Haaga, D. A. F., & Davison, G. C. (1993). An appraisal of rational-emotive therapy. *Journal of Consulting and Clinical Psychology, 61,* 215–220.

Hadley, S. W., & Strupp, H. H. (1977). Evaluations of treatment in psychotherapy: Naivete or necessity? *Professional Psychology, 8,* 478–490.

Hagen, M. L. (1997). *Whores of the court: The fraud of psychiatric testimony and the rape of American justice.* New York: HarperCollins.

Hahlweg, K., & Markman, H. J. (1988). Effectiveness of behavioral techniques in preventing and alleviating marital distress. *Journal of Consulting and Clinical Psychology, 56,* 440–447.

Hahlweg, K., Revenstorf, D., & Schindler, L. (1984). Effects of behavioral marital therapy on couples' communication and problem-solving skills. *Journal of Consulting and Clinical Psychology, 52,* 553–566.

Haley, J. (1971). *Changing families: A family therapy reader.* New York: Grune and Stratton.

Haley, W. E., McDaniel, S. H., Bray, J. H., Frank, R. G., Heldring, M., Johnson, S. B., Lu, E. G., Reed, G. M.,

& Wiggins, J. G. (1998). Psychological practice in primary care settings: Practical tips for clinicians. *Professional Psychology: Research and Practice, 29,* 237–244.

Hall, G. C. N., & Malony, H. N. (1983). Cultural control in psychotherapy with minority clients. *Psychotherapy: Theory, Research, and Practice, 20,* 131–142.

Hall, H. V. (1982). Dangerousness predictions and the maligned forensic professional. *Criminal Justice and Behavior, 9,* 3–12.

Hall, R. V., Lund, D., & Jackson, D. (1968). Effects of teacher attention on study behavior. *Journal of Applied Behavior Analysis, 1,* 1–12.

Halstead, W. C. (1947). *Brain and intelligence.* Chicago: University of Chicago Press.

Hammond, K. R., & Allen, J. M. (1953). *Writing clinical reports.* Englewood Cliffs, NJ: Prentice-Hall.

Handelsman, M. M. (1990). Do written consent forms influence clients' impressions of therapists? *Professional Psychology: Research and Practice, 21,* 451–454.

Handelsman, M. M., & Galvin, M. D. (1988). Facilitating informed consent for outpatient psychotherapy: A suggested written format. *Professional Psychology: Research and Practice, 19,* 223–225.

Handler, L. (1988). Monkey see, monkey do: The prescription-writing controversy. *Clinical Psychologist, 41,* 44–49.

Hanley, I., & Gilhooly, M. (Eds.). (1986) *Psychological therapies for the elderly.* New York: New York University Press.

Hare-Mustin, R. T. (1983). An appraisal of the relationship between women and psychotherapy. *American Psychologist, 38,* 593–601.

Harris, D. B. (1963). *Children's drawings as measures of intellectual maturity: A revision and extension of the Goodenough Draw-A-Man Test.* New York: Harcourt, Brace and World.

Harrison, R. (1965). Thematic apperceptive methods. In B. B. Wolman (Ed.), *Handbook of clinical psychology.* New York: McGraw-Hill.

Hart, J. T., & Tomlinson, T. M. (Eds.). (1970). *New directions in client-centered therapy.* Boston: Houghton Mifflin.

Hartlage, L. C. (1987). Neuropsychology: Definition and history. In L. C. Hartlage, M. J. Asken, & J. L. Homshy (Eds.), *Essentials of neuropsychological assessment.* New York: Springer.

Hartmann, D. P., Roper, B. L., & Bradford, D. C. (1979). Some relationships between behavioral and traditional assessment. *Journal of Behavioral Assessment, 1,* 3–21.

Hartmann, H. (1939). Psychoanalysis and the concept of health. *International Journal of Psychoanalysis, 20,* 308–321.

Hartnett, J., Simonetta, L., & Mahoney, J. (1989). Perceptions of nonclinical psychologists toward clinical psychology and clinical psychologists. *Professional Psychology: Research and Practice, 20,* 187–189.

Hartshorne, H., & May, M. A. (1928). *Studies in deceit.* New York: Macmillan.

Hartshorne, H., May, M. A., & Maller, J. B. (1929). *Studies in service and self-control.* New York: Macmillan.

Hartshorne, H., May, M. A., & Shuttleworth, F. K. (1930). *Studies in the organization of character.* New York: Macmillan.

Hathaway, S. R. (1943). *The Minnesota Multiphasic Personality Inventory.* Minneapolis: University of Minnesota Press.

Hathaway, S. R. (1972). Where have we gone wrong? The mystery of the missing progress. In J. N. Butcher (Ed.), *Objective personality assessment: Changing perspectives.* New York: Academic Press.

Hathaway, S. R., & McKinley, J. C. (1943). *Manual for the Minnesota Multiphasic Personality Inventory.* New York: Psychological Corporation.

Hattie, J. A., Sharpley, C. F., & Rogers, H. J. (1984). Comparative effectiveness of professional and paraprofessional helpers. *Psychological Bulletin, 95,* 534–541.

Havens, R. A., Colliver, J. A., Dimond, R. E., & Wesley, R. M. (1982). Ph.D. and M.A. clinical psychologists and MSWs in public mental health settings: A nationwide comparison. *Professional Psychology, 13,* 654–660.

Hawkins, J. D., & Catalano, R. F. (1992). *Communities that care.* San Francisco: Jossey-Bass.

Hayes, S. C., & Heiby, E. (1996). Psychology's drug problem: Do we need a fix or should we just say no? *American Psychologist, 51,* 198–206.

Hayes, S. C., Nelson, R. O., & Jarrett, R. B. (1987). The treatment utility of assessment: A functional approach to evaluating assessment quality. *American Psychologist, 42,* 963–974.

Haynes, S. N. (1998). The changing nature of behavioral assessment. In A. S. Bellack & M. Hersen (Eds.), *Behavioral assessment: A practical handbook* (4th ed.). (pp. 1–21). Boston: Allyn & Bacon.

Haynes, S. N., & O'Brien, W. H. (1990). Functional analysis in behavior therapy. *Clinical Psychology Review, 10,* 649–668.

Haynes, S. N., Richard, D. C. S., & Kubany, E. S. (1995). Content validity in psychological assessment: A functional approach to concepts and methods. *Psychological Assessment, 7,* 238–247.

Hazelrigg, M. D., Cooper, H. M., & Borduin, C. M. (1987). Evaluating the effectiveness of family therapies: An integrative review and analysis. *Psychological Bulletin, 101,* 428–442.

Heaton, R. K. (1981). *A manual for the card sorting test.* Odessa, FL: Psychological Assessment Resources.

Heaton, R. K., Baade, L. E., & Johnson, K. L. (1978). Neuropsychological test results associated with psychiatric disorders in adults. *Psychological Bulletin, 85,* 141–162.

Hebb, D. O. (1978). Open letter: To a friend who thinks the IQ is a social evil [Comment]. *American Psychologist, 33,* 1143–1144.

Heitler, J. B. (1976). Preparatory techniques in initiating expressive psychotherapy with lower-class, unsophisticated patients. *Psychological Bulletin, 83,* 339–352.

Heller, K. (1990). Social and community intervention. In M. R. Rosenzweig & L. W. Porter (Eds.), *Annual review of psychology.* Palo Alto, CA: Annual Reviews.

Heller, K., & Monahan, J. (1977). *Psychology and community change.* Pacific Grove, CA: Brooks/Cole.

Heller, K., Price, R. H., Reinharz, S., Riger, S., & Wandersman, A. (1984). *Psychology and community change: Challenges of the future.* Pacific Grove, CA: Brooks/Cole.

Helmes, E., & Reddon, J. R. (1993). A perspective on developments in assessing psychopathology: A critical review of the MMPI and MMPI-2. *Psychological Bulletin, 113,* 453–471.

Henderson, D., & Gillespie, R. D. (1950). *A text-book of psychiatry for students and practitioners* (7th ed.). Oxford: Oxford University Press.

Henggeler, S.W. (1994). A consensus: Conclusions of the APA Task Force Report on innovative models of mental health services for children, adolescents, and their families. *Journal of Clinical Child Psychology, 23* (Suppl.), 3–6.

Henricks, W. H., & Stiles, W. B. (1989). Verbal processes on psychological call-in programs: Comparisons with other help-intended interactions. *Professional Psychology: Research and Practice, 20,* 315–321.

Henry, B., Moffitt, T. E., Caspi, A., Langley, J., & Silva, P. A. (1994). On the "remembrance of things past": A longitudinal evaluation of the retrospective method. *Psychological Assessment, 6,* 92–101.

Henry, E. M., & Rotter, J. B. (1956). Situational influences on Rorschach responses. *Journal of Consulting Psychology, 20,* 457–462.

Henry, W. P., Strupp, H. H., Schacht, T. E., & Gaston, L. (1994). Psychodynamic approaches. In A. E. Bergin & S. L. Garfield (Eds.), *Handbook of psychotherapy and behavior change* (4th ed.) (pp. 467–508). New York: Wiley.

Herbert, D. L., Nelson, R. O., & Herbert, J. D. (1988). Effects of psychodiagnostic labels, depression, severity, and instructions on assessment. *Professional Psychology: Research and Practice, 19,* 496–502.

Herrnstein, R. J., & Murray, C. A. (1994). *The bell curve: Intelligence and class structure in American life.* New York: Free Press.

Herron, W. G. (1962). The process-reactive classification of schizophrenia. *Psychological Bulletin, 59,* 329–343.

Hershey, J. M., Kopplin, D. A., & Cornell, J. E. (1991). Doctors of psychology: Their career experiences and attitudes toward degree and training. *Professional Psychology: Research and Practice, 22,* 351–356.

Hess, A. K. (1999). Serving as an expert witness. In A. K. Hess & I. B. Weiner (Eds.), *The handbook of forensic psychology* (2nd ed.) (pp. 521–555). Danvers, MA: Wiley.

Hill, C. E. (1990). Exploratory in-session process research in individual psychotherapy: A review. *Journal of Consulting and Clinical Psychology, 58,* 288–294.

Hoag, M. J., & Burlingame, G. M. (1997). Evaluating the effectiveness of child and adolescent group treatment: A meta-analytic review. *Journal of Clinical Child Psychology, 26,* 234–246.

Hobbs, N. (1964). Mental health's third revolution. *American Journal of Orthopsychiatry, 34,* 822–833.

Hodges, K., Kline, J., Fitch, P., McKnew, D., & Cytryn, L. (1981). The Child Assessment Schedule: A diagnostic interview for research and clinical use. *Catalogue of Selected Documents in Psychology, 11,* 56.

Hokanson, J. E. (1983). *Introduction to the therapeutic process.* Reading, MA: Addison-Wesley.

Holden, W. W., Deichmann, M. M., & Levy, J. D. (1999). Empirically supported treatments in pediatric psychology: Recurrent pediatric headache. *Journal of Pediatric Psychology, 24,* 91–109.

Hollingshead, A. B., & Redlich, F. C. (1958). *Social class and mental illness: A community study.* New York: Wiley.

Hollon, S. D., & Beck, A. T. (1994). Cognitive and cognitive-behavioral therapies. In A. E. Bergin & S. L. Garfield (Eds.), *Handbook of psychotherapy and behavior change* (4th ed.) (pp. 428–466). New York: Wiley.

Holmes, D. S. (1974). The conscious control of thematic projection. *Journal of Consulting and Clinical Psychology, 42,* 323–329.

Holmes, T. H., & Rahe, R. H. (1967). The Social Readjustment Scale. *Journal of Psychosomatic Research, 11,* 213–218.

Holroyd, K. A., & Andrasik, F. (1982). A cognitive-behavioral approach to recurrent tension and migraine headache. In P. E. Kendell (Ed.), *Advances in cognitive-behavioral research and therapy* (Vol. 1). New York: Academic Press.

Holt, R. R. (1958). Clinical and statistical prediction: A reformulation and some new data. *Journal of Abnormal and Social Psychology, 56,* 1–12.

Holt, R. R., & Luborsky, L. (1958). *Personality patterns of psychiatrists* (Vols. 1 and 2). New York: Basic Books.

Holtzman, W. H. (1975). New developments in Holtzman Inkblot Technique. In P. McReynolds (Ed.), *Advances in psychological assessment* (Vol. 3). San Francisco: Jossey-Bass.

Holtzman, W. H., Thorpe, J. W., Swartz, J. D., & Herron, E. W. (1961). *Inkblot perception and personality: Holtzman Inkblot Technique.* Austin: University of Texas Press.

Holub, E. A., & Lee, S. S. (1990). Therapists' use of non-erotic physical contact: Ethical concerns. *Professional Psychology: Research and Practice, 21,* 115–117.

Honaker, L. M. (1988). The equivalency of computerized and conventional MMPI administration: A critical review. *Clinical Psychology Review, 8,* 561–577.

Hooper, S. R., & Hynd, G. W. (1993). The neuropsychological basis of disorders affecting children and adolescents: An introduction. *Journal of Clinical Child Psychology, 22,* 138–140.

Horney, K. (1945). *Our inner conflicts.* New York: Norton.

Horney, K. (1967). *Feminine psychology.* New York: Norton.

Horowitz, I. A., & Willging, T. E. (1984). *The psychology of law: Integrations and applications.* Boston: Little, Brown.

Horvath, P. (1988). Placebos and common factors in two decades of psychotherapy research. *Psychological Bulletin, 104,* 214–225.

Hothersall, D. (1984). *History of psychology* (2nd ed.). New York: McGraw-Hill.

House, J. S., Landis, K. R., & Umberson, D. (1988). Social relationships and health. *Science, 241,* 540–545.

Houts, A. C., & Krasner, L. (1980). Slicing the ethical Gordian knot: A response to Kitchener. *Journal of Consulting and Clinical Psychology, 48,* 8–10.

Huber, C. H., & Baruth, L. G. (1987). *Ethical, legal, and professional issues in the practice of marriage and family therapy.* Columbus, OH: Merrill.

Huber, P. W. (1993). *Galileo's revenge: Junk science in the courtroom.* New York: Basic Books.

Huessy, H. (1972). Tactics and targets in the rural setting. In S. E. Golann & C. Eisdorfer (Eds.), *Handbook of community mental health.* New York: Appleton-Century-Crofts.

Hunsley, J. (1988). Conceptions and misconceptions about the context of paradoxical therapy. *Professional Psychology: Research and Practice, 19,* 553–559.

Hunsley, J., & Bailey, J. M. (1999). The clinical utility of the Rorschach: Unfulfilled promises and an uncertain future. *Psychological Assessment, 11,* 266–277.

Hunt, R. G. (1960). Social class and mental illness: Some implications for clinical theory and practice. *American Journal of Psychiatry, 116,* 1065.

Hunt, W. A., & Matarazzo, J. D. (1970). Habit mechanisms in smoking. In W. A. Hunt (Ed.), *Learning mechanisms in smoking.* Chicago: Aldine-Atherton.

Hunt, W. A., Wittson, C. L., & Hunt, E. B. (1953). A theoretical and practical analysis of the diagnostic process. In P. H. Hoch & J. Zubin (Eds.), *Current problems in psychiatric diagnosis.* New York: Grune and Stratton.

Hunter, J. E., & Hunter, R. F. (1984). Validity and utility of alternative predictors of job performance. *Psychological Bulletin, 96,* 72–98.

Insel, P. M., & Moos, R. H. (1974). Psychological environments: Expanding the scope of human ecology. *American Psychologist, 29,* 179–188.

Institute of Medicine. (1994). *Summary: Reducing risks for mental disorders: Frontiers for preventive intervention research.* Washington, DC: National Academy Press.

Isaacs, K. S., & Haggard, E. A. (1966). Some methods used in the study of affect in psychotherapy. In L. A. Gottschalk & A. H. Auerbach (Eds.), *Methods of research in psychotherapy.* New York: Appleton-Century-Crofts.

Isaacs, M. R., & Benjamin, M. P. (1991). *Toward a cultural competent system of care* (Vol. 2). Washington, DC: Georgetown University Child Development Center.

Iscoe, I. (1982). Toward a viable community health psychology: Caveats from the experiences of the community mental health movement. *American Psychologist, 37,* 961–965.

Iscoe, I., & Harris, L. C. (1984). Social and community interventions. In M. R. Rosenzweig & L. W. Porter (Eds.), *Annual review of psychology.* Palo Alto, CA: Annual Reviews.

Jackson, D. D. (1957). The question of family homeostasis. *Psychiatric Quarterly Supplement, 31,* 79–90.

Jackson, D. D., & Weakland, J. H. (1961). Conjoint family therapy: Some considerations on theory, technique, and results. *Psychiatry, 24,* 30–45.

Jacobson, E. (1938). *Progressive relaxation.* Chicago: University of Chicago Press.

Jacobson, N. S., Follette, W. C., Revenstorf, D., Baucom, D. H., Hahlweg, K., & Margolin, G. (1984). Variability in outcome and clinical significance of behavioral marital therapy: A reanalysis of outcome data. *Journal of Consulting and Clinical Psychology, 52,* 497–504.

Jacobson, N. S., & Hollon, S. D. (1996). Cognitive-behavior therapy versus pharmacotherapy: Now that the jury's returned its verdict, it's time to present the rest of the evidence. *Journal of Consulting and Clinical Psychology, 64,* 74–80.

Jacobson, N. S., & Margolin, G. (1979). *Marital therapy: Strategies based on social learning and behavior exchange principles.* New York: Brunner/Mazel.

James, W. H. (1890). *The principles of psychology* (Vol. 1). New York: Holt, Rinehart and Winston.

Jampala, V., Sierles, F., & Taylor, M. (1988). The use of DSM-III in the United States: A case of not going by the book. *Comprehensive Psychiatry, 29,* 39–47.

Janicke, D. M., & Finney, J. W. (1999). Empirically supported treatments in pediatric psychology: Recurrent abdominal pain. *Journal of Pediatric Psychology, 24,* 115–127.

Janis, I. L. (1958). *Psychological stress.* New York: Wiley.

Jeffrey, N. A. (1998, January 5). A new balancing act for psychotherapy: Therapists opt for self-review of costs to keep outsiders at bay. *Wall Street Journal,* pp. B1, B6.

Jelalian, E., & Saelens, B. E. (1999). Empirically supported treatments in pediatric psychology: Pediatric obesity. *Journal of Pediatric Psychology, 24,* 223–248.

Jenkins v. *United States,* 307 F.2d 637 (D.C. Cir. 1962).

Jensen, J. P., Bergin, A. E., & Greaves, D. W. (1990). The meaning of eclecticism: New survey and analysis of components. *Professional Psychology: Research and Practice, 21,* 124–130.

Jesness, C. F. (1975). Comparative effectiveness of behavior modification and transactional analysis programs for delinquents. *Journal of Consulting and Clinical Psychology, 43,* 758–779.

Jessor, R., Liverant, S., & Opochinsky, S. (1963). Imbalance in need structure and maladjustment. *Journal of Abnormal and Social Psychology, 66,* 271–275.

Johnson, S. M., & Greenberg, L. S. (1985). Differential effects of experiential and problem-solving interventions in resolving marital conflict. *Journal of Consulting and Clinical Psychology, 53,* 175–184.

Johnson, S. M., Hunsley, J., Greenberg, L., & Schindler, D. (1999). Emotionally focused couples therapy: Status and challenges. *Clinical Psychology: Science and Practice, 6,* 67–79.

Johnson, W. R. (1981). Basic interviewing skills. In C. E. Walker (Ed.), *Clinical practice of psychology.* New York: Pergamon Press.

Johnstone, B., & Frank, R. G. (1995). Neuropsychological assessment in rehabilitation: Current limitations and applications. *NeuroRehabilitation, 5,* 75–86.

Jones, A. (1991). Psychological functioning in African Americans: A conceptual guide for use in psychotherapy. In R. L. Jones (Ed.), *Black psychology* (3rd ed.) (pp. 577–589). Berkeley, CA: Cobb & Henry.

Jones, B. P., & Butters, N. (1991). Neuropsychological assessment. In M. Hersen, A. E. Kazdin, & A. S. Bellack (Eds.), *The clinical psychology handbook* (2nd ed.) (pp. 406–429). New York: Pergamon Press.

Jones, M. C. (1924). The elimination of children's fears. *Journal of Experimental Psychology, 7,* 383–390.

Jones, R. R., Reid, J. B., & Patterson, G. R. (1975). Naturalistic observation in clinical assessment. In P. McReynolds (Ed.). *Advances in psychological assessment* (Vol. 3). San Francisco: Jossey-Bass.

Jourard, S. M. (1971). *Self-disclosure. An experimental analysis of the transparent self* New York: Wiley.

Kagehiro, D. K. (1990). Psycholegal research on the Fourth Amendment. *Psychological Science, 1,* 187–193.

Kahneman, D., & Tversky, A. (1973). On the psychology of prediction. *Psychological Review, 80,* 237–251.

Kamphaus, R. W. (1993). *Clinical assessment of children's intelligence: A handbook for professional practice.* Boston: Allyn & Bacon.

Kane, M. T. (1982). The validity of licensure examinations. *American Psychologist, 37,* 911–918.

Kane, R. L., Parsons, O. A., Goldstein, G., & Moses, J. A., Jr. (1987). Diagnostic accuracy of the Halstead-Reitan and Luria-Nebraska neuropsychological batteries: Performance of clinical raters. *Journal of Consulting and Clinical Psychology, 55,* 783–784.

Kanfer, F. H., & Phillips, J. S. (1970). *Learning foundations of behavior therapy.* New York: Wiley.

Kanfer, R., Eyberg, S., & Krahn, G. L. (1992). Interviewing strategies in child assessment. In C. E. Walker, & M. C. Roberts (Eds.), *Handbook of clinical child psychology* (2nd ed.) (pp. 49–62). New York: Wiley.

Kaplan, E., Fine, D., Morris, R., & Delis, D. C. (1991). *WAIS-R NI: Manual.* San Antonio, TX: Psychological Corporation.

Kaplan, L. M., & Reich, W. (1991). *Manual for Diagnostic Interview for Children and Adolescents–Revised (DICA-R).* St. Louis, MO: Washington University.

Kaplan, M. (1983). A woman's view of DSM-III. *American Psychologist, 38,* 786–792.

Kaslow, N. J., & Thompson, M. P. (1998). Applying the criteria for empirically supported treatments to studies of psychosocial interventions for child and adolescent depression. *Journal of Clinical Child Psychology, 27,* 146–155.

Kass, F., Spitzer, R. L., & Williams, J. B. (1983). An empirical study of the issue of sex bias in the diagnostic criteria of DSM-III Axis II personality disorders. *American Psychologist, 38,* 799–801.

Kassin, S. M., & Wrightsman, L. S. (1979). On the requirements of proof: The timing of judicial instruction and mock juror verdicts. *Journal of Personality and Social Psychology, 37,* 1877–1887.

Kassin, S. M., & Wrightsman, L. S. (1988). *The American jury on trial: Psychological perspectives.* New York: Hemisphere.

Katkin, E. S., & Hastrup, J. (1982). Psychophysiological methods in clinical research. In P. C. Kendall & J. N. Butcher (Eds.), *Handbook of research methods in clinical psychology.* New York: Wiley.

Katz, A. E. (1981). Self-help and mutual aid: An emerging social movement. *Annual Review of Sociology, 7,* 129–155.

Kaufman, A. S. (1990). *Assessing adolescent and adult intelligence.* Boston: Allyn & Bacon.

Kaufman, K. L., Holden, E. W., & Walker, C. E. (1989). Future directions in pediatric and clinical child psychology. *Professional Psychology: Research and Practice, 20,* 148–152.

Kausler, D. H. (1991). *Experimental psychology, cognition, and human aging* (2nd ed.). New York: Springer-Verlag.

Kazdin, A. E. (1977). *The token economy: A review and evaluation.* New York: Plenum Press.

Kazdin, A. E. (1978). Evaluating the generality of findings in analogue therapy research. *Journal of Consulting and Clinical Psychology, 46,* 673–686.

Kazdin, A. E. (1979). Nonspecific treatment factors in psychotherapy outcome research. *Journal of Consulting and Clinical Psychology, 47,* 846–851.

Kazdin, A. E. (1980). *Research design in clinical psychology.* New York: Harper and Row.

Kazdin, A. E. (1981). Drawing valid inferences from case studies. *Journal of Consulting and Clinical Psychology, 49,* 183–192.

Kazdin, A. E. (1985). Selection of target behaviors: The relationship of the treatment focus to clinical dysfunction. *Behavioral Assessment, 7,* 33–47.

Kazdin, A. E. (1987). Treatment of antisocial behavior in children: Current status and future directions. *Psychological Bulletin, 102,* 187–203.

Kazdin, A. E. (1988). *Child psychotherapy: Developing and identifying effective treatments.* Elmsford, NY: Pergamon Press.

Kazdin, A. E. (1990). Psychotherapy for children and adolescents. *Annual Review of Psychology, 41,* 21–54.

Kazdin, A. E. (1992). *Methodological issues and strategies in clinical research.* Washington, DC: American Psychological Association.

Kazdin, A. E. (1994). Methodology, design, and evaluation in psychotherapy research. In A. E. Bergin & S. L. Garfield (Eds.), *Handbook of psychotherapy and behavior change* (4th ed.) (pp. 19–71). New York: Wiley.

Kazdin, A. E. (1998). *Research design in clinical psychology* (3rd ed.). New York: Harper and Row.

Kazdin, A. E., & Bass, D. (1989). Power to detect differences between alternative treatments in comparative psychotherapy outcome research. *Journal of Consulting and Clinical Psychology, 57,* 138–147.

Kazdin, A. E., Bass, D., Ayers, W. A., & Rodgers, A. (1990). Empirical and clinical focus of child and adolescent psychotherapy research. *Journal of Consulting and Clinical Psychology, 58,* 729–740.

Kazdin, A. E., & Bootzin, R. R. (1972). The token economy: An evaluative review. *Journal of Applied Behavior Analysis, 5,* 343–372.

Kazdin, A. E., & Crowley, M. (1997). Moderators of treatment outcome in cognitively based treatment of antisocial children. *Cognitive Therapy and Research, 21,* 185–207.

Kazdin, A. E., & Weisz, J. R. (1998). Identifying and developing empirically supported child and adolescent treatments. *Journal of Consulting and Clinical Psychology, 66,* 19–36.

Keefe, R. S. E. (1995). The contribution of neuropsychology to psychiatry. *American Journal of Psychiatry, 152,* 6–15.

Keith-Spiegel, P., & Koocher, G. P. (1985). *Ethics in psychology: Professional standards and cases.* New York: Random House.

Kelly, E. L., & Fiske, D. W. (1951). *The prediction of performance in clinical psychology.* Ann Arbor: University of Michigan Press.

Kelly, G. A. (1955). *The psychology of personal constructs* (Vols. 1 and 2). New York: Norton.

Kelly, J. G., Snowden, L. R., & Munoz, R. F. (1977). Social and community interventions. In M. R. Rosenzweig & L. W. Porter (Eds.), *Annual review of psychology.* Palo Alto, CA: Annual Reviews.

Kempler, W. (1973). Gestalt therapy. In R. J. Corsini (Ed.), *Current psychotherapies.* Itasca, IL: Peacock.

Kendall, P. C. (1993). Cognitive-behavioral therapies with youth: Guiding theory, current status, and emerging developments. *Journal of Consulting and Clinical Psychology, 61,* 235–247.

Kendall, P. C. (1994). Treating anxiety disorders in youth: Results of a randomized clinical trial. *Journal of Consulting and Clinical Psychology, 62,* 100–110.

Kendall, P. C., & Butcher, J. N. (Eds.). (1982). *Handbook of research methods in clinical psychology.* New York: Wiley.

Kendall, P. C., & Hollon, S. D. (Eds.). (1979). *Cognitive behavioral interventions: Theory, research, and procedures.* New York: Academic Press.

Kendall, P. C., & Hollon, S. D. (Eds.). (1981). *Assessment strategies for cognitive-behavioral interventions.* New York: Academic Press.

Kendell, R. E. (1975). *The role of diagnosis in psychiatry.* Oxford, England: Blackwell Scientific.

Kent, R. N., & Foster, S. L. (1977). Direct observational procedures: Methodological issues in naturalistic settings. In A. R. Ciminero, K. S. Calhoun, & H. E. Adams (Eds.), *Handbook of behavioral assessment.* New York: Wiley.

Kernberg, O. F. (1973). Summary and conclusions of "Psychotherapy and psychoanalysis: Final report of the Menninger Foundation's Psychotherapy Research Project." *International Journal of Psychiatry, 11,* 62–77.

Kessler, M., & Albee, G. W. (1975). Primary prevention. In M. R. Rosenzweig & L. W. Porter (Eds.), *Annual review of psychology.* Palo Alto, CA: Annual Reviews.

Kessler, R. C., McGonagle, K. A., Zhao, S., Nelson, C. B., Hughes, M., Eshleman, S., Wittchen, H., & Kendler, K. S. (1994). Lifetime and 12-month prevalence of DSM-III-R psychiatric disorders in the United States. *Archives of General Psychiatry, 51,* 8–19.

Kiesler, C. A. (1977). The training of psychiatrists and psychologists. [Editorial], *American Psychologist, 32,* 107–108.

Kiesler, C. A., & Morton, T. L. (1988). Psychology and public policy in the "health care revolution." *American Psychologist, 43,* 993–1003.

Kiesler, D. J. (1966). Some myths of psychotherapy research and the search for a paradigm. *Psychological Bulletin, 65,* 110–136.

Kinney, J. M., Madsen, B., Fleming, T., & Haapala, D. A. (1977). Homebuilders: Keeping families together. *Journal of Consulting and Clinical Psychology, 45,* 667–683.

Kitchener, R. F. (1980). Ethical relativism and behavior therapy. *Journal of Consulting and Clinical Psychology, 48,* 1–7.

Klein, D. K. (1996). Preventing hung juries about therapy studies. *Journal of Consulting and Clinical Psychology, 64,* 81–87.

Klein, N. C., Alexander, J. F., & Parsons, B. V. (1977). Impact of family systems intervention on recidivism and sibling delinquency: A model of primary prevention and program evaluation. *Journal of Consulting and Clinical Psychology, 45,* 469–474.

Kleinmuntz, B. (1972). *Computers in personality assessment.* Morristown, NJ: General Learning Press.

Kleinmuntz, B. (1982). *Personality and psychological assessment.* New York: St. Martin's Press.

Kleinmuntz, B. (1990). Why we still use our heads instead of formulas: Toward an integrative approach. *Psychological Bulletin, 107,* 296–310.

Klerman, G. L., Weissman, M. M., Rounsaville, B. J., & Chevron, E. S. (1984). *Interpersonal psychotherapy of depression.* New York: Basic Books.

Klingman, A. (1987). A school-based emergency crisis intervention in a mass school disaster. *Professional Psychology: Research and Practice, 18,* 604–612.

Klopfer, W. (1960). *The psychological report.* New York: Grune and Stratton.

Klopfer, W. G., & Taulbee, E. S. (1976). Projective tests. In M. R. Rosenzweig & L. W. Porter (Eds.), *Annual review of psychology.* Palo Alto, CA: Annual Reviews.

Knapp, S., & VandeCreek, L. (1990). Application of the duty to protect HIV-positive patients. *Professional Psychology: Research and Practice, 21,* 161–166.

Knapp, S., & VandeCreek, L. (1997). *Jaffe v. Redmond:* The Supreme Court recognizes a psychotherapist-patient privilege in federal courts. *Professional Psychology: Research and Practice, 28,* 567–572.

Kneisel, P. J., & Richards, G. P. (1988). Crisis intervention after the suicide of a teacher. *Professional Psychology: Research and Practice, 19,* 165–169.

Knell, S. M. (1998). Cognitive-behavioral play therapy. *Journal of Clinical Child Psychology, 27,* 28–33.

Knight, B. (1986). *Psychotherapy with older adults.* Newbury Park, CA: Sage.

Knoff, H. M. (Ed.). (1986). *The assessment of child and adolescent personality.* New York: Guilford Press.

Kobak, K. A., Greist, J. H., Jefferson, J. W., & Katzelnick, D. J. (1996). Computer-assisted clinical rating scales: A review. *Psychopharmacology, 127,* 291–301.

Kobasa, S. C., & Maddi, S. R. (1977). Existential personality theory. In R. J. Corsini (Ed.), *Current personality theories.* Itasca, IL: Peacock.

Kohut, H. (1971). *The analysis of the self.* New York: International Universities Press.

Kohut, H. (1977). *The restoration of the self.* New York: International Universities Press.

Koocher, G. P. (1979). Credentialing in psychology: Close encounters with competence? *American Psychologist, 34,* 696–702.

Koocher, G. P., & Keith-Speigel, P. C. (1998). *Ethics in pyschology: Professional standards and cases* (2nd ed.). New York: Oxford University Press.

Kopel, S., & Arkowitz, H. (1975). The role of attribution and self-perception in behavior change: Implications for behavior therapy. *Genetic Psychological Monographs, 95,* 175–212.

Koppitz, E. M. (1968). *Psychological evaluation of children's human figure drawings.* New York: Grune and Stratton.

Korchin, S. J. (1976). *Modern clinical psychology.* New York: Basic Books.

Korchin, S. J., & Sands, S. H. (1983). Principles common to all psychotherapies. In C. E. Walker (Ed.), *The handbook of clinical psychology: Theory, research, and practice* (Vol. 1). Pacific Grove, CA: Brooks/Cole.

Korman, A. K. (1968). The prediction of managerial performance: A review. *Personnel Psychology, 21,* 295–322.

Korsch, B., & Negrete, V. (1972). Doctor-patient communication. *Scientific American, 227,* 66–78.

Koss, M. P., & Shiang, J. (1994). Research on brief psychotherapy. In A. E. Bergin & S. L. Garfield (Eds.), *Handbook of psychotherapy and behavior change* (4th ed.) (pp. 664–700). New York: Wiley.

Koss, M. P., Butcher, J. N., & Strupp, H. H. (1986). Brief psychotherapy methods in clinical research. *Journal of Consulting and Clinical Psychology, 54,* 60–67.

Kostlan, A. (1954). A method for the empirical study of psychodiagnosis. *Journal of Consulting Psychology, 18,* 83–88.

Kraepelin, E. (1913). *Lectures on clinical psychiatry.* London: Bailliere, Tindall, and Cox.

Kramer, J. H., & Delis, D. C. (1997). Neuropsychological assessment of memory. In G. Goldstein, P. D. Nussbaum, & S. R. Beers (Eds.), *Neuropsychology* (pp. 333–356). New York: Plenum Press.

Krantz, D. S., Grunberg, N. E., & Baum, A. (1985). Health psychology. In M. R. Rosenzweig & L. W. Porter (Eds.), *Annual review of psychology* (Vol. 36). Palo Alto, CA: Annual Reviews.

Krasner, L. (1963). *The therapist as a social reinforcer: Man or machine.* Paper presented at the meeting of the American Psychological Association, Philadelphia.

Krasner, L. (1971). The operant approach in behavior therapy. In A. E. Bergin & S. L. Garfield (Eds.), *Handbook of psychotherapy and behavior change.* New York: Wiley.

Krech, D. (1962). Cortical localization of function. In L. Postman (Ed.), *Psychology in the making.* New York: Knopf.

Kris, E. (1950). On preconscious mental processes. *Psychoanalytic Quarterly, 19,* 540–560.

Kroger, R. O., & Turnbull, W. (1975). Invalidity of validity scales: The use of the MMPI. *Journal of Consulting and Clinical Psychology, 43,* 48–55.

Kurke, M. I. (1980). Forensic psychology: A threat and a response. *Professional Psychology, 11,* 72–77.

Kusché, C. A., Cook, E. T., & Greenberg, M.T. (1993). Neuropsychological and cognitive functioning in children with anxiety, externalizing, and comorbid psychopathology. *Journal of Clinical Child Psychology, 22,* 172–195.

L'Abate, L., & McHenry, S. (1983). *Handbook of marital interventions.* New York: Grune and Stratton.

L'Abate, L., & Weinstein, S. E. (1987). *Structured enrichment programs for couples and families.* New York: Brunner/Mazel.

Ladkin, J. F., & Levine, L. (1976). Interpreting psychological test results to the hospitalized consumer. *Professional Psychology, 7,* 161–166.

Lafferty, P., Beutler, L. E., & Crago, M. (1989). Differences between more and less effective psychotherapists: A study of select therapist variables. *Journal of Consulting and Clinical Psychology, 57,* 76–80.

La Greca, A. M., & Stone, W. L. (1992). Assessing children through interviews and behavioral observations. In C. E. Walker & M. C. Roberts (Eds.), *Handbook of clinical child psychology* (2nd ed.) (pp. 63–83). New York: Wiley.

Lahey, B. B., Hart, E. L., Pliska, S., Applegate, B., & McBurnett, K. (1993). Neurophysiological correlates of conduct disorder: A rationale and review of research. *Journal of Clinical Child Psychology, 22,* 141–153.

Lahey, B. B., Hynd, G. W., Stone, P. A., Piacentini, J. C., & Frick, P. J. (1989). Neuropsychological test performance and the attention deficit disorders: Clinical utility of the Luria-Nebraska Neuropsychological Battery Children's Revision. *Journal of Consulting and Clinical Psychology, 57,* 112–116.

Lamb, D. H., Clark, C., Drumheller, P., Frizzell, K., & Surrey, L. (1989). Applying *Tarasoff* to AIDS-related psychotherapy issues. *Professional Psychology: Research and Practice, 20,* 37–43.

Lambert, L. E., & Wertheimer, M. (1988). Is diagnostic ability related to relevant training and experience? *Professional Psychology: Research and Practice, 19,* 50–52.

Lambert, M. J., & Bergin, A. E. (1983). Therapist characteristics and their contribution to psychotherapy outcome. In C. E. Walker (Ed.), *The handbook of clinical psychology: Theory, research, and practice* (Vol. 1). Pacific Grove, CA: Brooks/Cole.

Lambert, M. J., & Bergin, A. E. (1994). The effectiveness of psychotherapy. In A. E. Bergin & S. L. Garfield (Eds.), *Handbook of psychotherapy and behavior change* (4th ed.) (pp. 143–189). New York: Wiley.

Lambert, M. J., Christensen, E. R., & DeJulio, S. S. (Eds.). (1983). *The assessment of psychotherapy.* New York: Wiley.

Lambert, M. J., DeJulio, S. S., & Stein, D. M. (1978). Therapist interpersonal skills: Process, outcome, methodological considerations and recommendations for future research. *Psychological Bulletin, 85,* 467–489.

Lambert, M. J., Shapiro, D. A., & Bergin, A. E. (1986). The effectiveness of psychotherapy. In S. L. Garfield & A. E. Bergin (Eds.), *Handbook of psychotherapy and behavior change* (3rd ed.). New York: Wiley.

Lambert, N. (1981). Psychological evidence in *Larry P. v. Wilson Riles:* An evaluation by a witness for the defense. *American Psychologist, 36,* 937–952.

Lamiell, J. T. (1987). *The psychology of personality: An epistemological inquiry.* New York: Columbia University Press.

Landman, J. T., & Dawes, R. M. (1982). Psychotherapy outcome: Smith and Glass' conclusions stand up under scrutiny. *American Psychologist, 37,* 504–516.

Landy, F. J., & Trumbo, D. A. (1980). *Psychology of work behavior* (rev. ed.). Pacific Grove, CA: Brooks/Cole.

Lang, A. R., & Marlatt, G. A. (1982). Problem drinking: A social learning perspective. In R. J. Gatchel, A. Baum, & J. E. Singer (Eds.), *Handbook of psychology and health* (Vol. 1). Hillsdale, NJ: Erlbaum.

Lang, P. J., & Lazovik, A. D. (1963). Experimental desensitization of a phobia. *Journal of Abnormal and Social Psychology, 66,* 519–525.

Langer, E. J., & Rodin, J. (1976). The effects of choice and enhanced personal responsibility for the aged: A field experiment in an institutional setting. *Journal of Personality and Social Psychology, 34,* 191–198.

Lanyon, R. I., & Goodstein, L. D. (1982). *Personality assessment* (2nd ed.). New York: Wiley.

Larry P. v. Riles, 343 F. Supp. 1306 (N.D. Cal. 1972) (preliminary injunction), *affirmed,* 502F. 2d 963 (9th Cir. 1974), opinion issued No. C-71-2270 RFP (N.D. Cal. October 16, 1979).

Lasch, C. (1979). *The culture of narcissism: American life in an age of diminishing expectations.* New York: Norton.

Lassen, C. L. (1973). Effect of proximity on anxiety and communication in the initial psychiatric interview. *Journal of Abnormal Psychology, 81,* 226–232.

Laurent, J., Swerdlik, M., & Ryburn, M. (1992). Review of the validity research on the Stanford-Binet Intelligence Scale–Fourth Edition. *Psychological Assessment, 4,* 102–112.

Lavin, D. E. (1965). *The prediction of academic performance: A theoretical analysis and review of research.* New York: Russell Sage Foundation.

Lazarus, A. A. (1961). Group therapy of phobic disorders by systematic desensitization. *Journal of Abnormal and Social Psychology, 63,* 504–510.

Lazarus, A. A. (1971a). *Behavior therapy and beyond.* New York: McGraw-Hill.

Lazarus, A. A. (1971b). Where do behavior therapists take their troubles? *Psychological Reports, 28,* 349–350.

Lazarus, A. A. (1975). Multimodal behavioral therapy. In G. M. Gazda (Ed.), *Basic approaches to group psychotherapy and group counseling* (2nd ed.). Springfield, IL: Charles C Thomas.

Lazarus, A. A. (1980). Toward delineating some causes of change in psychotherapy. *Professional Psychology, 11,* 863–870.

Lazarus, A. A., & Davison, G. C. (1971). Clinical innovation in research and practice. In A. E. Bergin & S. L. Garfield (Eds.), *Handbook of psychotherapy and behavior change: An experimental analysis.* New York: Wiley.

Lazarus, R. S. (1984). Puzzles in the study of daily hassles. *Journal of Behavioral Medicine, 7,* 375–389.

Lefcourt, H. M. (1982). *Locus of control: Current trends in theory and research* (2nd ed.). Hillsdale, NJ: Erlbaum.

Lehman, A. K., & Salovey, P. (1990). Psychotherapist orientation and expectations for liked and disliked patients. *Professional Psychology: Research and Practice, 21,* 385–391.

Lehrer, P. M., Carr, R., Sargunaraj, D., & Woolfolk, R. L. (1994). Stress management techniques: Are they all equivalent, or do they have specific effects? *Biofeedback and Self-Regulation, 19,* 353–401.

Leitenberg, H., Agras, W. S., Barlow, D. H., & Oliveau, D. C. (1969). Contribution of selective positive reinforcement and therapeutic instructions to systematic desensitization therapy. *Journal of Abnormal Psychology, 74,* 113–118.

Leonberger, F. T. (1989). The question of organicity: Is it still functional? *Professional Psychology: Research and Practice, 20,* 411–414.

Lesser, G. S. (1957). The relationship between overt and fantasy aggression as a function of maternal response to aggression. *Journal of Abnormal and Social Psychology, 55,* 218–222.

Levin, M. R., Ashmore-Callahan, S., Kendall, P. C., & Ichii, M. (1996). Treatment of separation anxiety disorder. In M. A. Reinecke et al. (Eds.), *Cognitive therapy with children and adolescents* (pp. 153–174). New York: Guilford Press.

Levine, M., & Perkins, D. V. (1997). *Principles of community psychology: Perspectives and applications* (2nd ed.). New York: Oxford University Press.

Levitsky, A., & Perls, F. S. (1970). The rules and games of Gestalt therapy. In J. Fagan & I. L. Sheperd (Eds.), *Gestalt therapy now.* Palo Alto, CA: Science and Behavior Books.

Levitt, E. E., & French, J. (1992). Projective testing of children. In C. E. Walker & M. C. Roberts (Eds.), *Handbook of clinical child psychology* (2nd ed.) (pp. 149–162). New York: Wiley.

Levy, D. A. (1989). Social support and the media: Analysis of responses by radio psychology talk show hosts. *Professional Psychology: Research and Practice, 20,* 73–78.

Levy, J. (1938). Relationship therapy. *American Journal of Orthopsychiatry, 8,* 64–69.

Levy, L. H. (1963). *Psychological interpretation.* New York: Holt, Rinehart and Winston.

Levy, L. H. (1984). The metamorphosis of clinical psychology: Toward a new charter as human services psychology. *American Psychologist, 39,* 486–494.

Lewin, K. (1936). *Principles of topological psychology.* New York: McGraw-Hill.

Lewit, E. M., & Baker, L. G. (1994). Race and ethnicity: Changes for children. *Future of Children, 4*(3), 134–144.

Lezak, M. D. (1995). *Neuropsychological assessment* (3rd ed.). New York: Oxford University Press.

Liberman, R. P. (1970). Behavioral approaches to family and couple therapy. *American Journal of Orthopsychiatry, 40,* 106–118.

Liberman, R. P. (1972). Behavioral modification of schizophrenia: A review. *Psychological Bulletin, 1,* 37–48.

Lidz, T., Cornelison, A., Fleck, S., & Terry, D. (1957a). Intrafamilial environment of the schizophrenic patient: 1. The father. *Psychiatry, 20,* 329–342.

Lidz, T., Cornelison, A., Fleck, S., & Terry, D. (1957b). Intrafamilial environment of schizophrenic patients: 2. Marital schism and marital skew. *American Journal of Psychiatry, 114,* 241–248.

Lieberman, M. A. (1976). Change induction in small groups. In M. R. Rosenzweig & L. W. Porter (Eds.), *Annual review of psychology.* Palo Alto, CA: Annual Reviews.

Lindsley, O. R., & Skinner, B. F. (1954). A method for the experimental analysis of the behavior of psychotic patients. *American Psychologist, 9,* 419–420.

Lindzey, G. (1961). *Projective techniques and cross-cultural research.* New York: Appleton-Century-Crofts.

Lindzey, G. (1965). Seer versus sign. *Journal of Experimental Research in Personality, 1,* 17–26.

Lindzey, G., Bradford, J., Tejessy, C., & Davids, A. (1959). Thematic Apperception Test: An interpretive lexicon for clinician and investigator. *Journal of Clinical Psychology Monograph Supplement* (No. 12).

Linscott, J., & DiGiuseppe, R. (1998). Cognitive assessment. In A. S. Bellack & M. Hersen (Eds.), *Behavioral assessment: A practical handbook* (4th ed.) (pp. 104–125). Boston: Allyn & Bacon.

Lipsky, M. J., Kassinove, H., & Miller, N. J. (1980). Effects of rational-emotive therapy, rational role reversal, and rational-emotive imagery on the emotional adjustment of community mental health center patients. *Journal of Consulting and Clinical Psychology, 48,* 366–374.

Littell, W. M. (1960). The Wechsler Intelligence Scale for Children: Review of a decade of research. *Psychological Bulletin, 57,* 132–156.

Little, K. B., & Shneidman, E. S. (1959). Congruencies among interpretations of psychological test and anamnestic data. *Psychological Monographs, 73* (6, Whole No. 476).

Liverant, S. (1960). Intelligence: A concept in need of reexamination. *Journal of Consulting Psychology, 24,* 101–110.

Liverant, S. (1963). Learning theory and clinical psychology. In E. Abt & B. F. Reiss (Eds.), *Progress in clinical psychology* (Vol. 5). New York: Grune and Stratton.

Livermore, J. M., Malmquist, C. P., & Meehl, P. E. (1968). On the justifications for civil commitment. *University of Pennsylvania Law Review, 117,* 75–96.

Locke, E. A. (1971). Is "behavior therapy" behavioristic? An analysis of Wolpe's psychotherapeutic methods. *Psychological Bulletin, 76,* 318–327.

Lodge, G. T. (1953). How to write a psychological report. *Journal of Clinical Psychology, 9,* 400–404.

Loehlin, J. C., Willerman, L., & Horn, J. M. (1988). Human behavior genetics. In M. R. Rosenzweig & L. W. Porter (Eds.), *Annual review of psychology.* Palo Alto, CA: Annual Reviews.

Loftus, E. F. (1979). *Eyewitness testimony.* Cambridge, MA: Harvard University Press.

Loftus, E. F. (1983). Silence is not golden. *American Psychologist, 38,* 564–572.

Loftus, E. F., Miller, D. G., & Burns, E. J. (1978). Semantic integration of verbal information into a visual memory. *Journal of Experimental Psychology, 4,* 19–31.

Logue, M. B., Sher, K. J., & Frensch, P. A. (1992). Purported characteristics of adult children of alcoholics: A possible "Barnum effect." *Professional Psychology: Research and Practice, 23,* 226–232.

Loh, W. D. (1984). *Social research in the judicial process: Cases, readings, and text.* New York: Russell Sage Foundation.

Lomont, J. F., & Brock, L. (1971). Cognitive factors in systematic desensitization. *Behavior Research and Therapy, 9,* 187–195.

London, P. (1964). *The modes and morals of psychotherapy.* New York: Holt, Rinehart and Winston.

Lopez, S. R., Grover, K. P., Holland, D., Johnson, M. J., Kain, C. D., Kanel, K., Mellins, C. A., & Rhyne, M. C. (1989). Development of culturally sensitive psychotherapists. *Professional Psychology: Research and Practice, 20,* 369–376.

Lorion, R. P. (1974). Patient and therapist variables in the treatment of low-income patients. *Psychological Bulletin, 81,* 344–354.

Lorr, M. (Ed.). (1966). *Explorations in typing psychotics.* Oxford: Pergamon Press.

Lorr, M. (1986). Classifying psychotics: Dimensional and categorical approaches. In T. Millon & G. L. Klerman (Eds.), *Contemporary directions in psychopathology: Toward the DSM-IV.* New York: Guilford Press.

Louttit, C. M. (1936). *Clinical psychology.* New York: Harper.

Lubin, B. (1976). Group therapy. In I. B. Weiner (Ed.), *Clinical methods in psychology.* New York: Wiley-Interscience.

Ludwick-Rosenthal, R., & Neufeld, R.W.J. (1988). Stress management during noxious medical procedures: An evaluative review of outcome studies. *Psychological Bulletin, 104,* 326–342.

Luria, A. R. (1973). *The working brain.* New York: Basic Books.

MacFarlane, J. W., & Tuddenham, R. D. (1951). Problems in the validation of projective techniques. In H. H. Anderson & G. L. Anderson (Eds.), *An introduction to projective techniques.* Englewood Cliffs, NJ: Prentice-Hall.

MacGregor, R., Ritchie, A. M., Serrano, A. C., & Schuster, F. P. (1964). *Multiple impact therapy with families.* New York: McGraw-Hill.

Machover, K. (1949). *Personality projection in the drawing of the human figure.* Springfield, IL: Charles C Thomas.

MacKenzie, K. R. (1994). Where is here and when is now? The adaptational challenge of mental health reform for group psychotherapy. *International Journal of Group Psychotherapy, 44,* 407–428.

MacLeod, R. B. (1964). Phenomenology: A challenge to experimental psychology. In T. W. Wann (Ed.), *Behaviorism and phenomenology: Contrasting bases for modern psychology.* Chicago: University of Chicago Press.

Maddi, S. R. (1989). *Personality theories: A comparative analysis* (5th ed.). Pacific Grove, CA: Brooks/Cole.

Maddux, J. E., Brawley, L., & Boykin, A. (1995). Self-efficacy and healthy behavior: Prevention, promotion, and detection. In J. E. Maddux (Ed.), *Self-efficacy, adaptation, and adjustment: Theory, research, and application* (pp. 173–202). New York: Plenum Press.

Magaro, P. (1969). A prescription treatment model based upon social class and pre-morbid adjustment. *Psychotherapy, 6,* 57–70.

Magoon, T. M., Golann, S. E., & Freeman, R. W. (1969). *Mental health counselors at work.* New York: Pergamon Press.

Mahl, G. F. (1968). Gestures and body movement in interviews. In J. Schlein (Ed.), *Research in psychotherapy* (Vol. 3). Washington, DC: American Psychological Association.

Mahoney, M. J. (1977a). Reflections on the cognitive-learning trend in psychotherapy. *American Psychologist, 32,* 5–13.

Mahoney, M. J. (1977b). Some applied issues in self-monitoring. In J. D. Cone & R. P. Hawkins (Eds.), *Behavioral assessment: New directions in clinical psychology.* New York: Brunner/Mazel.

Mahoney, M. J., & Arnkoff, D. B. (1979). Self-management. In 0. F. Pomerleau & J. P. Brady (Eds.), *Behavioral medicine: Theory and practice.* Baltimore: Williams and Wilkins.

Malan, D. H. (1973). The outcome problem in psychotherapy research: A historical review. *Archives of General Psychiatry, 29,* 719–729.

Maloney, M. P. (1985). *A clinician's guide to forensic assessment.* New York: Free Press.

Maloney, M. P., & Ward, M. P. (1976). *Psychological assessment: A conceptual approach.* New York: Oxford University Press.

Mann, J. M. (1991). Global AIDS: Critical issues for prevention in the 1990s. *International Journal of Health Sciences, 21,* 553–559.

Mann, P. A. (1978). *Community psychology: Concepts and applications.* New York: Free Press.

Manne, S. L., Redd, W. H., Jacobsen, P. B., Gorfinkle, K., Schorr, O., & Rapkin, B. (1990). Behavioral intervention to reduce child and parent distress during venipuncture. *Journal of Consulting and Clinical Psychology, 58,* 565–572.

Margolin, G. (1982). Ethical and legal considerations in marital and family therapy. *American Psychologist, 37,* 788–801.

Margraf, J., Ehlers, A., Roth, W. T., Clark, D. B., Sheikh, J., Agras, W. S., & Taylor, C. B. (1991). How "blind" are double-blind studies? *Journal of Consulting and Clinical Psychology, 59,* 184–187.

Mariotto, M. J., & Paul, G. L. (1974). A multimethod validation of the Inpatient Multidimensional Psychiatric Scale with chronically institutionalized patients. *Journal of Consulting and Clinical Psychology, 42,* 497–508.

Maris, R. W., & Connor, H. E. (1973). Do crisis services work? A follow-up of a psychiatric outpatient sample. *Journal of Health and Social Behavior, 14,* 311–322.

Markowitz, J. C. (1998). *Interpersonal psychotherapy.* Washington, DC: American Psychiatric Press.

Markus, H., & Worf, E. (1987). The dynamic self-concept: A social psychological perspective. In M. R. Rosenzweig & L. W. Porter (Eds.), *Annual review of psychology.* Palo Alto, CA: Annual Reviews.

Marlatt, G. A. (1975). *Addictions: A cognitive behavioral treatment approach* [Cassette recording]. New York: Guilford Press, BMA Audio Cassettes.

Marlatt, G. A., & Gordon, J. R. (1985). *Relapse prevention maintenance strategies in the treatment of addictive behaviors.* New York: Guilford Press.

Marmar, C. R. (1990). Psychotherapy process research: Progress, dilemmas, and future directions. *Journal of Consulting and Clinical Psychology, 58,* 265–272.

Marques, C. (1998). Manual-based treatment and clinical practice. *Clinical Psychology: Science and Practice, 5,* 400–402.

Martin, S. (1995). APA to pursue prescription privileges. *APA Monitor, 26,* 6.

Marx, A. J., Test, M. A., & Stein, L. I. (1973). Extra-hospital management of severe mental illness. *Archives of General Psychiatry, 29,* 505–511.

Mash, E. J., & Wolfe, D. A. (1999). *Abnormal child psychology.* Pacific Grove, CA: Wadsworth.

Masling, J. (1960). The influence of situational and interpersonal variables in projective testing. *Psychological Bulletin, 57,* 65–85.

Maslow, A. H. (1962). *Toward a psychology of being.* Princeton, NJ: Van Nostrand.

Maslow, A. H. (1965). Some basic propositions of a growth and self-actualization psychology. In G. Lindzey & C. Hall (Eds.), *Theories of personality: Primary sources and research.* New York: Wiley.

Maslow, A. H. (1968). *Toward a psychology of being* (2nd ed.). Princeton, NJ: Van Nostrand.

Masserman, J. H. (1943). *Behavior and neurosis: An experimental psycho-analytic approach to psychobiologic principles.* Chicago: University of Chicago Press.

Masten, A. S., & Coatsworth, J. D. (1998). The development of competence in favorable and unfavorable environments: Lessons from research on successful children. *American Psychologist, 53,* 205–220.

Masterpasqua, F. (1989). A competence paradigm for psychological practice. *American Psychologist, 44,* 1366–1371.

Masters, W. H., & Johnson, V. E. (1970). *Human sexual inadequacy.* Boston: Little, Brown.

Matarazzo, J. (1965). The interview. In B. Wolman (Ed.), *Handbook of clinical psychology.* New York: McGraw-Hill.

Matarazzo, J. D. (1972). *Wechsler's measurement and appraisal of adult intelligence* (5th and enlarged ed.). Baltimore: Williams and Wilkins.

Matarazzo, J. D. (1980). Behavioral health and behavioral medicine: Frontiers for a new health psychology. *American Psychologist, 35,* 807–817.

Matarazzo, J. D. (1983). The reliability of psychiatric and psychological diagnosis. *Clinical Psychology Review, 3,* 103–145.

Matarazzo, J. D. (1986). Computerized clinical psychological test interpretations: Unvalidated plus all mean and no sigma. *American Psychologist, 41,* 14–24.

Matarazzo, J. D. (1987). There is only one psychology, no specialties, but many applications. *American Psychologist, 42,* 893–903.

Matarazzo, J. D. (1990). Psychological assessment versus psychological testing. *American Psychologist, 45,* 999–1017.

Matarazzo, J. D., & Wiens, A. N. (1972). *The interview: Research on its anatomy and structure.* Chicago: Aldine-Atherton.

Mathews, A. M. (1971). Psychophysiological approaches to the integration of desensitization and related procedures. *Psychological Bulletin, 76,* 73–91.

Maton, K. (1988). Social support, organizational characteristics, psychological well-being, and group appraisal in three self-help group populations. *American Journal of Community Psychology, 16,* 53–78.

Mayne, T. J., Norcross, J. C., & Sayette, M. A. (1994a). Admission requirements, acceptance rates, and financial assistance in clinical psychology programs: Diversity across the practice-research continuum. *American Psychologist, 49,* 806–811.

Mayne, T. J., Norcross, J. C., & Sayette, M. A. (1994b). *Insider's guide to graduate programs in clinical psychology: 1994/1995 edition.* New York: Guilford Press.

Mays, D. T., & Franks, C. M. (1980). Getting worse: Psychotherapy or no treatment—the jury should still be out. *Professional Psychology, 11,* 78–92.

Mays, D. T., & Franks, C. M. (Eds.). (1985). *Negative outcomes in psychotherapy and what to do about it.* New York: Springer.

McBurnett, K., Harris, S. M., Swanson, J. M., Pfiffner, L. J., Tamm, L., & Freeland, D. (1993). Neuropsychological and physiological differentiation of inattention/overactivity and aggression/defiance symptom groups. *Journal of Clinical Child Psychology, 22,* 165–171.

McClelland, D. C. (1961). *The achieving society.* Princeton, NJ: Van Nostrand.

McConaughy, S. H. (1992). Objective assessment of children's behavioral and emotional problems. In C. E. Walker & M.C. Roberts (Eds.), *Handbook of clinical child psychology* (2nd ed.) (pp. 163–180). New York: Wiley.

McConnell, S. C. (1984). Doctor of Psychology degree: From hibernation to reality. *Professional Psychology: Research and Practice, 15,* 362–370.

McCord, J. (1978). A thirty-year follow-up of treatment effects. *American Psychologist, 33,* 284–289.

McCrae, R. R., & John, O. P. (1992). An introduction to the Five-Factor Model and its applications. *Journal of Personality, 60,* 175–215.

McFall, R. M. (1991). Manifesto for a science of clinical psychology. *Clinical Psychologist, 44,* 75–88.

McFall, R. M., & Lillesand, D. V. (1971). Behavior rehearsal with modeling and coaching in assertive training. *Journal of Abnormal Psychology, 77,* 313–323.

McGee, R. K. (1974). *Crisis intervention in the community.* Baltimore: University Park Press.

McGinley, L. (1998, September 15). U. S. health costs are expected to double by 2007. *Wall Street Journal,* pp. A2, A4.

McGlynn, F. D. (1971). Experimental desensitization under two conditions of induced expectancy. *Behavior Research and Therapy, 9,* 367–369.

McGue, M., Bouchard, T. J., Jr., Iacono, W. G., & Lykken, D. T. (1993). Behavioral genetics of cognitive ability: A life-span perspective. In R. Plomin & G. E. McClearn (Eds.), *Nature, nurture, and psychology* (pp. 59–76). Washington, DC: American Psychological Association.

McLean, P. D., Woody, S., Taylor, S., & Koch, W. J. (1998). Comorbid panic disorder and major depression: Implications for cognitive-behavioral therapy. *Journal of Consulting and Clinical Psychology, 66,* 240–247.

McMullen, S., & Rosen, R. C. (1979). Self-administered masturbation training in the treatment of primary orgasmic dysfunction. *Journal of Consulting and Clinical Psychology, 47,* 912–918.

McNair, D. M., Lorr, M., Young, H. H., Roth, I., & Boyd, R. W. (1964). A three-year follow-up of psychotherapy patients. *Journal of Clinical Psychology, 20,* 258–264.

McQuaid, E. L., & Nassau, J. H. (1999). Empirically supported treatments of disease-related symptoms in pediatric psychology: Asthma, diabetes, and cancer. *Journal of Pediatric Psychology, 24,* 305–328.

McReynolds, P. (1975). Historical antecedents of personality assessment. In P. McReynolds (Ed.), *Advances in psychological assessment* (Vol. 3). San Francisco: Jossey-Bass.

McReynolds, P. (1987). Lightner Witmer: Little-known founder of clinical psychology. *American Psychologist, 42,* 849–858.

McReynolds, P. (1989). Diagnosis and clinical assessment: Current status and major issues. In M. R. Rosenzweig & L. W. Porter (Eds.), *Annual review of psychology.* Palo Alto, CA: Annual Reviews.

McReynolds, P. (1996). Lightner Witmer: A centennial tribute. *American Psychologist, 51,* 237–240.

Meador, B. D., & Rogers, C. R. (1984). Client-centered therapy. In R. J. Corsini (Ed.), *Current psychotherapies* (2nd ed.). Itasca, IL: Peacock.

Medway, F. J., & Updike, J. F. (1985). Meta-analysis of consultation outcome studies. *American Journal of Community Psychology, 13,* 489–505.

Meehl, P. E. (1945). An investigation of a general normality or control factor in personality testing. *Psychological Monographs, 59*(4, Whole No. 274).

Meehl, P. E. (1954). *Clinical versus statistical prediction.* Minneapolis: University of Minnesota Press.

Meehl, P. E. (1956). Wanted—A good cookbook. *American Psychologist, 11,* 263–272.

Meehl, P. E. (1957). When shall we use our heads instead of the formula? *Journal of Counseling Psychology, 4,* 268–273.

Meehl, P. E. (1959). Some ruminations on the validation of clinical procedures. *Canadian Journal of Psychology, 13,* 102–128.

Meehl, P. E. (1965). Seer over sign: The first good example. *Journal of Experimental Research in Personality, 1,* 27–32.

Meehl, P. E. (1977). Why I do not attend case conferences. In P. E. Meehl (Ed.), *Psychodiagnosis: Selected papers* (pp. 225–302). New York: Norton. (First published by the University of Minnesota, 1973)

Meehl, P. E. (1986). Causes and effects of my disturbing little book. *Journal of Personality Assessment, 50,* 370–375.

Meehl, P. E., & Rosen, A. (1955). Antecedent probability and the efficiency of psychometric signs, patterns, or cutting scores. *Psychological Bulletin, 52,* 194–216.

Megargee, E. I. (1970). The prediction of violence with psychological tests. In C. Spielberger (Ed.), *Current topics in clinical and community psychology.* New York: Academic Press.

Megargee, E. 1. (1980). The prediction of dangerous behavior. In G. Cooke (Ed.), *The role of the forensic psychologist.* Springfield, IL: Charles C Thomas.

Mehlman, B. (1952). The reliability of psychiatric diagnosis. *Journal of Abnormal and Social Psychology, 47,* 577–578.

Mehrabian, A. (1972). *Nonverbal communication.* Chicago: Aldine-Atherton.

Mehta, M. (1990). A comparative study of family-based and patient-based behavioral management in obsessive-compulsive disorder. *British Journal of Psychiatry, 157,* 133–135.

Meichenbaum, D. (1977). *Cognitive-behavior modification: An integrative approach.* New York: Plenum Press.

Meichenbaum, D. (1996). Stress inoculation training for coping with stressors. *Clinical Psychologist, 49,* 4–7.

Meier, M. J. (1997). The establishment of clinical neuropsychology as a psychological specialty. In M. E. Maruish & J. A. Moses (Eds.), *Clinical neuropsychology: Theoretical foundations for practitioners* (pp. 1–31). Mahwah, NJ: LEA.

Melamed, B. G., & Siegel, L. J. (1975). Reduction of anxiety in children facing hospitalization and surgery by use of filmed modeling. *Journal of Consulting and Clinical Psychology, 43,* 511–521.

Mellsop, G., Varghese, F., Joshua, S., & Hicks, A. (1982). The reliability of Axis II of DSM-III. *American Journal of Psychiatry, 139,* 1360–1361.

Melton, G. B., Huss, M. T., & Tomkins, A. J. (1999). Training in forensic psychology and the law. In A. K. Hess & I. B. Weiner (Eds.), *The handbook of forensic psychology* (2nd ed.) (pp. 700–720). Danvers, MA: Wiley.

Meltzoff, J. (1984). Research training for clinical psychologists: Point-counterpoint. *Professional Psychology: Research and Practice, 15,* 203–209.

Meltzoff, J., & Kornreich, M. (1970). *Research on psychotherapy.* New York: Atherton.

Menditto, A. A., Beck, N. C., Stuve, P., Fisher, J. A., Stacy, M., Logue, M. B., & Baldwin, L. J. (1996). Effectiveness of clozapine and a social learning program for severely disabled psychiatric inpatients. *Psychiatric Services, 47,* 46–51.

Menniger, K. (1963). *The vital balance: The life process in mental health and illness.* New York: Viking Press.

Mental health: Does therapy help? (1995, November). *Consumer Reports,* pp. 734–739.

Meyer, A. E. (1981). The Hamburg Short Psychotherapy Comparison Experiment. *Psychotherapy and Psychosomatics, 35,* 81–207.

Meyer, G. J. (1997a). Assessing reliability: Critical corrections for a critical examination of the Rorschach Comprehensive System. *Psychological Assessment, 9,* 480–489.

Meyer, G. J. (1997b). Thinking clearly about reliability: More critical corrections regarding the Rorschach Comprehensive System. *Psychological Assessment, 9,* 480–489.

Meyer, G. J. (1999). Introduction to the Special Series on the utility of the Rorschach for clinical assessment. *Psychological Assessment, 11,* 235–239.

Meyer, J. M., & Stunkard, A. J. (1993). Genetics and human obesity. In A. J. Stunkard & T. A. Wadden (Eds.), *Obesity: Theory and therapy* (pp. 137–149). New York: Raven Press.

Meyerowitz, B. E., Richardson, J., Hudson, S., & Leedham, B. (1998). Ethnicity and cancer outcomes: Behavioral and psychosocial considerations. *Psychological Bulletin, 123,* 47–70.

Meyers, H. F., Kagawa-Singer, M., Kumanyika, S. K., Lex, B. W., & Markides, K. S. (1995). Behavioral risk factors related to chronic diseases in ethnic minorities. *Health Psychology, 14,* 613–621.

Miller, J. O., & Gross, S. J. (1973). Curvilinear trends in outcome research. *Journal of Consulting Psychology, 41,* 242–244.

Miller, N. E. (1983). Behavioral medicine: Symbiosis between laboratory and clinic. In M. R. Rosenzweig & L. W. Porter(Eds.), *Annual review of psychology* (Vol. 34). Palo Alto, CA: Annual Reviews.

Millon, T. (1975). Reflections on Rosenhan's "On being sane in insane places." *Journal of Abnormal Psychology, 84,* 456–461.

Minuchin, C. F. (1974). *Families and family therapy.* Cambridge, MA: Harvard University Press.

Mio, J. S., & Morris, D. R. (1990). Cross-cultural issues in psychology training programs: An invitation for discussion. *Professional Psychology: Research and Practice, 21,* 434–441.

Mischel, W. (1968). *Personality and assessment.* New York: Wiley.

Mischel, W. (1973). Toward a cognitive social learning reconceptualization of personality. *Psychological Review, 80,* 252–283.

Mischel, W. (1986). *Introduction to personality* (4th ed.). New York: Holt, Rinehart and Winston.

Mittenberg, W., Hammeke, T. A., & Rao, S. M. (1989). Intrasubtest scatter on the WAIS-R as a pathognomonic sign of brain injury. *Psychological Assessment: A Journal of Consulting and Clinical Psychology, 1,* 273–276.

Monahan, J. (1976). The prevention of violence. In J. Monahan (Ed.), *Community mental health and the criminal justice system.* New York: Pergamon Press.

Monroe, S. M., & Simons, A. D. (1991). Diathesis-stress theories in the context of life stress research: Implications for the depressive disorders. *Psychological Bulletin, 110,* 406–425.

Moos, R. H. (1975). *Evaluating and changing community settings.* Paper presented at the meeting of the American Psychological Association, Chicago.

Moos, R., & Moos, B. (1981). *Family environment scale manual.* Palo Alto, CA: Consulting Psychologist Press.

Mora, C. D., & Bornstein, R. A. (1997). Evaluation of cerebrovascular disease. In G. Goldstein, P. D. Nussbaum, & S. R. Beers (Eds.), *Neuropsychology* (pp. 171–186). New York: Plenum Press.

Moras, K., Telfer, L. A., & Barlow, D. H. (1993). Efficacy and specific effects data on new treatments: A case study strategy with mixed anxiety-depression. *Journal of Consulting and Clinical Psychology, 61,* 412–420.

Moreland, K. L. (1985). Validation of computer-based test interpretations: Problems and prospects. *Journal of Consulting and Clinical Psychology, 53,* 816–825.

Moreno, J. L. (1946). *Psychodrama* (2nd ed.) (Vol. 1). New York: Beacon House.

Moreno, J. L. (1947). *The theatre of spontaneity.* New York: Beacon House.

Moreno, J. L. (1959). Psychodrama. In S. Arieti (Ed.), *American handbook of psychiatry* (Vol. 2). New York: Basic Books.

Morey, L., & Ochoa, E. (1989). An investigation of adherence to diagnostic criteria: Clinical diagnosis of the DSM-III personality disorders. *Journal of Personality Disorders, 3,* 180–192.

Morgan, C. D., & Murray, H. A. (1935). A method for investigating fantasies: The Thematic Apperception Test. *Archives of Neurology and Psychiatry, 34,* 289–306.

Morrison, C. F. (1989). AIDS: Ethical implications for psychological intervention. *Professional Psychology: Research and Practice, 20,* 166–171.

Morrison, J. K. (1976). An argument for mental patient advisory boards. *Professional Psychology, 7,* 127–131.

Morrison, R. L. (1988). Structured interviews and rating scales. In A. S. Bellack & M. Hersen (Eds.), *Behavioral assessment: A practical handbook* (pp. 252–277). New York: Pergamon Press.

Mosak, H. H. (1984). Adlerian psychotherapy. In R. Corsini (Ed.), *Current psychotherapies* (3rd ed.). Itasca, IL: Peacock.

Mowrer, O. H. (Ed.). (1953). *Psychotherapy: Theory and research.* New York: McGraw-Hill.

Munroe, R. L. (1955). *Schools of psychoanalytic thought.* New York: Dryden Press.

Munsterberg, H. (1908). *On the witness stand.* New York: Doubleday, Page.

Murray, B. (1995). Master's program growth spurs educational concerns. *APA Monitor, 26,* 47.

Murray, D. M., Richards, P. S., Luepker, R. V., & Johnson, C. A. (1987). The prevention of cigarette smoking in children: Two- and three-year follow-up comparisons of four prevention strategies. *Journal of Behavioral Medicine, 10,* 596–611.

Murray, H. A. (1943). *Thematic Apperception Test manual.* Cambridge, MA: Harvard University Press.

Murray, H. A. (1938). *Explorations in personality: A clinical and experimental study of fifty men of college age.* New York: Oxford University Press.

Murstein, B. I. (1958). Nonprojective determinants of perception on the TAT. *Journal of Consulting Psychology, 22,* 195–198.

Murstein, B. I. (1963). *Theory and research in projective techniques (emphasizing the TAT).* New York: Wiley.

Mussen, P. H., & Scodel, A. (1955). The effects of sexual stimulation under varying conditions on TAT sexual responsiveness. *Journal of Consulting Psychology, 19,* 90.

Myers, J. K., & Schaffer, L. (1954). Social stratification and psychiatric practice. *American Sociological Review, 19,* 307–310.

Naranjo, C. (1970). Present-centeredness: Technique, prescription, and ideal. In J. Fagan & I. Sheperd (Eds.), *Gestalt therapy now.* Palo Alto, CA: Science and Behavior Books.

Nash, E. H., Hoehn-Saric, R., Battle, C. C., Stone, A. R., Imber, S. D., & Frank, J. D. (1965). Systematic preparation of patients for short-term psychotherapy: 2. Relation to characteristics of patient, therapist, and the psychotherapeutic process. *Journal of Nervous and Mental Disease, 140,* 388–399.

Nathan, P. E. (1998). Practice guidelines: Not ideal yet. *American Psychologist, 53,* 290–299.

Nathan, P. E., & Gorman, J. M. (1998). Treatments that work—and what convinces us they do. In P. E. Nathan & J. M. Gorman (Eds.), *A guide to treatments that work* (pp. 1–25). New York: Oxford University Press.

National Institute of Alcohol Abuse and Alcoholism. (1978). *Alcohol and health: Third report to Congress.* Washington, DC: U.S. Government Printing Office.

Neimeyer, R. A., & Neimeyer, G. J. (Eds.). (1987). *Personal construct therapy casebook.* New York: Springer.

Neisser, U. (1979). The concept of intelligence. In R. J. Sternberg & D. K. Dettermen (Eds.), *Human intelligence: Perspectives on its theory and measurement.* Norwood, NJ: Ablex.

Neisser, U., Boodoo, G., Bouchard, T. J., Jr., Boykin, A. W., Brody, N., Ceci, S. J., Halpern, D. F., Loehlin, J. C., Perloff, R., Sternberg, R. J., & Urbina, S. (1996). Intelligence: Knowns and unknowns. *American Psychologist, 51,* 77–101.

Newmark, C. S., Woody, G. G., Finch, A. J., Jr., & Ziff, D. R. (1980). MMPI short forms: A different perspective. *Journal of Consulting and Clinical Psychology, 48,* 279–283.

Nicholson, R. A., & Berman, J. S. (1983). Is follow-up necessary in evaluating psychotherapy? *Psychological Bulletin, 93,* 261–278.

Nickelson, D. W. (1995). The future of professional psychology in a changing health care marketplace: A conversation with Russ Newman. *Professional Psychology: Research and Practice, 26,* 366–370.

Nietzel, M. T., & Dillehay, R. C. (1986). *Psychological consultation in the courtroom.* New York: Pergamon Press.

Nietzel, M. T., & Fisher, S. G. (1981). Effectiveness of professional and paraprofessional helpers: A comment on Durlak. *Psychological Bulletin, 89,* 555–565.

Nietzel, M. T., Winett, R. A., MacDonald, M. L., & Davidson, W. S. (1977). *Behavioral approaches to community psychology.* New York: Pergamon Press.

Nisbett, R. E., & Ross, L. (1980). *Human inference: Strategies and shortcomings of social judgment.* Englewood Cliffs, NJ: Prentice Hall.

Noll, J. O. (1974). Needed—A bill of rights for clients. *Professional Psychology, 5,* 3–12.

Norcross, J. C., Karg, R. S., & Prochaska, J. O. (1997a). Clinical psychologists in the 1990s: Part I. *Clinical Psychologist, 50*(2), 4–9.

Norcross, J. C., Karg, R. S., & Prochaska, J. O. (1997b). Clinical psychologists in the 1990s: Part II. *Clinical Psychologist, 50*(3), 4–11.

Norcross, J. C., & Prochaska, J. O. (1982). A national survey of clinical psychologists: Characteristics and activities. *Clinical Psychologist, 35,* 1, 5–8.

Norcross, J. C., & Prochaska, J. O. (1988). A study of eclectic (and integrative) views revisited. *Professional Psychology Research and Practice, 19,* 170–174.

Norcross, J. C., Prochaska, J. O., & Gallagher, K. M. (1989a). Clinical psychologists in the 1980s: I. Demographics, affiliations, and satisfactions. *Clinical Psychologist, 42,* 29–39.

Norcross, J. C., Prochaska, J. O., & Gallagher, K. M. (1989b). Clinical psychologists in the 1980s: II. Theory, research, and practice. *Clinical Psychologist, 42,* 45–53.

Norcross, J. C., Sayette, M. A., Mayne, T. J., Karg, R. S., & Turkson, M. A. (1998). Selecting a doctoral program in professional psychology: Some comparisons among Ph.D. counseling, Ph.D. clinical, and Psy.D. clinical psychology programs. *Professional Psychology: Research and Practice, 29,* 609–614.

Novaco, R. W. (1977). Stress inoculation: A cognitive therapy for anger and its application to a case of depression. *Journal of Consulting and Clinical Psychology, 45,* 600–608.

Nunnally, J. C., & Bernstein, I. H. (1994). *Psychometric theory* (3rd ed.). New York: McGraw-Hill.

Oakland, T., & Glutting, J. J. (1990). Examiner observations of children's WISC-R test-related behaviors:

Possible socioeconomic status, race, and gender effects. *Psychological Assessment: A Journal of Consulting and Clinical Psychology, 2,* 86–90.

Office of Demographic, Employment, and Educational Research (ODEER), American Psychological Association. (1993). *Surveys of licensed psychologists, PhDs and PsyDs in clinical psychology, lists of professional schools, and characteristics of 1993 doctorate recipients in psychology.* Washington, DC: Author.

Ogloff, J. R. P. (1991). A comparison of insanity defense standards on juror decision making. *Law and Human Behavior, 15,* 509–531.

Olbrisch, M. E., Kurz, R. B., & Matarazzo, J. D. (1981). Internships in health psychology: Or bolder than Boulder. *Health Psychologist, 3*(1).

Olbrisch, M. E., & Sechrest, L. (1979). Educating health psychologists in traditional graduate training programs. *Professional Psychology, 10,* 589–596.

Ollendick, T. H., & Hersen, M. (1998). *Handbook of child psychopathology* (3rd ed.). Thousand Oaks, CA: Sage.

Ollendick, T. H., & King, N. J. (1998). Empirically supported treatments for children with phobic and anxiety disorders: Current status. *Journal of Clinical Child Psychology, 27,* 156–167.

Olson, R. P., Ganley, R., Devine, V. T., & Dorsey, G. C., Jr. (1981). Long-term effects of behavioral versus insight-oriented therapy with inpatient alcoholics. *Journal of Consulting and Clinical Psychology, 49,* 866–877.

Olson, D. H., Portner, J., & Lavee, Y. (1985). *FACES III.* Unpublished manuscript, Department of Family Social Science, University of Minnesota.

O'Malley, S. S., Foley, S. H., Rounsaville, B. J., Watkins, J. T., Sotsky, S. M., Imber, S. D., & Elkin, I. (1988). Therapist competence and patient outcome in interpersonal psychotherapy of depression. *Journal of Consulting and Clinical Psychology, 56,* 496–501.

Orford, J. (1992). *Community psychology: Theory and practice.* New York: Wiley.

Orne, M., & Wender, P. (1968). Anticipatory socialization for psychotherapy: Method and rationale. *American Journal of Psychiatry, 124,* 88–98.

Oskamp, S. (1965). Overconfidence in case-study judgments. *Journal of Consulting Psychology, 29,* 261–265.

OSS Assessment Staff. (1948). *Assessment of men: Selection of personnel for the Office of Strategic Services.* New York: Rinehart.

Overall, J. E., & Gorham, D. R. (1962). The brief psychiatric rating scale. *Psychological Reports, 10,* 799–812.

Overall, J. E., & Hollister, L. E. (1982). Decision rules for phenomenological classification of psychiatric patients. *Journal of Consulting and Clinical Psychology, 50,* 535–545.

Overholser, J. C., & Fine, M. A. (1990). Defining the boundaries of professional competence: Managing subtle cases of clinical competence. *Professional Psychology: Research and Practice, 21,* 462–469.

Ownby, R. L. (1987). *Psychological reports: A guide to report writing in professional psychology.* Brandon, VT: Clinical Psychology.

Pace, T. M., Chaney, J. M., Mullins, L. L., & Olson, R. A. (1995). Psychological consultation with primary care physicians: Obstacles and opportunities in the medical setting. *Professional Psychology: Research and Practice, 26,* 123–131.

Padawer-Singer, A. M., & Barton, A. H. (1975). The impact of pretrial publicity on jurors' verdicts. In R. J. Simon (Ed.), *The jury system in America.* Newbury Park, CA: Sage.

Paniagua, F. A. (1998). *Assessing and treating culturally diverse clients: A practical guide* (2nd ed.). Thousand Oaks, CA: Sage.

Parker, K. C. H. (1983). A meta-analysis of the reliability and validity of the Rorschach. *Journal of Personality Assessment, 47,* 227–231.

Parker, K. C. H., Hanson, R. K., & Hunsley, J. (1988). MMPI, Rorschach, and WAIS: A meta-analytic comparison of reliability, stability, and validity. *Psychological Bulletin, 103,* 367–373.

Parks, C. W., Jr., & Hollon, S. D. (1988). Cognitive assessment. In A. S. Bellack & M. Hersen (Eds.), *Behavioral assessment: A practical handbook* (pp. 161–212). New York: Pergamon Press.

Parloff, M. B. (1986). Placebo controls in psychotherapy research: A sine qua non or a placebo for research? *Journal of Consulting and Clinical Psychology, 54,* 79–87.

Parloff, M. B., Kelman, H. C., & Frank, J. D. (1954). Comfort, effectiveness, and self-awareness as criteria of improvement in psychotherapy. *American Journal of Psychiatry, 111,* 343–351.

Parloff, M. B., London, P., & Wolfe, B. (1986). Individual psychotherapy and behavior change. In M. R. Rosenzweig & L. W. Porter (Eds.), *Annual review of psychology* (Vol. 37). Palo Alto, CA: Annual Reviews.

Parsons, O. A. (1986). Overview of the Halstead-Reitan Battery. In T. Incagndi, G. Goldstein, & C. J. Golden (Eds.), *Clinical application of neuropsychological test batteries.* New York: Plenum Press.

Pasamanick, B., Dintz, S., & Lefton, M. (1959). Psychiatric orientation and its relation to diagnosis and treatment in a mental hospital. *American Journal of Psychiatry, 116,* 127–132.

Patterson, G. R. (1971). *Families: Applications of social learning to family life.* Champaign, IL: Research Press.

Patterson, G. R. (1977). Naturalistic observation in clinical assessment. *Journal of Abnormal Child Psychology, 5,* 307–322.

Patterson, G. R., & Forgatch, M. S. (1995). Predicting future clinical adjustment from treatment outcome and process variables. *Psychological Assessment, 7,* 275–285.

Paul, G. L. (1967). Strategy of outcome research in psychotherapy. *Journal of Consulting Psychology, 31,* 109–118.

Paul, G. L., & Lentz, R. J. (1977). *Psychosocial treatment of chronic mental patients: Milieu versus social learning programs.* Cambridge, MA: Harvard University Press.

Paul, G. L., & Shannon, D. T. (1966). Treatment of anxiety through systematic desensitization in therapy groups. *Journal of Abnormal Psychology, 71,* 124–135.

Pavkov, T. W., Lewis, D. A., & Lyons, J. S. (1989). Psychiatric diagnoses and racial bias: An empirical investigation. *Professional Psychology: Research and Practice, 20,* 364–368.

Pearl, A. (1970). The poverty of psychology—An indictment. In V. L. Allen (Ed.), *Psychological factors in poverty.* Chicago: Markham.

Pedersen, N. L., Plomin, R., Nesselroade, J. R., & McClearn, G. E. (1992). A quantitative genetic analysis of cognitive abilities during the second half of the life span. *Psychological Science, 3,* 346–353.

Pedersen, P. B., & Marsella, A. J. (1982). The ethical crisis for cross-cultural counseling and therapy. *Professional Psychology, 13,* 492–500.

Pedro-Carroll, J. (1997). The children of divorce intervention program: Fostering resilient outcomes for school-aged children. In G. W. Albee & T. P. Gullotta (Eds.), *Primary prevention works* (pp. 213–238). Thousand Oaks, CA: Sage.

Pelham, W. E. (1993). Pharmacotherapy for children with attention-deficit hyperactivity disorder. *School Psychology Review, 22,* 199–227.

Pelham, W. E., & Hinshaw, S. P. (1992). Behavioral intervention for attention-deficit hyperactivity disorder. In S. M. Turner, K. S. Calhoun, & H. E. Adams (Eds.), *Handbook of clinical behavior therapy* (2nd ed.) (pp. 259–283). New York: Wiley.

Pelham, W. E., Wheeler, T., & Chronis, A. (1998). Empirically supported treatments for attention deficit hyperactivity disorder. *Journal of Clinical Child Psychology, 27,* 190–205.

Penn, N. E., Snehendu, K., Kramer, J., Skinner, J., & Zambrana, R. (1995). Panel IV: Ethnic minorities, health care systems, and behavior. *Health Psychology, 14,* 641–646.

Perls, F. S. (1947). *Ego, hunger, and aggression.* London: Allen and Unwin.

Perls, F. S. (1969a). *Gestalt therapy verbatim.* Lafayette, CA: Real People Press.

Perls, F. S. (1969b). *In and out the garbage pail.* Palo Alto, CA: Science and Behavior Books.

Perls, F. S. (1970). Four lectures. In J. Fagan & I. L. Sheperd (Eds.), *Gestalt therapy now.* Palo Alto, CA: Science and Behavior Books.

Perls, F. S. (1973). *The Gestalt approach and eyewitness to therapy.* Palo Alto, CA: Science and Behavior Books.

Perls, F. S., Hefferline, R. F., & Goodman, P. (1951). *Gestalt therapy.* New York: Julian Press.

Persons, J. B. (1991). Psychotherapy outcome studies do not accurately represent current models of psychotherapy. *American Psychologist, 46,* 99–106.

Persons, J. B. (1995). Why practicing psychologists are slow to adopt empirically validated treatments. In S. C. Hayes, V. M. Follette, R. M. Dawes, & K. E. Grady (Eds.), *Scientific standards of psychological practice: Issues and recommendations* (pp. 141–157). Reno, NV: Context Press.

Pervin, L. A. (1960). Existentialism, psychology, and psychotherapy. *American Psychologist, 15,* 305–309.

Peterson, D. R. (1968). The doctor of psychology program at the University of Illinois. *American Psychologist, 23,* 511–516.

Peterson, D. R. (1971). Status of the Doctor of Psychology program. *Professional Psychology, 2,* 271–275.

Peterson, D. R., Eaton, M. M., Levine, A. R., & Snepp, F. P. (1982). Career experiences of Doctors of Psychology. *Professional Psychology, 13,* 268–276.

Peterson, J. (1995). How are psychologists perceived by the public? *APA Monitor, 26,* 31.

Peterson, L. (1989). Special series: Coping with medical illness and medical procedures. *Journal of Consulting and Clinical Psychology, 57,* 331–332.

Peterson, L., & Bell-Dolan, D. (1995). Treatment outcome research in child psychology: Realistic coping with the "Ten Commandments of Methodology." *Journal of Clinical Child Psychology, 24,* 149–162.

Peterson, L., & Brown, D. (1994). Integrating child injury and abuse-neglect research: Common histories, etiologies, and solutions. *Psychological Bulletin, 116,* 293–315.

Peterson, L., & Roberts, M. C. (1992). Complacency, misdirection, and effective prevention of children's injuries. *American Psychologist, 47,* 1040–1044.

Peterson, L., & Sobell, L. (1994). Introduction to the state-of-the-art review series: Research contributions to clinical assessment. *Behavior Therapy, 25,* 523–531.

Peterson, L., Zink, M., & Farmer, J. (1992). Prevention of disorders in children. In C. E. Walker & M. C. Roberts (Eds.), *Handbook of clinical child psychology* (2nd ed.) (pp. 951–965). New York: Wiley.

Peterson, R. L., Peterson, D. R., Abrams, J. C., & Stricker, G. (1997). The National Council of Schools and Programs of Professional Psychology educational model. *Professional Psychology, 28,* 373–386.

Pettit, I. B., Pettit, T. F., & Welkowitz, J. (1974). Relationship between values, social class, and duration of psychotherapy. *Journal of Consulting and Clinical Psychology, 42,* 482–490.

Pfohl, B., Blum, N., & Zimmerman, M. (1994). *Structured interview for DSM-IV personality: SIDP-IV.* Iowa City, IA: Author.

Phares, E. J. (1967). The deviant personality. In H. Helson & W. Bevan (Eds.), *Contemporary approaches to psychology*. Princeton, NJ: Van Nostrand.

Phares, E. J. (1976). *Focus of control in personality*. Morristown, NJ: General Learning Press.

Phares, E. J. (1980). Rotter's social learning theory. In G. M. Gazda & R. J. Corsini (Eds.), *Theories of learning: A comparative approach*. Itasca, IL: Peacock.

Phares, E. J. (1991). *Introduction to personality* (3rd ed.). New York: HarperCollins.

Phares, E. J., Stewart, L. M., & Foster, J. M. (1960). Instruction variation and Rorschach performance. *Journal of Projective Techniques, 24,* 28–31.

Philipson, I. J. (1993). *On the shoulders of women: The feminization of psychotherapy*. New York: Guilford Press.

Piacentini, J. C., Cohen, P., & Cohen, J. (1992). Combining discrepant diagnostic information from multiple sources: Are complex algorithms better than simple ones? *Journal of Abnormal Child Psychology, 20,* 51–63.

Piedmont, R. L., Sokolove, R. L., & Fleming, M. Z. (1989). An examination of some diagnostic strategies involving the Wechsler scales. *Psychological Assessment: A Journal of Consulting and Clinical Psychology, 1,* 181–185.

Piotrowski, C. (1985). Clinical assessment: Attitudes of the Society for Personality Assessment membership. *Southern Psychologist, 2,* 80–83.

Piotrowski, C., Sherry, D., & Keller, J. W. (1985). Psychodiagnostic test usage: A survey of the Society for Personality Assessment. *Journal of Personality Assessment, 49,* 115–119.

Pipes, R. B., & Davenport, D. S. (1990). *Introduction to psychotherapy: Common clinical wisdom*. Englewood Cliffs, NJ: Prentice-Hall.

Plomin, R., DeFries, J. C., & McClearn, G. E. (1990). *Behavioral genetics: A primer* (2nd ed.). New York: Freeman.

Pollock, E. J. (1998, January 5). With "case rates," cures come fast or the doctor incurs a loss. *Wall Street Journal*, pp. B1, B6.

Polyson, J. A., Miller, H. L., & Shank, S. R. (1987). Axis IV: An experiment in progress. *Professional Psychology: Research and Practice, 18,* 447–451.

Pope, K. S. (1990). Therapist-patient sexual involvement: A review of the research. *Clinical Psychology Review, 10,* 477–490.

Pope, K. S., & Vetter, V. A. (1992). Ethical dilemmas encountered by members of the American Psychological Association: A national survey. *American Psychologist, 47,* 397–411.

Poser, E. G. (1966). The effect of therapist training on group therapeutic outcome. *Journal of Consulting Psychology, 30,* 283–289.

Powers, C. W. (1999). Empirically supported treatments in pediatric psychology: Procedure-related pain. *Journal of Pediatric Psychology, 24,* 131–145.

Powers, P. S. (1980). *Obesity: The regulation of weight*. Baltimore: Williams and Wilkins.

Poythress, N. G., Jr. (1979). A proposal for training in forensic psychology. *American Psychologist, 34,* 612–621.

Premack, D. (1959). Toward empirical behavior laws: I. Positive reinforcement. *Psychological Review, 66,* 219–233.

Price, R. H., Cowen, E. L., Lorion, R. P., & Ramos-McKay, J. (Eds.). (1988). *14 ounces of prevention: A casebook for practitioners*. Washington, DC: American Psychological Association.

Price, R. H., & Lynn, S. J. (1981). *Abnormal psychology in the human context*. Pacific Grove, CA: Brooks/Cole.

Prinz, R. J., & Kent, R. N. (1978). Recording parent-adolescent interactions without the use of frequency or interval-by-interval coding. *Behavior Therapy, 9,* 602–604.

Pritchard, D. A., & Rosenblatt, A. (1980). Racial bias in the MMPI: A methodological review. *Journal of Consulting and Clinical Psychology, 48,* 263–267.

Pruitt, S. D., & Elliott, C. H. (1992). Pediatric psychology: Current issues and developments. In C. E. Walker & M.C. Roberts (Eds.), *Handbook of clinical child psychology* (2nd ed.) (pp. 859–872). New York: Wiley.

Psychological Corporation. (1997). *WAIS-III/WMS-III: Technical manual*. San Antonio, TX: Author.

Quereshi, M. Y., & Kuchan, A. M. (1988). The master's degree in clinical psychology. *Professional Psychology: Research and Practice, 19,* 594–599.

Rabin, A. I. (1965). Diagnostic use of intelligence tests. In B. Wolman (Ed.), *Handbook of clinical psychology*. New York: McGraw-Hill.

Rachman, S. (1973). The effects of psychotherapy. In H. J. Eysenck (Ed.), *Handbook of abnormal psychology*. San Diego: Knapp.

Raimy, V. C. (Ed.). (1950). *Training in clinical psychology*. Englewood Cliffs, NJ: Prentice-Hall.

Rapaport, D. (1946). *Diagnostic psychological testing* (Vol. 2). Chicago: Yearbook Publishers.

Rapaport, D. (1953). On the psychoanalytic theory of affects. *International Journal of Psycho-Analysis, 34,* 177–198.

Rappaport, J. (1977). *Community psychology: Values, research, and action*. New York: Holt, Rinehart and Winston.

Rappaport, J. (1981). In praise of paradox: A social policy of empowerment over prevention. *American Journal of Community Psychology, 9,* 1–25.

Rappaport, J. (1987). Terms of empowerment/exemplars of prevention: Toward a theory for community psychology. *American Journal of Community Psychology, 15,* 121–148.

Rappaport, J., Chinsky, J. M., & Cowen, E. L. (1971). *Innovations in helping chronic patients: College students in a mental institution*. New York: Academic Press.

Rappaport, J., & Seidman, E. (in press). *Handbook of community psychology.* New York: Plenum Press.

Rathus, S. A. (1973). A 30-item schedule for assessing assertive behavior. *Behavior Therapy, 4,* 398–406.

Raviv, A., Raviv, A., & Yunovitz, R. (1989). Radio psychology and psychotherapy: Comparison of client attitudes and expectations. *Professional Psychology: Research and Practice, 20,* 67–72.

Reid, J. B. (1970). Reliability assessment of observation data: A possible methodological problem. *Child Development, 41,* 1143–1150.

Reisman, J. M. (1976). *A history of clinical psychology* (enlarged ed.). New York: Irvington.

Reitan, R. M. (1969). *Manual for administration of neuropsychological test batteries for adults and children.* Indianapolis: Author.

Reitan, R. M., & Davison, L. A. (1974). *Clinical neuropsychology: Current status and application.* New York: Winston/Wiley.

Reitan, R. M., & Wolfson, D. (1993). *The Halstead-Reitan neuropsychological test battery: Theory and clinical interpretation* (2nd ed.). Tucson, AZ: Neuropsychology Press.

Reitan, R. M., & Wolfson, D. (1996). The question of validity of neuropsychological test scores among head-injured litigants: Development of a dissimulation index. *Archives of Clinical Neuropsychology, 11,* 573–580.

Repucci, N. D., & Saunders, J. T. (1974). Social psychology of behavior modification: Problems of implementation in natural settings. *American Psychologist, 29,* 649–660.

Resnick, J. H. (1991). Finally, a definition of clinical psychology: A message from the President, Division 12. *Clinical Psychologist, 44,* 3–11.

Resnick, R. J. (1985). The case against the Blues: The Virginia challenge. *American Psychologist, 40,* 975–983.

Resnick, R. J. (1997). A brief history of practice—expanded. *American Psychologist, 52,* 463–468.

Rice, P. L. (1998). *Health psychology.* Pacific Grove, CA: Brooks/Cole.

Rice, S. (1929). Contagious bias in the interview: A methodological note. *American Journal of Sociology, 35,* 420–423.

Richardson, F. C., & Suinn, R. M. (1973). A comparison of traditional systematic desensitization, accelerated massed desensitization, and anxiety management training in the treatment of mathematics anxiety. *Behavior Therapy, 4,* 212–218.

Richters, J., & Pellegrini, D. (1989). Depressed mothers' judgments about their children: An examination of the depression-distortion hypothesis. *Child Development, 60,* 1068–1075.

Rie, H. E., & Rie, E. D. (Eds.). (1980). *Handbook of minimal brain dysfunctions: A critical view.* New York: Wiley.

Riley, W. T., Elliott, R. L., & Thomas, J. R. (1992). Impact of prescription privileging on psychology training: Training directors' survey. *Clinical Psychologist, 45,* 63–71.

Rimm, D. C., & Masters, J. C. (1979). *Behavior therapy: Techniques and empirical findings* (2nd ed.). New York: Academic Press.

Rioch, M. J. (1967). Pilot projects in training mental health counselors. In E. L. Cowen, E. A. Gardner, & M. Zax (Eds.), *Emergent approaches to mental health problems.* New York: Appleton-Century-Crofts.

Riskin, J., & Faunce, E. E. (1972). An evaluative review of family interaction research. *Family Process, 11,* 365–455.

Riva, M. T., & Smith, R. D. (1997). Looking into the future of group research: Where do we go from here? *Journal for Specialists in Group Work, 22,* 266–276.

Roberts, A. H. (1985). Biofeedback: Research, training and clinical roles. *American Psychologist, 40,* 938–941.

Roberts, M. C. (1986). *Pediatric psychology: Psychological interventions and strategies for pediatric problems.* New York: Pergamon Press.

Roberts, M. C. (1994). Models of service delivery in children's mental health: Common characteristics. *Journal of Clinical Child Psychology, 23,* 212–219.

Roberts, M. C., Carlson, C. I., Erickson, M. T., Friedman, R. M., La Greca, A. M., Lemanek, K. L., Russ, S. W., Schroeder, C. S., Vargas, L. A., & Wohlford, P. F. (1998). A model for training psychologists to provide services for children and adolescents. *Professional Psychology: Research and Practice, 29,* 293–299.

Roberts, M. C., Maddux, J., & Wright, L. (1984). The development perspective in behavioral health. In J. D. Matarazzo, N. E. Miller, S. Weiss, J. A. Herd, & S. Weiss (Eds.), *Behavioral health: A handbook of health enhancement and disease prevention.* New York: Wiley.

Roberts, M. C., & Walker, C. E. (Eds.). (1991). *Casebook of child and pediatric psychology.* New York: Guilford Press.

Robiner, W. N. (1991). How many psychologists are needed? A call for a national psychology human resource agenda. *Professional Psychology: Research and Practice, 22,* 427–440.

Robins, C. J. (1990). Congruence of personality and life events in depression. *Journal of Abnormal Psychology, 99,* 393–397.

Robins, L. N. (1985). Epidemiology: Reflections on testing the validity of psychiatric interviews. *Archives of General Psychiatry, 42,* 918–924.

Robins, L. N., & Guze, S. B. (1970). Establishment of diagnostic validity in psychiatric illness: Its application to schizophrenia. *American Journal of Psychiatry, 126,* 107–111.

Robins, L. N., & Helzer, J. E. (1986). Diagnosis and clinical assessment: The current state of psychiatric diagnosis. In M. R. Rosenzweig & L. W. Porter (Eds.), *Annual review of psychology* (Vol. 37). Palo Alto, CA: Annual Reviews.

Robinson, H. B., & Robinson, N. M. (1965). *The mentally retarded child.* New York: McGraw-Hill.

Robinson, L. A., Berman, J. S., & Neimeyer, R. A. (1990). Psychotherapy for the treatment of depression: A comprehensive review of controlled outcome research. *Psychological Bulletin, 108,* 30–49.

Rock, D. L., Bransford, J. D., Maisto, S. A., & Morey, L. (1987). The study of clinical judgment: An ecological approach. *Clinical Psychology Review, 7,* 645–661.

Roe, A. (1953). A psychological study of eminent psychologists and anthropologists, and a comparison with biological and physical scientists. *Psychological Monographs General and Applied, 67*(No. 352).

Rogers, C. R. (1939). *The clinical treatment of the problem child.* Boston: Houghton Mifflin.

Rogers, C. R. (1942). *Counseling and psychotherapy.* Boston: Houghton Mifflin.

Rogers, C. R. (1946). Significant aspects of client-centered therapy. *American Psychologist, 1,* 415–422.

Rogers, C. R. (1951). *Client-centered therapy.* Boston: Houghton Mifflin.

Rogers, C. R. (1956). Intellectualized psychotherapy. *Contemporary Psychology, 1,* 357–358.

Rogers, C. R. (1957). The necessary and sufficient conditions of therapeutic personality change. *Journal of Consulting Psychology, 21,* 95–103.

Rogers, C. R. (1959). A theory of therapy, personality, and interpersonal relationships, as developed in the client-centered framework. In S. Koch (Ed.), *Psychology: A study of a science* (Vol. 3). New York: McGraw-Hill.

Rogers, C. R. (1961). *On becoming a person.* Boston: Houghton Mifflin.

Rogers, C. R. (1967). Autobiography. In E. Boring & G. Lindzey (Eds.), *A history of psychology in autobiography* (Vol. 5). New York: Appleton-Century-Crofts.

Rogers, C. R. (1970). *On encounter groups.* New York: Harper and Row.

Rogers, C. R. (1974). In retrospect: Forty-six years. *American Psychologist, 29,* 115–123.

Rogers, C. R. (1980). *A way of being.* Boston: Houghton Mifflin.

Rogers, C. R., & Dymond, R. F. (1954). *Psychotherapy and personality change.* Chicago: University of Chicago Press.

Rogers, C. R., Gendlin, E. T., Kiesler, D. J., & Truax, C. B. (1967). *The therapeutic relationship and its impact.* Madison: University of Wisconsin Press.

Rogers, R. (1995). *Diagnostic and structured interviewing: A handbook for psychologists.* Odessa, FL: Psychological Assessment Resources.

Rogers, R., Bagby, R., & Chakraborty, D. (1993). Feigning schizophrenic disorders on the MMPI-2: Detection of coached simulators. *Journal of Personality Assessment, 60,* 215–226.

Rogers, R., Harrell, E., & Liff, C. (1993). Feigning neuropsychological impairment: A critical review of methodological and clinical considerations. *Clinical Psychology Review, 13,* 255–274.

Rogers, R. W. (1975). A protection motivation theory of fear appeals and attitude change. *Journal of Psychology, 91,* 93–114.

Rogler, L. H., Malgady, R. G., Constantino, G., & Blumenthal, R. (1987). What do culturally sensitive mental health services mean? The case of Hispanics. *American Psychologist, 42,* 565–570.

Ronan, K., Kendall, P. C., & Rowe, M. (1994). Negative affectivity in children: Development and validation of a self-statement questionnaire. *Cognitive Therapy and Research, 18,* 509–528.

Rorschach, H. (1921). *Psychodiagnostik.* Bern, Switzerland: Huber.

Rose, S. D. (1991). The development and practice of group treatment. In M. Hersen, A. E. Kazdin, & A. Bellack (Eds.), *The clinical psychology handbook* (2nd ed.) (pp. 627–642). New York: Pergamon Press.

Rosen, C. E. (1977). Why clients relinquish their rights to privacy under sign-away pressure. *Professional Psychology, 8,* 17–24.

Rosen, G. M. (1974). Therapy set: Its effects on subjects' involvement in systematic desensitization and treatment outcome. *Journal of Abnormal Psychology, 83,* 291–300.

Rosen, R. C., & Kopel, S. A. (1977). Penile plethysmography and biofeedback in the treatment of a transvestite-exhibitionist. *Journal of Consulting and Clinical Psychology, 45,* 908–916.

Rosenbaum, M. (1965). Group psychotherapy and psychodrama. In B. B. Wolman (Ed.), *Handbook of clinical psychology.* New York: McGraw-Hill.

Rosenhan, D. L. (1973). On being sane in insane places. *Science, 179,* 250–258.

Rosenman, R. H. (1978). The interview method of assessment of the coronary-prone behavior pattern. In T. M. Dembroski, S. M. Weiss, J. L. Shields, S. G. Haynes, & M. Feinleib (Eds.), *Coronary-prone behavior.* New York: Springer-Verlag.

Rosenstock, I. M. (1974). The health belief model and preventive health behavior. *Health Psychology Monographs, 2,* 354–386.

Rosenstock, I. M., Strecher, V. J., & Becker, M. H. (1988). Social learning theory and the health belief model. *Health Education Quarterly, 15,* 175–183.

Rosenthal, D., & Kety, S. (Eds.). (1968). *The transmission of schizophrenia.* New York: Pergamon Press.

Rosenthal, R. (1966). *Experimenter effects in behavioral research.* New York: Appleton-Century-Crofts.

Rosewater, L. B., & Walker, L. E. A. (Eds.). (1985). *Handbook of feminist therapy: Women's issues in psychotherapy.* New York: Springer.

Ross, A. O. (1959). *The practice of clinical child psychology.* New York: Grune and Stratton.

Rotgers, F., & Barrett, D. (1996). *Daubert* v. *Merrell Dow* and expert testimony by clinical psychologists: Implications and recommendations for practice. *Professional Psychology: Research and Practice, 27,* 467–474.

Rotter, J. B. (1946). Thematic Apperception Tests: Suggestions for administration and interpretation. *Journal of Personality, 15,* 70–92.

Rotter, J. B. (1954). *Social learning and clinical psychology.* Englewood Cliffs, NJ: Prentice Hall.

Rotter, J. B. (1960). Some implications of a social learning theory for the prediction of goal directed behavior from testing procedures. *Psychological Review, 67,* 301–316.

Rotter, J. B. (1966). Generalized expectancies for internal versus external control of reinforcement. *Psychological Monographs, 80*(1, Whole No. 609).

Rotter, J. B. (1970). Some implications of a social learning theory for the practice of psychotherapy. In D. J. Levis (Ed.), *Learning approaches to therapeutic behavior change.* Chicago: Aldine. (Also reprinted in Rotter, Chance, & Phares, 1972)

Rotter, J. B. (1971a). *Clinical psychology* (2nd ed.). Englewood Cliffs, NJ: Prentice-Hall.

Rotter, J. B. (1971b). Generalized expectancies for interpersonal trust. *American Psychologist, 26,* 443–452.

Rotter, J. B. (1975). Some problems and misconceptions related to the construct of internal versus external control of reinforcement. *Journal of Consulting and Clinical Psychology, 43,* 56–67.

Rotter, J. B. (1982). *The development and application of social learning theory: Selected papers.* New York: Praeger.

Rotter, J. B. (1990). Internal versus external control of reinforcement: A case history of a variable. *American Psychologist, 45,* 489–493.

Rotter, J. B., Chance, J. E., & Phares, E. J. (Eds.). (1972). *Applications of a social learning theory of personality.* New York: Holt, Rinehart and Winston.

Rotter, J. B., & Rafferty, J. E. (1950). *Manual for the Rotter Incomplete Sentences Black, college form.* New York: Psychological Corporation.

Rotter, J. B., & Wickens, D. D. (1948). The consistency and generality of ratings of "social aggressiveness" made from observations of role playing situations. *Journal of Consulting Psychology, 12,* 234–239.

Routh, D. K. (1988). Prevention and life style in child health psychology. In B. G. Melamed, K. A. Matthews, D. K. Routh, B. Stabler, & N. Schneiderman (Eds.), *Child health psychology.* Hillsdale, NJ: Erlbaum.

Routh, D. K. (1996). Lightner Witmer and the first 100 years of clinical psychology. *American Psychologist, 51,* 244–247.

Russo, N. F. (1990). Overview: Forging research priorities for women's mental health. *American Psychologist, 45,* 368–373.

Ryan, W. (1971). *Blaming the victim.* New York: Random House.

Saal, F. E., & Knight, P. A. (1988). *Industrial/organizational psychology: Science and practice.* Pacific Grove, CA: Brooks/Cole.

Sales, B. D., & Elwork, A. (1980). Issues in training forensic psychologists. In G. Cooke (Ed.), *The role of the forensic psychologist.* Springfield, IL: Charles C Thomas.

Salter, A. (1949). *Conditioned reflex therapy.* New York: Farrar, Straus.

Sanchez, P. N., & Kahn, M. W. (1991). Differentiating medical from psychological disorders: How do medically and non-medically trained clinicians differ? *Professional Psychology: Research and Practice, 22,* 124–126.

Sanford, N. (1965). The prevention of mental illness. In B. B. Wolman (Ed.), *Handbook of clinical psychology.* New York: McGraw-Hill.

Sarason, I. G., & Sarason, B. R. (Eds.). (1985). *Social support: Theory, research, and applications.* Dordrecht, The Netherlands: Martinus Nijhoff.

Sarbin, T. R. (1943). A contribution to the study of actuarial and individual methods of prediction. *American Journal of Sociology, 48,* 593–602.

Satir, V. (1967a). *Conjoint family therapy* (2nd rev. ed.). Palo Alto, CA: Science and Behavior Books.

Satir, V. (1967b). A family of angels. In J. Haley & L. Hoffman (Eds.), *Techniques of family therapy.* New York: Basic Books.

Satir, V. (1975). You as a change agent. In V. Satir, J. Stachowiak, & H. A. Taschman (Eds.), *Helping families to change.* New York: Jason Aronson.

Sattler, J. M. (1970). Racial "experimenter effects" in experimentation, testing, interviewing, and psychotherapy. *Psychological Bulletin, 73,* 137–160.

Sattler, J. M. (1992). Assessing of children's intelligence. In C. E. Walker & M. C. Roberts (Eds.), *Handbook of clinical child psychology* (2nd ed.) (pp. 85–100). New York: Wiley.

Sattler, J. M., & Gwynne, J. (1982). White examiners generally do not impede the intelligence test performance of black children: To debunk a myth. *Journal of Consulting and Clinical Psychology, 50,* 196–208.

Saunders, T. R. (1979). A critical analysis of the minimal brain dysfunction syndrome. *Professional Psychology, 10,* 293–306.

Sawyer, J. (1966). Measurement *and* prediction, clinical *and* statistical. *Psychological Bulletin, 66,* 178–200.

Sayette, M. A., & Mayne, T. J. (1990). Survey of current clinical and research trends in clinical psychology. *American Psychologist, 45,* 1263–1266.

Sayette, M. A., Mayne, T. J., & Norcross, J. C. (1998). *Insider's guide to graduate programs in clinical and counseling psychology.* New York: Guilford Press.

Schaefer, H. H., & Martin, P. L. (1969). *Behavior therapy.* New York: McGraw-Hill.

Schein, E. H., & Bennis, W. G. (1965). *Personal and organizational change through group methods: The laboratory approach.* New York: Wiley.

Scherer, K. R., & Ekman, P. (Eds.). (1982). *Handbook of methods in nonverbal behavior research.* Cambridge, England: Cambridge University Press.

Schilling, R. F., & McAlister, A. L. (1990). Preventing drug use in adolescents through media interventions. *Journal of Consulting and Clinical Psychology, 58,* 416–424.

Schmideberg, M. (1970). Psychotherapy with failures of psychoanalysis. *British Journal of Psychiatry, 116,* 195–200.

Schmitt, N. (1976). Social and situational determinants of interview decisions: Implications for the employment interview. *Personnel Psychology, 29,* 79–101.

Schneider, S. F. (1990). Psychology at the crossroads. *American Psychologist, 45,* 521–529.

Schneider, S. F. (1991). No fluoride in our future. *Professional Psychology: Research and Practice, 22,* 456–460.

Schofield, W. (1964). *Psychotherapy: The purchase of friendship.* Englewood Cliffs, NJ: Prentice-Hall.

Schroeder, M. L., Wormworth, J. A., & Livesley, W. J. (1992). Dimensions of personality disorder and their relationships to the Big Five dimensions of personality. *Psychological Assessment, 4,* 47–53.

Schuerger, J. M., & Witt, A. C. (1989). The temporal stability of individually tested intelligence. *Journal of Clinical Psychology, 45,* 294–302.

Schulberg, H. C., & Killelea, M. (Eds.). (1982). *The modern practice of community mental health.* San Francisco: Jossey-Bass.

Schwartz, G. E., & Weiss, S. (1977). What is behavioral medicine? *Psychosomatic Medicine, 36,* 377–381.

Schwartz, R. M., & Gottman, J. M. (1976). Toward a task analysis of assertive behavior. *Journal of Consulting and Clinical Psychology, 44,* 910–920.

Schweinhart, L. J., & Weikart, D. B. (1988). The High Scope/Perry Preschool Program. In R. H. Price, E. L., Cowen, R. P. Lorion, & J. Ramos-McKay (Eds.), *Fourteen ounces of prevention: A casebook for practitioners.* Washington, DC: American Psychological Association.

Schwitzgebel, R. L., & Schwitzgebel, R. K. (1980). *Law and psychological practice.* New York: Wiley.

Scogin, F., & McElreath, L. (1994). Efficacy of psychosocial treatments for geriatric depression: A quantitative review. *Journal of Consulting and Clinical Psychology, 62,* 69–74.

Scott, N. E., & Borodovsky, L. G. (1990). Effective use of cultural role taking. *Professional Psychology: Research and Practice, 21,* 167–170.

Scott, W. A. (1958). Research definitions of mental health and mental illness. *Psychological Bulletin, 55,* 29–45.

Sears, J. D., Hirt, M. L., & Hall, R. W. (1984). A cross-validation of the Luria-Nebraska Neuropsychological Battery. *Journal of Consulting and Clinical Psychology, 52,* 309–310.

Sechrest, L. (1963). Incremental validity: A recommendation. *Educational and Psychological Measurement, 23,* 153–158.

Sechrest, L. (1977). Personal constructs theory. In R. J. Corsini (Ed.), *Current personality theories.* Itasca, IL: Peacock.

Sechrest, L., & Bootzin, R. (1975). Preliminary evaluation of psychologists in encounter groups. *Professional Psychology, 6,* 69–79.

Segraves, R. T. (1982). *Marital therapy: A combined psychodynamic-behavioral approach.* New York: Plenum Medical.

Seidman, E., & Rappaport, J. (1974). The educational pyramid: A paradigm for research, training, and manpower utilization in community psychology. *American Journal of Community Psychology, 2,* 119–130.

Seifer, R. (1988). Assessment of children's temperament. In P. Karoly (Ed.), *Handbook of child health assessment: Biopsychosocial perspectives.* New York: Wiley-Interscience.

Seligman, M. E. P. (1994). *What you can change and what you can't.* New York: Knopf.

Seligman, M. E. P. (1995). The effectiveness of psychotherapy: The *Consumer Reports* study. *American Psychologist, 50,* 965–974.

Seligman, M. E. P., Castellon, C., Cacciola, J., Schulman, P., Luborsky, L., Ollove, M., & Downing, R. (1988). Explanatory style change during cognitive therapy for unipolar depression. *Journal of Abnormal Psychology, 97,* 13–18.

Seligman, M. E. P., Reivich, K., Jaycox, L., & Gillham, J. (1995). *The optimistic child.* New York: Houghton Mifflin.

Semenoff, B. (1976). *Projective techniques.* New York: Wiley.

Severance, L. J., & Loftus, E. F. (1982). Improving the ability to comprehend and apply criminal jury instructions. *Law and Society Review, 17,* 153–198.

Shadish, W. R., Jr., Doherty, M., & Montgomery, L. (1989). How many studies are in the file drawer? An estimate from the family/marital psychotherapy literature. *Clinical Psychology Review, 9,* 589–603.

Shadish, W. R., Montgomery, L. M., Wilson, P., Wilson, M. R., Bright, I., & Okwumabua, T. (1993). Effects of family and marital psychotherapies: A meta-analysis. *Journal of Consulting and Clinical Psychology, 61,* 992–1002.

Shaffer, G. W., & Lazarus, R. S. (1952). *Fundamental concepts in clinical psychology.* New York: McGraw-Hill.

Shah, S. A. (1978). Dangerousness: A paradigm for exploring some issues in law and psychology. *American Psychologist, 33,* 224–238.

Shah, S. A., & McGarry, A. L. (1986). Legal psychiatry and psychology: Review of programs, training, and qualifications. In W. J. Curran, A. L. McGarry, & S. A. Shah (Eds.), *Forensic psychiatry and psychology: Perspectives and standards for interdisciplinary practice.* Philadelphia: Davis.

Shapiro, A. E., & Wiggins, J. G. (1994). A PsyD degree for every practitioner: Truth in labeling. *American Psychologist, 49,* 207–210.

Shapiro, D. A., & Shapiro, D. (1982). Meta-analysis of comparative therapy outcome studies: A replication and refinement. *Psychological Bulletin, 92,* 581–604.

Shapiro, D. A., & Shapiro, D. (1983). Comparative therapy outcome research: Methodological implications of meta-analysis. *Journal of Consulting and Clinical Psychology, 51,* 42–53.

Shapiro, T. (1989). Psychoanalytic classification and empiricism with borderline personality disorder as a model. *Journal of Consulting and Clinical Psychology, 57,* 187–194.

Shea, S. C. (1998). *Psychiatric interviewing: The art of understanding* (2nd ed.). Philadelphia: Saunders.

Sheldon, W. H. (with the collaboration of S. S. Stevens). (1942). *The varieties of temperament: A psychology of constitutional differences.* New York: Harper and Row.

Shepherd, M., Oppenheim, B., & Mitchell, S. (1971). *Childhood behavior and mental health.* New York: Grune and Stratton.

Sher, K. S., & Trull, T. J. (1996). Methodological issues in psychopathology research. *Annual Review of Psychology, 47,* 371–400.

Sher, K. S., Walitzer, K. S., Wood, P. K., & Brent, E. E. (1991). Characteristics of children of alcoholics: Putative risk factors, substance use and abuse, and psychopathology. *Journal of Abnormal Psychology, 100,* 427–448.

Shiang, J., Kjellander, C., Huang, K., & Bogumill, S. (1998). Developing cultural competency in clinical practice: Treatment considerations for Chinese cultural groups in the United States. *Clinical Psychology: Science and Practice, 5,* 182–210.

Shneidman, E. S. (1951). *Thematic test analysis.* New York: Grune and Stratton.

Shneidman, E. S. (1952). *The Make a Picture Story Test.* New York: Psychological Corporation.

Shneidman, E. S. (1965). Projective techniques. In B. Wolman (Ed.), *Handbook of clinical psychology.* New York: McGraw-Hill.

Shneidman, E. S., & Farberow, N. L. (1965). The Los Angeles suicide prevention center: A demonstration of public health feasibilities. *American Journal of Public Health, 55,* 21–26.

Shoham-Salomon, V., & Rosenthal, R. (1987). Paradoxical interventions: A meta-analysis. *Journal of Consulting and Clinical Psychology, 55,* 22–28.

Shrout, P. E., & Fleiss, J. L. (1979). Intraclass correlations: Uses in assessing rater reliability. *Psychological Bulletin, 86,* 420–428.

Sierles, F. S., & Taylor, M. A. (1995). Decline of U.S. medical student career choice of psychiatry and what to do about it. *American Journal of Psychiatry, 152,* 1416–1426.

Sifneos, P. E. (1972). *Short-term psychotherapy and emotional crisis.* Cambridge, MA: Harvard University Press.

Silverman, L. H. (1976). Psychoanalytic theory: The reports of my death are greatly exaggerated. *American Psychologist, 31,* 621–637.

Silverman, W. H. (1989). Whatever happened to the therapeutic team? *Clinical Psychologist, 42,* 11–14.

Silverman, W. K., & Serafini, L. T. (1998). Assessment of child behavior problems: Internalizing disorders. In A. S. Bellack & M. Hersen (Eds.), *Behavioral assessment: A practical handbook* (4th ed.) (pp. 342–360). Boston: Allyn & Bacon.

Simon, R. J., & Aaronson, D. E. (1988). *The insanity defense: A critical assessment of law and policy in the post-Hinckley era.* New York: Praeger.

Sines, L. K. (1959). The relative contribution of four kinds of data to accuracy in personality assessment. *Journal of Consulting Psychology, 23,* 483–495.

Singer, E. (1965). *Key concepts in psychotherapy.* New York: Random House.

Skinner, B. F. (1953). *Science and human behavior.* New York: Macmillan.

Skinner, B. F. (1971). *Beyond freedom and dignity.* New York: Knopf.

Skinner, H. A., Steinhauer, P. D., & Santa-Barbara, J. (1983). The Family Assessment Measure. *Canadian Journal of Community Mental Health, 2,* 91–103.

Sleek, S. (1995a). Managed care sharpens master's-degree debate. *APA Monitor, 26,* 8–9.

Sleek, S. (1995b). So talk shows exploit the profession? *APA Monitor, 26,* 6.

Sloane, R. B., Staples, F. R., Cristol, A. H., Yorkston, N. J., & Whipple, K. (1975a). *Psychotherapy versus behavior therapy.* Cambridge, MA: Harvard University Press.

Sloane, R. B., Staples, F. R., Cristol, A. H., Yorkston, N. J., & Whipple, K. (1975b). Short-term analytically oriented psychotherapy versus behavior therapy. *American Journal of Psychiatry, 132,* 373–377.

Smith, E. W. L. (Ed.). (1976). *The growing edge of Gestalt therapy.* New York: Brunner/Mazel.

Smith, G. T., & McCarthy, D. M. (1995). Methodological considerations in the refinement of clinical assessment instruments. *Psychological Assessment, 7,* 300–308.

Smith, M. B., & Hobbs, N. (1966). The community and the community mental health center. *American Psychologist, 21,* 499–509.

Smith, M. L., & Glass, G. V. (1977). Meta-analysis of psychotherapy outcome studies. *American Psychologist, 32,* 752–760.

Smith, M. L., Glass, G. V., & Miller, T. I. (1980). *The benefits of psychotherapy.* Baltimore: Johns Hopkins University Press.

Smith, R. J., Barth, J. T., Diamond, R., & Giuliano, A. J. (1997). Evaluation of head trauma. In G. Goldstein, P. D. Nussbaum, & S. R. Beers (Eds.), *Neuropsychology* (pp. 135–170). New York: Plenum Press.

Smith, T. W. (1992). Hostility and health: Current status of a psychosomatic hypothesis. *Health Psychology, 11,* 139–150.

Smyer, M. A., Balster, R. L., Egli, D., Johnson, D. L., Kilbey, M. M., Leith, N. J., & Puente, A. E. (1993). Summary of the report of the Ad Hoc Task Force on Psychopharmacology of the American Psychological Association. *Professional Psychology: Research and Practice, 24,* 394–403.

Snepp, F. P., & Peterson, D. R. (1988). Evaluative comparison of PsyD and PhD students by clinical internship supervisors. *Professional Psychology: Research and Practice, 19,* 180–183.

Snyder, C. R. (1974). Acceptance of personality interpretations as a function of assessment procedures. *Journal of Consulting and Clinical Psychology, 42,* 150.

Snyder, D. K., Widiger, T. A., & Hoover, D. (1990). Methodological considerations in validating computer-based test interpretations: Controlling for response bias. *Psychological Assessment: A Journal of Consulting and Clinical Psychology, 2,* 470–477.

Snyder, D. K., Wills, R. M., & Grady-Fletcher, A. Long-term effects of behavioral versus insight-oriented marital therapy: A 4-year follow-up study. *Journal of Consulting and Clinical Psychology, 59,* 138–141.

Snyder, W. U. (Ed.). (1947). *Casebook of nondirective counseling.* Boston: Houghton Mifflin.

Snyder, W. U. (1961). *The psychotherapy relationship.* New York: Macmillan.

Snygg, D., & Combs, C. W. (1949). *Individual behavior.* New York: Harper and Row.

Snyderman, M., & Rothman, S. (1990). *The IQ controversy, the media, and public policy.* New Brunswick, NJ: Transaction.

Sobel, S. B., & Cummings, N. A. (1981). The role of professional psychologists in promoting equality. *Professional Psychology, 12,* 171–179.

Sobell, M. B., & Sobell, L. C. (1978). *Behavioral treatment of alcohol problems: Individualized therapy and controlled drinking.* New York: Plenum Press.

Soldz, S., Budman, S., Demby, A., & Merry, J. (1993). Representation of personality disorders in circumplex and five-factor space: Explorations with a clinical sample. *Psychological Assessment, 5,* 41–52.

Solomon, J. C. (1955). Play technique and the integrative process. *Journal of Orthopsychiatry, 25,* 591–600.

Sontag, L. W., Baker, C. T., & Nelson, V. L. (1958). Mental growth and personality development: A longitudinal study. *Monograph of the Society for Research in Child Development, 23* (No. 68).

Soskin, W. F. (1959). Influence of four types of data on diagnostic conceptualization in psychological testing. *Journal of Abnormal and Social Psychology, 58,* 69–78.

Spearman, C. (1927). *The abilities of man.* New York: Macmillan.

Speck, R. V., & Attneave, C. L. (1971). Social network intervention. In J. Haley (Ed.), *Changing families.* New York: Grune and Stratton.

Spitzer, R. L. (1975). On pseudoscience in science, logic in remission, and psychiatric diagnosis: A critique of Rosenhan's "On being sane in insane places." *Journal of Abnormal Psychology, 84,* 442–452.

Spitzer, R. L. (1981). The diagnostic status of homosexuality in DSM-III: A reformulation of the issues. *American Journal of Psychiatry, 138,* 210–215.

Spitzer, R. L., & Williams, J.D.W. (1985). *Structured clinical interview for DSM-III-R: Patient version.* New York: New York State Psychiatric Institute, Biometrics Research Division.

Stampfl, T. G., & Levis, D. J. (1967). The essentials of implosive therapy: A learning-theory-based psychodynamic behavioral therapy. *Journal of Abnormal Psychology, 72,* 496–503.

Stampfl, T. G., & Levis, D. J. (1976). Implosive therapy: Theory and technique. In J. T. Spence, R. C. Carson, & J. W. Thibaut (Eds.), *Behavior approaches to therapy.* Morristown, NJ: General Learning Press.

Stanton, M. D. (1975). Family therapy training: Academic and internship opportunities for psychologists. *Family Process, 14,* 433–439.

Staples, F. R., Sloane, R. B., Whipple, K., Cristol, A. H., & Yorkston, N. (1976). Process and outcome in psychotherapy and behavior therapy. *Journal of Consulting and Clinical Psychology, 44,* 340–350.

Steenbarger, B. N., & Budman, S. H. (1996). Group psychotherapy and managed behavioral health care: Current trends and future challenges. *International Journal of Group Psychotherapy, 46,* 297–309.

Stein, D. J., Dodman, N. H., Borchelt, P., & Hollander, E. (1994). Behavioral disorders in veterinary practice: Relevance to psychiatry. *Comprehensive Psychiatry, 35,* 275–285.

Stein, M. I. (1948). *The Thematic Apperception Test: An introductory manual for its clinical use with adult males.* Cambridge, MA: Addison-Wesley.

Sterling, M. E. (1982). Must psychology lose its soul? *Professional Psychology, 13,* 789–796.

Stern, W. (1938). *General psychology from the personalistic point of view.* New York: Macmillan.

Sternberg, R. J. (1985). *Beyond IQ: A triarchic theory of human intelligence.* Cambridge, England: Cambridge University Press.

Sternberg, R. J. (Ed.). (1988). *The nature of creativity: Contemporary psychological perspectives.* New York: Cambridge University Press.

Sternberg, R. J. (1991). Theory-based testing of intellectual abilities: Rationale for the triarchic abilities test. In H. A. Rowe (Ed.), *Intelligence: Reconceptualization and measurement* (pp. 183–202). Hillsdale, NJ: LEA.

Sternberg, R. J., & Salter, W. (1982). Conceptions of intelligence. In R. J. Sternberg (Ed.), *Handbook of human intelligence.* New York: Cambridge University Press.

Sternberg, R. J., & Wagner, R. K. (Eds.). (1986). *Practical intelligence: Nature and origins of competence in the everyday world.* New York: Cambridge University Press.

Stewart, A. E., & Stewart, E. A. (1998). Trends in postdoctoral education: Requirements for licensure and training opportunities. *Professional Psychology: Research and Practice, 29,* 273–283.

Stoller, F. (1968). Accelerated interaction: A time-limited approach based on the brief intensive group. *International Journal of Group Psychotherapy, 18,* 220–235.

Stone, A. R., Frank, J. D., Nash, E. H., & Imber, S. D. (1961). An intensive five-year follow-up study of treated psychiatric outpatients. *Journal of Nervous and Mental Disease, 133,* 410–422.

Stone, G. C. (1979). Psychology and the health system. In G. C. Stone, F. Cohen, & N. E. Adler (Eds.), *Health psychology.* San Francisco: Jossey-Bass.

Strauss, J. S. (1973). Diagnostic models and the nature of psychiatric disorder. *Archives of General Psychiatry, 29,* 445–449.

Strelnick, A. H. (1977). Multiple family group therapy: A review of the literature. *Family Process, 16,* 307–323.

Stricker, G. (1977). Implications of research for psychotherapeutic treatment of women. *American Psychologist, 32,* 14–22.

Stricker, G., & Gold, J. R. (1999). The Rorschach: Toward a nomothetically based, idiographically applicable configurational model. *Psychological Assessment, 11,* 240–250.

Strickland, B. R. (1979). Internal-external expectancies and cardiovascular functioning. In L. C. Perlmuter & R. A. Monty (Eds.), *Choice and perceived control.* Hillsdale, NJ: Erlbaum.

Strickland, B. R. (1988). Clinical psychology comes of age. *American Psychologist, 43,* 104–107.

Stroebe, W., & Stroebe, M. S. (1995). *Social psychology and health.* Pacific Grove, CA: Brooks/Cole.

Strosahl, K. (1998). The dissemination of manual-based psychotherapies in managed care: Promises, problems, and prospects. *Clinical Psychology: Science and Practice, 5,* 382–386.

Strupp, H. H. (1955a). An objective comparison of Rogerian and psychoanalytic techniques. *Journal of Consulting Psychology, 19,* 1–7.

Strupp, H. H. (1955b). Psychotherapeutic techniques, professional affiliation, and experience level. *Journal of Consulting Psychology, 19,* 97–102.

Strupp, H. H. (1958). The performance of psychoanalytic and client-centered psychotherapists in an initial interview. *Journal of Consulting Psychology, 14,* 219–226.

Strupp, H. H. (1971). *Psychotherapy and the modification of abnormal behavior.* New York: McGraw-Hill.

Strupp, H. H. (1990). Reflections on my career in clinical psychology. In C. E. Walker (Ed.), *The history of clinical psychology in autobiography* (Vol. 1, pp. 293–329). Pacific Grove, CA: Brooks/Cole.

Strupp, H. H., & Bergin, A. E. (1969). Some empirical and conceptual bases for coordinated research in psychotherapy: A critical review of issues, trends, and evidence. *International Journal of Psychiatry, 7,* 18–90.

Strupp, H. H., & Binder, J. L. (1984). *Psychotherapy in a new key: A guide to time-limited dynamic therapy.* New York: Basic Books.

Strupp, H. H., & Hadley, S. W. (1977). A tripartite model of mental health and therapeutic outcomes: With special reference to negative effects in psychotherapy. *American Psychologist, 32,* 187–196.

Stuart, R. B. (1969). Operant interpersonal treatment for marital discord. *Journal of Consulting and Clinical Psychology, 33,* 675–682.

Stuart, R. B. (1980). *Helping couples change: A social learning approach to marital therapy.* New York: Guilford Press.

Stunkard, A. J. (1979). Behavioral medicine and beyond: The example of obesity. In O. Pomerleau & J. Brady (Eds.), *Behavioral medicine: Theory and practice.* Baltimore: Williams and Wilkins.

Sturdivant, S. (1980). *Therapy with women: A feminist philosophy of treatment.* New York: Springer.

Sturges, J. W., & Rogers, R. W. (1996). Preventive health psychology from a developmental perspective: An extension of protection motivation theory. *Health Psychology, 15,* 158–166.

Sturgis, E. T., & Gramling, S. (1988). Psychophysiological assessment. In A. S. Bellack & M. Hersen (Eds.), *Behavioral assessment: A practical handbook* (pp. 213–251). New York: Pergamon Press.

Sue, D. W. (1990). Culture-specific strategies in counseling: A conceptual framework. *Professional Psychology: Research and Practice, 21,* 424–433.

Sue, S. (1988). Psychotherapeutic services for ethnic minorities: Two decades of research findings. *American Psychologist, 43,* 301–308.

Sue, S. (1998). In search of cultural competence in psychotherapy and counseling. *American Psychologist, 53*, 440–448.

Sue, S., Zane, N., & Young, K. (1994). Research on psychotherapy with culturally diverse populations. In A. E. Bergin & S. L. Garfield (Eds.), *Handbook of psychotherapy and behavior change* (4th ed.) (pp. 783–817). New York: Wiley.

Sullivan, B. J., & Denney, D. R. (1977). Expectancy and phobic level: Effects on desensitization. *Journal of Consulting and Clinical Psychology, 45*, 763–771.

Sullivan, H. S. (1953). *The interpersonal theory of psychiatry.* New York: Norton.

Sullivan, H. S. (1954). *The psychiatric interview.* New York: Norton.

Suls, J., & Wan, C. K. (1989). Effects of sensory and procedural information on coping with stressful medical procedures and pain: A meta-analysis. *Journal of Consulting and Clinical Psychology, 57*, 372–379.

Sundberg, N. D. (1977). *Assessment of persons.* Englewood Cliffs, NJ: Prentice-Hall.

Sundberg, N. D., Tyler, L. E., & Taplin, J. R. (1973). *Clinical psychology: Expanding horizons* (2nd ed.). Englewood Cliffs, NJ: Prentice-Hall.

Sundland, D. M., & Baker, E. U. (1962). The orientations of therapists. *Journal of Consulting Psychology, 26*, 201–212.

Suomi, S. J. (1982). Relevance of animal models for clinical psychology. In P. C. Kendall & J. N. Butcher (Eds.), *Handbook of research methods in clinical psychology.* New York: Wiley.

Surgeon General. (1964). *Smoking and health.* Washington, DC: U.S. Government Printing Office.

Sutton, R. G., & Kessler, M. (1986). National study of the effects of clients' socioeconomic status on clinical psychologists' professional judgments. *Journal of Consulting and Clinical Psychology, 54*, 275–276.

Svartberg, M., & Stiles, T. C. (1991). Comparative effects of short-term psychodynamic psychotherapy: A meta-analysis. *Journal of Consulting and Clinical Psychology, 59*, 704–714.

Swan, G. E., Piccione, A., & Anderson, D. C. (1980). Internship training in behavioral medicine: Program description, issues, and guidelines. *Professional Psychology, 11*, 339–346.

Sweet, J. J., Moberg, P. J., & Tovian, S. M. (1990). Evaluation of Wechsler Adult Intelligence Scale–Revised premorbid IQ formulas in clinical populations. *Psychological Assessment: A Journal of Consulting and Clinical Psychology, 2*, 41–44.

Swenson, C. H. (1957). Empirical evaluations of human figure drawings. *Psychological Bulletin, 54*, 431–466.

Swenson, C. H. (1968). Empirical evaluations of human figure drawings: 1957–1966. *Psychological Bulletin, 70*, 20–44

Swenson, C. H. (1971). Commitment and the personality of the successful therapist. *Psychotherapy: Theory, Research, and Practice, 8*, 31–36.

Swisher, J. D., Warner, R. W., & Hern, J. (1972). Experimental comparisons of four approaches to drug abuse prevention among 9th and 11th graders. *Journal of Counseling Psychology, 19*, 328–332.

Symonds, P. M. (1949). *Adolescent fantasy: An investigation of the picture-story method of personality study.* New York: Columbia University Press.

Szasz, T. S. (1961). *The myth of mental illness: Foundations of a theory of personal conduct.* New York: Harper-Hoeber.

Szasz, T. S. (1970). *The manufacture of madness.* New York: Harper and Row.

Taft, R. (1955). The ability to judge people. *Psychological Bulletin, 52*, 1–28.

Talbert, F. S., & Pipes, R. B. (1988). Informed consent for psychotherapy: Content analysis of selected forms. *Professional Psychology: Research and Practice, 19*, 131–132.

Talland, G. A. (1963). Psychology's concern with brain damage. *Journal of Nervous and Mental Disease, 136*, 344–351.

Tallent, N. (1958). On individualizing the psychologist's clinical evaluation. *Journal of Clinical Psychology, 14*, 243–244.

Tallent, N. (1960). Psychological consultation in psychiatry. *Diseases of the Nervous System, 21*, 1–7.

Tallent, N. (1983). *Psychological report writing* (2nd ed.). Englewood Cliffs, NJ: Prentice-Hall.

Tarullo, L. B., Richardson, D. T., Radke-Yarrow, M., & Martinez, P. E. (1995). Multiple sources in child diagnosis: Parent-child concordance in affectively ill and well families. *Journal of Clinical Child Psychology, 24*, 173–183.

Task Force on Promotion and Dissemination of Psychological Procedures. (1995). Training in and dissemination of empirically validated psychological treatments. *Clinical Psychologist, 48*, 3–23.

Tauer, C. A. (1979). Freud and female inferiority. *International Journal of Women's Studies, 2*, 287–304.

Taylor, H. G., Barry, C. T., & Schatschneider, C. (1993). School-age consequences of *Haemophilus influenzae* Type B meningitis. *Journal of Clinical Child Psychology, 22*, 196–206.

Taylor, L., & Adelman, H. S. (1989). Reframing the confidentiality dilemma to work in children's best interests. *Professional Psychology: Research and Practice, 20*, 79–83.

Taylor, S. E. (1984). The developing field of health psychology. In A. Baum, S. E. Taylor, & J. E. Singer (Eds.), *Handbook of psychology and health* (Vol. 4). Hillsdale, NJ: Erlbaum.

Taylor, S. E. (1987). The progress and prospects of health psychology: Tasks of a maturing discipline. *Health Psychology, 6*, 73–87.

Taylor, S. E. (1999). *Health psychology* (4th ed.). Boston: McGraw-Hill.

Telch, M. J. (1981). The present status of outcome studies: A reply to Frank. *Journal of Consulting and Clinical Psychology, 49,* 472–475.

Tellegen, A. (1993). Folk concepts and psychological concepts of personality and personality disorder. *Psychological Inquiry, 4,* 122–130.

Tellegen, A., & Ben-Porath, Y. S. (1992). The new uniform T-scores for the MMPI-2: Rationale, derivation, and appraisal. *Psychological Assessment, 4,* 145–155.

Terestman, N., Miller, J., & Weber, J. (1974). Blue-collar patients at a psychoanalytic clinic. *American Journal of Psychiatry, 131,* 261–266.

Terman, L. M., & Merrill, M. A. (1937). *Measuring intelligence.* Boston: Houghton Mifflin.

Terman, L. M., & Merrill, M. A. (1960). *Stanford-Binet Intelligence Scale.* Boston: Houghton Mifflin.

Thigpen, C. H., & Cleckley, H. (1957). *The three faces of Eve.* New York: McGraw-Hill.

Thomas, A., Chess, S., & Birch, H. G. (1968). *Temperament and behavior disorders in children.* New York: Brunner/Mazel.

Thorndike, R. L., Hagen, E. P., & Sattler, J. M. (1986). *Stanford-Binet Intelligence Scale: Guide for administering and scoring the fourth edition.* Chicago: Riverside Publishing.

Thorndike, R. M. (1997). The early history of intelligence testing. In D. P. Flanagan, J. L. Genshaft, & P. L. Harrison (Eds.), *Contemporary intellectual assessment: Theories, tests, and issues* (pp. 3–16). New York: Guilford Press.

Thorpe, G. L., & Olson, S. L. (1997). *Behavior therapy: Concepts, procedures, and applications* (2nd ed.). Boston: Allyn and Bacon.

Thurstone, L. L. (1938). Primary mental abilities. *Psychometric Monographs* (No. 1).

Timbrook, R. E., & Graham, J. R. (1994). Ethnic differences on the MMPI-2? *Psychological Assessment, 6,* 212–217.

Tipton, R. M. (1983). Clinical and counseling psychology: A study of roles and functions. *Professional Psychology: Research and Practice, 14,* 837–846.

Tischler, G. L. (Ed.). (1987). *Diagnosis and classification in psychiatry: A critical appraisal of DSM-III.* New York: Cambridge University Press.

Tolan, P. H., Gorman-Smith, D., Huesmann, L. R., & Zelli, A. (1997). Assessment of family relationship characteristics: A measure to explain risk for antisocial behavior and depression among urban youth. *Psychological Assessment, 9,* 212–223.

Tomarken, A. J. (1995). A psychometric perspective on psychophysiological measures. *Psychological Assessment, 7,* 387–395.

Totten, G., Lamb, D. H., & Reeder, G. D. (1990). *Tarasoff* and confidentiality in AIDS-related psychotherapy.
Professional Psychology: Research and Practice, 21, 155–160.

Tracy, J. J. (1977). Impact of intake procedures upon client attrition in a community mental health center. *Journal of Consulting and Clinical Psychology, 45,* 192–195.

Truax, C. B., & Carkhuff, R. R. (1967). *Toward effective counseling and psychotherapy.* Chicago: Aldine Atherton.

Truax, C. B., & Mitchell, K. M. (1971). Research on certain therapist interpersonal skills in relation to process and outcome. In A. E. Bergin & S. L. Garfield (Eds.), *Handbook of psychotherapy and behavior change: An empirical analysis.* New York: Wiley.

Trull, T. J. (1992). DSM-III-R personality disorders and the Five-Factor Model of personality: An empirical comparison. *Journal of Abnormal Psychology, 101,* 553–560.

Trull, T. J., & Sher, K. J. (1994). Relationship between the Five-Factor Model of personality and Axis I disorders in a nonclinical sample. *Journal of Abnormal Psychology, 103,* 350–360.

Trull, T. J., Useda, J. D., Costa, P. T., Jr., & McCrae, R. R. (1995). Comparison of the MMPI-2 Personality Psychopathology Five (PSY-5), the NEO-PI, and the NEO-PI-R. *Psychological Assessment, 7,* 508–516.

Trull, T. J., & Widiger, T. A. (1997). *Structured Interview for the Five-Factor Model of Personality (SIFFM): Professional manual.* Odessa, FL: Psychological Assessment Resources.

Trull, T. J., Widiger, T. A., & Guthrie, P. (1990). Categorical versus dimensional status of borderline personality disorder. *Journal of Abnormal Psychology, 99,* 40–48.

Tryon, W. W. (1998). Behavioral observation. In A. S. Bellack & M. Hersen (Eds.), *Behavioral assessment: A practical handbook* (4th ed.). *(pp. 79–103).* Boston: Allyn and Bacon.

Tuma, J. M. (1989). Traditional therapies with children. In T. H. Ollendick & M. Hersen (Eds.), *Handbook of child psychopathology* (2nd ed.). New York: Plenum Press.

Twentyman, C. T., & McFall, R. M. (1975). Behavioral training of social skills in shy males. *Journal of Consulting and Clinical Psychology, 43,* 384–395.

Tyler, L. E. (1969). *The work of the counselor* (3rd ed.). New York: Appleton-Century-Crofts.

Tyler, L. E. (1976). The intelligence we test—An evolving concept. In L. B. Resnick (Ed.), *The nature of intelligence.* Hillsdale, NJ: Erlbaum.

Ullman, L. P., & Krasner, L. (Eds.). (1965). *Case studies in behavior modification.* New York: Holt, Rinehart and Winston.

Ullman, L. P., & Krasner, L. (1969). *A psychological approach to abnormal behavior.* Englewood Cliffs, NJ: Prentice-Hall.

U.S. Department of Health and Human Services. (1993). *Eighth special report to the U.S. Congress on alcohol and health.* Rockville, MD: U.S. Public Health Service.

U.S. Department of Health and Human Services. (1997). *Ninth special report to the U.S. Congress on alcohol and health.* Rockville, MD: U.S. Public Health Service.

Valins, S., & Ray, A. A. (1967). Effects of cognitive desensitization on avoidance behavior. *Journal of Personality and Social Psychology, 7,* 345–350.

VandenBos, G. R., Nelson, S., Stapp, J., Olmedo, E., Coates, D., & Batchelor, W. (1979). *APA input to NIMH planning for mental health personnel development.* Washington, DC: American Psychological Association.

Van Kaam, A. (1966). *Existential foundations of psychology.* Pittsburgh: Duquesne University Press.

Vaux, A. (1988). *Social support: Theory, research, and intervention.* New York: Praeger.

Vernon, P. E. (1950). The validation of civil service selection board procedures. *Occupational Psychology, 24,* 75–95.

Vernon, P. E. (1960). *The structure of human abilities* (rev. ed.). London: Methuen.

Viglione, D. J. (1999). A review of recent research addressing the utility of the Rorschach. *Psychological Assessment, 11,* 251–265.

Vinson, J. S. (1987). Use of complaint procedures in cases of therapist-patient sexual conduct. *Professional Psychology: Research and Practice, 18,* 159–164.

Vischi, T. R., Jones, K. R., Shank, E. D., & Lima, L. H. (1980). *The alcohol, drug abuse, and mental health national data book* (Stock No. 017-024-00983-1). Washington, DC: U.S. Government Printing Office.

Voegtlin, W., & Lemere, F. (1942). The treatment of alcohol addiction. *Quarterly Journal of Studies on Alcohol, 2,* 717–803.

Wallace, J. (1966). An abilities conception of personality. Some implications for personality measurement. *American Psychologist, 21,* 132–138.

Wallach, M. A. (1971). *The intelligence/creativity distinction.* Morristown, NJ: General Learning Press.

Wallerstein, R. S. (Ed.). (1981). *Becoming a psychoanalyst: A study of psychoanalytic supervision.* New York: International Universities Press.

Wallerstein, R. S. (1989). The psychotherapy research project of the Menninger Foundation: An overview. *Journal of Consulting and Clinical Psychology, 57,* 195–205.

Wallston, B. S., & Wallston, K. A. (1984). Social psychological models of health behavior: An examination and integration. In A. Baum, S. E. Taylor, & J. E. Singer (Eds.), *Handbook of psychology and health* (Vol. 4). Hillsdale, NJ: Erlbaum.

Walsh, K., & Darby, D. (1999). *Neuropsychology: A clinical approach* (4th ed.). New York: Churchill Livingstone.

Ward, C. H., Beck, A. T., Mendelson, M., Mock, J. E., & Erbauch, J. K. (1962). The psychiatric nomenclature. *Archives of General Psychiatry, 7,* 198–205.

Washington v. Harper, 494 U.S. 210 (1990).

Watkins, C. E., Jr., Campbell, V. L., Nieberding, R., & Hallmark, R. (1995). Contemporary practice of psychological assessment by clinical psychologists. *Professional Psychology: Research and Practice, 26,* 54–60.

Watson, J. B., & Rayner, R. (1920). Conditioned emotional reactions. *Journal of Experimental Psychology, 3,* 114.

Watson, R. I. (1959). Historical review of objective personality testing: The search for objectivity. In B. M. Bass & I. A. Berg (Eds.), *Objective approaches to personality assessment.* Princeton, NJ: Van Nostrand.

Wechsler, D. (1939). *The measurement of adult intelligence.* Baltimore: Williams and Wilkins.

Wechsler, D. (1945). A standardized memory scale for clinical use. *Journal of Psychology, 19,* 87–95.

Wechsler, D. (1949). *Wechsler Intelligence Scale for Children.* New York: Psychological Corporation.

Wechsler, D. (1955). *Manual for the Wechsler Adult Intelligence Scale.* New York: Psychological Corporation.

Wechsler, D. (1958). *Measurement and appraisal of adult intelligence* (4th ed.). Baltimore: Williams and Wilkins.

Wechsler, D. (1967). *Manual for the Wechsler Preschool and Primary Scale of Intelligence.* New York: Psychological Corporation.

Wechsler, D. (1974). *Manual: Wechsler Intelligence Scale for Children–Revised.* New York: Psychological Corporation.

Wechsler, D. (1991). *WISC-III: Wechsler Intelligence Scale for Children–Third Edition manual.* San Antonio, TX: Psychological Corporation.

Wechsler, D. (1997a). *WAIS-III: Administration and scoring manual.* San Antonio, TX: Psychological Corporation.

Wechsler, D. (1997b). *Wechsler Memory Scale–Third Edition.* San Antonio, TX: Psychological Corporation.

Weidner, G., & Chesney, M. A. (1985). Stress, Type A behavior, and coronary heart disease. In W. E. Connor & J. D. Bristow (Eds.), *Coronary heart disease: Prevention, complications, and treatment.* Philadelphia: Lippincott.

Weinberg, R. A. (1989). Intelligence and IQ: Landmark issues and great debates. *American Psychologist, 44,* 98–104.

Weiner, I. B. (1975). *Principles of psychotherapy.* New York: Wiley-Interscience.

Weiner, I. B. (1991). Editor's note: Inter-scorer agreement in Rorschach research. *Journal of Personality Assessment, 56,* 1.

Weiner, I. B. (1994). The Rorschach Inkblot Method (RIM) is not a test: Implications for theory and practice. *Journal of Personality Assessment, 62,* 498–504.

Weiner, I. B. (1995). Methodological considerations in Rorschach research. *Psychological Assessment, 7,* 330–337.

Weiner, I. B., & Bordin, E. S. (1983). Individual psychotherapy. In I. B. Weiner (Ed.), *Clinical methods in psychology* (2nd ed.). New York: Wiley-Interscience.

Weiner, J. P. (1994). Forecasting the effects of health care reform on U.S. physician workforce requirements: Evidence from HMO staffing patterns. *Journal of the American Medical Association, 272,* 222–229.

Weiner, V. (1975). "On being sane in insane places": A process (attributional) analysis and critique. *Journal of Abnormal Psychology, 84,* 433–441.

Weiss, B., Catron, T., Harris, V., & Phung, T. M. (1999). The effectiveness of traditional child psychotherapy. *Journal of Consulting and Clinical Psychology, 67,* 82–94.

Weiss, R., & Margolin, G. (1977). Marital conflict and accord. In A. R. Ciminero, K. S. Calhoun, & H. E. Adams (Eds.), *Handbook of behavioral assessment.* New York: Wiley.

Weiss, R. L., Hops, H., & Patterson, G. R. (1973). A framework for conceptualizing marital conflict, technology for altering it, some data for evaluating it. In L. A. Hamerlynck, L. C. Handy, & E. J. Mash (Eds.), *Behavior change: Methodology, concepts, and practice* (pp. 309–342). Champaign, IL: Research Press.

Weissman, M. M., & Markowitz, J. C. (1994). Interpersonal psychotherapy: Current status. *Archives of General Psychiatry, 51,* 599–606.

Weissman, M. M., & Markowitz, J. C. (1998). An overview of interpersonal psychotherapy. In J. C. Markowitz (Ed.), *Interpersonal psychotherapy* (pp. 1–33). Washington, DC: American Psychiatric Press.

Weisz, J. R., Donenberg, G. R., Han, S. S., & Weiss, B. (1995). Bridging the gap between laboratory and clinic in child and adolescent psychotherapy. *Journal of Consulting and Clinical Psychology, 63,* 688–701.

Weisz, J. R., Weiss, B., Alicke, M. D., & Klotz, M. L. (1987). Effectiveness of psychotherapy with children and adolescents: A meta-analysis for clinicians. *Journal of Consulting and Clinical Psychology, 55,* 542–549.

Weisz, J. R., Weiss, B., Han, S. S., Granger, D. A., & Morton, T. (1995). Effects of psychotherapy with children and adolescents revisited: A meta-analysis of treatment outcome studies. *Psychological Bulletin, 117,* 450–468.

Wells, G. L. (1995). Scientific study of witness memory: Implications for public and legal policy. *Psychology, Public Policy, and Law, 1,* 726–731.

Wells, G. L., Small, M., Penrod, S., Malpass, R. S., Fulero, S. M., & Brimacombe, C. A. E. (1998). Eyewitness identification procedures: Recommendations for lineups and photospreads. *Law and Human Behavior, 22,* 603–647.

Wells, R. A., Dilkes, T. C., & Trivelli, N. (1972). The results of family therapy: A critical review of the literature. *Family Process, 11,* 189–207.

Westermeyer, J. (1987). Cultural factors in clinical assessment. *Journal of Consulting and Clinical Psychology, 55,* 471–478.

Wetter, M., Baer, R., Berry, D., Robison, L., & Sumpter, J. (1993). MMPI-2 profiles of motivated fakers given specific symptom information. *Psychological Assessment, 5,* 317–323.

Wetter, M., Baer, R., Berry, D., Smith, G., & Larsen, L. (1992). Sensitivity of MMPI-2 validity scales to random responding and malingering. *Psychological Assessment, 4,* 369–374.

Wexler, D. A., & Rice, L. N. (Eds.). (1974). *Innovations in client-centered therapy.* New York: Wiley.

White, L., Tursky, B., & Schwartz, G. E. (Eds.). (1985). *Placebo: Theory, research, and mechanisms.* New York: Guilford Press.

White, R. W. (1976). *The enterprise of living: A view of personal growth* (2nd ed.). New York: Holt, Rinehart and Winston.

Widiger, T. A. (1991). Personality disorder dimensional models proposed for DSM-IV. *Journal of Personality Disorders, 5,* 386–398.

Widiger, T. A., Mangine, S., Corbitt, E. M., Ellis, C. G., & Thomas, G. V. (1995). *Personality Disorder Interview–IV: A semistructured interview for the assessment of personality disorders.* Odessa, FL: Psychological Assessment Resources.

Widiger, T. A., & Settle, S. (1987). Broverman et al. revisited: An artifactual sex bias. *Journal of Personality and Social Psychology, 53,* 463–469.

Widiger. T. A., & Spitzer, R. L. (1991). Sex bias in the diagnosis of personality disorders: Conceptual and methodological issues. *Clinical Psychology Review, 11,* 1–22.

Widiger, T. A., & Trull, T. J. (1991). Diagnosis and clinical assessment. *Annual Review of Psychology, 42,* 109–133.

Wiener, M., Devoe, S., Rubinow, S., & Geller, J. (1972). Nonverbal behavior and nonverbal communication. *Psychological Review, 79,* 185–214.

Wiens, A. N. (1983). The assessment interview. In I. B. Weiner (Ed.), *Clinical methods in psychology* (2nd ed.). New York: Wiley-Interscience.

Wierson, M., & Forehand, R. (1994). Introduction to the Special Section: The role of longitudinal data with child psychopathology and treatment: Preliminary comments and issues. *Journal of Consulting and Clinical Psychology, 62,* 883–886.

Wiggins, J. S. (1973). *Personality and prediction: Principles of personality assessment.* Reading, MA: Addison-Wesley.

Wiggins, J. S., & Pincus, A. L. (1989). Conceptions of personality disorders and dimensions of personality. *Psychological Assessment: A Journal of Consulting and Clinical Psychology, 1*, 305–316.

Wigmore, J. H. (1909). Professor Munsterberg and the psychology of testimony: Being a report of the case of *Cokestone* v. *Munsterberg*. *Illinois Law Review, 3*, 399–445.

Wilkins, W. (1973). Expectancy of therapeutic gain: An empirical and conceptual critique. *Journal of Consulting and Clinical Psychology, 40*, 69–77.

Wilkins, W. (1986). Placebo problems in psychotherapy research: Social-psychological alternatives to chemotherapy concepts. *American Psychologist, 41*, 551–556.

Williams, C. L., & Butcher, J. N. (1989a). An MMPI study of adolescents: 1. Empirical validity of the standard scales. *Psychological Assessment: A Journal of Consulting and Clinical Psychology, 1*, 251–259.

Williams, C. L., & Butcher, J. N. (1989b). An MMPI study of adolescents: 2. Verification and limitations of code type classifications. *Psychological Assessment: A Journal of Consulting and Clinical Psychology, 1*, 260–265.

Williams, R. B., Barefoot, J. C., Califf, R. M., Haney, T. L., Saunders, W. B., Pryor, D. B., Hlatky, M. A., Siegler, I. C., & Mark, D. B. (1992). Prognostic importance of social resources among patients with CAD. *Journal of the American Medical Association, 267*, 520–524.

Willis, D. J. (1989). Expanding psychological practice to American Indians. *Clinical Psychologist, 42*, 5–8.

Wills, K. E. (1993). Neuropsychological functioning in children with spina bifida and/or hydrocephalus. *Journal of Clinical Child Psychology, 22*, 247–265.

Wilson, G. L., Bornstein, P. H., & Wilson, L. J. (1988). Treatment of relationship dysfunction: An empirical evaluation of group and conjoint behavioral marital therapy. *Journal of Consulting and Clinical Psychology, 56*, 929–931.

Wilson, G. T. (1981). Behavior therapy as a short-term therapeutic approach. In S. H. Budman (Ed.), *Forms of brief therapy*. New York: Guilford Press.

Wilson, G. T. (1997). Behavior therapy at century close. *Behavior Therapy, 28*, 449–457.

Wilson, G. T. (1998). Manual-based treatment and clinical practice. *Clinical Psychology: Science and Practice, 5*, 363–375.

Wilson, G. T., & Davison, G. C. (1971). Processes of fear reduction in systematic desensitization: Animal studies. *Psychological Bulletin, 76*, 1–14.

Wilson, G. T., & Lawson, D. M. (1976a). Effects of alcohol on sexual arousal in women. *Journal of Abnormal Psychology, 85*, 489–497.

Wilson, G. T., & Lawson, D. M. (1976b). Expectancies, alcohol, and sexual arousal in male social drinkers. *Journal of Abnormal Psychology, 85*, 587–594.

Wilson, G. T., & O'Leary, K. D (1980). *Principles of behavior therapy*. Englewood Cliffs, NJ: Prentice-Hall.

Wilson, G. T., & Rachman, S. J. (1983). Meta-analysis and the evaluation of psychotherapy outcome: Limitations and liabilities. *Journal of Consulting and Clinical Psychology, 51*, 54–64.

Windholz, M. I, & Silberschatz, G. (1988). Vanderbilt Psychotherapy Process Scale: A replication with adult outpatients. *Journal of Consulting and Clinical Psychology, 56*, 56–60.

Winett, R. A., Riley, A. W, King, A. C, & Altman, D. G. (1989). Prevention in mental health: A proactive-developmental-ecological perspective. In T. H. Ollendick & M. Hersen (Eds.), *Handbook of child psychopathology* (2nd ed.). New York: Plenum Press.

Winslow, R. (1998, January 20). Health-care inflation kept in check last year. *Wall Street Journal*, pp. B1, B4.

Witmer, L. (1907). Clinical psychology [Editorial]. *The Psychological Clinic, 1*, 1.

Wolberg, L. R. (1967). *The technique of psychotherapy* (2nd ed.). New York: Grune and Stratton.

Wolf, A. (1975). Psychoanalysis in groups. In G. M. Gazda (Ed.), *Basic approaches to group psychotherapy and group counseling* (2nd ed.). Springfield, IL: Charles C Thomas.

Wolpe, J. (1958). *Psychotherapy by reciprocal inhibition*. Stanford, CA: Stanford University Press.

Wolpe, J. (1973). *The practice of behavior therapy* (2nd ed.). New York: Pergamon Press.

Wolpe, J. (1981). Behavioral therapy versus psychoanalysis: Therapeutic and social implications. *American Psychologist, 36*, 159–164.

Wolpe, J., & Lazarus, A. A. (1966). *Behavior therapy techniques*. New York: Pergamon Press.

Wood, J. M., Nezworski, M. T., & Stejskal, W. J. (1996). The Comprehensive System for the Rorschach: A critical examination. *Psychological Science, 7*, 3–10.

Wood, J. M., Nezworski, M. T., & Stejskal, W. J. (1997). The reliability of the Comprehensive System for the Rorschach: A comment on Meyer (1997). *Psychological Assessment, 9*, 3–10.

Woodruff, R. A., Goodwin, D. W., & Guze, S. B. (1974). *Psychiatric diagnosis*. London: Oxford University Press.

Woodruff-Pak, D. (1988). *Psychology and aging*. Englewood Cliffs, NJ: Prentice Hall.

Woolfolk, A. E., Woolfolk, R. L., & Wilson, G. T. (1977). A rose by any other name . . . : Labeling bias and attitudes toward behavior modification. *Journal of Consulting and Clinical Psychology, 45*, 184–191.

World Health Organization. (1948). *Manual of the international statistical classification of diseases, injuries, and causes of death*. Geneva: Author.

Wright, L. (1967). The pediatric psychologist: A role model. *American Psychologist, 22*, 323–325.

Wrightsman, L. S., Nietzel, M. T., & Fortune, W. H. (1998). *Psychology and the legal system* (4th ed.). Pacific Grove, CA: Brooks/Cole.

Yalom, I. D. (1975). *The theory and practice of group psychotherapy.* New York: Basic Books.

Yates, A. J. (1966). Psychological deficit. In P. R. Earnsworth, O. McNemar, & Q. McNemar (Eds.), *Annual review of psychology.* Palo Alto, CA: Annual Reviews.

Yoken, C., & Berman, J. S. (1987). Third-party payment and the outcome of psychotherapy. *Journal of Consulting and Clinical Psychology, 55,* 571–576.

Yoshikawa, H. (1995). Long-term effects of early childhood programs on social outcomes and delinquency. In R. E. Behrman (Ed.), *The Future of Children: Long-Term Outcomes of Early Childhood Programs* (Vol. 5, No. 3, pp. 51–75). Los Altos, CA: Center for the Future of Children.

Yule, W. (1989). An introduction to investigation in clinical child psychology. In S. Lindsay & G. Powell (Eds.), *An introduction to clinical child psychology.* Aldershot, England: Gower.

Zarin, D. A., Pincus, H. A., Peterson, B. D., West, J. C., Suarez, A. P., Marcus, S. C., & McIntyre, J. S. (1998). Characterizing psychiatry with findings from the 1996 national survey of psychiatric practice. *American Journal of Psychiatry, 155,* 397–404.

Zax, M., & Specter, G. A. (1974). *An introduction to community psychology.* New York: Wiley.

Zelin, M. L. (1971). Validity of the MMPI scales for measuring twenty psychiatric dimensions. *Journal of Consulting and Clinical Psychology, 37,* 286–290.

Zigler, E., & Phillips, L. (1961). Psychiatric diagnosis: A critique. *Journal of Abnormal and Social Psychology, 63,* 607–618.

Zigler, E., & Phillips, L. (1962). Social competence and the process-reactive distinction in psychopathology. *Journal of Abnormal and Social Psychology, 65,* 215–222.

Zilboorg, G., & Henry, G. W. (1941). *A history of medical psychology.* New York: Norton.

Zimet, C. N. (1989). The mental health care revolution. *American Psychologist, 44,* 703–708.

Zook, A., II, & Walton, J. M. (1989). Theoretical orientations and work settings of clinical and counseling psychologists: A current perspective. *Professional Psychology: Research and Practice, 20,* 23–31.

Zubin, J., Eron, L. D., & Schumer, F. (1965). *An experimental approach to projective techniques.* New York: Wiley.

NAME INDEX

609

SUBJECT INDEX